PRAPAÑCASĀRA TANTRA

प्रपञ्चसारतन्त्रम्

प्रपञ्चसारतन्त्रम्

श्रीशङ्कराचार्यविरचितम्

तच्छिष्यपद्मपादाचार्यविरचितविवरणोपेतम्
प्रयोगक्रमदीपिकाख्यविवरणविवृतिसमेतम्

श्री आर्थर एवेलनेन पर्यवेक्षितम्
श्रीअटलानन्दसरस्वतीमहोदयैः सम्पादितम्

MOTILAL BANARSIDASS
PUBLISHING HOUSE • DELHI
Email: naraina@mlbd.in • Website: www.mlbd.in
@mlbdofficial

PRAPAÑCASĀRA TANTRA

OF

ŚAṄKARĀCĀRYA

With the Commentary Vivaraṇa by Padmapādācārya and Prayogakramadīpikā—a Vṛtti on the Vivaraṇa

Revised and documented with exhaustive Introduction
by

ARTHUR AVALON

Edited by

AṬALĀNANDA SARASVATĪ

PARTS I, II in one Vol.

MOTILAL BANARSIDASS PUBLISHING HOUSE • SINCE 1903

MOTILAL BANARSIDASS
PUBLISHING HOUSE • DELHI

Email: naraina@mlbd.in • Website: www.mlbd.in

@mlbdofficial

*4th Reprint : Delhi, **2023***
First Edition : Calcutta, 1935

ISBN: 978-93-5760-321-8 (Hardcover)
ISBN: 978-93-5760-319-5 (Paperback)

Printed & Published by
Rajendra P Jain *for*
Motilal Banarsidass Publishing House
A-44, Naraina Industrial Area, Phase I,
New Delhi–110 028 (INDIA)
Email: naraina@mlbd.in Website: www.mlbd.in
Tel.: (+91-11)4751 1592
Showroom:
4637/20, F-2, Hari Sadan, First Floor, Ansari Road, Daryaganj
Delhi–110 002 (Opp. Fire Station) ***Tel.*** : (+91-11)4559 7999

सूचीपत्रम्

* चिह्निताष्टोकोक्ताविषया:

विषय:	पृष्ठाङ्क:
शुद्धिपत्रम्	xvii
पाठभेद	xviii
Introduction	xxi
मङ्गलाचरणम	१
* तन्त्रावतारप्रयोजनम्	,,
* ग्रन्थविषयस्य पाञ्चविध्यम्	२
* स्वरव्यञ्जनपारायणम्	३
* मन्त्रभेदेन पारायणक्रमभेद:	४
* शारदाशब्दव्युत्पत्ति:	५
* आणव-शाक्त-शाम्भवदोक्षाप्रकार:	,,
ब्रह्मादीनामत्पत्ति:	६
भगवत: मायिन: स्थानमूर्त्यादि:	७
भगवत्समीपे ब्रह्मण: प्रश्न:	९
तत्र प्रमिताक्षरोक्ति:	,,
अक्षरस्वरूपम्	१०
हकारस्य सर्वात्मत्व-स्वरूप-व्याप्ति-कथनम्	११
लवादिप्रलयान्तकालभेदकथनम्	१२
ब्रह्मायु:परिमाणम्	१३
* आणवादियोग:	१४
तत्त्वविकृतिक्रम:	१६
बिन्दोर्बिन्दुनादबीजोत्पत्ति:	,,
प्रकृतेरिच्छासत्त्वादिरूपत्वम्	,,
रवोत्पत्ति:	१७
शब्दब्रह्मस्वरूपम्	,,
महदादिधरान्ततत्त्वोत्पत्ति:	,,
पञ्चभूतस्वरूपम्	१८
पञ्चभूतकला:	,,
* अपञ्चीकृतबीजोद्धार:	,,
* पञ्चीकृतबीजाद्धार:	,,
पञ्चीकरणम्	१९
पञ्चविंशतितत्त्वम्	१९
प्रकृतिविकृतिविभाग:	,,
प्रकृतेर्गुणत्रयात्मकत्वम्	२०
* ग्रन्थस्य सर्वागमसारत्वोक्ति:	,,
* शैवशाक्तादितत्त्वसमन्वयोक्ति:	,,
अर्थसृष्ट्युपसंहार:	२१
अर्थसृष्टे: प्रयोजनम्	,,
शब्दब्रह्मोपदेश:	२२
चतुर्विधदेहोत्पत्ति:	२३
जरायुजोत्पत्ति:	,,
मायीयादिमलत्रयम्	२४
जन्तो: स्त्रीपुंनपुंसकत्वे हेतु:	,,
जन्तोरुत्पत्तिप्रकार:	,,
सुषुम्नादिनाड़ीनामानि	,,
देहेऽहोरात्रादिक्रम:	२६
चेतनाधातोरागति:	,,
तत्र मतभेदा:	,,
तत्र स्वसिद्धान्त:	२७
मनोबुद्धाहङ्कारचित्तानां भेदा:	,,
शब्दब्रह्मणोऽभिव्यक्ति:	२८

द्वितीय: पटल:

विषय:	पृष्ठाङ्क:
गर्भवासवर्णनम्	२९
देहे प्राणादिदशवायूनां क्रिया	३०
वाय्वग्निदोषदूष्यादि	,,
प्राणादीनां धर्मा:	३१
षडूर्मय:। षट्कोशा:	,,
ओजोधातूत्पत्ति:	,,

विषयः	पृष्ठाङ्कः
राश्यधिपतिन्यासः	५८
राशिवेधादिन्यासः	६०
नक्षत्रवेधन्यासः	६१
नक्षत्रवेधन्यासक्रमः	६२
नक्षत्रवृक्षकथनम्	६३
नक्षत्रदेवतान्यासः	,,
तिथ्यादिन्यासः	६४
करणन्यासः । हृल्लेखाव्याप्तिः	६५
हृल्लेखाज्ञानेन विष्णुप्राप्तिः	६६
* राशिनक्षत्रनामार्णानुकूल्यम्	,,
* कुलाकुलर्णधनविभागः	६७
* मन्त्रशुद्धिक्रमः	,,
पञ्चमः पटलः	
दीक्षाप्रकरणम्	
दीक्षामन्त्रशब्दयोर्निर्वचनम्	६८
आचार्यनियमः	,,
वास्तुमण्डलमानम्	६९
वास्तुदेवार्चनक्रमः	,,
वास्तुबलिः । दीक्षामण्डपादि	७०
चतुरस्रकुण्डमेखलायोनिमानादिकथनम्	७२
षष्ठः पटलः	
ऋषिच्छन्दोदेवतानिरुक्तिः	७९
षड़ङ्गन्यासे हृदयादिशब्दार्थः	८०
पञ्चाङ्गन्यासपक्षे नेत्रत्यागः	८१
उपकरणस्थापननियमः	८२
देवतानां पूजानियमः	,,
कुम्भस्थापनविधिः	८३
गन्धाष्टकत्रैविध्यम्	८३
अष्टत्रिंशत्कलाविनियोगः	,,
ऋकपञ्चकेन कुम्भपूरणम्	८४
प्राणप्रतिष्ठामन्त्रः । उपचारभेदाः	८५
* उपचारमन्त्राः	८७
त्रैलोक्यमोहनप्रयोगः	८८
षड़ङ्गदेवताध्यानम्	९०
लोकपालास्त्रवर्णादीनि	,,
होमप्रकरणम्	९१
अग्निज्वालनमन्त्रः	,,
अग्निजिह्वानां सात्त्विकादिभेदाः	९२
तन्नामानि	,,
अग्नेरङ्गमूर्त्यादि	९३
अग्निमन्त्रः । अग्निध्यानम्	,,
व्याहृतिपूर्वकमनुना होमः	९४
गर्भाधानादिकर्मसु प्रणवेन होमः	,,
* होमद्रव्यपरिमाणविधिः	९५
ब्रह्मार्पणमनुः	९६
नक्षत्रादिबलिः	९७
अष्टाङ्ग-पञ्चाङ्ग-प्रणामः	,,
अभिषेकः	९८
सप्तमः पटलः	
मातृकाप्रकरणम्	
मातृकाविधानम्	१०१
मातृकामन्त्रर्ष्यादि	,,
भारतीध्यानम्	१०२
पुरश्चरणादि । यन्त्रम्	,,
नवशक्तिनामानि	१०३

विषयः	पृष्ठाङ्कः
इन्द्रियाणामर्थविशेषनियमहेतुः	३१
ग्रहणीकथनम्	३२
मूलाधारनिर्णयः	"
षड्रसाः । अन्नपाकप्रकारः	"
वस्तिनिरूपणम्	३३
गर्भस्थजन्तूत्पत्तिः	"
परापश्यन्त्यादिभावकथनम्	"
* एषां विवृतिः	"
कुण्डलिनीव्याप्तिप्रकरणम्	
वर्णव्यक्तिः । अहङ्कारोत्पत्तिः	३४
जन्तोः संसारक्रमः	"
* भावानां साप्तविध्यकथनम्	"
कुण्डलिन्याः सर्वात्मत्वम्	३५
कुण्डलिनीविभूतिः	"
गुणनप्रकरणम्	३६
* त्रिगुणादिव्याशयः	३७

तृतीयः पटलः

विषयः	पृष्ठाङ्कः
वर्णविभूतिप्रकरणम्	
वर्णानामग्नीषोमसूर्यात्मकत्वम्	३८
स्वरस्पर्शव्यापकवर्णनिरूपणम्	"
स्वराणां स्त्रीपुंनपुंसकत्वम्	३९
वर्णवीर्योद्भवकालः	"
बिन्दुसर्गयोः शशिसूर्यरूपत्वम्	४०
स्पर्शानां पाञ्चविध्यम्	"
व्यापकोदयक्रमः	"
कलानाम-कथनम्	४१
प्रणवकलाः	"
केशवादिमूर्त्तितच्छक्तिनामानि	४२
श्रीकण्ठादिमूर्त्तितच्छक्तिनामानि	४३
वर्णौषधिः	४४
वर्णानामीरणादिप्रकारः	"
वर्णस्वरूपनिष्पत्तिप्रकारः	४५
वर्णानां पुंप्रकृतिवाचकमन्त्रत्वम्	"
हंसस्वरूपसूचना	४६
हकारस्य सर्ववर्णादिकारणत्वम्	"
स्तम्भनादिप्रयोगप्रकारः	४७

चतुर्थः पटलः

विषयः	पृष्ठाङ्कः
हकारस्य विश्वयोनित्वम्	४८
षोडशाङ्गन्यासः	"
हकारादीनां गुणाः	"
गुणचतुष्टयकथनम् । न्यासक्रमः	५०
* पिपासादिन्यासभेदाः	५१
षडध्वन्यासस्सूचनम्	५२
लिङ्गशक्त्यादिन्यासः	"
स्वरपारायणन्यासः	५३
कुण्डलिनीन्यासस्थानकथनम्	"
हकारतो ब्रह्मादीनामुत्पत्तिः	५४
अजपादिन्यासः	"
हंसस्वरूपकथनम्	५५
परमात्ममन्त्रोद्धारः	"
तारविभूतिः	५६
ग्रहाणां सूर्यात्मकसंविद्दशाप्यत्वम्	५७
अहोरात्रादिन्यासः	"
राशिमण्डलम्	५८
राशीनां चरादिभेदः	५९
राशीनां ब्राह्मणादिवर्णोक्तिः	"

विषयः	पृष्ठाङ्कः
अष्टमातरः। जपादिफलकथनम्	१०३
कवितासिद्धिकरब्राह्मीष्टतम्	१०४
अभिषेकफलम्	„
* मुद्रादिन्यासभेदाः	१०५
तारकलान्यासविधिः	१०६
केशवादिन्यासविधिः	१०७
अर्द्धनारीश्वरध्यानादि	„
प्रपञ्चयागविधिः	„
सप्तग्रहन्यासस्थानम्	१०८
तत्र मन्त्रपञ्चकम्	१०९
* नवग्रहन्यासः	„
प्रपञ्चयागमन्त्रार्थादि	„
तारादिपञ्चमनूनां स्वरूपव्याप्ती	११०
स्वाहाशब्दनिरुक्तिः	„
परमात्ममन्त्रार्थः	„
शक्तिबीज-नेत्रास्त्रमन्त्रार्थः	१११
प्रपञ्चयागन्यासक्रमः	„
होमप्रकारः	११३
जपादावधिकारिनिर्णयः	„
दशविधन्यासफलकथनम्	११५
प्रपञ्चयागस्य भुक्तिमुक्तिहेतुता	„
होमद्रव्याणि	„
होमविधिः	११६
तिलकधारणफलम्	११७

अष्टमः पटलः

विषयः	पृष्ठाङ्कः
प्राणाग्निहोत्रप्रकरणम्	
प्राणाग्निहोत्रविधिः	११८
पञ्चकुण्डेषु वर्णहोमः	„
समन्त्रोद्धारनवग्रहहोमः	११९
भूतमन्त्रैर्होमः। भूतमन्त्रोद्धारः	„
हंसस्वरूपवर्णनम्	१२०
अशनकाले प्राणाग्निहोत्राधिकारः	„
* प्राणाग्निहोमक्रमः	„
होमफलम्	१२३
दशाक्षरसरस्वतीमन्त्रः	„
ध्यानम्। पुरश्चरणपूजाप्रयोगाः	१२४
मन्त्रान्तरम्	१२५
ध्यानम्। पुरश्चरणपूजाप्रयोगाः	„
वाग्देवीस्तोत्रम्	१२६

नवमः पटलः

विषयः	पृष्ठाङ्कः
त्रिपुराप्रकरणम्	
त्रिपुराशब्दनिर्वचनम्	१२८
त्रिपुरामन्त्रः	„
न्यासभेदाः	१२९
* पादुकासप्तकादिन्यासः	१३०
ध्यानम्	१३१
पुरश्चरणपूजाप्रयोगाः	१३२
वेधकप्राणायामः	„
नवयोनिचक्रम्	१३३
अष्टौ मातरः भैरवाश्च	१३४
वाग्भवसाधनक्रमः	„
जपादिनियमस्तत्फलञ्च	१३५
कामराजादिसाधनम्	१३७

दशमः पटलः

विषयः	पृष्ठाङ्कः
भुवनेश्वरीप्रकरणम्	
भुवनेश्वरीमन्त्रः	१३९

विषयः	पृष्ठाङ्कः
ऋष्यादिन्यासः	१३८
भूतशुद्धिक्रमः	१४०
दिव्यदेहसृष्टिक्रमः	१४१
* आवरणादिन्यासः	१४२
ध्यानम्	१४३
पाशाङ्कुशशब्दनिरुक्तिः	"
वराभयशब्दनिरुक्तिः	"
त्रिगुणितयन्त्रम्	"
हृल्लेखादीनां न्यासस्थानानि	१४४
ब्रह्माण्यादीनां न्यासस्थानानि	"
नवशक्तिनामानि	"
* पीठमन्त्रः। मूर्तिमन्त्रः	"
घटस्थापनपूरणक्रमः	१४५
कुम्भपूरणद्रव्याणि	"
गायत्र्यादीनां ध्यानम्	१४६
घटभेदे देवताभेदः	"
अभिषेकः। पुरश्चरणम्	"
व्यापिन्यादिध्यानम्	१४७
होमविधिः	"
योगिनामन्त्रःपूजायाः कर्त्तव्यता	"
अभिषेकादिफलम्	१४८
षड्गुणितयन्त्रनिर्माणप्रकारः	"
यन्त्रे पूजाप्रयोगः	१५०

एकादशः पटलः

द्वादशगुणितयन्त्रविधानम्	१५१
षोडश-द्वात्रिंश-चतुःषष्टिशक्तयः	१५२
घटार्गलयन्त्रम्	१५४
पाशाङ्कुशबीजम्	१५५
शक्तिमन्त्रः। पूजाप्रयोगादि	१५५
* कलशशब्दनिर्वचनम्	"
पुरश्चरणम्	१५६
यन्त्रलेखनद्रव्याणि	"
भुवनेश्वरीस्तोत्रम्	"

द्वादशः पटलः

लक्ष्मीप्रकरणम्	
लक्ष्मीमन्त्रः। ऋष्यादिन्यासः	१६०
ध्यानम्। पुरश्चरणम्	"
होमद्रव्याणि	१६१
पीठशक्तयः। आवरणदेवताः	"
चतुर्व्यूहः। अष्टशक्तिनामानि	"
अलक्ष्मीनाशकरहोमः	१६२
मन्त्रान्तरम्	"
ध्यानम्। पुरश्चरणादि	१६३
महालक्ष्मीमन्त्रः	१६४
ध्यानम्। पुरश्चरणम्	"
श्रीसूक्तविनियोगविधिः	१६५
ध्यानम्। पूजा-पुरश्चरणादि	"
द्वात्रिंशन्मन्त्रदेवतानामानि	१६७
श्रीसाधकवर्जनीयानि	"
श्रीसाधककर्त्तव्यानि	१६८

त्रयोदशः पटलः

त्रिपुटाप्रकरणम्	
त्रिपुटामन्त्रः। तदृष्यादि	१६९
ध्यानम्। पुरश्चरणम्	"
होमद्रव्याणि। भुवनवश्ययोगः	१७०
धरणीमन्त्रः। ऋष्यादि	"

विषयः	पृष्ठाङ्कः
ध्यानम्। होमादिविधिः	१७१
त्वरिताप्रकरणम्	१७२
त्वरिताशब्दनिर्वचनम्	"
त्वरितामन्त्रः। अङ्गन्यासादि	"
ध्यानम्। पुरश्चरणपूजाप्रयोगाः	१७३
होमद्रव्याणि	१७४
द्वादशरेखा-दशरेखा-यन्त्रम्	१७५
यन्त्रलेख्यमन्त्राः	"
नवरेखायन्त्रम्	१७६
यन्त्रलेख्यमनुः	१७७
अस्य श्रीकरत्वम्	"
कुम्भयन्त्रम्	"
नित्यामन्त्रः	१७८
ध्यानम्। पुरश्चरणादि	"
नित्याशक्तिनामानि	"
नित्यक्लिन्नामन्त्रः	१७९
ध्यानम्। पुरश्चरणादि	"
यन्त्रम्	१८०

चतुर्दशः पटलः

विषयः	पृष्ठाङ्कः
दुर्गाप्रकरणम्	
दुर्गामन्त्रः। ध्यानम्	१८१
पुरश्चरणम्। शक्तिनामानि	"
महासिंहमन्त्रः	"
वनदुर्गामन्त्रः। ऋष्यादि	१८२
ध्यानम्। पुरश्चरणम्	१८३
शक्तिनामानि। पूजाप्रयोगादि	१८४
शूलिनीदुर्गामन्त्रः	१८७
ऋष्यादि। ध्यानम्। पुरश्चर्यादि	१८८
विषापहननादिप्रयोगाः	१८९

पञ्चदशः पटलः

विषयः	पृष्ठाङ्कः
सौरप्रकरणम्	
सूर्यमन्त्रः। ऋष्यादि	१९१
ध्यानम्। पुरश्चरणादि	"
नवशक्तिनामानि	१९२
पीठमन्त्रः। अर्घ्यदानप्रकारः	"
अजपामन्त्रः। ऋष्यादि	१९३
ध्यानम्। पुरश्चरणम्। योगभेदाः	१९४
प्रयोजनतिलकमन्त्रः	१९५
ध्यानम्। पुरश्चरणादि	१९६
अर्घ्यद्रव्याणि	१९७
ग्रहशान्तिविधानम्	"
होमे समिन्नियमः	"
सौराष्टाक्षरमन्त्रः	१९८
ध्यानम्। पुरश्चरणप्रयोगादि	"

षोड़शः पटलः

विषयः	पृष्ठाङ्कः
चन्द्रप्रकरणम्	
चन्द्रमन्त्रः	२००
ध्यानम्। पुरश्चरणादि	"
विद्यामन्त्रः। अग्निमन्त्रः	२०२
ध्यानम्। पुरश्चरणादि	"
शक्त्यादिकथनम्	२०३
अग्न्यावाहनमन्त्रः। ऋष्यादि	"
पुरश्चरणादि	२०४
चतुर्विंशाक्षरमन्त्रः	"
ध्यानम्। पुरश्चरणादि	२०५

विषयः पृष्ठाङ्कः

सप्तदशः पटलः

महागणपतिप्रकरणम्
महागणपतिमन्त्रः २०८
ऋष्यादि „
ध्यानम्। पूजाविधिः २०९
पुरश्चरणादि २१०
शक्तिनामानि २११
आसनमन्त्रः। तर्पणभेदाः „
राजार्थिनृपतिकर्त्तव्यम् २१२
होमभेदाः „
स्तम्भनकरभूबीजम् २१४
मन्त्रान्तरम् „
ध्यानम्। पुरश्चरणादि „
क्षिप्रप्रसादनमन्त्रः। ऋष्यादि २१६
ध्यानम्। पुरश्चरणादि „
* गणेशगायत्री „
तर्पणप्रकारः २१७

अष्टादशः पटलः

मन्मथप्रकरणम्
मन्मथमन्त्रः। ऋष्यादि २१८
ध्यानम्। पुरश्चरणादि „
शक्तिनामानि। मन्मथयन्त्रम् „
गायत्री। मालामन्त्रः २१९
मदनविधानम् २२०
ध्यानम्। शक्त्यावरणदेवतादि „
प्रयोगयन्त्रम्। होमादि २२१
अष्टादशाक्षरश्रीकृष्णमन्त्रः २२२
ध्यानम्। पुरश्चरणादि „

विषयः पृष्ठाङ्कः

प्रातर्मध्याह्नादिभेदेन ध्यानभेदः २२२
पूजाप्रयोगादि २२३

एकोनविंशः पटलः

प्रणवप्रकरणम्
मोक्षप्रधानप्रणवमन्त्रः २२४
विष्णुध्यानम्। पुरश्चरणादि २२५
चतुर्व्यूहः। शक्तिनामानि „
योगलक्षणम् २२६
यमनियमादीनां लक्षणम् „
* पद्मासनभद्रासनवज्रासन-
लक्षणम् „
प्राणायामे पक्षान्तरम् २२७
सकलीकरणप्रकारः „
पञ्चाशन्मात्राधारणे प्रतिपत्तिः „
* वीरासनम् „
शोषणदहनादिप्रकारः २२८
योगप्रयोगेऽवस्थादेशादिनियमः „
सुषुम्नामध्यगतप्रणवध्यानम् „
प्रणवनामन्यासः २२९
प्रणवस्य वेदादित्वोपपादनम् „
* न्यासक्रमः। प्रणवनामानि „
मोक्षप्रधानयोगः २३०
मोक्षसाधनयोगभेदाः „
योगिनामवस्थाभेदाः २३१
जागरादिपञ्चावस्थालक्षणम् „
जपकाले प्रतिपत्त्यव्ययोगः २३२
योगक्रमः „
योगसिद्धिसूचकावस्थाः २३३

विषयः	पृष्ठाङ्कः
अणिमाद्यष्टैश्वर्याणि	२३३

विंशः पटलः

नारायणाष्टाक्षरमन्त्रः	२३४
अष्टाक्षरार्थः । ध्यानम्	"
मन्त्रवर्णन्यासक्रमः	२३५
अष्टाक्षरे द्वादशाक्षर-मन्त्रान्तर्भावः	२३६
अक्षरतत्त्व-मूर्त्तिपञ्जरन्यासौ	"
किरीटादिमन्त्राः	"
संक्षेपदीक्षाविधानम्	२३७
शक्त्यस्त्रादीनां नामानि	"
पञ्चावरणविष्णुविधानम्	२३८
पूजाप्रयोगादि	"

एकविंशः पटलः

मासयन्त्रप्रकरणम्	
मासयन्त्राणां सामान्यलक्षणम्	२४१
चरस्थिरोभयराशिकथनम्	"
त्रि-षड्-द्वादश-गुणितयन्त्रम्	"
द्वादशभानुनामानि	२४२
केशवादिपूजामन्त्रः	"
* केशवादित्यादिगायत्रीकथनम्	२४३
द्वादशराशियन्त्रम् । तत्पूजा	२४४
श्रीहरिस्तोत्रम्	२५०

द्वाविंशः पटलः

वासुदेवप्रकरणम्	
वासुदेवमन्त्रः	२५३
न्यासक्रमेण संहारसृष्टिस्थितयः	"

विषयः	पृष्ठाङ्कः
ध्यानम् । पुरश्चरणादि	२५३
सुदर्शनमन्त्रः	२५४
दिग्बन्धमन्त्रः	"
अग्निप्राकारमन्त्रः । वर्णन्यासः	"
सुदर्शनध्यानम् । गायत्री	२५५
रक्षाकरमन्त्रः । चक्रयन्त्रम्	"
मन्त्रः । कुम्भपूरणम्	२५६
आयुधवर्णाः । शक्तिनामानि	"
प्रयोगविधिः । स्थाननिर्देशः	"
बलिमन्त्रः	२५७
* रक्षोघ्नमन्त्रः	"
रक्षाकरयन्त्रम्	२५८
रक्षोघ्नमन्त्रः	"
यन्त्ररचनाविधिः	२६०

त्रयोविंशः पटलः

श्रीपुरुषोत्तमप्रकरणम्	
श्रीपुरुषोत्तममन्त्रः	२६१
* द्वादशाङ्गमन्त्रप्रयोगक्रमः	२६३
* मारणादिप्रयोगमन्त्राः	"
ऋष्यादि । षडङ्गमन्त्रः	२६४
व्यापकमन्त्रः	"
चक्राद्यायुधाष्टकमन्त्राः	२६५
गरुडमन्त्रः	"
त्रैलोक्यमोहनगायत्री	"
श्रीमन्त्रः	"
शक्त्यादीनां मन्त्राः	"
त्रैलोक्यमोहनध्यानम्	२६६
पुरश्चरणादि । होमः	२६७

विषय:	पृष्ठाङ्क:
चतुर्विंश: पटल:	
श्रीकरप्रकरणम्	
श्रीकरमन्त्र: । ऋष्यादि । ध्यानम्	२७०
पुरश्चरणम् । पूजाप्रयोगादि	२७१
महावराहमन्त्र:	"
ऋष्यादि । ध्यानभेदा:	२७२
पूजाप्रयोग: । पुरश्चरणादि	२७३
वराहयन्त्रम्	२७५
पञ्चविंश: पटल:	
नृसिंहप्रकरणम्	
नृसिंहानुष्टुब्मन्त्र: । ऋष्यादि	२७६
प्रसन्ना प्रतिपत्ति:	"
क्रूरा प्रतिपत्ति:	२७७
मानसपूजा	"
पुरश्चरणम् । प्रयोगादि	"
* गरुडमन्त्र: । अनन्तमन्त्र:	"
नृसिंहबीजम् । ऋष्यादि	२७८
होमादिविधि:	२७९
षडक्षरमन्त्र: । ध्यानम्	२८०
नृसिंहयन्त्रम् । रक्षायन्त्रम्	२८१
प्रयोगादि	"
षड्विंश: पटल:	
विष्णुपञ्जरविधि:	२८३
विष्णुपञ्जरयन्त्रम्	"
विश्वरूपमन्त्र:	"
षोडशाक्षरसर्वार्थसाधकमन्त्र:	"
चक्रादिमन्त्रेषु षोडशाक्षरयोग:	"
चक्रादिमन्त्रकथनम्	२८४
विश्वरूपध्यानम् । प्रयोगादि	२८६
जपविधि: । प्रयोगक्रम:	२८८
चक्रमन्त्र: । प्रतिपत्ति:	२८९
गीतादिमन्त्रयोगविधि:	"
रक्षादिप्रयोगा:	२९०
* मन्त्रप्रयोगक्रम:	"
सप्तविंश: पटल:	
प्रासादप्रकरणम्	
प्रासादशब्दनिर्वचनम्	२९३
प्रासादमन्त्र: । ऋष्यादि	"
ध्यानम् । मन्त्रदेवतानामानि	"
मूर्तिन्यास: । पुरश्चरणम्	२९४
पीठार्चनविधि:	"
नवपीठशक्तिनामादि	"
सद्योजात-वामाघोरध्यानानि	"
तत्पुरुषेशानध्यानकथनम्	२९५
पञ्चब्रह्मविधानम्	"
षडङ्गमन्त्र:	२९६
अष्टत्रिंशत्कलान्यास:	"
* ईशानादीनां श्रौतमन्त्रा:	"
न्यासक्रम: । विनियोगविधि:	२९७
शैवपञ्चाक्षरमन्त्र: । ऋष्यादि	२९८
न्यास: । ध्यानम् । पुरश्चर्यादि	"
विधानान्तरम्	"
गोलकन्यास: । जप्यमन्त्रा:	२९९
श्रीशिवस्तव:	"
शक्तिपञ्चाक्षरविधानम्	३००

विषयः पृष्ठाङ्कः

ध्यानम्। पूजाप्रयोगादि ३०१

शैवाष्टाक्षरमन्त्रः ”

ध्यानम्। ऋष्यादि ”

अष्टाविंशः पटलः

दक्षिणामूर्तिमन्त्रः ३०२

ऋष्यादि। ध्यानम् ”

पुरश्चर्यादि। आग्नेयमन्त्रः ३०३

ऋष्यादि। अघोरध्यानम् ”

पूजायन्त्रम्। प्रयोगादि ३०४

ऊर्ध्ववक्त्रप्रधानमन्त्रः ३०५

ऋष्यादि। ध्यानम् ”

पुरश्चर्यादि। प्रणवप्रधानयोगः ३०६

बाह्यप्रयोगाङ्गयन्त्रम् ३०७

मध्यबीजप्रधानान्तरयोगः ”

तृतीयबीजप्रधानयोगादिकम् ३०८

एकोनत्रिंशः पटलः

चिन्तामणिमन्त्रः ३१०

उमेशदेवताध्यानम् ”

अर्धनारीश्वरध्यानम् ”

क्रूरप्रयोगे ध्यानम्। पुरश्चर्यादि ”

रोगाद्युपशान्तौ प्रयोगभेदाः ३११

रक्षाकरयन्त्रम्। चण्डेश्वरमन्त्रः ३१४

ध्यानम्। पुरश्चरणम् ३१५

चण्डगायत्री। पूजाप्रयोगादि ”

त्रिंशः पटलः

गायत्रीमन्त्रविधिकथनम् ३१७

जपाद्यधिकारनियमः ”

विषयः पृष्ठाङ्कः

प्रणवस्य सानुभवसाधनकथनम् ३१८

व्याहृत्यर्थकथनम् ३१९

प्रणवव्याहृतिसम्बन्धः ”

अन्तःप्रणवव्याहृति-
पक्षे प्रणवाद्यर्थकथनम् ३२०

ध्येयस्वरूपध्यानप्रकारौ ३२१

रसशब्दार्थः ३२२

गायत्रीजपविधिः ”

निराकारध्यानम् ३२४

बहिर्जपक्रमः ”

गायत्रीमन्त्रवर्णपदन्यासः ३२५

गायत्रीध्यानम्। प्रयोगादि ”

एकत्रिंशः पटलः

त्रिष्टुब्विद्याप्रकरणम्

ऋष्यादि। ध्यानम् ३२७

प्रयोगादि। नवशक्तिनामानि ३२८

अक्षरशक्तिनामानि ”

अस्त्रमन्त्रः। पादविभागः ३२९

मन्त्रदेवताङ्गकल्पना ३३०

अतिदुर्गामन्त्रजपनियमः ”

प्रतिलोममन्त्रसाधनविधिः ३३१

मन्त्रवर्णदेवताव्याप्तिः ”

आवरणदेवताभेदाः ”

दिनास्त्रलक्षणम् ३३२

कृत्यास्त्रलक्षणम् ३३३

प्रयोगप्रकारः ३३४

अनुलोमप्रतिलोम-
ध्यानभेदकथनम् ३३५

विषयः	पृष्ठाङ्कः
स्तम्भनादिविधिः	३३६
मूर्तिवर्णकथनम्	,,
विविधप्रयोगविधिः	३३७

द्वात्रिंशः पटलः

लवणमन्त्रः	३४१
* चिटिमन्त्रः	,,
अग्निध्यानम् । यामवतीध्यानम्	३४२
कात्यायनीध्यानम्	,,
भद्रकालीध्यानम् । पुरश्चर्यादि	,,
पुत्तलीप्रयोगादि	,,
उपस्थानमन्त्राः	३४४
प्रयोगभेदाः	३४५
बलिमन्त्रः	३४६
बलिदानप्रकारः	३४७

त्रयस्त्रिंशः पटलः

अनुष्टुप्प्रकरणम्	
आयुःप्रदोऽनुष्टुब्मन्त्रः	३४८
ऋष्यादि । ध्यानम्	,,
आवरणदेवताः	३४९
मन्त्रवर्णशक्तिदेवताः	,,
पुरश्चर्यादि । होमादिविधिः	,,
शताक्षरमन्त्रः । ऋष्यादि	३५०
ध्यानम् । पुरश्चर्यादि	३५१
संवादसूक्तविधानम्	३५२
ऋष्यादि । ध्यानम्	,,
पुरश्चरणम् । होमादिविधिः	३५३
* अनुकूलमन्त्रः	,,
* मन्त्रयोगक्रमः	३५४

विषयः	पृष्ठाङ्कः
ऋग्वारुणीविधानम्	३५६
ऋष्यादि । ध्यानम्	,,
पुरश्चरणम् । होमादिविधिः	,,
* नवशक्तिनामानि	,,

चतुस्त्रिंशः पटलः

दीर्घायुःप्रदयन्त्रम्	३५८
ज्वरार्त्तिहरयन्त्रम्	,,
वश्यकरयन्त्रम्	,,
आकर्षकरयन्त्रम्	३५९
षड्गुणितप्रयोगः	,,
द्वादशगुणितमन्त्रविशेषः	,,
आकर्षकरघटार्गलयन्त्रम्	३६०
स्त्रीवश्यकृद्यन्त्रम्	३६१
यन्त्रान्तरम्	,,
वश्यकृदपरयन्त्राणि	,,
आकर्षकरयन्त्रम्	३६२
ब्रह्मश्रीमन्त्रः	,,
ध्यानम् । पुरश्चरणम्	,,
राजमुखीमन्त्रः	३६३
वश्यकरप्रयोगान्तरम्	,,
अन्नाधिपतिमन्त्रः	,,
मन्त्रमूर्तिः । अन्नपूर्णामन्त्रः	३६४
ध्यानम् । पूजाप्रयोगः	,,
बृहस्पतिमन्त्रः	३६५
शुक्रमन्त्रः । व्यासमन्त्रः	,,
ध्यानम्	३६६
शत्रुजयोपायमन्त्रः । ध्यानम्	३६६
अश्वारूढामन्त्रः	,,

विषयः	पृष्ठाङ्कः	विषयः	पृष्ठाङ्कः
पुरश्चरणादि । ध्यानम्	३६६	सर्वाकृष्ट्यादिकरयोगः	३७३
अमठन्यासः	३६७		
पञ्चत्रिंशः पटलः		**षट्त्रिंशः पटलः**	
प्राणप्रतिष्ठाप्रकरणम्		पुत्रोत्पत्तिकरप्रयोगः	३७४
प्राणप्रतिष्ठामन्त्रः	३६८	अपत्यहीननिन्दा	„
न्यासभेदास्तत्स्थानानि	„	अपत्योत्पत्तिकरयागः	„
प्राणशक्तिध्यानम्	३६९	हुताहुतिसंख्या	३७६
पुरश्चरणादि । प्रयोगमन्त्रः	„	सङ्कोचमन्त्रः । भूतमन्त्रः	„
दूतीमन्त्राः । प्राणप्रतिष्ठा	३७०	गुरुलक्षणम्	३७७
प्राणप्रतिष्ठाकालः	३७१	ग्राह्यशिष्यलक्षणम्	३७८
मृतादिदूतीनां स्थानम्	„	वर्ज्यशिष्यलक्षणम्	„
स्वहृदये विशेषप्रयोगः	३७२	दीक्षितशिष्यस्याचारः	३७९
मारणे विशेषप्रयोगः	„	तन्त्रस्य पाञ्चविध्यम्	३८०

प्रयोगक्रमदीपिकासूची

प्रथमः पटलः	३८१	चतुर्थः पटलः	४६०
द्वितीयः पटलः	४३०	पञ्चमः पटलः	४९३
तृतीयः पटलः	४४५	षष्ठः पटलः	५०४

सप्तमः पटलः ५३४

अष्टमः पटलः ५५६

नवमः पटलः ५६४

शिवपञ्चाक्षरीभाष्यम् ५६५

श्लोकानुक्रमणिका ५९७

शुद्धिपत्रम्

पृष्ठे	पंक्तौ	अशुद्धम्	शुद्धम्
५	२४	रूपाऽणवो	रूपाणवो
७	२	ग्रङ्क	ग्रङ्क
८	१३	वभासिन:	वाभासिन:
२३	२	औदुभिज:	औदुभिद:
२५	१६	स्त्रिय:	स्त्रिया:
३३	२८	वैखर्या	वैखर्या
३७	८	सोषुम्न	सौषुम्न
३८	२१	साममय	सोममय
४०	१४	सर्गस्लेषित	सर्ग: स्लेषित
४०	१७	भूतेन्दिय	भूतेन्द्रिय
४६	२८	छेदा:	छेद:
४७	५	जदुगदादि	जददुगादि
४७	६	दृष्ट्वैव	दृष्ट्वै
६१	१६	मृगीर्षायै	मृगशीर्षायै
७३	२७	सूत्रद्विगुणितं	सूत्रं द्विगुणितं
८१	२१	चणैरव	चणैरेव
८३	१८	मकणाप्ता	मकणप्ता
८४	२०	संग्रन्थि	सग्रन्थि
९८	३	परमात्वनि	परमत्मानि
९८	२५	तम्बाऽ	तचाऽ
१०१	५	रन्तस्थिते:	रन्त:स्थिते
१०४	२१	जुंसं	जूंस:
११५	५	विपत्	वियत्
११९	२	पुष्य	पुष्प
१२१	३	स्तियगू	स्तिर्यगू
१२६	२७	वाक्सूत्वादि	वाक्सूत्रादि
१३१	६	वैशद्य	धीवैशद्य
१३७	२७	पुनर्वैश्य	पुनर्वंश्य
१४०	२४	तदुद्दल	तदुदल
१५५	१८	करिरेनं	कविरेनं
२१२	२३	मूविनायक	भूविनायक
२४९	८	अर्चयितणा	अर्चयितृणा
२९४	१४	यात् ब्रू	ब्रूयात्
३१५	११	चेत्युक्ता	चेत्युक्ता
३२०	१५	क्रमिते	क्रमते
३२१	२९	मितरेष	मितरेषां
३३१	२५	कस्या	कस्या:

पाठभेदाः

पृष्ठे	पङ्क्तौ	पाठः	पाठान्तरम्
८	२५	व्यक्तं मायित्वहेतुत्व	व्यक्तौ मायित्वं हेतु
११	८	नोपलभ्यते	तेनोपलभ्यते
१६	१२	तद्रूपत्वात्	तद्रूपत्वम्
१८	३	तेऽ-	ते
१८	१४	असिते	सिते
१८	१०	विंशतिस्तथा	विंशतिकस्तथा
२०	३	देवाश्च श्रुतयः	देवाः सश्रुतयः
२८	१३	तस्याः	तस्यां
३३	२८	अध्यात्म	अध्यात्मं
३७	६	सुषिरोदर	सुषिरोदित
४०	२७	मण्डलमन्त्रैः	मण्डलत्रयमन्त्रैः
४८	१३	संस्थितिः, संस्थिति	संस्थितेः, संस्थिते
५४	६	समुत्पत्त्या	समुद्भूत्या
५८	१२	बलौ	बलेः
६१	४	स्यादन्यो	स्यादतो
८२	११	प्रोक्ताः	शुक्ला
८२	१२	समानवर्णा	समाने
८३	१२	क्रमशो	कलशे
८३	२८	सवितृ	सवितुः
८५	६	मनसावुदीर्य	मनसो उदीर्यं
८८	५	शिखया	शिखाथो
९०	२१	पत्रान्तरम्	पत्रद्वयम्
९०	२२	निवेद्य । पात्र	निवेद्यपात्र
९०	२३	निवेद्य । जातं	निवेद्यजातं
९२	१४	पादि	सादि
९३	१४	ततोऽग्निमनुना तेन	ततोऽग्निं मनुनाऽनेन

पृष्ठे	पङ्क्तौ	पाठः	पाठान्तरम्
१०१	४	मन्त्रेषु	तन्त्रेषु
१०२	८	जठरानलयो	जठराननयो
१०५	२	ध्यानेन	ध्यानैश्च
११०	१५	तेजस्त्वमह	तेजस्त्वह
११५	१४	ततोऽर्धं	तदर्धं
१२२	८	भुवनान्त	भुवनात्म
१३१	२२	ब्सूं स्त्रौं	ब्लूं स्त्रौं
१३२	१०	मिति परा	मिति परपरा
१३४	६	परपरा	परावरा
१३६	३	विंल्वभव	बिंल्वदल
१३८	३	मुखेनाऽनारत	मुखे नानारस
१५१	४	कोणान्तदुर्वी	कोणान्तदुं वी
१७५	८	द्वादशा	वा दशा
२८५	६	वाराहे विष्णवभि	वराहविष्णवभि
३१८	२९	भक्तान्	भक्तात्
३१८	२८	सत्यादा	सेत्यादा
३२१	१८	रादित्यो	रादित्ये

मूलेऽपि क्वचित् क्वचित् पाठभेदा बन्धनीमध्यगता द्रष्टव्याः ।

INTRODUCTION.

THE Prapancha is the extended universe composed of the five elements (Mahābhūta) or "Ether," "Air," "Fire," "Water," "Earth." The title of the work, therefore, means the essence, or the account, of the Prapancha.

This celebrated text is attributed to the great philosopher and devotee Shaṁkarāchārya. At the time printing was commenced it had not been previously published but after the receipt of the Text from the press and when this Introduction was being prepared, the nineteenth and twentieth volumes of the collected works of Shaṁkara were published by the Vā*n*ī Vilāsa Press, at Srirangam, Madras, containing the present work. An examination, however, of its text has shown it to contain some errors and therefore this present edition, even apart from the Introduction which follows, will not prove to be unnecessary.

In preparing this edition use has been made of three manuscripts : one in the possession of the Asiatic Society of Bengal ; another the property of the Varendra Anusandhāna Samiti of Rajshahi ; and a third belonging to Sj. Ak*sh*aya Kumāra Maitra. This third manuscript was formerly the property of the late Achalānanda Swāmī and is, according to the information of one of his Shi*sh*yas, in the Guru's own handwriting.

As I have said this work is in India currently attributed to Shaṁkara the author of the Shārīrakabhā*sh*ya and was, therefore, included in the collection above mentioned. The author of the Prapanchasāravivara*n*a states that Shiva is the author of this work through his incarnation (Avatāra) the philosopher Shaṁkara. The names of other Shaṁkaras occur in Tantrik literature such as the son or Kamalākara the author of the Vāsanātattvabodhinī or Tārārahasyav*ri*ttikā, and the Shaṁkara who is a commentator upon the *Shat*chakranirūpa*n*a published as the second volume of this series. The colophon at the end of the Madras edition refers to its composer as Bhagavān Shaṁkarāchārya, a title which is only applied to the author of the Shārīrakabhāshya who is believed to have been an incarnation of Shiva Himself. It is not stated, however, whether that colophon appears in the manuscript from which the Madras edition was prepared. In the three manuscripts on which this edition is based there is no such colophon. Whether, however, the work is rightly accredited is another question. It is common knowledge that in the history of all religions, works are attributed to great names to gain for them an authority which their real author could not perhaps have achieved. Doubtless some writings which pass under the great name of Shaṁkara are not really his. I have pointed this out in connection with one of the hymns attributed to him and which I have published (1) in collaboration with my wife Ellen Avalon. So again we find the Tārāpajjhaṭikā Stotra (which is given in the Tantrik compendium the Tārārahasyavṛittikā above mentioned) attributed to Shaṁkarāchārya though the same hymn is elsewhere in another manuscript ascribed to the Atharvanīyo Upanishad (2). In support of the accredited authorship I have been referred, in addition to the general style, and authoritative tone of the work, to the 59th verse of the 20th Paṭala where in enumerating the different Avatāras the name of Buddha is omitted. Now Buddha has been recognised as one of the ten Avatāras from the days of the Purāṇas to those of Jayadeva. It has, therefore, been suggested that only an author of the authority of Shaṁkarāchārya who in particular strongly combated the Buddhist doctrines would have presumed thus to run counter to such a recognised tradition. On the other hand, in one of the smaller hymns attributed to Shaṁkarā chārya Buddha is recognised as one of the Avatāras. Further in support of the accredited authorship we have the fact that both Rāghave Bhaṭṭa in his commentary on the Shāradātilaka and Kālīcharaṇa in his *Shaṭ*chakranirūpaṇa refer to the author of the Prapanchasāra as Shrīmadāchārya by which term the great Shaṁkara alone is meant. I leave however others, who may think that the contents of the work itself notwithstanding its authoritative tone and general style tell against the tradition as to its authorship, the developement of their thesis.

Whoever the author may be the Tantrik character of the text admits of no doubt. It is constantly cited as an

1. Hymns to the Goddess, page 95.
2. The name of the Upanishad is given as it appears in the manuscript.

authority in other Tantrik works, notably by Rāghava Bhaṭṭa, one of the greatest of Tantrik commentators, the author of the Bhāshya on the celebrated Shāradātilaka of Lakshmaṇāchārya. It is also referred to by Kālīcharaṇa in his notes on the *Shaṭchakranirūpaṇa* and by Vishvanātha in the *Shaṭchakravivṛiti* and by many others. The work is not only frequently quoted, but it has been the subject of several commentaries, among others the Prapanchasārasambandhadīpikā, the Prapanchasāravivaraṇa, and the Prapanchasārasārasaṁgraha; the last two dealing chiefly with ritual and Mantra. Further than this, the philosophical doctrine relating to sound-creation, the general terminology, Devatās of worship and the ritual character of its contents from the sixth chapter to the end of the work make any further elaboration of this point unnecessary which will be obvious to any one who is conversant with the Tantras and the present text. For others I need only for example draw particular attention to the reference to the Tantrik Bhūtashuddhi rite; the detailed account in the ninth chapter of the worship of Tripurāvidyā and to Japa, Bīja, Yantra, Mudrā and so forth which, as H. H. Wilson (1) long ago pointed out, are distinguishing marks of Tantrik ritual.

Having, however, regard to the alleged authorship the question may be asked, whether the work should be described as a Tantra or Tantrik text, such as, for instance the Shāradātilaka, Shāktānandataraṁgiṇī and like works. If it be not an original Tantra then the authoritative style and form of the work would render it more akin to the Shāradā than to the Shāktānandataraṁgiṇī. Tantrasāra, and other similar works which do not profess to be anything but compendia. The Madras edition says—Bhagavat Shrī Shaṁkarāchārya-virachita; that is, "composed or compiled by Bhagavān Shaṁkarāchārya." If it be the fact that it is the original composition of Shaṁkarāchārya then unless we can regard the work as the teaching of Shiva in his Avatāra as the great philosopher it would not be a Tantra in the proper sense of the term. For such a view however there is the authority of the statement of the Prapanchasāravivaraṇa to which I have referred. Still less would the text be such a Tantra if the author was some other Shaṁkara. On the other hand, the form in which the work appears is that of a discourse of the Mahāvishṇu in answer to questionings by

(1) Essays II. 33.

Brahmā. An old and learned Orissan Pa*nd*it to whom this question was referred stated to me his opinion to be that Shaṁkara was not the author of the work but its redactor or compiler, thus occupying the same position in regard to it as the *Rishis* did to the Vaidik Shruti. The question has importance because, amongst other reasons, of the fact that the Mahāsiddhasāra Tantra includes a Tantra called the Prapanchasāra amongst the group of 64 assigned to the Rathakrāntā (1). Whether the Tantra there referred to is the text before us I cannot say. It may be another of the same name. Thus we find in the group of Tantras mentioned by the Mahāsiddhasāra the Panchadashī. All are aware that the Panchadashī is not a Tantra but a Vedāntik treatise. It is possible, however, that a Tantra was also so-called just as there is one which is entitled Matsyasūkta. I have been informed, though I have not yet seen any such manuscript, that there was an ancient Tantra called Prapanchapanchaka, and it has been suggested that the text before us is a summary of that work. The title is not inconsistent with such view. For " sāra " may here refer either to the essence of the material world (prapancha) or to a summary of the Prapanchapanchaka though in that case the title would more properly be Prapanchapanchakasāra in the sense of the world " sāra " as used in the title of the well-known treatise of K*rishn*ānanda, the Tantrasāra.

Whatever be the authorship, the question last discussed seems to be concluded by the statement contained in the work itself. For at v. 62, Chapter 36, Mahāvi*shn*u says, "Oh Lotus-born ! in this Tantra (Tantre' smin) I have shown thee the Prapancha in its five-fold aspect" (2).

The text is a very important one and service would be rendered by its complete translation. A summary of the work which deals with the worship of all the Devatās is as follows :—

---

1. see Introduction to my edition of the first part of "Principles of Tantra".

2. It must however be noted that the word Tantra is sometimes used in a wider sense, that is, in a sense in which it is not an original Tantra *e. g.*, the Shāradā speaks of itself as a Tantra. See Introduction to my "Principle of Tantra," Vol. I.

[Padmapāda says the five-fold aspects are ;—Sthūla, Sūk*sh*ma, Kāra*n*a, Sāmānya, Sāk*sh*i.]

CHAPTER I.

At the close of the period of dissolution (Pralaya) Brahmā Vi*sh*nu and Rudra (1) who are respectively distinguished by the Gu*n*as (Gu*n*aprabhinna) Rajas, Sattva and Tamas, appeared. Wondering how it was that they came into being and the object thereof, they approached Nārāya*n*a (here the Mahāvi*sh*nu) then resting in the Ocean of Nectar and began to sing His praises. Pleased thereat He displayed to Them His great and beauteous form ; the sight whereof awed and astounded them.

Brahmā then said "Oh Lord, be merciful and tell us who we are and whence we have sprung ; what is our cause and what is that which we are to do (Kriyā)".

Nārāya*n*a replied "You have been brought forth by the Eternal Imperishable (Ak*sh*ara). Your respective work is to create, to preserve and to destroy".

Brahmā then asked "What is the Eternal Imperishable ; what is Its nature ; whence has It come ?"

Nārāya*n*a replies with a discourse on the creation of the world and teaches Brahmā, Vi*sh*nu, and Rudra the nature of Puru*sh*a and Prak*ri*ti (2) or Pradhāna (3) the two supreme Tattvas (4). Of the twenty-five Tattvas, Puru*sh*a and Prak*ri*ti are stated by the Mahāvi*sh*nu to be eternal (Nitya) Prak*ri*ti extending over and enveloping the whole universe "including Thee Oh Brahmā and Myself Nārāya*n*a." Of Prak*ri*ti the latter says "She knows Herself. None know Her but I as Kāla only." "Kāla it is," He says, "who effects Vik*ri*ti or change in Prak*ri*ti with Her three gu*n*as, Sattva, Rajas and Tamas (5) which exist throughout the whole universe and permeate all the Vikāra*s* (6)". The Mahāvi*sh*nu continues His discourse of which the following is a summary.

---

1. For they are the effect of the working of Prak*ri*ti and manifest Her gu*n*as though in different proportions according to their specific activities.

2. See note at p. 29 *post*.

3. See note at p. 29 *post*.

4. Prak*ri*ti is the invisible ultimate source as *noumenal* matter of all manifestation through whose contact with Puru*sh*a the whole universe arises.

5. With their characteristics of happiness, sorrow, and delusion and functions of revealing, inciting to activity and veiling or suppressing, respectively. Gu*n*a is that which works for another as they do for Puru*sh*a. See my Introduction to the Mahānirva*n*a Tantra under the heading "Gu*n*a." (1st Ed.).

6. Or effect or transformations of Prak*ri*ti.

Prakriti by contact with the light (Jyotih) (1) is Chinmātrā (2). In the desire to create She "solidifies" or "thickens" (Vichikīrshur ghanībhūtā) and appears as Bindu (3). Through the instrumentality of Kāla the Bindu divides itself into three, *viz.*, Sthūla (gross) Sūkshma (subtle) and Para (supreme). These are Bīja, Nāda (4) and Bindu (5) respectively. On this self-division of the supreme Bindu there arises an inarticulate sound (Avyaktarava) (6) which is the Shabda-Brahman or Sound Brahman (7). The latter is beyond speech (Avāchya) and is understandable to Itself alone (Svasaṁvedyasvarūpa) (8). The wise know "sound" to be the Shabda-Brahman. It permeates all substance and in the animal body exists as the five "elements" (Panchabhūtātmakadeha).

From this sound originates Mahat (9) or Buddhi and from the latter Ahaṁkāra which is threefold: Vaikārika,

---

1. Purusha.

2. That is, She who is in the first place Tattva (mere "thatness") quickens under the influence of Chit or consciousness which according to the Sāṁkhya system She reflects ; then She longs to create (Vichikīrshu) and "solidifies" (Ghanībhūtā) and appears as Bindu. *See* post and notes. The verse is quoted variously and reads also Chinmātra referring to the Light.

3. That is the Kārana or Causal Bindu which the Brahman becomes after passing from its state in Pralaya to that called Vichikīrshā when Karma ripens. As to the meaning of this, see Arthur Avalon's Introduction to "The Serpent Power."

4. Sā tattvasaṁjnā chinmātrā jyotishah sannidhestadā.
Vichikīrshurghanībhūtā kvachidabhyeti bindutām.
Kālena bhidyamānastu sa bindurbhavati tridhā.
Sthūla-sūkshma-paratvena tasya traividhyamishyate.
Sa bindur nādabījatvabhedena cha nigadyate.

Ch. 1. 41, *et Seq.*

5. That is, the Kārya or effect Bindu as Nāda is the Kriyā Bindu.

Another reading, given by Kālicharana, substitutes dvidhā for tridhā in the third line and the remaining lines also differ. According to this version the division is twofold into Hang and Sah (*See* Vol. II, Tantrik Texts, p. 66), the combination being Hangsah.

See Woodroffe's Shakti and Shākta and Garland of Letters.

6. *See* as to this, Rāghavabhatta's commentary on the Shāradātilaka and Woodroffe's Shakti and Shākta.

7. So also the Shāradātilaka says :-

Bhidyamānāt parādvindoravyaktātmā ravo'bhavat.
Shabdabrahmeti taṁ prāhuh.

Ch. 1. 11, 12.

8. Thus, (to illustrate the meaning of this term), whereas others may see in me a man I alone really know what a man is, and what I am. One must be a thing to know what it is. The existence of Prakriti is only inferrible from Her effects which exist in their cause.

9. It is said that this word does not, as is generally supposed, mean "great" but is derived from Maghas which means Light (Jyotih).

Taijasika, and Bhautika (1). From Ahaṁkāra issued the five Tanmātras (2); from which were developed the five gross elements (Mahābhūtas) (3) *viz.*, "ether," "air," "fire," "water," "earth" (4). From Ahaṁkāra through Shakti with Guṇa and Doṣha (5) urged by Kāla, sound is produced and from sound, ether (Ākāsha); from ether, air (Vāyu); from air, fire (Agni); from fire, water (Jala); and from water, earth (Pṛithivī). The Maṇḍala of ether is circular and of air hexagonal (6); of fire triangular; that of water resembles a crescent moon and that of earth is square. Ether contains air, and air, fire; fire contains water, and water, earth; and in earth is all that is moving and motionless in the universe (7). From Ahaṁkāra also issue the five organs of action (Karmendriya), namely the anus, feet, genitals, mouth and hands the functions of which are excretion, walking, procreation, speech and the power to hold; the five organs of knowledge (Jnānendriya), *viz.*, eye, ear, nose, tongue and skin; and the internal sense (Manas).

(From the combination of these elements the whole material world or Prapancha is produced) (8). Mūlaprakṛiti is Prakṛiti only; but Mahat, Ahaṁkāra and the five Tanmātras, these seven are both Prakṛiti and Vikṛiti (9). The remaining sixteen Tattvas, *viz.*, the ten Indriyas, Manas, and

---

1. That is the pure, passional, and dark or elemental aspects of Ahaṁkāra in which the guṇas Sattva, Rajas and Tamas predominate, respectively. According to the Sāṁkhya the first produces the eleven senses, the last the Tanmātras or causes of the gross elements (bhūta). and the second produces both. According to the Shaiva school the first is said to produce Manas, the second the ten senses, and the third as above. *See* Bhāskararāya's Comm. on Lalitāsahasranāma v. 397.

2. The subtle, imperceivable (to ordinary sense), "thing in itself," of which there are five, *viz.*, Shabda (sound), Sparsha (touch), Rūpa (form and sight), Rasa (taste), Gandha (smell) : that is, sound as such, touch as such etc..

3. Perceivable by the senses in those products which are made up of them.

4. So ether (Ākāsha) arises from the Shabda-Tanmātra and its Guṇa is Shabda. The word "element" is here retained for default of any better term though the "ether" etc., here spoken of are not to be confounded with the elements air, fire, earth, and water, in an English sense.

5. *See* post, p. 11 *et seq.*

6. Not in the ordinary sense of a hexagon but of a figure with six points which is formed by two equilateral triangles (one reversed) superimposed.

7. That is, all things may be resolved into "earth" : the latter is sublimed into water, and water into fire and so on, until ether is reached which potentially contains them all.

8. The parentheses in English here and later on are added to the text in a form which gives continuity to the summary.

9. That is both cause and effect : they are each the effect of the preceding cause and the cause of the succeeding effect. Prakṛiti is Cause. "The seven" or Mahat,

the five Mahābhūtas are purely Vikriti. They are called the sixteen Vikāras. The eight Prakritis are Avyakta (1), Mahat, Ahamkāra and the five Tanmātras the last seven being also Vikritis of Prakriti. The Karanas (2) are Buddhi, Ahamkāra, Chitta and the Indriyas both Jnāna and Karma (3).

Nārāyana then gives the divisions of time from the minutest, namely the Lava to the duration of Brahmā's life (or a period of 36,000 days and nights, each of 8,640,000,000 human years duration) as follows :—

1 Lava = the time it takes to pierce a lotus leaf with a needle.
30 Lavas = 1 Truti.
30 Trutis = 1 Kalā
30 Kalās = 1 Kāshthā.
30 Kāshthās = 1 Nimesha.
8 Nimeshas = 1 Mātrā which is equal to one breath (Shvāsa).
360 Shvāsas = 1 Danda or Nādikā.
2 Nādikās = 1 Muhūrtta.
30 Muhūrtas = 1 day and night.
30 days and nights = 1 month.
12 months = 1 human year.

1 human year = 1 day and night of the Devas.
360 days of the Devas = 1 celestial year.
12,000 celestal years = 1 age (Four Yugas).
1,000 Yugas = 1 day of Brahmā.
1,000 Yugas = 1 night of Brahmā.
30 such days and nights of Brahmā = 1 month of Brahmā.
12 months of Brahmā = 1 year of Brahmā.
100 years of Brahmā } = the period of the life of Brahmā.
The duration of Brahmā's life } = that of the outgoing breath (nishvāsa) of Kāla, (Nārāyana).

The sun, moon, fire and all Devatās are in constant movement for the preservation of the world. (The close of the day of Brahmā or Kalpa is followed by a night of Brahmā and this is what is called the intermediate dissolution or Pralaya of which there are as many as there are nights in the life of Brahmā. At the close of Brahmā's life with the in-drawn breath of Kāla there is the great dissolution or Mahā-pralaya). "At the time of dissolution", says Nārāyana, "all the universe re-enters Prakriti".

Nārāyana then treats of the generation of bodies. In Prakriti when moved by Kāla, there are four kinds of bodies, namely, those which spring from the ground (Audbhida) those from moisture (Svedaja) ; those which issue from eggs (Andottha) and lastly such as have their origin in the

---

Ahamkāra and the five Tanmātras are both cause and effect ; and the "sixteen" or the eleven senses (Indriya) including Manas and the five elements (bhūtas) are effects only. Purusha is neither cause nor effect. All effects exist in their causes. Prakriti and Purusha have themselves no cause.

1. Mūlaprakriti or unmanifested Prakriti whom the Pancharātra Agama calls "the one Mother of the universe the Mother of the Scriptures, Sarasvatī who has no origin." Vyakta on the other hand is Mahat and the other categories for they are manifested.

2. A Karana is that by which another thing is done, an instrument or agent.

3. The inner agents (antah-karana) are Buddhi, Ahamkāra, Chitta and Manas which sums up in itself and presides over the ten outer agents or senses (Indriyas) of knowledge and action.

uterus. Motionless things (such as trees, *etc.*), are called Audbhidas as they pierce through the ground. The Svedajas originate from the combination of the five elements. The A*nd*ajas or A*nd*otthas are produced by Shukra (semen) and Sho*n*ita (female ovum), and are formed into a ball. The Jarāyuja sprung from the uterus is the result of sexual intercourse. It is born with a body which contains the twentyfour Tattvas. Vāyu ("air") or nerve force takes the discharged semen and then mingles it with the seed of the Sho*n*ita. The seed of the female is called Māyīya and that of the male is Kārmaka. The uterine air nourishes the united seeds (Bīja) which are called Ā*n*ava and in which, in subtle forms, the twentyfour Tattvas exist. If there be a preponderance of Sho*n*ita the child becomes a female; if the proportions are even the child becomes a hermaphrodite and when Shukra predominates then the child becomes a male. The combined seeds in the course of the day by the action of air, fire and water solidify into a body the size of the mother's thumb Next day the embryo becomes a frothy body (budbudākāra). In the course of fifteen days it becomes quadrangular in shape and draws nourishment from the food taken by the mother. In time by the action of Vāyu (in the uterus) a straight long Nā*d*ī (nerve or artery) called Su*sh*umnā is produced.. The mouth of the Nā*d*ī is downward (that is, in the Mūlādhāra). There is a Nā*d*ī on each side of it. That on the left is I*d*ā and that on the right is Piṁgalā. With these seven other Nā*d*īs are connected. I*d*ā, connected with the left scrotum, encircles Su*sh*umnā, passes by the right hip, goes to the heart—and thence passing by the left shoulder proceeds to the right nostril. Piṁgalā originating from the right scrotum goes in a similar way to the left nostril.

The other Dhamanīs (Nā*d*īs) above mentioned are Gāndhārī, Hastijihvā, Pu*sh*ā, Alambu*sh*ā, Yashasvinī, Shaṁkhinī and Kuhu. These are ramified all over the body. The embryo continues to increase drawing its nourishment from the food taken by the mother through a Nā*d*ī which is attached to the wall of the uterus. As it goes on increasing it receives a part (Kalā) of the Supreme Light (Paraṁ jyoti*h*) and this Kalā is consciousness (K*sh*etrajnatā). The body which is thus possessed of consciousness is compounded of the elements (Bhautika) and has qualities of its own (Sagu*n*a). In the case of the male the testicles fully exist; but in the case of the hermaphrodite only slightly. The female embryo has none.

Besides the central Nā*d*ī Su*sh*umnā there are various other Nā*d*īs with branches and sub-branches and altogether they are 350,000 in number. Vāyu (v. *post* p. 11) passes through the body by means of these Shirās (Nā*d*īs). Vāyu is spread all over the body from the Mūlādhāra upwards proceeding along I*d*ā and Pimgalā towards the nostrils and thereafter stops at a distance of twelve fingers breadth therefrom. There is a constant upward and downward movement of Vāyu along the paths of the sun and the moon (1). Vāyu goes to the north by the left ; to the south by the right. Different views are held about this consciousness (Chetanā). Some speak of it as the effect of Shukra and Sho*n*ita ; others as produced by the food taken by the mother. Others again say that it is the product of the Rasa (essence, juice) of the food or lymph chyle. Some speak of it as the effect of Karma ; others as a manifestation (Vyāpti) of the Paraṁ Dhāma (Supreme Light). Some again say that the body and the Ātmā of the father repeatedly act and re-act the one upon the other with the result that the lustrous Supreme Light is communicated by Māruta (Vāyu) to the Shukra as it were the light from one lamp to another. Others say that when the material body of elements (Bhautika) is born the Jīvātmā comes from somewhere and enters it (2).

Nārāya*n*a then says that the great (Mahīyasī) Prak*ri*ti is distinguished by the Gu*n*as (Gu*n*abhinnā) and is Trido*sh*ā (v. *post*). She pervades and possesses the qualities (Gu*n*a) of the five elements. The seven substances or fundamental principles (v. *post*) are Her characteristics. She is Saptadhātubhinnā. She is in the Indriyas : both in the five Karmendriyas, and in the five Jnānendriyas. She is Panchabuddhiprabhāvinī. She issues from the unmanifested state when quickened by Her proximity to the Supreme Light. When She is well awakened by the Supreme Light then She is Manas and of great power and is in the state of certainty-uncertainty (Saṁkalpavikalpak*ri*tyā). When in the act of determining with certainty (nishchinute) then She is called Buddhi or determination. When She knows Herself as the knower She is Ahaṁk*ri*ti (Ahaṁkāra). When She withdraws into Herself (abhilīyate) She is Herself alone. When She the Great One moves to manifest Herself in Her different ways then the sound which issues upon the bursting of the Bindu becomes clearly perceptible.

---

1. That is, I*d*ā and Pimgalā.
2. These views are rejected by Nārāya*n*a.

CHAPTER II.

Matured in this way the embryo goes on increasing at every moment of time. It is first composed of six parts, *viz.*, head, two hands, two legs, and the middle portion. Consciousness then enters these six parts. If the three Dos*h*as *viz.*, Vāta or Vāyu, Pitta, Kapha are favourable then eyes, nose, mouth, ears, cheeks, chin, chest, belly, breasts and so forth are formed.

[At this point it is necessary to make an explanatory digression. These three terms are generally translated air, bile, and phlegm. While, however, they have this significator they, however, mean a great deal more (1). Vāyu is not atmospheric air nor is it an effete material such as gas generated during the process of digestion. Sushruta defines it as a force which sets the whole organism in motion. It is the principal factor which determines the genesis, continuance and disintegration of the living body. Its vibration takes a course as the controller of the correlative functions of the system. Taking into consideration the various functions which the living body has to perform this Vāyu is classified into Prā*n*a, Apāna, Samāna, Vyāna and Udāna which are said to correspond with the divisions of functions performed by the cerebro-spinal and sympathetic nerves of Western physiology. The Tantras abound in description of the Nā*dī*chakras (nerve plexuses) and give detailed accounts of the motor, sensory, and mixed nerves according to differences in their functions and relations.

In Chapter XV of the Sūtrasthānam of the Sushruta it is said that the imparting of motion to the body (Praspandanam), the carrying of the sensations of the respective sense organs (Udvahanam), the passing down of food to its proper receptacles (Pūra*n*am), the separation of excretions from the assimilated food matter (Viveka), and the retention and evacuation of urine, semen, etc., (Dhāra*n*am) should be ascribed to the functions of the five kinds of Vāyu which support the body.

---

1. For what follows on the medical side I am indebted and refer my reader to the Sushruta Saṁhitā, an English translation of which with a very useful introduction has been published at Calcutta by Kavirāja Kunjalāla Bhis*h*agratna.

In short the term Vāyu not only means nerve-force but is extended to include any kind of electro-motor or molecular force (as when we speak of the Vāyu of the soil) though the term is now loosely applied to signify gas or air.

The functions of the Pitta consists in metamorphosing the chyle to protoplasmic substance and is thus said to correspond to the metabolism of Western physiology. It means both bile and metabolism of tissues as well as the bodily heat which is the product of the latter. All metabolic processes in the organism whether constructive or destructive are called Pitta which is said to be in the products of those processes whether serum, bile, blood, albumen, *etc.*, which are either essential to the substance of the body or to the proper performance of any organic function. It also has five sub-divisions according to functions and locations, *viz* :— Pāchaka, Ranjaka, Sādhaka, Ālochaka and Bhrājaka ; or digestive heat or bile ; pigment ; rhythmic cardiac contractions ; the Pitta of sight and in the skin. The Sushruta Samhitā in the Chapter cited says that pigmentation (Ranjaka), digestion and metabolism of tissues (Pāchaka), the vitalisation and nutrition of protoplasmic cells (Oja*h*k*ri*t), origination of the faculty of intellection (1) (Medhāk*ri*t) (these last two coming under the common heading Sādhaka), the origination and preservation of eyesight (Ālochaka) and the germination of heat and maintenance of bodily temperature (Bhrājaka) are the functions of the five kinds of Pitta which contribute to the preservation of the body through its fiery or thermogenetic potency (Agni-karma).

Kapha or Shle*sh*mā is also of five kinds the functions of which according to Sushruta are the lubrication of the interior of the joints ; contributing to the gloss of the body, to the formation of healthy granules in sores , to the size of the body ; building fresh tissues ; imparting a pleasant or soothing sensation to the body ; increasing its strength and giving firmness to the limbs and thereby contributing to the welfare of the body by supplying it with its watery element.

---

1. The Editor of the work last cited, after stating that Sādhaka which is situated in the heart indirectly assists in the performance of cognitive functions by keeping up the rhythmic cardiac contractions, says that it was perhaps this view of the heart's construction which predisposed many ancient Indian physiologists to hold it to be the seat of cognition (Buddhisthānam).

At every moment the animal body dies. The etymological significance of the term Sharīra (body) which comes from the root Sh*ri* "to wither up" testifies to ancient knowledge of the combustion which is taking place at every moment in the human system. The internal fires would unduly feed upon its constituent principles were it not for the cooling and watery principle of Shles*h*mā which surcharging it with its own essential humidity keeps intact the integration of its component molecules. The Rasa or lymph chyle which is formed out of the ingested food prevents the internal bodily fires from preying upon the vitals by coursing freely throughout the whole organism. The Rasa thus generated undergoes a kind of purification, the purified portion being called Prasādabhūta and the excreted portion Malabhūta. Kapha or Shles*h*mā is that portion of Rasa which fills all the intercellular spaces of the body thus holding them together in a kind of cooling embrace (1) and prevents the combustion which would otherwise have been caused by organic heat.

Thus "air" is the correlative, as "fire" and "water" are the sustentative functions which, with generation, constitute the threefold activities of living matter. The lymph chyle or Rasa produced by the digested food potentially contains the elements (Dhātu) which build up the human organism through physiological metamorphosis. Vāyu, Pitta and Kapha are thus fundamental principles of the human economy or the primary subtle dynamics of organic life, when in virtue of their correlative and sustentative functions, they ensure an equipoise among the different vital and physiological processes, essential to its perfect health. But when the equilibrium is disturbed, pathological conditions arise which form the *esse* of disease and then they are said to be transfromed into Dos*h*as or morbific diathesis (2). They are denominated as Malas when observed in grosser or superficial principles of the organism producing those excretions or organic lesions which are the sphere of morbid anatomy. Thus Vāyu, Pitta and Kapha embrace both the biological and pathological principles of the organism. The same

---

1. The root Shli*sh* means "to embrace." Vāyu comes from the root Vā (be move) and Pitta according to the auther cited comes from "tap" (to burn) from which he says it should be inferred that motion, heat, and union and integration are the respective attributes of the vital Vāyu, Pitta and Kapha or Shles*h*mā, (Vol. I. P. 195.)

2 Thus blood which is a fundamental substance (dhātu) of the organism may be designated a dos*h*a when owing to congestion it produces a pathological condition.

principles which sustain the organism are transformed into the dynamics of disease and the grosser excretory changes and organic lesions which form the subject of morbid anatomy and are sometimes confounded with the disease itself. It is, therefore, incorrect to translate Vāyu, Pitta and Kapha as "air", "bile" and "phlegm" except under those circumstances in which they are transfromed into Malas but they are not "air", "bile" and "phlegm" in those planes of their functions which determine the genesis, growth and continuance of the organism as well as its death, decay and disintegration. These principles thus embrace the whole sphere of organic existence (1).]

The text then continues as follows : The embryo is moved by Vāyu at the time of delivery, It issues with its head downwards causing great pain to its mother. At that time its eyes and nose are (in the uterus which is itself steeped) in the filth of the mother's intestines and it repeatedly thinks of the thousands of sins committed by itself in previous births (which have caused it to be thus re-born). It is tormented by the heat of the mother's body and is smeared with her secretions. Its body which is rolled up into a ball is agitated by Vāyus moving in all directions. It is at this time that it longs for Liberation (Moks*h*a).

Before this period Prā*n*a and other Vāyus had lodged themselves in its body, Apāna and Prā*n*a now pull against one another. When Samāna fans the fire of digestion then Vyāna goes with the extract produced thereby (Rasa) all over the body. Udāna accompanies Prā*n*a. Nāga causes belching. Kūrmaka causes movement of the eyelids (1), K*ri*karaka causes hunger ; Devadatta yawning ; and Dhananjaya causes various sounds (Rava) meaning apparently motions in the body and does not leave it even after death. As there are ten airs, so there are ten fires in the body, Of these, seven fires are in the seven substances (Dhātus) and three in sweat (Sveda), phlegm (Kleda) and entrails (Antra). The Dhātus are skin (Tvak), blood (As*ri*k), fat (Meda), bone (2) (Asthi), flesh (Māṁsa), marrow (Majjā) and semen (Shukra). They are called Dū*sh*ya or that which is affected.

---

1 *op cit* of Kavirāja Kunjalāla Bhis*h*agratna whose exposition I have above condensed and re-arranged.

2. According to the Kāmikāgama cited by Bhāskararāya (Lalitā V. 116) the first five Dhātus are derived from Devī ; and the last two together with breath and vitality (Jīva) from Shiva. The tenth substance is called Parāshakti.

Dos*h*a is that which affects and the Dos*h*as are Vāta, Pitta and Kapha (1). The universal spirit (Vishvātmā) is Samavāyī (2). Action shows whether it affects or is affected. Hunger and thirst, grief and ignorance, decay and death are known as the six Ūrmis and exist in Prā*n*a, Buddhi, and as characteristics of the body (Dehadharma). From semen originate marrow (Majjā), bone (Asthi) and nerve (Snāyu); from female ovum come skin (Tvak), flesh (Māṁsa) and blood (Sho*n*ita). These are the six (3) Kos*h*as of the body. In the Dhātus Rasa and so forth is matured (Pāka). With maturity Ojas is produced which is the eighth product (Dashā). [It is said in Part I of the Bhāvaprakāsha that "health and strength reside latent in the Oja*h* Dhātu as butter (Gh*ri*tam) lies latent in milk." What it is, is not certain. According to some it is albumen or glycogen. But the medical Editor of the Sushruta already cited says (Vol I., p. LIII) that the term has been used to denote that vital principle in the organism which is essential to the maintenance of a healthy combustion in its tissues and to the due performance of their normal functions and activities, no matter whether that principle is patent in the form of protoplasm, protoplasmic albumen, glycogen, or mucosin in accordance with the difference of their functions, geneses, and conditions of protoplasmic metabolism]. This Ojas according to the text seeks to attach consciousness (Ks*h*etrajnatā) to itself as oil seeks union with the lamp or the firmament the splendour of the thunderbolt. When fire is covered by a pot which has holes in it, the lustre of its flame issues through these apertures and illumines the surrounding space. In the same way the lustrous consciousness (Ks*h*etrajnatā) although covered by the body gathers knowledge through the different senses. Ether is in the ears, air in the skin, fire in the eye, water in the tongue and earth in the nostrils. This is how knowledge is acquired.

When Pitta moved by Vāyu dissolves the Dhātus and is itself dissolved, it also dissolves blood in Lasikā (4) and the

---

1. That is, they are the things which affect the Dhātus as above explained. In Āyurveda it is said that these three acting on the body in different ways produce various results.

2. This word is an adjective of samavāya, which means an intimate and inseparable connection between things such as that which exists between a thing and the material of which it is made.

3. External.

4. Described by Charaka as the fluid which is between the skin and the flesh.

dissolved Lasikā working forward in the direction of the skin issues in the form of particles of perspiration. When Kapha is moved upward by Vāyu and Pitta then there is Praseka of the mouth and nose—that is, apparently these organs function by salivation, dribbling, running at the nose and so forth.

Here follow some verses dealing with diseases and their causes. Thus from the taking of unwholesome food discharge from the penis (Prameha), strangury (Mūtrak*ri*chhra), diarrhœa (Graha*n*i) and other diseases arise.

It is next stated that after food of the six different tastes is introduced into the mouth it is made palatable by Kapha. The six kinds of taste of edible things are sweet, sour, salt, bitter, hot and astringent. Food first goes to the stomach (Āmāshaya) and then to the seat of bile (Pittāshaya) and through contact with it becomes pungent (Ka*t*uka). Entering the intestines it is matured by the bile. The essence (Rasa) which is produced by the process of digestion assumes the form of blood and so forth and is carried through the body by Vāyu. The refuse is collected by Anila (air). This is called the excretion. It passes into the small intestines (Graha*n*ī) and remains there for some time when it passes out by way of the anus. In a similar manner the watery part passes through the thin Nā*d*īs which spread all over the body into the bladder (Vasti). Vasti is the recipient (Ashaya) of urine (Mūtra) and is bent in shape like a bow. The water which passes out of it is called urine.

The embryo (Jantu) covered by the caul (Jarāyu) is moved by the Vāyu into the uterine passage. It is the way of all sinful beings that they strive hard to come out of the womb. "Oh Lotus-born (Brahmā)" says Nārāya*n*a, "the ways (V*ri*tti) of men are various and wonderful". It is then born and shakes with fear. It yawns and suffers from fever. It breathes heavily and cries through its terror.

The text then proceeds to deal with what is called the Bhāvas or states of sound (1). The Bhāva which first arises in the lowest Tāttvik centre, the Mūlādhāra, is called

---

1, The whole of this verse occurs in the Alaṁkara-Kaustubha as quoted in the Shabdakalpadruma with the difference that the word Tāra is substituted fo Bhāvu.

[The text epeaks of four states of sound. Acording to Padmapāda the first state Parā is divisible into four parts (pada), namely, Shūnyā, Saṁvit, Sūks*h*mā and Parā—*See* page 34 of Text.]

Parā (1). In its next state it is Pashyantī (2). When it reaches the heart (Hṛidaya) and is united with Mā or Buddhi it is called Madhyamā (3). Then in the mouth and with the desire for utterence it is known as Vaikharī (4) or uttered speech. From this last arises by the action of air (Pavana) all the letters (5).

The letters are not clearly manifested because the necessary apertures have not appeared such as the throat and the like. Until these come into existence and become the seats of pronunciation the letters remain in their place of origin (Varṇavyaktisthānasaṁstha). When the embryo reaches the stage (Bhāva) in which the thought arises, "I am knower" or "It is I who know (Jnātā'smi)" it acquires Buddhi, Ahaṁkāra and Manas. Consciousness thus increases by degrees and causes the child to become attached to its mother, father and kinsmen. Drinking abundantly of the mother's milk it cries out when it desires to suck the breasts again. The sight of father, brother and uncles makes the child happy. Through this arising attachment to the world (Saṁsāra) the child forgets its actions in previous births, the agony endured in the mother's womb, and the pain caused on its delivery therefrom. When troubled it calls to its mother in half-formed words. These words are indistinct like the confused murmur of Kuṇḍalinī (6) in the Mūlādhāra (7).

The aspects of Kuṇḍalinī are various. She, in Her threefold aspect, is the imperceptible omnipresent Shakti who is Kāma (ई), Agni (र), Nāda (ॱ). She is Tāra (8). Some call Her Shakti, others the Paramātmā (9).

1, In the bodily aspect (Adhyātma) the Kāraṇabindu resides in the Mūlādhāra as the Shakti Piṇḍa Kuṇḍalinī. Here it is in its non-differentiated condition. The Shabdabrahman remaining here is called Parā sound.

[Padmapāda says that there are seven stages of sound.]

2. That is when it proceeds with slight motion (Sāmānyaspanda) from the motionless (niḥspanda) state as far as the navel chakra (Maṇipūra) and is associated with Manas. According to some accounts the Svādhiṣhṭhāna is substituted for Maṇipūra. Bhāskararāya Lalitā, v. 80.

3. As the former sounds possessed the nature of the Kāraṇa and Kārya Bindus respectively, it is here in the Nāda state endowed with more definite motion (Visheṣhaspanda). *ib.*

4. Here it is in the nature of the Bīja aspect with quite distinct motion (Spaṣhṭatara). *ib.*

5. Which exist in a latent or unexpressed state in the Suṣhumnā.

6. Known as Piṇḍa or She in whom all energies (Shakti) are stored (Piṇḍita).

7. The basic plexus. *See ib.* and Author's "The Serpent Power."

8. Another name for "Oṁ," (= A + U + M)

9. For the two are the same.

Her threefold aspect is that of the three Gu*n*as, the three Dos*h*as (1), three colours (2) ; Trayī (3), the three Lokas (4), the three lines (Trirekhā) (5). She is Tāra because She saves (Tāra*n*a), and Shakti because She is the support (Dh*ri*ti) of all.

In Her fourfold aspect She manifests as the Sūk-*sh*ma Kara*n*as (6) ; Jāgrat *etc.* (7).

In Her fivefold aspect She is represented by all things which are classified by five ; such as the five groups (Vargas) of letters ; the five colours (8) and the five Vāyus. (9)

In Her sixfold aspect She is the six Ko*sh*as (10), six Ūrmis (11), and six Rasas (12). She it is who forms the divisions of the six-chambered Yantra (*Shad*gu*n*ita Yantra).

In Her sevenfold aspect She is the component parts of Tāra (13), namely, A, U, M, Bindu, Nāda, Shakti and Shānta, and the component parts of H*ri*llekhā (14) or H, R, Ī, Bindu, Nāda, Shakti and Shānta. In Her sevenfold aspect—She is the regions (Lokas), Mountains (Adris), Islands (Dvīpas), Pātālas (Nether Regions), Oceans (Sindhus) (15), Planets (Grahas) (16), the Sages (Munis) (17), the Tones (Svaras) and Substances (Dhātus) (18), and all things which have a sevenfold existence.

---

1. V. *ante*, p. 11.
2. That is three colours of the three Gu*n*as—white, red, black.
3. The three Vedas—*Ri*k, Yajus and Sāman.
4. Bhū*h*, Bhuva*h*, Sva*h*, or the terrestial, upper and celestial worlds.
5. The three lines of the Akathādi triangle, *viz.* Vahni, Indu and Arka. *See* Arthur Avalon's "The Serpent Power".
6. Buddhi, Ahaṁkāra, Manas and Chitta.
7. Jāgrat Svapna, Sus*h*upti and Turīya.
8. The five elements are coloured ; transparency (ether), black (air), red (fire), white (water), yellow (earth).
9. Prā*n*a, Apāna, Samāna, Udāna, Vyāna.
10. V. *ante*, p. 11.
11. V. *ante*, p. 15.
12. Or tastes, V. *ante*, p. 16.
13. The Mantra Ong.
14. A name for the Bīja "Hrīng." As to Shakti and Shānta See p. 39, *n* 1. *post.*
15. V. *post*, notes to p. 36.
16. That is the seven planets which give their names to the days of the week. Omitting out of the nine planets Rāhu and Ketu, *viz* : Ravi or Sūrya (Sun), Soma or Chandra (Moon), Maṅgala (Mars), Budha (Mercury), V*ri*haspati (Jupiter), Shukra (Venus), Shani (Saturn). [Rahu and Ketu are not recognised as planets in Astronomical works].
17. See *post*, p. 36.
18. *Ib.*

In Her eightfold aspect She is the eight Prak*ri*tis (1), the eight Vasus (2), the eight points of the compass (3) and the eight Mothers (A*sht*amātara*h*) (4). The text then continues with the ten-fold aspect as manifested in the ten directions (5) and so forth ; the twelve-fold aspect as in the signs of Zodiac and the great twelve syllabled Mantra. Finally Shakti manifests in the fifty-fold form as the fifty letters of the Sanskrit alphabet.

CHAPTER III.

This Chapter deals with the letters of the Alphabet, which are of a three-fold character, lunar (Saumya), solar (Saura), and fiery (Āgneya). The vowels are lunar, the consonants (Sparsha) other than the Vyāpakas (6) are solar and the latter are fiery.

The letters A (अ) to Visarga (:) are vowels (Svara) some of which are short and others long. The short (Hrasva) vowels are, A (अ) I (इ) U (उ) *Ri* (ऋ) *Lri* (ऌ) and Bindu (°). The long (Dīrgha) vowels are Ā (आ) Ī (ई) Ū (ऊ) *Rrī* (ॠ) *Llri* (ॡ) and Visarga (:). The vowels E (ए) Ai (ऐ) O (ओ) and Au (औ) are not mentioned in the text probably because E (ए) is formed by long or short A (अ,आ) with long or short Ī (इ,ई) ; (ऐ) Ai by long or short A with E (ए) ; O by long or short A with long or short U ; and Au (औ) by long or short A with O. The short vowels A (अ) I (इ) U (उ) and Bindu (°) are masculine (Puṁ) : the long vowels Ā (आ) Ī (ई) and Ū (ऊ) and Visarga (:) are feminine (Strī); and the vowels *Ri* (ऋ) *Rri* (ॠ) *Lri* (ऌ) and *Llri* (ॡ) are neuter (Napuṁsaka). The text mentions the last four and the Prapanchasārasambandhadīpikā the other vowels (7).

---

1. *See ante*, p. 8.
2. Āditya, Marut, Ashvin, Indra, U*sh*as, Rudra, Vāyu and Kuvera.
3. N-S. E. & W., N-E. (Ishāna), N-W. (Vāyu), S-W. (Nairr*i*ta), S-E. (Agni),
4. *See post*, p. 35 *n*1 and p. 27.
5. *See* note (3) adding above and below.
6. That is the letters Ya (य) Ra (र) La (ल) Va (व) tālavya Sha (श), mūrdhanya *Sh*a (ष), Sa (स) Ha(ह) Lla (ळ) and K*sh*a (क्ष).
7. According to the Dīpikā these four appear (ayanasthiti) in Su*sh*umnā when Prā*n*avāyu is in that Nā*d*ī ; and by *Ri* and *Lri* there is outgoing breath (dak*shin*āyana) and by *Rri* and *Llri* ingoing breath (uttarāya*n*a).

These four exist in two states according as they are in the right or left nostril. When Prā*n*a is in the right nostril there is what is called Dak*sh*i*n*āyana and outgoing breath, and when in the left nostril Uttarāya*n*a and ingoing breath. The five short vowels manifest (1) when Prā*n*a is in the right, and the five long vowels when it is in the left nostril (2). Bindu and Visarga whose manifestations are dealt with later are the Sun and Moon respectively.

The Sparsha Var*n*as the last letter of which *viz.*, Ma (म) is the Sun and the Ātmā (3), are divided into five groups (Varga) of five letters each. The twenty-four letters (4) are the twenty-four Tattvas. The whole twenty-five letters are therefore both solar as governed by Ma the sun and elemental (Pānchabhautika).

The Vyāpakas are divided into two groups of five letters each (5), and are Fiery (Āgneya) and Pānchabhautika. They are so called because in union with the vowels (Svara) they emanate from "moon" (Shashī), "sun" (Ina) and "fire" (Agni).

From the letters of the alphabet there arise thirty-eight Kalās (6) ; Sixteen lunar (Saumya) Kalās come from the vowels ; twelve solar (Saura) Kalās come from the twenty-four conjoined Sparshas ; and ten fiery (Vahnija) Kalās from the Vyāpakas. From these Kalās the Sādhaka attains his

---

1. In other words Prā*n*a is in the south (right) with the utterance of the five short vowels.

2. *See* Dīpikā ; which also says that the short vowels are bhautika (elemental) and the long ones are of the nature of the five Kalās,—Niv*ri*tti, Prati*sh*t*h*ā, Vidyā, Shānti and Shāntyatītā. *See* also Shāradā Tilaka. Chapter 1. Pimgalāyām sthitā hrasvā i*d*āyām samgatā*h* pare. *Ib.*, Chapter 2.

3. For Ma is Bindu and the Sun or Ātmā among the letters. The Dīpikā says that by the Ātmā is meant all the animate world as a whole (jīva-samas*h*t*i) and the Supreme Spirit dwelling therein (tadantaryāmi). Shruti says 'the Sun is the Soul of the universe" (Sūrya ātmā jagatastasthu*sh*ashcha).

4. That is the Sparsha Var*n*as other than Ma.

5. That is Ya (य) Ra (र) La (ल) Va (व) and Sha (श) ; and *Sh*a (ष) Sa (स) Ha (ह) Lla (ळ) K*sh*a (क्ष).

6. Kalā means "part" ; according to the Commentary on the Ha*th*ayogapradīpikā (Ch. IV, v. I.) Kalā is a part of Nāda (Kalā nādaikadesha*h*). The Kalās are the various parts into which the Prak*ri*tic substance is considered as being divided. In every creation of the world it is said that Mūlaprak*ri*ti assumes the different gradations of Amsharūpi*n*i, Kalārūpi*n*i and Kalāmsharūpi*n*ī or manifests Herself in portions, (such as Durgā, Lak*sh*mī, Sarasvatī), in parts (such as Pu*sh*t*i, Tu*sh*ti and other secondary Devīs) and portions of parts and further sub-divisions such as all women-kind who are all venerable as manifestations of the Mahāprak*ri*ti. See H. H. Wilson's Essays on the Religion of the Hindus, pp. 245, 246, Vol. I. Here the connection between the various (letters) and the Kalās is shown and these Kalās are unfolding qualities of their cause.

desired aim. From the letters of the Tāra (1) originate the all pervading fifty Kalās which can be divided according to the five elements (Bhūtas). From these (2) originate the Shaktis and Māt*ri*s (3) and Mūrtis of Vi*sh*nu and Rudra respectively ; as also the herbs and vegetable substances (O*sh*adhi) (4).

The lunar Kalās arising from the vowels and which grant the fulfilment of desires (Kāmadāyinī) are Am*ri*tā, Mānadā, Pu*sh*ā, Tu*sht*i, Pu*sht*i, Rati, Dh*ri*ti, Shashinī, Chandrikā, Kānti, Jyotsnā, Shrī, Prīti, Aṁgadā, Pūr*n*ā, Pūr*n*ām*ri*tā.

The twelve solar Kalās which give wealth (Vasudā) connected with the letters commencing with Ka bha (कभ) and ending with *Th*a-*d*a (ठड) (5) are Tapanī, Tāpanī, Dhūmrā, Marīchi, Jvālinī, Ruchi, Su*sh*umnā, Bhogadā, Vishvā, Bodhanī, Dhāri*n*ī K*sh*amā.

The ten Kalās issuing from "fire" which are connected with the Vyāpakas and which grant Dharma (Dharmapradā) are Dhūmrā, Archi*h*, U*sh*mā, Jvalinī, Jvālinī, Visphuliṁginī, Sushrī, Surūpā, Kapilā, Havyakavyavahā. These make 38 Kalās for the fifty letters.

The text then proceeds to deal with Kalās of the Pra*n*ava. The ten Kalās which arise from Akāra (अ) (6) (Akāraprabhavā) which are Brahmā-born (Brahmajātā) and creative are *Srisht*i *Ri*ddhi, Sm*ri*ti, Medhā, Kānti, Lak*sh*mī, Dh*ri*ti, Sthirā, Sthiti, Siddhi.

The ten Kalās arising from Ukāra (उ) (Ukārotthā) which are Vi*sh*nu-born (Vi*shn*u-jātā) and preservative are Jarā, Pālinī, Shānti, Aishvarī, Rati, Kāmikā Varadā, Hlādinī, Prīti, Dīrghā.

The ten Kalās issuing from Makāra (म) are Rudra-born (Rudrajātā) and destructive and are Tīk*shn*ā, Raudrī, Bhayā, Nidrā, Tandrā, K*sh*ut, Krodhinī, Kriyā, Utkārī, M*ri*tyu.

---

1. Oṁkāra from which all the letters have originated.

These Kalās of Tāra according to the Dīpikā manifest in the workings of Prak*ri*ti (Sarvagā*h* prak*ri*tikāryavyāpinya*h*).

2. There are variant readings, *viz.*, tebhya*h* and tābhya*h* ; if the first then the letters are meant and if the second the Kalās.

3. The Shaktis and Mothers of the various manifestations of Vi*shn*u and Rudra ; the Shaktis of the latter being called Māt*ri*s.

4. V. *post.*

5. That is the first and last letter other than Ma, the second and last but one and so on are taken together, there being in all 24 letters. Thus :—Ka-Bha कभ) ; Kha-Ba (खब) ; Ga-Pha (गफ) ; Gha-pa घप) ; Nga-na (ङन) ! Cha-Dha (चध) ; Chha-Da (छद) ; Ja-Tha (जथ); Jha-Ta (झत) ; Nya-*n*a : (ञण) ; *T*a-*Dh*a (टढ) ; *Th*a-*D*a (ठड).

6. Which is in Oṁkāra which represent Brahmā just as Ukāra, and Makāra dealt with *post* stand for Vi*shn*u and Rudra.

Bindu has four Kalās, *viz.*, Pītā, Shvetā, Aru*n*ā and Asitā.

The sixteen Kalās issuing from Nāda are Niv*ri*tti, Pratishth*ā*, Vidyā, Shānti, Indhikā, Dīpikā, Rechikā, Mochikā, Parā, Sūk*sh*mā, Sūk*sh*māmritā, Jnānām*ri*tā, Āpyāyinī, Vyāpinī, Vyomarūpā, Anantā. These make 50 in all.

The text then proceeds to deal with the Vi*shn*u-mūrtis and Shaktis which have Vai*shn*ava names and the Rudra-mūrtis and Māt*ris* with Shaiva names. The Vai*shn*ava forms (Mūrtis) of the Vyanjana Var*n*as (1) are thirty-five in number, *viz.*, Chakrī, Gadī, Shārṁgī, Kha*d*gī, Shaṁkhī, Halī, Mu*sh*alī, Shūlī, Pāshī, Aṁkushī, Mukunda, Nandaja, Nandī, Nara, Narakajit, Hari, K*rishn*a, Satya, Sātvata, Shauri, Shūra, Janārdana, Bhūdhara, Vishvamūrti, Vaiku*nth*a, Puru*sh*ottama, Balī, Balānuja, Bāla, V*rish*aghna, V*rish*a, Haṁsa, Varāha, Vimala and N*ri*siṁha.

The Vai*shn*ava Shaktis (2) of the consonants are Jayā, Durgā, Prabhā, Satyā, Cha*nd*ā, Vā*n*ī, Vilāsinī, Virajā, Vijayā, Vishvā, Vinadā, Sūtadā, Sm*ri*ti, *Ri*ddhi, Sam*ri*ddhi, Shuddhi, Bhukti, Mukti, Mati, K*sh*amā, Ramā, Umā, Kledinī, Klinnā, Vasudā, Vasudhā, Parā, Parāparāya*n*ā, Sūk*sh*mā, Sandhyā, Prajnā, Prabhā, Nishā, Amoghā and Vidyutā.

The Vai*shn*ava-mūrtis of the vowels are Keshava, Nārāya*n*a, Mādhava, Govinda, Vi*shn*u, Madhusūdana, Trivikrama, Vāmana, Shrīdhara, H*rish*īkesha, Padmanābha, Dāmodara. Vāsudeva, Saṁkar*sh*a*n*a, Pradyumna, Aniruddha ; 16 in all. The Vai*shn*ava Shaktis of the vowels are Kīrti, Kānti, Tu*sht*i, Pu*sht*i, Dh*ri*ti, K*sh*ānti, Kriyā, Dayā, Medhā, Har*sh*ā, Shraddhā, Lajjā, Lak*sh*mī, Sarasvatī, Prīti, Rati ; 16 in all.

The Rudra-mūrtis of the vowels are Shrīka*nth*a, Ananta, Sūk*sh*ma, Trimūrti, Amareshvara, Arghīsha, Bhāvabhūti, Tithi, Sthā*n*u, Hara, Jhi*nt*īsha, Bhautika, Sadyojāta, Anugraheshvara, Akrūra, Mahāsena ; sixteen in all.

The Rudra-mūrtis, of the consonants are Krodhīsha Cha*nd*esha, Panchāntaka, Shivottama, Ekarudra, Kūrma, Ekanetra, Chaturānana, Ajesha, Sharva, Someshvara, Lāṁgalī, Dāruka. Ardhanārīshvara, Umākānta, Ā*sh*ā*dh*ī, Da*nd*ī, Adri, Mīna, Me*sh*a, Lohita, Shikhī, Chhagala*nd*a, Dvira*nd*a, Mahākāla, Kapālī, Bhujaṁgesha, Pi*n*ākī, Kha*d*gīsha, Vaka, Shveta, Bh*ri*gu, Nakulī, Shiva, Sambartaka ; 35 in all.

---

1. That is the letters other than the vowels : the consonants both **Sparsha** and **Vyāpaka.**

The Rudramātris of the vowels are Pūrnodarī, Virajā, Shālmalī, Lolākshī, Vartulākshī, Dīrghaghonā Sudīrghamukhī, Gomukhī, Dīrghajihvikā, Kundodarī, Ūrdhvakeshi, Vikritamukhī, Jvālāmukhī, Ulkāmukhī, Shrīmukhī, Vidyāmukhī, or 16 in all.

The Rudra-mātris of the consonants are Mahākālī, Sarasvatī, Sarvasiddhi, Gaurī, Trailokyavidyā, Mantrātmashaktī, Bhūtamātā, Lambodarī, Drāvinī, Nāgarī, Vaikharī, Manjarī, Rūpinī, Vīrinī, Kotarī, Pūtanā, Bhadrakālī, Yoginī, Shaṁkhinī, Garjinī, Kālarātri, Kurdinī, Kapardinī, Mahāvajrā, Jayā, Sumukeshvarī, Revatī, Mādhavī, Vārunī, Vāyavī, Rakshopadhārinī, Sahajā, Lakshmī, Vyāpinī, Māyā ; 35 in all.

The text here says that three kinds of Nyāsa (1) [with the Kalās and Mūrtis named] have been described as above.

Then follows the names of the fifty Oshadhis (herbs) such as Chandana (sandal), Kuchandana (red sandal), Aguru (fragrant aloe), Karpūra (camphor) and so forth.

The letters are expelled through the Sushumnā channel by air through the mouth by means of the throat and other organs (2). Utterance is of three kinds Udātta, Anudātta, and Svarita (3). also classed as Hrasva, Dīrgha and Pluta according to Mātrā

CHAPTER IV.

This Chapter deals with the Bīja Hrīṁ (which is commonly known as the Māyā Bīja). This Bīja is also called Nāda, Prāna, Jīva, Ghosha, Hrillekhā, *etc.* It is composed of the letters Ha (ह) (4), Ra (र), Ī (ई) (5) and Bindu (°) (6).

1. The Kalās are (*a*) the 38 (*b*) the 50 in Oṁkāra named and the Mūrtis (*c*) the Vaishnavamūrtis and Shaktis and the Rudramūrtis and Mātris.

2. Kanthādisthānaghattitāh ; throat (Kantha), chest (Uras) head (Shiras) root of the tongue (Jihvāmūla), teeth (Danta), nose (Nāsikā), lips (*Oshtha*), and palate (Tālu).

3. The Dīpikā cites authority to show that the first kind burns up sins (dahati pāpāni) ; the second grants moksha (mokshapradāyaka) and the last gives pleasure to the mind (āpyāyana). *See* Shāradā tilaka ch. I. 66 and ch. II. 5 and notes thereunder.

4. The Prapanchasārasambandhadīpikā referred to *post* as the Dīpikā says the Ha is Kritakritya, *i.e.*, all pervading.

5. Kāryakāranavāchimāyā according to the Dīpikā, "Māyā manifesting instrument and effect."

6. Satataṁ : or "the over existing one" according to the Dīpikā. Bhāskā-

Hakāra Bīja is Prā*n*ātmaka because it con notes the Paramātmā in conjunction with Māyā which is implied by the word Prā*n*a (1).

From Hakāra originate the vowels A (अ) to Ū (ऊ) and the six Ūrmis (2). The Mahāvi*sh*nu adds "From Hakāra have you (that is, Brahmā, Hari or Vi*sh*nu, Īshvara or Shiva) originated and it exists in all animate beings enveloping and permeating the Brahmā*nd*a (universe) with all that is moving and motionless therein." From Repha or Rakāra (र) originate the letters *Ri* (ऋ), *Rrī* (ॠ), *Lri* (ऌ), *Llrī* (ॡ) and the four Gu*n*as (3). From Īkāra (ई come the remaining six vowels including Bindu and Visarga and its Gu*n*as are the four Kara*n*as (4), Saṁghāta (5) and Chetanā. (6)

From the vowels the consonants from Ka to K*sh*a (क—क्ष) originated.

The Mahāvi*sh*nu proceeds to establish the identity of the Devatā of this Bīja (that is, Bhubaneshvarī) (7) with Ku*nd*alī and Haṁsa*h* and then to the realization of the Mahāvākya "So' haṁ" (सोऽहम्) (8). He then says that if Sa (स) and Ha (ह) of "So' haṁ" be eliminated we then get Oṁ (ओं) or the Pra*n*ava. If the latter be disjoined into its component parts then from its end (म) we get the elements beginning with Kha (ether) ; from its middle (उ) the sun and other lustrous substances ; and from the first part (अ) all sounds. This Shakti (Ku*nd*alī or Bhuvanesvarī) is the Parameshvari Shakti and produces all sounds and their meanings and therefore comprises all the 24 Tattvas. She is Savitā or the

---

rarāya citing the Mahāsvachchhanda Tantra says (Comm. Lalitā. v. 70) that there are eight notes (var*n*a) above the Bindu which in the order given are more and more subtle, *viz.*, Bodhinī, Nāda. Nādānta, Mahānāda, Vyāpikā Shakti, Ānjī, Samanī, Unmanī.

1. So the Devī is addressed in the Lalitā as Hrīṁkārī where the Commontator *loc. cit.* says (citing the Svatantra Tantra) "She it is who does creation, preservation and destruction."

2. Hunger, thirst, sorrow, ignorance (moha) decay and death.

3. Touch (sparsha), Form or Sight (rūpa), Taste (rasa) and Smell (gandha).

4 Manas, Buddhi, Ahaṁkāra and Chitta.

5. This is according to the Dīpikā—Deha or body.

6 Kāryārtha-kāra*n*a-samūha-gata chidābhāsa, that is, apparently the Chit-quickening Prak*ri*ti to be the cause of all functioning.

7. Ruler of the fourteen worlds (Bhuvanas). The Deity indicated by the Mantra Hrīṁ. *See* as to other meanings Bhāskararāya's Comm. Lalitā. v. 69 citing Tripurā. siddhānta and the Gha*t*ārgalayantra Chapter in the Dak*sh*i*n*āmūrti Saṁhitā.

8. In this connection reference may be made to pp. 66, 78 and 102 of vol. II of this series of Tantrik Texts.

Creatrix of the world (Jagatprasavakāri*n*ī). She is Gāyatrī since it is She who saves (Trā*n*ana) the singer (Gāyaka). As the embodiment of the seven groups of letters (1), She is the seven planets. The Sun is the Lord of the vowels and Maṁgala, Shukra, Budha, V*ri*haspati, Shani (2) and the Moon are the Lords of the Ka-varga (क), Cha-varga (च), Ta-varga (ट), Ta-varga (त) Pa-varga (प) and Ya-varga (य), respectively.

As all the other letters originate from the vowels so the six planets (Grahas) originate from the Sun (Savit*ri*). As the six Vargas disappear in the vowels so the six components of Hrīṁ (3) and the six chambered Yantra disappear in Bhuvaneshvarī. She is the eternal, all-pervading Shakti who shines by Her own effulgence in the Sun (4).

From Her have originated the signs of the Zodiac. The Mahāvi*sh*nu then proceeds to show how from the different letters the different signs of the Zodiac have originated. In the same way He deals with the 27 Nak*sh*atras (5) or Lunar Zodiac, Ashvinī and others.

He concludes by saying that to know Her is to be freed from all the bonds of Karma (Karmabandha) and to attain the supreme state of Vi*sh*nu (Vi*sh*no*h* paraṁ padaṁ prayāti).

CHAPTERS V & VI.

Henceforward the work deals largely with ritual which can only be described in an abbreviated form. These two Chapters deal with the subject of initiation (Dīk*sh*ā). It is so called because it produces a divine state of mind and body (Divyabhāva) and destroys (K*shin*uyāt) all evils (Duritāni). Mantra is so called because it gives understanding of the Tattva and saves (Trāyate) from fear.

1. The vowels and the vargas commencing with Ka-varga, v. *post.*
2. That is, Mars, Venus, Mercury, Jupiter, Saturn.
3. That is, Ha, Ra, Māyā (Ī), Nāda, Bindu and Shakti.
4. The Dīpikā says that here Her identity with Bharga is pointed out.
5. The system of the Nak*sh*atras or Asterisms was originally based upon the Sidereal revolution of the moon in about 27 days according to which a lunar zodiac of 27 asterisms near the ecliptic was made, so that in each night of the Sidereal month the moon entered a different asterism. Time was thus marked by defining the position of the moon without regard to its phases. *See* Dr. Barnett's Antiquities of India, p. 191, where the 27 Nak*sh*atras are fully given.

Then follows detailed rules regarding the selection of proper time and place for initiation, worship of the Vāstu Purusha (1), sacrifice (Bali), offerings and so forth. The conclusion is that Guru, Devatā and Mantra should be realised as being one and the same (Aikyaṁ).

CHAPTER VII.

This portion of the work deals with rules relating to the Sādhanā of the Devī of Speech and the Japa of Her Mantra (2). Japa is preceded by Mātrikānyāsa (2). The *Rishi* of this Mātrikāmantra (3) is Brahmā. The metre (Chhandah) is Gāyatrī. Sarasvatī is the Devatā and Her six limbs are the letters of the alphabet.

With the words, " I bow to Her the Bhāratī " (4) follows a Dhyāna or description of the Goddess (Devī) as She, in her gross (sthūla) form, is to be meditated on. She is seated on a lotus, three-eyed and of a transparent brilliancy. She is white as the moon and the jasmine flowers. The fifty different letters make Her face, hands, feet, belly and breasts which with Her buttocks are very large. On Her head are coils of hair and the crescent moon. She holds in Her right upper hand a rosary of Rudraksha beads (5) and with Her lower right hand makes Chintā-mudrā (6). In the left upper hand She holds a jar (of nectar) and in the lower left hand a book (7).

The nine Shaktis of Bhāratī are Medhā (understanding), Prajnā (wisdom), Prabhā (radiance), Vidyā (learning), Dhī (intelligence), Dhriti (constancy or steadiness), Smriti (memory), Buddhi (power of conception), Vidyeshvarī (sovereignty of all learning).

The Sādhaka with revernt devotion should worship Bhāratī, Her Shaktis and Āvarana Devatās (8) with fine perfume and flowers, incense and food.

---

1 The Genius of the ground where the Dīkshā takes place.

2. See Introduction to my book " The Serpent Power ".

3. That is, the letters A to Ksha with the Bindu superimposed.

4. The Dīpikā says that the word Bhāratī here indicates that She is subtle and Nādātmaka (in the nature of Nāda) and the word " Her " (tām) indicates that She is the Parachidātmikā Bhuvaneshvarī.

5. Seeds of the Eleocarpus ganitrus with which Japa is done.

6. A name for the jnāna-mudrā or munual gesture so called.

7. Cf. verse II of Hymn to Bhuvaneshvarī in Arthur and Ellen Avalon's " Hymns to the Goddess " at P. 35.

8. That is, attendant Devatās.

The eight Mothers are Brahmā*n*ī, Māheshī, Kaumārī, Vai*shn*avī, Vārāhī, Indrā*n*ī, Chāmu*nd*ā, Mahālak*sh*mī.

CHAPTER VIII.

The first part deals with Prā*n*āgni Homa. It commences by directing the Sādhaka as to his posture and then to meditate on the Mūlādhāra (1) in the middle of which is the "essence of Shakti" (Shaktisattva) that is Ku*nd*alinī and is surrounded by Māyā Bījas (2). Inside the Mūlādhāra is a triangle and five Ku*nd*as (fire pits) in which are the five fires Āvasathaja, Sabhya, Āhavanīya, Anvāhārya and Gārhapatya. In these five Ku*nd*as the letters are mentally offered in Homa. The Vyanjanas are divided into 7 groups and the vowels into 2 groups of eight each. Each of these groups is called after one of the nine gems (Ratna) and directions are given as to which letters should be cast into which Ku*nd*a. By these offerings the Sādhaka realises his subtle body. Details are then given of the ritual of this Homa in which mental offerings of the senses (Indriyas) and so forth are made.

The second portion after the 26th verse deals with the worship of Sarasvatī ; Her Nyāsa, Pūjā, Japa, Homa and so forth. A Hymn to Sarasvatī is given in vv. 47-60.

CHAPTER IX.

Deals with the worship of the Devī Tripurā. She is called Tripurā, because, She is the Creatrix of the three Mūrtis (3) ; and is in the three Vedas ; She too on the dissolution of the three worlds fills all space ; and existed before the Three (4) were. Her Bīja*s* are Aiṁ and Klīṁ (5).

---

1. The Chakra in the basic plexus. *See* my book "The Serpent Power" a translation of the *Shat*chakra-nirūpa*n*a published in the second volume of this series.

2. That is "Hrīṁ" v. *ante*.

3. So according to the Kālikā Purā*n*a, She is so-called because through the operation of Pradhāna Her b[illegible] became threefold as Brahmā, Vi*shn*u, Rudra. She is also threefold because the Ma*nd*ala is triangular ; the Mantra has three syllables ; there are three states (avasthā) and so forth. Some other meanings are given in the commentary to v. 178 of the Lalitā where She is addressed as Tripurāmbikā. Similarly in the *Shod*a-shistotra, She is addressed as Tripurādhivāsinī and Tristhā or "residing in the three" that is, the threefold worlds, body, states of consciousness and so forth.

4. That is, existed before the three Devas of the Trimūrti.

5. The Vāgbhava and Kāma Bījas. She has other Bījas also.

The Dhyāna is given at v. 8. The Sādhaka is directed to worship the Pīṭha, the Shaktis Vāmā and others and to draw the Navayoni-chakra and to then place a Kalasha (jar) on the Chakra and invoke the Devī therein. The Chakra is then described. The Shaktis and Mātṛkās and Bhairavas who are to be worshipped are named.

In vv. 23, 24, a description is given of a worship which has the effect of producing such amorous passion in the celestial female Spirits and Genii, Suras, Asuras, Siddhas, Yakshas, Vidyādharas, Gandharvas, Bhujaṁgas (1) and Chāraṇas (2) that they come to the Sādhaka "with gazelle-like eyes, breathing heavily, their bodies quivering with, and moist with the pearly sweat of, passion ; and throwing away their ornaments and letting their clothes fall from about them, bow themselves before him and offer to do his will".

CHAPTER X

Is concerned with the worship of Mūlaprakṛiti, Her Mantra, Homa, Abhisheka, Japa and Archana (3). For the purpose of worship She is materialised as Ambikā according to the directions of a Dhyāna which is given. She is there described as holding Pāsha (noose), Aṁkusha (goad) (4), Ishṭa (making the Varamudrā), Abhaya (making the Mudrā of that name) (5). An explanation is given of these four.

The rest of the Chapter is concerned with the ritual.

CHAPTER XI

Continues the same subject, and gives a description of Her Yantra (6), Gāyatrī, 16 Shaktis (7), 32 Shaktis (8), and 64 Shaktis (9) which are named.

1. That Nāgas or Serpent divinities.
2. The Siddhas and names following are various classes of Devayoni.
3. *See* these described in my "Shakti and Shākta" and "Garland of Letters".
4. *See* Arthur and Ellen Avalon's "Hymns to the Goddess.
5. The gestures of granting boons and dispelling fear.
6. Diagram used in worship.
7. Vv. 11, 12.
8. Vv. 12-16, including Sinībālī, Kālarātri, Mahārātri, Kapālinī, Mahishamardinī, Indrāṇī, Rudrāṇī.
9. Vv. 16-24, including Prakṛiti, Vikṛiti, Sṛishṭi, Sthiti, Saṁhṛiti, Svāhā, Svadhā, Gāyatrī, Sāvitrī, Vimalā, Bahurūpā, Satī, Bahushishnā, Madanāturā Akshobhyā, Satyavādinī.

Some further details regarding Her worship are set forth and then in verses 49-68 the following fine Hymn to Prak*ri*ti is given.

HYMN TO PRAK*RI*TI (1)

1

Be gracious to me, Oh Pradhānā (2)
Who art Prak*ri*ti (3) in the form of the elemental world (4)
Life (5) of all that lives,
With folded hands I make obeisance to Thee Our Lady (6)
Whose very nature and will it is to do (7)
That which we cannot understand (8).

2

A hymn is composed of sentences
And these of words with their terminations (9),

---

1. The primordial Shakti ; *see* note 3 below.

2. Pra + dhā + ana*t* = pradhatte sarvam ātmani or that which contains all things in itself ; the source and receptacle of all matter and form.

3. Pra + k*ri*ti, that is, She by whom all actions, that is, creation (*srishti*) maintenance (sthiti) and destruction (laya) are done. Prak*ri*yate kāryādikam anayā. Pradhāna and Prak*ri*ti are one and the same under different aspects. Prak*ri*ti also means before (Pra) creation (k*ri*ti), k*ri*te*h* prārambho yasyā*h*-She from whom creation begins. The first is the one as the container of the material which goes to the making of the world of form and Prak*ri*ti is the One in its active aspect moulding into form the materia prima (to use an analogous though not altogether accurate term) of which as Pradhāna, It is the container.

4. Prapancha, that is, the Universe as composed of the five gross "elements" (mahābhūta) or ether (ākāsha), air (vāyu), fire (tejas), water (ap), earth (p*ri*thivī).

5. Prā*n*a which manifests in the breath of breathing things (prā*n*ī).

6. Prabho ; the meaning of which is "one who can confer favours and show disfavour" (nigrahānugrahasamarthā).

7. It is Her very nature (prak*ri*ti) to be and to do, what She is and does. She cannot be otherwise and be Herself. She acts, and to do so is Her will and Her will is what She is.

8. The action of Prak*ri*ti is apratarkya, beyond all human discussion and conception, known only to Prak*ri*ti-Puru*sh*a and not to ourselves, who are but transformations (vik*ri*ti) and but limited manifestations of the immanent yet transcendent Cause.

9. In Sanskrit the root is not considered a word. It becomes only a word (padam) when the case or verbal termination is added. Thus bhū the root of the verb "to be" is not a pada but, bhavati, the third person singular present tense is such ; Rāma is not a pada, but Rāma*h*, Rāmaṁ, Rāme*n*a, *etc.*, are padas.

Words again consist of letters
And Thou Thyself, Oh Supreme Queen, art the letter (1),
Thus art Thou both the Hymn and those who hymn Thee (2).

3

Even Aja (3) Adhok*sh*aja (4) and Trīk*sh*a*n*a (5),
Know not Thy Supreme form which is Māyā (6),
But pray to Thee in Thy gross form as Ruler (7),
Therefore so must I pray to Thee (8).

4

Salutation to Thee our Lady supreme over all (9),
Who art Bindu (10),
Obeisance to Thee the Paratattva (11),

---

1. Ak*sh*ara or lettered sound is the gross manifestation of subtle sound or dhvani. Dhvani is Devī as Kulaku*nd*alinī. Mantra is therefore Devatā not only in its collective form, but in each of the letters which compose it. Ak*sh*ara also means 'imperishable'.

2. *Lit.* "the Devī praises Herself with letters which are Herself because the power of speech is Herself." The Hymnist and the Hymn are but manifestation of the Supreme whom they invoke. The Jīva worships its inner ground or Paramātmā.

3. Aja "the unborn one" is an epithet applicable to Brahmā, Vi*shn*u and Rudra but is generally and here used as a title of Brahmā the creative aspect of the trinity (trimūrti).

4. Adhok*sh*aja ; which means "He from whom there is no fall (rebirth) when once attained" ; or "He who is beyond the perception of the senses" (ak*sh*a= indriya) ; Vāchaspatya Dict. It here means Vi*shn*u.

5. Trīk*sh*a*n*a or "three-eyed" a term generally applied to Shiva who bears in His forehead the third eye of wisdom (jnāna-chak*sh*u*h*).

6. That by which the Brahman as Avyakta creating the Universe is able to make Itself appear to be different from what It really is.

7. Īshi tāṁ. She is the ineffable Lord (Īshvarī) ruling the Universe Her creation. This ruling aspect which involves relation is Her gross aspect.

8. That is, if even these three great Devas can only worship the gross aspect, of greater necessity it is that the hymnist should do so. 9. Samasteshi.

10. From the Sachchidānanda Parameshvara with Prak*ri*ti issued Shakti from Shakti came Nāda and from Nāda was born Bindu (Shāradātilaka, Ch. 1). This Bindu again has two aspects the Bindu or Puru*sh*a aspect or "Haṁ" manifesting in breathing creatures (Prā*n*ī) as expiration and the visarga or Prak*ri*ti aspect or "Sa*h*" manifesting as inspiration ; the current of the life wave being called Hang cha sa*h* or the motion of Ha and Sa. *See* my book "The Serpent Power".

11. *Lit.* the supreme Tattva or prak*ri*ti. In this edition the alternative reading "Ravatvena" has been preferred. As such the meaning is She is the Rava or sound which arises on the bursting of the Bindu. *See ante* p. 6.

Who art Pradhānā (1) and Mahattva (2),
Salutation to Thee Who art in the form of Ahaṁkāra (3).

5

Obeisance to Thee in the form of sound and ether,
Salutation to Thee in the form of touch and air,
Obeisance to Thee in the form of sight and fire,
Salutation to Thee in the form of taste and water,
Obeisance to Thee in the form of earth with its quality of smell (4).

6

Salutation to Thee in the form of the ear, skin, eyes, tongue, and nose (5),
And in the form of mouth, speech, arms, legs, organs of excretion and generation (6),
Salutation to Thee, Manas, Buddhi, Ahaṁkāra and Chitta (7),
Obeisance to Thee Who art in the form of the whole Universe:

---

1. *See* v. 1 note 2, p. 29.

2. Mahattva (Mahat-tattva) is that state of the vik*ri*ti of mūlaprak*ri*ti which when individualised is called Buddhi. The latter is one of the fourfold aspects of the anta*h*kara*n*a or mental organ, *viz.*, manas (lower mind or sensorium), buddhi (higher mind the function of which is determination ; nishchayakāri*n*ī), ahaṁkāra (egoity, self-consciousness) and chitta (v. post, v. 6, n. 7).

3. *See* last note. The ahaṁkāra here referred to is however to be distinguished from that mentioned in verse 6. It is ahaṁkāra thought of as before its divisions into Taijasa, Vaikārika, and Bhautika.

4. Ether, air, fire, water, earth are the five gross elements (mahābhūta). They each have certain qualities or gu*n*a. These are sound, touch, sight (by and of light) taste and smell. Mahābhūta is the container or supporter (ādhāra) and that which is called its gu*n*a is the supported or contained (ādheya). It is through its gu*n*a that the mahābhūta is perceived by the senses (indriya). Thus, sound is that by which the invisible ākāsha is known. The Mahābhūta and its gu*n*a represent the objective and subjective aspects. As the world is the creation of mind, the shabda, sparsha, rūpa, rasa and gandha (sound, touch, sight, taste, smell) tanmātras are the cause of the mahābhūtas the former themselves deriving from the tāmasa ahaṁkāra.

5. The organs of sense (indriya) are of two kinds *viz.*, Jnānendriyas or organs of sensation through which knowledge of the external world is obtained, *viz.*, those mentioned in this line and Karmendriyas or organs of action by which that knowledge is applied, namely, those mentioned in the second line.

6. *See* last note.

7. *See* n. 2. These four are vik*ri*tis of the Devī.

Chittam is that by which one knows (Chetati anena iti chittam). According to the Vedānta it is the faculty of the mental organ (anta*h*karana) which contemplates and investigates into the subject-matter of thought—anusandhānātmikā anta*h*kara*n*a- v*ri*tti*h* iti vedānta*h*.

Who pervadest all
And yet art formless (1).

7

Thou art the Antarātmā (2),
Who by the Sun (3) upholdest all living creatures,
And Who by the Moon ever nourishes them.
Again assuming the appearance of Fire the carrier of oblations (4) Thou burnest :
Oh Mahādevī, verily do these three lights (5) and fires issue from Thee.

8

Assuming the form of Brahmā with active quality (6)
The four-headed one, seated on a shining white swan,
Thou dost create the world
Of which thou becomest the Mother.
Who is there indeed, Oh Supreme Ruler (7),
Who can imagine Thy supreme state (8) ?

9

Adorned with crown,
Resplendent with conch and discus (9)

---

1. The forms of the Mother of the Universe are threefold. There is first the supreme (para) form of which, as the Vi*sh*n*u*yāmala says, "none know" (see Ch. III, Shāktānanda Taramgi*n*ī); next Her subtle form as mantra or sound ; and thirdly Her gross form in the visible universe and in those embodied aspects or spiritual avatāras in which She presents Herself, for the benefit of the sādhaka who can only worship Her in such form See Author's "Shakti and Shākta" and "Hymns to the Goddess."

2. Ātmā derived from āt + manin, is that which continues to exist in all states (avasthā) commencing with jāgrat and following on in the others : svapna, su*sh*upti, and turīya, that is, the eternal Spirit. Āt = sātatya-gamane or that which is continually going ; that is, which never ceases to exist. But as the term ātmā has also other meanings in Sanskrit (such as effort, patience, buddhi, nature, manas, son, jiva, sun, hutāsana (fire) vāyu, body) the term which specifically describes the Spirit as the inner substance of all things is antarātmā or inner ātmā.

3. The Sanskrit expression is finer but untranslatable—ravitvena bhutvā antarātmā dadhāsi ; that is, who upholds "by Thy sun-ness." In the same way later we have chandramastvena "by Thy moon-ness."

4. Fire it is which while consuming oblations in their gross form carries them as nourishing food in subtle form to the Devas.

5. That is Sun, Moon and Fire corresponding with the Kriyā, Ichchhā and Jnāna Shaktis.

6. That is the rajas gu*n*a.

7. Īshī.

8. *Lit.* "You (alone) think upon (or know) Your supreme state."

9. Chakra. Both conch and discus are white and shining.

As Nārāyana with quality of manifestation (1),
Thou dost maintain the world ;
For He also is part of Thee.

10

Again in the form of the three-eyed Rudra
Carrying axe and a rosary (2),
On whose matted hair are moon, serpent and Ganges (3),
He with the quality which veils (4)
Thou dost at the end of the Kalpa (5) destroy the whole universe,
And then alone shinest (6).

11

Thou, Oh Supreme Lady (7), art Sarasvatī (8),
The presiding Goddess of Speech,
Clad in white raiment (9),
Holding a rosary of Rudrāksha beads, a pen, and a jar of nectar,
Thou maketh the Chintā gesture (10)
Thou art The Three-eyed One
Bearing upon Thy matted hair (11)
The shining crescent moon.

12

Thou art, Oh Queen, the uncreated changeless One,
Thou art Durgā (12)
With shining conch and discus

---

1. Sattvaguna. *Lit.* "He who maintains is part of Thee".
2. Made of rudrāksha seed or human skull or bones.
3. When Gamgā was called down from heaven by Bhagīratha, She first fell into the matted hair (jatā) of Shiva.
4. Tamo-guna.
5. The period of time between two epochs of dissolution (pralaya) or 4,320,000,000 years. Then Shiva withdraws creation into Himself.
6. For what is there when all is gone but the unmanifest Prakriti ? *See* Yoginīhridaya Ch. 1. 7. Īshī.
8. Goddess of speech, learning and wisdom.
9. The colour of Sarasvatī is white. Thus She is represented as white holding the vīnā ; adorned with white flowers, holding a white rosary, besmeared with white sandal paste, clad in white raiment. *See* note to Sarasvatī stotra in Tantrasāra quoted in author's "Hymns to the Goddess." 10. The Jnāna-mudrā.
11. Kaparda as is worn by Shiva.
12. One of the greatest names of the Devī ; that is, Sā yā durgatim harati.

Formidable with whirling sword ;
She who with high and glittering crown
Is borne upon a roaring lion (1).
The crowd of Daityas (2) Thou dost destroy,
But Siddhas (3) worship Thee.

13

Truly, Oh Supreme Ruler (4), Thou art The (one) Mother,
Who art the half of the body of the enemy of Tripura (5),
Shining forth as the spouse of Bhava (6),
And again as Daughter of the King of Mountains (7),
Oh good and (8) supreme Queen,
Great Yogins salute Thee.

14

Great Goddess (9), I know Thee to be Shrī (10)
The only Mistress of all peoples,
Dear to the world,
She who lives in the sky-blue (11) breast of the enemy of Kaiṭabha (12),
Beauteous with the glittering splendour of the Kaustubha gem (13).

15

Oh great Goddess (14) and all-pervading One (15),
The seven shining Mothers
Are parts and forms of Thee,

---

1. The vehicle of Durgā. 2, Demonic spirits. [Esoterically the sense of duality in the sādhaka].

3. That is, here not the Devayoni of that name but the Perfect with all accomplishment ; those who are possessed of Siddhi. 4. Maheshī.

5. That is, Shiva. More stricly She and Shiva are halves of one whole as according to Hindu ideas man and wife form one completed being. Each is imperfect without the other. *See post* Ch. 27 Hymn to Shiva, verse 9 note.

6. Shiva in the watery form of the Ashṭamūrti.

7. Himālaya who was the father of Pārvatī. 8. Sunāthā. 9. Mahādevī.

10. Lakshmī. 11. Vyomanīle.

12. Vishnu destroyed the Asuras Madhu and Kaiṭabha. Madhu is tamoguna and Kaiṭabha is rajoguna. *See* Mārkandeya Chandī, Ch. 1.

13. Gem worn by Vishnu. The word means destruction of all evils, or worldlymindedness, or sense of smallness or limitation. *See post* p. 48.

14. Mahādevī. 15. Vibhu.

They who bear the signs, implements, and weapons
Of Aja, Adrī*t*, Guha, Abjāk*sh*a,
Potrī, Indraka, and Mahābhairava (1).

16

Thy lustre is that of a thousand rising suns
In the endless spaces of the Universe.
Upon Thy head is the crescent moon (2)
Thou holdeth the noose and goad (3)
And maketh the gestures of granting blessing and of dispelling fear (4).

17

Thou, Oh Ruler (5), art light, fame and beauty,
Day, evening and night,
Action, hope, darkness and hunger,
Intelligence (6), memory, patience,
Speech, mind (7) and knowledge (8)
Beauty and splendour
And all other powers (9).

18

Oh Destructress of ills (10),
Thou Who Art
Bindu and Nāda :

---

1. That is Brahmā, Girisha, Kārtikeya, Vi*sh*n*u, Varāha, Indra and Mahābhairava. Therefore the Mat*ri*kās are Brahmā*n*ī, Rudrā*n*i, Kaumārī, Vai*sh*n*avī, Vārāhī, Aindrī and Mahābhairavī or Chāmu*nd*ā. The Māt*ri*kās who issued from Durgā during her battle with Shumbha and Nishumbha are variously enumerated ; usually eight are spoken of and sometimes nine ; others being Aparājitā and Nārasimhī. *See* Cha*n*ai, Ch. VIII.

2. The Devī as spouse of Shiva bears (as He does) the crescent moon.

3. These with the arrow and bow are Her weapons. The Yoginīh*ri*daya says, "the noose is Ichchhāshkti, the goad Jnānashakti, and the bow and arrows Kriyāshakti." But the Tantrarāja says "Mind is the bow of sugarcane, desire the noose, attachment (rāga) the goad and the tanmatras the five arrows of flowers."

4. That is, She makes with her hands the two gestures (mudrā) called vara (or here abhī*sh*t*a) and abhaya. 5. Īshī.

6. Buddhi, see page 41.

7. Mati ; here the acting manas.

8. Sammati which also means agreement, consent, opinion, love, affection, also read Sannati (obeisance) and for Kānti (splendour) Bhakti (Faith, devotion) is read.

9. Shaktiprabheda ; that is, the various different manifestations of Her shakti.

10. Hare : that is, remover of sin and pain.

Shakti and Shānta (1)
Thou art in the form of the seven
Regions (2), nether worlds (3), mountains (4) and oceans (5),
Stars (6), islands (7), substances (8) and tones (9).

19

Salutation to Thee Oh great Queen (10)
Who art all (11)
And in the form of all (12),
Who art the power in all things (13),

---

1. Bhedaprabhinnai*h* abhinne bindunādai*h* sashaktyākhyashāntai*h*. Shakti and Shānta are parts of the Bīja and are states of the Brahman which in its various aspects the mantra is. When referrible to the sādhaka of the mantra, Shakti is that allpervading allembracing energy which appears in him in the stage leading to and immediately preceding Shānta where all his wishes are realised without will or effort for he is himself that by which they are done. Shānta is ordinarily understood as implying that state in which there is neither happiness nor unhappiness, attachment or desire ; but the Shānta here spoken of is the essence (tanmātra) of that : and which appears in the Mok*sh*a stage when the supreme Ātmā is realised. As Comm, to v. 52 of the *Shat*chakranirūpa*n*a says Shānta is the Chidātmā.

2. Bhū*h*, Bhuva*h*, Sva*h*, Maha*h*, Jana*h*, Tapa*h*, Satyam.

3. Tala, Atala, Vitala, Sutala, Talātala, Mahātala, Rasātala.

4. The seven mountains called Kula Parvatas are Mahendra, Malaya, Sahya, Shuktimān, *Rik*sha, Vindhya, Pāripātra.

5. Of Salt (Lava*n*a), Sugarcane juice (Ik*sh*u), Wine (Surā or Madhu), Ghee (Ājya, Sarpi*h*), Curd (Dadhi), Milk (K*sh*īra or Dugdha) and Sweet Water (Udaka).

6. Which are the seven sages, Marīchi, Atri, Angirā*h*, Pulastya, Pulaha, Kratu and Vashi*shth*a. Or grahas are the seven planets excluding Rāhu and Ketu.

7. Jambu, Plak*sh*a, Shālmali, Kusha, Krauncha, Shāka and Pu*sh*kara of which the world is composed.

8. Dhātu : that is, chyle (rasa), blood (as*ri*k), flesh (māmsa), fat (meda), bone (asthi), marrow (majjā) and semen (shukra) of the physical body.

9. Svara. The text here refers to *Shad*ja, *Rish*abha, Gāndhāra, Madhyama. Panchama, Dhaivata, Ni*sh*āda located in the Vishuddha chakra. *See* Introduction to "The Serpent Power". Tāntrik doctrine is expressed in terms of sound (shabda) and music is merely a species of it or grossly manifested sweet melodious sound. Musically considered the svaras are Sa, ri, ga, ma, pa, dha, ni (corresponding with the European scale c, d, e, f, g, a, b) which constitute the grāma or gamut. The intervals between these are the sub-tones or shrutis of which there are 22. The grāmas are threefold—low, middle and high or udārā, mudārā, tārā corresponding with the three svaras udātta, anudātta, and svarit ; pronounced from the navel, chest and head and called by the Mohammedan musicians nābhi (navel). bak*sh*a (chest), kapāla (head). As there are 7 tones and 3 grāmas there are 21 mūrchchhanās.

10. Maheshī. 11. Samaste. 12. Samastasvarūpe.

13. Samaste*sh*u vastu*sh*u anusyūtashakte ; *lit.* the power (shakti) which is "sewn into" or interweaved with all things. For nothing is or acts but by Her power and this existence and action is Her power that is Herself.

Who dost assume forms both gross and subtle
Thou art spoken of as memory and knowledge
And as the want thereof (1).

20

Let all our thoughts be ever of Thee,
Oh our Great Lady (2),
May all our speech be of, and all our hymn to, Thee,
May all we do (3) be homage to Thee.
Be ever gracious to and pardon me (4).

CHAPTER XII.

This Chapter gives an exposition of the worship of Shrī or Lak*sh*mī and states Her Bīja (5) and Dhyāna and the Japa and Homa in her Sādhana. Her nine Shaktis (6) are to be invoked round Her Pī*th*a. Verse 29 gives a Dhyāna of Her as Ramā and 32 Shaktis of Ramā are enumerated who should also be worshipped. The worship of Shrī leads to purity; bodily perfection and beauty, intelligence and devotion to Vi*sh*nu ; and not only the Sādhaka but his bed and all other things belonging to him are purified.

CHAPTER XIII.

At the commencement the Tripu*t*ā (7) Mantra is indicated. After doing Aṁganyāsa with that Mantra the

---

1. For Devī is avidyā (ignorance) as She is also vidyā (knowledge). Through the first She binds and by the second She liberates.

2. Maheshī.

3. That is all bodily action, eating, drinking, sexual intercourse, walking, sleeping *etc.*, which should be offered to Her and thus divinised. In the same way the Hymn to Vi*sh*nu in the 21st Chapter of this work contains the fine line—Devesha karmasarvaṁ me bhavedārādhanaṁ tava—"Oh Lord of Devas, all my actions should be worship of Thee."

4. The Prapanchasāra then recites the fruits of this Hymn saying that he who does japa, pūjā and recites this hymn with reverence attains that which is the supreme wealth and abode. Whoever serves the injunctions becomes both yogī and bhogī, that is, he has according to Tantra both liberation and enjoyment.

5. Shrīṁ.

6. Verse 8.

7. An antargatā Devī of Tripurā. *See* Tripu*t*āsrotra in Tantrasāra, translated with commentary at page 172 of Arthur and Ellen Avalon's "Hymns to the Goddess."

Sādhaka should meditate on the Devī as on a lotus seat in the heart lotus (1). After Pūjā to Her, Her Āvara*n*a Devatās should be worshipped. Her Japa is done 1,200,000 times (twelve lakhs). In vv. 4 and 5 Her Dhyāna is given. In v. 10, the Dhara*n*ī Bīja is indicated. The *Rish*i is Varāha, the Chhanda*h* is Niv*ri*t, and the Devatā is Dhara*n*ī. Then follows Tvaritā Vidyā who is so-called because She grants success to Her worshippers very speedily. The worshipper of this Tvaritā mantra is tempted by celestial damsels. If the Sādhaka overcomes these temptations then Devī Tvaritā grants all his desires. Totalāvidhi is described in vv. 64-66. Then Nityā Mantra is indicated and the mode of Her worship laid down. V. 84 says that (amongst other fruit secured by this Mantra) if he who is initiated therein thinks of a woman and makes Japa of this Mantra a thousand times, even when lying on his bed (2), then that woman becomes so maddened by the arrows of Madana the God of love that she comes running to him.

CHAPTER XIV

Deals with the worship of Durgā. Her Dhyāna is given in v. 4 In v. 7, Her nine Shaktis are given. Vv. 11 and 12 enumerate Her weapons, and another set of Shaktis. Again in v. 31 further Shaktis are given. One of the fruits of Her pūjā is declared to be the power to bring under control even the wives of Kings. Some warrior Shaktis are given in v. 72.

CHAPTER XV

Is concerned with the details of the ritual of the worship of Sārya (Sun) the Sāttvika aspect of Bhuvaneshvarī.

CHAPTER XVI

Indicates the Mantra of Chandra (Moon) and deals with His worship. V. 8 gives nine Shaktis of Chandra. At v. 25,

1. That is, not anāhata but the small I*sht*adevatā lotus below it.

2. That is, the mantra is so powerful that it may be recited with success under the easiest conditions.

the Agni mantra is indicated ; and at v. 30, the nine Shaktis of Agni are enumerated. The rest of the Chapter is largely concerned with the fruits of the various forms of worship. Chandra is the Rājasa and Agni the Tāmasa aspect of the Devī.

CHAPTER XVII

Treats of the worship of Mahāga*n*esha. Vv. 5-17 give the Dhyāna. V. 22 gives His nine Shaktis. These include Tīvrā, Jvālinī, Bhogadā, Kāmarūpi*n*ī, Ugrā, Tejovatī, Satyā, Vighnanāshinī.

CHAPTER XVIII

Contains the Manmatha (1) Mantra. The Dhyāna is in v. 4. His nine Shaktis (v. 6) are Mohanī (She who charms). Ks*h*obha*n*ī (She who perturbs), Trāsī (She who causes anxiety), Stambhanī (She who paralyzes). Ākars*h*i*n*ī (She who attracts), Drāvi*n*ī (She who softens), Āhlādinī (She who causes joy), Klinnā (She who moves the heart), Kledinī (She who moistens) (2). His Gāyatrī is given in v. 11, as follows :—Kāmadevāya vidmahe: Pus*h*pavā*n*āya dhīmahi: tānno' naṁga*h* prachodayāt. (3) The Mantra is at vv. 12-14 The 16 Āvara*n*a Shaktis are given at vv. 19-21. They are Yuvati (Youthfulness), Vipralambhā (Deception), Jyotsnā (Moonlight or Splendour), Subhrū (Beautiful eyebrows), Madadravā (Soften ing state of love), Suratā (Amorous play). Vāru*n*ī (Shakti of Varu*n*a) (4), Lolā (Agitation) (5), Kānti (Beauty) Saudāminī (Lightning), Kāmachhatrā (6) (all which induce passion)

---

1. "He who agitates the mind" or Kāmadeva "Deva of desire" the God of sexual desire whose mantra is Klīṁ. Other names of this Deity are Pradyumna "the powerful one" or "He who overcomes all," Kandarpa "He who fills the mind with happiness," Smara "He who pertubs or inflames" and (*see pos.*) Anaṁga "The bodiless one." At marriage and when a wife leaves her father's house to go to her husband for the first time petitions ware addressed to Him for children and marital happiness,

2. The above and the āvara*n*a Shaktis are simple examples of what is meant by a Devatā's Shaktis and are for this purpose enumerated.

3. "Let us know Kāma Deva ; let us meditate on Him the arrows of whose bow are made of flowers. May that Bodiless One direct us." Kāma is called the "Bodiless one" as He was consumed by the fire of Shiva when he sought to distract the latter from His yoga.

4. Quære.

5. Or fickle, lustiul : it may also mean the male genitals, as yoni is given post.

6. Chhatra ordinarily means umbrella ; or all covering things thus the season of spring or the sight of a beautiful woman would be Kāmachhatrā.

Chandralekhā (The Digits of the moon) (1), Shukī (a female parrot (2), Madanā (Passion of love), Yoni (The female genitals), Māyāvatī (She who deludes). At v. 21 His sixteen servants are given, namely, Shoka (Heat or anguish), Moha (Delusion), Vilāsa (Coquetry or play with women), Vibhrama (Perturbation or confusion or amorous gestures), Madanātura (Helpless state induced by passion), Apatrapa (Shamelessness), Yuvā (Male youthfulness) (3), Kāmī (Amorousness), Chyutapu*sh*pa (Mango blossom) (4), Ratipriya (Pleasant coition), Grī*sh*ma (summer) (5), Tapānta (Rainy season) (6), Ūrja (Autumn), Hemanta (Dewy season) (7), Shishira (winter), Mada (Spring). The text at vv. 24 and 25 says that at the corners of the Yantra of Madana should be worshipped the play of the amorous sidelong glances (8), the sensuous movements of woman's body (9), the Mādhavī creeper (10), Mālatī flower (11), the gazelle-like eye (Hari*n*āk*sh*ī) and the entrance-ment of passion (12).

The text then describes (vv. 27 *et. seq.*) the union of husband and wife (13). The body of man is a manifestation of Ahaṁ-

---

1. Taken collectively as the source of light.

2. A lovesick person as described in the Alaṁkārashāstra keeps a parrot to whom he or she tells his feelings.

3. As yuvatī is a youthful woman.

4. Mangoes blossom mostly in spring the season of love, and one of the God's arrows is made of them. Jayadeva says :—"In spring the cuckoo gladdened by the sight of the mango buds calls sweetly in every forest Kuhu Kuhu. The wind from the Malaya mountain wafts the fragrance of cloves. To wound the heart of woman spring advances with Kāma whose bow is formed of flowers, his bowstring a row of bees, his arrow the budding mango shoot: K*r*ish*n*a now gambols, but the separated lovers endure severe misery."

5. The seasons are companions of Kāmadeva ; v. *post*.

See brief discriptions of the six seasons extracted from different Sanskrit authors in Ward's View of the History, etc., of the Hindoos, (1818), Vol. I. p. 519. "In summer the earth through the fierceness of the heat is like a widowed woman in the bloom of youth (tormented by desire). The scorching wind is as the breath of the serpent Ananta at the churning of the ocean. The sun is like the countenance of one puffed up with riches. The world is motionless like the eyes of the yogi in the meditation (Sūktikar*n*ām*r*ita).

6. This season the delight of the amorous comes like a king sitting on a cloud formed maddened elephant ; the lightning his flag and the thunder his large kettle drum" (Kalidāsa).

7. Kārtika, Agrahāya*n*a : from middle of October to middle of December.

8. Apāṁgabhrūvilāsa.

9. Hāvabhāva, the movements a person makes which indicate desire.

10. Creeper with sweet smelling flowers. married to the Mango tree.

11. A kind of jasmine.

12. Madotka*t*ā.

13. Nijāng vanitām ; the wife and not some other Shakti.

kāra (1) and is the abode of error (2). Woman is Buddhi (3). These two are united in the Chittayoni (4), that is, in that mental function of the Anta*h*kara*n*a which is here figuratively regarded as the Yoni or womb of Buddhi. Ahaṁkāra is thus united with Buddhi and husband with wife (5). The husband is to think of himself as Madana (6) in the form of fire and of his Shiva (7) as a flame of fire. Let him embrace her who is overspread by its flame and let him sip with his tongue the nectar of her teeth and tongue. Let him think of his beautiful wife (8) as the embodiment of nectar whose body (9) is as it were the butter (10) which is melted in that fire. Let him touch her arms thinking them to be the flowery arrows of Kāma. The Mantrin should keep his self-control and take care not to injure the Jīva (11). In all the stages of passion (rati) he should be self-controlled. Thus should one's own beloved be worshipped (bhajet). If it be done thus then she who is struck by the arrows of Kāma follows her husband like a shadow even in another world (12).

At v. 40 is given the Mantra of K*rishn*a ; the *Rish*i of which is Nārada, the metre (chhanda*h*) Gāyatrī (13) and the Devatā K*rishn*a. At v. 43 is the general Dhyāna of K*rishn*a and in v. 47 His Dhyāna as He should be meditated on in the morning is described. Then He is thought of as a child of the colour of a blue lotus with a girdle of little bells covering his waist, thighs and buttocks. His throat is adorned by large and shining tiger claws. His face smiles happily like a lotus. It is He who killed the demons Shaka*t*a (14) and Pūtanā (15).

---

1. Vilasadahaṁkāratanu.
2. Vibhramāspadībhūta, for it is tamogu*n*a.
3. Buddhisharīrā nārī.
4. Chittayonim adhigachchhet.
5. As in the Jīva the Ahaṁkāra and Buddhi which are in it unite in its own Chitta, so restraining the body let the Mantrin unite with his own wife alone.
6. He thinks of his v*ri*ttis as being the embodiment of Kāma the God of Love.
7. The liṅga.
8. *Lit.* the "slender one" —tanvītanu.
9. *Lit.* the Mandanāgāra.
10. Navanīta. In Homa clarified butter is poured into the fire and sexual union is one of the fire fires.
11. That is, he should not over-exert himself and thus injuriously affect his ajapāmantra, or vital breath. Padmapāda refers to Kāmashāstra.
12. Bhavāntare ; or (may be) another birth.
13. There is here the same divisions as in the ordinary Gāyatrī.
14. A demon who attempted to fall on and crush the infant K*rishn*a who with His foot killed him.
15. Kaṁsa sent Pūtanā, the milk of whose breasts was poison, to K*rishn*a ; but He sucked her life away. *See* Devībhāgavata Purā*n*a, IV. 24.

He is the Govinda to whom Shaṁkara, Indra and others do obeisance.

At v. 48 is the midday meditation (Dhyāna). Let the worshipper then think of Him as Mukunda lustrous as the full blown lotus, with eyes like blue lotuses, surrounded by cows and herdswomen (Gopīs), as one Who has conquered all His enemies, Whose pure smile is like the white jasmine and the Mandāra flowers. His head is adorned with peacock feathers. He is the strong lustrous One habited in yellow raiment. Those who thus worship Him gain wealth (1).

At v. 49 is given the evening Dhyāna. He is then contemplated upon as the unconquerable One Who by His valour has laid in the dust all His enemies and "has lightened the weight of this Earth" (2). Who is ever surrounded by great *Rishis* such as Nārada and others who desire to learn from him the true meaning of Tattva. He is pure, incomparable, imperishable and luminously blue. He is the Vāsudeva "Who steals (3) the creation and maintenance of the universe" and Who grants Liberation.

CHAPTER XIX

Deals with Yoga. The Pra*n*ava (Oṁ) is the Kalpa tree of all desires and the grantor of Liberation. The Dhyāna is given in v. 4 of Oṁkāra or the Pra*n*ava as representing Vi*shn*u. Vv. 8-12 give the Āvara*n*a devatās of Vi*shn*u and their respective Shaktis. At verse 14 Yoga is spoken of. Yoga is defined as the constant uninterrupted vision in oneself of the Ātmā which is without hands, feet, mouth or other limb or body (4).

The faults which are impediments (Dū*shan*a) of Yoga are enumerated, *viz.*:—Kāma (lust), Kopa (anger), Lobha (greed), Pramoha (ignorance), Mada (pride), Matsaratā (envy). In verse 16 the well known Aṁgas of Yoga such as Yama and so forth are given and then defined. The several names of Oṁkāra follow (v. 34).

---

1. This is the Rājasika form, as the morning form is Sāttvika from which no material fruit is gained but the gifts of the spirit only.

2. By the removal of iniquity.

3. That is, He destroys the world. This is the Rudramūrti.

4. Kara-pāda-mukhādivihīnam anāratad*ri*shyam ananyagam ātmapadam
Yamihātmani pashyati tattvavida stamimaṁ kila yogamiti bruvate.

V. 42 describes how the different parts of Omkāra are dissolved in Shānta. A is dissolved (Samharet) in U, U in M, M in Bindu, Bindu in Nāda, Nāda in Shakti and Shakti in Shānta.

Five states (Avasthās) of consciousness are given (v. 46) and not four, *viz.*:—Jāgrat (waking), Svapna (dream sleep), Sus*h*upti (dreamless slumber), Turīya (the fourth state) and Tadatīta (that which is above the fourth) (1). They are then defined. Jāgrat is that enjoyment which the Ātmā enjoys by the aid of its own senses (Indriyas) (2). Svapna is that feeling or perception (Anubhava) which exists through these senses when devoid of consciousness (Samjnā) (3); Sus*h*upti is that condition of quietude which is caused by the effortless state of the Ātmā (4). Turīya is the state when the Ātmā sees the Supreme with unclouded vision (Chetas) (5). The fifth state is that which immediately precedes Liberation (Mukti) and is defined as "that condition where the Yogī realises the inseparateness of Ātmā and Paramātmā. From this state Liberation is not far" (6). When Pavana (Vāyu) is in the subtle Pashyantī (7) and in Madhyamā (7) and Vaikharī (7) when at the end of Sus*h*umnā (8) then Jāgrat is the utterance of the Bīja, Bindu is Svapna, Sus*h*upti is Nāda, Shakti is Turīya and Shānta is Laya (absorption) which is beyond Turīya.

---

1. So the Devī, in the Lalitā, is addressed as Sarvāvasthāvivarjitā, that is, "transcending all the states." Three Sūtras in the Shiva Sūtras describe this state. *See* Bhāskararāya's Comm. on Lalitā V. 63.

2. Svair indriyair yadātmā bhumkte bhogān sa jāgaro bhavati. *See* Introduction to The Serpent Power.

3. Samjnārahitair api tair asyānubhavo bhavet puna*h* svapna*h* ; that is, apparently when the sense organs cease to act directly on new objects of their functioning and Ātmā is conscious of mental images generated by those senses when in the Jāgrat state.

4. Ātmanirudyuktatayā nairākulyam bhavet sus*h*uptir api.

5. Pashyati param yadātmā nistamasā chetasā turīyam tat.

6. Ātmaparamātmapadayor abhedato vyāpnuyād yadā yogī,

Tachcha turīyātītam tasyāpi bhavenna dūrato mukti*h*.

What is here referred to is that which is called Jīvanmukti. When the body is relinquished there follows complete or bodiless Mukti (Videha Kaivalya).

7. The subtle states (bhāva) of sound so named.

8. "At the end of Sus*h*umnā." The end is just below the twelve-petalled lotus which rests on the upper end of Sus*h*umnā. Here the meaning may be towards the end,

Sūks*h*mākhyāyām pashyantyām madhyamākhyavaikharyo*h*.

Sasus*h*umnāgragayor api yunjyājjāgradādil hi*h* pavanam.

Mahāvi*shn*u then says :—In leaving the body, entering another body and re-entering one's own body the places of exit and entry are the Aṁgu*shth*a (either thumb or great toe), Gulpha (the ankle), Jānu (knee), Guda (anus), Sīvanī (fræ-num of prepuce or *quære* glans penis), Me*dh*ra (penis), Nābhi (navel), H*ri*daya (heart), Grīvā (neck). Lambikāgra (tip of the tongue), Nāsā (nose), Bhrūmadhyalalā*t*āgra (middle of eyebrows on the forehead).

He then speaks of the conquest of, or power of control over, the five elements. This is done through their respective Shaktis and Bījas, with which the self is identified (1). Thus to control fire the self is made one with its Shakti and Bīja (v. 56). He then describes the three states (2) of Siddhi (power) and the eight Siddhis ; to possess all of which is to be Jīvanmukta.

CHAPTER XX.

Deals with the meaning of the eight-letter Mantra of Nārāya*n*a "Oṁ nama*h* Nārāya*n*āya. The meaning is that Tāra (Oṁ) arises from Shakti and means So'haṁ ("I am He"). Na and Ma*h* are negatives. Nā is water, Rā is fire, Ya is air, *N*a is earth ; and the last Ya is there as a case-ending (3). The *Rish*i of the Mantra is Sādhyanārāya*n*a, the metre is Gāyatrī and the Devatā is Paramātmā. Verse 7 gives the Dhyāna of Mukunda (4). In the Sādhana of this Mantra the body of the Sādhaka is the Pī*th*a. V. 12 says that when Nyāsa is done with the letters of this Mantra then the Mantrin becomes the object of his own worship for he is personally composed of the letters of the Mantra.

At v. 60 the Mahāvi*shn*u enumerates the ten Avātaras of Vi*shn*u omitting Buddha and substituting Balarāma (5).

1. Shaktibhish cha tadbījai*h* sārūpyam ātmanash cha pratinītvā ; that is (to translate literally) by inducing a state of sameness (sārūpyam ātmana*h*) of the self (of the operator) with the Shakti and Bīja (of the elements).

2. That is, signs of approaching Siddhi or possession of Siddhi. The three states are ; prasūchika ("indicative" *e. g.*, physical signs such as thrill, hair standing on end (pulaka), *etc*,); pratyaya ("conviction," *e. g.*, beatitude, restraint of breath, *etc.*), and the third is Siddhi itself which is of various kinds, the chief enumeration being eight.

3 No more is said in the text, but the meaning is "I am He and not the five elements (named)."

4. A title of Vi*shn*u as the Giver of Liberation.

5. Shākyamuni Gautama, it may be noted, was not, as is commonly supposed the first Buddha. He merely gave shape and systematised the teachings of other Buddhas who preceded him. Both Buddhistik and Brahmanik writings of old prove this.

Vv. 21-24 state the Kirīṭādi Mantra (1). The Shaktis of the Pīṭha given in v. 29 are Vimalā and others. The rest of the Chapter deals with placing of the jar, Japa, Archana and other ritual details.

CHAPTER XXI

Treats of the twelve Yantras or diagrams of the twelve Rāshis (signs of the Zodiac) (2).

At vv. 54-69 is given a fine Hymn to Vishṇu here translated which is directed to be sung for the pleasure of the Deities who are to be worshipped in these Yantras.

HYMN TO VISHṆU. (3)

1

Oh Bhagavan (4), be gracious to me
Whose mind is dulled with ignorance ;
Give me the gift of devotion
To the pollen of Thy lotus feet.

2

Oh Bhagavan, be gracious to me ;
Thou cannot be imagined,
Abode as Thou art of immeasurable lustre,
Be gracious, Oh best of Purushas (5),
Who allayeth all our pains.

---

1. The Mantra used in the worship of the ornaments of Vishṇu such as crown armlet, necklace, *etc.*,

2. Mesha (Aries), Vrishabha (Taurus), Mithuna (Gemini), Karkaṭaka (Cancer), Siṁha (Leo), Kanyā (Virgo), Tūlā (Libra), Vrishchika (Scorpio), Dhanuḥ (Sagittarius), Makara (Capricornus), Kumbha (Aquarius), Mīna (Pisces) ; the solar year beginning with the entrance of the sun into Mesha.

3. Ch. 21, v. 54.

4. The Brahman as the possessor of all powers (aishvarya) which belong to Īshvara. This is one of the Saguṇa aspects of the Brahman.

5. The individual spirit.

3

Oh Īsha (1), Oh Stainless One, be gracious to me,
Who art the self of the Universe (2)
And bliss itself (3) ;
Essence unimagined (4),
To Thyself art Thou known only (5).

4

Be gracious to me, Highest of the highest,
Who art the Deepest of the deepest :
Be gracious, Oh Goodness and Beauty,
Who art Majesty itself to the majestic.
Great Light, be gracious to me.

5

Be gracious, Unmanifested One (6),
Ever pervading in that which ever pervades :
Minutest of the minute, be gracious ;
Most loving of the loving, be gracious ;
Be gracious, Thou Who art the end of all ends.

6

Be gracious to me, Greatest of the Great,
Oh Lord of all, Unending One (7), be gracious,
Who art eternal, Māyā (8), Holder of the conch (9),
Be gracious to us mortals :
Oh Mādhava (10), may You be ever victorious.

7

Victory be to Thee, Oh beautiful One !
Victory be to Thee Who art gentleness itself !

---

1. Lord.
2. Vishvātman.
3. Ānandātman.
4. Achintyasāra.
5. Svasaṁvedyasvarūpātman.
6. Avyakta.
7. Ananta. If 'ananya' be read for 'ananta' the meaning will be "Who art inseparate from Thy creatures".
8. Māyātman ; *Lit.* one with or inseparate from Māyā His Shakti.
9. By Shaṁkha (conch), says Shaṁkarāchārya, is meant Bhūtādyahaṁkāra, *See* Vishnusahasranāma, Vol 15 of this series, for the true sense of the epithets used in this hymn.
10. A title of Vishnu as husband of Mā or Lakshmī.

May You conquer, Oh Keshava (1).
Holder of the bow, Destroyer of Keshin (2),
Oh Auspicious One, delighter of Nanda (3),
May Thou be ever victorious.

8

Victory to Thee
In Whose hands are discus and mace (4) ;
Unconquerable One, may You conquer !
Thy head is adorned with a crown set with varied gems,
Oh Janārdana (5), be ever victorious.

9

The shadow (of the great wings)
Of the King of Birds, Thy carrier (6), obscures the Sun ;
Oh Enemy of Hell (7), salutation to Thee !
Oh Madhusūdana (8), obeisance to Thee !
May Thou be over victorious.

10

Salutation to Thee, Oh Lotus-eyed !
Obeisance to Thee Who art collyrium to our eyes (9) !
Salutation to Thee, Destroyer of sin !

---

1. This epithet of Vis*h*nu has several significations one of which is indicated in the text, *viz.*, He who destroys the Daitya Keshin. Another common definition is Ke jale shava iva bhāti iti Keshava : that is, "he who looks like a corpse in water" referring to the time when after pralaya and at the commencement of the creation of the world Vis*h*nu lay in the ocean of milk (Ks*h*īra-samudra). Other definitions given in the Shabdakalpadruma are :—Ka = Brahmā : Īsha = Rudra : Va = Vayati or "He who at pralaya having surrendered the 3 forms" (mūrti of the Trinity) which are upādhis exists in the form of the one Paramātmā : or Ka—A—Īsha : Ka—Brahmā ; A = Vis*h*nu ; Isha = Shiva : Keshava is He who controls these three : or Ka—Īsha = "He to whom Brahmā and Shiva are son and grandson." *See* Vol. XV of this Series.

2. See last note. 3. Foster father of K*r*is*h*na.

4. Chakra and Gadā which are His implements.

5. Epithet of Vis*h*nu as destroyer of the Asuras called Jana who dwell in the ocean ; or it also means the "one who is prayed to for the attainment of Purus*h*ārtha (that is, Dharma, Artha, Kāma, Moks*h*a). Vāchaspatya Dict.

6. Garu*d*a who is the vehicle (vāhana) of Vis*h*nu.

7. Narakārāte. Naraka, usally translated to mean 'hell', means 'rebirth'.

8. Epithet of Vis*h*nu as slayer of the Asura Madhu, *i. e.* Tamo gu*n*a

9. Collyrium (anjana) is used to clear the eyes and sight. The Lord clears the spiritual vision of His worshippers and grants them spiritual knowledge.

Obeisance to Thee, Our Lord (1)!
Salutation to Thee, Dispeller of all fears !

11

Reverence to Thee,
Who dost absorb all things in Thyself,
Who hast secured the Kaustubha gem (2).
Obeisance to Thee,
Who art beyond all sight (3)
And beyond all speech.

12

Salutation to Thee
Who art beyond all remembrance ;
Obeisance to Thee
Oh Cause in three-fold form (4)
Of creation, maintenance and dissolution,
Knowable in Thy various partial appearances (5),
Salutation to Thee.

13

Salutation to Vi*shn*u
Conqueror of the enemies of the Tridasha (6) ;
Paramātmā and Sūrya (7)

---

1. Ishāna.

2. A dark gem with the lustre of millions or suns which is worn by Vi*shn*u on His breast. It was formerly in the great ocean but Vi*shn*u having desired it, the gem was on the churning of the ocean secured by Him. *See ante* p. 34.

3. Nayanātīta. 4. As Brahmā, Vi*shn*u and Rudra.

5. Vibhinnajneyāṁsha, *lit.* "Whose various or seperate parts are knowable." The One has in Itself no parts but It displays Itself in various ways in the world. Each of such displays is a partial manifestation. What is seen is in this sense a part of Him.

6. Tridasha is a term for the Devas. Various explanations are given of the word. The simplest is that which makes it equal to $10 \times 3 + 3$ or 33 according to the rule of madhyapadalopa samāsa. These 33 are the following Devas, *viz.*, 12 Suns (Āditya), 11 Rudras, 8 Vasus, 2 Vishvedevas. According to another interpretation the term includes all Devas ; meaning t*ri*tīyā yauvanākhyā dashā yasya. As there are three states called infancy, boyhood and youth, tridasha then means he who has attained the third state called yauvana (youth), for the Devas are ever youthful. Or tri means he who has the "three," *viz.*, birth, existence, destruction ; not in the sense in which these terms are applied to mortal men who have increase, change and decay ; but they come into existence and exist and when their merit (pu*n*ya) is exhausted they leave Heaven and thus cease to be devas. They are called immortals (amara) but only in the limited sense of beings who exist until pralaya.—Or tri=thet hree pains (tāpa) for they who are not affected by the three-fold division, of sorrow.

7. Chakrabandhave ; *lit.* "friend of Chakra" which according to Hemādri here means the Sun (Sūrya) : for He is the Bharga, the Hira*n*ya Puru*sh*a in that golden luminary. *See* Chhāndogya Upani*sh*ad, Adhyāya I, Kha*n*da VI. *R*ik, 6 and 7.

Who holdeth the discus (1) whereby
The array of Thine enemies is destroyed.

14

Thou art in the form of the whole Universe
And art worshipped by the whole Universe,
Thou art the self of all beings in the Universe (2),
Salutation to Thee !
Thou art meditated upon by Yogins.
To Thee Who art the Inner Self (3), obeisance.

15

Salutation to Thee Who art the Giver of enjoyment (4)
To Thy devotees !
Reverence to Thee Who art the Giver of Liberation (5)
The actions of my mind, word and body
Should be meditation on Thee, praise of Thee and obeisance to Thee (6).

16

Oh Lord of Devas (7) !
All my actions should be worship of Thee (8)
And my worldly longings oblation to Thee.

Phalashloka.

The Mantrin (9) who in this manner
Is devotedly attached to the worship of Vi*sh*n*u*
By the doing of Havana, Japa, and Archā (10),
Such an one having certainly obtained all fruits of desire
And being wholly satisfied (11)
Attains that final Liberation (12)
Which is freedom from birth and death.

---

1. Chakra. 2. Vishvabhūtātmane. 3. Adhyātmarūpi*n*e. 4. Bhukti. 5. Mukti.

6. The purposes to which mental, vocal and bodily action should be put are His worship. In meditation (dhyāna) the operation of mind is displayed ; in hymns of praise (stuti), and in bowing or genuflection to make salutation (namaskriyā) the powers of speech and body are respectively used. 7. Devesha.

8. A fine line. Devesha karmasarvaṁ me bhaved ārādhanaṁ tava. A line wanting in the former edition has been found and printed in this. The Hymn now contains 16 verses. The last line is indicative of renunciation.

9. Mantrin = mantro guptabhā*sh*a*n*am yasya asti. He who has the mantra or secret word. Here used in the general sense of the initiated dovotee.

10. That is, Homa, "recitation" of Mantra and worship with flowers and other upachāra.

11. *Lit.* "having his antarātmā fully satisfied." 12. Uttamāṁ muktim.

CHAPTER XXII

Gives the twelve-lettered Mantra (1) of Vi*shn*u ; and three kinds of Nyāsa are prescribed with the letters of this Mantra : *viz.*,—Saṁhāranyāsa in which Nyāsa begins from the feet and proceeds upwards to the knees, liṁga, navel, belly, heart, hands, throat, mouth, eyes, head and the crown lock (Shikhā) (2) ; S*rishti*nyāsa in which the rite begins with the Shikhā in the reverse way ; and lastly, Sthitinyāsa in which the Nyāsa commences in the middle with the heart, goes down to the feet and then from the hand goes to the Shikhā. The first is for the destruction of all Do*sh*a (fault) ; S*rishti* is for the creation or production of good ; and the object of Sthiti is to gain peace (Shānti).

The Mantras of Sudarshana are given. The Chapter continues with ritual detail. The fruit gained varies with the offering made. Thus by the offering of bael leaf with appropriate Mantras freedom from disease is attained.

CHAPTER XXIII.

Gives several Mantras including that of Vi*shn*u as "The Charmer of the whole Universe" (Trailokyamohana). A remarkable meditation on Him is given in terms of sensuous splendour at vv. 37-49 and which is as follows :—

MEDITATION ON VI*SHN*U.

Think of a beautiful garden of Kalpa trees fragrant with the scent of flowers and musical with the humming of big bees. Therein meditate upon Ramāpati (3), seated on Garu*d*a (4) who is on a red lotus. The husband of Shrī (5) is the colour of a full blown red hibiscus flower and shines with the radiance of ten million rising suns. He is in the full flush of beauteous youth shedding the nectar of His sweet scented presence and lovely form. Kind is He to all. He holds a conch shell, bow, club (Mu*sh*ala), noose (Pāsha), discus (Chakra), sword, mace (Gadā), goad (Aṁkusha). His eyes

1. Oṁ Nama*h* Bhagavate Vāsudevāya.

2. Thus Oṁ padbhyāṁ nama*h* (Oṁ, salutation to the feet) ; Naṁ jānubhyāṁ nama*h* (Naṁ, salutation to the knees) ; Ma*h* liṁgāya nama*h* (Ma*h*, salutation to the Liṁga) ; Bhang nābhaye nama*h* (Bhang, salutation to the navel) and so on, thinking the while of the body of the I*sht*adevatā into which the Sādhaka's body is being transformed.

3. The husband of Ramā or Shrī or Lak*sh*mī ; that is, Vi*shn*u.

4. The bird-king who is His vehicle (vāhana).

5. Lak*sh*mī.

are fixed in gaze upon the face of Shrī, His spouse who embraces him in the fullness of Her love (1). Shrī is of peerless beauty and like molten gold, joyous and decked with all jewels. She holds a lotus. Her eyes are like lotuses thirsty to drink the honey from His lotus mouth. Such is the thrill (romāncha) of Her passion that it has covered Her body with pearly beads of sweat. In attendance upon them are all the Devas with their attendants, Daityas, Rāk*sh*asas (2), Gandharvas, Yak*sh*as, Pannagas (3) and the foremost of sages (Muni). Encircling Vi*shn*u and His spouse are their househld women with heavy thighs, hips and breasts (4), sweetly smiling. They look with ardent longing upon Him making obeisance with their soft folded hands. Pierced by the arrows of Anaṁga (5) they move voluptuously (6). Their lips part but scarcely utter a sound for they are tremulous with passion. Their hair and clothes are in disorder. They are shameless with passion (7). Their whole body shakes. They breathe heavily. All steadiness is stolen from them. They are about to fall, rent as they are by the terrible arrows of Manmatha (8). But yet they do not fall being strengthened and raised by the beauteous glance of Vi*shn*u. Forming lotuses as it were with their hands (9) they go towards Him and worship His two feet and with the murmur of hardly uttered words and with eyes wet with tears of joy say to Him "Supreme Lord and Husband, be our Refuge" (10).

This meditation is of a typical Vai*shn*ava quality. It is based on the idea which is expressed in the words said by the Vai*shn*ava Gurus or Gossains to their disciples, "I am Shyāma (K*ri*sh*n*a) you are Rādhā."

In His manifestation as Rādhā He is both the fount of Emotion (Rasa) and Emotion itself which includes the sexual sensation (Sh*ri*ṁgāra) and the higher love (Madhura) which in the more spiritually evolved marriage is associated with it. The worshipper rises above the unconscious animal life and the evil consciousness so often accompanying this up-

1. Madotka*t*ā : *lit.* She is in the extreme entrancement of passion.

2. Demonic beings.

3. Various kinds of lesser divinities (Devayoni). *See* The Great Liberation p. 2 & Notes.

4. Spa*sht*a-kaksha-jaghanastanana-bhārā.

5. "The Bodiless One" a title of Kāma, God of sexual desire.

6. Hāva-bhāva. *See ante* p. 40 *n.* 9.

7. Madanavigatalajjai*h*.

8. A title of Kāma as he who agitates tho mind, *See ante*, p. 39, *n.* 1. and Ward's Hindoos, II, 177, 178.

9. The hands are put together, with the palms upward and curved like the hollow of a flower.

10. Bhava parameṣhvara pati*h* shara*n*aṁ na*h*.

ward movement in which the passions are regarded as things only of and for the limited self (1). The gratification of sense in serving self alone is a "sowing to the flesh". He therefore identifies himself with Rādhā and thus places himself under the direction of Her Lord with whom She is one and who as the Antaryāmin or indwelling Spirit guides and controls the body and its senses. Thus gross desire is purified by its direction towards that abode of Vi*sh*nu wherein He as Gopāla plays and becomes as it were the vehicle on which subtle aspiration is made to rest. This inner sentiment has been sometimes exteriorised in accordance with the principle of Hindu worship whereby thought being translated into action is, by an established psychological law, reinforced by it. This is exampled by the Sakhibhāva of the Vai*sh*-*n*ava and certain ritual details in the Rahasyapūjā of the Shākta. A radical analysis af these theories and rites will, I believe, disclose a common ground and object, namely, the control and spiritualization of those passions which if left to themselves become so formidable impediments of spiritual progress. There are of course differences in the methods and devotional concepts :—Thus Vai*shn*ava wor*s*hip being of a dualistic trend retains the ideal distinctions of sex and person. In Shakti worship the aim is more directly monistic and accordingly the Sādhaka regards himself as the Devī whom he worships and not as the spouse of the Devatā even though according to the true inner doctrine governing both modes of adoration the ultimate object of it is one and the same. In his utilization of passion the Hindu has had the sense to know that we must do our market with and according to the funds in our purse. I wish also to add that if the Hindu described that passion in what to the prudish may seem "immodest" detail it was because he found nothing to be ashamed or afraid of in this natural state or function in itself but in its abuse which his Scriptures like any other forbid (2).

The western initiate however in these matters may say that these observations do not exhaust the subject and do not

---

1. These are the states of what other Tantras call that of the Pashu ; thus to take an example, the Kulār*n*ava Tantra calls "drinking as one pleases", pashupāna or the drinking of a Pashu or beast. The Vai*shn*ava view is all given in "The Soul of India" by Bipin Chandra Pal to which I refer.

2. These observations are merely here made because to some this kind of devotion is objectionable. Where (as is the general case) it is not understood the dislike of the general Anglo-Saxon temperament is due not to grounds of general validity but to special reasons largely peculiar to the race and its circumstances. According to orthodox interpretation it is "the Church's love unto Christ" which is symbolised in the highly sensuous imagery of the "Song of Solomon"; and abundant material, of the same kind, may be found in the Catholic mystics, to which the same kind of criticism has been applied.

touch upon those other principles which have been asserted according to which sexual relations or interactions are typal of relations universally existent as well as of all action absolutely; the process of redemption (to use western parlance) moreover being according to this view the assimilation of the earthly to the heavenly planes, all physical, psychic and spiritual life being varying forms and degrees of intensity in the one universal stream of radiant Energy. Criticism however of these views or a further developement of the subject either from the Western or Indian stand-point would carry me beyond the scope of my present purpose.

The Chapter continues with an enunciation of the offerings which should be given and the rules relating to worship. The worshipper of this Mantra, it is said, acquires wealth and freedom from the oppression of his enemies and in the end attains to the abode of Vi*sh*n*u.

After the disjointed fashion of several other parts of the work, at v. 64 the magical rites of Stambhana, Māra*n*a and Uchchā*t*ana are again referred to though they seem to have no connection with the other subjects of this Chapter.

CHAPTER XXIV

Deals with the Varāha (1), another Vai*sh*n*ava Mantra. Verse 24 says Earth is in the tusks of Varāha; the Goddess of Speech is in the grunt of this Boar; Air in His breath and the Sun and Moon are in His right and left hands. In His belly are the Vasus (2); in His ear the points of the compass; the two Ashvins (2) are in His eyes; in His feet is the Lotus born (3); in His heart Hari (4); and in His mouth Shaṁkara (5). These should all be worshipped separately. The rest of the Chapter deals with the ritual, Nyāsa, Homa, Yantra and so forth connected with this particular Mantra.

CHAPTER XXV

Describes the N*ri*siṁha (6) Mantra and the ritual connected therewith. The Dhyāna will be found in v. 8.

---

1. The Varāha (boar) incarnation of Vi*sh*n*u was for the purpose of drawing up with His tusk the Earth which at one of the dissolutions had sunk into the waters.

2. The Devatās of those names. 3. Brahmā. 4. Vi*sh*n*u. 5. Shiva.

6. The man-lion incarnation of Vi*sh*n*u in which He destroyed the demon Hira*n*yakashipu. Hira*n*yakashipu (= mattress of gold) is pride of wealth and power.

CHAPTER XXVI

Deals with the Vi*shn*upanjara Mantra. In v. 21 the Dhyāna or formula of meditation on Vi*shn*u is given. The rest of the Chapter deals with the ritual.

CHAPTER XXVII

Gives the Prāsāda Mantra (1) which is so called because it purifies the mind. V. 4 gives the Dhyāna of Shiva. The five Devatās of this Mantra are the five faces of Shiva, *viz.* :— Īshāna, Tatpuru*sh*a, Aghora, Vāmadeva, Sadyojāta. The Dhyānas of these are given. The Pī*th*a Shaktis are Vāmā, Jye*shth*ā, Raudrī, Kālī, Kalavikari*n*ī, Balavikari*n*ī, Balapramathinī, Sarvabhūtadamanī and Manonmanī.

Dhyāna is given of the various aspects of Shiva (vv. 15, 16). As Sadyojāta He is white like the jasmine (Kunda) and Mandāra flowers. He is four-armed holding in His two hands the Veda and a rosary of Rudrāk*sh*a beads and in the other two he makes the gestures (Mudrā) which grant boons (Vara) and dispel fear (Abhaya).

The Vāma Shiva is red ; makes the same two gestures and holds an axe and Rudrāk*sh*a rosary.

Aghora Shiva who is the dread of the Bodiless One (2) is black with fierce fangs. He holds a Rudrāk*sh*a rosary, Veda, Noose, Goad, Drum (*D*amaru), a staff surmounted with a skull (Kha*t*vāṁga), spear and skull (3).

Tatpuru*sh*a is of the colour of ligntning and making the Vara and Abhaya Mudrās holds the Veda and an axe. All the above forms have four faces and four arms.

Īshāna or Īsha is of the colour of pearl but has five faces (4). He makes the gestures abovenamed and has the weapons in the hands of Aghora. These five are Brahmā, Vi*shn*u, Rudra, Īshvara and Shiva. All five forms have three eyes (5).

---

1. For the Parāprāsāda Mantra *See* Ch. IV. of Kulā*r*nava Tantra.

2. Kāma, the Deva of sexual desire. According to the reading now adopted, 'tanu' for 'tano', the meaning is 'Aghora Shiva is huge in shape, of a luminous black colour, terrific of aspect with fierce fangs.'

3. Another Dhyāna of Aghora is given at v. 18 of Ch. 28.

4. Where Shiva is meditated upon as Sadyojāta, Vāma, *etc.*, collectively He is thought of as with five faces in all. But when the Dhyāna is of one of these forms only then the Mūrti has four or five faces as stated in the text.

5. The central eye of wisdom (jnānachak*sh*u*h*) situated between the eyebrows.

There is a remarkable (1) Dhyāna of Shiva in v. 41 where He is described as of gracious aspect; seated on a lotus; as it were "a mountain of pearl dust mingled in nectar." He is clad in tiger's skin and decked with ornaments (2); upon His hair high coiled above His head is a digit (Kalā) of the moon (3). He makes the two Mudrās abovenamed and holds an axe and a deer (4). He has five faces.

At vv. 55-64 the following Hymn to Shiva is given.

HYMN TO SHIVA

Obeisance
To Paramātmā
Manifest as Brahmā, Vi*shn*u and Īsha (5)
Whose power it is to create, preserve and to destroy (6).

2

Obeisance
To Thee, the Lord of creatures, Holder of the trident.
Who seemeth terrible to all things born on earth in fourfold way (7)
And yet removes the burden of their worldly pain.

3

Obeisance to Thee
Who didst drink the shining deadly poison,
Nīlaka*nth*a, Whose throat is stained thereby (8)
And Who dost devour the Universe (9).

---

1. Because the ordinary picture of Shiva is that of an ascetic but as appears from the text the Dhyāna varies with the object of worship. When worshipped for prosperity He has fleshly beauty and is decked with all ornaments. He manifests the prosperity which the worshipper desires.

2. Sarvālamkāradīpta.

3. The crescent moon is here meant.

4. V. 22 of the Mahimnastava of Pu*sh*padanta refers to the incident of Brahmā's lusting after His own daughter Sandhyā and of his transforming Himself into a stag when she to avoid him changed into a hind. Shiva in anger at the act bent his bow against him. The deer which He holds is said by some to be Brahmā. According to others it refers to a gigantic deer sent out to kill Shiva, but which He took in his hand, *See* Shivajnāna Siddhiyār, Ed. by J. M. N. Pillai, p. 91. M*r*iga (=deer) means Veda. Shiva for the ordinary man holds a deer in His hand. But the higher Sādhaka sees the Veda or Brahmajnāna.

5. Rudra.

6. They are the embodiments of these principles.

7. That is, from the womb, (*e.g.*, mammals) from the egg (*e.g.*, birds), moisture (*e.g.*, insects) and the earth (*e.g.*, trees and plants). *See ante*, p. 8.

8. At the churning of the ocean by the Gods by means of the mountain Mandara and the serpent Vāsuki, there was produced amongst other things churned from the sea a poison which Shiva swallowed to save the world. This stained His neck dark blue whence he is called "Blue neck" (Nīlaka*nth*a).

9. At the dissolution of the world which He as Mahākāla effects.

4.

Obeisance to Shambhu (1)
Who didst destroy Kāma (2)
Flashing from His central eye dark shining flame,
On Whom meditate Yogīs
Freed of all mental pain (3).

5.

Obeisance
To Him Whose body is one with that of His Spouse (4),
Who destroyed the sacrifice of Daksha (5),
Grantor of the four-fold desires (6),
He Who is subtle (7), the possessor of Māyā (8).

6.

Obeisance to Him
In physical form (9) ; the Primal element (10)
Rending His enemies with His trident,
The Destroyer of Kāla (11)
Whose head the cresent moon adorns.

7.

Obeisance
To Him the Naked One
In Whose matted hair are Serpent, Moon and Ganges (12)
Whose feet are upon the heads of Devas, Daityas, and Lords of Asuras,

---

1. A form and title of Shiva. Meaning "from Him comes good" or "Who is Bliss." Comm. Ch. IV, v 18 Hathayogapradīpikā.

2. God of Desire. See A. & E. Avalon's Hymns to the Goddess, p 39 n (3).

3. In Yoga upon the supression of the activity of the intellectual function, the first and most subtle manifestation of Prakriti or Māyā, there arises the condition of samādhi in which the Ātmā exists in its own true state freed of all pains attendant on its conditioned state.

4. Ardhanārsihvara ; the androgyne form in which half of the body is Shiva and the other half Shakti.

5. *See* "Principles of Tantra" Vol. I. p. 104.

6. Dharma, Artha, Kāma and Moksha.

7. Anu : atom. So in Nyāya, ātmā is said to be as fine as an atom. In the next verse His gross aspect is sung.

8. Māyī. He is shaktimān ; *cf.* the line "māyāṁ cha prakritiṁ vidyāt māyinaṁ tu maheshvaram."

9. The gross in opposition to the subtle (sūkshma) aspect celebrated in the preceding verse. This body is Māyā or Prakriti which when it is the constituent of the physical world is gross (sthūla).

10. Mūlabhūta.

11. Death or time in which lies the seed of death.

12. The Ganges in its descent from heaven at the call of Bhagīratha was caught in the matted hair of Shiva. It is for this that She is called Bhāgīrathī. *See ante* p. 33.

8.

Obeisance, obeisance
To Shaṁkara (1) besmeared with ashes,
Who is both the manifest and unmanifest (2),
The Grantor both of enjoyment and of Liberation (3) to His devotees.

9.

Obeisance
To the Enemy of Death and Andhaka (4),
Who is the Destroyer of the cities (5);
Obeisance to Thee Who didst rend the tusked Boar (6),
Obeisance ever to Thee
Entwined with great poisonous serpents,
Who art borne upon a great bull (7).

10

Obeisance ever to the Omnipresent One,
Appearing as ether, air, fire, water, earth
Sun, sacrifier and moon with nectar rays (8) !
Dispeller of the dread of Hell,
Mayest Thou both now and here (9)
Destroy our wordly fear (10).

---

1. Shiva. Shaṁkara = Beneficence.

2. Vyaktāvyaktasvarūpāya Avyakta is what is unmanifested and vyakta what is manifested. According to Sāṁkhya, avyakta is mūlaprakriti and vyakta is a vikriti or transformation and manifestation of Prakriti. According to the Vedānta, Avyakta is Ātmā the Reality and Vyakta the World of appearance.

3. For the Tantra grants both.

4. A great Daitya, son of Hiranyāksha, brother of Hiranyakashipu father of Prahlāda. *See* Ch. 8. Vāmana Purāna 59, 70. The word also means tamoguna, ignorance.

5. Shiva is Tripurāri exoterically as the destroyer of the Tripura or the three cities of the Asuras, Kamalāksha, Tārakāksha and Vidyunmālī. As the Kālikā Purāna says He is called Tripura because the three gunas are in him. His body becoming triple upon the three-fold manifestation of Brahmā, Vishnu and Rudra. He dissoloves these and He is Destroyer of the three bodies, Sthūla, Sūkshma and Kārana.

6. The Varāha Avatāra of Vishnu slain by Shiva in the form of the animal called Sharabha. Kālikā Purāna, Ch. 29.

7. The Vāhana of Shiva. The bull of Shiva is Vishnu who assumed that form to support Shiva at the time the latter killed Tripura. Shiva had for the purpose of the combat to assume so great a size using as his arrow the Sumeru Mountain that the Earth could not support Him, on which Vishnu assumed the form of a Bull to uphold Him. Vrishabha (Bull) means Dharma. Shiva (Beneficence) rests on Dharma.

8. The eight forms (Ashtamūrti) of Shiva. 9. In this world.

10. Bhavabhaya : that is, fear at the thought that we may be born again to suffer miseries which are the necessary attendants of all life in this world.

The rest of the Chapter deals with ritual, v. 68 giving an invocation to Shiva as Hara. Verse 68 says :—

"I adore Hara Who holds a spear and skull and makes the gestures of granting boons and dispelling fear. The Daughter of the Mountain holding in Her left hand a red lotus is seated on His left thigh and with Her right arm clasps His lustrous body."

Verse 71 says that in order to gain prosperity the Lord of Pārvatī should be meditated upon as being as beautiful as the God of Desire (Kāma) ; with the lustre of gold ; seated on a lotus decked with all manner of ornaments. He holds an axe and deer and makes the gesture (Mudrā) of granting boons. His left hand is placed upon the breast of His beloved, Whose right hand rests on His right thigh, and Whose left hand holds a red lotus.

CHAPTER XXVIII

Opens with the Mantra and description of Dak*shin*āmūrti, an aspect of Shiva. He is seated under a fig tree (Va*t*a) with one hand on His knee. He is white as milk (K*sh*īra). A great serpent is coiled around His waist. The crescent moon is on His matted hair. He holds an axe and deer and makes the auspicious (Bhadra) gesture (1). He is surrounded by Shuka and other Munis. "May Bhava grant ye purity of mind (Bhāvashuddhi)." Then follows some ritual in His worship.

Verses 12, 13 give the Mantra of Aghora Rudra and is followed in v. 18 by this invocation. "May Aghora destroy all that is evil to you. He is of fierce mien with three eyes and terrific to behold ; dark like the black clouds and clad in red raiment. Great serpents cover His body. He holds an axe, drum, sword, shield, bow, arrow, spear and skull. He it is Who devours inimical Nāgas (2) and evil planets. He ever grants good (that is, to His worshipper)".

The ritual is dealt with up to v. 30. The next verse gives the M*ri*tyunjayamantra ; and the Dhyāna of this aspect is at v. 33. The remainder of the Chapter deals with Yantra and other ritual details.

---

1. That is, Jnānamudrā. 2. Serpent Divinities.

CHAPTER XXIX

Commences with the Mantra of Ardhanārīshvara (1). The Dhyāna of Umesha is thus given at v. 3 after the invocation "May Isha ever protect you." His Shakti forms the (left) half of His body. He is three-eyed. On the coils of His matted hair are a serpent, moon and Ganges (2). He holds serpent, axe, spear, sword, fire (3), skull, arrow and bow. All the Devas lower their heads at His feet,

For the attainment of powers (Vibhūti) the Devatā should be meditated upon (v. 4.) as being in one half of His body, a man of ferocious aspect and in the other half as a voluptuous woman (4), holding in His and Her hands a noose, a red lotus a skull and spear ; or (v. 5) She should be thought of as the three-eyed One Who is red of colour, clothed in red raiment, adorned with red ornaments holding a spear in each of Her sixteen uplifted hands.

Rules are then given for Japa, Homa and so forth.

The colour of the Deva varies according to the object of worship (v. 13). When worshipped for Pu*sh*t*i*karma (5) and Shāntikarma (6), He is white ; for Ākar*sh*a*n*a and Vashīkara*n*a (7), red ; for K*sh*obha and Saṁstobhana (8), He is the colour of gold ; in rites done to drive away (9), torment of the body (10), the colour of smoke (Dhūmra) ; in rites performed to paralyze (11) , yellow ; and to gain Liberation, crytalline white (12).

The ritual in the worship of Ardhanārīshvara is dealt with up to v, 30. At v. 31 the Cha*nd*a Mantra and at vv. 36, 37 the Cha*nd*a Gāyatrī are given. The Chapter concludes with other details as to the worship of the fierce aspect of Shiva called Cha*nd*a.

---

1. The androgyne form of Shiva in which half the body is male (Himself) and half or the body of His spouse (Shakti)is female. *See* Shāradātilaka, XIX. v. 55 and notes.

2. *See* p. 56. *n* 12. 3. Vahni.

4. Hāva-bhāva-lalitārdhanārikaṁ. This is the Dhyāna of Ardhanārīshvara ; the Dhyāna in v. 5 is for Krūraprayoga.

5. Ritual done to produce nourishment, growth, increase, advance, prosperity, *etc.*

6. Ritual done to gain peace of mind and body.

7. Rites done to attract and control respectively. These and the following are magical rites ; portions of the *shat*karma, *etc.*

8. That is, for causing perturbation of the mind and for restraining speech and power of expression. 9. Uchchā*t*ana. 10. Aṁgārdana. 11. Stambhana.

12. It should be noted that in every case the Mantra also changes.

CHAPTER XXX.

This is an important Chapter dealing with the Gāyatrī Mantra. In v. 5 it is explained how the Pra*n*ava (1) produced by Prak*ri*ti-vik*ri*ti is like the humming of bees in the Mūlādhāra (2) and goes upwards along the channel of the Su*sh*umnā (3) in seven stages (4) to the head. V. 6 enumerates the seven Vyāh*ri*tis (5). In vv. 7-10 Mahāvi*shn*u teaches what these denote. Bhū*h* is mere existence alone (Sanmātra). Bhuva*h* is elements (Bhūta) and Cause (Kāra*n*a) Sva*h* is the Guide and the Ātmā of all that is (6) ; Maha*h* implies Greatness and Light (7); Tat, (Brahman) is Jana*h* because It is all (8). Tapa*h* denotes Jnānatā (All knowledge) and Tāpatā (9). Satyam implies Supremacy and Ātmatva or the natural state of Ātmā, that is, Ātmā in itself, and eternal Wisdom (Anantajnāna). The exoteric "worlds" are thus described as stages of being. The letters of the Pra*n*ava are then identified with them. A is Bhu*h*, U is Bhuva*h*, M is Sva*h*, Maha*h* is Bindu, Nāda is Jana*h*, Shakti is Tapa*h*, and Shānta is Satyam the highest of these states (vv. 11, 12).

Having dealt with Oṁ, Mahāvi*shn*u deals with each of the words of the Gāyatrī Mantra (10).

Tat is in the accusative singular. By it reference is made to the first Cause of all substance (Vastu). It exists in the form of fire and energy (Tejorūpa) in the disc of the Sun (Ādityama*nd*ala). It means the ever-blissful and Supreme Brahman. *Savituh* is in the genitive singular and is derived from a root which means to bring forth By this word is implied the source of all animate beings. It is called *Vareny-*

1. Oṁ. *See* Shāradātilaka XXI. vv. 1-31 and notes thereto. Rāghava in his Commentary under verse 18 gives the fourth pāda of the Gāyatrī which is recited by the seeker of Liberation. It is Parorajase sāvadoṁ.

2. The lowest of the centres (*Shat*chakra). *See* A. Avalon's "The Serpent Power."

3. The nerve (Nādī) of that name v. *ib.*

4. The six Chakras and the Sahasrāra. *See ante* p. 43 for the seven parts of the Pra*n*ava, also below.

5. That is, the seven upper worlds—Bhū*h*, Bhuva*h*, Sva*h*, Maha*h*, Jana*h*, Tapa*h*, Satyam.

6. Sarvasya svīra*n*āt svātmatayā.

7. Mahattvāt cha mahastvāt cha,

8. Tadeva sarvajanatā tasmāt tad vyāh*ri*tirjana*h*. Janatā=Janasamūha*h*.

9. This word which is here not translated literally means heating, suffering, and comes from the same root as does tapas or austerity, It means here the sum of distress and suffering to which, through ignorance, humanity is liable. The text here shows that the Gāyatrī mantra as a whole and in its parts is one with the Brahman.

10. Tat savitur vare*n*yam bhargo devasya dhīmahi dhiyo yo na*h* prachodayāt.

am because it is the Excellent One to Whom service should be rendered, adoration offered, and prayer said. The text reads these three words as composed of eight letters (Ak*sh*ara) and says that their Vyāh*ri*ti is Bhū*h*.

Bharga is so called because It destroys sin and is propitious to the devotee. *Devasya* implies that It has the luminous quality of light and is possessed of the power of giving rain and the like. *Dhīmahi* is derived from the root *dhyai* which means to think. "Let us here remember that the Deva who can be seen by the celestial eyes of Nigama (1) and knowledge (Vidyā) is golden (Hira*n*maya) and ever in the Sun, His lustre knows no diminution. Ever should we think what is subtle that I am (ya*h* sūk*sh*ma*h* so ham)." Bhuva*h* is the Vyāh*ri*ti of these second three words composed of eight letters.

Dhiyo (2) means Buddhi in the accusative plural. *Yo* is Ya*h*, the masculine gender being here used for the neuter (3) for the sake of the metre. It therefore stands for Yat. This Yat is the incomparable Energy (Tejas) which pervades all the Vedas. It destroys the sin of the devotee. *Na*h (our) is the genitive plural of Asmad. *Prachodayāt* means "May it send us in the path of prayer" (Prārthanā) (4). *Sva*h is the Vyāh*ri*ti of the third set of eight letters (vv. 13-26).

This Mantra of ten words is thus divided into three sections of eight letters each ; but it can also be divided into four sections of six letters each. The Mahāvi*sh*nu concludes by saying "May the excellent and Supreme Spirit (Bharga) of the Creative Lord (Deva Savitā) on Whom we meditate ever guide and direct our minds."

He then proceeds to speak of the Shira*h* (head) of Gāyatrī. Āpa*h*, Jyoti*h*, Rasa are the energy (Tejas) of Soma and Agni (5). The Universe is in the nature of this (Tadātmakam). It is Nectar (Am*ri*ta) because it is undestructible. By reason of this and His multiplicity or all-pervadingness Brahman is so called. Brahman who is Bliss itself (Ānandātmaka) and Satya (Truth) (6) and Jnāna (Knowledge or Consciousness) is Bhū*h*

1. A term for the Veda, and in the special sense Tantra.

2. Dhiya*h*, changed by the rule of Sandhi.

3. Yat as corresponding with Tat.

4. Ordinarily it is said "in the path of dharma, artha, kāma, mok*sh*a" But if prayer is made to God it must be for these for they include all man's aims.

5. By Soma and Agni, Prak*ri*ti and Puru*sh*a are meant. The Shira*h* of the Gāyatrī is:—Oṁ āpo jyotī raso'm*ri*taṁ bhūrbhuva*h* svaroṁ.

6. Sat is existence and truth (Satya) alone exists. Here the existence of the Brahman who is Sat, Chit, Ānanda is meant. The text is capable of other interpretations.

Bhuva*h*, Sva*h*, It has already been shown that "So'haṁ" "I am He" is Oṁ. Thus this Mantra is the Shira*h* of the Gāyatrī (1). Thus concluding the exposition of the points (Lak*shana*) of the Mantra, Mahāvi*shn*u says that the faithful Sādhaka who worships with desire (2) obtains the fulfilment thereof and he who seeks Liberation gets it.

Then follow rules of ablutions in Gāyatrī Sādhana. Vv. 40-45 deal with the *Rishis*, Devatās and metre of Pra*n*ava, the Vyāh*ri*tis and the Gāyatrī. The mode of doing Nyāsa is also stated. Verses 46-50 describe the way Upāsanā, Japa, Svādhyāya (3), Prā*n*āyāma and Dhyāna in Her subtle form, of the Gāyatri are to be done. V. 60 gives a Dhyāna of Tāri*nī* (Gāyatrī) (4), in her gross form with four faces which are white, yellow, red and black ; Her body being composed of the 24 letters of the Gāyatrī. V. 61 speaks of the worship of the Sun and His Shaktis. Mahāvi*shn*u concludes by saying "I have now spoken of the secret of the Vedas knowable only by very pure Yogīs. He who in his Japa, Homa. and Dhyāna worships Oṁkāra in this way is freed of all Karma and attains Liberation."

CHAPTER XXXI

Commences with the Tri*sht*ubh Mantra (5) which is Vedīk ; the Dhyāna of the Adhi-Devī of the Mantra who is Kātyāyanī is given in v. 9 and Her nine Shaktis in vv. 13, 14. In vv. 18-23 are to be found the names of the Shaktis of the letters of the Mantra. It is noted that the number of Japa prescribed (v. 25.) for this Mantra is twice that of the Gāyatrī. The Mantra which is composed of 44 letters, if reversed, becomes the (v. 29) Astra (weapon) mantra and is divided into eight sections which are identified with various things, the senses of knowledge, the senses of action, the five elements and so forth (vv. 30-34). From these 44 letters issue 44 Vahni Devatās, each of whom is attended by 5 Shaktis ; each of whom is attended by five handmaidens ; each of whom is again attended by 16 handmaidens ; each of whom again is attended by millions upon millions of handmaidens (40-43).

---

1. The Mantra at p. 61 *n*. 5 always precedes the Gāyatrī.
2. That is Sakāma Sādhana or worship done to gain an object.
3. Rite whereby oneness of the Mantra with the Devatā thereof is realised.
4. She who saves : for that is what of the Gāyatrī mantra does to its singer.
5. *See* Shāradātilaka, Ch. xxi, vv, 32 *et. seq.* Rāghava gives the Mantra and other details. The Devatā of the Mantra is Agni.

In v. 48 the Nak*sh*atras (1) are divided into three classes ; human (Mānu*sh*a), demonic (Asura) and celestial (Daiva). Their place in magical rites is also shown.

From verse 55 to the end of the Chapter Mahāvi*shn*u speaks of the magical rites relating to Stambhana, Vashīkara*n*a, Ākar*sh*a*n*a, Vidve*sh*a*n*a, Vimohana, Māra*n*a, Aṁgahānikara*n*a (2) and so forth ; and the means to be taken to counteract these operations when done by others. It is noteworthy here and in many other places that the most diverse matters are placed together. This is also the case with many verses which seem hardly in their proper place, suggesting a doubt as to the accuracy of the order in which the copying has been done.

CHAPTER XXXII

Deals with the Lava*n*a Mantra and Māra*n*a, Vashīkara*n*a and other magical rites. Verse 8 gives the Dhyāna of Kātyāyanī a form of Durgā. Her body is like the "friend of air" (3). She has three eyes and wears a bright crown. She holds discus (Chakra), conch, sword and spear and is the Destructress of many Daityas. Dhyānas are also given of Rātri (night), Agni and Bhadrakālī with prayers to these Deities. The fifth Mantra, it is said, is from the Atharva Veda.

CHAPTER XXXIII

Deals with the Anu*sht*ubh Mantra (4) of 32 letters which is Vedik ; the Dhyāna of the Deva of the Mantra who is Rudra is given in v. 8 and the 32 Shaktis in vv. 12-14. Then follow ritual details. At vv. 27, 28, a Mantra of a 100 letters (Shatāk*sh*ara) is mentioned. It is formed by the junction of Gāyatrī, Tri*sht*ubh and Anu*sht*ubh Mantras. These three Mantras are respectively Sun, Fire and Moon. The Devatā of the combined Mantra is (v. 31) the supreme Maha*h* who grants Liberation and of whom Shruti speaks. Vv. 60 *et seq* give the Nyāsa and other rites in connection

1. See p. 25, *n*, 5 *ante*.

2. Paralyzing, bringing under control, attracting, causing dissension, bewildering, killing, limb-destroying. Thus if Homa is done to Black Durgā in the manner described an enemy is killed and so forth.

3. Pavanasakha : Fire is so called.

4. The Shāradātilaka, Ch. xxiii, deals with this Mantra and Rāghava cites it.

with this Mantra. This is followed by (vv. 43-47) the Saṁvādasūkta a Mantra of Saṁvā*da*-saṁjnānāgni and the rites relating thereto. At v. 56 is given the *Ri*k and at v. 59 Dhyāna of Varu*n*a the predominating colour which the meditation seeks to excite being white. Ritual details as regards His worship follow.

CHAPTER XXXIV

Commences with rules relating to the drawing of diagrams (Yantra). Verse 33 describes a Yantra whereby the Sādhaka can make a woman desire him. Vv. 34-36 gives the Brahmashrī Mantra the Devatā of which is Gaurī. At v. 38 is a Dhyāna of Pārvatī. This is followed by a number of Mantras and Dhyānas of the Devatās thereof : the Rājamukhī (43-45) ; the Annapradāyaka (v. 51) ; Annapūr*n*ā (v. 54) ; V*ri*haspati (v. 60) ; Shukra (v. 63) and Vyása (v. 65) Mantras. In verse 66 the Dhyāna of Vyāsa is given. Verse 72 gives the Mantra and v. 74 the Dhyāna of Ādyā as Ashvārū*dh*ā (Seated on a horse).

CHAPTER XXXV

Gives the Prā*n*aprati*shth*ā Mantra used in the invocation of the Devatā into the Yantra or image to be worshipped.

At v. 7, a Dhyāna of Prā*n*ashakti is given in which She is represented as of the colour of the rising sun with three eyes and large full rounded breasts (1) seated on a full blown lotus which is on a boat in an ocean of blood (Raktāmbhodhi) ; holding a noose, a bow of sugarcane, a goad, five arrows (2) and As*ri*k-kapāla (3). Her Dūtīs or Shaktis are stated in verse 12.

CHAPTER XXXVI

Begins with some verses as to the causes of childlessness which are put down to want of faith, worship, charity, decrying

1. Pīnavak*sh*oruhā*dh*yā.
2. See A. & E. Avalon's "Hymns to the Goddess", p. 28, *n*. 9.
3. Skull full of blood.

(Nindaka) one's wife and so forth : and vv. 8-21 deal with the rites to be performed to cure this defect. Then follows an enunciation of the proper characteristics of a Guru (vv. 22-32) and of a disciple (vv. 32-41). If the disciple has the defects which are mentioned in vv. 42-48 he should be rejected and if a Guru received such a person as his disciple then the fault (Dos*h*a) of the latter affects the Guru just as that of the minister affects the king, and the sins of a wife affect her husband. If through either cupidity or affection a Guru initiates such a faulty disciple then the curse of the Devatā falls upon both (vv. 49 51).

Mahāvis*hn*u then speaks of the devotion which a disciple should exhibit towards his Guru or spiritual director and which is to be like that which should be shown to mother and father, to Vis*hn*u and Shiva (vv. 51-52). One should not cross anything belonging to, or connected with the Guru, not even his shadow ; nor should there be association with his enemy. Great reverence and selfrestraint should be shown whilst in his house. Therein there should be no anger and quarelling, lust, loud talk, lies, sloth and idle disputation ; nor any easing of nature, sexual intercourse, spitting, vomiting ; or traffic by way of buying, selling, or lending (vv. 53-55). The Guru's command should not be disobeyed. What he orders, that the disciple should do at once and unhesitatingly and without attempting to discuss whether it is right or wrong (1). In short the disciple should by action, mind and speech, worship his Guru with a guileless and faithful heart. At v. 59 it is said that one should never do anything which offends others, however much we may desire it even in so small a matter as dress.

At v. 62 Mahāvis*hn*u addressing Brahmā says "Oh Lotus-born One, in this Tantra (2) I have shown thee the Prapancha (3) in its five-fold aspect."

This Chapter and the work concludes with the following invocation.

---

1. Is*ht*aṁ vānis*ht*am ādis*ht*aṁ guru*n*ā yattu gurvapi,
Tvarayā parayā kuryād buddhyā samyag ajihmayā (V. 56).

This appears to solve in an extreme sense a point raised by St. Alphonsus Liguori as to the duties of a penitent towards his spiritual director, but possibly as in the case of all general rules there may be some exception here.

2. Tantre'smin. *See ante* p 4

3. *See ante* p. 1.

Obeisance to Him
Who is Energy and Light (1) itself
In Whom are the products of Prak*ri*ti (2),
Sun, Moon and Fire (3)
Which have sprung from the Tāra and other Bījas (4)
And which have their motion and increase
In Him.

CALCUTTA ;
The 24th January 1914.

ARTHUR AVALON.

---

1. Tejas.

2. *Lit.* the Vik*ri*tis of Prak*ri*ti. *See ante* p. 7.

3. Not merely the luminaries and elements so named but that also for which they stand as symbols.

4. That is, from Oṁ and other "Seed-mantras."

POSTSCRIPT

In the present edition the text has been rearranged. This has been done in accordance with the Commentary by Padmapādāchārya, now published for the first time. The two manuscripts available to the editor at the time the book was first published as Vol. III in this series, had the chapters in the order as in the book then published. There were some misgivings as to the correctness of the order in which the chapters were placed. Chapter 36 of that edition is devoted to Vi*shn*u rituals and its proper place, it was felt, was with the group of chapters dealing with the Vi*shn*u aspect of the Supreme Being. In the same way Chapter 33 in that edition should, it was felt, come at the end of the Book. But editors of any Shāstra have to be very reluctant to interfere with the text of their own motion as a rule, and should be more so in the case of Mantra-shāstra. It was on this account that the book was printed as it was in the manuscripts. Almost simultaneously with the publication by us of the Prapanchasāra, there was another recension published as part of the collected works of Shaṁkarāchārya from Srirangam. This publication received the support of the Sringeri Ma*tha*. In the Srirangam edition, the text of the Prapanchasāra is divided into 33 chapters, but the matter contained in it is almost identical with that contained in our publication, with this exception, that chapter 36 which is chapter 23 in the present edition is omitted. The reason for the omission may be explained by the fact that the manuscript available to the editors did not contain the chapter. It is called the Gupta Pa*t*ala or Secret Doctrine by Rāghava Bha*tt*a in his commentary of the Shāradātilaka (Ch. 17. 1). The editor of the Srirangam publication has also followed the wise method of not interfering with the text. It has evidently been printed as contained in the manuscript and even some palpable errors have not been set right. The editor, it may reasonably be presumed, hoped that in a subsequent edition the mistakes would be corrected with the help of other manuscripts. In the present edition, the following re-arrangement has been made. Chapter 36 of the first edition is here printed as 23, 34 as 32, 33 as 36, 32 as 34 and Chapter 31 as 33.

Padmapāda was one of the immediate disciples of Saṁkarāchārya and there can be no greater authority than he, as to the order in which the chapters are to be placed. His commentary named the "Vivara*n*a" is printed here for the first time. The only other works by him, so far known, are the Panchapādikā which deals with the Vedānta Sūtras and a commentary on the well-known Mantra of five letters of Shiva, (Shivapanchāk*sh*ara) printed at the end of this book.

It cannot be claimed that the text as published is complete and free from all blemishes. We had a copy of this furnished by the Adyar Library where there are two copies of the Vivara*n*a. A copy was obtained from the manuscript in the collection of the Madras Government. The Asiatic Society of Bengal has a fragment of the Vivara*n*a which contains the commentary of the first eight chapters of the book. The press copy was further read by Mr. Shrīnivāsa Aiyer who compared it with a manuscript in his possession.

The Prayoga-krama dīpikā is a gloss on Padmapāda's Vivara*n*a. Unfortunately, a complete copy of this could not be obtained inspite of all the efforts made. It ends with the ninth chapter of the book. It was felt that as it contained all the chapters dealing with the general principles of Mantra-shāstra, as also the chapters on Sarasvatī and Tripurā, the best thing to do would be to publish it as found. H. H The late Mahārājādhirāja Rameswar Singh of Darbhanga who glanced through it, considered that in spite of its defective readings in several places, it is of great practical value and supported the view taken by the editor. The Prayoga-krama-dīpikā is meant for the Sādhaka, but even the ordinary reader, whose quest is to trace the philosophical principles underlying the ritualistic practices of the Brahmanik faiths will find much of very great interest to himself.

The Vivara*n*a and the Prayoga-krama dīpikā will help to show him that Brahmanism is not as is commonly, in ignorance, supposed to be a mass of conflicting religious faiths. In Brahmanism, there is one goal for all different forms of Sādhanā and that goal is the Brahman. Unlike the followers of other forms of of religion, the follower of the Brahmanik faith has no quarrel with any one. He is aware that all men cannot have the same temperament and therefore cannot view things in the same way and it is on this account that even within the Brahmanik fold, there are quite a number of different forms of worship or Sādhanā. These are primarily divided into five classes, *viz.* Shaiva, Shākta, Vai*shn*ava, Saura and Gā*n*apatya. All these five aspects are dealt with in this book. The Prapanchasāra is the first book of its kind. Other eminent writers followed the great master ; the most noticeable among these being Lakshmana Deshikendra, Ishānashiva, Krishnānanda and many others less known.

The Vivarana does not give details like Rāghava Bhatta for instance, in his commentary on the Shāradātilaka, and Bhāskararāya in the works commented on by him. It is possible that at the time the book was written great details were not needed, as the men of those days were better informed. Or it may be, that he meant it only for that class of readers who did not require any greater help for the understanding of the text. The author of the Prayoga-krama dīpikā, which was evidently written at a much later age, has given these details and made the Vivarana intelligible in places which are obscure for present day learners. We know nothing about the author of the Dīpikā not even his name, but it is evident from his writings that his knowledge of the Shāstra was great and he believed Shaṁkarāchārya to be the author of the Prapanchasāra and Padmapāda, of the Vivarana.

There are several other commentaries of the Prapanchasāra by various writers written at different times. Rāghava Bhatta mentions one by name, *viz.*, the Vijnāna-chandrikā. This book is not so far available. There is another commentary called the Sambandhadīpikā by Uttamabodha. This must have been written after Lakshmanāchārya's Shāradātilaka became well known as an authoritative work. Pandit Gurupada Haldar places Lakshmanāchārya in the tenth century of the Christian era. This is the view of western Missionary writers also. There is another book by Gīrvānendra Sarasvatī named Prapanchasāra-sāra-saṁgraha. Gīrvānendra says that his Summary of Shaṁkarāchārya's teachings in the Praparchasāra follows the interpretation of a commentary named Sat-sampradāya-sarvasva. Other commentaries are :— (1) Prapanchasāra-vyākhyā, (2) Prapanchasāradīpa by Nārāyana, (3) Tattva-dīpikā by Nāgasvāmī, (4) Prapanchasāragūdhārtha-dīpikā by Nityānanda, (5) Vijnāna-dyotinī, (6) Prapanchasāra-vivriti, (7) Prapanchasāra-prayoga-vidhi, (8) Prapanchasāra-sambandha-tīkā and (9) Prapanchasāra-vrītti. These are preserved in the Madras Government manuscript Library. They all say that the book is by Shaṁkarāchārya. The Tanjore Library, it is said, contains some books, but no details of the same could be obtained. The fact that so many Sādhakas and scholars devoted themselves to the exposition of this book is a sure indication that it must have been written by a man entitled to very great reverence. The Nepal manuscript of the Prapanchasāra, in its colophon, states that the author of the book was Āchārya the word being in the plural. And that is how Shaṁkarāchārya is always designated.

When this book made its first appearance it was noticed in some periodicals and the reviewers occupied themselves merely in trying to prove that the author of the book could not have been Shaṁkarāchārya. One of these tried to make out that it was the work of the Vai*shn*ava teacher Shaṁkaradeva of Assam. This cannot be accepted, as he flourished about the time of Chaitanyadeva, which is less than 500 years from now. Another critic has attempted to make out that Vi*shn*u-svāmī, the Guru of Vidyāra*ny*a, was the author of this book and Vi*shn*u-svāmī flourished in the 13th century. This also cannot be accepted, as Amalānanda-yati, the author of the Kalpataru, has cited texts from the Prapanchasāra as the word of Shaṁkarāchārya and Amalānanda belonged to an age prior to that of Vi*shn*u-svāmī. As an instance of the un informed way the Shāstra is spoken of may be cited the case of H. P. Shāstrī who (Catalogue of Nepal Mss. Vol. 1) says that this book is an original Vai*shn*ava Tantra.

Critics of this type evidently cannot reconcile themselves to the fact that Shaṁkarāchārya, the Great Monist, could write a work on Mantra-shāstra. They seem to be labouring under the obsession that being a monist, Shaṁkarāchārya could not have written anything which advocates Sādhanā, as Sādhanā implies dualism, for in it there must be an object of Sādhanā. Orthodox exponents feel that these gentlemen look upon Shaṁkarāchārya as the holder of a chair in a modern University, whose duty it is to deliver a course of lectures on Monism as a theory, or perhaps, that he was a speculator like some German or other European philosopher who devotes himself to theorise and speculate about transcendental matters. This is mainly due to the fact of their having lost their Indian mind. Western philosophers have not succeeded in moulding the religious life of their countrymen like Shaṁkarāchārya, and even lesser men did in India.

It is not realised that Shaṁkarāchārya was not a mere theorist but a Teacher in the right sense of the word, a Guru who sought, and that successfully, not merely to uplift and enlighten the intellect but the very nature of the Sādhaka.

He established four Ma*th*as where the aspirants have, not merely to read the commentaries on the Brahma Sūtras and Upani*sh*ads, but to qualify themselves by Sādhanā for an experiential realisation of the teachings of the Vedānta.

His place as an authority on Mantrashāstra is recognised by all eminent writers of old. Even that abstruse logician Bhāskararāya begins his commentary on the Saptashatī Cha*nd*ī with a salutation of Shaṁkarāchārya and his four great disciples the foremost among whom was Padmapāda. There Bhāskararāya speaks of Shaṁkarāchārya as the Guru of the Gurus. His position is not fully understood by the majority of present day scholars who write or speak about him.

As against the opinion of present day critics presumably affected by westernism, we get the testimony of Amalānandayati already cited, the great Rāghava Bha*tt*a author of the Padārthādarsha, Bhāskararāya, an abstruse logician and one of the most authoritative commentators on Mantrashāstra, Mādhavāchārya, whose excellent commentary on the Sūtasaṁhitā is well-known, Nilaka*nth*a author of the Commentary on the Devī Bhāgavata and a whole host of other eminent authorities too numerous to mention. It is not realised that the teachings of Mantrashāstra are most jealously guarded and it is not possible to interpolate anything, much less substitute the name of one author for another. It is hard to believe that the great men whose names have been given above and who are great not merely as scholars but also as Sādhakas, should be misled. All the men whose names have been given, were men of great critical ability and some of them masters of Nyāya-Darshana. A careful perusal of this book, in spite of some of the defects from which it has not been possible to make it free, will convince the dispassionate reader that there can be no doubt about Shaṁkara being its author. This book will also give him a true conception of the Mantrashāstra.

With Indians, as the people of Bhāratavar*sh*a, are called, Vedānta is not mere speculation, but is something which is implanted into the life of the people. Tantra Shāstra is Sādhana Shāstra, and the object of it is to reach the highest Truth, which is the Brahman, the attributeless, impartite Tattva, which is without beginning or end and is the highest Bliss. The Sādhaka has, it is true, in the earlier stages, to have recourse to initiation by the Guru into his Mantra, Devatā and other accessories but he is repeatedly told to realise his oneness with the Guru, the Mantra, the Devatā of his worship and so forth. All the rituals that he has got to perform point to this one end. The image that is selected for him by his Guru as the object of worship, is his image of the Brahman (Svakīyā Brahmamūrti). It is through that image that he realises the Brahman and the image is not an end in itself. The different images used by the five classes of worshippers previously mentioned and the many sub-divisions of these five classes, are all images of the Brahman ; each class of Sādhaka having its own particular form according to competency (Adhikāra). This fact has been known even to western scholars, as is evident from a book published in the 18th century (Sketches of the Hindus, 2nd Ed. 1792 A. D.) It is there said "Amidst the multiplicity of their idols, all adoration is ultimately directed to Brahman, the Supreme, the Invisible." (Vol. II, page 256). The Sādhaka rises from the gross (Sthūla) to the subtle (Sūk*sh*ma) and then to the transcendent (Para) conception of the Supremes Being.

But in spite of this, it is a common pastime among western and westernised critics to make out that the Hindu is an idolator and a polytheist and as a result he is degenerate. Some may say this in ignorance, others with deliberation. Any religion which has a special place of worship is in that sense idolatorous. Primitive races have no images to worship and do not build Churches or temples with that object. It is a well-known fact that the Hos and the Mundaries of Chota-Nagpur, the aboriginal races of the Phillipines do not have images for their worship. The Hindu does not worship many gods. What he does is that he has the same respect for the faith of others as he has for his own.

Although followers of other religious faiths may decry them, the Hindus are prohibited from saying anything in disparagement of the Teachers and Sacred Books of other forms of Sādhanā. They do not also believe in proselytising. They however, at the same time, do not turn away the earnest seeker.

Whatever views may be entertained as to the authorship of this book it should be borne in mind that in his country the position of Shaṁkarāchārya as a Guru is higher than his position as scholar and philosopher. Others have written commentaries and books on the Vedānta Sūtras and the Upani*sh*ads but there is none who is venerated as Shaṁkara is all over the sacred land of Bhāratavar*sh*a. It may be noted here that even a Roman Catholic Missionary has discovered the harmony of Vedānta with Christian Philosophy ("Vedānta Vindicated" by Rev. J. F. Pessein) and has, so far as his dogmas have permitted him, accepted Shaṁkara's exposition. The Prapanchasāra, as has already been said, is the first book of its kind and has shown that all the different forms of Sādhanā which these days go under the generic name of Hinduism are in harmony with Vedānta and that all Mantras are meant for the realisation of the Supreme Brahman.

The Introduction has been re arranged to follow the arrangement of the text in the present edition.

The proofs were read and the table of contents and the alphabetical index of the verses made by Sj. Panchānana Sāṁkhya-Vyākara*n*atīrtha.

June 1935. A. A.

श्रीश्रीप्रपञ्चसारतन्त्रम्

भगवत्पाद-श्रीमच्छङ्कराचार्यविरचितम्

तच्छिष्य-पद्मपादाचार्यविरचित-विवरणोपेतम्

प्रयोगक्रमदीपिकाख्यविवरणविवृतिसमेतञ्च ।

पद्मपादाचार्यविरचित-शिवपञ्चाक्षरीभाष्यम् ।

श्रीआर्थारएवेलनेन प्रवर्त्तितं पर्यवेक्षितञ्च ।

श्रीश्रीमज्जगदम्बिकाम्बासरस्वतीश्रीचरणकमलाश्रित-

श्रीअटलानन्दसरस्वतीसम्पादितम् ।

आदितः विंशपटलान्तम् ।

कलिकातानगर्यां

२७।१ नं कर्णओयालिस् ष्ट्रीट्स्थ-

संस्कृतप्रेस डिपजिटरी-भवनात् प्रकाशितम् ।

लण्डनराजधान्यां लुज्याक् एण्ड कों कार्तृकेण

प्रकाशितम् ।

संवत्—१९८२

ॐ

श्रीप्रपञ्चसारतन्त्रम्

श्रीश्रीगुरवे नमः ।

प्रथमः पटलः ।

अकचटतपयाद्यैः सप्तभिर्वर्णवर्ग-
विरचितमुखबाहापादमध्याख्यहृत्का ।
सकलजगदधीशा शाश्वता विश्वयोनि-
र्वितरतु परिशुद्धिं चेतसः शारदा वः ॥ १

प्रपञ्चसारविवरणम्

ॐ श्रीगुरुचरणारविन्दाभ्यां नमः ॥

ॐ श्रीगणेशाय नमः ॥

अवर्णविग्रहं देवं वर्णविग्रहवर्जितम् ।
वर्णविग्रहवेत्तारं नमामि स्तौमि संश्रये ॥

इह खलु लोकानुग्रहैकरसतया कृतशरीरपरिग्रहो भगवान् शङ्कराचार्यः अपरोक्षीकृतपरदेवतात्मतत्त्वः परमां विभूतिकाष्ठां प्राप्तः स्वयमेकाकिसम्पदा लज्जमानो दुःखीकृतजनकारुण्याक्रान्तमानसश्च सन् तदनुग्रहाय समस्तागमसारसंग्रहप्रपञ्चागमसारसंग्रहरूपं ग्रन्थं चिकीर्षुः अभिमतसकलप्रयोजनसिद्धये प्रथमतः परदेवतातत्त्वानुस्मरणलक्षणम् आशीर्लक्षणं च मङ्गलमाचरन् ग्रन्थारम्भौपयिकं विषयादिकमपि अर्थात् सूचयति—अकचटतपयाद्यैरित्यादिना ।

शारदा वः चेतसः परिशुद्धिं वितरत्वित्यन्वयः । चित्तादिसङ्घातव्यतिरिक्तायाः शारदायाः सत्त्वे सिद्धे सम्भवतीयमाशीः । तदेव कुत इति विश्वकार्यकारणत्वेनाऽनुमानादित्याह—विश्वयोनिरिति । अपूर्वपरिणामत्वाभ्युपगमात् विश्वस्य कर्मणोऽपि विश्वयोनित्वसम्भवान्न शारदासाधकमनुमानमिति चेन्न । कर्मणः कार्यत्वेनाऽनित्यत्वात् जगन्मूलकारणत्वानुपपत्तेः । अतो नित्यं किञ्चित् जगदुपादानं वक्तव्यम् । नित्यत्वञ्च सर्वसाक्षिण्याः शारदाया एव सम्भवतीत्यभि-

प्रेत्याह—शाश्वतेति। सांख्यराद्धान्तसिद्धप्रधानस्यापि नित्यत्वात् तदेवास्तु जगद्योनिरिति चेन्न। अचेतनस्य प्रधानादेश्चेतनानधिष्ठितस्य कारणत्वानुपपत्तेः। अतश्चिद्रूपिणी सर्वाधिष्ठानसमर्था शारदैव विश्वयोनिरित्यभिप्रेत्याह—सकलेति। सकलं कारणं कलाभिः शक्तिभिः सह वर्त्तत इति जगत् कार्यं तयोः सकल-जगतोरधीश्वरीत्यर्थः। अस्तु तर्हि शारदाधिष्ठितस्य परमार्थसत्त्वस्य प्रधानस्य जगदुपादानत्वं शारदायाः तन्निमित्तमात्रत्वमेवेति सेश्वरसांख्यादिपक्षमाशङ्क्य सर्ववर्णतदर्थसमष्ट्यात्मकस्य प्रधानस्य शारदारूपचैतन्येऽध्यस्तत्वेन तदव्यतिरेकेणा-सत्त्वात् शारदैव तद्द्वारेण जगदुपादानं निमित्तं चेत्यभिप्रेत्य वर्णानां तद्विग्रहत्वेन तच्छ्लेषत्वमाह अकचटतपयाद्यैरित्यादिना। शरीरवत्त्वेनाऽस्मदाद्यविशेषमाशङ्क्य शरीरग्रहणे स्वातन्त्र्यं विशेष उक्तो विरचितेति। स्वातन्त्र्ये हेतुमाह—सकल-जगदधीशेति। तर्ह्यधिष्ठातृत्वेन विकारित्वात् अनित्यत्वादिदोषप्रसक्तिरिति चेन्न इत्याह—शाश्वतेति। तर्हि नित्यैकरूपिण्याः शारदाया अधिष्ठातृत्वं कारणत्वं वा नास्तीत्याशङ्क्य परमार्थतः तदभावेऽपि मायाद्वारेणाऽस्या एव तदभ्युपगन्तव्यम्। पक्षान्तरेषु एवंविधकारणत्वस्यापि अनुपपत्तेरित्यभिप्रेत्याह—विश्वयोनिरिति। अतः चित्तादिसङ्घातव्यतिरिक्तायाः चिन्मात्रविग्रहायाः शार-दायाः सत्त्वं तस्याः चित्तशुद्धिवितरणसामर्थ्यं च सिद्धमिति मङ्गलाचारप्रकारः।

स्थूलसूक्ष्मकारणसामान्यसाक्षिलक्षणः पञ्चविधोऽस्य ग्रन्थस्य विषयः। तत्र वैखरीतदर्थात्मकं विराड्रूपं स्थूलं विषयमाह प्रथमार्धेन। आद्यैरिति पदम् आद्यैः काद्यैश्चाद्यैरित्यादिप्रकारेण प्रत्येकं सम्बध्यते। मातृकाक्षरन्यासस्थानं वदन् विराजोऽवयवक्लृप्तिमाह—विरचितमुखबाह्वित्यादिना। मध्यशब्दः पवर्ग-न्यासस्थानार्थः। आख्याशब्देन त्वगादिधातव उक्ताः। आख्यायन्त एभिरिति। हृच्छब्देन हृत्स्थबुद्धिवाचिना ज्ञानक्रियाशक्त्यात्मकः प्राणस्तत्कारणभूता माया-शक्तिश्चाऽभिहिता। कशब्देन सुखार्थेन परमात्मोक्त इति। यादिन्यासस्थानानि तेषां याथात्म्यं यादिन्यासस्थानं धात्वादियोगः सर्वमन्त्रजपादेः शेषतया न्यासस्य सूचितः।

ननु त्वगादिपरमात्मान्तस्य देवतात्मनो यादिन्यासेनैव साधकशरीरे सन्निधाने सति किमवशिष्टाक्षरन्यासेनेति। देवतावयवविशेषकल्पनार्थमिति ब्रूमः।

न च प्रथमं सामान्यकल्पना पुनः विशेषकल्पनेति नियमोऽस्ति। येन लिपि-न्यासस्य चकारादित्वं स्यात्। सर्वत्र नित्यमेव सामान्यविशेषरूपं हि देवता-शरीरम्। तस्य साधकशरीरे सन्निधिर्न्यासेनोत्पाद्यते। अतः प्रथममकारादि-

न्यासेनाऽवयवविशेषसन्निधिस्मरणे न कश्चिद्दोषः।

न च संहारक्रमेण मातृकान्यासे प्रथमं सामान्यसंहारः पश्चाद्विशेषसंहार इति क्रमकोपः। उभयोरप्यात्मन्येव संहारात्।

न च सामान्यसंहारेणैव संहृतत्वाद्विशेषाणां पृथक्संहरणम् अनर्थकम्। विशेषसंहारक्रमचिन्तायाः कर्तव्यत्वात्।

ननु वैखर्यात्मकस्थूलकथने प्रस्तुते प्राणादिरूपसूक्ष्मादिकथनमनुपपन्नम्। न। तेन विना स्थूलमात्रेण व्यवहारासिद्धेः विराजोऽपि सर्वात्मत्वात्। अथवा प्राणशक्त्यात्मशब्दैरपि प्राणबुद्धिजीवस्थितिकराः स्थूलांशा एव अन्ना[धात्वा]दिशब्द-वाच्याः कथिताः। अस्मिन् पक्षेऽक्षरगतबिन्दुनादादिभिः विराट्शरीरानुगत-सूक्ष्मादिकथनमित्यवगन्तव्यम्।

ननु अकचटतपयाद्यैः विरचितमुखबाह्वित्यादिनैवाऽभिहितस्थूलविषयसिद्धौ किमधिकोक्त्येति। नैष दोषः। सौस्थानिकौत्थानिकस्नानाद्यनुष्ठानेषु लिपिन्यास-भेदसूचनार्थत्वात्। सौस्थानिकानुष्ठान एकपञ्चाशद्वर्णानां प्रत्येकं न्यासः सूचितोऽकचटतपयाद्यैः विरचितमुखबाह्वित्यादिना। औत्थानिके वर्गमात्रस्य मुखबाहुपादद्वयनाभिहृत्सु व्यापकत्वेन न्यासः सप्तभिः विरचितमुखबाह्वित्यादिना। स्नानादौ अकचादिवर्गत्रयस्य मुखमध्यपादेषु वर्गैर्विरचितेति। भोजनकाले समस्तस्य मस्तकादिपादान्तन्यासः सूचितो वर्णैः विरचितेति। देशकालाद्य-पेक्षया सर्वं वा सर्वत्र प्रयोक्तव्या इत्यभिप्रायः।

अथवा समस्तमन्त्रपारायणोद्धारार्थाधिकोक्तिः। तथाहि अकचटतपयाद्यैः अकचटतपयवर्गसम्बन्धिभिः अकाराद्यैः षोड़शस्वरैः विरचितमुखबाहापाद-मध्याख्यहृत्केति पञ्चाशद्वर्णानां प्रत्येकं षोड़शस्वरयोग उक्तः। लिपिन्यासस्थानेषु षोड़शदलानि पद्मानि सञ्चिन्त्य कर्णिकासु तं तं प्रधानं वर्णं विन्यस्य दलेषु तत्तद्वर्णानुबन्धषोड़शस्वरान् न्यसेत् न्यासप्रियो जपेच्च जपप्रियो ध्यायेच्च ध्यानप्रिय इत्यर्थः। ओं अं ओं नम इत्यकाराब्जकर्णिकायां विन्यस्य ओं अं अं नमः। ओं अं आं नमः। ओं अं इं नम इत्यादिकं दलेषु विन्यस्य आकारपद्मकर्णिकायाम् ओं आं ओं नम इति न्यसित्वा ओं आं अं नमः। ओं आं आं नमः। ओं आं इं नम इत्यादिकं दलेषु विन्यस्याऽवशिष्टाक्षर-पद्मेष्वपि एवमेव न्यसेदिति स्वरपारायणन्यासादिमन्त्रक्रमः।

अथ व्यञ्जनपारायणक्रमः। अकचटतपयाद्यैरक्तैः विरचितमुखबाहापाद-मध्याख्यहृत्केति विविधरचनम्। ओं अं अं नमः। ओं अं कं नमः।

ओं अं खं नम इत्यादि चान्तमूहयेत्। पूर्वोक्ताकारपद्मदलस्थाकारपरिवारत्वेन एषां न्यासः। आं अं नमः। आं कं नमः। आं खं नमः। इत्याद्याकारपरिवारत्वेन। इं अं नमः। इं कं नमः। इं खं नमः। इत्यादीकारपरिवारत्वेन। इत्यादि विसर्गान्तं समानम्। पुनः कं अं नमः। कं कं नमः। कं खं नमः। कं गं नमः। इत्यादि ककाराम्बुजदलस्थककारपरिवारत्वेन। पुनः कां अं नमः। कां कं नमः। कां खं नमः। कां गं नमः। इत्यादि काकारपरिवारत्वेन समानम्। पुनः खं अं नमः। खं कं नमः। खं खं नमः। खं गं नमः। इत्यादि खाम्बुजदलगतखकारपरिवारत्वेन सर्वमूह्यम्। इति ब्रह्मब्रह्मपारायणक्रमः। अं आं नमः। अं कां नमः। अं खां नमः। इत्यादिरूपो ब्रह्मविष्णुपारायणक्रमः। अं इं नमः। अं किं नमः। अं खिं नमः। इत्यादिरूपो ब्रह्मरुद्रपारायणक्रमः। अं ईं नमः। अं कीं नमः। इत्यादि विष्णुब्रह्मणः। अं उं नमः। अं कुं नमः इत्यादि विष्णुविष्णोः। अं ऊं नमः। अं कूं नमः। इत्यादि विष्णुरुद्रस्य। अं ऋं नमः। अं कृं नम इत्यादि रुद्रब्रह्मणः। अं ॠं नमः। अं कॄं नमः इत्यादि रुद्रविष्णोः। अं ऌं नमः। अं कॢं नमः। इत्यादि रुद्ररुद्रस्य। अं ॡं नमः। अं कॣं नमः इत्यादि ब्रह्मसर्वेश्वरस्य। अं एं नमः। अं कें नमः। इत्यादि विष्णुसर्वेश्वरस्य। अं ऐं नमः। अं कैं नमः इत्यादि रुद्रसर्वेश्वरस्य। अं ओं नमः। अं कों नमः इत्यादि सर्वेश्वरस्य। अं औं नमः। अं कौं नमः इत्यादि चतुर्मूर्त्तेः। अं अं नमः। अं कं नमः इत्यादि साक्षिणः। अं अः नमः। अं कः नमः इत्यादि परब्रह्मण इति पारायणक्रमः। पारायणक्रमवन्मन्त्रभेदानामपि अक्षरविरचनारूपत्वात् सोऽपि विरचितेत्यनेनैव सूचितः।

अथ तत्तन्मन्त्रभेदेन पारायणक्रमभेदमाह—अकचटतपयाद्यैरित्यादिना। अकचटतपयाद्यैरुक्तैः सप्तभिश्च वर्णवर्गैः मन्त्रवर्गैः विरचितमुखबाह्वित्यादि समानम्। तत्र ब्रह्मसरस्वतीविष्णुश्रीरुद्रोमासर्वेश्वरसप्तमन्त्रवर्गाः। उक्तपारायणमन्त्रान्ते तांस्तान्मन्त्रानुच्चार्य न्यासादिकं कर्त्तव्यम् इत्यलम् अनन्तवैखरीतदर्थरूपस्थूलप्रपञ्चनेन।

अथ मध्यमातदर्थहिरण्यगर्भबिन्दुरूपं सूक्ष्मं विषयमाह—सकलजगदधीशेति। कलाभिरवयवैः तत्त्वभुवनकलावर्णपदमन्त्ररूपैः संहताः सन्तो जायन्त इति सकलजा जीवाः तेषां गदधियोः शेते इति सकलजगदधीशा। गदशब्देन वाग्वाचिना तन्निवर्तकः प्राणः क्रियाशक्तिमात्रात्मोच्यते। धीशब्देन ज्ञानशक्तिमात्रं

तयोः शयनं च तदनुगतस्वातन्त्र्यात्मकेच्छाशक्त्यात्मना ततश्चेच्छाक्रियाज्ञानशक्त्यात्मको हिरण्यगर्भः प्रकाश्यप्रकाशकरूपाभ्यां मध्यमा वाक् तदर्थात्मा सूक्ष्मरूपो विषय इति उक्तं भवति। अत्र सकलशब्देनैव मध्यमान्तर्भूतानि शून्यस्पर्शनादध्वनिबिन्दुशक्तिबीजाक्षराणि उक्तानि। तानि मूलाधारलिङ्गमूलनाभिहृत्कण्ठलम्बिकाभ्रूमध्यललाटेषु न्यस्तव्यानीति। इच्छादित्रितयं शिरोदक्षिणवामस्तनेषु। शान्तिर्मूलाधारे वामा ज्येष्ठा रौद्र्यम्बिकाश्च तेष्वेवं न्यस्तव्याः। वैखरीन्यासात् पूर्वमेवेति मध्यमान्यासप्रकारः।

अथ पश्यन्तीतदर्थात्मकं तपउपचयादिशब्दवाच्यं कारणात्मनः सृष्ट्याद्युन्मुखं रूपं कारणशब्दोक्तं नादात्मकं प्रकाश्यप्रकाशकरूपेण वागर्थात्मकं विषयमाह—शाश्वतेति। आदिसर्गादिमहाप्रलयान्तमवस्थानात् सदादिरूपत्वाच्च शाश्वतत्वमवगन्तव्यम्। महासत्तायै नमः। महासंविदे नमः। महानन्दायै नमः। महेश्वर्यै नमः। इति मूर्धस्तनद्वयमूलाधारेषु पश्यन्तीन्यासोऽनेन सूचितः।

अथ परातदर्थात्मकं सामान्यरूपम् आत्माविभक्तान्तर्मुखकारणात्मकं शक्तिरूपं विषयमाह—विश्वयोनिरिति। व्यापकत्वेनाऽस्या न्यासः। एवं वागर्थात्मकचतुर्विधविषयकथनेनैवाऽवशिष्टमव्यवहार्यं विषयं लक्षणयोक्तम् अवगन्तव्यम्। भुक्तिमुक्तिलक्षणं प्रयोजनमाह—शारदेति। शीर्यत इति शारं स्थूलादिलक्षणं कर्मफलं तद्ददातीति शारदा। तत् तत्कारणं च ब्रह्मविद्याधिरूढा सती द्यति खण्डयतीति च शारदा इति। शारदेति पदं प्रयोजनद्वयपरतया व्याख्येयम्। प्रयोजनकथनेनैव सामान्यतस्तत्कामिन्यधिकारिणि सिद्धे अधिकारिविशेषः सूचितः। वितरत्वित्यादिना शुद्धान्तःकरणो गुरुणा केनचिद्दीक्षाप्रकारेणाऽनुगृहीतोऽधिकारीत्याशीर्लक्षणवाचिकदीक्षाकरणेनोक्तं भवति।

तत्र आणवी दीक्षा अणुभिः मन्त्रैः क्रियमाणा अनेकविधा। तत्रोक्तचतुर्विधलिपिन्यासानामेकेन शिष्यशरीरमशुद्धं संहृत्य शुद्धं सृजेदिति न्यासरूपाऽणवीदीक्षाप्रकारः। होमादिपूर्वकं तूत्तरत्र भविष्यति। स्वशक्तिसूत्रेण शिष्यदेहं प्रविश्य तत्त्वसंहारं कृत्वा तं परदेवतारूपं भावयेदिति शाक्तदीक्षाप्रकारः सकलजगदधीशेत्यादिपदत्रयेण सूचितः। सा च बहुप्रकारा चाक्षुषी स्पार्शी वाचिकी मानसीत्यादिद्वारभेदात्। शाम्भवदीक्षा केवलस्वरूपस्थितिमात्रेण शिष्यसर्वदेहग्रसनरूपा शारदेत्यनेनोक्ता।

सम्बन्धस्तु विषयकथनेनैव विषयविषयिभावः सूचित इति ॥ १ ॥

अथाऽभवन् ब्रह्महरीश्वराख्याः पुरा प्रधानात् प्रलयावसाने ।
गुणप्रभिन्ना जगतोऽस्य सृष्टिस्थितिक्षयस्पष्टनिविष्टचेष्टाः ॥ २

विषयादिमत्त्वात् ग्रन्थस्यारम्भणीयत्वे सिद्धे अयमुत्तरश्लोकावतारः। शारदा जगद्योनिरित्युक्तम् तदनुपपन्नं। पुराणादिषु त्रिमूर्तीनां जगत्सृष्ट्यादिहेतुत्वावगमात् इत्याशङ्क्य पुराणादिष्वेव मूर्तीनां सृज्यत्वावगमात् परमकारणत्वानुपपत्तेः तद्व्यतिरिक्तया शारदया परमकारणभूतया भाव्यमिति मन्वानः त्रिमूर्तीनां ततः उत्पत्तिं वदन् विद्यास्तुत्यादिप्रयोजनया आख्यायिकया ग्रन्थमारभते—अथेति।

सृष्टिहेतुकर्मोन्मुख्यानन्तर्यार्थकोऽयमथशब्दः। ब्रह्महरीश्वरास्तदाख्याश्चेति समासः। तेषामौपाधिकी उत्पत्तिः न पारमार्थिकीत्याह—पुराऽभवन्निति। शरीरेणेत्यर्थः। प्रथितमत्तीति प्रधानशब्देन प्रकृतिपुरुषकालाः तद्वाचको हकारश्चोक्तः। कदा सृष्ट्युन्मुख्यं कर्मण इति तदाह—प्रलयावसाने इति। उत्पत्तिवद्भेदोऽपि औपाधिकस्तेषामित्याह—गुणेति। तेषामुत्पत्तिप्रयोजनमाह—जगत इति। अस्येति कार्यत्वेन सृष्ट्याद्यपेक्षत्वं सूचितम्। एकैकस्यापि त्रितयहेतुत्वश्रुतेः कथमेकैकहेतुत्वोक्तिरिति तत्राह—स्पष्टेति। प्राधान्येनेत्यर्थः।

सृष्ट्यादौ विनियुक्ताः चतुर्मूर्तिवाचका मन्त्राश्चात्रोद्दिष्टाः। तथाहि—ब्रह्महरीश्वराख्या इति ब्रह्मविष्णुसदाशिवसर्वेश्वरशब्दाः मूर्तिमन्त्रान्तर्गताः सूचिताः। पुरेति। स्थूलविराट्शरीराय विश्ववैश्वानरात्मने सूक्ष्महिरण्यगर्भशरीराय तैजससूत्रात्मने सौषुप्ताज्ञानशरीराय प्राज्ञेश्वरात्मने व्याकृताव्याकृतशरीराय प्रत्यग्ब्रह्मात्मने नम इति मन्त्रपदानि सूचितानि। अत्र पुरावचनेनैव पुराभिमानिनामपि ग्रहणं कृतम्। तयोः नित्यसम्बन्धत्वात्। प्रधानादिति मन्त्राणां शक्त्यानन्तर्यं सूचितम्। प्रलयावसान इति शक्तेः व्यस्तसमस्तप्रणवानन्तर्यम्। गुणप्रभिन्ना इति स्थूलादिपदात् पूर्वं रजउपाधये सत्त्वोपाधये तमउपाधये गुणसाम्योपाधये इति। मूर्तीनां पुरस्तात् सरस्वतीसहिताय सर्वज्ञाय सदात्मनेऽसङ्गाखण्डसंविदे परमात्मने नमः। लक्ष्मीसहिताय सर्वज्ञाय आनन्दात्मनेऽसङ्गाद्वयसंविदे परमात्मने नमः। उमासहिताय सर्वज्ञाय चिदात्मनेऽसङ्गापरोक्षसंविदे परमात्मने नमः। मूलप्रकृतिमायासहिताय सर्वज्ञाय सदानन्दचिदात्मनेऽसङ्गाखण्डाद्वयापरोक्षसंविदे परमात्मने नम इति च योगः सूचितः।

अत्र परमात्मपदात् पूर्वमिष्टदेवतानाम योज्यम्। जगतोऽस्येति मूर्तीनां पूर्वभागे सर्वस्रष्ट्रे सर्वपालकाय सर्वसंहर्त्रे सर्वोत्पत्तिस्थितिसंहारकर्त्रे इति योगः

स्वनिष्पत्तिञ्च कृत्यञ्च ते विचिन्त्य समाविदन् ।
वक्तारमजमव्यक्तमरूपं मायिनं विभुम् ॥ ३
मूर्त्याभासेन दुग्धाब्धौ झषशङ्खसमाकुले ।
मरुत्संघट्टनोत्कीर्णलहरीकणशीतले ॥ ४

सूचितः । मूर्त्यपवादमन्त्रस्वारोपमात्रसूचनादेव सूचितः । ओं क्लीं ओं ओं ओं निरवद्यनिर्गुणायाऽशेर्याशरीरायाऽसङ्गप्रत्यगद्वयाय स्वाभासावभासिततत्त्वायाऽसङ्गबोधायाऽखण्डाद्वयापरोक्षसदानन्दचिदात्मने स्वबोधध्वस्तानर्थाद्वैतायाऽनिरालम्बलक्ष्विबिम्बायाऽहीनमहोदयाय परमात्मने नमः इत्यपवादमन्त्रः । प्रधानादभवन्नाख्या गुणप्रभिन्ना इति पदैः विशिष्टकुले प्रसूता गर्भाधानजातकर्मनामकरणादिसंस्कारविशिष्टा गुणिनो जगदुपकारका वक्ष्यमाणविद्यास्वधिकारिण इति विद्यास्तुतिः कृताऽवबोद्धव्या ॥ २ ॥

ते किमकुर्वन्नित्याकाङ्क्षायां तद्वृत्तान्तं वदन् अज्ञत्वादपि न तेषां परमकारणत्वमित्याह—स्वनिष्पत्तिमिति ।

निष्पद्यते तस्मादित्युपादानं निष्पत्तिः । निमित्तार्थश्चशब्दः । कृत्यं चेति चशब्दः स्वरूपार्थः । ते विचिन्त्याऽज्ञत्वेन स्वयं निर्णेतुमशक्ता गुणसाम्योपाधिं मायिनं वक्तारं समाविदन्नित्यर्थः । तस्य निर्णयसामर्थ्ये मूर्तिवैलक्षण्यं हेतुमाह—अजमिति । अजत्वे हेतुरव्यक्तमिति । अरूपत्वं तत्र । एवं निर्विशेषस्य तथा कथं वक्तृत्वमिति मायासम्बन्धात् कथञ्चित् सविशेषत्वं प्राप्येत्याह—मायिनमिति । तत्पारवश्यादज्ञत्वेन वक्तृत्वासामर्थ्यमाशङ्क्य निराचष्टे—विभुमिति । विचारक्षमा गुरूपसदनादियुक्तास्त्वाऽधिकारिणः । गुरुश्च निग्रहानुग्रहादिशक्तिमानित्येतत् सूचितम् ॥ ३ ॥

अत्र मायिनोऽपि स्थानमूर्तिविशेषादिसम्बन्धाभावेऽवक्तृत्वमाशङ्क्य क्रमेण तत्सर्वं सम्पादयति—मूर्त्येत्यादिना । मूर्तिर्माया शक्तिबीजम् । आ समन्ताद्भासते इत्याभासः प्रणवः । तेन मन्त्रेण विग्रहभूतेन दुग्धाब्धौ अनन्तभोगे शयितमित्यन्वयः । सर्वेश्वरप्रणवौपाधिकमित्यर्थः । ह्रौमिति सर्वेश्वरप्रणवः । ते समाविदन्निति । त्रिमूर्तयोऽस्य मुनयः सूचिताः । छन्दश्च देवी गायत्री गायकत्राणकथनात् सूचितम् । स्वामिन् प्रमोद विश्वेशेति देवतां च सूचयिष्यति । मूर्त्याभासेनेत्यङ्गदेहन्यासौ सूचितौ । तथाहि मूर्तिसम्बन्धित्वेनाभासन्त इति मूर्त्याभासा क्रामादिकाः सप्रणवा अङ्गानीत्यङ्गसूचनाप्रकारः । मूर्तौ मूर्तिभूते मूलमन्त्रे अनुगततया भासन्त इति मूर्त्याभासा अस्त्रसर्वेश्वरादि-

उद्यदादित्यकिरणप्रशान्तशिशिरोदये ।
पूर्णचन्द्रकरामर्शप्रतिक्षुब्धजलाशये ॥ ५
अनन्तभोगविमले फणायुतविराजिते ।
शयितं शार्ङ्गिणं शर्वशौरिपद्मभुवस्तदा ॥ ६
तुष्टुवुर्हृष्टमनसो विष्टरश्रवसं विभुम् ।
सूक्तिभिः स्तुतिभिः प्रीतः स्वमूर्त्तिं स व्यदर्शयत् ॥ ७
नीलोत्पलदलप्रख्यां नीलकुञ्चितमूर्द्धजाम् ।
अष्टमीचन्द्रविम्बाभललाटामायतभ्रुवम् ॥ ८

मन्त्राः ह्रीं ह्रीं क्रोमित्येवंरूपाः । नाभिहृद्भ्रूमध्येष्वेषां न्यासः । मूलाधारमूर्ध्नोः मूलन्यासः । ध्यानप्रकारस्तु दुग्धाब्धावित्यादिनोक्तः । तस्य च यथाश्रुतोऽर्थः स्पष्टः ।

अथान्योऽर्थः । मूर्तिर्माया । आभासस्तदभिव्यक्तश्चैतन्याभासः । स्वच्छत्वगम्भीरत्वगुणयोगात् दुग्धाब्धिशब्दोदितत्रिमूर्तिबुद्धावभासिनः शयितम् । आभासस्य द्वारत्वं तृतीयार्थः । तस्य तद्बुद्धौ सद्भावे गमकमाह—झषेति । झषशङ्खशब्दाभ्यां क्रियाज्ञानशक्ती ब्रह्मोपलक्षणभूतेऽक्षोभकत्वसाम्येन लक्ष्येते । तस्य तत्र सद्भावे तत्स्वरूपलक्षणभूतसुखाद्यभिव्यक्तिं हेत्वन्तरमाह—मरुदिति । मरुतोऽन्तर्यामिणः प्रेरणेनोद्भूताः सुखव्यञ्जिताश्चित्तवृत्तयो लहर्यः तासु यन्तैः सुखलवैर्निस्ताप इत्यर्थः ॥ ४ ॥

बुद्धौ ईश्वरसद्भावमुपपाद्य तत्र तदभिव्यक्तिविशेषकारणमाह—उद्यदिति । उद्यतो विवेकादित्यस्य प्रचारप्रकाशैः प्रशान्तसंसारोदय इत्यर्थः । विवेकज्ञानबिलं संसारं मान्द्यमभिधाय तत्फलभूतामानन्दाभिव्यक्तिमाह—पूर्णेति । परमानन्दाकारसम्बन्धेन प्रतिक्षुब्धजलाशये प्रातिलोम्येन विषयापरित्यागेनाऽन्तर्मुखतया क्षुब्धाः प्रवृत्ता जलविषया आशया वृत्तयो यस्मिन् स तथोक्तः ॥ ५ ॥

अतएवाऽनन्तं ब्रह्म भुङ्क्ते इत्यनन्तभोगः । अनन्ताकारचित्तवृत्तयः पुनः पुनराविर्भवन्त्यः फणायुतशब्दार्थः । शयितमभिव्यक्तम् । तत्राभिव्यक्तं मायित्वहेतुत्वमाह—शार्ङ्गिणमिति । शरणाद्रमणाद्गमनाच्च माया शार्ङ्गं तद्वान्श्शार्ङ्गी ॥६॥

विष्टरश्रवसं विस्तरा वेदास्तेषु श्रवः श्रवणं यस्य स तथोक्तः । विस्तीर्णकीर्त्तिर्वा । स्तोतव्यत्वमाह—विभुमिति । सूक्तिभिरुक्तैर्मन्त्रैः स्तुतिभिश्च प्रीत इत्यर्थः ।

॥ ७ ॥ ८ ॥ ९ ॥ १० ॥ ११ ॥ १२ ॥ १३ ॥ १४ ॥

रक्तारविन्दनयनामुन्नसीमरुणाधराम् ।
मन्दस्मिताधरमुखीं लसन्मकरकुण्डलाम् ॥ ९

कम्बुग्रीवां पृथुद्वंसविसरद्भुजमण्डलाम् ।
अनन्तरत्नप्रत्युप्तवलयाङ्गदमुद्रिकाम् ॥ १०

हारतारावलीराजत्पृथूरोव्योममण्डलाम् ।
कौस्तुभोद्भासितोरस्कां श्रीवत्सद्युतिदीपिताम् ॥ ११

लसदौदरिकाबन्धभास्वरां संवृतोदरीम् ।
गम्भीरनाभिं विपुलजघनां पीतवाससम् ॥ १२

पृथुवृत्तोरुमापूर्णजानुमण्डलबन्धुराम् ।
वृत्तजङ्घां गूढगुल्फां प्रपदाजितकच्छपाम् ॥ १३

तनुदीर्घाङ्गुलीभास्वन्नखराजिविराजिताम् ।
चक्रस्वस्तिकशङ्खाब्जध्वजाङ्कितपदद्वयाम् ॥ १४

तां दृष्ट्वा तरलात्मानो विध्यधोक्षजशङ्कराः ।
अतिष्ठन्नितिकर्तव्यमूढास्तत्राऽब्रवीदजः ॥ १५

स्वामिन् प्रसीद विश्वेश के वयं केन भाविताः ।
किंमूलाः किंक्रियाः सर्वमस्मभ्यं वक्तुमर्हसि ॥ १६

इति पृष्टं परं ज्योतिरुवाच प्रमिताक्षरम् ।
यूयमक्षरसम्भूताः सृष्टिस्थित्यन्तहेतवः ॥ १७

तरलात्मानो भक्तिपरवशचित्ताः । अजोऽकारजः ॥ १५ ॥

स्वामिन्निति प्रसादकर्तव्यतासूचनम् । प्रसादे स्वातन्त्र्यं प्रसन्नस्याऽभीष्टदानसामर्थ्यं च सूचितम् विश्वेशेति । के वयमिति । किं नित्याः उताऽनित्याः इत्यर्थः । यदि नित्यास्तर्हि के वयं किं स्वरूपा इत्यावृत्त्या योज्यम् । यद्यनित्यास्तर्हि केन निमित्तकारणेन भाविताः । किंमूलाः किमुपादानाः । किंक्रियाः किंव्यापाराः ॥ १६ ॥

स्वरूपेण नित्यानामप्यौपाधिकं कार्यत्वमस्तीति अनित्यत्वपक्षमाश्रित्य शार्ङ्गी निमित्तोपादानादिकं संग्रहेणोक्तवानित्याह—इति पृष्टमिति । प्रमिताक्षरमिति । प्रकर्षेण मीयते ज्ञायते मिनोति जानाति प्रमिनोति परिच्छिनत्तीति

तैरेव विकृतिं यातास्तेषु वो जायते लयः ।
इति तस्य वचः श्रुत्वा तमपृच्छत्सरोजभूः ॥ १८
अक्षरं नाम किं नाथ कुतो जातं किमात्मकम् ।
इति पृष्टो हरिस्तेन सरोजोदरयोनिना ॥ १९
मूलार्णमर्णविकृतीर्विकृतेर्विकृतीरपि ।
तत्प्रभिन्नानि मन्त्राणि प्रयोगांश्च पृथग्विधान् ॥ २०

क्रमेण प्रकृतिपुरुषकालाः प्रमिताः। प्रमितानां वाचकमक्षरं तदभिन्नं प्रमिताक्षरं परा वाक्। सतत्त्वहकारमित्यर्थः। तस्य बीजबिन्दुनादरूपेण प्रकृत्यादिवाचकत्वं द्रष्टव्यम्। अहमेलनरूपेण वा। तत्र प्रकृतिः उपादानम् इतरौ निमित्तमिति शार्ङ्गिणोऽभिप्रायः। हेतिसंग्रहेणोक्तेऽपि उत्तरे तेषामप्रतिपत्तिमालक्ष्य शार्ङ्गी स्वाभिप्रायं विवृणोति—यूयमिति। उपादान-प्रश्नोत्तरं यूयमिति। कार्यप्रश्नोत्तरं सृष्टीति। निमित्तप्रश्नोत्तरं तैरिति। एकैकस्य केवलस्योपादानत्वाद्यनुपपत्तेः मिलित्वैव तेषां कारणत्वमिति उक्तम् तैरेवेति। उपादानत्वमुपपादयति—तेष्विति। अत्र तैरेवेति बहुवचनप्रयोगात् यूयमक्षरेत्यत्रापि प्रकृतिपुरुषकालहकारा उत्तरत्र वक्ष्यमाणा न क्षरन्ति इति व्युत्पत्त्या रूढ्या चाऽक्षरशब्देनोच्यन्त इति गम्यते ॥ १७ ॥ १८ ॥

अक्षरशब्दोक्तं सर्वमेकीकृत्य पृच्छति—अक्षरं नामेति। किं नित्यमुताऽनित्य-मिति प्रश्नार्थः। अनित्यत्वे कुतो जातं नित्यत्वे किमात्मकमित्यर्थः ॥ १९ ॥

सर्वेषां नित्यत्वपक्षमाश्रित्य वाचकस्य तावन्नित्यसमस्तशब्दानुगतं स्वरूपमाह—मूलार्णमिति। अथवा वाचकप्राधान्यमाश्रित्य वाच्यवाचकाभेदमाश्रित्य वा सर्वेषामेव नित्यत्वं स्वरूपमाह संग्रहेण—मूलार्णमिति।

प्रकृतमक्षरशब्दं परित्यज्याऽर्णशब्दप्रयोगादन्ते हकारप्रयोगाच्च वाचकसर्वात्मक-त्वादिकमेवाऽत्रोच्यत इति गम्यते। वाच्यानामुत्तरत्र पृथक् सर्वात्मकत्वकथनाच्च। मूलार्णं शक्तिबीजं केवलमर्थसहितं वा। एवमुत्तरत्रापि। अर्णविकृतीर्हकार-रेफमायार्णविकृतित्वेन वक्ष्यमाणाः स्वराः। विकृतीनां स्वराणां विकृतिः। कादिक्षान्ता विकृतेर्विकृतयः। तत्प्रभिन्नानि तेभ्यो वर्णेभ्यो निष्पन्नानि मन्त्राणि। तेषामङ्गत्वेन प्रयुज्यन्त इति प्रयोगाः। अङ्गन्यासादिपूजामन्त्राः षट्कर्मलक्षणा वा प्रयोगाः। तान् सर्वान् ह इतीत्थमाहेत्यन्वयः। हकारो हि अकारहकारात्मा। तयोश्चाद्यन्ताक्षरयोः प्रत्याहारग्रहणन्यायेन गृहीतेतर-

वैदिकांस्तान्त्रिकांश्चाऽपि सर्वानित्थमुवाच ह ।
प्रकृतिः पुरुषश्चैव नित्यौ कालश्च सत्तम ॥ २१
अणोरणीयसी स्थूलात् स्थूला व्याप्तचराचरा ।
आदित्येन्द्वग्नितेजोमद्‌द्व्यद्द्व्यत्तत्तन्मयी विभुः ॥ २२
न श्वेतरक्तपीतादिवर्णैर्निर्धार्यं चोच्यते ।
न गुणेषु न भूतेषु विशेषेण व्यवस्थिता ॥ २३
अन्तरान्तर्बहिश्चैव देहिनां देहपूरणी ।
स्वसंवेद्यस्वरूपा सा दृश्या देशिकदर्शितैः ॥ २४
ययाकाशस्तमो वापि लब्धया नोपलभ्यते ।
पुंनपुंसकयोस्तुल्याऽप्यङ्गनासु विशिष्यते ॥ २५

वर्णयोः नादाकाररूपेण बुद्धिप्राणरूपेण ज्ञानक्रियाशक्तिरूपेण प्रकाशविमर्शरूपेण चिदानन्दरूपेण वा सर्ववर्णाद्यनुगमात् सर्वशब्दार्थसमध्यात्मकपरावागात्मत्वेन सर्वात्मत्वात् प्रकृतिपुरुषकालात्मत्वं नित्यत्वं चाऽवगन्तव्यम् ।

एवं वाचकस्याऽक्षरस्य नित्यत्वं सर्वात्मत्वं स्वरूपं चाभिधाय वाच्याक्षराणामपि तत्क्रमेण प्रतिपादयति—प्रकृतिरित्यादिना। चकारौ पुरुषकालादिसम्बन्धभेद-समुच्चयार्थौ। कालस्य पृथक् ग्रहणं निमित्तत्वावद्योतनार्थम्। प्रकृतिपुरुषकाला द्विविधाः परापरभेदेन। 'विचिकीर्षुः' 'स्वसंवेद्यस्वरूपा' 'या युष्मानपि' 'बहुना किं परं पुंसः' 'सा तु कालात्मना' 'लवादिप्रलयान्त' इत्यादिवाक्यविशेषात्। सत्तमेति। नित्यत्वे उपपत्तिः। विपर्ययेऽनवस्थालक्षणा त्वयैव प्रतिपत्तव्येति उक्तम्॥ २०॥ २१॥

प्रकृतेः स्वरूपं व्याप्तिं चाह—अणोरित्यादिना। अण्वादिषु सामान्यतो व्याप्तिमाह—व्याप्तेति। अधिज्यौतिषमधिविषयमधिगुणमधिभूतमध्यात्मं च क्रमेण व्याप्तिमाह—आदित्येत्यादिना॥ २२॥ २३॥

अन्तरा मध्ये इन्द्रियरूपेण। अन्तः अन्तःकरणप्राणादिरूपेण। बहिः सप्तधातुरूपेण देहिनां देहपूरणीत्यर्थः। कथं तर्हि एवं निर्विशेषाया असाधारणं रूपमुपलब्धुं शक्यत इति देशिकेनाचार्येण दर्शितैः उपायैः अपरप्रकृतिरूपसाक्षि-स्वरूपिणीत्याह—स्वसंवेद्येति॥ २४॥

सा लब्धेत्यत्र लब्धुः स्वात्मप्रत्यक्षो[यो]पपादकं गमकमाह—ययेति। आकाशं कार्यमात्रोपलक्षणम्। तमः कारणं जड़रूपा परा शक्तिः। वापीति सत्त्वादयः

प्रधानमिति यामाहुर्या शक्तिरिति कथ्यते ।
या युष्मानपि मां नित्यमवष्टभ्याऽतिवर्तते ॥ २६

साऽहं यूयं तथैवाऽन्यद् यद्वेद्यं तत्तु सा स्मृता ।
प्रलये व्याप्यते तस्यां चराचरमिदं जगत् ॥ २७

सैव स्वां वेत्ति परमा तस्या नान्योऽस्ति वेदिता ।
सा तु कालात्मना सम्यक् मयैव ज्ञायते सदा ॥ २८

लवादिप्रलयान्तोऽयं कालः प्रस्तूयते द्विज ।
नलिनीपत्रसंहत्यां सूक्ष्मसूच्यभिभेदने ॥ २९

दले दले तु यः कालः स कालो लववाचकः ।
लवैस्त्रुटिः स्यात्त्रिंशद्भिः कलां तावत् त्रुटिं विदुः ॥ ३०

इच्छादयस्त्वोक्ताः । तस्याः त्रिलिङ्गव्याप्तिमाह—पुंनपुंसकयोरिति । त्रिषु तुल्याऽपीत्यर्थः । अङ्गनासु प्रसवधर्मित्वाद्विशेषः ॥ २५ ॥

गुणभूतादिरूपेण त्रिष्वपि तुल्यत्वम् । शब्दतोऽपि त्रयात्मकत्वं गम्यत इत्याह — प्रधानमिति । पुंलिङ्गवाचकानामपि उपलक्षणमेतत् । किं बहुना जगत्कारणभूतान् युष्मानपि मदवष्टम्भात् कवलीकरोति सेत्याह—या युष्मानपीति । मां नित्यमवष्टभ्य या युष्मानप्यतिवर्तत इत्यन्वयः ॥ २६ ॥

त्वदनतिक्रमे किं कारणमित्याशङ्क्य मयि कल्पितत्वेन तस्या मद्व्यतिरेकेणाभावादिति वदन् परं पुरुषमाह—साऽहमिति । अस्मदतिक्रमे किं कारणमित्याशङ्क्य युष्माकं विषयवत् प्रकृतिकार्यत्वेन तस्यां कल्पितत्वादित्याह—यूयमिति । तत्र गमकमाह—प्रलय इति ॥ २७ ॥

ननु प्रलयेऽपि तस्याः साधकं बुद्ध्यादिकमभ्युपगन्तव्यमिति नेत्याह—सैवेति । सैव परमा साक्षिलक्षणा परा प्रकृतिः पूर्वोक्ता स्वसंवेद्यस्वरूपेति । स्वां स्वसम्बन्धिनीमपरां शक्तिं वेत्ति । तस्या नान्यो बुद्ध्यादिलक्षणो वेदिताऽस्तीत्यर्थः । अथवा तस्याः पराया अन्यो वेदिता नास्तीत्यर्थः । अस्त्वेवं प्रलयकाले स्थितिकाले तु वैपरीत्येन तत्राऽपराया बुद्ध्यादिविशिष्टतया बोधशक्तिमत्त्वादिति नेत्याह—सा त्विति । तुशब्दोऽपराया जडत्वलक्षणविशेषद्योतकः । कालात्मना ज्ञानात्मना । सम्यक् साक्षितयाऽव्यवधानेन ॥ २८ ॥

एवं परकालस्यापि स्वरूपमभिधायाऽपरं कालं प्रस्तौति—लवेति ॥ २९ ॥

॥ ३० ॥ ३१ ॥ ३२ ॥ ३३ ॥ ३४ ॥ ३५ ॥

काष्ठा तावत् कला ज्ञेया तावत् काष्ठा निमेषकः ।
सोऽङ्गुलिस्फोटतुल्यः स्यान्मात्राऽष्टाभिस्तु तैः स्मृता ॥ ३१
कालेन यावता स्वीयो हस्तः स्वं जानुमण्डलम् ।
पर्येति मात्रा सा तुल्या स्वीयैकश्वासमात्रया ॥ ३२
षष्ट्युत्तरैस्तु त्रिशतैर्निश्वासैर्नाड़िका स्मृता ।
द्विनाड़िको मुहूर्तः स्यात् त्रिंशद्भिस्तैरहर्निशम् ॥ ३३
त्रिंशद्भिरप्यहोरात्रैर्मासो द्वादशभिस्तु तैः ।
संवत्सरो मानुषोऽयमहोरात्रं दिवौकसाम् ॥ ३४
तथा दिव्यैरहोरात्रैस्त्रिशतैः षष्टिसंयुतैः ।
दिव्यः संवत्सरो ज्ञेयो दिव्यैः संवत्सरैस्तु तैः ॥ ३५
भवेद्द्वादशसाहस्रैर्भिन्नैरेकं चतुर्युगम् ।
तैः सहस्रैः शतानन्द तवैकं दिनमिष्यते ॥ ३६
तावती तव रात्रिश्च कथिता कालवेदिभिः ।
तथाविधैरहोरात्रैस्त्रिंशद्भिर्मासमृच्छसि ॥ ३७
तथाविधैर्द्वादशभिर्मासैरब्दस्तव स्मृतः ।
तथाविधानामब्दानां शतं त्वमपि जीवसि ॥ ३८
त्वदायुर्मम निश्वासः कालेनैवं प्रचोद्यते ।
स जानाति विपाकांश्च तस्यां सम्यग्व्यवस्थितान् ॥ ३९
सोऽन्वीच्य त्वादृशामायुः परिपाकं प्रयच्छति ।
प्रकृतेश्च क्वचित् कालो विकृतिं प्रतिपादयेत् ॥ ४०

भिन्नैरिति चतुस्त्रिद्व्येकसहस्रैः कृतादियुगकल्पना। तेषां सन्धिसन्ध्यंशौ तावच्छतैरित्यर्थः। त्वमपीति। एतौ हरिहरावपीत्यर्थः। तेषां जीवनकालस्य अल्पत्वमाह वैराग्यार्थकत्वम्—आयुरिति। निश्वासादिमतस्तवापि तर्हि उत्क्रमेण कालपरिच्छेदः स्यादिति न। कालस्य कालान्तरायोगादित्याह—कालेनेति। अथवा एवं विषममायुः कल्पयतः कालस्य वैषम्यनैर्घृण्ये स्यातामिति।

न। पुरुषकर्मानुसारेण तस्य प्रेरकत्वादित्याह—कालेनेति। वक्ष्यमाण-प्रकारेण प्रचोद्यत इति वार्थः ॥ ३५ ॥ ३६ ॥ ३७ ॥ ३८ ॥ ३९ ॥ ४० ॥

प्रकृतिः पुरुषश्चेत्यादेरन्योऽर्थः। प्रकृतिपुरुषकाला अकारोकारमकाराः। हकाररेफमाया वा। ते नित्याः वक्ष्यमाणप्रयोगेषु नियमेन प्रयोज्या इत्यर्थः। सत्तमेति योगौचित्येन बिन्द्वादियोगः सूचितः ॥ २१ ॥

आणवं योगमाह—अणोरणीयसीति। मूलाधारगतत्रिकोणमध्ये परमाणोरपि अणीयसी प्रकृतिः ध्येयाऽकाराकारेणेत्यर्थः। ततस्तस्याः प्रभारूपेण आकाशादेरपि व्यापक उकारश्चिन्त्य इत्याह—स्थूलादिति। ततः सर्वं जगत् मकाराकारेण तत्र मज्जनोयमित्याह—व्याप्तेति। धामक्रमयोगमाह—आदित्येति। चिदग्निव्याप्त-सौषुम्नमार्गमणिपूरकानाहताज्ञाब्रह्मरन्ध्रेषु अग्निसूर्यसोमब्रह्मधामानि सञ्चिन्त्य सर्वानुगतां कुण्डलिनीं ध्यायन् क्रमेण विलाप्य बिन्दुनादादिना व्यापिन्यादिद्वारेण विभुर्भवेदित्यर्थः ॥ २२ ॥

गुणयोगं भूतयोगं चोत्तरस्मिन् श्लोके वदन् तयोः गुणभूतयोः वर्णानां नामनियममाह—न खेतेति। गुणादियोगमाह—न गुणेष्विति। पूर्वोक्तमण्डल-स्थानेषु सत्त्वादिगुणगणम् एकवर्णं ज्योतिर्लिङ्गवत् ध्यायन् पूर्ववत् स्वरूपस्थो भवेदिति गुणयोगः। हृत्कण्ठतालुभ्रूमध्यब्रह्मरन्ध्रद्वादशान्तेषु मण्डलबीजा-धिष्ठात्वसहितान् पृथिव्यादिकारणान्तान् कुण्डलिनीप्रभावेन एकवर्णं ध्यात्वा संयोजयेत्। अयं भूतयोगः ॥ २३ ॥

अस्यैव योगस्य स्वरूपपर्यन्तव्याप्तिक्रममाह—अन्तरेति। समस्तरन्ध्रद्वारेण सबाह्याभ्यन्तरं व्याप्य उन्मन्यन्तं गत्वा देहिनां देहसंहर्त्रीत्यर्थः। एवं देशिक-दर्शितैरुपायैः परमात्मस्वरूपेण स्वानुभवनीया न पृथक्केनेत्याह—स्वसंवेद्येति ॥ २४ ॥

तदनुभवस्य परमपुरुषार्थत्वमाह—ययेति। अथ शक्तियोगमाह—पुंन-पुंसकयोरिति। पुंनपुंसकयोः प्राणमनसोः वाचि चेच्छादिशक्तिरूपेण तुल्याऽपि प्रणवोच्चारणसमये हि क्रमेण इच्छाक्रियाज्ञानशक्तिरूपाणां मनःप्राणवाचां निविड-तेजोध्वनिरूपमन्त्रात्मना एकत्वं तुल्यत्वं भवति। तस्मिन् साम्ये तेजसि स्थितासु अङ्गनासु अपरच[प]राच[प]रकुण्डलिनीषु विशिष्यते। सकलेच्छादिशक्तिरूपेण विशिष्टा भवतीत्यर्थः ॥ २५ ॥

ततस्तासां संहारमाह—प्रधानमिति। प्रथितं त्रयमकारादित्रयेणाऽत्ति। ततो बिन्दु कला निरोधिका रूपमनआदिकं निविड़तेजोरूपमत्ति। ततो नाद-नादान्तरूपा प्रभामत्तीति प्रधानम्। ततः परं या सर्वव्यापिनीसमन्युन्मनीशक्तिरिति

कथ्यत इत्यर्थः। अथ चतुर्मूर्त्यादिचतुर्दशयोगान् क्रमेणाह—या युष्मानिति। युष्मान् मामपि ब्रह्मविष्णुरुद्रसर्वेश्वरान् नाभिहृद्भ्रूमध्यद्वादशान्तस्थितान् अमृतमयान् अवष्टभ्याऽतिवर्तत इत्यर्थः। इति चतुर्मूर्तियोगः सूचितः। ब्रह्म विष्णु रुद्र-भेदाभेद लिङ्ग चिदवष्टम्भयोगा अपि अनेनैव सूचिताः। तत्र युष्मानतिवर्तत इति ब्रह्मादियोगत्रयं चतुर्ष्वपि स्थानेषु सपरिवारं ब्रह्माणं सञ्चिन्त्य संपूज्य तेजोरूपांस्तान् प्रणवेन एकीकृत्याऽमृतमास्रावयेदिति ब्रह्मयोगः। एवमेव विष्ण्वादियोगा द्रष्टव्याः। भेदयोगे स्थानेषु भिन्नशरीरमूर्त्तित्रयं ध्येयम्। अभेदयोगेऽभिन्नरूपम्। लिङ्गयोगे लिङ्गरूपम्। भेदादियोगत्रयं चापिशब्देन सूचितम्। अतिवर्तत इति चिदवष्टम्भयोगः। तेजसा बाह्यं स्थूलादिशरीरं व्याप्याऽतिक्रम्य वर्तनं ह्यतिवर्तनम्॥ २६॥

चिदवष्टम्भयोगानन्तरम् अध्यात्माधिदैवादिभेदं परित्यज्य स्थूलादिशरीरात्मकमेकमेव पिण्डं सर्वं ध्येयमित्याह—साऽहमिति। सा पूर्वमध्यात्मं कुण्डलिनीरूपेण स्थिता। अहं द्वादशान्ते स्थितः। यूयं नाभ्यादौ स्थिताः। अन्यच्च परिवारजातं वेद्यं बाह्यं च। तत् तु सा तत् सर्वं सैव। या हि नः स्थूलादिशरीररूपिणी स्मृता। विराट्हिरण्यगर्भकारणरूपिणीत्यर्थः।

इदानीं गुणसंहारोन्मानुज्ञात्रनुज्ञानिर्विकल्पयोगानाह—प्रलय इति। प्रलये प्रणवे वाचके। तस्यां च वाच्यात्मिकायां व्याप्यते संक्षियते चराचरमिदं जगत्। पूर्वं पूर्वं वाच्यवाचकरूपम् उत्तरो त्तरवाच्यवाचकरूपिण्यां तस्यां विलाप्यत इत्यर्थः। अकारोकार मकार बिन्दु नाद शक्ति शान्तानां विराट् हिरण्यगर्भ कारणगुण सामान्यगुणबीज गुणाभाव गुणसाक्षिणां च स्थूलत्व सूक्ष्मत्व कारणत्व समत्व बीजत्वनिर्विशेषत्व शान्तत्वगुणैः एकत्वचिन्तनं गुणयोगः। संहारयोगः तेषां क्रमेण संहारः। एवमधिष्ठानस्थस्य अतिसूक्ष्मस्य जगतः तत्सच्चिद्रूपव्याप्तिचिन्तनमोतयोगः। ततः स्वतः सत्ताद्यभावात् तस्य आत्माधीनत्वचिन्तनमनुज्ञात्रयोगः। आत्मव्यतिरेकेणाऽभावचिन्तनमनुज्ञायोगः। तत आत्मनो निर्विशेषत्वचिन्तनं निर्विकल्पयोगः॥ २७॥

ततो वाक्यार्थप्रतिपत्तिमाह—सैवेति। सा परापरशक्तिरविद्यया प्रपञ्चरूपतां प्राप्ता उक्तविवेकप्रकारेण स्वां वेत्ति। ब्रह्मात्मरूपतां वेदनफलमाह—परमेति। संसारनिवृत्तिं चाह—तस्या इति। वेद्यवेदितृवेदनादिकं नासीदस्ति भविष्यति इत्यर्थः। अथ कालयोगमाह—सा त्विति। कालस्याऽपरस्य पञ्चदशधा भिन्नस्यापि आत्मा कालात्मा। तेनोन्मनीरूपेण कालेन मया पञ्चदशकालाभिमानिनी

सा तत्त्वसंज्ञा चिन्मात्रा ज्योतिषः सन्निधेस्तदा ।
विचिकीर्षुर्घनीभूता क्वचिदभ्येति बिन्दुताम् ॥ ४१
कालेन भिद्यमानस्तु स बिन्दुर्भवति त्रिधा ।
स्थूलसूक्ष्मपरत्वेन तस्य त्रैविध्यमिष्यते ॥ ४२

सम्यगभेदेन ज्ञायत इत्यर्थः । लव त्रुटि कला काष्ठा निमेष मात्रा नाडिका मुहूर्ता-होरात्र मास संवत्सर युग कल्प महाकल्प परार्ध कालपर्वाणि अकारोकार मकार-बिन्दु कला निरोधिका नाद नादान्त शक्ति व्यापिनी व्योमरूपान्तनादान् आश्रिता समनीलचणप्रणवमात्रासु मूलाधारम् आरभ्याद्वादशान्तं व्यवस्थितासु सञ्चिन्त्य क्रमेण संहृत्य अकालकलिकायाम् उन्मन्यां व्यवतिष्ठेतेत्यर्थः ॥ २८ ॥

इदानीमुन्मन्यामवस्थितस्याऽप्रयत्नेनैव जपादनन्तं जपफलं दर्शयितुं लवादि-कालपर्वकथनाय चोपक्रमते लवादीति । त्वदायुर्मम निश्वास इत्यहोरात्रपक्ष-संवत्सरादियोगान् श्वासोच्छ्वासस्थान् दर्शयति । श्वासस्याऽऽयुषोऽपि तद्रूपत्वात् कालेनैवं प्रचोद्यत इति । अहोरात्रादियोगे साक्षितया सत्तामात्रेणात्मा प्रेरको ध्येयः । नतु कालमध्यवर्तितयेति उक्तम् ॥ २९ ॥ ३० ॥ ३१ ॥ ३२ ॥ ३३ ॥ ३४ ॥ ॥ ३५ ॥ ॥ ३६ ॥ ३७ ॥ ३८ ॥ ३९ ॥

कालः कर्मापेक्षया प्रेरक एव केवलमित्युक्तं पूर्वस्मिन् व्याख्याने तत् कथं प्रलये सर्वसंहारादित्याशङ्क्य प्रलयेऽपि सूक्ष्मरूपेण कर्मणामवस्थितिमीश्वरस्य सर्वज्ञतां चाह—स जानातीति । स अनन्तरोक्तः । सा तु कालात्मनेति व्यवहितत्वेन उक्तो वा । वाचकशब्दात् तां चेत्यर्थः । परिपक्वानि कर्माणि जात्यायुर्भोगांश्च विपाकांश्च सम्यगासां कार्येण सर्वदा प्रकृतौ कर्मणां सत्त्वे कथं कादाचित्की सृष्टिरित्याशङ्क्य ईश्वरापरकालादिवशादित्याह—प्रकृतेरिति ॥ ४० ॥

तत्त्वविकृतिक्रममाह—सा तत्त्वेति । सा प्रकृतिः तत्त्वस्य पारमार्थिकस्य संज्ञेव संज्ञा यस्याः तदविभक्तत्वात् सा तथोक्ता । सा तत्त्वात्मकताम् अन्तर्मुखताम् अपरित्यज्यैव क्वचिद्देशे बिन्दुतां किञ्चित् बहिर्मुखतया सृष्ट्युन्मुखकर्माविभक्ततया तरङ्गमूलभूतसूक्ष्मवायुव्याप्तसमुद्रवलनवत् किञ्चित् स्थौल्यं प्राप्नोतीत्यर्थः । परिपक्व-कर्माभेदात् घनीभावस्तदर्थं व्यापारो विचिकीर्षा । बिन्दुः कर्माभिन्नं रूपम् ॥४१॥

एवं परस्मादुत्पन्नस्य प्रकृतितत्त्वस्योत्तरसृष्टिनिर्वाहार्थम् इच्छासत्त्वादिरूप-तामाह—कालेनेति । भिद्यमानः सम्बध्यमानः विभज्यमानश्च । नहि चित्सम्बन्धं विनाऽचिद्रूपस्य ज्ञानादिरूपत्वं सम्भवति । इच्छादीनामेकैकस्य मायातच्छक्तितद्गत-

स बिन्दुनादबीजत्वभेदेन च निगद्यते ।
तद्विस्तारप्रकारोऽयं यथा वक्ष्यामि साम्प्रतम् ॥ ४३

बिन्दोस्तस्माद्भिद्यमानाद्रवोऽव्यक्तात्मको भवेत् ।
स रवः श्रुतिसम्पन्नैः शब्दब्रह्मेति कथ्यते ॥ ४४

अव्यक्तादन्तरुदितत्रिभेदगहनात्मकम् ।
महन्नाम भवेत्तत्त्वं महतोऽहङ्कृतिस्तथा ॥ ४५

भूतादिकवैकारिकतैजसभेदक्रमादहङ्कारात् ।
कालप्रेरितया गुणघोषयुजा शब्दसृष्टिरथ शक्त्या ॥ ४६

शब्दाद् व्योम स्पर्शतस्तेन वायु-
स्ताभ्यां रूपाद्वह्निरेतैः रसाच्च ।
अम्भांस्येतैर्गन्धतो भूर्धराद्या
भूताः पञ्च स्युर्गुणोनाः क्रमेण ॥ ४७

प्राणिकर्मविषयभेदेन त्रिरूपतामाह—स्थूलेति ॥ ४२ ॥

नवानामपि भेदानां तत्त्वमाह मन्त्रिहिताय—स बिन्द्विति। बिन्दुरीश्वरः। नादस्तस्याः चिन्मिश्रं रूपं पुरुषाख्यम्। बीजमचिदंशः। एतन्मन्त्रावृत्तिसमये स्वानुभवेनाऽनुगन्तव्यम्। स्वरूपस्थेन वक्ष्यति हि शब्दावगम्यमर्थमिति ॥ ४३ ॥

एवमर्थरूपस्य प्रकृतितत्त्वस्य सृष्टिमभिधाय एतामेवाऽर्थसृष्टिं शब्दसृष्टित्वेनाऽप्याह अत्र शब्दार्थभेदाभावात्—बिन्दोरिति। बिन्दुरुक्तः परमपुरुष एव। तस्माद्बीजरूपयोक्तया प्रकृत्या सम्बध्यमानात् उभयाभेदलक्षणो देदीप्यमानः परापश्यन्त्यात्मको रवोऽभवत्। स एव च कुण्डल्यादिशब्दैरभिलप्यते।

कोऽसौ रव इति तदाह—स रव इति ॥ ४४ ॥

त्रिभेदा इच्छासत्त्वादयः। अहङ्कृतिस्तथेति। इच्छासत्त्वादिरूपैवेत्यर्थः। अत्र महन् नाम ज्ञानसत्त्वप्रधानः परिणामः। सर्वजगदाश्रयभूत ईक्षणादिशब्दार्थः। ईक्षितुस्तदभिमानिनोऽहङ्कारस्तमःप्रधानः परिणामः ॥ ४५ ॥

कालप्रेरितयेति। कालो द्विविधः। गुणाः सत्त्वादयः। घोषः पूर्वोक्तो रवः शब्दब्रह्म। शक्तिस्तत्त्वसंज्ञेत्युक्ता। तस्माद्धराद्या भूता उत्पन्नाः शब्दादीनामेव काठिन्यावस्थारूपत्वाद् व्योमादीनां शब्दाद् व्योम इत्याद्यभिहितं त्रिभेदगहनात्मकम् ॥ ४६ ॥ ४७ ॥

खमपि सुषिरचिह्नमीरणः स्या-
च्चलनपरः परिपाकवान् कृशानुः ।
जलमपि रसवद् घना धरा तेऽ-
सितशितिपाटलशुभ्रपीतभासः ॥ ४८

वृत्तं व्योम्नो बिन्दुषट्कान्वितं त-
द्वायोरग्नेः स्वस्तिकोद्यत्त्रिकोणम् ।
अब्जोपेतार्द्धेन्दुमद्बिम्बमाप्यं
स्याद्वज्रोद्यच्चातुरस्रं धरायाः ॥ ४९

निवृत्तिसंज्ञा च तथा प्रतिष्ठा
विद्याह्वया शान्तिसशान्त्यतीते ।
स्युः शक्तयः पञ्च धरादिभूत-
प्रोत्थाः क्रमान्नादकलादिभूताः ॥ ५०

तथेति च महदहङ्कारयोः स्वरूपस्योक्तत्वादाकाशादेः स्वरूपमाह—खमपीति । न्यासप्रयोगादिविशेषतया आकाशादीनां रूपमाह—असितेत्यादिना ॥ ४८ ॥

वृत्तं ठकारवद् व्योम्नो बिम्बम् । तदेव वृत्तं बिन्दुषट्कान्वितं वायोः । स्वस्तिकं चतुर्वक्त्रं परस्परसम्बद्धं रेखाद्वयं कोणत्रयगतम् । भूताभिमानिनी बिन्दुतत्त्वनिर्गता शक्तिः ॥ ४९ ॥

प्रयोगाद्यार्थमेवाह—निवृत्तीति । तासां स्थूलवाचकांशमाह—नादकलादि-भूता इति । नादो हकारः कः अनुस्वारः । के ऊर्ध्वे येषां लादीनां ते तथोक्ताः । लस्यादौ लादौ रयौ लः आदिर्यस्य वकारस्य लश्चादिश्चेति त्रिधा योज्यम् । लवरयहा इत्यर्थः । कशब्देनैव बिन्दुयोगोऽप्येषां द्रष्टव्यः । इति तन्मात्राभि-मानिनीबीजोद्धारः ।

अथ अपञ्चीकृतबीजोद्धारः । नादः हकारः के येषां लादीनां सर्वेषामादीनां च ते तथोक्ताः । लादिशब्दार्थः पूर्ववत् व्याख्येयः । अत्र ल आदिर्यस्येति व्युत्पत्त्या हकारोऽपि ग्राह्यः । नादशब्दोक्तस्य हकारस्य सर्वसम्बन्धात् । आदयः आं ईं ऊं ऐं औं इत्येते । ततः ह्लां ह्वीं ह्रूं ह्यैं हौं इत्येतत् सिद्धं भवति ।

अथ पञ्चीकृतबीजानि उच्यन्ते । नादः के यस्य लकारस्य इत्यर्थः । स नाद-कलः ह्ल इत्यर्थः । नादकलाश्च आदिश्च नादकलादयः तेभ्यो भूताः तदात्म-तयाऽभिव्यक्ताः निवृत्त्याद्या इत्यर्थः । ततश्च ह्लां ह्लीं ह्लूं ह्लैं ह्लौं इति सिद्धं

पुटयोरुभयोश्च दण्डसंस्था पृथिवी तोयमधः कृशानुरूर्ध्वम् ।
पवनस्त्वथ पार्श्वगोऽथ मध्ये गगनं भूतगतिस्तनूद्भवेयम् ॥ ५१

व्योम्नि मरुद्च दहनस्तत्रापस्तासु संस्थिता पृथिवी ।
सचराचरात्मकानि तानि तस्यां जातानि सर्वभूतानि ॥ ५२

श्रोत्रत्वगक्षिजिह्वाघ्राणान्यपि चेन्द्रियाणि बुद्धेः स्युः ।
वाक्पाणिपादपायूपस्थानि च कर्मसंज्ञकानि तथा ॥ ५३

वचनादाने सगती सविसर्गानन्दकौ च संप्रोक्ताः ।
वागाद्यर्थाः समनो बुद्धिरहङ्कारश्चित्तमपि करणम् ॥ ५४

भूतेन्द्रियेन्द्रियार्थैरुद्दिष्टस्तत्त्वपञ्चविंशतिकः ।
व्यानन्दकैश्च तैरपि तत्त्वचतुर्विंशतिस्तथा प्रोक्ता ॥ ५५

करणोपेतैरेतैस्तत्त्वान्युक्तानि रहितवचनाद्यैः ।
भूतानीन्द्रियदशकं समनः प्रोक्तो विकारषोड़शकः ॥ ५६

अव्यक्तमहदहङ्कृतिभूतानि प्रकृतयः स्युरष्टौ च ।
तन्मात्राहङ्काराः समहान्तः प्रकृतिविकृतयः सप्त ॥ ५७

भवति । भूतगतिकथनमपि प्रयोगाद्यर्थमेव ॥ ५० ॥ ५१ ॥

प्रासङ्गिकं पञ्चीकरणमाह—व्योम्नि मरुदिति । अत्रेति तत्रेति च आकाश इत्यर्थः । तास्विति तत्सम्बन्ध आकाश इत्यर्थः । मरुति व्योमाऽत्राऽग्निस्तत्रापः तासु संस्थिता पृथिवीत्याद्यपि द्रष्टव्यम् । अथवा सूक्ष्मभूतानामेव लयाद्युपयोगितया व्याप्यव्यापकतामाह—व्योम्नीति ॥ ५२ ॥

एवं भूतादिकाहङ्कारकार्यमभिधाय तैजसवैकारिकाहङ्कारयोः भूतानुगतयोः क्रमेण कार्यमाह—श्रोत्रेति ॥ ५३ ॥ ५४ ॥

तत्त्वपञ्चविंशतिक इति । अत्र तत्त्वकल्पनायाः कुत्सितत्वं सूचितम् । कुत्सितोऽपसिद्धान्त इत्यर्थः । तथा प्रोक्ता इति । अत्र तथाशब्देनापि कुत्सितत्वं सूचितम् । विरक्तंमन्यमानानामपि तत्त्वकल्पना कुत्सितैवेत्यर्थः ॥ ५५ ॥

तत्त्वानि उक्तानीति केवलमुक्तान्येव न तु तत्त्वानि तानि । यदि चित्तशब्देन प्रकृतिः नोच्यत इत्यर्थः । ततः प्रकृत्यन्तानि चतुर्विंशतितत्त्वानि पुरुषान्तानि पञ्चविंशतितत्त्वानि ईश्वरान्तानि षड्विंशतितत्त्वानीति सिद्धं भवति । उत्तरत्र व्यवहारशेषतया केषाञ्चिन्मन्त्राणां वर्णतत्त्वन्यासयोगादिशेषतया च षोडश-

सत्त्वं रजस्तम इति संप्रोक्ताश्च त्रयो गुणास्तस्याः ।
तत्सम्बन्धात् विकृतैर्भेदचितयैस्ततं जगत् सकलम् ॥ ५८

देवाश्च श्रुतयः स्वराः समरुतो लोकाः सवैश्वानराः
कालाः शक्तियुतत्रिवर्गसहितास्तिस्रस्तथा वृत्तयः ।
नाड्योऽन्यच्च जगत्त्रयेऽत्र नियतं यद्वस्तु सम्बध्य त-
द्विश्वेषां स्थितये चरन्त्यविरतं सूर्येन्दुवैश्वानराः ॥ ५९

विकारादि कथनमवगन्तव्यम् ॥ ५६ ॥ ५७ ॥

तस्या इति मूलकारणभूतायाः प्रकृतेरित्यर्थः । तस्याः त्रिगुणात्मकत्वे प्रमाणमाह—तत्सम्बन्धादिति । ततं व्याप्तम् ॥ ५८ ॥

तदेव प्रपञ्चयति न्यासयोगविशेषांश्च प्रणवादिषु कामनानुरूपेण दर्शयन्—देवा इति । वृत्तयो जाग्रदाद्या याजनाद्या वा । नाड्यो योगस्थानभूताः सुषुम्नाचित्रावज्राख्याः प्रसिद्धा वा । न्यासयोगादिकं मण्डलत्रयोपेतमेव कार्यमित्याह—संबध्येत्यादिना । चरन्ति नाभ्यादिस्थिताः संभूय ऊर्ध्वं गच्छन्ति । परमानन्दं भक्षयन्ति चेत्यर्थः ॥ ५८ ॥

* ननु सर्वमन्त्रसमानत्वेन सर्वागमसारत्वादस्य ग्रन्थस्य शैवशाक्तादि तत्त्वान्यप्यत्र वक्तव्यानि । सत्यमुक्तानि तानि कथं शृणु । सा तत्त्वसंज्ञेत्यत्र चिन्मात्रज्योतिःशब्दाभ्याम् अधिष्ठानसाक्षिलक्षणौ अनाहतशिवशक्ती अकारलक्षितार्थौ कथ्येते । तत्त्वसंज्ञेति आहतशिवोऽकारवाच्यार्थः । अभ्येति बिन्दुतामित्यन्तेन आहतशक्तिः उकारवाच्या । स बिन्दुर्भवति त्रिधेति । इच्छाक्रियाज्ञानलक्षणानि इह सवाचकानि सदाशिवेश्वरशुद्धविद्यातत्त्वानि । एतच्छुद्धतत्त्वपञ्चकम् वैष्णवे तत्त्वे वासुदेवादिशब्दवाच्यमित्येव विशेषः । पोयरावलाश्च तत्र वर्णाः परमेष्ठिपुंविश्वनिवृत्ति सर्वात्मसहिताश्च । विद्यातत्त्वानन्तरं शैवे मायातत्त्वं स्वरूपाच्छादनविक्षेपात्मकम् । शुद्धपञ्चके त्वाच्छादनं नास्ति । तस्येश्वररूपत्वात् विद्यावत्त्वेन । मायादिकं तु जीवोपकरणभूतम् । एकैव शक्तिः अन्तर्मुखतया विकसन्ती विद्यादितत्त्वरूपिणी बहिर्मुखतया संकुचन्ती मायादितत्त्वरूपिणी । तदुपहितः शिव एव जीव इति हि तेषां सिद्धान्तः । माया विक्षेपे कालपरिच्छेदे हेतुः । कालतत्त्वं तत एव । देश काल कर्म फलादि नियतहेतुः ईश्वरेच्छा एव नियतितत्त्वम् । कला त्वेवं परिच्छिन्नस्य पशोः किञ्चित्कर्तृत्वशक्तिः । तस्यैव किञ्चिदज्ञत्वशक्तिः अशुद्धविद्या । तस्याः पूर्णमन्यता रागतत्त्वम् । एतत्षट्कविशिष्टः परमशिवो

एष सर्गः समुत्पन्न इत्थं विश्वं प्रतीयते।
विश्वप्रतीतौ हि यतः प्रपञ्चस्त्ववगम्यते ॥ ६०

जीवः। स पुरुषतत्त्वम्। अस्य च सप्तकस्य षादिमान्ता वर्णाः। वैष्णवे तु जीवतत्व एव एतत् सर्वमन्तर्भूतम्। पुरुषात्परं शैवे प्रकृतितत्त्वं पशोः सुखदुःखमोहलक्षणं भकारवाच्यम्। वैष्णवे प्राणतत्त्वेनैव गता प्रकृतिः। बिन्दोः तस्माद्भिद्यमानादित्यनेनैतत् तत्त्वगणमुक्तम्। बिन्दुः शिवः। तस्मात् आहतशिवशक्त्यादिरूपादेवमुक्तेन प्रकारेण मायादिरूपेण भिद्यमानात् परिणम्यमानात् अभिन्नो रवो वाचकांशः वाच्येन सह अव्यक्तात्मकः प्रकृतितत्त्वात्मकोऽभवत्। स रवः प्रकृतितत्त्वपर्यन्तः शब्दब्रह्मेति कथ्यत इति। महदादिकं तु सर्वत्र समानमिति। निवृत्तिसंज्ञा चेत्यत्र शाक्तमपि तत्त्वं निवृत्ति प्रतिष्ठा विद्या शान्तिशान्त्यतीत बिन्दु कला निरोधिका नाद नादान्त शक्ति व्यापिनीव्योमरूपानन्तानाथानाश्रिता समन्युन्मनीलक्षणं सूचितम्। स्युः पञ्च शक्तयः। नादकलादिभूताश्च त्रयोदश स्युरिति हि तस्यार्थः। नादो नाद एव कला बिन्दुः तावादिभूतौ येषामिति विग्रहः ॥ * ॥

एवं तत्त्वसृष्टिमभिधाय उपसंहरति—एष इति। सृज्यत इति सर्गः। तत्त्वगणः। इत्थमुक्तेन प्रकारेण समुत्पन्न इत्युपसंहारः। सृष्टेः व्यवहारलक्षणम् अवान्तरप्रयोजनमाह—इत्थमिति। इत्थमेवं सृष्टौ सत्यां विश्वं प्रतीयते। प्रतीतिः क्रियाया अप्युपलक्षणार्था। ज्ञानक्रियात्मको हि व्यवहारः।

अर्थसृष्टेः परमप्रयोजनमाह—विश्वेति। विश्वस्य कार्यस्य प्रतीतौ शक्त्यां सत्यां हि यस्मात् यतः परब्रह्मण उक्तः प्रपञ्चः समुत्पन्नः तद्ब्रह्माऽवगम्यते। नान्यथा। तस्मात् सृष्टिरर्थवतीत्यर्थः।

अथवा एषः सर्वप्रत्यक्षसिद्धः परमात्मा सर्गं सृजतीति स एव योऽसौ स्रष्टा परमात्मा स एव उक्ततत्त्वरूपेण समुत्पन्न इत्यर्थः। कुतः यत इत्थं परमात्मरूपेण घटः सन् घटः प्रकाशत इति च विश्वं सर्वं तन्मयं प्रतीयते। किमित्यसावेवमुत्पन्न इति स्वात्मप्रकाशनायेत्याह—विश्वेति। विश्वप्रतीतौ घटाद्याकारबुद्धिवृत्तौ तत्साक्षितया। हि यस्मादित्यादि समानम्।

एतदेव पद्यं त्रैपुरतत्त्वपरत्वेन योज्यते। इत्थं समुत्पन्न एष शैवतत्त्वलक्षणः सर्गः। विश्वं प्रमेय प्रमाण प्रमातृरूपात्म विद्या शिवतत्त्वरूपं प्रतीयते। 'प्रमा प्रमाता प्रमितं च विश्वम्' इति हि लिङ्गसूक्तवाक्यम्। तत्र मायान्तं मेयरूपम् आत्मतत्त्वं सदाशिवान्तं ज्ञानरूपं विद्यातत्त्वम् आहतशिवान्तं प्रमातृरूपं

शब्दब्रह्मेति यत् प्रोक्तं तदुद्देशः प्रवर्त्त्यते ।
अतः परमवाच्यं हि स्वसंवेद्यस्वरूपतः ॥ ६१

शब्दब्रह्मेति शब्दावगम्यमर्थं विदुर्बुधाः ।
स्वतोऽर्थानवबोधत्वात् प्रोक्तो नैतादृशो रवः ॥ ६२

स तु सर्वत्र संस्यूतो जाते भूताकरे पुनः ।
आविर्भवति देहेषु प्राणिनामर्थविस्तृतः ॥ ६३

शिवतत्त्वम् इति द्रष्टव्यम् ।

अवशिष्टं सर्वतत्त्वमाह—विश्वेति । विश्वस्य तत्त्वत्रयात्मकस्य वेद्यस्य प्रतीतौ साक्षिणि सति यतः यस्मादधिष्ठानात् अनाहतशिवात् प्रपञ्च उक्तो भवति । सः परमशिवः सर्वतत्त्वरूपोऽवगम्यत इति ॥ ६० ॥

एवमर्थसृष्टिं शब्दसृष्टिं च मध्यमान्तामभिधाय वैखरीसृष्टिकथनार्थम् उक्तानुवादपूर्वकमुपक्रमते—शब्दब्रह्मेति । तत्र तत्त्वसंज्ञा परावाक् तदर्थरूपिणी प्रकृतितत्त्वान्तं पश्यन्ती तदर्थात्मकम् इन्द्रियान्तं मध्यमा तदर्थात्मकं पञ्चीकृतं वैखरी तदर्थात्मकमिति अवगन्तव्यम् । शब्दब्रह्मेति यत् प्रोक्तं स रवः श्रुतिसंपन्नैरित्यत्र तदुद्देशः । तस्य क्रमेण वैखरीरूपेणोद्देशः उपदेशः प्रवर्त्यते ।

ननु बैन्दवतत्त्वरूपशब्दब्रह्मणोऽपि ऊर्ध्वं परावाग्रूपायाः तत्त्वसंज्ञायाः तत्साक्षिणः तत्त्वस्य चोद्देशनं याथार्थ्योपदेशनमकृत्वा किमिति शब्दब्रह्मोद्देशः क्रियत इति तयोरुद्देष्टुमशक्यत्वादित्याह—अतः परमिति । अत्राच्यत्वे हेतुः—स्वसंवेद्येति । आत्मा स्वसंवेद्यत्वेन अवाच्यः । शक्तेरपि तदभिन्नत्वात् तद्व्यतिरेकेणाऽभावाद्वा अवाच्यत्वमेव । स्वयंप्रकाशत्वेन वचनापेक्षाभावादिति वार्थः ॥ ६१ ॥

ननु शब्दब्रह्मेति श्रोत्रग्राह्य एव सूक्ष्मो व्यापी शब्दः न बैन्दवं तत्त्वमिति केचिदिति न इत्याह—शब्दब्रह्मेति । शब्दोच्चारणकाले तत्साक्षितयाऽन्तरत्वेन अवगम्यमर्थं बिन्द्वात्मकमित्यर्थः ।

इतरस्य न प्रकाशकशब्दरहस्यत्वं ब्रह्मत्वं चेत्याह—स्वत इति । बिन्द्वात्मकप्रकाशात्मत्वं विनाऽनवबोधकत्वात् तत्प्रोक्तो रवो न शब्दब्रह्मेत्यर्थः ॥ ६२ ॥

स्वाभिप्रेतस्य शब्दस्य ब्रह्मत्वं प्रकाशकत्वं चास्तीत्याह—स त्विति । सः शब्दावगम्योऽर्थः पूर्वोक्तः सर्वत्र संस्यूतः कारणत्वात् । तुशब्दो विशेषावधारणार्थः । अतस्तस्य ब्रह्मत्वं प्रकाशकत्वं च युक्तमित्याह—जाते इति । प्राणिनां देहेषु वैखर्या तदभिमतया विनापि यावदर्थः व्याप्तः सङ्कल्पविकल्प-

प्रकृतौ कालनुन्नायां गुणान्तःकरणात्मनि ।
देहश्चतुर्विधो ज्ञेयो जन्तोरुत्पत्तिभेदतः ॥ ६४
औद्भिजः स्वेदजोऽण्डोत्थश्चतुर्थस्तु जरायुजः ।
उद्भिद्य भूमिं निर्गच्छत्यौद्भिदः स्थावरस्तु सः ॥ ६५
निर्दिष्टः स्कन्धविटपपत्रपुष्पफलादिभिः ।
पञ्चभूतात्मकः सर्वः क्ष्मामधिष्ठाय जायते ॥ ६६
अम्बुयोन्यग्नि[भूवारितेजः]पवननभसां समवायतः ।
स्वेदजः स्विद्यमानाभ्यो भवन्त्यार्द्राः प्रजायते ॥ ६७
यूकमत्कुणकीटाणुचियाद्याः क्षणभङ्गुराः ।
अण्डजो वर्त्तुलीभूताच्छुक्रशोणितसंपुटात् ॥ ६८
कालेन भिन्नात् पूर्णात्मा निर्गच्छन् प्रक्रमिष्यति ।
अहिगोधावयोभेक[द]शिशुमारादिकश्च सः ॥ ६९
जरायुजस्तु ग्राम्यातः क्रियातः स्रुतिसम्भवः ।
स जायते चतुर्विंशत्तत्त्वसंयुक्तदेहवान् ॥ ७०
स्वस्थानतश्च्युताच्छुक्राद्बिन्दुमादाय मारुतः ।
गर्भाशयं प्रविशति यदा तुल्यं तदापरः ॥ ७१

निश्चयविमर्शनात्मना आविर्भवतीत्यर्थः ॥ ६३ ॥

तस्याविर्भावप्रकारप्रदर्शनार्थं देहोत्पत्तिप्रकारं दर्शयन् तद्भेदं तावदाह—प्रकृताविति । गुणान्तःकरणात्मनीति सर्वतत्त्वात्मत्वोपलक्षणार्थम् । उत्पत्तिप्रकारभेदादेव देहानां भेदः न पञ्चभूतात्मकत्वेन इति उक्तमुत्पत्तिभेदत इति ॥ ६४ ॥

उत्पत्तिभेदमाह—उद्भिद्येति । उद्भिज्जमपि अप्राणिदेहं पाषाणादिकं व्यावर्त्तयन् उद्भिज्जस्य रूपमाह—स्थावर इति ।

स्थावरत्वमपि तेषामस्तीति अतो विशिनष्टि—स्कन्धेति । तेषां पृथिव्याश्रयत्वेन केवलपृथिव्यात्मत्वशङ्कां व्यावर्तयति—पञ्चेति । यद्यपि क्ष्मामधिष्ठाय जायते तथापि रसादिदर्शनात् पञ्चभूतात्मकत्वमेवेत्यर्थः ॥ ६५ ॥ ६६ ॥

अम्ब्वादीनामेकैकाभावेऽदर्शनादप्रधानेभ्यो भूतेभ्य एव स्वेदजोत्पत्तिरित्याह अम्ब्विति । चतुर्विंशदित्युपलक्षणम् । सर्वतत्त्वानाम् ।

संभवशब्दार्थमाह—स इति ॥ ६७ ॥ ६८ ॥ ६९ ॥ ७० ॥

आर्त्तवात् परमं बीजमादायाऽस्याश्च मूलतः ।
यदा गर्भाशयं नेष्यत्यथ संमिश्रयेन्मरुत् ॥ ७२
मायीयं नाम योषोत्थं पौरुषं कार्मकं मलम् ।
आणवं नाम संयुक्तं मिलितं तन्मलद्वयम् ॥ ७३
सूक्ष्मरूपाणि तत्त्वानि चतुर्विंशं मलद्वये ।
तत्र युक्तिं व्रजन्त्याशु ततस्तद्गर्भमारुतः ॥ ७४
संक्षोभ्य संवर्धयति तन्मलं शोणिताधिकम् ।
स्त्री स्याच्छुक्राधिकं ना स्यात् समबद्धं नपुंसकम् ॥ ७५
स्वगतैर्मरुदग्न्यद्भिः स्विद्यते क्वाथ्यते च तत् ।
मिश्रीभूतं तदह्नैव मातुरङ्गुष्ठसम्मितम् ॥ ७६
आयामि बुद्बुदाकारं परेऽहनि विजृम्भते ।
पक्षेण चतुरस्रं स्यान्मातुर्भुक्तरसात्मवत् ॥ ७७
मिलितादपि तस्मात्तु पृथगेव मलद्वयात् ।
किट्टीभूतं द्वयं पूर्वं बीजयुग्मं समुन्नमेत् ॥ ७८
ऊर्ध्वं तु मरुता नुन्नं तस्मादपि मलद्वयात् ।
उभयात्मिक्यधोवृत्ता नाड़ी दीर्घा भवेदृजुः ॥ ७९
अवाङ्मुखी सा तस्याश्च भवेत् पक्षद्वये द्वयम् ।
नाड्योस्तत्सन्निबद्धाः स्युः सप्तान्या नाड़िका मताः ॥ ८०

योषोत्थं रक्तं त्वगसृङ्मांसकारणत्वेन निःसारेऽपि शरीरे सारबुद्धिजनकत्वान्मायीयम् । पौरुषं शुक्रम् । अस्थ्यादिकारणत्वेन दार्ढ्यहेतुत्वात् देहस्य व्यापारक्षमत्वकरमिति कार्मकं कर्मसंस्कृतत्वाद्वा कार्मकम् । मिलितमनुशय्यणुत्वहेतुत्वादाणवम् । संयुक्तयोरपि परस्परम् एकत्वम् अप्राप्तयोः नानुशय्यणुत्वहेतुत्वमिति संयुक्तमिलितमित्युक्तम् ॥ ७१ ॥ ७२ ॥ ७३ ॥

तस्य पूयत्वाप्राप्तौ हेतुमाह—सूक्ष्मरूपाणीति । अनेन सर्वेषां सर्वोपाधित्वमुक्तं भवति । आशु पूयभावात् प्रागेव लब्धवृत्तीनि भवन्तीत्यर्थः ॥ ७४॥७५॥७६॥७७ ॥

किं तद्द्वयमुन्नतमित्याह --बीजयुग्ममिति ॥ ७८ ॥

उभयात्मिकीति । अग्नीषोमात्मिकी प्रकृतिपुरुषाख्यात्मिकी चेत्यर्थः ॥ ७९ ॥

अवाङ्मुखत्वमपि अस्तीत्यवाङ्मुखीत्युक्तम् ॥ ८० ॥ ८१ ॥

तत्र या प्रथमा नाड़ी सा सुषुम्नेति कथ्यते ।
या वामेड़ेति सा ज्ञेया दक्षिणा पिङ्गला स्मृता ॥ ८१
या वाममुष्कसम्बद्धा सा श्लिष्यन्ती सुषुम्नया ।
दक्षिणं जत्रुमाश्रित्य धनुर्वक्रा हृदि स्थिता ॥ ८२
वामांसजत्र्वन्तरगा दक्षिणां नासिकामियात् ।
तथा दक्षिणमुष्कोत्था नाड़ी या वामरन्ध्रगा ॥ ८३
अन्या धमन्यो याः प्रोक्ता गान्धारी हस्तिजिह्विका ।
सपुषाऽलम्बुषा चैव यशस्विन्यपि शङ्खिनी ॥ ८४
कुहूरिति च विद्वद्भिः प्रधाना व्यापिकास्तनौ ।
काचिन्नाड़ी बहिर्वक्रा या मातुर्हृदि बध्यते ॥ ८५
यया तत्पुष्टिमाप्नोति केदार इव कुल्यया ।
मातुराहाररसजैर्धातुभिः पुष्यते क्रमात् ॥ ८६
क्रमवृद्धौ परंज्योतिष्कला चेतन्नतामियात् ।
सचेतन्नं मलं तत् तु संभूतं सगुणं पुनः ॥ ८७
सदोषदूष्यसम्पन्नं जन्तुरित्यभिधीयते ।
फलकोशद्वयं तत् तु व्यक्तं पुंसो न तु स्त्रियः ॥ ८८
नपुंसकस्य किञ्चित् तु व्यक्तिरत्रोपलक्ष्यते ।
मध्यस्थायाः सुषुम्नायाः पर्वपञ्चकसम्भवाः ॥ ८९
शाखोपशाखतां प्राप्ताः शिरालक्षत्रयात् परम् ।
अर्द्धलक्षमिति प्राहुः शारीरार्थविशारदाः ॥ ९०

वाममुष्केति छेदे अदक्षिणामिति छेदः । दक्षिणमुष्कोत्थेति छेदे अवामरन्ध्रगेति छेदः ॥ ८२ ॥ ८३ ॥ ८४ ॥

मातुर्भुक्तरसात्मवदित्युक्तम् । तत्कथमिति । तदाह—काचिदिति ॥ ८५॥८६ ॥

वैराग्यार्थमाह—सचेतन्नमिति । बीजयुग्मं समुन्नमेदित्युक्तम् । न तत् सार्वत्रिकमित्याशङ्क्याह—फलेति ॥ ८७ ॥ ८८ ॥ ८९ ॥

अवशिष्टं नाड़ीचक्रं योगियोगाभिवृद्धये दर्शयति—मध्यस्थाया इति । मूलाधारनाभि हृदय गलमूल भ्रूमध्यानुसारीणि पञ्चपर्वाणि ॥ ८९ ॥ ९० ॥

तद्भेदांश्च बहूनाहुस्ताभिः सर्वाभिरेव च ।
व्याप्नोति सर्वतो वायुर्येन देहः प्रवर्त्यते ॥ ९१
देहेऽपि मूलाधारे तु समुदेति समीरणः ।
नासाभ्यामस्तमभ्येति प्राणतो द्विषड्ङ्गुले ॥ ९२
अहोरात्रमिनेन्दुभ्यामूर्ध्वाधोवृत्तिरिष्यते ।
वामदक्षिणनाड़ीभ्यां स्यादुदग्दक्षिणायनम् ॥ ९३
अत्रापि चेतनाधातोरागतिं बहुधा विदुः ।
रेतःशोणितजं प्राहुरेकेऽन्ये मातुराहृतात् ॥ ९४
आहाराद्रसजं प्राहुः केचित् कर्मफलं विदुः ।
केचिदस्य परं धाम्नो व्याप्तिमेव प्रचक्षते ॥ ९५
कश्चित् कर्मप्रकारज्ञः पितुर्देहात्मना सकृत् ।
सम्बध्य मथ[द]नोद्रेकविलीनाच्छुक्रधातुतः ॥ ९६
तत्परं धाम सौजस्कं संक्रान्तं मारुतेन तु ।
ब्रूते रक्तव्यतिक्रान्ताद्दीपाद्दीपान्तरं यथा ॥ ९७

वायुव्याप्तिफलमाह—येनेति ॥ ९१ ॥

ज्ञानयोगक्रियानिष्ठानां हिताय देहे अहोरात्रादिक्रममाह—देहेऽपीति । अपिशब्दोऽस्तुरुदयसमुच्चयार्थो बाह्योदयसमुच्चयार्थो वा । इनरूपेणोर्ध्वप्राणवृत्ति-रहः । इन्दुरूपेणेतरत् ॥ ९२ ॥ ९३ ॥

सचेतनं मलमिति उक्तम् । तत्कथं चेतनप्रवेश इति । तत्र मतभेदं दर्शयति—अत्रापीति । चेतनाधातुश्चिदेकरसः पुरुषः । अपिशब्देन विरोधार्थेन पक्षाणामनुपपत्तिः दर्शिता । नहि चिदेकरसस्य पुरुषस्य एवंविधाः प्रवेशा उपपद्यन्त इत्यर्थः । रेतःशोणितजमिति । पञ्चाधिकरणानां पक्षः । मातुराहृतात् आहाराद्यो रसः पाकजः तद्द्वारेण गर्भशरीरं विशतीति वार्षगणाः । कर्मफलमिति अपत्यार्थिनां यथोक्ताहारविहारश्रद्धाद्यतिशयात् गर्भं प्रविशतीत्यापस्त्या[त्रेया]दयः । परं धाम्नो व्याप्तिमिति विन्ध्यवासिपक्षः । सर्वगस्येन्द्रियाभिव्यक्तिनिमित्तं परिच्छेद इत्यर्थः । दीपात् दीपान्तरमिति पतञ्जलिधन्वन्तर्यादिपक्षः ।

तत्परं धाम तस्य पितुरात्मा कश्चिदेवं ब्रूत इत्युत्तरत्रान्वयः । रक्तव्यति-क्रान्तादिति स्त्र्यात्मनोऽपि संक्रान्तिः दर्शिता ॥ ९४ ॥ ९५ ॥ ९६ ॥ ९७ ॥

कश्चित्तु भौतिकव्याप्ते जन्मकाले वपुष्यथ ।
कुतश्चिदेत्य जीवात्मा निष्पन्न इति शंसति ॥ ९८

बहुना किं परं पुंसः सान्निध्यात्प्रविजृम्भिता ।
प्रकृतिर्गुणभिन्ना सा त्रिदोषात्मा महीयसी ॥ ९९

पञ्चभूतमयी सप्तधातुभिन्ना च भौतिकैः ।
पञ्चभिश्च गुणैर्युक्ता पञ्चेन्द्रियविचारिणी ॥ १००

पञ्चेन्द्रियार्थगा भूयः पञ्चबुद्धिप्रभाविनी ।
पञ्चकर्मेन्द्रियगता पञ्चत्वादाप्रवर्त्तते ॥ १०१

परेण धाम्ना समनुप्रबद्धा
मनस्तदा सा तु महाप्रभावा ।
यदा तु सङ्कल्पविकल्पकृत्या
यदा पुनर्निश्चिनुते तदा सा ॥ १०२

स्याद्बुद्धिसंज्ञा च यदा प्रवेत्ति
ज्ञातारमात्मानमहङ्कृतिः स्यात् ।
तदा यदा सा त्वभिलीयतेऽन्त-
श्चित्तञ्च निर्धारितमर्थमेषा ॥ १०३

भौतिकव्याप्त इति बार्हस्पत्यः पक्षः । कुतश्चिदित्यनिमित्तमेवेत्यर्थः ॥ ९८ ॥

स्वसिद्धान्तमाह—बहुनेति । सान्निध्यं नाम चैतन्याभासोदयः । तेन प्रकृतिः प्रकर्षेण विविधजृम्भणप्रकारमाह—गुणभिन्नेति । गुणसाम्यावस्थातोऽपि विषमदशां प्राप्ता इत्यादिना उक्तसंक्षेपः क्रियते । सैव महीयसी महत्त्वं प्राप्ता शरीरावस्थायां वातादिरूपदोषरूपेण वर्तत इत्याह—त्रिदोषेति ।

महत्त्वमेव दर्शयति—पञ्चभूतमयीति । श्रोत्रादिपञ्चेन्द्रियरूपेण विचारिणी । पञ्चकर्मेन्द्रियार्थरूपेण गच्छतीति तथोक्ता । श्रोत्रादिजन्य पञ्चबुद्धिरूपेण प्रभवति इति तथोक्ता । पञ्चकर्मेन्द्रियरूपेण गच्छति इति तथोक्ता । आ पञ्चत्वादा-मोक्षत्वादित्यर्थः ॥ ९९ ॥ १०० ॥ १०१ ॥

सैवान्तःकरणरूपेत्याह—परेणेति । साक्षितया कारणतयाऽन्तर्यामितया च सम्बन्धः । समनुप्रोपसर्गाणामर्थः । महाप्रभावेति परिणामसामर्थ्यमुक्तम् । अह-मेव ज्ञातेत्यविवेकतया ज्ञातुः स्वात्मत्वमात्रवेदनमहङ्कारः । चित्तः साक्षिणीत्यर्थः ।

यदा स्वयं व्यञ्जयितुं यतेत
महीयसौ सा करणैः क्रमेण ।
तदा तु बिन्दुस्फुटनोद्भवस्य
रवस्य सम्यक् प्रविजृम्भितं स्यात् ॥ १०४

इति श्रीप्रपञ्चसारे प्रथमः पटलः ।

एवं प्रकृतेः शरीरान्तं परिणामकदम्बं संग्रहेणाऽभिधाय शरीरे पूर्वोक्तस्य शब्द-ब्रह्मणो वैखरीरूपेणाऽभिव्यक्तिमपि संक्षेपेणाह—निर्धारितमर्थमित्यादिना । करणैः प्रयत्नविशेषैरितरैश्च । क्रमेणेति । पश्यन्त्यादिक्रमेणेत्यर्थः । प्रविजृम्भणं वैखरीपर्यन्तः स्थूलभावः ॥ १०२ ॥ १०३ ॥ १०४ ॥

इति श्रीपद्मपादाचार्यकृते प्रपञ्चसारविवरणे
प्रथमः पटलः ।

द्वितीयः पटलः ।

अथ व्यवस्थिते त्वेवं मासात् पक्षाद्दिनादपि ।
मुहूर्त्तान्नाडिकायाश्च क्षणादपि च वर्धते ॥ १
जन्तुः षड़ङ्गी पूर्वं स्याच्छिरः पादौ करावपि ।
अन्तराधि[दि]श्चेति पुनः षड़ङ्गेषु प्रवर्तते ॥ २
अक्षिनासास्यकर्णभ्रूकपोलचिबुकादिकम् ।
प्रकोष्ठकूर्परांसाद्यं कट्यूरुप्रपदादिकम् ॥ ३
उरःकुक्षिस्तनाद्यञ्च ततः सर्वाङ्गवान् विभुः ।
कालेन जन्तुर्भवति दोषास्त्वनुगुणा यदि ॥ ४
प्रसूतिसमये सोऽथ जननीं क्लेशयन् मुहुः ।
संवृतास्यसुषुम्नाख्योऽवाङ्मुखोऽनिलचोदितः ॥ ५
तस्या ग्रहण्यां शकृति मग्नवक्त्राक्षिनासिकः ।
पुरा कृतानां पापानामयुतं संस्मरन् मुहुः ॥ ६
तस्याः कायाग्निना दग्धः क्लेदैः क्लिन्नाङ्गबन्धनः ।
पू[प्र]त्युद्गारपरीतश्च तत्पायुद्वारगोचरः ॥ ७
तदा प्रक्षुभितैः स्वीयवायुभिर्दशधा गतैः ।
सम्पिण्डितशरीरस्तु मोक्षमेव किलेच्छति ॥ ८

उक्तमपि गर्भवासं सविशेषं विस्तरेण वैराग्यार्थं प्रपञ्चयितुं द्वितीयपटलारम्भः ।
अथेति—एवं चैतन्यप्रवेशे व्यवस्थिते गर्भो वर्धत इत्यर्थः ॥ १ ॥
षड़ङ्गान्याह—शिर इति । विभुः वपुश्चलनादौ समर्थः ।
क्लेदो गर्भजलम् । किलेति । परोक्षत्वात् इदानीं तदनुगुणप्रवृत्तिदर्शनाच्चोक्तम् ।
॥ २॥३॥४॥५॥६॥७॥८ ॥

प्राणाद्या वायवस्तस्मिन् पूर्वमेव कृतास्पदाः ।
परस्परमपानश्च प्राणश्च प्रतिबध्यते ॥ ९

प्रयात्यूर्ध्वं यदा प्राणस्तदाऽपानो नयत्यधः ।
यदा समानः कायाग्निं संधुक्षयति पाचितुम् ॥ १०

तदा तत्पक्वभुक्तान्तु रसमादाय धावति ।
व्यानो जन्तोस्तु तं देहमापादतलमस्तकम् ॥ ११

उदानः प्राणसहगो निमेषोन्मेषकारकः ।
उद्गारकारको नाग उन्मीलयति कूर्मकः ॥ १२

क्षुत्कृत् कृकरको देवदत्तो जृम्भणकर्मकृत् ।
धनञ्जयाख्यो देहेऽस्मिन् कुर्याद्बहुविधान् रवान् ॥ १३

स च लौकिकवायुत्वान्मृतञ्च न विमुञ्चति ।
इत्यमी मारुताः प्रोक्ता दश देहाधिगामिनः ॥ १४

वह्नयश्च दशाऽन्ये स्युस्तेषां सप्त तु धातुगाः ।
त्रयस्त्रिदोषगाः प्रोक्ताः स्वेदक्लेदान्त्रगाश्च ते ॥ १५

त्वगसृङ्मांसमेदोऽस्थिमज्जाशुक्राणि धातवः ।
ते दूष्याः कफपित्तेन दोषास्तत्प्रेरको मरुत् ॥ १६

समवायी स विश्वात्मा विश्वगो विश्वकर्मकृत् ।
स दोषो वा स दूष्यो वा क्रियातः संप्रधार्यते ॥ १७

स्वोयवायुप्रक्षोभं दर्शयति—परस्परमिति ॥ ९॥१०॥११॥१२॥१३॥१४ ॥

भ्राजक रञ्जक क्लेदक स्नेहक धारक बन्धक द्रावका धातुगा वह्नयः । व्यापक-पाचक श्लेष्मका वातादिदोषगाः । पित्त श्लेष्म वात विकार विशेषाः स्वेदादयः । ॥ १५ ॥ १६ ॥

मरुतो दोषदूष्यसंयोजनस्वभावत्वे कथमदुष्टं जीवनमिति । तत्राह—समवायीति । समं वयत इति समवायी । तत्र हेतुर्विश्वात्मेति । तत्र हेतुद्वयं विश्वग इत्यादि । वायोः समवयनस्वभावत्वे कथं रोगाद्युद्भव इति । विषम-वयनादित्याह—स दोष इति । तत् कथं ज्ञातं शक्यत इति । कार्यत इत्याह—क्रियात इति ॥ १७ ॥

बुभुक्षा च पिपासा च शोकमोहौ जरामृती ।
षडूर्मयः प्राणबुद्धिदेहधर्मेषु संस्थिताः ॥ १८
मज्जास्थिस्नायवः शुक्राद्रक्तात्त्वङ्मांसशोणितम् ।
इति षाट्कौशिकं नाम देहे भवति देहिनाम् ॥ १९
रसादितः क्रमात् पाकः शुक्रान्तेषु तु धातुषु ।
शुक्रपाकात् स्वयं भिद्येदोजो नामाऽष्टमी दशा ॥ २०
क्षेत्रज्ञस्य तदोजस्तु केवलाश्रयमिष्यते ।
यथा स्नेहः प्रदीपस्य यथाऽभ्रमशनित्विषः ॥ २१
बहुच्छिद्रेण कुम्भेन संवृतस्य हविर्भुजः ।
यथा तेजः प्रसरति समीपालोकशक्तिमत् ॥ २२
तथा देहावृतस्यापि क्षेत्रज्ञस्य महात्विषः ।
इन्द्रियैः सम्प्रवर्त्तन्ते स्वं स्वमर्थग्रहं प्रति ॥ २३
नभः श्रोत्रेऽनिलस्त्वर्मण्यग्निश्चक्षुष्यथोदकम् ।
जिह्वायामवनिर्घ्राण इत्यमर्थप्रवर्त्तनम् ॥ २४
यदा पित्तं मरुन्नुन्नम् विलीनं प्रविलापयेत् ।
धातूंस्तदा क्रमाद्रक्तं लसीकां द्रावयेत् क्षणात् ॥ २५
द्रुता सा तु लसीकाख्या रोमकूपैः प्रवर्त्तते ।
बहिः सर्वत्र कणशस्तदा स्वेदः प्रतीयते ॥ २६
यदा कफो मरुत्पित्तनुन्नो लीनः प्रवर्त्तते ।
ऊर्ध्वं द्रुतो द्रुतं बाष्पं प्रसेकञ्च प्रवर्त्तयेत् ॥ २७

वायुप्रसङ्गेन प्राणादिधर्मानाह—बुभुक्षेति । धर्मेषु धर्मत्वेनेत्यर्थः ॥ १८ ॥

ऊर्मिप्रसङ्गेन कोशानाह—मज्जेति ॥ १९ ॥

धातुगत्वेन उक्तानाम् अग्नीनां प्रयोजनमाह—रसादित इति । स्वयमिति प्रधानमित्यर्थः । प्राधान्यमाह—क्षेत्रज्ञस्येति ॥ २० ॥ २१ ॥ २२ ॥ २३ ॥

इन्द्रियाणाम् अर्थविशेषनियमहेतुमाह—नभ इति । इत्थमिति । एतत्सम्बन्धानुसारेणेत्यर्थः ॥ २४ ॥

कार्यतः सम्प्रधार्यत इत्युक्तम् । तदाह—यदेति । विलीनं द्रवीभावं प्राप्तं धातून् प्रविलापयेत् व्यापयेत् । लसीकां रक्तत्वचोरन्तरालस्थाम् । प्रसेकं लालाम् ।

कफात्मिकास्तु विकृतीः कर्णशष्कुलिपूर्वकान् ।
गण्डमालादिकान् वापि कुर्याज्जन्तोस्तु कर्मजान् ॥ २८
ग्रहणी नाम सा प्राची प्रसृताञ्जलिसन्निभा ।
अधस्तस्याः प्रधानाग्निः स समानेन नुद्यते ॥ २९
तस्याऽधस्तात्त्रिकोणाभं ज्योतिराधारमुत्तमम् ।
विद्यते स्थानमेतद्धि मूलाधारं विदुर्बुधाः ॥ ३०
अथाहृतं षड्रसं वाऽप्याहारं कण्ठमार्गगम् ।
श्लेष्मणाऽनुगतं तस्य प्रभावान्मधुरीभवेत् ॥ ३१
तत्र स्वाद्वम्ललवण तिक्तोषण कषायकाः ।
षड्रसाः कथिता भूतविकृत्या द्रव्यमाश्रिताः ॥ ३२
तथैवामाशयगतं पश्चात्पित्ताशयं व्रजेत् ।
तदा तस्याऽनुगमनात् कटुकत्वं प्रपद्यते ॥ ३३
तत्राल्लान्तरसंश्लिष्टं पच्यते पित्तवारिणा ।
पच्यमानाद्रसं भिन्नं वायू रक्तादिकं नयेत् ॥ ३४
तत्र किट्टमसृग्भिन्नं ग्रहण्यां चिनुतेऽनिलः ।
तच्चीयमानं विस्राम ग्रहणीं पूरयेन्मुहुः ॥ ३५
सा तया शकृता पूर्णा वलिता प्रतिमुञ्चति ।
पुरीषं पायुमार्गेण तत्पाकिऽच्छाम्भसस्ततः ॥ ३६
अङ्गस्वेदवदभ्यन्तर्व्याप्तैः सूक्ष्मैः शिरामुखैः ।
वस्तिमापूरयेद्वायुः पूर्णां मुञ्चति धारया ॥ ३७

॥ २५॥२६॥२७॥२८ ॥

तस्यां ग्रहण्यां शकृतीत्युक्तम् । का सेति । तत्राह—ग्रहणीति । प्रधानाग्निः जाठराग्निः ।

तत्कारणमाह—तस्याऽधस्तादिति ॥ २९ ॥ ३० ॥

दोषत्रयं क्रमेण युक्त्या साधयति—अथाहृतमिति । अत्राधिक्ये माधुर्यं वाय्वाधिक्ये अम्लः भूवाय्वाधिक्ये लवणः । वाय्वग्न्याधिक्ये तिक्तः । अग्न्याधिक्ये उष्णः । वायुखाधिक्ये कषायः । 'क्ष्माम्भोऽग्नि क्ष्माम्बुतेजः खवाय्वग्न्यनिलगोऽनिलैः' इत्युक्तक्रमेण वा रसनिष्पत्तिः ॥ ३१॥३२॥३३॥३४॥३५॥३६॥३७॥३८॥३९ ॥

मूत्राशया धनुर्वक्रो वस्तिरित्यभिधीयते ।
मूत्रमित्याहुरुदकं वस्तेर्मेहननिर्गतम् ॥ ३८

अपथ्यभाजामनयोर्मार्गयोर्दोषदुष्टयोः ।
प्रमेहमूत्रकृच्छ्रादिर्ग्रहण्यादेश्च सम्भवः ॥ ३९

इत्थम्भूतः स जन्तुस्तु जरायुच्छन्नगात्रवान् ।
अपत्यवर्त्म संगम्य सज्यते वायुना मुहुः ॥ ४०

अथ पापकृतां शरीरभाजामुदरान्निष्क्रमितुं महान् प्रयासः ।
नलिनोद्भव हे विचित्रवृत्ता नितरां कर्मगतिस्तु मानुषाणाम् ॥ ४१

जायतेऽधिकसंविग्नो जृम्भतेऽङ्गैः प्रकम्पितैः ।
जर्त्योल्वणं निःश्वसिति भीत्या च परिरोदिति ॥ ४२

मूलाधारात् प्रथममुदितो यस्तु भावः पराख्यः
पश्चात् पश्यन्त्यथ हृदयगो बुद्धियुङ्मध्यमाख्यः ।
वक्त्रे वैखर्यथ रुरुदिषोरस्य जन्तोः सुषुम्ना-
बद्धस्तस्माद्भवति पवनप्रेरितो वर्णसङ्घः ॥ ४३

ऽर्तिः ज्वरः ॥ ४०॥४१॥४२ ॥

यदर्थो महान् प्रयासः तद्दर्शयति—मूलाधारादिति । मूलं जगन्मूलभूता परिणामिनी मायाशक्तिः । तस्या आधारभूतश्चिदात्मा मूलाधारः । सर्वगस्यापि तस्याऽभिव्यक्तिस्थानत्वात् गुदमेढमध्योऽपि मूलाधारः । तस्मात् प्रथममुदितः चैतन्याभासः भावश्च यः जगद्भावयतीति मायाशक्तिर्भावः स पराख्यः । चैतन्याभासविशिष्टतया प्रकाशिका माया निष्पन्दा परा वागित्यर्थः । सस्पन्दावस्थाः पश्यन्त्याद्याः । तत्र सामान्यस्पन्दप्रकाशरूपिणीं नादतत्त्वात्मिकाम् अध्यात्ममूलाधारादिनाभ्यन्तम् अभिव्यज्यमानां पश्यन्तीमाह—पश्चात् पश्यन्तीति । सामान्यज्ञानात्मकत्वात् पश्यन्ती सा । अथ बाह्यान्तःकरणाद्यात्मिकां हिरण्यगर्भरूपिणीं बिन्दुतत्त्वमयीं नाभ्यादिहृदयान्ताभिव्यक्तिस्थानां विशेषस्पन्दसङ्कल्पादिसतत्त्वात् मध्यमां वाचमाह —अथ हृदयग इति । मध्ये सा बुद्धिर्यस्याः सा मध्यमा । भाव एव विशेष्यः । अथ विराड्रूपिणीं बीजात्मिकां हृदयादास्यान्तम् अभिव्यज्यमानां शब्दसामान्यात्मिकां वैखरीमाह वक्त्र इति । विशेषेण खरत्वाद्वैखरी ।

सामान्यशब्दात् विशेषशब्दनिष्पत्तिमाह—तस्मादिति । तस्मात् वैखर्यात्मकात्

स्रोतोमार्गस्याऽविभक्तत्वहेतोस्तत्राऽर्णानां जायते न प्रकाशः ।
तावत् यावत् कण्ठमूर्धादिभेदो वर्णव्यक्तिः स्थानसंस्था यतोऽतः ॥ ४४

ज्ञाताऽस्मीति यदा भावो मनोऽहङ्कारबुद्धिमान् ।
जातश्चित्पूर्वको जन्तोः स भावः क्रमवर्धितः ॥ ४५

बध्नाति मातापित्रोस्तु ततो बन्धुषु च क्रमात् ।
स पीत्वा बहुशः स्तन्यं मातरं स्तन्यदायिनीम् ॥ ४६

इच्छन् रोदिति तां वीक्ष्य तत्र स्यादितरेतरम् ।
बन्धस्तदाऽधिकर्त्तारमतिस्निग्धमनन्यगम् ॥ ४७

पितरं वीक्ष्य तत्रापि तथा भ्रातरमेव च ।
पितृव्यमातुलादींश्च समुद्वीक्ष्य प्रमोदते ॥ ४८

एवं संबद्धसंसारबान्धवो विस्मरिष्यति ।
पूर्वकर्म च गर्भस्थमुद्भूतिक्लेशमेव च ॥ ४९

अथ स्वमुत्तारयितुमाह्वयेज्जननीं मुहुः ।
अवैशद्यान्मुखस्रोतोमार्गस्याऽविशदाक्षरम् ॥ ५०

भावादित्यर्थः । पवनशब्देन प्रेरकवर्गः सर्वोऽप्युक्तः ।

अथवा सूक्ष्मा परा पश्यन्ती मध्यमा वैखरीति पञ्चपदीं वाचमाश्रित्याह—मूलाधारादिति । सप्तपद्यपि वागनेनैव सूचिता । शून्य संवित् सूक्ष्मादीनि सप्तपदानि । तत्राऽनुत्पन्ना निष्पन्दा शून्या । वागुत्पित्सुः संवित् । उत्पत्त्यवस्था सूक्ष्मा । मूलाधारात् प्रथममुदिता परेति विभागः ॥ ४३ ॥

जातेन शिशुना रोदनव्याजेन एवं किमप्युच्यते चेत् कथं वर्णानभिव्यक्तिरिति तत्राह—स्रोत इति । अक्षराभिव्यक्तिस्थानस्येत्यर्थः ॥ ४४ ॥

गर्भे विवेकवतोऽप्यस्य मायाप्रभाववशात् अविवेकपूर्वकं संसारक्रममाह—ज्ञातास्मीति यदाऽस्य भावो भवति तदाऽहङ्कारादौ आत्मबुद्धिः दृढतरा जातेत्यर्थः । अहंभावबद्धस्य ममभावप्रकारमाह—चित्पूर्वक इत्यादिना । चिच्छब्देन उक्ता मनआदयः कथ्यन्ते । अहङ्कारपूर्वको भाव इत्यर्थः ।

पितरं वीक्ष्य तत्रापि ममत्वबन्ध इत्यर्थः । मायाभावस्य विक्षेपशक्तिविलसितमभिधाय आच्छादनशक्तेरप्याह—एवमिति ॥ ४५ ॥ ४६ ॥ ४७ ॥ ४८ ॥ ४९ ॥

विविधं सरणं विसरणं विविधपद्मादिरूपेणाऽवस्थानमित्यर्थः । सुषुम्ना-

अप्यव्यक्तं प्रलपति यदा कुण्डलिनी तदा ।
मूलाधारे विसरति सुषुम्नावेष्टनी मुहुः ॥ ५१

त्रिचतुःपञ्चषट्सप्त चाऽष्टशो दशशोऽपि च ।
अथ द्वादशपञ्चाशद्भेदेन गुणयेत् क्रमात् ॥ ५२

यदा त्रिशोऽथ गुणयेत्तदा त्रिगुणिता विभुः ।
शक्तिः कामाग्निनादात्मा गूढमूर्त्तिः प्रतीयते ॥ ५३

तदा तां तारमित्याहुरोमात्मेति बहुश्रुताः ।
तामेव शक्तिं ब्रुवते हरेमात्मेति चापरे ॥ ५४

त्रिगुणा सा त्रिदोषा सा त्रिवर्णा सा त्रयी च सा ।
त्रिलोका सा त्रिमूर्त्तिः सा त्रिरेखा सा विशिष्यते ॥ ५५

एतेषां तारणात्तारः शक्तिस्तद्भृतिशक्तितः ।
यदा चतुर्धा गुणिता सूक्ष्मादिस्थानवाचिकी ॥ ५६

वाचिका जाग्रदादीनां करणानाञ्च सा तदा ।
सा यदा पञ्चगुणिता पञ्चपञ्चविभेदिनी ॥ ५७

वेष्टनीति । सुषुम्नायामात्मानं विविधपद्मादिरूपेण वेष्टयति गुणयति स्थापयतीत्यर्थः । ॥ ५० ॥ ५१ ॥

मुहुः वेष्टनमेव दर्शयति—त्रिचतुरिति ॥ ५२ ॥

एवमात्मानं गुणयन्ती कुण्डलिन्येव यन्त्र मन्त्र देवतादि सकलजगन्मयीत्याह—यदेत्यादिना । त्रिगुणिता त्रिगुणितयन्त्रस्वरूपिणीत्यर्थः । त्रिकोणसम्बन्धान् त्रिबीजात्मकान् मन्त्रानस्या विभूतित्वेन कथयति—शक्तिरिति । गूढमूर्तिः शक्तिस्तदा प्रतीयत इत्यन्वयः । गूढमूर्तिः गुप्तमूर्तिः । मूर्तिं विशिनष्टि—कामाग्निनादात्मेति । कामः कामराजबीजं मध्यमबीजानीत्यर्थः । अग्निर्वाग्भवः प्रथमबीजानीत्यर्थः । नादः नादप्रधानानि तृतीयबीजानीत्यर्थः । कामाग्नि-नादात्मेति मूर्तिमन्त्रोद्धारो वा दर्शितः । कामः ईकारः । अग्नी रेफः । नादो हकारः । आत्मा बिन्दुः । ह्रीं हरिहर इत्येवं तल्लिङ्गं भवति । ओमात्मेति । अकारोकारमकारात्मेत्यर्थः । हरेमात्मेति । हकाररेफेमात्मेत्यर्थः ॥ ५३॥५४ ॥

विभूत्यन्तराण्युक्तविद्यार्थरूपाण्याह—त्रिगुणा सेति । त्रिरेखास्त्रिकोणरेखाः । सूक्ष्मादीति । परादीत्यर्थः । पञ्चपञ्चेति पञ्चविंशतितत्त्वादिकम् उक्तम् ।

पञ्चानामक्षराणाञ्च वर्णानां मरुतां तथा ।
गुणिता सा यदा षोढ़ा कोशोर्मिरसभेदिनी ॥ ५८

तदा षड्गुणिताख्यस्य यन्त्रस्य च विभेदिनी ।
यदा सा सप्तगुणिता तारहृल्लेखयोस्तदा ॥ ५९

भेदैरहाद्यैः शान्तान्तैर्भिद्यते सप्तभिः पृथक् ।
अकारश्चाऽप्युकारश्च मकारो बिन्दुरेव च ॥ ६०

नादश्च शक्तिः शान्तश्च तारभेदाः समीरिताः ।
हकारो रेफमाये च बिन्दुनादौ तथैव च ॥ ६१

शक्तिशान्तौ च सम्प्रोक्ताः शक्तेर्भेदाश्च सप्तधा ।
अङ्गेभ्योऽस्याश्च सप्तभ्यः सप्तधा भिद्यते जगत् ॥ ६२

लोकाद्रिद्वीपपातालसिन्धुग्रहमुनिस्वरैः ।
धात्वादिभिस्तथाऽन्यैश्च सप्तसंख्याप्रभेदकैः ॥ ६३

यदाऽष्टधा सा गुणिता तदा प्रकृतिभेदिनी ।
अष्टाक्षरा हि वस्वाशामातृमूर्तिविभेदिनी ॥ ६४

दशधा गुणिता नाड़ीमर्माशादिविभेदिनी ।
द्वादशात्मिक्यपि यदा तदा राश्यर्कमूर्तियुक् ॥ ६५

वर्णानां पोतादिभूतवर्णानामित्यर्थः । मरुतां प्राणादीनाम् ॥ ५५॥५६॥५७॥५८ ॥

लोका भूम्यादयः । मेरु निषध हेमकूट हिमवन्नील श्वेत शृङ्गिणः पर्वताः । जम्बू प्लक्ष शाल्मली कुश क्रौञ्च शाक पुष्करा द्वीपाः । अतल वितल सुतल गभस्तिमन्महातल नितल पातालाः सप्त । क्षारेक्षु सुरा घृत दधि क्षीर शुद्धोदाः सिन्धवः । ग्रहाः सूर्यादयः । भरद्वाज काश्यप गौतमात्रि विश्वामित्र जमदग्नि वसिष्ठा मुनयः । षड्जर्षभ गान्धार धैवत मध्यम पञ्चम निषधाः स्वराः । धातवः त्वगादयः । आवहादिकमादिशब्दार्थः । अत्र सप्तात्मकात् तारादेः सप्तविधजगदुत्पत्तिकथनं सर्वत्र तत्तद्गुणितसंख्यात्मनः तत्तदात्मकजगदुत्पत्तेरुपलक्षणम् ॥५९॥६०॥ ६१॥६२॥६३॥

प्रकृतयोऽष्टप्रकृतयः । अनन्त वासुकि तक्षक कर्कोटक पद्म महापद्म शङ्खपाल गुलिका अहयः । धरध्रुवसोमापाग्निवायुप्रत्युषप्रभासा वसवः । मातरो ब्रह्माण्यादयः । शर्व भव रुद्रोग्र भीमेशान महादेव पशुपतयो मूर्तयः ॥ ६४ ॥

नाड्यः सुषुम्नाद्याः । हृद् गुह्य तालु वदनोदर नेत्र कण्ठभ्रूमध्य शङ्ख गुदा

मन्त्रश्च द्वादशार्णोऽह्वमभिधत्ते स्वरानपि ।
तत्संख्यश्च तथा यन्त्रं शक्तेस्तद्गुणितात्मकम् ।
पञ्चाशद्वा प्रगुणिता पञ्चाशद्वर्णभेदिनी ॥ ६६

पञ्चाशदंशगुणिताऽथ यदा भवेत् सा
देवी तदात्मविनिवेशितदिव्यभावा ।
सोषुम्नवर्त्मसुषिरोदरनादसङ्गात्
पञ्चाशदीरयति पंक्तिश एव वर्णान् ॥ ६७

इति श्रीप्रपञ्चसारे द्वितीयः पटलः ।

मर्माणि । आदिशब्देन वाय्वग्निदशकादिकं ग्राह्यम् ।

अर्का धात्वादयः । मूर्तयः केशवाद्याः । स्वरा अपिनपुंसकाः ॥ ६५॥६६ ॥

* त्रिगुणादिषु अयमाशयः— मूलाधार स्वाधिष्ठान मणिपुरकानाहत विशुद्धि-लम्बिकाज्ञा कला ब्रह्मरन्ध्रेषु त्रिचतुष्पञ्च षट्सप्ताष्ट दश द्वादश पञ्चाशद्दलानि पद्मानि सञ्चिन्त्य तेषु इ न्म ऐ ख भ झ य र ह्ल ल इत्यन्तान् सर्वांश्च वर्णान् स्मृत्वा कर्णिकासु अकारोकार मकार बिन्दु नाद शक्ति शान्त शान्त्यतीत निर्विकल्पान् इष्टदेवताकारान् स्मृत्वा । दलेषु तत्परिवारत्वेनोक्तां विभूतिं स्मृत्वा । अमृतमयैरुपहारैः संपूज्य संहृत्य अमृतमास्रावयेदिति ॥ * ॥

एवं शिष्यवाक्यगताक्षरानुसारेण कुण्डल्यवस्थानविशेषमभिधाय नित्यसिद्ध-मातृकाक्षररूपेणापि वदन् उपसंहरति—पञ्चाशदंशेति ।

कथं देवीत्वमिति तदाह—आत्मेति । प्राप्तचिदानन्दरूपपुरुषभावेत्यर्थः । नादसङ्गः पश्यन्ती मध्यमात्मभावः ॥ ६७ ॥

इति श्रीपद्मपादाचार्यकृते प्रपञ्चसारविवरणे
द्वितीयः पटलः ।

तृतीयः पटलः ।

अथोभयात्मका वर्णाः स्युरग्नीषोमभेदतः ।
त एव स्युस्त्रिधा भूयः सोमेनाग्निविभागतः ॥ १

स्वराख्याः षोडश प्रोक्ताः स्पर्शाख्याः पञ्चविंशतिः ।
व्यापकाश्च दशैते स्युः सोमेनाग्न्यात्मकाः क्रमात् ॥ २

एषु स्वरा ह्रस्वदीर्घभेदेन द्विविधा मताः ।
पूर्वौ ह्रस्वः परो दीर्घो बिन्दुसर्गान्तिकौ च तौ ॥ ३

एवं वर्णनिष्पत्तिप्रकारमभिधाय तद्विभूतिकथनाय तृतीयपटलारम्भः ।

अथेति । अथशब्दो हेत्वर्थः । यस्मात् प्राप्तचिदग्नीन्दुभावात् शक्त्यमृतदीधितेः जाता वर्णाः तस्मादित्यर्थः । सर्ववर्णेषु अकारांशोऽग्न्यात्मकः पुरुषांशः । इतरः प्रकृत्यात्मकः सोमांशः । प्रकाशप्रकाश्यांशाभ्यां वाऽग्नीषोमात्मकत्वं स्वरव्यञ्जनभेदेन वा समविभागतो वा । अनेन च प्रपञ्चयागादिषु अग्नीषोममन्त्रौ सूचितौ । सतारशक्त्यादिपूर्वकम् आदिठान्तमुक्त्वा सोममण्डलाय नमः स्वः स्वाहा इति वा सोममन्त्रः । इतरोऽवशिष्टः ।

पुनरप्यक्षराणां व्याप्त्यन्तरमाह त एवेति । मिश्रं रूपमिनात्मकमिति द्रष्टव्यम् । अग्नीषोमात्मकत्वं पूर्ववदेव स्वरस्पर्शव्यापकभेदेन वा सोमेनाग्न्यात्मकत्वम् । अनेन च प्रपञ्चयागादिषु मण्डलत्रयमन्त्राः सूचिताः ।

स्वरानुक्त्वा सोममण्डलाय नमः स्वाहेति वा सोममण्डलमन्त्रः । इतरत् द्वयमूह्यम् ॥ १ ॥

अष्टत्रिंशत्कलान्यासे तत्प्राणप्रतिष्ठामन्त्रांशप्रदर्शनार्थं तद्व्यापकमन्त्रांशोद्धारार्थं चाह—स्वराख्याः षोडशेति ।

अं सोममण्डलाय षोडशकामकलात्मने साममयमण्डलात्मने अन्तरात्मने परमात्मने नमः । उं सूर्यमण्डलाय द्वादशार्ककलात्मने यजुर्मयेत्यादि समानम् । मं वह्निमण्डलाय दशधर्मकलात्मने ऋङ्मयेत्यादि समानम् । इत्येते मण्डलमन्त्राः ।

असूचितमंशान्तरम् उत्तरत्र किञ्चित् सूचयिष्यति ॥ २ ॥

स्वराणामेव पृथग्व्याप्तिं दर्शयन् तेषाम् अष्टमूर्तितच्छक्त्यादिवाचकत्वाय द्विप्रकारत्वमाह—एष्विति ॥ ३ ॥

आद्यन्तस्वरषट्कस्य मध्यमं यच्चतुष्टयम् ।
वर्णानामागमधनैस्तन्नपुंसकमीरितम् ॥ ४

तच्चतुष्कं सुषुम्नास्थे कुर्यात् प्राणेऽयनस्थितिम् ।
दक्षोत्तरस्थे प्राणाख्ये स्यातां दक्षोत्तरायणे ॥ ५

दक्षसव्यस्थिते ह्रस्वदीर्घाः पञ्चोदयन्ति च ।
भूतभूतकलाभिस्तदुदयः प्रागुदीरितः ॥ ६

स्वराणां स्त्रीपुंनपुंसकात्मकत्वमाह—आद्यन्तेति। अवशिष्टह्रस्वपञ्चकस्य पुरुषत्वं दीर्घपञ्चकस्य स्त्रीत्वं चाऽवगन्तव्यम्। बिन्दुविसर्गौ च स्त्रीपुरुषाद्यनुगतौ।

आगमधनैरित्ययमर्थः—अनुत्तराकार पुरुषस्य आनन्दाकारशक्तीच्छेकारेशने-कारोन्मेषोकारानन्तरमूनतोकारावस्थायां पृथिव्यादिविलयादवशिष्टानि तत्त्वा-वस्थारूपाणि अक्षराण्यकिञ्चित्कराणीति नपुंसकशब्देनागमेषु उच्यन्त इति ॥ ४ ॥

स्त्रीपुरुषभागयोर्मध्यस्थत्वं नपुंसकत्वे हेत्वन्तरत्वं वदन् तेषां विनियोगमाह—तच्चतुष्कमिति। सुषुम्नास्थे सति प्राणे अयनसंक्रान्तिरूपां स्थितिं कुर्यादित्यर्थः। तदानीं तेषामुदयस्तत्प्रधानानां च मन्त्राणां तत्रापि ह्रस्वद्वयस्य दक्षिणसंक्रमणे। दीर्घयोरितरसंक्रमण इत्यवगन्तव्यम्।

अनयनेऽपि अयनकार्यसिद्ध्यर्थम् आध्यात्मिकमयनमाह—दक्षोत्तरस्थ इति। बाह्यघटिकापञ्चकेन आध्यात्मिकमयनम् उक्तविधविलम्बस्यापि अनुपपत्तौ श्वासोच्छ्वासयोरेव कालावयवसम्पादनं द्रष्टव्यम्। तत्र श्वासोच्छ्वासात्मकानि अहोरात्रपक्षमासायनानि द्रष्टव्यानि। अहोरात्रात्मकौ वा श्वासोच्छ्वासौ। पक्षात्मकौ वा अयनात्मकौ वा इच्छावशेन ज्ञातव्यौ ॥ ५ ॥

ह्रस्वदीर्घाणां तत्प्रधानानाम् अग्नीषोमस्त्रीपुरुषाद्यात्मकानां च मन्त्राणाम् अयनयोरुदयं वदन् तेषां वीर्योद्भवकालं सूचयति—दक्षसव्यस्थित इति। चशब्दः तत्प्रधान मन्त्रग्रहनक्षत्राद्युदयसमुच्चयार्थः। तत्र हुहरादिप्रधाना आग्नेयमन्त्राः। वौषडादिप्रधानाः सौम्याः। हुंफडन्ताः पुरुषाः। स्वाहान्ताः स्त्रियः। नमोऽन्ता नपुंसकाः। ते च वश्य शान्ति क्रूरकर्मसु प्रायेण प्रशस्ताः। भूतभूत-कलाभिः सहोदयन्तीति सम्बन्धः। भूतकला निवृत्त्याद्याः। तत्र राशिषु एकैकघटिकायां वाय्वग्निभूजलाकाशभूतानामुदयः।

केन प्रकारेणोदय इति पुटयोरुभयोरित्यादिनोक्तः। स इत्याह—तदुदय इति ॥ ६ ॥

बिन्दुसर्गौ च यौ प्रोक्तौ तौ सूर्यशशिनौ क्रमात् ।
तयोर्विकारविस्तारः पुरस्तात् संप्रवक्ष्यते ॥ ७
स्पर्शाख्या अपि ये वर्णाः पञ्चपञ्चविभेदतः ।
भवन्ति पञ्चवर्गास्तदन्त्यश्चात्मा रविः स्मृतः ॥ ८
चतुर्विंशतितत्त्वाख्यास्तस्माद्वर्णाः परे क्रमात् ।
तेन स्पर्शाक्षराः सौराः प्राणाग्नीलाम्बुखात्मकाः ॥ ९
व्यापकाश्च द्विवर्गाः स्युस्तथा पञ्चविभेदतः ।
शशीनाग्न्युत्थिता यस्मात् स्वरस्पृग्व्यापकाक्षराः ॥ १०
तत्त्रिभेदसमुद्भूता अष्टात्रिंशत्कला मताः ।
स्वरैः सौम्याः स्पर्शयुग्मैः सौरा याद्याश्च वह्निजाः ॥ ११

स्वराणां सौम्यत्वे हेतुं वदन् बिन्दुसर्गयोस्तत्त्वं कालनिवर्तकत्वेन इतरस्वरवत् कालसम्बन्धं चाह—बिन्दुसर्गाविति । अनेन इतरस्वराणां कालरूपतिथ्यात्मकत्वं कार्यानुसारेण विसर्गादियोगश्च सूचितः ।

पुरस्तादिति । सः सर्गश्लेषित इत्यादिनेत्यर्थः । अथवाऽजपापटलेऽन्येषु वा बिन्दुविसर्गान्वितेषु मन्त्रेष्वित्यर्थः ॥ ७ ॥

एवं स्वराणां व्याप्तिं सौम्यत्वं चाभिधाय स्पर्शानां सौरत्वं व्याप्तिं च वदंस्तेषां भूतेन्द्रियमात्रादिसम्बन्धयोग्यत्वाय पाञ्चविध्यमप्याह—स्पर्शाख्या इति । अन्त्यो मकारः पुरुषः । सूर्यः जीवः । भादयः प्रकृतिबुद्ध्यहंकारमनांसि । तन्मात्र-श्रोत्रवागाकाशादय इतरा वर्णा इति क्रमेण चतुर्विंशतितत्त्वयोगः । स्पर्शानामन्त्य आत्मा रविः स्वावयवेषु अनुगतो यस्मात् तेन स्पर्शाक्षराः सौरा इत्यर्थः । प्राणाग्नी-लाम्बुखात्मका इति न चतुर्विंशतितत्त्वसम्बन्धक्रमः । किन्तु स्पर्शानामाध्यात्मं स्वरवत् भूतैः सह उदयक्रम उक्त इत्यवगन्तव्यम् ॥ ८ ॥ ९ ॥

व्यापकानामप्युदयक्रमं वदन् पञ्चशो वर्गद्वयत्वमाह—व्यापका इति । तथेति प्राणाम्ब्वादिक्रमः सूचितः । आग्नेयत्वं तु व्यापकानां नृसिंहाख्यकालाग्निरूप-क्षकारान्तत्वेन वक्ष्यति भुवनं कषत इति । अत्र पञ्चाशद्वर्णेभ्यः कथमष्टत्रिंशत्कलो-त्पत्तिरित्याशङ्क्य शश्यादिकलारूपतिथिमासभ्राजकादिसंबन्धेन वर्णानामष्ट-त्रिंशत्संख्यत्वादिति वदन् न्यासे मण्डलमन्त्रैः व्यापकं कलानां वर्णयोगं च सूचयति—शशीति ॥ १० ॥

सम्बन्धविशेषमाह—स्वरैरित्यादिना ॥ ११ ॥

षोड़श द्वादश दश संख्याः स्युः क्रमशः कलाः ।
वर्णेभ्य एव तारस्य पञ्चभेदैस्तु भूतगैः ॥ १२

सर्वगाश्च समुत्पन्नाः पञ्चाशत्संख्यकाः कलाः ।
तेभ्य एव तु तावत्यः शक्तिभिर्विष्णुमूर्तयः ॥ १३

तावत्यो मातृभिः सार्द्धं तेभ्यः स्यू रुद्रमूर्तयः ।
तेभ्य एव तु पञ्चाशत् स्युरोषधय ईरिताः ॥ १४

याभिस्तु मन्त्रिणः सिद्धिं प्राप्नुयुर्वाञ्छितार्थदाम् ।
अमृता मानदा पूषा तुष्टिः पुष्टी रतिर्धृतिः ॥ १५

शशिनी चन्द्रिका कान्तिर्ज्योत्स्ना श्रीः प्रीतिरङ्गदा ।
पूर्णा पूर्णामृता कामदायिन्यः स्वरजाः कलाः ॥ १६

तप[पि]नी ताप[पि]नी धूम्रा मरीचिर्ज्वालिनी रुचिः ।
सुषुम्ना भोगदा विश्वा बोध[धि]नी धार[रि]णी क्षमा ॥ १७

कभाद्या वसुदाः सौराष्ठडान्ता द्वादशेरिताः ।
धूम्रार्चिरुष्मा ज्वलिनी ज्वालिनी विस्फुलिङ्गिनी ॥ १८

सुश्रीः सुरूपा कपिला हव्यकव्यवहे अपि ।
याद्यार्णयुक्ता वह्न्युत्था दश धर्मप्रदाः कलाः ॥ १९

सृष्टिर्ऋद्धिः स्मृतिर्मेधा कान्तिर्लक्ष्मीर्धृतिः स्थिरा ।
स्थितिः सिद्धिरकारोत्थाः कला दश समीरिताः ॥ २०

अकारप्रभवा ब्रह्मजाताः स्युः सृष्टये कलाः ।
जरा च पालिनी शान्तिरैश्वरी रतिकामिके ॥ २१

वरदा ह्लादिनी प्रीतिर्दीर्घाश्चोकारजाः कलाः ।
उकारप्रभवा विष्णुजाताः स्युः स्थितये कलाः ॥ २२

पञ्चाशत्कलान्यासे वर्णप्रणवांशभूततत्त्वव्यष्टिसर्वयोगं च सूचयति—वर्णेभ्य इति। कामदायिन्य इति मण्डलमन्त्रांशः सूचितः। उत्तरयोः वसुदा धर्मदा इति पदाभ्यासः सूचितः ॥ १२ ॥ १३ ॥ १४ ॥ १५ ॥ १६ ॥ १७ ॥ १८ ॥ १९ ॥

अकारोत्था इत्यकारयोगः तत्कलान्यासे। ब्रह्मजाता इत्यादिनापि तत्तद्योगः।

तीक्ष्णा रौद्री भया निद्रा तन्द्रा क्षुत् क्रोधिनी क्रिया ।
उत्कारी चैव मृत्युश्च मकाराक्षरजाः कलाः ॥ २३

मकारप्रभवा रुद्रजाताः संहृतये कलाः ।
बिन्दोरपि चतस्रः स्युः पीता श्वेताऽरुणाऽसिता ॥ २४

निवृत्तिश्च प्रतिष्ठा च विद्या शान्तिस्तथैव च ।
इन्धिका दीपिका चैव रेचिका मोचिका परा ॥ २५

सूक्ष्मा सूक्ष्मामृता ज्ञानामृता चाप्यायिनी तथा ।
व्यापिनी व्योमरूपा स्यात् अनन्ता नादसम्भवा ॥ २६

नादजाः षोडश प्रोक्ता भुक्तिमुक्तिप्रदायिकाः ।
केशव नारायण माधव गोविन्द विष्णवः ॥ २७

मधुसूदनसंज्ञश्च सप्तमः स्यात्त्रिविक्रमः ।
वामनः श्रीधराख्यश्च हृषीकेशस्त्वनन्तरः ॥ २८

पद्मनाभस्तथा दामोदराह्वो वासुदेवयुक् ।
सङ्कर्षणश्च प्रद्युम्नः सानिरुद्धः स्वरोद्भवाः ॥ २९

ततश्चक्री गदी शार्ङ्गी खड्गी शङ्खी हली तथा ।
मुषली शूलिसंज्ञश्च भूयः पाशी तथाऽङ्कुशी ॥ ३०

मुकुन्दो नन्दजो नन्दी नरो नरकजिद्धरिः ।
कृष्णः सत्यः सात्वतश्च शौरिः शूरो जनार्दनः ॥ ३१

भूधरो विश्वमूर्तिश्च वैकुण्ठः पुरुषोत्तमः ।
बली बलानुजो बालो वृषघ्नश्च वृषस्तथा ॥ ३२

हंसो [सिंहो] वराहो विमलो नृसिंहो मूर्तयो हलाम् ।
कीर्त्तिः कान्तिस्तुष्टिपुष्टी धृतिः क्षान्तिः क्रिया दया ॥ ३३

मेधा च हर्षा श्रद्धाह्वा लज्जा लक्ष्मीः सरस्वती ।
प्रीती रतिश्च संप्रोक्ताः क्रमेण स्वरशक्तयः ॥ ३४

बिन्दुजा ईशजाः नादजाः सदाशिवजा इति द्रष्टव्यम् । भुक्तिर्बिन्दुकलासु योज्या ॥ २०—५२ ॥

जया दुर्गा प्रभा सत्या चण्डा वाणी विलासिनी ।
विरजा विजया विश्वा विनदा सुतदा स्मृतिः ॥ ३५
ऋद्धिः समृद्धिः शुद्धिश्च भुक्तिर्मुक्तिर्मतिः क्षमा ।
रमोमा क्लेदिनी क्लिन्ना वसुदा वसुधाऽपरा ॥ ३६
परा परायणा सूक्ष्मा सन्ध्या प्रज्ञा प्रभा निशा ।
अमोघा विद्युता चेति शक्तयः सर्वकामदाः ॥ ३७
इमाः पञ्चाशदुद्दिष्टा नमोऽन्ता वर्णपूर्विकाः ।
सधातुप्राणशक्त्यात्मयुक्ता यादिषु मूर्तयः ॥ ३८
श्रीकण्ठोऽनन्तसूक्ष्मौ च त्रिमूर्तिरमरेश्वरः ।
अर्घीशो भावभूतिश्च तिथिः स्थाणुर्हराह्वयः ॥ ३९
झिण्टीशो भौतिकः सद्योजातश्चाऽनुग्रहेश्वरः ।
अक्रूरश्च महासेनः स्युरेताः स्वरमूर्तयः ॥ ४०
ततः क्रोधीश चण्डेश पञ्चान्तक शिवोत्तमाः ।
तथैकरुद्र कूर्मैकनेत्राख्यचतुराननाः ॥ ४१
अजेश शर्व सोमेश्वराह्वा लाङ्गलिदारुकौ ।
अर्द्धनारीश्वरश्चोमाकान्तश्चाषाढिदण्डिनौ ॥ ४२
अद्रिर्मीनश्च मेषश्च लोहितश्च शिखी तथा ।
छगलण्डद्विरण्डौ च महाकालकपालिनौ ॥ ४३
भुजङ्गेशः पिनाकी च खड्गीशश्च बकस्तथा ।
श्वेतो भृगुश्च नकुली शिवः संवर्त्तकस्ततः ॥ ४४
पूर्णोदरी च विरजा तृतीया शाल्मली तथा ।
लोलाक्षी वर्त्तुलाक्षी च दीर्घघोणा तथैव च ॥ ४५
सुदीर्घमुखिगोमुख्यौ नवमी दीर्घजिह्विका ।
कुण्डोदर्यूर्ध्वकेश्यौ च मुखी विकृतपूर्विका ॥ ४६
सज्वालोल्काश्रिया विद्यामुख्यः स्युः स्वरशक्तयः ।
महाकालीसरस्वत्यौ सर्वसिद्धिसमन्विते ॥ ४७

गौरी त्रैलोक्यविद्या च तथा मन्त्रात्मशक्तिके ।
भूतमाता लम्बोदरी द्राविणी नागरी तथा ॥ ४८

वैखरी मञ्जरी चैव रूपिणी वीरिणी तथा ।
कोटरी पूतना भद्रकाली योगिन्य एव च ॥ ४९

शङ्खिनी गर्जिनी कालरात्रि कुर्दि[ज्जि]न्य एव च ।
कपर्दिनी महावज्रा जया च सुमुखेश्वरी ॥ ५०

रेवती माधवी चैव वारुणी वायवी तथा ।
रक्तोपधारिणी चाऽन्या तथैव सहजाह्वया ॥ ५१

लक्ष्मीश्च व्यापिनी मायेत्याख्याता वर्णशक्तयः ।
इत्युक्तस्त्रिविधो न्यासः क्रमात् सर्वसमृद्धिदः ॥ ५२

चन्दनकुचन्दनागुरुकर्पूरोशीररोगजलघुसृणाः ।
कक्कोलजातिमांसीमुराचोरग्रन्थिरोचनापत्राः ॥ ५३

पिप्पलबिल्वगुहारुणतृणकलवङ्गाह्वकुम्भिवन्दिन्यः ।
सोडुम्बरीकाश्मरिकास्थिराञ्जदरपुष्पिकामयूरशिखाः ॥ ५४

प्लक्षाग्निमन्थसिंहीकुशाह्वदर्भाश्च कृष्णहरपुष्पी ।
रोहिणलुगडुकबृहतीपाटलचिञ्चातुलस्यपामार्गाः ॥ ५५

शतमूलिलताद्विरेफा विष्णुक्रान्ता मुषल्यथाञ्जलिनी ।
दूर्वा श्रीदेवीसहे तथैव लक्ष्मीसदाभद्रे ॥ ५६

आदीनामिति कथिता वर्णानां क्रमवशादथौषधयः ।
गुलिकाकषायभसितप्रभेदतो निखिलसिद्धिदायिन्यः ॥ ५७

यथा भवन्ति देहान्तरमी पञ्चाशदक्षराः ।
येन येन प्रकारेण तथा वक्ष्यामि तत्त्वतः ॥ ५८

ओषधिकथनप्रयोजनमाह—गुलिकेति । भसितादिकरणप्रकारास्तु उत्तरत्र उच्यन्ते ॥ ५३ ॥ ५४ ॥ ५५ ॥ ५६ ॥ ५७ ॥

पञ्चाशदंशगुणितेत्यत्र पञ्चाशदीरयति पंक्तिश एव वर्णान् इत्युक्तानां वर्णानां विभूतिमभिधाय तदीरणादिप्रकारं वक्तुमुपक्रमते—यथेति । स्वरूपतो यथा

समीरिताः समीरेण सुषुम्नारन्ध्रनिर्गताः ।
व्यक्तिं प्रयान्ति वदने कण्ठादिस्थानघट्टिताः ॥ ५९

उच्चैरुन्मार्गगो वायुरुदात्तं कुरुते स्वरम् ।
नीचैर्गतोऽनुदात्तञ्च स्वरितं तिर्यगागतः ॥ ६०

अर्धैकद्वित्रिसंख्याभिर्मात्राभिर्लिपयः क्रमात् ।
सव्यञ्जना ह्रस्वदीर्घप्लुतसंज्ञा भवन्ति ताः ॥ ६१

अकारेकारयोर्योगादेकारो वर्ण इष्यते ।
तस्यैवैकारयोगेन स्यादैकाराक्षरं तथा ॥ ६२

उकारयोगात्तस्यैव स्यादोकाराह्वयः स्वरः ।
तस्यैवौकारयोगेन स्यादौकाराह्वयः स्वरः ॥ ६३

सन्ध्यक्षराः स्युश्चत्वारो मन्त्राः सर्वार्थसाधकाः ।
ऌवर्णॠवर्णयोर्व्यक्तिः लरोः सम्यक् प्रदृश्यते ॥ ६४

भवन्ति स्वरमात्रासन्धिस्थानप्रयत्नभूतषट्कर्मसु च येन येन प्रकारेण भवन्ति तथाच वक्ष्यामीत्यर्थः ॥ ५८ ॥

स्वरूपनिष्पत्तिप्रकारमाह—समीरिता इति ॥ ५९ ॥

वर्णानां पुरुषप्रकृत्युभयवाचकतया प्रयोगे स्वरविशेषं विवक्षन्नाह—उच्चैरिति । उन्मार्गग इत्युच्चैरित्यस्य व्याख्यानम् । तिर्यक् आगतः मध्यतः प्रसरन्नित्यर्थः ॥६०॥

पापक्षयमोक्षाप्यायनविनियोगे वर्णानां मात्राभेदं सूचयन्नाह—अर्धेति ॥ ६१ ॥

सर्वेषामेव वर्णानां प्रकृतिपुरुषवाचकत्वसिद्धये अध्यात्मकत्वम् अभिप्रेत्य केषाञ्चित्सन्धिं वदन् द्व्यात्मकतामाह—अकारेकारयोरिति ॥ ६२ ॥ ६३ ॥

तेषां प्रकृतिपुरुषवाचकमन्त्रत्वमाह—सन्ध्यक्षरा इति । प्रकृतिपुरुषात्मकोऽर्थः सर्वार्थस्तस्य साधकाः तद्वाचका इत्यर्थः । एषामृषिश्छन्दसी मातृकोक्ते । देवता परमात्मा । तत्तद्वर्णादियुतैः स्वरैरङ्गानि । मुद्राभयशुकवरदकरो द्विभुजः शुक्लरक्तभागद्वयः प्रकृतिपुरुषात्मकः कोऽपि देवो ध्येयः । ऌवर्णं ॠवर्णयोरङ्गविशेषं वदन्नितरेष्वपि तं सूचयति—ऌवर्णॠवर्णयोरिति । ऌवर्णॠवर्णयोर्मन्त्रयोः व्यक्तिः व्यज्यते अनेनेति व्यक्तिशब्देनाऽङ्गसामान्यमुच्यते । लरोः लकाररेफयोः । सम्यक् लां लीं रां रीमित्यादिप्रकारेण प्रदृश्यते । मूलागमेष्वित्यर्थः । इ उ ए ऐ ओ औ वर्णानां यकारवकारयोः विन्दुसर्गयोगो द्रष्टव्यः ॥ ६४ ॥

बिन्दुसर्गात्मनोर्व्यक्तिममसोरजपां वदेत् ।
कण्ठात्तु निःसरन् सर्गः प्रायोऽचामेकतः परः ॥ ६५

नश्वरः सर्ग एव स्यात् सोष्मा सप्राणकस्तु हः ।
स सर्गः प्रेषितः कण्ठे वायुनाऽकादिमीरयेत् ॥ ६६

वर्गं स्पर्शनमात्रेण कं स्वरस्पर्शनात् तु खम् ।
स्तोकगम्भीरसंस्पर्शात् गघौ ङश्च बहिर्गतः ॥ ६७

विसर्गस्तालुगः सोष्मेशं चवर्गञ्च यं यथा ।
ऋटुरेफषकारांश्च मूर्धगो दन्तगस्तथा ॥ ६८

लृतवर्गलसानोष्ठादुपूपध्मानसंज्ञकान् ।
दन्तौष्ठाभ्यां वञ्च तत्तत्स्थानगोऽर्णान् समीरयेत् ॥ ६९

बिन्दुसर्गाङ्गेषु हकारसकारयोगमाह—बिन्दुसर्गात्मनोरिति । बिन्दुसर्गात्मनोः अमसोरिति सम्बन्धः । हकारसकारयोः बिन्दुसर्गयोश्च क्रमेण पुरुषात्मकत्वं प्रकृत्यात्मकत्वं च सम्बन्धहेतुः । स्थानसाम्यमकारयोगस्य । अतोऽकाराङ्गेष्वपि हकारयोगो द्रष्टव्यः ।

ननु सर्वसमान बिन्दुविसर्गमन्त्रयोः स्थाने कथमकारोच्चारः । ततश्च कथं तयोः हकारसकारसंयोग इति । नैष दोषः । तयोरभिव्यक्त्यर्थत्वेनाकार-सम्बन्धोपपत्तेरित्याह—कण्ठादिति । तुशब्दः शङ्काव्यावृत्त्यर्थः । प्रायः सृष्टिरूप-प्रकृतिप्रतिभटः संहारात्मकः पुरुषः प्रायः तद्वाचको बिन्दुरित्यर्थः । सर्ग-स्तत्प्रतिभटबिन्दुश्च अचामेकतः प्रधानतः अकारात् पर इत्यर्थः ॥ ६५ ॥

अतत्परत्वेऽनभिव्यक्तिदोषमाह—नश्वर इति । सर्ग एव चेत् केवलः स्यात् तर्हि नश्वरः स्यादित्यर्थः । बिन्दोरपि उपलक्षणार्थमेतत् । यद्येवं सकारहकारौ प्रकृतिपुरुषवाचकौ । कथं तर्हि हकारस्यैव पूर्वं सर्ववाचकत्वमुक्तमिति । नायं दोषः । हकारस्यापि उभयात्मकत्वादित्याह—सोष्मा सप्राणकस्तु ह इति । उष्मा बलं शक्तिः प्रकृतिः स एव प्राणः कः प्राणस्य प्राणः पुरुषः ।

एवं हकारस्य प्रकृतिपुरुषात्मकत्वमभिधाय तदेव प्रपञ्चयन् तस्य प्रकृति-प्राधान्यमाश्रित्य सर्ववर्णादिकारणत्वमाह—स सर्ग इति । अकादिं वर्गमिति छेदः । तत्रैव वर्णविशेषाभिव्यञ्जकं प्रयत्नविशेषमाह—स्पर्शनमात्रेणेति । सोष्मा साग्निः । ईश शश्चेति छेदाः । उपसंहरति—तत्तदिति ॥ ६६॥६७॥६८॥६९ ॥

ह्रस्वाः पञ्च परे च सन्धिविकृताः पञ्चाथ बिन्द्वन्तिका
काद्याः प्राणहुताशभूकखमया याद्याश्च शार्णान्तिकाः ।
हान्ताः षच्चलसाः क्रमेण कथिता भूतात्मकास्ते पृथक्
तैस्तैः पञ्चभिरेव वर्णदशकैः स्युः स्तम्भनाद्याः क्रियाः ॥ ७०

ऊदृगदाद्विलला: कोर्नसौ चतुर्थार्णका वसौ वारः ।
इष्टर्ध्यैव द्वितीयरच्छा वह्नेरद्वन्द्वयोनिकादियषाः ॥ ७१

मरुतः कपोलबिन्दुकपञ्चमवर्णाः शहौ तथा व्योम्नः ।
मनुषु परेष्वपि मन्त्री करोतु कर्म्माणि तस्य संसिद्धै ॥ ७२

स्तम्भनाद्यमथ पार्थिवैरपामक्षरैश्च परिवर्षणादिकम् ।
दाहशोषणसशून्यतादिकान् वह्निवायुवियदक्षरैश्चरेत् ॥ ७३

दशभिर्दशभिरमीभिर्नमोऽन्तिकैर्द्वन्द्वशश्च बिन्दुयुतैः ।
योनेर्मध्ये कोणत्रितये मध्ये च संयजेन्मन्त्री ॥ ७४

वर्णानामुक्तमेव भूतसम्बन्धं विशदयन् तान् स्तम्भनादिषु विनियुङ्क्ते—ह्रस्वा इति। अ इ उ ऋ ऌ इति ह्रस्वाः। परे च दीर्घाः। आदयः पञ्च। ए ऐ ओ औ अं एते बिन्द्वन्ताः सन्धिविकृताः। ष च ल स ह इत्यन्त्यो वर्गः॥ ७० ॥
॥ ७१ ॥ ७२ ॥ ७३ ॥

स्तम्भनादिप्रयोगप्रकारमाह—दशभिरिति। अं आं नमः। एं कं नमः। चं टं नमः। तं पं नमः। यं षं नमः। इत्यादि मन्त्रप्रयोगप्रकारः। योनिस्त्रिकोणं तस्य मध्ये प्रथमो मन्त्रः। द्वितीयतृतीयचतुर्थाः अग्रादिकोणेषु। पञ्चमो मध्य एव संयजेत्। संलिख्य सञ्चिन्त्य वा पूजयेत्। मन्त्रीति सिद्धमन्त्रस्यायं प्रयोग इति सूचितः। मध्ये पञ्चोक्तभूतबीजं लिखित्वा तद्विन्दूर्ध्वाधोभागादिषु साधकसाध्यकर्मयोगो यन्त्रजीवादियोगश्च सूचितः। एतच्च यन्त्रं पार्थिवमण्डलगतं स्तम्भने। परिवर्षणादिष्वपि आप्यादिमण्डलगतानि यन्त्राणि। ह्सौः इति यन्त्रजीवं मध्यबीजाधोभागे न्यसेत्। हंसः संह इति मध्यजीवबीजचतुर्दिक्षु मध्याभिमुखं यन्त्रप्राणं लिखेत्। यन्त्रराजाय विद्महे वरप्रदाय धीमहि तन्नो यन्त्रः प्रचोदयात् इति गायत्री। गुणशोऽष्टदिक्षु पद्मवत्सु यन्त्रेषु दलेषु लेख्या। तद्बहिर्दशदिक्षु लं रं लं चं वं शं सं हं क्रों अं इति यन्त्रहृदयम्। ततो यथावकाशं प्राणप्रतिष्ठामन्त्रः। यन्त्रसामान्यमपि मन्त्रीत्यनेन सूचितम् ॥ ७४ ॥

पूर्वोक्ताद्बिन्दुमात्रात् स्वयमथ खतन्मात्रतामभ्युपेता-
ऽकारादीन् द्व्यष्ट कादीनपि तदनुगतान् पञ्चविंशत्तथैव।
यादीन् संयुक्तधातूनपि गुणसहितैः पञ्चभूतैश्च ताभि-
स्तन्मात्राभिर्व्यतीत्य प्रकृतिरथ हसंज्ञा भवेद्व्याप्य विश्वम् ॥ ७५

इति श्रीप्रपञ्चसारे तृतीयः पटलः ॥

एवं पटलत्रयोक्तां सृष्टिं संक्षेपेणाऽनुवदन् संहारमाह—पूर्वोक्तादिति। स्वयमिति। निस्तरङ्गा तत्त्वसंज्ञा प्रकृतिः सा स्वयमेव बिन्दुतत्त्वद्वारा खतन्मात्रतां शब्दब्रह्मात्मकतामभ्युपेता प्राप्ता सती अकारादीन् षोडश स्वरान् कादीनपि पञ्चविंशत् स्वरानुगतानभ्युपेता संयुक्तधातून् यादीनपि अभ्युपेतेत्यर्थः। अर्थात्मकतामुक्तामाह—गुणसहितैरिति। तन्मात्राभिः सह यादीनभ्युपेतेति सम्बन्धः।

संहारमाह—व्यतीत्येति। कार्यंजातमुक्तम्। स्वात्मन्येव संहृत्येत्यर्थः। विश्वं सर्वं ब्रह्म तद् व्याप्य तेनाऽभिन्नतां प्राप्येत्यर्थः ॥ ७५ ॥

इति श्रीपद्मपादाचार्यकृते प्रपञ्चसारविवरणे
तृतीयः पटलः।

चतुर्थः पटलः ।

अथ व्यवस्थिते त्वेवमस्य शक्तित्वमिष्यते ।
कृतकृत्यस्य जगति सततं रूढसंस्थितेः ॥ १

प्राणात्मकं हकाराख्यं बीजं तेन तदुद्भवाः ।
षडूर्मयः स्यू रेफोत्था गुणास्त्वार एव च ॥ २

एवं हकारस्य केवलस्य विश्वयोनित्वमभिधायादौ मूलार्णशब्दोक्तहृल्लेखात्मतां प्राप्तस्य विश्वयोनित्वं वक्तुं चतुर्थपटलारम्भः ।

अथेति । अथशब्दो हेत्वर्थः । हेतुत्वेन विवक्षितमर्थं स्वयमेव दर्शयति—जगत्येवं व्यवस्थित इति । एवमुक्तेन प्रकारेण जगति कार्ये कारणत्वेन व्यवस्थित इत्यर्थः । तुशब्दोऽवधारणार्थः । अस्य हकारस्य शक्तित्वं शक्तिवाचकमन्त्रत्वमिष्यते । कथमेकरूपस्य हकारस्य गुणत्रयात्मकशक्तिवाचकत्वमिति । नैष दोषः । वर्णान्तरसंयोगः कृतः कर्त्तव्यो यस्य तस्यैव मन्त्रत्वेष्टेरित्याह—कृतकृत्यस्येति । कर्तव्यमेव दर्शयन् हकारं विशिनष्टि—रूढसंस्थितेरिति । रेफोढो रूढः संभूय स्थित ई यस्मिन् हकारे स संस्थितिः रूढश्चासौ संस्थितिश्चेति विग्रहः । तस्य रूढसंस्थितेः ईकाररेफसंयुक्तस्येत्यर्थः । बिन्द्वादियोगार्थं रूढसंस्थितिं विशिनष्टि—सततमिति । ततः सहितं यथा भवति तथा रूढसंस्थितेरित्यर्थः । ततः बिन्दुः । व्याप्तत्वात्तस्य ।

अन्योऽर्थः । जातस्य शिशोः मुखान्निर्गतानां वर्णानां व्याप्त्यादिकमभिहितं तृतीये पटले । अथैवं वर्णानां तत्त्वे व्यवस्थिते अस्य वर्णोच्चारकस्य पुरुषस्य शक्तित्वं जगन्मूलकारणात्मकशक्त्यात्मकत्वमिष्यते ।

प्राकृतस्य परिच्छिन्नस्याऽस्य उक्तशक्त्यात्मकत्वम् अनुपपन्नमिति चेन्न । न्यासध्यानयोगादिभिः योग्यत्वस्य सम्पाद्यमानत्वात् सम्पादितत्वाच्च इत्याह—कृतकृत्यस्य जगतीति । जगति सर्वतत्त्वात्मके शरीरे यन्न्यासादिकं कर्तव्यं तत् कृतं यस्य साधकस्य स तथोक्तः । अतएव सततं रूढसंस्थिते रूढा प्रसिद्धा संविद्रूपप्रकृत्यात्मकत्वेन स्थितिर्यस्य स तथोक्तः ॥ १ ॥

उक्तस्याऽक्षरत्रयस्य व्याप्तिं वदन् साधकस्य प्रकृत्यात्मकत्वसिद्धये षोढ़शाङ्गन्यासमाह—प्राणात्मकमिति । प्राणे सत्येव मनोदेहयोः शोकजरादिधर्मवत्त्वदर्शनात् तदात्मकहकारधर्मत्वं षडूर्मीणामुक्तम् ॥ २ ॥

पवनाद्याः पृथिव्यन्ताः स्पर्शाद्यैश्च गुणैः सह ।
करणान्यपि चत्वारि सङ्घातश्चेतनेति च ॥ ३

ईकारस्य गुणाः प्रोक्ताः षड़िति क्रमशो बुधैः ।
ऊकारान्तास्त्वकाराद्याः षड्वर्णाः षड्भ्य एव च ॥ ४

प्रभेदेभ्यः समुत्पन्ना हकारस्य महात्मनः ।
ऋकाराद्यास्तु चत्वारो रेफोत्था लृपराः स्मृताः ॥ ५

एकारादिविसर्गान्तं वर्णानां षट्कमुद्गतम् ।
ईकारस्य षड़ङ्गेभ्य इतीदं षोड़शाङ्गवत् ॥ ६

गुणचतुष्टयमाह—पवनाद्या इति। तेषां गुणशब्दवाच्यत्वे हेतुः—स्पर्शाद्यैरिति। पारतन्त्र्यशाद्वा गुणशब्दः। तेषु करणानि मनआदीनि। संघातोऽवशिष्टकार्यकारणसंघातः। चेतना चैतन्याभ्यासः। चेतनालक्षणा बुद्धिवृत्तिर्वा।

अयमत्र न्यासक्रमः। प्राणात्मकं प्राणशरीरं हकाराख्यं बीजं बिन्दुसहितम्। हं प्राणात्मने नम इति प्राणबुद्ध्या व्यापयेदित्यर्थः। तेन प्राणात्मकेन हकारेण सह तदुद्भवाः षडूर्मयः स्वाधारेषु न्यस्तव्याः। हं बुभुक्षायै नमः। हं पिपासायै नमः। हं शोकाय नमः। हं मोहाय नमः। हं जरायै नमः। हं मृत्यवे नमः। इति प्राणबुद्धिर्देहेषु यथायोग्यं न्यसेदित्यर्थः। रेफोत्था गुणा इति चशब्दादाकाशशब्दौ गृह्येते। रं आकाशशब्दाभ्यां नम इति मूर्ध्नि न्यस्य। रं वायुस्पर्शाभ्यां नमः। रं तेजोरूपाभ्यां नमः। रं अब्रसाभ्यां नमः। रं पृथिवीगन्धाभ्यां नमः। इति वक्त्रहृद्गुह्यपादेषु न्यसेदित्यर्थः। करणान्यपीति। ईं ज्ञानशक्त्यै नम इति व्यापकं न्यस्य ईं मनसे नमः। ईं बुद्धेय नमः। ईं अहङ्काराय नमः। ईं चित्ताय नमः। ईं संघाताय नमः। ईं चेतनायै नमः। इति मनआदिषु न्यसेदित्यर्थः। बुधैरिति प्रणवशक्तिभ्यां व्यापकं सूचितम्।

अस्यैव न्यासस्य षोड़शस्वरयोगमाह—ऊकारान्ता इति। तुशब्दस्तत्तदक्षरयुक्तस्वरयोगं सूचयति। हं बुभुक्षायै नमः। हां पिपासायै नमः इत्यादि। ऋं वायुस्पर्शाभ्यां नमः। यें मनसे। यैं बुद्धये नम इत्यादयो मन्त्राः।

हकारस्य महात्मन इति। तत्तद्वर्गन्यासानन्तरं तैस्तैर्वर्गैः सहितेन तेन तेन वर्णेन व्यापकं सूचितम्। हं हां हिं हीं हुं हूं हकारात्मने नम इत्यादयो व्यापकमन्त्रा इति। इदं षोड़शाङ्गवदिति। तत्तद्बीजयुतषोड़शस्वरानुक्त्वाऽन्ते

एभ्यः संजज्ञिरेऽङ्गेभ्यः स्वराः षोडश सर्वगाः ।
तेभ्यो वर्णान्तराः सर्वे ततो मूलमिदं विदुः ॥ ७

ह्रीं इत्युच्चार्य व्यापकं सूचितमिति । एतैरुक्तैः स्वरैरिदं बीजं साधकशरीरं च षोडशाङ्गवदित्यर्थः ॥ ३ ॥ ४ ॥ ५ ॥ ६ ॥

पुनरप्यस्यैव न्यासस्य विशेषमाह—एभ्य इति । एभ्य उक्तेभ्यो हकारादि-विशिष्टेभ्यः स्वरेभ्यो बुभुक्षादिभ्यश्चाङ्गेभ्यः । सर्वगाः सर्ववर्णानुगताः स्वराः अकखादिक्षान्ताक्षरसंयुक्ताः स्वराः संजज्ञिर इत्यर्थः ।

अयमत्र प्रयोगक्रमः । हं अं बुभुक्षायै नमः । हां आं पिपासायै नमः । हिं इं शोकाय नमः । इत्यादि स्थानं व्यापकादिकं पूर्ववदेव । अथवा पूर्वोक्तस्वरपारायण न्यासवदेव न्यासः कार्य इति । षट्त्रिंशन्न्यासभेदा गताः ।

पुनरप्यस्यैव न्यासस्य भेदं सूचयति—तेभ्यो वर्णान्तराः सर्वं इति । तेभ्यः हकारादिविशिष्टाकखगघादिसंयुक्तषोडशस्वरेभ्यो बुभुक्षादिभ्यश्च वर्णान्तरा अकखादिषट्त्रिंशद्वर्णाः संजज्ञिर इत्यर्थः ।

अयमत्र प्रयोगक्रमः । हं अं बुभुक्षायै नमः । हं अं कं बुभुक्षायै नमः । हं कं खं बुभुक्षायै नमः । इत्यादि क्षान्तं समानम् । हं आं अं बुभुक्षायै नमः । हं आं कं बुभुक्षायै नमः । इत्यादि क्षान्तमेवमेव । हं अः अं बुभुक्षायै नमः । हं अः कं बुभुक्षायै नमः । हं अः खं बुभुक्षायै नमः । इत्यन्तं द्रष्टव्यम् । अकारपद्मदलेषु वृत्ताकारेणैषां न्यासः । पुनः हं कं अं बुभुक्षायै नमः । हं कं कं बुभुक्षायै नमः इत्यादि षोडशपर्यायाः काम्बुजदलेषु वृत्ताकारेण न्यस्तव्याः । पुनः हं खं अं बुभुक्षायै नमः । हं खं कं बुभुक्षायै । हं खं खं बुभुक्षायै नमः । इत्यादिका ब्रह्मब्रह्मपारायणवत् खाद्यम्बुजदलेषु न्यस्तव्या इति बुभुक्षान्यासभेदाः ।

अथ पिपासादिन्यासभेदाः । अथादौ हां हीमादियुता ब्रह्मब्रह्मपारायणवत् आदिक्रस्वैरेव संयोज्याऽकाराद्यम्बुजदलेषु न्यस्तव्याः । अथवा ब्रह्मविष्णवादि-पारायणवद् द्वितीयदीर्घादिसंयुक्ता न्यस्तव्याः । हां अं अं पिपासायै नमः । तथा हां अं कं पिपासायै नम इत्यादिक्षान्तम् । हां आं अं पिपासायै नमः । हां आं कं पिपासायै नमः इत्यादि विसर्गान्तमूह्यम् । हां अं कं पिपासायै । हां कं कं पिपासायै । हां कं खं पिपासायै इत्याद्यूह्यम् । पुनः हां खं अं पिपासायै । हां खं कं पिपासायै । हां खं खं पिपासायै इत्याद्यूह्यं सर्वम् । ततो मूलमिदं विदुरिति प्रतिपर्यायं मूलेन व्यापकन्यासाः सूचिताः ॥ ७ ॥

गतो वो बीजतामेष प्राणिष्वेवं व्यवस्थितः ।
ब्रह्माण्डं ग्रस्तमेतेन व्याप्तं स्थावरजङ्गमम् ॥ ८

नादः प्राणश्च जीवश्च घोषश्चेत्यादि कथ्यते ।
एष पुंस्त्रीनियमितैर्लिङ्गैश्च सनपुंसकैः ॥ ९

रेफो माया बीजमिति त्रिधा समभिधीयते ।
शक्तिः श्रीः सन्नतिः कान्तिर्लक्ष्मीर्मेधा सरस्वती ॥ १०

गतो वो बीजतामित्यादिना षडध्वन्यासः सूचितः । वो युष्माकं ब्रह्मविष्णुरुद्राणां बीजतां वाचकतामितीश्वरसदाशिवयोरपि उपलक्षणमेतत् । प्राणिषु अध्वषट्कविशिष्टेषु जीवेषु एवमुक्तेन प्रकारेण पञ्चमूर्त्यात्मकत्वे सति अध्वाभिमानित्वेन व्यवस्थितः । अध्वोपाधिकप्राणिनियामक पञ्चमूर्त्यात्मना व्यवस्थित इत्यर्थः । तत्राऽध्वानः संग्रहेणोच्यन्ते । विस्तारस्याऽशक्यत्वात् । अध्वानो द्विविधाः । वाच्यवाचकभेदेन । वाचको वर्णपदमन्त्रभेदेन त्रिविधः । वाच्यं च तत्त्वभुवनकलाभेदात् । हं हिं हुं हें होमिति वर्णाः । ओं क्षौं हौं नमः शिवाय शिवायै इति वा पदपञ्चकम् । सद्योजातादयो मन्त्राः । पृथिव्यादीनि तत्त्वानि । ब्रह्मलोकादीनि भुवनानि । ब्रह्माद्याः मूर्तयः कलाः । इति मूर्तिस्थानेषु न्यासः । अक्षरतत्त्वपदभुवनमन्त्रकलाक्रमेण न्यासः । हं नमः पृथिव्यै नमः । ओं नमो ब्रह्मलोकाय नमः । सद्योजाताय नमः । ब्रह्मणे नमः । इत्यादिक्रमेण मन्त्रप्रयोगो द्रष्टव्यः । प्रणवेनैतान् क्रमेण संहृत्य योगः कार्य इत्याह—ब्रह्माण्डमिति । ब्रह्माण्डमित्युपलक्षणम् । सर्वस्याऽध्वजातस्य । व्याप्तं स्थावरजङ्गममिति मूर्त्यधिष्ठेयतया ध्यातस्य तत्तत्तत्त्वादिवर्तिनः प्राणिजातस्यापि लय इत्युक्तः ॥ ८ ॥

नाद इत्यादिना मूर्तिलयानन्तरं मात्रान्यासयोगावाह । हों नादात्मने । हौं प्राणात्मने । एवं घोषजीव बिन्दुकला निरोधिका नादनादान्तादयोऽपि पादावारभ्य व्यापकत्वेन न्यस्तव्याः ।

लिङ्गन्यासमाह—एष इति । रं पुरुषात्मने नमः । ईं स्त्र्यात्मने नमः । ह्रं नपुंसकात्मने नमः । क्षौं अलिङ्गात्मने नमः । इत्येते मन्त्राः सूचिताः । दक्षिणोत्तरमध्यभागव्यापकेषु न्यासः । एष इत्यनेन व्यापकमन्त्रः सूचितः ।

शक्त्यादिन्यासं सूचयन् व्याप्तिमाह—शक्तिरिति । शक्तिः श्रीरित्येताभिः शक्तिभिः । आद्यैश्चाऽकारादिक्षकारान्तैर्वर्णैः सह मातृकास्थानेषु न्यसेदित्यर्थः । अं शक्त्यै नमः । आं शक्त्यै नमः । इत्यादयो मन्त्राः । एवं अं श्रियै नमः ।

क्षान्तिः पुष्टिः स्मृतिः शान्तिरित्याद्यैः स्वार्थवाचकैः ।
नानाविकारतां प्राप्तैः स्वैः स्वैर्भावैर्विकल्पितैः ॥ ११

तामेनां कुण्डलीत्येके सन्तो हृदयगां विदुः ।
सा रौति सततं देवी भृङ्गीसङ्गीतकध्वनिः ॥ १२

आकृतिं स्वेन भावेन पिण्डितां बहुधा विदुः ।
कुण्डली सर्वथा ज्ञेया सुषुम्नानुगतैव सा ॥ १३

इत्यादि दशपर्याया ऊह्याः । एतेषामेव न्यासानां विशेषमाह—स्वार्थवाचकैरिति । स्वार्थशब्देन कुण्डलिनी उच्यते । तस्या वाचकास्तदक्षराः त्रिबीजात्मकाश्च मन्त्राः विद्याश्च । तैश्च सह शक्त्यादिन्यासं कुर्यात् । प्रथममेकैकं बीजं संयोज्य शक्त्यैकादशकं न्यसेत् । पुनः द्वितीय तृतीय समस्तसंयोगेनापि तथा न्यसेदित्यर्थः ।

उक्तबीजसंयुक्त एव न्यासे मन्त्रान्तरसंयोगमाह—नानाविकारतां प्राप्तैरिति । उक्तत्रिबीजमन्त्राणां विकारत्वं नानाविधत्वं प्राप्ता ये ब्रह्मसरस्वती विष्णुलक्ष्मी-रुद्रोमा गणेशदुर्गादयः तेषां मन्त्रैरित्यर्थः । तैश्च सहोक्तमेव न्यासं कुर्यादिति सर्वमन्त्राणां शक्त्यादिन्यासः सूचितः । ओं अं ऐं नमो ब्रह्मणे शक्त्यै नमः । ओं अं ऐं नमः सरस्वत्यै शक्त्यै नमः । ओं अं ऐं नमो विष्णवे शक्त्यै नमः । ओं अं ऐं नमो लक्ष्म्यै शक्त्यै नमः । ओं अं ऐं नमः शिवाय शक्त्यै नमः । ओं अं ऐं नम उमायै शक्त्यै नमः । ओं अं ऐं गं नमः क्षिप्रप्रसादनाय शक्त्यै नमः । ओं अं ऐं ओं ह्रौं दुं नमो दुर्गायै शक्त्यै नमः । इत्यादि प्रकारेण सर्वमूलमौलिकमन्त्रेषु प्रयोगा द्रष्टव्याः ।

अथैवं विधानामेवैषां सर्वेषां स्वरपारायणन्यासमाह—स्वैः स्वैर्भावैरिति । स्वैः स्वैरकारककारादिसम्बन्धिभिः भावैः षोड़शस्वरैः सह न्यसेदित्यर्थः । न्यासस्तु षोड़शदलेषु कार्यः । व्यञ्जनपारायणन्यासमाह—विकल्पितैरिति । पुर्वोक्त-विरचनावत् विकल्पोऽवगन्तव्यः ॥ ८ ॥ १० ॥ ११ ॥

कुण्डलीन्यासं वक्तुं स्थानं सूचयति—तामेनामिति । अन्ये मूलाधार-नाभिभ्रूमध्यद्वादशान्तेषु विदुरिति स्थानसूचनमेतत् । सा रौतीति सर्वस्थानानु-गतनादज्योतिश्चिन्तनमुक्तम् ॥ १२ ॥

कुण्डलिनीन्यासमाह—आकृतिमिति । स्वेन भावेन च कुण्डलिनीवाचकहकारेण कुण्डलिनीबीजेन च पिण्डितामाकृतिं ब्रह्मब्रह्मादिरूपेण सर्वस्थानेषु बहुधा विदुरित्यर्थः । अयं भावः । ह्स्रां ह्स्रोमिति कुण्डलिनीबीजं नाभौ त्रिकोणमध्ये

चराचरस्य जगतो बीजत्वाद्बीजमेव तत् ।
मूलस्य बिन्दुयोगेन शतानन्द त्वदुद्भवः ॥ १४

रेफान्वितेकाराकारयोगादुत्पत्तिरेतयोः ।
हङ्काराख्यो भवांस्तेन हरिरित्येष शब्द्यते ॥ १५

हरत्वमस्य तेनैव सर्वात्मत्वं ममापि च ।
अस्य बिन्दोः समुत्पत्त्या तदन्तोऽसौ हमुच्यते ॥ १६

न्यसेत् । ब्रह्माणं सरस्वतीं च सञ्चिन्त्य हं परब्रह्मणे पराशक्त्यै नमः । हं साचिषे साचिष्यै नमः । इत्यपि मध्य एव व्यापकत्वेन विन्यसेत् । ह्रौं चतुर्मूर्तये चतुर्मूर्त्यै नमः । इत्यपि व्याप्य ह्रों सर्वेश्वराय मूलप्रकृत्यै नमः । ह्रैं रुद्रसर्वेश्वराय उमामूलप्रकृत्यै नमः । ह्रें विष्णुसर्वेश्वराय लक्ष्मीमूलप्रकृत्यै नमः । ह्रां ह्रॄं ब्रह्मसर्वेश्वराय सरस्वतीमूलप्रकृत्यै नम इति द्वादशान्त भ्रूमध्य हृदय नाभिषु त्रिकोणमध्यकोणत्रयेषु वा न्यसित्वा तेषां परिवारत्वेन वक्ष्यमाणान् मन्त्रान् न्यसेत् । ह्रॄं रुद्ररुद्रायोमोमायै । ह्रॄं रुद्रविष्णवे उमालक्ष्म्यै । ह्रं रुद्रब्रह्मणे उमासरस्वत्यै नमः । इति रुद्रसर्वेश्वरपरितः । हूं विष्णुरुद्राय लक्ष्म्युमायै । हुं विष्णुविष्णवे लक्ष्मीलक्ष्म्यै । ह्रीं विष्णुब्रह्मणे लक्ष्मीसरस्वत्यै नमः । इति विष्णुसर्वेश्वरपरितः । हिं ब्रह्मरुद्राय सरस्वत्युमायै । हां ब्रह्मविष्णवे सरस्वतीलक्ष्म्यै । हं ब्रह्मब्रह्मणे सरस्वतीसरस्वत्यै नमः । इति ब्रह्मसर्वेश्वरपरितः इति ।

एवं नाभौ न्यसित्वा हृदयादिषु मध्ये विष्ण्वादीन् सञ्चिन्त्योक्तप्रकारेण षोडशमूर्तिन्यासं कुर्यात् । कुण्डली सर्वथा ज्ञेया इति चतुर्मूर्तियोगादि-निर्विकल्पयोगान्तान् योगानुक्तान् सूचयति ॥ १३ ॥

केन मन्त्रेण एवं कुण्डली ज्ञेयेति ह्रोमिति सहकारेण प्रणवेनेत्याह—चराचरस्येति । न केवलं प्रणव एव चराचरस्येदं बीजं यतस्तदपि शब्दब्रह्म हकारो बीजमेवेत्यर्थः । बीजत्वमेव प्रपञ्चयन् मूर्तिन्यासमाह—मूलस्येति ॥ १४ ॥

रेफान्वितेन इकारेण योगाद्विष्णोरुत्पत्तिः । रेफान्वितेनाऽकारेण योगाद्रुद्रस्य । उक्तेऽर्थे गमकमाह—हङ्काराख्य इति । सर्वात्मत्वं मम सर्वसंयोगादित्यर्थः । हं ब्रह्मणे नमः इति । हरिः विष्णवे नमः । हरः रुद्राय नमः । ह्रीं सर्वेश्वराय नम इति नाभ्यादिषु न्यसेदित्यर्थः । एतदेव मन्त्रचतुष्टयं प्रणवसंयुक्तं पिण्डीकृतं प्रणवचतुष्टयं भवति । ह्रों ह्यों ह्रीं ह्योमिति ।

विभूत्यन्तरं दर्शयन् अजपापरमात्मप्रणवन्यासानाह—अस्येति । अस्य हस्य

स हंकारः पुमान् प्रोक्तः स इति प्रकृतिः स्मृता ।
अजपेयं मता शक्तिस्तथा दक्षिणवामतः ॥ १७

बिन्दुर्दक्षिणभागस्तु वामभागो विसर्गकः ।
तेन दक्षिणवामाख्यौ भागौ पुंस्त्रीविशेषितौ ॥ १८

बिन्दुः पुरुष इत्युक्तो विसर्गः प्रकृतिर्मता ।
पुंप्रकृत्यात्मको हंसस्तदात्मकमिदं जगत् ॥ १९

पुंरूपं सा विदित्वा स्वं सोऽहम्भावमुपागता ।
स एष परमात्माख्यो मनुरस्य महामनोः ॥ २०

सकारश्च हकारश्च लोपयित्वा प्रयोजयेत् ।
सन्धिं वै पूर्वरूपाख्यं ततोऽसौ प्रणवो भवेत् ॥ २१

बिन्दुतत्त्वादभिव्यक्तः तदन्तः तच्छिरस्कोऽसौ हः हमित्युच्यते। इत्यजपा-प्रथमबीजोद्धारः ॥ १५॥१६ ॥

द्वितीयबीजस्वरूपमाह—स इति। उद्धृतयोर्बीजयोस्तत्त्वं वदन् न्यास-मन्त्रावाह—हंकार इति। हं पुरुषात्मने नमः। सः प्रकृत्यात्मने नमः। इति मन्त्रौ सूचितौ। देवतात्वेन शक्तिरेव ध्येयेत्याह—अजपेति। न्यासस्थानमाह—तथा दक्षिणवामत इति। यथा मूलशिरसोर्न्यासः प्रसिद्धः। तथा दक्षिण-वामयोरपि न्यस्तव्यावित्यर्थः ॥ १७ ॥

न्यासे नियममाह—बिन्दुरिति। बिन्दुविसर्गयुक्तौ हकारसकारौ बिन्दुविसर्ग-शब्दार्थौ। भागनियमे गमकमाह—तेनेति। देवानां सर्वेषां चेत्यर्थः ॥ १८ ॥

तेन कथं पुंस्त्रीविशेषितत्वमिति। तत्राह—बिन्दुरिति। अतोऽर्धनारीश्वर-देवत्यो हंसमन्त्रः तथा ध्येय इत्याह—पुंप्रकृतीति। तस्य सर्वात्मकत्वं वदन् न्यास-फलमाह—तदात्मकमिति। अयमत्र द्वितीयो न्यासप्रकारः। उक्तमन्त्राभ्यां शिरो ललाट भ्रूनेत्र श्रोत्रनासा गण्ड गलांस बाहु मूलोपबाहु कूर्पर प्रकोष्ठ मणिबन्ध-तलाङ्गुल्युरःकक्ष स्तनोदर पार्श्व नाभि जठर स्फिग्वृषणपादमूलोरु जानु जङ्घागुल्फ-प्रपदाङ्गुलिद्वयेषु न्यसित्वा। हंसः प्रकृतिपुरुषात्मने नम इति व्यापयेदिति। पुंप्रकृत्यात्मको हंस इत्यनेनैव सूचितो व्यापकमन्त्रः ॥ १९ ॥

एवं प्रत्यगात्मनो ब्रह्मणैकत्वप्रतिपादकं मनुमभिधाय तस्याऽनेन तत्प्रतिपादकं परमात्ममन्त्रमुद्धरति—पुंरूपमिति। सा तदुपाधिको जीव इत्यर्थः। अस्यापि

ताराद्विभक्ताच्चरमांशतः स्युर्भूतानि खादीन्यथ मध्यमांशात् ।
इनादितेजांसि च पूर्वभागाच्छन्दाः समस्ताः प्रभवन्ति लोके ॥ २२

एवमेषा जगत्सूतिः सवितेत्यभिधीयते ।
यदा तदेति स्वैस्तत्त्वैश्चतुर्विंशतिधा भिदाम् ॥ २३

तद्वर्णभिन्ना गायत्री गायकत्राणनाद्भवेत् ।
सप्तग्रहात्मिका प्रोक्ता यदेयं सप्तभेदिनी ॥ २४

तदा स्वरेशः सूर्योऽयं कवर्गेशस्तु लोहितः ।
चवर्गप्रभवः काव्यष्टवर्गाद् बुधसम्भवः ॥ २५

तवर्गोत्थः सुरगुरुः पवर्गोत्थः शनैश्चरः ।
यवर्गजोऽयं शीतांशुरिति सप्तगुणा त्वियम् ॥ २६

मन्त्रस्य न्यासादिकमुक्तप्रायम् । पुनरेकत्वानुभवसाधनं प्रणवमुद्धरति—अस्य महामनोरिति ॥ २० ॥ २१ ॥

उद्धृतस्य तारस्य न्यासयोगादिकं वदन् विभूतिमाह—तारादिति । मं आकाशात्मने नमः । मं वाय्वात्मने नमः । मं तेज आत्मने नमः । मं अबात्मने नमः । मं पृथिव्यात्मने नमः इति मूर्धादिषु न्यसेदिति मकारन्यासः । उं सूर्याय नमः । उं सोमाय नमः । उं अग्नये नमः । इति हृन्मूर्धमूलाधारेषु उकारन्यासः । अं शब्दब्रह्मणे नम इति व्यापयेत् । इत्यकारन्यासः ॥ २२ ॥

गायत्रीतत्त्वन्यासं सूचयन् गायत्रीदेवतापि एषैव शक्तिरिति सहेतुकमाह—एवमिति । तत्त्वन्यासं सूचयति—यदा तदेति ॥ २३ ॥

तत्त्वन्यासे गायत्रीवर्णसान्निध्यमाह—तद्वर्णेति । तच्छब्दस्तत्त्ववाचकः । तत्त्वसंख्यवर्णसंयुक्तेत्यर्थः । सप्तग्रहात्मकत्वं वदन् सप्तग्रहन्यासं सूचयति—सप्तग्रहात्मिकेति । हकारादिशान्तान्तैः यदा सप्तभेदिनी तदा सप्तग्रहात्मिका इति न्यासमन्त्रेषु हकारात्मने नम इत्यादियोगः सूचितः ॥ २४ ॥

मन्त्रशेषं सूचयति—तदा स्वरेश इति । अं आं इं ईं उं ऊं ऋं ॠं ऌं ॡं एं ऐं ओं औं अं अः स्वराधिपतये सूर्याय भगवते हकारात्मने नमः । कं खं गं घं ङं कवर्गाधिपतये अङ्गारकाय भगवते रेफात्मने नमः । चं छं जं झं ञं चवर्गाधिपतये शुक्राय भगवते ईकारात्मने नमः । टं ठं डं ढं णं टवर्गाधिपतये बुधाय भगवते बिन्द्वात्मने नमः । तं थं दं धं नं तवर्गाधिपतये बृहस्पतये भगवते

यथा स्वरेभ्यो नाऽन्ये स्युर्वर्णाः षड्वर्गभेदिताः ।
तथा सवित्रनुस्यूतं ग्रहषट्कं न संशयः ॥ २७

इति संलीनसूर्यांशे वर्गषट्के तु षड्गुणा ।
हृल्लेखियं तथा यन्त्रं स्मर्यते स्मृतिकोविदैः ॥ २८

सर्वव्याप्ता हि सा शक्तिः शश्वद्भास्कररूपिणी ।
स्वभासा क्रमते यत्र तत्राऽस्याः स्थितिरिष्यते ॥ २९

अस्यास्तु रजसा चैव तमसा च दिवानिशम् ।
सत्त्वावष्टब्धबिन्द्वात्मा मेरुं पर्येति भास्करः ॥ ३०

अस्या विकाराद्वर्णेभ्यो जाता द्वादश राशयः ।
लवादिकालोपचितैस्तैः स्याच्चक्रगतिस्त्रिधा ॥ ३१

ऋक्षराश्यादियुतया चक्रगत्या जगत्स्थितिः ।
वक्ष्यामि चक्ररूपञ्च प्रबद्धं राशिभिर्यथा ॥ ३२

नादात्मने नमः । पं फं बं भं मं पवर्गाधिपतये शनैश्चराय भगवते शक्त्यात्मने नमः । यं रं लं वं शं षं सं हं लं क्षं यवर्गाधिपतये सोमाय भगवते शान्तात्मने नमः । इति मन्त्राः सूचिताः । इति सप्तगुणा त्वियमिति । ह्रीं अं क्षं सर्वाधिपतये सर्वैश्वर्य संविदे नमः । इति व्यापकमन्त्रः सूचितः ॥ २५ ॥ २६ ॥

तस्या व्यापकत्वं सूचयन् ग्रहाणां सूर्यात्मकत्वं विद्व्याप्यत्वमाह – यथेति । उक्तं हि स्वरकार्यत्वं वर्णान्तराणां तेभ्यो वर्णान्तरा इति । अत्र सप्तग्रहन्यासार्थं षड्गुणितयन्त्रं सूचयति—यन्त्रमिति । स्मृतिकोविदैरिति स्मृतिप्रकारः सूचितः । हृदयमध्य गुह्य जान्वंसमूर्धांम जानुकोणं स्मरन्तीत्यर्थः ॥ २७ ॥ २८ ॥

अस्य न्यासस्य ध्यानं देवताव्याप्तिं च दर्शयति—सर्वेति ॥ २९ ॥

अहोरात्रन्यासमाह—अस्यास्त्विति । रेफेकारहकारा रजआदयः । रं अह्ने नमः । ईं रात्र्यै नमः । हं भैरवे नमः । ह्रीं भास्कराय नमः । इति मन्त्रा मूर्धमूलाधारसुषुम्नाहृत्सु न्यस्तव्या इत्यर्थः ॥ ३० ॥

राशिव्याप्तिं वदन् राशिन्यासे वर्णयोगं सूचयति—अस्या इति ।

कालचक्रमध्ये लवादिन्यासं राशिन्यासं च सूचयति—लवादीति ॥ ३१ ॥

चक्रसंहारेण स्वरूपस्थितिं सूचयति—ऋक्षेति । चक्रस्य गतिः संहारः । जगतः परमात्मरूपेण स्थितिरित्यर्थः । वक्ष्यामीति सुबोधम् ॥ ३२ ॥

अन्तर्बहिर्विभागेन रचयेद्राशिमण्डलम् ।
भूचक्र एष मेषादिः प्रविज्ञेयोऽथ मानुषः ॥ ३३
आद्यैर्मेषाह्वयो राशिरीकारान्तैः प्रजायते ।
ऋकारान्तैरुकाराद्यैर्वृषो युग्मं ततस्त्रिभिः ॥ ३४
एदैतोः कर्कटो राशिरोदौतोः सिंहसम्भवः ।
अमःशवर्गलेभ्यश्च सञ्जाता कन्यका मता ॥ ३५
षड्भ्यः कचटतेभ्यश्च पयाभ्याश्च प्रजज्ञिरे ।
वणिगाद्याश्च मीनान्ता राशयः शक्तिजृम्भणात् ॥ ३६
चतुर्भिर्यादिभिः सार्द्धं स्यात् क्षकारस्तु मीनगः ।
स्यातामर्धाधिकौ पञ्चनाड़िकौ चापकर्कटौ ॥ ३७

अन्तर्बहिरिति । अयमर्थः । चतुरस्रत्रयात्मकं सकोणसूत्रं राशिमण्डलं मूलाधारे मनसा लिखित्वा । तन्मध्ये षट्कोणं देव्यधिष्ठितमध्यं लवत्रुटिकला-काष्ठानिमेषमात्राधिष्ठित षट्कोणं स्मृत्वा राशिचक्रे प्रतित्रिकोणं चतुरस्रं लिखित्वा तेषां मध्ये त्रिकोणानि लिखेत् । तत्र चतुरस्रकोणेषु त्रिकोणकोणेषु च घटिका-न्यासः । राशिव्यापकमन्त्रैः वक्ष्यमाणैः तस्मिन् तस्मिन् राशौ व्यापकम् । ततः त्रिकोणमध्ये राशिवर्णैः सह धात्राद्यादित्यन्यासः । ततो वक्ष्यमाणमन्त्रैः राशि-वेधन्यासः । ततस्तदधिपतिवेधन्यासः । पुनः राशिचक्रात् बहिः वृत्तं लिखित्वा तत्र परितः सप्तविंशति त्रिकोणान्यपि लिखित्वा तेषु नक्षत्रन्यासं नक्षत्रदेवतान्यासं नक्षत्रवेधन्यासं च कृत्वा तद्बहिरपि वृत्तं विधाय तत्र त्रिंशत्त्रिकोणात्मकं तिथि-चक्रं लिखित्वा तेषु तिथिन्यासं तिथिदेवतान्यासं च कृत्वा मेषमीनान्तराले तिथिचक्रे वा करणन्यासं कृत्वा समष्टिमन्त्रेण व्यापयेत् । अथवा राशिचक्र एव नक्षत्रतिथिन्यासोऽपि । तथा चेत् राशिमण्डल एव नक्षत्रमण्डलं तिथिमण्डलं च कार्यम् । इत्यन्तर्बहिर्विभागेन राश्यादिमण्डलरचनाप्रकारो न्यासप्रकारश्चोक्तः ।

अथ मन्त्रविशेषप्रदर्शनार्थं ग्रन्थे व्याख्यायते—भूचक्र इति । समष्टिमन्त्रे भूचक्राय नमः । इति योगो दर्शितः । मेषादिरिति न्यासोपक्रमस्थानं दर्शितम् । मानुष इति । राशिव्यापकमन्त्रेषु लग्नादेः पूर्वं मानुषपदयोगो दर्शितः ॥ ३३ ॥

तेषामेव प्रथमतोऽक्षरयोगक्रमं दर्शयति—आद्यैरिति ॥ ३४॥३५॥३६॥३७ ॥

वर्णानामुपरि राशिनाड़िकासंख्यायोगं दर्शयति—स्यातामिति । अनेनैव नाड़िकान्यासोऽपि दर्शितः ॥ ३७॥३८॥३९ ॥

पादाधिका मकरयुक्सिंहवृश्चिकसंज्ञकाः ।
पादोनौ कुम्भवृषभौ वणिक्कन्ये च पञ्चके ॥ ३८

त्रिपादोनौ मीनमेषौ संख्योक्ता राशिसंश्रिता ।
चापो नीरगयुक्कन्याः पीताः स्युरुभयास्त्वमी ॥ ३९

वणिङ्मकरमेषाह्वकुलीरा रक्तरोचिषः ।
चरा वशिष्टाश्चत्वारः स्थिराः श्वेताः पृथङ्मताः ॥ ४०

स्युः कर्कटो वृश्चिकमीनराशी विप्रा नृपाः सिंहधनुश्च मेषः ।
तुला सकुम्भा मिथुनश्च वैश्याः कन्यावृषौ द्वौ मकरश्च शूद्राः ॥ ४१

आङ्गारावजवृश्चिकौ वृषतुले शुक्रस्य युक्कन्यके
बौधे कर्कटकाह्वयो हिमरुचेः सिंहस्तथा गोपतेः ।
चापाङ्गावपि धैषणौ मकरकुम्भाख्यौ च मान्दौ ग्रहाः
प्रोक्ता राश्यधिपा बलौ च कलशे सोऽयं क्रमो दर्शितः ॥ ४२

लग्नो धनं भ्रातृबन्धुपुत्रशत्रुकलत्रकाः ।
मरणं धर्मकर्मायव्यया द्वादश राशयः ॥ ४३

संख्यायाः परस्ताच्चरस्थिरोभयपदं पीतादिपदं च दर्शयति– चाप इति ॥ ॥ ३८॥४० ॥

चरादिपीताद्योर्मध्ये ब्राह्मणादि पदं दर्शयति—स्युरिति ॥ ४१ ॥

राश्यधिपतिन्यासं दर्शयति—आङ्गाराविति ॥ ४२ ॥

राशिनाम्नः पूर्वं लग्नादियोगं दर्शयति—लग्न इति । अयमत्र प्रयोगक्रमः । क्रीं समस्तकालसाक्षिण्ये संविदे नम इति षट्कोणमध्ये न्यसेत् । क्रीं लवाय नमः । क्रीं त्रुट्यै नमः । क्रीं कलायै नमः । क्रीं काष्ठायै नमः । क्रीं निमिषाय नमः । क्रीं मात्रायै नमः । इति षट्कोणेषु । क्रीं मेषराशि-प्रथमघटिकायै नमः । क्रीं मेषराशिद्वितीयघटिकायै नमः । एवं तृतीय चतुर्थ-घटिकायै नम इति । राशिमध्यचतुरस्रकोष्ठेषु न्यसित्वा । मेषराशिपादाय नम इति चतुरस्रमध्यगतत्रिकोणाग्रकोणे न्यसेत् । एवं सर्वत्र घटिकान्यासो द्रष्टव्यः ।

घटिकान्यासानन्तरं राशिमन्त्रैः तं तं राशिं व्यापयेत् । क्रीं अं आं इं ईं सपादचतुर्घटिकात्मने चरात्मने नृपवर्णात्मने रक्तवर्णाय मनुष्यलग्नाय मेषराशये नमः । उं ऊं ऋं पादोनपञ्चघटिकात्मने स्थिरात्मने शूद्रवर्णात्मने

ततस्तदूर्ध्वभागस्थो भुवश्चक्रः समस्तथा ।
स तु सिंहादिको यस्मिन् पैतृको नियता गतिः ॥ ४४

तदूर्ध्वभागसंस्थः स्यात् स्वश्चक्रश्चाऽपि तादृशः ।
स तु चापादिको दैवश्चक्रस्त्वैनाभिकस्तु सः ॥ ४५

श्वेतवर्णाय मनुष्यधनाय ऋषभराशये नमः । ऋं ॠं लृं ॡं पादाधिकपञ्चघटिकात्मने उभयात्मने वैश्यवर्णात्मने पीतवर्णाय मनुष्यभ्रात्रे मिथुनराशये नमः । एं ऐं अर्धाधिकपञ्चघटिकात्मने चरात्मने ब्राह्मणवर्णात्मने रक्तवर्णाय मनुष्यबन्धवे कर्कटराशये नमः । ओं औं पादाधिकपञ्चघटिकात्मने स्थिरात्मने नृपवर्णात्मने श्वेतवर्णाय मनुष्यपुत्राय सिंहराशये नमः । अं अः शं षं सं हं लं पञ्चघटिकात्मने उभयात्मने शूद्रवर्णात्मने पीतवर्णाय मनुष्यशत्रवे कन्याराशये नमः । कं खं गं घं ङं पञ्चघटिकात्मने चरात्मने वैश्यवर्णात्मने रक्तवर्णाय मनुष्यकलत्राय तुलाराशये नमः । चं छं जं झं ञं पादाधिकपञ्चघटिकात्मने स्थिरात्मने ब्राह्मणवर्णात्मने श्वेतवर्णाय मनुष्यमरणाय वृश्चिकराशये नमः । टं ठं डं ढं णं अर्धाधिक-पञ्चघटिकात्मने उभयात्मने नृपवर्णात्मने पीतवर्णाय मनुष्यधर्माय धनूराशये नमः । तं थं दं धं नं पादाधिकपञ्चघटिकात्मने चरात्मने शूद्रवर्णात्मने रक्तवर्णाय मनुष्यकर्मणे मकरराशये नमः । पं फं बं भं मं पादोनपञ्चघटिकात्मने स्थिरात्मने वैश्यवर्णात्मने श्वेतवर्णाय मनुष्यायाय कुम्भराशये नमः । यं रं लं वं क्षं त्रिपादोनपञ्चघटिकात्मने उभयात्मने ब्राह्मणवर्णात्मने पीतवर्णाय मनुष्यव्ययाय मीनराशये नमः इति व्यापकमन्त्राः ।

अथ धात्रादिन्यासः । मेषराशये नम इत्यादिषु मेषराश्यधिपतये धात्रे नम इत्यादि योज्यं धात्रादि न्यासे ।

अथ राशिविधन्यासः । राशिव्यापकमन्त्रैरेव विध्युर्धनुर्मेषसिंहा इति वक्ष्यमाण-प्रकारेण न्यासः ।

अथ राश्यधिपग्रहन्यासः । तत्र मेषराश्यधिपतये धात्रे नम इत्यादि स्थानेषु मेषराश्यधिपतये अङ्गारकाय नमः । इत्यादिकं प्रक्षिप्य न्यासः कार्यः । अधिपतयश्च आङ्गारकावजवृश्चिकावित्यादिनोक्ताः ॥ ४३ ॥

मूलाधारचक्रवदेव हृच्चक्रेऽपि न्यासः कर्तव्यः । इत्याह—ततस्तदूर्ध्व इति । तत्र न्यासः सिंहादिक इत्याह—स त्विति । लग्नादयश्च पितृलग्नाय सिंहराशये नमः । इत्येवं क्रमेण योज्या इत्याह—यस्मिन्निति ॥ ४४ ॥

मूर्धस्थस्वश्चक्रेऽपि समो न्यास इत्याह—तदूर्ध्व इति । तत्र चापादिको न्यास

धनुस्तु देवलग्नत्वात् समासाल्लग्नमुच्यते ।
विध्युर्धनुर्मेषसिंहा मकरर्षभकन्यकाः ॥ ४६
सकुम्भयुग्मवणिजो मीनवृश्चिककर्कटाः ।
अयन्तु राशिवेधः स्यादन्यो वेधस्तु भात्मकः ॥ ४७
मूलाश्विनीमघाज्येष्ठारेवत्यश्लेषकास्तथा ।
याम्यपूर्वानुपूर्वाहिर्बुध्नपुष्यानुराधकाः ॥ ४८
स्वाती शतभिषार्द्रा च श्रोणारोहिणिहस्तकाः ।
पादं पादत्रयैर्विध्याद् योजयेदधमर्धकैः ॥ ४९

इत्याह स त्विति। चक्रत्रयन्यासानन्तरं त्रैनाभिकाय कालचक्राय नम इति व्यापकमाह—चक्रस्त्रैनाभिक इति ॥ ४५ ॥

धनुर्मासाय देवलग्नाय धनूराशये नम इत्यादि क्रमेण मन्त्रः प्रयोक्तव्य इत्याह—धनुस्त्विति। मासादूर्ध्वं लग्नादिकमुच्यत इत्यर्थः। वेधन्यासप्रकार-मुक्तमाह—विध्युरिति ॥ ४६ ॥ ४७ ॥

नक्षत्रन्यासं वदन् वेधसाम्यात् प्रथमं नक्षत्रवेधन्यासमाह—मूलेति। न्यासक्रमस्तूच्यते। क्ष्रौं अं आं अश्विन्यै नमः। इं भरण्यै नमः। ईं उं ऊं कृत्तिकायै नमः। ऋं ॠं ऌं ॡं रोहिण्यै नमः। एं मृगशीर्षायै नमः। ऐं आर्द्रायै नमः। ओं औं पुनर्वसवे नमः। कं पुष्यायै नमः। खं गं अश्लेषायै नमः। घं ङं मघायै नमः। चं पूर्वफल्गुन्यै नमः। छं जं उत्तरफल्गुन्यै नमः। झं ञं हस्तायै नमः। टं ठं चित्रायै नमः। डं स्वात्यै नमः। ढं णं विशाखायै नमः। तं थं दं अनुराधायै नमः। धं ज्येष्ठायै नमः। नं पं फं मूलायै नमः। बं पूर्वाषाढ़ायै नमः। भं उत्तराषाढ़ायै नमः। मं श्रवणायै नमः। यं रं श्रविष्ठायै नमः। लं शतभिषजे नमः। वं शं पूर्वभाद्रपदायै नमः। षं सं हं उत्तरभाद्रपदायै नमः। लं क्षं अं अः रेवत्यै नमः। इति नक्षत्रचक्रे न्यसेत्।

पुनस्तत्रैव नक्षत्रदेवतान्यासं कुर्यात्। अं आं अश्विन्यधिपतिभ्यामश्विभ्यां नम इत्यादि क्रमेण मन्त्राः द्रष्टव्याः। पुनरेभिरेव मन्त्रैः नक्षत्रवेधन्यासः। स च मूलाश्विन्यादिक्रमेण न्यस्तव्यः। राशिचक्र एव चेत् नक्षत्रन्यासः तदा राश्यर्णैः राशिभिश्च सह न्यासः कार्यः। अं आं इं ईं अश्विनीभरणीकृत्तिकापादात्मने मेषराशये नम इत्यादिक्रमेण मन्त्रा द्रष्टव्याः। एवं उं ऊं ऋं कृत्तिकापादत्रय-रोहिणी मृगशीर्षा पूर्वार्धात्मने वृषभराशये नमः। ॠं ऌं ॡं मृगशीर्षोत्तरा-

चरस्थिरोभयात्मानश्चातुर्वर्ण्यगुणात्मकाः ।
राशिं राश्यधिपास्त्वेवं विध्युर्वेधविधानतः ॥ ५०

एभ्य एव तु राशिभ्यो नक्षत्राणाञ्च सम्भवः ।
स चाऽप्यक्षरभेदेन सप्तविंशतिधा भवेत् ॥ ५१

आभ्यामश्वयुगेर्जाता भरणी कृत्तिका पुनः ।
लिपित्रयाद्रोहिणी च तत्पुरस्ताच्चतुष्टयात् ॥ ५२

एदैतोर्मृगशीर्षार्द्रे तदन्याभ्यां पुनर्वसुः ।
अमसोः केवलो योगो रेवत्यर्थं पृथङ्मतः ॥ ५३

कतस्तिष्यस्तथाऽश्लेषा खगयोर्घङ्योर्मघा ।
चतः पूर्वाऽथ छजयोरुत्तरा झञयोस्तथा ॥ ५४

हस्तश्चित्रा च टठयोः स्वाती डादक्षरादभूत् ।
विशाखा तु ढणोद्भूता तथदेभ्योऽनुराधिका ॥ ५५

र्धार्द्रापुनर्वसुत्रिपादात्मने मिथुनराशये नमः। एं ऐं पुनर्वसुपादपुष्याश्लेषात्मने कर्कटकराशये नमः। ओं औं मघापूर्वोत्तरपादात्मने सिंहराशये नमः। अं अः शं षं सं हं लं उत्तरात्रिपादहस्ताचित्रापूर्वार्धात्मने कन्याराशये नमः। कं खं गं घं ङं चित्रोत्तरार्धस्वातीविशाखात्रिपादात्मने तुलाराशये नमः। चं छं जं झं ञं विशाखापादानुराधाज्येष्ठात्मने वृश्चिकराशये नमः। टं ठं डं ढं णं मूलापूर्वाषाढोत्तराषाढापादात्मने धनूराशये नमः। तं थं दं धं नं उत्तराषाढात्रिपादश्रवणाश्रविष्ठा पूर्वार्धात्मने मकरराशये नमः। पं फं बं भं मं श्रविष्ठोत्तरार्धशतभिषक्पूर्वभाद्रत्रिपादात्मने कुम्भराशये नमः। यं रं लं वं क्षं पूर्वभाद्रपादोत्तरभाद्ररेवत्यात्मने मीनराशये नमः। इति मन्त्रांशाः। प्रथमं राशिगतपूर्वपादत्रिपादार्धत्रिकोणेषु नक्षत्रन्यासं कृत्वोक्तैः मन्त्रैः व्यापयेद्वा ।

नक्षत्रवेधन्यासक्रमं दर्शयति—मूलाश्विनीति। मूलाश्विनीमघा विध्युः। एवं ज्येष्ठा रेवत्यश्लेषकाद्याः ॥ ४८ ॥ ४९ ॥

पूर्वोक्तराशिव्यापकमन्त्रक्रमं सूचयति—चरेति। राश्यधिपन्यासे राशिवेधन्यासे चोक्तमेव मन्त्रं सविशेषं सूचयति—राश्यधिपास्त्विति ॥ ५० ॥

नक्षत्रन्यासेऽक्षरयोगक्रममाह—एभ्य एव त्विति ॥५१॥५२॥५३॥५४॥५५॥५६॥
॥५७॥५८॥५९॥

ज्येष्ठा धकारान्मूलाख्या नफफेभ्यो बतस्तथा ।
पूर्वाषाढ़ा भतोऽन्या च संजाता श्रवणा मतः ॥ ५६

श्रविष्ठाख्या च यरयोस्तथा शतभिषा लतः ।
वशयोः प्रोष्ठपत्संज्ञा षसहेभ्यः परा स्मृता ॥ ५७

ताभ्याममोभ्यां लार्णोऽयं यदा वै सह वत्स्यते ।
तदेन्दुसूर्ययोर्योगादमावास्या प्रकीर्त्यते ॥ ५८

कषतो भुवनं मत्तः कषयोः सङ्गमो भवेत् ।
ततः क्षकारः सञ्जातो नृसिंहस्तस्य देवता ॥ ५९

स पुनः षसहैः सार्द्धं परप्रोष्ठपदं गतः ।
कारस्कराख्यामलकोदुम्बरा जम्बुसंज्ञकः ॥ ६०

खदिरः कृष्णवंशौ च पिप्पलो नागरोहिणौ ।
पलाशप्लक्षकाम्बष्ठबिल्वार्जुनविकङ्कताः ॥ ६१

वकुलः सरलः सर्जो वञ्जुलः पनसार्ककौ ।
शमीकदम्बाम्रनिम्बमधूकान्ता दिनाङ्घ्रिपाः ॥ ६२

आयुष्कामः स्वर्क्षवृक्षं छेदयेन्न कदाचन ।
सिञ्चयेद्वर्धयेच्चापि पूजयेत् प्रणमेत्तथा ॥ ६३

तिथिनक्षत्रवारेषु तेषु मन्त्रजपो वरः ।
तस्मादेषां दिनानाञ्च वक्ष्यन्ते देवतादयः ॥ ६४

अश्वियमानलधातृशशिरुद्रादितिसुरेज्यसर्पाश्च
पित्र्यर्यमभगदिनकृत्त्वष्टारो मरुतस्तथेन्द्राग्नी ।

मित्रेन्द्रौ निर्ऋतिजले विश्वेदेवा हरिस्तथा वसवः
वरुणोऽजैकपादहिर्बुध्नः पूषा च देवता भानाम् ॥ ६५

अश्वेभाजभुजङ्गसर्पसरमामार्जारिकाजाकुली
मूषा मूषिकरुद्रयानमहिषीव्याघ्रा यमारोहणम् ।

नक्षत्रवृक्षकथनम् उत्तरत्र प्रयोगार्थम् ॥ ६०॥६१॥६२॥६३ ॥

नक्षत्रदेवतान्यासं सूचयति—अश्वीति ॥ ६४॥६५॥६६ ॥

व्याघ्रेणी हरिणी प्लवानरपशुः शाखामृगः स्त्री हयो
मर्त्यो गौः करिणीति साधु कथिता नक्षत्रयोन्यः क्रमात् ॥ ६६

एभ्योऽमावास्यान्ता वर्त्तन्ते प्रतिपदादिकास्तिथयः ।
राशिभ्योऽत्र तिथीनामध्यर्धयुगन्तु राशिरेकः स्यात् ॥ ६७

तेन त्रिंशत्तिथयो द्वादशधा वर्णभेदतो भिन्नाः ।
ता एव स्युर्द्वेधा पुनरपि पूर्वान्त्यपक्षभेदेन ॥ ६८

पक्षः पञ्चदशाहः स्यात् पूर्वः प्रतिपदादिकः शुक्लः ।
तद्वज्ज्ञेयोऽप्यपरः पक्षः कृष्णः प्रतिपदादिकः प्रोक्तः ॥ ६९

संज्ञासाम्ये सत्यपि सौम्यात्तु ह्रासवृद्धितस्तिथयः ।
न समाः पक्षद्वितये त्रिंशद्भेदं तथाहि संप्राप्ताः ॥ ७०

अग्न्यश्विमाः सविघ्ननागा गुहसवित्रमातरो दुर्गा ।
ककुभो धनपतिविष्णुयमहरचन्द्राः क्रमेण तिथ्यधिपाः ॥ ७१

तिथिन्यासं सूचयति—एभ्य इति। हं शुक्लपक्षाय नमः। सः कृष्णपक्षाय नमः। इति तिथिमण्डलदक्षिणवामभागयोः न्यसेदिति पक्षन्यासः। हं अं शुक्लप्रथमाकलायै नमः इत्यादि। हं अं शुक्लपञ्चदशीकलायै नम इत्यन्तं तिथिमण्डलवामभागे विन्यस्य। सः कं खं कृष्णप्रथमाकलायै नमः। सः गं घं कृष्णद्वितीयाकलायै नमः। एवं सः ङं चं कृष्णतृतीयाकलायै नम इत्यारभ्य सः वं शं षं कृष्णपञ्चदशीकलायै नम इत्यन्तं दक्षिणभागे न्यसेत्।

पुनः तिथ्यधिपतिन्यासं कुर्यात्। हं अं शुक्लप्रथमाकलाधिपतयेऽग्नये नम इत्यादिमन्त्रैस्तिथ्यधिपतिन्यासः। पक्षद्वयेऽप्यग्न्याद्या एव वक्ष्यमाणा देवताः।

राशिचक्र एव वा पूर्वार्धत्रिपादक्रोणेषु तिथ्यादिन्यासः। अथवा तिथिचक्रे तिथिन्यासं कृत्वा। राशिचक्रे तिथिन्यासं कुर्यात्। अं आं इं ईं शुक्लप्रथमाद्वितीयातृतीयार्धकलात्मने मेषराशये नम इत्यादिमन्त्रैः तत्तद्राशिस्थानेषु व्यापयेदिति न्यासप्रकारः।

एभ्योऽमावास्यान्ता वर्तन्त इत्यनेन राशिचक्रे तिथिन्यासो दर्शितः ॥ ६७ ॥

वर्णभेदतो भिन्ना इति। तिथिचक्रन्यासे वर्णविशेषयोगमाह। ता एवेति पक्षन्यासः सूचितः ॥ ६८ ॥

प्रतिपदादिकः शुक्ल इति न्यासमन्त्रांशाः सूचिताः ॥ ६९ ॥ ७० ॥

राशिभ्यः सदिनेभ्यः सतिथिभ्यः शक्तिजृम्भणसमुत्थात् ।
अक्षरभेदविकारात् करणानि च सप्तभेदकान्यभवन् ॥ ७२

सिंहव्याघ्रवराहाः खरगजवृषकुक्कुराः प्रतिपदर्धात् ।
अन्त्यात्तिथ्यर्धार्धं तिष्ठन्त्याकृष्णगोश्चतुर्दश्याः ॥ ७३

एवं सग्रहराशिकदिनतिथिकरणप्रभेदकाः कथिताः ।
अस्मात् पञ्चविभागाद्विज्ञेया पञ्चवर्णनिष्पत्तिः ।
वर्णाः पीतश्वेतारुणासितश्यामकास्तथा क्वाद्याः ॥ ७४

इति मूलाक्षरविकृतं
कथितमिदं वर्णविकृतिबाहुल्यम् ।
सचराचरस्य जगतो
मूलत्वान्मूलताऽस्य बीजस्य ॥ ७५

अग्न्यश्वेति । तिथ्यधिपतिन्यासः उक्तः ॥ ७१ ॥

करणन्यासं सूचयति—राशिभ्य इति । करणपञ्चकन्यासे गते तिथियुक्त-राशिमन्त्रेण व्यापकं सूचितम् । सदिनेभ्य इति प्रतिपर्यायं सप्तग्रहयोगः सूचितः । सतिथिभ्य इति तत्तत्तिथ्यर्धयोगः सूचितः । न्यासस्थानं च तिथिमण्डलं सूचितम् । शक्तिजृम्भणसमुत्थादित्यादिना शक्तिसहितानां षष्टिसंख्यानां वर्णानां योगः सूचितः ।

क्लीं सूर्यात्मने सिंहकरणाय शुक्लप्रतिपदप[दुत्त]रार्धात्मने नम इति प्रतिपच्चक्रापरार्धे विन्यस्य । क्लीं अं सोमात्मने व्याघ्रकरणाय शुक्लद्वितीया-प्रथमार्धात्मने नम इति द्वितीयाचक्रप्रथमार्धे न्यसेत् । इत्यादिक्रमेण न्यासमन्त्रा ऊह्याः । पश्चिमृगसर्पकीटकरणानि अवशिष्टानि केतुराहुग्रहौ ॥ ७२॥७३ ॥

कालसमष्टिमन्त्रव्यापकं सूचयति - एवमिति । क्लीं राशिग्रहनक्षत्रतिथि-करणात्मने पृथिव्यप्तेजोवाय्वाकाशात्मने त्रैनाभिकाय कालचक्राय नम इति मन्त्रः ॥ ७४ ॥

सर्वमन्त्रेषु शक्तियोगं सूचयति—इतीति ।

व्याप्तिन्यासकथनफलम् उपसंहरन् अवसाने हृल्लेखया व्यापकमाह—सचरा-चरस्येति । अस्य साधकस्यैव न्यस्तविग्रहस्य बीजस्य मन्त्रस्य मूलकारणात्मता एवं सिद्धेत्यर्थः ॥ ७५ ॥

यां ज्ञात्वा सकलमपास्य कर्मबन्धं
तद्विष्णोः परमपदं प्रयाति लोकः ।
तामेतां त्रिजगति जन्तुजीवभूतां
हृल्लेखां जपत च नित्यमर्चयीत ॥ ७६

इति श्रीप्रपञ्चसारे चतुर्थः पटलः ।

कालचक्रयोगं दर्शयन् पटलमुपसंहरति—यामिति । न्यासानन्तरं जपादिकं चानेनैव सूचितम् । त्रिजगतीति चक्रात्मके जगत्त्रये ये जन्तवः तेषां जीवभूतां तेषु प्रविश्य जीवात्मतां प्राप्तां परां चिन्मात्ररूपामिति कालचक्रयोगक्रमः सूचितः । सकलं हृल्लेखां ज्ञात्वा जपतेति हृद्यम् ॥ ७६ ॥

* अत्र लग्न इत्यादिना राश्यानुकूल्यस्य सूचितत्वात् राशिनक्षत्रनामार्णानुकूल्यं संक्षेपत उच्यते । यस्मिन् राश्यक्षरगणे साधकस्य नामाद्यक्षरं दृष्टं तं राशिमारभ्य मन्त्रस्याद्यक्षरसम्बन्धराश्यन्तं लग्नादिभिर्गणयेत् । तत्र धनभ्रातृबन्धुपुत्रकलत्रधर्मायानाम् अन्यतमरूपा ये मन्त्राक्षरयुक्तराशिवर्णास्ते ग्राह्या इति ।

राश्यानुकूल्यमन्यथाऽपि उच्यते । प्रथमपञ्चमनवमा बान्धवः । द्वितीयषष्ठदशमाः सेवकाः । तृतीयसप्तमैकादशाः पोषकाः । द्वादशाष्टमचतुर्था घातकाः । स्वराशिमारभ्य गणनं त्रिनवखण्डं मण्डलं कृत्वा तेषु अश्विन्याद्यक्षराण्यग्रकोष्ठादारभ्य लिखित्वा

जन्म सम्पत् विपत् क्षेमः प्रत्यरिः साधको बधः ।
मैत्रं परममैत्रं च जन्मादिषु पुनः पुनः ॥

इत्युक्तप्रकारेण स्वनामाक्षरं स्वनक्षत्राक्षरं चारभ्य मन्त्राक्षरपर्यन्तं गणिते सम्पत्क्षेमसाधकमैत्र परममैत्राणाम् अन्यतमं चेत् भवति तर्हि शोभनम् ।

अथ नामानुकूल्यं षोडशकोष्ठं मण्डलमालिख्य ईशानकोष्ठमारभ्य एकैकान्तरितम् अकारादिक्षकारान्तानि अक्षराणि तत्र लिखित्वा । नामाद्यक्षरयुक्तं खण्डचतुष्टयम् आरभ्य सिद्धसाध्यसुसिद्धारित्वेन जानीयात् । सिद्धसिद्धो यथोक्तजपादिना सिध्यति । सिद्धसाध्यो द्विगुणात् । सिद्धसुसिद्धोऽर्धेन । सिद्धारिर्बान्धवान् हन्ति । साध्यसिद्धादयो विघ्नैरर्थक्षयस्त्रीनाशगोत्रनाशान् प्रयच्छन्ति । सुसिद्धसिद्धोऽर्धजपात् । तत्साध्यः त्रि[द्वि]गुणजपात् । तत्सुसिद्धो ग्रहणादेव सिद्धिदः । तदरिर्ज्ञातिहानिदः । अरिसिद्धादयः पुत्रपुत्रीपत्न्यात्महानिदाः ।

नृसिंहार्कवराहाणां प्रासादप्रणवस्य च वैदिके पिण्डमन्त्रे च न सिद्धादि-परीक्षणमावश्यकम्।

अथ कुलाकुलविभागः।

मन्त्रनामाद्यक्षरयोः एकभूतसम्बन्धित्वे एककुलता। पार्थिवानाम् आप्यानि मित्राणि। आग्नेयानां मारुतानि मित्राणि। पार्थिवाप्यानां मारुतानि शत्रवः। आग्नेयानाम् आप्यानि शत्रवः। आप्यानां तैजसानि च शत्रवः। नाभसानि सर्वाविरुद्धानीति।

अथ ऋणधनविभागः। साधकनामाक्षराणि मन्त्राक्षराणि च अजभक्तिविभागेन गणित्वाऽष्टभ्यः परित्यक्ते यस्याऽक्षरमधिकं भवति सोऽधमर्णः। अन्यः उत्तमर्णः। साधकाक्षरस्योत्तमर्णत्वे शोभनम्।

शत्रुमरणादिशब्देन मन्त्रदोषाणामपि सूचितत्वात् तच्छुद्धये प्रयोगः कथ्यते। योनिबन्धपूर्वकं बीजबिन्द्वादिक्रमेण उन्मन्यन्तं गत्वा तत्रस्थो यं मन्त्रं सहस्रवारमावर्तयेत् स शुद्धो निर्दोषो भवति।

मातृकापद्मं लिखित्वा स्वेष्टमन्त्रं तत उद्धरेत्। इदं जननम्। प्रणवान्तरितान् मन्त्रवर्णान् जपेत् शतावृत्त्या। एतज्जीवनम्। भूर्जे मन्त्रवर्णानालिख्य वायुबीजेन प्रत्येकं शतं शतं ताडयेत्। एतत्ताडनम्। तथैव लिखित्वा मन्त्रवर्णसंख्यं करवीरपुष्पैरग्निबीजेन ताडयेत्। एतत् बोधनम्। स्वतन्त्रोक्तप्रकारेणाऽश्वत्थपल्लवेनाऽष्टशतमभिषिञ्चेत्। अयमभिषेकः। सञ्चिन्त्य मनसा मन्त्रान् ज्योतिर्मन्त्रेण मलत्रयं संदहेत्। एतद्विमलीकरणम्। ओं ह्रौं नम इति ज्योतिर्मन्त्रः। स्वजप्तेन कुशोदकेन प्रतिवर्णप्रोक्षणम् आप्यायनम्। नाम्ना स्वेन तर्पणं तर्पणम्। तारमाया रमायोगो दीपनम्। अन्येषामप्रकाशनं गोपनम्। इत्थं दशधा शोधिते छिन्ना रुद्धा इत्यादयो दोषाः नश्यन्ति। *

इति श्रीपद्मपादाचार्यकृते प्रपञ्चसारविवरणे
चतुर्थः पटलः।

पञ्चमः पटलः ।

अथ प्रवक्ष्ये विधिवन्मनूनां दीक्षाविधानं जगतो हिताय ।
येनोपलब्धेन समाप्नुवन्ति सिद्धिं परत्रेह च साधकेशाः ॥ १

दद्याच्च दिव्यभावं क्षिणुयाद्दुरितान्यतो भवेद्दीक्षा ।
मननात्तत्त्वपदस्य त्रायते इति मन्त्रमुच्यते भयतः ॥ २

दैवादिकस्याऽप्यथ मानुषादेः पित्र्यादिकस्याऽप्यथ वत्सरस्य ।
आदिं समारभ्य समग्रसम्पद्‌यत्नेन दीक्षाविधिमारभेत ॥ ३

शुभकर्मणि दीक्षायां मण्डपकरणे गृहादिविधिषु तथा ।
विहितो वास्तुबलिः स्याद्रक्षोविघ्नोपशान्तिसम्पद्भ्यः ॥ ४

अभवत् पुराऽथ किल वास्तुपुमानिति विश्रुतो जगदुपद्रवकृत् ।
चतुरस्रसंस्थितिरसौ निहतो निहितः क्षितौ सुरगणैर्दितिजः ॥ ५

अदीक्षितानामुक्तन्यासादिषु अनधिकारात् तत्सिद्धये साङ्गोपाङ्गदीक्षाकथनाय पञ्चम षष्ठपटलारम्भः ।

अतोऽथशब्दो हेत्वर्थः । विधिवदिति वेदाविरुद्धत्वमुक्तम् । जगतो हितार्थत्वमेव दर्शयति—येनेति । न केवलं दीक्षालाभमात्रेण ऐहिकामुष्मिक पुरुषार्थलाभः । किन्तु तत्पूर्वकमन्त्रसाधनादेव इत्याह—साधकेशा इति ॥ १ ॥

दीक्षाशब्दनिर्वचनेन दीक्षायाः सिद्धिदानसामर्थ्यं दर्शयति—दद्यादिति । दाञ् दाने । क्षि क्षये । इति धातुद्वयनिष्पन्नत्वात् दीक्षाशब्दस्येत्यर्थः । दीक्षाया अपि मन्त्रयोगः सामर्थ्यहेतुरिति वदन् मनुशब्दपर्यायं मन्त्रपदं निर्वक्ति—मननादिति ॥ २ ॥

दीक्षाकालं नियमयन्नाचार्यस्य नियममाह—दैवादिकस्येति । दैवशब्दादय आदौ येषां वत्सराणां ते तथोक्ताः । आदिं पूर्वपक्षमित्यर्थः । देवा ब्रह्माद्याः पञ्चमूर्तयो हृदादिस्थानगताः । मानुषः साधकः पिता आचार्यः । एषामादिभूतस्य वत्सरस्य वत्सान् देवादीन् व्याप्य रौतीति वत्सरः । तस्यादिं सर्वव्यापिन्यादिशक्तिं समालभ्य समः शिष्यात्मनः अग्रसम्पत्तिः परमपदप्राप्तिस्तत्साधकेन यत्नविशेषेण युक्तः सन् आचार्यो दीक्षाविधिमारभेत् इत्याचार्यस्य नियम उक्तः ॥ ३ ॥

तद्देहसंस्थिता ये देवास्ते विश्रुतास्त्रिपञ्चाशत् ।
मण्डलमध्येऽभ्यर्च्या यथा तथोक्तक्रमेण वक्ष्यन्ते ॥ ६

कृत्वाऽवनिं समतलां चतुरस्रकृप्ता-
मष्टाष्टकोद्यतपदाञ्च सकोणसूत्राम् ।
तस्यां चतुष्पदसमन्वितमध्यकोष्ठे
ब्रह्मा तु साधकवरेण समर्चनीयः ॥ ७

प्रागयाम्यवारुणोदग्दिक्कोष्ठचतुष्पदेषु समभियजेत् ।
आर्यकमथ सविवस्वत्संज्ञमथ मित्रं महीधरं क्रमशः ॥ ८
कोणद्वयार्धकोष्ठेष्वर्च्याः सावित्रसवित्रशक्राह्वाः ।
सेन्द्रजयरुद्रतज्जयसापश्च वत्सकस्तथाऽग्न्याद्याः ॥ ९
अस्त्रे पार्श्वोत्थपदे द्वन्द्वे शर्वं गुहार्यमणौ च यजेत् ।
जम्भकपिलिपिच्छाख्यौ चरकिविदार्यौ च पूतना प्रोक्ता ॥ १०
अर्धपदाद्यन्तासु च चतसृषु दिक्षु क्रमेण बहिरर्च्याः ।
वासवयमजलेशशशिनामष्टावष्टौ च मन्त्रिणा विधिना ॥ ११
ईशानाख्यः सपर्जन्यो जयन्तः शक्रभास्करौ ।
सत्यो वृषोऽन्तरिक्षश्च देवताः प्रागुदीरिताः ॥ १२
अग्निः पूषा च वितथो यमश्च गृहरक्षकः ।
गन्धर्वो भृङ्गराजश्च मृगो दक्षदिगाश्रिताः ॥ १३
निर्ऋतिर्दौवारिकश्च सुग्रीवो वरुणस्तथा ।
पुष्पदन्तासुरौ शेषोरगौ प्रत्यग्दिगाश्रिताः ॥ १४

उद्यतपदाञ्चेति चकारेण कोणचतुष्के कोष्ठचतुष्कमपरं गुरुगणेशदुर्गाक्षेत्रेश-यजनार्थं सूचितम्। ब्रह्मा त्विति तस्य सरस्वतीसाहित्यमुक्तम् । साधकवरेणेति। मध्ये ब्रह्मपीठादिपूजनमुक्तम् । अणिमादिसर्वसिद्ध्यन्ता ब्रह्मनवशक्तयः। ओं सर्वज्ञानक्रियाव्यक्तकमलासनाय योगपीठाय नम इति पीठमन्त्रः। ओं नमो ब्रह्मण इति मूलमन्त्रः। प्रजापतिः ऋषिः। पंक्तिश्छन्दः। ब्रह्मा देवता। अक्षरैरङ्गानि। स्रुक्स्रुवदण्डकमण्डलुधरो ब्रह्मा ध्येयः ॥ ४॥५॥६॥७ ॥

कोणेषु स्थितमर्धकोष्ठद्वयं कोणद्वयार्धकोष्ठं तेष्वित्यर्थः ॥ ८॥९॥१० ॥

मन्त्रिणेति। ब्रह्मणः पार्श्वयोः विष्णुरुद्रयोः स्वस्वमन्त्रेण पूजनमुक्तम् ।

वायुर्नागश्च मुख्यश्च सोमो भल्लाट एव च ।
अर्गलाख्यो दितिस्तद्वददितिः सौम्यदिग्गताः ॥ १५
इतीरितानामपि देवतानां चित्राणि कृत्वा रजसा पदानि ।
पयोऽम्भसा साधु बलिः प्रदेयो द्रव्यैश्च वा तन्त्रविशेषसिद्धैः ॥ १६
भूयो भूमितले समे विरहिते रोमास्थिलोष्टादिभिः
कर्तव्यं नवसप्तपञ्चकमितैर्हस्तैः परीणाहतः ।
युक्तं द्वारचतुष्ककल्पितपयोभूरुट्चतुस्तोरणं
दर्भस्रक्परिवीतमुज्ज्वलतरं स्यात् संवृतं मण्डपम् ॥ १७
सप्ताहतो वा नवरात्रतो वा प्रागेव दीक्षादिवसाद् यथावत् ।
सपालिकापञ्चमुखीशरावचतुष्टये बीजनिवापमुक्तम् ॥ १८
अन्यस्मिन् भवने सुसंवृततरे शुद्धे स्थले मण्डलं
कुर्यात् प्राग्वरुणायतं पदचतुष्कोपेतभानूदरम् ।

विधिनेति । पीठादिपूजापूर्वकमित्यर्थः ॥ ११॥१२॥१३॥१४॥१५ ॥

इतीरितानामपीति अपिशब्दः क्षेत्रपालादिसूचनार्थः । साध्विति मुष्टिमात्रैः दर्भाग्रैः सकूर्चैः पदानि आस्तीर्य तां तां देवतामावाह्य जलादिभिः सम्पूज्य प्रणवशक्तिपूर्वैः नमोऽन्तैः नामभिः बलिर्देय इत्यर्थः । द्रव्यैश्च वा तन्त्रेति । दध्याज्यगुडमिश्रमन्नं ब्रह्मणः पायसक्रसरमाषान्नमुद्गान्नगुलान्नघृतान्नदध्यन्नैरेकैकस्य वर्गस्य बलिरित्यर्थः ॥ १६ ॥

रोमादिकमुद्धृत्य पुण्याहं वाचयित्वा शुभनक्षत्रादियुते काले मण्डपं विधातव्यम् । एककलशपक्षे पञ्चहस्तं मण्डपम् । नवकलशपक्षे सप्तहस्तम् । अष्टोत्तरशतपक्षे नवहस्तम् । सहस्रपक्षे सप्तपञ्चकमितम् । पञ्चत्रिंशद्धस्तमानमित्यर्थः । स च षोडशस्तम्भयुतः । मध्ये चत्वारः प्रान्तेऽवशिष्टाः । मध्या अष्टहस्तप्रमाणाः । अन्ये पञ्चहस्तप्रमाणाः । तेषां पञ्चमोंऽशो भूमौ खातव्यः । तोरणस्तम्भाः सप्तहस्ताः । तदर्धाः फलकाः । शूलानि हस्तमानानि । ध्वजाष्टकं लोकपालप्रभम् । मध्येऽरत्निमात्रोन्नतं मण्डलार्थं स्थानं कल्पयेत् ॥ १७ ॥

दीक्षादिवसात् यथावदिति । पुण्याहादिपुरःसरमित्यर्थः ॥ १८ ॥

अन्यस्मिन् भवने दीक्षामण्डपोत्तरभागस्थ इत्यर्थः । पदचतुष्केति । पञ्चहस्तप्रमाणानि द्वादशाङ्गुलान्तराणि पूर्वापरायतानि पञ्च सूत्राणि निपात्य । दक्षिणोत्तरसूत्राण्येकादशाऽर्पयित्वा । पङ्क्त्या सर्वतो वीथ्यो विधातव्याः ।

पीतारक्तसितासितं प्रतिपदं वज्राद्यदिशर्वान्तिमं
याम्योदीच्यसमायतं प्रणिगदन्त्यन्ये च तन्मन्त्रिणः ॥ १९
वैष्णव्यस्त्वथ पालिका अपि चतुर्विंशाङ्गुलोच्छ्रायका
वैरिञ्च्यो घटिकास्तु पञ्चवदना द्वाष्टाङ्गुलोत्सेधकाः ।
शैवाः स्युर्द्विषड़ङ्गुला अपि शरावाह्वा जलक्षालिताः
सूत्रैश्च प्रकलय्य पङ्क्तिषु च ताः प्रोक्तक्रमाद्विन्यसेत् ॥ २०
पृथगपि शालीतण्डुलपूर्णासु सदर्भबद्धकूर्चासु ।
मृद्वालुकाकरीषैः क्रमेण पूर्णानि तानि पात्राणि ॥ २१
शालीकङ्गुश्यामाकतिलसर्षपमुद्गमाषनिष्पावाः ।
खल्वाढकिसमेता बीजानि विदुः प्ररोहयोग्यानि ॥ २२
प्रक्षाल्य तानि निवपेदभिमन्त्र्य मूल-
बीजेन साधकवरस्त्वथ पात्रकेषु ।
विप्राशिषा च विधिवत् प्रतिपाद्यमान-
शङ्खादिमुख्यतरपञ्चमहास्वनैश्च ॥ २३
हारिद्राद्भिः सम्यगभ्युक्ष्य वस्त्रैराच्छाद्याऽद्भिः सिच्यतां पञ्चघोषैः ।
सायंप्रातःशर्वरीषु प्रदद्यादुक्तैर्द्रव्यैस्तद्बलिं साधकेशः ॥ २४
भूतपितृयक्षनागब्रह्मशिवा देवताश्च विष्ण्वन्ताः ।
ताभ्यः क्रमेण रात्रिषु सप्तसु नवसु वा तद्बलिर्देयः ॥ २५

ततश्चोक्तरजसाऽऽपूर्य वीथ्यः श्यामेन पूरणीयाः इत्यर्थः ॥ १९ ॥

अपि चतुर्विंशाङ्गुलोच्छ्रायका इति तदर्धमुखविस्तारः सूचितः । मुखार्धाधोविस्तारश्च । घटिकास्त्विति । षड़ङ्गुलमुखपरिमाणत्वं तावत् परिमाणपृष्ठत्वं चोक्तम् । द्विषड़ङ्गुला अपीति । द्वादशाङ्गुलमुखत्वं तदर्धाधोभागत्वं चोक्तम् । पङ्क्तिषु चेति पश्चिमादि विन्यसेदित्यर्थः । प्रोक्तक्रमो वज्राद्यदिशर्वान्तिकः ॥ २०॥२१॥२२ ॥

साधकवर इति प्रक्षालनायाऽमृतबीजं सूचितम् । दुन्दुभ्यादयस्तालादयो वीणादयो मुखवाद्यादयः शङ्खादयश्च पञ्चमहाशब्दाः । विधिवत् प्रतिपाद्यमानेति । उचिततालशब्द विशेषेणेत्यर्थः ॥ २३ ॥

तद्बलिं साधकेश इति । प्रागादिदिक्षु दानं सूचितम् ॥ २४—२८ ॥

लाजातिलनक्तरजोदधिशक्त्वन्नानि भूतक्रूराख्यम् ।
पैत्रं तिलतण्डुलकं सोडुम्बरिकधानलाजकं याम्यम् ॥ २६
क्षीरोदशक्तुपिष्टं नागं पद्माद्यतश्च वैरिञ्चम् ।
अन्नापूपं शैवं गुडौदनं वैष्णवं च दौग्धान्नम् ॥ २७
कृशरश्च वैष्णवेयं यदि नवरात्रं क्रमेण बलिरुक्तः ।
तारादिकैर्नमोऽन्तैः स्वैः स्वैरपि नामभिश्च बलिमन्त्रः ॥ २८
पात्राणि वि[वि]विधान्यपि परितः पुनरष्टदिक्षु बलिकॢप्तिः ।
बीजारोपणकर्म प्रथितमिदं सार्वकामिकं भवति ॥ २९

प्रागेव लक्षणयुतानि च मण्डपेऽस्मिन्
कुण्डानि कारयतु सम्यगथो दिशासु ।
आखण्डलार्कसुतवारिधनाधिपानां
दोर्माचकाणि विलसद्गुणमेखलानि ॥ ३०

चतुरस्रमर्धशशिबिम्बविलसितमथ त्रिकोणकम् ।
पद्मदलरुचिरवृत्तमिति ब्रुवते बुधा विधिषु कुण्डलक्षणम् ॥ ३१

विंशत्या चतुरधिकाभिरङ्गुलीभिः
सूत्रेणाऽप्यथ परिसूत्र्य भूमिभागम् ।
ताभिश्च प्रखनतु तावतीभिरेकां
त्यक्त्वा चाऽङ्गुलिमपि मेखलाश्च कार्याः ॥ ३२

सत्त्वपूर्वकगुणान्विताः क्रमात् द्वादशाष्टचतुरङ्गुलोच्छ्रिताः ।
सर्वतोऽङ्गुलिचतुष्कविस्तृता मेखलाः सकलसिद्धिदा मताः ॥ ३३

योनिस्तत्पश्चिमायामथ दिशि चतुरस्रस्थलारब्धनाला
तन्मध्योल्लासिरन्ध्रोपरि परिविततश्वत्थपत्रानुकारा ।

प्रागेवेति मण्डलनिर्माणादित्यर्थः ॥ ३० ॥ ३१ ॥

ताभिश्च प्रखनत्विति । मेखलोच्छ्रायेण सार्धमिति द्रष्टव्यम् । तावतीभिः मेखलाश्च कार्या इति । मेखलाविस्तारः समुच्चित्योक्तः । तत्राधो मेखलाविस्तारो द्वादशाङ्गुलः । मध्यमेखलाया अष्टाङ्गुलः । ऊर्ध्वमेखलायाश्चतुरङ्गुलः । इति मिलित्वा चतुर्विंशाङ्गुलविस्तारत्वं विवक्षितम् । उच्छ्रायश्चैवमेव द्रष्टव्यः । ॥ ३२ ॥ ३३ ॥

उत्सेधायामकाभ्यां प्रकृतिविकृतिसंज्ञाङ्गुलाऽष्टाङ्गुला स्या-
द्विस्तृत्या द्वादशार्धाङ्गुलामतनमिताग्रा निविष्टैव कुण्डे ॥ ३४
अथवा दिशि कुण्डमुत्तरस्यां प्रविदध्याच्चतुरस्रमेकमेव ।
गदितैरपि लक्षणैः समेतापघनं दृष्टिमनोहरञ्च कान्त्या ॥ ३५

ततो मण्डपमध्ये तु स्थण्डिलं गोमयाम्बुना ।
उपलिप्य यथान्यायं तस्य मध्ये निधापयेत् ॥ ३६
सूत्रं प्राक्प्रत्यगात्ताग्रं विप्राशीर्वचनैः सह ।
गुणितेनाऽभितो मत्स्यौ मध्यादारभ्य विन्यसेत् ॥ ३७
तन्मध्यस्थितयाम्योदगग्रं सूत्रं निधापयेत् ।
ततो मध्यात् सपञ्चहस्तमानेन च दिशं प्रति ॥ ३८

चतुरस्रस्थलेति । पृथिवीस्थानारब्धनालेत्यर्थः । तन्मध्योल्लासिरन्ध्र इति । तस्य नालस्य मध्यमेखलाया वा मध्ये विलसितरन्ध्रेत्यर्थः । उत्सेधायामका-भ्यामिति । उत्सेधेन आयामेन च प्रकृतिविकृतिसंज्ञाङ्गुलाऽष्टाङ्गुला च प्रत्येकं पञ्चदशाङ्गुलेत्यर्थः । द्वादशार्धाङ्गुलेति । उपक्रमे द्व्यङ्गुला । ततो दशाङ्गुला । मध्ये पञ्चाङ्गुला । अवसानेऽङ्गुलविस्तृतेत्यर्थः । शतार्धहोमे मुष्टिमितानि कुण्डानि । शतहोमेऽरत्निमितानि । सहस्रहोमे पञ्चाङ्गुलाधिकारत्निमितानि । अयुतहोमे दशाङ्गुलाधिकारत्निमितानि । अर्धलक्षहोमे पञ्चदशाङ्गुलाधिकारत्निमितानि । लक्षहोमे विंशत्यङ्गुलाधिका-रत्निमितानि । पञ्चाशल्लक्षहोमे कोटिहोमे च कराष्टकमितानि । सर्वेष्वपि कुण्डेषु प्रथममेखलोच्छ्रायेण तुल्यं खातम् । कण्ठोऽष्टयवैः हस्तमात्रे अरत्निमात्रे षड्भिः मुष्टिमिते चतुर्भिः अन्येषु अङ्गुलिद्वयवृद्ध्या कण्ठः कर्तव्यः । मुष्टिमिते प्रथमा मेखला दशाङ्गुला । द्वितीयतृतीये त्र्यंशे अरत्निमिते प्रथमा द्वादशाङ्गुला । द्वितीयतृतीये त्र्यंशे हस्तमानेऽपि प्रथमा मेखला द्वादशाङ्गुला । अन्ये पूर्ववत् । अन्येषां कुण्डानामङ्गुलिद्वयवृद्धितः प्रथमा मेखला । अन्ये त्र्यंशे कार्ये । सर्वत्र कण्ठमानेनाऽन्तःप्रविष्टा योनिः कार्या ॥ ३४ ॥ ३५ ॥

यथान्यायमिति । ईशानकोणावसानत्वमभ्युक्षणादिकं च सूचितम् ॥ ३६ ॥

गुणितेनेति । सूत्रद्विगुणितं कृत्वा तेन गुणितेन सूत्रेण प्राक्प्रसृतसूत्रस्या-ऽभितो मध्याद् द्विगुणितस्यापि उभयतो मध्यादारभ्य उभयतो मत्स्यौ विन्यसेदित्यर्थः । सपञ्चहस्तेत्यत्र पादशब्दश्च षट् त्रिंशदङ्गुलवचनः । "पादः षट्

सूत्रेषु मकरान् न्यसेत् स्पष्टानन्योन्यतः समान् ।
सूत्राग्रमकरेभ्यस्तु न्यसेत् कोणेषु मत्स्यकान् ॥ ३९

कोणमत्स्यस्थिताग्राणि दिक्षु सूत्राणि पातयेत् ।
ततो भवेच्चतुष्कोष्ठं चतुरस्रञ्च मण्डलम् ॥ ४०

तत्राऽग्निमारुतं सूत्रं नैर्ऋतेशञ्च पातयेत् ।
प्राग्याम्यवारुणोदीच्यसूत्राग्रमकरेषु च ॥ ४१

निहिताग्रयुगं सूत्रचतुष्कं प्रतिपादयेत् ।
कृते एवं भवेयुस्ते कोणकोष्ठेषु मत्स्यकाः ॥ ४२

तेषु प्राग्वारुणांस्तन्तून् याम्योदीच्यान्निपातयेत् ।
षट्पञ्चाशत्पदानि स्युरधिकानि शतद्वयात् ॥ ४३

यदा तदाऽथो विभजेत् पदानि क्रमशः सुधीः ।
पदैः षोड़शभिर्मध्ये पद्मं वृत्तत्रयान्वितम् ॥ ४४

अष्टचत्वारिंशता तै राशिः स्याद्वीथ्यशीतिभिः ।
सद्वादशैः शतपदैः शोभायुग्द्वारकोणकम् ॥ ४५

द्वाराणि पदषट्कानि शोभाख्याः स्युश्चतुष्पदाः ।
चतुष्पदाश्चोपशोभाः षट्पदं कोणकं भवेत् ॥ ४६

वृत्तवीथ्योरारचयेन्मध्ये सूत्रचतुष्टयम् ।
प्राग्याम्यवारुणोदीच्यं भवेत्तद्राशिमण्डलम् ॥ ४७

कर्णिकायाः केसराणां दलसन्धेर्दलस्य च ।
दलाग्रवृत्तराशीनां वीथ्याः शोभोपशोभयोः ॥ ४८

कृतानि चतुरस्राणि व्यक्तं स्थानानि कल्पयेत् ।
भवेन्मण्डलमध्यार्धे कर्णिका चतुरङ्गुला ॥ ४९

द्व्यङ्गुलाः केसराश्च स्युः सन्धिश्च चतुरङ्गुलः ।
तथा दलानां मानन्तदग्रं द्व्यङ्गुलकं भवेत् ॥ ५०

त्रिंशदङ्गुलः" इत्याप्तवचनात् । यथा यथा स्थित एवार्थः ॥ ३७—४८ ॥

मण्डलमध्यार्धं इति । मण्डलस्य मध्यं मण्डलमध्यं राशिमण्डलान्तः ।

अन्तरालं पृथग्वृत्तत्रये द्व्यङ्गुलमुच्यते ।
ततश्च राशिचक्रं स्यात् स्वस्ववर्णविभूषितम् ॥ ५१

राशिमङ्गुलकैः कुर्यात् षड्भिर्नवभिरेव वा ।
द्वात्रिंशदङ्गुलं ह्येतत् परस्तात्तावदिष्यते ॥ ५२

वृत्तं चक्रमुशन्त्येके चतुरस्रञ्च तद्विदः ।
यदि वा वर्त्तुलमराः स्युश्च द्वादश राशयः ॥ ५३

ते स्युः पिपीलिकामध्या मातुलुङ्गनिभा अपि ।
चक्रं च चतुरस्रं च त्रास्रा द्वादश राशयः ॥ ५४

भवेयुः पङ्कजदलनिभा वा कथिता बुधैः ।
तद्बही रुचिरान् कुर्यात् चतुरः कल्पशाखिनः ॥ ५५

ललितान् रूढकुसुमान् फलपल्लवशोभितान् ।
जलजैः स्थलजैर्वापि सुमनोभिः समन्वितान् ॥ ५६

हंससारसकारण्डशुकभ्रमरकोकिलैः ।
मयूरचक्रवाकाद्यैरारूढविटपानतान् ॥ ५७

सर्वर्तुनिर्वृतिकरान् विलोचनमनोहरान् ।
तद्बहिः पार्थिवं कुर्यान्मण्डलं कृष्णकोणकम् ॥ ५८

मण्डलानि तु तत्त्वज्ञो राश्यन्तान्येव कारयेत् ।
राशावन्यत्र रचयेत् प्रमोहादन्यमण्डलम् ॥ ५९

आवाह्य देवतामन्यामर्चयंस्त्वन्यदेवताम् ।
उभाभ्यां लभते शापं मन्त्री तरलदुर्मतिः ॥ ६०

कालात्मकस्य देवस्य राशेर्व्यक्तिमजानता ।
कृतं समस्तं व्यर्थं स्यादज्ञेन ज्ञानमानिना ॥ ६१

तस्मात् सर्वप्रयत्नेन राशीन् साधिपतीन् क्रमात् ।
अवगम्याऽनुरूपाणि मण्डलानि च नान्यधीः ॥ ६२

तस्याप्यर्धं मध्य इत्यर्थः ॥ ४९ ॥ ५० ॥ ५१ ॥

षड्भिः नवभिरेव वेति । वृत्तराशिपक्षे षड्भिः । त्रास्रराशिपक्षे नवभि-

उपक्रमेदर्चयितुं होतुं वा सर्वदेवताः ।
रजांसि पञ्चवर्णानि पञ्चद्रव्यात्मकानि च ॥ ६३

पीतशुक्लारुणशितिश्यामान्येतानि भूतशः ।
हारिद्रं स्याद्रजः पीतं ताण्डुलञ्च सितं भवेत् ॥ ६४

तथा दोषारजः क्षारसंयुक्तं रक्तमुच्यते ।
कृष्णं दग्धपुलाकोत्थं श्यामं बिल्वदलादिकम् ॥ ६५

सितेन रजसा कार्याः सीमारेखा विपश्चिता ।
अङ्गुलोत्सेधविस्ताराः सर्वा मण्डलकर्मसु ॥ ६६

पीता स्यात् कर्णिका शुक्लपीतरक्ताश्च केसराः ।
दलान्यच्छान्यन्तरालं श्यामचूर्णेन पूरयेत् ॥ ६७

सितरक्तासितैर्वर्णैर्वृत्तत्रयमुदीरितम् ।
नानावर्णविचित्राः स्युश्चित्राकाराश्च वीथयः ॥ ६८

द्वारशोभोपशोभास्राः सितरक्तनिशासिताः ।
राशिचक्रावशिष्टानि कोणान्यस्त्रिषु यानि वै ।
पीठपादानि तानि स्युररुणान्यसितानि च ॥ ६९

अथवाऽरुणानि दलानि च तथा दलसन्धिरप्यसितरुग्भवति ।
असितारुणाच्छरजसा विहितान्यपि वर्त्तुलानि कथयन्त्यपरे ॥ ७०

इति श्रीप्रपञ्चसारे पञ्चमः पटलः ।

रित्यर्थः । द्वात्रिंशदङ्गुलमिति । पादः षट् त्रिंशदङ्गुल इत्यस्मिन् पक्षे पक्षान्तरे अपि त्रिंशद्द्वयाङ्गुलं षष्ठ्यङ्गुलमित्यर्थः ॥ ५२—६८ ॥

राशिचक्रावशिष्टानीति वृत्तराशिपक्षे द्रष्टव्यम् ॥ ६९ ॥

अथवाऽरुणानीति वैष्णवादौ विशेषोऽभिहितः ॥ ७० ॥

इति श्रीपद्मपादाचार्यकृते प्रपञ्चसारविवरणे
पञ्चमः पटलः

षष्ठः पटलः ।

अथ पुनराचम्य गुरुः प्राग्वदनो विष्टरोपविष्टः सन् ।
प्राणायामं सलिपिन्यासं कृत्वा न्यसेत्तदृष्यादीन् ॥ १

अथ पुनरिति । एवं साधनसंपत्त्यानन्तर्यमथशब्दार्थः । पुनराचम्येति । नित्याचमनव्यतिरेकेण पुनराचमनविधानात् । स्नानपूजादिकमपि नित्यानन्तरं पृथक् कर्तव्यमिति सूचितम् । अतस्तदुच्यते । ब्राह्मे मुहूर्त्ते उत्थाय । देवतां ध्यात्वा । कर्मसमर्पणं विधाय । हंसपूजां संकल्प्य । सुशुद्धः । स्वाचान्तः । सकलीकृत्य अस्त्रेण मृदं खनित्वा । हृदयेनादाय । शिरसा जलतीरेऽस्त्रशोधिते धृत्वा । शिखया शर्करादिकमुद्धृत्याऽस्त्रेण संप्रोक्ष्य । नेत्रेण संवीक्ष्य । कवचेन त्रिधा विभज्य । मूलेनाऽभिमन्त्र्य । भागेनाऽस्त्रमन्त्रेणाऽङ्गानि प्रक्षाल्य । भागान्तरमापादतलमस्तकमालिप्य । तीर्थमवगाह्य । निमज्याऽस्त्रमन्त्रं शक्त्यावर्त्य । उन्मज्य आचम्याऽपरं मृद्भागं त्रिधा विभज्याऽस्त्राङ्गमूलैरेकैकमभिमन्त्र्य अस्त्र-जप्तं दिक्षु रक्षार्थं निक्षिप्याऽङ्गजप्तेनात्मानमालभ्याऽपरं हृन्मन्त्रानीते तीर्थे मूलेन विलोड्य । निमज्य मूलं शक्तितोऽनुसन्धाय । साङ्गेन मूलेनाऽभिषिच्य । तीरमागत्या-चम्य । अस्त्रप्रोक्षितं वासः परिधायाचम्य । सकलीकृत्य । पूजाक्रमेण सन्तर्प्योद्वास्य । द्वास्थः सूर्यमुपस्थाय । यागमण्डपं गत्वा । वेदमन्त्रैः आचम्याथर्वाङ्गाग्निभिः संमृज्य । चक्षुरादिकं तत्तद्देवतामन्त्रैरुपस्पृशेत् । पुनः सवित्रेऽर्घ्यं दत्त्वा । सामान्यार्घ्येण द्वारपूजां कुर्यात् । अस्त्रजप्तोदकेन द्वारं संप्रोक्ष्य । गं गणपतये । श्रीं लक्ष्म्यै । सां सरस्वत्यै नम इत्यूर्ध्वभागे संपूज्य । गं गणपतये । क्षं क्षेत्रपालाय । गं गङ्गायै । यं यमुनायै नम इति दक्षसव्यभागयोः । ततो देहल्यामस्त्रं संपूज्याऽस्त्रदृष्ट्यस्त्रोदकास्त्र-पार्ष्णिघातैर्दिव्यादिव्यविघ्नान् उत्सार्य वामशाखाश्रयेण देहलीं लङ्घयित्वा । निर्ऋतिकोणे वास्त्वीशं ब्रह्माणं च संपूज्य । पञ्चगव्यार्घ्यतोयाभ्याम् अस्त्रेण मण्डलमभ्युक्ष्य । मूलमन्त्रेण संवीक्ष्याऽस्त्रेण संप्रोक्ष्य । तेनैव दर्भैः सन्ताड्य । वर्मणाऽभ्युक्ष्य । तेनैव चन्दनागरुकर्पूरैः सन्धूप्य । लाजाचन्दनसिद्धार्थभस्म-दूर्वाकुशाक्षतान् अस्त्रेण सप्तजप्तान्मण्डपे विकीर्याऽस्त्रजप्तदर्भमुष्टिना तान् संमार्ज्य । ईशानकोणे वर्धन्यासनत्वेन तानि सङ्कल्पयेत् । पुण्याहं वाचयित्वाऽत्र ब्राह्मणान् भोजयित्वा तत्र मण्डलमुक्तलक्षणं कर्तव्यमित्येतत् सर्वमुक्तं—गुरुरिति ।

पुनरक्षप्रोक्षिते शुद्धे विष्टरे लिपिपद्ममध्यगप्रणवबिन्दौ प्राङ्मुख उदङ्मुखो वा बद्धासन उपविशेदित्याह—प्राग्वदन इत्यादिना।

विष्टरोपविष्ट इत्यनेनैव गुर्वादिवन्दनस्य अङ्गुलिकरशोधनस्य अपरिच्छिन्नताया जीवरक्षायाश्च सूचितत्वात्। तदुच्यते। विष्टरे परमात्मनि समष्ट्यात्मनि अस्त्रतेजसि गुर्वादिषु च मानसोपवेशो हि विष्टरोपवेशः। श्रीं ह्रीं परमात्माद्यशेषपारम्पर्यक्रमेण स्वगुरुपादाम्बुजं यावत्तावत् प्रणौमि इति शिरसि गुरुपरम्परां नत्वा। गं अस्मद्गुरुभ्यो नमः। गं गणपतये नमः। दुं दुर्गायै नमः। सां सरस्वत्यै नमः। चं क्षेत्रपालाय नमः। पं परमात्मने नमः। इति अंसोर्वंग्रहस्तु नत्वाऽस्त्रेण अङ्गुलिकरशोधनतालत्रयदिग्बन्धनाग्निप्राकारवेष्टनानि विधिवत् विधायाकारादिमन्त्रैः पादादिमस्तकान्तं व्यापकं कुर्वन्। अपरिच्छिन्नतनुर्भूत्वा। जीवरक्षां कुर्यात्। लृं वृं रृं यृं हृं इति पादगुह्यहृन्मुखमस्तकेषु न्यसन्। भूतपारवश्यं हित्वा। ह्रीं स्रं श्रीं इति पादादिमस्तकान्तं व्यापकत्रयं कुर्वन्। कारणबन्धत्यागं चिद्रूपत्वोद्भावनं ब्रह्मलक्षणलक्षितत्वं च स्मृत्वा। हंसः सोऽहमिति मूलादिमस्तकान्तं मस्तकादिमूलान्तं च व्यापयन्। ब्रह्मात्मनोरैक्यं भावयेदिति जीवरक्षाप्रकारः।

अथ प्राणायामः कर्तव्य इत्याह—प्राणायामं सलिपिन्यासमिति। प्रथमं तावत् परिच्छिन्नं वायुं दक्षिणनासापुटेन विरेच्य। वामनासापुटेनापूर्य च सूर्यमण्डलस्थं वायुमण्डलं सबीजं धूम्रवर्णं सञ्चिन्त्य। सूर्यमण्डले स्पर्शवर्णान् विन्यस्य। पूरककाले तयोर्नाभावैक्यं सञ्चिन्त्य। कुम्भककाले शोषयित्वा। दक्षिणनासया विरेच्य। तस्यामेव सवायुमण्डलम् अग्निमण्डलं सञ्चिन्त्याऽग्निमण्डले व्यापकाक्षराणि विन्यस्य। हृदयस्थेनाऽग्निमण्डलेन पूरयन् एकीकृत्य। कुम्भककाले सन्दह्य। वामनासिकया विरेच्य। तस्याममृतमण्डलं सञ्चिन्त्य। तत्र स्वरान् विन्यस्य। तन्मूर्धस्थेनाऽमृतमण्डलेन एकीकृत्य। प्लावनं कुर्यात् इति प्राणायामप्रकारः।

अथवा यादिदशकं सधातुप्राणशक्त्यात्मसु न्यसन् तान् पञ्चीकृतभूतेषु संहरेत्।

अत्र प्राणशब्देनेन्द्रियादि प्रवृत्तिकारणमात्रम् उच्यते। शक्तिशब्देन ज्ञानवृद्धिकरमात्रम्। आत्मशब्देन जीवस्थितिकारणमात्रमिति विभागः। यादिन्यासेन तान् सञ्चिन्त्य। हंस्रौमिति उत्क्रम्य। पञ्चीकृतबीजानि मूर्धादिषु न्यसन् तान् तेषु संयोज्य। क्ष्रौमिति आप्याय्य। पञ्चीकृतपृथिव्यादिसंहाराय प्राणायामपञ्चकं विधाय। समानधनञ्जयान्तःकरणवाक्श्रोत्रपञ्चकेषु मनणअङादिपञ्चकान् न्यसन्

ऋषिर्गुरुत्वाच्छिरसैव धार्यः छन्दोऽक्षरत्वाद्रसनागतं स्यात् ।
धियाऽवगन्तव्यतया सदैव हृदि प्रदिष्टा मनुदेवता च ॥ २

ऋषिवर्षादिकौ धातू स्तो गत्या प्रापणेन च ।
याभ्यामाभ्यां यत्स्वरूपं स गुरुः स्यादृषिवाचकः ॥ ३

इच्छादानार्थकौ धातू स्तश्छदादयश्च दादिकः ।
तयोरिच्छां ददातीति छन्दो मन्त्रार्णवाचकम् ॥ ४

आत्मनो देवताभावप्रदानाद्देवतेति च ।
पदं समस्ततन्त्रेषु विद्वद्भिः समुदीरितम् ॥ ५

हृदयशिरसोः शिखायां कवचाच्यस्त्रेषु सहचतुर्थीषु ।
नत्या हुत्या च वषड् हुं वौषट् फट्पदैः षडङ्गविधिः ॥ ६

तान् सञ्चिन्त्य । यमोमिति उत्क्रम्याऽपञ्चीकृतबीजानि मूर्धादिषु न्यसन् तेषु संयोज्य । ह्रोमित्याप्याय्याऽपञ्चीकृतभूतलयार्थं प्राणायामपञ्चकं विधायाऽकारादिविसर्गान्तं नाभ्यादिगतब्रह्मब्रह्मादिषु न्यसित्वा । ह्रौमिति तानुत्क्रम्य । ह्रीमित्याप्यायनं कुर्वन् । कारणे संयोज्य । सत्वरजस्तमःसाम्यबीजतद्वासनाः संहरन् । प्राणायामषट्कं कृत्वा । कञ्चित्कालं स्वात्मन्यवस्थाय । निरवद्यादिमन्त्रैः व्यापयन् । सर्वं सृष्ट्वा । मातृकान्यासं विधाय । वक्ष्यमाणक्रमेण पीठन्यासं कृत्वा । तत्तन्मूर्तिमन्त्रेण मूर्तिं सङ्कल्प्य । आवाहन स्थापनासन प्रतिष्ठा सन्निधानसन्निरोध स्वयं स्वागत सुस्वागताभिमुख्यावगुण्ठनानि विधाय । करन्यासाङ्गुलिन्यासव्यापकवर्णन्यासादिकान् न्यासान् विधायाङ्गर्ष्यादिकं न्यसेदित्यभिप्रायः ॥ १ ॥

ऋ गतौ । षिङ् प्रापणे । इति एतौ ऋषिवर्षादिकौ धातू गत्या प्रापणेन चार्थेन युक्तौ । आभ्यां निष्पन्न ऋषिशब्दः ।

अथावयवार्थमभिधाय समुदायार्थमाह—यत्स्वरूपं याति स गुरुः स्यादृषिवाचक इति । यस्य परमात्मनः स्वरूपं याति । शिष्यो गुरुश्च सः परमात्मैव गुरुरूपेण स्थितः ऋषिवाचकः । ऋषिशब्दो वाचको यस्य स तथोक्तः इति देवतागुर्वात्मनामैक्यमुक्तम् ॥ २॥३ ॥

छदु इच्छायां दाण् दाने इतीच्छादानार्थौ धातू । तयो रूपं छन्दःशब्दः । समुदायार्थमाह—इच्छां ददातीति ॥ ४ ॥

दिव् क्रीड़ा विजिगीषा व्यवहार द्युति स्तुति मोद मदस्वप्नकान्तिगतिषु तनुलघु तनुकरणे इति धातुद्वयनिष्पन्नो देवताशब्दः ॥ ५ ॥

हृदयं बुद्धिगम्यत्वात् प्रणामः स्यान्नमःपदम् ।
क्रियते हृदयेनाऽतो बुद्धिगम्या नमस्क्रिया ॥ ७
तुङ्गार्थं स्याच्छिरः स्वे स्वे विषयाहरणे द्विठः ।
शिरोमन्त्रेण चोत्तुङ्गविषयाहृतिरीरिता ॥ ८
शिखा तेजः समुद्दिष्टा वषड़ित्यङ्गमुच्यते ।
तत्तेजोऽस्य तनुः प्रोक्ता शिखामन्त्रेण मन्त्रिणः ॥ ९
कव ग्रहण इत्यस्माद्धातोः कवचसम्भवः ।
हुन्तेजस्तेजसा देहो गृह्यते कवचं ततः ॥ १०
नेत्रं दृष्टिः समुद्दिष्टा वौषड्दर्शनमुच्यते ।
दर्शनं दृशि येन स्यात्तत्तेजो नेत्रवाचकम् ॥ ११
असुवसादिकौ धातू स्तः क्षेपचलनार्थकौ ।
ताभ्यामनिष्टमाक्षिप्य चालयेत् फट् पदाग्निना ॥ १२

हृदयमिति परमात्मोच्यते। कथं हृत्स्थबुद्धिगम्यत्वादिति योज्यम्। समुदायार्थमाह—क्रियत इति। हृदयमन्त्रेणान्वयव्यतिरेकैरनात्मनो विविच्यात्मप्रतिपत्तिः क्रियत इत्यर्थः ॥ ६ ॥ ७ ॥

तुङ्गार्थमुत्कृष्टपरमात्मार्थं स्यात्। शिरःशब्दस्तस्मै सर्वविषयाहरणे स्वाहाशब्दो वर्तते। समुदायार्थमाह—शिर इति। उत्तुङ्गे परमात्मनि विषयस्य हृदमन्त्रेण विविक्तस्याहृतिर्विलापनमुक्तम्। शिरोमन्त्रेणेत्यर्थः ॥ ८ ॥

एवमपवादं कृत्वाऽध्यारोपाय शिखामन्त्र इत्याह—शिखेति। तेजश्चिदात्मकं शिखेत्युपदिष्टम्। अङ्गं कार्यकरणात्मकं शरीरं वषड़ित्युच्यते। समुदायार्थमाह—तदिति। अस्य मन्त्रिणः स्वरूपभूतं तेजस्तनुः प्रोक्ता। तमोस्तत्र अध्यस्तत्वादित्यर्थः ॥ ९ ॥

आत्मन्यनात्माध्यासमभिधाय आत्मनोऽनात्मन्यध्यासमाह कवचेन - कव ग्रहण इति। तेजसा चैतन्येन देहः पूर्वोक्तो गृह्यते व्याप्यते यतस्ततः कवचमित्युच्यत इत्यर्थः ॥ १० ॥

अथाध्यासनिवर्तकं ज्ञानमाह नेत्रमन्त्रेण—नेत्रमिति दृष्टिः। दृष्टेः दृष्टिः परमात्मा। दर्शनं तदाकारं ज्ञानम्। समुदायार्थमाह—दर्शनमिति। दृष्टिरूपे परमात्मनीत्यर्थः ॥ ११ ॥

उत्पन्नज्ञानस्य संसारनिवृत्तिमाह अस्त्रेण—असुवसादीति। असुक्षेपणे

अङ्गमन्त्रा इमे प्रोक्ताः सर्वतन्त्रेषु मन्त्रिभिः ।
पञ्चैव यस्य मन्त्रस्य भवन्त्यङ्गानि मन्त्रिणः ॥ १३
सर्वेष्वपि च मन्त्रेषु नेत्रलोपो विधीयते ।
अङ्गुलीषु क्रमादङ्गैरङ्गुष्ठादिषु विन्यसेत् ॥ १४
कनिष्ठान्तासु तद्बाह्यतलयोः करयोः सुधीः ।
अस्त्रेण तालत्रितयं कृत्वा तेनैव बन्धयेत् ॥ १५
दिशो दश क्रमादङ्गषट्कं वा पञ्चकं न्यसेत् ।
जपारम्भे मननान्तु सामान्येयं प्रकल्पना ॥ १६
शङ्खं सगन्धपुष्पाक्षततोयं वामतः प्रविन्यस्य ।
साङ्गं मन्त्रं पूजामूर्तौ न्यसेद् गुरूपदेशेन ॥ १७

त्रस चलन इति धातू स्तः ॥ १२ ॥

मन्त्रिभिरिति सर्वज्ञादिपदयोगः सूचितः। तैश्च ज्ञानानन्दादिमात्रं लक्ष्यं निष्कलनिष्ठस्य। सकलनिष्ठस्य तु सर्वज्ञत्वादिशक्त्यात्मकत्वं तैरुच्यते। हृदयादि-शब्दैरपि परिच्छिन्नापरिच्छिन्नसर्वज्ञत्वादिशक्त्यैक्यमुच्यते। सकलनिष्ठस्य त्वङ्गैक्य-मेव उच्यत इति विभागः।

मन्त्रिण इति नेत्रमन्त्रलोपेऽपि न मन्त्रित्वहानिरित्यर्थः ॥ १३॥१४ ॥

सुधीरिति। कस्यचित् कनिष्ठादिक्रमत्वं नमस्कारान्तत्वम् अङ्गुलीनाम् असंयोजनन्यासक्रमं च सूचितवान् ॥ १४॥१५ ॥

दिशो दश क्रमादिति च क्रमोऽन्य इति सूचितः ॥ १६ ॥

बाह्यपूजार्थं शङ्खपूरणक्रममाह— शङ्खमिति। न्यासानन्तरं ध्यात्वा। अर्घ्यादिभि-रुपचारैः मनसा संपूज्य। किञ्चिज्जपित्वा। वामश्वासाग्रतोऽर्घ्यमण्डलं सामान्यार्घ्यजलेन विधाय अस्त्रेणाऽर्घ्यपात्राधारं प्रक्षाल्य। रमित्यर्घ्यमण्डले प्रति-ष्ठाप्य। तत्र व्यापककला न्यसित्वा अग्निमण्डलमन्त्रेणाऽभिमन्त्र्य। अर्घ्यपात्र-मध्यस्त्रेण प्रक्षाल्य। ह्रमिति सूर्यमण्डलं बुद्ध्याधारे संस्थाप्य। तत्र स्पर्शकला न्यसित्वा। सूर्यमण्डलमन्त्रेणाऽभिमृश्य। मूलेन गन्धाक्षतादिकं निक्षिप्य। समूलेन हृन्मन्त्रेण सामान्यार्घ्यजलैरापूर्य। गामिति गालिनीं प्रदर्श्य। ठं अमृतीभव वं निर्विषीभव च्लौं सं इति अमृतीकरणनिर्विषीकरणगरुडसुरभिमुद्राः प्रदर्श्य।

गङ्गे च यमुने चैव गोदावरि सरस्वति।
नर्मदे सिन्धु कावेरि जलेऽस्मिन् सन्निधिं कुरु ॥

न्यसेच्च दक्षभागे सुमनःपात्रं तथाऽभितो दीपान् ।
अन्यत्साधनमखिलं पुरतो गन्धाक्षतादिकं मन्त्री ॥ १८

प्रथमं निजसव्यतो यथावत् प्रयजेद्देवमयान् महागुरून् स्वान् ।
गणनायकमन्यतश्च पाशाङ्कुशदन्ताभयहस्तमुज्ज्वलाङ्गम् ॥ १९

रक्तं धर्मं वृषतनुमथाऽग्नौ हरिं श्यामवर्णं
ज्ञानं रक्षोदिशि मरुति पीतञ्च वैराग्यसंज्ञम् ।
भूताकारं द्विरदतनुमैश्वर्यमीशे च कृष्णं
नञ्पूर्वैस्तैर्यजतु दिशि चित्राणि गात्राणि पीठे ॥ २०

मध्येऽनन्तं पद्ममस्मिंश्च सूर्यं सोमं वह्निं तारवर्णैर्विभक्तैः ।
सत्त्वादींश्च त्रीन् गुणानात्मयुक्ताञ्छक्तीः किञ्जल्केषु मध्ये यजेच्च ॥

श्वेताकृष्णारक्तापीताश्यामानलोपमाः प्रोक्ताः ।
अञ्जनजपासमानवर्णास्तेजोरूपाश्च शक्तयः प्रोक्ताः ॥ २२

इति तीर्थमावाह्य । तत्र स्वरकला न्यसित्वा । सोममण्डलमन्त्रेणाऽभिमृश्य । हृदयेनाऽष्टगन्धादिकं निक्षिप्य । शिरसा धेनुमुद्रां बद्ध्वा । शिखया लोलिन्याऽऽलोड्य । नेत्रेणाऽवलोक्य । कवचेनाऽवगुण्ठ्याऽस्त्रेण सतालत्रयं दिशो बद्ध्वा । आधारादिकम् अग्न्यादिमण्डलमन्त्रैः जलादिभिरभ्यर्च्य । पीठमन्त्रेण पुष्पाञ्जलिं कृत्वा । जलमध्ये देवमावाह्य । सकलीकृत्य । जलादिभिः संपूज्य अङ्गमन्त्रैरपि जलादिभिरर्चयित्वा । भगवन्तं मूलेन व्यापयन्निष्कलीकृत्याऽऽनन्दरूपेणाऽर्घ्यजलात्मनाऽवस्थितं भावयित्वा । समूलेन दक्षिणकरतलेन पात्रमुखमाच्छादयेत् । अष्टवारं मूलं जपित्वा । तदर्घ्यं करकोदके प्रक्षिप्य । ततः किञ्चिदादाय समूलेन करतले अर्घ्योदकं किञ्चिदादाय समूलेन वामतलेन पिधायाऽष्टवारं जपित्वा अन्ते पूजोपकरणमात्मानं च त्रिधा प्रोक्षयित्वा सर्वं सच्चिदानन्दरूपं भावयेदित्युक्तं गुरूपदेशेनेति ॥ १७ ॥

गन्धाक्षतादिकं मन्त्रीति मूलहृदयाग्रां तेषामभिमर्शनमुक्तम् ॥ १८ ॥

निजसव्यतो यथावदिति । प्रथमं न्यासस्थानेषु जलादिभिरात्मपूजां कृत्वा आत्मानमलङ्कृत्य सासनमूर्तिपूजापूर्वकं गुरुगणेशावर्चयेदित्यर्थः । देवमयानिति गुरुध्यानमुक्तम् । गुं परमगुरुभ्यो नमः । गुं परापरगुरुभ्यो नमः । गुं अपरगुरुभ्यो नमः । गुं अस्मद्गुरुभ्यो नमः । इति मन्त्रा महागुर्वादिपदसूचिताः । तत आधारशक्ति मूलप्रकृत्यनन्त पृथिवी कल्पकवृक्ष रत्नमण्डपमन्त्रैः मध्ये

विन्यस्य कर्णिकोपरि शालींस्तदुपरि तण्डुलांश्च तथा ॥
तेषामुपरि च दर्भान् दर्भोपरि कूर्चमक्षतोपेतम् ॥ २३
त्रिगुणेन च तन्तुरूपभाजा परितोऽथो परिवेष्टितं यथावत् ।
लघुनाऽलघु धूपितञ्च कूर्चोपरि कुम्भं निदधातु तारजापी ॥ २४
न्यस्य दर्भमयकूर्चमक्षताद्यन्वितं सनवरत्नकं घटे ।
पूरयेत् सह कषादिकान्तगैरक्षरौषधिविपाचितैर्जलैः ॥ २५
अथवा दशमूलपुष्पदुग्धाङ्घ्रिपचर्मोत्क्वथितैः कषायतोयैः ।
स्तनजद्रुमचर्मसाधितैर्वा सलिलैः संयतधीः शुभोदकैर्वा ॥ २६
शङ्खे कषायोदकपूरिते च विलोड्य सम्यग्विधिनाऽष्टगन्धम् ।
कलाः समावाह्य विनिक्षिपेत्तत्क्वाथोदकापूर्णमुखे च कुम्भे ॥ २७
त्रिविधं गन्धाष्टकमपि शाक्तेयं वैष्णवञ्च शैवमपि ।
गन्धाष्टकेन शक्तिः स्यात् क्रमशो मन्त्रिणा कृतेऽनन्ता ॥ २८
चन्दनकर्पूरागुरुकुङ्कुमकपिमांसिरोचनाचोराः ।
गन्धाष्टकमपि शक्तेः सान्निध्यकरञ्च लोकरञ्जनकृत् ॥ २९
चन्दनह्रीवेरागुरुकुष्ठासृगुशीरमांसिमुरमपरम् ।
चन्दनकर्पूरागुरुदलरुधिरकुशीतरोगजमपरम् ॥ ३०
अष्टत्रिंशत्प्रभेदेन याः कलाः प्रागुदीरिताः ।
गुरूपदेशक्रमतस्ता विद्वान् विनियोजयेत् ॥ ३१

संपूज्य धर्मादिकमुक्तस्थानेषु पूजयेत् । मध्ये यजेच्च इति चशब्दः पीठसमष्टि-मन्त्रपुष्पाञ्जलिसूचनार्थः ॥ १८॥२०॥२१॥२२ ॥

शालिविन्यसनादिकं पीठपूजायाः पूर्वमेव ॥ २३॥२४ ॥

सह कषादिकान्तगैरिति त्रिशः प्रतिलोमपठितेन मन्त्रेण सहेत्यर्थः ॥ २५ ॥

संयतधीः शुभोदकैर्वेति । विनाऽप्यौषधैस्तज्जन्यसामर्थ्यापादनक्षम इत्यर्थः ।

विलोड्य सम्यग्विधिनेति । समूलेन हृदयेनापूर्य । हृदयेनाऽष्टगन्धं निक्षिप्य । शिरसा धेनुमुद्रां प्रदर्श्य इत्यादिकं सूचितम् ॥ २६ ॥ २७ ॥

मन्त्रिणा कृतेऽनन्तेति । गन्धद्वारामिति मन्त्रस्य जपः सूचितः ॥२८॥२९॥३०॥

कलाः समावाह्येत्येतत् विवृणोति—अष्टत्रिंशदिति । गुरूपदेशक्रमत इति । आग्नेयसौरसौम्यक्रमेणेत्यर्थः । विद्वानिति । मण्डलमन्त्राणां जातवेदसे तत्सवितु

याः पञ्चाशत्कलास्तारपञ्चभेदसमुत्थिताः ।
पञ्चपञ्चकसम्भिन्ना विदुस्तास्तत्त्ववेदिनः ॥ ३२

सप्तात्मकस्य तारस्य परौ द्वौ तु परौ यतः ।
ततस्तु शक्तिशान्ताख्यौ पठ्यते न परैः सह ॥ ३३

प्रथमं प्रकृतेर्हंसः प्रतद्विष्णुरनन्तरः ।
त्रैयम्बकं तृतीयं स्यात् चतुर्थस्तत्पदादिकः ॥ ३४

विष्णुर्योनिरितीत्यादिः पञ्चमः कल्प्यतां मनुः ।
चतुर्नवतिमन्त्रात्मा देवतावाह्य पूर्यताम् ॥ ३५

अत्र याः पञ्च संप्रोक्ता ऋचस्तारस्य पञ्चभिः ।
कलाप्रभेदैश्च मिथो युज्यन्ते ताः पृथक् क्रमात् ॥ ३६

त्र्यम्बक इत्यृचां च क्रमेण संयोगं जानन्नित्यर्थः ॥ ३१ ॥

तारपञ्चभेदसमुत्थिता इत्यकारादिकलान्यासानन्तरम् अं ब्रह्मणे नमः उं विष्णवे नमः । मं रुद्राय नमः । ओं बिन्द्वात्मने ईश्वराय नमः । ओं नादात्मने सदाशिवाय नम इति मन्त्राणामावाहनं सूचितम् । पञ्चपञ्चकसंभिन्ना इति । लं पृथिव्यात्मने गन्धतन्मात्रात्मने घ्राणात्मने उपस्थानन्दात्मने निवृत्त्यात्मने नमः । तथा वं अबात्मने रसतन्मात्रात्मने रसनात्मने पायुविसर्गात्मने प्रतिष्ठात्मने नमः । तथा रं अग्न्यात्मने रूपतन्मात्रात्मने चक्षुरात्मने पादगमनात्मने विद्यात्मने नमः । तथा यं वाय्वात्मने स्पर्शतन्मात्रात्मने त्वगात्मने पाण्यादानात्मने शान्त्यात्मने नमः । तथा हं आकाशात्मने शब्दतन्मात्रात्मने श्रोत्रात्मने वाग्वचनात्मने शान्त्यतीतात्मने नमः । इति पञ्चपञ्चकावाहनमुक्तम् ॥ ३२ ॥

शक्तिशान्तिकलावाहनं सूचयति—सप्तात्मकस्येति । नादकलान्यासानन्तरम् इच्छाशक्तये नमः । क्रियाशक्तये नमः । ज्ञानशक्तये नमः । इति शक्तिकला आवाह्य । चिदात्मने नमः । आनन्दात्मने नमः । इति शान्तिकलावाहनम् । एवं चतुर्नवतिकलावाहनमपि सिद्धं भवति । विनापि मन्त्रैरित्यर्थः ।

न पठ्यते परैः सहेति । तत्र पञ्चकादिसंभेदो नास्तीत्यर्थः । ओं शक्त्यात्मने शान्तात्मने नम इति तु योज्यम् । चतुर्नवतीति त्रिनवतिकलावाहनानन्तरं मूलमन्त्रमपि सकृज्जप्त्वा पूरयेदित्यर्थः ॥ ३३ ॥

कलाप्रभेदैश्च मिथ इति । एकैककलावाहनान्तरं युज्यन्त इत्यर्थः । क्रमादिति । हंस इति अकारकलादिषु । प्रतद्विष्णुरिति उकारकलादिष्वित्यादि-

कुर्यात् प्राणप्रतिष्ठाञ्च तत्र तत्र समाहितः ।
प्राणप्रतिष्ठामन्त्रेण पुनस्तोयं कलात्मकम् ।
उच्चारयन् मूलमन्त्रं कलशे सन्निधापयेत् ॥ ३७

प्रोक्त्वापूर्वममुष्य शब्दमथ च प्राणा इह प्राणका-
स्तद्वज्जीव इह स्थितेति च तथा सर्वेन्द्रियाणीति च ।
तद्वद्वाङ्मनसावुदीर्य तदनु प्राणा इहायान्त्विति
स्वाहान्तं प्रजपेन्मनुं निशितधीः प्राणान् प्रतिष्ठापयेत् ॥ ३८

अश्वत्थचूतपनसस्तवकैः सुत्रामवल्लरीतण्डुलैः[युक्तैः] ।
सुरतरुधिया पिधाय कुम्भमुखं वेष्टयीत वासोभ्याम् ॥ ३९

पुनस्तोयगतं देवं साध्यमन्त्रानुरूपतः ।
सकलीकृत्य च गुरुरुपचारान् समाचरेत् ॥ ४०
आसनस्वागते सार्घ्यपाद्ये साचमनीयके ।
मधुपर्काचमस्नानवसनाभरणान्यपि ॥ ४१
सुगन्धसुमनोधूपदीपान्नैवेद्यवन्दने ।
प्रयोजयेदर्चनायामुपचारांस्तु षोडश ॥ ४२

क्रमेण योग इत्यर्थः ॥ ३४॥३५॥३६ ॥

प्रोक्त्वापूर्वमिति । आपूर्वं प्रोक्त्वा आं ह्रीं क्रों यं रं लं वं शं षं सं हों क्षं सः हंसः ह्रीं ह्रोमिति प्रोक्त्वा इत्यर्थः । अत्रामुष्येति साध्यनामग्रहणमुक्तम् । तद्वज्जीव इति पूर्ववदापूर्वमेवेत्यर्थः । चशब्दो जीवपदात् पूर्वं तत्तत्पदद्योतनार्थः । तथा सर्वेन्द्रियाणीत्यपि । तथा तद्वदित्यपि तथा वाङ्मनसग्रहणं चक्षुःश्रोत्रघ्राणानामुपलक्षणार्थम् । निशितधीरिति । पाशेन देवताः सर्वगा व्याप्य ह्रींकारेणोपस्थाय क्रोमित्याभिमुख्यं संभाव्य यादिभिर्देवतां सकलां सञ्चिन्त्याऽवशिष्टेन तदनुज्ञया सान्निध्यमापादयेदित्यर्थः ॥ ३७॥३८ ॥

सुत्रामवल्लरी कल्पलतारूपा ध्येया । तण्डुलानि तत्फलपुष्परूपाणि । वासः छायारूपम् ॥ ३८ ॥

सकलीकृत्येति । आवाहनादिन्यासान्तं कृत्वा । विश्रमपूजां च कृत्वाऽनुज्ञामादाय उपचारान् कल्पयेदित्यर्थः । गुरुरिति शङ्खपूरणवदर्घ्यादिक्रमो द्रव्यदेवतासम्बन्धश्चैकात्म्यलक्षणः सूचितः ॥ ४० ५२ ॥

अर्घ्यपाद्याचमनमधुपर्काचमनान्यपि ।
गन्धादयो निवेद्यान्ता उपचारा दश क्रमात् ॥ ४३

गन्धादिका निवेद्यान्ता पूजा पञ्चोपचारिकी ।
सपर्याः त्रिविधाः प्रोक्तास्तासामेकां समाचरेत् ॥ ४४

गन्धपुष्पाक्षतयवकुशाग्रतिलसर्षपाः ।
दूर्वा चेति क्रमादर्घ्यद्रव्याष्टकमुदीरितम् ॥ ४५

पाद्यं श्यामाकदूर्वाब्जविष्णुक्रान्ताभिरुच्यते ।
जातीलवङ्गकक्कोलैर्मतमाचमनीयकम् ॥ ४६

मधुपर्कञ्च सक्षौद्रं दधि प्रोक्तं मनीषिभिः ।
शुद्धाभिरद्भिर्विहितं पुनराचमनीयकम् ॥ ४७

चन्दनागुरुकर्पूरपङ्कं गन्धमिहेष्यते ।
अथवा लघुकाश्मीरपटीरमृगनाभिजम् ॥ ४८

तुलस्यौ पङ्कजे जात्यौ केतक्यौ करवीरकौ ।
शस्तानि दश पुष्पाणि तथा रक्तोत्पलानि च ॥ ४९

उत्पलानि च नीलानि कुमुदानि च मालती ।
मल्लिका कुन्दमन्दारनन्द्यावर्तादिकानि च ॥ ५०

पलाशपाटलीपार्थपारन्त्यावर्तकानि च ।
चम्पकानि सनागानि रक्तमन्दारकाणि च ॥ ५१

अशोकोद्भवबिल्वोत्थकर्णिकारोद्भवानि च ।
सुगन्धानि सुरूपाणि स्वागमोक्तानि यानि च ॥ ५२

मुकुलैः पतितैर्म्लानैः शीर्णैर्वा जन्तुदूषितैः ।
आघ्रातैरङ्गसंस्पृष्टैरुषितैरपि नाऽर्चयेत् ॥ ५३

सगुग्गुल्वगुरूशीरसिताज्यमधुचन्दनैः ।
साराङ्गारे विनिक्षिप्तैर्मन्त्री नीचैः प्रधूपयेत् ॥ ५४

मन्त्री नीचैरिति धूपे गन्धविशेषं सूचयन् गन्धादिष्वपि सूचयति । ओं लं क्षीं ओं नमः पराय गन्धतन्मात्रप्रकृत्यानन्दात्मकं गन्धं कल्पयामि नम

गोसर्पिषा वा तैलेन वर्त्त्या च लघुगर्भया ।
दीपितं सुरभिं शुद्धं दीपमुच्चैः प्रदीपयेत् ॥ ५५

इत्यादयो मन्त्रा देवस्य गन्धादिदाने। आवरणानां तु तत्तन्नाममन्त्रैरेव देयम्। अथवा आगमोक्तैः श्लोकैरेवावाहनादयः कर्तव्या इति सूचितः।

स्वात्मसंस्थमजं शुद्धं त्वामद्य परमेश्वर ।
अरण्यामिव हव्याशं मूर्तावावाहयाम्यहम् ॥ नमः ।
तवेयं महिमा मूर्तिस्तस्यां त्वां सर्वगं प्रभो ।
भक्तिस्नेहसमाकृष्टं दीपवत् स्थापयाम्यहम् ॥ नमः ।
सर्वान्तर्यामिणे देव सर्वबीजमयं शुभम् ।
स्वात्मस्थाय परं शुद्धमासनं कल्पयाम्यहम् ॥ नमः ।
अस्मिन् वरासने देव सुखमास्वाऽक्षरात्मके ।
प्रतिष्ठितो भवाऽस्मिंस्त्वं प्रसीद परमेश्वर ॥ नमः ।
अनन्या तव देवेश मूर्तिः शक्तिरियं प्रभो ।
सान्निध्यं कुरु तस्यां त्वं भक्तानुग्रहतत्पर ॥ नमः ।
आज्ञया तव देवेश कृपाम्भोधे गुणाम्बुधे ।
स्वात्मानन्दैकतृप्तं त्वां निरुणध्मि पितर्गुरो ॥ नमः ।
दृष्ट्या पीयूषवर्षिण्या पूरयन् यज्ञविप्लवम् ।
मूर्तौ वा यज्ञसम्पत्त्यै स्थिरो भव महेश्वर ॥ नमः ।
यस्य दर्शनमिच्छन्ति देवाः स्वाभीष्टसिद्धये ।
तस्मै ते परमेशाय स्वागतं स्वागतं च मे ॥ नमः ।
कृतार्थोऽनुगृहीतोऽस्मि सफलं जीवितं मम ।
यदागतोऽसि देवेश सुस्वागतमिदं पुनः ॥ नमः ।
अज्ञानाद्वा प्रमादाद्वा वैकल्यात्साधनस्य वा ।
यदाऽपूर्णं भवेत् कृत्यं तदाऽप्यभिमुखो भव ॥ नमः ।
अभक्तवाङ्मनश्चक्षुःश्रोत्रदूराऽमितद्युते ।
त्वत्तेजःपञ्जरेणेश वेष्टितो भव सर्वतः ॥ नमः ।
तापत्रयहरं दिव्यं परमानन्दलक्षणम् ।
तापत्रयविनिर्मुक्तं तवाऽर्घ्यं कल्पयाम्यहम् ॥ नमः ।
यद्भक्तिलेशसंपर्कात् परमानन्दसंभवः ।
तस्मै ते चरणाब्जाय पाद्यं शुद्धाय कल्पये ॥ नमः ।

सुशितेन सुशुद्धेन पायसेन सुसर्पिषा ।
सितोपदंशकदलीदध्याद्यैश्च निवेदयेत् ॥ ५६

वेदानामपि वेदाय देवानां देवतात्मने ।
आचामं कल्पयामीश शुद्धानां शुद्धिहेतवे ॥ नमः ।
सर्वकालुष्यहीनाय परिपूर्णसुखात्मकम् ।
मधुपर्कमिदं देव कल्पयामि प्रसीद मे ॥ नमः ।

वेदानामपि वेदायेत्यादिरेव पुनराचमनमन्त्रः ।

परमानन्दबोधाब्धिनिमग्ननिजमूर्तये ।
साङ्गोपाङ्गमिदं स्नानं कल्पयामीश ते पुनः ॥ नमः ।

अयमत्र स्नानक्रमः । उत्तरभागे स्नानशालां निर्माय । यानेन सोपचारं देवं तत्र नीत्वा । यानादवरोप्य । पादुकाभ्यामन्तः नीत्वा । पीठं समर्प्य अर्घ्यादिकं दत्त्वा केशप्रसाधनाङ्गमर्दनाभ्यङ्गामलकचूर्ण कुङ्कुमानुलेप कषायोदक-स्नान पञ्चगव्य पञ्चामृत स्नान गन्धानुलेपन गन्धोदकस्नानाष्टगन्धानुलेपाष्टगन्धोदक-स्नान दिव्यगन्धानुलेप दिव्यगन्धोदकस्नानपुष्पफलस्वर्ण रत्नमन्त्रोदकस्नानानि अर्घ्या-दिपूर्वकं प्रयच्छेदिति ।

मायाचित्रपटाच्छन्न निजगुह्योरुतेजसे ।
निरावरणविज्ञान वस्त्रं ते कल्पयाम्यहम् ॥ नमः ।
यमाश्रित्य महामाया जगत्संमोहिनी सदा ।
तस्मै ते परमेशाय कल्पयाम्युत्तरीयकम् ॥ नमः ।
यस्य शक्तित्रयेणेदं संप्रोतमखिलं जगत् ।
यज्ञसूत्राय तस्मै ते यज्ञसूत्रं प्रकल्पये ॥ नमः ।
स्वभावसुन्दराङ्गाय नानाशक्त्याश्रयाय ते ।
भूषणानि विचित्राणि कल्पयाम्यमरार्चित ॥ नमः ।

इति भूषणन्यासान्तरम् ।

समस्तदेवदेवेश सर्वतृप्तिकरं परम ।
अखण्डानन्दसंपूर्ण गृहाण जलमुत्तमम् । नमः ॥
परमानन्दसौरभ्यपूर्णा[परि]पूर्णदिगन्तरम् ।
गृहाण परमं गन्धं कृपया परमेश्वर । नमः ॥
तुरीयवनसंभूतं नानागुणमनोहरम् ।
आनन्दसौरभं पुष्पं गृह्यतामिदमुत्तमम् । नमः ॥

वर्णैर्मनुप्रपुटितैः क्रमशः शतार्ध-
न्यासक्रमादभियजेत् सकलासु मन्त्री ।
गन्धादिभिः प्रथमतो मनुदेवतासु
त्रैलोक्यमोहनमिति प्रथितः प्रयोगः ॥ ५७

हृदयं सशिरस्तथा शिखया कवचञ्चेत्यनलादिकास्विषु ।
पुरतो नयनं दिशासु मन्त्री पुनरस्त्रञ्च समर्चयेत् क्रमात् ॥ ५८

वनस्पतिरसोपेतो गन्धाढ्यो गन्ध उत्तमः ।
आघ्रेयः सर्वदेवानां धूपोऽयं परिगृह्यताम् । नमः ॥
सुप्रकाशो महादीपः सर्वतस्तिमिरापहः ।
सबाह्याभ्यन्तरज्योतिः दीपोऽयं परिगृह्यताम् । नमः ॥५४॥५५॥५६॥

पुनः पुष्पाञ्जलिं विधाय प्रसरपुष्पाञ्जलिमेकाक्षरादिमन्त्रैः कुर्यादित्याह—वर्णैर्मनुप्रपुटितैरिति । न्यासक्रमात् लिपिन्यासक्रमात् । क्रमश इति परादिक्रमः सूचितः । सकलास्विति परादि कलायोगः । मन्त्री इति एकाक्षरादिमन्त्रयोगः । प्रथमत इत्यावरणपूजायाः पूर्वमित्यर्थः ।

अयमत्र प्रयोगक्रमः । ओं नमः । अहं नमः । विश्वयोन्यै नमः । इति परापुष्पाञ्जलिः । महासत्तायै नमः । महाचिते नमः । महानन्दायै नमः । महेश्वर्यै नमः । अं नमः । वामायै ज्येष्ठायै रौद्र्यै अम्बिकायै नमः । इति मूर्धवामदक्षिणभागमूलाधारेषु पूजयेत् । हं नमः । इच्छायै नमः । क्रियायै नमः । ज्ञानायै नमः । शान्तायै नम इत्यपि तथेति पश्यन्तीपुष्पाञ्जलिः । शून्यात्मने स्पर्शात्मने नादात्मने ध्वन्यात्मने बिन्द्वात्मने शक्त्यात्मने बीजात्मने अक्षरात्मने नमः । इति मध्यमापुष्पाञ्जलिः । ततो मनुप्रपुटितैर्वर्णैः वर्णस्थाने वैखरीपुष्पाञ्जलिः । ओं नमः । मं नमः । उं नमः । इत्येकाक्षरमन्त्रैः मूर्धादिषु । अहं हरिहर नमः । हर नमः । हरि नमः । अं नमः । इति द्व्यक्षरैरपि तेष्वेव । ओं नमो ब्रह्मणे विष्णवे शिवाय नमः । ओं नमः शिवाय ओं नमो विष्णवे ओं नमो ब्रह्मणे इति षडक्षरैरपि तेष्वेव । ओं क्रीं हंसः सोहं स्वाहा । ओं नमो नारायणाय । ह्रौं नमः शिवाय नमः । ओं क्रीं ह्रौं नमः शिवाय । ओं नमो नारायणाय । ओं क्रीं हंसः सोहं स्वाहा । इत्यपि तेष्वेव । ओं तत्सत् नमो ब्रह्मणे तत्सत् नमः । ओं नमो भगवते वासुदेवाय क्रीं क्रौं नमः शिवाय । हंसः सोहं नमः । ओं क्रीं ह्रौं नमः शिवाय

हारस्फटिककलायाञ्जनपिङ्गलवह्निरोचिषो ललनाः ।
अभयवरोद्यतहस्ताः प्रधानतनवोऽङ्गदेवताः कथिताः ॥ ५९
आदावङ्गावरणं तन्त्वत्वादीरितं विधानेषु ।
अन्ते च लोकपालावृतिरथ कुलिशादिकानाञ्च ॥ ६०
इन्द्राग्नियमनिशाचरवरुणानिलधनेशशिवाहिपतिविधयः ।
जात्यधिपहेतिवाहनपरिवारान्ताः क्रमेण यष्टव्याः ॥ ६१
पीतः पिङ्गः कृष्णो धूम्रः श्वेतश्च धूम्रसितशुक्लाः ।
काशारुणाम्बुजाभा लोकेशा वासवादयः प्रोक्ताः ॥ ६२
वज्र सशक्तिर्दण्डः खड्गः पाशाङ्कुशौ गदाशूलौ ।
रथचरणनलिनसंज्ञौ प्रोक्तान्यस्त्राणि लोकपालानाम् ॥ ६३
पीतहिमजलदगगनाचिरप्रभारक्तकुन्दनोलरुचः ।
करविन्दारुणवर्णाः प्रोक्ताः स्युर्वर्णतोऽपि वज्राद्याः ॥ ६४

हंसः सोऽहं ओं नमो भगवते वासुदेवाय ओं तत्सत् नमो ब्रह्मणे तत्सत् नमः इत्यपि । तथा पुनः समस्तव्यस्तगायत्रनुष्टप्त्रयेण च तेष्वेव ।

नारायणाय विद्महे वासुदेवाय धीमहि । तन्नो विष्णुः प्रचोदयात् । इति विष्णुगायत्री ।

तत्पुरुषाय विद्महे महादेवाय धीमहि । तन्नो रुद्रः प्रचोदयात् । इति रौद्री ।

हंसात्मकोऽयमपामग्नेस्तेजसा दीप्यमानः स नो मृत्योस्त्रायतां नमो ब्रह्मणे विश्वनाभिरिति ब्रह्मानुष्टुप । इतरत् द्वयं वक्ष्यति । तत आवरणस्थाने तत्सामान्यमन्त्रैः पुष्पाञ्जलिं कुर्यादिति प्रसरपुष्पाञ्जलिः ॥ ५७॥५८ ॥

प्रधानतनव इति पचान्तरम् । आवरणपूजानन्तरं प्रसरपुष्पाञ्जलिवैलोम्येन संकोचपुष्पाञ्जलिं कृत्वा । अर्घ्याद्यष्टकं दत्त्वा । निवेद्य । पात्रमस्त्रमन्त्रेण संशोध्य । तस्मिन् मूलमन्त्रतेजसि निवेद्य । जातं संपाद्य अमृतीकरणं निर्विषीकरणं द्वयं विधाय । मूलेनाऽभिमन्त्र्य । कवचास्त्राभ्यां संरक्ष्य । परिषेकादिकं कृत्वा । नेत्रेण नेत्रयोः पुष्पाञ्जलिं विधाय ।

सत्पात्रतद्धविःसौकर्थ्यविविधानेकभक्षणम् ।
निवेदयामि देवेश सानुगाय गृहाण तत् ॥ नमः ।

इति निवेद्य सुरभिसंहारग्रासप्राणादिसुरभिसंहारमुद्राः प्रदर्श्य मूलं किञ्चित् जपेत् ॥ ५९॥६०॥६१॥६२॥६ ॥६४ ॥

कृते निवेद्ये च ततो मण्डलं परितः क्रमात् ।
मङ्गलाऽङ्कुरपात्राणि स्थापनीयानि मन्त्रिणा ॥ ६५

उपलिप्य कुण्डमत्र स्वचरणयोग्या विलिख्य रेखाश्च ।
अभ्युक्ष्य प्रणवेन प्रकल्पयेद् योगविष्टरं मन्त्री ॥ ६६

अथवा षट्कोणावृतत्रिकोणके गुरुजनोपदेशेन ।
प्राणाग्निहोत्रविधिनाऽप्यावसथीयाह्वयेऽनलस्थाने ॥ ६७

तत्राथो सद्दतुमतीमतीन्द्रियाभां
संस्मृत्य सकलजगन्मयीञ्च शक्तिम् ।
तद्योनौ मणिभवमारणेयकं वा
तारेणाक्षिपतु गृहोत्थमेव वाऽग्निम् ॥ ६८

चित्पिङ्गलपदमुक्त्वा हनदहपचयुग्मकानि सर्वज्ञम् ।
आज्ञापयाग्निजाये प्रभाष्य मनुनाऽमुनाऽनलं ज्वालयेत् ॥ ६९

मण्डलं परितः क्रमादिति अङ्कुरार्पणगत क्रमेणेत्यर्थः । मन्त्रिणेति विष्णवे नम इत्यादिमन्त्रैरित्यर्थः ॥ ६५ ॥

उपलिप्य कुण्डमत्र चेति चकारेण कुण्डसंस्काराः सूचिताः । प्रथमं मूलेन वीक्षणं कुर्यात् । ततोऽस्त्रेण प्रोक्षणम् । तेनैव दर्भैः संमार्जनम् । वर्मणा अभ्युक्षणम् । अस्त्रेण खननोद्धारौ । पूरणं हृदा । समीकरणमस्त्रेण । वर्मणा सेचनम् । अस्त्रेण कुट्टनम् । वर्मणा मार्जनं विलेपनं कलारूपतत्त्वकल्पनं त्रिसूत्रवेष्टनं च । हृदयेन अर्चनम् । अस्त्रेण वज्रीकरणम् । हृदयेन चतुष्पथीकरणम् । कवचेनाऽक्षपाटनमिति कुण्डसंस्काराः । अथवा वीक्षणप्रोक्षणताड़नाभ्युक्षणैरेव संस्कुर्यात् । योगविष्टरं मन्त्रीति । ओं ह्रीं वागीश्वरी वागीश्वरासनाय नम इति मन्त्रेण पूजयेदित्यर्थः ॥ ६६ ॥

गुरुजनोपदेशेनेति । गुरूक्तविधिना महागणपतिपटलोक्तविधिना वा त्रिकोणत्रयं मन्त्रविशेषानुसारेण लिखेदित्यर्थः । मूलाधारेऽपि त्रिकोणमध्याग्नौ योगविष्टरं कल्पनीयमित्याह—प्राणाग्नीति ॥ ६७ ॥

उभयत्रापि वागीश्वरी कल्पनीयावित्याह—तत्रेति । सद्दतुमतीं बाह्ये वागीश्वरीं अतीन्द्रियाभां मूलाधार इति विशेषः । चशब्दः शक्तिमत्समुच्चयार्थः । मण्यादिजमग्निं पात्रेण आनीयाऽस्त्रेण क्रव्यादांशं परित्यज्य ।

अग्निं प्रज्वलितं वन्दे जातवेदं हुताशनम् ।
सुवर्णवर्णममलं समिद्धं विश्वतोमुखम् ॥ ७०
अनेन ज्वलितं मन्त्रेणोपतिष्ठेद्धुताशनम् ।
ततः प्रविन्यसेद्देहे जिह्वामन्त्रैर्विभावसोः ॥ ७१
सलिङ्गगुदमूर्द्धास्यनासानेत्रेषु च क्रमात् ।
ससर्वाङ्गेषु जिह्वाश्च वक्ष्यन्ते त्रिविधात्मिकाः ॥ ७२
हिरण्या गगना रक्ता कृष्णा चैव तु सुप्रभा ।
बहुरूपाऽतिरक्ता च जिह्वाः सप्तेति सात्त्विकाः ॥ ७३
पद्मरागा सुवर्णा च तृतीया भद्रलोहिता ।
लोहिताख्या तथा श्वेता धूमिनी सकरालिका ॥ ७४
राजस्यः कथिता जिह्वाः क्रमात् कल्याणरेतसः ।
विश्वमूर्त्तिस्फुलिङ्गिन्यौ धूम्रवर्णा मनोजवा ॥ ७५
लोहिता च करालाख्या काली तामसजिह्विकाः ।
अनलेरार्घिबिन्द्वन्ताः पादियान्ताक्षरान्विताः ॥ ७६
सात्त्विका दिव्यपूजासु राजस्यः काम्यकर्मसु ।
तामस्यः क्रूरकार्येषु प्रयोक्तव्या विपश्चिता ॥ ७७
सुराः सपितृगन्धर्वयक्षनागपिशाचकाः ।
राक्षसाश्च क्रमादग्नेराश्रिता रसनास्त्वमी ॥ ७८
जिह्वासु त्रिदशादीनां तत्तत्कार्यसमाप्तये ।
जुहुयाद्वाञ्छितां सिद्धिं दद्युस्ता देवता मताः ॥ ७९
स्वनामसदृशाकाराः प्रायो जिह्वा हविर्भुजः ।
मन्त्री प्रविन्यसेद्भूयो वह्नेरङ्गानि वै क्रमात् ॥ ८०

वीक्षणादिभिः संस्कृत्य । तमग्निं नासिकाद्वारेण मूलाधारं नीत्वा शिवशक्त्यात्मककुण्डलिन्या एकीकृत्य । तत्र प्राणाग्निहोत्रविधिना सकृत् वर्णहोमं विधाय । तमग्निं प्रणवेन बैन्दवाग्निना एकीकृत्य अमृतमास्राव्य । तमग्निं रं अग्निचैतन्याय नमः इति पात्राग्नौ संस्थाप्य । तारेणाऽभिमन्त्र्य । सुरभ्या अमृतीकृत्य । अस्त्रेण संरक्ष्य । कवचेनाऽवगुण्ठ्य । रं अग्नये नम इत्यभ्यर्च्य । कुण्डोपरि त्रिः प्रणवेन परिभ्राम्य । तारेण शिवबीजबुद्ध्या देव्या योनौ क्षिपेदित्यर्थः ॥ ६८—७९ ॥

सहस्रार्चिः स्वस्तिपूर्णं उत्तिष्ठपुरुषस्तथा ।
धूमव्यापी सप्तजिह्वो धनुर्द्धर इतीरितः ॥ ८१
अङ्गमन्त्रान् क्रमादष्टमूर्तीश्चाऽथ प्रविन्यसेत् ।
मूर्धांसपार्श्वकट्यन्धुकटिपार्श्वांसकेषु च ॥ ८२
प्रादक्षिण्येन विन्यस्येद् यथावद्देशिकोत्तमः ।
जातवेदाः सप्तजिह्वो हव्यवाहन एव च ॥ ८३
अश्वोदरजसंज्ञश्च सवैश्वानर एव च ।
कौमारतेजाश्च तथा विश्वदेवमुखाह्वयौ ॥ ८४
स्युरष्टमूर्तयो वह्नेरग्नये पदपूर्विकाः ।
प्रणवादिनमोऽन्ताश्च पुनर्दर्भचतुष्टयैः ॥ ८५
दिक्क्रमात् संपरिस्तीर्य सम्यग्गन्धादिभिर्यजेत् ।
मध्ये च कोणषट्के च जिह्वाभिः केसरेषु च ॥ ८६
अङ्गमन्त्रैस्ततो बाह्ये चाऽष्टभिर्मूर्तिभिः क्रमात् ।
ततोऽग्निमनुना तेन मन्त्री मध्ये च सयजेत् ॥ ८७
वैश्वानरं जातवेदमुक्त्वा चेहावहेति च ।
लोहिताक्षपदं सर्वकर्माणीति समीरयेत् ।
ब्रूयाच्च साधयेत्यन्ते वह्निजायान्तिको मनुः ॥ ८८
त्रिनयनमरुणाप्ताबद्धमौलि सुशुक्लां-
शुकमरुणमनेकाकल्पमम्भोजसंस्थम् ।

मन्त्री प्रविन्यसेदिति । ज्ञानादिसर्वज्ञादियोगः सूचितः । पीठमूर्ति-पूजादिकं चाङ्गन्यासात् पूर्वम् ॥ ८०॥८१ ॥

यथावत् देशिकोत्तम इति । अग्न्यादिपादाष्टकयोगः शक्तियोगश्च सूचितः । ॥ ८२॥८३॥८४ ॥

संपरिस्तीर्य सम्यगिति । परिषेचनपूर्वकत्वं परिस्तरणानन्तरं परिधि-निधानम् । तेषु प्रागादि क्रमेण ब्रह्मादिमूर्तिचतुष्टयपूजाश्च सूचिताः । पुनः वैश्वानरमन्त्रेणाऽग्निं संपूज्य जिह्वाद्यावरणपूजा च कार्या । मूर्तिबाह्ये मातृभैरवावृतिरपि पूज्या इति केचित् । तद्बहिर्लोकपालाः पूज्याः ॥ ८५॥८६ ॥

मनुना तेन मन्त्रीति प्रणवशक्तियोगः सूचितः । समृद्धिमन्त्रोक्ता ऋष्यादयः ।

अभिमतवरशक्तिस्वस्तिकाभीतिहस्तं
नमत कनकमालालङ्कृतांस कृशानुम् ॥ ८९

जिह्वा ज्वालारुचः प्रोक्ता वराभययुतानि च ।
अङ्गानि मूर्तयः शक्तिस्वस्तिकोद्यतदोर्द्वयाः ॥ ९०

संस्कृतेन घृतेनाऽभिद्योतनोद्योतितेन च ।
व्याहृत्यनन्तरं तेन मनुना जुहुयात्त्रिशः ॥ ९१

गर्भाधानादिका वह्नेः समुद्वाहावसानिकाः ।
क्रियास्तारेण वै कुर्यादाज्याहुत्यष्टकैः पृथक् ॥ ९२

क्लीं बीजं । स्वाहा शक्तिः ॥ ८७॥८८॥८९॥९० ॥

आवरण पूजानन्तरं स्रुक्स्रुवौ पाणिभ्यामादाय अधोमुखं त्रिशः प्रताप्य । दर्भैः अग्रादिक्रमेण संमार्ज्य । सव्यहस्तेन गृहीत्वा दक्षिणेन प्रोक्षयित्वाऽस्त्रेण पुनः प्रताप्य । दर्भानग्नौ प्रक्षिप्याऽऽत्मदक्षभागे कुशास्तरे संस्थाप्याऽऽज्यस्थालोमस्त्रेण संप्रोक्ष्य । वोक्षणादि संस्कृतमाज्यं तस्मिन्निक्षिप्य । निरुह्य वायव्येऽङ्गारान् हृदा तेषु संस्थापयेत् । इदं तापनं नाम आज्यसंस्कारः । दर्भद्वयं संदोप्याज्ये क्षिप्त्वा । वह्नौ क्षिपेत् । हृदयेन इदं पवित्रोकरणम् । दोप्तेन दर्भद्वयेन नोराज्य कवचेनाग्नौ क्षिपेत् । इदमभिद्योतनम् । घृतं प्रज्वलितान् दर्भान् प्रदर्श्य अस्त्रमन्त्रेणाऽग्नौ प्रक्षिपेत् । इदमुद्योतनम् । आहृत्याज्यं बहिर्वह्नावङ्गारान् संयोज्य । हस्तौ प्रक्षाल्य । प्रादेशमात्रौ कुशावङ्गुष्ठोपकनिष्ठिकाभ्यां धृत्वा अस्त्रेणोत्पुनोयात् । इदमुत्पवनम् । एतदेवात्माभिमुखं कुर्यात् । संप्लवनमिदम् । प्रादेशमात्रं संग्रन्थ्य दर्भयुग्ममाज्ये विन्यस्य । स्रुवेण दक्षिणभागादाज्यमादाय । हृदा सह अग्नये स्वाहेति अग्नेः दक्षिणनेत्रे हुत्वा । भागान्तरात् इतरनेत्रे सोमाय स्वाहेति हुत्वा । मध्यादादायाऽग्नोषोमाभ्यां स्वाहेति ललाटनेत्रे हुत्वा । दक्षिणभागादादाय अग्नये स्विष्टकृते स्वाहेति वह्नौ जुहुयात् । सहृदया एव सर्वे मन्त्राः । स्वाहेति तत्तद्भागे संपातं च कुर्यात् । इदं नेत्रवह्न्योद्घाटनम् । एतत् सर्वमुक्तं—संस्कृतेन घृतेनेत्यादिना ।

व्याहृत्यनन्तरमिति प्रणवानन्तर्यस्याप्युपलक्षणम् । गर्भाधान पुंसवन सोमन्तोन्नयन जातकर्म नामकरणोपनिष्क्रमणान्नप्राशन चौलोपनयनवेदव्रतचतुष्टयसमावर्तविवाहाग्न्याधानादिकाः । तत्तत्कर्मसमाप्तये चतुर्गृहीतेन पूर्णाहुतोस्तिष्ठत्वौषडन्तेन मूलेन जुहुयात् । ततः पितरौ संपूज्य आत्महृदये स्थापयित्वा समिधो

जिह्वाङ्गमूर्तिमनुभिरेकाहुत्या हुनेत्ततः ।
जिह्वायां मध्यसंस्थायां मन्त्री ज्वालावलीतनौ ॥ ९३
ताराद्यैर्दशभिर्भेदैः पूर्वपूर्वसमन्वितैः ।
मनुना गणपत्येन हुनेत्पूर्वं दशाहुतीः ॥ ९४
जुहुयाच्च चतुर्वार समस्तेनैव तेन तु ।
आज्येन साध्यमनुना पञ्चविंशतिसंख्यकम् ॥ ९५
जुहुयात् सर्वहोमेषु सुधीरनलतृप्तये ।
तान्त्रिकाणामयं न्यायो हुतानां समुदीरितः ॥ ९६
पुनः साध्येन मनुना हुनेदष्टसहस्रकम् ।
अथवाऽष्टशतं सर्पिःसंयुक्तेन पयोऽन्धसा ॥ ९७
द्रव्यैर्विधानप्रोक्तैर्वा महाव्याहृतिपश्चिमम् ।
पुनः समापयेद्धोमं परिषिकावसानकम् ॥ ९८

जुहुयात् ॥ ९१॥९२ ॥

मन्त्री ज्वालावली तनाविति समस्ताग्निमन्त्रैः होमः सूचितः । गणपतये इत्यन्तः सप्तमः । वरवरदे इत्यन्तोऽष्टमः । सर्वजनं मे इत्यन्तो नवमः । ततः चर्वर्धमग्निं प्राक् स्थापयित्वा । साध्यमन्त्रस्य पीठपूजादिकं कृत्वा । बाह्याग्निरूपान्तामभ्यर्च्य साध्यमनुना अग्निमुखे पञ्चविंशतिवारं जुहुयात् । इदं वह्नीकोकरणम् ॥ ९३॥९४ ॥

सुधीरित्यग्निदेवतैक्यं जानन्नित्यर्थः । आत्मनि देवतैक्यं भावयन् मूलेनैकादश जुहुयादिति । नाडीसन्धानमेतत् । अथ जिह्वाङ्गादिमन्त्रैरपि हुत्वा । कुण्डान्तरेष्वग्निं पूर्वादितो विहृत्य सावरणां देवतां तेषु संपूज्य मूलेनाऽष्टनवपञ्चविंशतिसंख्यं हुत्वा आज्येन साध्यचरुणा वा पुनः साध्येन मनुना हुनेदित्यादि सकलकुण्डेषु समानम् ॥ ९५॥९६ ॥

द्रव्यैर्विधानप्रोक्तैरित्यत्रायं द्रव्यपरिमाणविधिः । कर्षमानं घृतम् । शुक्तिमात्रं पयः । पञ्चगव्यमधूनि तत्समानानि । दुग्धान्नमक्षमात्रम् । दधि प्रसृतम् । मुष्टिर्लाजं । पृथुकमक्तवः । गुलशर्करे पलार्धे । ग्रासार्धाश्चरवः । इक्षुः पर्वान्तः । पत्रपुष्पापूपकदलीनारङ्गफलानि एकैकशः । मातुलुङ्गं चतुःखण्डम् । पनसं दशखण्डम् । नालिकेरम् अष्टखण्डम् । बिल्वं त्रिखण्डम् । त्रिखण्डं कपित्थम् । उर्वारुकं त्रिखण्डम् । फलान्यन्यानि अखण्डानि । समिधो दशाङ्गुलाः । दूर्वा-

भूर्भुवःस्वर्भूर्भुवःस्वःपूर्वं स्वाहान्तमेव च ।
अग्नये च पृथिव्यै च महते च समन्वितम् ॥ ९९

वायवे चाऽन्तरिक्षाय महते च समन्वितम् ।
आदित्याय च वै दिवे महते च समन्वितम् ॥ १००
चन्द्रमसे नक्षत्रेभ्यो दिग्भ्यश्च महतेऽन्वितम् ।
महाव्याहृतयस्त्वेताः सर्वशो देवतामयाः ॥ १०१
ब्रह्मार्पणाख्यमनुना पुनरष्टावथाहुतीः ।
जुहुयान्मन्त्रवर्येण कर्मबन्धविमुक्तये ॥ १०२
इतः पूर्वं प्राणबुद्धिदेहधर्माधिकारतः ।
जाग्रत्स्वप्नसुषुप्तीनामन्तेऽवस्थास्वितीरयेत् ॥ १०३
ततश्च मनसा वाचा कर्मणेति प्रभाषयेत् ।
हस्ताभ्याञ्च तथा पद्भ्यामुदरेणेति भाषयेत् ॥ १०४
शिश्ना च यत् स्मृतं प्रोक्ता यदुक्तं यत्कृतं तथा ।
तत्सर्वमिति संभाष्य ब्रह्मार्पणपदं वदेत् ॥ १०५
भवत्वन्ते द्विठश्चाऽयं ब्रह्मार्पणमनुर्मतः ।
हुते तु देशिकः पश्चान्मण्डले बलिमारभेत् ॥ १०६

त्रिकयुता। गल्ची चतुरङ्गुला। व्रीहिमुद्गमाषयवकोद्रवगोधूमाः मुष्टिमात्राः। तण्डुलाः तदर्धतः। तिलसर्षपाः चुलुकमानाः। शुक्तिमात्रं लवणम्। मरिचान्येकविंशतिः। पुरं बदरमात्रम्। चन्दनागरुकर्पूरकस्तूरीकुङ्कुमानि तिन्तिणीफलमानानि।

समिद्धोमेऽग्निं स्थितं ध्यायेत्। शयानमाज्यहोमेषु। निषण्णं शेषहोमेषु। अग्नेरास्ये होतव्यम्। स्वर्णसिन्दूरबालार्ककुङ्कुमक्षौद्रवर्णोऽग्निः शुभदः। भेरीवारिदहस्तिध्वनिः शुभदः। नागचम्पकपुन्नागपाटलीयूथिकापद्मेन्दीवरकह्लारसर्पिर्गुग्गुलुगन्धोऽग्निः शुभदः। प्रदक्षिणाग्निर्निष्कम्पः शुभः। कुन्देन्दुधवलो धूमः शुभदः। कृष्णवर्णोऽग्निर्यजमानं नाशयेत्। श्वेतो वायसस्वरो राष्ट्रं नाशयेत्। झर्झरस्वरः सर्वनाशकः। पूतिगन्धो होतृदुःखप्रदः। छिन्नावृत्ताशिखा धनक्षयं मृत्युं च कुर्यात्। शुकपारावतनिभोऽग्निः तुरङ्गगोहानिकृत्। एवंविधेषु दोषेषु मूलेनाज्येन प्रायश्चित्ताय पञ्चविंशतिवारं जुहुयात् ॥ ९७—१०६ ॥

नक्षत्राणां सराशीनां सवाराणां यथाक्रमम् ।
दद्याद्बलिं गन्धपुष्पधूपदीपकमादरात् ॥ १०७
ताराणामश्विनादीनां राशिः पादाधिकं द्वयम् ।
मेषादिमुक्त्वा नक्षत्रसंज्ञापूर्वमनन्तरम् ॥ १०८
देवताभ्यः पदं प्रोक्त्वा दिवानक्तं पदं वदेत् ।
चारिभ्यश्चाऽथ सर्वेभ्यो भूतेभ्यश्च नमो वदेत् ॥ १०९
एवं राशौ तु सम्पूर्णे तस्मिंस्तद्वत् प्रयोजयेत् ।
तथा राश्यधिपानाञ्च ग्रहाणां तत्र तत्र तु ॥ ११०
सप्तानां करणानाञ्च दद्यान्मीनाद्यमेषयोः ।
अन्तराले बलिस्त्वेवं संप्रोक्तः कलशात्मकः ॥ १११
पुनर्निवेद्यमुद्धृत्य पुरावत् परिपूज्य च ।
मुखवासादिकं दत्त्वा स्तुत्वा तद्युक्तया पुनः ॥ ११२
स्तुत्वा यथावत् प्रणमेद्भक्तियुक्तस्तु साधकः ।
अष्टाङ्गं वापि पञ्चाङ्गमुभाभ्यां वा समाहितः ॥ ११३
दोर्भ्यां पदाभ्यां जानुभ्यामुरसा शिरसा दृशा ।
वचसा मनसा चेति प्रणामोऽष्टाङ्ग ईरितः ॥ ११४
बाहुभ्याञ्च सजानुभ्यां शिरसा वचसा धिया ।
पञ्चाङ्गकः प्रणामः स्यात् पूजासु प्रवराविमौ ॥ ११५

गुर्वाद्यास्तारादिका यागमन्त्रा लोकेशान्तास्ते चतुर्थीनमोऽन्ताः ।
पूजायामप्यग्निकार्ये द्विठान्ता बीजैः पूजा स्याद्विभक्त्या वियुक्तैः ॥

मेषादिमुक्तेति । बलिमन्त्रोद्धारः । नक्षत्रसंज्ञां पूर्वमुक्त्वा । मेषादिराशिसंज्ञामनन्तरमुक्त्वा । देवताभ्य इत्यादि वदेदित्यन्वयः । अश्विनी भरणी कृत्तिकापादनक्षत्रमेषराशिदेवताभ्यो दिवानक्तञ्चारिभ्यः सर्वेभ्यो भूतेभ्यो नम इत्यादयो मन्त्राः । राश्यधिपबलिमन्त्रेषु तत्तद्राश्यधिपतिनामसंयोगश्च विशेषः ॥ १०७ ॥
॥ १०८॥१०९॥११०॥१११ ॥

पुनर्निवेद्यमुद्धृत्येति । पानीयं समर्प्य यथाविधानं जलं दत्त्वा गण्डूषदन्तधावनादिकं समर्प्य । अर्घ्याद्यष्टकं दत्त्वा प्रसरपुष्पाञ्जलिं विधाय दर्पणादिकं तैर्मन्त्रैः प्रयच्छेत् ।

वाससी च पुनरङ्गुलिभूषां होमकृत् सुमुखजप्रवरेषु ।
ईश्वरार्पणमिति प्रति दत्त्वा वर्धितो द्विजमुखैरितवाग्भिः ॥ ११७

नत्वा ततस्तनुभृते परमात्मने स्वं
द्रव्यार्धमेव गुरवे चतुरंशकं वा ।
दत्त्वा दशांशमथवापि च वित्तशाठ्यं
हित्वाऽर्पयेन्निजतनुं तदधीनचेताः ॥ ११८

बुद्धिः सवासना क्लृप्ता दर्पणं मङ्गलानि च ।
मनो वृत्तिर्विचित्रा ते नृत्यरूपेण कल्पिता ॥
ध्वनयो गीतिरूपेण शब्दा वाद्यप्रभेदतः ।
छत्राणि तव पद्मानि कल्पितानि मया प्रभो ॥
सुषुम्ना ध्वजरूपेण प्राणाद्याश्चामरात्मना ।
अहङ्कारो गजत्वेन क्लृप्तो देहो रथात्मना ॥
इन्द्रियाण्यश्वरूपाणि शब्दादि रथवर्त्मना ।
मनः प्रग्रहरूपेण बुद्धिः सारथिरूपतः ॥
सर्वमन्यन्मया क्लृप्तं तवोपकरणात्मना ॥

इति राजोपचारान् दत्त्वा। पुष्पाञ्जलिं विधाय। प्रसन्नार्घ्यं दत्त्वा। मूलमन्त्रं शक्त्यनुसारेण जप्त्वा। समर्प्य। प्रदक्षिणस्तुतिनमस्कारादिकं विधाय। देवतानुज्ञया तूत्तरतः कर्करीं स्थापयेत्। ईशानकोणे पूर्वसङ्क्षिते विकिरे हेमवस्त्रादिसंयुक्तां तोयपूर्णां कर्करीं स्थाप्य। तस्यां सिंहस्थां खड्गखेटकधारिणीं घोररूपां पश्चिमास्यामस्त्रदेवतां संपूज्य। चलासनेन प्रदक्षिणं नालमुक्तवारिणा सार्धं नयन् रक्षतेति लोकपालानां देवाज्ञां श्रावयित्वाऽस्त्रमन्त्रेण यथापूर्वं स्थापयेत्। पूजयेच्च। पुनश्चर्वर्थं स्थापितेऽग्नौ पुनश्चरुं पाचयेत्। पात्रमस्त्रेण प्रक्षाल्य। मूलजप्तानां तण्डूलानां प्रसृतिपञ्चदशकं तत्राऽस्त्रेण निक्षिप्य। प्रक्षाल्य। गव्यपयसा संपूर्य। कवचेन तन्मुखं पिधाय। प्राङ्मुखो मूलमन्त्रं जपन् पचेत्। मूलेन तत्राऽभिघारं दत्त्वा कवचेनाऽवतार्याऽस्त्रजप्ते कुशास्तीर्णे मण्डले संस्थाप्य। त्रिधा विभज्य। देवायाऽग्नये च भागद्वयं दत्त्वा। परं शिष्येण सार्धं भुक्त्वाऽऽचाम्याऽऽचान्तं शिष्यमानीय। सकलीकृत्य। तालप्रमाणं हृज्जप्तं दन्तकाष्ठं तस्मै दद्यात्। स तेन दन्तान् संशोध्य। प्रक्षाल्य। विसृज्याऽऽचम्याऽऽगच्छेत्। तं शिखाबन्धाभिरक्षितं कृत्वा। वेद्यां दर्भास्तरे तेन सार्धं शयीतेत्यधिवासः।

अथ पटुरवमुख्यवाद्यघोषैर्द्विजमुखनिष्पतदाशिषां रवेण ।
सुनियतमपि सुस्थितं च शिष्यं कलशजलैरभिषेचयेद् यथावत् ॥ ११९

यथा पुरा पूरितमन्त्रवरैर्घटैः सुधामयैः शिष्यतनौ तथैव तैः ।
प्रपूरयन्मन्त्रिवरोऽभिषेचयेदवाप्तये मङ्क्षु यथेष्टसम्पदाम् ॥ १२०

विमले परिधाय वाससी पुनराचम्य गुरुं प्रणम्य च ।
निकटे समुपासते वदेदपि शिष्याय मनुं विशो गुरुः ॥ १२१

ततः प्रातरुत्थाय कृतनित्यपूजो नैमित्तिकीमपि जपादिसमर्पणान्तं विधाय शुद्धं शिष्यमानीय । पञ्चगव्यं प्राशयित्वा । तं कुण्डसमीपे नीत्वा तं दिव्यदृष्ट्या विलोक्य । तच्चैतन्यं स्वहृदये संयोज्य । संक्षेपतो विस्तरतो वाऽध्वशोधनं कुर्यात् ॥ ११२ ॥ ११३ ॥ ११४ ॥ ११५ ॥ ११६ ॥ ११७ ॥ ११८ ॥

मन्त्रवर्णपदभुवनतत्त्वकलाध्वनः पदाम्बुनाभिहृद्भालमूर्धसु स्मृत्वा आचार्यकुण्डे सघृतैस्तिलैरमुकमध्वानं शोधयामि स्वाहेति प्रत्येकमध्वनामाहुत्यष्टकं शुद्ध्यर्थं हुत्वा । क्रमेण विलाप्य । सृष्टिक्रमेणोत्पाद्य । स्वहृत्स्थं चैतन्यं तत्र नियोज्य । मूलेन पूर्णां हुत्वा । देवतां कलश उद्वास्य । पुनर्व्याहृति जिह्वाङ्गादीनां हुत्वा परिषिच्यात्मनि अग्निमुद्वास्य । नेत्रमन्त्रेण शिष्यनेत्रे बद्ध्वा । तं मण्डलमानीय । तेन कलशस्थे देवे पुष्पाञ्जलिं कारयित्वा । नेत्रवस्त्रं विसृज्य । सर्वस्वादिक्रमेण दत्तदक्षिणं तं दर्भसंस्तरे स्थापयित्वा आत्मयागक्रमेण तं संहृत्य । उत्पाद्य । साध्यमन्त्रन्यासादिकं तच्छरीरे विधाय । कलशस्थदेवाय पुष्पाञ्जलिं विधाय । तं निष्कलीकृत्योद्धृत्य धृत्वा अभिषिञ्चतो गुरोर्भावनाप्रकारमाह—अथ पटुरवेति । पटुरवाणां मुखे भवा या उन्मनी साक्षिरूपिणी तेन वाद्या समनी तस्या घोषैः द्वारभूतैः शिष्यशरीरं प्रविश्य । तदु द्विजमुखात् कुण्डलीमुखान्निष्पततामाशिषामिच्छाशरीराणां ब्रह्मादिपञ्चमूर्तीनां कारणभूतेन रवेण द्वारभूतेन सर्वसंव्यापिनी समनीद्वारेण परमपदं प्राप्य । सुनियतमपि शिष्यं देवताविग्रहरूपेण सुस्थितं ध्यात्वा । कलशजलैः कला यस्मिन् शेरते परमात्मनि तद्रूपैः जलैः यथावदभेदेनाऽभिषेचयेत् इत्यर्थः ॥ ११९ ॥

अभिषेककाले मातृका मनसा अनुलोमेन जप्तव्येत्याह—यथा पुरेति । मन्त्रिवर इति । मातृकानन्तरं मूलं विरुच्चरन् अभिषेचयेत् । तदनन्तरं न्यासादिकं च कुर्यादिति उक्तम् ॥ १२० ॥

विशो गुरुरिति । शिष्यहृत्पुण्डरीकस्थां देवतां संपूज्य । तस्य दक्षिणकर्णे

गुरुणा समनुगृहीतं मन्त्रं सद्यो जपेच्छताद्यात्या ।

गुरुदेवतामनूनामैक्यं सम्भावयन् धिया शिष्यः ॥ १२२

मन्त्रे मन्त्रगुरावपि मन्त्री मन्त्रस्य देवतायां च ।

त्रिषु विहितसततभक्तिः प्रेत्येह निजेप्सितं फलं लभते ॥ १२३

सङ्क्षेपादिति गदिता हिताय दीक्षा

जन्तूनां प्रवरफलप्रदाऽचिराय ।

प्राप्यैनां जपविधिरादरेण कार्यो

विद्वद्भिः सहुतविधिर्निजेष्टसिद्ध्यै ॥ १२४

प्रोक्तेनैवं कलशविधिनैकेन वाऽनेककुम्भै-

र्भक्त्या यो वा सुमतिरभिषिञ्चेन्नरो मन्त्रजापी ।

कामान् प्राप्नोत्ययमिह परत्रापि किं तत्र चित्रं

लोकैश्चिन्त्यो न खलु मणिमन्त्रौषधीनां प्रभावः ॥ १२५

इति श्रीप्रपञ्चसारे षष्ठः पटलः ॥

सर्षिच्छन्दोदेवतं त्रिश उच्चार्य । सोदकं दत्त्वा । स्वयं च निजशक्तिहान्यनवासये जपेदित्यर्थः ॥ १२१ ॥ १२२ ॥ १२३ ॥ १२४ ॥ १२५ ॥

इति श्रीपद्मपादाचार्यकृते प्रपञ्चसारविवरणे

षष्ठः पटलः ।

सप्तमः पटलः ।

अथाऽक्षराणामधिदेवतायाः समस्तबोधस्थितिदीपिकायाः ।
अशेषदुःखप्रशमाय नृणां वक्ष्ये जपादेः प्रवरं विधानम् ॥ १

ब्रह्माऽस्या ऋषिरीरितः सुमतिभिर्गायत्रमुक्तञ्च त-
च्छन्दस्त्वेव सरस्वती निगदिता मन्त्रेषु तद्देवता ।
आद्यन्तस्वरषट्कलघुपरयोरन्तस्थितैः कादिभि-
र्वर्गैर्यान्तगतैः क्रमेण कथिता न्यस्याः षडङ्गानि च ॥ २

सर्वमन्त्रजपादेः लिपिन्यासादिपूर्वकत्वात् सर्वमन्त्रमयज्ञानशक्तिरूपत्वेन प्राधान्याच्च प्रथमतो मातृकाविधानं वक्तुमारभते—अथेति । सर्वमन्त्रसामान्यदीक्षाकथनानन्तर्यमथशब्दार्थः । समस्तबोधस्थितिदीपिकाया इत्यक्षराधिदेवतात्वोपपादनम् । बोधानां ज्ञानशक्तिप्रसरात्मकानां शब्दानां स्थितयः वैखरी मध्यमापश्यन्ती परा लक्षणाः । तासां दीपिका उन्मनीशक्तिरित्यर्थः ।

अथवा समस्तानां बोधानां स्थितिः पर्यवसानं यस्मिन् परमात्मनि तस्य प्रकाशिकाया इत्यर्थः । अस्ति हि सर्ववर्णानां वाक्यरूपत्वेन ब्रह्मात्मबोधकत्वम् । अथवा समस्ता बोधास्तिष्ठन्ति येषु विषयेषु तस्य सर्वस्य दीपिकाया इत्यर्थः । शब्दानुविद्धं हि सर्वं विज्ञानजातम् । अशेषदुःखप्रशमायेति विनियोगोक्तिः । बिन्दुविसर्गौ बीजशक्ती । हसावित्यन्ये । ततो हमिति बीजं स इति शक्तिः । इत्युभयाविरोधेन सिद्धं भवति । अथाऽनन्तरमक्षराणाम् अधिदेवताया मातृकाया जपादेः प्रवरं विधानं वक्ष्य इत्यन्वयः ।

कस्यानन्तरमिति आह—अधिदेवताया इति । भुवनाधिपतेरित्यर्थः । वाग्भवानन्तर्यमप्याह—समस्तेति ।

प्रणवानन्तर्यमप्याह—जपादेरिति । प्रणववाग्भवशक्त्यनन्तरं नमोऽन्ता वर्णा जपादौ प्रयोक्तव्या इत्यर्थः ॥ १ ॥

सुमतिभिरिति विधिपदयोगः सूचितः । उक्तं चेति देवीपदयोगः सूचितः । मातृका सरस्वती देवता । क्रमेण कथिता न्यस्या इति । क्रमादियोग उक्तः । भुवनेश्वर्यादि योगे चायं विशेषः ॥ २ ॥

पञ्चाशद्वर्णभेदैर्विहितवदनदोःपादयुक्कुक्षिवक्षो-
देशां भास्वत्कपर्दाकलितशशिकलामिन्दुकुन्दावदाताम् ।
अक्षस्रक्कुम्भचिन्तालिखितवरकरां त्रीक्षणां पद्मसंस्था-
मच्छाकल्पामतुच्छस्तनजघनभरां भारतीं तां नमामि ॥ ३

काननवृत्तदृगक्षिश्रुतिनोगण्डौष्ठदन्तमूर्धास्ये ।
दोःपत्सन्ध्यग्रकेषु च पार्श्वद्वयपृष्ठनाभिजठरेषु ॥ ४
हृद्दोर्मूलापरगलकक्षेषु हृदादिपाणिपादयुगे ।
जठरानलयोर्व्यापकसंज्ञान्न्यस्येदथो वर्णान् क्रमशः ॥ ५

संदीक्षितो विमलधीर्गुरुणाऽनुशिष्टो
लक्षं न्यसेत् सुनियतः प्रजपेच्च तावत् ।
अन्तेऽयुतं प्रतिहुनेन्मधुरत्रयाक्तैः
शुद्धैस्तिलैरपि यजेद्दिनशोऽक्षरेशीम् ॥ ६

व्योमाविःसचतुर्दशस्वरविसर्गान्तस्फुरत्कर्णिकं
किञ्जल्कालिखितस्वरं प्रतिदलं प्रारब्धवर्गाष्टकम् ।
क्ष्माबिम्बेन च सप्तमार्णवयुजाऽऽस्राशासु संवेष्टितं
वर्णाब्जं शिरसि स्मृतं विषगदप्रध्वंसि मृत्युञ्जयम् ॥

भारतीमिति नादाद्यात्मकं सूक्ष्मरूपं कथितम्। तामिति परं चिदात्मकं भारतीं तां भुवनेश्वरीरूपिणीमिति। स्थूलध्यानेऽपि पाशाङ्कुशपुस्तकाक्षवलययोगः सूचितः ॥ ३ ॥

विमलधीरिति तत्तदक्षरन्यासे तत्पारायणादि व्यास्यविस्मरणं सूचितम्। गुरुणाऽनुशिष्ट इति करन्यासादिकं सूचितम्। आदिषट्कं तलादिषु न्यसित्वा ककारादिदशकं दक्षकनिष्ठाद्यङ्गुलीषु व्यापकादिकमङ्गुलीपर्वसु न्यस्याङ्गमन्त्रैरपि न्यसेदिति करन्यासः। सामान्यपटलोक्ता न्यासाः सर्वत्र कार्या इति। सुनियत इति ब्रह्मचर्यस्थानासनादिनियमाः सूचिताः। अपि यजेदिति तर्पणाभिषेकोपस्थानादिकम् उक्तम् ॥ ४ ॥ ५ ॥ ६ ॥

व्योमाविःसेति। हकारसकाराबुद्धृतौ। प्रतिदलं प्रारब्धेति। पारायणाक्षराणां शक्त्यनुसारेण लेखनं सूचितम्। ऋग्वेदादिगतवर्गप्रश्नादीनां च सप्तमार्णः ठकारः। विषध्वंसे गारुडयोगः। गदध्वंसे नारसिंहयोगः। मृत्युञ्जये

प्रविधाय पद्ममथ पीठमथो कथितक्रमेण विधिनाऽभियजेत् ।
नवभिश्च शक्तिभिरमुत्र सहावरणैः समर्चयतु वर्णतनुम् ॥ ८

मेधा प्रज्ञा प्रभा विद्या धीर्धृतिस्मृतिबुद्धयः ।
विद्येश्वरीति संप्रोक्ता भारत्या नव शक्तयः ॥ ९

अङ्गान्यादौ तदनु च कलायुग्मशश्चाऽष्टवर्गान्
ब्रह्माण्याद्याः शतमखमुखाद्यानथो लोकपालान् ।
मुख्यैर्गन्धैः प्रवरकुसुमैर्धूपदीपैर्निवेद्यै-
र्वर्णान् जापी यजतु दिनशो भारतीं भक्तिनम्रः ॥ १०

ब्रह्माणी माहेशी कौमारी वैष्णवी च वाराही ।
इन्द्राणी चामुण्डा समहालक्ष्मीश्च मातरः प्रोक्ताः ॥ ११

वर्गस्वरयाद्यंशाः क्रमेण कलधौतरजतताम्राः स्युः ।
इति रचितं रुचकमिदं साधकसर्वार्थदायि सततं स्यात् ॥ १२

विवारमम्भः परिजप्तमेतया पिबेद्दिनादावपि विद्यया सुधीः ।
अनेडमूकोऽपि कवित्वगर्वितः पराञ्च सिद्धिं लभतेऽर्कमासतः ॥ १३

सद्योगः [रुद्रयोगः] ॥ ७ ॥

विधिनाऽभियजेदिति : पृथिव्यनन्तरं विद्याब्धियोगः सूचितः । प्रविधायेति यन्त्रजीवादियोगः । अमुत्रेति । ओं ह्रीं वर्णाब्जाय सरस्वत्यासनाय नमः इति पीठमन्त्रः सूचितः । वर्णतनुमिति मातृकया मूर्तिपूजा ॥ ८ ॥ ९ ॥

चाऽष्टवर्गानिति चशब्देन व्यापिन्यादिशक्तिभिश्चतुर्थमावरणं सूचितम् । व्यापिनी पालिनी वाचिनी क्लेदिनी धारिणी मालिनी हंसिनी शान्तिन्यः शक्तयः । ताश्च श्वेताः अक्षवलयपुस्तकधारिण्यः । ब्रह्माणी कनकवर्णा अक्षसूत्र-कमण्डलुवरदाभयधरा । शूलपरशुडुन्दुभिकपालधरा माहेश्वरी । अङ्कुशदण्ड-खट्वाङ्गपाशधरा कौमारी । चक्रघण्टाकपालशङ्खधरा वैष्णवी । मुसलखड्गखेटका-भयधरा वाराही । अङ्कुशतोमरपाशकुलिशधरा इन्द्राणी । शूलकृपाण-नृशिरःकपालधरा चामुण्डा रक्ता । अक्षस्रक् बीजापूर कपाल पङ्कजधरा महालक्ष्मीः । शतमखमुखाद्यानिति--शतमखमुखाः लं रं टं क्षं वं यं सं हं क्रीं क्षमिति बीजानि । तान्यादौ येषां लोकपालानां ते तथोक्ताः । वर्णान्-जापीति वर्णजापी वेत्यर्थः ॥ १० ॥ ११ ॥ १२ ॥

कमलोद्भवौषधिरसेन वचया पयसा च पक्वमथ सर्पिरपि ।
अयुताभिजप्तममुना दिनशो लिहतां कविर्भवति वत्सरतः ॥ १४

वर्णौषध्या शृताभिः कलशममलधीरद्भिरापूर्य नूनं
प्रातस्तेनाऽभिषिञ्चेद्दशशतपरिजप्तेन यं वापि मासम् ।
स स्यान्मेधेन्दिरायुः प्रशमकवियशो विश्वसंवादयुक्तो
नारी बन्ध्याऽपि नानागुणगणनिलयं पुत्रवर्यं प्रसूते ॥ १५

आधारोद्यच्छक्तिविन्दूत्थिताया वक्त्रे मूर्धेन्दुं ग्रसन्त्याः प्रभायाः ।
क्षाद्यान्तार्णान् पातयेद्वह्निसोमप्रोतान्मन्त्री मुच्यते रोगजातैः ॥

अपि विद्ययेति । कर्णिकाबीजयोगः सूचितः । अथवा अपिशब्देन दशाक्षरीयोगः विद्याशब्देन त्रिपुराणामन्यतमयोः योगः सूचितः । सुधीरित्याधारेषु पञ्चवर्णादिचिन्तनम् । अयमत्र प्रयोगक्रमः । स्वयं देवताविग्रहो भूत्वा । लिपिपद्मे हस्ते संकल्प्य । तस्मिन् जलमादाय । ऐं क्लीं सौः अः वद वद वाग्वादिनि स्वाहा अः सौः क्लीं ऐं एवं क्षकारान्तं जपित्वा । क्षाद्यकारान्तमेव सबिन्दुकं जपित्वा । एवमेव सबिन्दुविसर्गम् अकारादिक्षान्तं जपित्वा पिबन् । मूलाधाराद्याधारेषु चतुःषड् दश द्वादश षोडश द्विदलपद्मेषु वर्णानां वादि बादि-डादि कादि आदि हादीनां दीपशिखावदुव्याप्तिं ध्यायेत् । पुनरप्येवं द्विवारं पिबन् वर्णानामास्यान्तरम् उद्गमनम् आस्याच्छास्त्राद्याकारेण निर्गमनं च ध्यायेत् । सप्तत्यैकवर्गैर्वा त्रिवारजप इति ।

अप्ययुताभिजप्तमिति पूजाहोमादिकमुक्तम् ॥ १३ ॥ १४ ॥

कलशममलधीरिति कामनानुगुणबीजयोगादिकं सूचितम् । मेधाकामस्य श्रीयोगः । इन्दिराकामस्य तद्योगः । आयुषि जुंसंयोगः । प्रशमे प्रणवयोगः । कवित्वे वाग्भवयोगः । यशसि अजपायोगः । विश्वसंवादे शक्तियोगः । नानागुणाश्रयपुत्रकामे सर्वयोग इति ।

अथवा भानुवारे मध्यप्रागादि दिक्षु नवकलशान् मुक्तामाणिक्यवैडूर्यगोमेद-वज्रविद्रुमपुष्परागमरकतनीलरत्नयुतान् संपूज्याऽभिषिञ्चेत् । तत्र मध्ये सर्वैः बीजैः देवीं संपूज्य । दलकुम्भेषु ह्लौः इत्यादिभिः व्यापिन्याद्याः पूज्याः । शान्तिन्या दुर्गाबीजेन पूजा त्रिलोहमुद्रिका नवरत्नमुद्रिका वा कलितसङ्गता कार्या । कलशजपपूजा होमसहिता ॥ १५ ॥

- वह्निसोमप्रोतानिति । अग्नीषोमात्मकानित्यर्थः । मन्त्रीति । ओं क्षीं

विन्यासैरथ सजपैर्हुतार्चनाद्यै-
र्ध्यानैर्न प्रभजति भारतीं नरो यः।
स श्रीमान् पुनरचिरेण काव्यकर्ता
क्ष्वेलादीन् जयति जरापमृत्युरोगैः॥ १७

ॡं क्षं नमः। ओं क्लीं लॣं ळं नमः। ओं क्लीं ॠं ह्रं नम इत्यादिक्रमेण पातयेदित्यर्थः॥ १६॥

विन्यासैरिति। शुद्ध सविसर्ग सबिन्दुविसर्ग सबिन्दु सकल सकेशवादि-सश्रीकण्ठादि सशक्तिकमलामार समारकमलाशक्ति सशक्ति सकमल समारन्यासैरन्यै-श्चेत्यर्थः। जपाश्चैवंविधाः। हुतार्चनाविधी मातृकोक्तौ।

शुद्धन्यासे अङ्गर्षिध्यानादिकं मातृकायामुक्तप्रकारेण द्रष्टव्यम्। सरस्वती एव देवता।

विसर्गन्यासे विसर्गान्तान्यङ्गानीत्येव विशेषः। ध्यानपूजादिकं समानम्। सृष्टिसरस्वती देवता।

बिन्दुविसर्गयोगे तथाविधानि अङ्गानि। स्थितिसरस्वती देवता। ध्याने तु विशेषः। सिन्दूरवर्णं वराक्षसूत्रमृगपुस्तकधरं देवं ध्यात्वा। तत्पार्श्वे काञ्चनाभां पुस्तकाक्षमालाधरां देवीं ध्यायेदिति।

सबिन्दुन्यासे संहारसरस्वती देवता। रक्तवर्णाम् अक्षमालाटङ्कमृगपुस्तकधरां ध्यायेत्।

सकलन्यासे प्रजापतिः ऋषिः। गायत्री छन्दः। कला सरस्वती देवता। ह्रस्वदीर्घास्वरस्थैः प्रणवैरङ्गानि। पद्म चक्र शूलमृगाक्षसूत्र पुस्तक टङ्क कपालशङ्ख-कलशधरा मुक्ताविद्युत्पयोद स्फटिक जपावर्णपञ्चवदना शुक्लवर्णा ध्येया।

केशवादियुतन्यासे प्रजापतिः ऋषिः। गायत्री छन्दः। अर्धलक्ष्मीनारायणो देवता। दीर्घषट्कयुक्तेन कामेनाऽङ्गानि। अथवा ओं नमो क्लीं नमो नारायणाय हंसः सोऽहं अं कं खं गं घं ङं आं ओं नमो नारायणाय हंसः सोऽहं देव्यै हृदयाय नमः। इत्यादिमन्त्रैरङ्गानि कुर्यात्। पद्मिनी विष्णुपत्नी वरदा कमलरूपा-शूलिन्योऽवशिष्टाः शक्तयः। पद्म गदा शङ्ख चक्र पुस्तक पद्मादर्श रत्नकलशधरो विद्युत्पयोदवर्णो ध्येयः।

श्रीकण्ठादियुतन्यासेऽम्बरीष ऋषिः। अनुष्टुप् छन्दः। अर्धनारीश्वरो देवता। दक्षिणामूर्तिगायत्री ऋषिच्छन्दसी इत्यन्ये। षड्दीर्घयुजा हसाऽङ्गानि। अथवा

कला: कला नादभवा वदन्त्यजा: कचादिवर्णानुभवाष्टतादिकान् ।
पयादिकान्माचरजाश्च बिन्दुजा: क्रमादनन्तावधिकास्तु षादिकान् ॥
कुर्यात् कलाभिराभिर्मन्त्री दिनशस्तनौ कलान्यासम् ।
सान्निध्यकृत् स मर्त्य: प्रतिमाकलशादिषु प्रविज्ञेय: ॥ १९

ओं नमो भगवति ब्रह्माणि रक्ष रक्ष पद्महस्ते मां रक्ष रक्ष अं कं खं गं घं ङं आं क्रौं ह्सौ: सञ्जीवनि सञ्जीवनि हृदयाय नम: । ओं नमो भगवति माहेश्वरि रक्ष रक्ष त्रिशूलहस्ते मां रक्ष रक्ष इं चं छं जं झं ञं ईं क्रौं ह्सौ: ऊर्ध्वकेशिनि शिरसे स्वाहा । ओं नमो भगवति कौमारि रक्ष रक्ष शक्तिहस्ते मां रक्ष रक्ष उं टं ठं डं ढं णं ऊं क्रौं ह्सौ: जटिलकेशिनि शिखायै वषट् । ओं नमो भगवति वैष्णवि रक्ष रक्ष चक्रहस्ते मां रक्ष रक्ष एं तं थं दं धं नं ऐं क्रौं ह्सौ: मायात्रैलोक्यरूपिणि सहस्रपरिवर्तिनि कवचाय हुं । ओं नमो भगवति वाराहि रक्ष रक्ष दंष्ट्रहस्ते मां रक्ष रक्ष ओं पं फं बं भं मं औं क्रौं ह्सौ: ताराक्षिणि नेत्रत्रयाय वौषट् । ओं नमो भगवति इन्द्राणि रक्ष रक्ष वज्रहस्ते मां रक्ष रक्ष अं यं रं लं वं शं षं सं हं लं क्षं अ: क्रौं ह्सौ: मारय मारय अस्त्राय फट् । ओं नमो भगवति चामुण्डे रक्ष रक्ष पाशहस्ते मां रक्ष रक्ष अं इत्यादि ह्रस्वाष्टकं कादिक्षान्तं दीर्घाष्टकं चोक्त्वा सर्वाङ्गं रक्ष रक्ष सर्वाङ्गव्यापिनि स्वाहा इति मन्त्रैरङ्गानि व्यापकं च कुर्यात् । बन्धूककाञ्चननिभोऽक्षमालाङ्कुशपाशवरदधरो ध्येय: ।

शक्तिकमलामारयोगे शक्ते: ऋष्यादिकं न्यसेत् । द्विरुक्तैर्बीजैरङ्गानि । अक्षस्रक्पञ्चशर पद्माङ्कुश पाशपद्मेक्षुधनु: पुस्तकधरा अरुणा ध्येया ।

समारकमलाशक्तिन्यासे सम्मोहनगायत्रीजगज्जनन्य ऋष्यादय: । द्विरुक्तैर्बीजैरङ्गानि । पञ्चबाण पद्माङ्कुशाक्षमाला पुस्तकपाशपद्मधनुर्धरा ध्येया ।

सशक्तिन्यासे शक्तिवदङ्गर्ष्यादिकम् । अक्षस्रगङ्कुशपाशपुस्तकधरा ध्येया ।

सश्रीन्यासे श्रीबीजवदङ्गर्ष्यादिकम् । अक्षस्रक्कमलद्वयपुस्तकधरा ध्येया ।

सकामन्यासे कामबीजवदङ्गर्ष्यादिकम् । अक्षस्रक्शरचापपुस्तकधरा ध्येया ।

स श्रीमानिति । केशवादियोगे श्रीबीजयोगे च श्रीरेव फलम् । कलायोगे काव्यकर्तृत्वम् । श्रीकण्ठादियोगे क्ष्वेलादिजय: । जरापमृत्युरोगादिजयोऽन्येषाम् । सर्वं सर्वत्र वा ॥ १७ ॥

कला: कला इति कलान्यासे वर्णयोगक्रममाह । प्रसङ्गाच्चान्यत् ॥ १८ ॥

मन्त्रीति । कलान्यासे पाशाङ्कुशत्र्यक्षरादियोग: सूचित: ॥ १९ ॥

मन्त्रोद्धारविधानेन वर्णव्यत्यासक्लृप्तिरुद्दिष्टा ।
आभिः श्रीकण्ठादिप्रोक्तैर्वा नामभिर्वा विशेषज्ञैः ॥ २०

अष्टाक्षरोक्तमनुवर्यविशिष्टमूर्त्तिं
संस्मृत्य विष्णुमपि मन्त्रितमो यथावत् ।
वर्णैर्न्यसेदपि पुरेव च केशवादि-
मूर्त्या युतैर्वपुषि भक्तिभरावनम्रः ॥ २१

रुद्रादीन् शक्तियुतान् न्यसेद् याद्यांस्त्वगादिसप्तधातुयुतान् ।
श्रीकण्ठादौ विद्वान् वर्णान् प्राग्बीजसंयुतांश्चापि ॥ २२

सिन्दूरकाञ्चनसमोभयभागमर्ध-
नारीश्वरं गिरिसुताहरचिह्नभूषम् ।
पाशाभयाक्षवलयेष्टदहस्तमेवं
स्मृत्वा न्यसेत् सकलवाञ्छितवस्तुसिद्ध्यै ॥ २३

शक्त्या शक्तिश्रीभ्यां शक्तिश्रीक्लीभिरन्वितैर्वर्णैः ।
श्रीशक्त्या युगस्मराद्यैरथवा विहितः समृद्धये न्यासः ॥ २४

अथाऽनया पञ्चविभेदभिन्नया प्रपञ्चयागस्य विधिः प्रकथ्यते ।
कृते तु यस्मिन्निह साधकोत्तमाः प्रयान्ति निर्वाणपदं तदव्ययम् ॥ २५

विशेषज्ञैरिति । उद्धारस्य मलसंहाररूपत्वं जानद्भिरित्यर्थः ॥ २० ॥

केशवादिन्यासे विशेषमाह—अष्टाक्षरेति । अष्टाक्षरपटल उक्तो यो मनुवर्यस्तेन विशिष्टमूर्तिं विष्णुमिति । वर्णोर्ध्वभागेऽष्टाक्षरयोगोऽप्युक्तः । विष्णुमपीति श्रियमपीत्यर्थः । मन्त्रितम इति वर्णादौ त्रिपुटादियोगः सूचितः । यथावदित्यर्धलक्ष्मीनारायणध्येयत्वं सूचितम् । न्यसेदपीति पूजादिकमपि कुर्यादित्यर्थः ॥ २१ ॥

रुद्रादीनिति । रुद्राणां श्रीकण्ठादिमूर्तीनामादौ स्थितान् वर्णान् शक्तियुतान् मूर्त्यन्ते पूर्णोदर्यादिशक्तियुतान् । याद्यैस्त्वगादिधातुयोगः सर्वन्यासेषु समानः । श्रीकण्ठादौ विद्वानिति । श्रीकण्ठादिमूर्तीनामादौ वर्णानामुपरि पञ्चाक्षरीविद्यायोगः उक्तः । प्राग् बीजसंयुतानिति वर्णादौ प्रणवशक्तिप्रासादयोग उक्तः । अपीत्यजपादियोगः ॥ २२॥२३॥२४ ॥

पञ्चविभेदभिन्नयेति । पञ्चाशत् सप्त त्रि द्वेऽकमन्त्रसम्बद्धयेत्यर्थः । सप्तशक्ति-

पूर्वं महागणपतिं स्वविधानसिद्ध-
रूपञ्च साङ्गमपि सावरणं विचिन्त्य ।
बीजेन संयुतमृचा प्रजपेत माला-
मन्त्रं निजेष्टविधयेऽवहितो यथावत् ॥ २६

सचतुश्चत्वारिंशद्वारं बीजं तथैकवारमृचम् ।
प्रजपेच्चतुरावृत्त्या मालापूर्वं मनुञ्च मन्त्रितमः ॥ २७

समुनिच्छन्दो दैवतमपि साङ्गमातृकां च विन्यसेत् ।
प्रागभिहितेन विधिना वारत्रितयं ग्रहांश्च सप्त तथा ॥ २८

वदने च बाहुपादद्वितये जठरे च वक्षसि यथावत् ।
अर्काद्यान् विन्यसेत् क्रमेण मन्त्री स्वरादिवर्गेशान् ॥ २९

कमलामार समारकमलाशक्ति सशक्तिकमला सशक्ति समारपञ्चन्यासभेदयुतयेति वार्थः । साधकोत्तमा इति प्रपञ्चयागादौ तत्त्वस्पृहामधिकार उक्तः ॥ २५ ॥

पूर्वमिति । लिपिन्यासात् पूर्वं नित्यलिपिन्यासादुत्तरमित्यर्थः । अवहित इति बीजादीनां ध्यानभेदः सूचितः । यथावदित्यङ्गादिन्यासपूर्वकत्वम् ॥ २६ ॥

मन्त्रितम इति विभूतिमन्त्रजपः । बीजषट्कानन्तरं महाविभूते वरे वरदे सर्वजनविमर्दिनीत्यादिर्विभूतिमन्त्रः ॥ २७ ॥

ग्रहांश्च सप्तेति नवग्रहन्यासः सूचितः ॥ २८ ॥

प्राणाग्निहोत्रार्थं सप्तग्रहन्यासस्थानमाह— वदन इति । अयमत्र न्यासक्रमः । स्वरस्थाने स्वरान् विन्यस्य । तानुक्त्वा । स्वराधिपतये सूर्याय भगवते नमः । इति स्वरस्थाने व्यापयेत् । कवर्गं न्यसित्वा । तानुक्त्वा । कवर्गाधिपतये मङ्गलाय भगवते नमः । चवर्गाधिपतये शुक्राय नमः । इत्यादयो व्यापकमन्त्राः ज्ञातव्याः । यथावदिति प्रणवशक्तिमूलमन्त्रादियोगो व्यापकन्यासश्च सूचितः ।

मन्त्री स्वरादिवर्गेशानिति । भगवत्पदस्य तत्तदधिपतिपदस्य च योग उक्तः । स्वरानुक्त्वा सोममण्डलाय नम इति मूर्धादिगलपर्यन्तं व्याप्य । स्पर्शानुक्त्वा सूर्यमण्डलाय नम इति गलादिनाभिपर्यन्तं व्याप्य । यादिकमुक्त्वा अग्निमण्डलाय नम इति नाभ्यादिपादान्तं न्यसेदिति मण्डलत्रयन्यासः । आदिठान्तमुक्त्वा सोममण्डलाय नम इति मूर्धादिहृदयान्तं न्यसित्वा । डादिक्षान्तमुक्त्वाऽग्नि-मण्डलायेति हृदादिपादान्तं न्यसेदिति अग्नीषोमन्यासः । आदिक्षान्तमुक्त्वा

तारश्च शक्तिरजपा परमात्मबीजं
वह्नेः प्रिया च गदिता इति पञ्च मन्त्राः ।
एभिस्तृतीयलिपिभिः कथितः प्रपञ्च-
यागाह्वयो हुतविधिः सकलार्थदायी ॥ ३०

ब्रह्मा स्यादृषिरस्य च छन्दः परमान्विता च गायत्री ।
सकलपदार्थसदर्थपरिपूर्णं देवता परं ज्योतिः ॥ ३१

जायाऽग्नेर्हृदयमथो शिरश्च सोऽहं
हंसात्मा त्वथ च शिखा स्वयञ्च वर्म ।
ताराख्यं समुदितमीच्चणं तथाऽस्त्रं
प्रोक्तं स्याद्वरिहरवर्णमङ्गमेवम् ॥ ३२

हंसः पुरुषात्मने नम इति व्यापकत्वेन हंसन्यासः । एते चाऽन्याश्च यथावदित्यनेन सूचिताः । तथेति वा ।

अथ नवग्रहन्यासः । चं लं हं सं षं मरकतवर्णाय केतवे भगवते नमः । शं वं लं रं यं गोमेदवर्णाय राहवे भगवते नमः । मं भं बं फं पं नीलवर्णाय शनैश्चराय भगवते नमः । नं धं दं थं तं विद्रुमवर्णाय बृहस्पतये भगवते नमः । णं ढं डं ठं टं वज्रवर्णाय बुधाय भगवते नमः । ञं झं जं छं चं पुष्परागवर्णाय शुक्राय भगवते नमः । ङं घं गं खं कं वैडूर्यवर्णाय अङ्गारकाय भगवते नमः । अः अं औं ओं ऐं एं ॡं ऌं मुक्तावर्णाय सोमाय भगवते नमः । ॠं ऋं ऊं उं ईं इं आं अं माणिक्यवर्णाय सूर्याय भगवते नम इति मूलाधार लिङ्गमूल नाभि हृदय गल लम्बिका भ्रूमध्य ललाट ब्रह्मरन्ध्रेषु न्यसित्वा । मण्डलत्रयाग्नीषोमहंसन्यासान् पूर्वोक्तवैपरीत्येन न्यसेदिति । 'कृत्वा महात्माऽथ शतार्धसंख्यं विन्यस्य तावच्च'इति प्राणाग्निहोत्रस्य प्राथम्यं वक्ष्यति ।

अतः प्रथमं नवग्रहमण्डलत्रयादिन्यासं कृत्वा । सप्तग्रहमण्डलत्रयादि-न्यासः कर्तव्यः ॥ २९ ॥

ब्रह्मा स्यादृषिरस्य प्रपञ्चयागमन्त्रस्य । प्राणाग्निहोत्रस्य तु स्वयंभूरित्यर्थः । परमान्विता चेति । स्वयमन्विता या गायत्री प्राणाग्निहोत्रस्येत्यर्थः । स्वयंज्योतिः प्राणाग्निहोत्रदेवता ॥ ३०॥३१ ॥

शिरश्च सोऽहमिति । प्राणाग्निहोत्रे हंसस्य शिरस्त्वमुक्तम् । अथ च शिखेति । प्राणाग्निहोत्रे सोऽहमित्यस्य शिखात्वं सूचितम् । स्वयं च वर्मेति । शक्तेः ध्येयत्वं

अत्राऽकारहकाराद्यावाद्यौ शान्तान्तिकौ मनू ।
हकारस्याऽप्यकारस्य बिन्दुः सर्गौ च साक्षरः ॥ ३३
साकारस्यात्ममन्त्रः षड़िन्द्रियात्मक उच्यते ।
सकारौकारहकारा बिन्दुः पञ्चार्णको मनुः ॥ ३४
करणात्मसमायुक्तः परमात्माह्वयो मनुः ।
सवाकारैर्हदीर्घाभ्यां वह्निजायामनुर्मतः ॥ ३५
वागादीन्द्रियसम्भिन्नः सोऽयं पञ्चाक्षरात्मकः ।
तस्मादेभिः कृतो न्यासो विशेषादवरोहकृत् ॥ ३६
ब्रह्मा बृहत्तया स्यात् परमपदेन प्रकाशितः प्रवरः ।
गायकसन्त्राणनतो गायत्रं समुदीरितं छन्दः ॥ ३७
परमन्यदतिशयं वा ज्योतिस्तेजो निरूपितेऽन्यद् यत् ।
अतिशायि च नितरामिति कथितैवं देवता परं ज्योतिः ॥ ३८
स्वेति स्वर्गः स्वेति चात्मा समुक्तो हेत्याहुतिर्हेति विद्याद् गतिञ्च ।
स्वर्गात्मावध्याततता धामशाखा वह्नेर्जाया यत्र हूयेत सर्वम् ॥ ३९
स इति परिततं परन्तु तेजस्त्वमहमिति मय्युदिते मनोऽस्य यत्र ।
तदिति सकलचित्प्रकाशरूपं कथितमिदं शिरसोऽपि मन्त्रमेवम् ॥

सूचितम् । मन्त्राणां व्याप्तिकथनेन न्यासविशेषाः सूचिताः । ते च गुर्वादिवन्दनं कृत्वा अस्त्रेण करशुद्ध्यादिकं प्राणायामादिकं च कृत्वा न्यस्तव्याः ॥ ३२॥३३ ॥ ॥ ३४॥३५॥३६॥३७॥३८ ॥

हेत्याहुतिरिति स्वर्गशब्दार्थस्य परमात्मनः स्वशब्दार्थप्रत्यगात्मन्याह्वान-मित्यर्थः । हेति विद्यात् गतिं चेति । आत्मनः परमात्मनि गतिमित्यर्थः । हृदयमन्त्रेण जीवात्मपरमात्मनोः परस्परमेकत्वम् उक्तमिति । तात्पर्यमाह—स्वर्गात्मेति । अयमेवार्थं इत्यत्रोपपत्तिमाह—यत्र हूयेतेति ॥ ३९ ॥

परमात्ममन्त्रस्य त्वंपदार्थपर्यन्तं तत्पदार्थत्वमाह—स इति । अहमिति मय्युदिते मनोऽस्य यत्रेति । देहेन्द्रियादिभ्य उद्गते मयि साक्षिणि परमात्मन्यस्य साधकस्य मनो यत्र वर्तते साक्षितया सोऽहंशब्दार्थ इत्यर्थः ।

वाक्यार्थमाह—तदिति । सकलः परिपूर्णः चित्प्रकाशश्च तं रूपयतीति सकलचित्प्रकाशरूपो मन्त्रः ॥ ४० ॥

हमिति प्रकाशितोऽहं स इति च सकलप्रकाशनिर्वाणम् ।
अतुलमनुष्णमशीतं यत्तदितीत्थं प्रकाशितेह शिखा ॥ ४१

प्रतिमथ्य गुणत्रयानुबद्धं सकलं स्थावरजङ्गमाभिपूर्णम् ।
स्वगुणैर्निजबिन्दुसन्ततात्माखिललोकस्थितिवर्ममन्त्र उक्तः ॥ ४२

आद्यैस्त्रिभेदैस्तपनान्तिकैर्यत् सृजत्यजस्रं जगतोऽस्य भावम् ।
तेजस्तदेतन्मनुवर्यकस्य नेत्रत्रयं सन्त उदाहरन्ति ॥ ४३

हुङ्काराख्यो धातुर्हरणार्थे साधकानभीष्टान् ।
संहरतीति यदेतत्तेजोरूपं तदस्त्रमन्त्रः स्यात् ॥ ४४
यदा लिपिविभिन्नोऽयं तदात्माष्टाक्षरः स्मृतः ।
एतत् सर्वप्रपञ्चस्य मूलमष्टाक्षरं स्मृतम् ॥ ४५
प्रपञ्चयागस्त्वमुना कृतो न्यासविधिर्मतः ।
वर्णैर्देहेऽनले द्रव्यैर्विद्याहुतविधिं द्विधा ॥ ४६
मातृकान्यासवत्साधं लिपिनाऽष्टाक्षरेण तु ।
नित्यं न्यसेत् संयतात्मा पञ्चाशद्वारमुत्तमम् ॥ ४७

अजपायास्तत्पदार्थपर्यन्त त्वंपदार्थतामाह—हमिति । अतुलमिति वाक्यार्थकथनम् ॥ ४१ ॥

एवं होमाधिकरणाग्निशोधनार्थयोः परमात्माजपामन्त्रयोरर्थमभिधाय । द्रव्यसंशोधनार्थस्य शक्तिबीजस्यार्थमाह—प्रतिमथ्येति । प्रतिमथ्य संहृत्य गुणत्रयव्याप्तं सकलं जगत् स्वगुणैः हकारादिरूपैः तांश्च हकारादीन् बिन्दौ गुणसाम्यात्मनि संहृत्य । सर्वलोकाश्रयापरप्रकृत्यमृतात्मनाऽवस्थितः कवचमन्त्र इत्यर्थः ॥ ४२ ॥

प्रणवस्याऽमृतरूपद्रव्योत्पादकत्वेन विनियोगं वदन् नेत्रमन्त्रार्थमाह—आद्यैरिति । अजस्रमिति प्रतिहोममित्यर्थः ॥ ४३ ॥ ४४ ॥ ४५ ॥ ४६ ॥

पञ्चाशन्मन्त्रैः प्रपञ्चयागक्रममाह—मातृकान्यासवदिति । सप्तग्रहमण्डलत्रयादिहोमं सूचयति । अयमत्र क्रियाक्रमः । प्राणाग्निहोत्रप्रपञ्चयागयोः ऋष्यादिकं विन्यस्य । शक्तिरूपमात्मानं ध्यात्वा । अष्टाक्षरद्वयमष्टवारमावर्त्त्य । हयरौं ययरौं रयरौं वयरौं लयरौं इति मूलाधारत्रिकोणशक्ति बिन्दुमध्यप्राग्वारुणसौम्य दक्षिणदिग्गतकुण्डेष्वग्नीनुज्ज्वाल्य । चाद्यकारान्तमुच्चरन् । पादादिमस्तकान्तं व्याप्य । स्वशरीरात्मकं सर्वं जगत् परमामृतेनैकीकृत्य । ओं क्रीं

चं परंज्योतिषि जुहोमि सोऽहं हंसः स्वाहा। ओं क्लीं लं परंज्योतिषि जुहोमि सोऽहं हंसः स्वाहा। ओं क्लीं हं परंज्योतिषि जुहोमि सोऽहं हंसः स्वाहा। ओं क्लीं सं परंज्योतिषि जुहोमि सोऽहं हंसः स्वाहा। ओं क्लीं षं परंज्योतिषि जुहोमि सोऽहं हंसः स्वाहा। इति मध्यादिकुण्डेषु हुत्वा। शाद्यकारान्तमेवं हुत्वा अकारमवशेषयेत्। पुनः प्रणवशक्तिबीजाभ्यां शरीरमुत्पाद्य। शुद्धन्यासेन सकलीकृत्य। चाद्यकारान्तं व्यापकत्वेन पूर्ववदमृतीकृत्य। पुनः चं शं मं नं णं जं ङं अः एं ऊं आकाशशब्दतन्मात्र श्रोत्र वागात्म शान्त्यतीत नादतुरीयातीतानुग्रह सदाशिवेशानवासुदेवान् परंज्योतिषीत्यादि मध्ये। ओं क्लीं लं वं भं धं ढं झं घं ओं लृं उं वायुस्पर्शतन्मात्र स्पर्शपाणिप्रकृति शान्तिबिन्दुतुरीयतिरोधानेश्वरतत्पुरुष संकर्षणान् परंज्योतिषीत्यादि पूर्वकुण्डे। ओं क्लीं हं लं वं दं डं जं गं औं ऌं ईं तेजोरूपतन्मात्र चक्षुःपादाहंकार विद्यामकार सुषुप्ति संहाररुद्राघोर प्रद्युम्नान् परंज्योतिषीत्यादि पश्चिमे। ओं क्लीं सं रं फं थं ठं छं खं ओं ॠं इं अब्रसतन्मात्र रसनपायु मनःप्रतिष्ठोकार स्वप्नस्थिति विष्णुवामदेवानिरुद्धान् परंज्योतिषीत्यादि सौम्ये। ओं क्लीं षं यं पं तं टं चं कं ऐं ऋं आं पृथिवीगन्धतन्मात्रघ्राणोपस्थ बुद्धि निवृत्त्यकार जाग्रत्सृष्टि ब्रह्मसद्योजातनारायणान् परंज्यतिषीत्यादि दक्षिणे कुण्डे हुनेत्। पुनः लरियों वरियों ररियों यरियों हरियोमित्यग्नीनेकीकृत्य। पुनः पूर्ववदुत्पाद्य। सबिन्दुकेन सकलीकृत्य। पूर्ववदमृतीकृत्य। ओं क्लीं अं परंज्योतिषीत्यादिना हुत्वा। पूर्ववदुत्पाद्य। सविसर्गेण सकलीकृत्याऽमृतीकृत्य। ओं क्लीं चं परंज्योतिषीत्यारभ्याऽकारान्तं हुत्वा। पूर्ववदुत्पाद्य। सबिन्दुसविसर्गेण सकलीकृत्य। नवग्रहन्यासमन्त्रैः विधिवत् हुत्वा। पूर्ववदुत्पाद्य। सकलन्यासेन सकलीकृत्याऽमृतीकृत्याऽग्न्यादिमण्डलत्रयन्यासमन्त्रैः विधिवत् हुत्वोत्पाद्य। सकेशवादिन्यासेन सकलीकृत्याऽमृतीकृत्याऽग्नीषोमन्यासमन्त्राभ्यां हुत्वोत्पाद्य। श्रीकण्ठादिन्यासेन सकलीकृत्याऽमृतीकृत्य हंसन्यासमन्त्रेण हुत्वोत्पाद्य। सशक्ति कमला मारन्यासेन सकलीकृत्य प्रपञ्चयागं कुर्यात्। ओं क्लीं अं परंज्योतिषि जुहोमि हंसः सोऽहं स्वाहेत्यादि चकारान्तं वर्णस्थानेषु न्यस्य हुत्वा। पूर्ववदुत्पाद्य। समार कमला शक्तिन्यासेन सकलीकृत्य। सप्तग्रहन्यासवत् हुत्वा। पूर्ववदुत्पाद्य। सशक्तिन्यासेन सकलीकृत्य। सोमादिमण्डलत्रयन्यासवत् हुत्वा। पूर्ववत् समुत्पाद्य सकमलान्यासेन सकलीकृत्याऽग्नीषोमन्यासवत् हुत्वोत्पाद्य। समारन्यासेन सकलीकृत्य। हंसन्यासवत् हुत्वा। प्रणवेन स्वात्मस्थो भवेदिति प्रपञ्चयागः॥ ४७॥

पञ्चज्ञानेन्द्रियाबद्धाः सर्वास्तु लिपयो मताः ।
ताभिरारात्तनं सर्वं तत्तदिन्द्रियगोचरम् ॥ ४८
स्मर्तव्याशेषलोकान्तर्वर्त्ति यत्तेज ऐश्वरम् ।
ब्रह्माग्नौ जुहुयात्तस्मिन् सदा सर्वत्र वर्तिनि ॥ ४९
ब्रह्मात्मभिर्महामन्त्रैर्ब्रह्मविद्भिः समाहितैः ।
ब्रह्माग्नौ ब्रह्महविषा हुतं ब्रह्मार्पणं स्मृतम् ॥ ५०
एवं वर्णविभेदभिन्नमदृढं मांसास्थि[त्व]मज्जावृतं
देहं तत् चरमचरे सुविशदे सर्वत्र वर्तिन्यथ ।
हुत्वा ब्रह्महुताशने विमलधीस्तेजःस्वरूपी स्वयं
भूत्वा सर्वमनून् जपेदभियजेद्ध्यायेत्तथा तर्पयेत् ॥ ५१

एवं समन्त्रकं प्रपञ्चयागमभिधायाऽमन्त्रकं विदुषामयत्नसाध्यं प्रपञ्चयागमाह— पञ्चज्ञानेन्द्रियेति। वाचकवर्गस्य इन्द्रियसम्बन्धमभिधाय तद्द्वारेण वाच्यस्यापि तत्त्वगणस्य तदाह—त्विति।

अथ होमप्रकारमाह—ताभिरिति। ताभिर्लिपिभिः सह तत्तदिन्द्रियगोचरं ब्रह्माग्नौ जुहुयादित्यन्वयः। आरात्तनं दूरमन्तिकं च अध्यात्ममधिदैवतं चेत्यर्थः। अयं होमप्रकारः। सर्वसाक्षित्वेन स्वयमवाच्यमवाचकं ब्रह्म भूत्वा घटादिविषयदर्शनसमये स्वस्मादुत्पद्यमानस्य तत्त्वगणस्य स्वस्मिन्नेव लयं दर्शनावसाने भावयेदिति। तत्राहतशिवतत्त्वं प्रमाताऽकारार्थः। परिणामिन्यपरशक्तिरित्यर्थः। तस्य परिणामसामर्थ्यमाहतशक्तिः चकारतदर्थरूपिणी विमर्शप्रकाशाभ्यां वा शक्तिशिवतत्त्वभेदः। तदिच्छाक्रियाज्ञानानि सदाशिवेश्वरविद्यातत्त्वानि। तत्तद्विक्षेपे तदाच्छादने च मायातत्त्वम् अवस्थितम्। कालस्तत्काले। नियतिः तस्य देशादिनियमे। कला किञ्चित्कर्तृत्वे। अविद्या किञ्चिज्ज्ञत्वे। रागः तत्पूर्णतायाम्। पुरुषः तज्ज्ञत्वाभिमानित्वे। प्रकृतिः सुखदुःखादौ। अहंकारादित्रयम् अहंकारनिश्चयसंकल्पादौ। श्रोत्रादिकं शब्दस्पर्शरूपास्वादपरिमलेषु। वागादिकं वचनादानगमनविसर्गानन्देषु। शब्दाकाशादिकं तु सर्वविषयेषु प्रसिद्धमेव ॥ ४८ ॥ ४९ ॥

अमन्त्रके समन्त्रके च कथिते होमे पृथक् ब्रह्मार्पणं न कर्तव्यमित्याह— ब्रह्मात्मभिरिति ॥ ५० ॥

एवं प्राणाग्निहोत्रप्रपञ्चयागाभ्यां शुद्धस्य सकलीकरणन्यासेन आत्मसात्कृत-

देवताविग्रहस्यैव जपादौ अधिकार इत्याह—एवं वर्णेति। तेजःस्वरूपी स्वयं भूत्वेति सकलीकरणन्यासेन चतुर्नवति मन्त्रात्मक देवताविग्रहो भूत्वेत्यर्थः।

अयं न्यासक्रमः। प्रपञ्चयागानन्तरम् अपरिच्छिन्ने परतेजसि प्रणवशक्तिभ्यां व्यापयन् अपरं जीवात्मकं तेजः सञ्चिन्त्य ताभ्यामेव सुषुम्नां कारणशक्तिकवलीकृतजीवां स्मृत्वा तदग्रे ताभ्यामेव सहस्रदलं कारणात्मकं पद्मं प्रतिपाद्य तस्मात् ताभ्यामेव वर्णात्मकसमृतपिण्डं सुषुम्नाकवलनक्रमेण उत्पाद्य विसर्गान्वितमातृकान्यासेन सकलीकृत्य मूलाधार हृद् भ्रूमध्येषु दश द्वादश षोडशप्रणवजपेन तावद्दलानि पद्मानि सञ्चिन्त्य दशदलेषु व्यापककला न्यसित्वा कर्णिकायां मं वह्निमण्डलाय दशधर्मकलात्मने नमः इत्यादि मन्त्रं जातवेदस इति ऋचं च जपित्वा तत्रैव व्यापककलानामग्नेश्च प्राणप्रतिष्ठां कुर्यात्। पुनः द्वादशदलेषु स्पर्शकला न्यसित्वा कर्णिकायां अं सूर्यमण्डलायेत्यादि मन्त्रं तत्सवितुरिति ऋचं च जपित्वा तत्रैव स्पर्शकलानां सूर्यस्य च प्राणप्रतिष्ठां विधाय। षोडशदलेषु स्वरकला न्यसित्वा कर्णिकायां उं सोममण्डलायेति मन्त्रं त्र्यम्बकमिति ऋचं च जपित्वा तत्रैव स्वरकलानां सोमस्य च प्राणप्रतिष्ठां कुर्यात्।

पुनः पञ्चाशत्कला न्यसेत्। कं सृष्ट्यै नमः इत्यादि दशकं पादयोर्न्यस्य लं पृथिवीगन्धतन्मात्रेत्यादि मन्त्रेण पादयोर्व्यापकत्वेन न्यसेत्। अं ब्रह्मणे नमः लं पृथिव्यै नमः इत्यादिमन्त्रैः षष्ठपटलोक्तैर्वा यथास्थानं न्यसेत्। एवमेवोकारादिकलान्यासेष्वपि द्विधा पञ्चकन्यासो द्रष्टव्यः। पुनः पादयोः हंसः शुचिषदिति ऋचं च जपित्वा तत्रैवाऽकारकलानां ब्रह्मणश्च प्राणप्रतिष्ठां कुर्यात्। पुनः टं जरायै नम इत्याद्या उकारकला हस्तयोः न्यस्य अप्पञ्चकं विन्यस्य हस्तयोः प्रतद्विष्णुरिति ऋचं जपित्वा तत्रैव उकारकलानां विष्णोश्च प्राणप्रतिष्ठां कुर्यात्। पुनः पं तीक्ष्णायै नम इत्यादि मकारकला मूलाण्डगुह्यनाभिहृत्स्तनपार्श्वद्वयपृष्ठककुत्सु न्यसित्वा तेजःपञ्चकं विन्यस्य हृदये त्र्यम्बकमिति ऋचं विन्यस्य तत्रैव मकारकलानां रुद्रस्य च प्राणप्रतिष्ठां कुर्यात्। पुनः षं पीतायै नम इत्यादि बिन्दुकला गलास्यनेत्रादिषु न्यसित्वा वायुपञ्चकं विन्यस्य भ्रूमध्ये तत्सवितुरिति ऋचं न्यसित्वा तत्रैव बिन्दुकलानामीश्वरस्य च प्राणप्रतिष्ठां कुर्यात्। पुनः अं निवृत्त्यै नमः इत्यादिनादकला विसर्गाद्यकारान्तस्थानेषु विन्यस्याऽऽकाशपञ्चकं न्यसित्वा शिरसि विष्णुर्योनिमिति ऋचं च विन्यस्य तत्र नादकलानां सदाशिवस्य च प्राणप्रतिष्ठां कुर्यात्।

पुनर्जीवकलाः सकला मातृकान्यासवत् विन्यस्य हृदये जीवकलानां प्राणप्रतिष्ठां

शुद्धस्याऽपि सबिन्दुकस्त्वथ कलायुक्तेशवाद्यैर्युतः
श्रीकण्ठादियुतश्च शक्तिकमलामारैश्च चैकैकशः।
न्यासास्ते दशधा पृथङ्निगदिताः स्युर्ब्रह्मयागान्तिकाः
सर्वे साधकसिद्धिसाधनविधौ सङ्कल्पकल्पद्रुमाः॥ ५२

प्रपञ्चयागस्तु विशेषतो विपत्प्रपञ्चसंसारविशेषयापकः।
परश्च नित्यं भजतामयत्नतः परस्य चार्थस्य निवेदकः सदा॥ ५३

द्रव्यैर्यथा यैः क्रियते प्रपञ्चयागक्रिया तानि तथैव सम्यक्।
यास्वप्यवस्थासु च ताश्च कृत्वा प्राप्नोति यत्तत् कथयामि सर्वम्॥ ५४

प्रोक्तक्रमेण विघ्नान्तिकमपि हुत्वा घृतेन मन्त्रितमः।
एकावृत्त्या जुहुयात् प्रपञ्चयागाह्वयं घृतेन ततः॥ ५५

अश्वत्थोडुम्बरप्लक्षन्यग्रोधसम्भवाः समिधः।
तिलसर्षपदौग्धघृतान्यष्टद्रव्याणि संप्रदिष्टानि॥ ५६

एतैर्जुहोति अ[नि]युताधिकलक्षसंख्यं
मन्त्री ततोऽर्धमथवापि तदर्धकं यः।
स त्वैहिकीं सकलसिद्धिमवाप्य वाञ्छा-
योग्यां पदं परतरं च परत्र याति॥ ५७

विधाय हृदये परमात्मकला दश प्रणवलक्षणा न्यस्य तत्रैव तासां प्राणप्रतिष्ठां कुर्यात्। पाशाङ्कुशत्र्यक्षरमूलमन्त्राभ्यां सहैदं सकलीकरणं कर्तव्यम्। पुनस्त्रिवारं मातृकां न्यस्य इष्टमन्त्रन्यासादिकं कुर्यादिति सकलीकरणप्रकारः॥ ५१॥

शुद्धादिन्यासानां प्राणाग्निहोत्रप्रपञ्चयागशेषत्वेन तत्फलत्वेन फलवत्त्वमभिधाय स्वातन्त्र्येणापि फलसम्बन्धमाह—शुद्धस्यापीति॥ ५२॥

समन्त्रकप्रपञ्चयागस्य विशेषतो भुक्तिमुक्तिहेतुत्वमाह—प्रपञ्चयागस्त्विति। विपत्प्रपञ्चयापनं विलापनं मोक्ष इत्यर्थः। संसारविशेषयापनं निर्वाहः भुक्तिरित्यर्थः। अमन्त्रकप्रपञ्चयागस्याऽयत्नेन केवलमोक्षहेतुत्वमाह—परश्चेति। परः अन्यः प्रपञ्चयागः। अमन्त्रक इत्यर्थः॥ ५३॥ ५४॥

प्रोक्तक्रमेणेति। षष्ठपटलोक्तक्रमेणेत्यर्थः। मन्त्रितम इति बीजेन च ऋचा मूलहोमं सूचयति॥ ५५॥ ५६॥

लक्षसंख्यं मन्त्रीति। सिद्धिकामस्य श्रीबीजयोगं मुक्तिकामस्य प्रणवपुटितत्वं

एकद्विकत्रिकचतुष्कशताभिवृत्त्या
तां तां समीक्ष्य विकृतिं प्रजुहोतु मन्त्री ।
क्षुद्रज्वरादिविषमग्रहभूतयक्ष-
रक्षःपिशाचजनिते महति प्रकोपे ॥ ५८

द्वादशसहस्रमथवा तद्द्विगुणं वा चतुर्गुणं वाथो ।
जुहुयात् क्षुद्रग्रह रिपु विषमज्वर भूतसम्भवे कोपे ॥ ५९

अयथाप्रतिपत्ति मन्त्रकाणां प्रजपात् स्यादिह विस्मृतिर्नराणाम् ।
शमयेदचिरात् सहस्रवृत्त्या मतिमान् वस्तुभिरेभिरेव जुह्वन् ॥ ६०

एतैः सहस्रत्रितयाभिवृत्त्या जुहोति यस्तु क्रमशो यथावत् ।
जयेत् क्षणेनैव स विस्मृतिञ्च सापस्मृतिं शापभवांश्च दोषान् ॥ ६१

मधुरत्रयावसिक्तैरेतैर्लक्षं जुहोति यो मन्त्री ।
तस्य सुराधिपविभवो महद्भ्रूपा तृणलवायते न चिरात् ॥ ६२

लक्षं तदर्धकं वा मधुरत्रयसंयुतैर्हुनेदेतैः ।
अब्दत्रयादथाऽर्वाक् त्रिभुवनमखिलं वशीकुरुते ॥ ६३

वश्यादिकानि कर्माण्यभिकाङ्क्षन्नेभिरेव सद्रव्यैः ।
जुहुयाच्च कार्यगुरुतालाघवमभिवीक्ष्य योग्यपरिमाणम् ॥ ६४

लक्षं तिलैर्वा जुहुयादघानां शान्त्यै श्रियेऽथो नलिनैर्यथावत् ।
दौग्धेन पुष्ट्यै यशसे घृतेन वश्याय जातीकुसुमैश्च लोणैः ॥ ६५

च सूचयति ॥ ५७ ॥

प्रजुहोतु मन्त्रीति । नृसिंहबीजयोगः सूचितः ॥ ५८ ॥

होमविधिमाह—द्वादशसहस्रमिति ॥ ५९ ॥

मतिमान् वस्तुभिरिति । दशांशेनाभिषेकः पञ्चब्रह्मभिर्योजितपञ्चगव्यप्राशनं च प्रातःकाले मध्याह्ने हृदयमात्रजले स्थित्वा सूर्यमन्त्रजपः रात्रौ तिलहोमश्च सूचितः ॥ ६० ॥

क्रमशो यथावदित्यमृतध्यानं नृसिंहयोगश्च सूचितः ॥ ६१ ॥

मन्त्रीति श्रीयोगः ॥ ६२ ॥ ६३ ॥

सद्रव्यैरिति । तत्तत्कर्मयोग्यो व्यञ्जनयोग उक्तः ॥ ६४ ॥ ६५ ॥

शालीतण्डुलचूर्णकैस्त्रिमधुरासिक्तैः स्वसाध्याकृतिं
कृत्वाऽष्टोर्ध्वशताख्यमस्य शितधीः प्राणान् प्रतिष्ठाप्य च ।
न्यासोक्तक्रमतो निशासु जुहुयात्तां सप्तरात्रं नरो
नारी वा वशमेति मङ्क्षु विधिना तेनैव लोणेन वा ॥ ६६

पञ्चाशदोषधिविपाचितपञ्चगव्य-
जाते घृतेन शतवृत्ति हुनेद् घटाग्नौ ।
तावत् प्रजप्य विधिनाऽभिसमर्च्य सिद्धं
भस्मादद‍ीत सकलाभ्युदयावहं तत् ॥ ६७

अनुदिनमनुलिम्पेत्तेन किञ्चित् समद्या-
त्तिलकमपि विदध्यादुत्तमाङ्गे क्षिपेच्च ।
अनुततदुरितापस्मारभूतापमृत्यु-
ग्रहविषरहितः स्यात् प्रीयते च प्रजाभिः ॥ ६८

एका दशार्धकणिकां वरकाञ्चनस्य
दद्यात्तदेव गुरवेऽथ सहस्रहोमे ।
अर्धोर्ध्वपञ्चकणिका द्विकणा च सार्धा
स्याद्दक्षिणेह कथिता मुनिभिस्त्रिधैवम् ॥ ६९

निजेप्सितं दिव्यजनैः सुरद्रुमात् समस्तमेव प्रतिलभ्यते यथा ।
प्रपञ्चयागादपि साधकैस्तथा करप्रचेयाः सकलार्थसिद्धयः ॥ ७०

इति श्रीप्रपञ्चसारे सप्तमः पटलः ।

सप्तरात्रमित्यष्टम्यादि चतुर्दश्यन्तमित्यर्थः ॥ ६६ ॥ ६७ ॥ ६८ ॥

एका दशार्धकणिकामिति । एका प्रधाना दक्षिणा सा दशार्धकणिकां वरकाञ्चनस्य दद्यादिति इत्यन्वयः । पलस्य सप्तमभागः कणिका ॥ ६९ ॥ ७० ॥

इति श्रीपद्मपादाचार्यकृते प्रपञ्चसारविवरणे
सप्तमः पटलः ।

अष्टमः पटलः।

अथ हितविधये विदुषां वक्ष्ये प्राणाग्निहोत्रविहितविधिम्।
बद्ध्वा पद्मासनमृजुकायो मन्त्री विशेत् पुरोवदनः॥ १

शक्तेः सत्त्वनिबद्धमध्यमथ तन्मायारजोवेष्टितं
प्रायश्चोऽनिलदिग्गताश्रिजठरं मध्ये च नाभेरधः।
मध्ये प्राग्वरुणेन्द्रयाम्यलसितैः कुण्डैर्ज्वलद्वह्निभि-
र्मूलाधारमनारतं समतलं योगी स्मरेत् सिद्धये॥ २

मध्येन्द्रवरुणशशियमदिग्भवानि क्रमेण कुण्डानि।
आवसथजसभ्याहवनीयान्वाहार्यगार्हपत्यानि॥ ३

चिद्रूपात् सकलप्रभाप्रभवकान्मूलप्रकृत्यात्मनः
कल्पार्कात् प्रतिलोमतोऽमृतमयीं ज्योतीरुचाऽच्छां धिया।
स्पृष्टामक्षरमालिकां तु जुहुयात् कुण्डेषु तेषु क्रमात्
कल्पान्ताग्निशिखास्फुरत्कुहरकेष्वासाविता वर्णशः॥ ४

प्रपञ्चयागात् पूर्वमेव कर्तव्यमपि प्राणाग्निहोत्रं क्रमगोपनार्थम् अनन्तरमाह—अथेति। विदुषामिति। शुद्धसच्चिदानन्दादिमातृकाभेदसंयोगक्रमविदामित्यर्थः। मन्त्री विशेदिति। आधारशक्तिकमलासनाय नम इति स्वासनपूजनं सूचितम्॥ १॥

जठरं मध्य इति अशनकाले कुण्डानां स्थानमुक्तम्। नाभेरध इति योगकाले नाभिर्लिङ्गं तस्य द्व्यङ्गुलाध इत्यर्थः। ज्वलद्वह्निभिरिति। हयरोमित्यादिमन्त्रैः अग्निज्वलनमुक्तम्। अनारतमिति अनेन प्राणेन क्रियादिशक्त्यात्मना भारतमित्यर्थः। समो जीवस्य अस्य च परस्य स्थानत्वात् समतलमित्युक्तम्। कुण्डनामकथनमशनकाले मन्त्रेषु तदुयोगार्थम्॥ २॥ ३॥

पश्चाशद्वर्णैः पञ्चकुण्डेषु क्रमेण होमं दर्शयति—चिद्रूपादिति। अर्कत्वे हेतुः सकलप्रभेति। तत्र हेतुः मूलप्रकृत्यात्मन इति। अमृतमयीमानन्दमयीमित्यर्थः। ज्योतीरुचा स्पृष्टामित्यन्वयः। कुण्डलीस्पर्शाभिव्यक्तामित्यर्थः। धिया जुहुयादित्यन्वयः। त्विति तृतीयहोमार्थमकारावशेषं सूचयति। कल्पान्ताग्निः मूलाधारस्थोऽग्निः॥ ४॥

च्चाद्यास्ते सप्तवर्गा मरकतपशुमेदाह्वनीलाभ्रवर्णा
भूयः स्युर्विद्रुमाभाः कुलिशसमरुचः पुष्यवैदूर्यभासः ।
सर्वे ते पञ्चशोऽभिस्रवदमृतमया व्यापकस्पर्शसंज्ञा
मुक्तामाणिक्यरूपाः सुमतिभिरुदिताश्चाऽष्टशः स्युः स्वराख्याः ॥ ५

एतानि केतोरमृताकरारेर्मन्दस्य जीवस्य च सोमजस्य ।
शुक्रारसोमांशुमतां क्रमेण नवैव रत्नानि विदुर्नवानाम् ॥ ६

इत्येवं हुतविधिमन्वहं दिनादौ
ये सम्यग्विदधति मन्त्रिणः शतार्धम् ।
ते रत्नैरपि कनकांशुकैः सधान्यैः
सम्पन्नाः सकलजगत्प्रिया भवन्ति ॥ ७

अन्त्यशवर्गान्त्यासिवामश्रवणान्यथावसथजाते ।
असितावववर्गचतुर्थांसूक्ष्माः सत्याह्वये च सश्रोत्राः ॥ ८

हलयुतवर्गतृतीयोपराः सशान्तीश्च पश्चिमे वह्नौ ।
भृगुरेफफादिपञ्चकसद्योऽतिथिलोचनानि सभ्येऽग्नौ ॥ ९

मज्जात्वग्वर्गादिकभौतिकभावाह्वयप्रतिष्ठाश्च ।
गार्हपत्ये जुहुयादित्युक्तं होमकर्म वर्णानाम् ॥ १०

व्योम्ना मध्योत्थितेऽग्नावखिलमविरतं शब्दमैन्द्रेऽनिलेन
स्पर्शं स्वेनैव रूपं पुनरपरभवे सोमजेऽब्धौ रसञ्च ।
याम्ये गन्धं पृथिव्योभयरुचिरुचिरेष्वचरौघैर्हुनेद् यो
मन्त्री स्यात् सर्ववेद्यप्रतिमथनसमुद्भासितप्रत्यगात्मा ॥ ११

नवग्रहहोमं पञ्चमं समन्त्रोद्धारं दर्शयति—च्चाद्या इति । व्यापकेत्यादिपदैः मण्डलत्रयहोमः षष्ठः सूचितः । सुमतिभिरिति । परमानन्दतत्त्वविद्भिरित्यर्थः ॥ ५ ॥ ६ ॥

सम्यग्विदधतीति । अस्माभिः पूर्वोक्तः क्रमः सूचितः । मन्त्रिण इति मूलमन्त्रादियोगः । ते रत्नैरित्येतद् गुणफलम् ॥ ७ ॥

दशभिर्दशभिर्वर्णैः सह भूतमन्त्रैः होमं द्वितीयं दर्शयति—अन्त्यशवर्गान्त्या इति ॥ ८ ॥ ९ ॥ १० ॥

व्योम्नेत्यादिना भूतमन्त्रोद्धारः कृतः । अखिलमविरतमिति पदाभ्यां

सतारशक्त्याद्यजपान्तमेवं हुत्वा महात्माऽथ शतार्धसंख्यम् ।
विन्यस्य तावच्च तथैव सूक्ष्मात्राकृतिर्नित्यतनुश्च भूयात् ॥ १२

कल्पादित्यमुखः स्वमूलविलसत्कल्पानलान्तःस्फुर-
चन्द्रार्कग्रहकालभूतभुवनब्रह्मेशविष्ण्वादिकः ।
अव्यक्तोऽक्षरसंज्ञकोऽमृतमयस्तेजोद्वयोद्यत्प्रभो-
नित्यानन्दमयस्त्वनादिनिधनो यः स्यात् स हंसात्मकः ॥ १३

अनुदिनममुना भजतां विधिनाहारक्रियासु मन्त्रविदाम् ।
प्राणाद्याः स्युर्मरुतो गार्हपत्यादिकानि कुण्डानि ॥ १४
सप्तम्यन्तां च कुण्डाख्यामाख्यां च मरुतामपि ।
हिरण्यागगनारक्ताकृष्णाभिर्वर्णमीरयेत् ॥ १५

शब्दविशेषाः तदनुगतं सामान्यं चोक्तम् । अविरतं निरन्तरमनुगतमित्यर्थः । उभयत्रचित्रचिरेष्विति । चिदानन्दात्मककल्पकाग्न्यर्कप्रकाशविशिष्टेष्वित्यर्थः । उभयत्रचित्रचिरेषु अक्षरौवैरिति पदाभ्यां सप्तमाष्टमहोमौ सूचितौ । मन्त्रीति अवशिष्टाः होममन्त्राः सूचिताः ॥ ११ ॥

प्राणाग्निहोत्रे प्रणवशक्त्याद्यनन्तरं परमात्ममन्त्रम् अभिधाय अजपा-स्वाहाकारौ प्रयोक्तव्यौ इत्याह—सतारेति । महात्मेति अक्षुद्रचित्ततया मन्त्रार्थस्मरणसमर्थ इत्यर्थः । विन्यस्य तावच्चेति । प्रपञ्चयागं च शतार्धवारं कृत्वा इत्यर्थः । सूक्ष्मात्राकृतिरिति सकलनिष्कलध्यानमुक्तम् । नित्यतनुरिति निष्कलध्यानम् । स्थूलध्यानं तु पूर्वमेवोक्तम् । स्वयं च वर्मेति ध्यातस्यैव फलत्वाफलत्वमपि अनेनैवोक्तम् ॥ १२ ॥

अथ स्थूलादिध्यानं समुच्चित्य वदन् सफलं प्राणाग्निहोत्रमुपसंहरति—कल्पादित्यमुख इति । विष्ण्वादिक इत्यन्तेन स्थूलं रूपमुक्तम् । तेजोद्वयोद्यत्प्रभ इत्यन्तेन सूक्ष्मम् । अवशिष्टेन परमिति विभागः ॥ १३ ॥

उक्तः प्राणाग्निहोत्रकर्तॄणाम् अशनकाले प्राणाग्निहोत्राधिकार इत्याह—अनुदिनमिति । मन्त्रविदामित्यनेन प्राणाग्निहोत्रशेषभूताः केचन मन्त्राः सूचिताः ।

अयमत्र होमक्रमः । स्वेष्टदेवस्य सकलीकरणं विधाय । तं ध्यात्वा ओं श्रद्धायां प्राणे निविष्टोऽमृतं जुहोमि इत्यारभ्य । श्रद्धायां ब्रह्मणि मात्मानिविष्टोऽमृतं जुहोमि इत्यन्तैर्मन्त्रैः दक्षिणोत्तरपश्चिमपूर्वमध्यकुण्डेषु अग्नीन् उज्ज्वाल्य सप्रणवे शिपिपष्टे हविरादाय । अयं प्राणमवमपानमाहुः । अन्नं मृत्युं तमु जीवातुमाहुः ।

समुप्रभाभिः सहितं शुचयः पावका इति ।
अग्निं विहृत्य चेत्येवमात्मानमुपचर्यं च ॥ १६

ऊर्ध्वाधस्तिर्यगूर्ध्वाधस्तिर्यक्समममथो वदेत् ।
गच्छतूक्त्वा ठयुग्मं च पञ्चाग्नीन् संस्मरेत्ततः ॥ १७

हुताहुतिसमुद्दीप्तशिखासंयुक्तरोचिषः ।
गार्हपत्यादिकं भूय उपचर्यान्तमेव च ॥ १८

अन्नं ब्रह्मणो जवसं वदन्ति । अन्नमाहुः प्रजननं प्रजानाम् । इति उपस्थाय सद्यप्रणवगायत्र्या त्रिवारमभिमन्त्र्य । विद्युदसि विद्य मे पाप्मानम् । इति हस्तप्रक्षालनं विधाय । परिषिच्य । उपस्पृश्य । ओं तद्ब्रह्म । ओं तद्वायुः । ओं तदात्मा । ओं तत्सत्यम् । ओं तत्सर्वम् । ओं तत्पुरो नमः ।

ओं अन्तश्चरति भूतेषु गुहायां विश्वमूर्तिषु ।
त्वं यज्ञस्त्वं वषट्कारस्त्वं विष्णुः पुरुषः परः ॥
त्वमापः आपोज्योतीरसोऽमृतं ब्रह्म भूर्भुवःस्वरोम् ॥

अमृतोपस्तरणमसि इत्याचम्य । चितिः स्रुक् । चित्तमाज्यम् । वाग वेदिः । आधीतं बर्हिः । केतो अग्निः । विज्ञातमग्निः । वाक्पतिर्होता । मन उपवक्ता । प्राणो हविः । सामाध्वर्युः । वाचस्पते विधे नामन् विधेम ते नामविधे त्वमस्माकं नाम । वाचस्पतिः सोमं पिबत्वास्मा नृम्णं ध्यात् स्वाहेति जपित्वा । ओं गार्हपत्ये प्राणे हिरण्यवर्णाः शुचयः पावकाः अग्निं विहृत्य आत्मानमुपचर्योर्ध्वं गच्छतु स्वाहा । श्रद्धायां प्राणे निविष्टोऽमृतं जुहोमि । शिवोमाविशाप्रदाहाय प्राणात्मने नारायणाय मह्यं मह्यं स्वाहेति दक्षिणाग्नौ हुत्वा । ओमन्वाहार्ये अपाने गगनवर्णाः शुचयः पावकाः अग्निं विहृत्यात्मानमुपचर्याऽधो गच्छतु स्वाहा । श्रद्धायामपाने निविष्टोऽमृतं जुहोमि । शिवोमाविशाप्रदाहायाऽपानात्मने नारायणाय मह्यं मह्यं स्वाहेति उत्तरे हुत्वा । ओमाहवनीये व्याने रक्तवर्णाः शुचयः पावकाः अग्निं विहृत्यात्मानमुपचर्य तिर्यग् गच्छतु स्वाहा । श्रद्धायां व्याने निविष्टोऽमृतं जुहोमि । शिवोमाविशाप्रदाहाय व्यानात्मने नारायणाय मह्यं मह्यं स्वाहा इति पश्चिमे हुत्वा । ओं सभ्ये उदाने कृष्णवर्णाः शुचयः पावकाः अग्निं विहृत्यात्मानमुपचर्योर्ध्वाधस्तिर्यग गच्छतु स्वाहा । श्रद्धायामुदाने निविष्टोऽमृतं जुहोमि । शिवोमाविशाप्रदाहाय उदानात्मने नारायणाय मह्यं मह्यं स्वाहा इति पूर्वं हुत्वा । ओं आवसथीये समाने सुप्रभावर्णाः शुचयः पावकाः अग्निं विहृत्यात्मानमुपचर्य

मन्त्रं सर्वमनुक्रम्य जिह्वाः संस्मृत्य सर्वशः ।
बहुरूपां तु सङ्कल्प्य पञ्चानलशिखायुताम् ॥ १९

अहं वैश्वानरो भूत्वा जुहोम्यन्नं चतुर्विधम् ।
पचाम्येवं विधामेनेत्यापूर्णं संयतेन्द्रियः ॥ २०

तूष्णीं हुत्वा पिधायाऽद्भिरुपस्पृश्य विधानतः ।
आरभ्य मूलाधारं स्वमामस्तकमनुस्मरेत् ॥ २१

क्षेत्रज्ञसंज्ञकममुं प्रकृतिस्थमाद्यं
व्याप्तद्विसप्तभुवनान्तमनन्यमेकम् ।
पञ्चाननाग्निरसनापरिदत्तशुद्ध-
सान्नाय्यतर्पितमतर्कितमात्मरूपम् ॥ २२

संचिन्त्य चरितामृताच्चरशतार्धाम्भोऽवसिक्तं हवि-
स्तेजंप्राऽकुटिलान्तराधिरधिकं संदीप्तपञ्चानलः ।

समं गच्छतु स्वाहा। श्रद्धायां समाने निविष्टोऽमृतं जुहोमि। शिवोमाविशा-प्रदाहाय समानात्मने नारायणाय मह्यं मह्यं स्वाहेति मध्ये हुत्वा। अग्नीनेकीकृत्य। ओं गार्हपत्यान्वाहार्याहवनीयसभ्यावसथीयेषु प्राणापानव्यानोदानसमानेषु हिरण्य-गगन रक्त कृष्ण सुप्रभा वर्णाः शुचयः पावका अग्निं विहृत्यात्मानमुपचर्योर्ध्वाधस्ति-र्यगूर्ध्वाधस्तिर्यक्समं गच्छतु स्वाहा। अहं वैश्वानरो भूत्वा जुहोम्यन्नं चतुर्विधं पचामि। श्रद्धायां ब्रह्मणि म आत्मा निविष्टोऽमृतं जुहोमि। शिवोमाविशा-प्रदाहाय क्षेत्रज्ञात्मने नारायणाय मह्यं मह्यं स्वाहेति हुत्वा आपूर्णं तूष्णीं हुत्वा। अद्भिः पिधाय। गण्डूषादिकं कृत्वा। आचम्य। तृप्तिरसि तृप्तमे पाप्मानममृतात्मत्वमुपागामिति हस्तप्रक्षालनं कृत्वा। प्राणानां ग्रन्थिरसि रुद्रोमाविशान्तकस्तेनाऽन्नेनाऽऽप्यायस्व।

अङ्गुष्ठमात्रः पुरुषोऽङ्गुष्ठं च समाश्रितः ।
ईशः सर्वस्य जगतः प्रभुः प्रीणाति विश्वभुक् ॥

इति दक्षिणपादाङ्गुष्ठे जलधारामासिच्य। उद्वयं चित्रमित्यादिनोपतिष्ठेदिति।

अथ प्रणवेन अमृतमास्रावयेदित्याह—आरभ्येत्यादिना ॥ १४ ॥ १५ ॥ १६ ॥ ॥ १७ ॥ १८ ॥ १९ ॥ २० ॥ २१ ॥

मातृकयापि अमृतं स्रावणीयमित्याह—सञ्चिन्त्येति। ततः श्रद्धायां प्राणे

सायं प्रातरनेन होमविधिना भोज्यानि नित्यं भजन्
प्राणी न प्रमदोदरं प्रविशति प्राणाग्निहोत्री पुनः ॥ २३

इति तव षडङ्गवेदशास्त्राद्युपहितसर्वविकारसङ्गमातुः ।
तनुरियमुदिता विरिञ्च विश्वस्थितिलयसृष्टिकरोह वर्णमाला ॥ २४

इति जगदनुषक्तां तामिमां वर्णमालां
न्यसत जपत भक्त्या जुह्वताऽभ्यर्चयीत ।
निरुपमकवितायुःकीर्तिकान्तीन्दिराप्त्यै
सकलदुरितदुःखोच्छित्तये मुक्तये च ॥ २५

इतीरिता सकलजगत्प्रभाविनी
क्रमोत्क्रमक्रमगुणितार्णमालिका ।
अभीष्टसाधनविधये च मन्त्रिणां
भवेन्मनुप्रतिपुटिताक्षमालिका ॥ २६

मध्ये वद्यक्षरयोः सदवदवाग्वार्णिका निचन्द्रयुगे ।
प्रोक्ता दशाक्षरीयं कण्वविराजौ च वागृषिप्रमुखाः ॥ २७

कर्णोक्षनयननासावदनाम्बुगुदेषु विन्यसेद्वर्णान् ।
स्वरपुटितैरथ हल्भिः कुर्यादङ्गानि षट् क्रमान्मन्त्री ॥ २८

निविश्याऽमृतं हुतं प्राणमन्नेनाऽऽप्यायस्व इत्यारभ्य श्रद्धायां ब्रह्मणि म आत्मा निविश्याऽमृतं हुतं ब्रह्माणमन्नेनाप्यायस्व इत्यन्तैराप्याय्य अङ्गुष्ठादि न्यसित्वा उपसंहरेत् ॥ २२॥२३ ॥

शार्ङ्गी ब्रह्माणं प्रत्याह--इति तवेति ॥ २४ ॥

सर्वान् प्रत्याह—इति जगदनुषक्तामिति । अक्षमालाया मध्यस्थः क्षकारो मेरुत्वेन ज्ञेयः । अतस्तेन मन्त्रयोगो न कार्यः ॥ २५ ॥ २६ ॥

सरस्वतीदैवत्यां लिपिमभिधाय सरस्वतीदैवत्यं मन्त्रान्तरमाह—मध्ये वद्यक्षरयोरिति ॥ २७ ॥

अङ्गानि षट् क्रमान्मन्त्रीति । वद हृदयाय नमः । वद शिरसे स्वाहा । वाक् शिखायै वषट् । वादिनि कवचाय हुम् । स्वाहा नेत्रत्रयाय वौषट् । समस्तेनास्त्रम् इत्यङ्गेषु मन्त्रयोगः सूचितः । ऐं बीजम् । स्वाहा शक्तिः । अत्र

अमलकमलसंस्था लेखनीपुस्तकोद्यत्-
करयुगलसरोजा कुन्दमन्दारगौरी ।
धृतशशधरखण्डोल्लासिकोटीरचूडा
भवतु भवभयानां भञ्जिनी भारती वः ॥ २९

अक्षरलक्षजपान्ते जुहुयात्कमलैः सितैः पयोऽभ्यक्तैः ।
त्रिमधुरयुतैः सुशुद्धैरयुतं नियतात्मकस्तिलैरथवा ॥ ३०

मातृकोक्तविधिनाऽक्षराम्बुजे शक्तिभिश्च विनियुज्य पूर्ववत् ।
पीठमत्र वचसां महेश्वरीं पूजयेत् प्रथममङ्गमन्त्रकैः ॥ ३१

योगा सत्या विमला ज्ञाना बुद्धिः स्मृतिस्तथा मेधा ।
प्रज्ञेत्यष्टाभिर्मातृभिरपि लोकेशैः प्रपूजयेत् क्रमशः ॥ ३२

इति सिद्धमनुर्मनोजदूरो न चिरादेव कविर्भवेन्मनस्वी ।
जपहोमरतः सदावगच्छन् वनितां वागधिपतिर्गौरवेण ॥ ३३

न्यासान्वितं निशितधीः प्रजपेत् सहस्र-
मक्षो मुखेऽनुदिवसं प्रपिबेत्तथापः ।
तन्मन्त्रिताः पुनरयन्त्रितमेव वाचां
सिद्धिर्भवेदभिमता परिवत्सरेण ॥ ३४

हृदयह्रयसि स्थितोऽथ तोये रविबिम्बे प्रतिपद्य वागधीशाम् ।
जपतस्त्रिसहस्रसंख्यमर्वाक् कवितामण्डलतो भवेत् प्रभुता ॥ ३५

पलाशबिल्वप्रसवैस्तयोश्च समिद्वरैः स्वादुयुतैश्च होमः ।
कवित्वसौभाग्यकरः समृद्धिलक्ष्मीप्रदो रञ्जनकृच्चिराय ॥ ३६

चतुरङ्गुलजैः समित्प्रसूनैर्जुहुयाद् यो मधुरत्रयावसिक्तैः ।
मनुजः समवाप्य धीविलासानचिरात्काव्यकृतां भवेत् पुरोगः ॥ ३७

सुविमलनखदन्तपाणिपादो मुदितमना: परदूषणेषु मौनी ।
हरिहरकमलोद्भवाङ्घ्रिभक्तो भवति चिराय सरस्वतीनिवासः ॥ ३८

वचसां महेश्वरीमिति मातृकायामिव पीठमूर्तिमन्त्रावित्युक्तम् ॥ २८॥२९ ॥ ३० ॥
॥ ३१ ॥ ३२ ॥ ३३ ॥

न्यासान्वितं निशितधीरिति बालया सह न्यसेत् जपेदपपानमपि तथैव

आद्यन्तप्रणवगशक्तिमध्यसंस्था
वाग्भूयो भवति सरस्वती च ङेन्ता ।
नत्यन्तो मनुरयमीशसंख्यवर्णः
संप्रोक्तो भुवि भजमानपारिजातः ॥ ३९

सौषुम्नाग्रे भ्रूयुगमध्ये नवके तथैव रन्ध्राणाम् ।
विन्यस्य मन्त्रवर्णान् कुर्यादङ्गानि षट् क्रमाद्वाचा ॥ ४०

हंसारूढा हरहसितहारेन्दुकुन्दावदाता
वाणी मन्दस्मितयुतमुखी मौलिबद्धेन्दुरेखा ।
विद्यावीणामृतमयघटाक्षस्रगादीप्तहस्ता
शुभ्राब्जस्था भवदभिमतप्राप्तये भारती स्यात् ॥ ४१

दिनकरलक्षं प्रजपेन्मन्त्रमिमं संयतेन्द्रियो मन्त्री ।
द्वादशसहस्रकमथो सितसरसिजनागचम्पकैर्जुहुयात् ॥ ४२

पूजायां पार्श्वयुगे ससंस्कृता प्राकृता च वाग्देव्याः ।
केवलवाङ्मयरूपे संपूज्याऽङ्गैश्च शक्तिभिस्तदनु ॥ ४३

प्रज्ञा मेधा श्रुतिरपि शक्तिः स्मृत्याह्वया च वागीशी ।
सुमतिः स्वस्तिरिहाभिर्मातृभिराशेश्वरैः क्रमात् प्रयजेत् ॥ ४४

इति निगदितो वागीश्वर्याः सहोमजपार्चना-
विधिरनुदिनं मन्त्री त्वेनां भजन् परिमुच्यते ।
सकलदुरितैर्मेधालक्ष्मीयशोभिरवाप्यते
परमपरमां भक्तिं प्राप्योभयत्र च मोदते ॥ ४५

कुर्यात् । ध्यानं च तद्वत् कुर्यादित्यर्थः ॥ ३४ ॥ ३५ ॥ ३६ ॥ ३७ ॥ ३८ ॥

अङ्गानि षट् क्रमाद् वाचेति । ऐं क्लां हृदयाय नमः इत्यादि क्रमेणेत्यर्थः । ऐं बीजम् । क्लीं शक्तिः । ऋष्यादिकं पूर्ववत् ॥ ३९ ॥ ४० ॥

हंसारूढा वाणीति वाग्भवे हंसयोग उक्तः । विद्यावीणेति । विद्या-पुस्तकम् । ['भसितहरहासेन्दु' इत्यपि पाठः ।] संयतेन्द्रियो मन्त्रीति बालायोग उक्तः ॥ ४१ ॥ ४२ ॥ ४३ ॥ ४४ ॥

मन्त्री त्वेनां जपन्निति । दुरितमोक्षे नृसिंहस्य लक्ष्म्यास्तद्बीजस्य यशसेऽज-

इति मातृकाविभेदान् प्रजपन्मन्त्रद्वयञ्च मन्त्रितमः ।
प्रजपेदेनां स्तुतिमपि दिनशो वाग्देव्यनुग्रहाय बुधः ॥ ४६
अमलकमलाधिवासिनि मनसो वैमल्यदायिनि मनोज्ञे ।
सुन्दरगात्रि सुशीले तव चरणाम्भोरुहं नमामि सदा ॥ ४७
अचलात्मजा च दुर्गा कमला त्रिपुरेति भेदिता जगति ।
या सा त्वमेव वाचामीश्वरि सर्वात्मना प्रसीद मम ॥ ४८
त्वच्चरणाम्भोरुहयोः प्रणामहीनः पुनर्द्विजातिरपि ।
भूयादनेडमूकस्त्वद्भक्तो भवति देवि सर्वज्ञः ॥ ४९
मूलाधारमुखोद्गतविसतन्तुनिभप्रभाप्रभावतया ।
विसृतलिपिव्राताहितमुखकरचरणादिके प्रसीद मम ॥ ५०
वर्णतनोऽमृतवर्णैं नियतमतिभिर्वर्णितेऽपि योगीन्द्रैः ।
निर्णीतिकरणदूरे वर्णयितुं देहि देवि सामर्थ्यम् ॥ ५१
ससुरासुरमौलिलसन्मणिप्रभादीपिताङ्घ्रियुगनलिने ।
सकलागमस्वरूपे सर्वेश्वरि सन्निधिं विधेहि मयि ॥ ५२
पुस्तकजपवटहस्ते वरदाभयचिह्नचारुबाहुलते ।
कर्पूरामलदेहे वागीश्वरि विशोधयाऽऽशु मम चेतः ॥ ५३
क्षौमाम्बरपरिधाने मुक्तामणिविभूषणे मुदावासे ।
स्मितचन्द्रिकाविकसितमुखेन्दुबिम्बेऽम्बिके प्रसीद मम ॥ ५४
विद्यारूपेऽविद्याविनाशिनि विद्योतितेऽन्तरात्मविदाम् ।
गद्यैः सपद्यजातैराद्यैर्मुनिभिः स्तुते प्रसीद मम ॥ ५५
त्रिमुखि त्रयीस्वरूपे त्रिपुरे त्रिदशाभिवन्दिताङ्घ्रियुगे ।
त्रीक्षणविलसितवक्त्रे त्रिमूर्तिमूलात्मिके प्रसीद मम ॥ ५६
वेदात्मिके निरुक्तज्योतिर्व्याकरणकल्पशिक्षाभिः ।
सच्छन्दोभिः सन्ततक्लृप्तषडङ्गेन्द्रिये प्रसीद मम ॥ ५७

पाया योगः सूचितः ॥ ४५ ॥

मन्त्रद्वयं चेति । मन्त्रान्तरेष्वपि सारस्वतेषु स्तोत्रविनियोगार्थः । मन्त्रितम इति प्रतिज्ञोक्तं वाग्भवयोगः सूचितः । वाक्सूत्रादिजपो वा । बुध इति

त्वच्चरणसरसि जन्मस्थितिमहितधियां न लिप्यते दोषः ।
भगवति भक्तिमतस्त्वयि परमां परमेश्वरि प्रसीद मम ॥ ५८
बोधात्मिके बुधानां हृदयाम्बुजचारुरङ्गनटनपरे ।
भगवति भवभङ्गकरीं भक्तिं भद्रार्थदे प्रसीद मम ॥ ५९
वागीशीस्तवमिति यो जपार्चनाहवनवृत्तिषु प्रजपेत् ।
स तु विमलचित्तवृत्तिर्देहापदि नित्यशुद्धमेति पदम् ॥ ६०

इति श्रीप्रपञ्चसारे अष्टमः पटलः ।

ध्यानम् ॥ ४६—६० ॥

इति श्रीपद्मपादाचार्यकृते प्रपञ्चसारविवरणे
अष्टमः पटलः ।

नवमः पटलः ।

अथ प्रवक्ष्यामि सुदुर्लभाप्तिं विद्यां विशिष्टां त्रिपुराभिधानाम् ।
या सा त्रिभेदाऽपि जगत्यवाप्तत्रिंशत्प्रकारा त्रिदशाभिवन्द्या ॥ १

त्रिमूर्तिसर्गाच्च पुराभवत्वात्त्रयीमयत्वाच्च पुरैव देव्याः ।
लये त्रिलोक्या अपि पूरणत्वात् प्रायोऽम्बिकायास्त्रिपुरेति नाम ॥ २

व्योमेन्दुवक्त्राधरबिन्दुभिरेकमन्य-
द्रक्ताच्छकेन्द्रशिखिभिः सरमार्धचन्द्रैः ।

एवं ज्ञानशक्तिप्रधानान् मन्त्रान् अभिधाय क्रियाशक्तिप्रधानान् त्रैपुरान् मन्त्रान् प्रस्तौति—अथेति । बीजत्रयरूपेण त्रिभेदत्वम् । त्रिंशत्प्रकारत्वं तु तद्गतबीजबिन्द्वादिभिः । अथवा सुलभा दुर्लभा चाप्तिर्व्याप्तिरुच्चारणं यस्याः सा तथोक्ता । तत्र केवला बिन्द्वन्ता मकारान्ता विसर्गान्ता च सुवचा । बिन्दुविसर्गान्ता दुर्वचा । कूटस्थपृथग्गतौ वा सुदुर्वाच्यौ मन्त्राविति कूटाकूटपक्षयोरपि पञ्चपञ्चप्रकारौ सिद्धौ । पुनश्च

आदिमादिमनादिञ्च मध्यं मध्यममध्यमम् ।
अन्त्यमन्त्यमनन्त्यञ्च त्रिपुरा शीघ्रसिद्धिदा ॥

इति न्यायेन कूटपक्षे अकूटपक्षेऽपि त्रिंशत्प्रकारत्वं सिद्धम् । सर्वेषां त्रिबीजात्मकत्वेन त्रिप्रकारत्वं च सिद्धम् । विशिष्टामिति विद्याभेदमाह । अविशिष्टा शुद्धा बाला । विशिष्टा हकारादिव्यञ्जनविशिष्टा । सभेदानामेव एतेषां मन्त्राणां कुटाकूटत्वं सुदुर्वचत्वम् । 'आदिमादिमनादिं च' इत्यादि समानमिति सर्वेषां त्रिंशत्प्रकारत्वं त्रिप्रकारत्वं च सिद्धम् । पारायणभेदेन चाऽनन्तप्रकारत्वम् । पुनरपि मन्त्रान्तरयोगनिमित्तं भेदमाह—त्रिपुराभिधानामिति । त्रिपुराः सत्त्वादिशरीराः विष्ण्वादयः तेषामभिधानरूपां तत्तन्मन्त्रसंयोगिनेत्यर्थः । प्रकारान्तरेण त्रयस्त्रिंशत्प्रकारत्वं त्रिप्रकारत्वं च सिद्धम् । पारायणभेदेन चानन्तप्रकारत्वमाह अस्या विद्यायाः—या त्रिभेदापीति । कादिहान्ताक्षराद्यत्वेन त्रयस्त्रिंशत्प्रकारेत्यर्थः ॥ १ ॥

त्रिमूर्तिमन्त्रेषु विद्यासंयोग उपपत्तिमाह—त्रिमूर्तीति । पुरैव त्रयीमयत्वं सच्चिदानन्दरूपत्वं गुणसाम्यात्मकत्वं वा ॥ २ ॥

सरमार्धचन्द्रैरिति । सकाररूपिणी शक्तिर्यस्मिन् हकारे शिवे रमते स ह-

अन्यद्द्वयं शीतकरपावकमन्वमन्ते-
बीजैरमीभिरुदिता त्रिपुरेति विद्या ॥ ३

वागैश्वर्यातिशयदतया वाग्भवं बीजमुक्तं
त्रैलोक्यक्षोभणसवशताकृष्टिदं कामराजम् ।
शाक्तं क्ष्वेलापहरकविताकारकं मन्त्रमेतत्
प्रोक्तं धर्मद्रविणसुखमोक्षप्रदं साधकानाम् ॥ ४

नाभेरथाचरणमाहृदयाच्च नाभिं
मूर्ध्नस्तथा हृदयमित्यमुना क्रमेण ।
बीजैस्त्रिभिर्न्यसतु हस्ततले च सव्ये
दक्षाह्वये द्वितयमप्युभयोस्तृतीयम् ॥ ५

मूर्धनि गुह्यहृदोरपि नेत्रत्रितये च कर्णयोरास्ये ।
अंसद्वये च पृष्ठे कौर्परयोर्नाभिमण्डले न्यसेत् ॥ ६

कारः सरः । मा श्रोः ईकारः । अर्धचन्द्रो बिन्दुरिति निष्कीलविद्योद्धारप्रकारः ॥३॥

व्यस्तविनियोगोक्तिर्वागैश्वर्येति । धर्मेति समस्तविनियोगोक्तिः । आदि-नाथदेवीगायत्रीत्रिपुराभैरव्यः ऋष्यादयः । वाग्भवकामराजौ बीजशक्ती । शाक्तं वा शक्तिः ॥ ४ ॥

नाभेरथाचरणमिति । पीठमूर्तिन्यासावाहनादि कराङ्गुलिन्यास व्यापक-लिपिश्रीकण्ठादिन्यासानन्तरमित्यर्थः । तत्र पीठन्यासे आधारशक्तिमूल-प्रकृत्यनन्त पृथिव्यमृतार्णव रत्नद्वीप रत्नमण्डप कल्पकतरु श्वेतच्छत्राणि हृदि विन्यस्य । धर्मादिकं वरदान्तं दक्षिणकर्णांसपार्श्वकटिपादेषु । अधर्मादिकं वामकर्णादिषु । इच्छा ज्ञाना क्रिया कामा कामिनी कामदायिनी रतिप्रियानन्दा-मनोन्मन्यो नव शक्तयः । नवशक्तिन्यासानन्तरं नवयोनिचक्रासनाय नमः इति व्याप्य नवयोनिन्यासमाचरेत् । मूलबीजैः श्रोत्रद्वयचिबुकेषु प्रथमः पर्यायः । शङ्खद्वयास्येषु द्वितीयः । दृग्द्वयघ्राणेषु तृतीयः । अंसद्वयहृत्सु चतुर्थः । कूर्परद्वयकुक्षिषु पञ्चमः । जानुद्वयाण्डेषु षष्ठः । पादद्वयगुह्येषु सप्तमः । पार्श्वद्वयहृत्सु अष्टमः । स्तनद्वयकण्ठेषु नवम इति । पुनर्द्वादश-शक्तिन्यासः । ऐं वामायै नमः । ज्येष्ठायै नमः । रौद्र्यै नमः । अम्बिकायै नमः । हृत्त्रिकोणरेखात्रये मध्ये च । इच्छायै ज्ञानायै क्रियायै कुब्जिकायै ।

वाग्भवेन पुनरङ्गुलीष्वथो विन्यसेच्च पुनरुक्तमार्गतः।
अङ्गषट्कममुना विधाय तद्देवतां विशदधीर्विचिन्तयेत्॥ ७

कोणबाह्येषु मध्ये च। प्रह्वैर विषण्णैर दूतर्यै सर्वानन्दायै। कोणत्रितये मध्ये चेति। पुनश्चतुष्पीठन्यासः। ऐं क्लीं सौः ओड्याणपीठाय नमः। ऐं जालन्धरपीठाय नमः। क्लीं पूर्णगिरिपीठाय नमः। सौः कामरूपपीठाय नमः। इति शिरोललाटहृदयगुह्येषु पीठन्यासः। ऐं परायै। क्लीं अपरायै। सौः परापरायै। ह्सौः सदाशिवमहाप्रेतपद्मासनाय नमः। इति पीठसमष्टिमन्त्रेण व्याप्य। पादुकासप्तकं न्यसेत्। ऐं अण्डजे अङ्गजानन्ददेवि [श्रीपादुकाभ्यो नमः इतीत्यपि क्वचिदधिकः] अह्निकरि आज्ञां पूजयामि नमः। ऐं परायै श्रीगुरुपादुकापङ्क्त्यै नमः। क्लीं अपरायै श्रीगुरुपादुकापङ्क्त्यै नमः। सौः परापरायै श्रीगुरुपादुकापङ्क्त्यै नमः। ऐं श्रीअनन्तनाथदेव श्रीअनन्तनाथदेवि श्रीगुरुपादुकाभ्यो नमः। एवमेव क्लीं श्रीअवतारनाथदेव श्रीअवतारनाथदेवि श्रीपादुकापद्मेभ्यो नमः। सौः श्रीसिद्धनाथदेव श्रीसिद्धनाथ देवि श्रीपादुकाभ्यो नमः इति शिरसि। ऐं क्लीं ह्सौः त्रिपुराभैरवीमूर्तये नमः। इति मूर्तिन्यासः।

तत आवाहनादिकम्। ततः करन्यासाङ्गुलिन्यासौ। तत्राऽङ्गुलिन्यासे मध्यबीजस्थक्लकारेण विनपुंसकक्लस्वयुतैः ईशानादिमूर्तिभिः सहितैरङ्गुष्ठादिषु न्यसेत्। क्लां ईशानमनोभवाङ्गुष्ठाभ्यां नमः। क्लें तत्पुरुषमकरध्वजतर्जनीभ्यां नमः। क्लुं अघोरकुमारकन्दर्पमध्यमाभ्यां नमः। क्लिं वामदेवमन्मथानामिकाभ्यां नमः। क्लं सद्योजातकामदेवकनिष्ठिकाभ्यां नमः। पुनः षडङ्गेन सवाग्भवमध्यदीर्घेणाऽङ्गुलिं न्यसित्वा। बाणपञ्चकं न्यसेत्। द्रां शोषणबाणाङ्गुष्ठाभ्यां नमः। एवमेव द्रीं मोहन। क्लीं सन्दीपन। ब्लूं तापन। सः मादनबाणकनिष्ठिकाभ्यां नमः। इति बाणान् न्यसित्वा। मूलेन देहे त्रिशो व्याप्य। मूलपुटितमातृकां न्यसित्वा। श्रीकण्ठादिन्यासं कुर्यात्॥ ५॥ ६॥

वाग्भवेन पुनरिति। मूलबीजमध्यमबीजदीर्घानन्तरमित्यर्थः। ह्स्रैं हसकलह्रां ह्स्रैं हृदयाय नमः। हसकलह्रीं हसकलह्रीं ह्स्रैं शिरसे स्वाहा। ह्स्रौः हसकलह्रूं ह्स्रैं शिखायै वषट्। ह्स्रैं हसकलह्रैं ह्स्रैं कवचाय हुं। हसकलह्रौं हसकलह्रौं ह्स्रैं नेत्रत्रयाय वौषट्। ह्स्रौः हसकलह्रः ह्स्रैं अस्त्राय फट्। पुनरुक्तिः पुनर्वचनम्। चशब्देन करयोः

आताम्रार्कायुताभां कलितशशिकलारञ्जितप्नां त्रिनेत्रां
देवीं पूर्णेन्दुवक्त्रां विधृतजपवटीपुस्तकाभीत्यभीष्टाम् ।
पीनोत्तुङ्गस्तनार्तां बलिलसितविलग्नामसृक्पङ्कराज-
न्मुण्डस्रङ्मण्डिताङ्गीमरुणतरदुकूलानुलेपां नमामि ॥ ८

बाणादिन्यासाः सूचिताः ।

विशदधीरिति । वैशद्यहेतुभूताच्चरतत्त्वत्रिपञ्चनवावृत्त्यमृतेश्वर्यादि रत्यादि-मूर्त्यङ्गबाणसुभगामात्रादिभूषणन्यासाः सूचिताः । तत्र मूर्धाधारहृत्सु मूलवर्णन्यासः । ह्स्त्रैं आत्मतत्त्वेश्वर्यै त्रिपुराभैरव्यै नमः । हसकलह्रीं विद्यातत्त्वेश्वर्यै त्रिपुराभैरव्यै नमः । ह्स्रौः शिवतत्त्वेश्वर्यै त्रिपुराभैरव्यै नमः । समस्तान्ते सर्वतत्त्वेश्वर्यै त्रिपुराभैरव्यै नमः । नाभ्याद्यास्यान्तं गुह्यादिभ्रूमध्यान्तं मूलाधारादिमस्तकान्तं पादादिमस्तकान्तं च तत्त्वन्यासः । पाद जानु गुह्य नाभि हृत्कण्ठास्य भ्रूमस्तकेषु त्रयावृत्तिन्यासः । मूर्धगुह्यहृत्सु दक्षिणवामोर्ध्वनेत्रेषु कर्णद्वयास्येषु अंसद्वयपृष्ठेषु कोर्परद्वयनाभिषु पञ्चा-वृत्तिन्यासः । नवावृत्तिन्यासो नवयोनिन्यासवत् । ह्स्त्रौः अमृतेश्वर्यै नमः । मध्यमान्ते योगेश्वर्यै नमः । ह्स्त्रैं विश्वयोन्यै नमः । भ्रूमध्य हृदय मूलाधारेषु इत्यमृतेश्वर्यादिन्यासः । ह्स्त्रैं रत्यै नमः । मध्यमान्ते प्रीत्यै नमः । ह्स्त्रौः मनोभवायै नमः । इति मूलाधारादिषु रत्यादिन्यासः । मूर्तय ईशान-मनोभवाद्या मूर्धास्यहृद्गुह्यपादनामभिः ऊर्ध्वप्राग्दक्षिणोत्तरपश्चिमवक्त्राणां नामभिश्च संयोज्य तेष्वेव न्यस्तव्याः । ह्स्त्रौं ईशानमनोभवाय मूर्ध्ने नमः । ह्स्त्रौं ईशानमनोभवायोर्ध्ववक्त्राय नमः । इत्यादि प्रयोगक्रमः । पुनरङ्गानि विन्यस्य मूर्तिन्यासवद् बाणन्यासं विधाय । ततः सुभगादिन्यासं ललाट-भ्रूमध्याद्यष्टाधारेषु ऐं क्लीं ब्लूं स्त्रीं सः इति बीजैः सह विन्यस्य । मूलाधारा-द्यष्टाधारेषु आं क्षामादिदीर्घयुता ब्रह्माण्याद्या अं क्षमादिह्रस्वयुतैः भैरवैः सह विन्यस्य । शिरसि मूलमन्त्रं न्यसित्वा । व्याप्य । अङ्गुष्ठादिकं विन्यस्य । भूषणन्यासं विधाय । आताम्रार्कायुताभामित्युक्तप्रकारेण विशदधीः ध्यायेदित्यर्थः ।

शिरो ललाटभ्रू कर्णद्वयाक्षिद्वय नासाद्वय गण्डद्वयौष्ठद्वय दन्तद्वयास्येषु स्वरान् गल कण्ठ पार्श्वद्वय स्तनद्वय पादबाहुद्वय कोर्परद्वय पाणितलतत्पृष्ठनाभिगुह्योरुद्वय-जानुद्वय जङ्घाद्वय स्फिक्पादतलद्वय पादाङ्गुष्ठद्वयेषु कादिरान्तं काञ्ची ग्रैवेय-

दीक्षां प्राप्य विशिष्टलक्षणयुजः सत्सम्प्रदायाद् गुरो-
र्लब्ध्वा मन्त्रममुं जपेत् सुनियतस्तत्त्वार्धलक्षावधि ।
स्वाद्वक्तैश्च नवैः पलाशकुसुमैः सम्यक् समिद्धेऽनले
मन्त्री भानुसहस्रकं प्रतिहुनेदश्वारिसूनैरपि ॥ ९

प्राणायामैः पवित्रीकृततनुरथ मन्त्री निजाधारराज-
द्योनिस्थां दिव्यरूपां प्रमुदितमनसाऽभ्यर्चयित्वोपचारैः ।

कटकहृदगुह्यकुण्डलद्वयमौलिषु वललक्षसषहान् न्यसेदिति भूषणन्यासः ।

असृक्पङ्कराजन्मुण्डस्त्रङ्मण्डिताङ्गीमिति । कुङ्कुमपङ्कवच्छोभमानाभिः मुण्डस्रग्भिः उत्तमाङ्गरूपाभिः स्रग्भिः शक्तिव्यापिनीसमनीभिर्मण्डितशरीरामिति परावरध्यानकथनमेतत् । अथवा असृक् अकारः स्रष्टा परः । तस्य पङ्कः सान्द्रीभावः आभास इत्यर्थः । तेन राजन्ती मुण्डा कुण्डलिनी । तस्याः स्रग्वद्विच्छिन्नतया वर्तमानाः शक्तिभेदाः मुण्डस्रजः । तैरलङ्कृतशरीरामित्यर्थः । यथाश्रुतो वार्थः । तस्मिन् पक्षे आताम्रेत्यनेनैव परादिरूपकथनं द्रष्टव्यम् । निष्कीलपञ्चकूटे पाशाङ्कुशपुस्तकाक्षस्रग्धरा वा देवी ध्येया । षट्कूटादिषु पाशाङ्कुशशूलकपालधरा वा ॥ ७।८ ॥

सत्सम्प्रदायादिति । वैदिकादित्यर्थः । परप्रकाशानन्दनाथश्रीपादुकां पूजयामि । तथा परविमर्शानन्द परमशिवानन्द कामेश्वर्यम्बाश्रीपादुकाम् । मोक्षानन्दकामानन्दामृतानन्दा दिव्यौघः । ईशः तत्पुरुषः अघोरः वामः सदानन्दः सिद्धौघः । उत्तमोद्भवानन्द परमानन्द सर्वज्ञानन्द शान्तानन्द-स्वच्छन्दानन्द सिद्धानन्द गोविन्दानन्द शङ्करानन्दाः स्वगुरुत्रयं च मानवौघः । इत्ययं वैदिकसम्प्रदायक्रमः । सुनियत इति । ब्रह्मचर्यादिमानित्यर्थः । तत्त्वानि तदर्धं च तत्त्वार्धं षट्त्रिंशदित्यर्थः । अनेन शुद्धादिचतुष्कूटान्तजपसंख्योक्ता । तत्त्वलक्षावधीति पञ्चकूटस्य तत्त्वार्धलक्षावधीति षट्कूटादेरित्यवगन्तव्यम् । चतुष्कूटान्तस्य पालाशैर्होमः । परमश्वारिजैः । अपिशब्देन सर्वत्रापि शतांशो होमः सूचितः । अथवा भानुसहस्रकमित्यनेनैव सर्वत्र शतांशहोमः सूचितः । भान्तीति भानवः षट्त्रिंशत्तत्त्वानि चतुर्विंशतितत्त्वानि द्वादशादित्याश्च तत्सहस्रकमिति हि तस्यार्थः । मन्त्रीति काम्यहोमेषु तत्तत्कामनोचितबीजयोगः ॥ ९ ॥

प्राणायामैः पवित्रीकृततनुरिति । वेधकप्राणायामसूचनम् । मूलेन

बद्ध्वाऽसौ योनिमुद्रामपि निजगुदलिङ्गान्तरस्थां प्रदीप्तां
भूयो द्रव्यैस्तु शुद्धैररुणरुचिभिरित्यारभेद्वाह्यपूजाम् ॥ १०

वामादिशक्तिसहितं परिपूज्य पीठं
तत्र प्रकल्प्य विधिवन्नवयोनिचक्रम् ।
योनौ निधाय कलशं त्वथ मध्यगाया-
मावाह्य तां भगवतीं प्रयजेत् क्रमेण ॥ ११

वह्नेः पुरद्वितयवासवयोनिमध्य-
सम्बद्धवह्निवरुणेशसमाश्रितास्त्रि ।
देव्यर्चनाय मुनिभिर्विहितं पुरैव
लोकेऽतिदुर्लभमिदं नवयोनिचक्रम् ॥ १२

रेचकं पूरकं च कृत्वा । कुम्भककाले मातृकां प्रतिलोमेन जपन् । अकारलक्ष्ये परे सर्वं संहरेदिति वर्णविधः । पुनस्तन्मात्रापञ्चीकृतबीजानि पञ्चभूतस्थानेषु न्यसन् । सर्वं सृष्ट्वा । पञ्चीकृतापञ्चीकृतबीजानि पृथिव्यादिस्थानेषु न्यसन् । तानि तन्मात्रासु संहृत्य । गन्धमात्राबीजं पादादिजानुपर्यन्तं तत् न्यसित्वा । मूलमेकवारं जपन् । प्राणमायच्छन् । गन्धतन्मात्रं रसतन्मात्रायां संहृत्य । इतरा अपि मात्रा यथाक्रमं संहरेदिति कलाविधः । पूर्वोक्तषडाधारयोगरूपप्राणायामैः सर्वं संहरेदिति योगिनोविधः । एवं प्राणायामत्रयं कृत्वा । प्राणायाममन्त्रैरेव व्युत्क्रमेण सृष्टिः कार्येत्याह—अथ मन्त्रीति । दिव्यरूपामिति । व्यापिन्यादिप्रभाभिर्व्याप्तामित्यर्थः । बाह्ये अभ्यन्तरे च योनिमुद्रा बन्धनीया । अपीति ओड्याणजालन्धरखेचरीबन्धार्थः । इत्यारभेदिति । वक्ष्यमाणप्रकारेणेत्यर्थः ॥ १० ॥

वामादिशक्तिसहितमित्यत्र वामादिशक्तिसाहित्यं नवयानिचक्रस्येत्यवगन्तव्यम् । विधिवन्नवयोनिचक्रमिति । मध्ययोनौ मूलस्य अवशिष्टयोनिषु गायत्र्यक्षरत्रयस्य दलेषु मातृभैरवबीजानां बहिर्मातृकावेष्टनस्य चतुरस्रे मध्यबीजलेखनस्य च सूचनं कृतम् । यन्त्रजीवादिकं तु सर्वत्र समानम् । त्रिपुरादेवी च विद्महे कामेश्वरी च धीमहि । तन्नः क्लिन्ना प्रचोदयादिति गायत्री ॥ ११ ॥

नवयोनिरचनाप्रकारमाह—वह्नेरिति । वाग्भवादित्वमुपलक्षणं कामराज-

वामा ज्येष्ठा रौद्रिका साम्बिकेच्छा
ज्ञानाभिख्या सक्रिया कुब्जिकाह्वा ।
प्रह्वी चान्या स्याद्विषघ्नी सदूतिः
सर्वानन्दा शक्तयः स्युः क्रमेण ॥ १३

प्राङ्मध्ययोन्योः पुनरन्तराले सम्पूजयेत् प्राग्गुरुपादपङ्क्तिम् ।
पराभिधानामपराह्वयाञ्च परापराख्यामपि वाग्भवादिम् ॥ १४

तेनैव चाङ्गानि विदिग्दिशासु मन्त्री यथोक्तक्रमतः प्रपूज्य ।
तन्मध्ययोनेरभितः शरांश्च संपूजयेत् पञ्चममग्रभागे ॥ १५

सुभगां भगां भगान्ते सर्पिणीं भगमालिनीमनङ्गाह्वाम् ।
तत्पूर्वकुसुमसंज्ञां तदादिकं चाथ मेखलामदने ॥ १६

ब्राह्मीमाहेश्वर्यौ कौमारी वैष्णवी च वाराही ।
इन्द्राणी चामुण्डा सचण्डिका चेति मातरः प्रोक्ताः ॥ १७

संपूज्य योनिषु च मातृगणं सचण्डि-
कान्तं दलेष्वभियजेदसिताङ्गकाद्यैः ।
तैर्भैरवैः सह सुगन्धकपुष्पधूप-
दीपादिकैर्भगवतीं प्रवरैर्निवेद्यैः ॥ १८

असिताङ्गाख्यो रुरुरपि चण्डक्रोधाह्वयौ तथोन्मत्तः ।
सकपालिभीषणाख्यौ संहारश्चाष्ट भैरवाः कथिताः ॥ १९

इति क्रमाप्त्या विहिताभिषेकः संपूजयित्वा द्रविणैर्गुरुंश्च ।
जप्त्वाऽर्चयित्वोक्ततयाऽथ हुत्वा युञ्जीत योगांश्च गुरूपदिष्टान् ॥ २०

अच्छाभः स्वच्छभूषो धरणिमयगृहे वाग्भवं लक्षमेकं
यो जप्यात्तद्दशांशं विहितहुतविधिर्मन्त्रजप्ताञ्जनादिः ।

प्राक्तादित्वे परावरादिपङ्क्त्योः । मन्त्री यथोक्तक्रमत इत्यत्र मन्त्रीत्यङ्गेषु मूलयोगो मध्यबीजदीर्घयोगश्चोक्तः ॥ १२ ॥ १३ ॥ १४ ॥ १५ ॥ १६ ॥

इति क्रमाप्तेरिति । गुरोर्जपपूजादिक्रमाप्तेरित्यर्थः । सहार्थे तृतीया । उक्ततयेति । केवलमुक्ततया न फलाकाङ्क्षयेत्यर्थः ॥ १७ ॥ १८ ॥ १९ ॥ २० ॥

समस्तसाधनमभिधाय फलविशेषकामस्य समस्तव्यस्तसाधनं वदन् वाग्भव-

काव्यैर्नानार्थवृत्तैर्भुवनमखिलमापूरयेत् स स्वकीयै-
र्मारार्त्या विह्वलाभिः पुनरयमनिशं सेव्यते सुन्दरीभिः ॥ २१

रक्ताकल्पारुणतरदुकूलात्तवालेपहृद्यो
मौनी भूसद्मनि सुखनिविष्टो जपेल्लक्षमेकम् ।
बीजं मन्त्री रतिपतिमयं प्रोक्तहोमावसाने
योऽसौ लोके स सुरमनुजैः सेव्यते पूज्यते च ॥ २२

ससुरासुरसिद्धयक्षविद्याधरगन्धर्वभुजङ्गचारणानाम् ।
प्रमदा मदवेगतो विकीर्णाभरणाः स्रस्तदुकूलकेशजालाः ॥ २३

अतिदुःसहमन्मथव्यथाभिर्व्यथितान्तःपरितापवेपिताङ्ग्यः ।
घनघर्मजतोयबिन्दुमुक्ताफलसक्तोरुकुचान्तबाहुमूलाः ॥ २४

रोमाञ्चकञ्चुकितगात्रलताघनोद्य-
दुत्तुङ्गपीनकुचकुम्भनिपीड़िताङ्ग्यः ।
औत्सुक्यभारपृथुवेपथुखेदखिन्न-
पादारविन्दचलनस्खलिताभिघाताः ॥ २५

मारसायकनिपातदारिता रागसागरनिमग्नमूर्त्तयः ।
श्वासमारुततरङ्गिताधरा वाष्पपूरभरविह्वलेक्षणाः ॥ २६

मस्तकारचितदोर्द्वयाञ्जलिप्राभृता हरिणशावलोचनाः ।
वाञ्छितार्थकरणोद्यताश्च तद्दृष्टिपातमपि संनमन्ति ताः ॥ २७

धरापवरके तथा जपतु लक्षमन्त्यं मनुं
सुशुक्लकुसुमांशुकाभरणलेपनाढ्यो वशी ।
अमुष्य वदनादनारततयोच्चरेद्भारती
विचित्रपदपद्धतिर्भवति चास्य लोको वशे ॥ २८

साधनक्रममाह—अच्छाभ इति। वाग्भवं लक्षमेकमिति। तदादिकं मन्त्रमित्यर्थः। होमः पालाशैरेव ॥ २१ ॥

बीजं मन्त्री रतिपतीति। मन्त्रस्य कामराजादित्वमुक्तम्। होमोऽश्वारिजे-दशांशः ॥ २२ ॥

मध्यबीजस्य क्षोभकत्वमाह—ससुरासुरेति। अन्त्यं मनुमिति। अन्त्य-बीजादिकं मनुमित्यर्थः। ह्सः हस्त्रां हसकलहरकीं क्लीं हरसरयोः इत्येवं क्रमेण

पलाशपुष्पैर्मधुरत्रयाक्तैर्होमं विदध्यादयुतावधिं यः ।
सरस्वतीमन्दिरमाशु भूयात् सौभाग्यलक्ष्म्योश्च स मन्त्रजापी ॥ २९
वाजीकरञ्जाह्वशमीवटोत्थैः समिद्वरैर्विल्वभवप्रसूनैः ।
त्रिस्वादयुक्तैर्हवनक्रियाऽऽशु नरेन्द्रनारीनररञ्जनी स्यात् ॥ ३०
मालतीवकुलजैर्द्दलद्दलैश्चन्दनाम्भसि घने निमज्जितैः ।
श्रीकरी कुसुमकैर्हुतक्रिया सैव चाशु कविताकरी मता ॥ ३१
अनुलोमविलोममन्त्रमध्यस्थितसाध्याह्वयुतं प्रजप्य मन्त्री ।
पटुसंयुतया जुहोतु वाज्या नरनारीनरपान् वशे विधातुम् ॥ ३२
मधुरत्रयेण सह विल्वजैः फलैर्हवनक्रियाऽऽशु जनतानुरञ्जनी ।
अपि सैव साधकसमृद्धिदायिनी दिनशो विशिष्टकमलाकरी मता ॥

खण्डैः सुधालतोत्थैस्त्रिमधुरसिक्तैर्जुहोतु मन्त्रितमः ।
सकलोपद्रवशान्त्यै ज्वरापमृत्युप्रणोदनाय वशी ॥ ३४

फुल्लैर्विल्वप्रसूनैस्तदभिनवदलै रक्तकह्लारपुष्पैः
प्रत्येकं बन्धुजीवैररुणसरसिजैरुत्पलैः कैरवाह्वैः ।
नन्द्यावर्तैः सकुन्दैर्नृपतरुकुसुमैः पाटलीनागपुष्पैः
स्वाद्वक्तैरिन्दिरायै प्रजुहुत दिनशः सर्पिषा पायसेन ॥ ३५

मूलाधारात् स्फुरन्तीं शिखिपुरपुटवीतां प्रभां विद्युदाभा-
मार्कात्तन्मध्यगेन्दोः स्रवदमृतमुचा धारया मन्त्रमय्या ।
सद्यः सम्पूर्यमाणां त्रिभुवनमखिलं तन्मयत्वेन मन्त्री
ध्यायेन्मुच्येत वैरूप्यकदुरितजरारोगदारिद्र्यदोषैः ॥ ३६

वक्ष्यमाणाः परिवारवर्णाः प्रतिबीजमत्रापि प्रयोक्तव्याः ॥ २३ ॥ २४ ॥ २५ ॥
॥ २६ ॥ २७ ॥ २८ ॥

समन्त्रजापीत्यनुजपः सूचितः । सर्वंच दलद्दलैः विकसद्दलैरित्यर्थः ।
॥ २९ ॥ ३० ॥ ३१ ॥

प्रजप्य मन्त्रीति कर्मसाधकयोरपि प्रयोगः सूचितः ॥ ३२ ॥ ३३ ॥

जुहोतु मन्त्रीतम इत्यन्त्यबीजादित्वममृतयोगो वा सूचितः ॥ ३४ ॥ ३५ ॥

पूर्वसूचितान् योगानाह—मूलाधारादिति । शिखिपुरपुटेषु द्विरावृत्त्या मन्त्रन्यासं बहिरष्टदले केशरस्थाने स्वरयोगं दलेषु अष्टवर्गयोगं भूपुरे मध्यम-बीजयोगं बीजविशेषयोगं चाह—मन्त्री ध्यायेदिति ॥ ३६ ॥

वह्नेर्बिम्बद्वयपरिवृताधारसंस्थं समुद्यद्-
बालार्काभं स्वरगणसमावेष्टितं वाग्भवाख्यम् ।
वाण्या स्वीयाद्वदनकुहरात् सन्ततं निःसरन्त्या
ध्यायेन्मन्त्री प्रततकिरणप्रावृतं दुःखशान्त्यै ॥ ३७

हृत्पद्मस्थितभानुबिम्बविलसद्योन्यन्तरालोत्थितं
मध्याह्नार्कसमप्रभं परिवृतं वर्णैः कभाद्यान्तकैः ।
ध्यातं मन्मथबीजराजमखिलब्रह्माण्डविक्षोभकं
राज्यैश्वर्यविमर्दिनीमपि रमां दत्त्वा जगद्रञ्जयेत् ॥ ३८

मूर्ध्नोऽथ द्वादशान्तोदितशशधरबिम्बस्थयोनौ स्फुरन्तं
संवीतं व्यापकार्णैर्धवलरुचि मकारस्थितं बीजमन्त्यम् ।
ध्यात्वा सारस्वताच्छामृतजललुलितं दिव्यकाव्यादिकर्ता
नित्यं क्ष्वेलापमृत्युग्रहदुरितविकारान्निहन्त्याशु मन्त्री ॥ ३९

योनेः परिभ्रमितकुण्डलिरूपिणीं तां
रक्तामृतद्रवमुचा निजतेजसैव ।
व्योमस्थलं सकलमप्यभिपूर्य तस्मि-
न्नाविश्य मङ्क्षु वशयेद्वनिता नरांश्च ॥ ४०

गुह्यस्थितं वा मदनस्य बीजं
जवारुणं रक्तसुधां स्रवन्तम् ।
विचिन्त्य तस्मिन् विनिवेश्य साध्यं
वशीकरोत्येव विदग्धलोकः ॥ ४१

वाग्भवयोगमाह—वह्नेर्बिम्बेति । षट्कोणेषु वाग्भवयोगमाह—ध्याये-न्मन्त्रीति ॥ ३७ ॥

मध्यमबीजयोगमाह—हृत्पद्मेति । योनिः षटकोणम् । अत्र कोणेषु मध्यमबीजयोगमुक्त्वा योन्यन्तरालोत्थितमित्यनेनैव अन्त्यबीजयोगमाह ॥ ३८ ॥

मूर्ध्न इति । योनिः षट्कोणमेव नवयोनिर्वा । मकारस्थितमिति च्छेदः । आशु मन्त्रीति । योनिष्वन्त्यबीजयोग उक्तः ॥ ३९ ॥

पुनर्वैश्यप्रधानं रक्तवर्णध्यानयुक्तं वाग्भवयोगमाह—योनेरिति ॥ ४० ॥

मध्यमबीजस्य स्थानभेदेन योगान्तरमाह—गुह्यस्थितमित्यादिना ॥ ४१ ॥

अन्त्यं बीजमथेन्दुकुन्दविशदं संचिन्त्य चित्ताम्बुजे
तद्भूतां धृतपुस्तकाक्षवलयां देवीं मुहुस्तन्मुखात् ।
उद्यन्तं निखिलाक्षरं निजमुखेनाऽनारतस्रोतसा
निर्यान्तञ्च निरस्तसंसृतिभयो भूयात् स वाग्वल्लभः ॥ ४२

सङ्क्षेपतो निगदिता त्रिपुराभिधाना
विद्या सजापहवना सविधानपूजा ।
सोपासना च सकलाभ्युदयप्रसिद्धै-
वाणीरमाप्तिविधये जगतो हिताय ॥ ४३

विद्येशीं त्रिपुरामिति प्रतिभजेद् यो वा जपेन्नित्यशः
तद्वक्त्रादथ नूतनार्थविशदा वाणी मुदा निःसरेत् ।
सम्पत्त्या नृपनन्दिनी ततयशःपूरा भवेदिन्दिरा
तस्याऽसौ प्रतियाति सर्वमुनिभिः संप्रार्थनीयं पदम् ॥ ४४

इति श्रीप्रपञ्चसारे नवमः पटलः ।

अन्त्यबीजस्य सकलयोगमितरबीजयोरपि उपलक्षणार्थमाह—अन्त्यमिति ।
॥ ४२ ॥ ४३ ॥ ४४ ॥

इति श्रीपद्मपादाचार्यकृते प्रपञ्चसारविवरणे
नवमः पटलः ।

दशमः पटलः ।

अथाभिवक्ष्ये सकलप्रपञ्चमूलात्मिकायाः प्रकृतेर्यथावत् ।
मन्त्रं तु साङ्गं सहुताभिषिकं जपार्चनाढ्यं सकलार्थसिद्धै ॥ १

घनवर्त्मकृशागतिशान्तिबिन्दुभिः
कथितः परप्रकृतिवाचको मनुः ।
दुरितापहोऽर्थसुखधर्ममोक्षदो
भजतामशेषजनरञ्जनक्षमः ॥ २

शक्तिः स्यादृषिरस्य तु गायत्री चोदिता मनोश्छन्दः ।
बोधस्वरूपवाची संवित्प्रोक्ता च देवता गुरुभिः ॥ ३

नेत्रकरणर्तुदिनकरभुवनदिक्कारस्वराग्निबिन्दुयुजा ।
व्योम्ना षड़ङ्गक्लृप्तिर्जातिविभिन्नेन चापि संप्रोक्ता ॥ ४

अथेच्छाशक्तिप्रधानां भुवनेश्वरीमाह—अथाऽभिवक्ष्य इति । सकलप्रपञ्चमूलात्मिकाया इति । पूर्वोक्तनिष्कीलविद्यामध्यमबीजसारभूताया इत्यर्थः । अतोऽस्यास्तद्योगः सूचितः ।

अथवा सकलः प्रणवः पञ्चाशत्कलात्मकत्वात् । तस्य प्रपञ्चो विस्तारः विभूतिः श्रीरित्यर्थः । मूलं कामं वाक् च । एतेषामात्मभूताया मध्यस्थायाः प्रकृतेरित्येतेषामेकैकेन समस्तैश्च पुटितत्वं शक्तेः सूचितम् । यथावदिति । अनुलोमप्रतिलोमक्रमः सूचितः । साङ्गं त्विति । अङ्गेषु तत्तद्बीजदीर्घादियोगः सूचितः । सकलार्थसिद्धैर इति । प्रणवयोगे मोक्षस्य श्रीयोगेऽर्थस्य कामयोगे कामस्य वाग्योगे धर्मज्ञानादेः सर्वयोगे सर्वस्य सिद्धिरित्यर्थः ॥ १ ॥

केवलस्यापि सकलपुरुषार्थसाधनत्वमाह—दुरितापह इति ॥ २ ॥

बोधस्वरूपवाचीति । बोधस्वरूपं परमात्मानं वक्ति प्रकाशयतीति बोधस्वरूपवाची ब्रह्मात्मैकत्वविद्या निरूढ़ा संविदित्यर्थः । गुरुभिः प्रोक्तेति । श्रीदुर्गादिमन्त्रदेवताः सूचिताः ॥ ३ ॥

जातिविभिन्नेनेति । हृदयाय नम इत्यादियुक्तेनेत्यर्थः । अपिना सर्वज्ञादियोग उक्तः । ह्रं बीजम् । ईं शक्तिः ॥ ४ ॥

अग्नीन्दुयोगविकृता लिपयो हि सृष्टा-
स्ताभिर्विलोमपठिताभिरिदं शरीरम् ।
भूतात्मकं त्वगसृगादियुतं समस्तं
संव्यापयेन्निशितधीर्विधिना यथावत् ॥ ५

अन्त्यावुष्मस्वमून् वादिषु मलिपिषु तांस्तांश्चतुर्वर्गवर्णो-
ष्वेतानस्यम्यदस्तद्दृदति तदपि परेषु क्रमेणाऽवचिन्त्य ।
संहृत्य स्थानयुक्तं क्षपितसकलदेहो ललाटस्थितान्तः-
प्राप्तिव्याप्तद्विसप्ताधिकभुवनतलो यातु मद्भावमेव ॥ ६

दिग्बन्धाद्यनन्तरं भूतशुद्धिक्रममाह—अग्नीन्दिति। अग्नीन्दुशब्दाभ्यां प्रकृतिपुरुषावुच्येते। योगस्तयोः सम्बन्धः। तेन परापश्यन्तीतदर्थादिरूपेण विकृता लिपयो वैखरीतदर्थरूपेण सृष्टा हि यस्मात् तस्मात्ताभिः सहेदं शरीरं तदर्थात्मकं तत्र व्यापयेत् संहरेत्। कथमित्याह—प्रतिलोमपठिताभिरिति। प्रतिलोमेन न्यस्ताभिरित्यर्थः। शरीरस्य अशुद्धत्वेन संहरणीयत्वमाह—भूतात्मकमिति। प्रतिलोममातृकान्यासेन वैखरीतदर्थात्मकं स्थूलं बिन्दुं मध्यमात्मके सूक्ष्मे संहृत्य बुद्ध्यैव सूक्ष्मादिकं संहर्तव्यमित्याह—निशितधीरिति। विधिनेति। प्राणायामैरित्यर्थः। तत्र प्रथमप्राणायामेन बिन्दुं सूक्ष्मात्मकं नादे कारणे पश्यन्त्यां विलापयेत्। द्वितीयेन नादं कारणं सामान्ये परायां शक्तौ। तृतीयेन शक्तिं शान्तौ इति विधिनेति सूचितम्। यथावदिति। नादाद्यन्तं मूलोच्चारणेनित्यर्थः ॥ ५ ॥

प्रकारान्तरेण भूतशुद्धिमाह—अन्त्यावुष्मस्विति। मूलाधार लिङ्गमूल नाभि हृदय गल तालु भ्रूमध्य ललाट मस्तकेषु द्विचतुश्चतुःपञ्चपञ्चपञ्चपञ्चषोडश-दलानि पद्मानि अष्टप्रकृतीश्वराधिष्ठितानि स्मृत्वा तत्संहारेण स्वयं परो भवेदिति श्लोकार्थः।

तत्र मूलाधारपद्मे चलौ दलत्वेन स्मृत्वा। तद्द्वलद्वयं पृथिवीविकारात्मकं चं स्वाहा लं स्वाहेति कर्णिकागतपृथिव्यां विलाप्य। साऽपि लिङ्गमूलस्थवसषश-चतुर्दलपद्मकर्णिकागतापसु संहार्या इत्याह—अन्त्यावुष्मस्विति। तत्रापि दलात्मकाब्विकारान् पूर्ववत् अप्सु हुत्वा ता अपि नाभिस्थवादिचतुर्दलपद्म-कर्णिकास्थतेजसि संहार्या इत्याह—अमून् वादिष्विति। तदपि तेजः सविकारं हृद्गते पञ्चदले पवर्गात्मके वायुरूपे संहार्यमित्याह—मलिपिषु तानिति।

मूलाधारात् स्फुरिततड़िदाभा प्रभा सूक्ष्मरूपोद्-
गच्छन्त्यामस्तकमणुतरा तेजसां मूलभूता ।
सौषुम्नाध्वाचरणनिपुणा सा सविद्यानुबद्धा
ध्याता सद्योऽमृतमथ रवेः स्रावयेत् सार्धसोमात् ॥ ७

शिरसि निपतिता या बिन्दुधारा सुधाया
भवति लिपिमयी सा ताभिरङ्गं मुखाद्यम् ।
विरचयतु समस्तं पातितान्तश्च तेज-
स्यनल इव घृतस्योद्दीपयेदात्मतेजः ॥ ८

अनेनैव क्रमेणोत्तरं पद्मचतुष्कं तवर्गाद्यात्मकं पञ्चपञ्चदलं साधिष्ठातृकं मूर्धस्थे षोडशदले स्वरात्मनि ईश्वरात्मके संहरणीयमित्याह—तांश्चतुरिति । एतान् असि विसर्गे विसर्गात्मनीश्वर इत्यर्थः । ईश्वरैश्वर्यात्मक दलषोडशकमीश्वरे संहार्य-मित्याह—अम्यद इत्यादिना । अमि बिन्दौ । अदः विसर्गम् । बिन्द्वात्मनि ईश्वरे विसर्गदलं संहरेदित्यर्थः । तद् दति दन्तसम्बन्धिन्यौकारे तदात्मके ईश्वर इत्यर्थः । एवमुत्तरत्रापि । स्थानयुक्तमिति । प्रथमं संहारन्यासेन स्थूलं संहृत्य पश्चादनेन योगेन सूक्ष्माणि स्थानानि संहरेदित्यर्थः । ललाटस्थित इति । ललाटे प्रकृत्यब्जे तदभिन्नतया स्थितो जीवः । अतोऽकारार्थस्येश्वरस्य मूर्धस्थस्य प्राप्त्या व्याप्तद्विसप्ताधिकभुवनतलः संहृतसकलसंसारः स मद्भावं प्रत्यगीश्वरतामेव यात्विति शार्ङ्गिणो वचनमेतत् ।

स्रष्टृत्व स्थापकत्व संहर्तृत्व तिरोधायकत्वानुग्राहकत्व सर्वज्ञत्व सर्वैश्वरत्व सर्व-शक्तित्व सर्वान्तर्यामित्व सर्वात्मत्व सदानन्दचित्पूर्णात्मत्वाद्वयत्वानि ईश्वरगुणाः स्व-रार्थभूताः । सत्त्वरजस्तमःसाम्यबीजानि प्रकृतेर्गुणाः । शब्दादिपञ्चकनिश्चयाः महतः । तन्निश्चयकर्तृत्वाभिमानपञ्चकम् अहङ्कारस्य । पञ्चविधशब्दपरिणाम-सामर्थ्यमाकाशस्य । पञ्चस्पर्शरूपेण परिणामसामर्थ्यं वायोः । आकाशवायुरूपा-वेकीकृत्य चतुर्विधरूपपरिणामसामर्थ्यं तेजसः । तथा चतुर्विधरसपरिणाम-सामर्थ्यमपाम् । सुरभ्यसुरभिगन्धरूपेण परिणामसामर्थ्यं पृथिव्याः गुणद्वयम् । पृथिव्यादीनामेवंविधगुणविभागमभिसन्धाय द्विदलादिपद्मकल्पना कृता इत्यव-गन्तव्यम् ॥ ६ ॥

ततो दिव्यदेहसृष्टिक्रममाह—मूलाधारादिति । अधिष्ठानमेव मूलाधारः । प्रभा कुण्डलिनीमस्तकम् । मस्तकमपि परब्रह्मैव । तदेव ब्रह्म संविद्रूपिण्या

संहृत्य चोत्पाद्य शरीरमेवं
तेजोमयं व्याप्तसमस्तलोकम् ।
सङ्कल्प्य शक्त्यात्मकमात्मरूपं
तच्चिह्नमात्मन्यथ संदधीत ॥ ९

प्रकृत्या सह सार्धंसोमो रविश्च मायित्वात् । प्रणवशक्त्युच्चारणेन पूर्ववत्तेजः-सुषुम्नापद्मामृतपिण्डान् स्मृत्वा निरवद्यादिमन्त्रैर्व्याप्य अक्षरन्यासेन शरीरं रचयेदित्यर्थः ॥ ७ ॥ ८ ॥

व्याप्तसमस्तलोकमिति । व्यापिन्यादिक्रमेण स्वरूपपर्यन्तं व्याप्तमित्यर्थः । सङ्कल्प्य शक्त्यात्मकमिति । शक्त्यात्मकत्वसिद्धये सामान्यपटले कथिता इह वक्ष्यमाणाश्च न्यासाः सूचिताः । तच्चिह्नमिति । भूषणायुधादिन्यासः सूचितः ।

अयं न्यासक्रमः । पीठन्यासमूर्तिन्यासानन्तरम् आवाहनाद्यवगुण्ठनान्तं विधाय । मातृकां विन्यस्य । मूलेन करन्यासं कृत्वा । मूलतदक्षरमूल-तदङ्गहृल्लेखादिकम् अङ्गुलिषु विन्यस्य । मूलेन देहे त्रिशो व्याप्य । मूलपुटितां मातृकां विन्यस्य । शैवतत्त्वन्यास शक्तिश्रीसन्नतिरित्यादिन्यास-बुभुत्वादिन्यास श्रीकण्ठादिन्यासमूलतद्वर्णैः मूर्धहृदयनाभिषु सृष्ट्यादिन्यास शाक्त-तत्त्वन्यासाहोरात्रादित्रिलिङ्गाजपापरमात्मप्रणवन्यासान् विधाय । अष्टमात्रया शक्त्याष्टाक्षरदशाङ्गन्यासवत् दशाङ्गन्यासाङ्गर्थादिकन्यासान् कृत्वा । त्रिपुरोक्त-क्रमेण भूषणन्यासमाचरेत् ।

अथ आवरणन्यासः । क्रों क्रें क्रुं क्रिं क्रं इति बीजसहिता हृल्लेखाद्या मूर्धादिषु भूतस्थानेषु ऊर्ध्वादिवक्त्रेषु च विन्यस्य । गायत्र्यादित्रयं ललाटवाम-दक्षिणगण्डेषु न्यसित्वा । ब्रह्मादित्रयं सव्यकर्णास्यवामकर्णेषु न्यसित्वा । गलसव्यस्तनवामस्तनेषु गायत्र्याद्या अपि विन्यस्य । सव्यांस हृदय वामांसेषु ब्रह्मादिकं न्यसेत् । पुनर्नाभिवामदक्षिणोरुषु गायत्र्याद्यान् न्यसित्वा । वामस्फिगाधारदक्षिणस्फिक्षु ब्रह्मादिकं न्यसेत् । ह्रां ह्रीं ह्रूं इति गायत्र्यादीनां बीजानि । ह्रं ह्रिं ह्रुं इति ब्रह्मादीनाम् । पुनरलिकादिषु मातृभैरवन्यासः सबीजः । पुनर्ध्यात्वा संपूज्य पुनर्जपित्वा संयोगान् वक्ष्यमाणान् न्यासानाचरेत् । गुणितयोग षड्ध्वयोग लवादियुतराशि नक्षत्र तिथि करणन्यासयोग कुण्डलिनीहंस-हरिहरादिचतुःप्रणवप्राणापानयोः अहोरात्रमाससंवत्सरदेवाः सस्तुतयः स्वरा इत्यादियोग चतुर्दशयोगाजपापरमात्मप्रणवयोगन्यासान् विधायाऽण्ययोगेन जप्त्वा बाह्यपूजां कुर्यादिति न्यासक्रमः ॥ ९ ॥

उद्यद्भास्वत्समाभां विजितनवजवामिन्दुखण्डावनद्ध-
द्योतन्मौलिं त्रिनेत्रां विविधमणिलसत्कुण्डलां पद्मगाञ्च।
हारग्रैवेयकाञ्चीगुणमणिवलयाद्यैर्विचित्राम्बराढ्या-
मम्बां पाशाङ्कुशेष्टाभयकरकमलामम्बिकां तां नमामि ॥ १०

धातू द्वौ स्तो रक्षणव्यापकार्थौ पाद्योऽश्वाद्यस्तत्प्रभावात्तयोश्च।
सर्वं संरक्ष्याऽथ सर्वात्मना यो व्याप्नोत्यंशः स्यादसौ पाशवाची ॥ ११
अं स्यादात्मा कुर्धरा कुस्तनुर्वा भागार्थः स्याच्छोऽथवाऽऽवृत्तिवाची।
भूश्चेद्गतान्यन्यथा चेच्छरीराण्याकृष्यात्मन्याहरेदङ्कुशाख्यः ॥ १२
स्मृते यथा संसृतिचक्रचङ्क्रमोद्भवाद्घनापायसमुत्थितादपि।
वियोजयत्यात्मतनुं नरं भयात्तथाऽभयस्याऽभयसंज्ञिता विभोः ॥ १३
मुख्यार्थवाची वरशब्द उक्तः स्याद्वाञ्छितार्थश्च वराभिधानः।
मुख्यं त्वभीष्टं स्मृतिमात्रकेण ददाति योऽसौ वरदोऽवगम्यः ॥ १४

दीक्षाकृत्यै पुरोक्ते रचयतु विधिवन्मण्डलं मण्डपे तद्-
व्यक्तं युक्तञ्च कान्त्या त्रिगुणितविलसत्कर्णिकं वर्णवीतम्।
आवीतं केसरेष्वारचितहरिहरार्णैश्च मध्ये समायै-
स्तैरग्रे मायया्ऽऽढ्यं कमलमथ बहिः प्रोक्तचिह्नैरुपेतम् ॥ १५

पद्मगां चेति। पद्ममध्यगत्रिकोणगां चेत्यर्थः। वलयाद्यैः सह विचित्राम्बराढ्यामित्यन्वयः। अम्बिकामिति सूक्ष्मध्यानमुक्तम्। तामिति परध्यानम् ॥१०॥

पा रक्षण इति पाद्यः। अशू व्याप्ताविति अश्वाद्यः तयोर्निष्पन्नः पाशशब्दः स्यात्। तत्प्रभावात् सर्वं संरक्षेदिति। अंशिन्याः शक्तेः प्रभावादित्यर्थः। पाशवाची पाशस्मारक इत्यर्थः ॥ ११ ॥

अङ्कुशावयवार्थमाह—अं स्यादिति। आवृत्तिः पौनःपुन्यम्। भूश्चेत् कुशब्दार्थ इति शेषः। अन्यथा चेदिति तन्वर्थपक्षोऽनूदितः ॥ १२ ॥

यथातथाशब्दौ यस्मात्तस्मादर्थौ ॥ १३ ॥ १४ ॥

वर्णवीतमिति। उत्तरश्लोके वक्ष्यमाणप्रकारेण वीतमित्यर्थः। आवीतं केसरेष्विति। मध्ये समायैर्मध्ये मायासहितैः हरिहरार्णैः हरिहर इत्येतैरर्णैः केसरेषु वेष्टितमित्यर्थः। ह रि ह्रीं ह र ह्रीं इत्येवं लेखनप्रकारः। मध्ये समायैस्तैरिति। मध्ये दलमध्ये समायैरीकारसहितैः तैर्हरिहरार्णैः आवीत-

शक्त्याविःसाध्यमिन्द्रानिलनिर्ऋतिगबीजाभिबद्धं पुरोऽग्ने-
स्तत्कोणोल्लासिमायं हरिहरविलसद्गण्डमेभिः समायैः ।
वर्णैश्चावेष्टितं तत्त्रिगुणितमिति विख्यातमेतत् सुयन्त्रं
स्यादायुष्यञ्च वश्यं धनकरममितश्रीप्रदं कीर्तिदञ्च ॥ १६

हृल्लेखाख्यां गगनां रक्तां च करालिकां महोच्छुष्माम् ।
मूर्धनि वदने हृदये गुह्ये पदयोर्न्यसेत्तदङ्गैश्च ॥ १७

गायत्रीं न्यसतु गले स्तने तु सव्ये सावित्रीं पुनरपरे सरस्वतीञ्च ।
सव्येऽंसे सरसिजसम्भवं मुकुन्दं हृद्देशे पुनरपरांसके शिवञ्च ॥ १८

अलिकांसपार्श्वकुक्षिषु पार्श्वांसापरगलहृत्सु च क्रमशः ।
ब्रह्माण्याद्या विधिवन्न्यस्तव्या मातरोऽष्ट मन्त्रितमैः ॥ १९

सजया विजया तथा जिताह्वया चाऽपराजिता नित्या ।
तदनु विलासिनीदोग्ध्र्यौ साघोरा मङ्गला नव प्रोक्ताः ॥ २०

एवं संपूज्य पीठं तदनु नव घटान् पञ्च वा कर्णिकायां
पत्राग्रेषु न्यसेत् काञ्चनरजतताम्रोद्भवान्मार्त्तिकान् वा ।

मित्यर्थः। तैरग्रे मायया$\S$ऽऽढ्यमिति। तैर्हरिहरार्णैः। अग्रे दलाग्रे मायया ईकारेणाऽऽढ्यं यथा भवति तथा आवीतमिति योजना। एतत्त्रयं षड्गुणित-द्वादशगुणितयोरपि समानम् ॥ १५ ॥

शक्त्याविःसाध्यमिति पूर्वश्लोकस्य व्याख्या। शक्तिस्त्रिकोणमध्यस्था हृल्लेखा। तस्यामग्निविभागे आविर्भूतसाध्यम्। लिखितसाध्यनामेत्यर्थः। साधककर्मनाम्नो-र्मायाभागादौ लेखनस्योपलक्षणमेतत्। बीजानि शक्तिबीजानि। तत्-कोणोल्लासिमायमिति। त्रिकोणकोणेषु ईकारलेखनमुक्तम्। एभिः समायैरा-वेष्टितमिति। ह रि ई ह र ई इति शक्तिवेष्टनाद् बहिर्वेष्टितं तद्बहिर्वर्णै-र्मातृकाक्षरैश्चावेष्टितमित्यर्थः। आयुष्ये मध्यमबीजं मृत्युञ्जयेन वेष्टयेत्। वश्ये शक्त्या। धनश्रियोः श्रिया। कीर्त्तावजपया। यन्त्रजीवादिलेखनं तु सर्वत्र समानम् ॥ १६ ॥ १७ ॥ १८ ॥

ब्रह्माण्याद्या विधिवदिति। भैरवयोगः सूचितः। मन्त्रितमैरिति। आं ह्रां अं क्षम् इत्यादिबीजयोगः सूचितः ॥ १९ ॥

नवशक्तीराह—सजयेति। ह्रीं श्रीं भुवनेश्वर्यासनाय नम इति पीठमन्त्रः।

एकं वा कर्णिकायां सुमतिरथ विनिःक्षिप्य कुम्भं यथावत्
संपूर्याऽऽवाहयेत्त्रिष्वपि विधिषु पुनर्वक्ष्यमाणक्रमेण ॥ २१
मधुना महता रवेण साकं विधिना मध्यगतं प्रपूर्य कुम्भम् ।
अभिवाद्य कलाः प्रवेष्टयीत प्रवराभ्यामथ तं नवांशुकाभ्याम् ॥

ऐन्द्रं घृतेन यमदिक्प्रभवञ्च दध्ना
क्षीरेण वारुणमथो तिलजेन सौम्यम् ।
क्षीरद्रुचर्मदशमूलकपुष्पसिद्ध-
क्वाथेन कोणनिहितानपि पूरयेच्च ॥ २३

मूत्रेणैन्द्रं गोमयेनापि याम्यं क्षीरेणाप्यं सौम्यजञ्चैव दध्ना ।
मध्यप्रोत्थं सर्पिषा पञ्च कुम्भाः स्युश्चेदेवं पूरणीयाः क्रमेण ॥ २४

गोमूत्रगोमयोदकपयोदधिघृतांशकाः क्रमात् प्रोक्ताः ।
एकार्धधातुसत्त्वाद्येक्षि सर्वाणि वा समानि स्युः ॥ २५
तारभवाभिरथर्ग्भिः क्रमेण संयोजयेत् पञ्चगव्यानि ।
आत्माष्टाक्षरमन्त्रैरथ वा योज्यानि पञ्चभिः पञ्च ॥ २६

यद्येककलशक्लृप्तौ विधिरपि पञ्चाशदोषधिक्वाथैः ।
पूरयतु पञ्चभिर्वा गव्यैस्तोयात्मकैःऽष्टगन्धाद्भिः ॥ २७
अत्रोत्तरस्यां दिशि पङ्कजे च पलाशचर्मक्वथितैः पयोभिः ।
सम्पूरणीयः कलशो यथावत् सुवर्णवस्त्रादियुतः सुशुद्धः ॥ २८
द्वारेषु मण्डपस्य द्वौ द्वौ कुम्भौ सुशुद्धजलपूर्णौ ।
संस्थाप्य च वसनाद्यैः प्रवेष्टयित्वा हि पूजनीयाः स्युः ॥ २९
ऊर्ध्वेन्द्रयाम्यसौम्यप्रत्यग्दिक्षु च भूतवर्णकाः क्रमशः ।
हृल्लेखाद्यास्तदनु च पूर्ववदङ्गानि पूजनीयानि ॥ ३०

ह्रीं भुवनेश्वरीमूर्तये नम इति मूर्तिमन्त्रः ॥ २० ॥

सुमतिरिति । एकस्मिन्नेव कुम्भेनैककुम्भशक्त्यापादनसमर्थ इत्यर्थः । यथावदिति पूर्वोक्तपूरणक्रमः सूचितः ॥ २१ ॥

नवघटपक्षे पूरणमाह—मधुनेति ॥ २२ ॥ २३ ॥

पञ्चकुम्भपक्षे पूरणक्रममाह—मूत्रेणेति ॥ २४ ॥

पञ्चगव्ययोजनप्रकारमाह कलशान्तरार्थं—गोमूत्रेति । सर्वाणि वेति

गायत्रीं शतमखजे निशाचरोत्थे
सावित्रीं पवनगते सरस्वतीञ्च ।
ब्रह्माणं हुतभुजि वारुणे च विष्णुं
बीजेऽस्रे समभियजेत् तथेशमैशे ॥ ३१

रक्ता रक्ताकल्पा चतुर्मुखी कुण्डिकाक्षमालेऽब्जे ।
दधती प्राग्बीजस्था गायत्री तादृशोऽग्निगो ब्रह्मा ॥ ३२

अरिदरगदाब्जहस्ता किरीटकेयूरहारसम्भिन्ना ।
निशिचरबीजसमुत्था सावित्री वरुणगस्तथा विष्णुः ॥ ३३

टङ्काक्षाभयवरान् दधती च त्रीक्षणेन्दुकलितजटा ।
वाणी वायव्यस्था विशदाकल्पा तथेश्वरस्त्वैशे ॥ ३४

ब्रह्माण्याद्यास्तद्बहिरनन्तरं वासवादिकाशेशाः ।
पूज्याः पूर्वप्रोक्तैरुपचारैः सम्यगिति निजेष्टाप्त्यै ॥ ३५

यदि नव कलशास्तेष्वथ संपूज्या मातरोऽष्ट दिक्क्रमशः ।
हृल्लेखाद्याः पूज्या मध्यादिषु पञ्च चेद्भवन्ति घटाः ॥ ३६

प्रथमं घृतजं ततः कषायं दधि पश्चात् क्वथितं पयः कषायम् ।
अथ तैलकषायकौ मधूत्थं द्विजवृक्षात् क्वथितं ततोऽभिषिञ्चेत् ॥ ३७

द्वारगकुम्भधृतैरथ सलिलैः पुनरन्तरान्तरा सेकम् ।
कुर्यान्मुखकरचरणक्षालनमपि साचमादिकं मन्त्री ॥ ३८

विधिवदिति कृताभिषिको द्वात्रिंशल्लक्षमथ जपेन्मन्त्रम् ।
निजकरदत्तार्घ्यामृतजलपोषितभानुमत्प्रभोऽनुदिनम् ॥ ३९

पद्मान्तरोक्तिः ॥ २५ ॥ २६ ॥ २७ ॥ २८ ॥ २९ ॥ ३० ॥

बीजेऽस्रे समभियजेदिति । बीजानि त्रिकोणबहिष्ठानि वेष्टनबीजानि । तेषु गायत्र्याद्याः पूज्याः । अस्रेषु त्रिकोणकोणेषु ब्रह्मादिकं पूजनीयमित्यर्थः । ॥ ३१ ॥ ३२ ॥ ३३ ॥ ३४ ॥ ३५ ॥ ३६ ॥

अभिषेकक्रममाह—प्रथमं घृतजमिति ॥ ३७ ॥

साचमादिकं मन्त्रीति । मन्त्राचमनमुक्तम् ॥ ३८ ॥

निजकरदत्तार्घ्यामृत इति । स्वस्य करे रश्मिभिः सर्वनाडीद्वारा निःसृताभिरर्घ्यामृतविभक्ताभिः आदित्यमण्डलपर्यन्तं व्याप्ताभिरादित्याय दत्तानि यान्यर्घ्यं-

भूत्वा शक्तिः स्वयमथ दिनेशेन्दुवैश्वानराणा-
मैक्यं कुर्वन् प्रणवमनुना शक्तिबीजेन भूयः ।
आकृष्याऽन्तर्बहिरपि समाधाय बुद्ध्यैव तेजो
जप्यान्मन्त्रं ज्वलनहुतशिष्टान्नभुक् प्रोक्तसंख्यम् ॥ ४०

अथ तु हविष्यप्राशी नक्ताशी वा जपेन्मनुस्त्वेवम् ।
परिपूर्णायां नियमितजपसंख्यायां समारभेद्धोमम् ॥ ४१

जपाद्दशांशं जुहुयाद्‌थाऽष्टद्रव्यैर्गुडृक्षौद्रघृतावसिक्तैः ।
वर्णौषधीसिद्धजलाभिषिक्तं कृत्वा द्विजानभ्यवहारयेच्च ॥ ४२

ततोऽस्य प्रत्ययास्त्वेवं जायन्ते जपतो मनुम् ।
अधिष्ठितं निष्प्रदीपं निस्तमिस्रं गृहं भवेत् ॥ ४३

ततः कृत्वा जपन्यासं समुपासीत शक्तितः ।
युक्तात्मा नित्ययोगेन प्रागुक्तविधिनाऽर्चयेत् ॥ ४४

अश्वत्थविप्राङ्घ्रिपबिल्वनाम्नां तर्कारिकप्लक्षकसिव्यकानाम् ।
प्रसारणीकाश्मरिरोहिणीनामुडुम्बरीपाटलिडुण्डुकानाम् ॥ ४५

पलं पलार्धं त्वथ कर्षमर्धं तेषान्तु भागः कथितः क्रमेण ।
एतैः सृतेनाथ जलेन चासौ संपूरणीयः कलशो यथावत् ॥ ४६

जलामृतानि तैरादित्यभावमापन्नैरादित्येच्छया पुनरपि प्रत्यामृतैः पोषितः सन् स्वयमपि भानुवत् प्रभ इत्यर्थः । अर्घ्यदानप्रकारस्तु सौरपटले द्रष्टव्यः ॥ ३८ ॥

जपकाले ध्यानप्रकारमाह—भूत्वा शक्तिरिति । भूत्वा शक्तिः स्वयमिति विग्रहध्यानमुक्तम् । दिनेशेन्दुवैश्वानराणामैक्यं कुर्वन्नित्यान्तरं सूक्ष्मध्यानम् ।

व्यापिन्यादिध्यानमाह—शक्तिबीजेनेति । अन्तःस्थिततेजस्त्रयात्मकं तत् तेजः शक्तिबीजजपसमये बुद्ध्यैव आकृष्य बहिरपि व्यापिन्याद्यात्मना समाधाय जपेदित्यर्थः ॥ ४० ॥ ४१ ॥

अष्टभिर्द्रव्यैरिति । प्रपञ्चयागोक्तैरित्यर्थः ॥ ४२ ॥

जायन्त इति बहुवचनेन प्रतिभादिकमुक्तम् ॥ ४३ ॥

समुपासीतेति । युञ्ज्यादित्यर्थः । योगो नाम परापरशक्त्यैक्यद्वारा पूर्णभावः । योगिना बाह्यपूजाः परित्यज्याऽन्तरेव पूजा कार्येत्याह—युक्तात्मेति । परेण युक्तः संयुक्त एकीभूत आत्माऽन्तःकरणं यस्य स तथोक्तः । स नित्ययोगेन प्रत्यग्-

प्रत्यब्दसेकाद्भविता शतायुर्मेधेन्दिरावान् रहितश्च रोगैः ।
मासेषु जन्मस्वभिषिक्ततः स्यादुर्वीपतिर्मङ्क्षु महापृथिव्याः ॥ ४७

अर्काभस्तेजसाऽसौ भवति नलिनजा सन्ततं किङ्करी स्या-
द्रोगा नश्यन्ति दृष्ट्या तमथ च धनधान्याकुलं तत्समीपम् ।
देवा नित्यं नमोऽस्मै विदधति फणिनो नैव दंशन्ति पुत्राः
सम्पन्नाः स्युः सपुत्रास्तनुविपदि परं धाम विष्णोः स भूयात् ॥ ४८

शक्तिप्रग्रस्तसाध्यं हरशरकलमायावृतं वह्निगेह-
द्वन्द्वाश्रिप्राप्तमायं प्रतिविवरलसच्छक्तिबद्धं बहिश्च ।
कोणोद्यद्दण्डादण्डित्रिलिपिहरिहराबद्धगण्डं विलोमा-
र्णावीतं क्ष्मायुगाष्टोदरगनृहरिचिन्ताश्मकं षड्गुणाख्यम् ॥ ४९

षडङ्गुलप्रमाणेन वर्तुलं कर्तुरालिखेत् ।
षडङ्गुलावकाशेन तद्बहिश्च प्रवर्त्तयेत् ॥ ५०

ब्रह्मयोगरूपेण । प्रागुक्तविधिना विधीयत इति विधिः क्रम उपकरणजातं च सर्वं तेनाऽर्चयेत् अमृतमयैश्चित्पर्यन्तं व्याप्तैरुपहारैरन्तरेवाऽर्चयेदित्यर्थः ॥ ४४ ॥ ४५ ॥ ॥ ४६ ॥ ४७ ॥ ४८ ॥

बहिरर्चनस्य पूर्वमेव विहितत्वेन इहाऽविधेयत्वात् षड्गुणितं संगृह्णाति—शक्तिप्रग्रस्तेति । शक्तिर्मध्यस्था हृल्लेखा तया प्रग्रस्तसाध्यम् । तस्यां लिखितसाध्यमित्यर्थः । साध्यलेखनमुपलक्षणं साधककर्मलेखनस्यापि । हरशरकलमायाः ह्रीं श्रीं क्लींकाराः तैरावृतं पूर्वोक्तं शक्तिबीजम् । तत्र ह्रींबीजेन पञ्चधाऽऽवृत्तिरेका आवृत्तिः । पुनस्तदन्तराल एव श्रीबीजेन । तथैव तदन्तराले क्लींबीजेन । वह्निगेहद्वन्द्वाश्रिप्राप्तमायमिति । षट्कोणस्याऽवशिष्टांशे ईकारलेखनमुक्तम् । प्रतिविवरेति । षट्कोणान्तरालेष्वित्यर्थः । बहिरिति । द्वितीयवर्तुलाद् बहिरित्यर्थः । कोणोद्यदिति । कोणशब्देन षट्कोणान्युच्यन्ते । शक्तिश्रीकामाः त्रिलिपयः । दण्डित्वं सबिन्दुत्वम् । दण्डिबीजत्रयमूर्ध्वकोणत्रये । अदण्डिबीजत्रयमधःकोणत्रये । गण्डशब्देन षट्कोणान्तरालषट्कं विवक्षितम् । विलोमार्णावीतमिति । तृतीयवृत्तान्तर्बाह्यभागयोः अनुलोमविलोममातृकावर्णैः वेष्टितमित्यर्थः । विगता विलोमेन गता वर्णा अनुलोमगताश्च वर्णा विलोमार्णाः । क्ष्मायुगं पृथिवीमण्डलद्वयं पुटितं तस्याष्टोदरेषु कोणाष्टकेषु गतनृहरिचिन्ताश्मकं दिक्षु नृसिंहबीजं विदिक्षु चिन्तारत्नमिति विभागः ॥ ४९ ॥

वर्तुलं तावता भूयस्तद्बहिश्च तृतीयकम् ।
मध्यवर्तुलमध्ये तु हृल्लेखाबीजमालिखेत् ॥ ५१
द्वितीयवर्तुलाश्लिष्टमीषच्छ्लिष्टषडस्रकम् ।
पुटितं मण्डलं वह्नेरस्पृशन्मध्यवर्तुलम् ॥ ५२
इन्द्राग्निरक्षोवरुणवाय्वीशान्तास्रकं लिखेत् ।
षट्सु कोणान्तरालेषु हृल्लेखाषट्कमालिखेत् ॥ ५३
एकैकान्तरितास्तास्तु सम्बध्युरितरेतरम् ।
शिखाभिरन्तराभिस्तु बाह्याबाह्याभिरान्तराः ॥ ५४
मध्यवर्तुलसंस्थाया हृल्लेखायाः कपोलयोः ।
अधरे साध्यनामार्णं साधकस्योत्तरे लिखेत् ॥ ५५
अन्तराग्निश्रियोः कर्मं साधकांशे समालिखेत् ।
हरमायाः पञ्चकृत्वः स्युर्बहिर्गर्भवर्तुलम् ॥ ५६
तद्बहिः शरमायाश्च कलमायाश्च तद्बहिः ।
लिखेन्मायां बिन्दुमतीं वह्नेः कोणेषु षट्स्वपि ॥ ५७
वह्नेः कोणत्रये श्रीमत्पश्चीये वितयं लिखेत् ।
शक्तिश्रीकामबीजानां सदण्डं साधकार्णवत् ॥ ५८
वह्नेस्तु वह्निपश्चीये तान्येवाऽदण्डवन्ति च ।
ससाध्यनामवर्णानि स्पष्टनिष्ठानभाञ्जि च ॥ ५९
बाह्यरेखामन्तरा स्युर्वर्णाः क्रमगताः शुभाः ।
तद्बहिः प्रतिलोमाश्च ता स्युर्लेखकपाटवात् ॥ ६०
ततो विदर्भितं भूमेर्मण्डलद्वयमालिखेत् ।
महादिक्षु नृसिंहार्णं चिन्तारत्नाश्रितास्रकम् ॥ ६१
बहिः षोड़शशूलाङ्कं शोभनं व्यक्तवर्णवत् ।
एतद्यन्त्रं समालिख्य पद्ममारचयेत्ततः ॥ ६२
रुचिरं द्वादशदलं षट्त्रिंशत्केसरोज्ज्वलम् ।
विवृत्तराशिवीथ्याद्यैः पार्थिवान्तञ्च मण्डलम् ॥ ६३

अस्य श्लोकस्य व्याख्यानं—षडङ्गुलेत्यादि । बहिर्गर्भवर्तुलमिति । गर्भवर्तुलं

पूर्वोक्तलक्षणोपेतं शुभं दृष्टिमनोहरम् ।
एवं कृते षड्गुणिते मण्डले सुमनोहरे ।
प्राग्वत् सङ्कल्प्य कलशमर्चयेत् सुसमाहितः ॥ ६४

अभ्यर्च्य पीठं नवशक्तिकान्तमङ्गानि बीजेषु च षट्सु भूयः ।
गायत्रसावित्रसरस्वतीश्च यजेदथ श्रीरतिपुष्टिसंज्ञाः ॥ ६५

ब्रह्माणमथ च विष्णुं महेश्वरं धनदमदनगणनाथान् ।
अभ्यर्चयेत् षट्स्वपि वह्नेः कोणेषु तद्बहिः क्रमशः ॥ ६६

रक्तामनङ्गकुसुमां कुसुमातुरां च
नित्यामनङ्गमदनां मदनातुराख्याम् ।
गौरीं तथैव गगनां गगनस्य रेखां
पद्मां भवप्रमथिनीं शशिशेखरां च ॥ ६७

एता द्विषट् प्रतिदलं प्रतिपूज्य शक्ती-
स्तद्बाह्यतो यजतु मातृगणं क्रमेण ।
इन्द्रादिकान् बहिरतश्च तदायुधानि
संपूज्य पूर्वविधिनाऽमुमथाऽभिषिञ्चेत् ॥ ६८

योऽमुमर्चयति मुख्यविधानं सिद्धशक्तिरपि संजपहोमैः ।
स श्रियो निलयनं त्रिदशानां वन्द्यतां व्रजति विष्णुसमानः ॥ ६९

इति श्रीप्रपञ्चसारे दशमः पटलः ।

बहिर्यथा भवति तथा स्युरित्यर्थः ॥ ५०—६४ ॥

षड्गुणितविधाने षट्कोणन्यासे प्रथमं गायत्र्यादिषट्कं न्यसित्वा एष्वेव कोणेषु ब्रह्मादिकमपि विन्यस्य शङ्खकपोलगलजत्रुस्तनपार्श्वेषु प्रादक्षिण्येन रक्तानङ्गकुसुमादिकां विन्यस्य मातृकक्रमार्गेण न्यसेदिति ॥ ६५॥६६॥६७॥६८ ॥

इति श्रीपद्मपादाचार्यकृते प्रपञ्चसारविवरणे
दशमः पटलः ।

एकादशः पटलः ।

अथ वक्ष्ये संग्रहतो द्वादशगुणिताख्यमहायन्त्रवरम् ।
संपूज्य येन शक्तिं भुक्तेर्मुक्तेर्व्रजेन्नरोऽनुभवम् ॥ १

व्याहृत्यावीतशक्तिज्वलनपुरयुगद्वन्द्वसन्ध्युत्थशक्त्या-
वीतं कोणात्तदुर्बीजकमनु च कपोलात्तगायत्रिमन्त्रम् ।
आग्नेय्यावीतमर्णैर्वृतमनुविगतैर्भूपुराभ्याञ्च रन्ध्रे
ह्रीं चिन्तारत्नकं द्वादशगुणितमिदं यन्त्रमिष्टार्थदायि ॥ २

पूर्वोक्तमानक्लृप्ता मन्त्री त्रितयं विलिख्य वृत्तानाम् ।
विलिखेदन्तर्वर्तुलमनु शक्तिं स्पष्टबिन्दुनिष्ठानाम् ॥ ३

द्वादशमध्यमवर्तुलरेखाया बहिरालिखेच्च शक्तीनाम् ।
हरियमवरुणधनाधिपदिक्षु द्वे द्वे च ताः क्रमेण स्युः ॥ ४

ईशाग्निनिर्ऋतिमरुतां दिक्ष्वेकैकं विलिख्य भूयश्च ।
बीजान्तरालनिर्गतशूलाङ्कितकोणषट्कयुगमग्नेः ॥ ५

मण्डलयुगयुगलं स्यादस्रशदान्तरितवर्तुलं विशदम् ।
शक्तिं प्रवेष्टयेच्च प्रतिलोमव्याहृतिभिरन्तःस्थाम् ॥ ६

रविकोणेषु दुरन्तां मायां विलिखेदथाऽत्र बिन्दुमतीम् ।
एकैकान्तरितास्ताः परस्परं शक्तयश्च सम्बध्युः ॥ ७

षड्गुणितविधानानन्तरं द्वादशगुणितविधानमाह—अथ वक्ष्य इति । आद्येति पाठेऽयमर्थः । श्रीबीजप्रधानषड्गुणितपूजया प्राप्तविभूतेः पुरुषस्य दुर्गाबीजप्रधानं रक्षायां प्रशस्तं विधानमुच्यत इति । मुक्तेः प्रणवयोगः ॥ १ ॥

व्याहृत्यावीतशक्तीति । प्रतिलोमसप्तव्याहृतिवेष्टितमध्यशक्तीत्यर्थः । कोणात्तदुर्बीजकमिति । द्वादशकोणानामवशिष्टांशे लिखितदुर्गाबीजम् अन्तर्गतांशे लिखितमायाबीजं चेत्यर्थः । कपोलयोर्गायत्र्यक्षरद्वयं प्रतिलोमतो लेख्यम् । शक्तिवेष्टनाद् बहिराग्नेयेनापि प्रतिलोमेनावीतम् अनुविगतवर्णवेष्टनं पूर्ववत् ॥२॥

अस्य पद्यस्य व्याख्या—पूर्वोक्तेति । मन्त्रीति । स्थानशोधनादिमन्त्रज्ञ इत्यर्थः । स्पष्टबिन्दुनिष्ठानामिति । स्पष्टबिन्द्ववयवसंस्थानामित्यर्थः ॥ ३—७ ॥

गायत्रीं प्रतिलोमतः प्रविलिखेद्दक्षैः कपोलं बहि-
र्द्वे द्वे चैव लिपी बहिश्च रचयेद् भूयस्तथा त्रिष्टुभम् ।
वर्णान् प्रानुगतांश्च भूपुरयुगे सिंहाख्यचिन्तामणिं
लिख्याद् यन्त्रमशेषदुःखशमनायोक्तं पुरा देशिकैः ॥ ८

बहिरथ षोडशपत्रं वृत्तविचित्रं च राशिवीथियुतम् ।
विरचय्य मण्डलं पुनरत्र यथोक्तं निधापयेत् कलशम् ॥ ९

आदावङ्गावरणमनु हृल्लेखिकाद्याश्चतस्रो
ब्राह्म्याद्याः षोडश च विकृतीर्द्वन्द्वसंख्याः क्रमेण ।
सार्धं भूयश्चतसृभिरथो षष्टिभिर्लोकपालै-
र्वज्राद्यैरष्टममपि समभ्यर्चयेद्भक्तिनम्रः ॥ १०

कराली विकराली च उमा देवी सरस्वती ।
दुर्गा शची उषा लक्ष्मी श्रु[र]तिः स्मृतिधृती तथा ॥ ११

श्रद्धा मेधा मतिः कान्तिरार्या षोडश शक्तयः ।
विद्याश्रीपुष्टयः प्रज्ञा सिनीवाली कुहूस्तथा ॥ १२

रुद्रवीर्या प्रभा नन्दा पोषणी ऋद्धिदा शुभा ।
कालरात्रिर्महारात्रिर्भद्रकाली कपालिनी ॥ १३

विकृतिर्दण्डिमुण्डिन्यौ सेन्दुखण्डा शिखण्डिनी ।
निशुम्भशुम्भमथिनी महिषासुरमर्दिनी ॥ १४

इन्द्राणी चैव रुद्राणी शङ्करार्धशरीरिणी ।
नारी नारायणी चैव त्रिशूलिन्यपि पालिनी ॥ १५

अम्बिका ह्लादिनी चैव द्वात्रिंशच्छक्तयो मताः ।
पिङ्गलाक्षी विशालाक्षी समृद्धिर्बुद्धिरेव च ॥ १६

श्रद्धा स्वाहा स्वधाख्या च मायाभिख्या वसुन्धरा ।
त्रिलोकधात्री गायत्री सावित्री त्रिदशेश्वरी ॥ १७

बहिश्चेति । शक्तिवेष्टनाद् बहिरित्यर्थः । भूयस्तथा त्रिष्टुभमिति । प्रतिलोमेनेत्यर्थः ॥ ८ ॥ ९ ॥

हृल्लेखिकाद्याश्चतस्र इति । हृल्लेखा तदाद्याश्चतस्रश्चेत्यर्थः ॥ १०—२१ ॥

सुरूपा बहुरूपा च स्कन्दमाताऽच्युतप्रिया ।
विमला सामला चैव अरुणी वारुणी तथा ॥ १८

प्रकृतिर्विकृतिः सृष्टिः स्थितिः संहृतिरेव च ।
सन्ध्या माता सती हंसी मर्दिका वज्रिका परा ॥ १९

देवमाता भगवती देवकी कमलासना ।
त्रिमुखीसप्तमुख्यौ च सुरासुरविमर्दिनी ॥ २०

सुलम्बोष्ठ्यूर्ध्वकेश्यौ च बहुशिरा वृकोदरी ।
रथरेखाह्वया चैव शशिरेखा तथाऽपरा ॥ २१

पुनर्गगनवेगाख्या वेगा च पवनादिका ।
भूयो भुवनपालाख्या तथैव मदनातुरा ॥ २२

अनङ्गाऽनङ्गमदना भूयश्चाऽनङ्गमेखला ।
अनङ्गकुसुमा विश्वरूपाऽसुरभयङ्करी ॥ २३

अक्षोभ्यासत्यवादिन्यौ वज्ररूपा शुचिव्रता ।
वरदा चैव वागीशी चतुःषष्टिः प्रकीर्त्तिताः ॥ २४

दृष्ट्वा यथोक्तमिति तं कलशं निजं वा
पुत्रं तथाऽऽप्तमपि शिष्यमथाऽभिषिञ्चेत् ।
आस्तिक्ययुक्तमथ सत्यरतं वदान्यं
विप्रप्रियं कुलकरञ्च नृपोत्तमं वा ॥ २५

विधानमेतत् सकलार्थसिद्धिकरं परं पावनमिन्दिरादम् ।
आयुःप्रदं वश्यकरं रिपूणां भुक्तिप्रदं मुक्तिफलप्रदञ्च ॥ २६

पाशाङ्कुशमध्यगया शक्त्याऽथ जपार्चनहुतादियुतम् ।
वक्ष्ये यन्त्रविधानं त्रैलोक्यप्राभृतायमानमिदम् ॥ २७

शक्तेर्विधानमभिधाय तस्या एव स्वायुधबीजपुटिताया विधानं वक्तुमारभते— पाशाङ्कुशेति । चतुरस्रद्वयात्मकमष्टकोणं लिखित्वा कोणाष्टकगतमृजुरेखाद्वयमृजु प्रसारयेत् । यथा रेखाद्वयं मध्ये परस्परलग्नं क्षुद्रदुन्दुभ्याकारं भवति तथा प्रसार्य दुन्दुभिमध्योभयभागयोः वृत्तद्वयं विधाय बहिष्ठवृत्तस्पृष्टदुन्दुभ्यग्ररेखाद्वयादारभ्य अर्गलसमाग्राण्यष्टदलानि विरच्य वृत्तद्वयात् बहिरम्बुजपुटितं घटं च रचयेत् । इति यन्त्रशरीरनिर्माणप्रकारः ॥ २७ ॥

अष्टाशात्तार्गलाविर्हलयवरयुताच्पूर्वपाश्चात्यषट्कं
कोष्ठोद्यत्स्वाङ्गसाष्टाक्षरयुगयुगलाष्टाक्षराख्यं बहिश्च ।
मायोपेतात्मयुग्मस्वरमिलितलसत्केसरं साष्टपत्रं
पद्मं तन्मध्यपङ्क्तित्रितयपरिलसत्पाशशक्त्यङ्कुशार्णम् ॥ २८

पाशाङ्कुशावृतमनुप्रतिलोमकैश्च
वर्णैः सरोजपुटितेन घटेन चापि ।
आवीतमिष्टफलभद्रघटं तदेतद्-
यन्त्रोत्तमं त्विति वटार्गलनामधेयम् ॥ २९

प्राक्प्रत्यगर्गले हलमथ पुनराग्नेयमारुते च हयम् ।
दक्षोत्तरे हवार्णं नैर्ऋतशैवे हरं द्विपङ्क्तिशो विलिखेत् ॥ ३०
विलिखेच्च कर्णिकायां पाशाङ्कुशसाध्ययुतां शक्तिम् ।
अभ्यन्तराष्टकोष्ठेष्वङ्गान्यवशेषितेषु चाऽष्टार्णौ ॥ ३१
कोष्ठेषु षोड़शस्वथ षोड़शवर्णं मनुं तथा मन्त्री ।
पद्मस्य केसरेषु च युगस्वरात्मान्वितां तथा मायाम् ॥ ३२
एकैकेषु दलेषु त्रिशस्त्रिशः कर्णिकागतान्मन्त्रान् ।
पाशाङ्कुशबीजाभ्यां प्रवेष्टयेद्बाह्यतश्च नलिनस्य ॥ ३३

तत्राक्षरलेखनक्रममाह—अष्टाशेति । अर्गलशब्देन बृहत्कोष्ठाष्टकमुच्यते । तेष्वाविर्भवतां हलहयहवहरैः युतानामचां पूर्वषट्कं ह्लं ह्लां ह्लिं ह्लीं ह्लुं ह्लूं इत्यादि । पाश्चात्यषट्कं ह्लें ह्लैं ह्लों ह्लौं ह्लं ह्लः इत्यादि । कोष्ठोद्यदिति । चतुरस्रसम्बन्धाष्टकोष्ठेषु अङ्गानि तदनन्तरकोष्ठेषु पाशाद्यष्टाक्षरम् । तदनन्तर-कोष्ठेषु कामिन्याद्यष्टाक्षरम् । तदनन्तरकोष्ठद्वन्द्वेषु दुन्दुभ्याकारेषु युगलाष्टाक्षरं षोड़शाष्टाक्षरमित्यर्थः । बहिश्चेति । कर्णिकाबहिरित्यर्थः । मायोपेतात्मयुग्म-स्वरमिलितलसत्केसरमिति । माया ई । आत्मा हंसः । मायोपेतात्मना युग्मस्वरेण चेत्यर्थः । तत्र युग्मस्वरा दलमूलग्रन्थिषु लेखनीयाः । ग्रन्थ्योर्मध्ये हकारसकारौ तयोर्मध्ये मायेति लेखनप्रकारः । पद्मबाह्ये पाशाङ्कुशावृतिः । इष्टं फलं भद्रं घटयतीति, इष्टफलभद्रघटम् ॥ २८ ॥ २९ ॥

प्राक् प्रत्यगिति व्याख्यानम् ॥ ३० ॥ ३१ ॥

तथा मन्त्रीति यन्त्रजीवादिसूचनम् ॥ ३२ ॥ ३३ ॥ ३४ ॥

अनुलोमविलोमगतैः प्रवेष्टयेदक्षरैश्च तद्वाह्ये ।
तदनु घटेन सरोजस्थितेन तद्वक्त्रकोऽम्बुजश्च लिखेत् ॥ ३४
बिन्दूत्तिका प्रतिष्ठा सन्दिष्टा पाशबीजमिति मुनिभिः ।
निजभूर्दहनाप्यायिनीशशधरखण्डान्वितोऽङ्कुशो भवति ॥ ३५
पाशश्रीशक्तिस्मरमन्मथशक्तीन्दिराङ्कुशाश्चेति ।
एकं कामिनि रञ्जिनि ठद्वयमपरं त्विहाष्टवर्णं स्यात् ॥ ३६
अथ गौरि रुद्रदयिते योगेश्वरि सकवचास्त्रठद्वितयैः ।
बीजादिकमिदमुक्तं शाक्तेयं षोड़शाक्षरं मन्त्रम् ॥ ३७
इति कृतदलसुभूषितमतिरुचिरं लोकनयनचित्तहरम् ।
कृत्वोज्ज्वलमथ मण्डलमपि पीठाद्यं पुरेव परिपूज्य ॥ ३८
पूर्वप्रोक्तैः क्वाथैरेभिनापूर्य पूजयेत् कलशम् ।
हृल्लेखाद्यङ्गाद्यो मातृसुरेशादिकी सकुलिशाद्यी ॥ ३९
एवं संपूज्य देवीं कलशमनु शुभैर्गन्धपुष्पादिकैस्तां
दध्याज्यक्षौद्रसिक्तैस्त्रिशतमथ पृथग् दुग्धवीरुत्समिद्भिः ।
हुत्वा दत्त्वा सुवर्णांशुकपशुधरणीर्दक्षिणार्थं द्विजेभ्यः
संपूज्याऽऽचार्यवर्यं वसुभिरमलधीः संयतात्माऽभिषिञ्चेत् ॥ ४०

इति कृतकलशोऽयं सिच्यते येन पुंसा
स भवति कविरेनं नित्यमालिङ्गति श्रीः ।
धनदिनरजनीशैस्तुल्यतेजा महिम्ना
निरुपमचरितोऽसौ देहिनां स्यात् पुरोगः ॥ ४१

निजभूः ककारः ॥ ३५ ॥ ३६ ॥

बीजादिकमिति शक्तिबीजादिकमित्यर्थः ॥ ३७ ॥ ३८ ॥ ३९ ॥ ४० ॥

इति कृतकलशोऽयमिति । इत्थं कृतकलशोऽयमाचार्यो येन साधकेन सिच्यते सेच्यते इत्यर्थः । अन्तर्भाविण्यर्थत्वात् । अथवा इति इत्थं कृतः आवाहितः कलशो यस्मिन् घटे स तथोक्तः । कलाः शेरते यस्मिन् परे संविद्रूपे तेजसि स कलशः । इत्थं कृतकलशोऽयं घटः सिच्यते स्वात्मनि येन पुंसा स भवति कविरित्यादिक्रमेण योज्यम् । शिष्यस्यैव ह्यभिषेककर्तृत्वम् । आचार्यस्तु तेन प्रयुक्तः करोति ॥ ४१ ॥

जपेच्चतुर्विंशतिलक्षमेवं सुयन्त्रितो मन्त्रवरं यथावत् ।
हविष्यभोजी परिपूर्णसंख्ये जपे पुनर्होमविधिर्विधेयः ॥ ४२

पयोद्रुमाणाञ्च समित्सहस्रषट्कं दधिक्षौद्रघृतावसिक्तम् ।
तिलैश्च तावज्जुहुयात्पयोक्तैर्द्विजोत्तमानभ्यवहारयेच्च ॥ ४३

गुरुमपि परिपूज्य काञ्चनाद्यै-
र्जपतु च मन्त्रमथो सहस्रमात्रम् ।
भजतु च दिनशोऽमुमर्चनाया
विधिविहितं विधिमादरेण भूयः ॥ ४४

संक्षेपतो निगदितो विधिरर्चनायाः
शक्तेरयं सकलसंसृतिमोचनाय ।
कान्त्यै श्रियै च यशसे जनरञ्जनाय
सिद्ध्यै प्रसिद्धमहसोऽस्य परस्य धाम्नः ॥ ४५

गजमृगमदकाश्मीरैर्मन्त्रितमः सुरभिरोचनोपेतैः ।
विलिखेदलक्तकरसालुलितैर्यन्त्राणि सकलकार्यार्थी ॥ ४६

राज्या पटुसंयुतया सपाशशक्त्यङ्कुशेन मन्त्रेण ।
साद्रक्तयाऽभिजुह्वन् निश्युर्वशीमथो वशी वशयेत् ॥ ४७

एभिर्विधानैर्भुवनेश्वरीं तां समर्च्य सिद्ध्यै तु जपंश्च मन्त्री ।
स्तुत्याऽनया स्तौतु सदा समग्रप्रीत्यै समस्तार्त्तिविभञ्जिकायाः ॥ ४८

सुयन्त्रितो नियतः । मन्त्रवरं यथावदिति । प्रणवादित्वम् अतिद्रुतत्वादि-वर्जनं चोक्तम् ॥ ४२॥४३ ॥

जपतु च मन्त्रमथो सहस्रमात्रमिति नित्यजप उक्तः । विधिविहितं शास्त्र-विहितम् ॥ ४४ ॥ ४५ ॥

यन्त्रलेखनद्रव्याण्याचष्टे—गजमृगेति । मृगमदः कस्तूरिका । काश्मीरं कुङ्-कुमम् । मन्त्रितम इति द्रव्याणि संयोज्य मूलेन जपपूजादिकमुक्तम् ॥ ४६॥४७ ॥

इति समीरितविधानानन्तरं सकलदुःखनाशिनीं परसंविद्रूपां शक्तिमचलया भक्त्या समर्च्य मन्त्री स्तुतिमपि पठेदित्याह—एभिर्विधानैरिति । मन्त्रीति प्रतिश्लोकं बीजयोगः सूचितः ॥ ४८—७० ॥

इति श्रीपद्मपादाचार्यकृते प्रपञ्चसारविवरणे
एकादशः पटलः ।

प्रसीद प्रपञ्चस्वरूपे प्रधाने प्रकृत्यात्मिके प्राणिनां प्राणसंज्ञे ।
प्रणोतुं प्रभो प्रारभे प्राञ्जलिस्त्वां प्रकृत्याऽप्रतर्क्यं प्रकामप्रवृत्ते ॥ ४९

स्तुतिर्वाक्यबद्धा पदात्मैव वाक्यं
पदं त्वक्षरात्माऽक्षरं त्वं महेशि ।
ध्रुवं त्वां त्वमेवाऽक्षरैस्त्वन्मयैस्तो-
ष्यसि त्वन्मयी वाक्प्रवृत्तिर्यतः स्यात् ॥ ५०

अजाधोक्षजत्र्यक्षणाख्याऽपि रूपं
परं नाभिजानन्ति मायामयं ते ।
स्तुवन्तीशि तां त्वाममी स्थूलरूपां
तदेतावदम्बेह युक्तं ममापि ॥ ५१

नमस्ते समस्तेशि बिन्दुस्वरूपे
नमस्ते रव[पर]त्वेन तत्त्वाभिधाने ।
नमस्ते महत्त्वं प्रपन्ने प्रधाने
नमस्ते त्वहङ्कारतत्त्वस्वरूपे ॥ ५२

नमः शब्दरूपे नमो व्योमरूपे
नमः स्पर्शरूपे नमो वायुरूपे ।
नमो रूपतेजोरसाम्भःस्वरूपे
नमस्तेऽस्तु गन्धात्मिके भूस्वरूपे ॥ ५३

नमः श्रोत्रचर्माक्षिजिह्वाख्यनासा-
स्यवाक्पाणिपत्पायुसोपस्थरूपे ।
मनोबुद्ध्यहङ्कारचित्तस्वरूपे
विरूपे नमस्ते विभो विश्वरूपे ॥ ५४

रवित्वेन भूत्वाऽन्तरात्मा दधासि
प्रजाश्चन्द्रमस्त्वेन पुष्णासि भूयः ।
दहस्यग्निमूर्तिं वहन्त्याहुतिं वा
महादेवि तेजस्त्वयं त्वत्त एव ॥ ५५

चतुर्वक्त्रयुक्ता लसद्धंसवाहा
रजःसंश्रिता ब्रह्मसंज्ञां दधाना ।
जगत्सृष्टिकार्यां जगन्मातृभूते
परं त्वत्पदं ध्यायसीशि त्वमेव ॥ ५६

विराजत्किरीटा लसच्चक्रशङ्खा
वहन्ती च नारायणाख्यां जगत्सु ।
गुणं सत्त्वमास्थाय विश्वस्थितिं यः
करोतीह सोऽंशोऽपि देवि त्वमेव ॥ ५७

जटाबद्धचन्द्राहिगङ्गा त्रिनेत्रा
जगत्संहरन्ती च कल्पावसाने ।
तमःसंश्रिता रुद्रसंज्ञां दधाना
वहन्ती परश्वक्षमाले विभासि ॥ ५८

सचिन्ताक्षमाला सुधाकुम्भलेखाधरा वीक्षणार्धेन्दुराजत्कपर्दा ।
सुशुक्लांशुकाकल्पदेहा सरस्वत्यपि त्वन्मयैवेशि वाचामधीशा ॥ ५९

लसच्छङ्खचक्रा चलत्खड्गभीमा
नदत्सिंहवाहा ज्वलत्तुङ्गमौलिः ।
द्रवद्दैत्यवर्गा स्तुवत्सिद्धसङ्घा
त्वमेवेशि दुर्गाऽपि सर्गादिहीने ॥ ६०

पुरारातिदेहार्धभागा भवानी
गिरीन्द्रात्मजात्वेन येषा विभाति ।
महायोगिवन्द्या महेशा सुनाथा
महेश्यम्बिका तत्त्वतस्त्वन्मयैव ॥ ६१

लसत्कौस्तुभोद्भासिते व्योमनीले
वसन्तीश्च वक्षःस्थले कैटभारेः ।
जगद्वल्लभां सर्वलोकैकनाथां श्रियं
तां महादेव्यहं त्वामवैमि ॥ ६२

अजाद्रीड्गुहाब्जाच्चपोत्वीन्द्रकाणां
महाभैरवस्यापि चिह्नं वहन्त्यः ।
विभो मातरः सप्त तद्रूपरूपाः
स्फुरन्त्यस्त्वदंशा महादेवि तास्च ॥ ६३

समुद्यद्दिवाकृत्सहस्राभभासा सदा सन्तताशेषविश्वावकाशे ।
लसन्मौलिबद्धेन्दुलेखे सपाशाङ्कुशाभीत्यभीष्टात्तहस्ते नमस्ते ॥ ६४

प्रभा कीर्तिकान्ती दिवारात्रिसन्ध्याः
क्रियाशा तमिस्रा क्षुधाबुद्धिमेधाः ।
धृतिर्वाङ्मतिः सन्नतिः श्रीश्च भ[श]क्ति-
स्त्वमेवेशि येऽन्ये च शक्तिप्रभेदाः ॥ ६५

हरे बिन्दुनादैः सशक्त्याख्यशान्तैर्नमः तेऽस्तु भेदप्रभिन्नैरभिन्ने ।
सदा सप्तपाताललोकाचलाब्धिग्रहद्वीपधातुस्वरादिस्वरूपे ॥ ६६

नमस्ते समस्ते समस्तस्वरूपे समस्तेषु वस्तुष्वनुस्यूतशक्ते ।
श्रितस्थूलसूक्ष्मस्वरूपे महेशि स्मृते बोधरूपेऽप्यबोधस्वरूपे ॥ ६७

मनोवृत्तिरस्तु स्मृतिस्ते समस्ता
तथा वाक्प्रवृत्तिः स्तुतिः स्यान्महेशि ।
शरीरप्रवृत्तिः प्रणामक्रिया स्यात्
प्रसीद क्षमस्व प्रभो सन्ततं मे ॥ ६८

हृल्लेखाजपविधिमर्चनाविशेषा-
नेतांस्तां स्तुतिमपि नित्यमादरेण ।
योऽभ्यस्येत् स खलु परां श्रियञ्च गत्वा
शुद्धं तद् व्रजति पदं परस्य धाम्नः ॥ ६९

इति हृल्लेखाविहितो विधिरुक्तः संग्रहेण सकलोऽयम् ।
योऽस्मिन्नियतमना मन्त्री योगी स्यात् स एव भोगी च ॥ ७०

इति श्रीप्रपञ्चसारे एकादशः पटलः ।

द्वादशः पटलः ।

अथ श्रियो मन्त्रविधिः समासतो जगद्धिताय प्रतिवक्ष्यतेऽधुना ।
सहाऽङ्गभेदैः सजपार्चनाहुतक्रमैः समभ्युद्धरणाय दुर्गतेः ॥ १

वियत्तुरीयस्तु विलोमतोऽनलप्रदीपितो वामविलोचनान्वितः ।
सचन्द्रखण्डः कथितो रमामनुर्मनोरथावाप्तिमहासुरद्रुमः ॥ २

ऋषिर्भृगुश्छन्दसि चोदिता निवृत्
समीरिता श्रीरपि देवता पुनः ।
दृगन्तिकर्णेनमनुस्वरानला-
न्वितेन चाऽस्या विहितं षडङ्गकम् ॥ ३

भूयाद् भूयो द्विपद्माभयवरदकरा तप्तकार्तस्वराभा
शुभ्राभ्राभेभयुग्मद्वयकरधृतकुम्भाद्भिरासिच्यमाना ।
रत्नौघाबद्धमौलिर्विमलतरदुकूलार्तवालेपनाढ्या
पद्माक्षी पद्मनाभोरसि कृतवसतिः पद्मगा श्रीः श्रियै वः ॥ ४

संदीक्षितोऽथ गुरुणा मनुवर्यमेनं
सम्यग् जपेन्निशितधीर्दिननाथलक्षम् ।

इच्छाशक्तिप्रधानभुवनेश्वर्यनन्तरं पुनरपि क्रियाशक्तिप्रधानामेकबीजात्मिकां पूर्वविधानेषु प्रसक्तां च श्रियं वक्तुमारभते—अथेति । अथाऽनन्तरम् । कस्य । समासतोऽनन्तरम् । समासशब्देन सर्वत्रानुगम्यमानाः प्रणवशक्तिवाक्कामाः सूचिताः । समासतः संक्षेपत इत्यनेन सामान्यपटलोक्तन्यासादिविस्तारः शक्तिवदस्यापि सूचितः । सहाङ्गभेदैरिति । शक्तिकामयोगे तद्दीर्घयोगं वाक्प्रणवयोगे तद्योगं चाङ्गानामाह । विनियोगमाह—समभ्युद्धरणायेति । अधर्मनिःस्वतादयो दुर्गतयः ॥ १ ॥

केवलस्यापि सर्वपुरुषार्थेषु विनियोगमाह—मनोरथावाप्तिरिति ॥ २ ॥

श्रीरपि देवतेति । प्रणवादियोगे तद्देवतानामुपसर्जनत्वं श्रियः सूचितम् । परमात्मस्वरूपिणी श्रीर्देवतेत्यादिप्रकारेण । शं बीजम् । ईं शक्तिः ॥ ३ ॥ ४ ॥

सम्यग् जपेदिति । कामानुसारेण उक्तबीजपुटिततया जप उक्तः ।

अभ्यर्चयन्नहरहः श्रियमादरेण
मन्त्री सुशुद्धचरितो रहितो वधूभिः ॥ ५
जपावसाने दिनकृत्सहस्रसंख्यैः सरोजैर्मधुरत्रयाक्तैः ।
हुनेत्तिलैर्वा विधिनाऽथ बैल्वैः समिद्वरैर्मन्त्रिवरस्त्रिभिर्वा ॥ ६
रुचिराष्टपत्रमथ वारिरुहं गुणवृत्तराशिचतुरस्रयुतम् ।
प्रविधाय पीठमपि तत्र यजेन्नवशक्तिभिः सह रमाञ्च ततः ॥ ७
विभूतिरुन्नतिः कान्तिः सृष्टिः कीर्त्तिश्च सन्नतिः ।
व्युष्टिरुत्कृष्टिर्ऋद्धिश्च रमाया नव शक्तयः ॥ ८
आवाह्य सम्यक् कलशे यथावत् समर्चनीया विधिना रमा सा ।
जप्त्वा यथाशक्ति पुनर्गुरुस्तु तं सेचयेत् संयतमात्मशिष्यम् ॥ ९
अङ्गैः प्रथमावृतिरपि मूर्तीभचतुष्कनिधियुगैरपरा ।
शक्त्यष्टकेन चाऽन्या चरमा ककुबीश्वरैः समभ्यर्च्या ॥ १०
वासुदेवः सङ्कर्षणः प्रद्युम्नश्चाऽनिरुद्धकः ।
दमकः सलिलश्चैव गुग्गुलुश्च कुरुण्टकः ॥ ११
वलाकी विमला चैव कमला वनमालिका ।
विभीषिका मालिका च शङ्करी वसुमालिका ॥ १२

निश्चितधीरिति। तत्तद्बीजदेवतानुसारेण ध्यानम्। श्रियमादरेण मन्त्रीति। तच्छ्लेषतया अष्टाक्षर जप उक्तः ॥ ५ ॥

तिलैर्वा विधिनेति। अग्निसंस्कारो विधिः। मन्त्रिवरस्त्रिभिरिति। कमलवासिनीमहालक्ष्मीश्रीसूक्तैः सकृत् सकृत् हुत्वा पुनः मूलेन होतव्यमित्युक्तम् ॥ ६ ॥

रुचिराष्टपत्रमिति। कर्णिकामध्ये श्रीबीजयोगो रुचिरत्वम्। तत्र यजेदिति। पीठमन्त्रः सूचितः। रमाञ्चेति। मूर्तिपूजा सूचिता। श्रीं श्रीदेव्यासनाय नमः। श्रीं श्रीदेवीमूर्तये नमः। इति पीठमूर्तिमन्त्रौ ॥ ७ ॥

रमाया नव शक्तय इति। तासु श्रीबीजयोग उक्तः ॥ ८ ॥

आवाह्य सम्यगिति। मूर्तिं हृदयकमले तदभेदेनेत्यर्थः। यथावदिति। आवाहनादिश्लोकेषु स्त्रीलिङ्गयोगो मुद्रायोगश्चोक्तः। विधिनेति। विश्रमपूजादिकमुक्तम् ॥ ९ ॥ १० ॥ ११ ॥ १२ ॥

अनयैव च पूर्वसेवया परितुष्टा कमला प्रसीदति ।
धनधान्यसमृद्धिसंकुलामचिरादेव च मन्त्रिणे श्रियम् ॥ १३
अम्भस्युरोजद्वयसेऽभितिष्ठंस्त्रिलक्षमेनं प्रजपेच्च मन्त्री ।
श्रियं विचिन्त्याऽर्कगतां यथावद् दरिद्रताया भवति प्रमुक्तः ॥ १४
वसतावुपविश्य कैटभारेः कमलावृक्षतले तथा त्रिलक्षम् ।
जपतोऽपि भवेच्च काङ्क्षितार्थादधिको वत्सरतो वसुप्रपञ्चः ॥ १५
जुहुयादशोकदहने सघृतैरपि तण्डुलैः सकलवश्यतमम् ।
खदिरानले त्रिमधुरैरपि तैर्धनदश्च राजकुलवश्यमपि ॥ १६

समधुरनलिनानां लक्षहोमादलक्ष्मी-
परिगतमपि जन्तुं प्राप्नुयाच्छ्रीः समग्रा ।
धनविभवसमृद्ध्या नित्यमाह्लादयन्ती
त्यजति न करुणार्द्रा तस्य सा सन्ततिश्च ॥ १७

बिल्वं श्रीसूक्तजापी निजभुवि मुखजो वर्द्धयित्वाऽस्य पूर्वं
पत्रैस्त्रिस्वादुयुक्तैः कुसुमफलसमिद्भिस्ततः स्कन्धभेदैः ।
तन्मूलैर्मण्डलात् प्राक् सुनियतचरितोऽसौ हुलान्निर्मलात्मा
रूपं पश्येद्रमायाः कथमपि च पुनस्तत्कुले स्यादलक्ष्मीः ॥ १८
हृदयकमलवर्णतः परस्तादमृतमनन्तयुतं ततश्च सिन्यै ।
हुतवहदयितेत्यसौ रमायाः प्रवरधनार्थिभिरर्थितो हि मन्त्रः ॥ १९

मन्त्रभेदेष्वपि समानेयं पूजेत्याह—अनयैवेति । मन्त्रिणे श्रियमिति । तत्तन्मन्त्रानुरूपां श्रियमित्यर्थः ॥ १३ ॥

प्रजपेच्च मन्त्रीति । श्रीं रत्नगर्भायै नमः इति मन्त्रस्य शतांशजप उक्तः । चशब्देन तर्पणादिकमुक्तम् । अर्कगतां यथावदिति । अभयवरदकराभ्यां रत्नकुम्भधरामित्यर्थः ॥ १४ ॥ १५ ॥

जुहुयादशोकेति । सकामेन प्रयोगः । खदिरानलेऽपि तेनैव केवलेन वा । ॥ १६ ॥ १७ ॥

मुखज इति । ब्राह्मणस्यैव श्रीसूक्ते विधानेऽधिकारः सूचितः ॥ १८ ॥

प्रवरधनार्थिभिरिति । सर्वपुरुषार्थेषु विनियोग उक्तः । श्रों श्रीं बीजम् । स्वाहा शक्तिः ॥ १९ ॥ २० ॥

दक्षोऽस्य स्यादृषिश्छन्दसि सुमतिभिरुक्ता विराड् देवता च
श्रीर्देवीपद्मिनीभ्यां हृदयकशिरसी विष्णुपत्न्या शिखा च ।
मेदोरेफाद्वर्णैरपि च कमलरूपाच्च रैवर्म चाऽस्त्रं
ताराद्याभिर्नमोऽन्ताभिरपि निगदितं जातियुक्ताभिरङ्गम् ॥ २०
पद्मस्था पद्मनेत्रा कमलयुगवराभीतियुग्दो:सरोजा
देहोत्थाभिः प्रभाभिस्त्रिभुवनविवरं भास्वरा भासयन्ती ।
मुक्ताहाराभिरामोन्नतकुचकलशा रत्नमञ्जीरकाञ्ची-
ग्रैवेयोर्म्यङ्गदाढ्या धृतमणिमुकुटा श्रेयसे श्रीर्भवेद्व: ॥ २१

ध्यात्वैवं श्रियमपि पूर्वक्लृप्तपीठे
पद्मादौ प्रथममथाऽर्चयेत्तदङ्गैः ।
अष्टाभिर्दलमनु शक्तिभिस्तदन्ते
लोकेशैरिति विधिनाऽर्चयेत् समृद्ध्यै ॥ २२
दीक्षातो जपतु रमारमेशभक्तो
लक्षाणां दशकममुं मनुं नियत्या ।
स श्रीमान् बहुधनधान्यसङ्कुलः स-
न्मेधावी भवति च वत्सरेण मन्त्री ॥ २३

इति मन्त्रजपाद्दतधीर्मधुरक्तिर्यैरयुतं जुहुयात् कमलैः ।
परिशुद्धमना न चिरात् स पुनर्लभते निजवाञ्छितमर्थचयम् ॥ २४
समुद्रगायामवतीर्य नद्यां स्वकण्ठमात्रे पयसि स्थितः सन् ।
त्रिलक्षजाप्याढ्यतमोऽब्दमात्रान्मन्त्री भवेन्नात्र विचारणीयम् ॥ २५

नन्द्यावर्तैर्जुहुत भगभेऽभ्यर्च्य लक्ष्मीं सहस्रं
तावद्बैल्वैस्त्रिमधुरयुतैर्वा फलैः पौर्णमास्याम् ।
पञ्चम्यां वा सितसरसिजैः शुक्रवारेऽच्छपुष्पै-
रन्यैर्मासं प्रतिहुतविधिर्वत्सरात् स्याद्धनाढ्यः ॥ २६

श्रियमपीति । बीजविशेषयोगे ध्यानविशेषः सूचितः । अथवा श्रीपति-
मपीत्यर्थः । अत्रापि अष्टाक्षरस्य जप्तव्यत्वात् ॥ २१ ॥ २२ ॥

वत्सरेण मन्त्रीति । दशांशेन अष्टाक्षरजप उक्तः ॥ २३ ॥ २४ ॥

तारारमामायाः श्रीः कमले कमलालये प्रसीदयुगम् ।
बीजानि तानि पुनरपि समहालक्ष्म्यै हृदिन्दिरामन्त्रः ॥ २७

त्रिभिस्तु वर्णैर्हृदयं शिरोऽपि स्यात् पञ्चभिश्चाऽथ शिखा त्रिवर्णैः ।
त्रिभिस्तथा वर्म चतुर्भिरस्त्रं पृथक् त्रिबीजापुटितैस्तदङ्गम् ॥ २८

हस्तोद्यद्वसुपात्रपङ्कजयुगादर्शा स्फुरन्नूपुरा
ग्रैवेयाङ्गदहारकङ्कणमहामौलिर्ज्वलत्कुण्डला ।
पद्मस्था परिचारिकापरिवृता शुक्लाङ्गरागांशुका
देवी दिव्यगणार्चिता भवदघप्रध्वंसिनी स्याद्रमा ॥ २९

लक्षं जपेन्मनुमिमं मधुरत्रयाक्त-
बल्वैः फलैः प्रतिहुनेदयुतं तदन्ते ।
आराधयेदनुदिनं प्रतिवक्ष्यमाण-
मार्गेण दुर्गतिभयाद्रहितो भवेत् सः ॥ ३०

श्रीधरश्च हृषीकेशो वैकुण्ठो विश्वरूपकः ।
वासुदेवादयश्चाऽङ्गावरणात् समनन्तरम् ॥ ३१
भारतीपार्वतीचान्द्रीशचीभिरपि संयुता ।
दमकादिभिस्तृतीयाऽनुरागाद्यैश्चतुर्थ्यपि ॥ ३२
अनुरागो विसंवादो विजयो वल्लभो मदः ।
हर्षो बलश्च तेजश्चेत्यष्टौ बाणा महाश्रियः ॥ ३३
अनन्तब्रह्मपर्यन्तैः पञ्चमीन्द्रादिभिर्मता ।
चक्रपद्मान्तिकैः षष्ठी वज्राद्यैरावृतिः श्रियः ॥ ३४
संपूज्यैवं श्रियमनुदिनं यो जपेन्मन्त्रमेनं
प्रोक्तां संख्यां सहुतविधिमप्युक्षितां प्राप्य लक्ष्मीम् ।
द्विजादर्वागवनिपशुपुत्रादिभोगैः समृद्धो
वर्षाद्देहापदि च पदमप्येति नित्यं स विष्णोः ॥ ३५

मन्त्री भवेदिति। रत्नगर्भामन्त्रजपः सूचितः ॥ २५ ॥ २६ ॥

महालक्ष्मीमन्त्रस्य श्रीं बीजम् क्लीं शक्तिः। पूर्ववद्दृष्यादि पीठमूर्तिश्च ॥२७॥

॥ २८ ॥ २९ ॥ ३० ॥ ३१ ॥ ३२ ॥ ३३ ॥ ३४ ॥ ३५ ॥

श्रीमन्त्रेष्विति गदितेषु भक्तियुक्तः
श्रीसूक्तान्यपि च जपेद् यजेद्धुनेच्च ।
सूक्तेषु प्रथमतरे स्वयं मुनिः स्या-
दन्येषां मुनय इमे भवन्ति भूयः ॥ ३६

आनन्दः कर्दमश्चैव चिक्लीतश्चेन्दिरासुतः ।
ऋचामथो तदन्यासामृषयः समुदीरिताः ॥ ३७

आद्ये सूक्तत्रये छन्दोऽनुष्टुप् कांसि वृहत्यपि ।
तदन्त्ययोस्त्रिष्टुबाख्यं परस्तादष्टकी पुनः ॥ ३८

अनुष्टुबन्त्ये प्रस्तारपङ्क्तिश्छन्दांसि वै क्रमात् ।
श्राग्नी स्यातां देवते च न्यासाङ्गविधिरुच्यते ॥ ३९

मूर्धाक्षिकर्णनासामुखगलदोर्हृदयनाभिगुह्येषु ।
पायूरुजानुजङ्घाचरणेषु न्यसतु सूक्तकैः क्रमशः ॥ ४०

सहिरण्मयी च चन्द्रा रजतहिरण्यस्रजे हिरण्याख्या ।
अङ्गानि जातियुञ्जि त्वथ च हिरण्यवर्णाह्वया तथाऽस्त्रं स्यात् ॥ ४१

अरुणकमलसंस्था तद्रजःपुञ्जवर्णा-
करकमलधृतेष्टाभीतियुग्माम्बुजा च ।
मणिमुकुटविचित्रालङ्कृताऽऽकल्पजातै-
र्भवतु भुवनमाता सन्ततं श्रीः श्रिये वः ॥ ४२

आरभ्याच्छां प्रतिपदमथ प्राप्तदीक्षो वियुक्त-
स्त्वङ्गीभिस्तनुविमलवासाः सुधौतद्विजाढ्यः ।
एकादश्यामथ परिसमाप्याऽर्कसाहस्रिकान्तं
जापं मन्त्री प्रयजतु रमां प्राक्तनप्रोक्तपीठे ॥ ४३

प्राकरणिकश्रीमन्त्रशेषत्वेन श्रीसूक्तं विनियुङ्क्ते—श्रीमन्त्रेष्विति। जपहोमादिकं सकृत् सकृत् कार्यम्। यजेदिति। पुष्पाञ्जलिश्च कार्यं इत्यर्थः। स्वप्रधानत्वेनापि जपादिकं सूक्तानां विवक्षुस्तेषामृष्यादिकमाह—सूक्तेष्विति। स्वयं श्रीरित्यर्थः। हिरण्यवर्णामिति ऋग्बीजम्। कांसोऽस्मीति ऋक्शक्तिः। [सूक्तमिदं पञ्चदशर्चात्मकं श्रौतम्] ॥ ३६ ॥ ३७ ॥ ३८ ॥ ३९ ॥ ४० ॥ ४१ ॥ ४२ ॥

मन्त्रीति। प्रत्यृचं श्रीबीजयोग उक्तः ॥ ४३ ॥ ४४ ॥ ४५ ॥

पद्मा सपद्मवर्णा पद्मस्थार्द्रा च तर्पयन्त्यभिधा ।
तृप्ता ज्वलन्त्यभिख्या स्वर्णप्राकारसंज्ञका चेति ॥ ४४
मध्ये दिशाधिपाङ्गावृत्त्योरेतास्ततश्च वज्रादीन् ।
प्रयजेच्चतुरावरणं निगदितमिति सूक्तकल्पितं विधानम् ॥ ४५
अन्नघृताभ्यां जुहुयादनुदिनमष्टोत्तरं शतं मन्त्री ।
आवाहनासनार्घ्यकपाद्याचमनमधुपर्कसेकानि ॥ ४६
वासोभूषणगन्धान् सुमनोयुतधूपदीपभोज्यानि ।
सोद्वासनानि कुर्याद्भक्तियुक्तः पञ्चदशभिरथ मनुभिः ॥ ४७
व्यस्तैरपि च समस्तैः पूजायां संयतात्मकः सिद्धै ।
पद्मैर्बिल्वसमिद्भिः पयोऽन्धसा सर्पिषा क्रमाज्जुहुयात् ॥ ४८
एकैकं त्रिस्त्रिशतं द्वादश्यां भोजयीत विप्रांश्च ।
मन्दारकुन्दकुमुदकनन्द्यावर्ताख्यमालतीजात्यः ।
कह्लारपद्मरक्तोत्पलकेतकचम्पकादयो ग्राह्याः ॥ ४९
परिषिञ्चेत्त्रिशो नित्यं सूक्तैस्तैः स्नानकर्मणि ।
आदित्याभिमुखो जप्याद् यावत्तावच्च तर्पयेत् ॥ ५०
अर्चयेद्विधिनाऽनेन दिनशो जुहुयात्त्रिशः ।
एवं करोति षण्मासं योऽसौ स्यादिन्दिरापतिः ॥ ५१
उद्बुद्धमात्रे नलिने नवनीतं विनिक्षिपेत् ।
सकर्णिके सकिञ्जल्कोदरे पत्रान्तरालये ॥ ५२
पुनस्तत् पद्ममुद्धृत्य सुसमिद्धे विभावसौ ।
जुहुयादन्यया ऽर्चा शतमष्टोत्तरं जपन् ।

अष्टोत्तरशतं मन्त्रीति । सूक्तानां सप्तवारजपान्तेऽन्यस्य सूक्तस्य त्रिरावृत्तिर्विवक्षिता । मन्त्रीति । प्राकरणिकमन्त्रैः सकृत् सकृत् प्रथमतो होमस्य सूचितः ॥ ४६ ॥ ४७ ॥

व्यस्तैः समस्तैरित्यत्र व्यस्तैश्चतुर्दशभिः निवेद्यान्तं दत्त्वा श्रीबीजेन चतुर्दशेनैव वा गण्डूषोपचारादिकं समर्प्य समस्तेन सूक्तेन प्रदक्षिणस्तुतिनमस्कारान् विधाय शेषं श्रीबीजेन कृत्वा अन्त्ये चोद्वासयेदित्यर्थः । पद्महोमेऽष्टोत्तरशतजपः ।

चत्वारिंशच्छुक्रवारैर्महाश्रीस्तस्य जायते ॥ ५३

कांसोऽस्मीत्यनया सम्यगेकादश घृताहुतीः ।
षण्मासं जुह्वतो नित्यं भूयात् प्रायो महेन्दिरा ॥ ५४

सूक्तैरेतैर्जपतु जुहुयादर्चयीताऽवगाहेत्
सिञ्चेद्वक्त्रे दिनमनु तथा संयतस्तर्पयीत ।
संशुद्धात्मा विविधधनधान्याकुलाभ्यन्तरोऽसौ
मन्त्री सर्वैर्भुवि बहुमतः श्रीमतां स्यात् पुरोगः ॥ ५५

श्रीर्लक्ष्मीर्वरदा विष्णुपत्नी च सवसुप्रदा ।
हिरण्यरूपा सस्वर्णमालिनी रजतस्रजा ॥ ५६

समुवर्णगृहा[प्रभा] स्वर्णप्राकारा पद्मवासिनी ।
पद्महस्ता पद्मपूर्वप्रिया मुक्तापदादिका ॥ ५७

अलङ्कारा तथा सूर्या चन्द्रा बिल्वप्रियेश्वरी ।
भुक्तिः प्रपूर्वा मुक्तिश्च विभूत्यृद्धिसमृद्धयः ॥ ५८

तुष्टिः पुष्टिश्च धनदा तथाऽन्या तु धनेश्वरी ।
शु[श्र]द्धा सम्भोगिनी भोगदात्री धात्रविधात्रके ॥ ५९

द्वात्रिंशदेताः श्रीदेव्या ये मन्त्राः समुदीरिताः ।
तारादिका नमोऽन्ताश्च तैरर्चासु बलिं हरेत् ।
तर्पयेच्च महादेवीं दिनादौ मन्त्रवित्तमः ॥ ६०

नाभ्यक्तोऽद्यान्न नग्नः सलिलमवतरेन्न स्वपेद्वाऽशुचिः स-
न्नाऽभ्यञ्ज्यान्नैव चाऽद्यात्तिलरुहलवणे केवलेनैव दोषाम् ।
वक्त्रे लिम्पेद्वदेन्नाऽनृतमपि मलिनः स्यान्न बिल्वाम्बुजन्म-
द्रोणान्नो धारयेत् के भुवमपि न वृथैवाऽऽलिखेदिन्दिरार्थी ॥ ६१

पूर्ववत् सर्वाणि वा सूक्तान्यष्टोत्तरशतं जप्यानि ॥ ४८—५३ ॥

सम्यगेकादशेति । प्रणव व्याहृति प्राकरणिक मन्त्राद्यन्तत्वं मन्त्रस्योक्तम् ॥५४॥

मन्त्री सर्वैरिति । ऋचः श्रीबीजपुटितत्वं होमतर्पणादौ स्वाहा तर्पयाम्यन्तत्वं चोक्तम् ॥ ५५॥५६॥५७॥५८॥५९ ॥

दिनादौ मन्त्रवित्तम इति । प्राकरणिकमन्त्राणामेकं साङ्गं जानन्नित्यर्थः ।

सुविमलचरितः स्याच्छुद्धमाल्यानुलेपा-
भरणवसनदेहो मुख्यगन्धोत्तमाङ्गः ।
सुविशदनखदन्तः शुद्धधीर्विष्णुभक्तो
विमलरुचिरशय्यः स्याच्चिरायेन्दिरार्थी ॥ ६२

दुष्टां कष्टान्ववायां कलहकलुषितां मार्गदुष्टामनिष्टा-
मन्यासक्तामसक्तामतिविपुलकृशाङ्गीमतिह्रस्वदीर्घाम् ।
रोगार्तां भोगलोलां प्रतिपुरुषचलां राजकान्तामकान्तां
काकाक्षीमेकचारां गृ[ग्र]हकुसुमयुतां न स्पृशेदिन्दिरार्थी ॥ ६२

शान्तः शश्वत्स्मितमधुरपूर्वाभिभाषी दयार्द्रो
देवाचार्यातिथिदहनपूजारतः पुण्यशीलः ।
नित्यस्नायी नियमनिरतः प्रत्यगाशामुखाशी
मन्त्री वर्णाश्रमदृढरतिः स्याच्चिरायेन्दिरार्थी ॥ ६४

श्रीमन्त्रभक्तः श्रितविष्णुदीक्षः श्रीसूक्तजापी सितधीः सुशीलः ।
स्वदारतुष्टो मितभाषणाशी लोकप्रियः स्याच्चिरमिन्दिरार्थी ॥ ६५

इति श्रीप्रपञ्चसारे द्वादशः पटलः ।

॥ ६०॥६१॥६२॥६३॥६४॥६५॥

इति श्रीपद्मपादाचार्यकृते प्रपञ्चसारविवरणे

द्वादशः पटलः ।

त्रयोदशः पटलः।

अथ रमाभुवनेशिमनोभवैस्त्रिपुटसंज्ञकमन्त्रमुदीरितम्।
सकलवर्गफलाप्तियशस्करं जगति रञ्जनदं कविताकरम्॥ १
बीजैस्त्रिभिर्द्विरुक्तैः कुर्यादङ्गानि साधकः सिद्ध्यै।
पूर्वतरेरितयोर्वा द्वयोरप्येकं तदङ्गयोः प्रभजेत्॥ २
नवकनकभासुरोर्वीविरचितमणिकुट्टिमे सकल्पतरौ।
रत्नवरबद्धसिंहासननिहितसरोरुहे समासीनाम्॥ ३

आबद्धरत्नमुकुटां मणिकुण्डलोद्यत्-
केयूरकोर्मिरसनाद्वयनूपुराढ्याम्।
ध्यायेद्धृताब्जयुगपाशवराङ्कुशेक्षु-
चापां सपुष्पविशिखां नवहेमवर्णाम्॥ ४

चामरमुकुरसमुद्गकताम्बूलकरङ्कवाहिनीभिश्च।
दूतीभिः समभिवृतां पश्यन्तीं साधकं प्रसन्नदृशा॥ ५

लोकेश्वरीमिति विचिन्त्य जपेच्च मन्त्र-
मादित्यलक्षमथ मन्त्रितमो जपान्ते।

क्रियाशक्तिप्रधानानामेव केषाञ्चिन्मन्त्राणां विधिं वक्तुमारभते—अथ रमेति। तत्र प्रथमं भुवनेशीपटले प्रस्तुतायास्त्रिपुटाया विधानमुच्यते। विनियोगमाह—सकलेति। रमादित्वे सकलवर्गफलाप्तिः। शक्त्यादित्वे यशस्करम्। कामादित्वे रञ्जनदम्। वाग्भवयोगे कविताकरमिति द्रष्टव्यम्॥ १॥

अङ्गानि साधक इति। त्रिबीजसंयुतैः सामान्यपटलोक्तन्यासैरात्मानं देवतारूपत्वेन साधयतीति साधकः इति न्यासाः सूचिताः। मन्त्रविशेषाणामङ्गविशेषं सूचयति—पूर्वतरेति। पूर्वतरवक्ष्यमाणकामबीजाङ्गानामेकं वा कुर्यादित्यर्थः। यद्बीजादिको मन्त्रस्तस्याऽङ्गानि कुर्यादिति भावः। संमोहन ऋषिः। गायत्री छन्दः। त्रिपुटादेवी देवता। श्रीं बीजं क्लीं वा। ह्रीं शक्तिः। मूलेन सह पीठमूर्तिपूजा। घृणिनी सूर्याऽऽदित्या प्रभावती इत्येता दूत्यः॥ २॥

मन्त्रितमो जपान्त इति। श्रीवृक्षसमिदादिहोमेषु मन्त्रस्य श्रीबीजाद्यादित्व-

श्रीराजवृक्षसमिधां सजवार्त्तवानां
तावत् सहस्रसमितं मधुरैर्जुहोतु ॥ ६
अङ्गैर्लक्ष्मीहरिगिरिसुताशर्वरत्यङ्गजातैः
षट्कोणस्थैर्निधियुगयुतैस्तद्वहिर्मातृभिश्च ।
योषिद्रूपैर्बहिरपि यजेल्लोकपालैस्तदेतत्
प्रोक्तं देव्या अपि सुरगणैः पूजनीयं विधानम् ॥ ७
लक्ष्मीगौरीमनसिशयबीजानि कृत्वा कलायां
तां वा बिन्दौ तमपि गगने तच्च सिन्दूरवर्णम् ।
स्मृत्वा बुद्ध्वा भुवनमखिलं तन्मयत्वेन मन्त्री
देवान् वश्यानपि वितनुते किं पुनर्मर्त्यजातीन् ॥ ८
य इमं भजते मनुं मनस्वी विधिना वा पुनरर्चयेद्विधानम् ।
स तु सम्यगवाप्य इष्टभोगान् परतस्तत्परमैशमेति धाम ॥ ६

सहृदयभगवत्यै दान्तरण्यैधराणाः
सणिधरशिवधाणारिद्विठान्ता ध्रुवाद्याः ।
गदितमिति धराया मन्त्रमुत्कृष्टधात्री-
सुखसुतधनधान्यप्राप्तिदं कीर्त्तिदञ्च ॥ १०
ऋषिरपि वराह उक्तश्छन्दो निवृदस्य देवता धरणी ।
मनुनाऽमुनैव च पदैः षोढ़ाभिन्नेन निगदितोऽङ्गविधिः ॥ ११

मुक्तम् । [योगेश्वरीमिति वा पाठः] ॥ ३ ॥ ४ ॥ ५ ॥ ६ ॥ ७ ॥

योगमाह—लक्ष्मीगौरीति । कला ईकारः सर्वबीजानुगतः त्रिशक्त्यात्मा । तां वा बिन्दाविति । तां च कलां निविड़तेजोबिन्दौ कृत्वा तं बिन्दुं गगने नादे प्रभारूपे । तच्च गगनं सिन्दूरवर्णं शक्तितत्त्वं स्मृत्वेत्यर्थः । मन्त्रीति । एवं मन्त्रवीर्यात्मतां प्राप्त इत्यर्थः । अथवाऽमुकं वशयेति क्रमोत्क्रममन्त्रमध्ये योजयेदिति मन्त्रीशब्दार्थः ॥ ८ ॥ ६ ॥

क्रियाशक्तिप्रधानायाः श्रियः श्रीबीजप्रधानायाः त्रिपुटायाश्च विधानमभिधाय इच्छाशक्तिप्रधानाया भुवो मन्त्रमाह—सहृदयेति । विनियोगमाह—उत्कृष्टेति । ग्लौं भूबीजयोगे धात्रीदम् । प्रणवयोगे परमसुखदम् । कामयोगे सुतदम् । श्रीबीजयोगे धनधान्यदम् । ह्रीं योगे कीर्तिदमित्यर्थः । षोढ़ाभिन्नेनेति । त्रिचतुस्त्रि-

मुख्याम्भोजे निविष्टारुणचरणतला श्यामलाङ्गी मनोज्ञा
चञ्चच्छाल्यग्रचुम्बच्छुकलसितकरा प्राप्तनीलोत्पला च ।
रत्नाकल्पाभिरामा मणिमयमुकुटा चित्रवस्त्रा प्रसन्ना
दिश्याद्विश्वम्भरा वः सततमभिमतं वल्लभा कैटभारेः ॥ १२

लक्षायता च सदशांशहुतावसाना
प्रोक्ता धराहृदयमन्त्रजपक्रिया स्यात् ।
सर्पिष्मता सुविमलेन पयोऽन्धसाऽस्य
होमे विधिः सकलसिद्धिकरः किलाऽयम् ॥ १३

पीठे विष्णोः पूजयेत् पूर्वमङ्गैर्भूवह्न्यम्बुप्राणसंज्ञैश्च भूतैः ।
शान्त्यन्ताभिः शक्तिभिः साकमाशापालैः पृथ्वीं संयतात्मोपचारैः ॥

पुष्पैः प्रियङ्गोर्मधुरत्रयाक्तैर्नीलोत्पलैर्वाऽपि तथाऽरुणैस्तैः ।
सहस्रमानं प्रतिजुह्वतः स्याद्गोर्गोमती शस्यकुलाकुला च ॥ १५

पिञ्जरां पृथुलशालिमञ्जरीं यो जुहोति मधुरत्रयोक्षिताम् ।
नित्यशः शतमथाऽस्य मण्डलाद्वस्तगा भवति विस्तृता मही ॥ १६

भृगोस्तु वारे निजसाध्यभूमृद्विलोड़िताम्भःपरिपक्वमन्धः ।
पयोघृताक्तं जुहुयात् सहस्रं दुग्धेन वाऽन्नेन दिनावतारे ॥ १७

षण्मासादनुभृगुवारमेष होमः
सम्पन्नान् समुपनयेद्धराप्रदेशान् ।
पुत्रान् वा पशुमहिषिष्टजुष्टपुष्टा-
मिष्टामप्यनुदिनमिन्दिरां समग्राम् ॥ १८

संक्षेपतो हृदयमन्त्रविधिर्धरायाः
प्रोक्तो हिताय जगतां रहितक्षमाणाम् ।

पञ्चद्विद्विवर्णैः षोढाभिन्नैरित्यर्थः । ग्लौं बीजम् । स्वाहा शक्तिः । न्यासास्तु ग्लौंबीजेन सह सामान्यपटलोक्ताः कर्तव्याः ॥ १० ॥ ११ ॥

रत्नाम्भोजं मुख्याम्भोजम् । ग्लौं पृथिवीमूर्तये नमः इति मूर्तिमन्त्रः ॥ १२ ॥
॥ १३ ॥ १४ ॥ १५ ॥ १६ ॥

भृगोस्तु वार इति । प्रयोगो वराहपटलोक्तक्रमेण द्रष्टव्यः । तद्बीजयुतश्च ।
॥ १७ ॥ १८ ॥ १९ ॥

एनं भजन्निति धराकमलासमृद्धः
स्यादत्र सिद्धिमपरत्र परां प्रयाति ॥ १९

अथ पुरुषार्थचतुष्टयसिद्धिकरी मन्त्रजापनिरतानाम् ।
त्वरिताख्येयं विद्या निगद्यते जपहुतार्चनविधिभिः ॥ २०
भक्तियुतानां त्वरया सिद्धिकरी चेति मन्त्रिणां सततम् ।
देव्यास्त्वरिताख्या स्यात्त्वरितं क्ष्वेलग्रहादिहरणतया ॥ २१
वर्मद्ध्यें च तदन्त्यः शिवयुक् चरमाङ्गनाद्युसार्घिलवम् ।
अन्त्यः सयोनिरस्त्रान्तिकः सतारो मनुर्दशार्णयुतः ॥ २२
तारान्तेऽस्यादावपि मायाबीजं प्रयोजयेन्मन्त्री ।
तेन हि काङ्क्षितसिद्धिर्भूयादचिरेण मन्त्रविदाम् ॥ २३
कूर्मादिभ्यां द्वाभ्यां द्वाभ्यामपि पूर्वपूर्वहीनाभ्याम् ।
कुर्यात् सप्तभिरर्णैरङ्गानि च षट् क्रमेण मन्त्रज्ञः ॥ २४
कालिकगलहृन्नाभिकगुह्योरुषु जानुजङ्घयोः पदयोः ।
देहन्यासं कुर्यान्मन्त्रेण व्यापकं समस्तेन ॥ २५

पुनरपि क्रियाशक्तिप्रधानायास्त्वरिताया विधानं वक्तुमारभते—अथेति । विनियोगमाह—पुरुषार्थेति । वक्ष्यमाणशक्तियोगवत् प्रणवयोगि मुक्तिकरी तद्वत् कामयोगि कामकरी श्रीयोगेऽर्थकरी वाग्योगि धर्मज्ञानकरी शक्तियोगि सर्वकरीति विभागः ॥ २० ॥

मन्त्रिणां सततमिति । किङ्करमन्त्रजपः सूचितः । प्रणवशक्तिनमोऽन्ते चतुर्थ्यां भगवच्छ्वरमहाकिरातरूपकङ्कालधरपदान्ते कवचास्त्रठद्वययुक्तः किरातमन्त्रः ॥ २१ ॥

वर्म हुं । ऋद्धिः खं । ए ए एव । च इति च एव । तदन्त्यश्छकारः । शिव एकारः । चरमः क्षकार । अङ्गना स्त्री । सार्घिलवोद्युः हूं । मायाबीजं प्रयोजयेन्मन्त्रीति । कुण्डलिनीबीजरूपमायाप्रयोग उक्तः । क्लीमिति कुण्डलिनीबीजम् । मन्त्रविदामित्यस्यादौ क्लीमिति मायाबीजप्रयोग उक्तः ॥ २२ ॥ २३ ॥

मन्त्रज्ञ इत्यङ्गेषु मायादीर्घयोग उक्तः । उपरितनमायां विना सप्तभिरक्षरैरङ्गमन्त्रज्ञ इति चार्थः । अथवा सर्वज्ञादियोगः सूचितः । अत्र शक्तिबीजेन सार्धं सामान्यपटलोक्ता न्यासाः कर्तव्याः । अर्जुनविराट्त्वरिता ऋष्यादयः । हुं बीजम् । क्लीं शक्तिः ॥ २४ ॥ २५ ॥

श्यामलतनुमरुणपङ्कजचरणतलां वृषलनागमञ्जीराम् ।
पर्णांशुकपरिधानां वैश्याहिद्वन्द्वमेखलाकलिताम् ॥ २६

तनुमध्यनतां पृथुलस्तनयुगलां करविराजदभयवराम् ।
शिखिपिच्छनालवलयां गुञ्जाफलगुणितभूषितारुणिताम् ॥ २७

नृपफणिकृतकेयूरां तां गलविलसद्विविधमणियुताभरणाम् ।
द्विजनागविहितकुण्डलमण्डितगण्डद्वयीमुकुरशोभाम् ॥ २८

शोणतराधरपल्लवविद्रुममणिभासुरां प्रसन्नाञ्च ।
पूर्णशशिबिम्बवदनामरुणायतलोचनत्रयीनलिनाम् ॥ २९

कुञ्चितकुन्तलविलसन्मुकुटाघटिताहिवैरिपिञ्छयुताम् ।
कैरातीं वनकुसुमोज्ज्वलां मयूरातपत्रकेतनिकाम् ॥ ३०

सुरुचिरसिंहासनगां विभ्रमसमुदायमन्दिरां तरुणीम् ।
तामेनां त्वरिताख्यां ध्यात्वा कुर्याज्जपार्चनाहोमान् ॥ ३१

दीक्षां प्राप्य गुरोरथ लक्षं जप्याद्दशांशकं जुहुयात् ।
बिल्वसमिद्भिस्त्रिमधुरसिक्ताभिः साधकः सुसंयतधीः ॥ ३२

अष्टहरिविधृतसिंहासने समावाह्य सरसिजे देवीम् ।
अङ्गैः सह प्रणीतां गायत्रीं पूजयेद्दिशां क्रमतः ॥ ३३

हुङ्काराख्या खेचरिचण्डे सच्छेदनी तथा क्षपणी ।
भूयः स्त्रियाह्वयाहुङ्कारीसक्षेमकारिकाः पूज्याः ॥ ३४

सश्रीबीजा लोकेशायुधभूषान्विता दलाग्रेषु ।
फट्कारी चाप्यग्रे शरा सशरधारिणी च तद्बाह्ये ॥ ३५

सस्वर्णवेत्रयष्ट्यौ द्वाःस्थे पूज्ये पुनर्जयाविजये ।
कृष्णो वर्वरकेशो लगुडधरः किङ्करश्च तत्पुरतः ॥ ३६

अरुणैश्चन्दनकुसुमैर्वनजैरपि धूपदीपनैवेद्यैः ।
प्रवरैश्च नृत्यगीतैः समर्चयेद्भक्तिभरावनम्रतनुः ॥ ३७

कर्कोटकपद्मौ शूद्रौ । तक्षकमहापद्मौ वैश्यौ । वासुकिशङ्खपालौ नृपौ । अनन्तकुलिकौ ब्राह्मणौ । शाक्ते पीठे पूजा । दीर्घपटलोक्त आसनमन्त्रः । मूलेन मूर्तिपूजा ॥ २६—३७ ॥

जपहुतपूजाभेदैरिति सिद्धे मन्त्रजापिनो मन्त्रे ।
नारीनरनरपतयः कुर्वन्ति सदा नमस्क्रियामस्मै ॥ ३८
विद्याधर्यो यक्ष्यः समुरासुरसिद्धचारणप्रमदाः ।
अप्सरसश्च विशिष्टाः साधकसक्तेन चेतसाकुलिताः ॥ ३९
स्मरशरविह्वलिताङ्ग्यो रोमाञ्चितगात्रवल्लरीललिताः ।
घनघर्मबिन्दुमौक्तिकविलसत्कुचगण्डमण्डलद्युतयः ॥ ४०
विस्पष्टजघनवक्षोरुहदोर्मूलाः प्रस्खलत्पदन्यासाः ।
मुकुलितनयनसरोजाः प्रस्पन्दितदशनवसनसंभिन्नाः ॥ ४१
स्रथमानांशुकचिकुरा मदविवशस्खलितमन्दभाषिण्यः ।
मृदुतरमस्तकविरचितनत्यञ्जलयः प्रसादकाङ्क्षिण्यः ॥ ४२
ईक्षस्व देहि वाचं परिरम्भणपरमसौख्यमस्माकम् ।
एहि सुरोद्यानादिषु रंस्यामः स्वेच्छया निरातङ्कम् ॥ ४३
इत्यादिवादि[नि]नीभिः प्रलोभ्यमानो यदा न विक्रियते ।
मन्त्री तदैव वाञ्छितमखिलं तस्मै ददाति सा देवी ॥ ४४

योनिं कुण्डस्यान्तः प्रकल्प्य तत्राऽनलं समाधाय ।
संपूज्य पूर्वविधिना जुहुयात् सर्वार्थसिद्धये मन्त्री ॥ ४५
इक्षुशकलैः समृद्ध्यै दूर्वाभिस्त्वायुषे श्रियै धान्यैः ।
धान्याय यवैः पुष्ट्यै गोधूमैर्ऋद्धये तिलैर्जुहुयात् ॥ ४६
जम्बूभिः स्वर्णाप्त्यै राजीभिः शत्रुशान्तये तथाऽक्षतकैः ।
अक्षयसिद्ध्यै वकुलैः कीर्त्यै कुमुदैर्महोदयाय तथा ॥ ४७
अरुणोत्पलैश्च पुष्ट्यै मधूकजैरिष्टसिद्धयेऽशोकैः ।
पुत्राप्त्यै पाटलजैः स्त्रीसिद्ध्यै निम्बजैश्च विद्विष्ट्यै ॥ ४८
तुष्ट्यै नीलोत्पलकैः सचम्पकैः कनकसिद्धये पद्मैः ।
सहकिंशुकैश्च सर्वोपद्रवशान्त्यै स साधको जुहुयात् ॥ ४९

मन्त्रजापिन इति । ओं क्लीं नमो नित्ये स्वाहेति त्वरितामन्त्रस्य दशाङ्ग उक्तः । मन्त्री तदैवेति क्षोभनिवृत्त्यर्थं पञ्चाक्षरस्य किङ्करस्य च जपः सूचितः ॥ ३८—४४ ॥

योनिं कुण्डस्येति । योनिकुण्डं विरच्येत्यर्थः । सर्वार्थसिद्धये मन्त्रीति । तत्तत्प्रयोगानुरूपबीजयोगः किङ्करपञ्चाक्षराभ्यां होमश्चोक्तः ॥ ४५॥४६॥४७।४८॥४९ ॥

हुतसंख्या साहस्री त्रियुता वाथाऽयुतान्तिकी भवति ।
यावत्संख्यो होमस्तावज्जप्यश्च मन्त्रिणा मन्त्रः ॥ ५०
मनुमन्त्रितैश्च वारिभिरासिक्तः क्ष्वेलशान्तिकृद्भवति ।
तज्जप्तयष्टिघातो मन्त्रितचुलुकोदकाहतिश्च तथा ॥ ५१
तत्कर्णरन्ध्रजापात् सद्यो नश्युर्विषग्रहादिरुजः ।
तद्यन्त्रस्थापनमपि विषभूतादिप्रशान्तिकृत् प्रोक्तम् ॥ ५२
आख्यां मध्ये सतारे मनुमथ शतसंयुक्तविंशत्पुटेषु
प्रादक्षिण्येन शर्वादिकमनुविलिखेद् द्वादशावृत्ति मन्त्री ।
विंशद्द्वन्द्वाष्टशूलाकलितविरचितं यन्त्रमेतत् सुजप्तं
बद्धं क्ष्वेलग्रहार्त्तिं हरति विजयलक्ष्मीप्रदं कीर्त्तिदञ्च ॥ ५३
आख्यां मध्यगतानले लिखतु दिक्पंक्तिष्वथ स्युः सङ्क्रूं
च्चं च्चं क्षूं करणादिषष्टिपदकैः शैवादि कालीमनुम् ।
१० १२ १२
नैर्ऋत्यादि तथा क्रमाद्द्वयमवृतं बाह्येऽनलेनावृतं
प्रोक्तं निग्रहचक्रमन्तकपुरप्राप्तिप्रदं वैरिणाम् ॥ ५४

कालीमाररमालीका लीनमोच्चचमोनली ।
मामोदिततदेमोमा रच्चतत्त्वत्त्वतच्चर ॥ ५५
यमापाटटपामाय माटमोटटमोटमा ।
पामोभूरिरिभूमोपा टटरीस्त्वस्त्वरीटट ॥ ५६

वङ्क्षेविंगन्निम्बनिर्यासकविषमसिभिः सीसपट्टेऽशुभे वा
शावे पाषाणके वा विलिखतु मतिमान् काकपक्षेण यन्त्रम् ।

मन्त्रिणा मन्त्र इत्यनुजपेऽपि तदेवोक्तम् ॥ ५० ॥ ५१ ॥ ५२ ॥

आख्यां मध्य इति । द्वादशरेखात्मकं यन्त्रम् । साधकसाध्यकर्मणामाख्या आख्याशब्दार्थः । त्वरिते अमुकस्याऽमुकं वशयेत्याद्या आख्या । द्वादशावृत्ति मन्त्रीति । क्ष्वेलहरणे गरुडबीजाक्षराणि लिखेत् । ग्रहार्तिहरणे नारसिंहे विजये दौर्गे लक्ष्म्यां श्रीबीजे कान्तौ कामे सर्वार्थे शक्तौ ॥ ५३ ॥

आख्यां मध्यगतानल इति । दशरेखायन्त्रम् । अनललेखनं सर्वपङ्क्तिषु समानम् ॥ ५४ ॥ ५५ ॥ ५६ ॥

वङ्क्षेविंडङ्गारः शावः । सूरण चित्रक लोण पिण्डोन्मत्त त्रिकटुक गृहधूमा विषाः ।

वल्मीके चत्वरे वाऽक्षकतरुविवरे वा निदध्याद्‌राति-
र्मृत्युं प्राप्नोति भूयादवयवविकलो व्याधितः पातितो वा ॥ ५७
चक्रे चाऽष्टाष्टपदे कालीशिवयातुधानखण्डाद्यम् ।
यमदहनानिलवीतं विलिख्य विषदण्डमर्कटीलिप्तम् ॥ ५८
जप्तमधोमुखमेतद् यन्त्रं यत्र तु देशे विनिक्षिपेन्मन्त्री ।
तत्रोपद्रवमखिलं दिनशः सर्वात्मना भवति ॥ ५९

खण्डेष्वेकाशीतिषु मध्येन्दुगसाध्यं
जूंसः पूर्वं दिक्स्थचतुःपङ्क्तिषु शैखम् ।
लिख्याल्लक्ष्मीं शिष्टचतुःषष्टिषु विद्वा-
नीशाद्यं कन्यादि च बाह्ये त्वरिताख्याम् ॥ ६०
दिग्दिक्संस्थामस्त्रपदाविर्वषडन्तां
मेदोमालावेष्टितबिम्बं घटवीतम् ।
पद्मस्थं तत्पङ्कजराजद्वदनाग्र्यं
प्रोक्तं चक्रं सम्यगथाऽनुग्रहसंज्ञम् ॥ ६१

तैर्नरादितैलेन शूलारूढशवपटवर्त्या मसिः कार्या । सोसोऽपि देवताजातिहस्तगतो ग्राह्यः । शवांशुकः शूलारूढस्य ग्राह्यः । पाषाणो रजकपाषाणः । मतिमानिति । देशकालादिज्ञ इत्यर्थः । अर्धरात्रिसन्ध्यादयः कालाः । देशः शवाङ्गणादिः । वल्मीकेऽवयववैकल्यं भवति । चत्वरे व्याधिः । अक्षतरुविवरे मरणमिति भेदाः ॥ ५७ ॥

चक्रे चेति । नवरेखायन्त्रम् । दण्डो ब्रह्मदण्डी । विनिक्षिपेत् मन्त्रीति । मन्त्राक्षरशक्तीनां काकोलूकपाषाणाङ्गारद्रव्यात्मना ध्यानं सूचितम् ॥ ५८ ॥ ५९ ॥

खण्डेष्वेकाशीतिष्विति । दशरेखायन्त्रमनुग्रहाख्यम् । इन्दुः ठकारवकारौ सर्वखण्डेषु च समानावेतौ । जूंसः पूर्वं दिक्स्थचतुःपङ्क्तिषु शैखमिति । मध्यसन्निहितदिक्पङ्क्तिषु जूं तदन्तरासु सः ततो वं ततो षडित्येकः प्रकारः । सर्वं सर्वत्रेत्यपरः । शैखं शिखासम्बन्धि वषडित्यर्थः । विद्वानिति । अक्षराणां श्रीबीजमध्यस्थत्वमुक्तम् ॥ ६० ॥

अस्त्रपदाविर्वषडन्तामिति । फडिति परित्यज्य तत्र वषडन्वितामित्यर्थः । मेदोवेष्टितबिम्बमिति । मेदसा वेष्टितं बिम्बं यस्य स तथोक्तः । यन्त्रस्य बहिश्चन्द्रबिम्बं लिखित्वा तद्गतमेदोभिः वकारैः वेष्टयेदित्यर्थः ॥ ६१ ॥

श्री सा माया यामा सा श्री सा नो यान्ते ज्ञेया नो सा ।
माया लीला लाली यामा यान्ते लाली लीला ज्ञेया ॥ ६२

लाक्षाभिः कुङ्कुमैर्वा विलिखतु धवले चांऽशुके स्वर्णपट्टे
लेखन्या स्वर्णमय्या दृढमपि गुलिकीकृत्य सन्धारयेद् यः ।
कृत्यातो मृत्युतो वा ग्रहविषदुरितेभ्योऽपि मुक्तः स धन्यो
जीवेत् स्वैः पुत्रपौत्रैरपरिमितमहासम्पदा दीर्घकालम् ॥ ६३

चतुःषष्ठ्यंशे वा क्रमविदथ लक्ष्मीमनुममुं
शिवाद्यं नैर्ऋत्यादिकमपि च तूर्णामृतवृतम् ।
बहिः स्वच्छे पट्टे कनकविहिते पूर्वविधिना
लिखित्वा जप्त्वा निक्षिपतु शितधीर्यत्र तदिदम् ॥ ६४

चक्रमनुग्रहसंज्ञं मन्त्री देशेऽत्र सम्पदोऽविरतम् ।
शुभतरफलदायिन्यो भवन्ति शस्यर्द्धिकालवृष्ट्याद्याः ॥ ६५

हुङ्कारे साध्यसंज्ञां विलिखतु तदधः कर्णिकायाञ्च शिष्टा-
नष्टौ वर्णान् दलेष्वारचयतु हरमायां त्रिशो वेष्टयीत ।
कुम्भस्थं यन्त्रमेतत् सरसिजपुटितं सर्वरक्षाप्रसिद्ध्यै
क्लृप्तं रक्षोपसर्गप्रशमनफलदं श्रीकरं वश्यकारि ॥ ६६

इति निगदितक्लृप्त्या पूजयेत्तोतलाया
मनुमनुदिनमेनमानयेन्मानवो यः ।
स तु जगति समग्रां सम्पदं प्राप्य देहा-
पदि मुदिततरात्मा युक्तधीर्मुक्तिमेति ॥ ६७

चतुःषष्ठ्यंश इति । नवरेखायन्त्रम् । क्रमविदिति । अमृतबीजयोः श्रीबीजस्य च लेखने प्रोक्तक्रमविदित्यर्थः । तूर्णा त्वरिता । अमृतं ठवौ ताभ्यां वहिर्वृतमित्यर्थः । शितधीरिति । मन्त्राक्षरशक्तीनाममृतरत्नपुष्पादिवेष्टितया ध्यानमुक्तम् ॥ ६२ ॥ ६३ ॥ ६४ ॥

मन्त्रीति । वषडन्तत्वमुक्तम् ॥ ६५ ॥

कुम्भस्थयन्त्रमाह—हुंकार इति । तारे शक्तौ हुंकारो लेख्यः । पद्मबाह्ये वृत्तेषु हकाररेफमायावेष्टनं रक्षोपसर्गप्रशमनयोस्तारं दुर्गाबीजेन वेष्टयेत् । श्रीवेष्टितं श्रीकरम् । शक्तिवेष्टितं वश्यकारि ॥ ६६ ॥ ६७ ॥

स्मरदीर्घेऽधरकाग्न्यों दीर्घे त्यद्वेलदद्रलान्त्यशिवाः ।
अभितः शक्तिनिरुद्धो द्वादशवर्णोऽयमीरितो मन्त्रः ॥ ६८
द्वाभ्यां वा चैकेन द्वाभ्यां द्वाभ्यां तथा पुनर्द्वाभ्याम् ।
मन्त्राक्षरैर्विदध्यादङ्गविधिं जातिसंयुतैर्मन्त्री ॥ ६९

इन्दुकलाकलितोज्ज्वलमौलिर्मारमदाकुलिताऽयुगनेत्रा ।
शोणितसिन्धुतरङ्गितपोतद्योतितभानुदलाम्बुजसंस्था ॥ ७०
दोर्धृतदाड़िमसायकपाशा साङ्कुशचापकपालसमेता ।
शोणदुकूलविलेपनमाल्या शोणतरा भवतोऽवतु देवी ॥ ७१
स्मृत्वा नित्यां देवीमेवं प्रजपेन्मनुं शतसहस्रम् ।
अयुतं जुहुयादन्ते नृपतरुसमिधा घृतेन वा सिद्ध्यै ॥ ७२
शक्तिपीठे पूज्या देवी कुसुमानुलेपनैररुणैः ।
स्वयमप्यलङ्कृताङ्गः सधूपदीपैर्निवेद्यताम्बूलैः ॥ ७३

हृल्लेखा क्लेदिनी नन्दा क्षोभणी मदनातुरा ।
निरञ्जना रागवती क्लिन्ना च मदनावती ॥ ७४
मेखला द्राविणी चैव तथाऽन्या वेगवत्यपि ।
सस्मरा द्वादश प्रोक्ताः शक्तयः पञ्चसंस्थिताः ॥ ७५
अङ्गैः शक्तिभिराभिर्मातृभिराशाधिपैः क्रमात् पूज्याः ।
भक्तिभरानतवपुषा भवभयभङ्गाय मन्त्रिणाऽहरहः ॥ ७६

स्मरं कामबीजम् । दीर्घा नकारः । दीर्घा च एकारस्य दीर्घैकारः । ततश्च क्लिन्ने इति सिद्धं भवति । अधर ऐकारः । को बिन्दुः ककारस्य । अग्नौ रेफः । ओमिति स्वरूपम् । अतः ऐं क्रोमिति सिद्धं भवति । दीर्घा च ह्रस्व दीर्घे । त्य इति स्वरूपम् । ततश्च नित्य इति सिद्धम् । ह्वेलो मकारः । दद्रेति स्वरूपग्रहणम । लान्त्यो वकारः । शिव एकारः । ततश्च मदद्रवे इति सिद्धम् ॥ ६८ ॥

मन्त्रीति । क्रामादियोग उक्तोऽङ्गेषु । अङ्गिरात्रिष्टुब्वज्रप्रस्तारिण्य ऋष्याद्याः । क्लीं बीजम् । ऐं शक्तिः । न्यासः सामान्यपटलोक्तः ॥ ६९॥७० ॥ ॥ ७१॥७२॥७३॥७४॥७५ ॥

मन्त्रिणेति । प्रणवादित्वमुक्तम् । दारिद्र्यास्पर्शे श्रीयोगः । रोगास्पर्शे

दारिद्र्यरोगदुःखैर्दौर्भाग्यजरापमृत्युदोषैश्च ।
अस्पृष्टो निरपायो जीवति मन्त्री भजन्निमं मनुजः ॥ ७७

इतीरिता लोकहिताय वश्यप्रस्तारिणी मन्दिरमिन्दिरायाः ।
या सर्वनारीनरराजवर्गसम्मोहिनी मोहनबाणभूता ॥ ७८

निद्रयोरन्तरा त्वक्लिन्नेमदाः स्युश्च वै शिरः ।
मायादिकस्तथा वर्णद्वन्द्वैश्चाऽङ्गविधिः स्मृतः ॥ ७९

रक्ता रक्तांशुककुसुमविलेपादिका सेन्दुमौलिः
स्विद्यद्वक्त्रा मदविवशसमाघूर्णितचीक्षणा च ।
दोर्भिः पाशाङ्कुशयुतकपालाभया पद्मसंस्था
देवी पायादमितफलदा नित्यशः पार्वती वः ॥ ८०

दीक्षितः प्रजपेल्लक्षं मनुमेनं हुनेत्ततः ।
मधूकपुष्पैः स्वाद्वक्तैरयुतं हविषाऽथवा ॥ ८१

पीठं पूर्ववदभ्यर्च्य तत्रावाह्याऽभिपूजयेत् ।
अङ्गैश्च शक्तिभिर्लोकपालैर्देवीं समाहितः ॥ ८२
नित्या निरञ्जना क्लिन्ना क्लेदिनी मदनातुरा ।
मदद्रवा द्राविणी च द्रविणा शक्तयो मताः ॥ ८३

प्रजपेत् प्रमदां विचिन्त्य यां वा
शयनस्थो मनुवित् सहस्रमानम् ।
निशि मारशिलीमुखाहताङ्गी
न चिरात् सा मदविह्वला समेति ॥ ८४
नित्याभिः सदृशतरा न सन्ति लोके
लक्ष्मीदा जगदनुरञ्जनाश्च मन्त्राः ।

दुर्गायोगः । दुःखदौर्भाग्यास्पर्शे कामयोगः । जरापमृत्युरोगास्पर्शे मृत्युञ्जय-योगः ॥ ७६ ॥ ७७ ॥ ७८ ॥

नित्यक्लिन्नायाः संमोहननित्यक्लिन्नादेव्य ऋष्याद्याः । क्लीं बीजं स्वाहा शक्तिः । वर्णद्वन्द्वैश्चेति । क्लामादियोगः उक्तः ॥ ७९ ॥ ८० ॥ ८१ ॥ ८२ ॥ ८३ ॥

मनुविदिति । मदद्रवे इत्यस्मात् पूर्वं साध्यनामयोग उक्त इति ॥ ८४॥८५ ॥

तस्मात्ताः शुभमतयो भजन्तु नित्यं
जापार्चाहुतसमुपासनाविशेषैः ॥ ८५

स्वर्णपट्टेऽथवा भूर्जे पाशबीजेन वेष्टयेत् ।
शक्तिबीजं साध्यनाम तन्मध्ये परिकल्पयेत् ॥ ८६

केसरेषु लिखेत् पाशशूलिबीजे प्रदक्षिणम् ।
मन्त्रवर्णांशनित्यादीन् दलमध्येषु बाह्यतः ॥ ८७

वृते स्वाहापदेनापि षोडशाक्षरविद्यया ।
पाशाङ्कुशाढ्यया पूर्वं प्रोक्तया वेष्टयेदपि ॥ ८८

एतद्यन्त्रं मदालिप्तं मृगमातङ्गयोः परम् ।
सर्वार्थसाधकं मूर्ध्नि करे वा विधृतं भवेत् ॥ ८९

अङ्कुशस्मरबाणानां बीजाद्यं शक्तिपाशयोः ।
सहस्रं प्रजपेदेनां विद्येशीं वीरमानसः ॥ ९०

इति श्रीप्रपञ्चसारे त्रयोदशः पटलः ।

[स्वर्णेत्यादि वीरमानस इत्यन्तं श्लोकपञ्चकं क्वचिन्न दृश्यते ।] ॥ ८६—९० ॥

इति श्रीपद्मपादाचार्यकृते प्रपञ्चसारविवरणे

त्रयोदशः पटलः ।

चतुर्दशः पटलः ।

अथ वक्ष्यामि दुर्गाया मन्त्रान् साङ्गान् सदैवतान् ।
सजपार्चाहुतविधीन् प्रीत्यर्थं मन्त्रजापिनाम् ॥ १

तारो मायाऽमरेशोऽद्रिपीठो बिन्दुसमन्वितः ।
स एव च विसर्गान्तो गायै नत्यन्तिको मनुः ॥ २

दुर्गाऽस्य देवता छन्दो गायत्रं नारदो मुनिः ।
तारो माया च दुर्गायै क्रामाद्यन्ताङ्गकल्पना ॥ ३

शङ्खारिचापशरभिन्नकरां त्रिनेत्रां
तिग्मेतरांशुकलया विलसत्किरीटाम् ।
सिंहस्थितां सकलसिद्धनुताञ्च दुर्गां
दूर्वानिभां दुरितवर्गहरां नमामि ॥ ४

कृताभिषिकदीक्षस्तु वसुलक्षं जपेन्मनुम् ।
तदन्ते जुहुयात् सर्पिः संयुतेन पयोऽन्धसा ॥ ५

अष्टसाहस्रसंख्येन तिलैर्वा मधुराप्लुतैः ।
पीठार्चायां प्रयष्टव्याः क्रमात्तच्छक्तयो नव ॥ ६

प्रभा माया जया सूक्ष्मा विशुद्धा नन्दिनी तथा ।
सुप्रभा विजया सर्वसिद्धिदा नवमी तथा ॥ ७

अर्च्या ह्रस्वत्रयक्लीबरहितैश्च स्वरैरिमाः ।
तारान्ते वज्रमाभाष्य नखदंष्ट्रायुधाय च ॥ ८

महासिंहाय चेत्युक्त्वा वर्मास्त्रनतयः क्रमात् ।
सिंहमन्त्रोऽयमित्येवं संप्रोक्ता पीठकल्पना ॥ ९

इच्छोपसर्जनां क्रियाशक्तिमभिधाय ज्ञानोपसर्जनक्रियाशक्तिरूपाया दुर्गाया विधानं वक्तुमारभते— अथेति । दुं बीजम् । ह्रीं शक्तिः । मूलेन मूर्तिकल्पना । ह्रींकारसहिता न्यासाः । कर्णिकायां बीजम् । दलेषु वर्णाष्टकम् । मातृकया च बहिर्वेष्टनम् । भूबिम्बकोणेषु नृसिंहबीजमित्यस्मिन्

अङ्गैः स्यादावृतिः पूर्वा द्वितीया शक्तिभिः स्मृता ।
अष्टायुधैस्तृतीया स्याल्लोकपालैश्चतुर्थ्यपि ॥ १०
तदायुधैः पञ्चमी च दुर्गायजनमीदृशम् ।
जया च विजया कीर्तिः प्रीतिश्चाथ प्रभाह्वया ॥ ११
श्रद्धा मेधा श्रुतिरपि शक्तयः स्वाचरादिकाः ।
चक्रशङ्खगदाखड्गपाशाङ्कुशशरा धनुः ॥ १२
क्रमादष्टायुधाः प्रोक्ता दौर्गा दुर्गतिहारिणः ।
इत्थं दुर्गामनौ जापहुतार्चाभिः प्रसाधिते ॥ १३
मन्त्रीन्दिरावान् भवति दीर्घायुर्दुरितान् जयेत् ।
यान् यानिच्छति कामान् स तांस्तानाप्नोत्ययत्नतः ॥ १४
विधाय विधिना तेन कलशं त्वभिषिचयेत् ।
यमसौ भूतवेतालपिशाचाद्यैर्विमुच्यते ।
राजाऽभिषिक्तो विधिना सपत्नानमुना जयेत् ॥ १५
अमुना विधिना कृताभिषिक्ता ललना पुत्रमवाप्नुयाद्विनीतम् ।
हवनात्तिलसर्षपैः सहस्रद्वितयैराशु भवेच्च गर्भरक्षा ॥ १६
अनयैव जपाभिषिक्तहोमक्रियया स्यादनुरञ्जनं जनानाम् ।
भजतां सकलार्थसाधनार्थं मुनिवर्यैः परिकल्पितोऽयमादौ ॥ १७
उत्तिष्ठपदं प्रथमं पुरुषि ततः किंपदं स्वपिषियुतम् ।
भयमपि मेऽन्ते समुपस्थितमित्युच्चार्य यदिपदं प्रवदेत् ॥ १८
शक्यमशक्यं वोक्त्वा तन्मे भगवति निगद्य शमयपदम् ।
प्रोक्त्वा ठद्वितययुतं सप्तत्रिंशाक्षरो मनुः प्रोक्तः ॥ १९
आरण्यकोऽस्त्यनुष्टुब्वनदुर्गाख्याः क्रमेण भगवत्याः ।
ऋष्यादिकाः स्वमनुना विहितान्यङ्गानि वाक्यभिन्नेन ॥ २०

यन्त्रे पूजयेत् ॥ १—१३ ॥

मन्त्रीन्दिरावान् भवतीति । इन्दिरायोगः सूचितः । मृत्युञ्जययोगे दीर्घायुः । शक्त्यनन्तरं तु योगः । सिंहयोगे दुरितां जयेत् । शक्तिपुटितत्वे सर्वकामाप्तिः । कामयोगे पुत्रावाप्तिः ॥ १४॥१५॥१६॥१७ ॥

वनदुर्गायाः दुं बीजम् । स्वाहा शक्तिः । वा तन्म इत्यक्षराणि कीलानि ।

षड्भिश्चतुर्भिरष्टभिरष्टार्णैः षड्भिरपि च पञ्चार्णैः ।
जातियुतैश्च विदध्यादङ्गान्यपि षट् क्रमेण विशदमतिः ॥ २१
पद्द्वयसन्धिगुदाम्बुधारोदरपार्श्वहृत्स्तनेषु गले ।
दोःसन्धिवदननासाकपोलदृक्कर्णयुग्भ्रुक्षि न्यस्येत् ॥ २२
हेमप्रख्यामिन्दुखण्डात्तमौलिं शङ्खारीष्टाभीतिहस्तां त्रिनेत्राम् ।
हेमाब्जस्थां पीतवस्त्रां प्रसन्नां देवीं दुर्गां दिव्यरूपां नमामि ॥ २३
अरिशङ्खकृपाणखेटबाणान् सधनुःशूलकतर्जनीर्दधाना ।
भवतां महिषोत्तमाङ्गसंस्था नवदूर्वासदृशी श्रियेऽस्तु दुर्गा ॥ २४

चक्रदरखड्गखेटकशरकार्मुकशूलसंज्ञककपालैः ।
ऋष्टिमुसलकुन्तनन्दकवलयगदाभिन्दिपालशक्त्याख्यैः ॥ २५
उद्यद्विकृतिभुजाढ्या माहिषके सजलजलदसङ्काशा ।
सिंहस्था वाऽग्निनिभा पद्मस्था वाथ मरकतश्यामा ॥ २६
व्याघ्रत्वक्परिधाना सर्वाभरणान्विता त्रिनेत्रा च ।
अहिकलितनीलकुञ्चितकुन्तलविलसत्किरीटशशिशकला ॥ २७
सर्पमयवलयनूपुरकाञ्चीकेयूरहारसम्भिन्ना ।
सुरदितिजाभयभयदा ध्येया कात्यायनी प्रयोगविधौ ॥ २८
संयतचित्तो लक्षचतुष्कं जप्त्वा हुनेद्दशांशेन ।
व्रीहितिलाज्यहविर्भिः सम्यक् संचिन्त्य भगवतीमनले ॥ २९

हुं दुं दुर्गे इति अकीलाक्षराणि । क्रमेण विशदमतिरिति । सामान्यपटलोक्त-न्यासक्रमस्मरणकुशल इत्यर्थः । अथवा प्रणवशक्ति नरसिंहदुर्गाबीजादियोगेऽङ्गेषु विशेषज्ञ इत्यर्थः । अथवा विष्णुदैवत्यपक्षे नैतन्मन्त्रस्य पञ्चार्णत्वम् इत्यर्थः ॥ १८॥१९॥२०॥२१॥२२ ॥

हेमप्रख्येति । साधने ध्यानम् । अरिशङ्खेति । रक्षादौ । चक्रदरेति । युद्धमारणादौ । सिंहस्थाऽप्यष्टभुजा रक्षादौ प्रशस्ता । पद्मस्थापि द्विभुजा वरदाभयकरा । सहस्राक्षी शाकम्भरी ॥ २३ ॥ २४ ॥ २५ ॥ २६ ॥

षोडशभुजाया विशेषणं व्याघ्रत्वगित्यादि । प्रयोगविधाविति मारणोच्चाटन-योरित्यर्थः । प्रतिलोमयोगविधाविति चार्थः ॥ २७॥२८ ॥

सम्यक् संचिन्त्येत्यग्निभेदेनेत्यर्थः । पूर्वविधानवद्यथोदितं शेषमिति । यक्तीनां

पीठे पूर्वप्रोक्ते पूज्याऽङ्गैः शक्तिभिस्तथाऽष्टाभिः ।
अष्टायुधैश्च मातृभिराशेशैः क्रमश एव दुर्गेयम् ॥ ३०

आर्या दुर्गा भद्रा सभद्रकाली तथाऽम्बिकाख्या च ।
क्षेमा सवेदगर्भा क्षेमङ्करी चेति शक्तयः प्रोक्ताः ॥ ३१

अरिदरकृपाणखेटकबाणधनुःशूलपाण्डरकपालाः ।
अष्टायुधाः क्रमेणोक्ताः पूर्वविधानवद्यथोदितं शेषम् ॥ ३२

इत्थं जपार्चनाहुतसिद्धमनोर्मन्त्रिणः प्रयोगविधिः ।
विहितो जपः प्रतिदिनं निजरक्षायै शतं सहस्रं वा ॥ ३३

उद्दिश्य यद्यदेनं मनुं जपेदथ सहस्रमयुतं वा ।
तत्तन्मन्त्री लभ्येदचिरात्तदनुग्रहादसाध्यमपि ॥ ३४

स्नात्वार्काभिमुखः सन्नाभिसमकेऽम्भसि स्थितो मन्त्री ।
अष्टोर्ध्वशतं प्रजपेन्निजवाञ्छितसिद्धये च लक्ष्म्यै च ॥ ३५

ध्यात्वा त्रिशूलहस्तां ज्वरसर्पग्रहविपत्सु जन्तूनाम् ।
संस्पृश्य शिरसि जप्यात्तज्जन्योपद्रवं द्रुतं शमयेत् ॥ ३६

अयुतं तिलैर्वनोत्थै राजीभिर्वा हुनेत् समिद्भिर्वा ।
मायूरकीभिरचिरात्सापस्मारादिकांश्च नाशयति ॥ ३७

स्वाक्षरादित्वं संकोचविकाशादिकं मातॄणां बीजसाहित्यमित्याद्यतिदिष्टमिति द्रष्टव्यम् । कर्णिकायां बीजम् । पत्रेषु पदद्वयम् । त्रिष्टुभा मातृकया च बहिर्वेष्टनं बहिः पार्थिवबिम्बे दुंबीजमित्यस्मिन् पूजयेत् ॥ २९॥३०॥३१॥३२ ॥

मन्त्रिणः प्रयोगविधिरिति । तत्तत्प्रयोगौचित्येन बीजयोग उक्तः । तत्तन्मन्त्री लभ्येदिति । चोरभयं मे समुपस्थितं व्याघ्रभयं मे समुपस्थितं रोगभयं मे समुपस्थितमित्यादियोगः सूचितः ॥ ३३ ॥ ३४ ॥

अम्भसि स्थितो मन्त्रीत्यनेनादौ चतुरक्षरयोगः सूचितः । लक्ष्म्यै चेल्लक्ष्मी-योगः कार्यः ॥ ३५ ॥

ध्यात्वा त्रिशूलेति । प्रतिलोमप्रयोगः । एवमन्यत्रापि निग्रहप्रयोगाः प्रतिलोमेनेति ज्ञातव्याः । दुंबीजप्रधानेनाऽनुलोमेनैव वा क्रूरकर्म कुर्यात् ॥३६॥ ॥ ३७ ॥

जुहुयाद्रोहिणसमिधामयुतं मन्त्री पुनः सशुङ्गानाम् ।
सर्वापदां विमुक्त्यै सर्वसमृद्ध्यै ग्रहादिशान्त्यै च ॥ ३८
आर्कैः समित्सहस्रैः प्रतिजुहुयादर्कवारमारभ्य ।
दशदिनतोऽर्वाग्वाञ्छितसिद्धिर्देव्याः प्रसादतो भवति ॥ ३९
शुद्धैः सारैरिध्मैस्त्रिदिनं वा सप्तरात्रकं वापि ।
प्रतिशकलं प्रतिजुहुयान्मनुना निजवाञ्छिताप्तये मन्त्री ॥ ४०
विशिखानां त्रिंशत्कं पुरो निधायाऽथ तीक्ष्णतैलेन ।
जुहुयात् सहस्रकं वाऽयुतमपि संख्यासु पूरितासु पुनः ॥ ४१
सम्पातिततैलेन च शरान् समभ्युत्य पूर्ववज्जुहुयात् ।
तानथ शूरो धन्वी शुद्धाचारः प्रवेश[ध]येद् बाणान् ॥ ४२
प्रतिसेनाया मध्ये सा धावति सद्य एव सम्भ्रान्ता ।
भूयो गुरुं धनैरपि धान्यैः परिपूजयेच्च कारयिता ॥ ४३
अष्टोत्तरशतजप्तं यच्छिरसि प्रक्षिपेच्चिताभस्म ।
स तु विद्विष्टो लोकैर्देशाद्देशान्तरं परिभ्रमति ॥ ४४
कारस्करस्य पत्रैरष्टसहस्रैर्निपातितैर्मरुता ।
जुहुयात् सपादपांशुभिरुच्चाटकरं भवेद्रिपोः सद्यः ॥ ४५
सेनां संस्तम्भयितुं विषतरुसुमनःसहस्रकं जुहुयात् ।
तावद्भिस्तत्पत्रैर्मन्त्री च तां निवर्त्तयति ॥ ४६
विषतरुमयीञ्च शत्रोः प्रतिकृतिमसकृत्प्रतिष्ठितप्राणाम् ।
छित्त्वा छित्त्वा काकोलूकवसाक्तैः सहस्रमष्टौ च ॥ ४७

मन्त्री पुनः सशुङ्गानामिति। प्राकरणिकैरन्यैर्मन्त्रैः प्रतिलोमतो होम उक्तः ॥ ३८ ॥ ३९ ॥

शुद्धैः सारैरिध्मैरिति। असनसारोत्थैरिध्मैरित्यर्थः। प्रतिशकलं प्रतिलोमशकलम्। प्रतिजुहुयात्। पृष्ठाग्रं प्रतिलोमेन जुहुयात्। अथवा प्रतिशकलमिध्महोमं कुर्यादित्यर्थः। शकलं शकलं प्रत्येकेकेन प्रतिलोमेन जुहुयादिति वा। निजवाञ्छिताप्तये मन्त्रीति। गायत्र्या जप उक्तः ॥ ४०॥४१॥४२॥४३॥४४॥४५ ॥

तत्पत्रैर्मन्त्रीति। वायुबीजयोग उक्तः। संस्तम्भने पृथिवीबीजयोगः। ॥ ४६—५६ ॥

असितचतुर्दश्यां तन्नामैर्जुहुयादरण्यकेऽर्द्धनिशि ।
त्रिचतुर्दशीप्रयोगादर्वाङ्म्रियते रिपुर्न सन्देहः ॥ ४८
खवसारक्तोपेतैर्जुहुयात्पत्रैरुलूकवायसयोः ।
म्रियतेऽरातिर्मत्तः स्यादुन्मत्तसमित्सहस्रहोमेन ॥ ४९
संस्थापितानिलां तां प्रतिकृतिमुष्णोदके विनिःक्षिप्य ।
प्रजपेदुन्मादः स्याच्छ्वोर्दुग्धाभिषिक्ततः शान्तिः ॥ ५०
रविबिम्बगतामरुणां करयुगपरिक्लृप्तशूलतर्जनिकाम् ।
ध्यात्वाऽयुतं प्रजप्यान्मारयितुं सद्य एव रिपुनिवहम् ॥ ५१
असिखेटकराऽर्कस्था क्रुद्धा मारयति सैव जपविधिना ।
सिंहस्था बाणधनुःकरा समुच्चाटयेदरीनचिरात् ॥ ५२
विषतरुसमिदयुतहुतादथ करिणो रोगिणो भवन्त्यचिरात् ।
तत्पर्णैश्च विनाशस्तेषामुच्चाटनञ्च तत्पुष्पैः ॥ ५३
आनित्यकसमिद्धोमाद्रोगा नश्यन्ति दन्तिनामचिरात् ।
तत्पुष्पैर्मधुराक्तैर्होमाच्च वशीभवन्ति मातङ्गाः ॥ ५४
त्रिमधुरयुतैरानित्यकपत्रैर्मत्ता भवन्ति ते सद्यः ।
रक्षाकरस्तु करिणां तज्जापितपञ्चगव्यलेपः स्यात् ॥ ५५
आज्यतिलराज्यानित्यकदुग्धौदनपञ्चगव्यतण्डुलकैः ।
सघृतैश्च प्रत्येकं सहस्रहवनं गजाश्ववर्धनकृत् ॥ ५६
द्विजभूरुहं महान्तं छित्त्वा निर्भिद्य पञ्चधा भूयः ।
आशाक्रमेण पञ्चायुधा विधेयाश्च साधु शिल्पविदा ॥ ५७
शङ्खः सनन्दकोऽरिः शार्ङ्गः कौमोदकी दिशां क्रमशः ।
पञ्चेति पञ्चगव्ये निधाय जप्याच्च पञ्चसाहस्रम् ॥ ५८
तावद्घृतेन जुहुयात्तेष्वथ सम्पात्य साधु सम्पातम् ।
पुनरपि तावज्जप्त्वा मध्याद्यवटेषु पञ्चगव्ययुतम् ॥ ५९
संस्थाप्य समीकृत्य च बलिं हरेत्तत्र तत्र तन्मन्त्रैः ।
पुरराष्ट्रग्रामाणां कार्या रक्षैवमेव मन्त्रविदा ॥ ६०

तत्र तत्र तन्मन्त्रैरिति । विष्णुपञ्जरसिद्धैः शङ्खादिमन्त्रैरित्यर्थः । रक्षैवमेव

यस्मिन् देशे विहिता रक्षेयं तत्र वर्धते लक्ष्मीः ।
धनधान्यसमृद्धिः स्याद्रिपुचोराद्याश्च नैव बाधन्ते ॥ ६१
पद्मोत्पलकुमुदहुतैर्नृपपत्नीर्ब्राह्मणान् वशीकुरुते ।
कह्लारलवणहोमैर्विट्शूद्रौ जातिभिस्तथा ग्रामम् ॥ ६२
अथ वारिदरगदाम्बुजकरं मुकुन्दं विचिन्त्य रविबिम्बे ।
व्यत्यस्तपुरुषभगवत्पदं मनुं भजतु सर्वसिद्धिकरम् ॥ ६३
साध्याख्याक्षरदर्भितं मनुमिमं पत्रे लिखित्वा च त-
च्चक्रीहस्तमृदा कृतप्रतिकृतेर्विन्यस्य मन्त्री हृदि ।
सप्ताहं त्वथ पुत्तलीमभिमुखे संस्थाप्य सन्ध्यात्रये
जप्यादष्टशतं चिराय वशतां गच्छत्यसौ निश्चयः ॥ ६४
व्रीहीणां जुहुयान्नरोऽष्टशतकं सम्वत्सराट् व्रीहिमान्
गोदुग्धैः पशुमान् घृतैः कनकवान् दध्ना च सर्वर्द्धिमान् ।
अन्नैरन्नसमृद्धिमांश्च मधुभिः स्याद्रत्नवान् दूर्वयाऽ-
प्यायुष्मान् प्रतिपङ्कजेन महतीं सद्यः श्रियं प्राप्नुयात् ॥ ६५

क्रान्तं मरुत्तुरियवर्णयुतं सवाद्यं
संवीप्स्य शूलिनिपदञ्च सदुष्टशब्दम् ।
पश्चान्तकं सदहनं परिभाष्य हान्तं
हूं फट् द्विठान्तमिति शूलिनिमन्त्रमेव ॥ ६६

मन्त्रविदेति । मूलमन्त्रवत्तेषामायुधानां ध्यानपूजादिकं सूचितम् ॥ ५७॥५८ ॥
॥ ५८ ॥ ६० ॥ ६१ ॥ ६२ ॥ ६३ ॥

साध्याख्याक्षरदर्भितमिति । मन्त्राक्षराभ्यामेकैकनामाक्षरयोजनं विदर्भः । वश्याकर्षणपौष्टिकेषु विनियोगोऽस्य । सर्वत्रैवमेव प्रयोगः कर्तव्यः । समस्तमन्त्रान्ते समस्तनामयोजनं पल्लवः । मारणेऽस्य विनियोगः । नामान्ते मन्त्रयोजनं योगः । संस्तम्भनोच्चाटनविद्वेषेषु विनियोगः । मन्त्राद्यन्तयोर्नामयोजनं रोधः । संमोहने विनियोगः । मन्त्रनामाक्षरयोरेकैकान्तरितयोः योजनं ग्रथनम् । शान्तिके विनियोगः । नामाद्यन्तयोर्मनुयोजनं संपुटम् । कीलने विनियोगः । विन्यस्य मन्त्रीति । प्रतिकृतौ प्रातिलोम्येन मन्त्रन्यासादिकं सूचयति ॥६४॥६५॥

शूलिन्या हुं बीजं स्वाहा शक्तिः ॥ ६६ ॥

ऋषिर्दीर्घतपाश्छन्दः ककुब्दुर्गा च देवता ।
दुर्गा हृद्वरदा शीर्षं शिखा स्याद्विन्ध्यवासिनी ॥ ६७
वर्माऽसुरमर्दिनि च युद्धपूर्वप्रिये तथा ।
त्रासयद्वितयश्चाऽस्त्रं देवसिद्धसुपूजिते ॥ ६८
नन्दिन्यन्ते रक्षयुगं महायोगेश्वरीति च ।
शूलिन्याद्यन्तु पञ्चाङ्गं हूं फड़न्तमितीरितम् ।
अङ्गकमैव रक्षाकृत् प्रोक्तं ग्रहनिवारणम् ॥ ६९
बिभ्राणा शूल बाणास्यरि सदर गदा चाप पाशान् कराब्जै-
र्मेघश्यामा किरीटोल्लसितशशिकला भीषणा भूषणाढ्या ।
सिंहस्कन्धाधिरूढ़ा चतसृभिरसिखेटान्विताभिः परीता
कन्याभिर्भिन्नदैत्या भवतु भवभयध्वंसिनी शूलिनी वः ॥ ७०

एवं विचिन्त्य पुनरक्षरलक्षमेनं
मन्त्री जपेत् प्रजुहुयाच्च दशांशतोऽन्ते ।
प्राज्येन साज्यहविषा प्रयजेच्च देवी-
मङ्गाष्टशक्तिनिजहेतिदिशाधिनाथैः ॥ ७१

दुर्गा च वरदा विन्ध्यवासिन्यसुरमर्दिनी ।
युद्धप्रिया देवसिद्धपूजिता नन्दिनी तथा ।
महायोगेश्वरी चाष्ट शक्तयः समुदीरिताः ॥ ७२
रथाङ्गशङ्खासिगदाबाणकार्मुकसंज्ञकाः ।
सशूलपाशा यष्टव्या दिक्क्रमादष्ट हेतयः ॥ ७३
दीक्षाजपहुतार्चाभिः सिद्धः कर्म समाचरेत् ।
आमयोन्मादभूतापस्मारक्ष्वेलशमादिकम् ॥ ७४

असुरमर्दिनि युद्धप्रिये त्रासय त्रासयेति कवचम् । अस्त्रं देवसिद्धेत्यादि । शूलिन्याद्यं त्विति । शूलिनि दुर्गे हुं फट हृदयाय नमः । शूलिनि वरदे हुं फट् शिरसे स्वाहा । इत्याद्यमित्यर्थः । त्विति । बीजान्तरयोगेऽङ्गविशेषं सूचयति ॥ ६७ ॥ ६८ ॥ ६९ ॥

चतसृभिरिति । जया विजया भद्रा शूलिनीकात्यायन्याख्याभिरित्यर्थः ॥७०॥

मन्त्री जपेदिति । प्रणवशक्तिनृसिंहदुर्गाबीजपुटितं जपेदित्यर्थः ॥७१—७६॥

उद्गूर्णैः प्रहरणकैरुदीर्णवेगैः
शूलाद्यैर्निजमथ शूलिनीं विचिन्त्य ।
आविश्य क्षणमिव जप्यमानमन्त्र-
स्यावृत्त्या द्रुतमपयान्ति भूतसङ्घाः ॥ ७५

अन्तराऽथ पुनरात्मरोगिणोरम्बिकामपि निजायुधाकुलाम् ।
संविचिन्त्य जपतोऽरिमुद्रया विद्रवन्त्यवशविग्रहा ग्रहाः ॥ ७६
अहिमूषिकवृश्चिकादिजं वा बहुपात्कुक्कुरलूतिकोद्भवं वा ।
विषमाशु विनाशयेन्नराणां प्रतिपत्त्यैव च विन्ध्यवासिनी सा ॥ ७७
आधाय बाणे निशिते च देवीं क्षेमङ्करीमन्त्रमिमं जपित्वा ।
तद्वेधनादेव विपक्षसेना दिशो दिशो धावति नष्टसंज्ञा ॥ ७८
आत्मानमार्यां प्रतिपद्य शूलपाशान्वितां वैरिबलं प्रविश्य ।
मन्त्रं जपन्नाशु परायुधानि गृह्णाति मुष्णाति च बोधमेषाम् ॥ ७९
तिलसिद्धार्थैर्जुहुयाल्लक्षं मन्त्री सपत्ननामयुतम् ।
स तु रोगाभिहतात्मा मृतिमेति न तत्र सन्देहः ॥ ८०
त्रिमधुरसिक्तैश्च तिलैरष्टसहस्रं जुहोति योऽनुदिनम् ।
अप्रतिहताऽस्य शक्तिर्भूयात् प्रागेव वत्सरतः ॥ ८१
सर्पिषाऽष्टशतहोमतोऽमुना वाञ्छितं सकलमब्दतो भवेत् ।
दूर्वया त्रिकयुजेप्सितं लभेत् सम्यगष्टशतसंख्यया हुतात् ॥ ८२
क्षुरिकाकृपाणखरा मन्त्रेणाऽनेन साधु संजप्ताः ।
सम्पाताज्यसुसिक्ता अप्रतिहतशक्तयो भवन्ति युधि ॥ ८३
गोमयविहितां गुलिकां जुहुयाच्छतमष्टपूर्वकं मन्त्री ।
दिवसैः सप्तभिरिष्टौ द्विष्टौ मिथो वियोगिनौ भवतः ॥ ८४
अस्पृष्टकुं गोमयमन्तरिक्षे संगृह्य जप्त्वा त्रिसहस्रमानम् ।
यियासतां वै निखनेन्नराणां संस्तम्भनं द्वारि चमूमुखे च ॥ ८५

प्रतिपत्त्यैवेति । अमृताभिषेकप्रतिपत्त्येत्यर्थः ॥ ७७॥७८॥७९ ॥
मन्त्री सपत्नेति । पल्लवः सूचितः ॥ ८० ॥ ८१ ॥ ८२ ॥ ८३ ॥
शतमष्टपूर्वकं मन्त्रीति । वायुबीजसम्बन्धयोगप्रयोगश्च सूचितः ॥ ८४ ॥
॥ ८५ ॥

पानीयान्धःपाशिमार्यां प्रसन्नां ध्यात्वा ग्रामं वा पुरं वापि गच्छन् ।
जप्त्वा मन्त्रं तर्पयित्वा प्रविष्टो मृष्टं भोज्यं प्राप्नुयाद्भृत्यवर्गैः ॥ ८६

आर्कैर्मन्त्री त्रिमधुरयुतैरर्कसाहस्रमिध्मै-
राश्वत्थैर्वा त्वतिविशदचेतास्तिलैर्वा जुहोति ।
यानुद्दिश्य त्ववहितमनास्तन्मये सम्यगग्नौ
ते वश्याः स्युर्विधुरितधियो नात्र कार्यो विचारः ॥ ८७

कुर्यात् प्रयोगानपि दावदुर्गाकल्पोदितान् वै मनुनाऽमुना च ।
मन्त्री जपार्चाहुततर्पणान्तान्नाल्पो हि मन्त्रोरनयोर्विशेषः ॥ ८८

इति श्रीप्रपञ्चसारे चतुर्दशः पटलः ॥

आर्कैर्मन्त्रीति । शक्तियोगो विदर्भप्रयोगश्च सूचितः । अतिविशदचेता इति पाशाङ्कुशधनुर्धराया रक्तवर्णाभायाः ध्यानं सूचितम् । अवहितमना इति । पाशेन बद्ध्वाऽङ्कुशेनाकर्षणादिकं सूचितम् । तन्मये अर्ककाष्ठमय इत्यर्थः ॥ ८६॥८७ ॥

अमुना चेति । अत्रोक्तानमुना च कुर्यादित्यर्थः । मन्त्रीति । शान्तिप्रयोगेषु शूलिन्या वषडन्तत्वमुक्तमिति ॥ ८८ ॥

इति श्रीपद्मपादाचार्यकृते प्रपञ्चसारविवरणे
चतुर्दशः पटलः ।

पञ्चदशः पटलः ।

अथ कथयिष्ये मन्त्रं चतुरक्षरसंज्ञकं समासेन ।
प्रणवो भुवनाधीशाद्गण्डिखमस्यादिको विसर्गान्तः ॥ १
ऋषिरस्याऽजश्छन्दो गायत्रञ्च देवता च भुवनेशी ।
अङ्गानि षट् क्रमेण प्रोक्तानि प्रणवशक्तिबीजाभ्याम् ॥ २
भास्वद्रत्नौघमौलिस्फुरदमृतरुचो रञ्जयच्चारुरेखां
सद्यः सन्तप्तकार्त्तस्वरकमलजवाभासुराभिः प्रभाभिः ।
विश्वाकाशावकाशं ज्वलयदशिशिरं धर्तृ पाशाङ्कुशेष्टा-
भीतीनां भङ्गितुङ्गस्तनमवतु जगन् मातुरार्कं वपुर्वः ॥ ३
संदीक्षितोऽथ प्रजपेच्च मन्त्रं मन्त्री पुनर्लक्षचतुष्कमेनम् ।
पुष्पैस्तदन्ते द्विजवृक्षजातैः स्वादुप्लुतैर्वा जुहुयात् सरोजैः ॥ ४
मनोरथार्कात्मतया त्वनेन प्रवर्त्स्यतेऽर्घ्योपहिता प्रपूजा ।
समे सुमृष्टे रचयेद्विविक्ते शुद्धे तले स्थण्डिलमङ्गणस्य ॥ ५
प्रयजेदथ प्रभूतां विमलां साराह्वयां समाराध्याम् ।
परमसुखामग्न्यादिष्वस्त्रिषु मध्ये च पीठकृप्तेः प्राक् ॥ ६
ह्रस्वत्रयक्लीबवियोजिताभिः क्रमात् कृशान् बिन्दुयुताभिरज्भिः ।
सहाऽभिपूज्या नव शक्तयः स्युः प्रद्योतनाः प्राज्यतरप्रभावाः ॥ ७

एवं त्रिशक्त्यात्मकान् मन्त्रानभिधाय त्रिगुणात्मकानां सूर्यसोमाग्नीनां मन्त्रान् वदन् सत्त्वात्मकस्य सूर्यस्य मन्त्रं वक्तुमारभते—अथेति । ओं बीजम् । ह्रीं शक्तिः । हंसौ वा बीजशक्ती ॥ १ ॥

अङ्गानि षट्क्रमेणेति । शक्तिदीर्घाणामङ्गेषु क्रमेण शक्तियोगः सूचितः । अत्रापि शक्तिबीजेन सह सामान्यन्यासाः कर्तव्याः । आदित्यादीनां पञ्चानां धात्रादीनां द्वादशानां नवसप्तग्रहाणां च न्यासाः कर्तव्याः ॥ २

समनोव्यापिन्यादिशक्तयः कार्तस्वरादिवर्णाः । अशिशिरमित्याग्ने[दिति]-यमित्यर्थः । स्तनयोर्भङ्गित्वं निरन्तरत्वम् ॥ ३ ॥

मन्त्री पुनरिति । अजपान्ते परमात्ममन्त्रयोग उक्तः ॥ ४॥५॥६॥७॥८ ॥

दीप्ता सूक्ष्मा जया भद्रा विभूतिर्विमला तथा ।
अमोघा विद्युता चैव नवमी सर्वतोमुखी ॥ ८
ब्रह्मविष्णुशिवात्मकं समीर्य सौराय योगपीठाय ।
प्रोक्त्वेति नतिमपि पुनः समापयेत् पीठमन्त्रमहिमरुचेः ॥ ९
आवाह्य हार्ल्लेखिकमर्कमर्घ्यपाद्याचमाद्यैर्मधुपर्कयुक्तैः ।
प्रपूजयेदावरणैः समस्तसम्पत्त्यवाप्त्यै तदधीनचेताः ॥ १०
हृल्लेखाद्याः पञ्च यष्टव्यास्त्वङ्गैस्तदनु मातृभिः पश्चात् ।
अङ्गाराद्यैराशापालैरभ्यर्चयेत् क्रमान्मन्त्री ॥ ११
प्रतिपूज्य शक्तिमपि तत्र पुरः प्रणिधाय ताम्ररचितं चषकम् ।
प्रजपन्मनुं प्रतिगतक्रमतः प्रतिपूरयेत् सुविमलैः सलिलैः ॥ १२
अक्षतयवकुशदूर्वातिलसर्षपकुसुमचन्दनोपेतैः ।
प्रस्थयाह्यच्छिद्रं स्वैक्यं सम्भावयन् समाहितधीः ॥ १३

दृष्ट्वा दिनेशमथ पीठगतं तथैव
व्योमस्थितं परिवृतावरणं विलोक्य ।
अष्टोत्तरशतमथ प्रजपेन्मनुं तं
पूर्णोदकं निजकरेण पिधाय पात्रम् ॥ १४

भूयोऽभ्यर्च्य सुधामये जलमथो तद्गन्धपुष्पादिभि-
र्जानुभ्यामवनिं गतश्चषकमप्यामस्तकं प्रोद्धरन् ।
दद्यान्मण्डलबद्धदृष्टिहृदयो भक्त्याऽर्घ्यमोजोबल-
ज्योतिर्दीप्तियशोधृतिस्मृतिकरं लक्ष्मीप्रदं भास्वते ॥ १५

नतिमपि पुनः समापयेदिति । हृल्लेखार्कासनाय नमः इत्येवं मन्त्रसमापनमुक्तम् । मूर्तिर्मूलेन खं खखो[घं घर्णी]ल्काय नमः इत्यन्तेन देया ॥ ८ ॥

हार्ल्लेखिकमर्कमिति । हृल्लेखार्को देवतेति देवताविशेष उक्तः ॥ १० ॥

अर्चयेत् क्रमान्मन्त्रीति । सोम बुध बृहस्पति शुक्राङ्गारक शनैश्वर राहु केतुक्रमं ग्रहमन्त्राणां स्वाक्षरबीजाद्यत्वं चाह ॥ ११ ॥

प्रतिपूज्य शक्तिमपीति । पूर्वमेव मण्डलाकारस्यादित्यस्यापि पूजनमुक्तम् । प्रतिपूरयेत् सुविमलैरिति । अर्घ्यपूरणक्रमेण पूरणमवगन्तव्यम् । ओजो मानसं बलम् । ज्योतिः शरीरकान्तिः । दीप्ती रश्मयः ॥ १२ ॥ १३ ॥ १४ ॥ १५ ॥

अथ कृतपुष्पाञ्जलिरपि पुनरष्टशतं जपेन्मनुमिमं मन्त्री ।
यावद्रश्मिषु भानोर्व्याप्नोत्यम्भः सुधामयं तदपि ॥ १६

अमृतमयजलावसिक्तगात्रो दिनपतिरप्यमृतत्वमातनोति ।
धनविभवसुदारपुत्रमित्रपशुगणजुष्टमनन्तभोगयोगि ॥ १७

तस्मादिनाय दिनशो ददताद्दिनादौ
दैन्यापनोदितनवे दिनवल्लभाय ।
अर्घ्यं समग्रविभवस्त्वथ वाऽर्कवारे
पारं स गच्छति भवाह्वयवारिराशेः ॥ १८

अनुदिनमर्चयितव्यं पुंसां विधिनाऽमुनाऽथवा रवये ।
दद्यादर्घ्यद्वयमपि कुर्याद्वाञ्छितार्थसमवाप्त्यै ॥ १९

एकीकृत्य समस्तवस्त्वनुगतानादित्यचन्द्रानलान्
वेदाद्येन गुणात्मकेन सगुणानाकृष्य हृल्लेखया ।
सर्वं सत्प्रतिमथ्य तामपि समावष्टभ्य हंसात्मना
नित्यं शुद्धमनन्यमक्षरपदं मन्त्री भवेद् योगतः ॥ २०

अथ वदाम्यजपामनुमुत्तमं सकलसंसृतियापनसाधनम् ।
दुरितरोगविषापहरं नृणामिह परत्र च वाञ्छितसिद्धिदम् ॥ २१

विष्णुपदं ससुधाकरखण्डं चन्द्रयुगावधिकं वतुरीयम् ।
चेत्रविदो मनुरेष समुक्तो यं प्रजपत्यपि सन्ततमात्मा ॥ २२

ऋष्याद्या ब्रह्मदेव्यादिगायत्रीपरमात्मकाः ।
हसाऽक्लीबकलादीर्घयुजाऽङ्गानि समाचरेत् ॥ २३

अष्टोत्तरशतं मन्त्रीति । सोऽहमन्त्रत्वमुक्तम् । जपकाले ध्यानप्रकारमाह—यावदिति । अपिशब्द आत्मनोऽपि व्याप्तिं सूचयति ॥ १६ ॥

धनविभवेत्यादि । दृष्टं फलम् ॥ १७ ॥ १८ ॥ १९ ॥

योगमाह—एकीकृत्येति । तामपि शक्तिमात्मत्वेनाऽवष्टभ्य प्रतिपद्येत्यर्थः । प्रतिपत्तिप्रकारस्तु प्रपञ्चयागे कथितः । मन्त्री भवेदिति । सोऽहं योग उक्तः ॥२०॥

अजपाविनियोगमाह—सकलसंसृतीति । यापनं समापनं निर्वाहश्च । तत्रापि तत्तत्कार्यानुगुणबीजयोगोऽवगन्तव्यः ॥ २१ ॥

विष्णुपदमाकाशं हकारः । क्षेत्रज्ञबीजत्वमुपपादयति—यं प्रजपत्यपीति । हं

अरुणकनकवर्णं पद्मसंस्थञ्च गौरी-
हरनियमितचिह्नं सौम्यतानूनपातम् ।
भवतु भवदभीष्टप्राप्तये पाशटङ्का-
भयवरदविचित्रं रूपमर्द्धाम्बिकेशम् ॥ २४

प्रजपेद्द्वादशलक्षं मनुमिममाज्यान्वितैश्च दौग्धान्नैः ।
तावत् सहस्रमानं जुहुयात् सौरे समर्चनापीठे ॥ २५
निक्षिप्य कलशमस्मिन् पूर्वोक्तानामपामथैकेन ।
आपूर्य चोपचर्य च विद्वानङ्गैः प्रपूजयेत् पूर्वम् ॥ २६
ऋतवसुवरनरसंज्ञास्तथर्तगोऽब्द्रिपूर्विका जान्ताः ।
आशोमाशास्थेयास्ततो दिशापास्ततश्च वज्राद्याः ॥ २७
इति परिपूज्य च कलशं पुनरभिषिच्याऽथ नियमतोऽर्घ्यमपि ।
दद्याद्दिनाय चैहिकपारत्रिकसिद्धये चिरं मन्त्री ॥ २८

इन्दुद्वयोदितसुधारसपूर्णसार्ण-
सम्बद्धबिन्दुसुसमेधितमादिबीजम् ।
संचिन्त्य यो मनुमिमं भजते मनस्वी
स्वात्मैक्यतोऽथ दुरितैः प्रतिमुच्यतेऽसौ ॥ २९
व्योमानुगेन वसुधाम्बुमुचा सदाऽमा
प्रद्योतमानसविनिःसृतशीतरुग्भ्याम् ।
आराधिता दहनचन्द्रलसन्महोभ्यां
रोगापमृत्युविषदाहरुजः प्रयान्ति ॥ ३०

बीजम् । सः शक्तिः । चिरं मन्त्रीति । सोऽहंयोग उक्तः ॥ २२ ॥ २३ ॥ २४ ॥ ॥ २५ ॥ २६ ॥ २७ ॥ २८ ॥

योगमाह—इन्दुद्वयेति । इन्दुद्वयं विसर्गस्थबिन्दुद्वयं द्वादशान्तस्थं तस्मादुद्गतेन सुधारसेन पूर्णो यः सार्णः भ्रूमध्यस्थः तेन सम्बद्धो यो बिन्दुः हृत्स्थः तेन सुष्ठु दीपितमादिबीजं हकारो मूलाधारस्थ इति न्यासक्रमोऽप्यनेनैव सूचितः । विसर्गात्मने नम इत्यादयो न्यासमन्त्राः ॥ २९ ॥

अनुलोमयोगमाह उक्तेष्वेव स्थानेषु—व्योमानुगेनेति । अमा बिन्दुना । सविनिःसृतेति । सकारान्निःसृतविसर्गशीतरुग्भ्यामित्यर्थः । दहनचन्द्र-

हंसाण्डाकाररूपं स्रुतपरमसुधं मूर्धचन्द्राज्ज्वलन्तं
नीत्वा सौषुम्नमार्गं निशितमतिरथ व्याप्तदेहोपगात्रम् ।
स्मृत्वा संजप्य मन्त्रं पलितविषशिरोरुग्ज्वरोन्मादभूता-
पस्मारादींश्च मन्त्री हरति दुरितदौर्भाग्यदारिद्र्यदोषैः ॥ ३१

विधाय लिपिपङ्कजं मनुयुतोल्लसत्कर्णिकं
निधाय घटमत्र पूरयतु वारिणा तन्मुखम् ।
पिधाय शशिनात्ममन्त्रयुतवामदोष्णा पुनः
सुधायितरसैः स्वसाध्यमभिषिचयेत्तज्जलैः ॥ ३२

नारी नरो वा विधिनाऽभिषिक्तो मन्त्रेण तेनेति विषद्वयोत्थैः ।
रोगैस्तथाधिप्रभवैर्विमुक्तश्चिराय जीवेत् करणैर्विशुद्धैः ॥ ३३
करेण तेनैव जलाभिपूर्णं प्रजप्य मन्त्री करकं पिधाय ।
सुधायितैस्तैर्विषिणं निषिञ्चेद्विषं निहन्यादपि कालकूटम् ॥ ३४

गदितं निजपाणितलं विषिणः
शिरसि प्रविधाय जपेज्जलैः शितधीः ।
अचिरात् प्रतिमोचयते विषतो
मतिमानथ तक्षकदष्टमपि ॥ ३५

इत्यजपामन्त्रविधिः सम्प्रोक्तः संग्रहेण मन्त्रिवराः ।
यं प्राप्य सकलवसुसुखधर्मयशोभुक्तिमुक्तिभाजः स्युः ॥ ३६
अरुणा शिखिदीर्घयुता हृल्लेखा श्वेतया युताऽनन्ता ।
प्रोक्तः प्रयोजनानां तिलकस्तु यथार्थवाचको मन्त्रः ॥ ३७

लसम्महोभ्यामिति । चिदानन्दामृतात्मत्वमुक्तम् ॥ ३० ॥

पिण्डयोगमाह—हंसाण्डेति । भूतापस्मारादींश्च मन्त्रीति । योग्यबीजयोग उक्तः ॥ ३१॥३२॥३३ ॥

उक्तमेव प्रयोगं निर्यन्त्रमाह—जलाभिपूर्णमिति । मन्त्रीति । गरुडबीजयोग उक्तः ॥ ३४ ॥

शितधीरिति । पाणितलद्वयेऽप्यमृतध्यानकुशल इत्यर्थः । मतिमानिति । जीवरक्षा हंसःसोहंपुटमध्यस्थसंस्थापनलक्षणा सूचिता ॥ ३५॥३६ ॥

प्रयोजनतिलकमन्त्रमाह—अरुणेति ॥ ३७ ॥

गुह्यादाचरणतलं कण्ठादागुह्यमागलं कान्तात् ।
विन्यस्य मन्त्रवर्णान् क्रमेण मन्त्री करोतु चाऽङ्गानि ॥ ३८
मन्त्रस्य मध्यमनुना दीर्घयुजाऽङ्गानि चेह कथितानि ।
ध्यायेत् पुनरहिमकरं मन्त्री निजवाञ्छितार्थलाभाय ॥ ३९
अरुणसरोरुहसंस्थस्त्रिदृगरुणोऽरुणसरोजयुगलधरः ।
करकलिताभयवरदो द्युतिबिम्बोऽमितभूषणस्त्विनोऽवतु वः ॥ ४०
कृतसन्दीक्षो मन्त्री दिनकरलक्षं मनुं जपेज्जुहुयात् ।
तावत्सहस्रमन्नैः सघृतैर्वा त्रिमधुराप्लुतैश्च तिलैः ॥ ४१
प्रागभिहितेन विधिना पीठाद्यं प्रतिविधाय तत्र पुनः ।
विन्यस्य कलशमस्मिन् प्रपूजयेत्तरणिमपि सावरणम् ॥ ४२
अङ्गैः प्रथमावरणं ग्रहैर्द्वितीयं तृतीयमाशेशैः ।
मुख्यतरगन्धसुमनोधूपाद्यैः कृतभक्तिनम्रमनाः ॥ ४३
प्रागादिदिशासंस्थाः शशिबुधगुरुभार्गवाः क्रमेण स्युः ।
आग्नेयादिष्वस्रिषु धरणिजमन्दाहिकेतवः पूज्याः ॥ ४४
शुभ्रसितपीतशुक्ला रक्तासितधूम्रकृष्णकाः क्रमशः ।
चन्द्राद्याः केत्वन्ता वामोरुन्यस्तवामकरलसिताः ॥ ४५
अपरकराभयमुद्रा विकृतमुखोऽहिः कराहिताञ्जलियुक् ।
दंष्ट्रोग्रास्यो मन्दः सवर्णसदृशांशुकादिभूषश्च ॥ ४६
संपूज्यैवं विधिना विधिवद् गोरोचनादिकैर्द्रव्यैः ।
दद्यादर्घ्यं रवये मन्त्री निजवाञ्छिताप्तये भक्त्या ॥ ४७

क्रमेण मन्त्री करोतु चाङ्गानीति । हृल्लेखादि आदित्यादि पञ्चमूर्तिद्वादशादित्यग्रहन्यासाः सूचिताः ॥ ३८ ॥

मन्त्री निजवाञ्छितेति । बीजविशेषयोगे ध्यानविशेषाः सूचिताः । ह्रीं बीजम् । सं शक्तिः ॥ ३९॥४० ॥

मन्त्री दिनकरलक्षमिति । जपे प्रणवादित्वं सूचितम् ॥ ४१॥४२॥४३॥४४ ॥ ॥ ४५॥४६ ॥

मन्त्री निजवाञ्छिताप्तये इत्यर्घ्येऽपि बीजविशेषः हंसःसोऽहंयोगावुक्तौ । ॥ ४७॥४८ ॥

गोरोचनासतिलवैणवराजिरक्त-
शीताख्यशालिकरवीरजवाकुशाग्रान् ।
श्यामाकतण्डुलयुतांश्च यथाप्रलाभं
संयोज्य भक्तिभरतोऽर्घ्यविधिर्विधेयः ॥ ४८

कृत्वा मण्डलमष्टपत्रलसितं तत्कर्णिकायां तथा
पत्राग्रेषु विधाय कुम्भनवकं तत्पूरयित्वा जलैः ।
आवाह्य क्रमशो ग्रहानभिसमाराध्याऽभिषेकक्रियां
कुर्याद्द् यो ग्रहवैकृतानि विलयं यान्त्यस्य लक्ष्मीर्भवेत् ॥ ४९

ग्रहपरिवृतमिष्ट्वा पूर्वक्लृप्त्या दिनेशं
प्रतिजुहुत निजर्क्षे वैकृते वै ग्रहाणाम् ।
शुभमतिरुपरागे चन्द्रभान्वोः स्वभे वा
रिपुनृपजभये वा घोररूपे गदे वा ॥ ५०

अर्कद्विजाङ्घ्रिपमयूरकपिप्पलाह्वाः
सोदुम्बराः खदिरशम्यभिधाः सदूर्वाः ।
दर्भाह्वयाश्च समिधोऽष्टशतं क्रमेण
सर्पिर्हविर्घृतयुताः पृथगेव च स्युः ॥ ५१

सोमादीनां दिशि दिशि समाधाय वह्निं यथाव-
द्धोमे सम्यक्कृतवति मुदं यान्ति सर्वे ग्रहाश्च ।
युद्धे सम्यग्जयमपि रुजः शान्तिमायुश्च दीर्घं
कृत्याशान्तिं व्रजति पुनरेकत्र वा सर्वहोमः ॥ ५२

ग्रहशान्तिमाह—कृत्वा मण्डलमिति ॥ ४९ ॥

उक्त एव प्रयोगे कालविशेषं होमविशेषं च विवक्षन्नाह—ग्रहपरिवृतमिति । शुभमतिरुपराग इति । पूर्वोक्तग्रहमन्त्राविस्मरणमुक्तम् ॥ ५० ॥

होमे समिन्नियममाह—अर्केति । सर्पिर्हविर्घृतयुता इति । प्रथमं सर्पिः । ततः समित् । ततो घृतम् । ततो हविः । ततो घृतमिति क्रमः । अष्टशतमेव होमसंख्या । आज्याहुत्या त्वादावन्ते च व्याहृतिभिरपि जुहुयात् ॥ ५१ ॥

सर्वेषां सोमादीनां यथावद्धोमे कृत इति । वरुणवायुमध्यस्थे सूर्यकुण्डेऽग्नि-जननादिकं कृत्वा सोमादिककुण्डेषु प्रागादिदिक्स्थेषु अग्निं विहृत्य तत्राऽग्नि-

अमुना विधिनाऽर्चनाहुताद्यैः प्रभजेद्यो दिनशो नरो दिनेशम् ।
मणिभिः स धनैश्च धान्यवर्गैः परिपूर्णावसथो भवेच्चिराय ॥ ५३

त्यद्यन्त आर्यसूण्यर्णा मेधा रेचिकया गुणः ।
व्यत्ययोऽष्टाक्षरः प्रोक्तः सौरः सर्वार्थसाधकः ॥ ५४
देवभाग ऋषिस्तस्य गायत्री छन्द उच्यते ।
आदित्यो देवता चाऽस्य कथ्यन्तेऽङ्गान्यतो मनोः ॥ ५५
सत्यब्रह्मविष्णुरुद्रैः साग्निभिः सर्वसंयुतैः ।
तेजोज्वालामणिहुंफट्स्वाहान्तैरङ्गमाचरेत् ॥ ५६

आदित्यं रविभानू भास्करसूर्यौ न्यसेत् स्वरैर्लघुभिः ।
सशिरोमुखहृद्गुह्यकचरणेषु क्रमश एव मन्त्रितमः ॥ ५७
सशिरोमुखगलहृदयोदरनाभिशिश्नाङ्घ्रिषु प्रविन्यस्येत् ।
प्रणवाद्यैरष्टार्णैः क्रमेण सोऽयं तदक्षरन्यासः ॥ ५८
अरुणोऽरुणपङ्कजे निषण्णः कमलेऽभीतिवरौ करैर्दधानः ।
स्वरुचाहितमण्डलस्त्रिनेत्रो रविराकल्पशताकुलोऽवताद्वः ॥ ५९

संदीक्षितोऽथ मन्त्री मन्त्रं प्रजपेच्च वर्णलक्षान्तम् ।
जुहुयात्त्रिमधुरसिक्तैर्दुग्धतरुसमिद्वरैर्वसुसहस्रम् ॥ ६०
अथवा सघृतैरन्नैः समर्चयेन्नित्यशोऽर्घ्यमपि दद्यात् ।
पूर्वोक्त एव पीठे कुम्भं प्रणिधाय साधु संपूर्य ॥ ६१
शुद्धाद्भिररुणवासोयुगेन संवेष्ट्य पूजयेत् क्रमशः ।
अङ्गावृतेः परस्तादादित्याद्यैरुषादिशक्तियुतैः ॥ ६२

मुखमात्रं कृत्वा होमे कृत इत्यर्थः । एकत्र होमपक्षेऽपि प्रथमं सूर्यहोमं कृत्वा तं कुम्भे विसृज्य सोममावाह्य तद्धोमं विधाय तद्विसृज्य बुधादि होममप्येवमेव कुर्यात् ॥ ५२॥५३ ॥

अष्टाक्षरस्य ओं बीजम् । क्लीं शक्तिः ॥ ५४॥५५॥५६ ॥

क्रमश एव मन्त्रितम इति । क्लोमित्यादिक्रमेणादित्यादिबीजानां सम्बन्ध उक्तः । द्वादशादित्यादिन्यासश्च ॥ ५७॥५८॥५९ ॥

मन्त्री मन्त्रमिति । शक्तियोग उक्तः ॥ ६०॥६१ ॥

आदित्याद्यैरुषादिशक्तियुतैरिति । आदित्यं मध्ये संपूज्य रव्यादिचतुष्टयं

मातृभिररुणान्ताभिः सग्रहैः सुरैश्चाऽन्ते सूर्यपार्षद्भिः ।
सोषा सप्रज्ञा सप्रभा सन्ध्या च शक्तयः प्रोक्ताः ॥ ६३

संपूज्यैवं दिनेशं पटुमतिरथ जप्त्वा च हुत्वाऽभिषेकं
कृत्वा दत्त्वेनसंख्यं वसुमपि गुरवे सांशुकं भोजयेच्च ।
विप्रानादित्यसंख्यानिति विहितमनुर्नित्यशोऽर्घ्यञ्च दद्यात्
वारे वा भास्करीये शुभतरचरितो वल्लभाय ग्रहाणाम् ॥ ६४

इतीह दिनकृन्मनुं भजति नित्यशो भक्तिमान्
य एष निचितेन्द्रिरो भवति नीरुजो वत्सरात् ।
समस्तदुरितापमृत्युरिपुभूतपीडादिका-
नपास्य स सुखी स जीवति परञ्च भूयात् पदम् ॥ ६५

इति श्रीप्रपञ्चसारे पञ्चदशः पटलः ॥

दिक्षु उषादिचतुष्टयं कोणेषु पूजयेदित्यर्थः ॥ ६२ ॥

अरुणान्ताभिरिति । मन्त्रानन्तरमग्रेऽरुणमपि पूजयेदित्यर्थः ॥६३॥६४॥६५॥

इति श्रीपद्मपादाचार्यकृते प्रपञ्चसारविवरणे
पञ्चदशः पटलः ।

षोडशः पटलः ।

अथ चन्द्रमनुं वक्ष्ये सजपार्चाहुतादिकम् ।
हिताय मन्त्रिणां साध्यविधानञ्च समासतः ॥ १

भृगुः ससद्यः सार्द्धेन्दुर्बिन्दुहीनः पुनश्च सः ।
विषानन्तौ मान्तनतौ मन्त्रोऽयं सोमदैवतः ॥ २
दीर्घभाजा स्वबीजेन कुर्यादङ्गानि वै क्रमात् ।
विचिन्तयेत् पुनर्मन्त्री यथावन्मन्त्रदेवताम् ॥ ३

विमलकमलसंस्थः सुप्रसन्नाननेन्दु-
र्वरदकुमुदहस्तश्चारुहारादिभूषः ।
स्फटिकरजतवर्णो वाञ्छितप्राप्तये वो
भवतु भवदभीष्टद्योतिताङ्कः शशाङ्कः ॥ ४

दीक्षितः प्रजपेन्मन्त्री रसलक्षं मनुं वशी ।
पञ्चमी दशमी पञ्चदशीषु तु विशेषतः ॥ ५
अयुतं प्रजपेन्मन्त्री सायाह्नेऽभ्यर्च्य भाधिपम् ।
पयोऽन्नेन हुनेद्भूयः सघृतेन सहस्रकम् ॥ ६
ससर्पिषा पायसेन षट्सहस्रं हुनेत् पुनः ।
पीठक्लृप्तौ तु सोमान्तं परिपूज्याऽर्चयेद्विधुम् ॥ ७

सात्त्विकसूर्यविधिमभिधाय राजसस्य सोमस्य विधिमाह—अथ चन्द्रेति ॥१॥

अत्रिः ऋषिः । पङ्क्तिश्छन्दः । सोमो देवता । सौं बीजम् । भाय शक्तिः ॥ २ ॥

पुनर्मन्त्रीति । प्रणवादित्वमुक्तम् । यथावदिति । सोममण्डल इत्यर्थः । ॥ ३॥४ ॥

प्रजपेन्मन्त्रीति । ओं सौं स्वौं] पुटत्वमुक्तम् ॥ ५ ॥ ६ ॥

पीठक्लृप्तौ सोमान्तमिति । अं सूर्यमण्डलाय नमः । मं वह्निमण्डलाय नमः । उं सोममण्डलाय नमः । इति पीठपूजायां मण्डलं पूजयेदित्यर्थः ।

राका कुमुद्वती नन्दा सुधा संजीवनी क्षमा ।
आप्यायिनी चन्द्रिका च ह्लादिनी नव शक्तयः ॥

केसरेष्वङ्गपूजा स्याच्छक्तीस्तद्बहिरर्चयेत् ।
रोहिणीं कृत्तिकाख्याञ्च रेवतीं भरणीं तथा ।
रात्रिमार्द्राह्वयां ज्योत्स्नां कलाञ्च क्रमतोऽर्चयेत् ॥ ८

दलाग्रेषु ग्रहानष्टौ दिशानाथाननन्तरम् ।
सुसितैर्गन्धकुसुमैः पात्रे रूप्यमयैस्तथा ॥ ९
शक्तयः फुल्लकुन्दाभास्तारहारविभूषणाः ।
सितमाल्याम्बरालेपा रचिताञ्जलयो मताः ॥ १०

इति सिद्धमनुर्मन्त्री शशिनं मूर्ध्नि चिन्तयन् ।
त्रिसहस्रं जपेद्रात्रौ मासान्मृत्युञ्जयो भवेत् ॥ ११
हृदयाम्भोजसंस्थं तं भावयन् प्रजपेन्मनुम् ।
राज्यैश्वर्यं वत्सरेण प्राप्नुयादप्यकिञ्चनः ॥ १२
आहाराचारनियतो जपेल्लक्षचतुष्टयम् ।
असंशयतरं तेन निधानादि च लभ्यते ॥ १३
घोरज्वरगराः शीर्षरोगाः कृत्याश्च कामलाः ।
तन्मन्त्रायुतजापेन नश्यन्ति सकलापदः ॥ १४

नित्यशः प्रजपेन्मन्त्रं पूर्णासु विजितेन्द्रियः ।
जपेन्मनुं यथाशक्ति लक्ष्मीसौभाग्यसिद्धये ॥ १५
त्रितयं मण्डलानान्तु कृत्वा पाश्चात्यपौर्विकम् ।
आसीनः पश्चिमे मध्यसंस्थे द्रव्याणि विन्यसेत् ॥ १६
पूर्वस्मिन् पङ्कजोपेते पूर्ववत् सोममर्चयेत् ।
राकायामुदये राज्ञो निजकार्यं विचिन्तयेत् ॥ १७
संस्थाप्य राजतं तत्र चषकं परिपूरयेत्
गव्येन शुद्धपयसा स्पृष्टपात्रो जपेन्मनुम् ॥ १८

पूर्वादिक्रमतो मन्त्री नत्यन्ताः पूजयेदिमाः ॥ ७॥८॥९॥१०॥

सिद्धमनुर्मन्त्रीति । ओं सौं पुटितं मन्त्रमित्यर्थः । राज्यैश्वर्ये श्रीपुटो मन्त्रः ॥ ११॥१२॥१३॥१४॥१५ ॥

अर्घ्यदानप्रकारमाह—त्रितयमिति ॥ १६॥१७॥१८ ॥

अष्टोत्तरशतावृत्त्या दद्यादर्घ्यमथेन्दवे ।
विद्यामन्त्रेण मन्त्रज्ञो यथावत्तद्गतात्मना ॥ १९
विद्येविद्यापदे प्रोक्त्वा मालिनीति च चन्द्रिणि ।
चन्द्रमुख्यग्निजायाश्च निगदेत् प्रणवादिकम् ॥ २०
प्रतिमासश्च षण्मासात् सिद्धिमेष्यति काङ्क्षिताम् ।
इष्टाय दीयते कन्या कन्यां विन्देन्निजेप्सिताम् ॥ २१
अमितां श्रियमाप्नोति कान्तिं पुत्रान् यशः पशून् ।
सोमार्घ्यदाता लभते दीर्घमायुश्च विन्दति ॥ २२
इति सोममन्त्रविधिः प्रणिगदितः संग्रहेण मन्त्रविदाम् ।
उपकृतयेऽमितलक्ष्म्यै मेधायै प्रेत्य चेह सम्पत्त्यै ॥ २३

अथाऽग्निमन्त्रानखिलार्थसिद्धिप्रदान् प्रवक्ष्ये जगतो हिताय ।
सप्ताचिरादीनपि साङ्गभेदान् सार्चाविशेषान् सजपादिकांश्च ॥ २४
वियतो दशमोऽर्धिसर्गयुक्तो भुवसर्गौ भृगुलान्तषोडशाद्यः ।
हुतभुग्दयिता ध्रुवादिकोऽयं मनुरुक्तः सुसमृद्धिदः कृशानोः ॥ २५
भृगुरपि तदृषिश्छन्दो गायत्री देवताऽग्निरुद्दिष्टः ।
प्राक्प्रोक्तान्यङ्गानि द्विशः समुक्तैश्च मन्त्रवाक्यैर्वा ॥ २६
शक्तिस्वस्तिकपाशान् साङ्कुशवरदाभयान् दधत्त्रिमुखः ।
मुकुटादिविविधभूषोऽवताच्चिरं पावकः प्रसन्नो वः ॥ २७

जपेदिमं मनुमृतुलक्षमादरा-
द्दशांशतः प्रतिजुहुयात् पयोऽन्धसा ।
ससर्पिषाऽप्यसिततरैश्च षाष्टिकैः
समर्चयेदथ विधिवद्विभावसुम् ॥ २८

मन्त्रज्ञो यथावदिति । विद्यामन्त्रस्य प्रणवबीजादित्वं मूलमन्त्रात्मत्वमात्म-मण्डलस्थदिविष्ठसोमार्घ्यामृतानामैक्यध्यानं चोक्तम् । अन्यच्च जपादिकम् ॥ १९ ॥

विद्यामन्त्रमुद्धरति—विद्येविद्येति । संग्रहेण मन्त्रविदामिति । अमितलक्ष्म्यै श्रीयोगं मेधायै वाग्भवयोगं लोकद्वयसम्पदे प्रणवयोगं चाह ॥ २०॥२१॥२२॥२३॥

तमोगुणप्रधानानाग्नेयान् मन्त्रान् सविनियोगानाह—अथाऽग्नीति । ओं बीजम् । स्वाहा शक्तिः । प्राक्प्रोक्तानीत्यग्निजनने प्रोक्तानि । सहस्रार्चिः

पीता श्वेताऽरुणा कृष्णा धूम्रा तीव्रा स्फुलिङ्गिनी ।
रुचिरा ज्वालिनी चेति कृशानोर्नव शक्तयः ॥ २९
पीठे तनूनपातः प्रागङ्गैरष्टमूर्तिभिस्तदनु ।
भूयश्च शतमखाद्यैर्विधिनाऽथ हिरण्यरेतसं प्रयजेत् ॥ ३०
आज्यैरष्टोर्ध्वशतं प्रतिपदमारभ्य मन्त्रविद्दिनशः ।
चतुरो मासान् जुहुयात् लक्ष्मीरत्यायता भवेत्तस्य ॥ ३१
शुक्लाभिः शालीभिर्दिनमनुजुहुयादथाऽब्दमात्रेण ।
शालीशालि गृहं स्याद्गोमहिष्याद्यैश्च संकुलं तस्य ॥ ३२
शुक्लान्नैर्घृतसिक्तैः प्रतिदिनमग्नौ समेधिते जुहुयात् ।
अन्नसमृद्धिर्महती स्यादस्य निकेतनेऽब्दमात्रेण ॥ ३३
जुहुयात्तिलैः सुशुद्धैः षण्मासाज्जायते महालक्ष्मीः ।
कुमुदैः सकह्लारैरपि जातीकुसुमैश्च जायते सिद्धिः ॥ ३४
पालाशैः पुनरिध्मकैः सरसिजैर्बैल्वैश्च रक्तोत्पलै-
र्दुग्धैर्वीरुहसम्भवैः खदिरजैर्व्याघातवृक्षोद्भवैः ।
दूर्वाख्यैश्च शमीविकङ्कतभवैरष्टोर्ध्वयुक्तं शतं
नित्यं वा जुहुयात् प्रतिप्रतिपदं मन्त्री महासिद्धये ॥ ३५
तारव्याहृतयश्चाऽग्ने जातवेद इहावह ।
सर्वकर्माणि चेत्युक्त्वा साधयाऽग्निवधूर्मनुः ॥ ३६
ऋष्याद्याः पूर्वोक्ता मन्त्रेणाऽङ्गानि वर्णभिन्नेन ।
भूततुंकरणसेन्द्रियगुणयुग्मैर्मन्त्रवर्णकैस्तदपि ॥ ३७
अथवा शक्तिस्वस्तिकदर्भाञ्चसक्स्रुवस्रुगभयवरान् ।
दधदमिताकल्पो वो वसुरवतात् कनकमालिकालसितः ॥ ३८

स्वस्तिपूर्ण इत्यादिनित्यर्थः । जिह्वासप्तकमूर्त्यष्टकन्यासौ सामान्यपटलोक्तन्यासाश्च कर्तव्याः । मूलेनैव पीठमूर्तिकल्पना ॥ २४॥२५॥२६॥२७॥२८॥२९॥३० ॥

मन्त्रविद्दिनश इति । श्रीबीजयोग उक्तः । मन्त्री महासिद्धय इत्यपि श्रीबीजयोग एव । प्रतिदिनमेकैकेन द्रव्येण षण्मासं जुहुयात् । कह्लार-कुसुदाववशिष्टौ द्रव्यौ प्रतिपदि वा सर्वैर्जुहुयात् ॥ ३१॥३२॥३३॥३४॥३५ ॥

तारं व्याहृतय इति । श्रीं बीजम् । स्वाहा शक्तिः ॥ ३६॥३७ ॥

वत्सरादेश्चतुर्दश्यां दिनादाविव दीक्षितः ।
मन्त्रं द्वादशसाहस्रं जपेत् सम्यगुपोषितः ॥ ३९

अर्चयेदङ्गमूर्तीश्च लोकेशकुलिशादिभिः ।
समिदाज्यममायां हि परिशोध्य यथाविधि ॥ ४०

ब्राह्मणान् भोजयित्वाऽथ स्वयं भुक्त्वा समाहितः ।
परेऽह्नि प्रतिपद्येतैर्जुहुयादर्चितेऽनले ॥ ४१

मन्त्री वटसमिद्व्रीहितिलराजीहविर्घृतैः ।
अष्टोत्तरशतावृत्त्या हुनेदेकैकशः क्रमात् ॥ ४२

दशाहमेवं हुत्वा तु पुनरेकादशीतिथौ ।
शक्त्या प्रतर्प्य विप्रांश्च प्रदद्याद् गुरुदक्षिणाम् ॥ ४३

सुवर्णवासोधान्यानि शोणां गाञ्च सतर्णकाम् ।
पुनरष्टोत्तरं मन्त्री सहस्रं दिनशो जपेत् ॥ ४४

विधिनेति विधातुरग्निपूजामचिरेणैव भवेन्महासमृद्धिः ।
धनधान्यसुवर्णरत्नपूर्णा धरणी गोवृषपुत्रमित्रकीर्णा ॥ ४५

प्रजपेदथवा सहस्रसंख्यं दिनशो वत्सरतो भवेन्महाश्रीः ।
जुहुयात् प्रतिवासरं शताख्यं हविषाऽब्देन भवेन्महासमृद्धिः ॥ ४६

पालाशैः कुसुमैर्हुनेद्दधिघृतक्षौद्राप्लुतैर्मण्डलं
नित्यं साष्टशतैस्तथैव करवीरोत्थैः समृद्ध्या हुनेत् ।
षण्मासं कपिलाघृतेन दिनशोऽप्यष्टौ सहस्रं तथा
होतव्यं लभते स राज्यसदृशीं लक्ष्मीं यशो वा महत् ॥ ४७

उत्पूर्वात्तिष्ठशब्दात् पुरुषहरिपदे पिङ्गलान्ते निगद्य
प्रोच्याऽथो लोहिताक्षं पुनरपि च वदेत् देहिमेदान् क्रमेण ।
भूयो ब्रूयात्तथा दापयशशियुगलार्णांश्चतुर्विंशदर्णः
प्रोक्तो मन्त्रोऽखिलेष्टप्रतरणसुरसद्माङ्घ्रिपः स्यात् कृशानोः ॥ ४८

अथवेति । पूर्वमन्त्रोक्तध्यानविकल्पार्थः ॥ ३८॥३९॥४०॥४१ ॥

मन्त्री वटसमिदिति । होमे मन्त्रान्तेऽपि व्याहृतित्रययोगार्थः ॥ ४२॥४३ ॥

अष्टोत्तरं मन्त्रीति । प्रणवशक्तिपुटितत्वमुक्तम् ॥ ४४॥४५॥४६॥४७ ॥

ऋष्याद्याः स्युः पूर्ववद्दतुभूतदिशातिकरणयुगलार्णैः ।
मूलमनुनाऽथ कुर्यादङ्गानि क्रमश एव मन्त्रितमः ॥ ४९
हैमाश्वत्थसुरद्रुमोदरभुवो निर्यान्तमश्वाकृतिं
वर्षन्तं धनधान्यरत्ननिचयान् रश्मैः स्वकैः सन्ततम् ।
ज्वालापल्लवितस्वरोमविवरं भक्तार्तिसम्भेदनं
वन्दे धर्मसुखार्थमोक्षफलदं दिव्याकृतिं पावकम् ॥ ५०
जप्याच्च लक्षमानं मन्त्री संदीक्षितोऽथ मनुमेनम् ।
जुहुयाच्च तदवसाने घृतसिक्तैः पायसैर्दशांशेन ॥ ५१
अङ्गैर्हुतवहमूर्तिभिराशेशैः संयजेत्तदस्त्रैश्च ।
पावकमिति मन्त्रितमो गन्धाद्यैरनुदिनं तमुपहारैः ॥ ५२
दिनावतारे मनुमेनमन्वहं जपेत् सहस्रं नियमेन मन्त्रवित् ।
अधृष्यतायै यशसे श्रियै रुजां विमुक्तये युक्तमतिस्तथाऽऽयुषे ॥ ५३
शालीतण्डुलकैः सितैश्च पयसा हुत्वा हविः पावकं
गन्धाद्यैः परिपूज्य तेन हविषा संवर्त्य पिण्डं महत् ।
आज्यालोड़ितमेकमेव जुहुयाज्जप्त्वा मनुं मन्त्रवित्
साष्टोर्ध्वं प्रतिपद्यथो शतमतः स्यादिन्दिरा वत्सरात् ॥ ५४

अष्टोत्तरं शतमथो मृगमुद्रयैव
मन्त्री प्रतिप्रतिपदं जुहुयात्पयोऽन्नैः ।
साज्यैर्भवेन्न खलु तत्र विचारणीयं
संवत्सरात् स च निकेतनमिन्दिरायाः ॥ ५५

उत्पूर्वादिति । श्रीं बीजम् । स्वाहा शक्तिः ॥ ४८ ॥

क्रमश एव मन्त्रितम इति । बीजान्तरयोगेऽङ्गविशेषाः कथिताः ॥ ४९॥५० ॥

लक्षमानं मन्त्रीति । प्रणवयोग उक्तः ॥ ५१ ॥

पावकमिति मन्त्रितम इति । पुष्पाञ्जल्यादिमन्त्रश्च इत्यर्थः ॥ ५२ ॥

नियमेन मन्त्रविदिति । अधृष्यतायै नृसिंहबीजयोगं यशसेऽजपायोगं श्रियै तद्योगं रुजां विमुक्तये दुर्गायोगमायुषे मृत्युञ्जययोगं चाह । युक्तमतिरिति । तत्तद्बीजोदितध्यानमाह ॥ ५३ ॥

जप्त्वा मनुं मन्त्रविदिति श्रीयोगं देहि मे इत्यत्र साध्ययोगं चाह ।

अष्टोर्ध्वं शतं हविषा मन्त्रेणाऽनेन नित्यशो जुहुयात् ।
षण्मासादाढ्यतमो भवति नरो नात्र सन्देहः ॥ ५६

शालीभिः शुद्धाभिः प्रतिदिनमष्टोत्तरं शतं जुहुयात् ।
धनधान्यसमृद्धः स्यान्मन्त्री संवत्सरार्द्धमात्रेण ॥ ५७

आज्यैरयुतं जुहुयात् प्रतिमासं प्रतिपदं समारभ्य ।
अतिमहती लक्ष्मीः स्यात्तस्य तु षण्मासतो न सन्देहः ॥ ५८

अरुणैः पुनरुत्पलैः शतं यो मधुराक्तैः प्रजुहोति वत्सरार्द्धम् ।
मनुनाऽप्यमुना शताधिकं स प्रलभेन्मङ्क्षु महत्तराञ्च लक्ष्मीम् ॥ ५९

जातीपलाशकरवीरजवाख्यविल्व-
व्याघातकेसरकुरण्टभवैः प्रसूनैः ।
एकैकशः शतमथो मधुरत्रयाक्तै-
र्जुह्वन् प्रतिप्रतिपदं श्रियमेति वर्षात् ॥ ६०

खण्डैश्च सप्तदिनमप्यमृतालतोत्थै-
र्मन्त्री हुनेद्गुणसहस्रमथो पयोऽक्तैः ।
सम्यक् समर्च्य दहनं त्वचिरेण जन्तु-
श्चातुर्थिकादिविषमज्वरतो वियुञ्ज्यात् ॥ ६१

क्षीरद्रुमत्वगभिपक्वजलैर्यथाव-
त्संपूर्य कुम्भमभिपूज्य कृशानुमत्र ।
जप्त्वा मनुं पुनरमुं त्रिसहस्रमात्रं
सेकक्रिया ज्वरहरी ग्रहवैकृतघ्नी ॥ ६२

पयसि हृदयदघ्ने भानुमालोक्य तिष्ठन्
प्रजपतु च सहस्रं नित्यशो मन्त्रमेनम् ।
स दुरितमपमृत्युं रोगजातञ्च हित्वा
व्रजति नियतसौख्यं वत्सराद्दीर्घमायुः ॥ ६३

उक्तमन्त्रद्वयग्रहणेऽप्ययमेवार्थः ॥ ५४॥५५॥५६॥५७॥५८॥५९॥६० ॥

मन्त्री हुनेद् गुणसहस्रमिति । अमृतबीजयुतत्वमुक्तम् ॥ ६१॥६२॥६३॥६४ ॥

मनुनाऽमुनाऽष्टशतजप्तमथ प्रपिबेज्जलं ज्वलनदीपनकृत् ।
गुरुभुक्तमप्युदरगं त्वमुना परिजापितं पचति कुक्ष्यनलः ॥ ६४

जुहुयादरुणपङ्कजैस्त्रिमधुराप्लुतैर्नित्यशः
सहस्रमृतुमासतः पृथुतरा रमा जायते ।
प्रतिप्रतिपदं जुहेदिति बुधोऽथवा संवत्सरं
विनष्टवसुरप्यसौ भवति चेन्दिरामन्दिरम् ॥ ६५

इति श्रीप्रपञ्चसारे षोडशः पटलः ॥

बुधोऽथवेति । प्रतिपन्मात्रहोमे होमसंख्याधिक्यं सूचितम् ॥ ६५ ॥

इति श्रीपद्मपादाचार्यकृते प्रपञ्चसारविवरणे
षोडशः पटलः ।

सप्तदशः पटलः ।

अथ संगृह्यैव कथयामि मनुमपि महागणेशितुः ।

यं समवहितधियः सुधियः समुपास्य सिद्धिमधिकां प्रपेदिरे ॥ १

तारः श्रीशक्तिमारावनिगणपतिबीजानि दण्डीनि चोक्त्वा

पश्चाद्विघ्नं चतुर्थ्या वरवरदमथो सर्वयुक्तं जनञ्च ।

आभाष्य क्ष्वेलमेन्तं वशमिति च तथैवाऽऽनयेति द्विठान्तः

प्रोक्तोऽयं गाणपत्यो मनुरखिलविभूतिप्रदः कल्पशाखी ॥ २

ऋषिरपि गणकोऽस्य स्याच्छन्दो निवृदन्विता च गायत्री ।

सकलसुरासुरवन्दितचरणयुगो देवता गणाधिपतिः ॥ ३

प्रणवादिबीजपीठस्थितेन दीर्घस्वरान्वितेन सता ।

अङ्गानि षड्विदध्यान्मन्त्री विघ्नेश्वरस्य बीजेन ॥ ४

समृद्धिमन्त्रानन्तरं महासमृद्धिदस्य विधानं वक्तुमारभते—अथेति । समवहितधियः स्वाश्रमधर्मादप्रमत्ताः सुधियो मन्त्रज्ञा ध्यानविशेषज्ञाः ॥ १॥२॥३ ॥

मन्त्री विघ्नेश्वरस्य इति । अङ्गमन्त्रेषु सर्वज्ञादियोग उक्तः । न्यासविशेषैः मन्त्रात्मत्वमपि सूचितम् । प्रणवपुटितैः पञ्चबीजैरङ्गुलीषु विन्यस्याऽवशिष्टेन करयोः व्याप्य अङ्गान्यङ्गुलीषु विन्यस्य मूलेन देहे त्रिशो व्याप्य प्रणवपुटितं बीजपञ्चकं मूर्धादिषु विन्यस्याऽवशिष्टेन तत्रैव व्याप्य तथैव पञ्चवक्त्रेषु दोःपत्सन्ध्यग्रेषु कटिद्वयांसद्वयहृत्सु च प्रादक्षिण्येन न्यसित्वा पदाष्टकमष्टाधारेषु न्यसेत् । पदचतुर्दशकं चेत् चतुर्दशाधारेषु । नवकं चेत् नवाधारेषु । दशकं चेद् दशाधारेषु । मूलाधार वृषण लिङ्गमूल जठर नाभ्युदर हृदयोरो गललम्बिका भ्रूमध्य ललाटकेशान्त मूर्धानः चतुर्दशाधाराः । वृषणजठरोदरोरोवर्ज्या दशाधाराः । केशान्तवर्ज्या नवाधाराः । ललाटवर्ज्या अष्टाधाराः । बीजषट्कं पदषट्कम् । वरदेत्यन्तं सप्तममवशिष्टम् अष्टममित्यष्टपदपक्षः । नवपदपक्षे गणपतये इत्यन्तं सप्तमं वरदान्तमष्टमम् अवशिष्टं नवमम् । दशपदपक्षे सर्वजनं मे इत्यन्तं नवममवशिष्टं दशमम् । चतुर्दशपदपक्षे वरवरदेति च पदद्वयमवगन्तव्यम् । मूर्धभ्रूमध्याक्षिद्वयास्य करपत्सन्ध्यग्र गलहृत्सु वर्णन्यासः पदन्यासात् पूर्वमेव । मूर्धभ्रूमध्याक्षिद्वयास्येषु बीजपञ्चकं सर्वजनं मे वशमानय स्वाहेति अनेन सहितं न्यसेत् । तथा करपत्-

मन्दाराद्यैः कल्पकवृक्षविशेषैर्विशिष्टतरफलदैः ।
शिशिरितचतुराशेऽन्तर्बालातपचन्द्रिकाकुले च तले ॥ ५
ऐक्षवजलनिधिलहरीकणजालकवाहिना च गन्धवहेन ।
संसेविते च सुरतरुसुमनःश्रितमधुपपक्षचलनपरेण ॥ ६
रत्नमये मणिवज्रप्रवालफलपुष्पपल्लवस्य सतः ।
महतोऽधस्तादृतुभिर्युगपत्संसेवितस्य कल्पतरोः ॥ ७
सिंहमुखपादपीठगलिपिमयपद्मे त्रिषट्कोणोल्लसिते ।
आसीनस्त्वेकरदो बृहदुदरो दशभुजोऽरुणो गजवदनः ॥ ८

बीजापूरगदेक्षुकार्मुकरुजाचक्राब्जपाशोत्पल-
व्रीह्यग्रस्वविषाणरत्नकलशप्रोद्यत्कराम्भोरुहः ।
ध्येयो वल्लभया च पद्मकरयाश्लिष्टो ज्वलद्भूषया
विश्वोत्पत्तिविनाशसंस्थितिकरो विघ्नो विशिष्टार्थदः ॥ ९

करपुष्करधृतकलशस्रुतमणिमुक्ताप्रवालवर्षेण ।
अविरतधारां विकिरन् परितः साधकसमग्रसम्पत्त्यै ॥ १०
मदजललोलुपमधुकरमालां निजकर्णतालताड़नया ।
निर्वासयन् मुहुर्मुहुरमरैरसुरैश्च सेवितो युपगत् ॥ ११

अग्रेऽथ बिल्वमभितश्च रमारमेशौ
तद्दक्षिणे वटजुषौ गिरिजावृषाङ्कौ ।
पृष्ठेऽथ पिप्पलजुषौ रतिपुष्पबाणौ
सव्ये प्रियङ्गुमभितश्च महीवराहौ ॥ १२

सन्ध्यग्रेष्वपि कक्षद्वयसहृत्स्वपि जानुद्वयगुल्फद्वयनाभिष्वपि स्तनद्वयकण्ठपृष्ठ-ककुत्स्वपि । एष विभूतिन्यासः । पुनः बीजपञ्चकमेव मूर्धभ्रूमध्याक्षिवदनेषु सर्वजनमित्यादि व्यापकत्वेन न्यसेत् । रमारमेशादिकं मूर्धादिपञ्चभूतस्थानेषु नाभितत्पार्श्वकण्ठतत्पार्श्वेषु विघ्नषट्कं सशक्तिकं निधिद्वयं च स्तनद्वयाधः पुनः अश्वाख्यादिकमलिकादिषूक्तेषु स्थानेषु च । सामान्यपटलोक्तन्यासाश्च कार्या इति । गं बीजम् । श्रीं शक्तिः ॥ ४ ॥

लिपिमयपद्मे त्रिषडिति । त्रिकोणमध्ये प्रणवे गमिति साध्याख्यादियुतं लिखित्वा श्रीं ह्रीं क्लीं ग्लौं बीजैस्तत् संवेष्ट्य षट्कोणेषु बीजषट्कं तदन्तरालेषु

ध्येयौ च पद्मयुगचक्रदरैः पुरोक्तौ
पाशाङ्कुशाख्यपरशुत्रिशिखैरथाऽन्यौ ।
युग्मोत्पलेक्षुमयचापशरैस्तृतीया-
वन्त्यौ शुकाब्जकलमाग्रगदारथाङ्गैः ॥ १३

ध्येयाः षट्कोणास्त्रिषु परितः पाशाङ्कुशाभयेष्टकराः ।
सप्रमदा गणपतयो रक्ताकाराः प्रभिन्नमदविवशाः ॥ १४
अथासन्नावामोदः प्रमोदसुमुखौ च तमभितोऽस्त्रियुगे ।
पृष्ठे च दुर्मुखाख्यस्त्वमुमभितो विघ्नाविघ्नकर्तारौ ॥ १५
सव्यापसव्यभागे तस्य ध्येयौ च शङ्खपद्मनिधी ।
मौक्तिकमाणिक्याभौ वर्षन्तौ धारया धनानि सदा ॥ १६
सिद्धिसमृद्धौ चान्या कान्तिर्मदनावती मदद्रवया ।
द्राविणिवसुधाराख्ये वसुमत्यपि विघ्ननिधियुगप्रमदाः ॥ १७
ध्यात्वैवं विघ्नपतिं चत्वारिंशत्सहस्रसंयुक्तम् ।
प्रजपेल्लक्षचतुष्कं चतुःसहस्रञ्च दीक्षितो मन्त्री ॥ १८
दिनमनु सचतुश्चत्वारिंशत्संख्यं सन्तर्पयेद्विघ्नम् ।
उक्तजपान्ते मन्त्री जुहुयाच्च दशांशतोऽष्टभिर्द्रव्यैः ॥ १९
मोदकपृथुकसलाजाः सशक्तवः सेक्षुनारिकेलतिलाः ।
कदलीफलसहितानीत्यष्ट द्रव्याणि संप्रदिष्टानि ॥ २०
अनुदिनमर्चयितव्यो जपता मनुमपि च मन्त्रिणा गणपः ।
प्राक्प्रोक्तपद्मपीठे सशक्तिके सासिकामनो विधिना ॥ २१

अङ्गषट्कम् अष्टदलेषु पदाष्टकं तद्बहिर्वृत्तत्रये मातृकापाशाङ्कुशार्णान् विलिख्य तद्बहिःभूपुरद्वये आं क्रों इति लिखेदित्यर्थः ॥ ५—१३ ॥

सप्रमदा इति । सिद्धि समृद्धि कान्ति मदनावती मदद्रवा द्राविणीभिः सहिता इत्यर्थः । वसुधारावसुमत्यौ निध्योः शक्तिः ॥ १४ ॥ १५ ॥ १६ ॥ १७ ॥

दीक्षितो मन्त्रीति । चतुर्थीं परित्यज्य सम्बुद्धिस्वीकार उक्तः । मिथुन-मन्त्राणां दशांशजपश्च उक्तः । मन्त्री जुहुयादित्यपि तथा ॥ १८ ॥ १९ ॥ २० ॥

जपता मनुमपि मन्त्रिणेति । विभूतिमन्त्रजप उक्तः । पूर्वोक्तार्चनामन्त्राश्च । आसिकामनुरासनमन्त्रः । विधिनेति । इक्षुसमुद्रादियोगः ॥ २१॥२२॥२३॥२४ ॥

तीव्रा ज्वालिनी नन्दा सभोगदा कामरूपिणी चोग्रा ।
तेजोवती च स[नि]त्या संप्रोक्ता विघ्ननाशिनी नवमी ॥ २२
सर्वयुतं शक्तिपदं प्रोक्त्वा कमलासनाय नम इति च ।
आसनमन्त्रः प्रोक्तो नवशक्त्यन्ते समर्चयेदमुना ॥ २३
आद्या मिथुनैरावृतिरपरा सनिधिभिरपि च षड्विघ्नैः ।
अङ्गैरन्या मातृभिरपरेन्द्राद्यैश्च पञ्चमी पूज्या ॥ २४
दीक्षाभिषेकयुक्तः प्रजपेत् संपूजयेदिति गणेशम् ।
अभिधीयतेऽस्य च पुनर्गुर्वादेशेन मन्त्रिणो दीक्षा ॥ २५
मध्ये च दिग्दलानां चतुष्टयाग्रे प्रविन्यसेत् कलशान् ।
क्षीरद्रुबिल्वरोहिणपिप्पलफलिनीत्वगुद्भवैः क्वाथैः ॥ २६
संपूरयेद्यथावत् क्रमात् समावाह्य गणपतिमिथुनानि ।
अभ्यर्च्य चोपचारैर्हुत्वा विधिवत् पुनः समभिषिञ्चेत् ॥ २७
इति जपहुतार्चनाद्यैः सिद्धो मन्त्रेण कर्म कुर्वीत ।
अष्टद्रव्यैर्वाऽन्यैर्हुनेच्च तत्तत्प्रयोजनावाप्त्यै ॥ २८

स्वर्णाप्त्यै मधुना च गव्यपयसा गोसिद्धये सर्पिषा
लक्ष्म्यै शर्करया जुहोतु यशसे दध्ना च सर्वर्द्धये ।
अन्नैरन्नसमृद्धये च सतिलैर्द्रव्याप्तये तण्डुलै-
र्लाजाभिः पतये कुसुम्भकुसुमैः साम्बारिभिर्वाससे ॥ २९

पद्मैर्भूपतिमुत्पलैर्नृपवधूं तन्मन्त्रिणः कैरवै-
रश्वत्थादिसमिद्भिरग्रजमुखान् वर्णान् वधूः पिष्टजैः ।
पुत्तल्यादिभिरन्वहं च वशयेज्जुह्वन्नवावृष्टये
लोणैर्वृष्टिसमृद्धये च जुहुयान्मन्त्री पुनर्वेतसैः ॥ ३०

मन्त्रेणाऽथ पुराऽमुनैव चतुरावृत्त्या समातर्प्य च
श्रीशक्तिस्मरभूविनायकरतीर्नाम्नैव बीजादिकम् ।

गुर्वादेशेन मन्त्रीति । दीक्षाया असाधारण्यमाह ॥ २५ ॥
यथावत् क्रमादिति । कलशावाहनादिकम् । विधिवदित्यभिषेकक्रमम् ॥२६॥२७॥
मन्त्री पुनर्वेतसैरित्यमृतबीजयोगमाह ॥ २८ ॥ २९ ॥ ३० ॥

आमोदादिनिधिद्वयञ्च सचतुःपूर्वं चतुर्वारकं
मन्त्री तर्पणतत्परोऽभिलषितं संप्राप्नुयान्मण्डलात् ॥ ३१

बीजानन्तरञ्चतुरावृत्तितर्पणमाह—मन्त्रेणाऽथेति। मन्त्रेणेति। मूलमन्त्र उक्तः। अथ अनन्तरम्। पुरा शक्तिमन्त्रेणेत्यर्थः। चतुरावृत्त्येति जले पीठमूर्तिपूजादिपूर्वकं देवमावाह्य निवेद्यान्तानुपचारान् दत्त्वा निवेद्यकाले साष्टद्रव्यत्रिमधुररूपेणाऽमृतबीजेनाऽमृतीकृतेन पीठमन्त्रैः सकृत् सकृत् सन्तर्प्य मूलेन चतुःपूर्वं चतुर्वारं देवाय सन्तर्प्य पुनरपि मूलेन चतुर्वारं देवाय सन्तर्प्य विभूतिमन्त्रेण देवीं चतुर्वारं तर्पयेत्। एवं वक्ष्यमाणमन्त्रैरपि मूलेन देवाय चतुर्वारपूर्वकं तर्पयेदिति भावः। श्री शक्ति स्मर भू विनायक रतीरिति। श्रीबीजादिबीजचतुष्टयसंबन्धा विनायकाः स्वामिनः रतयश्च ते तथोक्ताः। रमारमेशादय इत्यर्थः। तान् नाम्नैव स्वस्वबीजादिकं चतुःपूर्वं चतुर्वारं तर्पयेत्। श्रीं रमारमेशौ तर्पयामि। ह्रीं उमामहेश्वरौ तर्पयामि। क्लीं रतिपुष्पबाणौ तर्पयामि। ग्लौं महीवराहौ तर्पयामीति मन्त्राः। तत ईशानभागे स्वबीजसम्बन्धि मिथुनतर्पणमिति सूचयितुञ्च विनायकरतिग्रहणम्। गं पुष्टिविनायकौ तर्पयामीति तन्मन्त्राङ्ग बीजदेवतातर्पणमपि चतुःपूर्वं कार्यम्। पुनरामोदादिकं निधिद्वयं च चतुःपूर्वकं चतुर्वारं सन्तर्प्य। मूलेन देवाय चतुर्वारं तर्पयेत्। एवं तर्पिते चतुर्विंशत्यधिकं शतं भवति।

अथ प्रकारान्तरेण तर्पणमुच्यते—मन्त्रेणेति। देवस्य मूलमन्त्रेणेत्यर्थः। तेन च दशधा विभज्य तर्पणीयम्। अथानन्तरम्। पुरा शरीरेण देवस्य शरीरसम्बन्धिभिः बीजापूरादिभिरित्यर्थः। बीजापूरादिरत्नकलशान्तैर्मन्त्रैरेकादशभिः बीजापूरं तर्पयामीत्याद्यैः तर्पयेदित्यर्थः। तत एकविंशन्मन्त्रा आगताः। अमुनेति। क्षिप्रमन्त्रे विघ्नादिदशनामयुतेन मूलेनेत्यर्थः। गणपत इत्यस्मात् पूर्वं तु योगः। तत एकविंशन्मन्त्रा आगताः। श्रीशक्तिस्मरभूविनायकरतीर्नाम्नैव बीजादिकमित्यष्टौ मन्त्राः कथिताः। तत एकोनचत्वारिंशन्मन्त्रा आगताः। आमोदादिनिधिद्वयं चेति। षोडशमन्त्रा उक्ताः। ततः पञ्चपञ्चाशन्मन्त्राः सिद्धाः। तैश्चतुःपूर्वं चतुर्वारं सन्तर्प्य मूलेन चतुर्वारं तर्पयेत्। आरम्भकाल एव वा मूलेन चतुर्वारं तर्पयेत्। ततश्चतुश्चत्वारिंशदधिकं चतुःशतं भवति। ततोऽवशिष्टानामावरणानामेकैकवारं सन्तर्प्य पूजाशेषं समापयेदिति।

अथवा सशक्तिकं निधिद्वयं परित्यज्य मूलं विभूतिमन्त्रं पुष्टिविनायकमन्त्रौ च स्वीकृत्य प्रकृतां संख्यां पूरयेत्। अथवा सर्वमप्येतत् स्वीकृत्य षट्सप्तत्यधिकं

अथ गजलिप्सुर्नृपतिर्गजवनमध्ये प्रसाधयेद्वारि ।
तन्निकटे सुविशालं चतुरस्रं कारयेच्च गृहवर्यम् ॥ ३२
परिवीतदृढावरणं तच्च चतुर्द्वारतोरणोल्लसितम् ।
तस्मिन्मण्डपवर्ये चतुरस्रामुन्नतां स्थलीं कृत्वा ॥ ३३
उत्तरभागे तस्याः कुण्डं रचयेद्यथा पुरा तत्र ।
चापजहरिभवमेषजचक्रप्रोक्तानथाऽक्षरान्मन्त्री ॥ ३४
ऊर्ध्वादिमेखलासु क्रमेण विलिखेन्निजेष्टसमवाप्त्यै ।
संप्रोक्तलक्षणयुतं प्रविरचयेन्मण्डलं स्थलीमध्ये ॥ ३५
आवाह्य विघ्नेश्वरमर्चयित्वा प्रागुक्तया तन्त्रविधानक्लृप्त्या ।
निवेद्य चाथो सह भक्ष्यलेह्यैः प्राज्यैश्च साज्यैरपि भोज्यजातैः ॥ ३६
आधाय वैश्वानरमत्र कुण्डे समर्च्य मन्त्रैः क्रमशः कृशानोः ।
तैरेव पूर्वं जुहुयाद्घृतेन मन्त्री समृद्ध्या च ततस्त्रिवारम् ॥ ३७
तारेण लक्ष्म्यद्रिसुतास्मरक्ष्माविघ्नेशबीजैः क्रमशोऽनुबद्धैः ।
पदत्रयेणापि च मन्त्रराजं विभज्य मन्त्री नवधा जुहोतु ॥ ३८
पुनः समस्तेन च मन्त्रवर्णसंख्यं प्रजुह्वन्नपि सर्पिषैव ।
पूर्वप्रदिष्टैर्जुहुयादथाऽष्टद्रव्यैः प्रसिक्तैर्मधुरत्रयेण ॥ ३९
सचतुश्चत्वारिंशत्सहस्रसंख्यैश्चतुःशतैश्चतुर्भिश्च ।
दशकैश्चतुर्भिरपि हुताच्चतुश्चत्वारिंशद्दिनैरतो हि ॥ ४०
करिकलभाः करिणीभिः संपाद्य[त्य]न्तेऽवटेऽत्र गणपतिना ।
प्रतिदिनमभ्यवहार्यं च विप्रान् संवर्धितस्तदाशीर्भिः ॥ ४१

चतुःशतं तर्पयेत् । मन्त्री तर्पणेति । तर्पणमन्त्रा उक्ताः ॥ ३१ ॥

वारि अवटम् । चापजेति । चापादिवृश्चिकान्तराश्यक्षराणि ऊर्ध्वमेखलायां सिंहादिकर्कटान्तराश्यक्षराणि मध्यमेखलायां मेषादिमीनान्तराश्यक्षराणि अधोमेखलायां लिखेदित्यर्थः । मन्त्रीति । तत्तद्राशिनामसंयोगः सूचितः ॥
॥ ३२ ॥ ३३ ॥ ३४ ॥ ३५ ॥

समर्च्य मन्त्रैः क्रमशः कृशानोरिति । षष्ठपटलोक्तमूलजिह्वाष्टमूर्तिमन्त्रैरित्यर्थः । मन्त्री समृद्ध्या चेति । अग्निप्रकरणोक्तसमृद्धिमन्त्रत्रयेणेत्यर्थः ॥ ३६॥३७ ॥

मन्त्री नवधेति । विभूतिमन्त्रेणाऽपि नवधा होम उक्तः ॥ ३८— ४२ ॥

तेषां मातङ्गानां दद्यात् पञ्चाशद्दक्षिणां गुरवे ।
तद्विक्रीतं वसु वा प्रसादितायाऽथ तद्दशांशं वा ॥ ४२
मिथुनानां गणपानां निध्योश्च तथाऽङ्गमातृलोकेशानाम् ।
मन्त्रैर्घृतेन हुत्वाऽभ्यर्च्य च होमं समाप्य सम्यङ्मन्त्री ॥ ४३
पुनरुद्धृत्य निवेद्यादिकं समभ्यर्च्य गणपतिं सावरणम् ।
उद्वास्य स्वे हृदये विहरेदित्यर्चनाक्रमो निर्दिष्टः ॥ ४४
प्रोक्तस्त्वेवं दशभुजमनुः संग्रहेणाऽत्र भक्तो
दीक्षां लब्ध्वा विधिवदभिजप्याथ हुत्वाऽर्चयित्वा ।
नत्वा नुत्वा दिनमनु तथा तर्पयित्वा स्वकामान्
लब्ध्वा चान्ते व्रजति मुनिभिः प्रार्थनीयं पदं तत् ॥ ४५

स्मृतिपीठः पिनाकी सानुग्रहो बिन्दुसंयुतः ।
बीजमेतत् भुवः प्रोक्तं संस्तम्भनकरं परम् ॥ ४६
च-तुरीयो विलोमेन तारादिर्बिन्दुसंयुतः ।
वैघ्नो मन्त्रो हृदन्तोऽर्चाविधौ होमे द्विठान्तकः ॥ ४७
गणकः स्यादृषिश्छन्दो निवृद्विघ्नोऽस्य देवता ।
बीजेन दीर्घयुक्तेन दण्डिनाऽङ्गक्रियेरिता ॥ ४८

रक्तो रक्ताङ्गरागांशुककुसुमयुतस्तुन्दिलश्चन्द्रमौलि-
र्नेत्रैर्युक्तस्त्रिभिर्वामनकरचरणो बीजपूरात्तनासः ।
हस्ताग्राक्लृप्तपाशाङ्कुशरदवरदो नागवक्त्रोऽहिभूषो
देवः पद्मासनो वो भवतु सुरनतो भूतये विघ्नराजः ॥ ४९

दीक्षितः प्रजपेल्लक्षचतुष्कं प्राक्समीरितैः ।
जुहुयादष्टभिर्द्रव्यैर्यथापूर्वं दशांशतः ॥ ५०
पीठे तीव्रादिभिः पद्मकर्णिकायां विनायकम् ।
आवाह्य पूजयेद्दिक्षु चतुर्ष्वपि यजेत् पुनः ॥ ५१
गणाधिपं गणेशञ्च गणनायकमेव च ।
गणक्रीडं कर्णिकायामङ्गैः किञ्जल्कसंस्थितैः ॥ ५२

मन्त्री पुनरुद्धृत्येति । तत्र तत्रापेक्षिता मन्त्रविशेषाः सूचिताः ॥४१—४६॥

वक्रतुण्डैकदंष्ट्रौ च महोदरगजाननौ ।
लम्बोदराख्यविकटौ विघ्नराड्धूम्रवर्णकौ ॥ ५३
समर्चयेन्मातृवर्गं बाह्ये लोकेश्वरानपि ।
इति प्रोक्ता संग्रहेण गाणेशीयसमर्चना ॥ ५४
नारिकेलान्वितैर्मन्त्री शक्तुलाजतिलैर्हुनेत् ।
आरभ्याच्छां प्रतिपदं चतुर्थ्यन्तं चतुःशतम् ॥ ५५
दिनशः सर्ववश्यं स्यात् सर्वकामप्रदं नृणाम् ।
तिलतण्डुलकैर्लक्ष्मीवश्यकृच्च यशस्करम् ॥ ५६
मधुरत्रयसिक्ताभिर्लाजाभिः सप्तवासरम् ।
जुहुयात् कन्यकार्थी वा कन्यका वा वरार्थिनी ॥ ५७
चतुर्थ्यां नारिकेलैस्तु होमः सद्यः श्रियावहः ।
हविषा घृतसिक्तेन सर्वकार्यार्थदो हुतः ॥ ५८
दध्यक्तलोणमुद्राभिर्हुनेन्निशि चतुर्दिनम् ।
दुष्टार्थसिद्ध्यै मतिमान् सद्यः संवादसिद्धये ॥ ५९
ईदृशं गणपं ध्यात्वा मन्त्री तोयैः सुधामयैः ।
दिनादौ दिनशस्तस्य तर्पयेन्मस्तके सुधीः ॥ ६०
चत्वारिंशच्चतुःपूर्वं तत्पूर्वं वा चतुःशतम् ।
चत्वारिंशद्दिनात्तस्य काङ्क्षिता सिद्धिरेष्यति ॥ ६१
नवनीते नवे लिख्यादनुलोमविलोमकम् ।
उदरस्थितसाध्याख्यं तद्बीजं तत्प्रवेष्टितम् ॥ ६२

बीजस्य श्रं बीजम् । गं शक्तिः ॥ ४७—५५ ॥

नारिकेलान्वितैः मन्त्रीति । शक्तियोग उक्तः ॥ ५५ ॥ ५६ ॥ ५७ ॥ ५८ ॥

मतिमानिति । विपरीतबुद्धिं पाशेन बद्ध्वा अङ्कुशेनानयन् ध्यायेत् । शक्तिबीजं च योजयेदित्युक्तम् । ईदृशमित्युक्तलक्षणमित्यर्थः । मन्त्री तोयैरिति । पीठावरणमन्त्रैः सकृत् सकृत् तर्पणमुक्तम् । मस्तके प्रथमतश्चतुर्वारं तर्पयेत् । सुधीरिति । चतुर्वारतर्पणे देवस्य बोधनप्रतिपत्तिरुक्ता ॥ ५९ ॥ ६० ॥ ६१ ॥

अनुलोमविलोमगमिति । कर्णिकायां षट्कोणमध्ये परस्परविमुखं गकारद्वयमालिख्य मध्ये बिन्दुभागयोः साध्यादिकं विलिख्य बीजैः संवेष्ट्य षट्कोणेष्व-

समीरणं प्रतिष्ठाप्य जप्त्वाऽष्टशतसंख्यकम् ।
तूष्णीं प्रभक्षयेदेतत् सप्तरात्राद्वशीकरम् ॥ ६३
अन्त्यासनोऽथ सूक्ष्मो लोहितगोऽग्निः पुनः स एव स्यात् ।
सादान्ते नायार्णौ नत्यन्तो मनुरयं स्वबीजाद्यः ॥ ६४
ऋषिदेवते तु पूर्वे छन्दस्तु विराडमुष्य संप्रोक्तम् ।
बीजेन दीर्घभाजा कथितोऽङ्गविधिः क्रमेण बिन्दुमता ॥ ६५
धृतपाशाङ्कुशकल्पलतिकास्वरदश्च बीजपूरयुतः ।
शशिशकलकलितमौलिस्त्रिलोचनोऽरुणतनुश्च गजवदनः ॥ ६६
भासुरभूषणदीप्तो बृहदुदरः पद्मविष्टरो ललितः ।
ध्येयोऽनायतदोःपत्सरसिरुहः सम्पदे सदा मनुजैः ॥ ६७
दीक्षायुक्तः प्रजपेल्लक्षं मनुमेनमथ तिलैरयुतम् ।
त्रिमधुरयुतैर्जुहुयात् पूर्वोक्तैर्वाथवाऽष्टभिर्द्रव्यैः ॥ ६८
विघ्नविनायकवीराः सशूरवरदेभवक्त्रैकरदाः ।
लम्बोदरश्च मातृङ्गात्त्र्योरन्तराथ लोकेशाः ॥ ६९
पूज्याः सितघृतपायसहवनात्सञ्जायते महालक्ष्मीः ।
केवलघृतहुतमुदितो विघ्नः सद्यो वशीकरोति जगत् ॥ ७०
एकमपि नारिकेलं सचर्मलोष्टेन्धनं हुनेन्मन्त्री ।
दिनशश्चत्वारिंशद्दिनतः स तु वाञ्छितार्थमभ्येति ॥ ७१
सपृथुकशक्तुकलाजातिलैरभीष्टार्थसिद्धये जुहुयात् ।
सापूपनारिकेलेक्षुकदलीभिस्तथा समधुराभिः ॥ ७२

षट्कं लिखित्वा केसरेषु स्वरान् दलेषु गायत्रीवर्णत्रयं बाह्ये व्यञ्जनावेष्टितं चतुरस्रहृदये भूबीजं लिखित्वा यन्त्रसामान्यमन्त्रांश्च लिखित्वा प्राणप्रतिष्ठादिकं कुर्यादित्यर्थः ॥ ६२॥६३ ॥

क्षिप्रस्य गं बीजम्। नमः शक्तिः। कर्णिकायां षट्कोणे बीजसाध्यादिकं लिखेत्। तेनैव वेष्टयेत्। केसरेषु स्वरान् क्षिप्रेति पूर्वदले प्रप्र इत्याग्नेये प्रसा इति दक्षिणे इत्यादिक्रमेण लिखित्वा तद्बहिः गायत्रीव्यञ्जनादिकं पूर्ववल्लिखेत्। एकदंष्ट्राय विद्महे वक्रतुण्डाय धीमहि तन्नो विघ्नः प्रचोदयादिति गायत्री। अस्मिन् यन्त्रे देवं पूजयेत् ॥ ६४—७० ॥

अष्टभिरेतैर्विहितो होमः सर्वार्थसाधको भवति ।
दिनशः सघृतान्नहुतो गृहयात्राप्रापको गृहस्थानाम् ॥ ७३

अन्वहमङ्घ्रामादौ गणपं सन्तर्पयेच्चतुःपूर्वम् ।
चत्वारिंशद्वारं सशुद्धजलैरिन्दिराप्तये मन्त्री ॥ ७४

समहागणपतियुक्तैर्विघ्नाद्यैर्दशभिराह्वयैर्दिनशः ।
तर्पणपूजाहुतविधिरपि वाञ्छितसिद्धिदायको भवति ॥ ७५

बिम्बादम्बुदवत् समेत्य सवितुः सोपानकै राजते-
स्तोयं तोयजविष्टरं धृतलतादन्तं सपाशाङ्कुशम् ।
नासां साध्यनृक्षे निधाय सुधया तद्रन्ध्रनिर्यातया
सिञ्चन्तं पुनरन्वहं गणपतिं स्मृत्वाऽमृतैस्तर्पयेत् ॥ ७६

प्राग्भाषितानपि विधीन् विधिवद्विदध्या-
न्मन्त्री विशेषविदथाऽन्वहमादरेण ।
एकत्र वा गणपतौ मनुजाः स्वरुच्या
नामानुरूपमनुमेनममी भजन्तु ॥ ७७

इति जपहुतपूजातर्पणैर्विघ्नराजं
प्रभजति मनुजो यस्तस्य सिद्धिर्विशाला ।
भवति सधनधान्यैः पुत्रमित्रादियुक्ता
विगतसकलविघ्ना विश्वसंवादिनी च ॥ ७८

इति श्रीप्रपञ्चसारे सप्तदशः पटलः ।

इनेमन्त्रीति । श्रीबीजादियोग उक्तः ॥ ७१ ॥ ७२ ॥ ७३ ॥

इन्दिराप्तये मन्त्रीति । इन्दिरायोगः । दशभिरिति । क्षिप्रेण सहाभिधान-दशकं भवति ॥ ७४ ॥ ७५ ॥

तर्पणप्रकारमाह—बिम्बादम्बुदवदिति ॥ ७६ ॥

विधिवद् विदध्यादिति । महागणपतिप्रकरणोक्तध्यानादिपूर्वकं विदध्यादि-त्यर्थः । मन्त्रीति । अत्रापि बीजषट्कादियोग उक्तः । विशेषविदिति । कार्यानुगुणबीजादित्वमिहोक्तम् । मन्त्रान्तरेऽपि कुर्यादित्याह—एकत्र वेति । अनेकमन्त्र कथनतात्पर्यमाह—नामानुरूपेति ॥ ७७ ॥ ७८ ॥

इति श्रीपद्मपादाचार्यकृते प्रपञ्चसारविवरणे सप्तदशः पटलः ।

अष्टादशः पटलः ।

अथ मन्मथमन्त्रविधिं विधिना कथयामि सहोमविधिं सजपम् ।
मथनस्य पुरामपि मोहकरं व्यथिताखिलसिद्धसुरादिगणम् ॥ १
अजकलाप्रथमावनिशान्तिभिर्युतसुधाकरखण्डविकाशिभिः ।
निगदितो मनुरेष मनोभुवः सकलधर्मसुखार्थयशोवहः ॥ २

ऋष्यादिकाश्च सम्मोहनगायत्रीमनोभुवः प्रोक्ताः ।
बीजेन दीर्घभाजा विहितान्यङ्गान्यमुष्य जातियुजा ॥ ३

अरुणमरुणवासोमाल्यदामाङ्गरागं
स्वकरकलितपाशं साङ्कुशास्त्रेषुचापम् ।
मणिमयमुकुटाद्यैर्दीप्तमाकल्पजाते-
रुणनलिनसंस्थं चिन्तयेदङ्गयोनिम् ॥ ४

तरणिलक्षममुं मनुमादरात् समभिजप्य हुनेच्च दशांशतः ।
तदनु किंशुकजैः प्रसवैः शुभैस्त्रिमधुरार्द्रतरैर्निजसिद्धये ॥ ५

मोहनी क्षोभणी त्रासी स्तम्भन्याकर्षणी तथा ।
द्राविण्याह्लादिनी क्लिन्ना क्लेदिनी स्मरशक्तयः ॥ ६
आशान्तिद्वयवामश्रुतिसर्गान् द्रयुगकलबलैश्च ससैः ।
शोषणमोहनसन्दीपनतापनमादनान् यजेत् क्रमशः ॥ ७

अनङ्गरूपा सानङ्गमदनाऽनङ्गमन्मथा ।
अनङ्गकुसुमाऽनङ्गकुसुमातुरसंज्ञका ॥ ८
अनङ्गशिशिराऽनङ्गमेखलाऽनङ्गदीपिका ।
अङ्गाशापालयोर्मध्ये बाणानङ्गाद्वतीर्यजेत् ॥ ९

आलिख्यात् कर्णिकायामनलपुरयुगे मारबीजं ससाध्यं
तद्रन्ध्रेष्वङ्गषट्कं बहिरपि गुणशो मारगायत्रिवर्णान् ।

पूर्वमन्त्रे प्रस्तुतस्य कामप्रधानत्वेन च गतमन्त्रसदृशस्य काममन्त्रस्य विधिं वक्तुमारमते—अथ मन्मथेति ॥ १ ॥

क्लीं बीजम् । ह्रीं शक्तिः ॥ २—१५ ॥

मालामन्त्रं दलाग्रेष्वपि गुहमुखशः पार्थिवास्त्रिष्वनङ्गं
कुर्याद्यन्त्रं तदेतद्भुवनमपि वशे का कथा मानवेषु ॥ १०

प्रोक्त्वाऽथ कामदेवाय विद्महे तदनु पुष्पबाणाय ।
तथा धीमह्यन्ते तन्नोऽनङ्गः प्रचोदयाच्च गायत्री ॥ ११

नत्यन्ते कामदेवाय चोक्त्वा सर्वजनं वदेत् ।
प्रियायेति तथा सर्वजनसंमोहनाय च ॥ १२

दीप्यायित्वा ज्वलपदं प्रज्वलश्च प्रभाषयेत् ।
पुनः सर्वजनस्येति हृदयं मम चेत्यथ ॥ १३

वशमुक्त्वा कुरु वीप्सा कथयेद्वह्निवल्लभाम् ।
प्रोक्तो मदनमन्त्रोऽष्टचत्वारिंशद्भिरक्षरैः ॥ १४

इति यन्त्रकृप्तकलशो बहुशः कतमं नरं न परिमोहयति ।
प्रमदावनीश्वरसभानगरादिकमीश्वरानपि वशीकुरुते ॥ १५

वक्ष्ये विधानमन्यन्मनोभवस्याऽथ मोहनं जगतः ।
येनार्चितः स देवो वाञ्छितमखिलं करोति मन्त्रविदाम् ॥ १६

अमृतोद्भवो मकरकेतनः सङ्कल्पजन्माह्वयाच्चतरूपौ ।
इक्षुधनुर्धरपुष्पशराख्यावङ्गानि च वह्निजायान्तानि ॥ १७

अरुणतरवसनमाल्यानुलेपनाभरणमिक्षुशरासनधरम् ।
न्यस्तशरबीजदेहो ध्यायेदात्मानमङ्गजं रुचिरम् ॥ १८

अङ्गबाणावृतेरूर्ध्वं पूज्याः षोडश शक्तयः ।
युवतिर्विप्रलब्धा च ज्योत्स्ना सुभ्रूर्मदद्रवा ॥ १९

सुरता वारुणी लोला कान्तिः सौदामिनी तथा ।
कामच्छत्रा चन्द्रलेखा शुकी च मदनाह्वया ॥ २०

योनिर्मायावती चेति शक्तयः स्युर्मनोभुवः ।
शोको मोहो विलासश्च विभ्रमो मदनातुरः ॥ २१

अपत्रपो युवा कामी चूतपुष्पो रतिप्रियः ।
ग्रीष्मस्तपान्त ऊर्जश्च हेमन्तः शिशिरो मदः ॥ २२

करोति मन्त्रविदामिति । इक्लीमिति मन्त्र उक्तः ॥ १६—२६ ॥

चतुर्थ्यामावृतौ पूज्याः स्युर्मारपरिचारकाः ।
परभृत्सारसौ चैव शुकमेघाह्वयौ तथा ॥ २३

अपाङ्गभ्रूविलासौ च हावभावौ स्मरप्रियाः ।
माधवी मालती चैव हरिणाक्षी मदोत्कटा ।
एताश्चामरहस्ताः स्युः पूज्याः कोणेषु संस्थिताः ॥ २४

हृल्लेखया स्वनाम्ना च शक्त्यादीनां समर्चनम् ।
इन्द्राद्यैः सप्तमी पूज्या स्मरार्चाविधिरीदृशः ॥ २५

मदनविधानमितीत्थं प्रोक्तं योऽनेन पूजयेद्विधिना ।
स तु सकललोकपूज्यो भवेन्मनोज्ञश्च मन्दिरं लक्ष्म्याः ॥ २६

विलसदहङ्कारतनुर्मनःशिवो विभ्रमास्पदीभूतः ।
बुद्धिशरीरां नारीं नरः सदा चित्तयोनिमधिगच्छेत् ॥ २७

इति मदनयोगक्लृप्त्या यो रमयेन्नित्यशो निजां वनिताम् ।
स तु भुक्तिमुक्तिगामी वनिताजनहृदयमोहनो भवति ॥ २८

आत्मानं मदनं ध्यायेदाशुशुक्षणिरूपकम् ।
तद्बीजाग्रं शिवज्वालातनुं तन्वीतनुं तथा ॥ २९

सुधामयीञ्च तद्योनिं नवनीतमयीं स्मरेत् ।
संगच्छेच्च शिवज्वालालीढं तद्धृदयादिकम् ॥ ३०

विलसदहङ्कारतनुरिति । समनीपर्यन्तं व्याप्याहङ्कारतनुः समनीस्थक्रियाशक्त्यात्मकसूर्यशरीरस्थ इत्यर्थः । मनोऽध्यात्ममवस्थितं परिच्छिन्नं शिवो लिङ्गं यस्य स तथोक्तः । तात्कालिकं शिवं विशिनष्टि—विभ्रमेति । विविधं भ्रमणं विभ्रमः । समन्यामिव ज्ञानशक्त्यात्मकः सोमांशः पत्न्याः शरीरं कल्पनीयमित्याह—बुद्धीति । चित्ताध्यात्मपरिच्छिन्नं योनिर्यस्या सा तथोक्ता । तामधिगच्छेदिति । अधोऽपहासं कुर्यादित्यर्थः ॥ २७ ॥

एवं विदुषोऽधोऽपहासकर्तुः फलमाह—इतीति ॥ २८ ॥

अहङ्कारशब्देनाऽग्न्यात्मा सूर्यो विवक्षित इत्येतदाह—आत्मानमिति । मदनं मदनबीजात्मकमित्यर्थः । मदनाकारमिति चार्थः । तद्बीजाग्रं मदनबीजाग्रं बिन्दुरूपं शिवज्वालातनुं लिङ्गलक्षणज्वालाशरीरं ध्यायेत् । तन्वीतनुं पत्नीशरीरम् । सुधामयीं चन्द्रमयीं ध्यायेत् । शिवज्वालालीढं तदधृदयादिकं यथा

आलिङ्गेदग्निसंस्पर्शद्रुतं तद्रूपकामृतम् ।
रसनाशिखयाकर्षेत् तद्दन्तरसनामृतम् ।
कुसुमास्त्रधिया बाहौ स्पृशेत् कररुहैरपि ॥ ३१
हानिं न कुर्याज्जीवस्य मन्त्री विशदमानसः ।
रतावधोऽधोमध्योर्ध्वक्रमेणैवं समाहितः ॥ ३२
निजां प्रियां भजेदेवं सा मारशरविह्वला ।
छायेवाऽनुगता तस्य भवेदपि भवान्तरे ॥ ३३
साध्याख्याकामवर्णैः प्रतिपुटितलसत्कर्णिकं पत्रराज-
त्तारर्त्विक्पञ्चजाष्टादशसमिदृतुगण्डान्तगान्ताक्षराढ्यम् ।
आशाशूलाङ्कितं तद्विपतिरिपुदले सम्यगालिख्य सैरं
मारं जाप्याऽस्य यामाशयति वशगता सा भवेत् सद्य एव ॥ ३४
हंसारूढो मदनस्त्रैलोक्यक्षोभको भवेदाशु ।
द्यु[ह]युतो रञ्जनकृत् स्याज्जीवोपेतस्तथाऽऽयुषि शस्तः ॥ ३५
तारयुजा त्वमुनाऽग्नौ हुत्वा सम्पातितेन चाज्येन ।
सम्भोजयेत् पतिं स्वं वनिता स नितान्तरञ्जितो भवति ॥ ३६

भवति तथा संगच्छेदिति । क्रियाविशेषणमेतत् ॥ २९ ॥ ३० ॥

आलिङ्गेदग्निसंस्पर्शद्रुतं तद्रूपकामृतमिति । स्वलिङ्गाग्निसंस्पर्शेन द्रुतं द्रवीभूतं तत्तद्रूपकममृतं यथा भवति तथाऽऽलिङ्गेदित्यर्थः ॥ ३१ ॥

हानिं न कुर्याज्जीवस्य इति । सहसा रेतोविसर्गं न कुर्यादित्यर्थः । तदुपायं मन्त्रध्यानं च सूचयति—मन्त्री विशदमानस इति । सोष्मणो घोषवतो नादवतो ओंकारस्य बिन्द्वाद्युन्मन्यन्तमात्रायुतस्योच्चारणमुपाय इत्यर्थः । ऊरु-मध्यमातिप्रमाणलिङ्गसाध्या रतयोऽधोमध्यमोर्ध्वरतय इत्यवगन्तव्यम् ॥ ३२॥३३ ॥

प्रयोगयन्त्रमाह—साध्याख्येति । तारः ईकारः । ऋत्विक् षोडशस्वरः । पञ्चः पञ्चदशस्वरः । जाष्टादशो मकारः । समिदेकविंशवर्णः ङकारः । ऋतुः षष्ठस्वरः । गण्डान्त एकारः । गान्तो घकारः । एतान् पत्रेषु लिखेत् । आशाशूलाङ्कित-मिति । पत्राग्रेषु त्रिशूलान् रचयेदित्यर्थः । सम्यगिति । यन्त्रहृदयादिकं सूचितम् ॥ ३४ ॥ ३५ ॥

तारयुजेति । ईकार एव भवति ॥ ३६ ॥ ३७ ॥ ३८ ॥

दध्यक्ताभिर्जुहुयाल्लाजाभिः कन्यकां समाकाङ्क्षन् ।
कन्याऽपि वरं लभते विधिना नित्यानुरक्तममुनैव ॥ ३७

अभिनवैः सुमनोभिरशोकजैर्दधियुतैर्विहिता हवनक्रिया ।
परमवश्यकरी परिकाङ्क्षितामभिवहेदचिरादिव कन्यकाम् ॥ ३८

अभीष्टदायी स्मरणादपि स्मरस्तथा जपादर्चनया विशेषतः ।
प्रसादतोऽस्याखिललोकवर्तिनश्चिराय वश्याश्च भवन्ति मन्त्रिणः ॥ ३९

क्रन्दामध्यगताः षायगोव्यर्णा यल्लमध्यगाः ।
गोपीजनवकाराः स्युर्भाय स्वाहा स्मरादिकाः ॥ ४०

ऋषिश्च नारदोऽस्य स्याद्गायत्रं छन्द उच्यते ।
मन्त्रस्य देवता कृष्णस्तदङ्गविधिरुच्यते ॥ ४१

मूलमन्त्रचतुर्वर्णचतुष्केण द्विकेन च ।
प्रोक्तान्यङ्गानि भूयोऽमुं चिन्तयेद्देवकीसुतम् ॥ ४२

अव्यान्मीलत्कलापद्युतिरहिरिपुपिच्छोल्लसत्केशजालो
गोपीनेत्रोत्पलाराधितललितवपुर्गोपगोवृन्दवीतः ।
श्रीमद्वक्त्रारविन्दप्रतिहसितशशाङ्काकृतिः पीतवासा
देवोऽसौ वेणुवाद्यक्षपितजनधृतिर्देवकीनन्दनो वः ॥ ४३

अयुतद्वितयावधिर्जपः स्यादरुणैरम्बुरुहैर्हुनेद्दशांशम् ।
मुरजिद्विहिते तु पीठवर्ये दिनशो नन्दसुतः समर्चनीयः ॥ ४४

अङ्गाशेड्वज्राद्यैः परिपूज्य च पायसेन सुसितेन ।
हैयङ्गवीनकदलीफलदधिभिः प्रीणयेच्च गोविन्दम् ॥ ४५

जुहुयाद्दुग्धहविर्भिर्विमलैः सर्पिः सितोपलोपेतैः ।
इष्टां तुष्टो लक्ष्मीं समावहेत् सद्य एव गोविन्दः ॥ ४६

बालं नीलाम्बुदाभं नवमणिविरणत्किङ्किणीजालबद्ध-
श्रोणीजङ्घान्तयुग्मं विपुलरुरुनखप्रोल्लसत्कण्ठभूषम् ।
फुल्लाम्भोजाभवक्त्रं हतशकटपतत्पूतनाद्यं प्रसन्नं
गोविन्दं वन्दितेन्द्राद्यमरवरमजं पूजयेद्वासरादौ ॥ ४७

मन्त्रिण इति । अग्नियोग उक्तः ॥ ३८ ॥

स्मरानुविद्धं कामपितुः कृष्णस्य मन्त्रमाह—क्रन्देति । क्लीं बीजम् ।

वन्द्यं देवैर्मुकुन्दं विकसितकरविन्दाभमिन्दीवराक्षं
गोगोपीवृन्दवीतं जितरिपुनिवहं कुन्दमन्दारहासम् ।
नीलग्रीवाग्रपिच्छाकलनसुविलसत्कुन्तलं भानुमन्तं
देवं पीताम्बराढ्यं यजतु च दिनशो मध्यमेऽह्नो रमायै ॥ ४८

विक्रान्त्या ध्वस्तवैरिव्रजमजितमपास्तावनीभारमाद्यै-
रावीतं नारदाद्यैर्मुनिभिरनुदिनं तत्त्वनिर्णीतिहेतोः ।
सायाह्ने निर्मलं तं निरुपममजरं पूजयेन्नीलभासं
मन्त्री विश्वोदयस्थित्यपहरणपरं मुक्तिदं वासुदेवम् ॥ ४९

त्रिकालमेवं परिचिन्त्य शार्ङ्गिणं प्रपूजयेद्यो मनुजो महामनाः ।
स धर्ममर्थं ससुखं श्रियं परामवाप्य देहापदि मुक्तिमाप्नुयात् ॥ ५०

ग्रामं गच्छन्नगरमपि वा मन्त्रजापी मनुष्यो
देवेशं तं मुखमनु मुहुस्तर्पयेद्दुग्धबुद्ध्या ।
शुद्धैस्तोयैः स तु बहुरसोपेतमाहारजातं
दद्यान्नित्यं प्रचुरधनधान्यांशुकाद्यैर्मुकुन्दः ॥ ५१

भिक्षावृत्तिर्दिनमनु तमेवं विचिन्त्यात्मरूपं
गोपस्त्रीभ्यो मुहुरपहरन्तं मनोभिः सहैव ।
लीलावृत्त्या ललितललितैश्चेष्टितैर्दुग्धसर्पि-
र्दध्यन्नाद्यं स पुनरमितामेति भिक्षां गृहेभ्यः ॥ ५२

ध्यानी मन्त्री मन्त्रजापी च नित्यं यद्यद्वाञ्छन् यत्र यत्र प्रयाति ।
तत्तल्लब्ध्वा तत्र तत्र प्रकामं प्रीतः क्रीडेद्देववन्मानुषेषु ॥ ५३

एवं देवं पूजयन्मन्त्रमेनं जप्यान्मन्त्री सर्वलोकप्रियः स्यात् ।
इष्टान् कामान् प्राप्य सम्पन्नवृत्तिर्नित्यं शुद्धं तत्परं धाम भूयात् ॥ ५४

इति श्रीप्रपञ्चसारे अष्टादशः पटलः ।

स्पष्टा ग्रन्थिः ॥ ४०॥४१॥४२॥४३॥४४॥४५॥४६॥४७॥४८ ॥

मन्त्री विश्वेति । प्रणवपुटितत्वमुक्तम् ॥ ४९॥५०॥५१॥५२ ॥

ध्यानी मन्त्रीति । प्रयोगानुसारेण ध्यानभेदा मन्त्रभेदाश्चोक्ताः ॥ ५३ ॥

मन्त्री सर्वलोकेति । त्रिपुटापुटितत्वमुक्तमिति ॥ ५४ ॥

इति श्रीपद्मपादाचार्यकृते प्रपञ्चसारविवरणे अष्टादशः पटलः ।

एकोनविंशः पटलः ।

अथ प्रणवसंज्ञकं प्रतिवदामि मन्त्रं परं
सजापमपि सार्चनं सहुतक्लृप्ति सोपासनम् ।
अशेषदुरितापहं विविधकामकल्पद्रुमं
विमुक्तिफलसिद्धिदं विमलयोगिसंसेवितम् ॥ १

आद्यः स्वरः समेतोऽमरेण सधसप्तमार्णबिन्दुयुतः ।
प्रोक्तः स्यात्प्रणवमनुस्त्रिमात्रकः सर्वमन्त्रसमवायी ॥ २

मन्त्रस्याऽस्य मुनिः प्रजापतिरथ छन्दश्च देव्यादिका
गायत्री गदिता जगत्सु परमात्माख्यस्तथा देवता ।

कामप्रधानं मन्त्रमभिधाय मोक्षप्रधानं मन्त्रमाह—अथ प्रणवेति। परत्वमुपपादयन् विनियोगमाह—अशेषेति। ह्रस्वस्य पापक्षये विनियोगः। स च मकारान्तः। तत्र च केवलाग्निशिखावत् ध्यानम्। स एव ह्रस्वः। कामप्रदो भवति। दीपशिखामध्ये तं तं काममम्मृतेनाभिषिञ्चतः स एव त्र्यक्षरात्मको ह्रस्वो मोक्षप्रदोऽपि भवति। समन्युन्मनीपरलक्षणसाक्ष्यसाक्षिब्रह्मार्थत्वे दीर्घप्लुतयोरेवमेव सर्वार्थत्वमगन्तव्यम्। अकारोकारमकारबिन्दुनादान्तो दीर्घः पूर्ववत् पापक्षयकाममोक्षार्थत्वे ध्यानभेदोऽवगन्तव्यः। मकारान्तः समनीवाचकः बिन्दुः साक्षिवाचकः नादो ब्रह्मवाचक इति मोक्षहेतुत्वे स्थितिः। शक्तिशान्तौ प्लुतिः। मकारान्तः समनीवाचकः। बिन्दुनादौ साक्षिवाचकौ शक्तिशान्तौ ब्रह्मण इति मोक्षार्थत्वे प्रतिपत्तिः। अस्य मन्त्रस्य मोक्षप्रधानत्वेन तद्धेतुत्वमुपपादयति—विमलेति ॥ १ ॥

बिन्दुयुत इति। नादादेरपि उपलक्षणार्थः। त्रयीमात्रसिद्धः प्रणवः त्रिमात्रक इत्युक्तः। तस्मिन् पक्षे तिसृष्वेवाऽवशिष्टमात्रान्तर्भावो ज्ञातव्यः। सर्वमन्त्रसमवायीति। सर्वमन्त्राधारत्वं वदन् मन्त्रन्यासमाह। अं अं नमो ब्रह्मणे नमः। आं उं नमो विष्णवे नमः। इं मं नमः शिवाय नमः। ईं अं नमो ब्रह्मणे नमः इत्यादि क्षकारान्तमेवं द्रष्टव्यम्। पुनरेवमेवाऽष्टाक्षरैः द्वादशाक्षरैरन्यैश्च मन्त्रैः संयोज्य मातृकास्थान एव मन्त्रन्यासः कार्यः। अं बीजम्। उं शक्तिः ॥ २ ॥

अक्लीबैर्युगमध्यगध्रुवयुतैरङ्गानि कुर्यात् स्वरै-
र्मन्त्री जातियुतैश्च सत्यरहितैर्वा व्याहृतीभिः क्रमात् ॥ ३
विष्णुं भास्वत्किरीटाङ्गदवलययुगाकल्पहारोदराङ्घ्रि-
श्रोणीभूषं सवक्षोमणिमकरमहाकुण्डलामण्डितांसम् ।
हस्तोद्यच्चक्रशङ्खाम्बुजगदममलं पीतकौशेयमाशा-
विद्योतद्भासमुद्यद्दिनकरसदृशं पद्मसंस्थं नमामि ॥ ४
दीक्षितो मनुमिमं शतलक्षं प्रजपेत्प्रतिहुनेच्च दशांशम् ।
पायसैर्घृतयुतैश्च तदन्ते विप्रभूरुहभवाः समिधो वा ॥ ५
सर्पिःपायसशालीतिलसमिदाज्यैरनेन यो जुहुयात् ।
ऐहिकपारत्रिकमपि स तु लभते वाञ्छितं फलं न चिरात् ॥ ६

अभ्यर्च्य वैष्णवमथो विधिनैव पीठ-
मावाह्य तत्र सकलार्थकरं मुकुन्दम् ।
अङ्गैः समूर्तियुगशक्तियुगैः सुरेन्द्र-
वज्रादिकैर्यजतु मन्त्रितमः क्रमेण ॥ ७
वासुदेवः सङ्कर्षणः प्रद्युम्नश्चाऽनिरुद्धकः ।
स्फटिकस्वर्णदूर्वेन्द्रनीलाकाराश्च वर्णतः ॥ ८
चतुर्भुजाश्चक्रशङ्खगदापङ्कजधारिणः ।
किरीटकेयूरिणश्च पीताम्बरधरा अपि ॥ ९
सशान्ती श्रीसरस्वत्यौ रतिश्चास्त्रिदलाश्रिताः ।
अच्छपद्मरजोदुग्धदूर्वावर्णाः स्वलङ्कृताः ॥ १०
आत्मान्तरात्मपरमज्ञानात्मानस्तु मूर्तयः ।
निवृत्तिश्च प्रतिष्ठाख्या विद्या शान्तिश्च शक्तयः ॥ ११
ज्वलज्ज्वालारुचः प्रोक्ता आत्माद्या मूर्तिशक्तयः ।
इति पञ्चावरणकं विधानं प्रणवोद्भवम् ॥ १२

स्वरैर्मन्त्रीति न्यासविशेषैः मन्त्रात्मा सन्नित्यर्थः । सत्यरहितैर्वा व्याहृतिभि-
रिति । वाशब्देन सत्यसहितैर्वा व्याहृतिभिरिति पञ्चाङ्गपक्षः सूचितः ॥३॥४॥५॥६॥
मन्त्रितमः क्रमेणेत्यावाहनादिमन्त्रश्च इत्यर्थः ॥ ७॥८॥९॥१०॥११॥१२ ॥

इत्थं मन्त्री तारमनुं जापहुतार्चा-
भेदैरङ्गीकृत्य च युञ्ज्यादपि योगान् ।
यैः संलब्ध्वा चेह समग्रां श्रियमन्ते
शुद्धं विष्णोर्धाम परं प्राप्नुयति योगी ॥ १३

करपादमुखादिविहीनमनारतदृश्यमनन्यगमात्मपदम् ।
यमिहात्मनि पश्यति तत्त्वविदस्तमिमं किल योगमिति ब्रुवते ॥ १४
योगाग्निदूषणपरं त्वथ कामकोपलोभप्रमोहमदमत्सरतेति षट्कम् ।
वैरं जयेत्सपदि योगविदेनमङ्गैर्योगस्य धीरमतिरष्टभिरिष्टदैश्च ॥ १५

यमनियमासनपवनायामाः प्रत्याहृतिश्च धारणया ।
ध्यानञ्चापि समाधिः प्रोक्तान्यङ्गानि योगयोग्यानि ॥ १६
सत्यमहिंसा समता धृतिरस्तेयं क्षमाऽऽर्जवञ्च तथा ।
वैराग्यमिति यमः स्यात् स्वाध्यायतपोऽर्चनाव्रतानि तथा ॥ १७
सन्तोषश्च सशौचो नियमः स्यादासनञ्च पञ्चविधम् ।
पद्मस्वस्तिकभद्रकवज्रकवीराह्वयाः क्रमात्तदपि ॥ १८
रेचकपूरककुम्भकभेदात्त्रिविधः प्रभञ्जनायामः ।
मुञ्चेद्दक्षिणयाऽनिलमथानयेद्वामया च मध्यगया ॥ १९

इत्थं मन्त्रीति । वासुदेवादिद्वादशाक्षराण्युक्तानि । अथवा बिन्दुनादशक्त्यादियुतस्य प्रणवस्य योगशेषत्वमुक्तम् । जपभेदा वाचिकादयः । बाह्याध्यात्मिकभेदात् हुतार्चनयोर्भेदः । योगप्रयोजनमाह—यैरिति ॥ १३॥१४ ॥

स्वशाखाजपः स्वाध्यायः । पद्मस्वस्तिकेति ।

ऊर्वोरुपरि विन्यस्य सम्यक् पादतले उभे ।
अङ्गुष्ठौ च निबध्नीयाद्धस्ताभ्यां व्यत्क्रमेण तु ॥ इदं पद्मासनम् ।
जानूर्वोरन्तरा सम्यक् कृत्वा पादतले उभे ।
ऋजुकायो विशेदेतदासनं स्वस्तिकं विदुः ॥
सीवन्याः पार्श्वयोर्न्यस्येत् गुल्फयुग्मं सुनिश्चलम् ।
वृषणाधः पार्श्वपादौ पाणिभ्यां परिबन्धयेत् ॥ इदं भद्रासनम् ।
ऊर्वोः पादौ क्रमान्न्यस्येत् जान्वोः प्रत्यङ्मुखाङ्गुलिः ।
करौ निदध्यादाख्यातं वज्रासनमनुत्तमम् ॥

संस्थापयेच्च नाड्येत्येवं प्रोक्तानि रेचकादीनि ।
षोडशतद्द्विद्विगुणचतुःषष्टिमात्रकाणि तानि च क्रमशः ॥ २०
चित्तात्मैक्यधृतस्य प्राणस्य स्यात् संहृतिः स्थानात् ।
प्रत्याहारो ज्ञेयश्चैतन्ययुतस्य सम्यगनिलस्य ॥ २१
स्थानस्थापनकर्म प्रोक्ता स्याद्धारणेति तत्त्वज्ञैः ।
यो मनसि देवताया भावः स्यादस्य मन्त्रिणः सम्यक् ॥ २२
संस्थापयेच्च तत्रेत्येवं ध्यानं विदन्ति तत्त्वविदः ।
सत्तामात्रं शुद्धं नित्यमपि निरञ्जनञ्च यत्प्रोक्तम् ॥ २३
तत्प्रविचिन्त्य च तस्मिंश्चित्तलयः स्यात् समाधिरुद्दिष्टः ।
अष्टाङ्गैरिति कथितैः पुनराशु निगृह्यतेऽरिरात्मविदा ॥ २४
अथवा शोषणदाहनप्लावनभेदेन शोधिते देहे ।
पञ्चाशद्भिर्मात्राभेदैर्विधिवत् समायमेत्प्राणान् ॥ २५
पञ्चाशदात्मकोऽपि च कलाप्रभेदेन तार उद्दिष्टः ।
तावन्मात्रायमनात्कलाश्च विधृता भवन्ति तत्त्वविदा ॥ २६

एकं पादमधः कृत्वा विन्यस्योरौ तथेतरम् ।
ऋजुकायो विशेद्योगी वीरासनमुदाहृतम् ॥ १५—२० ॥

चैतन्ययुतस्येति । चैतन्यशब्देन पूर्वोक्तौ चित्तात्मानावुच्येते ॥ २१ ॥

अस्य मन्त्रिण इति । समन्त्रकं ध्यानमुक्तम् ॥ २२ ॥

संस्थापयेदिति । निर्मन्त्रकं ध्यानमुक्तम् ॥ २३ ॥

तत् प्रविचिन्त्येति । संप्रज्ञातसमाधिरनायासेन वृत्तिसातत्यलक्षण उक्तः । सायाससातत्यं तु ध्यानमाहुः । तस्मिंश्चित्तलय इत्यसंप्रज्ञातसमाधिरुक्तः ॥ २४ ॥

भूतशुद्ध्यर्थे प्राणायामे पक्षान्तरं दर्शयति—अथवेति । पूर्वोक्तप्राणायामेनापि भूतशुद्धिर्भवति । तत्स्थरेचकादीनां सृष्टिसंहारस्वात्मस्थितिरूपत्वात् । भूतशुद्ध्यनन्तरं संग्रहेण सकलीकरणप्रकारमाह—पञ्चाशद्भिरिति । विधिवदिति । अकारादित्रयं प्रत्येकं दशमात्रं धारयेत् । बिन्दुं चतुर्मात्रम् । नादं षोडशमात्रमित्यर्थः । तत्र बिन्दुनादावर्तनार्थं तदन्तं प्रणवमावर्तयेत् ॥ २५ ॥

पञ्चाशन्मात्राधारणे प्रतिपत्तिमाह—पञ्चाशदात्मक इति । तत्त्वविदा तत्त्वसंख्यायमनात् तत्त्वानि च विधृतानि भवन्तीति सूचितम् । तत्त्वधारणायां

पूर्वमिडाया वदने विचिन्तयेद्धूम्रमानिलं बीजम् ।
तेनागतेन देहं प्रशोषयेत् सान्तराधिकरचरणम् ॥ २७

पिङ्गलया प्रतिमुञ्चेत्तथैव कार्शानवेन रक्तरुचा ।
प्रतिदह्य पूर्वविधिना मुञ्चेन्नैशाकरेण सुसितेन ॥ २८

संपूरयेत् सुधामयजलशीकरवर्षिणा तनुं सकलाम् ।
निर्माय मानसेन च परिपूर्णमनाश्चिरं भूयात् ॥ २९

सुजीर्णमितभोजनः सुखसमाप्तनिद्रादिकः
सुशुद्धतलसद्गृहे विरहिते च शीतादिभिः ।
पटाजिनकुशोत्तरे सुविशदे च मृद्वासने
निमीलितविलोचनः प्रतिविशेत्सुखं प्राङ्मुखः ॥ ३०

प्रसारितं वामकरं निजाङ्के निधाय तस्योपरि दक्षिणञ्च ।
ऋजुः प्रसन्नोऽवहितेन्द्रियः सन्नाधारमत्यन्तसमं स्मरेत् स्वम् ॥ ३१

तन्मध्यगतं प्रणवं प्रणवस्थं बिन्दुमपि च बिन्दुगतम् ।
नादं विचिन्त्य तारं यथावदुच्चार्य तन्नयेत् सुषुम्नान्तम् ॥ ३२

तन्मध्यगतं शुद्धं शब्दब्रह्माऽतिसूक्ष्मतन्तुनिभम् ।
तेजः स्मरेच्च तारात्मकमपि मूलं चराचरस्य सदा ॥ ३३

पृथिव्यादिसंबन्धतत्त्वसंख्यानुसारेण अकारादिकमावर्तनीयम् ॥ २६ ॥

शोषणादिप्रकारमाह—पूर्वमिति। तेनागतेनेति। नाभिगतवायुमण्डलं प्राप्तेनेत्यर्थः ॥ २७ ॥

तथैव कार्शानवेनेति। पिङ्गलाद्वारेण हृदयदेशस्थाग्निमण्डलं प्राप्तेनेत्यर्थः।

एवं कुक्षिमध्यगतं महापातकपञ्चाङ्गं पातकोपाङ्गसंयुतम् उपपातकरोमाणं कृष्णवर्णं पापपुरुषं स्वतनुं वा संशोष्य संदह्य वंकारेण प्लावनं कार्यमित्याह—नैशाकरेणेति। इडामार्गेण द्वादशान्तस्थामृतमण्डलेन पूरककाले बीजस्य मण्डलस्य वं बीजस्यैक्यं सञ्चिन्त्य कुम्भककाले प्लावयेदित्यर्थः ॥ २८ ॥ २९ ॥

योगप्रयोगेऽवस्थादेशादिनियममाह—सुजीर्णेति ॥ ३० ॥ ३१ ॥

प्रणवस्थं बिन्दुमिति। दीपशिखाकारं बिन्दुं नादं च तत्प्रभाकारं संचिन्त्येत्यर्थः। यथावदुच्चार्येति। अलिविरुतिवत् उन्मन्यन्तमुच्चार्य इत्यर्थः। सुषुम्नान्तं सुषुम्नाग्रं मध्यं वा सर्वथाप्युत्तरश्लोकः ॥ ३२ ॥

ॐकारो गुणबीजं प्रणवस्तारो ध्रुवश्च वेदादिः ।
आदिरुमध्यो मपरो नामान्यस्य त्रिमात्रकश्च तथा ॥ ३४
अस्य तु वेदादित्वात् सर्वमनूनां प्रयुज्यतेऽथादौ ।
योनिश्च सर्वदेहे भवति च स च ब्रह्म सर्वसंवादः ॥ ३५
ऋक् च तदाद्यादिः स्यात्तन्मध्यान्तं यजुश्च मान्तादिः ।
सामापि तस्य भेदा बहवः प्रोक्ता हि वेदलोकेषु ॥ ३६

सुषुम्नामध्यगतस्य प्रणवस्य ध्यानमाह—तन्मध्येति ॥ ३३ ॥

इदानीं प्रणवविभूतिं वदन्नामन्यासं प्रणवपुटितविन्यासानन्तरं प्रणवपुटितलिपिन्यासस्थान एव विधेयमाह—ओंकार इति । ॐकारादीनि दश नामानि । तत्र वेदादिरिति नामोपपादयन्न्यासमन्त्रान् सूचयति ॥ ३४ ॥

अस्य त्विति । न्यासमन्त्राणामादावन्ते च प्रणवः प्रयोक्तव्य इत्यर्थः । योनिश्चेति । नामचतुष्टयमुक्तम् । सर्वयोनये सर्वदेहाश्रयाय ब्रह्मणे सर्वसंवा[पा]दकायेति नामचतुष्टयमवगन्तव्यम् ॥ ३५ ॥

पूर्वोक्तं वेदादित्वमुपपादयति—ऋक् चेति । अग्निमील इत्यकारः ऋग्वेदादिः । समुद्रो बन्धुरित्युकारो यजुरन्तरः । मान्तादिः सामापीति । मान्तः मकारान्तः आदिः अकारादिश्च सामवेद इत्यर्थः । ज्योतिरुत्तममिति हि साससमाप्तिः । अग्न आयाहीति च तस्यादिः । अवशिष्टानि नामान्तराणि न्यासाय सूचयति । तस्य भेदा इति । अव रक्षण गति प्रीति तृप्त्यवगम कान्ति प्रवेश श्रवण स्वाम्य सामर्थ्य याचन क्रियेच्छा दीप्त्यवाप्त्यालिङ्गन हिंसा दहन भाव वृद्धिष्विति धातुनिष्पन्नानि लौकिकनामानि य उत्तरतः स ओंकार इत्यादि श्रुतिसिद्धानि वैदिकनामानीति विभागः ।

अयमत्र न्यासक्रमः । ओं अं ब्रह्मणे नमः । ओं आं विष्णवे नमः । ओं इं रुद्राय नमः । ओं ईं ओंकाराय नमः । ओं उं प्रणवाय नमः । इत्यादि क्षकारान्ता ऊह्याः । नाममात्रं तूच्यते । प्रणवः । सर्वव्यापी । अनन्तः । तारम् । सूक्ष्मः । शुक्लः । वैद्युतः । परं ब्रह्म । एकः । एकरुद्रः । ईशानः । भगवान् । महेश्वरः । महादेवः । सदाशिवः । सर्वरक्षिता । सर्वगतः । सर्वप्रियतमः । नित्यतृप्तः । सर्वावगमः । सर्वकान्तः । सर्वप्रविष्टः । सर्वश्रोता । सर्वस्वामी । सर्वसमर्थः । सर्वयाचकः । सर्वक्रियः । सर्वेच्छः । सर्वदीप्तः । सर्वावाप्तः । सर्वालिङ्गितः । सर्वहिंसकः ।

उच्चार्योच्चार्य च तं क्रमान्नयेदुपरि षड्द्वयान्तान्तम् ।
मनसा स्मृते यदाऽस्मिन्मनो लयं याति तावदभ्यस्येत् ॥ ३७
अथवा बिन्दुं वर्तुलमावर्तैस्त्रिभिरुपेतमेवमिव ।
प्रोतं रविबिम्बेन च समभ्यसेत् स्रुतसुधामयं तेजः ॥ ३८
अपमृत्युरोगपाप्मजिदचिरेण नृणां सिद्धिदो योगः ।
अथवा मूलाधारोत्थिता प्रभा बिसविभेदतन्तुनिभा ॥ ३९
वदनामृतकरबिम्बस्रुता ध्याताऽमृताम्बुलवलुलिता ।
स्थावरजङ्गमविषहृद्योगोऽयं नात्रसन्देहः ॥ ४०
अथवा त्रिवलयबिन्दुगधाम प्रणवेन समुन्नयेदूर्ध्वम् ।
पीतोर्णातन्तुनिभं सौषुम्नेनैव वर्त्मना योगी ॥ ४१
तस्मिन्निधाय चित्तं विलयं गमयेद्दिनेशसंख्याते ।
पुनरावृत्तिविहीनं निर्वाणपदं व्रजेत् समभ्यासात् ॥ ४२
अथवादिबीजमौ पुनरुमपि विषि तमपि संहरेद्बिन्दौ ।
बिन्दुं नादे तमपि शक्तौ शक्तिं तथैव शान्ताख्ये ॥ ४३

सर्वदाहकः । सर्वभावः । सर्वव्रजः । गुणबीजम् । ध्रुवः । वेदादिः । उमध्यः । मपरः । त्रिमात्रकः । योनिः । सर्वदेहाश्रयः । सर्वसंवाहकः । सर्वात्मेति नामानीति ॥ ३६ ॥

एवं नामविभेदैः प्रणवविभूतिं स्मृत्वोन्मन्यन्तं क्रमेण तं प्रणवं नयेदित्याह—उच्चार्येति ॥ ३७ ॥

बिन्दोः सूक्ष्मतन्तुनयनात्मकं योगमभिधाय बिन्दुस्वरूपनयनात्मकमप्याह—अथवा बिन्दुं वर्तुलमिति । प्रोतं रविबिम्बेनेति । द्वादशान्तस्थचिदर्कबिम्बेनेत्यर्थः ॥ ३८ ॥

पाप्मादिजयार्थं सौरं योगमभिधाय विषनिर्हरणाद्यर्थं सौम्यं योगतन्तूनयनात्मकमाह—अथवा मूलाधारेति । वदनशब्देन कारणमुच्यते । तद्गतेनानन्दलक्षणेनाऽमृतबिम्बेन स्रुतेत्यर्थः ॥ ३९ ॥ ४० ॥

रक्तसूत्रोन्नयनात्मकमावृत्तिहीनं मोक्षप्रधानं योगमाह—अथवा त्रिवलयेति । ॥ ४१ ॥ ४२ ॥

स्थूल सूक्ष्म कारण सामान्य बीज संविदभाव तद्वाचिकाकारादिमात्राणां च क्रमसंहारलक्षणं मोक्षसाधनयोगमाह—अथवादिबीजमिति ॥ ४३ ॥

तैजस्यनन्यगे चिति निर्द्वन्द्वे निष्कले सदानन्दे ।
सूक्ष्मे च सर्वतोमुखकरपदनयनादिलक्षणेऽलक्ष्ये ॥ ४४

स्वामिनि संहृत्यैवं करणेन्द्रियवर्गनिर्गमापितः ।
विलीनपुण्यपापो निरुच्छ्वसन् ब्रह्मभूत एव स्यात् ॥ ४५

अथवा योगोपेताः पञ्चावस्थाः क्रमेण विज्ञाय ।
ताभिर्युञ्जीत सदा योगी सद्यः प्रसिद्धये मुक्तेः ॥ ४६

जाग्रत् स्वप्नसुषुप्ती तुरीयतदतीतके च तास्तासु ।
स्वैरिन्द्रियैर्यदात्मा भुङ्क्ते भोगान् स जागरो भवति ॥ ४७

संज्ञारहितैरपि तैरस्याऽनुभवो भवेत् पुनः स्वप्नः ।
आत्मनिरुद्‌युक्ततया नैराकुल्यं भवेत् सुषुप्तिरपि ॥ ४८

इतरतेजसो वैलक्षण्यमाह—अनन्यग इति । अनन्यगत्वे हेतुश्चितीति । ज्ञानत्वेन प्राप्तं विषयजन्मादियोगं निराचष्टे—निर्द्वन्द्व इति । तत्र हेतुर्निष्कल इति । ततः सदानन्दत्वमस्ति चेत् एवंविधमानन्दं कुतो नोपलभ्यते सर्वैरिति । तत्राह—सूक्ष्म इति । कथं तर्हि अस्तित्वसिद्धिरिति । तत्राह—सर्वत इति । एवमप्यविषयत्वमाह—अलक्ष्य इति । करणेन्द्रियवर्गो यस्मादबोधान्निर्गच्छति उत्पद्यते स अपितः अपगतो यस्य स तथोक्तः । अत एव विलीनपुण्य-पापादित्वमपि संभवति ॥ ४४ ॥ ४५ ॥

सर्वव्यवहारेष्वपि कर्तुं बीज बिन्दु नाद शक्ति शान्तात्मक प्रणवसाधनम् उच्चारणादिरहितं स्वाभाविकं योगमाह—अथवा योगेति । योगोपेता समाधानविशेषोपेता इत्यर्थः ॥ ४६ ॥

अवस्था दर्शयति—जाग्रदिति । तासां विविच्य स्वरूपमाह—तास्वित्या-दिना । बुद्ध्यादि विषयव्याप्ति बीजरूपा जाग्रदवस्था विषयप्राधान्यपरित्यागेन बुद्धिप्राधान्यावस्था बिन्दुस्वप्नात्मिका सविषयाया बुद्धेः कारणात्मत्वावस्था नादसुषुप्त्यात्मिका कारणात्मिकाया बुद्धेः साक्ष्याकारावस्था शक्तितुरीयात्मिका ततस्तस्याः साक्षिणि लयावस्था शान्ततुरीयातीतेत्यर्थः ॥ ४७ ॥

संज्ञारहितैरिति । संज्ञाशब्देनेन्द्रियाणि उच्यन्ते । संज्ञायन्ते एभिरिति । जाग्रद्विवेकसामर्थ्यरहितैः इन्द्रियैः वासनात्मकैरित्यर्थः । मनोरूपैरिति भावः । आत्मनिरुद्‌युक्ततयेति । आत्मनो मनसो निःसंकल्पतया आत्मनो यन्नैराकुल्यं

पश्यति परं यदात्मा निस्तमसा चेतसा तुरीयं तत् ।
आत्मपरमात्मपदयोरभेदतो व्याप्नुयाद्यदा योगी ॥ ४९
तच्च तुरीयातीतं तस्यापि भवेन्न दूरतो मुक्तिः ।
अथवा सूक्ष्माख्यायां पश्यन्त्यां मध्यमाख्यवैखर्योः ॥ ५०
ससुषुम्नाग्रगयोरपि युञ्ज्याज्जाग्रदादिभिः पवनम् ।
बीजोच्चारो जाग्रद्बिन्दुः स्वप्नः सुषुप्तिरपि नादः ॥ ५१
शक्त्यात्मकं तुरीयं शान्ते लय आत्मनस्तुरीयान्तम् ।
अङ्गुष्ठगुल्फजानुद्वितयं च गुदश्च सीवनी मेढ्रम् ॥ ५२
नाभिर्हृदयं ग्रीवा सलम्बिकाग्रं तथैव नासा च ।
भ्रूमध्यललाटाग्रं सुषुम्नाग्रं द्वादशान्तमित्येवम् ॥ ५३
उत्क्रान्तौ परकायप्रवेशने चाऽऽगतौ च पुनः स्वतनौ ।
स्थानानि धारणायाः प्रोक्तानि मरुत्प्रयोगविधिनिपुणैः ॥ ५४
स्थानेष्वेष्वात्ममनःसंयोगसमीकरकर्मणोऽभ्यासात् ।
अचिरेणोत्क्रान्त्याद्या भवन्ति संसिद्धयः प्रसिद्धतराः ॥ ५५
कण्ठे भ्रूमध्ये हृदि नाभौ सर्वाङ्गके स्मरेत् क्रमशः ।
लवरसमीरहवर्णैरनिलममा कालवञ्चनेयं स्यात् ॥ ५६
अवनिजलानलमारुतविहायसां शक्तिभिश्च तद्बीजैः ।
सारूप्यमात्मनश्च प्रतिनीत्वा तत्तदाशु जयति सुधीः ॥ ५७

तत्सुषुप्तिरित्यर्थः ॥ ४८ ॥ ४९ ॥ ५० ॥

जपकाले प्रतिपत्तव्यं योगमाह—अथवा सूक्ष्माख्यायामिति। तत्र सूक्ष्मशब्देन सूक्ष्मा वागुक्ता। स्वमहिमस्था निश्चला। आख्याशब्देन परा किंचिच्चलिता मूलाधारस्था। पश्यन्ती सामान्यज्ञानरूपिणी नाभिस्था। मध्यमा विशेषज्ञानरूपा हृदि स्थिता। वैखरीशब्दरूपिणी मुखस्था। इति मन्त्रोत्पत्तिक्रमयोगमभिधाय लयक्रमयोगमभिदधाति—ससुषुम्नाग्रगयोरिति। सुषुम्नाया अग्रं सुषुम्नाग्रं तं गच्छन्तीति सुषुम्नाग्रगाः। वैखरीमध्यमापश्यन्तीपरासूक्ष्माख्याः। आस्यभ्रूमध्यमूर्ध्वद्वादशान्तषोडशान्तस्थाः वाग्भेदाः। तैः सहितयोः मध्यमाख्यवैखर्योरित्यर्थः। योगक्रममाह—बीजोच्चार इति। सृष्टिसंहारयोः जाग्रदवस्था एकैव अवगन्तव्या। बिन्दुः स्वप्न इति। भ्रूमध्यहृदयस्थमध्यमा-

एवं प्रोक्तैर्योगैरायोजयतोऽन्वहं तथाऽऽत्मानम् ।
अचिरेण भवति सिद्धिः समस्तसंसारमोचनी नित्या ॥ ५८

इति योगमार्गभेदैः प्रतिदिनमारूढयोगयुक्तधिया ।
सिद्धय उपलभ्यन्ते मुक्तिपुरीसंप्रवेशनद्वाराः ॥ ५९

कम्पः पुलकानन्दौ वैमल्यस्थैर्यलाघवानि तथा ।
सकलप्रकाशवित्ते इत्यष्टावस्थाः प्रसूचिकाः सिद्धेः ॥ ६०

त्रैकाल्यज्ञानोहौ मनोज्ञता च्छन्दतो मरुद्रोधः ।
नाड़ीसंक्रमणविधिर्वाक्सिद्धिर्देहतश्च देहाप्तिः ।
ज्योतिःप्रकाशनं चेत्यष्टौ स्युः प्रत्यया युजः सिद्धेः ॥ ६१

अणिमा महिमा च तथा गरिमा लघिमेशिता वशित्वञ्च ।
प्राप्तिः प्राकाम्यञ्चेत्यष्टैश्वर्याणि योगयुक्तस्य ॥ ६२

अष्टैश्वर्यसमेतो जीवन्मुक्तः प्रवच्यते योगी ।
योगानुभवमहामृतरसपानानन्दनिर्भरः सततम् ॥ ६३

इत्येवं प्रणवविधिः समीरितोऽयं
भक्त्या तं प्रभजति यो जपादिभेदैः ।
स प्राप्नोत्यनुततनित्यशुद्धबुद्धं
तद्विष्णोः परमतरं पदं नराग्र्यः ॥ ६४

इति श्रीप्रपञ्चसारे एकोनविंशः पटलः ।

द्वयात्मकबिन्दुद्वयात्मकं स्वप्नद्वयमित्यर्थः । एवमुत्तरत्रापि योज्यम् ॥ ५०—५८ ॥
सकलप्रकाशः सर्वस्य तेजोमयत्वेन प्रकाशः वित्ता वेत्तृता याथात्म्येनेत्यर्थः ॥
॥ ५८ ॥ ६० ॥
ज्योतिःप्रकाशनमिति । परं प्रत्यपि सर्वस्य ज्योतिर्मयत्वप्रकाशनमित्यर्थः ॥
॥ ६१ ॥ ६२ ॥ ६३ ॥ ६४ ॥

इति श्रीपद्मपादाचार्यकृते प्रपञ्चसारविवरणे
एकोनविंशः पटलः ।

विंशः पटलः ।

अथ पुनरभिवक्ष्ये मन्त्रमष्टाक्षराख्यं
सकलदुरितदुःखध्वान्तसम्भेदभानुम् ।
प्रणवहृदयनारावर्णतोऽन्ते यणार्णौ
मपर इति समुद्दिष्टोऽयमिष्टार्थदायी ॥ १

तारः शक्त्युत्थतया निर्दिष्टः सोऽहमर्थकः पूर्वम् ।
नार्णः प्रतिषिधार्थो मोकारस्त्वायमर्थको भवति ॥ २

सलिलानलपवनधराः क्रमेण नारायणाक्षराः प्रोक्ताः ।
चरमो यस्तु विभक्तिव्यक्त्यर्थं दर्शितस्तदर्थार्थे ॥ ३

ऋषिरस्य मनोः साध्यनारायण इतीरितः ।
छन्दश्च देवी गायत्री परमात्मा च देवता ॥ ४

अथ क्रुद्धमहावीरद्युसहस्रपदादिकैः ।
उल्कैर्जातियुतैः कुर्यात् पञ्चाङ्गानि मनोः क्रमात् ॥ ५

अष्टाक्षरेण व्यस्तेन कुर्यादष्टाङ्गकं सुधीः ।
सहृच्छिरःशिखावर्मनेत्रास्त्रोदरपृष्ठके ॥ ६

अर्कौघाभं किरीटान्वितमकरलसत्कुण्डलं दीप्तिराज-
त्केयूरं कौस्तुभाभाशबलरुचिरहारं सपीताम्बरञ्च ।
नानारत्नांशुभिन्नाभरणशतयुतं श्रीधराश्लिष्टपार्श्वं
वन्दे दोःसक्तचक्राम्बुरुहदरगदं विश्ववन्द्यं मुकुन्दम् ॥ ७

प्रणवमभिधाय प्रणवस्याष्टमात्रात्मकाष्टवर्णविशिष्टाक्षरविधिं वदन् विनियोगमाह --अथ पुनरिति। पूर्वमप्यष्टभेदप्रणवात्मना अष्टाक्षरस्यैवोक्तत्वात् पुनःशब्दः।

अष्टाक्षरस्यार्थमाह—तार इति। शक्त्युत्थतयेति। शक्त्युत्थोऽजपोत्थः। परमात्ममन्त्रसारतयेत्यर्थः। सोऽहं न तु पञ्चभूतसम्बन्धीदमिति मन्त्रार्थ इत्यर्थः॥ १॥ २॥ ३॥ ४॥

मनोः क्रमादित्युल्कान्ते स्वाहापदं प्रयोज्य पश्चाज् जातिः प्रयोक्तव्येति सूचितम्॥ ५॥

अष्टाङ्गकं सुधीरिति। न्यास एवाष्टाङ्गविनियोगः नतु पूजायामिति

संदीक्षितो मनुमिमं प्रतिजप्तुमिच्छन्
कुर्यान्निजेन वपुषैव तु योगपीठम् ।
अंसोरुयुग्मपदसाननाभिमूल-
पार्श्वद्वयैर्विहितगात्रसमुज्ज्वलश्च ॥ ८

मध्येऽनन्ताद्यैरपि संज्ञानात्मान्तिकैर्यजेन्मन्त्री ।
पीठाख्यमन्त्रपश्चिममथ गन्धाद्यैश्च सम्यगुपचारैः ॥ ९

प्रणवं हृदयञ्चैव प्रोक्त्वा भगवते पदम् ।
विष्णवे च समाभाष्य सर्वभूतात्मनेपदम् ॥ १०
वासुदेवाय सर्वात्मसंयोगपदमुच्चरेत् ।
योगपद्मपदे चोक्त्वा ततः पीठात्मने नमः ॥ ११
अस्त्रमन्त्रप्रबद्धाशो मन्त्रवर्णांस्तनौ न्यसेत् ।
विन्यस्तैर्यैर्भवेन्मन्त्री मन्त्रवर्णात्मको हरिः ॥ १२

आधारहृद्वदनदोःपदमूलनाभौ
कण्ठे सनाभिहृदयस्तनपार्श्वपृष्ठे ।
कास्येक्षणश्रवणगन्धवहे च दोःपत्-
सन्ध्यङ्गुलीषु हृदि धातुषु सानिलेषु ॥ १३
मूर्धेक्षणास्यहृदयोदरसोरुजङ्घा-
पादद्वयेषु लिपिशो न्यसतु क्रमेण ।
गण्डांसकोरुचरणेषु रथाङ्गशङ्ख-
श्रीमद्गदाम्बुजपदेषु समाहितात्मा ॥ १४

ततोऽष्टाक्षरपूर्त्यर्थं स्मर्तव्यो द्वादशाक्षरः ।
मन्त्रो द्वादश मूर्तीस्तु तत्प्रभिन्नास्तनौ न्यसेत् ॥ १५

विशेषश्च इत्यर्थः । श्रं बीजम् । आय शक्तिः ॥ ६ ॥ ७ ॥

यजेन्मन्त्रीति । तं तमसे नमः इत्यस्यानन्तरं मं मायायै नमः विं विद्यायै नमः इति मन्त्रद्वयं सूचयति ॥ ८ ॥ ९ ॥ १० ॥ ११ ॥

मन्त्रो मन्त्रवर्णेति । न्यासमन्त्राणां प्रणवपुटितत्वं प्रतिपर्यायं व्यापकन्यासश्चोक्तः ॥ १२ ॥ १३ ॥ १४ ॥

ततोऽष्टाक्षरपूर्त्यर्थमिति । यद्यप्यष्टाक्षराणाम् अष्टप्रकृत्यात्मकत्वेन जड़-

अष्टप्रकृत्यात्मकश्च संप्रोक्तोऽष्टाक्षरो मनुः ।
अष्टानां प्रकृतीनाञ्च चतुर्णामात्मनामपि ॥ १६

द्वादशानान्तु संयोगो मन्त्रः स्याद्द्वादशाक्षरः ।
आदित्या द्वादश प्रोक्ता युक्ता द्वादशमूर्तिभिः ॥ १७

केशवादिप्रदिष्टानां मूर्तीनां द्वादशादितः ।
आदिस्वरयुता न्यस्येत्ताः स्युर्द्वादश मूर्तयः ॥ १८

ललाटोदरहृत्कण्ठदक्षपार्श्वांसकेषु गले ।
तथा वामत्रये पृष्ठककुदोश्च यथाक्रमम् ॥ १९

द्वादशाक्षरमन्त्रञ्च मन्त्रविन्मूर्ध्नि विन्यसेत् ।
मूर्धस्थो वासुदेवस्तु व्याप्नोति सकलां तनुम् ॥ २०

पुनस्तत्प्रतिपत्त्यर्थं किरीटादिमनुं जपेत् ।
किरीटकेयूरहारपदान्याभाष्य मन्त्रवित् ॥ २१

मकरान्ते कुण्डलञ्च शङ्खचक्रगदादिकम् ।
अब्जहस्तपदं चोक्त्वा पीताम्बरधरेति च ॥ २२

श्रीवत्साङ्कितमाभाष्य वक्षःस्थलमथो वदेत् ।
श्रीभूमिसहितं स्वात्मज्योतिर्द्वयपदं वदेत् ॥ २३

वाचकत्वम् एवेति भाति मन्दानां तथापि लक्षणया चेतनस्याऽप्युक्तत्वात् बिन्दुनादशक्तिशान्तानाम् आत्मचतुष्टयवाचिनां सद्भावाद्वा पूर्णमेव स्वतोऽष्टाक्षरं तथापि तत्र स्पष्टमिति। तत्स्पष्टीकरणाय द्वादशाक्षरमन्त्रोऽष्टाक्षरेऽन्तर्भूतः स्मर्तव्यो न्यस्यव्यश्चेत्यर्थः ॥ १५ ॥

स्वतः पूर्तिं वदन् अक्षरतत्त्वन्यासं सूचयति—अष्टेति। द्वादशाक्षरयोगी पूर्तिं वदन् बिन्द्वादिभिः सार्धमात्मचतुष्टयन्यासं व्यापकत्वेनाह—अष्टानामिति। अत्र प्रणवेन सार्धं बिन्द्वादयः प्रयोक्तव्याः। तत्त्वन्यासो द्वादशाक्षरयोगोऽनेनैव सूचितः। मूर्तिपञ्जरन्यासमाह—आदित्या इति ॥ १६ ॥ १७ ॥

कास्ताः द्वादशमूर्तयः। किं विशिष्टाश्चेति। तदाह—केशवादीति। मन्त्रविन्मूर्ध्नीत्यष्टाक्षरेण सार्धमित्यर्थः। तत्र प्रतिपत्तिमाह—मूर्धस्थ इति ॥ १८ ॥ १९ ॥ २० ॥

मन्त्रविन्मकरान्ते कुण्डलमिति। मकरकुण्डलालङ्कृत इति पदाध्याहारः

दीप्तिमुक्ता करायेति सहस्रादित्यतेजसे ।
हृदन्तः प्रणवादिः स्यात् किरीटादिमनुस्त्वयम् ॥ २४
कृत्वा स्थण्डिलमस्मिन्निःक्षिप्य निजासिकां समुपविश्य ।
पीठादिकं निजाङ्के प्रपूज्य गन्धादिभिः सुशुद्धमनाः ॥ २५
सद्वादशाक्षरान्तं प्रपूज्य विधिवत् किरीटमन्त्रेण ।
कुर्यात् पुष्पाञ्जलिमपि निजदेहे पञ्चशोऽथवा त्रिशः ॥ २६
इति दीक्षितविहितविधिः संप्रोक्तोऽष्टाक्षरस्य मन्त्रस्य ।
शुद्धानां विमलधियां दीक्षा प्रतिवक्ष्यतेऽत्र संक्षेपात् ॥ २७
कृत्वा त्रिगुणितादीनामेकं मण्डलमुज्ज्वलम् ।
आत्मार्चनोक्तविधिना शक्तिभिः पीठमर्चयेत् ॥ २८
विमलोत्कर्षणी ज्ञाना क्रिया योगेति शक्तयः ।
प्रह्वी सत्या तथेशानाऽनुग्रहा नवमी स्मृता ॥ २९
निधाय कलशं तत्र पञ्चगव्येन पूरयेत् ।
पयोभिर्वा गवां प्रोक्तैः क्वाथैर्वा साष्टगन्धकैः ॥ ३०
अष्टाक्षराङ्गैरष्टार्णयुगैरष्टाक्षरान्वितैः ।
दलमूले यजेद्भूयो वासुदेवादिकान् क्रमात् ।
सशक्तिकांस्ततो बाह्ये सम्पूज्या हरिहेतयः ॥ ३१
चक्रशङ्खगदाम्बुजकौस्तुभमुसलाः सखड्गवनमालाः ।
रक्ताच्छपीतकनकश्यामलकृष्णाद्युशुक्लभासः स्युः ॥ ३२
ध्वजश्च वैनतेयश्च शङ्खपद्मौ दिशो गताः ।
विघ्नार्यकौ तथा दुर्गा विष्वक्सेनो विदिग्गताः ॥ ३३
ध्वजः श्यामो विपो रक्तो निधी शुक्लारुणप्रभौ ।
अरुणश्यामलश्यामपीता विघ्नादयो मताः ॥ ३४

सूचितः ॥ २१ ॥ २२ ॥ २३ ॥ २४ ॥

सुशुद्धमना इति । गन्धादीनां चित्पर्यन्तं व्याप्तिचिन्तनमुक्तम् ।

विधिवदिति । पुष्पाञ्जलेर्जलगन्धसंपुटत्वम् ॥ २५ ॥ २६ ॥ २७ ॥

अष्टाक्षराङ्गैरिति । पञ्चाङ्गैः प्रथमावरणमुक्तम् । अष्टार्णवर्णैरित्यक्षराष्टकेन द्वितीयम् । पञ्चावरणमित्यङ्गैः विनेत्यवगन्तव्यम् ॥ २८—४१ ॥

इन्द्राद्यस्तद्बहिश्च पूज्याः पूर्वादिभिः क्रमात् ।
इति विष्णोर्विधानन्तु पञ्चावरणमुच्यते ॥ ३५
एवमभ्यर्चिते विष्णावुपचारैस्तु पूर्ववत् ।
अग्निमाधाय कुण्डे तु ब्रह्मयागसमीरितैः ॥ ३६
जुहुयादष्टभिर्द्रव्यैर्मनुनाऽष्टाक्षरेण तु ।
पृथगष्टशतावृत्त्या हुत्वा दत्त्वा बलिं ततः ॥ ३७
अभिषिच्य गुरुः शिष्यं प्रवदेत् पूर्ववन्मनुम् ।
द्वात्रिंशल्लक्षमानेन स तु मन्त्रं जपेत्ततः ।
तदर्धसंख्यकं वापि शुद्धाचारो जितेन्द्रियः ॥ ३८
पद्मासनः प्राग्वदनोऽप्रलापी तन्मानसस्तर्जनिवर्जिताभिः ।
अक्षस्रजा वाङ्गुलिभिर्जपेत्तं नातिद्रुतं नातिविलम्बितञ्च ॥ ३९
प्रागीरितैरथ जुहोतु दशांशकं वा द्रव्यैः शुभैः सरसिजैर्मधुराप्लुतैर्वा ।
रत्नांशुकप्रवरकाञ्चनगोमहीभिर्धान्यैर्यथाविभवतः प्रयजेद्गुरुञ्च ॥ ४०
विप्रान् प्रतर्प्य विभवैरथ मन्त्रजापी
संक्रासयेज्जपविधिञ्च ततः क्रमेण ।
नित्यार्चना च विहिता विधिनाऽमुनैव
प्रोक्तक्रमेण विदधात्वथ चात्मपूजाम् ॥ ४१
इति जपहुतार्चनाद्यैर्मन्त्री योऽष्टाक्षरं समभ्यस्येत् ।
स त्वैहिकीञ्च सिद्धिं संप्राप्याऽन्ते प्रयाति परमं पदम् ॥ ४२
अङ्गानि पूर्वं त्वथ मूर्तिशक्तीः सकेशवादींश्च पुरन्दरादीन् ।
समर्चयेद्यस्तु विधानमेतन्नरोऽचिरात् काङ्क्षितमेति कामम् ॥ ४३
यष्टव्याः स्युर्वासुदेवादिरादौ चक्राद्याः कीत्वादिकाः केशवाद्याः ।
इन्द्राद्याश्चेत्येवमेव प्रदिष्टं पुष्ट्यायुःश्रीकीर्त्तिसिद्ध्यै विधानम् ॥ ४४
सवासुदेवादिकमर्चयित्वा भूयो ध्वजादींश्च पुरन्दरादीन् ।
क्रमेण विद्वान् विधिनाऽर्चयीतेत्यथं क्रमश्च त्रिदशाभिपूज्यः ॥ ४५

अर्चनाद्यैर्मन्त्रीति । ऐहिकसिद्धौ तद्योग्यबीजयोगादिकमुक्तम् ॥ ४२ ॥
॥ ४३ ॥ ४४ ॥

इत्युक्तविधिचतुष्के पूजयितुरथैकमपि यथाशक्ति ।
अचिरेण भवति लक्ष्मीर्हस्तगता सकलवर्गसिद्धिकरी ॥ ४६

अष्टाक्षराक्षराष्टकमूर्तिविधानानि भेदभिन्नानि ।
वक्ष्याम्यर्चयितॄणां वाञ्छितसकलार्थसिद्धिदानि सदा ॥ ४७

सिन्दूरकुन्दकरविन्दकबन्धुजीव-
काश्मीरपद्ममकरन्दरुचः क्रमेण ।
नीलोत्पलाम्बुरुहरागसमानरूपाः
स्युर्मूर्तयोऽष्ट कथिता मनुवर्णजाताः ॥ ४८

अरिदरगदाब्जहस्ताः सर्वास्तु नकारमोऽर्णयोर्मूर्ती ।
शङ्खारिगदाब्जकरे लक्षणमन्यत् समानरूपं स्यात् ॥ ४९

या मूर्तिरर्च्यतेऽस्य व्रजन्ति परिवारतां तदवशिष्टाः ।
अविशिष्टेऽन्तेऽप्यंशे स्वयञ्च परिवारतां प्रयाति तदा ॥ ५०

इयमेवावृतिरधिका ध्रुवजे ध्रुवजात् पुरा समुद्दिष्टात् ।
भवति विधानादिति पुनरेषां प्रथमविधानमुद्दिष्टम् ॥ ५१

अथ द्वितीयाक्षरजेऽङ्गतोऽन्ते वर्णाष्टमूर्तीरपि मूर्तिशक्तीः ।
यजेद्विधाने च सकेतुलोकपालादिकानन्यदथ प्रवक्ष्ये ॥ ५२

मोकारजे रतिधृती च सकान्तितुष्टि-
पुष्टिस्मृतीरपि च दीप्त्यभिधाञ्च कीर्त्तिम् ।

क्रमेण विद्यानित्यङ्गावरणयोग उक्तः ॥ ४५ ॥ ४६ ॥

भेदभिन्नानीत्यावरणभेदभिन्नानीत्यर्थः ॥ ४७ ॥

अम्बुरुहरागवर्णाः सर्वविधानेष्ववशिष्टान्त्या मूर्तिरिति ज्ञेया ॥ ४८ ॥

अरिदरगदाब्जहस्ताः सर्वा इति । दक्षिणोर्ध्वहस्तमारभ्य प्रादक्षिण्येनेत्यर्थः । इयमेवाक्षरमूर्त्यावृतिः प्रणवजे विधानेऽधिका भवति । तस्मात् पुरा प्रणवपटले उक्तात् प्रणवविधानादित्यर्थः । अङ्गवासुदेवाद्यात्मादीन्द्रवज्रादिभिर्हि प्रणवविधानमुद्दिष्टम् । अत्र तु क्रुद्धोल्कादिभिरङ्गपूजा तदनन्तरमक्षरमूर्तिपूजा ततो वासुदवादिकमिति । नकारादिविधानेषु ओं नं ओं नमो नारायणाय इत्यादयो मन्त्रा ज्ञातव्याः । सर्वत्र चाङ्गानन्तरं मूर्त्यावृतिद्वयं द्रष्टव्यम् ॥ ४९ ॥ ५० ॥ ५१ ॥ ५२ ॥

केशवादिकञ्च सशतक्रतुपूर्वकञ्च
सम्पूजयेद्विमलधीः पुनरङ्गतोऽन्ते ॥ ५३

नाकारजेऽङ्गतोऽन्ते प्रपूजयेन्मूर्तिशक्तिलोकेशान् ।
रावर्णजे तु मूर्तीः श्रीभूमायामनोन्मथनीश्च यजेत ॥ ५४

क्षीः श्री रतिः सपुष्टिर्मोहनिमाये महादियोगाद्ये ।
माये च तृतीयावृतिरन्यदशेषं पुरैव निर्दिष्टम् ॥ ५५

यकारजेऽरिशङ्खौ च सगदाहलशार्ङ्गकाः ।
मुसलः खड्गशूलौ च तृतीया णाक्षरोद्भवे ॥ ५६

शेषो वासुकितक्षककर्कोटकपङ्कजमहापद्माः ।
दरपालकुलिकाख्यौ तृतीयमन्यत् समं विधानेऽन्त्ये ॥ ५७

अङ्गैः प्रथमावरणं मूर्तिभिरपि शक्तिभिर्द्वितीयमपि ।
अन्ये केशवकेत्वादिभ्यां स्यात् पञ्चमञ्च मत्स्याद्यैः ॥ ५८

मत्स्यः कूर्मवराहौ नृसिंहकुब्जविरामकृष्णाश्च ।
कल्किः सानन्तात्मा पुनरमृतात्मा च षष्ठमहिपाद्यैः ॥ ५९

सप्तममपि लोकेशैरष्टममपि तदायुधैश्च संप्रोक्तम् ।
प्रागुक्तेषु विधानेष्वालक्ष्यं नोक्तमत्र यत्तदपि ॥ ६०

अष्टाक्षराक्षरविधानचतुष्कयुग्मं
प्रोक्तक्रमेण विधिनाऽभियजेद् य एनम् ।
भक्त्या मुकुन्दमनुजापरतो नराग्र्यः
प्राप्नोति वाञ्छितमयत्नत एव कामम् ॥ ६१

इति श्रीप्रपञ्चसारे विंशः पटलः ।

विमलधीरिति । मूर्त्यावरणमन्त्रभेदाः मूर्त्यावरणे तत्तदक्षरानन्तरमारभ्य पूजाक्रमश्च सूचितः ॥ ५३ ॥ ५४ ॥ ५५ ॥ ५६ ॥ ५७ ॥ ५८ ॥ ५९ ॥

आलक्ष्यमिति । किरीटमन्त्रपुष्पाञ्जल्यादिक्रमेष्वपि विधानेषु द्रष्टव्यमित्यर्थः ॥ ६० ॥ ६१ ॥

इति श्रीपद्मपादाचार्यकृते प्रपञ्चसारविवरणे
विंशतिः पटलः ।

एकविंशः पटलः ।

अथ प्रवक्ष्यामि च मासभेदभिन्नानि यन्त्राण्यपि संग्रहेण ।
रेखाक्रमद्युन्ति विचित्रवर्णलसन्ति विषोऽस्य विधानभाञ्जि ॥ १
यैः कुर्युरिष्टाग्निनिविष्टचेष्टा धरण्यनन्तादिकसंज्ञकानि ।
व्रतान्यभीष्टार्थदकल्पवृक्षैरनारतैनैव च साधकेशाः ॥ २
मेषादिकं यच्च चतुष्कमादौ मासेषु तद्वायुगृहावृतं स्यात् ।
सिंहादिकं भूगृहसंवृतञ्च चापादिकं पार्थिवयुग्मवीतम् ॥ ३
मेषादिकेषु त्रिगुणात्मकानि चराणि भास्वद्गुणितात्मकानि ।
स्थिराण्यथो षड्गुणितानि तज्ज्ञैरुक्तानि यन्त्राण्युभयात्मकानि ॥ ४
तानि त्रिषड्द्वादशकात्मकोक्तैः स्थूलैर्लक्षणैरप्यभिलक्षितानि ।
स्वैः स्वैश्च नामप्रविभक्तरूपभेदैर्बहिर्वेष्टितबिम्बकानि ॥ ५
त्रिगुणितमपि यन्त्रमष्टपत्रावृतमथ षड्गुणितं द्विषड्दलाख्यम् ।
स्थिरगतमपि चाष्टयुग्मपत्रं तदपि षड्युगपत्रशोभितं वा ॥ ६
पद्मं चरोभस्थिरसंज्ञकेषु रक्तप्रपीताच्छदलादिवर्णम् ।
मासेषु यन्त्रोदरकॢप्तत्तन्मासाभिधामूर्त्यभिधाक्षराढ्यम् ॥ ७
केशवमेषादीनां ये दीर्घा मूर्तिराशिवर्णानाम् ।
ते वृत्तानि भवन्ति च निगदितमिति यन्त्रकॢप्तिसामान्यम् ॥ ८

अथाष्टाक्षरस्यैव मासयन्त्रभेदेन विधानभेदं वक्तुमारभते—अथ प्रवक्ष्या-मीति । यन्त्रादिकथनप्रयोजनमाह—यैः कुर्युरिति ॥ १ ॥ २ ॥

मासयन्त्राणां सामान्यलक्षणं विभागश्च आह—मेषादिकमिति ॥ ३ ॥ ४ ॥

स्वैः स्वैश्च नामेति । स्वैः स्वै रूपैर्मेषवृषभादिलक्षणैः । कथंभूतैः । नामभिः मेषवृषभेत्यादिभिः ललाटलिखितैः सह प्रविभक्तं रूपं येषां ते तथोक्ताः । बिम्बशब्देन यन्त्रबाह्ये लिखितानि वायवादिमण्डलान्युच्यन्ते ॥ ५ ॥ ६ ॥

यन्त्रोदरकॢप्तेति । मध्यबीजस्य यानि वेष्टनान्युक्तानि त्रिगुणितादिषु तद्बाह्ये ओं मेषाधिपतये केशवाय नमः इत्यादिमन्त्रैर्वेष्टितानीत्यर्थः ॥ ७ ॥

वृत्तानि भवन्तीति । उक्तवेष्टनबाह्ये मेषाद्याकारबाह्ये इति केचित् ॥ ८ ॥

सुवर्णगोक्षीरजवाशिलालपीतेन्द्रनीलारुणकैरवाभाः ।
काश्मीरमेघाञ्जनरोचिषश्च क्रमेण वर्णैरपि केशवाद्याः ॥ ९
इतीरिताश्चापि किरीटहारकेयूरपीताम्बरकादितुल्याः ।
सचक्रशङ्खाः सगदाम्बुजाश्च संपूजनीयास्तपनैः क्रमेण ॥ १०

धात्रर्यममित्राख्यावरुणांशुभगा विवस्वदिन्द्रयुताः ।
पूषाह्वयपर्जन्यौ त्वष्टा विष्णुश्च भानवः प्रोक्ताः ॥ ११
प्रथमं केशवधात्रकमितरन्नारायणार्यमाख्यञ्च ।
अन्यन्माधवमैत्रं परमपि गोविन्दवारुणं प्रोक्तम् ॥ १२
पञ्चममपि विष्ण्वंशुं मधुसूदनभगञ्च षष्ठमपि ।
त्रिविक्रमविवस्वदाख्यं सप्तममन्यच्च वामनेन्द्रमपि ॥ १३
श्रीधरपौष्णं नवमं दशमञ्च हृषीकेशपार्जन्यम् ।
अम्बुजनाभं त्वाष्ट्रं दामोदरवैष्णवं विधानमिति ॥ १४

शिला मनःशिला । आलं हरितालम् । सचक्रशङ्खा इति ।

पद्मारिगदया शङ्खपद्मशङ्खगदारिभिः ।
गदारिशङ्खपद्मैश्च केशवाद्यास्त्रयोऽङ्किताः ॥
गदाचक्राब्जशङ्खैश्च गदाशङ्खारिपङ्कजैः ।
शङ्खचक्राब्जगदया गोविन्दादय अङ्किताः ॥
गदाब्जचक्रशङ्खैश्च चक्रशङ्खगदाम्बुजैः ।
चक्राम्बुजगदाशङ्खैः त्रिविक्रमपुरःसराः ॥
चक्रशैलाब्जशङ्खैश्च पद्मशैलारिशङ्खकैः ।
शङ्खचक्रगदापद्मैः हृषीकेशादयः क्रमात् ॥
उत्तराधरभेदेन दक्षवामक्रमात्तथा ।

इत्युक्तक्रमेणेत्यर्थः ॥ ९ ॥ १० ॥ ११ ॥

पूजामन्त्रान् कथयति—प्रथमं केशवेति । ओं अं केशवाय धात्रे नमः । मं आं नारायणाय अर्यम्णे नमः । इति द्वादशाक्षरद्वादशस्वरमूर्त्यादित्यनमस्कारयुता मन्त्रा इत्यर्थः । एते च पुष्पाञ्जलिन्यासादिमन्त्राः । मूलमन्त्रास्त्वेते । ओं श्रीं नमो भगवतेऽस्मै केशवाय ओं श्रीं ओं नम इति केशवमन्त्रः । ओं क्लीं नमो भगवतेऽस्मै नारायणाय ओं क्लीं ओं नमः ।

आदौ विधानेषु समेतमूर्तीः शक्तीश्चतस्रोऽभियजेद्यथावत् ।
राशिष्वथो भानुयुताश्च मूर्तीः प्रवक्ष्यमाणाश्च निरूप्य मन्त्री ॥ १५
वृषहरिवृश्चिककलशात्मकेष्वथो केतुकेशवाद्यैश्च ।
मत्स्यादिकशेषाद्यैः समभियजेदन्तरा समावरणम् ॥ १६

ओं ह्स्नौं (ह्स्नैः) नमो भगवते माधवाय ओं ह्स्नौं (ह्स्नैः) ओं नमः । ओं ह्र्यौं (ह्र्यैं) नमो भगवतेऽन्ते गोविन्दाय ओं ह्र्यौं (ह्र्यैं) ओं नमः । ओं मुक्तिष्ठश्रीकराय स्वाहान्ते विष्णवे नमः । ओं म्र्यौं मधुसूदनाय ओं म्र्यौं ओं नमः । ओं क्ष्रौं त्रिविक्रमाय ओं क्ष्रौं ओं नमः । ओं प्रौं वटुवामनाय ओं प्रौं ओं नमः । ओं क्लीं श्रीं क्लीं नमः श्रीधराय ओं क्लीं श्रीं क्लीं ओं नमः । ओं ऐं द्रीं द्रां हृषीकेशाय विष्णवे ओं ऐं द्रीं द्रां ओं नमः । ओं हुं ओं नमः पद्मनाभाय ओं हुं ओं नमः । ओं द्रं ओं नमो दामोदराय ओं द्रं ओं नम इत्यवशिष्टा मन्त्राः । एतैः सहितेनाऽष्टाक्षरेण पूजाः कार्याः ।

ओं केशवाय विद्महे जलधराय धीमहि तन्नो भुवः प्रचोदयात् । नारायणाय विद्महे भवोद्भवाय धीमहि तन्नो विश्वः प्रचोदयात् । श्रीं माधवाय विद्महे लक्ष्मीधराय धीमहि तन्नो विश्वः प्रचोदयात् । श्रीगोविन्दाय विद्महे विश्वेश्वराय धीमहि तन्नो विश्वः प्रचोदयात् । विष्णवेश्वराय विद्महे देवश्रेष्ठाय धीमहि तन्नो व्यापी प्रचोदयात् । मधुसूदनाय विद्महे लोकपालाय धीमहि तन्नो धीरः प्रचोदयात् । वामनेशाय विद्महे मायारूपाय धीमहि तन्नश्चित्तं प्रचोदयात् । श्रीधरेशाय विद्महे लक्ष्मीधराय धीमहि तन्नो जातः प्रचोदयात् । त्रिविक्रमाय विद्महे महाम्बुजाय धीमहि तन्नो जीवः प्रचोदयात् । हृषीकेशाय विद्महे महादेवाय धीमहि तन्नः साध्यः प्रचोदयात् । पद्मनाभाय विद्महे आकर्षज्ञानाय धीमहि तन्नो ब्रह्मा प्रचोदयात् । दामोदराय विद्महे स्तवप्रियाय धीमहि तन्नो दिव्यः प्रचोदयात् । इति गायत्रीभिर्वोपचारान् प्रयच्छेत् ॥ १२ ॥ १३ ॥ १४ ॥

आवरणेष्वपि सामान्यावरणान्याह—आदाविति । यथावदिति । अङ्गमन्त्रयम् । वासुदेवादीनां वासुदेवादिमन्त्रपूर्वकत्वं चाह—मन्त्रीति । या मूर्तिः मध्ये पूज्या तस्याः स्थाने वासुदेवमन्त्रेण पूजोक्ता । सा तु केतुकेशवाद्यैरिति । केत्वादेः पूर्वं मत्स्या[ध्या]द्यावरणं केशवादेः पूर्वं शेषाद्यावरणमित्यर्थः । अतः सर्वपूजासु केत्वाद्यावरणासितत्वमपि सिद्धम् ॥ १५ ॥ १६ ॥

प्रानुप्रोद्यत्स्वराष्टद्वितयवृतमहाबीजकं शक्तिलक्ष्मी-
कामैराप्ताग्निकोणं बहिरपि वृतसिंहान्वितक्रोडमन्त्रम् ।
बिन्दूनामन्तरालेष्वपि च विलिखितैः कादिवर्गैश्च युक्तं
षड्भिर्वायव्यगेहावृतमभिमतकामप्रदं मेषयन्त्रम् ॥ १७
गौरीन्दिरा रतिधृती वसुधा तुष्टिपुष्टिश्रमासरस्वत्यः ।
मूर्त्योश्च मध्यमावृतिराशेशात् प्राग्ध्वजादिभिरपि कथिता ॥ १८
हयगजरथभृत्यादीनरिपरिभवशौर्यादिसिद्धिश्च ।
तेजो यशश्च विपुलं पूजयितुर्वितनुते विधानमिदम् ॥ १९
वर्णैराद्यैरमन्तैः समभिवृतमहाबीजमञ्मध्यराजत्-
पान्तद्वाद्यच्चराढ्यं गुहनयनहुताशास्त्रिराजन्मथार्णम् ।
अस्रेर्गण्डद्वयोद्यत्पचलिपिपरिवीतञ्च नाद्यैश्च कान्तैः
काद्यैर्नान्तैश्च यन्त्रं बहुविधफलदं पूजितं स्याद्वृषोत्थम् ॥ २०

नित्यानन्दा[न्ता] व्यापिनी व्योमरूपा
शान्तिर्विद्यारूपिणी च प्रतिष्ठा ।
कल्पामोघा चण्डिका दीर्घजिह्वे-
त्येवं प्रोक्ता ह्यावृतिः स्यात्तृतीया ॥ २१

प्रानुप्रोद्यदिति। ऋकारादिस्वराष्टकं प्रतिलोमेन लृकाराद्यष्टकमनुलोमेन इत्यर्थः। ऋं लृं ऋं लृं अं एं इत्येवं क्रमेण पूर्वस्थितवेष्टनबाह्ये वेष्टयेदित्यर्थः। बहिरपीति। शक्तिवेष्टनाद् बहिरपीत्यर्थः। नृसिंहानुष्टुब्वराहमन्त्राभ्यां वृत्तद्वयं कार्यम्। बिन्दूनामन्तरालेष्विति। वायुमण्डलस्य बिन्दूनामन्तरालेष्वित्यर्थः। अभिमतकामप्रदमिति। मध्ये कामबीजस्य लेखनं सूचितम्। यन्त्रसामान्यमन्त्रास्त्वत्रापि समानाः ॥ १७ ॥

मूर्त्योरिति। वासुदेवादिकेशवाद्योरित्यर्थः। अङ्ग वासुदेव गौरी केशव-ध्वजेन्द्रवज्राद्यैः सप्तावरणा मेषयन्त्रपूजेत्यर्थः ॥ १८ ॥ १९ ॥

अञ्मध्यराजदिति। महाबीजवेष्टनाचां मध्ये राजद्भिः पान्तद्वाद्यच्चरै-राढ्यमित्यर्थः। अं चं आं लं इं हं इत्यादि क्रमेण वेष्टयेन्मध्यबीजमित्यर्थः। नाद्यैः कान्तैरिति। शक्तिवेष्टनाद् बाह्ये नं कं धं खं दं गमित्यादिक्रमेण वेष्टममवगन्तव्यम्। अङ्ग वासुदेव नित्यानन्दा केशव मत्स्य मेष ध्वजेन्द्र

सुरभिहयमहिषदासीदासाभरणांशुकादिसिद्धिकरम् ।
वृषजं विधानमेतद्देहान्ते सिद्धिकृत् परस्य सतः ॥ २२

प्रागच्छन्मातृभिख्यालिपिभिरभिवृतं तत् स्वरायुक्तवृत्तं
शाद्यैः क्षान्तैस्तदाद्यैरपि परिवृतगण्डान्तदस्रात्तजूंसम् ।
काद्यैर्भान्तैः प्रवीतं मयरलवहयुग्बिन्दुकं वायुगेहा-
वीतं वाञ्छाप्रदानप्रसवगुणयुतं युग्मजं यन्त्रमेतत् ॥ २३

इन्द्राणी कौमारिका ब्रह्मजाया
वाराह्याख्या वैष्णवी चाथ लक्ष्मीः ।
चामुण्डा माहेश्वरी स्यात्तृतीया
रक्षा प्रज्ञा श्रीप्रदं स्याद्विधानम् ॥ २४

पाशाद्यष्टाक्षरार्णप्रतिपुटितमहाष्टाक्षरार्णावृतान्त-
र्बीजं शाखान्तरूढेगगनन्हरिबीजात्तकोणं बहिश्च ।
कामिन्यष्टाक्षराद्यन्तगहरिहरबीजावृतं प्रत्यनूद्य-
द्वर्णाढ्यं वायुगेहे स्थितमिति गदितं कर्कटोत्यस्त्र यन्त्रम् ॥

वज्रादिभिः नवावरणा वृषयन्त्रपूजा ॥ २० ॥ २१ ॥ २२ ॥

प्रागच्छदिति। प्रातिलोम्येनागच्छद्भिः ब्रह्माण्यादिमातॄणामभिख्यालिपिभिः नामाक्षरैरभिवृतमध्यबीजमित्यर्थः। यदेवंभूतं यन्त्रं तद्युग्मजमित्युत्तरत्र यच्छब्दस्यान्वयः। मातृकाक्षरावृतिं विशिनष्टि—स्वरायुक्तवृत्तमिति। अः अं महालक्ष्मी औं ओं चण्डिके ऐं एं इन्द्राणी इत्यादिक्रमेण वेष्टनमवगन्तव्यम्। शाद्यैः क्षान्तैरिति। षड्गुणितस्य गण्डद्वादशकं भवति। तेषु शादिक्षान्तं क्षादिशान्तं च लिखेदित्यर्थः। तत्र दक्षिणभागगण्डेषु क्षादिकं वामेषु शादिकमित्यवगन्तव्यम्। तदस्रात्तेति। षट्स्वस्रेषु जूं स इति लिखेदित्यर्थः। काद्यैर्भान्तैरिति। शक्तिवेष्टनाद् बहिः कं भं खं बं गं फमित्यादि क्रमेण च लेखनीयम्। मयरलवहयुग्बिन्दुकमिति। वायुमण्डलबिन्दुष्वेतानि लिखेदित्यर्थः। अङ्ग वासुदेवेन्द्राणी केशव केलिन्द्र वज्रादिभिः सप्तावरणा मिथुनयन्त्रपूजा ॥ २३ ॥ २४ ॥

पाशाद्यष्टार्णेति। महाष्टाक्षरं वैष्णवाष्टाक्षरम्। शाखान्तरूढं गगनेति। शाखान्तं प्रणवः तस्मिन् रूढं ई शाखान्तरूढे गगनं हकारः न्हरिः क्ष्रौं

रक्ता रमा कराली कमला चण्डेन्दिरा महोच्छुष्मा ।
श्रीरिति मूर्तियुगलयोर्मध्यगता चावृतिरियञ्चापि ॥ २६
भूतिर्विभूतिरुन्नतिर्नतिर्धृतिररतिसंयतिद्युतयः ।
आवृतिरेषा प्रोक्ता श्रीवश्यकरं विधानमिति गदितम् ॥ २७

उष्मार्णाष्टाक्षरावेष्टितहृदयमथो द्वादशार्णात्तकोणं
सान्तःस्थात्माष्टवर्णैः क्रमगतविगतैरुल्लसत्तत्त्वगण्डम् ।
सिंहानुष्टुब्द्वयार्णान्तरितवृतकलालङ्कृतं चाथ वह्नि-
प्राणेशानक्षपाटास्विगकचटतपल्वक्शलं सिंहयन्त्रम् ॥ २८

पुष्टिस्तुष्टिर्धृतिरपि कृतिः शान्तिकान्ती प्रमोदा
मेधा हर्षा स्मृतिरभिमता चान्तिका स्यात्तृतीया ।
कृष्णः सत्यो नृहरिवरदौ विश्वमूर्तिर्वरेण्यः
शौरिः शूरो नरमुरजितौ विष्णुजिष्णू चतुर्थौ ॥ २९

विपक्षनिग्रहं तेजो यशश्च धनसङ्गमम् ।
करोत्यर्चयितॄणाञ्च विधानमिति सिंहजम् ॥ ३०

एतैरात्तकोणमित्यर्थः। बहिश्चेति। त्रिकोणात् बहिरित्यर्थः। का हरि मि ह र नि हरि इत्यादिक्रमेण वेष्टनम्। प्रत्यनूष्यद्वर्णाख्यमिति। शक्तिवेष्टनबाह्ये। अङ्ग वासुदेव रक्ता भूति केशव केलिन्द्र वज्रादिभिः अष्टावरणा कर्कटकपूजा ॥ २५॥२६॥२७ ॥

ऊष्मार्णेति। अत्रानुविगता ऊष्मार्णा ग्राह्याः। शं श्रों षं नं सं मों हं नां हं रां सं यं षं णां शं यं इति वेष्टनप्रकारः। द्वादशार्णं प्रसिद्धम्। सान्तस्थेति। क्रमगतात्माष्टाक्षरवर्णद्वयान्तरं क्रमगतान्तस्थवर्णानामेकैकं लिखित्वा विगतात्माष्टाक्षरवर्णद्वन्द्वान्तरं विगतान्तस्थवर्णानामेकैकं लिखित्वा विगतात्माष्टाक्षरवर्णद्वन्द्वान्तरं विगतान्तस्थवर्णानामेकैकं चतुर्विंशतिगण्डेषु लिखेदित्यर्थः। सिंहानुष्टुबिति। शक्तिवेष्टनाद् बहिः उं यं ॠं वीं रं आं इत्यादिप्रकारेण वेष्टनम्। वह्निप्राणेति। पृथिवीमण्डलस्य अग्निवाय्वीशाननिर्ऋतिकोणेषु कचटतवर्गान् पयशलवर्गांश्च लिखेदित्यर्थः। ल्वक्शब्देन यवर्ग उक्तः। अङ्ग वासुदेव पुष्टि कृष्णानन्त केशव मत्स्य केलिन्द्र वज्रादिभिर्दशावरणा सिंहपूजा ॥ २८ ॥ २९ ॥ ३० ॥

सर्गाद्यान्ताद्यमन्त्रैरभिवृतहृदयं दण्डिभिश्चाथ हाही-
हूहैहौहोभिरात्तास्त्रिकमथ तु शिखाद्योतिवर्गान्त्यवर्णम् ।
वर्णैः प्रत्यन्वितैः प्रावृतमवनिपुरास्त्रोल्लसत्कामबीजं
क्लिन्नेस्वाहार्णयुक्तं महिततरफलं कन्यकोत्थञ्च यन्त्रम् ॥ ३१

अत्राऽर्च्यो मधुसूदनस्त्वथ हृषीकेशाह्वयो मोहिनी
वैकुण्ठो विरजा हरिः सरसिजा शार्ङ्गी तमोहारिणी ।
ब्रह्माख्यः कमलावती च समुकुन्दाख्यो रमेति क्रमा-
न्मत्स्याद्यैश्च सुताश्वगोमहिषसौभाग्यप्रदं पावनम् ॥ ३२

आद्यैरावीतबीजं ग्रहवलययुतं हुंफड़ा युक्तकोणं
बाह्ये पाशाङ्कुशार्णावृतमथ युगषण्मूर्तिनामार्णमर्णैः ।
प्रत्यन्वेष्यद्भिरुद्यद्धरियुतहरवर्णैश्च वीतं धरायाः
कोणेष्वद्यन्नृसिंहाच्चरमिति कथितं स्यात्तुलायन्त्रमेतत् ॥ ३३

प्राक्प्रोक्तैश्चक्राद्यैरुक्तास्य समावृतिस्तृतीया स्यात् ।
पोतोपलब्धिमेतत्करोति वाणिज्यलाभञ्च ॥ ३४

सर्गाद्यान्ताद्यमन्त्रैरिति । विसर्गाद्याकारान्तैरकाराद्यमन्त्रैश्च वेष्टयेत् । अः अं आः आं इः इं ईः ईं इत्यादिप्रकारेण आत्तास्त्रिकमित्यस्त्रिशब्देन षट्कोणकोणान्युच्यन्ते । शिखाशब्देन षट्कोणाग्राणि । वर्गान्त्यः ङकारः । वर्णैः प्रत्यन्वितैरिति । शक्तिवेष्टनबाह्ये अवनिपुरकोणेषु एव क्लींक्लिन्नेस्वाहार्णाः । अङ्ग वासुदेव हृषीकेश मत्स्य केशव केत्विन्द्र वज्रादिभिरष्टावरणा कन्यका पूजा ।
॥ ३१ ॥ ३२ ॥

आद्यैरावीतमिति । ग्रहवलययुतं यथा भवति तथाद्यैः आवीतमध्यबीजमित्यर्थः । सूर्य अं आं सोम इं ईं अङ्गारक उं ऊं शुक्र ऋं ॠं बुधः लृं लॄं बृहस्पते एं ऐं शनैश्वर ओं औं राहो अं केतो अः इति वेष्टन प्रकारः । हुंफड़ायुक्तकोणमिति । हुंफड्युक्तत्रिकोणकोणमित्यर्थः । बाह्य इति । शक्तिवेष्टनाद् बाह्य इत्यर्थः । युगषण्मूर्तयः केशवाद्याः तेषां नामार्णैरेकावृतिः तद्बहिः प्रत्यन्वेष्यद्भिः मातृकावर्णैः आवृतिद्वयं तद्बहिः हरिहरवर्णैः । अङ्गवासुदेवचक्रकेशवकेत्विन्द्रवज्रादिभिः सप्तावरणा तुलापूजा ॥ ३३ ॥ ३४ ॥

अक्लीबद्वादशाजद्वादशलिपिवृतच्छ्ल्लेखमस्त्रिद्विषट्क-
प्रोक्तास्वष्टाक्षरोष्मार्णकमपि लिपिभिः कादिभिश्चाऽभिवीतम् ।
तद्बाह्ये चन्द्रबिम्बप्रपुटितवसुधामण्डलास्त्रिप्रराजत्-
क्लीबार्णं वृष्णिकोत्थं प्रवरतरफलप्राप्तिदं यन्त्रमेतत् ॥ ३५

चिद्रूपा चिन्मया चिन्तामणिः श्रीः चोणिसंज्ञका ।
रतिश्च पावनी धारा धरणी तारणी तथा ॥ ३६
द्राविणी मोहिनी चेति तृतीयेयं समावृतिः ।
अन्वयाप्तिं धर्मरतिं प्राप्नुयादस्य चाऽर्चनात् ॥ ३७

षट्कोणाबद्धबाणासनविवरलसन्नारसिंहं तदन्तः
शक्तेर्बाह्ये परानुप्रचितलघुसन्ध्यर्णयुक्पञ्चकाढ्यम् ।
अस्त्रिष्वाबद्धशिष्टस्वरमुपरिलसच्छूलकं प्राप्तवर्गं
भूमेरष्टास्त्रिकोद्यद्यदुजहुलवकं चापयन्त्रं तदेतत् ॥ ३८

हर्षाख्या सुनदारुणा सगगना घोरा रमा द्राविणी
वीरा वीरिणि हारिणी सहरिणी मन्दारिका द्वादश ।
प्रोक्तेयञ्च समावृतिः पुनरिदं संपूजयन् प्राप्नुया-
ल्लक्ष्मीसन्ततिबुद्धिवश्यपटुतां कान्तिञ्च भक्तिं शुभाम् ॥ ३९

अक्लीबेति । द्वादशलिपिर्द्वादशाक्षरम् । अं ओं आं नं उं मों इत्यादिप्रकारेण वेष्टनमवगन्तव्यम् । अस्त्रिद्विषट्केति । अष्टाक्षराक्षरद्वयं कोणद्वये लिखित्वा ऊष्मार्णानामेकैकं तृतीयकोणे विलिख्याऽवशिष्टकोणेष्वप्येवं क्रमेण लिखेदित्यर्थः । लिपिभिः कादिभिरिति । शक्तिवेष्टनबाह्ये । चन्द्रबिम्ब-प्रपुटितकेति । चन्द्रमण्डलं लिखित्वा तन्मध्ये भूमण्डलं विरच्य तत्कोणेषु नपुंसकाक्षराणि लिखेदित्यर्थः । अङ्ग वासुदेव चिद्रूपानन्त केशव मत्स्य केलिन्द्र-वज्रादिभिर्नवावरणा वृष्णिकपूजा ॥ ३५ ॥ ३६ ॥ ३७ ॥

बाणासनेति । बाणासनशब्देन धनुराकारं षट्कोणान्तरालमुच्यते । तदन्तरिति षट्कोणमध्य इत्यर्थः । युक्पञ्चकाढ्यं पञ्चकद्वयाढ्यं किं तत्पञ्चक द्वयमिति । तदाह—लघुसन्ध्यर्णेति । अ इ उ ऋ ऌ इत्येतल्लघुपञ्चकम् । ए ऐ ओ औ अं इत्येतत् सन्धिपञ्चकम् । वेष्टनक्रममाह—परानुप्रचितेति । ऌं एं ऋं ऐं उं ओं इं औं अं अं इति क्रमेण वेष्टयेदित्यर्थः । अस्त्रिष्विति ।

मध्यस्थायाः परीतो विलसदनुपरात्तस्वरप्राक्पराधं
सिंहार्णान्तास्त्रिगण्डस्फुरितहरिहराणां ग्रहार्णावृतञ्च ।
तद्बाह्ये षोडशार्णाचरवृतमुभकुद्योतितं कोणराजत्
सोऽहं हंसाचराढ्यं मकरभवमिदं यन्त्रमिष्टार्थदायि ॥ ४०

मेधा हर्षा श्रद्धा कृपा रतिर्वाक् सरस्वती प्रीतिः ।
वाणी चेति तृतीयावृतिरुक्ता मकरजे विधानेऽस्मिन् ॥ ४१
स्वच्छेववर्तिनः स्युर्ग्रहा क्रमात् केशवादिभिः सहिताः ।
अर्चयितणामेतद्धनधान्यसमृद्धिदं विधानं स्यात् ॥ ४२

शक्तिश्रीकामबीजैः पुटितहरिहरब्रह्मभिश्चावृतान्त-
र्बीजं कोणद्विषट्कस्फुरितनृहरिबीजप्रतिद्योतितञ्च ।
आदिक्षान्तैश्च वर्णैर्वृतमवनिगृहद्वन्द्वकोणान्तकाम-
श्रीशक्तिच्मार्णचिन्तामणिमनु तदिदं श्रीकरं कुम्भयन्त्रम् ॥ ४३
अच्युतकामिनिभानुमनोज्ञा विश्वतनुर्विमला हरिभद्रे ।
सूक्ष्मसरस्वतिनन्दनसन्ध्या स्यादिति मध्यगता वृतिरेषा ॥ ४४

षट्कोणेष्वित्यर्थः । आं ईं ऊं ऋं लॄं अः इत्येते शिष्टाः स्वराः । उपरि लसच्छूलप्राप्त वर्गमिति । षट्कोणाग्रान्निर्गच्छत्सु शूलेषु प्राप्त क च ट त प य वर्गमित्यर्थः । यदुजदुलवकं कामबीजद्वमित्यर्थः । अङ्ग वासुदेव हृषीकेश-केशव केलिन्द्र वज्रादिभिः सप्तावरणा चापपूजा ॥ ३८ ॥ ३९ ॥

अनुपरात्तस्वरप्राक्पराधमिति । अं अः आं अं इं औमित्यादिक्रमेणेत्यर्थः । सिंहार्णान्तास्त्रीति क्षौंकारविशिष्टकोणत्रयमित्यर्थः । ग्रहार्णावृतिः हरिहरबाह्ये । षोडशार्णावृतिश्च तत्रैव । षोडशार्णः सुदर्शने वक्ष्यमाणो ग्राह्यः । अत्र षोडशार्णा-चराभ्यां वृतमिति । शक्तिवेष्टनात् बहिर्मातृकावृतिरपि उक्ता । स्वच्छेववर्तिन इत्युक्तं ग्रहावरणं सर्वत्र समानमिति केचित् । सर्वथापि तत्र पृथग्-गणनार्थम् । केशवाद्यावरण एवाऽन्तर्भूतत्वादित्यवगन्तव्यम् । अङ्ग वासुदेव-मेधा केशव केलिन्द्र वज्रादिभिः सप्तावरणा मकरयन्त्रपूजा ॥ ४० ॥ ४१ ॥ ४२ ॥

शक्तिश्रीति । ह्रीं हरिः श्रीं हरः क्लीं ब्रह्मेति क्रमेणावृतिः कार्येत्यर्थः । आदिक्षान्तैरिति । शक्तिबाह्ये । अवनिगृहेति । दिग्गतकोणेषु क्षौमादयो लेख्याः । कोणगतकोणेषु चिन्तामणिमनुरिति विभागः । अङ्गवासुदेवाच्युता-

अवनिपशुपुत्रसम्पदमपि पितृसौख्यञ्च हृत्प्रबोधञ्च ।
कुरुते विधानमेतत् प्रयोक्तुरन्ते च निर्वृतिं परमाम् ॥ ४५

व्यन्वेष्यदृभ्रस्वदीर्घा समभिहतमहाबीजमस्त्रेषु षट्सु
द्योतत्सौर्मारलक्ष्मीगिरिदुहितृधराबीजकं प्रोंसमेतम् ।
वीतं काद्यैः क्षान्तैर्बहिरपि च कुक्षोणाष्टकोल्लासिहंसं
सर्वार्थान् साधकेभ्यो वितरति विधिवत्कल्पितं मीनयन्त्रम् ॥ ४६

हृष्टिर्व्युष्टिस्तुष्टिरिष्टा सपुष्टिः कान्तिर्मेधा मङ्गला वामसंज्ञा ।
दुर्गा प्रज्ञा भारती मध्यसंस्था वाक्सामर्थ्यश्रीकरं स्याद्विधानम् ॥

एभिर्विधानैर्धरणीव्रतादिदीक्षाविधीन् ये विधिना प्रकुर्युः ।
ते पुण्यभाजो नितरां समृद्ध्या सपुत्रदाराः सुखिनो भवन्ति ॥ ४८

दीर्घायुषो मुख्यतरेन्द्रियाश्च महाप्रभावास्त्वसमानवीर्याः ।
कलेवरान्ते विगताधयस्ते विष्णोरनन्यं पदमाप्नुवन्ति ॥ ४९

एभिर्विधेयाः कलशाश्च तत्तन्मासोक्तयन्त्रेषु नरैर्यथावत् ।
निजेप्सितं प्राप्य मनोरथन्ते भक्तेश्च मुक्तेरनुभावकाः स्युः ॥ ५०

कर्षोन्मिते च हाटकपट्टे यन्त्रं विलिख्य चतुरस्रे ।
तद्द्विवंशकृते वा कलशेषु विनिक्षिपेच्च दीक्षासु ॥ ५१

अभिषिच्य यन्त्रकलशं गुरवे प्रददातु संयतमतिः सुमतिः ।
दुरितापनोदविधये द्युतये यशसे श्रिये च मतिसंयतये ॥ ५२

एषां यागविधीनामेकेन तु पूजयंस्तदवसाने ।
तत्तन्मूर्तिं प्रीत्यै संस्तोतव्योऽनया हरिः स्तुत्या ॥ ५३

प्रसीद भगवन्मह्यमज्ञानात्कुण्ठितात्मने ।
तवाङ्घ्रिपङ्कजरजोरागिणीं भक्तिमुत्तमाम् ॥ ५४

नन्त केशव मत्स्य केलिन्द्र वज्रादिभिर्नवावरणा कुम्भपूजा ॥ ४३ ॥ ४४ ॥ ४५ ॥

व्यन्वेष्यदृभ्रस्वेति । अं आं ओं ईं ऐं जं लृं ऋं ॠं ॡं उं ऐं इं औं अं अः इति क्रमेणावृतिः कार्येत्यर्थः । विधिवत् कल्पितमिति । यन्त्रच्छदादिकं सूचयति । अङ्गवासुदेव हृषीकेश केशव केलिन्द्र वज्रादिभिः सप्तावरणा मीनपूजा ॥ ४६ ॥ ४७ ॥ ४८ ॥ ४९ ॥ ५० ॥ ५१ ॥ ५२ ॥

अज प्रसीद भगवन्नमितद्युतिपञ्जर ।
अप्रमेय प्रसीदाऽस्मद्दुःखहन् पुरुषोत्तम ॥ ५५
स्वसंवेद्यस्वरूपात्मन्नानन्दात्मन्ननामय ।
अचिन्त्यसार विश्वात्मन् प्रसीदेश निरञ्जन ॥ ५६
प्रसीद तुङ्ग तुङ्गानां प्रसीद शिव शोभन ।
प्रसीद स्पष्टगम्भीर गम्भीराणां महाद्युते ॥ ५७
प्रसीदाऽव्यक्त विस्तीर्ण विस्तीर्णानामणोरणो ।
प्रसीदार्द्राद्रंजातीनां प्रसीदाऽन्तान्तयायिनाम् ॥ ५८
गुरोर्गरीयः सर्वेश प्रसीदाऽनन्त[न्य] देहिनाम् ।
जय माधव मायात्मन् जय शाश्वत शङ्खभृत् ॥ ५९
जय सुन्दर सौम्यात्मन् जय केशव केशिहन् ।
जय शार्ङ्गधर श्रीमन् जय नन्दकनन्दन ॥ ६०
जय चक्रगदापाणे जयाऽजय्य जनार्दन ।
जय रत्नोत्करावद्धकिरीटाक्रान्तमस्तक ॥ ६१
जय पक्षिपतिच्छायानिरुद्धार्ककराकर ।
नमस्ते नरकाराते नमस्ते मधुसूदन ॥ ६२
नमस्ते नलिनापाङ्ग नमस्ते नयनाञ्जन ।
नमः पापहरेशान नमः सर्वभयापह ॥ ६३
नमः संहृतसर्वात्मन् नमः सम्भृतकौस्तुभ ।
नमस्ते नयनातीत नमोऽतिक्रान्तवाक्पथ ॥ ६४
नमो विभिन्नवेषांश नमः स्मृतिपथातिग ।
नमस्त्रिमूर्तिभेदेन सर्गस्थित्यन्तहेतवे ॥ ६५
विष्णवे त्रिदशारातिजिष्णवे परमात्मने ।
चक्रभिन्नारिचक्राय चक्रिणे चक्रबन्धवे ॥ ६६
विश्वाय विश्ववन्द्याय विश्वभूतात्मने नमः ।
नमोऽस्तु योगिध्येयाय नमोऽस्त्वध्यात्मरूपिणे ॥ ६७

स्तुतिमाह—प्रसीदेत्यादि षोडशभिः ॥ ५२—६९ ॥

भुक्तिप्रदाय भक्तानां नमस्ते मुक्तिदायिने ।
मनोवाक्कायचेष्टाः स्युर्ध्यानस्तुतिनमस्क्रियाः ॥ ६८

देवेश कर्म सर्वं मे भवेदाराधनं तव ।
विषयेष्वपि सङ्गो मे स्तुतं विष्णो तवाऽच्युत ॥ ६९

इति हवनजपार्चाभेदतो विष्णुपूजा-
निरतहृदयकर्मा यस्तु मन्त्री चिराय ।
स खलु सकलकामान् प्राप्य हृष्टान्तरात्मा
जननमृतिवियुक्तामुत्तमां मुक्तिमेति ॥ ७०

इति श्रीप्रपञ्चसारे एकविंशः पटलः ।

यस्तु मन्त्री चिरायेति । अतोक्तान् केशवादिमन्त्रान् सूचयति ॥ ६८ ॥

इति श्रीपद्मपादाचार्यकृते प्रपञ्चसारविवरणे
एकविंशः पटलः ।

द्वाविंशः पटलः ।

अथोच्यते द्वादशवर्णसंज्ञो मन्त्रस्तु साङ्गः सजपः सहोमः ।
विधानतो यं प्रतिजप्य भक्ता भुक्तेश्च मुक्तेश्च पदं भवेयुः ॥ १

तारं सहृदयं मध्ये गवते स्युर्भवार्णयोः ।
सुययोश्च तथा देवा मन्त्रोऽयं द्वादशाक्षरः ॥ २

ऋषिः प्रजापतिश्छन्दो गायत्री विष्णुरुच्यते ।
देवता हृद्ध्रुवेण स्यान्नमसा शिर उच्यते ॥ ३

चतुर्भिश्च शिखा वर्णैः पञ्चभिः कवचं भवेत् ।
प्रोक्तमस्त्रं समस्तेन पञ्चाङ्गविधिरीदृशः ॥ ४

सपादजानुयुगललिङ्गनाभ्युदरेषु च ।
हृद्दोर्गलास्यदृङ्मस्तशिखास्वक्षरतो न्यसेत् ॥ ५

शिखाललाटनेत्रास्यगलदोर्हृदयेष्वपि ।
सकुक्षिनाभिलिङ्गाख्यजानुपादेषु विन्यसेत् ॥ ६

हृत्कुक्षिनाभिषु तथा गुह्यजानुपदेष्वथ ।
करकण्ठास्यदृङ्मस्तशिखामूर्धसु विन्यसेत् ॥ ७

संहृतेर्दोषसंहारः सृष्टेश्च शुभपुष्टयः ।
स्थितेस्तु शान्तिविन्यासस्तस्मात्कार्यस्त्रिधा मतः ॥ ८

हरिमुज्ज्वलचक्रदराब्जगदाकुलदोःपरिघं सितपद्मगतम् ।
वलयाङ्गदहारकिरीटधरं नवकुन्दरुचं प्रणमामि सदा ॥ ९

विधिवदथ विहितदीक्षो जपेन्मनुं वर्णलक्षमानममुम् ।
शुद्धैश्च तिलैर्जुहुयाद्द्वादशसाहस्रसंख्यकं मन्त्री ॥ १०

द्वादशमूर्तिविधानानन्तरं तत्समष्टिवाचकस्य द्वादशाक्षरस्य विधानं वदन् विनियोगमाह—अथोच्यत इति। अं बीजम्। नमः शक्तिः ॥ १ ॥ २ ॥

पञ्चाङ्गविधिरीदृश इति। द्वादशाङ्गस्यापि सद्भावः सूचितः। तत्र द्वादशवर्णैः साधं पुरुष सत्याच्युत वासुदेवादिनारायण ब्रह्म विष्णु नरसिंह वराहाद्याभिः षडङ्गोदरपृष्ठबाहूरुजानुपादेषु कार्यम् ॥ ३॥४॥५॥६॥७॥८॥९ ॥

द्वादशसाहस्रकं मन्त्रीति। विशेष होमजपेषु बीजविशेष उक्तः ॥ १० ॥

पीठे हरेरथाङ्गैः सशक्तिभिर्मूर्तिभिस्तदनु यजेत् ।
केशवसुरनाथाद्यैरपि देवं भक्तिसंयुतो विद्वान् ॥ ११
समिधामथ दुग्धवृक्षजानां जुहुयादर्कसहस्रकं सदुग्धम् ।
मनसः परिशुद्धये मनस्वी सघृतेनापि पयोऽन्धसा सितेन ॥ १२
द्वादशाक्षरजपं तु सार्चनं यो भजेन्नियमतो दिने दिने ।
ऐहिकं समुपलभ्य वाञ्छितं प्रेत्य याति पदमक्षयं हरेः ॥ १३
अथ प्रवक्ष्यामि सुदर्शनस्य विधिं मनोः संग्रहतो जपादेः ।
यत्सिद्धितः सिद्धिमवापुरग्र्यां सिद्धा मुनीन्द्रा अपि सद्य एव ॥ १४
अन्त्यतुरीयतदादिकभृगुदहनानन्तवह्निवर्मास्त्रैः ।
तारादिर्मनुरुक्तः स्यादभिमतसिद्धिदो रथाङ्गाख्यः ॥ १५
ऋषिरस्याऽहिर्बुध्न्यश्छन्दोऽनुष्टुब्देवता च विष्णुः ।
चक्रपदैराविसुधीसंज्वालाद्यैः शिरोऽन्वितैरङ्गम् ॥ १६
ऐन्द्रीं समारभ्य दिशन्त्वधस्तादन्तं समुक्त्वा क्रमशो दशानाम् ।
चक्रेण बध्नामि नमस्तथोक्त्वा चक्राय शीर्षं च दिशां प्रबन्धः ॥ १७
त्रैलोक्यं रक्ष रक्षेति हुं फट् स्वाहेति चोदितः ।
तारादिकोऽयं मन्त्रः स्यादग्निप्राकारसंज्ञकः ॥ १८
तारन्तु मूर्ध्न्यथ सितारुणकृष्णवर्णां
मध्ये भ्रुवोश्च समथो वदने हकारम् ।
हृद्गुह्यजानुपदसन्धिषु चाऽवशिष्टान्
वर्णान्न्यसेदिति मनोः [तनौ] पुनरग्निवर्णान् ॥ १९

भक्तिसंयुतो विद्वानित्यष्टाक्षरोक्तं सर्वम् । विद्वानिति । मासयन्त्र-पूजादिक्रमत्रापि समानमित्युक्तम् ॥ ११ ॥ १२ ॥ १३ ॥ १४ ॥

सम्यग्विज्ञानविज्ञेयस्य वासुदेवस्य पूजामभिधाय चक्रात्मकज्ञानविशिष्टस्य तस्यैव विधानं वक्तुमारभते—अन्त्येति ॥ १५ ॥

देवता विष्णुरिति । सुदर्शनविष्णुरित्यर्थः । रं बीजम् । हुं शक्तिः ॥ १६ ॥

ऐन्द्रीं दिशं चक्रेण बध्नामि नमश्चक्राय स्वाहेत्याद्याः प्रयोगेषु रक्षार्थं दिग्बन्धनमन्त्राः । सुदर्शनमुद्रया सहाऽयं दिग्बन्धः कार्यः ॥ १७ ॥ १८ ॥

तारं तु मूर्ध्नीति वर्णन्यासः । अत्रापि समानाः सामान्यन्यासाः ॥ १९ ॥

अव्याद्भास्करसप्रभाभिरखिलाभाभिर्दिशो भासयन्
भीमाक्षः स्फुरदट्टहासविकसद्दंष्ट्राग्रदीप्तानन: ।
दोर्भिश्चक्रदरौ गदाब्जमुसलप्रासांश्च पाशाङ्कुशौ
बिभ्रत् पिङ्गशिरोरुहोऽथ भवतश्चक्राभिधानो हरिः ॥ २०

प्रोक्त्वा सुदर्शनायेति विद्महेऽन्ते महापदम् ।
ज्वालाय धीमहि प्रोक्त्वा तन्नश्चक्रः प्रचोदयात् ॥ २१
सौदर्शनीयं गायत्री जप्तव्या जप्तुमिच्छता ।
सान्निध्यकारिणीं मुद्रां दर्शयेदनया सुधीः ॥ २२
नमो भगवते प्रोक्त्वा महासुदर्शनाय च ।
महाचक्राय च तथा महाज्वालाय चेत्यपि ॥ २३
दीप्तरूपाय चेत्युक्त्वा सर्वतो रक्ष रक्ष माम् ।
महाबलाय स्वाहेति प्रोक्तस्तारादिको मनुः ।
रक्षाकरः प्रसिद्धोऽयं क्रियमाणेषु कर्मसु ॥ २४

षट्कोणान्तःस्थतारं विवरलिखितमन्त्राक्षरं सन्धिराजत्
स्वाङ्गं बाह्ये कलाकेसरमुदरगताष्टाक्षरञ्चाऽष्टपत्रम् ।
पद्मं वर्णैर्विराजत् विकृतिदललसत्षोड़शार्णं त्रिवीतं
व्योमान्त्यार्णं स्वनाम्ना विरचितगुणपाशाङ्कुशं चक्रयन्त्रम् ॥ २५

ध्यानमाह—अव्यादिति ॥ २० ॥

सुदर्शनगायत्रीमाह—प्रोक्त्वेति । सान्निध्यकारिणी मुद्रा सुदर्शनमुद्रा । सुधीरिति । सहस्रारस्य सुदर्शनस्य ध्यानमुक्तम् ॥ २१ ॥ २२ ॥

रक्षाकरमपरं मन्त्रमाह—नम इति ॥ २३ ॥ २४ ॥

पूजादौ प्रयोक्तव्यं यन्त्रमाह—षट्कोणेति । विवरशब्देन कोणषट्कमुक्तम् । बाह्य इति । वृत्तबाह्य इत्यर्थः । कलाः स्वराः । उदरं दलमध्यम् । वर्णैः विराजद्विकृतिदललसत्षोड़शार्णमिति । वर्णैः कादिसान्तैः द्विशः केसरस्थानलिखितैः विराजद्विकृतिसंख्यादलयुक्तपद्मदलस्थषोडशार्णमित्यर्थः । तद्बाह्यस्थवृत्तत्रयेति । त्रिवीतं व्योमान्त्यार्णं व्योमार्णं हकारः अन्त्यार्णः क्षकारः । तद्बाह्ये स्वनाम्ना सह विरचितगुणपाशाङ्कुशम् । गुणः प्रणवः । प्रथमं प्रणवः ततो नाम्नः प्रथममक्षरम् । ततः पाशः ततो नामद्वितीयाक्षरम् ।

प्रणवहृद्भगवद्युतङे महादिकरथाङ्गचतुर्थी हुमस्त्रकैः ।
निगदितस्त्विति षोडशवर्णको मनुवरो मुनिभिर्विहितादरः ॥ २६

क्वाथैः पयोभूरुहचर्मसिद्धैर्दुग्धेन गव्यैरपि पञ्चभिर्वा ।
मूत्रैः पशोर्वा प्रतिपूर्य कुम्भं समर्चयेच्चक्रहरिं क्रमेण ॥ २७

अङ्गैः प्रथमावृतिरपि च पूज्या चक्रादिभिर्द्वितीया च ।
लक्ष्म्यादिभिस्तृतीया क्रमात्तथेन्द्रादिभिश्चतुर्थी स्यात् ॥ २८

चक्रशङ्खगदापद्ममुसला धनुरेव च ।
पाशाङ्कुशौ पीतरक्तसितश्यामत्विषस्त्विमाः ॥ २९
लक्ष्मीः सरस्वती चाथ रतिः प्रीत्याह्वया ततः ।
कीर्त्तिः कान्तिस्तुष्टिपुष्टी क्रमेणैव तु शक्तयः ॥ ३०

संपूज्य चैवं विधिना हरिन्तु शिष्यं गुरुः प्रीततमोऽभिषिञ्चेत् ।
भक्त्या स्वशक्त्या विभवैर्द्विजातीन् सन्तर्प्य भूयो गुरुणाऽनुशिष्टः ॥ ३१
एकाग्रचित्तो रविलक्षसंख्यं जपेन्मनुं नित्यकृताभिपूजः ।
तावत् सहस्रं तिलसर्षपाब्जबिल्वाज्यदोग्धानि जुहोतु सम्यक् ॥ ३२
समुद्रतीरेऽप्यथवाऽद्रिशृङ्गे समुद्रगानां सरिताञ्च तीरे ।
जपेद्विविक्ते निज एव गेहे विष्णोर्गृहे वा पुरुषो मनस्वी ॥ ३३
यथोक्तसंख्यं विधिवत् प्रजप्ते मन्त्रे यथोक्तैश्च हुते हुताशे ।
द्रव्यैरथ स्वार्थपरार्थहेतोः कुर्यात् प्रयोगान् विधिना यथावत् ॥ ३४

पीताभा कर्णिका स्यादरुणतरमरं श्यामलञ्चाऽन्तरालं
नेमिः श्वेता च बाह्ये विरचितशिखरेखाकुलं पार्थिवान्तम् ।
चक्रद्वन्द्वं लिखित्वा विशदमतिरथो सौम्ययाम्यञ्च मन्त्री
कुम्भं संपूर्य सौम्ये प्रचयतु तथा दक्षिणे होमकर्म ॥ ३५

ततोऽङ्कुशमिति विरचनाप्रकारः ॥ २५ ॥ २६ ॥

पीतरक्तादिवर्णा लक्ष्म्याद्या ज्ञातव्याः २७ ॥ २८ ॥ २९ ॥ ३० ॥

सम्यगिति । द्रव्याणां समविभागं सूचयति ॥ ३१ ॥ ३२ ॥

मनस्वीति । ब्रह्मचर्यादिनियमवानित्यर्थः ॥ ३३ ॥

विधिना यथावदिति । विधिनेत्यग्निजननादिकमुक्तम् । यथावदिति । कार्यानुगुणबीजविशेषयोगः सूचितः ॥ ३४ ॥

षड्विंशच्छतसम्मितैरथ घृतापामार्गकैश्चाचतैः
सद्राजीतिलपायसैश्च सकलैर्गव्यैर्घृताक्तैः क्रमात् ।
हुत्वा तद्धुतशिष्टमत्र विधिवत् क्षिप्त्वा प्रतिद्रव्यकं
प्रस्थार्धान्नकृतञ्च पिण्डममलं कुम्भोदके मन्त्रवित् ॥ ३६
संस्थाप्य दक्षिणस्यां साध्यं कुम्भेन तेन नीराज्य ।
तमथ घटं सद्रव्यं बहिराराद्दृष्टमे क्षिपेद्राशौ ॥ ३७
अग्न्यादिकमपि सर्वं क्षिपेदथ घटस्य दक्षिणे भागे ।
हुतशेषान्नेन च बलिं मन्त्रेणाऽनेन मन्त्रवित् कुर्यात् ॥ ३८
हृदयान्ते विष्णुपदं प्रोक्त्वाऽथ गणेभ्य उच्चरेत् पूर्वम् ।
शान्तिकरेभ्यश्च बलिं गृह्णन्त्विति शान्तये नमोऽन्तः स्यात् ॥ ३९
ज्वरादिकां रोगपरम्परां वा विस्मृत्यपस्मारभवां रुजं वा ।
रक्षःपिशाचग्रहवैकृतं वा विधिस्त्वयं मङ्क्षु हरेद्विकारम् ॥ ४०
पालाशैर्वा स्तनजद्रुमजैर्वा पञ्जरे कृते फलकैः ।
संपूर्य पञ्चगव्यैस्तत्र तु संस्थाप्य शुद्धमपि गदिनम् ॥ ४१
पूर्वोद्दिष्टैर्दिक्षु च सजपं जुहुयुः पृथग्द्विजा वशिनः ।
द्रव्यैः सदक्षिणं तानभ्यर्च्य च मुच्यते रुजो जन्तुः ॥ ४२

विशदमतिरथो इति । चक्रयाथात्म्यज्ञत्वमुक्तम् । मन्त्रीति । चक्रस्य मूलमन्त्रतत्त्ववित् । कुम्भं संपूर्येति । शुद्धोदकेन संपूर्य तत्र देवमावाह्याऽभिपूज्येत्यर्थः ॥ ३५ ॥

विधिवत् क्षिप्त्वेति । दशांशं कलशे क्षिप्त्वेत्यर्थः । कुम्भोदक इति । कुम्भमुख इत्यर्थः । मन्त्रविदिति । वषडन्तमूलान्वित सुदर्शनगायत्र्या क्षिपेदित्यर्थः । मन्त्रविदित्यनेनैव दक्षिणभागस्थस्य साध्यस्य सकलीकरणं रक्षोघ्नमन्त्रेण नीराजनं चोक्तम् ।

ओं स्थाने हृषीकेश तव प्रकीर्त्याऽन्नो सह नमो जगत् प्रहृष्यत्यनुरज्यते चाऽस्ते स्मार नारा रक्षांसि भीतानि दिशो द्रवन्ति हुं फड् यणा सर्वे नमस्यन्ति च सिद्धसंघाः योमिति रक्षोघ्नमन्त्रः ॥ ३६ ॥ ३७ ॥

मन्त्रवित् कुर्यादिति । प्रणवग्रहणादित्वं मन्त्रस्य सूचितम् ॥ ३८॥३९॥४० ॥

शुद्धमपीत्यपिना सकलीकरणमुक्तम् ॥ ४१ ॥ ४२ ॥

विप्रचीरद्रुमत्वङ्मलयजपुरकाश्मीरकुष्ठवियामा-
बिल्वापामार्गराजीतिलतुलसियुगक्रान्तिदूर्वाजवार्कैः ।
लक्ष्मीदेवीकुशागोमयकमलवचारोचनापञ्चगव्यैः
सिद्धेऽग्नौ कुम्भसिद्धं मनुजपसहितं भस्म सर्वार्थदायि ॥ ४३

लक्ष्म्यायुष्करमतुलं पिशाचभूता-
पस्माराद्विकमचिरेण नाशयेच्च ।
क्षुद्रादीनपि विविधांस्तथोपसर्गा-
नेतस्मान्न परतरा समास्ति रक्षा ॥ ४४

जुहुयात् गुग्गुलुगुलिकासहस्रकं साष्टकं च मन्त्रितमः ।
त्रिदिनं चतुर्दिनं वा सर्वोपद्रवनिवारणं भवति ॥ ४५
खरमञ्जर्याः समिधामयुतं वा मन्त्रवित्तमो जुहुयात् ।
ज्वरभूतामयविस्मृत्यपस्मृतीः शमयितुं नियतचित्तः ॥ ४६
आज्याक्तैर्जुहुयाच्छ्रियै सरसिजैर्दूर्वाभिरप्यायुषे
मेधायै द्विजभूरुहैश्च कुमुदैः श्वेतैस्तथा वाससे ।
शुद्धाज्यैः पशवेऽप्युदुम्बरभवैः पुत्राय चाऽश्वत्थजै-
रेकाब्दं विधिवत् सहस्रसमितैरष्टोत्तरं मुक्तये ॥ ४७
चक्रस्य नाभिसंस्थं स्मृत्वाऽऽत्मानं जपेन्मनुं मन्त्री ।
स्वयमेकोऽपि न युद्धे मर्त्यैर्बहुभिः पराजितो भवति ॥ ४८
मन्त्री सुनियतचित्तश्चक्रस्थं भाव[भ्राम]येद्धिया ग्रस्तम् ।
आविश्य सकलं मुक्त्वा मुञ्चति दग्धोऽग्निनाऽऽशु नाभिभुवा ॥ ४९

सिद्धेऽग्नौ कुम्भसिद्धमिति। पूर्वोक्तविधानेनाऽग्निं संस्कृत्य पूर्वोक्तप्रकारेणैव कुम्भे पञ्चगव्यं संयोज्य तस्मिन् प्रोक्तमौषधजातं निक्षिप्य मूलमन्त्रं जपन् भर्जयेत्। ततः कुम्भमध्यगतौषधिष्वभिव्यक्तेऽग्नौ मूलेन शतं सहस्रं वा हुत्वा जपपूजादिना घटे सिद्धं भस्म सकलाभ्युदयदायीत्यर्थः ॥ ४३ ॥ ४४ ॥

साष्टकं च मन्त्रितम इति नृसिंहबीजयोग उक्तः ॥ ४५ ॥

मन्त्रवित्तमो जुहुयादित्यपि तथा वषट्कारयोगश्च ॥ ४६ ॥ ४७ ॥

मनुं जपेन्मन्त्रीति। रक्षोघ्नमन्त्रयुतमित्यर्थः ॥ ४८ ॥

मन्त्री सुनियतचित्त इति तथा दीप्तमित्यपि सहस्रारज्वालाकारा-

दीप्तं करालदहनप्रतिमस्य चक्रं
यस्य स्मरेच्छिरसि कस्यचिदप्रियस्य ।
सप्ताहतोऽस्य दहनप्रतिमो ज्वरः स्या-
त्त्रिंशद्दिनैश्च स परेतपुरं प्रयाति ॥ ५०

कलावृतं यादिपदाभिवेष्टितं
समक्षरं यच्छिरसि स्मरेत् सदा ।
दशाहतोऽसौ प्रति चाश्यते रिपु-
र्मृतिं तथा मण्डलतः प्रयाति ॥ ५१

सार्थं[न्तं] वायसवर्णं शत्रोः शिरसि स्मरेच्च सप्ताहम् ।
उच्चाटयति क्षिप्रं मारयति वा धियोऽस्य नैशित्यात् ॥ ५२

स्रवत्सुधावर्षिणमिन्दुसप्रभं
समक्षरं यच्छिरसि प्रचिन्तयेत् ।
क्षणात् समाप्यायितसर्वविग्रहो
भवेत् स मर्त्यः सुचिरञ्च जीवति ॥ ५३

मध्ये तारं तदनु च मनुं वर्णशः कोणषट्के
बाह्ये चाङ्गं लिखतु कनके रूप्यके चाऽथ ताम्रे ।
पाषाणे वा विधिवदभिजप्याऽथ संस्थापितं त-
च्चक्रं चोरग्रहरिपुभयध्वंसि रक्षाकरञ्च ॥ ५४

स्थाने हृषीकेशविदर्भितं च साष्टाक्षरञ्चाप्यभिजप्तमेतत् ।
रक्षां ग्रहादेः सततं विधत्ते यन्त्रं सुकृप्तञ्च मनुत्रयेण ॥ ५५

तत्त्वध्यानमुक्तम् ॥ ४९ ॥ ५० ॥

कलावृतमिति । यं यामित्यादिभिरावृतमित्यर्थः । शिरसि स्थितं समक्षरं वायसाकारं हृद्गतं जीवं ग्रसति चेन्मृतिं याति । धीनैशित्यमप्येतदेव ॥ ५१ ॥ ॥ ५२ ॥

स्रवत्सुधावर्षिणमिति प्रयोगोऽमृतमण्डले वं वामित्यादियुक्तश्च कार्यः ॥५३॥

विधिवदभिजप्येति । होमादिपूर्वकमित्यर्थः ॥ ५४ ॥

रक्षोघ्नमन्त्रमुद्धरति—स्थानेति ॥ ५५ ॥

अष्टाक्षरान्तरितपादचतुष्ककोष्ठं
कोष्ठत्रयोल्लिखितसाध्यसुदर्शनञ्च ।
रेखाभिरप्युभयतः श्रुतिशः प्रबद्धं
तत्सप्तकोष्ठमिति यन्त्रमिदं प्रशस्तम् ॥ ५६

भूर्जे वा क्षौमपट्टे तनुमसृणतरे कर्पटे वाऽस्य यन्त्रं
मन्त्री सम्यग्लिखित्वा पुनरपि गुलिकीकृत्य लाक्षाभिवीतम् ।
कृत्वा भस्मादिहोमप्रविहितघृतसम्पातपाताप्तशक्ति
जप्तं सम्यग्विदध्यात् प्रतिशममुपयान्त्येव सर्वे विकाराः ॥ ५७

इति जपहुतार्चनाभिर्यन्त्रविशेषैश्च साधु मन्त्रमिमम् ।
भजते योऽसौ मन्त्री लभते भुक्तिं सुखेन मुक्तिञ्च ॥ ५८

इति श्रीप्रपञ्चसारे द्वाविंशः पटलः ।

यन्त्ररचनाप्रकारमाह— अष्टाक्षरेति । रेखाष्टकं लिखित्वा एकान्तरितमुभयतो बद्ध्वा अष्टाक्षराक्षरद्वयान्तरितगीतात्रिष्टुप्पादचतुष्कयुतकोष्ठचतुष्कं कुर्यात् । प्रथमं पादद्वयमूर्ध्वभागस्थकोष्ठद्वये अपरद्वयमधोभागस्थकोष्ठद्वये मध्यकोष्ठोभयभागस्थकोष्ठद्वययोः सुदर्शनं मध्यकोष्ठगप्रणवे साध्यादिकं लिखेदिति यन्त्ररचनाप्रकारः । श्रुतिशः प्रबद्धमिति । तृतीयतृतीयरेखादिभिः बद्धमित्यर्थः ॥ ५६ ॥

मन्त्रीति । यन्त्रहृदयादिकमुक्तम् । भस्मादिना होमप्रविहितघृतसम्पातपातेन चात्तशक्तीत्यर्थः ॥ ५७ ॥ ५८ ॥

इति श्रीपद्मपादाचार्यकृते प्रपञ्चसारविवरणे
द्वाविंशः पटलः ।

त्रयोविंशः पटलः।

धर्मवित्तसुखमोक्षफलाप्तौ योषितामपि नृणां प्रवरं यत्।
मन्त्ररत्नमतिगुह्यमिदानीं वक्ष्यते मतिमतामपि रम्यम्॥ १

दौर्भाग्यव्याधिदारिद्र्यजराशोकभयातुराः।
भर्तृराजाभिभूताश्च स्त्रीविघ्नार्त्तास्तदीप्सवः॥ २

पुत्रभृत्यार्थिनो युद्धजयकामान्यवञ्चिताः।
भूतार्थाक्लिष्टसंसारवश्यसंवननार्थिनः॥ ३

बलिसिद्ध्यर्थिनश्चैव अन्तर्धानाभिकाङ्क्षिणः।
शत्रुभिः परिभूताश्च सर्वविघ्नैरुपद्रुताः॥ ४

मारणोच्चाटनद्वेषस्तम्भाकर्षणकाङ्क्षिणः।
भजेयुः सर्वथैवैनं मन्त्रं त्रैलोक्यमोहनम्॥ ५

हृदयपुरुषोत्तमान्ते त्वप्रतिरूपेति चापि संभाष्य।
लक्ष्मीनिवासपरतो जगदादौ सकल इत्युदाहृत्य॥ ६

क्षोभण सर्वपदान्ते स्त्रीहृदयविदारण त्रिभुवनेति।
समनोन्मादकरेति च सुरासुरान्ते वदेन्मनुजपदम्॥ ७

भूयश्च सुन्दरीजनमनांस्यथो तापयादिकान् वीप्स्य।
तापय दीपय शोषय मारय भृगुकामिकालवान्ते तु॥ ८

रक्षाप्रधानसुदर्शनमभिधाय रक्षितस्य शीघ्रं विभूतिसिद्धये श्रीपुरुषोत्तमविधिमाह—धर्मेति। अथवा चक्राधिरूढस्य भगवतो विधिमभिधाय गरुडाधिरूढस्य भगवतो विधिरभिधीयत इति सम्बन्धो वाच्यः। धर्मत्यादिना विनियोग उक्तः। योषितामपीति। स्त्रीणामप्यत्राऽधिकार उक्तः। मतिमतामिति। तत्तत्पुरुषार्थविनियोगे बीजविशेषज्ञानामित्यर्थः॥ १॥

भूतार्थाक्लिष्टसंसारेति। प्रभूतानां प्राणिनां प्रयोजनायाक्लिष्टसंसारनिर्वाहादिकमर्थयन्तीति तथोक्ताः॥ २॥ ३॥ ४॥

मारणोच्चाटनेत्यादिना स्वार्थप्रयोगकांक्षिणामप्यधिकार उक्तः॥ ५॥

मन्त्रमुद्धरति—हृदयेति। तन्द्री श्रीकण्ठाद्यं सम्प्रवणं कमिति अमुकमिति।

निद्रां बालिनमाभाष्य ब्रूयादपि ततः परम् ।
मोहय द्रावयेति च भूयश्चाकर्षयेत्युदीर्यान्तः ॥ ९
समस्तपरमसुभगं सर्वप्रदयोस्तु मध्यतः प्रवदेत् ।
सौभाग्यसृष्टिवह्नीन् ससर्वादिकं कामशब्दञ्च ॥ १०
तन्द्री श्रीकण्ठाद्यं सश्रवणं कं हनद्वयञ्च वदेत् ।
चक्रेण वाऽथ गदया खड्गेन च सर्वबाणैश्च ॥ ११
भिन्दद्वयञ्च पाशेनाऽन्ते घट्टयद्वयं समाभाष्य ।
भूयोऽङ्कुशेन ताड़य तु[कु]रुयुग्मकञ्च किञ्च प्रवदेत् ॥ १२
तिष्ठसि तावद्यावत् समोहितं मे समाभाष्य ।
सिद्धं भवतु च हुंफट् नमोऽन्तिकं मन्त्रमुद्धरेन्मन्त्री ।
मन्मथबीजोपेतं ताराद्यं सर्वसिद्धिदं भवति ॥ १३
मन्त्रपदानि द्वादश विद्यादाज्ञापदानि तावन्ति ।
सम्बुद्ध्यन्ता हुंफट्पदान्विताश्चेमे मन्त्राः स्युः ।
मध्यनरान्ते च परे गदिता मुनिभिर्मनोरमुष्य पुनः ॥ १४

अमुकशब्दं परित्यज्य तत्स्थाने साध्यनामयोग उक्तः । मन्त्रमुद्धरेन्मन्त्रीति । शक्ति-श्रीबीजयोग उक्तः ॥ ६ ॥ ७ ॥ ८ ॥ ९ ॥ १० ॥ ११ ॥ १२ ॥ १३ ॥

मन्त्रपदानीति । आमन्त्रणपदानि सम्बुद्ध्यन्तपदानीत्यर्थः । तानि द्वादश विद्यात् । द्वादशाङ्गन्यासपूजादिसाधनत्वेन जानीयादित्यर्थः । आज्ञापदानि प्रार्थनपदानीति भावः । तान्यपि तापयादीनि तावन्ति द्वादशसंख्यातानि विद्यात् । वश्याकर्षणक्रूरकर्मादिषु पुष्पाञ्जल्यर्थं जानीयादित्यर्थः ।

तत्र द्वादशाङ्गादिमन्त्राणां द्वादशमूर्तिसंयोगमाह—सम्बुद्ध्यन्ताः पुरुषाद्यन्ता इति सम्बुद्ध्यन्ता मन्त्रांशाः पुरुषाद्यन्ताः । सम्बुद्ध्यन्तानां पदानामुपरि पुरुषादयः प्रयोक्तव्या इत्यर्थः । पुरुष सत्याच्युत वासुदेव संकर्षण प्रद्युम्नानिरुद्ध नारायण-ब्रह्म विष्णु नरसिंह वराहाः पुरुषादयः ।

आज्ञापदान् विशिनष्टि—हुं फट्पदान्विता इति । आज्ञापदानामुपरि हुंफडिति प्रयोक्तव्यमित्यर्थः ।

पुनरपि मन्त्रणपदानां विशेषं दर्शयन् बीजप्रयोगक्रमं मन्त्रणपदानां द्वादश-संख्यानाञ्च पूरयति—मध्येति । मध्यनरान्ते परे सति मुनिभिः द्वादशमन्त्रा गदिताः स्युरित्यन्वयः । बीजचितये मध्यस्थो नरः पुरुषः पुरुषोत्तमः

कामबीजरूपी मध्यनर: तस्याऽन्ते पार्श्वे सति पार्श्वद्वयगतशक्तिश्रीबीजद्वये सतीत्यर्थ:। अनेन बीजानां प्रयोगक्रम उक्त:। आमन्त्रणपदानां बीजत्रयेण सार्धं द्वादशसंख्या च पूरिता।

अवशिष्टं मन्त्रांशमाह—परे सतीति। सम्बुद्ध्यन्तपदानामुपरि चतुर्थ्यन्ते परपदे च सतीत्यर्थ:। चशब्देन मन्त्राणामादिभूत प्रणवोपरि मन्त्रमध्यगतनम:पदयोग: सूचित:। आज्ञापदेष्वपि बीजत्रययोगं वदन् तेषामादौ पुरुषोत्तमपदसंयोग-माह—मध्यनरान्ते च पर इति। मध्यनरस्य मध्यमपुरुषस्याऽन्ते उत्तमपुरुषे पुरुषोत्तमे सति परे अन्ये आज्ञामन्त्रा: स्युरित्यर्थ:।

अत्रायं द्वादशाङ्गमन्त्रप्रयोगक्रम:। ओं नमो क्लीं पराय पुरुषात्मने हृदयाय नम:। ओं नम: क्लीं पराय सत्यात्मने शिरसे स्वाहा। ओं नम: श्रीं पराय अच्युतात्मने शिखायै वषट्। ओं नम: पुरुषोत्तमपराय वासुदेवात्मने कवचाय हुम्। ओं नम: अप्रतिरूपपराय संकर्षणात्मने नेत्राभ्यां वौषट्। ओं नमो लक्ष्मीनिवासपराय प्रद्युम्नात्मने अस्त्राय फट्। ओं नम: सकलजगत्-क्षोभणपराय अनिरुद्धात्मने उदराय नम:। ओं नम: सर्वस्त्रीहृदयविदारणपराय नारायणात्मने पृष्ठाय नम:। ओं नम: त्रिभुवनमनोन्मादकरपराय ब्रह्मणे बाहुभ्यां नम:। ओं नम: समस्तपरमसुभगपराय विष्ण्वात्मने ऊरुभ्यां नम:। ओं नम: सर्वसौभाग्यकर पराय नृसिंहात्मने जानुभ्यां नम:। ओं नम: सर्वकामप्रदपराय वराहात्मने पादाभ्यां नम:। इति द्वादशाङ्गन्यासादिमन्त्रा:।

द्वादशाङ्गन्यासानन्तरं लक्ष्म्याद्या: सुदर्शनोक्ता: शक्तयो मूर्धास्यहृद्गुह्य-कण्ठनाभ्यक्षिसर्वाङ्गेषु स्त्रां स्त्रीं स्त्रूं स्त्रें स्त्रैं स्त्रों स्त्रौं स्त्रं बीजयुता न्यस्तव्या:। अथाज्ञामन्त्रा वश्यादिक्रियासु पुष्पाञ्जल्यर्था उच्यन्ते। ओं क्लीं क्लीं श्रीं नम: पुरुषोत्तम अमुष्य सुरासुरमनुजसुन्दरीजनमनांसि तापय तापय हुं फट् तुरु तुरु किं तिष्ठसि तावत् यावत् समीहितं मे सिद्धं भवति हुं फण्नम: इति तापनमन्त्र:। एवमेव दीपन शोषण मारण स्तम्भन द्रावणाकर्षण मन्त्रेषु प्रणवादिबीजचतुष्टयस्य नमस: पुरुषोत्तमपरस्य अमुष्य सुरासुरमनुजसुन्दरीजन-मनांसीत्यस्य दीपयेत्यादिवीप्सायां हुंफट्पदयो: तुरु तुरु इत्यादेश्च प्रयोगो द्रष्टव्य:। एते च मन्त्रा वश्याकर्षणेषु प्राधान्येन प्रयोक्तव्या:। मारणमन्त्र-व्यतिरिक्ता: षण्मन्त्रा एव वश्यादौ प्रयोक्तव्या इत्यन्ये।

अथ मारणादौ प्रयोक्तव्या घट्टन ताडन भेदन हनन मारण मन्त्रा उच्यन्ते। ओं क्लीं क्लीं श्रीं नम: पुरुषोत्तम अमुकं पाशेन घट्टय द्वि: हुं फट् तुरु तुरु किं

ऋषिस्तु जैमिनिः प्रोक्तश्छन्दश्च जगतीष्यते ।
सर्वलोकशरण्योऽसौ देवता पुरुषोत्तमः ॥ १५
पुरुषोत्तमत्रिभुवनमनोन्मादकरेति च ।
हृदयं सकलान्ते च जगत्क्षोभण इत्यपि ॥ १६
सलक्ष्मीदयितेत्येवं शिरोमन्त्र उदाहृतः ।
मन्मथोत्तमशब्दान्ते अङ्गजे कामदीपिनि ॥ १७
शिखा सुभगशब्दन्तु परमाद्यन्तदन्ततः ।
सर्वसौभाग्य इत्यन्ते करमप्रतिरूपकम् ॥ १८
केशवस्मरवर्णान्ते जातिञ्च कवचं विदुः ।
सुरासुरहृदययोर्मध्ये मनुजसुन्दरी ॥ १९
विदारणपदं तस्मात् सर्वप्रहरणेति च ।
धरसर्वपदान्ते तु कामिकं हनयुग्मकम् ॥ २०
हृदयान्ते बन्धनानीत्यथाऽऽकर्षयं वीप्सयेत् ।
ततो महाबलेत्येतदस्त्रमन्त्रमुदीरितम् ॥ २१
त्रिभुवनेश्वरसर्वान्ते जनेत्युक्त्वा मनांसि च ।
हनदारययोर्युग्मं पृथङ्मे वशमानय ॥ २२
नेत्रं तारादिकाः सर्वे हुंफडन्ता नमोऽन्तिकाः ।
त्रैलोक्यमोहनान्ते तु हृषीकेशाऽप्रतीति च ॥ २३
रूपमन्मथ सर्वस्त्रीहृदयाकर्षणेति च ।
आगच्छाऽऽगच्छ च नमो मन्त्रः स्याद्व्यापकाह्वयः ॥ २४
आवाहादिविसर्गान्तेषूक्तोऽयं चापि सूरिभिः ॥ २५

तिष्ठेत्यादिर्घट्टनमन्त्रः । अथाऽङ्कुशेन ताडय ताडयेत्यादिस्ताडनमन्त्रः । श्रीं ह्रीं क्लीं श्रीं नमः पुरुषोत्तम अमुकं चक्रेण गदया खड्गेन सर्वबाणैः भिन्द भिन्द हुं फट् तुरु तुरु किं तिष्ठसीत्यादिर्भेदनमन्त्रः । तथा हनहनेत्यादि हननमन्त्रः । तथा मारय मारयेत्यादिर्मारणमन्त्रः इति ॥ १४ ॥

ऋष्यादिकमाह—ऋषिरिति ॥ १५—२४ ॥

उक्तोऽयं चापीति । पूर्वोक्तावाहनादिमन्त्रसमुच्चयार्थोऽपिशब्दः ॥ २५ ॥

सुदर्शन महाचक्रराजेत्युक्त्वा धमद्वयम् ।
सर्वदुष्टभयान्ते तु कुरुच्छिन्द्युगन्ततः ॥ २६
विदारयद्वयान्ते तु परमन्त्रान् ग्रस ग्रस ।
भक्षयद्वयभूतानि त्रासयद्वयवर्मफट् ॥ २७
चक्राय नम इत्येष चक्रमन्त्रः प्रकीर्तितः ।
शङ्खमन्त्रो जलचराय स्वाहेति परिकीर्तितः ॥ २८
कौमोदकि महान्ते तु बले सर्वासुरान्तकि ।
प्रसीद हुंफट् स्वाहेति गदामन्त्र उदाहृतः ॥ २९
संवर्त्तकान्ते मुसल पोथयद्वितयं ततः ।
हुंफट् स्वाहा मौसलकः शार्ङ्गाय सशराय च ॥ ३०
शार्ङ्गस्य खड्गतीक्ष्णान्ते छिन्द्युक् खड्गमन्त्रकः ।
अङ्कुशाद्यं घट्टयुगं चाऽङ्कुशस्य समीरितः ॥ ३१
सानन्तलोहितवक्रौ बन्धाकर्षयवीप्सकौ ।
वह्निजाया च पाशस्य स्वमुद्राभिर्न्यसेदिमान् ॥ ३२
स्वाहान्तः पक्षिराजाय तस्य मन्त्रः प्रकीर्त्तितः ।
त्रैलोक्यमोहनायान्ते विद्महे तु समुच्चरन् ॥ ३३
स्मराय धीमहीत्युक्त्वा तन्नो विष्णुः प्रचोदयात् ।
गायत्र्येषा तयाऽर्चासु स्थानद्रव्याणि शोधयेत् ॥ ३४
व्यस्तैर्द्वादशभिर्मन्त्रैर्नमोऽन्तैश्चाऽर्च्यते हरिः ।
भृगुः सबिन्दुः खड्गीशो देव्या मन्त्र उदाहृतः ॥ ३५
सूक्ष्मामरमहासेनक्लीबहीनैः स्वरैरसौ ।
लक्ष्म्यादीनान्तु शक्तीनां मन्त्राः पूजाविधौ स्मृताः ॥ ३६

चक्राद्यायुधाष्टकमन्त्रानुद्धरति—सुदर्शनेति। शङ्खादिमन्त्रेष्वपि महाशब्द । पाञ्चजन्याय नमः । कौमोदक्यै नमः । इत्यादि क योजनीयम् ॥ २६ २७ ॥ २८॥२९॥३०॥३१॥३२ ॥

गरुडमन्त्रमाह—स्वाहेति ॥ ३३॥३४ ॥

व्यस्तैर्द्वादशभिरिति । नित्यपूजासु सम्बुद्ध्यन्तैः द्वादशभि नामभि र्यथायोगमित्यर्थः । श्रीमन्त्रमाह—भृगुरिति ॥ ३५॥३६ ॥

उद्यद्दिनेन्दुपयोदभ्रमरपिकारावकुसुमसौरभ्ये ।
सुमनोहरे च कल्पकवृक्षोद्याने रमापतिं ध्यायेत् ॥ ३७
अरुणारविन्दकर्णिकामध्यगगरुडोपरि स्थितं देवम् ।
उद्यद्दिनकरकोटिप्रतिमं सिन्दूरनवजवाकान्तिम् ॥ ३८
दरचापमुसलपाशान् चक्रासिगदाङ्कुशान् भुजैर्दधानम् ।
अतिहृद्ययौवनोन्मुखसौन्दर्यातिशयसाम्यनिर्मुक्तम् ॥ ३९
अतिविह्वलं स्मरस्य शरैरतिरुचिरा + + ।
+ + + + ॥ ४०
औदार्यकान्तिसौरभलावण्यसुधारसैर्जगत् सकलम् ।
सिञ्चन्तमिव समस्तानुग्रहिणं श्रीमुखाब्जसक्तसुदृशम् ॥ ४१
वामोरुजङ्घगतयाऽऽलिङ्गितदेहं श्रिया मदोत्कटया ।
तद्वक्त्राम्बुरुहासवपिपासितभ्रान्तनेत्रषट्पदया ॥ ४२
रोमाञ्चहर्षनिर्गतजलमुक्तालङ्कृताङ्गया सततम् ।
वामकरस्थाम्बुजया प्रतप्तकनकाभयाऽतिसुन्दर्या ॥ ४३
अनुपमसौन्दर्येण च सर्वाभरणैरुपेतयाऽतिमुदा ।
विष्वग्बहुप्रकारानेकैः सपरिच्छदैश्च देवगणैः ॥ ४४
गन्धर्वदैत्यरक्षोयक्षपन्नगैर्मुनीन्द्रैश्च ।
संसेवितं पुरन्ध्रीवृन्दैश्चाऽनङ्गबाणसन्तप्तैः ॥ ४५
भावहावमधुरस्मितवक्त्रप्रेक्षणस्खलितभाषणजातैः ।
स्पष्टकक्षजघनस्तनभारैः स्रस्तवस्त्रचिकुरैर्मदलोलैः ॥ ४६

क्षरितमदनवारिस्वेदकम्रैर्विवस्त्रै-
र्मदनविगतलज्जैः स्पन्दमानाधरोष्ठैः ।
मृदुतरकरपद्माक्लृप्तनत्यञ्जलीकैः
शिरसि मुषितधैर्यैः कम्पिताशेषगात्रैः ॥ ४७

[ध्यानमाह—उद्यदिति सार्धैस्त्रयोदशभिः । मदनलुलितघूर्णितं ताम्रं च नेत्रपद्मं यस्य तम् । अनेकैः भूषणैः दिव्याभ्यामम्बराभ्यां गन्धपुष्पाभ्यां च समुज्ज्वलम् । इति सम्बन्धदीपिकाकारः ॥ ३७—५० ॥

ज्वरार्त्तैः श्वसद्भिः पतद्भिः शरीरैः
शरैर्दारितैर्मन्मथस्याऽतिघोरैः ।
समाप्यायितैस्तस्य लावण्यदृष्ट्या
समुत्थाय विष्णोस्तमेवाऽभियातैः ॥ ४८

करतलकल्पितकोकनदैस्तत्पदयुगलं च पुनः परिपूज्य ।
नयनजलैः सगद्गदवाक्यैर्भव परमेश्वर पतिः शरणं नः ॥ ४९

इत्थं संप्रार्थितं तं सकलसुरवरस्त्रीसहस्रैरजस्रं
दिव्यैर्भोगार्थिभिश्चाऽप्यखिलमुनिवरैर्भक्तितो मुक्तिकामैः ।
ध्यात्वा लक्षार्धसंख्यं जपतु मनुमिमं प्राप्तमन्त्रा[दीक्षोऽ]भिषिक्ता
द्रव्यैरेतैश्च जुह्वन् भवति मनुवरस्याऽधिकारी क्रियासु ॥ ५०

शतं दधि घृतं पयः पृथगथाऽयुतं साज्यहविषा
शृतेन पयसा हुनेद्द्रविमितं तथा साक्षततिलैः ।
तथा दशदशो[शतो]न्मितं त्रिमधुभिर्वरैश्चात्तवफलैः
पलाशसमिधां शतं समभितोषयेत् स्वं गुरुम् ॥ ५१

ततो लक्षत्रयं जप्त्वा कुण्डे चाऽर्धेन्दुसन्निभे ।
हुनेदम्भोरुहैर्जातिकुसुमैश्च यवैरपि ।
दशांशं वैष्णवे वह्नौ ब्राह्मणांश्चैव तोषयेत् ॥ ५२

अम्भोधाराः सदा भिन्ने सेतौ संसिद्धयोऽखिलाः ।
यथाऽम्भोनिधिमायान्ति तथा यान्ति निरन्तरम् ॥ ५३

मन्त्रिणः कृतकृत्यत्वं काङ्क्षमाणाः पुनः पुनः ।
पीठे तु वैष्णवे नित्यं पूजयेत् पुरुषोत्तमम् ॥ ५४

अङ्गानि कर्णिकायामग्न्यादिदलेषु चाऽष्ट लक्ष्म्याद्याः ।
ताश्च स्युर्लसरप्रीकीकातुप्वाद्याः सुदर्शने ज्ञेयाः ॥ ५५

कियत्संख्यो होमस्तदाह—शतमिति ॥ ५१॥५२॥५३ ॥

प्रथमावरणं प्रागादिदलेषु लक्ष्म्याद्यावरणं पूजयेत्। ताश्च लसरप्रीकीकातुप्वाद्याः स्युः। लादिः लक्ष्मीः। सादिः सरस्वती। रादी रतिः। प्रादिः प्रीतिः। कादिः कीर्तिः। कादिः कान्तिः। त्वादिस्तुष्टिः। प्वादिः पुष्टिः।
॥ ५४ ॥ ५५ ॥ ५६ ॥ ५७ ॥ ५८ ॥ ५९ ॥

दरचक्रगदामुसलाः पूर्वाद्याशासु चाऽथ कोणेषु ।
वह्न्यादिषु शार्ङ्गखड्गाङ्कुशपाशा दिशाधिपाः पूज्याः ॥ ५६
अङ्गानि देववर्णानि मदविवशाः शक्तयोऽष्ट लक्ष्म्याद्याः ।
चामरहस्ताः सर्वाः स्वलङ्कृताश्चाऽथ सुन्दर्यः ॥ ५७
योऽर्चयेत् सकृदप्येवं पुरुषः पुरुषोत्तमम् ।
प्राप्य राज्येप्सितां लक्ष्मीं प्राप्नोत्यमरवन्दिताम् ॥ ५८
दुर्भगो वसुसहस्रहुतेन स्यादतीव सुभगश्च मनोज्ञः ।
दीप्तिमत्प्रभवतैलवरेण व्याधिमोक्षणपरस्तु तथैव ॥ ५९
श्रीफलैः प्रजुहुयात्कमलैर्वाऽकिञ्चनोऽपि रविसहस्रमतोऽसौ ।
स्याद्धनाधिपसमोऽयुतसंख्यं जप्तुराधिरुपयाति विनाशम् ॥ ६०
यां प्रमदामभिकाङ्क्षति तस्या नामयुतं प्रजपेन्मनुमेतम् ।
पञ्चमहर्वदनेऽष्टसहस्रं सा वशमेति न तत्र विचारः ॥ ६१

हयारिकुसुमैर्हरिं समभिपूज्य चाऽष्टोत्तरं
सहस्रमपि जुह्वतः शशिभवप्रसूनैः शुभैः ।
भवन्त्यवशगा नृपास्त्रिदशभिर्दिनैः किङ्कराः
परैर्हृतधनस्तथा कटुभवेन तैलेन वा ॥ ६२
समिद्भिरथ बोधिजैर्दशशतं तथाऽष्टोत्तरं
त्रिमासमथवा जपेद्दशशतं तथा नित्यशः ।
स एव पुनरेत्य तद्वसु समाहृतं मन्त्रिणं
प्रणम्य पुनरर्पयेत्समभितोष्य चोपायनैः ॥ ६३

राजीश्चाऽष्टोत्तरशतं जप्त्वा शत्रुगृहे खनेत् ।
हयारिकुसुमं वापि पक्षे शुक्लेऽसिते क्रमात् ॥ ६४
शुक्लं रक्तं वेष्टितञ्च कीशैश्चाऽटनकृद्रिपोः ।
नित्यं नेत्रसमिद्भिस्तु चाऽष्टोत्तरसहस्रकम् ॥ ६५
षण्मासन्तु ततस्तेजोवत्यास्तैलं सहस्रकम् ।
जुह्वतो म्रियते शत्रुर्दष्टा मासचतुष्टयात् ॥ ६६

होमादीनां फलभेदानाचष्टे—श्रीफलैरिति ॥ ६०—७२ ॥

अनेन विधिना वाऽथ स्तम्भनं स्यात्तथैव च ।
तथैवाज्याक्तदूर्वाणां होमतो मुच्यते भयात् ॥ ६७

पयोव्रतोऽर्चाजपतत्परस्त्रिमासमङ्कोलघृतं सहस्रम् ।
नित्यं हुनेच्चैव ततस्त्रिमासि पूर्णे हुताशेऽपि च हूयमाने ॥ ६८

प्राप्ते च मध्ये दिवसस्य वह्नेः पार्श्वे शशाङ्कप्रतिमा सुदीप्ता ।
संदृश्यते वै गुलिका सभानुः सहस्रमष्टोत्तरमेव मन्त्रम् ॥ ६९

प्रतिमन्त्र्य च तां वहतो गुलिकाममरैरपि दर्शनमस्य भवेत् ।
इह सिद्धिरथाऽस्य भवत्यखिला वड़वामुखपुष्करयानमुखा ॥ ७०

इति सिद्धमुनीन्द्रयक्षविद्याधरगन्धर्वसमहाप्सरोरगाद्यैः ।
प्रतिसेवितमुत्तमं विधानं गदितं तत् पुरुषोत्तमस्य विष्णोः ॥ ७१

इति जपहुतपूजाध्यानकैः श्रीधरं यो
भजति स तु समग्रां सम्पदैश्वर्यलक्ष्मीम् ।
अधरकृतविपक्षां प्राप्य लोकैकवन्द्यो
व्रजति पदमनन्तं लोकवन्द्यस्य विष्णोः ॥ ७२

इति श्रीप्रपञ्चसारे त्रयोविंशः पटलः ।

इति श्रीपद्मपादाचार्यकृते प्रपञ्चसारविवरणे
त्रयोविंशः पटलः ।

चतुर्विंशः पटलः ।

अथोच्यते श्रीकरनामधेयमष्टाक्षरं लोकहिताय तावत् ।
येन प्रजप्तेन समर्चितेन हुतेन सिद्धिं समुपैति मन्त्री ॥ १
सर्गाद्यर्कः क्षतो विंशतियुगमियुतं शान्तगं चन्द्रबिम्बं
श्रीबाहुः शुक्रमेदोहरिशयनहकारा मनुः श्रीकराख्यः ।
ऋष्याद्या वामपङ्क्ती हरिरपि पुनरङ्गानि यान्तैर्हुमन्तै-
र्भीषत्रासप्रमर्दप्रसहितगदितध्वंसरक्षैर्हिरुक्तैः ॥ २

मूर्धाक्षिकण्ठहृदयोदरसोरुजानु-
पादद्वयेषु लिपिशो न्यसतु स्वदेहे ।
विप्रादिकान्मुखकरोरुपदेषु वर्णा-
श्चक्रादिकानपि करेषु ततस्तदस्त्रान् ॥ ३

दुग्धाब्धिद्वीपवर्यप्रविलसितसुरोद्यानकल्पद्रुमाधो-
भद्राम्भोजन्मपीठोपरिगतविनतानन्दनस्कन्धसंस्थः ।
दोर्भिर्बिभ्रद्रथाङ्गं सदरमथ गदापङ्कजे स्वर्णवर्णो
भास्वन्मौलिर्विचित्राभरणपरिगतः स्याच्छ्रिये वो मुकुन्दः ॥ ४

दिक्पत्रेषु श्रीरतिधृतिकान्तीः कोणगेषु मूर्तीश्च ।
इष्ट्वाऽभितो निधीशौ विष्वक्सेनञ्च दिक्पतीन् प्रयजेत् ॥ ५
आराध्य चैवं विधिनाऽथ विष्णुं मन्त्री पुनर्होमविधिं करोतु ।
श्रीवृक्षदुग्धोत्थसमिद्भिरब्जैः साज्येन दौग्धेन च सर्पिषा च ॥ ६

विभूतिप्रदश्रीपुरुषोत्तमानन्तरं तथाविधमेव श्रीकरं सविनियोगमाह—अथोच्यत इति । मन्त्रीति । तत्तल्लिङ्गरचितबीजयोग उक्तः ॥ १ ॥

श्रीबाहुः श्रीकरः । श्रीं बीजम् । स्वाहा शक्तिः । हरिरपीति । श्रीकरविष्णुरित्यर्थः । यान्तैर्हुमन्तैरिति । क्रमेणोभयान्तत्वं भीषादीनाम् विप्रादिन्यासोऽप्यक्षरैः सार्धमेव कार्यः ॥ २ ॥ ३ ॥

श्रिये वो मुकुन्द इत्यनेनैव श्रीदेव्या सह ध्यानमित्यवगन्तव्यम् ॥ ४ ॥ ५ ॥

मन्त्री पुनर्होमविधिमिति । जप पूजा होमादिषु प्रणवश्रीबीजयोग

पृथगष्टशतं क्रमेण हुत्वा कनकाद्यैरपि तर्पिते गुरौ च ।
अभिषिच्य तथाऽभिपूज्य विप्रान्मनुमेनं प्रजपेद्यथाऽष्टलक्षम् ॥ ७

द्रव्यैस्तैः प्रतिजुहुयाद्दशांशमानै-
राचार्यं पुनरपि पूजयेज्जपान्ते ।
स प्राप्नोत्यपरिमितां श्रियञ्च कीर्त्तिं
कान्तिञ्चाऽचिरमनुरज्यते च लोकैः ॥ ८

दूर्वां घृतप्रसिक्तां जुहुयादयुतं नरस्तु हुतशिष्टैः ।
आज्यैश्चरुमुपयुञ्ज्याद्दद्याद् गुरवे च दक्षिणां शक्त्या ॥ ९
परिभोजयेच्च विप्रांस्तेषु दिनेषु स्वशक्तितो भक्त्या ।
अपमृत्युरोगपापान् विजित्य स तु दीर्घमायुराप्नोति ॥ १०
अनुदिनमादित्याभिमुखः प्रजपेदूर्ध्वीकृतस्वबाहुयुगः ।
तस्य गृहेऽन्नसमृद्धिश्चिराय संजायते सुष्ठुतरा ॥ ११
एवं प्रोक्तैः प्रतिजपहुतार्चादिभिर्मन्त्रमेनं
भक्त्या यो वा भजति मनुजो नित्यशः सोऽचिरेण ।
दृष्टैः पुत्रैर्धनधरणिधान्यादिभिर्हृष्टचेताः
स्यादप्यन्ते परमपरिशुद्धं परं धाम विष्णोः ॥ १२
अथ कथयामि विधानं महावाराहाभिधानमन्त्रस्य ।
साङ्गं सजपं सहुताराधनमपि मन्त्रिणामभीष्टाप्त्यै ॥ १३
वाक्यं प्रोक्त्वा हृदाख्यं तदनु भगवते युग्वराहं च रूपा-
येत्युक्त्वा व्याहृतीनामुपरि च पतये भूपतित्वञ्च मेऽन्ते ।
देहीत्याभाष्य दान्तं सुमतिरथ पुनर्दापयस्वेति हान्तं
प्रोक्त्वा तारादिकं प्रोद्धरतु मनुवरं तं त्रयस्त्रिंशदर्णम् ॥ १४

उक्ताः ॥ ६ ॥ ७ ॥

द्रव्यैस्तैरिति । औदुम्बसमिदादिभिः दीक्षाहोमाय कथितैरित्यर्थः ॥ ८ ॥

॥ ९ ॥ १० ॥ ११ ॥ १२ ॥

विभूत्यतिशयार्थं वराहमन्त्रमाह—अथेति । मन्त्रिणामभीष्टाप्त्यै इति । अभीष्टविशेषेषु बीजविशेषयोगार्थः ॥ १३ ॥

सुमतिरिति । भूपतित्वमित्यत्र साध्यनामग्रहणमुक्तम् । हूं बीजम् ।

ऋषिस्तु भार्गवः प्रोक्तोऽनुष्टुप् छन्द उदीरितम् ।
वराहो देवता चाऽस्य कथ्यन्तेऽङ्गान्यतः परम् ॥ १५
अस्यैकशृङ्गो हृदयं शिरोऽपि व्योमोल्कतेजोऽधिपतो शिखा च ।
स्याद्विश्वरूपः कवचं महादिदंष्ट्रोऽस्त्रमुक्तं स्वयमेव चाऽङ्गम् ॥ १६
ससप्तभिः पुनः षड्भिः सप्तभिश्चाऽथ पञ्चभिः ।
अष्टभिर्मूलमन्त्रार्णैर्विदध्यादङ्गकल्पनाम् ॥ १७
जान्वोरापादमुद्यत्कनकमिव हिमप्रख्यमाजानु नाभेः
कण्ठादानाभि वह्निप्रभमथ शिरसश्चागलं नीलवर्णम् ।
मौलेर्व्योमाभमाकं करलसदरिशङ्खासिखेटं गदाश-
क्त्याख्येष्टाभीतिहस्तं प्रणमत वसुधोल्लासिदंष्ट्रं वराहम् ॥ १८
सजलाम्बुवाहनिभमुद्यतदोःपरिघं धराधरसमानतनुम् ।
सितदंष्ट्रिकाधृतभुवं त्वथवा प्रविचिन्तयेत् सपदि कोलममुम् ॥ १९
हेमप्रख्यं पार्थिवे मण्डले वा नीहाराभं नीरजेऽग्नेस्तदाभम् ।
वायोः कृष्णं द्युप्रभं वा दिविष्ठं क्रोडं व्याप्तं सत्यसंस्थं यजेद्वा ॥ २०
अष्टपत्रमथ पद्ममुल्लसत्कर्णिकं विधिवदारचय्य च ।
मण्डलं रविसहस्रसन्निभं शूकरं यजतु तव सिद्धये ॥ २१
प्राग्दक्षिणप्रत्यगुदग्दिशासु चत्वारि चाऽङ्गानि यजेत् क्रमेण ।
अस्त्रं विदिक्षूर्ध्वमधश्च चक्राद्यस्त्राणि पूज्यानि वराहमूर्त्तेः ॥ २२
अरिशङ्खकृपाणखेटकसंज्ञान् सगदाशक्तिवराभयाह्वयांश्च ।
अभिपूज्य दिशाधिपान् यथावद्वरगन्धाक्षतपुष्पधूपदीपैः ॥ २३

स्वाहा शक्तिः ॥ १४ ॥ १५ ॥ १६ ॥ १७ ॥ १८ ॥

सजलाम्बुवाहेति । द्विभुजस्य ध्यानमुक्तम् ॥ १९ ॥

स्तम्भनशान्तिकवश्याद्युच्चाटनशून्यताकरणादिषु पृथिव्यादिबीजयुक्तस्य ध्यानविशेषानाह—हेमप्रख्यमिति । एते च ध्यानविशेषाः सर्वमन्त्रेषु समानाः । सत्यसंस्थमिति । मुमुक्षोर्ध्यानमुक्तम् । स्वस्वमहिमस्थमित्यर्थः । प्राणसंस्थमिति चार्थः ॥ २० ॥

उल्लसत्कर्णिकमिति । वराहबीजविशिष्टकर्णिकमित्यर्थः । विधिवदारचय्येति । स्वरकेसरं चतुश्चतुर्वर्णलसद्दलाष्टकं बहिर्व्यञ्जनावेष्टितं

दंष्ट्रायां वसुधा सशैलनगरारण्यापगा हुंकृतौ
वागीशी श्वसितेऽनिलो रविविधू बाह्वोश्च दक्षान्ययोः।
कुक्षौ स्युर्वसवो दिशः श्रुतिपथे दस्रौ दृशोः पादयोः
पद्मोत्थो हृदये हरिः पृथगमी पूज्या मुखे शङ्करः॥ २४
एवं काले कोलमभ्यर्चयित्वा जप्यो मन्त्रोऽसौ पुनर्लक्षसंख्यम्।
होमं कृत्वा तद्दशांशैश्च पद्मैस्त्रिस्वाद्वक्तैः प्राप्नुयाद्भूसमृद्धिम्॥ २५
ध्यानादपि धनसिद्धिर्मन्त्रजपाच्चाऽधरो भवेत् सधरः।
जपपूजाहुतविधिभिर्मङ्क्षु नरो धनधरेन्दिरावान् स्यात्॥ २६
ध्यातः सन् भूगृहेऽसौ भुवमतुलतरां वारुणे शान्तिमुच्चै-
राग्नेये वश्यकृत्या[कीर्त्या]दिकमनिलपुरस्थोऽयमुच्चाटनादीन्।
रक्षां व्योम्नोऽरिभूतग्रहविषदुरितेभ्योऽनिलाग्न्योश्च पीडां
युद्धे वज्रीरयोर्वै जयमपि सुतरां संविधत्ते वराहः॥ २७

हरिस्थेऽर्केऽष्टम्यामथ सितरुचौ कोलवपुषा
सितां गन्धैः सर्वैर्युतमयुतजप्तामपि शिलाम्।
उदग्वक्त्रो मन्त्री मनुजपरतः स्थापयतु ता-
मयत्नं चेत्रेषु द्रुतमरिनिरोधं शमयति॥ २८

भौमे वारेऽथ भानूदयमनु जपवान् सन् गृहीत्वा मृदंशं
कोलात्मा वैरिरुद्धादपि च कुतलतस्तञ्च कृत्वा गुणांशम्।
एकं जातौ विलिम्पेद्यात् पुनरपरतरं पाकपात्रे तथाऽन्य-
त्तोये तस्मिन् सदुग्धे प्रतिपचतु हविः संस्कृते हव्यवाहे॥ २९
आराध्य चाऽष्टोर्ध्वशतं प्रमाणं साज्येन मन्त्री हविषाऽथ तेन।
सप्तारवारं जुहुयाद्यथावत् चेत्रोत्थितापत्प्रशमं प्रयाति॥ ३०

भूकोणस्थबीजमारचय्येत्यर्थः॥ २१॥ २२॥ २३॥ २४॥

एवं काले इति। प्रातरेवेत्यर्थः॥ २५॥

ध्यानजपादीनां फलभेदमाचष्टे—ध्यानादपीति। अधरः धरारहितः॥२६॥२७॥

सितां गन्धैरिति। दशपलमितां बिल्वादिपात्रस्थामित्यर्थः। मन्त्री मनुजपरत इति। भूबीजसाहित्यमुक्तम्॥ २८॥ २९॥

साज्येन मन्त्रीत्यपि तथैव॥ ३०॥ ३१॥ ३२॥

भृगुवारे च मुखेऽङ्कः संगृह्य मृदं हविः सुसम्पाद्य ।
जुहुयादीरितविधिना बलिमपि दद्यान्महीविरोधेषु ॥ ३१
हुतक्रियैवं दिवसैश्च सप्तभिः प्रणाशयेद्भूमिविवादसङ्कटम् ।
परेतवेतालपिशाचडाकिनीसमुत्थिताश्चाविकृतिं विधिस्त्वयम् ॥ ३२
विलोड्य तामेव मृदञ्च दुग्धे हुनेद्घृतेनाऽष्टयुतं सहस्रम् ।
त्रिमण्डलादेव मही महार्घ्या स्यान्मन्त्रिणोऽस्यैव तु निःसपत्ना ॥ ३३
नृपतरुसमिधामयुतं मन्त्रेणाऽनेन यो हुनेन्मन्त्री ।
गृहयात्राऽस्य न सीदेत् चैत्रादिकमपि वर्धते क्रमशः ॥ ३४
अष्टोर्ध्वशतं मन्त्री दिनशो यो वा जुहोति शालीभिः ।
स तु वत्सरेण मन्त्री विराजते व्रीहिपुञ्जपूर्णगृहः ॥ ३५
मन्त्रेणाऽनेन सर्पिर्जुहुत दशशतं मण्डलात् स्वर्णसिद्धिः
स्वादक्तेनाञ्जलिन्या अपि कुसुमसहस्रेण वा वाससाञ्च ।
लाजानां कन्यकाया अपि च मधुयुजां होमतो वाञ्छितायाः
सिद्धी रक्तोत्पलानामपि मधुरयुजां स्याद्धुताच्छ्रीः समग्रा ॥ ३६
दण्डार्घीशो व्योमासनस्तु वाराहमुच्यते बीजम् ।
अमुना तु साधितेन प्राप्नुवन्ति नराः सिद्धिमतुलतराम् ॥ ३७
तारेऽमुमपि लिखित्वा तद्बाह्येऽनलपुरं समापुटितम् ।
तद्बाह्ये चतुर्दलमब्जं स्यात्तद्बहिस्तथाऽष्टदलम् ॥ ३८
बाह्ये षोडशपत्रं मण्डलमाखण्डलीयमपि बाह्यम् ।
शूकरबीजे साध्यन्तेचाख्यञ्चक्रमन्त्रमस्त्रिषु च ॥ ३९
रन्ध्रेष्वङ्गमनूनपि दलमूलेऽष्टार्णकेसराणि लिखेत् ।
अष्टावष्टौ दलमनु शूकरमन्त्रस्य चाऽक्षरान् क्रमशः ॥ ४०

स्यान्मन्त्रिण इत्यपि एवमेव । हुनेन्मन्त्रीत्यपि । तथा शतं मन्त्रीति । वराहबीजयोगमाह । मन्त्री विराजत इत्यस्मिन्नेव प्रयोगे बीजयोग उक्तः ॥ ३३ ॥ ३४ ॥ ३५ ॥ ३६ ॥

अमुना तु साधितेनेति । ऋषिदेवते पूर्वोक्ते । गायत्री छन्दः । दीर्घयुजा स्वेनैवाऽङ्गानि । ऊं बीजम् । हं शक्तिः । ध्यानपूजादिकं पूर्ववत् ॥ ३७ ॥ ३८ ॥ ॥ ३९ ॥ ४० ॥ ४१ ॥ ४२ ॥ ४३ ॥

अन्तेऽवशिष्टमक्षरमथाऽष्टपत्रे स्वराख्यकिञ्जल्के।
वर्णांश्चतुश्चतुरपि तथाऽष्टमे पञ्च चालिखेत् पत्रे ॥ ४१
व्यञ्जनकिञ्जल्केऽन्त्ये द्वौ द्वौ त्रयमन्त्यके दले विलिखेत्।
तारमहीकोलार्णैः प्रवेष्टयेत् साध्यवर्णपरिपुटितैः ॥ ४२
तद्बाह्ये मनुवर्णैर्विदर्भिताभिश्च साध्यपदलिपिभिः।
क्ष्माबिम्बचतुष्कोणे गर्भगसाध्याक्षरं भूबीजम् ॥ ४३
अष्टसु शूलेषु तथा वाराहं वायुधेन संयुक्तम्।
लाक्षाकुङ्कुमचन्दनलघुकर्पूरैः सरोचनैर्विलिखेत्।
गोशकृदम्भोयुक्तैर्लेखन्या हैमया दिने प्रवरे ॥ ४४
सौवर्णे राज्यसिद्धिं रजतजफलके ग्रामसिद्धिश्च ताम्रे
साहस्रस्वर्णसिद्धिं भुजदललिखितं चाशु संसारयात्राम्।
क्षौमे लाभं धरायाः पिचुतरुफलके कार्यसिद्धिं निजेष्टां
मन्त्रं सञ्जप्तमेतद्घृतहुतकृतसम्पातपातं करोति ॥ ४५
मन्त्री समास्थाय वराहरूपं साध्यप्रदेशे निखनेच्च यन्त्रम्।
स्थिराख्यराशावभिवाह्य कोलमङ्गानि दिक्षु क्षिपतां यथावत् ॥ ४६
यन्त्रममुं रक्षायै रोगग्रहवैकृतेषु जन्तूनाम्।
संयज्य शिरसि बध्यात् स तु नीरोगस्त्वयत्नतो भवति ॥ ४७

इत्येवं प्रणिगदितो वराहमन्त्रो
यस्त्वेनं प्रभजति नित्यशो जपाद्यैः।
स प्राप्नोत्यखिलमहीसमृद्धिमस्मिन्
देहान्ते व्रजति हरेः परं पदं तत् ॥ ४८

इति श्रीप्रपञ्चसारे चतुर्विंशः पटलः ॥

तथा वराहमिति। साध्यादिनामसहितमित्यर्थः। [यन्त्रं संजप्तकृतमिति क्वचित्] ॥ ४४ ॥ ४५ ॥

निक्षिपतां यथावदिति। गर्तेषु सितपाषाणादिषु आवाह्य संपूजयेदित्यर्थः। ॥ ४६ ॥ ४७ ॥ ४८ ॥

इति श्रीपद्मपादाचार्यकृते प्रपञ्चसारविवरणे चतुर्विंशः पटलः।

पञ्चविंशः पटलः ।

अथ प्रवच्यामि नृसिंहमन्त्रस्याऽनुष्टुभः संग्रहतो विधानम् ।
साङ्गं सजापं सहुतक्रमञ्च सार्चाविधानं निजवाञ्छिताप्त्यै ॥ १

उग्रं वीरयुतं महान्तिकमथो विष्णुं ज्वलन्तान्वितं
संप्रोक्त्वाऽथ च सर्वतोमुखनृसिंहार्णांस्तथा भीषणम् ।
भद्रं मृत्युयुतं च मृत्युमपि तच्चोक्त्वा नमाम्या युतं
भूयोऽहम्पदमुद्धरेत् मनुमिमं मन्त्री समस्तार्थदम् ॥ २

ब्रह्मा प्रजापतिर्वा प्रोक्त ऋषिर्नारदश्च विद्वद्भिः ।
छन्दोऽनुष्टुबुदाहृतमथ विष्णुर्देवता नृसिंहाख्यः ॥ ३

वर्णैश्चतुर्भिरुदितं हृदयं शिरश्च
तावद्भिरष्टभिरथाऽस्य शिखा प्रदिष्टा ।
षड्भिश्च वर्म नयनञ्च चतुर्भिरस्त्रं
प्रोक्तं क्रमेण मनुनाऽक्षरशः षडङ्गम् ॥ ४

सशिरोललाटदृग्युगमुखकरपत्सन्धिकेषु साग्रेषु ।
उदरहृद्दोर्गलपार्श्वेष्वपरे ककुदि क्रमान्न्यसेद्वर्णान् ॥ ५

प्रतिपत्तिरस्य चोक्ता प्रसन्नताक्रूरताविशेषेण ।
द्विविधा प्रसन्नया स्यात् साधनपूजाऽन्यया प्रयोगविधिः ॥ ६

जान्वोरासक्ततीक्ष्णस्वनखरुचिलसद्बाहुसंस्पृष्टकेश-
श्चक्रं खड्गञ्च दोर्भ्यां दधदनलसमज्योतिषा ग्रस्तदैत्यः ।
ज्वालामालापरीतं रविशशिदहनवीक्षणं दीप्तजिह्वं
दंष्ट्रोग्रं धूतकेशं वदनमपि वहन् पातु वो नारसिंहः ॥ ७

वराहविधानानन्तरं नृसिंहविधानं वदन् विनियोगमाह—अथेति ॥ १ ॥

मन्त्री समस्तार्थदमिति । तत्तदर्थविशेषेषु बीजविशेषयोग उक्तः । हं बीजम् । ईं शक्तिः ॥ २ ॥ ३ ॥ ४ ॥ ५ ॥

प्रथमां प्रतिपत्तिमाह—जान्वोरिति । बाहुसंस्पृष्टकेश इति । कण्ठेशस्य केशौ । कौ ब्रह्मा । ईशो रुद्रश्च ॥ ६ ॥ ७ ॥

उद्यद्भास्वत्सहस्रप्रभमशनिनिभं चोत्तयं विद्यरन्तं
वह्नीनक्षाय विद्युत्ततिविततसटाभीषणं भूषणैश्च ।
दिव्यैराद्दीप्तदेहं निशितनखलसद्बाहुदण्डैरनेकैः
सम्भिन्नं भिन्नदैत्येश्वरतनुमतनुं नारसिंहं नमामि ॥ ८

नरसिंहममुं धियैव पूर्वं प्रणिपातार्घ्यकपाद्यसाचमाद्यैः ।
प्रयजेत् सहगन्धपुष्पधूपादिभिरेवं प्रवरैश्च नृत्यगीतैः ॥ ९

सुविशदमतिरथ बहिरपि सम्यक् संपूज्य वैष्णवं पीठम् ।
तत्रावाह्य च नरहरिमुपचारैः सम्यगर्चयेत्प्रवरैः ॥ १०

अङ्गैः प्रथमावृतिरपि पक्षीन्द्रानन्तशर्वकमलभवैः ।
सहश्रीह्रीधृतिपुष्टिभिरपरोक्ता लोकपालकैरन्या ॥ ११

प्राक्प्रत्यग्यमशशिनां दिगाश्रिता मूर्तयोऽनलादिषु च ।
स्युः शक्राय इत्येवं भक्त्या परया युतोऽर्चयेद्देवम् ॥ १२

द्वात्रिंशतिकसहस्रैरधिकृतिरयुतैर्भवेत् पुरश्चरणम् ।
तावद्भिस्तावद्भिर्लक्षैः सिद्धिः समीरिता चाऽस्य मनोः ॥ १३

विकृतिद्विगुणसहस्रैर्जुहुयादाज्यान्वितैश्च दुग्धान्नैः ।
जपपरिपूर्त्तौ मन्त्री दिनशः संपूजयेच्च नरसिंहम् ॥ १४

विधाय तद्बीजविशिष्टकर्णिकं चतुश्चतुर्वर्णलसद्दलाष्टकम् ।
सुलक्षितं मण्डलमन्यलक्षणैर्विधाय तस्मिन् कलशं प्रपूर्य च ॥ १५
यथोक्तमार्गेण समर्च्य साष्टकं सहस्रसंख्यं प्रजपेन्मनुं ततः ।
विरुच्चरन्मन्त्रमथाऽभिषिचयेद्दयमेष मृत्योः प्रतिमुच्यते मुखात् ॥ १६

क्रूरां प्रतिपत्तिमाह—उद्यदिति । अतनुमिति सूक्ष्मादिरूपमुक्तम् ॥ ८ ॥

नरसिंहममुमिति । मानसपूजा । सा च सर्वमन्त्रेषु समाना ॥ ९ ॥

विशदमतिरित्याधारशक्त्यादीनां ध्यानं सूचितम् । सम्यगिति । मूल-प्रकृत्यादिमन्त्रयोग उक्तः पीठपूजायाम् । स च सर्वत्र समानः ॥ १० ॥ ११ ॥ १२ ॥ १३ ॥

जपपरिपूर्त्तौ मन्त्रीति । ब्रह्म द्वादशाक्षर पञ्चाक्षर गरुडपञ्चाक्षरानन्तसप्ताक्षरादयः सूचिताः । [हं कमलासनाय नमः इति ब्राह्मनवाक्षरः इति सम्बन्धदीपिकाकारः] क्षिपान्ते तारं स्वाहेति गरुडपञ्चाक्षरम् । आमन्तेऽनन्ताय नम इत्यनन्तमन्त्रः ॥ १४ ॥ १५ ॥ १६ ॥

वर्णान्त्यानलभुवनबिन्दुभिरुक्तं नृसिंहबीजमिदम् ।
तन्नास्ति सम्यगमुना मन्त्रविदा साधितेन यदसाध्यम् ॥ १७

ऋष्यादिकमपि पूर्ववदङ्गं बीजेन दीर्घयुजा ।
ध्यानार्चनादिकमन्यदशेषं समानं स्यात् ॥ १८

विभवानुरूपतोऽस्मै दातव्या दक्षिणा च निजगुरवे ।
प्राणप्रदानकर्त्रे न च कार्यं वित्तशाठ्यममलधिया ॥ १९

संप्रीणयित्वा गुरुमात्मशक्त्या संपूजयेद्विप्रवरान् यथावत् ।
स त्वैहिकीं शुद्धिमवाप्य शुद्धं परं परत्रापि पदं समेति ॥ २०

दूर्वातिकैरष्टसहस्रसंख्यै-
राराध्य मन्त्री जुहुयादथाप्सु ।
शान्तिं प्रयान्त्येव तदोपसर्गा
आपो हि शान्ता इति च श्रुतिः स्यात् ॥ २१

उत्पाते सति महति क्षुद्रुपद्रवाणां
होमोऽयं भवति च शान्तिदो नराणाम् ।
यद्वाऽन्यन्निजमनसेप्सितञ्च कामं
तत्प्राप्नोत्यखिलनृणां प्रियश्च भूयात् ॥ २२

दुःस्वप्नेष्वपि दृष्टेष्ववशिष्टा जाग्रता निशा नेया ।
जपमानमलशक्त्या सुस्वप्नो भवति तत्क्षणादेव ॥ २३

चरन् वने दुष्टमृगाहिघोरव्यालाकुले मन्त्रमिमं जपेद्यः ।
असाधितं साधितमेव तस्य न विद्यते भीर्बहुरूपजाता ॥ २४

जप्तेनाऽष्टसहस्रं कलशेनाऽप्यहिविषार्त्तमभिषिञ्चेत् ।
अतिविषमेण विषेणाऽप्यसौ विमुक्तः सुखी भवति ॥ २५

सम्यगमुनेत्यङ्गर्ष्यादिकं सूचितम् । ब्रह्मा ऋषिः । गायत्री छन्दः । नृसिंहो देवता । दीर्घयुजा स्वेनाऽङ्गानि । क्ष्रौं बीजम् । षं शक्तिः । ध्यानादिकं पूर्ववत् । मन्त्रविदेति । तत्तत्साध्यानुरूपबीजयोग उक्तः [ऋष्यादिकमपीति श्लोकः क्वचिन्न दृश्यते] ॥ १७ ॥ १८ ॥ १९ ॥ २० ॥

मन्त्री जुहुयादथाप्स्विति । नृसिंहं भीषणमिति निष्कीलमन्त्रेणेत्यर्थः । ॥ २१॥२२॥२३॥२४॥२५॥२६॥२७॥२८॥२९॥३० ॥

मूषिकलूतावृश्चिकबहुपादाद्युद्भवं विषं शमयेत् ।
अष्टोत्तरशतजापान्मनुरयमभिमन्त्रितञ्च भस्माद्यम् ॥ २६
सशिरोऽक्षिकर्णहृद्गलकुक्षिरुजाज्वरविसर्पवमिहिक्काः ।
मन्त्रौषधाभिचारिककृतान् विकारानयं मनुः शमयेत् ॥ २७
नरहरिवपुषात्मना गृहीतं हरिणशिशुं निजवैरिणं विचिन्त्य ।
क्षिपतु गगनतः क्षितौ सुदूरं यमनुदिनं प्रतिचाल्यते स मासात् ॥ २८
याञ्च दिशं प्रति मनुनाक्षिप्तोऽसौ तां दिशं प्रयात्यचिरात् ।
पुत्रकलत्रधनादींस्त्यक्त्वा न पुनर्निवृत्तये सहसा ॥ २९
नरहरिवपुषात्मना निजारिं खरनखराग्रसमग्रभिन्नदेहम् ।
तृणमिव निहतं विचिन्त्य खादन्निव जपतां मनुमेष नाशमेति ॥ ३०
पूर्वतरे मृत्युपदे विधाय निजसाध्यनाम मन्त्रितमः ।
क्रूरेण चक्षुषा तं दहन्निवालोक्य जपतु सप्तदिनम् ॥ ३१
दिनशोऽष्टोर्ध्वंसहस्रं म्रियते रिपुरस्य नात्र सन्देहः ।
मारणकर्म न शस्तं क्रियते यद्ययुतमथ जपेच्छान्त्यै ॥ ३२
वश्याकृष्टिद्वेषणमोहोच्चाटादिकानि यदि वाञ्छेत ।
तदर्हया प्रतिपत्त्या तत्तत्कर्म प्रसाधयेन्मन्त्री ॥ ३३
दिनमनु दिननाथं पूजयित्वा दिनादौ
नरहरिमपि सम्यक् प्रोक्तमार्गेण मन्त्री ।
तदनु तदनुमत्या भस्मना मन्त्रितेन
प्रतिरचयतु राज्ञे वाऽप्यभीष्टाय रक्षाम् ॥ ३४
न्यासोक्तेषु स्थानेष्वपि न्यसेद्भस्मना च मन्त्रार्णान्
अखिलोपद्रवशान्त्यै सम्पत्त्यै वाञ्छितार्थसिद्ध्यै च ॥ ३५
अथ परराष्ट्रजयेच्छो राज्ञः कुर्यात्प्रयोगविधिमेवम् ।
नरहरिमपि विधिना तं हिरण्यकशिपुद्विषं समभ्यर्च्य ॥ ३६

साध्यनाम मन्त्रितम इति । चक्षुषि नृसिंहबीजन्यास उक्तः ॥ ३१ ॥ १२ ॥

साधयेन्मन्त्रीति । स्तम्भनादिषु पृथिवीबीजादियोग उक्तः ॥ ३३ ॥

प्रोक्तमार्गेण मन्त्रीति । रक्षायां नृसिंहबीजयोग उक्तः ॥ ३४ ॥ ३५ ॥ ३६ ॥
॥ ३७ ॥ ३८ ॥ ३९ ॥

तस्य पुरस्ताद्विधिवन्निधाय वह्निं बिभीतकतरुकाष्ठैः ।
उज्ज्वलिते च ज्वलने ससूलतूलैः शरैश्शतदशकैः ।
खादन्निवोच्चरेन्मनुमरींश्च भिन्दन्निव चिपेत् समिधः ॥ ३७
हुत्वा परराष्ट्रेभ्यः पृतनां सन्नाह्य सम्मुखे तस्याः ।
निघ्नन्तं रिपुसेनां स्मरेन्नृसिंहं पुरेव दितितनयान् ॥ ३८
यावज्जितारिरेष्यति नृपतिस्तावज्जपेत् स्मरन्देवम् ।
सेन्द्रसुरासुररक्षोयक्षानपि जयति का कथा मनुजे ॥ ३९
श्रीकामः श्रीप्रसूनैर्दशकमथ शतानां हुनेद्बिल्वकाष्ठै-
स्तत्पत्रैर्वा प्रसूनैः सुमतिरथ समिद्भिः फलैर्वा तदीयैः ।
पुत्रेप्सुः पुत्रजीवेन्धनचितदहने तत्फलैर्वा सहस्रै-
र्दूर्वाभिस्त्वायुषेऽब्दादभिमतमखिलं प्राप्नुयान्मन्त्रजापी ॥ ४०
ब्राह्मीं वचां वाऽष्टशताभिजप्तां प्रातः समद्यान्नृहरिं विचिन्त्य ।
संप्राप्य मेधां स तु वेदशास्त्रनिष्णातधीः स्यादपि वत्सरेण ॥ ४१

उक्तैः किमत्र बहुभिर्मनुनाऽमुनैव
संप्रार्थितं सकलमेव लभेद्विधिज्ञः ।
तस्मादमुं भजत तत्प्रतिपन्नचित्ताः
संसारसागरसमुत्तरणार्थिनो ये ॥ ४२
पाशाङ्कुशान्तरितशक्तिनृसिंहबीजे
वर्मास्त्रयुङ्मनुरयं कथितः षडर्णः ।
ऋष्यादिकाः स्वभवपङ्क्तिकनारसिंहा
वर्णैश्च मन्त्रनिहितैः कथितं षडङ्गम् ॥ ४३

भव्यान्निर्व्याजरौद्राकृतिरतिविकृतास्योल्लसत्तीव्रदंष्ट्र-
श्चक्रं शङ्खञ्च पाशाङ्कुशकुलिशगदादारणाख्यान्दधानः ।
रक्ताकारश्च नाभेरध उपरि सितो दिव्यभूषाविशेषो
देवोऽर्काग्नीन्दुनेत्रो निखिलसुखकरो नारसिंहश्चिरं वः ॥ ४४

सुमतिरिति । श्रीबीजयोगरत्नाभिषेकध्याने कथिते । प्राप्नुयान्मन्त्रजापीत्यनु-
जप उक्तः । षडक्षरस्य क्ष्रौं बीजम् । ह्रीं शक्तिः ॥ ४० ॥ ४१ ॥ ४२ ॥ ४३ ॥

षट्कोणस्थसुदर्शनं वसुदलप्रोल्लासिताष्टाक्षरं
बाह्ये द्वादशवर्णपत्रकमलं तत् षोड़शार्णच्छदम् ।
द्वात्रिंशन्मनुवर्णपत्रकमलं वृत्तोल्लसन्मातृकं
मध्योत्थं ध्रुवमूर्तिबीजवलयं चक्रं नृसिंहात्मकम् ॥ ४५
हृल्लेखान्तःस्थसाध्यं दहनपुरयुगास्रिस्थमन्त्रार्णमन्तः-
सिंहानुष्टुप्चतुर्वर्णकलसितदलाढ्यं कलाकेसरञ्च ।
वृत्तोद्यद्व्यञ्जनावेष्टितमवनिपुरान्तःस्थवृत्तो[चिन्तो]पलं तद्-
यन्त्रं रक्षःपिशाचामयरिपुविषविध्वंसनं नारसिंहम् ॥ ४६

इति विरचितयन्त्रप्रोज्ज्वले मण्डले प्राक्-
समभिहितकषायाम्भोभिरापूर्य कुम्भम् ।
प्रतियजतु तदङ्गैरस्त्रभेदैस्तदीयै-
स्तदनु शतमखाद्यैः साधु वज्रादिकैश्च ॥ ४७

रथचरणशङ्खपाशाङ्कुशकुलिशगदाह्वयानि चाऽस्त्राणि ।
दारणमुद्राकरयोर्ययोस्तदीयौ कृपाणखेटाख्यौ ॥ ४८
इति कृतदीक्षः प्रजपेदक्षरलक्षप्रमाणात्मकं मन्त्रम् ।
जुहुयाच्च षट्सहस्रं जपावसाने घृतेन शुद्धेन ॥ ४९
खरमञ्जरीसमुत्थं जुहुयादथ मञ्जरीसहस्रयुतम् ।
प्रस्नातपञ्चगव्यं सप्तदिनं भूतशान्तये मन्त्री ॥ ५०
छिन्नरुहां समिधां त्रिसहस्रं यश्च जुहोति चतुर्दिनमात्रम् ।
दुग्धयुतं नचिरान्मनुजानां होमविधिर्ज्वरशान्तिकरः स्यात् ॥ ५१
यस्य यन्त्रमभिलिख्य भूर्जके साधु वाऽथ तृणराजपत्रके ।
मन्त्रजप्तमथ शीर्षबन्धनाज्जूर्तिविभ्रमशिरोरुजापहम् ॥ ५२

रक्तोत्पलैः प्रतिदिनं मधुरत्रयाक्तै-
र्यो वा जुहोति नियमेन सहस्रसंख्यैः ।

ध्यानमाह—भव्यादिति । [षट्कोणस्थेति श्लोकः पुस्तकान्तरे नास्ति] ॥४४॥ ॥ ४५ ॥ ४६ ॥ ४७ ॥ ४८ ॥ ४९ ॥

भूतशान्तये मन्त्रीति । मन्त्रजप्तपञ्चगव्यप्राशनादिकं सूचितम् ॥५०॥५१॥५२॥

मासेन वाञ्छितमवाप्स्यति मन्त्रजापी
स्याद्वत्सरेण धनधान्यसमृद्धगेहः ॥ ५३

आरक्तैस्तरणिसहस्रकैः प्रफुल्लै-
रम्भोजैस्त्रिमधुरसंयुतैर्जुहोतु ।
लक्ष्मीः स्यादतिमहती महत्तथायुः
संप्राप्य सकलजगत्प्रियश्च भूयात् ॥ ५४

लाजाभिस्त्रिमधुरसंयुताभिरह्नो
मासार्धं प्रतिजुहुयान्मुखे सहस्रम् ।
कन्यार्थी प्रतिलभते वरोऽथ कन्यां
कन्या वा भवति वरार्थिनी वराढ्या ॥ ५५

तिलैः सराजीखरमञ्जरीसमिद्भिर्घृतैश्च द्विसहस्रसंख्यकैः ।
प्रजुह्वतो नैव रुजो ग्रहोद्भवा न वाऽभिचारक्षतिरस्य जायते ॥

दशाधिकशतैः पयोघृतयुतैश्च दूर्वाचयै-
र्हुनेद्दिनमुखे विभुं नरहरिं विचिन्त्याऽनले ।
अवाप्य स तु दीर्घमायुरखिलैर्विमुक्तो गदैः
सुखी भवति मानवो निजकलत्रपुत्रादिभिः ॥ ५७

विस्तारैः किं प्रतिजपति यो मन्त्रमेनं यथोक्तं
लब्ध्वा कामान् समभिलषितानाशु मन्त्री स भूयात् ।
द्रव्यैराढ्यो द्विजनृपवरैः पूजितः शान्तचेता
देहान्ते स्यात् परमपरिशुद्धं परं धाम विष्णोः ॥ ५८

इति श्रीप्रपञ्चसारे पञ्चविंशः पटलः ।

मन्त्रजापीति । श्रीबीजयोग उक्तः ॥ ५३ ॥ ५४ ॥ ५५ ॥ ५६ ॥ ५७ ॥
आशु मन्त्रीत्यभिलषितविशेषप्राप्तौ बीजविशेषयोग उक्तः ॥ ५८ ॥

इति श्रीपद्मपादाचार्यकृते प्रपञ्चसारविवरणे
पञ्चविंशः पटलः ।

षड्विंशः पटलः ।

अथ सम्प्रति विष्णुपञ्जरस्य प्रतिवक्ष्यामि समासतो विधानम् ।
जितवांस्त्रिपुरं हरोऽपि येन त्रिदशानामधिपो बलासुरञ्च ॥ १
शक्तेर्द्वादशगुणिते यन्त्रे मन्त्राणि मण्डलान्यपि च ।
बीजानि यानि चोक्तान्येभिः क्लृप्तन्तु पञ्जरं विष्णोः ॥ २
विष्णुं लिखेन्मध्यगशक्तिबिन्दौ कपोलयोः सिंहवराहबीजे ।
तद्विश्वरूपाह्वयमन्त्रवीतं प्रवेष्टयेत् षोड़शवर्णकेन ॥ ३
तारं हृदन्ते भगवत्पदं महाविष्णुवासुदेवौ च ङेऽन्तौ ।
विश्वादिरूप शरणं भव मे प्रभविष्णवे नमः स्यान्मन्त्रः ॥ ४
द्वादशाक्षरमन्त्रान्ते भवेतां कवचास्त्रकौ ।
स्वाहान्तः षोड़शार्णोऽयं मन्त्रः सर्वार्थसाधकः ॥ ५
क्रमेण तद्वर्णविकारजाताश्चक्रादिकाः षोड़श मूर्तयः स्युः ।
याभिस्तु विष्णोरिह पञ्जरस्य प्रवर्त्यते शक्तिरनेकरूपा ॥ ६

नृसिंहविधानानन्तरं रक्षाकरत्वसाम्यात् विष्णुपञ्जरविधानमाह—अथ संप्रतीति । रक्षाकरत्वमाह—जितवानिति ॥ १ ॥

विष्णुपञ्जरयन्त्रं तावदाह—शक्तेरिति । मण्डलानि वृत्तत्रिकोणचतुरस्राणि ॥ २ ॥

अधिकमंशमाह—विष्णुमिति । विष्णुमकारमित्यर्थः । तस्य बिन्दौ विश्वरूपविष्णुरपि लेखनीयः । तस्य हस्तेषु वक्ष्यमाणायुधधारणक्रमेण षोड़शाक्षराक्षराण्यपि लेखनीयानि । कपोलयोरिति । अकारहकारभागद्वयोरित्यर्थः । सिंहवराहशब्दाभ्यामेव तद्बीजे उक्ते । ते चाकारकपोलयोः लेखनीये । बीजे इति तु हकारकपोलयोः गरुड़चक्रबीजलेखनमुक्तम् । तद्विश्वरूपेति । तच्छब्देन मध्यमबीजमुक्तम् ॥ ३ ॥

विश्वरूपमन्त्रमुद्धरति—तारमिति । ओं बीजम् । नमः शक्तिः ॥ ४ ॥ ५ ॥

चक्रादिमन्त्रेषु षोड़शाक्षराक्षरयोगं सूचयति—तद्वर्णविकारजाता इति । याभिरिति । कारणसूक्ष्मस्थूलरूपाभिः भगवद्धस्तवेष्टनबीजपद्मदलादिस्थाभिरित्यर्थः ॥ ६ ॥

यन्त्रस्य बीजेषु चतुर्षु पूर्वं प्राग्दक्षिणप्रत्यगुदग्गतेषु ।
विद्वांस्तु चक्रञ्च गदाञ्च शार्ङ्गं खङ्गञ्च मन्त्रैः सहितं विलिख्यात् ॥
शङ्खहलमुसलशूलान्यग्न्याद्यग्निष्वथाऽष्टबीजेषु ।
विलिखेत् दण्डं कुन्तं शक्तिं
पाशाङ्कुशकुलिशपरशुशतमुखवह्नीन् ॥ ८
सप्रणवहृदयभगवद्विष्णुस्वाख्यानमूर्तिधरयुक्ताः ।
सेनापतिसहिता निजमन्त्रान्ता मूर्तयोऽत्र लिखितव्याः ॥ ९
सहस्रारपदं पूर्वं कौमोदकी ततो भवेत् ।
महाशार्ङ्गपदं पश्चात् महाखङ्गपदं पुनः ॥ १०

यन्त्रस्य बीजेष्विति । वेष्टनशक्तिबीजेष्वित्यर्थः । विद्वानिति । चित्रकर्मज्ञ इत्यर्थः । मन्त्रैः सहितमिति । ललाटे तत्तन्मन्त्रांश्च लिखेदित्यर्थः ॥ ७ ॥

अग्निष्विति । अग्निगतबीजबिन्दुष्वित्यर्थः । सिंहवराहमूर्त्योस्तु लेखनं शक्तिवेष्टनपूर्वापरभागयोः । गरुडचक्रमूर्त्योस्तु शक्तिवेष्टनबाह्ये नृसिंहस्याग्रे ॥८॥

चक्रादिमन्त्रानुद्धरति—सप्रणवेति । नमो योगादेव भगवद्विष्णुपदयोश्चतुर्थ्यन्तत्वमवगन्तव्यम् । स्वाख्यानं स्वस्य चक्रादेराख्यानम् । ततश्च ओं नमो भगवते विष्णवे चक्रायेत्येतत् सिद्धं भवति । स्वाख्यानमूर्तीति । स्वाभिमुख्यार्थमाख्यानं स्वाख्यानं तेन सहिता मूर्तिः स्वाख्यानमूर्तिः । सम्बुध्यन्तो मूर्तिशब्द इत्यर्थः । स्वस्य साधकस्य आख्यानं स्वाख्यानं शोभनप्राप्त्यर्थमाख्यानं स्वाख्यानं मां रक्षेत्याख्यानमित्यर्थः । सुतरामाख्यानं स्वाख्यानं रक्षरक्षेति वीप्सेत्यर्थः । ततश्च चक्रमूर्ते मां रक्ष रक्षेत्येतत् सिद्धं भवति । स्वाख्यानमूर्तिधरयुक्ताः सेनापतिसहिता इति । स्वाख्यानयुक्ताः । स्वाख्यानमूर्तियुक्ताः । स्वाख्यान मूर्तिधरयुक्ताः । स्वाख्यानमूर्तिधराः सेनापतिसहिता इत्यन्वयः । तत्र स्वाख्यानयुक्ता इत्यस्यायमर्थः । ओं नमो भगवते विष्णवे चक्रायेत्यादीनि स्वाख्यानानि तैः युक्ता इति । स्वाख्यानमूर्तियुक्ता इत्यस्यायमर्थः । उक्तमन्त्रान्ते चक्रमूर्तये इत्यादि योजयेदिति । ततः परं चक्रमूर्तिधरायेत्यादि योजयेत् । ततः परं चक्रमूर्तिधरसेनापतये इत्यादि योजयेदित्यवशिष्टस्यार्थः ॥ ९ ॥

निजमन्त्रानुद्धरति—सहस्रारेति । पोत्रं धृतधरं विद्वानिति । वराहबीजयोगविद्वानित्यर्थः । विष्णवभिख्ययोरन्तरेति । विष्णवे पोत्रधृतधराय महावराहायेति क्रमेणेत्यर्थः । मन्त्रीति । महावराहमन्त्रस्यान्ते योग इत्यर्थः ।

प्रोक्तानि वर्मास्त्रान्तानि निजमन्त्राणि वै क्रमात् ।
पूर्वं महापाशजन्यं महाहलमनन्तरम् ॥ ११
ततो महामुसलकं महाशूलं ततः परम् ।
स्वाहान्तानि च मन्त्राणि शङ्खादीनां क्रमाद्विदुः ॥ १२
दण्डादीनामथाऽष्टानामन्ते युज्यान्नमःपदम् ।
पोत्रं धृतधरं विद्वान् वाराहे विष्णुभिख्ययोः ॥ १३
अन्तरा योजयेन्मन्त्री नारसिंहे पुनः सुधीः ।
नखश्च दलितश्चैव रिपुविग्रहमेव च ॥ १४
योजयित्वा नृसिंहात् प्राक् सिंहमन्त्रं समापयेत् ।
विष्णोरन्ते महापक्षिराजाय च गरुत्मते ॥ १५
हरिपूर्वं वाहनाय प्राणात्मन इतीरयेत् ।
नमोऽन्तोऽसौ तु विद्वद्भिर्मन्त्रो गारुत्मतो मतः ॥ १६
सत्रिष्टुभा वह्निगृहेण पूर्वं सानुष्टुभेन्दोर्निलयेन चापि ।
गायत्रमन्त्रोल्लसितेन भूयः संवेष्टयेदर्कनिकेतनेन ॥ १७
अनुलोमविलोमगैश्च वर्णैरभिवीतं च सुधापुटद्वयेन ।
नलिनं बहिरष्टयुग्मपत्रं प्रविदध्यादथ मूर्तिमन्त्रयुक्तम् ॥ १८
तद्बहिर्मण्डलं सर्वलक्षणैरभिलक्षितम् ।
तस्मिन्नावाह्य विधिवद्विश्वरूपं हरिं यजेत् ॥ १९
अग्नीषोमात्मकमरिगदाशार्ङ्गखड्गैः सशङ्खै-
रुद्यद्बाहुं हलमुसलशूलैः सदण्डैः सकुन्तैः ।
शक्त्या पाशाङ्कुशकुलिशटङ्काग्निभिश्चाऽर्कवह्नि-
द्योतद्वक्त्राङ्घ्रिकसरसिजं तप्तकार्त्तस्वराभम् ॥ २०

नारसिंहे पुनः सुधीरिति । नृसिंहबीजयोगश्च इत्यर्थः । नृसिंहात् प्रागिति । महानृसिंहाय नमः इत्यतः पूर्वमित्यर्थः । नृसिंहमन्त्रं समापयेदित्यनुष्टुभोऽन्ते योग उक्तः । विष्णोरन्त इति । विष्णवे महापक्षिराजायेत्यादिक्रमेणो-च्चरेदित्यर्थः । विद्वद्भिरिति । महापदयोग उक्तः ॥ १०—१८ ॥

अग्नीषोमात्मकमिति । दक्षिणाधोहस्तमारभ्य पञ्चमे पञ्चमे हस्ते चक्रादिचतु-ष्टयं दक्षिणाधस्तृतीयहस्तमारभ्य पञ्चमे पञ्चमे शङ्खादिचतुष्टयं दक्षिणाधोद्वितीय-

विश्वं भास्वत्किरीटं मणिमुकुटकटीसूत्रकेयूरहार-
ग्रैवेयोर्म्यादिमुख्याभरणमणिगणोल्लासिदिव्याङ्गरागम् ।
विश्वाकाशावकाशप्रविततमयुतादित्यसङ्काशमुद्य-
द्दाक्षग्र्यव्यग्रनानायुधनिकरधरं विश्वरूपं नमामि ॥ २१

अभ्यर्च्य पूर्ववत् पीठं नवशक्तिसमन्वितम् ।
अर्चयेत् क्रमशो विद्वान् मूर्तिशक्तिचतुष्टयम् ॥ २२

चक्रञ्च चक्राङ्ककिरीटमौलिं सशङ्खचक्रं सगदं सशार्ङ्गम् ।
रक्ताम्बरं रक्ततनुं करालदंष्ट्राननं प्राग्दलकेऽर्चयीत ॥ २३

पूज्या गदा गदाङ्कितमौलिः सगदा सचक्रशङ्खधनुः ।
पीताम्बरानुलेपा पीता क्रुद्धा च याम्यसंस्थदले ॥ २४

शार्ङ्गं शार्ङ्गाङ्कितकं श्यामं शार्ङ्गारिदरगदाहस्तम् ।
रक्तांशुकानुलेपनमाल्यादि वारुणे यजेत् पत्रे ॥ २५

खड्गं सखड्गशिरसं खड्गारिगदाधनुःकरं धूम्रम् ।
विकृताम्बरानुलेपस्रजं समर्चयेदुदक्पत्रे ॥ २६

शङ्खं सशङ्खशिरसं शङ्खारिगदाधनुःकरं सुसितम् ।
सितवसनमाल्यभूषं यजेन्महानादमग्निसंस्थदले ॥ २७

शङ्खोक्तचिह्नभूषान् स्वास्त्रादिकधरचतुर्भुजानपरान् ।
हलमुसलशूलसंज्ञान् संयजेन्निशाटादिकोणेषु पत्रेषु ॥ २८

दण्डादिकांस्तथाऽष्टौ छिद्रदलेष्वर्चयीत रक्ताभान् ।
स्वस्वायुधप्रधानांश्चतुर्भुजाञ्कृतमुखानलान्तांश्च ॥ २९

दंष्ट्राग्रलग्नवसुधं सजलाम्बुवाह-
घोरत्विषं त्वभियजेदथ साष्टबाहुम् ।
चक्रासिबाणसगदादरचर्मशार्ङ्ग-
शक्त्याख्यकान् दधतमादिमहावराहम् ॥ ३०

चक्रमारभ्य एकैकान्तरितहस्तेषु दण्डाद्यष्टकमित्येवमायुधधारणक्रमः ॥ २०॥२१ ॥

क्रमशो विद्वानिति । वासुदेवादिमन्त्राः सूचिताः ॥ २२—३२ ॥

अर्कानलोज्ज्वलमुखं नयनैस्त्रिभिश्च
वह्निं वमन्तमवधूतसटाकलापम् ।
शुक्लाभभूषमरिशङ्खगदासिबाहुं
भूयोऽभिराधयतु खे च महान्टसिंहम् ॥ ३१
अग्रे समग्रबलमुग्रतनुं स्वपक्ष-
विक्षेपविक्षतविलक्षविपक्षपक्षम् ।
खड्ग[गड]ाग्रतुण्डममुमण्डजदण्डनाथ-
माराधयेदथ च पञ्जरकस्य विष्णोः ॥ ३२
भूयोऽपि केशवेन्द्रादिकान् समभ्यर्चयेच्चक्रवज्रादीन् ।
गन्धादिभिरुपचारैः पञ्चभिरथ संयतात्मको मन्त्री ॥ ३३
निजोदितो होमविधिश्च कार्यो दीक्षाविधानाभिहिते च वह्नौ ।
ससर्पिषाऽन्नेन तु वह्निमूर्तीर्हुत्वा तु विष्णोर्मनुना तथैव ॥ ३४
हुत्वा मनुवर्णसमं षोड़शवर्णं जुहोतु षोड़शशः ।
जुहुयाच्च वासुदेवादिकं शान्त्यादींश्चाऽथ रुद्रसंख्येन ॥ ३५
दुग्धतरूत्थाः समिधः क्रमेण चक्रादिभिश्चतुर्मन्त्रैः ।
जुहुयादष्टोर्ध्वशतं शङ्खाद्यैर्द्वादशभिरथ मनुभिः ॥ ३६
तिलसिद्धार्थैर्जुहुयाद्विकारसंख्यं पृथक् पृथङ्मन्त्री ।
त्रिष्टुबनुष्टुप्तत्पदमन्त्रैर्मन्त्रार्णसंख्यकं हविषा ॥ ३७
सघृतेन केशवाद्यैर्दिनकरसंख्यं तथेन्द्रवज्राद्यैः ।
जुहुयात् पृथगपि वसुमितमथ च महाव्याहृतीर्हुनेन्मतिमान् ॥ ३८
आराध्य च विसृज्याऽग्निमभिषिच्य सुसंयतः ।
विष्णोस्तु पञ्जरं कुर्याद्दृषी ब्रह्मबृहस्पती ॥ ३९
छन्दस्त्वनुष्टुप् त्रिष्टुप् च मुनिभिः समुदाहृते ।
विश्वरूपादिको विष्णुर्विष्णुपञ्जरदेवता ॥ ४०

संयतात्मको मन्त्रीति । केशवादीनामुक्ता मन्त्राः सूचिताः । वह्निमूर्तिग्रहणं जिह्वादीनामप्युपलक्षणम् । विष्णोर्मनुर्विश्वरूपमन्त्रः । [निजोदित इत्यप निवेदिते इत्यपि पाठः] ॥ ३३ ॥ ३४ ॥ ३५ ॥ ३६ ॥

पृथक् पृथङ्मन्त्रीति । वराहनृसिंहगरुड़मन्त्रैरपि होमं सूचयति ॥ ३७ ॥

अष्टार्णचक्रमनुमध्यगतैश्च पादै-
र्व्यस्तैस्तथा सुमतिरारचयेत् समस्तैः ।
गीतामनोः क्रमश एव तु जातियुग्भि
पञ्चाङ्गकानि हरिपञ्जरकल्पितानि ॥ ४१

विष्णुः प्राच्यादिकमथ जपेन्नारसिंहोऽम्बरान्तं
त्रींस्त्रीन् मन्त्रान् पुनरपि तथा पञ्चशस्त्वेकविंशम् ।
बुद्धिस्वास्थ्यप्रभृति च तथा पञ्चवारं त्रिगाथां
भूयो जप्याद्विमलशितधीश्चक्रमन्त्राभिधानम् ॥ ४२

हुनेन्मतिमानिति । आदौ प्रणवेन होम उक्तः ॥ ३८ ॥ ३९ ॥ ४० ॥

सुमतिरारचयेदिति । चक्रमनोरूर्ध्वं प्रणवशक्तियोगश्च इत्यर्थः ॥ ४१ ॥

विष्णुः प्राच्यादिकमथ जपेदिति । त्रिष्टुबनुष्टुब्गायत्रीगीतात्रिष्टुब्विश्वरूप-षोडशाक्षराणां सकृत् सकृत् जपानन्तरं शतानीक उवाचेत्यारभ्य तन्निबोध मह्यीपत इत्यन्तः सकृत् जप्त्वा त्रिष्टुबादिमन्त्रषट्कं त्रिवारमावर्त्याऽनन्तरमित्यथशब्दार्थः । षोडशाक्षराक्षरवराहनृसिंहगरुडचक्रबीजैः सप्रणवशक्तिभिः सह तेषां जपः कार्यः ।

अयमत्र प्रयोगक्रमः । ओं क्लीं ओं विष्णुः प्राच्यां स्थितश्चक्री । ओं क्लीं नं विष्णुर्दक्षिणतो गदी । ओं क्लीं मों प्रतीच्यां शार्ङ्गधृग्विष्णुः । ओं क्लीं भं विष्णुः खड्गी ममोत्तरे । ओं क्लीं गं हृषीकेशो विकोणेषु । ओं क्लीं वं हृषीकेशो विकोणेषु । ओं क्लीं तें हृषीकेशो विकोणेषु । ओं क्लीं वां हृषीकेशो विकोणेषु । ओं क्लीं सुं तच्छिद्रेषु जनार्दनः । ओं क्लीं दें तच्छिद्रेषु । ओं क्लीं वां तच्छिद्रे । ओं क्लीं यं तच्छिद्रे । ओं क्लीं हुं तच्छिद्रेषु । ओं क्लीं फट् ओं क्लीं तच्छिद्रेषु । स्वां तच्छिद्रेषु । ओं क्लीं हां तच्छिद्रेषु । ओं क्लीं हूं क्रोडरूपो हरिर्भूमौ । ओं क्लीं क्ष्रौं नरसिंहोम्बरे मम । ओं क्लीं चौं विष्णुरग्रे स्थितो गरुडः । ओं क्लीं रं विष्णुरग्रे स्थितं चक्रमिति विंशन्मन्त्रांस्त्रिवारं जपेत् ।

नरसिंहोऽम्बरान्तमिति । नृसिंहमन्त्रस्य पञ्जरकल्पनामन्त्रेष्वन्त्यत्वमुक्तम् । नतु ततः परं पञ्जररचकमन्त्राभावोऽन्तशब्देन सिध्यति । यतः तत्र पुनरपीति मन्त्रद्वयसद्भावं सूचयति । तथा पञ्चशस्त्वेकविंशमिति । विश्वरूपमन्त्रेण सार्धं चक्रादिचक्रान्तान् एकविंशतिमन्त्रान् पञ्च पञ्चवारं जपेदित्यर्थः । तत्र विश्वरूपमन्त्रं ओं नमो भगवते विष्णवे विश्वरूपमूर्ते मामित्यादिको ग्राह्यः ।

ॐ नमो भगवते सर्वजिष्णवे विश्वरूपिणे ।
वासुदेवाय चक्रादिसर्वायुधभृते नमः ॥ ४३

अर्केन्दुवह्निनिलयस्फुरितत्रिमन्त्र-
शक्तिप्रवृद्धमहसः परमस्य विष्णोः ।
पादारविन्दगलितामृतसिक्तगात्रं
साध्यं स्मरेज्जपविधावपि साधकेशः ॥ ४४

विष्णोः सान्निध्यलब्धोल्लसितचलचलद्वस्तदण्डोद्यतास्त्रै-
श्चक्राद्यैर्भीषणास्यैर्ज्वलनचरणवचोहासहुङ्कारघोरैः ।
उत्छिन्नाछिन्नकृत्तस्फुटितविदलितांश्चूर्णितध्वस्तगात्रान्
ध्यायेद्वेतालभूतग्रहदुरितपिशाचारिनागादिरोगान् ॥ ४५

पूर्वं स्थाने हृषीकेशमन्त्रयुक्तं विधानवित् ।
विश्वरूपात्मकं जप्याद्वैष्णवं मूलमन्त्रकम् ॥ ४६
योजयित्वा जपेत् पश्चात् चक्रादिषु यथाक्रमम् ।
चतुर्षु चतुरः पादान् गीतात्रिष्टुप्समुद्भवान् ॥ ४७
पूर्वेषु षोड़शस्वेवमाद्यं पादं वराहके ।
द्वितीयं नारसिंहे च तृतीयं गारुड़े पुनः ।
चतुर्थं चक्रमन्त्रे च योजयित्वा जपेत् सुधीः ॥ ४८

पूर्वोद्धृतविश्वरूपमन्त्रेण सहाऽयं पञ्चवारं प्रथमतो जप्यः । ततश्चक्रादिमन्त्राः । विमलयितमतिरिति । पञ्जराकाराणां तद्रूचकाकाराणामायुधादीनामाधारभूतानां त्रिष्टुबादीनां ध्यानमायुधानां मुद्रापूर्वकं जपः त्रिष्टुबादिप्रतिलोमजपश्चेत्यादि सूचितम् ॥ ४२ ॥

चक्रमन्त्रमुद्धरति—ओं नमः इति ॥ ४३ ॥

[प्रतिपत्तिमाह—अर्केन्द्विति द्वाभ्याम् । अर्केन्दुवह्नीनां निलयानि मण्डलानि । तेषु स्फुरितास्त्रिमन्त्राः गायत्र्यनुष्टुप्त्रिष्टुभः तेषां शक्तिभिः प्रवृद्धं समेधितमत्युर्जितं महस्तेजो यस्य स तथा तस्य विश्वरूपविष्णोः] ॥ ४४॥४५ ॥

विश्वरूपत्रिष्टुबादीनामपि पञ्चपञ्चवारं जपमाह—पूर्वमिति । विश्वरूपचक्रादिमन्त्रजपात् पूर्वमित्यर्थः । त्रिष्टुबादिजपक्रमं च सूचयति—विधानविदिति । चक्रादिमन्त्रेष्वपि गीतात्रिष्टुबादियोगमाह—योजयित्वेति ।

मन्त्रं सुदर्शनं चेत्थमिम[ष्ट]मष्टाक्षरं मनुम् ।
संयोज्य कृच्छ्रे महति जपेन्मन्त्री विधानवित् ॥ ४९
आग्नेये वक्ष्यमाणेन विधानेन समाहितः ।
सिकतोपलचर्वादीन् साधयेदथ तैः क्रियाम् ॥ ५०
वास्तौ पुरे वा ग्रामे वा विदध्याद्विषयेऽपि वा ।
मध्ये च षोड़शाशान्ते खनेदष्टादशाऽवटान् ॥ ५१
अष्टादशन्तु चक्रस्य विदध्यात् पुरतोऽवटम् ।
हस्तागाधांस्तथाऽऽयामांश्चतुरस्रान् समन्ततः ॥ ५२
अन्योन्यतश्चंक्रमार्थं शुद्धान् मार्गान् विधाय च ।
गोमयेनोपलिप्यैतानानीय स्थाप्य वस्त्वपि ॥ ५३

सुधीरिति । गाथाचक्रमन्त्रेष्वपि गीतात्रिष्टुबादियोगश्च इत्यर्थः ॥४६॥४७॥४८॥

पादपूर्वोत्तरभागयोरष्टाक्षरस्य च क्रमेण योगमाह—मन्त्रमिति । जपेन्मन्त्री विधानविदिति । सुदर्शनानन्तरं प्रणवशक्तिषोड़शाक्षराक्षरादिबीजस्तोत्रयोग इत्यादिकं दर्शितम् ।

अयमत्र मन्त्रप्रयोगक्रमः । ओं क्लीं रं विष्णुरग्रे स्थितं चक्रमित्यन्तमुक्त-प्रकारेण त्रिवारं जप्त्वा षोडशाक्षरादिमन्त्रषट्कं त्रिवारमावर्त्य क्षुरान्तमित्यादि विष्णुचक्ररयाहता इत्यन्तमेकवारं जप्त्वा षोडशाक्षरादिमन्त्रषट्कमप्येकैकवारं जपित्वा त्रिष्टुबादिमन्त्रषट्कं पञ्चवारमावर्त्य ओं नमो भगवते विष्णवे विश्वरूप-मूर्तें मामित्यादि विश्वरूपमन्त्रमपि पञ्चवारं जपित्वा चक्रादिचतुर्विंशतिमन्त्रान् पञ्चवारमावर्तयेत् । ओं नमो नारायणाय स्थाने हृषीकेश तव प्रकीर्त्या सहस्रार हुं फट् ओं क्लीं ओं विष्णुः प्राच्यां स्थितश्चक्री ओं नमो भगवते विष्णवे चक्रमूर्ते मां रक्ष रक्ष ओं नमो भगवते विष्णवे चक्राय चक्रमूर्तये चक्रमूर्ति-धराय चक्रमूर्तिधरसेनापतये सहस्रार हुं फडिति चक्रमन्त्रः । एवमन्येऽपि मन्त्रा ऊह्याः । एवं रक्षां कृत्वाऽङ्गर्ष्यादिकं विन्यस्योपसंहरेदिति ॥ ४९ ॥

शरीररक्षाप्रकारमभिधाय वास्त्वादिरक्षाप्रकारमाह—आग्नेये इति । विधान-प्रकारमाह—मध्य इति ॥ ५० ॥ ५१ ॥

हस्तागाधानिति । मध्यव्यतिरिक्तानां परिमाणकथनं मध्ये तु त्रिहस्तेन त्रिभौमी भाव्यम् । वराहनृसिंहयोरपि तत्रैव प्रतिष्ठाया वक्ष्यमाणत्वात्

शुक्लपुष्करपत्रेषु निदध्याद्विंशतिष्वपि ।
ततो मध्यगकुण्डस्य प्रविश्य पुरतो गुरुः ॥ ५४
तदन्तरिष्टा पीठस्य तत्र यन्त्रमनुस्मरन् ।
स्थापयेद्दैष्णवे स्थाने विश्वरूपधिया सुधीः ॥ ५५
ततः क्रमेण चक्रादीन् दिक्कुण्डेषु चतुर्ष्वपि ।
पुनः शङ्खादिकांस्तद्वत् कुण्डेष्वस्राश्रितेष्वपि ॥ ५६
तथा दण्डादिकानष्टौ छिद्राशासु प्रकल्पयेत् ।
मध्ये पुनरधश्चोर्ध्वे कोलकेसरिणौ यजेत् ॥ ५७
चक्रस्य प्राक्तने कुण्डे स्थापयेद्विनतासुतम् ।
ततः समस्थलीकृत्य क्रमात् समुपलिप्य च ॥ ५८
प्रत्यगासनमासीनो मध्यगस्थण्डिले स्थिते ।
यन्त्रे काञ्चनपट्टस्थे पूजयेत् पूर्ववत् प्रभुम् ॥ ५९
वादित्रघोषबहुलं निवेद्यान्तं यथाक्रमम् ।
हुनेच्च पूर्वसन्दिष्टैर्द्रव्यैः पूर्वोक्तमानतः ॥ ६०
आशोपाशान्तराशासु बलिं दद्यात्त्रिशस्त्रिशः ।
क्रमाच्चक्रादिमूर्तीनां पञ्चपूराऽम्भसा सुधीः ॥ ६१
तत उद्वास्य देवेशं पूजां परिसमाप्य च ।
दत्त्वा सुवर्णवासांसि गुरवे ब्राह्मणानपि ॥ ६२
प्रतर्प्य विभवैः सम्यक् भोजयेद्देवताधिया ।
तत्रोपसर्गा नश्यन्ति नरनारीमहीस्थिताः ॥ ६३

एकोनविंशतिकुण्डानि कार्याणि । चक्रस्य पुरतो गरुडस्यापि हि स्थापनमत्र विवक्षितम् । [पुष्करपत्रेण सहितान् तत्तन्मन्त्रैर्यथाविधि जप्तान् सिकतादीन् विश्वरूपविष्ण्वादिदेवताबुद्ध्या तत्तन्मन्त्रैस्तेषु तेषु अवटेषु उक्तक्रमेण स्थापयेदित्याह —स्थापयेदित्यादिना । मध्ये पुनरिति । मध्यमावटे विश्वरूपहरेरध ऊर्ध्वं च द्रव्यस्थापनपूर्वकं वराहनृसिंहौ पूजयेदित्यर्थः । चक्रस्य प्राक्तन इति । नृसिंह-प्रतिष्ठानन्तरं तत्पुरस्थितकुण्डे सुदर्शनचक्रं प्रतिष्ठाप्य तत्पुरस्थितकुण्डे गरुडं प्रतिष्ठापयेदित्यर्थः । पञ्चपूराम्भसेति । दधिसक्तुलाजतिलहरिद्रारजोन्वितमोदनं तेषु विष्णुपार्षदेभ्यो बलिं विकिरयेदित्यर्थः । इति सम्बन्धदीपिका·

ग्रहक्षुद्रपिशाचाद्या नेक्षन्ते तां दिशं भयात् ।
अश्मपातादिका ये च भया नश्यन्ति तेऽचिरात् ॥ ६४
यशःश्रीर्गोसमृद्धिश्च प्रजावृद्धिश्च जायते ।
धनधान्यसमृद्धिश्च वर्धते तत्कुलं क्रमात् ।
दारिद्र्यरोगनिर्मुक्तं सुखमाभूतसंप्लवम् ॥ ६५

रक्षोभिरक्षतबलैरसुरैश्च दैत्यैः
सर्वैः समुद्यतमहास्त्रधरैः परीतम् ।
विष्णोस्तु पञ्जरमिदं प्रभजन्तमव्यात्
साक्षादपौन्द्रमपरत्र नरे कथा का ॥ ६६

इति श्रीप्रपञ्चसारे षड्विंशः पटलः ॥

कारः] ॥ ५२—६५ ॥

अपरत्र नरे कथा केति । एवंविधशत्रुपरीतमिन्द्रमपि अरक्षत् । तत उत्पन्नशत्रुं नरं रक्षितुं सामर्थ्यमस्तीति का कथेत्यर्थः ॥ ६६ ॥

इति श्रीपद्मपादाचार्यकृते प्रपञ्चसारविवरणे
षड्विंशः पटलः ।

सप्तविंशः पटलः ।

अथाऽभिवक्ष्यामि मनुं समासात् प्रासादसंज्ञं जगतो हिताय ।
येन प्रजप्तेन यथाऽर्चितेन हुतेन सिद्धिं लभते यथेष्टाम् ॥ १
प्रसादनत्वान्मनसो यथावत् प्रासादसंज्ञाऽस्य मनोः प्रदिष्टा ।
अन्त्यात्तृतीयः प्रतिलोमतः स्यादनुग्रहार्धेन्दुयुतश्च मन्त्रः ॥ २
ऋषिरस्य वामदेवः पङ्क्तिश्छन्दश्च देवतेशः स्यात् ।
तेनैवाऽक्लीबकलादीर्घयुजाऽङ्गानि तस्य बीजेन ॥ ३
शूलाही टङ्कघण्टासिसृणिकुलिशपाशाग्न्यभीतीर्दधानं
दोर्भिः शीतांशुखण्डप्रतिघटितजटाभारमौलिं त्रिनेत्रम् ।
नानाकल्पाभिरामापघनमभिमतार्थप्रदं सुप्रसन्नं
पद्मस्थं पञ्चवक्त्रं स्फटिकमणिनिभं पार्वतीशं नमामि ॥ ४

ईशानादीन् मन्त्रवित् पञ्च मन्त्रा-
नङ्गुष्ठादिष्वङ्गुलीषु क्रमेण ।
न्यस्येदज्भिर्युतक्रमाद्व्योमगाभि-
र्हस्वाख्याभिस्ताभिरेवाऽङ्गुलीभिः ॥ ५

ईशानस्तत्पुरुषाघोराख्यौ वामदेवसंज्ञश्च ।
सद्योजाताह्वय इति मन्त्राणां देवताः क्रमात् पञ्च ॥ ६

वैष्णवविधानानन्तरं शैवं विधानं वदन् शैवागमसारस्य प्रासादस्य विधानं सप्रयोजनं वक्तुमुपक्रमते—अथेति ॥ १॥२ ॥

देवतेशः स्यादिति। सदाशिव इत्यर्थः ॥ ३॥४ ॥

मन्त्रवित् पञ्च मन्त्रानिति। अङ्गुष्ठाभ्यां नम इत्यादियोग उक्तः। ताभिरेवाङ्गुलीभिरित्यस्य मूर्धाननादिषु विन्यसेदिति उत्तरत्रान्वयः ॥ ५ ॥

ईशानादिमन्त्रान् विहाय देवतानामभिर्वा बीजसहितैः न्यास इति मन्त्रानो देवतानामानि कथयति—ईशान इति ॥ ६॥७॥८॥९ ॥

मूर्धाननहृद्गुह्यकपादेषु च नामभिः स्वबीजाद्यैः ।
ऊर्ध्वप्राग्दक्षोदक्पश्चिमगेष्वाननेषु विन्यस्येत् ॥ ७
प्रतिपाद्य निजं शरीरमेवं प्रजपेदिन्द्रियलक्षकं शिवात्मा ।
जुहुयाच्च दशांशतस्तदन्ते मधुराक्तैः करवीरजप्रसूनैः ॥ ८
अथवा कुसुमैर्जवासमुत्थैः कमलैर्वा विमलेन पायसेन ।
नृपवृक्षभवैः समिद्वरैर्वा जुहुयात् साधकसत्तमः समृद्ध्यै ॥ ९
अष्टपत्रगुणवृत्तराशिभिर्वीथिकल्पतरुभिः समावृतम् ।
मण्डलं प्रतिविधाय शूलिनः पीठमत्र नवशक्तिभिर्यजेत् ॥ १०
वामा ज्येष्ठा रौद्री काल्याख्या कलबलाद्यविकरिण्यौ ।
सबलप्रमथिनिसर्वभूतदमन्यौ मनोन्मनीश्च यजेत् ॥ ११
तारादिकं नतिमपि प्रोक्त्वा भगवत्पदं चतुर्थ्यन्तम् ।
सकलगुणात्मपदान्ते शक्तियुक्ताय चेति सम्भाष्य ॥ १२
भूयोऽनन्तायेति च योगान्ते पीठात्मने चेति ।
नमसा युक्तं यात् ब्रूपीठाख्योऽयं मनुः समुद्दिष्टः ॥ १३
न्यासक्रमेण देहे मन्त्री गन्धादिभिः समभ्यर्च्य ।
पूर्वोक्तदिक्षु मूर्तीर्विदिक्षु सनिवृत्तिपूर्विकाश्च यजेत् ॥ १४
सद्यो वेदाक्षमालाभयवरदकरः कुन्दमन्दारगौरो
वामः काश्मीरवर्णोऽभयवरदपरश्वक्षमालाविलासी ।
अक्षस्रग्वेदपाशाङ्कुशडमरुकखट्वाङ्गशूलान् कपालं
बिभ्राणो भीमदंष्ट्रोऽञ्जनरुचिरतनुर्भीतिदश्चाप्यघोरः ॥ १५

अष्टपत्रेति। मध्ये प्रासादिकं केसरेषु स्वरान् दलेष्वष्टाक्षरं तद्बहिः वृत्ते व्यञ्जनानि पार्थिवकोणेषु प्रासादं लिखेत्। तद्बहिः गुणवृत्तादिकं लिखेदित्यर्थः ॥ १० ॥

पीठशक्तीराह—वामेति ॥ ११॥१२॥१३ ॥

न्यासक्रमेण मन्त्रीति। पूजायां पञ्चाक्षर्यन्तत्वमुक्तम्। पूर्वोक्तदिक्ष्विति। ऊर्ध्वप्रागित्युक्तेत्यर्थः ॥ १४ ॥

प्रोक्ताः सर्व इति पञ्चान्तरम्। बाहुभिः खेटा[विदा]भयवरदकुठारधराश्चास्मिन् पक्षे शर्वो देवः स्वयमपि शूलडमरुकवराभयधरोऽस्मिन् पक्षे पक्षान्तरमाश्रित्य

विद्युद्वर्णोऽथ वेदाभयवरदकुठारान् दधत् पूरुषाख्यः
प्रोक्ताः सर्वे त्रिनेत्रा विधृतमुखचतुष्काश्चतुर्बाहवश्च ।
मुक्तागौरोऽभयेष्टाधिककरकमलोऽघोरतः पञ्चवक्त्र-
स्त्वीशो ध्येयोऽम्बुजन्मोद्भवमुररिपुरुद्रेश्वराः स्युः शिवान्ताः ॥ १६

भूतानां शक्तित्वाद्व्याप्तत्वाज्जगति वा निवृत्त्याद्याः ।
तेजोरूपाः करपदवर्णविहीना मनीषिभिः प्रोक्ताः ॥ १७
अनन्तसूक्ष्मौ च शिवोत्तमश्च तथैकपूर्वावपि नेत्ररुद्रौ ।
त्रिमूर्तिश्रीकण्ठशिखण्डिनश्च प्रागादिपत्रेषु समर्चनीयाः ॥ १८
शूलाशनिशरचापोल्लासिदोर्दण्डभीषणाः सर्वे ।
पद्मासनाश्च नानाविधभूषणभूषितास्त्रिनेत्राश्च ॥ १९
पाटलपीतसितारुणशितिरक्तशितिप्रभाश्च धूम्रान्ताः ।
कोटीरघटितविलसच्छशिकलायुताश्च मूर्तयः क्रमशः ॥ २०
उमा चण्डेश्वरो नन्दी महाकालो गणेश्वरः ।
वृषभृङ्गिरिटिस्कन्दाः संपूज्याश्चोत्तरादिकाः ॥ २१
कनकविदूरजविद्रुममरकतमुक्तासिताच्छरक्ताभाः ।
पद्मासनसंस्थाश्च क्रमादुमाद्या गुहान्तिकाः प्रोक्ताः ॥ २२
पुनराशेशास्तदनु च कुलिशाद्या दिक्क्रमेण संपूज्याः ।
प्रासादविधानमिदं निगदितमिति सकलवर्गसिद्धिकरम् ॥ २३
अमुना विधिना महेशपूजां दिनशो यः कुरुते समाहितात्मा ।
स तु सम्यगवाप्य दृष्टभोगान् परमन्ते परिपूर्णमेति धाम ॥ २४
वक्ष्यामि शैवागमसारमष्टत्रिंशत्कलान्यासविधिं यथावत् ।
सपञ्चभिर्ब्रह्मभिरीशपूर्वैः सर्घादिकैः साङ्गविशेषकैश्च ॥ २५

ईशानस्य ध्यानमाह—मुक्तागौर इति। सद्यादीनां स्वरूपमाह—अम्बुजन्मेति। मूर्त्यावरणाद्बहिरङ्गावरणं द्रष्टव्यम् ॥ १५—२४ ॥

प्रासादविधानमभिधाय तदवयवभूतानां पञ्चब्रह्मणां विधानमाह—वक्ष्यामीति। शशिन्यङ्गदेष्टदामरीच्यंशुमालिन्यः ईशानकलाः। निवृत्याद्याश्चतस्रस्तत्पुरुषकलाः। तमोमोहाक्षयानिद्राव्याधिर्मृत्युक्षुधातृषा इति अघोरकलाः।

ईशोऽनुष्टुबभूरीश्वरास्तत्पुरुषसंज्ञगायत्र्यापः ।
पुनरग्न्यनुष्टुबापो वामकृतिभगा हरस्त्वनुष्टुब्भगयुक् ॥ २६
इन्द्रियतारसमेतं सर्वज्ञायेति हृच्छिरस्त्वमृते ।
तेजोमालिनि पूर्वं त्वप्ताय ब्रह्मशिरस इति कथितम् ॥ २७
ज्वलितशिखिशिखान्ते त्वनादिबोधाय चाऽन्वितेह शिखा ।
वज्रिणे वज्रधराय स्वान्ते तन्त्रायेति वर्म नेत्रञ्च ॥ २८
स्रौं चौ[वौ] ह्रौ बिन्दुयुतं संप्रोक्ताऽलुप्तशक्तये च तथा ।
श्लौं पशु हुं फट् अनन्तशक्तये तथा चाऽस्त्रं स्यात् ।
समुनिच्छन्दोदैवतयुक्तं तदङ्गषट्कमिति कथितम् ॥ २९
करदेहमुखन्यासं मन्त्री पूर्ववदाचरेत् ।
कलाः प्रविन्यसेद्देहे वक्ष्यमाणक्रमेण तु ॥ ३०
ताः स्युः पञ्च चतस्रोऽष्टौ त्रयोदश चतुर्दयम् ।
अष्टत्रिंशत्कलाः सम्यक् न्यस्तव्या मन्त्रवित्तमैः ॥ ३१

रजा रक्षा रतिः पाल्या कामा संयमिनी क्षया [क्रिया] ।
वृद्धिः स्थिरा च रा।त्रिश्च भ्रामिणी मोहनी जरा ॥

इति वामदेवकलाः ।

वृद्धिः सिद्धिर्धुतिर्लक्ष्मीर्मेधा प्रज्ञा प्रभा सुधा ।

इति सद्योजातकलाः । एताश्च पञ्चब्रह्मकलाभिः साधं न्यस्तव्याः । अतस्तैः साधं वक्ष्यामीत्याह—सपञ्चभिरिति ॥ २५॥२६ ॥

इन्द्रियतारसमेतमिति । ऐं क्लीं श्रीं हसखफ्रें ह्सौः सर्वज्ञाय सर्वात्मने हृदयाय नमः इति हृन्मन्त्र इत्यर्थः । पञ्चप्रणवयोगः शिरआदिष्वपि समानः । त्वप्ताय इत्यतः पूर्वं नित्यपदं योज्यमित्याचार्याः । अस्त्रे ऽपि श्लौमित्यस्यानन्तरं क्लौमिति योज्यम् । मन्त्रवित्तमैरिति । प्रणवशक्तिप्रासादयोगः पदविभागश्च कथितः ।

ईशानः सर्वविद्यानामीश्वरः सर्वभूतानां ब्रह्माधिपतिर्ब्रह्मणोऽधिपतिर्ब्रह्मा शिवो मे अस्तु सदाशिवोम् ।

तत्पुरुषाय विद्महे महादेवाय धीमहि तन्नो रुद्रः प्रचोदयात् ।

अघोरेभ्योऽथ घोरेभ्यो घोरघोरतरेभ्यश्च सर्वतः सर्वशर्वेभ्यः नमस्ते अस्तु रुद्ररूपेभ्यः ।

दिक्षु प्राग्याम्यवारीड्वसुपनिजभुवामैन्द्रवाराकिंराज्ञां
हृद्ग्रीवांसद्वयीनाभ्युदरचरमवक्षःसु गुह्याण्डयोश्च ।
सोर्वोर्जान्वोः सजङ्घास्फिगुभयकटिपार्श्वे च पद्दोस्तलेषु
घ्राणे के बाहुयुग्मेष्वपि विशदमतिर्विन्यसेदङ्गुलीभिः ॥ ३२
विन्यासः प्रतिमाकृतौ च नितरां सान्निध्यकृत् स्यादयं
देहे वापि शरीरिणां निगदितः सामर्थ्यकारीति च ।
आस्ते यत्र तथाऽमुनैव दिनशो विन्यस्तदेहः पुमान्
क्षेत्रं देशममुष्य योजनमितं शैवागमज्ञा विदुः ॥ ३३
न्यस्यैवं पञ्चभिर्ब्रह्मभिरथ शिवमाराधयेद्दृग्भिराभि-
र्मध्यप्राग्याम्यसौम्यापरदिशि पुनरङ्गैरनन्तादिभिश्च ।
अन्योमाद्यैर्दिशापैः पुनरपि कुलिशाद्यैर्यजेदेवमुक्तं
पाञ्चब्राह्मं विधानं सकलसुखयशोभुक्तिमुक्तिप्रदञ्च ॥ ३४
पञ्चाक्षरविहितविधिं वक्ष्ये जपतामभीष्टसिद्धिकरम् ।
सिद्धेन येन देही प्रेत्येह च वाञ्छितं पदं लभते ॥ ३५

वामदेवाय नमः । ज्येष्ठाय नमः । रुद्राय नमः । कालाय नमः । कलविकलनाय नमः । बलाय नमः । बलविकलनाय नमः । बलप्रमथनाय नमः । सर्वभूतदमनाय नमः । मनोन्मनाय नमः ।

सद्योजातं प्रपद्यामि सद्योजाताय वै नमः । भवे अभवे अनादिभवे भजस्व मां भवोद्भवाय नमः ॥ २७॥२८॥२९॥३०॥३१ ॥

न्यासक्रममाह—दिक्ष्विति । शिरोदिक्ष्वित्यर्थः । ऐन्द्रेत्यादिना वक्त्राणि तत्पुरुषन्यासस्थानान्युच्यन्ते । हृदित्यादिना अघोरकलान्यासस्थानानि । गुह्येत्यादिना वामकलान्यासस्थानानि । पद्दोरित्यादिना सद्योजातकलान्यासस्थानानि । अङ्गुलीभिरित्यङ्गुष्ठाद्यङ्गुलीभिः क्रमेणेशानकलादि न्यसेदित्यर्थः । ओं क्लीं ह्रौं नमः शिवाय ईशानः सर्वविद्यानां शशिन्यै नमः इत्यादयो मन्त्राः ॥ ३२॥३३॥३४ ॥

पञ्चब्रह्मविधानमभिधाय तदात्मकस्य पञ्चात्मकस्य विधिं वदन् विनियोगमाह—पञ्चाक्षरेति । जगतामिति । पञ्चाक्षरमन्त्रे सर्वेषामधिकार उक्तः । न केवलं प्राप्तिमात्रेणेष्टसिद्धिः किन्तु साधितेनैवेत्याह—सिद्धेनेति ॥ ३५ ॥

दीर्घो विषो विसर्गी मृत्युः साक्षी च सवाक्षरः पवनः ।
तारात्भवति यदस्मात्तदादिरभिधीयते मनुप्रवरः ॥ ३६

अन्त्याऽक्षराण्यमूनि च पञ्च स्युः पञ्चभूतगानि तथा ।
जगदपि भूतारब्धं तेन हि जगदात्मतोदिताऽस्य मनोः ॥

प्रोक्तमृष्यादिकं पूर्वमङ्गवर्णैस्तु मन्त्रजैः ।
अङ्गुलीदेहवक्त्रेषु मूलमन्त्राक्षरादिकान् ॥ ३८

न्यसेत्तत्पुरुषाघोरसद्योवामेशसंज्ञकान् ।
सतर्जनीमध्यमान्त्यानामिकाङ्गुष्ठकेषु च ३९

वक्त्रहृत्पादगुह्याख्यमूर्धस्वपि च नामभिः ।
प्राग्याम्यवारुणोदीच्यवक्त्रष्वाप च मूर्धनि ॥ ४०

बिभ्रद्दोर्भिः कुठारं मृगमभयवरौ सुप्रसन्नो महेशः
सर्वालङ्कारदीप्तः सरसिजनिलयो व्याघ्रचर्मात्तवासाः ।
ध्येयो मुक्तापरागामृतरसकलिताद्रिप्रभः पञ्चवक्त्र-
स्त्र्यक्षः कोटीरकोटीघटिततुहिनरोचिःकलोत्तुङ्गमौलिः ॥ ४१

अक्षरलक्षचतुष्कं जप्यात्तावत्सहस्रमपि जुहुयात् ।
शुद्धैस्तिलैर्घृतैर्वा दुग्धान्नैर्दुग्धभूरुहेध्मैर्वा ॥ ४२

तत्पुरुषाद्याः सर्वे प्रधानसप्रोक्तबाहुहेतियुताः ।
उल्लसितमुखचतुष्कास्तेजोरूपो विलक्षणस्त्वीशः ॥ ४३

आवृतिराद्या मूर्तिभिरङ्गैरन्याऽपराऽप्यनन्ताद्यैः ।
अपरोमादिभिरपरेन्द्राद्यैरपरा तदायुधैः प्रोक्ता ॥ ४४

कथयामि मनोर्विधानमन्यन्मुनिपूज्यं प्रवरं पिनाकपाणेः ।
स्वतनौ परिकल्प्य पीठमङ्गान्यपि विन्यस्य तथैव मन्त्रवर्णान् ॥

हृन्मुखांसोरुयुग्मेषु षड्वर्णान् क्रमशो न्यसेत् ।
कण्ठमूले तथा नाभौ पार्श्वयुक्पृष्ठहृत्सु च ॥ ४६

प्रणवस्य भूतयोन्यात्मत्वमितरेषां भूतात्मत्वं च वदन् न्यासादौ मन्त्रविशेषान् आह—तारादिति । अनेन चाऽक्षरतत्त्वन्यासः सूचितः ॥ ३६॥३७ ॥

प्रोक्तं पूर्वमिति प्रासाद इत्यथः । अं बीजम् । आय शक्तिः ॥ ३८—४९ ॥

मूर्द्धास्यनेत्रघ्राणेषु दोःपत्सन्ध्यग्रकेषु च ।
सशिरोवक्त्रहृदयजठरोरुपदेष्वपि ॥ ४७
हृदाननपरश्चेणाभौल्याख्यवरदेषु च ।
मुखांसहृदयेषु त्रीन् परान् पादोरुकुक्षिषु ॥ ४८
ऊर्ध्वाधः क्रमशः कुर्याद्गोलकन्यासमुत्तमम् ।
पुनस्तत्पुरुषाघोरसद्योवामेशसंज्ञकान् ॥ ४९
ललाटजठरद्वंसहृदयेषु क्रमान्न्यसेत् ।
पुनस्तत्प्रतिपत्त्यर्थं जपेन्मन्त्रमिमं सुधीः ॥ ५०
नमोऽस्तु स्थाणुभूताय ज्योतिर्लिङ्गावृ[मृ]तात्मने ।
चतुर्मूर्तिवपुश्छायाभासिताङ्गाय शम्भवे ॥ ५१
कुर्यादनेन मन्त्रेण निजदेहे समाहितः ।
मन्त्री पुष्पाञ्जलिं सम्यक् त्रिशः पञ्चश एव च ॥ ५२
पूर्वोक्त एव पीठे प्रागङ्गैर्मूर्तिभिः शक्तिभिस्तदनु ।
वृषपालचण्डदुर्गागुहनन्दिगणपसैन्यपाः पूज्याः ॥ ५३
पूज्याश्च वासवाद्याः पुनरुपहारैः क्रमेण भक्तिमता ।
अभ्यर्चिते हुते च स्तोतव्यः संस्तवेन पुनरीशः ॥ ५४
नमो विरिञ्चिविष्णवीशभेदेन परमात्मने ।
सर्गसंस्थितिसंहारव्याहृति[वृत्ति]व्यक्तमूर्तये ॥ ५५
नमश्चतुर्धाप्रोद्भूतभूतभी[भू]तात्मने भुवः ।
भूरिभारार्तिसंहर्त्रे भूतनाथाय शूलिने ॥ ५६
विश्वग्रासाय विलसत्कालकूटविषाशिने ।
तत्कलङ्काङ्कितग्रीवनीलकण्ठाय ते नमः ॥ ५७
नमो ललाटनयनप्रोल्लसत्कृष्णवर्त्मना ।
ध्वस्तस्मरनिरस्ताधियोगिध्येयाय शम्भवे ॥ ५८

मन्त्रमिदं सुधीरिति । मन्त्रार्थगतमानस इत्यर्थः ॥ ५०॥५१॥५२ ॥

मन्त्री पुष्पाञ्जलिमिति । मूलमन्त्रयागमाह सम्यगिति । सप्रतिपत्तिकमित्यर्थः ॥ ५२—६६ ॥

नमो देहार्धकान्ताय दग्धदक्षाध्वराय च ।
चतुर्वर्गे[र्गे]ष्वभीष्टार्थदायिने मायिनेऽणवे ॥ ५९
स्थूलाय मूलभूताय शूलदारितविद्विषे ।
कालहन्त्रे नमश्चन्द्रखण्डमण्डितमौलये ॥ ६०
विवाससे कपर्दान्तर्भ्रान्ताहिसरिदिन्दवे ।
देवदैत्यासुरेन्द्राणां मौलिघृष्टाङ्घ्रये नमः ॥ ६१
भस्माभ्यक्ताय भक्तानां भुक्तिमुक्तिप्रदायिने ।
व्यक्ताव्यक्तस्वरूपाय शङ्कराय नमो नमः ॥ ६२

नमोऽन्तकान्धकरिपवे पुरद्विषे
नमोऽस्तु ते द्विरदवराहभेदिने ।
विषोल्लसत्फणिवरबद्धमूर्तये
नमः सदा वृषवरवाहनाय ते ॥ ६३
वियन्मरुद्धुतवहवार्वसुम्धरा-
मखिशरव्यमृतमयूखमूर्तये ।
नमः सदा नरकभयापभेदिने
भवेह नो भवभयभङ्गकृद्विभो ॥ ६४
स्तुत्वेन्दुखण्डपरिमण्डितमौलिमेव-
मुद्वासयेत् पुनरमुं हृदयाम्बुजे स्वे ।
अभ्यर्च्य देह[व]मपि संयतचित्तवृत्ति-
र्भूत्वा शिवो जपतु मन्त्रमहेशमेनम् ॥ ६५

सन्तर्प्य विप्रान् पुनरेवमेव संपूजयेदिन्दुकलावतंसम् ।
जपेद्‌यथाशक्ति शिवस्वरूपी भूत्वा तथाऽन्ते च शिवः स भूयात् ॥
अमुमेव मनुवरं मनुलक्षं हृल्लेखया अभितो निरुद्धम् ।
जप्त्वा नृपतरुसमिधां मधुरयुजां मनुसहस्रमपि जुहुयात् ॥ ६७

शक्तिपञ्चाक्षरविधानमाह—अमुमेवेति । ह्राङादियुतेन षडक्षरेण अङ्गानि । ऋष्यादिकं पूर्ववत् । ओं बीजम् । ह्रीं शक्तिः । अष्टाक्षरस्याऽप्येवमेव बीजशक्ती । पञ्चार्णोक्तान्यङ्गानि । इति ह्राङादियोगबाधकं न भवति ॥ ६७—७२ ॥

वन्दे हरं वरदशूलकपालहस्तं
साभीतिमद्रिसुतयोज्ज्वलदेहकान्तिम् ।
वामोरुपीठगतया निजवामहस्त-
न्यस्तारुणोत्पलयुजा परिरब्धदेहम् ॥ ६८

आवृतिरङ्गैराद्या हल्लेखाद्याभिरनु वृषाद्यैश्च ।
मातृभिरीशैरुक्तं पञ्चावरणं विधानमीशस्य ॥ ६९

आप्यायिनी शशियुताऽप्यरुणाऽग्निमाया-
बिन्द्वन्तिका च नकुली भुवनेन्दुयुक्ता ।
दीर्घी कलायुतविषश्च शिवायवर्णाः
स्याच्छूलिनो मनुरयं वसुवर्णयोगी ॥ ७०

वामाङ्कन्यस्तवामेतरकरकमलायास्तथा वामबाहु-
न्यस्तारक्तोत्पलायाः स्तनविधृतलसद्वामबाहुः प्रियायाः ।
सर्वाकल्पाभिरामो धृतपरशुमृगेष्टः करैः काञ्चनाभो
ध्येयः पद्मासनस्थः स्मरललिततनुः सम्पदे पार्वतीशः ॥ ७१

पञ्चार्णोक्ताङ्गाद्यः पञ्चब्रह्मप्रदिष्टपूजश्च ।
वसुमितलक्षजपोऽयं मन्त्रस्तावत्सहस्रहोमश्च ॥ ७२

इति जपहुतपूजाध्यानकैरीशयाजी
प्रियतरचरितः स्यात् सर्वतो देहभाजाम् ।
धनविभवयशःश्रीसम्पदा दीर्घजीवी
तनुविपदि च शैवं तत्परं धाम भूयात् ॥ ७३

इति श्रीप्रपञ्चसारे सप्तविंशः पटलः ।

इति श्रीपद्मपादाचार्यकृते प्रपञ्चसारविवरणे
सप्तविंशः पटलः ।

अष्टाविंशः पटलः।

अथ प्रवक्ष्यते मन्त्रो दक्षिणामूर्तिसंज्ञितः।
जपतामिष्टसंसिद्धिविधानसुरपादपः॥ १
अद्रिः क्षिणा कालकर्णकामिकायुग्मयेन्दराः।
तुभ्यामध्यगताः स्युर्भ्यं वटमूलनिवासिने॥ २
नैधात्वनिरताङ्गाय नमो रुद्राय शम्भवे।
तारशक्तिनिरुद्धोऽयं मन्त्रः षट्त्रिंशदक्षरः॥ ३
शुकः प्रोक्तो मुनिश्छन्दोऽप्यनुष्टुप् समुदाहृतम्।
दक्षिणामूर्तिरुद्रोऽस्य देवता समुदाहृता॥ ४
तारशक्त्यादिकैर्ङेङाद्यन्तैर्मन्त्राक्षरैः क्रमात्।
ऋत्वक्षिवसुवस्वग्निगुणवर्णैर्विभागशः।
मन्त्री कुर्यात् षडङ्गानि जातियुञ्जि समाहितः॥ ५
कालिकश्रुतिदृग्गण्डद्वयनासास्यके दश।
दोःसन्धिकण्ठाननहृन्नाभिकस्यन्धुषु क्रमात्॥ ६
पत्सन्धिषु पुनर्द्वाभ्यां मन्त्रविद्व्यापकं न्यसेत्।
एवं न्यस्तशरीरोऽथ चिन्तयेन्मन्त्रदेवताम्॥ ७
मुद्रां भद्रार्थदात्रीं सपरशुहरिणां बाहुभिर्बाहुमेकं
जान्वासक्तं दधानो भुजगवरसमाबद्धकक्षो वटाधः।
आसीनश्चन्द्रखण्डप्रतिघटितजटः क्षीरगौरस्त्रिनेत्रो
दद्यादाद्यैः शुकाद्यैर्मुनिभिरभिवृतो भावशुद्धिं भवो वः॥ ८

एवं पञ्चवक्त्रस्य शिवस्य मन्त्रानभिधाय दक्षिणवक्त्रप्रधानं सौम्यमन्त्रमाह—
अथ प्रवक्ष्यत इति। इष्टेति। विनियोग उक्तः। ओं बीजम्। ह्रीं
शक्तिः। मन्त्री कुर्यादिति। सर्वत्रादियोग उक्तः॥ १॥ २॥ ३॥ ४॥ ५॥

द्वाभ्यां मन्त्रविदिति। प्रणवशक्त्योः सर्वत्र योगं जानन्नित्यर्थः [आद्यन्त-
प्रणवशक्त्योरेकत्वं जानन्नित्यर्थ इति पदार्थादर्शोद्धृतपाठः]॥ ६॥ ७॥

ध्यानमाह—मुद्रामिति॥ ८॥

प्राक्प्रोक्तविधानेन च सम्यक् संपूज्य साधु कलशाद्यैः ।
कृतसंदीक्षो मन्त्री जप्यादेनं मनुं समाहितधीः ॥ ९
द्वात्रिंशदयुतमानं प्रतिजप्य जुहोतु तद्दशांशमितैः ।
दुग्धाक्तैस्तिलैर्वा साज्येन पयोऽम्भसा द्वयेनाऽपि ॥ १०

जप्त्वैवं मन्त्रमेनं दिनमनु गिरिशं पूजयित्वा च हुत्वा
स्तुत्वा नत्वा मनोवाक्तनुभिरवहितः प्राप्य कामानशेषान् ।
व्याख्याता चागमानां भुवि कविषु वरः साधु वेदान्तवेदी
वादीट् सोऽद्वैतविद्याफलममलतरं याति शैवं पदं तत् ॥ ११

जीवशिखिकर्णरेफान् प्रतिवीप्सा प्रादिकांश्च पुनरपि तान् ।
मेधाप्यायिनियान्तांस्तानेव तराऽन्तिकान् सतनुरूपान् ॥ १२
आभाष्य चटप्रचटौ सकहवमौ बन्धघातयौ वीप्सा ।
प्रोक्त्वा वर्मास्त्रावधि समुद्धरेच्छक्तिपूर्वकं मन्त्रम् ॥ १३
ऋषिरस्याऽघोराख्यः संप्रोक्तस्त्रिष्टुबुच्यते छन्दः ।
रुद्रोऽप्यघोरपूर्वः संप्रोक्ता देवताऽस्य मनोः ॥ १४
हृत् पञ्चभिस्तदर्णैः शिरोऽपि षड्भिः शिखा तथा दशभिः ।
तावद्भिरेव कवचं दृगष्टभिर्द्वादशभिरपि चाऽस्त्रम् ॥ १५
कदृगास्यकण्ठहृन्नाभ्यन्धूरुषु जानुजङ्घयोः पदयोः ।
एकादशधा भिन्नैर्मन्त्रार्णैर्न्यसतु विग्रहे मन्त्री ॥ १६
पञ्चभिरथो सषड्भिर्द्वाभ्यामप्यष्टभिश्चतुर्भिश्च ।
षड्भिश्चतुस्त्रयेण च षड्भिर्द्वाभ्यां च भेदितैः क्रमशः ॥ १७

कालाभ्राभः कराग्रैः परशुडमरुकौ खड्गखेटौ च बाणे-
ष्वासौ शूलं कपालं दधदतिभयदो भीषणास्यस्त्रिनेत्रः ।

कृतसंदीक्षो मन्त्रीति। शक्त्यनन्तरं पञ्चाक्षरयोग उक्तः [न्यासमन्त्रादौ प्रणवशक्तियोग उक्त इति पदार्थादर्शीद्धृतपाठः] ॥ ८ ॥

द्वयेनाऽपीत्यपिर्वार्थः ॥ १० ॥ ११ ॥

दक्षिणवक्त्रप्रधानमेवाग्नेयं मन्त्रमाह — जीवेति ॥ १२ ॥ १३ ॥ १४ ॥ १५ ॥

विग्रहे मन्त्रीति। न्यासमन्त्रेषु प्रणवशक्त्यादियोगार्थः। हुं बीजम्। ह्रीं शक्तिः ॥ १६॥१७॥१८॥१९॥२०॥

रक्ताकाराम्बरोऽहिप्रवरघटितगात्रोऽरिनागग्रहादीन्
खादन्निष्टार्थदायी भवदनभिमतोच्छित्तये स्यादघोरः ॥ १८
स्वच्छो मुमुक्षोस्तु भवेदघोरः काम्यक्रियायामपि रक्तवर्णः ।
कृष्णोऽभिचारे ग्रहवैकृते च प्रोक्तो जपः स्यादपि लक्षमानः ॥ १९
घृतावसिक्तैस्तिलतण्डुलैश्च जपावसाने जुहुयाद्दशांशम् ।
घृतप्लुतैर्वाऽथ हविर्भिरेव तावत्प्रजुह्वन् समुपैति कामान् ॥ २०
हृल्लेखास्थितसाध्याक्षरविलसत्कर्णिकं कलावीतम् ।
वर्गाष्टकान्तकेसरमन्त्ये सहलक्षयाक्षरोल्लसितम् ॥ २१
मन्त्राक्षरत्रयोद्यद्दलमध्यदलाग्रकस्च तद्बाह्ये ।
वह्निपुटास्त्रिसमाश्रितकवचास्त्रं प्रतिविलिख्य यन्त्रमिदम् ॥ २२
कृत्वा समाप्य मण्डलमत्र विनिःक्षिप्य पूरयेत् कलशम् ।
पीठे पिनाकपाणेर्गव्यैर्वा क्वाथकृप्ततोयैर्वा ॥ २३

अङ्गावृतेरनु च हेतिभिरीरिताभिः
पश्चाच्च मातृभिरथाऽपि दिशाधिनाथैः ।
संपूजयीत विधिनेति षडक्षरोत्थ-
मार्गेण वा मनुपरिस्फुरणाय मन्त्री ॥ २४

आज्यापामार्गसमित्तिलसर्षपपायसाज्यकैश्च पृथक् ।
रात्रौ सहस्रहोमाद्भूतापस्मारादिशान्तिरुद्दिष्टा ॥ २५
सितकिंशुकनिर्गुण्डीकनकापामार्गजन्मनां समिधाम् ।
पृथगपि सहस्रहोमान्निग्रहमोक्षोऽचिराद्ग्रहाणां स्यात् ॥ २६

पूजायन्त्रमाह—हृल्लेखेति । साध्याक्षरमिति । साधकाद्यक्षरस्योपलक्षणम् । कलावीतमिति । स्वरवेष्टितमध्यबीजमित्यर्थः । अन्त्ये सहलक्षयाक्षरोल्लसितमिति । अन्त्ये दले सहलक्षयाक्षरोल्लसितम् । क्षयाक्षरं क्षकारः । उक्तं हि भुवनं कषत इति । स एव लकारेण सह वर्तत इति सहलक्षयाक्षरं तेनोल्लसितमित्यर्थः । अथवा हकारलकाराभ्यां सह वर्तमानं क्षकारं तेनाऽन्त्येन उल्लसितमित्यन्त्यदलेऽक्षर-त्रयलेखनमनेन दर्शितम् । समाप्य मण्डलमिति । वृत्तराश्यादिकं बहिः कल्पयित्वेत्यर्थः ॥ २१ ॥ २२ ॥ २३ ॥

परिस्फुरणं सिद्धिः । मन्त्रीति । प्रणवशक्तिपुटितत्वमुक्तम् ॥ २४॥२५॥२६ ॥

गव्याक्तैर्जुहुयात् पृथग्दशशतं मन्त्री मयूरेभकै-
र्भूयस्तैश्चतुरङ्गुलैश्च शिवपञ्चम्यां निशायां हुनेत् ।
सर्पिर्मार्गसपञ्चगव्यचरुभि: सर्पि: ससंपातकं
हुत्वा तत् प्रतिभोजयेत् प्रतिशमं यान्त्येव सर्वे ग्रहा: ॥ २७
षट्कोणे कर्णिकायां स्फुरयुगलयुतां साध्यगर्भाञ्च शक्तिं
कोणाग्रे प्रस्फुरद्वन्द्वकमथ विलिखेन्मन्त्रवर्णान् दलेषु ।
षड्वेदद्वन्द्वषड्वेदकचतुर्युगषट्संख्यकान् बाह्यषट्के
वर्मास्त्राणां तदेतद्ग्रहगदभयहृद्यन्त्रमाघोरमाहु: ॥ २८
न च रिपवो न च रोगा न ग्रहपीडा न शस्त्रबाधा च ।
न दवेलरुजो मर्त्यान् स्पृशन्त्यघोरास्त्रमन्त्रजापरतान् ॥ २९
तस्मादघोरास्त्रमनुं प्रजप्यात् समर्चयेत्तद्विहितं विधानम् ।
हुनेच्च तेनैव समस्तवाञ्छासंसिद्धये चाऽथ विमुक्तये च ॥ ३०

खसप्तम: कर्णयुतोऽर्धचन्द्रवान्
कुपञ्चमो द्वीन्दुयुतो ध्रुवादिक: ।
मनुस्त्वयं मृत्युजयात्मक: स्फुटं
समीरित: साधकरक्षणाक्षम: ॥ ३१

ऋषिरस्य कहोलाख्यश्छन्दो देव्यादिका च गायत्री ।
स्याद्देवता च मृत्युञ्जयरुद्रोऽङ्गान्यथाचरेद्भृगुणा ॥ ३२

पुटितनलिनसंस्थं मौलिबद्धेन्दुरेखा-
गलदमृतजलार्द्रं चन्द्रवह्न्यर्कनेत्रम् ।
स्वकरकलितमुद्रापाशवेदाक्षमालं
स्फटिकरजतमुक्तागौरमीशं नमामि ॥ ३३

मन्त्री मयूरेति । शक्त्यनन्तरं चिन्तामणियोग उक्त: ॥ २७॥२८॥२९॥३० ॥

शिवस्यैवोर्ध्ववक्त्रप्रधानं मन्त्रवर्यमाह—खसप्तम इति ॥ ३१ ॥

अङ्गान्यथाचरेत् भृगुणेति । नाभिहृद्भ्रूमध्येषु अक्षरन्यासानन्तरं दीर्घ-
स्वरयुतेन भृगुणा अङ्गान्याचरेदित्यर्थ: । जूं बीजम् । स: शक्ति: ॥ ३२ ॥

स्फटिकरजतमुक्तावर्णमिति । एकैकाक्षरप्रधानेषु वक्ष्यमाणेषु ध्यानेष्वपि
वर्णविशेष उक्त: ॥ ३३ ॥

जप्तव्योऽयं मन्त्रवर्यस्त्रिलक्षं दीक्षापूर्वं होमकृत् स्यादृशांशैः ।
दुग्धाज्याक्तैः शुद्धखण्डैर्गुडूच्या गुर्वादेशात् साधको हव्यवाहे ॥ ३४
अर्चा कार्या नित्यशः शैवपीठे स्यादप्यङ्गैर्लोकपालैस्तदस्त्रैः ।
सम्यक् पूजावस्तुभिर्मन्त्रजापी प्रोक्तं ह्येतन्मृत्युजेतुर्विधानम् ॥ ३५
इति जपहुतार्चनादिभिः सिद्धो मन्त्रोक्तमूर्तिविहिततनुः ।
समाचरेन्निजान्तर्योगं कृत्यापमृत्युनाशकरम् ॥ ३६
तारनालमथ मध्यपत्रकं हाद्यकर्णिकयुतं क्रमोत्क्रमात् ।
चिन्तयेन्नियतमन्तरा शिवं नीरुजे च नियतायुषेऽञ्जयोः ॥ ३७

ऊर्ध्वाधः प्रोतपद्मद्वयदलनिचितैरक्षरैस्तैर्ध्रुवाद्यै-
रायन्तैर्मन्दमन्दप्रतिगलितसुधापूरसंसिच्यमानम् ।

गुर्वादेशादिति । द्रव्यदेवतैक्यज्ञत्वमुक्तम् ॥ ३४ ॥

सम्यक् पूजा वस्तुभिरिति । अमृतमयैरित्यर्थः । मन्त्रजापीति । मन्त्राज्ज्ञाता मन्त्रे वीता च । मन्त्रजापीत्यनेनाऽर्चां विशिनष्टि । शिवपदादाविर्भूय तत्रैव विलीनया माययाऽमृतमय्याऽर्चा कार्येत्यर्थः । वक्ष्यमाणमन्त्रेणाऽर्चा कार्येति भावः ॥ ३५ ॥

मन्त्रोक्तमूर्तिविहिततनुरिति । मन्त्रगततत्तदक्षरानुगतह्रस्वस्वरपञ्चकेन सार्धम् उक्तैरीशानादिमूर्तिभिर्विहिततनुरिति । प्रणवादिप्रधानयोगेषु न्यासविशेषाः कथिताः । तत्र प्रणवप्रधानयोगे ओं एं उं इं अं इति बीजैः सार्धमीशानादिमूर्तिभिः सूक्तवत्क्न्यासं कुर्यात् । वोमित्यादिभिः सार्धं वा । इतरयोस्तु योगयोर्ज्वीं सोमित्यादिभिः सार्धं न्यासः कार्यः । सर्वैः सार्धं समष्टिमूर्तेरित्यर्थसिद्धमेतत् ॥ ३६ ॥

प्रणवप्रधानं योगमाह—तारेति । क्रमोत्क्रमादिति । ऊर्ध्वाधोमुखपद्मद्वयं क्रमोत्क्रममन्त्रात्मकं चिन्तनीयमित्युक्तम् । चिन्तयेन्नियतमन्तरा शिवमिति । नियतमन्तरा नियतस्य नित्यस्य मायाबीजस्याऽनुलोमविलोममन्त्रमध्यस्थितस्य अन्तरा मध्ये शिवं पञ्चाक्षरमित्यर्थः । ततो ध्यानार्थमीं नमः शिवाय ईमिति मन्त्रः सूचितः अनुलोमविलोममध्ये । अत्र च शिवः स्फटिकनिभः स्त्रीरूपो वीणावादनपरो ध्येयः ॥ ३७ ॥

अस्मिन्नेव योगे मन्त्रान्तरं शिववाचकमाह—ऊर्ध्वाध इति । पूर्ववत् पद्मद्वयं सङ्कल्प्य दलेष्वपि अक्षरत्रयं लेख्यमित्याह—दलनिचितैरक्षरैरिति । स्वरविशिष्टा-

ईशानं सूक्ष्मरूपं विमलतरसुषुम्नान्तरा सन्निषण्णं
ध्यायन्नाप्नोति रोगैर्नियतपरिहृतस्तज्जपाद्दीर्घमायुः ॥ ३८
आदौ तारं विलिखतु ससाध्याह्वयं कर्णिकायां
दिक्पत्रेष्वप्यपरमपरं वाऽपि तत्कोणकेषु ।
भूयो भूमेः परमनु मृगाङ्कं तदस्रेषु टान्तं
जप्त्वा बन्धग्रहगदविषध्वंसि यन्त्रं तदेतत् ॥ ३९
इति कृतयन्त्रविभूषितमण्डलमध्ये निधाय कलशमपि ।
आपूर्य चाऽभिषिञ्चेच्छ्रीवश्यकरं ग्रहाभिचारहरम् ॥ ४०
ततश्छिन्नोद्भवानाञ्च समिद्भिश्चतुरङ्गुलैः ।
दुग्धसिक्तैः समिद्धेऽग्नौ षट्सहस्रद्वयं हुनेत् ॥ ४१
यस्तु वह्नौ जुहोत्येवं यावत्संख्येन साधकः ।
तावत्संख्यैः सुधाकुम्भैरग्निः प्रीणाति शङ्करम् ॥ ४२
आप्यायितोऽग्निना शर्वः साधकस्येप्सितान् वरान् ।
प्रदद्यादायुराद्यांश्च दुरन्तान् प्रलयान्तिकान् ॥ ४३
मन्त्रान्ते साध्याख्यां पालययुगलं प्रतीपमपि मन्त्रम् ।
प्रोक्त्वा समापयेन्मनुमयमपि मृत्युञ्जयाह्वयो मन्त्रः ॥ ४४

नामाक्षराणां लेखनं कर्तव्यमित्याह—आद्यन्तैरिति। अ आ इत्यादयः अन्ते येषामक्षराणां तान्याद्यन्तानि तैरित्यर्थः। तस्मात् प्रणवसम्बन्धिभिः स्वरैः केसरस्थाने संवेष्ट्य जकारसम्बन्धिभिः स्वरैः दलमध्ये वेष्टयित्वा सकारसम्बन्धिभिः स्वरैः दलाग्रे वेष्टयेदित्यर्थः। पूर्वोक्तपद्मेऽपि समानमेतत् वेष्टनत्रयम्। ईशानं सूक्ष्मरूपमिति मन्त्रविशेषमाह। इकारः सूक्ष्मशब्दार्थः। ततः ईं ईशानाय नमः इं इति मन्त्रः सिद्धः अनुलोमविलोममध्ये। अत्र तु शिवो वीणावादनपरो ध्येयः॥ ३८॥

बाह्यप्रयोगाङ्गं यन्त्रमाह—आदौ तारमिति॥ ३९॥ ४०॥ ४१॥

होमकाले प्रतिपत्तिमाह—तावत्संख्यैरिति॥ ४२॥ ४३॥

मध्यबीजप्रधानमान्तरं योगमाह—मन्त्रान्त इति। मन्त्रमपि प्रोक्त्वा प्रतीपं प्रतिलोमं समापयेदित्यन्वयः। पालयेत्यस्याऽन्ते ज्वीं नमः शिवाय ज्वोमित्येतन्मन्त्रमुक्त्वा प्रतिलोममुच्चरेदित्यर्थः। रजतवर्णा मुद्रापुस्तकधरा देव्यत्र

अथवाऽमलकमलपुटान्तरितं शिशुवेशभूषणं रुद्रम् ।
ध्यात्वा जप्याद् यथावद् भूतकृपया मृत्युनाशनं दृष्टम् ॥ ४५
चतुरङ्गुलिपरिमाणैरमृताखण्डैरथाऽर्कसाहस्रम् ।
जुहुयाच्च दुग्धसिक्तैरारोग्यायाऽऽयुषे च लक्ष्म्यै च ॥ ४६
अमृता वटतिलदूर्वाः पयो घृतं पायसं क्रमेणेति ।
सप्तद्रव्याण्युक्तान्येतैर्जुहुयात् पृथक् सहस्रतयम् ॥ ४७
तीव्रे ज्वरे घोरतरेऽभिचारे सोन्मादके दाहगदे च मोहे ।
तनोति शान्तिं न चिरेण होमः सञ्जीवनं चाऽब्दशतप्रमाणम् ॥ ४८
सम्भोजयेद्धोमदिनेषु विप्रान् सप्ताधिकान् स्वादुभिरन्नभोज्यैः ।
सतर्णका गाश्च हुतावसाने दद्याद् द्विजेभ्यो हुतकर्मकृद्भ्यः ॥ ४९
निजजन्मदिने शतं शतं यो जुहुयाद् द्रव्यवरैश्च सप्तसंख्यैः ।
मधुरैः प्रतिभोजयेच्च विप्रानभिवाञ्छन्नियमेन दीर्घमायुः ॥ ५०
अथवा सप्तभिरेतैर्द्रव्यैरेकेन वा सहस्रतयम् ।
जन्मर्क्षहोममावान्निरुपद्रवमुत्तमं व्रजेदायुः ॥ ५१
दूर्वात्रितयैर्जुहुयान्मन्त्रविदेकादशाहुतीर्दिनशः ।
जित्वाऽपमृत्युरोगान् प्रयात्यसावायुषश्च दैर्घ्यमपि ॥ ५२
जन्मर्क्षाणां त्रितये छिन्नाकाश्मर्यवकुलजैरिध्मैः ।
क्रमशो हुनेत् सहस्रं नश्यन्त्यपमृत्युरोगदुरितानि ॥ ५३

ध्येया। पुनः पूर्ववदक्षरत्रयविशिष्टषोडशस्वरयुक्तं पद्मद्वयं सञ्चिन्त्य तन्मध्ये मुद्रापुस्तकधरं शिवं सञ्चिन्त्य पालयान्ते ज्वौं ईशानाय नमः ज्वोमिति जपित्वा प्रतिलोमं जपेदिति मध्यबीजयोगः ॥ ४४ ॥

तृतीयबीजप्रधानं योगादिकमाह—अथवेति। कमलद्वयं वर्णत्रयं स्वरविशिष्टमवाप्यनुलोमविलोममन्त्रात्मकं द्रष्टव्यम्। स्विं नमः शिवाय स्वोमिति देवीमन्त्रः। स्विं ईशानाय नमः स्वोमिति देवमन्त्रः। तत्र त्रिवर्षं दिग्वाससं विचित्रकिङ्किण्याद्यलंकृतं वामहस्ते अर्धेन्दुधरं तमेव दक्षिणहस्तेन भक्षयन्तं मुक्तावर्णं देवं देवीं च ध्यायेत्। अर्धनारीश्वरो वा सर्वत्र ध्येय इति ॥ ४५ ॥
॥ ४६ ॥ ४७ ॥ ४८ ॥ ४९ ॥ ५० ॥ ५१ ॥

मन्त्रविदेकादशाहुतीरिति। पञ्चाक्षरयोग उक्तः ॥ ५२ ॥ ५३ ॥ ५४ ॥

सितसिद्धार्थैः सहस्राहुत्या नश्यन्त्युपद्रवा ज्वरजाः ।
तद्वदपामार्गहुतान्मृत्युञ्जयमप्यरोगतां लभते ॥ ५४

प्रोक्तैर्ध्याननिजपार्चनाहुतविधानाद्यैश्च मृत्युञ्जयं
यो मन्त्री प्रभजेन्मनुं प्रतिदिनं प्रातः प्रसन्नाशयः ।
तस्येष्टानि भवन्ति संस्मृतिरपि स्फीता च पुत्रादयः
सम्पन्नाः सुसुखी च जीवति चिरं देहापदि स्याच्छिवः ॥ ५५

इति श्रीप्रपञ्चसारे अष्टाविंशः पटलः ।

प्रभजेद् यो मन्त्रीति । प्रणवान्ते शक्तिबीजयोग उक्तः ॥ ५५ ॥

इति श्रीपद्मपादाचार्यकृते प्रपञ्चसारविवरणे
अष्टाविंशः पटलः ।

एकोनत्रिंशः पटलः ।

अथ सजपहुताद्यो वक्ष्यते साधुचिन्ता-

मणिरभिमतकामप्राप्तिकल्पद्रुमोऽयम् ।

अनलकषमरेफप्राणसत्यान्तवाम-

श्रुतिहिमरुचिखण्डैर्मण्डितो मन्त्रराजः ॥ १

ऋषिरपि काश्यप उक्तश्छन्दोऽनुष्टुप् च देवतोमेशः ।

यान्तैः षड्भिर्वर्णैरङ्गं वा देवताऽर्धनारीशः ॥ २

अहिशशधरगङ्गाबद्धतुङ्गात्ममौलि-

स्त्रिदशगणनताङ्घ्रिस्त्रीक्षणः स्त्रीविलासः ।

भुजगपरशुशूलान् खड्गवज्रौ कपालं

शरमपि धनुरीशो बिभ्रदव्याच्चिरं वः ॥ ३

हावभावललितार्धनारिकं भीषणार्धमथवा महेश्वरम् ।

पाशसोत्पलकपालशूलिनं चिन्तयेज्जपविधौ विभूतये ॥ ४

अथवा षोडशशूलव्यग्रभुजा त्रिनयनाहिनद्धाङ्गी ।

अरुणांशुकानुलेपनवर्णाभरणा च भगवती ध्येया ॥ ५

विहितार्चनविधिरथाऽनुदिनं प्रजपेद्दशायुतमितं मतिमान् ।

अयुतं हुनेत्त्रिमधुराद्रतरैस्तिलतण्डुलैस्तदवसानविधौ ॥ ६

शैवोक्तपीठाङ्गपदैर्यथावद् वृषेचदुर्गुर्नगसैर्मुखाद्यैः ।

समातृभिर्दिक्पतिभिर्महेशं पञ्चोपचारैर्विधिनाऽर्चयीत ॥ ७

ऊर्ध्ववक्त्रप्रधानमन्त्रानन्तरमुत्तरवक्त्रप्रधानं मन्त्रं वदन् विनियोगमाह—अथ सजपहुताद्य इति ॥ १ ॥ २ ॥

उमेशदेवतापक्षे ध्यानमाह—अहीति ॥ ३ ॥

अर्धनारीश्वरदेवतापक्षेऽप्याह—हावभावेति । पुरश्चरणे नित्यजपपूजादौ अर्धनारीश्वरध्यानं नियमयति—जपविधाविति ॥ ४ ॥

क्रूरप्रयोगे ध्यानमाह—अथवेति । रं बीजम् । औं शक्तिः ॥ ५ ॥

मतिमानिति । उन्मन्यन्तं व्याप्तचित्त इत्यर्थः ॥ ६ ॥

अङ्गपदैर्यथावदिति । सर्वज्ञादियुक्तैरित्यर्थः । मुखाद्यैरिति । वृं वृषभाय

आरभ्यादिज्वलनं दिक्संस्थैरष्टभिर्मनोर्वर्णैः ।
आराधयेच्च मातृभिरिति संप्रोक्तः प्रयोगविधिरपरः ॥ ८

कात्पूर्वं हसलिपिसंयुतं जपादौ
जप्तॄणां प्रवरमितीह केचिदाहुः ।
प्रासादाद्ययुतजपेन मङ्क्षु कुर्या-
दावेशादिकमपि नीरुजाच्च मन्त्रः ॥ ९

शिरसोऽवतरन्निशेशबिम्बस्थितमजभिर्वृतमागलत्सुधार्द्रम् ।
अपमृत्युहरं विषज्वरापस्मृतिविभ्रान्तिशिरोरुजापहच्च ॥ १०
निजवर्णविकीर्णकोणवैश्वानरगेहद्वितयावृतत्रिकोणम् ।
विगतस्वरवीतमुत्तमाङ्गे स्मृतमेतत् क्षपयेत् क्षणाद् ग्रहार्तिम् ॥ ११
वह्नेर्बिम्बे वह्निवत् प्रज्वलन्तं न्यस्त्वा बीजं मस्तके ग्रस्तजन्तोः ।
ध्यात्वाऽऽवेशं कारयेद्बन्धुजीवं तज्जप्तं वा सम्यगाघ्राणनेन ॥ १२
शुक्लादिः शुक्लभाः पौष्टिकशमनविधौ कृष्टिवश्येषु रक्तो
रक्तादिः क्षोभसंस्तोभनविधिषु हकारादिको हेमवर्णः ।
धूम्रोऽङ्गामर्दनोच्चाटनविधिषु समीरादिको मा[ऽदा]दिरुक्तः
पीताभः स्तम्भनादौ मनुरतिविमलो मुक्तिभाजामना[दा]दिः ॥ १३

कृष्णाभं प्राणगेहस्थितमथ नयने ध्यातमान्ध्यं विधत्ते
बाधिर्यं कर्णरन्ध्रेऽर्दितमपि वदने कुक्षिगं शूलमाशु ।
मर्मस्थाने समीरं सपदि शिरसि वा दुःसहं शीर्षरोगं
वायोर्धं कण्ठनालेऽवनिवृतमथ तन्मण्डले बीजमेतत् ॥ १४

नमः इत्यादिप्रकारेण मुखाक्षराद्यैरित्यर्थः । अथवा देवस्याऽग्रमारभ्य पूजयेदित्यर्थः ॥ ७ ॥

अर्धनारीश्वरध्यानपक्षे वृषभादिस्थान आवरणान्तरमाह—आरभ्येति ॥ ८ ॥

कात्पूर्वमिति । रेफं परित्यज्य तत्स्थाने इत्यर्थः । प्रासादादित्वमपि तथैव ॥ ९ ॥ १० ॥

निजवर्णविकीर्णेति । निजशब्देन वैश्वानरो मूलमन्त्रस्योक्तः । अतः सर्वकोणेष्वग्निबीजं लिखित्वा तेषु बीजेषु मूलाक्षराणि षट्कोणपूर्वकोणमारभ्य लिखित्वा मध्यगताग्निबीजे बिन्दौ मूलं लिखित्वा तत्र वक्ष्यमाणक्रमेण मकार-

प्रालेयत्विषि च स्वरावृतमिदं नेत्रे स्मृतं तद्रुजं
योनौ वामदृशोऽस्रविस्रुतिमथो कुक्षौ च शूलं जयेत्।
विस्फोटे सविषे ज्वरे तृषि तथा रक्तामये विभ्रमे
दाहे शीर्षगदे स्मरेद्विधिमिमं संतप्तये मन्त्रवित्॥ १५

साध्याया हृदयकुशेशयोदरस्थं
प्राणाख्यं दृढमभिबध्य बीजवर्णैः।
तेजस्तच्छिरसि विधुं विधाय वाते-
नाकर्षेदपि निजवाञ्छयैव मन्त्री॥ १६

पारिभद्रसुमनोदलभद्रं वह्निबिम्बगतमक्षरमेतत्।
संस्मरेच्छिरसि यस्य स वश्यो जायते न खलु तत्र विचारः॥ १७
निजनामगर्भमथ बीजमिदं प्रविचिन्त्य योनिसुषिरे सुदृशः।
वशयेत् क्षणाच्छ्रिततया मनसः स्रवयेच्च शुक्रमथवा रुधिरम्॥ १८
निजशिवशिरःश्रितं तद्बीजं स्मृत्वा प्रवेशयेद् योनौ।
यस्यास्तत्सम्पर्कात्ताश्च स्रवयेत् क्रमेण[क्षणेन] वशयेच्च॥ १९
पररेफगर्भधृतसाध्यपदं त्रिकगं हुताशयुगषट्कवृतम्।
विगतस्वरावृतमगारभुवि स्थितमेतदाशु वशयेद्रमणान्॥ २०

सम्बन्धरेफोदरे साध्यं कोदरे मोदरे वा साधकं साधकांशे कर्म च विलिखेदिति सिद्धम्॥ ११॥ १२॥ १३॥ १४॥

संतप्तये मन्त्रविदिति। वकारयोगेऽन्ते पञ्चाक्षरयोगश्चोक्तः॥ १५॥

वातेनेति। काकचञ्चुवातेनेत्यर्थः। निजवाञ्छयैव मन्त्रीति। मूलाधारगतमन्त्राग्नौ साध्यप्रक्षेप उक्तः॥ १६॥ १७॥

श्रिततया मनस इति। योनिस्थमन्त्ररज्ज्वाबद्धस्य तस्या मनसः स्वलिङ्गनिःसृतकुण्डलीशक्त्याकर्षणध्यानमुक्तम्। स्रवयेच्चेति। यस्य प्रतिबन्ध इष्टः। शुक्रस्य रक्तस्य वा तदाश्रये पृथिवीबीजस्थमर्णं चिन्तयेत्। इतरत्राऽग्निबीजस्थं तत इष्टं भवतीत्यर्थः॥ १८॥

उभयोरपि सहचरणार्थमन्यमृतस्थप्रयोगान्तरमाह—निजशिवेति। त्रिकगमिति। त्रिकोणगतमित्यर्थः। हुताशयुगात्मकं षट्कोणं हुताशयुगषट्कं तेन वृतमित्यर्थः। अत्राऽपि कोणेषु मन्त्राक्षरयोगो द्रष्टव्यः॥ १९॥ २०॥

मधुरत्रयसंयुतेन शालीरजसा पुत्तलिकां विधाय तेन ।
मनुना जुहुयात्तया[था] विभज्य त्रिदिनं यस्य कृते वशीभवेत् सः ॥

विषपावकोद्यदभिधानगदं ठगतं कुकोणाद्य[यु]तलाङ्गलिकम् ।
अहिपचक्रपमपरिजप्तमिदं शिरसो रुजं प्रशमयेददनात् ॥ २२

कण्ठे केनाऽवरुद्ध्याऽर्पितदहनयुजा मज्जया मेन वामं
दक्षं संवेष्ट्य वक्षोरुहमनलसमीरौभिरंसद्वयश्च ।
वक्त्रे नाभौ च दीर्घं सुमतिरथ विनिःक्षिप्य बिन्दुं निशेशं
वक्षस्याधाय बद्ध्वा चिरमिव विहरेत् कन्दुकैरात्मसाध्यैः ॥ २३

कृत्वा वह्नेः पुरमनु मनुं बन्धुजीवेन तस्मि-
न्नाधायाऽग्निं विधिवदभिसंपूज्य चाऽऽज्यैः शताख्यम् ।
त्रैलोहाख्ये प्रतिविहितसंपातमष्टोत्तरं त-
द्धुत्वा जप्तं दुरितविषवेतालभूतादिहारि ॥ २४

साध्याख्यागर्भमेनं लिख दहनपुरे कर्णिकायां षडस्रं
बाह्यास्त्रिष्वङ्गमन्त्रान् दलमनु परितो बीजवर्णान् विभज्य ।
भूयोऽचः कादियादींस्त्रिषु वृतिषु कुगेहास्रके नारसिंहं
तस्मिन् कार्यो यथावत्कलशविधिरयं सर्वरक्षाकरः स्यात् ॥ २५

तया विभज्येति । सव्यपाद सव्यपार्श्व सव्यहस्त शिरो दक्षिणहस्त दक्षिणपार्श्व-दक्षिणपादेर्जुहुयात् स्त्रीवश्ये । पुरुषवश्ये तु विपरीतमित्यर्थः ॥ २१ ॥

विषपावको मकारसम्बद्धो रेफः तस्मिन् उद्भूतेन साध्यसाधकाभिधानेन गदेन च संयुक्तमित्यर्थः ॥ २२ ॥

सुमतिरिति । बिन्दुलक्षणेन निशेशेन तस्य जीवं रक्षन्निक्षिप्येत्युक्तम् । [वश्यकरं प्रयोगमाह—कण्ठं केनेति । साध्यस्य कण्ठं रेफसहितककारेण बद्ध्वा मज्जया षकारेण मेन मकारेण च वामदक्षिणहस्तौ संवेष्ट्य अनलसमीरौभिः रेफयकारचतुर्दशस्वरैः ऊंसद्वयं वक्त्रं च बद्ध्वा ऊकारेण दीर्घरूपेण नाभिं बद्ध्वा सुमतिः बिन्दुलक्षणेन निशेशेन तस्य जीवं वक्षसि निक्षिप्य गृहीत्वा वश्यैः क्रीडासाधनैरिव विहरेदित्यर्थः । इति सम्बन्धदीपिकाकारः] ॥ २३ ॥

कृत्वा वह्नेः पुरमिति । बन्धुजीवपुष्परसेन भूमिं विलिप्य तत्र तद्रसेन तत्पुष्पेण त्रिकोणं लिखित्वा तन्मध्ये मन्त्रं च विलिख्य अग्न्याधानादिकं कुर्यादित्यर्थः । अत्र लोहत्रयमपि मूलाक्षरसंख्यं ग्राह्यम् ॥ २४ ॥ २५ ॥

टान्ते लिख्यात् कलाभिर्वृतमनुमनलावासयुग्मेन वह्नि-
द्योतत्कोणेन बाह्ये तदनु सवितृबिम्बेन काद्यर्णभाजा ।
तद्बाह्ये क्ष्मापुराभ्यां लिखितनृहरियुक्ताश्रकाभ्यां तदेतद्
यन्त्रं रक्षाकरं स्याद् ग्रहभयविषमक्ष्वेलजूर्त्यादिरोगे ॥ २६

बिम्बद्वन्द्वे कृशानोर्विलिखतु मनु[णि]मेनं ससाध्यं तदश्रि-
ष्वग्न्यादीन् व्यञ्जनार्णान् स्वरयुगलमथो सन्धिषट्के यथावत् ।
तारावीतश्च बाह्ये कुगृहपरिवृतं गोमयाब्रोचनाभ्यां
लाक्षाबद्धं निबध्याज्जपमहितमिदं साधु साध्योत्तमाङ्गे ॥ २७

लक्ष्म्यायु:पुष्टिकरं परञ्च सौभाग्यवश्यकृत् सततम् ।
चोरव्यालमहोरगभूतापस्मारहारि यन्त्रमिदम् ॥ २८

साध्याख्याकर्मयुक्तं दहनपुरयुगे मन्त्रमेनं तदश्रि-
ष्वग्निज्वालाश्च बाह्ये विषतरुविटपे साग्रशाखे लिखित्वा ।
जप्त्वाऽष्टोर्ध्वं सहस्रं नृहरिकृतधिया स्थापयेत् तत्र शत्रु-
व्याघ्रादिक्रोडचोरादिभिरपि च पिशाचादयो न व्रजन्ति ॥ २९

ससिद्धसुरपूजित: सकलवर्गसंसाधको
ग्रहज्वरविषापहो विविधकामकल्पद्रुम: ।
किमत्र बहुना नृणामभिमतार्थचिन्तामणि:
समुक्त इह संग्रहान्मनुवरस्तु चिन्तामणि: ॥ ३०

षष्ठस्वरो हुतवहस्तययोस्तुरीया-
वादिस्वरौ मनुरयं कथित: फडन्त: ।
अस्य त्रिको निगदितो मुनिरप्यनुष्टुप्
छन्दश्च चण्डसहितो मनुदेवतेश: ॥ ३१

रक्षाकरं यन्त्रमाह—टान्त इति ॥ २६ ॥

बिम्बद्वन्द्व इति । बिम्बद्वन्द्वमध्य इत्यर्थ: । तदश्रिष्वन्तरालेषु । यथावदिति । आवूकारेण सार्धमित्यर्थ: । कुगृहे च नृसिंहबीजं लिखितव्यम् ॥ २७॥२८ ॥

दहनपुरयुगे युगमध्य इत्यर्थ: । तदश्रिष्वन्तरालेषु चैनं पूर्ववल्लिखित्वा नेमिबाह्येऽग्निज्वालाश्च लिखेदित्यर्थ: ॥ २९ ॥ ३० ॥

महेश्वरस्य मन्त्रानभिधाय चण्डेश्वरस्य मन्त्रमाह—षष्ठेति । चं बीजम् ।

दीप्तज्वलज्ज्वालिनिभिस्तटेन च हनेन च ।
सर्वज्ज्वालिनिसंयुक्तैः फड़न्तैरङ्गमारभेत् ॥ ३२

अव्यात् कपर्दकलितेन्दुकलः करात्त-
शूलाक्षसूत्रककमण्डलुटङ्क ईशः ।
रक्ताभ्र[भ]वर्णवसनोऽरुणपङ्कजस्थो
नेत्रत्रयोल्लसितवक्त्रसरोरुहो वः ॥ ३३

कृतसंदीक्षो मन्त्री जप्याल्लक्षत्रयञ्च मन्त्रमिमम् ।
जुहुयात्त्रिमधुरयुक्तैः सतिलैरपि तण्डुलैर्दशांशेन ॥ ३४
व्याघातसमिद्भिर्वा मनुजापी तावतीभिरथ जुहुयात् ।
पूर्वोक्त एव पीठे गन्धाद्यैरर्चयेच्च चण्डेशम् ॥ ३५
चण्डचण्डाय चेत्युक्त्वा प्रवदेद् विद्महेपदम् ।
चण्डेश्वराय च प्रोक्त्वा धीमहिपदमुद्धरेत् ॥ ३६
तन्नश्चण्ड इति प्रोक्त्वा ब्रूयाद् भूयः प्रचोदयात् ।
एषा तु चण्डगायत्री जपात् सान्निध्यकारिणी ॥ ३७
अङ्गैः समातृभिर्मन्त्री लोकेशैः सम्प्रपूजयेत् ।
कूर्मो विष्णुयुतो दण्डी बीजमस्योच्यते बुधैः ॥ ३८
वदेच्चण्डेश्वरायेति बीजादिहृदयान्तिकम् ।
अर्चनादिष्विमं मन्त्रं यथावत् सम्प्रयोजयेत् ॥ ३९
एवं जपहुतार्चाभिः सिद्धे मन्त्रे तु मन्त्रिणः ।
वाञ्छितादधिकं लभेत् काञ्चनं नात्र संशयः ॥ ४०
त्र्यक्षरस्य जपो यावत्तावज्जप्यात् षड़क्षरम् ।
ऐहिकामुष्मिकीं सिद्धिं तथा हि लभते नरः ॥ ४१

कृत्वा पिष्टेन शाल्याः प्रतिकृतिमनलं चाऽपि काष्ठेश्चिताना-
माधायारभ्य पुंसस्त्रिमधुरलुलितं दक्षिणाङ्गुष्ठदेशात् ।

फट् शक्तिः ॥ ३१ ॥ ३२ ॥ ३३ ॥

मन्त्री जप्यादिति । प्रणवयोग उक्तः ॥ ३४ ॥ ३५ ॥ ३६ ॥ ३७ ॥

मन्त्री लोकेशैरिति । चण्डपार्षदायेति योगः सूचितः ॥ ३८ ॥

यथावदिति । प्रणवयोग उक्तः ॥ ३९॥४०॥४१॥४२॥४३॥४४॥४५॥४६ ॥

छित्वा छित्वाऽष्टयुक्तं शतमथ जुहुयाद् योषितो वामभागा-
द्विप्रादीनां चतुर्णां वशकरमनिशं मन्त्रमेतद्भुतान्तम् ॥ ४२
अनुदिनमष्टशतं यो जुहुयात् पुष्पैरनेन मन्त्रेण ।
सप्तदिनैः स तु लभते वासस्तद्वर्णसङ्काशम् ॥ ४३
अहरहरष्टशतं यो मन्त्रेणाऽनेन तर्पयेदीशम् ।
तस्य तु मासचतुष्कादर्वाक् सञ्जायते महालक्ष्मीः ॥ ४४
साध्यर्क्षाङ्घ्रिपचर्मणां सुमसृणां पिष्टैश्च लोणैः कृतां
छित्त्वा पुत्तलिकां प्रतिष्ठितचलां जप्त्वा च रात्रौ हुनेत् ।
सप्ताहं पुरुषोऽङ्गना यदि चिरं वश्यस्त्ववश्यं भवे-
दस्मिन् जन्मनि नाऽत्र चोद्यविषयो देहान्तरेऽसंशयः ॥ ४५
इति चण्डमन्त्रविहितं विधिवद्विधिमादरेण य इमं भजते ।
स तु वाञ्छितं पदमिहाप्य पुनः शिवरूपतामपि परत्र लभेत ॥ ४६

इति श्रीप्रपञ्चसारे एकोनत्रिंश पटलः ।

इति श्रीपद्मपादाचार्यकृते प्रपञ्चसारविवरणे

एकोनत्रिंशः पटलः ।

त्रिंशः पटलः ।

अथाऽखिलार्थानुगतैव शक्तिर्युक्ता चतुर्विंशतितत्त्वभेदैः ।
गायत्रिसंज्ञाऽप्यथ तद्विशेषान् सहप्रयोगान् कथयामि साङ्गान् ॥ १
ताराद्यवी व्याहृतयश्च सप्त गायत्रिमन्त्रः शिरसा समेतः ।
अन्वर्थकं मन्त्रमिमन्तु वेदसारं पुनर्वेदविदो वदन्ति ॥ २
जप्यः स्यादिह परलोकसिद्धिकामैर्मन्त्रोऽयं महिततरो द्विजैर्यथावत् ।
भूदेवा नरपतयस्तृतीयवर्णाः संप्रोक्ता द्विजवचनेन तेऽत्र भूयः ॥ ३
तेषां शुद्धकुलद्वयोत्थमहसामारभ्य तन्तुक्रियां
तारव्याहृतिसंयुता सहशिरो गायत्र्युपास्या परा ।
सन्ध्योपासनया जपेन च तथा स्वाध्यायभेदैरपि
प्राणायामविधानतो मतिमतां ध्यानैस्तथा नित्यशः ॥ ४

तान्त्रिकमन्त्रानन्तरं वैदिकमन्त्रान् वदन् वेदसाररूपिण्या गायत्र्या विधानं प्रथमतः प्रतिपादयन् तद्वाच्यदेवतायाः तत्त्वमाह—अथाऽखिलेति। अथशब्दस्तान्त्रिकानन्तर्यार्थः। अखिलार्थानुगता शक्तिरेव गायत्रीसंज्ञाऽपि भवेत्। अथ तद्विशेषानपि सहप्रयोगान् साङ्गान् प्रवदामीत्यन्वयः। त्रिसप्तव्याहृतिदशद्वादशप्रणवशक्तिश्रीबीजादियुक्ता गायत्र्या विशेषशब्दार्थः। अखिलार्थानुगताया एकरूपिण्याः शक्तेः कथं चतुर्विंशत्यक्षरात्मकगायत्र्यात्मकत्वमित्याशङ्क्य शक्तेरपि चतुर्विंशत्तत्त्वात्मता चतुर्विंशतिसंख्यायोगादिति वदन् गायत्र्यक्षरैः सार्धं तत्त्वन्यासं सूचयति—युक्ता चतुर्विंशतितत्त्वभेदैरिति ॥ १ ॥

वदामीति प्रतिज्ञातं विशेषमाह—ताराद्य इति। अन्वर्थकत्वं साधयति—वेदसारमिति ॥ २ ॥

जपादावधिकारनियममाह—जप्यः स्यादिति। यथावदिति उपनयनादिपूर्वकमित्यर्थः। द्विजशब्देन रूढिमाश्रित्य न ब्राह्मणमात्रं गृह्यते इत्याह—भूदेवा इति ॥ ३ ॥

द्विजेष्वपि शुद्धानामेव अधिकार इत्याह—तेषामिति। शुद्धानामपि उपनीतानामेवाऽधिकार इत्याह—आरभ्येति। उपासनप्रकारानाह—सन्ध्येति। सन्ध्योपासनादि प्रकारमुत्तरत्र वक्ष्यति ॥ ४ ॥

आदौ तारः प्रकृतिविकृतिप्रोत्थितोऽसौ च मूला-
धारादारादलिविरुतिराविश्य सौषुम्नमार्गम् ।
आद्यैः शान्तावधिभिरनुगो मात्रया सप्तभेदैः
शुद्धो मूर्धावधिपरिगतः शाश्वतोऽन्तर्बहिश्च ॥ ५

प्रकाशितादौ प्रणवप्रपञ्चता निगद्यते व्याहृतिसप्तकं पुनः ।
सभूर्भुवः स्वश्च महोजनस्तपःसमन्वितं सत्यमिति क्रमेण च ॥ ६

भूःपदाद्या व्याहृतयो भूःशब्दस्तदि वर्तते ।
तत्पदं सदिति प्रोक्तं सन्मात्रत्वात् तु भूरतः ॥ ७

अथ ध्यानार्थं सविशेषाया गायत्र्या अर्थं वदन् प्रणवस्याऽर्थं सानुभवसाधनमाह—आदाविति । आदौ भवो यस्तारः असौ प्रकृतिविकृतिप्रोत्थितः । प्रकृतिः निश्चला परावाग्रूपिणी परप्रणवात्मिका कुण्डलिनी शक्तिः । तस्या विकृतिर्विकारः पश्यन्त्यादिरूपः तद्रूपेण प्रोत्थितः अभिव्यक्तः । एवमुच्चारणात् पूर्वं पूर्णसंविदात्मना स्थितस्य परप्रणवस्य किञ्चिद् बहिर्मुखः सन् स्वातन्त्र्येच्छाज्ञानप्रयत्न शरीरस्पर्शतदन्तर्गत क्रियाज्ञानशक्तिरूप गुरुवक्त्र मनोन्मन्युन्मना समनाव्यापिनोस्पर्शशक्तिनादान्तनादावस्थाः प्राप्तस्य विशेषयत्नरूप निरोधिन्यात्मना ज्वालाप्रवाहशब्द भेदरूप कालबिन्दुबीजात्मना चोच्चारणसमये अभिव्यक्तस्य प्रणवस्य सुषुम्नाप्रवेशक्रमं दर्शयति तेन परानुभवप्रकारं दर्शयितुम्—असावित्यादिना । असावभिव्यक्तः प्रणवः । मूलाधारात् आमूलाधारम् उद्गतो य आरः । आ समन्तात् स्वप्रभया राति गच्छतीत्यारश्चिदग्निः ज्योतिर्लिङ्गाकारः तस्मादलिविरुतिः सन् सौषुम्नमार्गं प्रविश्य शाश्वतो भवतीत्यन्वयः । सौषुम्नमार्गं प्रविष्टे प्रणवे स्थानविशेषे वाचकरूपाकारादिसप्तभेदानुसन्धानं कर्तव्यमित्याह—आद्यैः शान्तावधिभिः सप्तभेदैरनुगत इति । वाचकभेदानुगतवद् वाच्यभेदानुगमोऽपि ध्यातव्य इत्याह—मात्रयेति । मात्रा कुण्डलिनी शक्तिः । तया च ब्रह्मविष्णुरुद्रेश्वरसदाशिवशक्तिपररूपिण्या अनुगत इत्यर्थः । उक्तवाच्यवाचकभेदे संहारेण शुद्धज्योतिर्मात्रप्रणवो ध्यातव्य इत्याह—शुद्ध इति । मूर्धशब्देन सर्वोत्कृष्टं द्वादशान्तस्थं तत्त्वमुच्यते । तत्पर्यन्तं व्यापिन्यादिद्वारेण गत्वा शाश्वतो भवति । अपरिच्छिन्नत्वेन शाश्वतत्वमुपपादयति—अन्तर्बहिश्चेति ॥ ५ ॥

एवं निर्विशेषब्रह्मार्थत्वं प्रणवस्योत्तमाधिकारिणां प्रदर्श्य मन्दानां सप्रपञ्चार्थमाह—प्रकाशितादाविति । ताराद्विभक्तान् त्रिगुणासत्यादावित्यच्चरार्थः ॥ ६ ॥

भूतत्वात् कारणत्वाच्च भुवःशब्दस्य सङ्गतिः ।
सर्वस्य स्वीरणात् स्वात्मतया च स्वरितीरितम् ॥ ८
महत्त्वाच्च महस्त्वाच्च महःशब्दः समीरितः ।
तदेव सर्वजनता तस्मात्तद्[त्तु]व्याहृतिर्जनः ॥ ९
तपो ज्ञानतया चैव तथा तापतया स्मृतम् ।
सत्यं परत्वादात्मत्वादनन्तज्ञानतः स्मृतम् ॥ १०
प्रणवस्य व्याहृतीनामतः सम्बन्ध उच्यते ।
अकारो भूरुकारस्तु भुवो मार्णः स्वरीरितः ॥ ११

एवं प्रणवस्य सगुणं निर्गुणं चाऽर्थमभिधाय व्याहृतीनामर्थं वदन् भूरित्यस्यार्थमाह—भूःशब्दस्तदीति तत्पदार्थं इत्यर्थः । भूःशब्दस्य कथं तत्र वृत्तिरिति तत्राह—तत्पदं सदिति । तदिति पदं यस्य ब्रह्मणः 'तत् सदेव सौम्य' 'ओं तत्सत्' इत्यादौ सदिति प्रोक्तम् । भूश्च सत्तार्थः । अतस्तस्य तदर्थत्वं तत्पदत्वं संभवतीत्यर्थः । अतः पूर्वोक्तस्य प्रणवार्थस्य सन्मात्रत्वात् भूःशब्देनापि तदेव लक्षणयोच्यते इत्याह—सन्मात्रत्वादिति । मन्दानां चादित्यानुगतं सदादिशब्दवाच्यं सगुणं ब्रह्म भूःशब्देन प्रतिपत्तव्यमिति उक्तम् ।

तुशब्देन भुव इत्यत्र भुइत्यस्य भूतात्मत्वं व इत्यस्य जगद्गमनात्मत्वं जगदुपादनात्मत्वं च स्वीकृत्याह—भूतत्वादिति । भूतत्वं नित्यसिद्धत्वं पारमार्थिकत्वं च । भुवःशब्दस्य रुंगतिरिति । प्रणवार्थेन लक्षणया मुख्यया वृत्त्या वा सम्बन्ध इत्यर्थः । एवमुत्तरपदानामपि प्रणवार्थेनैव संगतिः । स्वःशब्दस्य स्वर्गसुखात्मकत्वेनात्मार्थत्वं सुवहनार्थत्वं चादायाह—सर्वस्येति ॥ ७ ॥ ८ ॥

महत्त्वं त्रिविधं देशतः कालतो वस्तुतश्च । महस्त्वं चैतन्यं ज्योतिषि । इतश्च तदेव इति ब्रह्मैवेत्यर्थः । तस्मात्तद्व्याहृतिर्जन इति शब्दार्थयोरेकत्वमप्युक्तम् ॥ ९ ॥

तापतयेति । अज्ञानां संसारतापनिमित्तत्वादित्यर्थः । आदित्यानुगते तु तत्सत्त्वं प्रसिद्धमेव । सत्यं परत्वादिति । अनृतेभ्यः परत्वादित्यर्थः । तत् कथमित्याह—आत्मत्वादिति । तदपि कथमित्याह—अनन्तेति ॥ १० ॥

एवं केवलनिर्गुणनिष्ठानां केवलसगुणनिष्ठानां च प्रतिपत्तिप्रकारमभिधाय सगुणद्वारा निर्गुणपर्यन्तं गच्छतां प्रतिपत्तिप्रकारं वदन् प्रणवमात्राभिः व्याहृतीनां सम्बन्ध इत्याह—अकारो भूरिति । ब्रह्म विष्णु रुद्रेश्वर सदाशिव कारण साक्षि-

बिन्दुर्महस्तथा नादो जनः शक्तिस्तपः स्मृतम् ।
शान्तं सत्यमिति प्रोक्तं यत् स्यात् परतरं पदम् ॥ १२
प्रणवस्य व्याहृतीनां गायत्र्यैक्यमथोच्यते ।
अत्रापि तत्पदं पूर्वं प्रोक्तं तदनु वर्ण्यते ॥ १३
तद्द्वितीयैकवचनमनेनाऽखिलवस्तुनः ।
सृष्ट्यादिकारणं तेजोरूपमादित्यमण्डले ॥ १४
अभिध्येयं सदानन्दं परं ब्रह्माऽभिधीयते ।
यत्तत्सवितुरित्युक्तं षष्ठ्येकवचनात्मकम् ॥ १५
धातोरिह विनिष्पन्नं प्राणिप्रसववाचकात् ।
सर्वासां प्राणिजातीनामिति प्रसवितुः सदा ॥ १६
वरेण्यं वरणीयत्वात् सेवनीयतया तथा ।
भजनीयतया सर्वैः प्रार्थनीयतया स्मृतम् ॥ १७

णोऽकाराद्यर्थभूताः व्याहृतिभिरपि ध्येया इत्यर्थः ॥ ११ ॥ १२ ॥

एवं बहिःप्रणवव्याहृतिपञ्चमभिधायाऽन्तःप्रणवव्याहृतिपञ्चमाश्रित्य प्रणवाद्यर्थ-कथनायोपक्रमते—प्रणवस्येति। प्रणवस्त्रिमात्रः। व्याहृतयश्च तिस्रः। तेषां गायत्र्यैक्यं ओं भूर्भुवःस्वस्तत्सवितुर्वरेण्यमिति प्रकारेण अथवा ओं अं भूः तत् सवितुर्वरेण्यम् ओं उं भुवः भर्गो देवस्य धीमहि ओं मं स्वः धियो यो नः प्रचोदयात्। इत्यैक्यं स्वरूपतोऽर्थतश्चोच्यत इति।

अत्रापि तत्पदं पूर्वमिति। प्रथमपाद प्रथमस्याहृत्योरेकार्थत्वद्योतनायेति। अपिना ध्येयवाचकत्वेन द्वितीयैकवचनमुपपादयति—अनेनेति। आदित्यमण्डले इत्युपलक्षणम्। कारणमण्डलस्यापि।

धियो य इत्यत्र यच्छब्देन चास्य सम्बन्ध इत्याह—यत्तदिति। द्वितीयं पादं व्याचष्टे—तत् सवितुरिति। षूङ् प्राणिप्रसव इति धातुः। इति प्रसवितुर्यस्मात् संकोचकं नास्ति तस्मात् सर्वप्रसविता परमेश्वरोऽस्यार्थः। इति तात्पर्यकथनमेतत् ॥ १३ ॥ १४ ॥ १५ ॥ १६ ॥

परमपुरुषार्थरूपत्वात् वरणीयत्वम्। असेवितस्य वरणायोगात्। तदर्थं सेवनीयत्वमप्यस्त्यस्य। पूजाभिलक्षणभजनेन विना सेवायोगात् भजनीयत्व-मप्यस्ति। प्रार्थनया विना पूजादिलक्षणभजनस्याप्ययोगात् तदर्थं सर्वैः प्रार्थनीयत्वमप्यस्त्यस्य ॥ १७ ॥

पूर्वस्याऽष्टाक्षरस्यैवं व्याहृतिर्भूरिति स्मृता ।
पापस्य भर्जनाद्भर्गो भक्तस्निग्धतया तथा ॥ १८

देवस्य वृष्टिदानादिगुणयुक्तस्य नित्यश: ।
प्रभूतेन प्रकाशेन दीप्यमानस्य वै तथा ॥ १९

ध्यै चिन्तायामतो धातोर्निष्पन्नं धीमहीत्यद: ।
निगमाद्येन दिव्येन विद्यारूपेण चक्षुषा ॥ २०

दृश्यो हिरण्मयो देव आदित्ये नित्यसंस्थित: ।
हीनतारहितं तेजो यथा स्यात् स हिरण्मय: ॥ २१

य: सूक्ष्म: सोऽहमित्येवं चिन्तयाम: सदैव तु ।
द्वितीयाष्टाक्षरस्यैवं व्याहृतिर्भुव ईरिता ॥ २२

धियो बुद्धीर्मनोरस्य छान्दसत्वाद् य ईरित: ।
क्तस्य लिङ्गव्यत्यास: सूत्रात् सुप्तिङुपग्रहात् ॥ २३

यत् तु तेजो निरूपमं सर्ववेद[देव]मयात्मकम् ।
भजतां पापनाशस्य हेतुभूतमिहोच्यते ॥ २४

पूर्वस्याऽष्टाक्षरस्यैवमिति । एवमुक्तेन प्रकारेण यस्मात् सर्वजगत्कारणं सदात्मकं ब्रह्म प्रथमपादार्थ: तस्मात्तस्य भूरित्येव व्याहृतिरीरितेत्यर्थ: ।

भर्गश्चित्प्रकाश: । केन चिन्त्यत इति तदाह—निगमाद्येनेति । प्रथमं प्रणवेन संचिन्त्य पुनस्तदेव तदक्षरव्याहृतिपादैश्चिन्तनीयमित्यर्थ: ॥ १८ ॥ १९ ॥ २० ॥

अथ 'य एषोऽन्तरादित्यो हिरण्मय:' इत्यादिश्रुतिमाश्रित्य ध्येयस्वरूपं ध्यानप्रकारं चाह—दृश्यो हिरण्मय इति । द्वितीयाष्टाक्षरस्यैवमिति । एवमुक्तेन प्रकारेण द्वितीयपादद्वितीयव्याहृत्योरेकार्थत्वात् तयो: संगतिर्योग्येत्यर्थ: ॥२१॥२२॥

धियो यो न इति वक्तव्ये य इति वचनमनुपपन्नमिति तत्राह:—छान्दसत्वादिति । छन्दसि तु लिङ्गव्यत्यासादिकं सम्भवतीत्यत्र प्रमाणमाह—क्तस्येति । सुप्तिङुपग्रहलिङ्गनराणां कालहल स्वरकर्तृयङां च व्यत्ययमिच्छति शास्त्रकृदेषाम् सोऽपि च सिध्यति बाहुलकेन इति वचनादित्यर्थ: ॥ २३ ॥

यच्छब्दार्थ: क इति । भर्गशब्देनोक्त: प्रकाश इत्याह—यत्त्विति । निरूपममित्यनेन निर्गुणनिष्ठानां ध्येयं तेज इत्युक्तम् । सर्ववेदमयात्मकमिति । सगुणनिष्ठानां सर्ववेदमय: सूर्य: तदात्मकमित्यर्थ: । भर्गपदार्थस्य विशेष्यत्वमितरेष विशेषणत्वं च विवक्षन्नाह—पापनाशस्येति ॥ २४ ॥

न इति प्रोक्त आदेशः षष्ठ्यसौ युष्मदस्मदोः ।
तस्मादस्माकमित्यर्थः प्रार्थनायां प्रचोदयात् ॥ २५
तृतीयाष्टाक्षरस्याऽपि व्याहृतिः स्वरितोरिता ।
एवं दशपदान्यस्यास्त्रयश्चाऽष्टाक्षराः स्मृताः ॥ २६
षडक्षराश्च चत्वारः स्युश्चतुर्विंशदक्षराः ।
इत्थंभूतं यदेतस्य देवस्य सवितुर्विभाः ॥ २७
वरेण्यं भजतां पापविनाशनकरं परम् ।
भर्गोऽस्माभिरभिध्यातं धियस्तन्नः प्रचोदयात् ॥ २८
उक्त्वैवमत्र गायत्री पुनस्तच्छिर उच्यते ।
आपो ज्योती रस इति सोमाग्न्योस्तेज उच्यते ॥ २९
तदात्मकं जगत् सर्वं रसस्तेजोद्वयं युतम् ।
अमृतं तदनाशित्वाद्बृहत्वाद्ब्रह्म उच्यते ॥ ३०
यदानन्दात्मकं ब्रह्म सत्यज्ञानादिलक्षणम् ।
तद्भूर्भुवः स्वरित्युक्तं सोऽहमित्योमुदाहृतम् ॥ ३१
एतत् तु वेदसारस्य शिरस्त्वाच्छिर उच्यते ।
लक्षणैरिति निर्दिष्टे वेदसारे सुनिष्ठितः ॥ ३२
फलार्थी फलमाप्नोति मुमुक्षुर्मोक्षमृच्छति ।
उषस्युषसि चोत्थाय कृतशौचविधिर्द्विजः ॥ ३३

न इति षष्ठी । बहुवचनस्यादेशत्वात् षष्ठीबहुवचनमेवेत्याह—न इति । तस्य तदादेशे प्रमाणमाह—युष्मदस्मदोरिति । युष्मदस्मदोः षष्ठी । चतुर्थीद्वितीयार्थयोर्बहुवचनस्य वस्नसौ इत्येतावादेशौ भवतः । पदसंख्याकथनेन पदतस्त्वन्यासः सूचितः । पदाक्षरसंख्याकथनेन भूमिमन्तरिक्षं द्यौरित्यष्टावक्षराणीत्युक्तमुपासनं सूचितम् । चतुष्पात्त्वकथनेन 'पादोऽस्य विश्वा भूतानि' इत्युक्तं चिन्तनं सूचितम् । चतुर्विंशाक्षरत्वकथनेन चतुर्विंशतितत्त्वात्मनोपासनमुक्तम् ॥ २५ ॥ २६ ॥ २७ ॥

उक्तमर्थं संक्षिप्याह—इत्थमिति । सोमाग्निशब्दाभ्यां प्रकृतिपुरुषावुच्येते । न केवलं कारणमात्रमुच्यते किन्तु कारणात्मकं जगदप्युच्यते इत्याह—तदात्मकं जगदिति । रसशब्दार्थमाह—रस इति ॥ २७॥२८॥२९॥३०॥३१॥३२ ॥

वेदसारे सुनिष्ठित इत्युक्तां निष्ठां साङ्गमाह—उषस्युषसीति ॥ ३२—४९ ॥

दन्तानां धावनञ्चैव जिह्वानिर्लेखनादिकम् ।
कृत्वा स्नात्वा समाचम्य मन्त्रपूतेन वारिणा ॥ ३४
आपोहिष्ठामयाद्याभिर्ऋग्भिस्तिसृभिरेव च ।
अभ्युत्त्य शुद्धदेहः सन्नपः पीत्वा समाहितः ॥ ३५
सूर्यश्चेत्यनुवाकेन पुनराचम्य पूर्ववत् ।
अभ्युत्त्य शुद्धदेहः सन् गृहीत्वाऽञ्जलिना जलम् ॥ ३६
आदित्याभिमुखो भूत्वा तद्गतात्मोर्ध्वलोचनः ।
वेदसारं जपन् ज्योतिर्मूलभूतं परात्परम् ॥ ३७
हृत्स्थं सर्वस्य लोकस्य मण्डलान्तर्व्यवस्थितम् ।
चिन्तयन् परमात्मानमापस्तूर्ध्वं विनिःक्षिपेत् ॥ ३८
एनस्ताः प्रतिनिघ्नन्ति जगदाप्याययन्ति च ।
ततः प्रदक्षिणीकृत्य पुनराचम्य संयतः ॥ ३९
क्रमात्तारादिमन्त्राणामृष्यादीन् विन्यसेत् सुधीः ।
तत्र तु प्रणवस्याऽऽदावृषिरुक्तः प्रजापतिः ॥ ४०
छन्दस्तु देवी गायत्री परमात्मा च देवता ।
जमदग्निभरद्वाजभृगुगौतमकाश्यपाः ॥ ४१
विश्वामित्रो वसिष्ठाख्य ऋषयो व्याहृतीरिताः ।
गायत्र्युष्णिगनुष्टुप् च बृहती पङ्क्तिरेव च ॥ ४२
त्रिष्टब्जगत्यौ छन्दांसि कथ्यन्ते देवता अपि ।
सप्ताच्चिरनिलः सूर्यो वाक्पतिर्वरुणो वृषा ॥ ४३
विश्वेदेवा इति प्रोक्ताः सप्तव्याहृतिदेवताः ।
हृन्मुखांसोरुयुग्मेषु सोदरेषु क्रमान्न्यसेत् ॥ ४४
विश्वामित्रस्तु गायत्र्या ऋषिश्छन्दः स्वयं स्मृतम् ।
सविताऽस्या देवता च ब्रह्मा शिरऋषिः स्मृतः ।
छन्दस्तु देवी गायत्री परमात्मा च देवता ॥ ४५

सुधीरिति । ऋष्यादिन्यासस्थानमुक्तं स्मरन्नित्यर्थः । अथवा तारादिव्याप्तिं जानन्नित्यर्थः ॥ ३८ ॥ ४० ॥ ४१ ॥ ४२ ॥ ४३ ॥ ४४ ॥ ४५ ॥

स्थानेषु पूर्वमुक्तेषु सतारा व्याहृतीर्न्यसेत् ।
गायत्रीं शिरसा विद्वान् जप्यात्त्रिः स्यादुपासना ॥ ४६
हृदयेऽधस्तथोर्ध्वञ्च महादिक्ष्वपि संयतः
व्यापयेद्व्याहृतीः सम्यग्गायत्रीञ्च शिरोयुताम् ।
सार्थं संस्मृत्य संजप्यात्त्रिविधं जपलक्षणम् ॥ ४७
आत्मन्यधश्चोपरि च दिग्भ्यस्ताः समुपानयेत्
गायत्रीं पूर्ववज्जप्यात् स्वाध्यायविधिरीदृशः ॥ ४८
एतत्त्रयं त्रिशः कुर्यादृजुकायस्त्वनन्यधीः ।
निरुच्छ्वासः स विज्ञेयः प्राणायामो मनीषिभिः ॥ ४९
ध्यानस्य केवलस्याऽस्य व्याख्याने दर्शितः क्रमः ।
त्रिर्व्याहृत्यादिमभ्यस्येद्गायत्रीं सन्ध्ययोः सुधीः ॥ ५०
शतं वाऽथ सहस्रं वा मन्त्रार्थगतमानसः ।
पूर्वं प्रपञ्चयागोक्तान् गाणपत्यजपादिकान् ॥ ५१
लिपिन्यासादिकान् साङ्गान् ग्रहन्यासादिसंयुतान् ।
सनिजर्ष्यादिकान् सर्वान् विदध्याद्विधिवद्बुधः ॥ ५२
पादसन्धिचतुष्काम्बुनाभिहृद्गलदोर्द्वये ।
सन्ध्यास्यनासागण्डाक्षिकर्णभ्रूमस्तकेष्वपि ॥ ५३

पूर्वं कर्तव्यतया उक्तानुपासनाजपस्वाध्यायप्राणायामध्यानान् क्रमेण आह—स्थानेष्वित्यादिना। विद्वानर्थज्ञ इत्यर्थः ॥ ४६ ॥

व्याहृतीः सम्यगिति। बहिर्मुखाभिः मुद्राभिः जगत् सर्वं व्याहृतिभिः व्यापयन्नित्यर्थः। समुपानयनमन्तर्मुखमुद्राभिः न्यासं व्यापनमानयनं चेत्यर्थः। एतत्त्रयं त्रिश इति। अविच्छेदेन त्रयं कृत्वा पुनः व्याहृत्यादिसहितां गायत्रीं त्रिशः जपेत्। अयमेकः प्राणायामः। पुनरप्येवं द्विवारं कुर्यादित्यर्थः॥ ४७॥४८॥४९ ॥

ध्यानैस्तथा नित्यश इत्युक्ता ध्यानप्रकाराः कथं कर्तव्या इति तत्र निराकारध्यानप्रकार उक्त इत्याह—ध्यानस्येति। केवलस्येति। केवलस्य निराकारस्येत्यर्थः। अस्येति। प्राणायामादिभिः शुद्धस्येत्यर्थः। सुधीरिति। व्याहृतीनामादौ प्रणवेन स्वरूपध्यानमुक्तम् ॥ ५० ॥

बहिः जपक्रममाह—पूर्वमिति। मन्त्रवित्तम इति। प्रणवशक्त्यादियोगो

वारुणैन्द्रवयाम्यप्रागूर्ध्वगेषु मुखेषु च ।
क्रमेण वर्णान् विन्यस्येद्गायत्र्या मन्त्रवित्तमः ॥ ५४
शिरोभ्रूमध्यनयनवक्त्रकण्ठेषु वै क्रमात् ।
हृन्नाभिगुह्यजान्वाख्यपादेष्वपि पदान्न्यसेत् ॥ ५५
सब्रह्मविष्णुरुद्रैश्च सेश्वरैः ससदाशिवैः ।
ससर्वात्माह्वयैः कुर्यादङ्गन्यासं समाहितः ॥ ५६
एवं कृत्वा तु सिद्ध्यर्थं गायत्रीं दीक्षितो जपेत् ।
अथ त्रिगुणिते प्रोक्ते विचित्रे मण्डलोत्तमे ॥ ५७
शक्तिभिः प्राक्समुक्ताभिः सौरं पीठं समर्चयेत् ।
तत्र निःक्षिप्य कलशं यथापूर्वोपचारतः ॥ ५८
गव्यैर्वा पञ्चभिः क्वाथजलैर्वा पूरयेत्ततः ।
तस्मिन्नावाह्य कलशे शक्तिमित्थं विचिन्तयेत् ॥ ५९
मन्दाराह्वयरोचनाञ्जनजवाच्छाभैर्मुखैरिन्दुम-
द्रत्नोद्यन्मुकुटाङ्गसन्ततचतुर्विंशार्णचित्राऽतनुः ।
अब्जे चाऽरिगदाह्वयौ गुणकपालाख्यौ च पाशाङ्कुशे-
ष्टाभीतीर्दधती भवेद्भवदभीष्टोद्भाविनी तारिणी ॥ ६०
सञ्चिन्त्य भर्तारमिति प्रभाणां विशक्तिमूर्तीः प्रथमं समर्च्य ।
आदित्यशक्त्याख्यचतुष्टयेन यजेद्द्वितीयावरणे दिनेशम् ॥ ६१
प्रह्लादिनीं प्रभां नित्यां सविश्वम्भरसंज्ञिकाम् ।
विलासिनीप्रभावत्यौ जयां शान्तां क्रमाद्यजेत् ॥ ६२
कान्तां दुर्गासरस्वत्यौ विद्यां रूपाह्वयां तथा ।
विशालेशां व्यापिनीं च विमलाख्यां क्रमाद्यजेत् ॥ ६३
तमोऽपहारिणीं सूक्ष्मां विश्वयोनिं जयावहाम् ।
पद्मालयां परां शोभां पद्म[भद्र]रूपां तथा यजेत् ॥ ६४

धियमित्यस्य द्वित्वं चोक्तम् ॥ ५१॥५२॥५३॥५४ ५५॥५६॥५७॥५८॥५९॥६० ॥

विशक्तिमूर्तीर्ब्रह्माद्याः । आदित्यशक्त्याख्यचतुष्टयेनेति । आदित्यादि-पञ्चकसहितेनादित्यशक्तिचतुष्टयेनेत्यर्थः । तत्रादित्यो मध्ये रव्यादयो दिक्षु उषाद्या विदिक्षु ॥ ६१ ॥ ६२ ॥ ६३ ॥ ६४ ॥ ६५ ॥ ६६ ॥ ६७ ॥ ६८ ॥ ६९ ॥

मातृभिः सारुणान्ताभिः षष्ठ्यथो सप्तमी ग्रहैः ।
आदित्यपार्षदन्तैरप्यष्टमीन्द्रादिभिः सुरैः ॥ ६५
आवृतिः कथिता चेति विधानं परमीदृशम् ।
गन्धादिभिर्निवेद्यान्तैर्दिनेशं सम्यगर्चयेत् ॥ ६६

अथ पुनरमुमभिषिञ्चेत् संयतचित्तश्च देशिकः शिष्यम् ।
कृतहुतविधिमपि विधिवद्विहितबलिं दत्तदक्षिणं गुरवे ॥ ६७
भूयस्त्वक्षरलक्षं गायत्रीं संयतात्मको जप्त्वा ।
जुहुयात् पायसघृततिलदूर्वाभिर्दुग्धतरुसमिद्भिरपि ॥ ६८
एकैकं त्रिसहस्रं मन्त्री समभीष्टसिद्धये मुक्त्यै ।
अक्षरसहस्रसंख्यं मुख्यतरैः केवलैस्तिलैर्जुहुयात् ॥ ६९
दुरितोच्छेदनविधये मन्त्री दीर्घायुषि च विशदमतिः ।
आयुःकामो जुहुयात् पायसहविराज्यैः पीवलाज्यैश्च ।
दूर्वाभिः सतिलाभिः सर्वैस्त्रिसहस्रसंख्यकं मन्त्री ॥ ७०
अथवा त्रिमधुरसिक्तैररुणैर्जुहुयात् सरोरुहैरयुतम् ।
नष्टश्रीरपि भूयो भवति मनोज्ञः स मन्दिरं लक्ष्म्याः ॥ ७१
अन्नाद्यर्थ्यन्नैरपि पालाशैर्ब्रह्मवर्चसि जुहुयात् ।
सर्वैरेतैर्जुहुयात् सर्वफलाप्त्यै द्विजेश्वरो मतिमान् ॥ ७२

इति परमरहस्यं वेदसारस्य सारं
गदितमज मुमुक्षुैर्योगिभिर्ध्यानगम्यम् ।
अमुमथ जपहोमध्यानकाले य एवं
भजति स तु विमुक्तः कर्मभिर्मुक्तिमेति ॥ ७३

इति श्रीप्रपञ्चसारे त्रिंशः पटलः ॥

दुरितोच्छेदनविधये मन्त्रीति । दीर्घायुष्याय मृत्युञ्जयहंसयोग उक्तः । विशदमतिरिति । शुक्लध्यानमुक्तम् । त्रिसहस्रसंख्यकं मन्त्रीत्यपि तथा इति ॥ ७० ॥ ७१ ॥ ७२ ॥ ७३ ॥

इति श्रीपद्मपादाचार्यकृते प्रपञ्चसारविवरणे
त्रिंशत्पटलः ।

एकत्रिंशः पटलः ।

अथ वक्ष्यामि विद्यायास्त्रिष्टुभः प्रवरं विधिम् ।
ऋषिच्छन्दोदेवताभिरङ्गन्यासक्रमैः सह ॥ १
मरीचिः काश्यपो नाम ऋषिश्छन्दः स्वयं स्मृतम् ।
देवता जातवेदोऽग्निरुच्यन्तेऽङ्गान्यतो मनोः ॥ २
नवभिः सप्तभिः षड्भिः सप्तभिश्च तथाऽष्टभिः ।
सप्तभिर्मूलमन्त्रेण कुर्यादङ्गानि वर्णकैः ॥ ३
अङ्गुष्ठगुल्फजङ्घासु जानूरुकटिगुह्यके ।
सनाभिहृदयोरोजपार्श्वयुक्पृष्ठकेषु च ॥ ४
स्कन्धयोरुभयोर्मध्ये बाहुमूलोपबाहुषु ।
प्रकूर्परप्रकोष्ठेषु मणिबन्धतलेषु च ॥ ५
मुखनासाक्षिकर्णेषु मस्तमस्तिष्कमूर्धसु ।
विन्यसेदक्षरान्मन्त्री क्रमान्मन्त्रसमुद्भवान् ॥ ६
शिखाललाटदृक्कर्णयुगोष्ठरसनासु च ।
सकण्ठबाहुहृत्कुक्षिकटिगुह्योरुजानुषु ॥ ७
जङ्घाचरणयोर्न्यस्येत् पदानि त्रिष्टुभः सुधीः ।
इति विन्यस्तदेहस्तु कुर्याज्जप्यादिकाः क्रियाः ॥ ८

उद्यद्विद्युत्करालाकुलहरिगलसंस्थाऽरिशङ्खासिखेटे-
ष्विष्वासाख्यत्रिशूलानरिगणभयदां तर्जनीञ्चाऽऽदधाना ।
चर्मास्युद्दृप्तूर्णदोर्भिः प्रहरणनिपुणाभिर्वृता कन्यकाभि-
र्दद्यात्काशानवीष्टांस्त्रिनयनलसिता चापि कात्यायनी वः ॥ ९

सावित्र्या विधानमभिधाय आग्नेय्या विधानं वक्तुमारभते—अथ वक्ष्यामीति ।
[मन्त्रोऽयमृग्वेदोक्तः प्रसिद्धः तेनाऽत्र नोक्तः] ॥ १ ॥ २ ॥ ३ ॥ ४ ॥ ५ ॥

अक्षरान्मन्त्रीति । प्रणवशक्त्यादिपूर्वकानित्यर्थः । सुधीरित्यपि तथा । रं बीजम् । क्लीं शक्तिः ॥ ६ ॥ ७ ॥ ८ ॥ ९ ॥

दीक्षा प्रवर्त्यते पूर्वं यथावद्देशिकोत्तमैः ।
ततोऽस्त्रक्लृप्तिः सम्प्रोक्ता स्यात्प्रयोगविधिस्ततः ॥ १०
दीक्षकाख्याक्षराख्यादौ शक्त्यावेष्ट्य ततो बहिः ।
यन्त्रं षड्गुणितं कृत्वा दुर्वर्णलसितास्त्रकम् ॥ ११
बहिरष्टदलं पद्मं प्रोक्तलक्षणलक्षितम् ।
अत्र पीठं यजेन्मन्त्री क्रमात् सनवशक्तिकम् ॥ १२
जया सविजया भद्रा भद्रकाली सुदुर्मुखी ।
व्याघ्रसिंहमुखी दुर्गा त्रिष्टुभो नव शक्तयः ॥ १३
तत्राधाय घटं गव्यक्वाथमूत्रपयोऽम्भसाम् ।
एकेन पूरणं कृत्वा आवाह्य च विभावसुम् ॥ १४
आवृतेर्बहिरग्न्यादिपादाष्टकविनिःसृताः ।
मूर्तीरभ्यर्चयेदग्नेर्जातवेदादिकाः क्रमात् ॥ १५
पृथिव्यम्बुनलेरानप्यात्मनेपदसंयुतान् ।
अर्चयेद्दिक्षु कोणेषु निवृत्त्यादीर्यथाक्रमम् ॥ १६
दिक्ष्वेकादशसंख्याः स्युर्जार्णाद्या वर्णशक्तयः ।
लोकपालांश्च तद्बहिर्विधिनेति समर्चयेत् ॥ १७
जाग[ग्र]ता तपनी वेदगर्भा दहनरूपिणी ।
सेन्दुखण्डा शुम्भहन्त्री सनभश्चारिणी तथा ॥ १८
वागीश्वरी मदवहा सोमरूपा मनोजवा ।
मरुद्वेगा रात्रिसंज्ञा तीव्रकोपा यशोवती ॥ १९
तोयात्मिका तथा नित्या दयावत्यपि हारिणी ।
तिरस्क्रिया वेदमाता तथाऽन्या दमनप्रिया ॥ २०

यथावदिति । योजनान्तमित्यर्थः । अस्त्रक्लृप्तिः भविष्यतीति ॥ १० ॥

दीक्षकाख्येति । मध्यशक्तावाख्यादिकं लिखेदित्यर्थः । शक्त्येति । त्रिष्टुभेत्यर्थः ।
यजेन्मन्त्रीति । प्रणवशक्त्यादित्वं मन्त्राणामुक्तम् ॥ ११॥१२॥१३॥१४॥१५॥१६॥

वर्णशक्तीनां स्वाद्याक्षराद्यत्वमाह—जार्णाद्या इति । जाद्यर्णाद्या इत्यर्थः ।
[एकादशेति प्रतिदिशमेकादशेत्यर्थः] ॥ १७ ॥

षष्ठरशक्तीराह - जागता इति ॥१८ ॥ १९ ॥ २० ॥ २१ ॥ २२ ॥ २३ ॥

समाराध्या नन्दिनी च परा रिपुविमर्दिनी ।
षष्ठी च दण्डिनी तिग्मा दुर्गा गायत्रिसंज्ञिका ॥ २१
निरवद्या विशालाक्षी श्वासोद्वाहा च नादिनी ।
वेदना वह्निगर्भा च सिंहवाहाह्वया तथा ॥ २२
धुर्या दुर्विषहा चैव रिरंसा तापहारिणी ।
त्यक्तदोषा निःसपत्ना चत्वारिंशच्चतुर्युताः ॥ २३
अभिषिच्य पुनः शिष्यं कुम्भादीन् गुरुराहरेत् ।
ईदृशं यन्त्रमारुह्य जपेच्छिष्यः सुयन्त्रितः ॥ २४
मन्त्राक्षरसहस्रन्तु सिद्ध्यर्थं गुरुसन्निधौ ।
सर्वजापेषु चाग्नेय्या गायत्र्या द्विगुणो जपः ॥ २५
कर्तव्यो वाञ्छितावाप्त्यै रक्षायै कार्यसिद्धये ।
तिलराज्यनलक्षीरवृक्षेध्महविराज्यकैः ॥ २६
सर्पिःसिक्तैः क्रमाद्धोमः साधयेदीप्सितं नृणाम् ।
चत्वारि चत्वारिंशच्च चतुःशतसमन्वितम् ॥ २७
चतुःसहस्रसंयुक्तं प्रोक्तैर्द्रव्यैर्हुतक्रिया ।
एवं संसिद्धमन्त्रस्य स्युरस्त्राद्याः क्रिया मताः ॥ २८
चत्वारि चत्वारिंशच्च वर्णानामस्त्रमिष्यते ।
विलोमपाठो वर्णानामस्त्रमाहुर्मनीषिणः ॥ २९
पादाष्टकमिदं विद्यात्ततोऽष्टाङ्गो मनुस्त्वयम् ।
जप्तुकामो मनुन्त्वेनं पादांस्तु प्रतिलोमतः ॥ ३०
जपेत्तथा हि मन्त्रोऽयं चाल्यते दुष्टदूषितः ।
आद्याः पञ्चाक्षराः पादास्त्रयः सप्ताक्षरः परः ॥ ३१
पञ्चमश्चाऽथ षष्ठश्च द्वौ तु पादौ षडक्षरौ ।
पञ्चाक्षरौ तदन्त्यौ च तेषां भावो निगद्यते ॥ ३२

ईदृशमिति उक्तपूजायन्त्रग्रहणं कृतम् ॥ २४ ॥ २५ ॥ २६ ॥ २७ ॥ २८ ॥ २९ ॥

अष्टाङ्गो मनुस्त्विति । अष्टमूर्तिभिः सहाऽष्टपादन्यासः सूचितः । त्रिस्त्वेत्यारभ्य पादाक्षरगणना ।

तेषां भाव इत्यादिना तत्त्वन्यासं सूचयति । भावो याथात्म्यम् ॥३०॥३१॥३२॥

आ[ग्न्या]द्यं ज्ञानेन्द्रियं कामं द्वितीयं पाञ्चभौतिकम् ।
तृतीयं धातवः सप्त चतुर्थं वर्णसप्तकम् ॥ ३३

षडूर्मयः पञ्चमं स्यात् षष्ठः षाट्कौशिको मतः ।
सप्तमश्चाऽष्टमः पादः शब्दाद्यं वचनादिकम् ॥ ३४

साङ्गः सप्रतिपत्तिकः सगुरुपद्द्वन्द्वप्रणामक्रियो
जाप्योऽत्यादिषदन्तकोऽन्तविगतो वर्णप्रतीपस्तथा ।
गुर्वादेशविधानतश्च विधिवद्ध्यातो मनुर्मन्त्रिणा
तत्तत्कार्यसमाप्तयेऽखिलविपद्ध्वान्तौघभानूदयः ॥ ३५

अनुलोमजपेऽङ्गानामपि पाठोऽनुलोमकः ।
प्रतिलोमानि तानि स्युः प्रतिलोमविधौ तथा ॥ ३६

अन्तपादप्रतीपे हि तथा तानि भवन्ति हि ।
वर्णप्रतीपे हि तथा मात्रा च प्रतिलोमगा ॥ ३७

प्रतिपत्तिविशेषांश्च तत्र तत्र विचक्षणः ।
गुर्वादेशविधानेन प्रविद्ध्यान्न चाऽन्यथा ॥ ३८

आद्यपादत्रयं देव्या हैरण्यगर्भरूपार्थः। चतुर्थो देव्या वैराजरूपार्थः। तत्र धातुशब्देन पञ्चीकृतभूतानि तदनुगतनामरूपे चोक्ते। अवशिष्टपादचतुष्कं देव्येच्छया गृहीतव्यष्टिशरीरगतं तत्त्वजातम्।

पत्तिपरेशजीवप्रकृतितत्त्वानि क्लीं ह्रीं च्रौं टुभिः सह व्यापकत्वेन प्रथमत एव न्यस्तव्यानि ॥ ३३ ॥ ३४ ॥

अतिदुर्गापदपादवर्णप्रतिलोमानां जपे नियममाह—साङ्ग इति। प्रतिपत्तिरुत्तरत्र रक्तकर्मणि वक्ष्यमाणानामेका। अथवा उक्तैव अष्टभुजाऽतिक्रूरा ध्येया। सहस्रभुजा सहस्रनयना वा। प्रतिजपं देवतारूपो गुरुर्मनसा नमस्कार्य इत्याह—सगुरुपदिति। अत्यादिषदन्तकः अतिदुर्गा। अन्तविगतः अवसानादारभ्य विलोमेन गतः। पदपादप्रतिलोमावित्यर्थः। वर्णप्रतिलोमानां पृथग्ग्रहणात्। वक्ष्यमाणप्रयोगः प्रतिपत्तयश्च गुर्वादेशेनैव ज्ञातव्या इत्याह—गुर्वादेशेति। मन्त्रिणेति। तत्तत्कर्मोचितबीजादियोग उक्तः ॥ ३५ ॥

साङ्ग इत्युक्तमङ्गभेदमाह—अनुलोमेति। वर्णपदन्यासयोरपि समानोऽयं न्यासः। सकृत्प्रतिषेधमात्रेणाऽकार्यान्मन्दान्न निवर्तयितुं शक्य इति पुनरप्याह—प्रतिपत्तीति ॥ ३६ ॥ ३७ ॥ ३८ ॥

जपः पुरोक्तसंख्यः स्याद्हुतकॢप्तिस्तथा भवेत् ।
क्षीरवृक्षसमिद्द्राजीतिलहव्यघृतैः क्रमात् ॥ ३९
अथवा पञ्चगव्योत्थचरुणा हुतमुच्यते ।
प्रत्यङ्मुखेन कर्तव्यं प्रायोजपहुतादिकम् ॥ ४०
ततः स्युर्मन्त्रवर्णेभ्यस्तावत्यो वह्निदेवताः ।
प्रत्येकमावृतास्तास्तु पञ्चकेन नतभ्रुवाम् ॥ ४१
तत्पञ्चकञ्च प्रत्येकमावृतं पञ्चभिः पृथक् ।
प्रत्येकं पञ्चकानाञ्च षोड़शावृतिरिष्यते ॥ ४२
प्रत्येकं षोड़शानाञ्च कोटयः परिचारिकाः ।
इत्येकाक्षरजात् पूर्वादिकस्मात् षोड़शात्मकात् ॥ ४३
एतावत्यस्तु जातास्तद्विस्तारं पुनरूहयेत् ।
तत्र त्विन्द्रियजाः प्रोक्ता देवतास्तूर्ध्वदृष्टयः ॥ ४४
तिर्यञ्चो भौतिकाः प्रोक्ता धातूत्थास्तूभयाननाः ।
ऊर्मिजास्तूर्ध्ववदनास्तिर्यञ्चश्चाऽथ कोशजाः ॥ ४५

प्रतिलोममन्त्रस्य पृथक्साधनं कर्तव्यमित्याह—जपः पुरोक्तसंख्य इति। प्रायोजपहुतादिकं प्रतिलोमजपहुतादिकमित्यर्थः ॥ ३९ ॥ ४० ॥

प्रयोगार्थं मन्त्रवर्णदेवताव्याप्तिमाह—तत इति। सिद्धमन्त्रस्य सृत्यनन्तरमित्यर्थः। सर्वासां वर्णशक्तीनां पञ्चभूतात्मकत्वात् पञ्चकेनावृता इति उक्तम्। तासामपि पञ्चभूतात्मकत्वात् आह—तत्पञ्चकमिति। तासामपि भूतगतशब्दादिगुणभेदेन कारणसहितेन षोड़शधा भेदमाह—प्रत्येकमिति। कोटिभेदोऽपि शब्दादिवैचित्र्यादेव ज्ञातव्यः ॥ ४१ ॥ ४२ ॥ ४३ ॥

उक्तां विभूतिमनूद्य विभूत्यन्तरमाह—इत्येकाक्षरजादिति। इति इत्थम्। एकाक्षरजात् पञ्चकात् पूर्वं पूर्वं जातात् प्रत्येकं पञ्चकपरिवृतात् पुनरप्येकैकस्मात् षोड़शात्मकादेतावत्यो विभूतयो जाता इत्यर्थः। तद्विस्तारं पुनरूहयेदित्यस्याऽयमर्थः। कोटीनां मध्ये एकैकस्या पञ्चकोटयः परिचारिकाः। तासामेकैकस्याः पुनः पञ्च कोटयः। तासामेकैकस्याः षोड़शकोटयः। तासामेकैकस्याः कोटिकोटयः। इत्यादिप्रकारेणोहयेदिति ॥ ४३ ॥ ४४ ॥

इन्द्रियजानामूर्ध्वदृष्टित्वं केवलसमष्टिजत्वेन। प्रत्यङ्मुखत्वात् तिर्यञ्चः।

क्लीबा मुखद्वयोपेता गोचरोत्थाः स्त्रियो मताः ।
अधोमुखाश्च तिर्यञ्च इत्युक्तो मूर्तिसंग्रहः ॥ ४६

आभिः सर्वाभिरपि च शिखाभिर्जातवेदसः ।
व्याप्यते परराष्ट्रेषु वृक्षगुल्मलतादिकम् ॥ ४७

आरम्भे मानुषाणि स्युर्नक्षत्राण्याभिचारिणि ।
कर्मण्यासुरभानि स्युर्दैवानि स्युस्तथा हृतौ ॥ ४८

अन्त्याश्वीन्द्वर्कादितिगुरुहरिमित्रानिलाह्वया दैवाः ।
पूर्वोत्तरत्रयीयमहरविधयो मानुषाः परेऽसुरभाः ॥ ४९

नन्दास्वारभ्य रिक्तासु प्रयोज्याऽऽत्मनि संहरेत् ।
भद्रासु संग्रहं कुर्याज्जयासु तु विशेषतः ॥ ५०

आरेणारभ्य मन्देन प्रयोज्याऽऽदित्यवारके ।
संहरेत् संग्रहं कुर्याद्वारे त्वाचार्ययोः सुधीः ॥ ५१

चरैर्विसृज्योभयकैराहरेदभ्यसेत् स्थिरैः ।
दिनास्त्रं दिनकृद्युक्तं वारग्रहसमन्वितम् ॥ ५२

वराहसिंहादिवदना इत्यर्थः । उभयानना इति । द्विवदना ऊर्ध्वाधोमुखाश्चेत्यर्थः । पञ्चीकृतत्वेनोभयात्मकत्वात् तासाम् । ऊर्मिजानामूर्ध्ववदनत्वम् । तासामध्यात्म-स्थूलसूक्ष्मकारणसमष्टिरूपत्वेन विवचितत्वात् । तिर्यक्त्वं पूर्ववत् कोशजानाम् । क्लीबत्वं स्त्रीपुरुषमिश्रात्मकत्वात् । गोचरोत्थानां स्त्रीत्वं प्रकृतिप्रधानत्वात् । अधोमुखत्वं बहिर्मुख्यप्राधान्यात् ॥ ४४ ॥ ४५ ॥ ४६ ॥

प्रयोगे प्रतिपत्तिमाह—आभिरिति ॥ ४७ ॥ ४८ ॥ ४९ ॥ ५० ॥ ५१ ॥

[राशीनपि विदधाति—चरैरिति राशिभिः । इति दीपिकाकारः ।]

दिनास्त्रमिति । प्रतिदुर्गादिनास्त्रमेकादशाक्षरं च । दिनकृद्युक्तमिति । दिनकृच्छब्दो द्वादशसंख्यालक्षकः प्राणबुद्धिसहितेन्द्रियदशकयुतमन्त्र इत्यर्थः । आद्यन्तयोः द्वादशादित्यनामयुक्तमिति चाऽर्थः । आदित्यगतदेवताध्यानयुक्तमिति चाऽर्थः । वारग्रहसमन्वितमाद्यन्तयोर्वाराभिमानिग्रहनामभिः समन्वितमन्ते वार्यस्यावरणीयस्य ग्रहेण ग्रहणेन नाम्ना समन्वितं चादित्यमण्डलस्थादिभिः प्रधानाकाराभिर्वारग्रहाभिमानिदेवताभिः षट्कोणस्थाभिः समन्वितमिति त्रिधा योज्यम् ॥ ५२ ॥

कृत्तिकादि च कृत्यान्तं कृत्यास्त्रं जातवेदसः ।
नक्षत्रात्मा हुताशः स्यात्तिथ्यात्मेन्दुरुदाहृतः ॥ ५३

कृत्तिकादि चेति । युक्तमिति पदमत्रापि योज्यम् । कृत्तिकादि चादि च कृत्तिकादि । कृत्तिकादिशब्देन सप्तविंशतिनक्षत्राणि उक्तानि कृत्तिकादीनि । आदिशब्देन प्रथमाद्वितीयेत्यादि तिथिपञ्चदशकमुक्तम् । तदेव द्वयमाद्यन्तयोः युक्तमिति कृत्तिकादि चेत्यस्यैकोऽर्थः ।

कृत्तिका त्वक् । त्वक् च तदादि च कृत्तिकादि । इन्द्रियगणात् पूर्वं त्वगादि-धात्वष्टकयुक्तमित्यर्थः । कृत्यान्तं कृत्यावसानम् । साध्यनामान्ते मारय मारय दह दहेति वा क्रियायुक्तमित्यर्थः ।

कृत्तिका कुण्डलिनी तदादि च । कृत्यान्तं कृत्यापि कुण्डलिनी तदन्तं च दिनास्त्रम् । सर्पज्वालायुधादिरूपिणीं कुण्डलिनीमुत्थाप्य साध्यं ग्रसित्वा कुण्डलिन्यग्नावानीय दाहान्तं दिनास्त्रमध्यात्मप्रयोग इत्यर्थः ।

कृत्यास्त्रं जातवेदसः । कृत्यास्त्रं नाम प्रतिलोमास्त्रं पञ्चदशाक्षरं च । अतिदुर्गाप्रतिलोमास्त्रमेवेति केचित् । तदप्येवमेव प्रयोक्तव्यमिति शेषः ।

प्रयोगप्रकारं मन्त्रविशेषं चाह—नक्षत्रात्मा हुताशः स्यादिति । नक्षत्राणा-मात्मा आधारभूतः हुताशः स्यात् । द्वादशादित्य सप्तग्रह तिथीनामुपलक्षणं नक्षत्रग्रहणम् । आदित्यादीनां ग्रहणम् । आदित्य ग्रह नक्षत्र तिथीनामस्त्राद्यन्त-योः चतुर्थीसम्बुद्ध्यन्ततया स्थितानामादौ चतुर्थीसम्बुद्ध्यन्तः अग्निशब्दः प्रयोक्तव्य इत्यर्थः ।

अथाऽन्योऽर्थः । नक्षत्रादय आत्मा आधारो यस्य हुताशस्याऽनुलोमत्रिष्टुभः स तथोक्तः । चतुर्थ्यन्तनक्षत्रादीनामन्तेऽनुलोममन्त्रः प्रयोक्तव्य इत्यर्थः ।

अथाऽन्योऽर्थः । नक्षत्रात्मा सप्तविंशत्यात्मा हुताशः अग्निमन्त्रः स्यात् । अमुष्य त्वचं दह दहेत्यादिकृत्यान्ते रं रं रमित्याद्यग्निमन्त्रः सप्तविंशतिवारमा-वर्तनीयः इत्यर्थः ।

अन्योऽर्थः । नक्षत्रात्मा सप्तविंशतिज्वालारूपः हुताशः कुण्डल्यात्मा हुताश-मन्त्रोऽध्यात्मप्रयोगे ध्येयः । अधिदैवतप्रयोगे सप्तविंशत्यादित्यात्मा इति विशेषः ।

तिथ्यात्मेन्दुरुदाहृत इत्यनेनाऽस्त्रोपसंहारसमये मन्त्रविशेषं प्रतिपत्तिविशेषं चाह । अत्रापि तिथिग्रहणमुपलक्षणार्थम् आदित्यादीनां तिथ्यादीनामात्मा इन्दुः सोमः । चतुर्थीसम्बुद्ध्यन्तादित्य ग्रह नक्षत्र तिथीनामादौ तथाविधः सोमशब्दः प्रयोक्तव्य इत्यर्थः ।

ताभ्यां करोति दिनकृद्विसर्गादानकर्मणी ।
इत्येष निपुणो मन्त्री प्रयोगादन्यथात्महा ॥ ५४

अन्योऽर्थः । तिथ्यादय आत्मा यस्य सोमस्याऽनुलोममन्त्रस्य स तथोक्तः । चतुर्थ्यन्तसोमशब्दान्ते अनुलोममन्त्रः प्रयोक्तव्य इत्यर्थः ।

अन्योऽर्थः । तिथ्यात्मा इन्दुः सौम्यत्वात् गायत्रीन्दुः । स तिथ्यात्मा पञ्चदशात्मा । उपसंहारविधौ प्रतिलोमजपाभावात् तत्स्थाने गायत्रीपञ्चदशकं जप्तव्यमित्यर्थः ।

अन्योऽर्थः । तिथ्यात्मा पञ्चदशात्मा इन्दुः सोममन्त्रः वं वं वं वं वं वं वे वं व वै वं व व वं व व इत्युदाहृतः । सम्बुद्ध्यन्ते तिथ्यादीनामनन्तरपठितानां मम त्वचं पूरय पूरय इत्यादीनामन्ते अमृतमन्त्रः पञ्चदशवारमावर्तनीय इत्यर्थः ।

अन्योऽर्थः । तिथ्यात्मा पञ्चदशात्मा अमृतधारात्मा इन्दुः । परकुण्डल्यमृतरूपो मन्त्रोऽध्यात्मप्रयोगे अधिदैवते पञ्चदशचन्द्रात्मा उदाहृत इति ॥ ५२ ॥

इदानीं प्रयोगप्रकारमाह—ताभ्यामिति । ताभ्यां हुताशेन्दुभ्यां नाड़ीद्वय वर्तिभ्यां करोति दिनकृत् । आदित्यात्मा साधकः मध्यनाडीप्रधानः स विसर्गादानकर्मणी दक्षिणमार्गेणाऽग्निरूपेणाऽग्निरूपाणां देवतानां विसर्गं कृत्वा ता विसृष्टा देवतास्तत्रैव साध्यप्रदेशे संस्थाप्य तन्मूलभूतं कुण्डल्यात्मकं तेजः केवलं तेनैव मार्गेण मूलाधारपर्यन्तमादत्ते । पुनः सोममन्त्रोच्चारणसमये वाममार्गेण मध्यमार्गेण चातिसौम्यतेजोरूपेण कुण्डलिनीं विसृज्य पूर्वविसृष्टदेवतासंख्याभिः अमृतधाराभिस्तासामाप्यायनं वामनाड़ीद्वारेण कृत्वा मध्यनाड़ीद्वारेणात्मनोऽप्याप्यायनं विधाय तामपि कुण्डलिनीं वामनाड़ीद्वारेण गतां तेनैव मार्गेण मूलाधार एवादत्ते । मध्यगतां तु तां तथैव स्थापयतीत्यर्थः । प्रणवान्ते अग्नये धात्रे इति उक्त्वा अनुलोमत्रिष्टुबन्तेन दुर्गतिं कलौहच्च सचस्त्र औ इति दिनास्त्रम् सं साये य साये ययं साये ययंसायया इति कृत्यास्त्रं वोक्त्वा अतिदुर्गाप्रतिलोमं वोच्चार्य अग्ने धातरमुष्य त्वचं दह दह रं ररं रररं रैं रररं ररं ररमित्यग्निमन्त्रं सप्तविंशतिवारमावर्तयेत् । इत्यादयः प्रयोगमन्त्राः । प्रणवान्ते सोमाय धात्र इत्यस्यान्ते अनुलोमत्रिष्टुभमुच्चार्य गायत्रीं पञ्चदशवारमावर्त्य सोम धातः अमुष्य त्वचं पूरय पूरय इत्याद्यन्ते अमृतमन्त्रमपि पञ्चदशवारं जपेदित्यादय आदानमन्त्राः । एते च धात्रु सूर्य कृत्तिकाप्रतिपदाद्येकषष्टिमन्त्राः प्रयोगादानयोः त्वगादिषु विंशतिषु प्रत्येकं प्रयोक्तव्याः । व्यस्तप्रयोगे । समस्तप्रयोगे तु धात्रादीनां त्वगादीनां च नामानि सकृदेवोच्चार्य एक एव मन्त्रः प्रयोक्तव्यः । निरपेक्षादानसमये त्वेकषष्टिरेव प्रयोक्तव्यः । आगच्छागच्छेति च तत्र क्रिया एकप्रयोगपक्षे

रक्षानिग्रहकर्मणोरनुपराग्वक्त्राः प्रधानाकृति-
प्रख्या मन्त्रविधानविच्च दिशि दिश्येकादशैकादश ।
संस्थाप्य क्रमशोऽक्षरोदितरुचोः शक्तीर्जपेद्वा मनुं
सम्यग्वा जुहुयादनु प्रतिगतं सिद्ध्यै समाराधयेत् ॥ ५५
पीताऽयोमुष्टिगदाहस्ता महिषाज्यसंयुतपुलाकैः ।
वैभीतकारिष्टसमित्कोद्रवकैः स्तम्भयेच्च हुतविधिना ॥ ५६
सुसिता पाशाङ्कुशयुग्विगलद्वारिप्रवाहसम्भिन्ना ।
वैतससमिदाहुत्या मधुरयुजा मङ्क्षु वशयेद्दुर्गा ॥ ५७
रक्ता पाशाङ्कुशिनी निशि फलिनीकेसरोद्भवैः पुष्पैः ।
चन्दनरससंसिक्तैर्होमाद्दुर्गा वशीकरोति जगत् ॥ ५८
लवणैस्त्रिमधुरसिक्तैस्तत्कृतया वा जुहोतु पुत्तल्या ।
उडुतरुकाष्ठैर्नक्तं सप्ताहान्नृपतिमपि वशे कुरुते ॥ ५९
सकपालशूलपाशाङ्कुशहस्ताऽरुणतरा तथा दुर्गा ।
आकर्षयेच्च लावणपुत्तल्या त्रिमधुराक्तया होमात् ॥ ६०
ध्यात्वा धूम्रां मुसलत्रिशिखकरामस्थिभिश्च तीक्ष्णाक्तैः ।
कार्पासानां निम्बच्छदमेषघृतैर्हुताच्च विद्वेषः ॥ ६१
धूम्रा तर्जनिशूलाहितहस्ता विषदलैः समाहिषाज्यैः ।
होमाच्च मरिचसर्षपचरुभिरजारुधिरसेचितैरटयेत् ॥ ६२
शिखिशूलकराऽग्निनिभा सर्षपतैलाक्तमत्तबीजैश्च ।
मरिचैर्वा राजियुतैर्होमादहितान् विमोहयेद्दुर्गा ॥ ६३

एकेनैवोपसंहारः ॥ ५४ ॥

अनुलोमप्रतिलोमयोः कार्यभेदध्यानभेदं चाह—रक्षेति । अनुपराग्वक्त्रा इति उभयोरपि रक्षानिग्रहकर्मणोः अनुपराग्वक्त्रत्वं ज्ञातव्यम् । मन्त्रविधानविदिति । रक्षायां चतुश्चत्वारिंशदनुलोमविधानवित् । निग्रहे चतुश्चत्वारिंशत्प्रतिलोमविधानविदित्यर्थः । मूलोक्तमेव सर्वत्र विधानं प्रतिलोमविधानेषु आवरणपूजादिकमपि प्रातिलोम्येन कार्यमिति विशेषः । अक्षरोदितरुचोरिति । रुचयः शक्तयः । चतुश्चत्वारिंशदक्षराणां यावत्यः शक्तय उक्ताः । तावच्छक्ति-विशिष्टा एकैकाक्षरशक्तय इत्यर्थः । चतुश्चत्वारिंशत्तत्त्वानि पादाष्टकविभूति-

कृष्णा शूलासिकरा रिपुदिनवृक्षोद्भवैः समित्प्रवरैः ।
व्रणकृद्दुष्घृतसंसिक्तैर्होमान्मारयति मासतो दुर्गा ॥ ६४
नक्षत्रवृक्षसमिधो मरिचानि च तीक्ष्णहिङ्गुशकलानि ।
मारणकर्मणि विहितान्यारुष्करस्नेहसिक्तानि ॥ ६५
नक्षत्रवृक्षसमिधां विलिखितसाध्याभिधानकर्मवताम् ।
सचतुश्चत्वारिंशत्तत्त्वयुजां होमकर्म मारणकरम् ॥ ६६
मरिचं क्षौद्रसमेतं प्रत्यक्पुष्पीपरागसम्भिन्नम् ।
उष्णाम्भःपरिलुलितं प्रसिचयेद्वृक्षवृक्षपुत्तल्या ॥ ६७
हृदये वदने च रिपोः सम्मुखतः संप्रतिष्ठिते वायोः ।
ऊर्ध्वमभिभूतोऽरिः स्यात्तत्क्वथनात् पक्षमात्रकान्म्रियते ॥ ६८
सैव प्रतिकृतिरसकृत्तत्प्रतिष्ठितसमीरणा च विशदधिया ।
तीक्ष्णस्नेहालिप्ता विलोमजापेन तापनीयाऽग्नौ ॥ ६९
विधिना ज्वरविद्धः स्यादपघनहोमेन हानिरङ्गस्य ।
सर्वाहुत्या मरणं प्राप्नोति रिपुर्न तत्र सन्देहः ॥ ७०

प्राक्प्रोक्तान् भूतवर्णान् दशदशयुगशो बिन्दुयुक्तान्नमोऽन्तान्
योनेमध्यास्त्रिमध्येष्वपि पुनरथ संस्थाप्य भूताभवर्णान् ।
वर्णैस्तैः साकमग्नेर्मनुमपि कुलिशाद्यैः स्वचिह्नैः समेतं
कुर्यात् कर्माणि सम्यक् पटुविशदमतिः स्तम्भनाद्यानि मन्त्री ॥

ऊदन्नादिललाः कोनसौचतुर्थार्णका वसौ वारः ।
दृष्टैर्द्वितीयरक्षा वह्नेरहन्दुयोनिकादियषाः ॥ ७२

कथनेन कथितानि तद्बुद्ध्या जुहुयादित्यर्थः ॥ ५५ ७० ॥

अग्नेर्मनुमपीति । त्रिष्टुभमपीत्यर्थः । स तु मध्ये लेखनीयः । कुलिशाद्यैरिति स्तम्भनाद्युचित पृथिव्यादिमण्डलैरित्यर्थः । मन्त्रीति । तत्तत्प्रयोगोचितानुलोमविलोममन्त्रज्ञ इत्यर्थः । पटुविशदमतिरिति । पूर्वोक्तध्यानविशेषेष्वायत्तमतिरित्यर्थः । अतिदुर्गाप्रतिलोमैश्च मारणोच्चाटन विद्वेषणस्तम्भन मोहनादीनि । गाणविश्वाग्निदुर्गाभिः वश्यम् अग्निदुर्गया आकर्षणं सोमसिन्धुदुर्गाभ्यां सौम्यप्रयोग इत्यादिमन्त्रविनियोगज्ञ इत्यथः ॥ ७१ ॥

मूर्तिवर्णानाह—ऊदिति ।

मरुतः कपोलबिन्दुकपञ्चमवर्णाः शष्टौ तथा व्योम्नः ।
मनुषु परेष्वपि मन्त्री करोतु कर्माणि तस्य संसिद्ध्यै ॥ ७३
उन्मत्तज्वलनैवद्रुमभवसमिधां सप्तसाहस्रकान्तं
प्रत्येकं राजितैलालुलितमथ हुनेन्माहिषाज्याप्लुतं वा ।
कृष्णाष्टम्याद्यमेवं मुनियतचरितः सप्तरात्रं निशायां
निःसन्देहोऽस्य शत्रुस्त्यजति किल निजं देहमाविष्टमोहः ॥ ७४
सामुद्रे च सहिङ्गुजीरकविषैः साध्यर्क्षवृक्षाकृतिं
कृत्वाऽधोवदनां जले घटकटाहादिस्थिते क्वाथयेत् ।
सप्ताहं ज्वलनं जपन् विषतरोर्यष्ट्या शिरस्ताड़नं
कुर्वन् सप्तदिनान्तरे यमपुरक्रीड़ापरः स्यादरिः ॥ ७५
चर्मस्यन्दनबद्धपन्नगमुखग्रस्ताङ्घ्रिमाशाम्बरं
न्यग्वक्त्रं तिलजाप्लुतं विषहतं दीप्तं करैर्भास्वतः ।
वायुप्रेरितवह्निमण्डलमहाज्वालाकुलास्यादिकं
ध्यायन् वैरिणमुत्क्षिपेत् जलममुं मन्त्रं जपन् मृत्यवे ॥ ७६
आर्द्रांशुकोऽग्निमनुना त्वथ सप्तरात्रं
सिद्धार्थतैललुलितैर्मरिचैर्जुहोतु ।
आरभ्य विष्टिदिवसेऽरिनरः प्रलाप-
मूर्च्छान्वितेन विषमीक्रियते ज्वरेण ॥ ७७

[भूतवर्णान् विभजते—जदद्गादीति सार्धेन । उकारश्च ऊकारश्च ऊ । दत् दन्ताक्षरः ओकारः । गादयो गजडदबाः । लकारलकारौ च । एते दश कोः पृथिव्या वर्णाः । नसोः नासिकापुटयोरक्षरे ऋकारऋकारौ । औकारश्च । चतुर्थार्णकाः घझढधभाः । वकारसकारौ च । इत्येते दश वारः जलस्य वर्णाः । दृश्योरक्षरे इकारईकारौ । ऐकारश्च । द्वितीयाः खछठथफाः । रेफक्षकारौ च । एते दश अग्निवर्णाः । अहन्दमिति । अकारआकारौ । योनिरेकारः । कादयः कचटतपाः । यकारषकारौ च । इत्येतानि दश वायोरक्षराणि । कपोलयोरक्षरे लृकारलॄकारौ च । बिन्दुः पञ्चदशस्वरः । ङञणनमाः शकारहकारौ च । इत्येते दश आकाशस्य वर्णा इत्यर्थः । अयं विधिः सर्वमन्त्रसाधारण इति ब्रूते—मनुषु परेष्विति । इति सम्प्रदायदीपिकाकारः]।

मन्त्री करोत्विति । तत्सम्प्रदायोग इत्युक्तः ॥ ७२—८० ॥

तालस्य पत्रे भुजपत्रके वा
मध्ये लिखेत् साध्यनराभिधानम् ।
अथाऽभितो मन्त्रमिमं विलोमं
विलिख्य भूमौ विनिखन्य तत्र ॥ ७८

आधाय वैश्वानरमादरेण समर्च्य सम्यङ्मरिचैर्जुहोतु ।
तीव्रो ज्वरस्तस्य भवेत् पुनस्तत्तोये क्षिपेद्वश्यतमः स भूयात् ॥ ७९

सिंहस्थां शरनिकरैः कृशानुवक्त्रै-
र्धावन्तीं रिपुमनु धावमानमेनाम् ।
संचिन्त्य क्षिपतु जलं दिनेशबिम्बे
जप्त्वाऽमुं मनुमपि चाटनाय शीघ्रम् ॥ ८०

कृत्वा स्थण्डिलमङ्गणे भगवतीं न्यासक्रमादर्चयेद्-
गन्धाद्यैः पुनरम्भसा च विकिरेन्मन्त्री निशायां बलिम् ।
जप्त्वा मन्त्रममुञ्च रोगसहिताः कृत्या निकृत्या कृता-
स्तांस्तान् भूतपिशाचवैरिविहितान् दुःखानसौ नाशयेत् ॥ ८१

विधिवदभिज्वाल्याऽनलमन्वहमाराध्य गन्धपुष्पाद्यैः ।
सन्ध्यासु जपाच्च मनुरयमाकाङ्क्षितसर्वसिद्धिकल्पतरुः ॥ ८२

कुसुमरसलुलितलोणैर्वारुणवदनो जुहोतु सन्ध्यासु ।
मन्त्रार्णसंख्यमग्नेरैक्येन द्रावयेदरीनचिरात् ॥ ८३

शुद्धैश्च तण्डुलैरथ हविरपि निष्पाद्य पञ्चगव्यमपि ।
सघृतेन तेन जुहुयादष्टसहस्रं समेतसम्पातम् ॥ ८४

प्राशितसम्पातस्य स्याद्रक्षा सर्वथैव साध्यस्य ।
प्राङ्गणमन्दिरयोरपि निखनेत् द्वारेऽवशिष्टसम्पातम् ॥ ८५

कृत्या नश्यति तस्य वीक्षितेन ग्रहादयो भीत्या ।
कर्त्तारमेति कुपिता कृत्या सर्वात्मना च नाशयति ॥ ८६

ब्रह्मद्रुमफलकान्ते मन्त्रितमः सप्तसप्तकोष्ठयुते ।
कोणोदराणि हित्वा मायाबीजं सकामं मध्यगते ॥ ८७

मन्त्री निशायामिति । पञ्चदुर्गादिभिः बलिदानमुक्तम् ॥ ८१—८६ ॥

मन्त्रितमः सप्तेति । सर्वकोष्ठेषु मायाबीजलेखनमुक्तम् ॥ ८७—९४ ॥

विलिखेत् क्रमेण मन्त्राक्षरांश्च शिष्टेषु तेषु कोष्ठेषु ।
तत्र मरुतः प्रतिष्ठां विधाय निधाय वह्निमपि जुहुयात् ॥ ८८
आज्येनाऽष्टसहस्रं फलकोपरि सम्यगात्तसम्पातम् ।
विप्रतिपत्तिधरायां निखनेन्नश्यन्त्युपद्रवाः सद्यः ॥ ८९
सिकताचरुगव्याश्मकमृदां प्रतिष्ठा विधीयते सिद्ध्यै ।
प्रस्थाढकघटमाना गृहपुरराष्ट्राभिगुप्तये सिकताः ॥ ९०
मध्येऽष्टाशान्तासु च कुण्डानामारचय्य नवकमपि ।
विधिना निवपेत् क्रमशः सिंहधनुष्काणगयायिनि दिनेशे ॥ ९१
तिथिषु तु कालाष्टम्यां भेषु विशाखाग्निमूलभाग्ये[गे]षु ।
वारेषु मन्दवाक्पतिवर्ज्याः सर्वे प्रशस्यन्ते तथा ॥ ९२
हस्तश्रवणमघासु प्राजापत्ये च कर्म कुर्वीत ।
द्वादशसहस्रसंख्यं प्रजपेद्गायत्रमपि यथा प्रोक्तम् ॥ ९३
मध्ये च मूलमनुना तदायुधैरष्टदिक्षु चक्राद्यैः ।
सकपालान्तैः पृथगपि संस्थापनकर्म निगदितं विधिवत् ॥ ९४
तास्ताश्च देवता अपि परिपूज्य यथाक्रमेण मन्त्रितमः ।
कुर्याद्बलिं दिनग्रहकरणेभ्यो लोकपालराशिभ्यः ॥ ९५
सिकताषोड़शकुड़वं ब्रह्मद्रुमभाजनेऽन्नगव्याक्तम् ।
निर्वपति यदि विधिना तं देशं ग्रामं करोति चतुरब्दात् ॥ ९६
अर्केऽजस्थेऽब्धिगायामपरिमितजलायां समादाय शुद्धाः
सम्यक् संशोषयित्वातपमनु सिकताः शूर्पकोणैर्विशोध्य ।
संशुद्धे पञ्चगव्ये सुमतिरथ विनिःक्षिप्य ताः कुम्भसंस्था
मन्त्राग्नौ मन्त्रजापी द्विजतरुसमिधा भर्जयेत् कार्यहेतोः ॥ ९७
एवं मृदुपलयोरधः संस्थाप्यन्ते सपञ्चगव्यास्ताः ।
वसुधाविप्रतिपत्तिक्षयञ्च पुष्टिञ्च कुर्वते क्रमशः ॥ ९८

यथाक्रमेण मन्त्रितम इति । चक्रादिमन्त्रैः पूजनं सूचितम् । ग्रहादि-बलिमन्त्राश्च सूचिताः ॥ ८५ ॥ ८६ ॥

सिकतोपादानशोधनसंस्कारक्रममाह —अर्केऽजस्थ इति । सुमतिरिति । अग्निमन्त्रदेवतासिकतानामैक्यञ्च इत्यर्थः ॥ ८७ ॥ ८८ ॥ ८९ ॥ १०० ॥ १०१ ॥

रथचरणदरगदाम्बुजहस्ता निष्टप्तशातकुम्भनिभा ।
सघृतपयोऽन्धोहोमान्महतीं लक्ष्मीं समावहेद्दुर्गा ॥ ९९
व्रीहिभिरन्नैः क्षीरैः समिद्भिरपि दुग्धवीरुधामाज्यैः ।
मधुरत्रयमधुरैर्महतीमृद्धिं करोति हुतविधिना ॥ १००
यद्यद्वाञ्छति पुरुषस्तत्तदमुष्य प्रभावतः साध्यम् ।
सग्रहनक्षत्राढ्यां सगिरिपुरग्रामकाननां वसुधाम् ।
साब्धिझषोपलमुदधिं दहति हि मतिमानयत्नमेतेन ॥ १०१
एवं प्रोत्थापयति च मन्त्रेणाऽनेन निशितधीर्मन्त्री ।
पुंसा केन कियद्वा मन्त्रस्याख्यायतेऽस्य सामर्थ्यम् ॥ १०२

तस्मादेनं मनुवरमभीष्टाप्तये संयतात्मा
जप्यान्नित्यं सहुतविधिमप्यादरादर्चयीत ।
भक्त्या कुर्यात् सुमतिरभिषिकादिकं कर्मजातं
कर्तुं वाऽन्यत् प्रवणमतिरत्रैव भक्तः सदा स्यात् ॥ १०३

इति श्रीप्रपञ्चसारे एकत्रिंशः पटलः ।

निशितधीर्मन्त्रीति । पूर्वोक्तास्त्रप्रयोगध्यानज्ञताऽस्त्रमन्त्रप्रयोगज्ञता चोक्ता । ॥ १०२ ॥ १०३ ॥

इति श्रीपद्मपादाचार्यकृते प्रपञ्चसारविवरणे
एकत्रिंशत्पटलः ।

द्वाविंशः पटलः ।

अथ लवणमनुं वदामि साङ्गं सजपं सप्रतिपत्तिकं सहोमम् ।
विधिवद्विहितेन येन सर्वां जगतीमात्मवशे करोति मन्त्री ॥ १

लवणाम्भसि चेत्याद्या द्वितीया लवणेति च ।
दहेति तृतीया स्यात्तं दग्ध्वेति च चतुर्थ्यपि ।
ऋक् पञ्चमी च या ते स्याद्यथा प्रोक्तमथर्वणि ॥ २
ऋग्भिराभिस्तु पञ्चाङ्गं पञ्चभिर्वा समीरितम् ।
विद्याक्षरैः षडङ्गं वा प्रणवाद्यैर्निगद्यते ॥ ३
पञ्चभिश्च त्रिभिरपि पञ्चभिः करणाक्षरैः ।
सपञ्चभिर्युगार्णेन जातियुक्तैः समीरितम् ॥ ४
अङ्गिराः स्यादृषिश्छन्दोऽनुष्टुप्त्रिष्टुप् च देवताः ।
अग्नीरात्रिस्तथा दुर्गा भद्रकाली समीरिताः ॥ ५

अथाऽग्निदुर्गादिदैवत्यस्य लवणमन्त्रस्य विधानमाह—अथ लवणेति । करोति मन्त्रीति । चिटिमन्त्रवानित्यर्थः । तारपाशशक्त्यङ्कुश यं लं वं इति उक्त्वा लवणाम्भसि तीक्ष्णोऽसि उग्रोऽसि हृदयं तव लवणस्य पृथिवी माताऽस्ते लवणस्य वरुणः पिता । प्रथमा । लवणे हूयमाने तु पुनः कुतो निद्रा कुतो रतिः । लवणं पचति पाचयति । लवणं छिन्दति भिन्दति अमुकस्य दह गात्राणि दह मांसं दह त्वचम् । द्वितीया । दह त्वगसृङ्मांसमेदोऽस्थिभ्यो मज्जिकां दह यदि वसति योजनशते नदीनां वा शतान्तरे । तृतीया । तं दग्ध्वा नय मे शीघ्रमग्रे लवणस्य तेजसा लोहप्राकारे नगरे कृष्णसर्पद्वतार्गले अत्रैव वशमायातु । लवणमन्त्रपुरस्कृतः । चतुर्थी ।

या ते रात्रिः शल्यविद्धस्य शूलाग्रारोपितस्य च ।
या ते रात्रिर्महारात्रिः सा ते रात्रिर्महानिशा ॥ इति पञ्चमी ।

क्रों बीजम् । क्रीं शक्तिः ।

ॐ आं क्रीं क्रों चिटि चिटि चण्डालि महाचण्डालि अमुकं मे वशमानय स्वाहा । इति चिटिमन्त्रः । लवणवदेव बीजादिकमस्यापि ॥ १ ॥ २ ॥ ३ ॥ ॥ ४ ॥ ५ ॥ ६ ॥ ७ ॥ ८ ॥ ९ ॥

अरुणोऽरुणपङ्कजसन्निभः सुवशक्तिवराभययुक्तकरः ।
अमिताचिंरजात्तगतिर्विलसन्नयनत्रितयोऽवतु वो दहनः ॥ ६
नीलतरांशुककेशकलापा नीलतनुर्निविडस्तनभारा ।
साङ्कुशपाशसशूलकपाला यामवती भवतोऽवतु नित्यम् ॥ ७
करकमलविराजच्चक्रशङ्खासिशूला
परिलसितकिरीटा पातितानेकदैत्या ।
त्रिनयनलसिताङ्गी तिग्मरश्मिप्रकाशा
पवनसखनिभाङ्गी पातु कात्यायनी वः ॥ ८
सुरौद्रसितदंष्ट्रिका त्रिनयनोर्ध्वकेशोल्वणा
कपालपरशूलसड्डमरुकत्रिशूलाकुला ।
घनाघननिभा रणद्रुचिरकिङ्किणीमालिका
भवद्विभवसिद्धये भवतु भद्रकाली चिरम् ॥ ९
अयुतं नियतो मन्त्री मन्त्रमृक्पञ्चकान्वितम् ।
प्रजपेत्त्रिसहस्रं वा सम्यगेनं समाहितः ॥ १०
दशांशेन हुनेत्सिद्ध्यै हविषा घृतसंयुजा ।
एवं कृते प्रयोगार्हो मन्त्रो भूयान्न चाऽन्यथा ॥ ११
वह्निराची वरे स्यातां वश्याकर्षणकर्मणोः ।
दुर्गाभद्रे तथा देव्यौ शस्ते मारणकर्मणि ॥ १२
आरभ्य कर्मकृन्मन्त्री तृतीयां कृष्णपक्षजाम् ।
संदीक्षितो भवेत्पूते मन्दिरे मन्त्रजापवान् ॥ १३
निखन्यात्तत्र कुण्डञ्च दोर्मात्रं त्र्यस्रमेखलम् ।
चतुष्कं सुन्दराकारं पुत्तलीनाञ्च कारयेत् ॥ १४
एकां साध्यर्क्षवृक्षेण शालीपिष्टेन चाऽपराम् ।
चक्रिहस्तमृदा चाऽन्यां मधूच्छिष्टेन चाऽपराम् ॥ १५

अयुतं नियतो मन्त्रीति । प्रणवपाशाङ्कुशवायुपृथिव्यमृतयोग उक्तः । समन्वितं चिटिमन्त्रमिति शेषः ॥ १० ॥

मन्त्रो भूयान्न चाऽन्यथेति । मारणादिषु तदुचितबीजयोग उक्तः ॥ ११॥१२ ॥

आरभ्य कर्मकृन्मन्त्रीति । कर्म विशेषपूजादिकम् । मन्त्रीत्याग्नेये दीर्घे वा

तासु हृद्देशलिखितसाध्याख्यासु समाहितः ।
सम्यक् संस्थापयेत् प्राणान् साध्यादानीय साधकः ॥ १६
उत्तानां दारवीं कुण्डे खनेन्मन्त्राभिमन्त्रिताम् ।
पिष्टजां विष्टरस्याऽधः पादस्थाने च मृन्मयीम् ॥ १७
लम्बयेदम्बरे सिक्थमयीमूर्ध्वमधोमुखीम् ।
पुनः कृष्णाष्टमीरात्रौ पूर्वयामे गते सति ॥ १८
रक्तमाल्याम्बरो मन्त्री कृतरक्तानुलेपनः ।
सम्यक्कृतलिपिन्यासः प्राणायामादिकृच्छुचिः ॥ १९
कुड़वं पीतलवणं सुश्लक्ष्णं परिचूर्णितम् ।
दधिक्षौद्रघृतक्षीरैः प्रोक्षयित्वा सुशोधितम् ॥ २०
आलोड्य गुड़मध्वाज्यैर्विस्पष्टावयवामथ ।
तेन पुत्तलिकां मन्त्री चार्वङ्गीं कारयेद्बुधः ॥ २१
तस्याञ्च स्थापयेत्प्राणान् गुर्वादिशविधानतः ।
अष्टोर्ध्वशतसंख्यं वा तथाऽष्टोर्ध्वसहस्रकम् ॥ २२
एकक्पञ्चकं पञ्चविंशत्संख्यं प्रतिकृतिं स्पृशन् ।
जपित्वाऽङ्गानि विन्यस्येत् स्वाङ्गे प्रतिकृतावपि ॥ २३
सतारैश्चिटिमन्त्रार्णैश्चतुर्विंशतिसंख्यकैः ।
शिरोललाटदृक्कर्णनासास्यचिवुकेष्वपि ॥ २४
सकण्ठहृदयोरोजनाभिकुक्षिकटीषु च ।
मेढ्रपायूरुजान्वग्रजङ्घाङ्घ्रिषु च विन्यसेत् ॥ २५
अधोगुह्यादभेदः स्यादूर्ध्वं भेदो द्विकौ सति ।
आत्मन्येवं प्रविन्यस्य पुनः प्रतिकृतौ न्यसेत् ॥ २६

उक्तपूजामन्त्रकलापग्रहणमुक्तम् ॥ १३ ॥ १४ ॥ १५ ॥ १६ ॥ १७ ॥ १८ ॥

मन्त्री कृतरक्तानुलेपन इति न्यासादिभिः मन्त्रात्मत्वमुक्तम् ॥ १९ ॥ २० ॥

पुत्तलिकां मन्त्रीति । मन्त्रं जपता पुत्तलीका कार्येत्युक्तम् ॥ २१ ॥

गुर्वादिशविधानत इति । प्रतिकृतिहृदि प्राणप्रतिष्ठायन्त्रस्थापनपूर्वक-मित्यर्थः । वक्ष्यमाणादौ प्राणप्रतिष्ठाप्रकारभेदश्चाऽनेन सूचितः ॥ २२ ॥

स्वाङ्गे प्रतिकृतावपीति । स्वाङ्गे कर्मोपक्रम एव न्यासः कार्यः ॥ २३—३१ ॥

अङ्गुष्ठसन्धिप्रपदजङ्घाजानूरुपायुषु ।
सलिङ्गनाभिजठरहृदयेषु स्तनद्वये ॥ २७
कन्धराचिवुकास्येषु घ्राणदृक्कर्णयुग्मके ।
ललाटशिरसोर्न्यस्येत् प्रतिमायाञ्च संघशः ॥ २८
उपलिप्तेऽथ कुण्डेऽन्तर्बहिर्गोमयवारिणा ।
साध्यसंमुखमासीन आदध्याद्धव्यवाहनम् ॥ २९
प्रज्वाल्य साध्याङ्गुतरुकाष्ठैरभ्यर्च्य दिक्क्रमात् ।
राजीकुशीतपुष्पाद्भिस्त्रषके राजतादिके ॥ ३०
देवतां प्रति पाद्यार्घ्यं दत्त्वा कार्यार्थसिद्धये ।
उपतिष्ठेद्धुतस्यादावन्ते मन्त्रैरितीरितैः ॥ ३१
त्वमाननममित्रघ्न निशाया हव्यवाहन ।
हविषा मत्वदत्तेन तृप्तो भव तया सह ॥ ३२
जातवेदो महादेव तप्तजाम्बूनदप्रभ ।
स्वाहापते विश्वभक्ष लवणं दह शत्रुहन् ॥ ३३
ईशे शर्वरि शर्वाणि ग्रस्तं मुक्तं त्वया जगत् ।
महादेवि नमस्तुभ्यं वरदे कामदा भव ॥ ३४
तमोमयि महादेवि महादेवस्य सुव्रते ।
त्रियामे पुरुषं हृत्वा वशमानय देव्यु[हि]मे ॥ ३५
दुर्गे सर्गादिरहिते दुर्गसंरोधनार्गले ।
चक्रशङ्खधरे देवि दुष्टशत्रु[सत्त्व]भयङ्करि ॥ ३६
नमस्ते दह शत्रून् मे वशमानय चण्डिके ।
शाकम्भरि महादेवि शरणं मे भवाऽनघे ॥ ३७
भद्रकालि भवाभीष्टे भद्रसिद्धिप्रदायिनि ।
सपत्नान् मे हन हन दह शोषय तापय ॥ ३८
शूलासिशक्तिवज्राद्यैरुत्कृत्योत्कृत्य मारय ।
महादेवि महाकालि रक्षाऽस्मानक्षतात्मिके ॥ ३९

[उपस्थानमन्त्रं दर्शयति—त्वमाननमित्यष्टभिः । इति सम्बन्धदीपिकायाम् ।
क्वचित् 'त्रियामे' इत्यत्र 'स्त्रिया मे पुरुषं गत्वा' इति पाठः ।

पुनः प्रतिकृतेरङ्गसप्तकं निशितायसा ।
दक्षपादादिकं छित्त्वा पञ्चचं प्रजपेन्मनुम् ॥ ४०
साध्यं संस्मृत्य शितधीर्जुहुयात् सप्तसंख्यया ।
दक्षिणं चरणं पूर्वं ततो दक्षार्धकं पुनः ॥ ४१
दक्षहस्तं तृतीयं स्याद्गलादूर्ध्वं चतुर्थकम् ।
पञ्चमं वामहस्तं स्यात् षष्ठं वामार्धमेव च ॥ ४२
सप्तमं वामपादं स्यादन्याऽपि स्याद्दुतक्रिया ।
सप्त सप्त विभागो वा क्रमादङ्गेषु सप्तसु ॥ ४३
एकादशांशभिन्नैर्वा तदङ्गैः सप्तभिर्हुनेत् ।
होमोऽन्यथा वा पूर्वन्तु दक्षिणं चरणं भवेत् ॥ ४४
द्वितीयो दक्षिणकरस्तृतीयं शिर उच्यते ।
वामबाहुश्चतुर्थन्तु मध्यादूर्ध्वन्तु पञ्चमम् ॥ ४५
अधोभागस्तु षष्ठः स्याद्वामपादस्तु सप्तमः ।
हुत्वैवं पूर्वसंप्रोक्तैरुपस्थाय च मन्त्रकैः ॥ ४६
अर्चयित्वा दण्डदीर्घं प्रणमेद्धव्यवाहनम् ।
सस्वर्णाञ्च समुक्तां गां शोणां दद्यात् सतर्णकाम् ॥ ४७
दक्षिणां सप्तकर्षन्तु दद्यान्मारणकर्मणि ।
अंशुकं रुचकं धान्यं दत्त्वा संप्रीणयेद्गुरुम् ॥ ४८
एवं कृतेन मन्त्रीष्टं लभते होमकर्मणा ।
अथवा मारणाकाङ्क्षी साध्यवामाङ्घ्रिपांशुभिः ॥ ४९
सनिम्बतिलसिद्धार्थव्रणकृत्तैलसंयुतैः ।
हिङ्गुत्रिकटुकोपेतैर्महिषीमूत्रपेषितैः ॥ ५०
वराहपारावतयोः पुरीषेण समन्वितैः ।
एतैर्विमिश्रयित्वा तु लोणं पूर्वोक्तसंख्यकम् ॥ ५१
पूर्ववत् पुत्तलीं तेन लोणचूर्णेन कारयेत् ।
प्राणान् प्रतिष्ठापयेच्च तत्र पूर्वोक्तसंख्यया ॥ ५२

सस्वर्णाञ्च समुक्तामित्यत्र सकर्षस्वर्णयुक्तामिति क्वचित् । मूत्रपेषितैरित्यत्र मूत्रविड्विषैरिति क्वचित्] ॥ ३२—५६ ॥

पूर्वोक्ताभिः पुत्तलीभिः कुण्डे दक्षिणदिङ्मुखः ।
दुर्गां वा भद्रकालीं वा प्रणिपत्य यथोचितम् ॥ ५३
उपस्थितेऽर्धरात्रे तु सव्यपाणिस्थशस्त्रकः ।
वामपादं समारभ्य जुहुयात् पूर्वसंख्यया ॥ ५४
समापयेद्दक्षपादे विकारेणाऽयसो वशी ।
त्रिसप्ताहप्रयोगेण मारयेद्रिपुमात्मनः ॥ ५५
तस्यां रात्र्यामुपोष्याऽथ परेऽहनि तु साधकः ।
प्राणायामादिभिरपि गायत्रीजपहोमकैः ॥ ५६
विमुक्तपातको भूत्वा स पुनर्विहरेद्वशी ।
यां कल्पयन्त्यपामार्गराजीघृतहवींषि च ॥ ५७
पृथगष्टोत्तरशतावृत्त्या हुत्वा बलिं हरेत् ।
दशस्वाशासु दिवि च मन्त्रैरेतैर्यथाक्रमम् ॥ ५८

यो मे पूर्वगतः पाप्मा पापकेनेह कर्मणा इन्द्रस्त्वं देवो राजा जम्भयतु स्तम्भयतु मोहयतु वशयतु मारयतु नाशयतु बलिं तस्मै प्रयच्छतु कृतं मम शुभं मम शिवं मम शान्तिः स्वस्त्ययनं मम ।

यो मेऽग्निगतः । यो मे यमगतः । यो मे निर्ऋतिगतः । यो मे वरुणगतः । यो मे वायुगतः । यो मे सोमगतः । यो मे ईशानगतः । यो मे अधोगतः । यो मे ऊर्ध्वगतः । यो मे पातालगतः ।

यो मे दिवि गतः पाप्मा पापकेनेह कर्मणा सूर्यस्त्वं देवो राजा जम्भयतु स्तम्भयतु मोहयतु वशयतु मारयतु नाशयतु बलिं

यां कल्पयन्तीत्यस्य ब्रह्मानुष्टुप्प्रत्यङ्गिरस ऋष्याद्याः । ॐ बीजम् । क्लीं शक्तिः । अष्टचतुश्चतुश्चतुःषड्भिरक्षरैरङ्गानि । भ्रूमध्यनयनद्वयगलबाहुद्वयहृन्नाभिपार्श्वद्वयकटिद्वयाम्बुपादद्वयेषु न्यासः । खड्गचर्मधरा कृष्णा मुक्तकेशी दिगम्बरा सदंष्ट्रा ससर्पा[र्वा]भरणा भक्षितारिर्ध्येया ।

यां कल्पयन्ति नोऽरयः क्रूरां कृत्यां वधूमिव ।
तां ब्रह्मणाऽपनिर्नुद्मः प्रत्यक्कर्तारमृच्छतु ॥ इति मन्त्रः ॥ ५७ ॥ ५८ ॥

[अनेन मन्त्रेणोक्तद्रव्यैरुक्तसंख्यं हुत्वा बलिं दद्यादित्याह—यो इति ।

तस्मै प्रयच्छतु कृतं मम शुभं मम शिवं मम शान्ति: स्वस्त्ययनं मम । यो मे सर्वगत: ।

एवं दिशासु दशसु देवताभ्यो बलिं हरेत् ।
बलावेवं कृते शत्रोराशु कृत्या प्रणश्यति ॥ ६०

प्रणवयुगलं भूयुग्मान्तस्थितं ठगतञ्च
तद्वसुकुलिशगं तेषां मध्ये ध्रुवं भुवमन्तरा ।
अमरपतिदिक्कोणे ग्लौं पाशाङ्कुशान्तरमायया
वलयितमथो जम्भाद्यष्टौ लिखेत् कुरुते जडम् ॥ ६१

जम्भयस्तम्भयौ वीप्सा तथा बन्धयमोहयौ ।
इत्यनन्तास्तथा स्युस्ते जम्भाद्यष्टौ द्विठान्तिका: ॥ ६२

अथवा लवणै: परागभूतैर्मधुराक्तै: पुनरष्टमीनिशाद्यम् ।
जुहुयाच्च चतुर्दशीनिशान्तं कुड्वोन्मितमेभिरेव मन्त्रै: ॥ ६३

नारीं नरं वा नगरं नृपान् वा
ग्रामान् जनान् वा मनसोऽनुरूपम् ।
वशीकरोत्येव हुतक्रियेयं
चिराय नैवाऽत्र विचारणीयम् ॥ ६४

इति लवणमनोर्विधानमेवं प्रणिगदितं विविधप्रभेदभिन्नम् ।
विधिवदमुमादरेण संप्रयुञ्जन् व्रजति फलं निजवाञ्छितं चिराय ॥

इति श्रीप्रपञ्चसारे द्वात्रिंश: पटल: ।

इत्यादिमन्त्रेष्वाद्यन्तौ मन्त्रौ पूर्णपुटितौ । इतरेऽपि तथैव जप्या: ॥ ५८ ॥ ५९ ॥

बलिप्रदानप्रकारमाह—दशस्विति ॥ ६० ॥ ६१ ॥ ६२ ॥

मधुरत्रयावसिक्तलवणचूर्णमुद्राभि: वश्याकर्षणादिषु जुहुयादित्यभिधत्ते—अथवेति ॥ ६२ ॥ ६३ ॥

अस्य मन्त्रस्याऽन्येऽपि विविधभेदा: सन्तीति सूचयन् उपसंहरति—इति लवणमनोरिति । इति सम्बन्धदीपिकायाम् ॥ ६४ ॥

इति श्रीपद्मपादाचार्यकृते प्रपञ्चसारविवरणे
द्वात्रिंशत्पटल: ।

त्रयस्त्रिंशः पटलः ।

अथाऽभिवक्ष्ये महितस्य मन्त्रस्याऽनुष्टुभः संग्रहतो विधानम् ।
ऋष्यादिकैरङ्गपदैर्यथावद्दीक्षाजपार्चाहवनक्रमेण ॥ १
ऋषिरभिहितो वशिष्ठश्छन्दोऽनुष्टुप् च देवता रुद्रः ।
त्र्यम्बकपदादिकः स्यान्मनुनाऽमुनैव षड़ङ्गक्लृप्तिरिह कथिता ॥ २
त्रिभिस्तु वर्णैर्हृदयं शिरश्च चतुर्भिरष्टाभिरथो शिखा च ।
उक्तं नवार्णैः कवचं तथाऽक्षि पञ्चार्णकं त्र्यम्बकमस्त्रमाहुः ॥ ३
प्राक्प्रत्यग्याम्यसौम्ये शिरसि च वदनोरोगलांसेषु नाभौ
हृद्देशे पृष्ठकुक्ष्योरथ शिवगुदयोरूरुमूलान्तयोश्च ।
जान्वोस्तद्वृत्तयुग्मस्तनतटयुगपार्श्वेषु पत्पाणिनासा-
शीर्षेष्वप्यूर्ध्वतोऽर्णैर्न्यसतु पुनरधस्तोऽपि मन्त्री तथोर्ध्वम् ॥ ४
चरणाग्रसन्धिगुह्याधारोदरहृदयकन्धरासु पुनः ।
बाह्वोः सन्ध्यग्रास्यौष्ठघ्राणदृक्श्रुतिभ्रूशीर्षेषु ॥ ५
वर्णान् न्यस्य शिरोभ्रूदृग्वक्त्रगलहृदुदरगुह्येषु ।
ऊर्वोर्जान्वोः पदयोः पदैश्च मनुवित् क्रमेण विन्यस्येत् ॥ ६
वशिष्ठादिक्रमेणैव अङ्गन्यासं समाचरेत् ।
वशिष्ठस्त्र्यम्बकस्यैव त्रिनेत्रस्य तथैव च ।
अनुष्टुप्छन्दसे चेति जातियुक्तेन मन्त्रवित् ॥ ७
अच्छः स्वच्छारविन्दस्थितिरुभयकराङ्कस्थितं पूर्णकुम्भं
द्वाभ्यां वेदाक्षमाले निजकरकमलाभ्यां घटौ नित्यपूर्णौ ।
द्वाभ्यां तौ च स्रवन्तौ शिरसि शशिकलाबन्धुरे प्लावयन्तौ
देहं देवो दधानः प्रदिशतु विशदाकल्पजातः श्रियं वः ॥ ८

मारणवश्यादिकर्तुरायुःचयत्वसंभवादायुःप्रदं मन्त्रं वक्तुमारभते —अथाऽभिवक्ष्ये इति [मन्त्रोऽयं वैदिकत्वान्नोक्तः] ॥ १ ॥ २ ॥ ३ ॥

मन्त्री तथोर्ध्वमिति । प्रणवशक्तिप्रासादयोग उक्तः । ॐ बीजम् । ह्रौं शक्तिः ॥ ४ ॥ ५ ॥ ६ ॥

मन्त्रविदिति । पञ्चाक्षरप्रणवशक्तिबीजयोगः सूचितः ॥ ७ ॥ ८ ॥

प्रासादोक्ते च पीठे गव्यैर्वा दुग्धतरुकषायैर्वा ।
संपूर्य कलशमस्मिन् महेशमावाह्य पूजयेद्भक्त्या ॥ ९
अङ्गैराद्याऽर्काद्यैः पुनरावृतिरष्टभिर्द्वितीया स्यात् ।
मन्त्रार्णशक्तिभिः स्युः पुनश्चतस्रो दिशापवज्राद्यैः ॥ १०
अर्केन्दुधरणितोयानलैरवियदात्मसंज्ञकास्ते च ।
आनुष्टुभमित्यष्टावरणं प्रोक्तं विधानवरमेवम् ॥ ११
रमा राका प्रभा ज्योत्स्ना पूर्णोषा पूरणी सुधा ।
विश्वा विद्या सिता प्रह्वा सारा सन्ध्या शिवा निशा ॥ १२
आर्द्रा प्रज्ञा प्रभा मेधा कान्तिः शान्तिर्धृतिर्मतिः ।
धरोमा पावनी पद्मा शान्ताऽमोघा जयाऽमला ॥ १३
द्वात्रिंशदिति निर्दिष्टाः शक्तयोऽनुष्टुभः क्रमात् ।
शिवानुभावतो नित्यं जगदाप्याययन्ति याः ॥ १४
इति परिपूज्य महेशं कलशजलैः समभिषिचयेच्छिष्यम् ।
कनकांशुकरत्नाद्यैर्गुरुमपि परिपूज्य मनुमतः सिद्धैः ॥ १५
प्रजपेल्लक्षावृत्त्या द्रव्यैर्जुहुयाज्जपावसाने च ।
बिल्वपलाशौ खदिरवटसिद्धार्थदोग्धदुग्धानि ॥ १६
दधि दूर्वेति दशैतान्याज्यसमेतानि होमवस्तूनि ।
एकैकशः सहस्रं दशभिर्हुत्वा प्रतर्प्य विप्रांश्च ॥ १७
भवति नरः सिद्धमनुर्मन्त्रेण च सर्वकर्मकर्ता स्यात् ।
बिल्वैरयुतं हुत्वा महतीं लक्ष्मीमवाप्नुयाद्विप्रः ॥ १८
तावद्भिर्द्विजवृक्षैर्द्विजः श्रियं पुष्कलामवाप्नोति ।
खदिरसमिदयुतहोमात्तेजोबलपुष्टिमाप्नुयादिष्टाम् ॥ १९
न्यग्रोधायुतहोमाद्धनधान्यसमृद्धिमेति न चिरेण ।
अयुतं तिलैः प्रजुह्वन्नपमृत्योः पाप्मनो विमुक्तः स्यात् ॥ २०
सिद्धार्थायुतहोमैर्वैरिणमपमृत्युमपि विनाशयति ।
पायसहुतेन परमां रमामथायुर्यशो लभेन्मर्त्यः ॥ २१

प्रासादोक्ते पीठे कलशमापूर्य तस्मिन् भगवन्तमावाह्य पूजयेदित्याह—प्रासादोक्त इति। अष्टमूर्तीराह—अर्केति। मन्त्रवर्णशक्तीराह—रमेति। ['प्रभा'

दुग्धहुताच्छान्तिः स्यात् परकृत्या नश्यति श्रियं लभते ।
दधिहोमतोऽन्नवान् स्यात् संबलनकरं च तद्वदन्ति बुधाः ॥ २२
दूर्वायुतेन जुह्वन् रोगान्निर्वास्य सर्वमपमृत्युम् ।
गर्वितधीरब्दानां विप्रवरः सर्वथा शतं जीवेत् ॥ २३
निजजन्मदिने पयोऽम्बसा वा शतवीर्यात्रितयैः पयोघृताक्तैः ।
जुहुयाच्च शतं च विंशतिं यः स लभेदायुररोगितां चिराय ॥ २४
काश्मर्यदारुसमिधां त्रिशतं समेत-
सर्पिः पयोऽन्नसहितं त्रिदिनं जुहोतु ।
विप्रान् प्रतर्प्य च गुरून् परिपूज्य सम्य-
ग्दीर्घं विमुक्तगदमायुरवाप्तुकामः ॥ २५
स्नात्वा चाऽर्कमुखोऽम्भसि स्थित इमं मन्त्रं सहस्रं जपे-
दायुष्यं प्रतिपर्व दुग्धहविषा होमो महाश्रीप्रदः ।
लाजाभिर्निजवाञ्छिताय हवनात् कन्याशु संदीयते
स्याद्वक्तस्तनजद्रुहोमविधिना वर्णान् वशे स्थापयेत् ॥ २६
गायत्रिवर्णपरिपूर्णतनुश्च भानु-
स्त्रिष्टुब्विशिष्टमहिमा महितः कृशानुः ।
आनुष्टुभाक्षरसमग्ररुचिः शशाङ्को
दद्युः समुद्यतममी परिवाञ्छितं वः ॥ २७
एभिस्त्रिभिर्मनुवरैस्तु शताक्षराख्यो
मन्त्रोऽभिकाङ्क्षितफलाप्तिदकामधेनुः ।
प्रोक्तो हिताय जगतां मुनिभिः कृपार्द्र-
चित्तैर्यथोक्तमथ संग्रहतो वदामि ॥ २८
ऋष्याद्याः पूर्वोक्तास्त्रिविधाः स्युर्हृत्त्रयोदशभिर्वर्णैः ।
शिर एकादशभिश्च द्वाविंशद्भिस्तथा शिखा कवचम् ॥ २९

इत्यत्र परेति 'कान्ति'रित्यत्र कीर्तिरिति क्वचित्] ॥ ८—२६ ॥

आयुःप्रधानमेव शताक्षरमाह—गायत्रिवर्णेति । अनेनैव गायत्रीध्यानवदेवाऽस्य सकलस्य ध्यानमुक्तं भवति । त्रिष्टुबनुष्टुभौ तु तस्याः सान्निध्यजकामरूपाविति च ॥ २७ ॥ २८ ॥

नयनं पञ्चदशार्णैः ससप्तभिर्दशभिरस्त्रमङ्गविधिः ।
विन्यासस्त्र मनूनां मन्त्रज्ञः पूर्ववत् क्रमात् कुर्यात् ॥ ३०
स्मर्तव्याखिललोकवर्ति सततं यज्जङ्गमं स्थावरं
व्याप्तं येन च यत्प्रपञ्चविहितं मुक्तिश्च यत्सिद्धितः ।
यद्वा स्यात् प्रणवत्रिभेदगहनं श्रुत्या च यद्गीयते
तद्वः काङ्क्षितसिद्धयेऽस्तु परमं ज्योतिस्त्रयोत्थं महः ॥ ३१
लक्षायतो जपविधिः शताक्षरस्याऽथ होमविधिरुक्तः ।
अयुतावधिको द्रव्यं दौग्धान्नं सर्पिषा समायुक्तम् ॥ ३२
सौरे पीठे पूजा प्रोक्तैरङ्गैः समावृतिः प्रथमा ।
प्रह्लादिन्याद्याभिस्तिस्रः प्रोक्ताः क्रमात् समावृतयः ॥ ३३
पञ्चम्यावृतिरुक्ता त्रैष्टुभ इव जागतादिभिस्तदनु ।
स्याच्च रमादिभिरावृतिचतुष्कमुक्तं दशम्यथेन्द्राद्यैः ॥ ३४
इति शताक्षरमन्त्रसमर्चना निगदितेह दशावरणायुधैः ।
प्रभजतामभिकाङ्क्षितसिद्धये निखिलसंसृतिमोक्षपदाप्तये ॥ ३५
दुग्धाक्तैर्जुहुयात् सहस्रममृताकाण्डैस्तु दीर्घायुषि
दूर्वाणां चितयैस्तथा घृतपयःसिक्तैर्घृतेनैव वा ।
लक्ष्म्यै कोकनदैश्च शोणरुचिभिस्त्रिस्वादुयुक्तैस्तथा
रक्तैरुत्पलकैस्तदक्षि विकचैर्वैल्वैः प्रसूनैरपि ॥ ३६

अनुदिनमघशान्त्यै संयतात्मा सहस्रं
प्रतिजुहुतु तिलैर्वा मन्त्रविन्मासमेकम् ।
अपि दिनकरसंख्यान् भोजयीत द्विजातीन्
विविधरसविशिष्टैर्भक्तितो भोज्यजातैः ॥ ३७

शतं शतं प्रातरतन्द्रितोद्यतो जपेद्द्विजो मन्त्रममुं शताक्षरम् ।
आरोग्यजुष्टं बहुलेन्दिरायुतं शतं प्रजीवेच्छरदां सुखेन सः ॥ ३८

सर्वान् कामानवाप्नोति मन्त्रमेनं जपेत् तु यः ।
सर्वं साधयते मन्त्री अस्त्रशस्त्रादिलक्षणम् ॥ ३९

मन्त्रज्ञः पूर्ववदिति । अजपापरमात्मयोग उक्तः ॥ २८—३५ ॥
मन्त्रवित् मासमिति । मृत्युञ्जययोग उक्तः ॥ ३६ ॥ ३७ ॥ ३८ ॥ ३९ ॥

प्रणवव्याहृत्याद्या व्याहृतितारान्तिका च मन्त्रिवरैः ।
जप्या शताक्षरी स्यादिह परलोकप्रसिद्धये दिनशः ॥ ४०

मनुममुमथ शान्त्यै तत्पदाद्यं प्रजप्याद्-
गदगणरहितायाऽप्यायुषेऽनुष्टुबाद्यम् ।
विमलमतिररातिध्वंसने त्रिष्टुबाद्यं
दिनमनु दिनवक्त्रे वत्सरं संयतात्मा ॥ ४१

शताक्षरमनोरयं क्रम उदीरितः संग्रहा-
द्भजेदमुमतन्द्रितो दिनश एव मन्त्री रहः ।
अभीष्टफलसिद्धये सुयशसे च दीर्घायुषे-
ऽप्यशेषजनरञ्जनाय चिरमिन्दिरावाप्तये ॥ ४२

संवादसूक्तविहितं विधानमथ साङ्गदेवतारूपम् ।
वक्ष्यामि साधकानामनुदिनमभिवाञ्छितप्रदानकरम् ॥ ४३
ऋषिरपि संवलनोऽस्याऽनुष्टुप्सत्रिष्टुबुच्यते छन्दः ।
संवादाद्यः प्रोक्तः संज्ञानाद्यश्च देवता चाऽग्निः ॥ ४४

ब्रह्माख्यो हृदयमनुः शिरश्च विष्णू
रुद्रः स्यादिह तु शिखेश्वरश्च वर्म ।
नेत्रत्वे भवति सदाशिवस्तथाऽस्त्रं
सर्वात्मेत्यथ कथितं षडङ्गमेवम् ॥ ४५

धवलनलिनराजच्चन्द्रमध्ये निषण्णं
करविलसितपाशं साङ्कुशं साभयञ्च ।
सवरदममलेन्दुक्षीरगौरं त्रिनेत्रं
प्रणमत सुरवक्त्रं मङ्क्षु संवादयन्तम् ॥ ४६

मन्त्रिवरैरिति । व्याहृत्यनन्तरमजपामृत्युञ्जयपरमात्ममन्त्रयोग उक्तः ॥ ४० ॥

विमलमतिररातीति । तत्तन्मन्त्रादित्वे तत्तन्मन्त्रोक्तध्यानं सूचितम् ॥ ४१ ॥

मन्त्री रह इति । तत्तत्कार्यानुगुणबीजयोग उक्तः । गायत्र्यक्षराणि बीजानि । त्रिष्टुबक्षराणि शक्तयः ॥ ४२ ॥

सं समिद्युवस इत्याद्यृकचतुष्टयात्मकसंवादसूक्तविधानं वक्तुम् उपक्रमते— संवादेति । संवादस्य तृतीया ऋग् बीजम् । द्वितीया शक्तिः । संवादाद्य

सहस्रकाणां दशकैश्चतुर्भिरथो सहस्रैश्च चतुर्भिरन्वितम् ।
जपेन्मनुं सम्यगथाऽभिदीक्षितः पयोऽन्धसाऽन्ते जुहुयाद्दशांशकम् ॥
यजेत् पुराऽङ्गैश्च तदर्चनाविधौ पुनर्द्वितीयावरणेऽग्निमूर्तिभिः ।
अनन्तरञ्च चित्रशेश्वरादिभिः क्रमेण वह्निं विधिनेति पूजयेत् ॥
संवादसूक्ते विधिनेत्यनेन संसाधिते कर्म करोतु मन्त्री ।
चतुःशतञ्चापि दशोत्तरेण चतुश्चतुष्कं प्रजपेद्धुनेच्च ॥ ४९
पायसेन मधुरत्रयभाजा विप्रराजतरुजैः कुसुमैर्वा ।
सर्पिषा स्तनजवत्ससमिद्भिर्वाञ्छितार्थविधये प्रजुहोतु ॥ ५०
जुहुयात् कलाचतुष्कैः प्रत्यृचमायोज्य कादिवर्गचतुष्कैः ।
तद्वच्च पयशलाद्यैर्वर्गैः संयोज्य पूर्वसंख्यकं मतिमान् ॥ ५१
तद्वदृचं प्रतियोज्य त्रिष्टुप्पादांश्च पूर्वसंख्येन ।
जुहुयात् सर्पिःसिक्तं पायसमचिरेण कार्यसमवाप्त्यै ॥ ५२

इति । संवादसंज्ञानाग्निः देवतेत्यर्थः ॥ ४३॥४४॥४५॥४६॥४७ ॥

आग्नेये पीठे पूजा ॥ ४८ ॥

कर्म करोतु मन्त्रीति । होमतर्पणजपकर्मसु प्रयुज्यमानमन्त्राणां प्रणवशक्तिपूर्वकत्वमुच्यते । चतुःशतं चापीति । त्रिष्टुप् (स्वत्रिष्टुप्कस्वत्रिष्टुप्क) स्वत्रिष्टुप् त्रिष्टुबनुष्टुब् गायत्री महागणपति पादमन्त्र व्याहृत्यनुकूलमन्त्रैः सह सूक्तं दशधाऽऽवर्त्य वैश्वानर जातवेद इहावह लोहिताक्ष सर्वकर्माणि साधय स्वाहा । ॐ भूर्भुवःस्वः स्वाहा । ॐ भूर्भुवःस्वः अग्ने जातवेद इहावह सर्वकर्माणि साधय स्वाहा । उत्तिष्ठ पुरुष हरिपिङ्गल लोहिताक्ष सर्वकर्माणि साधय स्वाहा । इत्यग्निमन्त्रान् सकृत् सकृदावर्तयेदित्यर्थः । प्रतिकूलं मे नश्यत्वनुकूलं मे वशमानय स्वाहा । इत्यनुकूलमन्त्रः । होमादिकमप्येवमेव कार्यम् ॥ ४९॥५० ॥

कलाचतुष्कैः प्रति ऋचमायोज्येति । ॐ क्लीं अं आं इं ईं इति उक्त्वा सं समिद्युवस इत्युक्त्वा ऋचोऽन्ते स्वाहेति तर्पयामीति वा वदेत् । एवमेव ॐ क्लीं ॐ ऊं ऋं ॠं संगच्छध्वमित्यादिकमूहयेत् । एवं मातृकां सप्तत्रिंशद्वारमावर्तयेत् । एवं कृते संख्या पूर्णा भवति मिश्रहोमपक्षे । अमिश्रहोमपक्षे तु अष्टादशवारमेवमेव मातृकामावर्तयेत् । आदावन्ते च त्रिष्टुब्महागणपत्यग्निमन्त्रैः होमादिकमाचरेदित्यर्थः । एतत् सर्वं सूचितं मतिमानिति ॥ ५१ ॥

ऋचं प्रतियोज्य त्रिष्टुप्पादानिति । चतुष्पादा अष्टपादा वा त्रिष्टुप्पादाः ।

प्रतिपादमथर्क्पादं प्रतियोज्य जुहोतु पूर्ववन्मतिमान् ।
तेनाऽभीष्टावाप्तिर्न चिरेण नरस्य हस्तगता ॥ ५३
अक्षरपादत्रिष्टुब्युक्तैः सूक्तैस्तु पूर्वसंख्येन ।
जुहुयात् समाजरूपं संवादयितुं प्रतर्पयेद्वाऽद्भिः ॥ ५४

अत्रायं योगक्रमः। ॐ ह्रीं जातवेदसे सुनवाम सोममिति उक्त्वा सं समिद्युवसे इति ऋचम् अभिधाय होमादिकमाचरेत्। ॐ ह्रीं अरातीयतो निदहाति वेदः इत्यादिपादत्रयेण सार्धं सूक्तं समापयेत्। एवमेकादशोत्तरशतवारं सूक्ते आवर्तिते सति संख्या पूर्णा भवति मिश्रहोमपक्षे। अमिश्रहोमपक्षे तु पञ्चपञ्चाशद्वारमावर्त्याऽन्ते अग्निमन्त्रचतुष्टयेन होमादिकं कर्तव्यमिति चतुष्पादपक्षः। अष्टपादपक्षेऽपि मिश्रहोमपक्षे चतुष्पादपक्षामिश्रहोमवत् क्रमः। अमिश्रहोमपक्षे तु सप्तविंशतिवारमावर्तनीयम्। आदावन्ते च त्रिष्टुब्महागणपत्यग्निमन्त्रैः होमादिकं कर्तव्यमित्यर्थः॥ ५२॥

प्रतिपादमथ ऋक्पादमिति। पादं पादं प्रतिपादं प्रतिपादमन्त्रम् पादमन्त्रं प्रतीत्यर्थः। ऋचस्त्र तत्पादास्त्र ऋक्पादम् एकैकपादमन्त्रेण सार्धमेकैकाम् ऋचं जपेत्। अथवा एकैकेनैव पादमन्त्रेण चतुर्वारमावर्तितेन सह ऋक्चतुष्टयं जपेत्। पुनरप्यपरेणाऽप्येवं जपेत्। इति पादमन्त्राणाम् ऋचां च संयोगक्रमः। पादमन्त्राणामृक्पादषोडशकानां च संयोगक्रम एवमेव द्विधा विज्ञातव्यः। तत्र पादमन्त्राणामृचां च संयोगे पक्षद्वयेऽपि मिश्रहोमपक्षे सूक्तस्यैकादशोत्तरशतवारमावृत्तिः कार्या। अमिश्रहोमपक्षे तु पञ्चपञ्चाशद्वारमावृत्त्याऽन्तेऽग्निमन्त्रचतुष्टयेन होमादिकं कर्तव्यम्। पादमन्त्राणामृक्पादसंयोगपक्षद्वयेऽपि मिश्रहोमपक्षे सप्तविंशतिवारमावर्तनीयम्। आदावन्ते च त्रिष्टुब्महागणपत्यग्निमन्त्रैः होमादिकं कर्तव्यम। अमिश्रपक्षे तु त्रयोदशवारमावर्तनीयम्। आद्यन्तयोः त्रिष्टुबनुष्टुब् गायत्र्यग्निमन्त्रचतुष्टय गणपतिचतुर्मूर्ति प्रणवाजपापरमात्ममन्त्रैश्च होमादिकं कर्तव्यमित्यर्थः। भद्रं नो अपि वातय मनः। मरुतामोजसे स्वाहा। इन्द्रो विश्वस्य राजति। शन्नो भव द्विपदे शं चतुष्पदे। इति पादमन्त्राः। मतिमानिति। उक्तमन्त्रसंयोगज्ञ इत्यर्थः॥ ५३॥

अक्षरपादत्रिष्टुब्युक्तैरिति। पञ्चपञ्चाशदक्षराण्यक्षरशब्दार्थः। पादशब्देन पादमन्त्रा उक्ताः। पादत्रिष्टुब्युक्तैरिति। त्रिष्टुभः पादचतुष्टयेन युक्तैरित्यर्थः। अयमत्र क्रमः। ॐ ह्रीं अं भद्रं नो अपि वातय मनः। जातवेदसे सुनवाः

उद्दिश्य यद्यदिह मन्त्रितमो जुहोतु
सूक्तैरमा निगदितैस्त्रिविधैश्च मन्त्रैः ।
व्यस्तैर्यथाविभवतो विधिवत् समस्तै-
स्तत्तस्य सिध्यति समग्रमयत्नमेव ॥ ५५

सोममिति उक्त्वा सं समिद्युवसे इति ऋचमुक्त्वा तर्पणादिकं कुर्यात् । पुनः ॐ क्लीं श्रां मरुतामोजसे स्वाहा । अरातीयतो निदहाति वेदः । संगच्छध्वमित्याद्युक्त्वा तर्पणादिकं कुर्यात् । ॐ क्लीं इं इन्द्रो विश्वस्य राजति । स नः पर्षदति दुर्गाणि विश्वा । समानो मन्त्र इत्यादि । पुनः ॐ क्लीं ईं शन्नो भव द्विपदे शं चतुष्पदे । नावेव सिन्धुं दुरितात्यग्निः । समानो वः इत्यादि । पुनरप्येवमेव मातृकासमाप्तिपर्यन्तमावर्तयेत् । अन्त्यपर्याये अपेक्षिताक्षरस्थाने जिह्वामूलीयं योजयेत् । पुनरप्येवमेवावर्तयन् द्वितीय तृतीय चतुर्थपर्यायेषु उपध्मानीयं दुस्पृष्टाक्षरद्वयं चाऽन्त्ये पर्याये अवशिष्टाक्षरस्थाने योजयेत् । पुनरप्येवमेव मातृकां चतुर्वारमावर्तयेत् । मिश्रहोमपक्षे आद्यन्तयोश्च त्रिष्टुबनुष्टुबादि चतुर्दशमन्त्रान् उक्तान् योजयेत् । अमिश्रपक्षे तु जिह्वामूलीयोपध्मानीयाभ्यामेव संयोज्य मातृका द्विवारमावर्तनीया । आद्यन्तयोश्च त्रिष्टुबनुष्टुबादि चतुर्दशमन्त्रान् योजयेत् इति । ≍क इति जिह्वामूलीयम् । ≍प इति उपध्मानीयम् । ळ्भळ्भइत्येतद्द्वयं दुस्पृष्टाक्षरम् ॥ ५४ ॥

मन्त्रितमो जुहोतु सूक्तैरमा निगदितैस्त्रिविधैश्च मन्त्रैरिति । सूक्तैः संसमिदाद्यैः अमा निगदितैः सह पठितैः त्रिविधैर्मन्त्रैः त्रिप्रकारैः मन्त्रैः त्रैपुरैर्मन्त्रैरित्यर्थः । कथं तेषां सूक्तैः सहोच्चारणं कर्तव्यमिति तत्राह—व्यस्तैः समस्तैरिति । व्यस्तानां वाग्भवादिबीजानामाद्येन सूक्तत्रयेण संयोगः समस्तानां चाऽन्त्यसूक्तेनेत्यर्थः । एवं शुद्धाद्येकादशमन्त्रैः सार्धं दशवारमावर्तयेत् । मिश्रहोमपक्षे । अमिश्रहोमपक्षे पञ्चवारं प्रथमतश्च महागणपतिमन्त्रेण सकृत् तर्पणादिकं कुर्यात् । अन्ते च शैवद्वादशाक्षराष्टाक्षरपञ्चाक्षरैः सकृत् सकृत तर्पणादिकं कुर्यादित्यर्थः । यथाविभवत इति । प्रतिबन्धप्राबल्यानुसारेणेत्यर्थः । विधिवदिति । द्वादशाक्षरादिसंयोग उक्तः । आं ऽ॑ औं । ऐं ईं औं इति शुद्धा । ऐं क्लीं सौः इति बाला । ह्रैं ह्क्लीं ह्सौः । ह्सैं ह्सक्लीं ह्स्सौः । ह्स्रैं हस्कलरीं हस्रौः । हसरडैं हसकलरडीं हसरडसौः । हसरडसैं हसकलरडसीं हसरडस्सौः । हसरडसहैं हसकलरडसहीं हसरडसहसौः । हसरडसक्षैं हसकलरडसक्षीं हसरडसक्षसौः ।

ऋग्वारुणी ध्रुवाख्याद्या या सा त्रिष्टुब्निगद्यते ।
ऋषिर्वशिष्ठस्त्रिष्टुप् च छन्दो वारीट् च देवता ॥ ५६
अष्टभिः सप्तभिः षड्भिः पुनस्तावद्भिरक्षरैः ।
षडङ्गानि विधेयानि तन्मन्त्रसमुदीरितैः ॥ ५७
अङ्गुल्यग्रससन्धिपायुशिवसंज्ञाधारनाभिष्वथो
कुक्षौ पृष्ठहृदोरुरोजगलदोःसन्ध्यग्रवक्त्रेषु च ।
गण्डघ्राणविलोचनश्रवणयुग्भ्रूमध्यमस्तेषु धी
सर्वाङ्गेषु तथा न्यसेद्द्विशदधीर्वर्णैर्मनूत्थैः क्रमात् ॥ ५८
अच्छांशुकाभरणमाल्यविलेपनाढ्यः
पाशाङ्कुशाभयवरोद्यतदोःसरोजः ।
स्वच्छारविन्दवसतिः सुसितः प्रसन्नो
भूयाद्विभूतिविधये वरुणश्चिरं वः ॥ ५९
अङ्गैरष्टभिरहिभिर्दिशाधिपैः समभिपूज्य वारीशम् ।
कलशजलैः पुनरभिषिञ्चेत् परमगुरुर्मन्त्रजापिनं शिष्यम् ॥ ६०
वसुभिः प्रसाद्य देशिकमथ शिष्यो मनुमिमं जपेल्लक्षम् ।
जुहुयाच्च दुग्धपक्वैरन्नैरयुतं घृताप्लुतैर्मतिमान् ॥ ६१
ऋगियमृणमोचनी स्याज्जपैर्हुतैस्तर्पणैश्च मन्त्रविदः ।
संप्राप्तदुर्गतेरपि सद्यो ह्यद्याच्च संवहेल्लक्ष्मीम् ॥ ६२
दूर्वाः सितस्य शकलैर्घृतसिक्तैर्यश्चतुर्दिनं जुहुयात् ।
सकलोपद्रवशान्त्यै तथर्णमुक्त्यै च सम्पदे सुचिरम् ॥ ६३

हसरडसहरडैं हसकलरडसहरडीं हसरडसहरडसौः इति शुद्धाद्येकादशमन्त्राः। तद्वयुता तत्सयुता तद्रयुता तड्डयुता तत्सयुता तद्वयुता तद्रयुता तड्डयुता बालेवान्या विद्याविद्याः इत्युक्तत्वात् ॥ ५५ ॥

अथ वैदिकमेव ऋणमोचनफलदमनुं दर्शयति—ऋग्वारुणीति। [वैदिकत्वान्नोक्तः]। सुधा कुमुदिनी पूर्णा वारुणी विश्वतोमुखी तरङ्गिणी सुरसा सुशीता व्यापिन्यो वरुणनवशक्तयः ॥ ५६ ॥ ५७ ॥ ५८ ॥ ५९ ॥ ६० ॥ ६१ ॥

तर्पणैश्च मन्त्रविद इति। व्यस्मद्दृणपाशं वरुण इति योगः सूचितः। ॥ ६२॥६३॥६४॥६५॥६६॥६७॥६८॥६९ ॥

वेतससमिद्युतहुताद्वृष्टिमकालेऽपि वितनुते वरुणः ।
गव्यक्षीरसमेतात्त्रिदिनकृताह्निमुखेषु मुदितमनाः ॥ ६४
शतभिषजि समुदितेऽर्के चतुःशतं पायसं हुनेत् सघृतम् ।
ऋणमोचनाय लक्ष्म्यै जनसंवननाय शुक्रवारे च ॥ ६५
पाशनिबद्धं वैरिणमङ्कुशसंप्रोतमम्बुधेः पारे ।
ध्यायन् परे क्षिपन्तं वरुणं जुहुयाच्च तथा प्रजपेत् ॥ ६६
पाशनिबद्धं वैरिणमसिनाच्छिद्याशु नाशयन्तममुम् ।
ध्यायन् वेतससमिधो गोमूत्रयुता हुनेत्तदपहत्यै ॥ ६७
दौग्धान्नैर्भृगुवारे घृतसंसिक्तैः कृतस्य हवनविधिः ।
ऋणमोचदस्य विविधोपद्रवशमनकृद्रमाकरः प्रोक्तः ॥ ६८
पश्चिमसन्ध्यासमये पश्चिमवदनोऽनलं समाराध्य ।
ऋचमेनामभिजप्याच्चतुःशतं सकलदुःखशमनाय ॥ ६९
शालीर्घृतसंसिक्ताः सरिदन्तरितो जुहोतु परसेनाम् ।
संस्तम्भयितुं त्रिदिनं सुमना मन्त्री चतुःशतावृत्त्या ॥ ७०
प्रत्यङ्मुखोऽथ मन्त्री प्रतर्पयेद्वा जलैः सुशुद्धतरैः ।
यः स ह्युपद्रवाणां रुन्ध्यान्निचयं श्रियं समृच्छति च ॥ ७१
बहुना किमनेन मन्त्रिमुख्यो मनुनाशु प्रसाधयेदभीष्टम् ।
हवनक्रिययाऽथ तर्पणैर्वा सजपैः पाशभृतो महामहिम्नः ॥ ७२

इति श्रीप्रपञ्चसारे त्रयस्त्रिंशः पटलः ।

सुमना मन्त्रीति । मध्ये समुद्रध्यानं मन्त्रे पृथिवीयोगस्योक्तः ॥ ७० ॥
मन्त्री प्रतर्पयेदिति । उचितबीजयोग उक्तः ॥ ७१ ॥ ७२ ॥

इति श्रीपद्मपादाचार्यकृते प्रपञ्चसारविवरणे
त्रयस्त्रिंशत्पटलः ।

चतुस्त्रिंशः पटलः ।

अथ यन्त्रविरचनाभिर्मन्त्रविशेषान् बहुप्रकारयुतान् ।
कथयिष्ये मन्त्रविदामैहिकपारत्रिकाप्तये सुधियाम् ॥ १
त्रिगुणितसंज्ञे मायालङ्कृतकोणे तयाऽभिसंवीते च ।
या या विशेषक्लृप्तिस्तां तामपि संग्रहेण समभिदधे ॥ २
कोणोल्लसितसुधाक्षरगलदमृतस्फुरितवह्निपरिवीतात् ।
बिन्दोर्मध्यगतबीजस्थितां सुधाधारया परिस्रुतया ॥ ३
पूर्णसुषुम्नारन्ध्रां साध्यतनुं संस्मरञ्छिरसि बध्यात् ।
तेनाऽरोगी पुरुषः प्रज्ञावान् दीर्घमायुराप्नोति ॥ ४
शीतांशुमण्डलस्थं कूर्मचतुर्थाक्तकोणलसितमिदम् ।
शीतप्रलिप्तजप्तं कध्रुतं च शिरोरुजाज्वरार्तिहरम् ॥ ५
तद्द्वययन्त्रयुगं विलिखेदभिलषितसाध्यसाधकाख्ययुतम् ।
साध्यमधस्तात् कृत्वा बद्ध्वाऽत्र स्वपितु साधको नित्यम् ॥
विधिनाऽनेन तु सद्यः साध्योऽस्य वशी भवेद्यत्नेन ।
तत्तु खनित्वागारे तत्राऽन्नं सिद्धमत्तु वश्यकरम् ॥ ७

पूर्वोक्तानां त्रिगुणितादियन्त्राणां प्रयोगविशेषज्ञापनाय नानाविधमन्त्रविशेषज्ञापनाय नानाविधमन्त्रविशेषविधिप्रदर्शनाय च पटलान्तरमारभते—अथ यन्त्रेति । मन्त्रविदामिति । यन्त्रजीवादिविदामित्यर्थः । सुधियामिति । प्रयोगानुरूपध्यानविदामित्यर्थः ॥ १ ॥

अत्रोच्यमानविशेषेण पूर्वोक्तयन्त्राणां न बाधः किन्तु समुच्चय इत्याह—त्रिगुणितसंज्ञ इति ॥ २ ॥

कोणोल्लसितेति । त्रिगुणितस्य कोणेषु लिखितमायामध्ये उल्लसितसुधाक्षरात् वकारात् गलितामृतेन स्फुरितमध्यशक्तिवह्निना परिवीतात् बिन्दोः परिस्रुतया सुधाधारया पूर्णसुषुम्नारन्ध्रां साध्यतनुं स्मरन् शिरसि त्रिगुणितं बध्नीयादित्यर्थः । ॥ ३ ॥ ४ ॥

यन्त्रान्तरमाचष्टे—शीतांशुमण्डलस्थमिति ॥ ५ ॥

वश्यकरं यन्त्रमाह—तद्द्वययन्त्रयुगमिति ॥ ६ ॥ ७ ॥

साध्याख्यां शक्तिवक्त्री नरहरिमपि रन्ध्रत्रये च त्रिशक्तौ
कर्मालिख्याऽथ लोष्टे सततगमपि संस्थाप्य जप्त्वा स्वशक्त्या ।
आगारे स्थापयित्वा नरमुदकनिधेश्चित्रपत्रे लिखित्वा
दीपाग्नौ तापयित्वा स्त्रियममलधियः सम्यगाकर्षयेयुः ॥ ८
त्रिगुणितविहिता विधयः षड्गुणिते च प्रयोजनीयाः स्युः ।
रक्षाकर्मणि विहितं तत्प्रायः प्रचुरमन्त्रयुक्ततया ॥ ९
पाशाष्टाक्षरवीतशक्तिदहनप्रोल्लासि साध्याह्वयं
शक्तिश्रीस्मरसंवृतं कुयुगरन्ध्रावद्धचिन्तामणि ।
इत्थं षड्गुणितं विलिख्य जपितं मन्त्री दधानोऽसक्त-
द्राज्ञां वामदृशां प्रियो भवति संग्रामे पुरे वा चिरम् ॥ १०
चिन्तारत्नाश्रितास्त्रित्रियुगमथ नृसिंहावृतान्तःस्थबीजं
प्राद्युः साध्याभिधानं बहिरपि लिपिभिः प्रानुलोमाभिवीतम् ।
क्ष्माबिम्बद्वन्द्वरन्ध्रप्रचितचतुरर्णं ग्रहोन्मादभूत-
व्याधिघ्नं यन्त्रमस्मिन् कृतकलशविधिर्गर्भरक्षादिकारी ॥ ११
द्वादशगुणितेऽखिलसन्नृसिंहाबीजं महेन्द्रपुरवीतम् ।
शीतालिप्तं पुरलघुधूपितमन्तःप्रबद्धकर्मयुतम् ॥ १२
चतसृषु दिक्षु निखन्यात् सीमायां द्वारतोरणाधो वा ।
देशाभिगुप्तिरेषा गुप्ततमा सूरिभिः पुरा प्रोक्ता ॥ १३
अलदलनिशाकुशीतैर्मसृणे पट्टे विलिख्य यन्त्रमिदम् ।
सेरस्थापनकर्म प्रतिजप्तं प्राङ्गणे खनेन्मन्त्री ॥ १४

आकर्षकरं यन्त्रमाह—साध्याख्यामिति । शक्तिवक्त्राविति । मध्यशक्ति-वक्त्रावित्यर्थः । रन्ध्रत्रये कोणत्रय इत्यर्थः । त्रिशक्ताविति । वेष्टनशक्तिष्वित्यर्थः । अमलधिय इति । ध्यानसामर्थ्यमुक्तम् ॥ ८ ॥ ९ ॥

षड्गुणितप्रयोगमाह—पाशाष्टाक्षरेति । मन्त्रो दधान इति । धारयितुः शक्तिमत्त्वव्रता उक्ता । चतुरर्णं सूर्यचतुरक्षरम् ॥ १० ॥ ११ ॥

वास्तुरक्षाकरं द्वादशगुणितयन्त्रविशेषमाचष्टे—द्वादशगुणित इति ॥ १२॥१३ ॥

कुशीतैर्मन्त्रीति । लेखनद्रव्यस्य मूलेन पूजोक्ता । खनेन्मन्त्रीति । पूजावल्यादि मन्त्रज्ञ इत्यर्थः ॥ १४॥१५ ॥

तत्र विशन्ति न चौरा ग्रहकृत्याः स्यान्निकेतरक्षा च ।
अश्माभिपातवारणमभिवृद्धिः सम्पदाम्भवेदचिरात् ॥ १५
तद्वद् घटार्गलाख्यं यन्त्रं नीले विलिख्य पट्टवरे ।
मोचकसाध्यप्रतिकृतिहृदये गुलिकां विधाय निःक्षिप्य ॥ १६
त्रिमधुरयुक्ते पात्रे विन्यस्याऽभ्यर्च्य गन्धपुष्पाद्यैः ।
बलिमपि विकिरेद्रात्रिषु सप्ताहादानयेद्वधूमिष्टाम् ॥ १७
तामेवाथ प्रतिकृतिमग्नौ किञ्चित् प्रतापयेज्जपन् ।
शक्तिं पाशाङ्कुशमनुसाध्याह्वविदर्भितां समाहितधीः ॥ १८
विधिनाऽमुना त्रिरात्रान्नर्वितधियमपि सुराङ्गनां मन्त्री ।
आकर्षयेन्निजवाञ्छाप्रदायिनीं मदनबाणविह्वलिताम् ॥ १९
यन्त्रं तदेव लाक्षातास्रावीतं निधाय कलशजले ।
जप्त्वा भानुसहस्रकमभिषिञ्चेद्रजतकाञ्चनाभ्याञ्च ॥ २०
तद्वद्विधाय कलशं तद् यन्त्रं धारयेत् पुनर्नित्यम् ।
वाञ्छितसिद्धिं लभते भक्त्या प्रणमन्ति देवता अपि तम् ॥ २१
यन्त्रं तदेव मन्दिरभित्तावभिलिख्य पूजयेद्दिनशः ।
चौरादिभूतनागा अपि तं देशं न वीक्षितुं शक्ताः ॥ २२
आलिख्य वीरपट्टे यन्त्रमिदं स्वमस्तकार्पितं कृत्वा ।
युध्यन् प्रत्यर्थिनमपि हत्वा यात्यव्रणाङ्कितो योद्धा ॥ २३
गजमदविलिखितमेतद् यन्त्रं जप्तञ्च मस्तके न्यस्तम् ।
करिणीमपि मदयेत् द्राक् चण्डतरे का कथा करेणुवरे ॥ २४
बहुनेति भाषितेन किमेभ्यो मुख्यं न किमपि च यन्त्रेभ्यः ।
तस्मादमूनि सद्भिर्धार्याणि च विश्ववश्यमिच्छद्भिः ॥ २५
गजमृगमदकाश्मीरैर्मन्त्रितमः सुरभिरोचनायुक्तैः ।
विलिखेदलक्तकरसालुलितैर्यन्त्राणि सकलकार्यार्थी ॥ २६

मन्त्रजपादिसहितं घटार्गलयन्त्रमाकर्षणकरमित्याचष्टे—यद्वदिति ॥१६॥१७॥
सुराङ्गनां मन्त्रीति । घटार्गलोक्तषोडशाक्षरस्यापि जप उक्तः ॥ १८॥१९ ॥
रजतकाञ्चनाभ्यां चावीतमिति अनुषज्यते । प्रयोगान्तरं चैतत् ॥ २०—२५॥
मन्त्रितम इति । यन्त्रसामान्यमत्र इत्यर्थः ॥ २६ ॥

राज्या पटुसंयुतया सपाशशक्त्यङ्कुशेन मन्त्रेण ।
स्वादक्तयाऽभिजुह्वन् निश्युर्वीशांस्तथोर्वशीं वशयेत् ॥ २७

हृल्लेखाग्निस्थसाध्याह्वयमथ बहिरांक्रोंवृतं वह्निगेह-
द्वन्द्वास्रिस्वस्तिकाढ्यं प्रतिलिखतु दले यन्त्रकं नागवल्ल्याः ।
जप्त्वा शक्तिं तु पाशाङ्कुशलिपिसहितां तापयेद्दीपवह्नौ
नक्तं भक्त्या नताङ्गी स्मरशरविवशा प्रेमलोलाऽभियाति ॥ २८

शक्तिस्थं निजनाम वह्निभवनद्वन्द्वोदरे मान्मथं
बीजं साध्यविदर्भया परिवृतं शक्त्या बहिः पार्थिवम् ।
तत्कोणे स्मरमन्यपुष्टनयनप्रोत्थैः पुनः कण्टकै-
स्ताम्बूले लिखिताभिजप्तमदयेद्‌योषिन्मनोमोहनम् ॥ २९

शक्त्यन्तःस्थितसाध्यनाम परितो बीजैश्चतुर्भिः समा-
बद्धं शक्तिमनोभवाङ्कुशलिपिप्रोम्भिः समावेष्टितम् ।
शाल्युत्थे प्रतिलिख्य पिष्टविकृतौ प्राणान् प्रतिष्ठाप्य च
विस्वादौ परिभर्ज्य तत्समदतः साध्यो वशी तिष्ठति ॥ ३०

सान्तं शिखीलवयुतं दहनांशसाध्यं
मायांशसाधकमथाऽभिवृतं कलाभिः ।
मध्योल्लसद्‌द्विमुखशूलमिदन्तु भर्तु-
र्यन्त्राह्वयं नरनताङ्घ्रिवशीकरं स्यात् ॥ ३१

मृत्काराङ्गुलिकात्तया सक्रकलासान्तर्वसायुक्तया
साध्यस्याऽङ्घ्रिरजोयुजा मृदुमृदा क्लृप्तस्य शक्तिं हृदि ।
रूपस्याऽभिविलिख्य तद्विवरके साध्यं तदीरान् प्रति-
ष्ठाप्याजप्य निखन्य तत्र दिनशो मेहेच्चिरं वश्यकृत् ॥ ३२

स्त्रीवश्यकृद्यन्त्रमाह—हृल्लेखेति । बहिरिति । मध्यशक्तेः बहिरित्यर्थः ॥ २८ ॥

अन्यदप्याह—शक्तिस्थमिति ॥ २९ ॥

वश्यकृदपरं यन्त्रमाचष्टे—शक्त्यन्तरिति । समावेष्टितमिति । समाबद्धमित्यस्य व्याख्या ॥ ३० ॥

वश्यकरं यन्त्रविशेषमाचष्टे—सान्तमिति । शिखीलवेति । शिखी ई लवेति पदच्छेदः । यन्त्रान्तरमाह—मृत्कारेति ॥ ३१ ॥ ३२ ॥

वामाच्च्याः प्रतिलिख्य नाम निशया वामोरुदेशे निशा-
मध्ये वामकरेण संशितमतिः संछादयंस्तन्मनाः ।
पूर्वं रुद्रपदं ततश्च दयिते योगीश्वरि त्विन्दुम-
न्मन्त्रं जप्यति चेदनङ्गविवशां सद्यः प्रियामानयेत् ॥ ३३
मायाहृदोरथाऽन्ते ब्रह्मश्रीराजितेऽक्षरान् प्रोक्ता ।
राजयुतपूजितेऽर्णान् जये सविजये सगौरि गान्धारि ॥ ३४
त्रिभुवनवशङ्करीति च सर्वलोकान्तिके वशङ्करि च ।
सर्वस्त्रीपुरुषवशङ्करि सुदुघे वाक्षरान् प्रवीष्मत्र ततः ॥ ३५
मायाद्विठान्तिको मनुरेकाधिकषष्टिवर्णकः प्रोक्तः ।
ऋषिरस्याऽजो निवृच्छन्दो गौरी च देवता प्रोक्ता ॥ ३६
सचतुर्दशभिर्दशभिस्तथाऽष्टभिश्चाऽष्टभिस्तथा दशभिः ।
एकादशभिर्मन्त्राक्षरैः क्रमादुच्यते षडङ्गविधिः ॥ ३७

असकलशशिराजन्मौलिराबद्धपाशा-
ङ्कुशरुचिरकराब्जा बन्धुजीवारुणाङ्गी ।
अमरनिकरवन्द्या त्रीक्षणा शोणलेपां-
शुककुसुमयुता स्यात् सम्पदे पार्वती वः ॥ ३८

अयुतं प्रजपेज्जुहुयाद्घृतप्लुतैः पायसैर्दशांशेन ।
आराधयेत्तदङ्गैर्मातृभिराशाधिपैश्च निशितमनाः ॥ ३९
तिलतण्डुलकैर्लोणैस्त्रिमधुरसिक्तैः फलैश्च मधुरतरैः ।
आज्यैररुणकुवलयैस्त्रिदिनं हवनक्रियाशु वश्यकरी ॥ ४०
नित्यश्चादित्यगतां देवीं प्रविचिन्त्य तन्मुखो जप्यात् ।
अष्टोत्तरशतमङ्गामादौ भुवनं वशीकरोत्यचिरात् ॥ ४१
वार्णादर्वाङ्मन्त्री प्रयोजयेत् साध्यनामकर्मयुतम् ।
प्रजपेद्वा हवनविधौ वाञ्छितसिद्धिप्रदस्तथा मन्त्रः ॥ ४२

आकर्षकरं यन्त्रमाचष्टे— वामेति ॥ ३३ ॥

ब्रह्मश्रीमन्त्रमुद्धरति—मायेति । ब्रह्मश्रीमन्त्रस्य ह्रीं बीजम् । स्वाहा शक्तिः । शाक्ते पीठे पूजा । अङ्गब्रह्माणीन्द्रवज्रादिभिरावरणपूजा । वार्णादर्वाङ्मन्त्रीति । प्रणवशक्त्यादिकल्पमुक्तम् ॥ ३४॥३५॥३६॥३७॥३८॥३९॥४०॥४१॥४२ ॥

सताररराजमुख्यन्ते राजाभिमुखिवर्णकान् ।
आभाष्य वश्यमुखि च क्लींश्रींमारार्णकान् वदेत् ॥ ४३
वीप्सा देवि महादेविपदं देवाधिदेवि च ।
प्रोक्त्वा सर्वजनस्येति मुखं मम वशं वदेत् ॥ ४४
कुरु कुर्विति ठद्वन्द्वान्तिकं मन्त्रं समुद्धरेत् ।
सप्ताधिकैः सदशभिस्तथा त्रिंशद्भिरक्षरैः ॥ ४५
दशभिः सप्तभिश्चैव चतुर्भिः करणाक्षरैः ।
पञ्चभिः सप्तदशभिर्वर्णैरङ्गक्रिया मनोः ॥ ४६
ब्रह्मश्रीमन्त्रसंप्रोक्ता प्रतिपत्तिरमुष्य च ।
मन्त्रस्य जपक्लृप्तिश्च तथा होमविधिः स्मृतः ॥ ४७
मन्त्री सर्वजनस्थाने कुर्यात् साध्याह्वयं मनोः ।
प्रजपे हवने वाऽथ तथा तर्पणकर्मणि ॥ ४८

देवीध्याष्टशतं प्रसूनवदथ त्रिस्वादुयुक्तं हुनेत्
सप्ताहं भसितेन तेन विहितं पुण्ड्रादिकं वश्यकृत् ।
आज्यैस्तत्कृतहोमपातितसमाजप्तं घृतं प्राशयेत्
साध्यं निष्परिहारकश्च तदिदं वश्यम्भवेद्देहिनाम् ॥ ४९
शक्तिं साध्यर्क्षवृक्षप्रतिकृतिहृदि संलिख्य संस्थाप्य जीवं
जप्त्वा खन्याऽङ्गणेऽस्मिन्विधिवदनलमाधाय पुष्पैर्जवायाः ।
देवीमन्त्रेण रात्रौ दशपरशतसंख्यैस्तु काचन्दनाक्तै-
र्हुत्वा तां सप्तरात्रं सरिति निखननादुत्तमं वश्यकर्म ॥ ५०

अन्नं मह्य[व्य]न्नं मे देह्यन्नाधिपतये ममेत्युक्त्वा ।
अन्नं प्रदापयेति च ठद्वयान्तोऽन्नप्रदायको मन्त्रः ॥ ५१

राजमुखीमन्त्रमुद्धरति—सतारेति । राजमुखीमन्त्रस्यापि ब्रह्मश्रीमन्त्रवदेव बीजादिकं सर्वम् । क्लीं बीजम् । क्लीं शक्तिरिति वा ॥ ४३॥४४॥४५॥४६॥४७ ॥

मन्त्री सर्वजनस्थान इति शक्त्यादित्वमुक्तम् ॥ ४८ ॥ ४९ ॥

वश्यकरं प्रयोगान्तरमाचष्टे—शक्तिमिति ॥ ५० ॥

अन्नाधिपतिमन्त्रं दर्शयति—अन्नमिति । अन्नमन्त्रस्य वैश्रवण ऋषिः । अनुष्टुप्छन्दः । भूश्रियौ देवते । ग्लौं बीजम् । श्रीं शक्तिः । ग्लांश्रामादि-

करणेन्द्रियरसधातुद्वयवर्णैरङ्गमस्य मन्त्रपदैः ।
द्व्ययुतजपावधिरेष द्विसहस्रहुतश्च सर्पिरन्नाभ्याम् ॥ ५२
दुग्धाब्धौ रूप्यवप्रावृतकनकमयद्वीपवर्ये सुराढ्ये
कल्पद्रूद्यानकाधो मणिमयलसिते वित्तपस्याऽग्रभागे ।
आसीने भूश्रियौ वाञ्छितवसुनिचयं मन्त्रिणे संसृजन्त्यौ
मन्त्री संचिन्तयानो जपतु दिनमुखे सम्पदेऽन्नस्य मन्त्रम् ॥ ५३
नत्यादिभगवत्यन्ते माहेश्वरिपदं वदेत् ।
अन्नपूर्णेऽग्निजायान्तो मन्त्रोऽन्नप्रदसंज्ञकः ॥ ५४
मायाविहितषडङ्गो दिनमुखे जप्यश्च षोड़शसहस्रम् ।
प्रोक्तो जपावसाने सघृतैरन्नैर्दशांशको होमः ॥ ५५
रुद्रताण्डवविलोकनलोलां भद्रवक्त्रनयनां भवकान्ताम् ।
अन्नदाननिरतां जननीं तां संस्मरन् जपतु चित्रदुकूलाम् ॥ ५६
वैश्रवणः पक्षाशः पिङ्गलविविधौ तथैव वित्तेशः ।
सकुवेरः स्वाहान्ताः सव्याहृतयः समीरिता मन्त्राः ॥ ५७
वित्तेशस्याऽन्तराले दशवटसमिधः सर्पिषाक्ता विविक्ता
होतव्या द्रव्यसिद्धै कनकघटकरण्डात्तदोस्तुन्दिलोऽसौ ।
हेमाभो रत्नदीप्तो दरकमलनिधिद्योतितो रत्नपीठे
ध्येयो न्यग्रोधमूले हुतभुजि विदुषा वैश्वदेवावसाने ॥ ५८
मन्त्रैरेतैर्घृतयुतपायसहोमोऽपि मन्त्रिणां विहितः ।
लक्ष्म्यै सघृतैश्च तिलैर्बिल्वसमिद्धोमतस्तथैव फलम् ॥ ५९

युतैरन्त्यैरङ्गानि । वैष्णवे पीठे पूजा । अङ्गपृथिव्यादिवलाकाद्यैन्द्रवज्रादिभिरावरणपूजा ॥ ५१ ॥ ५२ ॥

मन्त्रमूर्तिं दर्शयति—दुग्धाब्धाविति । मन्त्री सञ्चिन्तयान इति । प्रणवश्रीपृथिव्यादित्वमुक्तम् ॥ ५३ ॥

अन्नपूर्णामन्त्रमुद्धरति—नत्यादीति । अन्नपूर्णाया ह्रीं बीजम् । स्वाहा शक्तिः । ब्रह्मा ऋषिः । अनुष्टुप् छन्दः । माहेश्वरी देवता । शाक्ते पीठे पूजा । अङ्गब्रह्माणीन्द्रवज्रादिभिरावरणपूजा ॥ ५४ ॥ ५५ ॥ ५६ ॥

मन्त्रिणो विहित इति । वैश्रवणमन्त्राणां प्रणवशक्त्यादित्वमुक्तम् ॥५७॥५८॥५९॥

भया भारेन्दुयुक् सैव विबिन्दुर्हंस्पताक्षरैः ।
बालिस्थयोनिनत्यन्तो वसुवर्णो मनुर्मतः ॥ ६०
वसुसाहस्रजापस्य तावच्छतहुतो मतः ।
होमः सर्पिष्मताऽन्नेन बीजेनाऽङ्गक्रिया मता ॥ ६१
रत्नस्वर्णांशुकादीन्निजकरकमलाद्दक्षिणादाकिरन्तं
वासोराशौ निधायाऽपरममरगुरुं पीतवस्त्रादिभूषम् ।
ध्यायन्नासीनमप्यापणभुवि शतसंख्यं सविंशत्कमेवं
भीतापुष्पैर्घृताक्तैस्त्रिदिनमथ हुनेत् स्वर्णवस्त्रादिसिद्ध्यै ॥ ६२
वययोरन्तरा स्वमेदेहिशुक्राक्षरा द्विठः ।
मन्त्रोऽयुतजपः सर्पिःसहस्रहवनक्रियः ॥ ६३
शुक्रास्ये शुक्लपुष्पैर्हुतभुजि गुणशः सप्तशोऽप्येकविंश-
द्वारं होतव्यमेषोऽप्यतिसितकुसुमालेपनो वामदोष्णा ।
वासोरत्नानि कार्त्तस्वरमपि सततं साधकाय प्रयच्छन्
ध्यातो व्याख्यानमुद्राकलितवरकरस्त्वापणालिन्दसंस्थः ॥ ६४
राजीरस्थोऽह्निपो दण्डी वेदान्तेऽसौ विदाहकः ।
सायान्ते नतिरप्यष्टवर्णो वैयासिको मनुः ॥ ६५

बृहस्पतिमन्त्रमाचष्टे—भयेति । बृहस्पतिमन्त्रस्य ब्रह्मानुष्टब्बृहस्पतय ऋष्यादयः । बृं बीजम् । नमः शक्तिः । बीजेनाऽङ्गानि । अङ्गेन्द्रवज्रादिभिरावरणपूजा ॥ ६० ॥ ६१ ॥ ६२ ॥

शुक्रमन्त्रमाह—वययोरिति । शुक्रमन्त्रस्य ब्रह्मविराट्शुक्राख्या ऋष्यादयः । ओं बीजम् । स्वाहा शक्तिः । बीजेनाऽङ्गानि मन्त्रपदैर्वा । अङ्गेन्द्रवज्रादिभिरावरणपूजा ।

गुणशः सप्तशोऽप्येकविंशद्वारमिति । तत्र गुणश एकविंशद्वारहोमः मालतीमल्लिकाजातिभिः । सप्तशः एकविंशद्धोमः पङ्कजकुमुदकह्लारकुन्दमन्दारनन्द्यावर्तसेवन्तिकाभिः । मिश्रहोमपक्षे द्विचत्वारिंशदाहुतिसंख्या । अमिश्रहोमपक्षे दशाधिकद्विशतसंख्या आहुतयः ॥ ६३ ॥ ६४ ॥

व्यासमन्त्रमाचष्टे—राजीरस्थ इति । व्यासमन्त्रस्य ब्रह्मानुष्टब्वेदव्यासाः ऋष्यादयः । व्यं बीजम् । नमः शक्तिः । बीजेनाङ्गानि ॥ ६५ ॥ ६६ ॥ ६७ ॥

मुनिव्रातावीतं विमलधियमम्भोदरुचिर-
द्युतिं व्याख्यामुद्राकलनविलसद्दक्षिणकरम् ।
परं जानौ कृत्वा दृढकलितकक्षैकविवरं
समासीनं व्यासं स्मरत निरतं पुण्यचरितम् ॥ ६६

प्रकृतिसहस्रजपोऽयं दशांशकृतपायसाज्यहवनविधिः ।
निरुपमकविताप्रज्ञाव्याख्याश्रीसम्पदावहो मन्त्रः ॥ ६७

करचरणपार्श्वमूलद्युलोहरेबिन्दुदंसरसनार्णाः ।
अलिकाद्यो वर्मास्त्रद्विठान्तिको मनुरयं ध्रुवादिः स्यात् ॥ ६८

अयुतं प्रजपेच्च षट्सहस्राधिकमन्ते जुहुयाद्दशांशमानैः ।
तिलसर्षपतण्डुलैः सशालीहविराज्यैः सुसमेधिते कृशानौ ॥ ६९

उत्तुङ्गाद्रिः प्रचेता अपि दहनसमीरौ धराव्योमसंज्ञे
प्राक्प्रत्यग्दक्षसौम्यास्वध उपरि च दिक्षु प्रबद्धप्रभाः स्युः ।
तन्मध्यस्थान्विपक्षादिकहरिरुरुदन्तीन्द्रनागान् सचोरान्
हन्त्येतैर्मन्त्रिमुख्यो मनुविहितबलव्याकुलान् सद्य एव ॥ ७०

निजरिपुमचलाद्यैस्तैः ससम्बाधवीतं
मनुविदथ हलोभ्यां रुद्धनिश्वासवेगम् ।
तदुपरिगतबीजैः साधुसंस्यूतवक्त्रं
दहतु सकवचास्त्रैर्दीन्दुभिः स्वेच्छयैव ॥ ७१

योनिर्वियत् सनेत्रं परमेवर्णास्तथाऽस्थिगं मेदः ।
रक्तस्थदृक् द्विठान्तस्ताराद्योऽयं मनुर्दशार्णयुतः ॥ ७२

शत्रुजयोपायमन्त्रमाह — करेति । महासङ्कोचकमन्त्रस्य दं बीजं क्लीं शक्तिः । ब्रह्मानुष्टुप्पर्वतादय ऋष्यादयः । अकचटतपैर्हलोंक्रामादियुक्तैरङ्गानि ॥ ६८ ॥ ६९ ॥

ध्यानमाह — उत्तुङ्गाद्रिरिति । मन्त्रिमुख्य इति प्रणवादित्वं मन्त्रस्योक्तम् ॥७०॥

मनुविदिति । साध्यादिपदयोग उक्तः ॥ ७१ ॥

अश्वारूढामन्त्रमुद्धरति — योनिरिति । अश्वारूढाया प्रणवानन्तरं पाशशक्त्य ङ्कुशत्र्यक्षरं योज्यम् । तथाच त्रयोदशार्णा भवन्ति । द्वाभ्यां हृदयम् । शक्त्या शिरः । अङ्कुशेन शिखा । पुनर्द्वाभ्यां कवचम् । पञ्चभिर्नेत्रम् । द्वाभ्यामस्त्रम् ।

अयुतं जपेन्मनुमिमं सहस्रवारं हुनेत्तथाज्येन ।
ध्याताऽपि गिरिसुतेयं जगतीं विश्वां वशीकरोत्यनिशम् ॥ ७३
अश्वारूढा कराग्रे नवकनकमयीं वेत्रयष्टिं दधाना
दक्षेऽन्येनानयन्ती स्फुरिततनुलता पाशबद्धां स्वसाध्याम् ।
देवी नित्यं प्रसन्ना नवशशधरबिम्बा त्रिनेत्राभिरामा
दद्यादाद्याऽनवद्यां प्रवरफलसुखप्राप्तिहृद्यां श्रियं वः ॥ ७४
विद्ययाऽनुदिनहृद्ययाऽनया होमकर्म वरहेमदायि तत् ।
कामितां सपदि वामलोचनामानयेदपि च मारपीड़िताम् ॥ ७५
हवनक्रिया सपदि वश्यकरी मधुरावसेकपटुना पटुना ।
सदृशो न कश्चन जगत्यपरो मनुनाऽमुनाऽऽनयनकर्मविधौ ॥ ७६
वाणी स्यात्ताररूपा शिरसि गिरिसुता शक्तिरूपा ललाटे
रव्यग्न्यक्ष्णोस्तथात्मा विधुरपि वदनावेष्टने टान्तरूपः ।
श्रीर्जिह्वायां स्वरूपाऽप्यभिमतकरिरूपौ स्वहौ दीर्घयुक्ता-
वेवं न्यासो मुखे श्रीविभवसुखयशःकान्तिमेधाकरः स्यात् ॥ ७७

इति श्रीप्रपञ्चसारे चतुस्त्रिंशः पटलः ।

ॐ बीजम् । क्लीं शक्तिः । स्वाहा वा शक्तिः । शाक्ते पीठे पूजा । पाशाङ्कुशत्वरत्वरविधानेन पूजा । षोड़शकोष्ठानि लिखित्वा मध्यचतुष्के प्रणवं ससाध्यं लिखेत् । अवशिष्टेष्ववशिष्टान् वर्णान् विलिखेत् । सर्ववश्यकरमिदं यन्त्रम् ॥ ७२ ॥ ७३ ॥ ३४ ॥ ३५ ॥ ७६ ॥

अमठन्यासमाह—वाणीति । लक्ष्मीनारायणत्वहतो श्रिय ऋष्यादयः । श्रीं बीजम् । क्लीं शक्तिः ॥ ७७ ॥

इति श्रीपद्मपादाचार्यकृते प्रपञ्चसारविवरणे

चतुस्त्रिंशत्पटलः ।

पञ्चत्रिंशः पटलः ।

प्राणप्रतिष्ठानमनोर्विधानं प्रवच्यते संप्रति सर्वसिद्ध्यै ।
यस्मादृतेऽमी कथिताः प्रयोगा व्यर्था भवेयुर्गतजीवकल्पाः ॥ १
प्रोक्तापूर्वममुष्यशब्दमथ च प्राणा इह प्राणका-
स्तद्वज्जीव इह स्थितेति च तथा सर्वेन्द्रियाणीति च ।
तद्वद्वाङ्मनसी दृशं श्रुतिमथो घ्राणञ्च सप्राणकं
सेविहागमथो त्वयुक् सुखचिरे तिष्ठन्तु ठद्वन्द्वयुक् ॥ २
मन्त्रस्याऽस्य विधिर्हरिश्च हर इत्येते मुनित्वे स्थिता-
श्छन्दश्चर्ग्यजुषं ससामकमथोऽतिच्छन्दसं वा भवेत् ।
स्रष्ट्री या जगतामनादिनिधना सर्वस्य चेष्टाकरी
प्राणाख्या प्रकृतिः क्रियामयवपुर्देवी परा देवता ॥ ३
प्रत्येकं कादिवर्गैः प्रतिगतलिपिभिर्बिन्दुयुक्तैर्धराद्यैः
शब्दाद्यैः श्रोत्रमुख्यैर्वदनकरमुखैस्तत्क्रियाभिः क्रमेण ।
बुद्ध्याद्यैश्चात्मनेऽन्तैरुपरि च विलसज्जातिभिः षड्भिरेवं
कुर्यादङ्गानि सम्यग्विशदमतिरथो विश्वरूपत्वसिद्ध्यै ॥ ४
नाभेर्देशादापदं पाशबीजं हृद्देशादानाभिदेशञ्च शक्तिम् ।
आहृद्देशं मस्तकादङ्कुशाख्यं न्यस्त्वा यादीन् धातुषु न्यस्य सप्त ॥
प्राणे जीवे चैव हंसद्वयाणं न्यस्येन्मूलं व्यापकं मस्तकादि ।
एवं न्यस्य प्राणशक्तिस्वरूपां विद्यां ध्यायेदात्मरूपाञ्च देवीम् ॥ ६

उक्तसर्वमन्त्रजीवभूतस्य प्राणप्रतिष्ठामन्त्रस्य विधानं वक्तुमारभते—प्राणप्रतिष्ठानेति ॥ १ ॥

प्रोक्तापूर्वममुष्येति । प्रोक्ता आपूर्वमिति पदच्छेदः । ॐ आं ह्रीं क्रों इति प्रोक्तेत्यर्थः । मूलमन्त्रस्यैवंरूपत्वात् । ब्रह्मविष्णुमहेश्वरा ऋषयः । ऋग्यजुःसामाथर्वाणि अतिच्छन्दांसि । श्रीमूलप्रकृतिः प्राणशक्तिर्देवता । आं बीजम् । क्रों शक्तिः ॥ २ ॥ ३ ॥

सम्यग्विशदमतिरिति । अङ्गमन्त्राणां स्वरपुटितत्वं सूचितम् । अं ङं घं

रक्ताम्भोधिस्थपोतोल्लसदरुणसरोजाधिरूढा कराब्जैः
पाशं कोदण्डमिक्षूद्भवमथ गुणमप्यङ्कुशं पञ्च बाणान् ।
बिभ्राणाऽसृक्कपालं त्रिनयनलसिता पीनवक्षोरुहाढ्या
देवी बालार्कवर्णा भवतु सुखकरी प्राणशक्तिः परा वः ॥ ७

ध्यात्वा देवीमेवं प्रजपेल्लक्षं मनुं समाहितधीः ।
आज्येनाऽन्ते जुहुयाच्चरुणा वा तद्दशांशतो मन्त्री ॥ ८
शाक्ते पीठे देवीं षट्कोणस्थैः प्रजेशहरिरुद्रैः ।
वाणीलक्ष्मीगिरिजासहितैरङ्गैश्च मातृलोकेशैः ॥ ९
प्रयजेच्चतुर्भिरेवं परिवारैर्नित्यमेव मन्त्रितमः ।
एवं संसिद्धमनुर्वश्याद्यान्यारभेत कर्माणि ॥ १०

पाशाङ्कुशान्तरितशक्तिमनोः परस्ता-
दुच्चार्य यादिवसुवर्णगुणं सहंसम् ।
पश्चादमुष्य पदमुच्चरतु प्रयोग-
मन्त्रोऽयमित्यमुदितो ग्रहसंख्यया वा ॥ ११

गं खं कं पृथिव्यप्तेजोवाय्वाकाशात्मने आं क्रों हृदयाय नमः । इत्यादिमन्त्रेण अङ्गमन्त्रा द्रष्टव्याः ॥ ४ ॥ ५ ॥ ६ ॥ ७ ॥

तद्दशांशतो मन्त्रीति । ॐ आं स्वाहा ॐ क्रीं स्वाहा ॐ क्रों स्वाहा ॐ यं मृतायै स्वाहा । एवं राद्यक्षरयुताभिः वैवस्वताद्याभिः सकृत्सकृद्धुत्वा ॐ चं सं हं सः क्रीं ॐ इत्यक्षरैरपि तथा हुत्वा मूलेनोक्तसंख्यं जुहुयादित्यर्थः ॥ ८ ॥

प्रजेशहरिरुद्राः ब्रह्मविष्णुरुद्राः । ते च षट्कोणस्य प्राङ्निर्ऋतिवायु-कोणस्थाः । वाण्याद्याः ईशानाग्निवरुणकोणस्थाः । मन्त्रितम इति । ब्रह्मादीनां स्वस्वबीजयोग इत्युक्तः ॥ ९ ॥ १० ॥

ग्रहसंख्यया वेति । प्राणप्रतिष्ठामन्त्रसंग्रह उक्तः । ग्रहशब्देन नवसंख्या लक्षिता । नवमन्त्रैर्वा प्राणप्रतिष्ठेत्यर्थः । यं रं लं वं शं षं सं हों हंसः इत्येभिरित्यर्थः । गुणशब्देन ॐ तेन होममिति । पाशादित्र्यक्षरयोगस्तु पदद्वयेऽपि समानः । अन्यथापूर्तः । अथवा ग्रहसंख्यया वेत्यस्यायमर्थः । यादिवसुवर्णगुणं ग्रहसंख्यया सप्तसंख्यया युक्तं वेति । याद्यष्टकानन्तरं प्रणवं चं सं हं सः क्रीं ॐ इति च संयोज्यमित्यर्थः [ग्रहसंख्ययैवेति राघवभट्टधृतपाठः] ॥ ११ ॥

मृता वैवस्वता चैव जीवहा प्राणहा तथा ।
आकृष्या मथना चैव प्रमादा विस्फुलिङ्गिनी ।
चेचन्नप्रतिहारीति प्राणदूत्यश्च यादिकाः ॥ १२
बद्ध्वा साध्यं पाशबीजेन शक्त्या
गृह्णन्नाकृष्याऽङ्कुशेनाऽथ यादीन् ।
दूतीश्चोक्त्वा साध्यनामाऽथ धातू-
नेवं मन्त्रो यावदात्मा सवीर्यः ॥ १३

दूतीमन्त्रानुद्धरति—मृतेत्यादिना । आं क्रीं क्रों यं रं लं वं शं षं सं हों ॐ चं सं हं सः ह्रीं ॐ यं मृते अमुष्य मृतात्मकान् प्राणान् इहाहर । अमुष्य मृतात्मकाः प्राणा इह प्राणा इति वा । इहैवागत्य सुखं चिरं तिष्ठन्तु स्वाहा ॐ चं सं हं सः क्रीं ओं इत्यभिधाय आं क्रोमित्यादि ओमन्तमुक्त्वा यं मृते अमुष्य मृतात्मकं जीवमिहाहर । अमुष्य मृतात्मकजीवः इह स्थित इति वा । इहैवेत्यादिक-मभिधाय आं क्रोमित्याद्योमन्तमुक्त्वा यं मृते अमुष्य मृतात्मकानि सर्वेन्द्रियाणि वाङ्मनश्चक्षुः श्रोत्र घ्राण प्राणानिहाहर । अमुष्य मृतात्मकानि सर्वेन्द्रियाणि वाङ्मनश्चक्षुः श्रोत्र घ्राण प्राणा इति वा । इहैवागत्य सुखं चिरं तिष्ठन्तु स्वाहा । ॐ चं सं हं सः क्रीं ओमिति वदेत् । एष मृतामन्त्रः । एवं वैवस्वतादिमन्त्रा ऊहनीयाः ॥ १२ ॥

प्राणप्रतिष्ठाप्रकारमाह—बद्ध्वेति । साध्यस्य शक्तिं पाशशक्तितेजोऽङ्कुशमहा-भ्रमरकालदण्डरूपेण पञ्चधा निःसार्य पाशबीजमुच्चरन् साध्यं पाशेन गले बद्ध्वा शक्तिबीजतेजसा तं स्ववशे कृत्वा अङ्कुशेनाकृष्याऽग्रतः संस्थाप्य याद्यष्टकमुच्चरन् साध्यस्य त्वगादीन् व्याप्याऽतिक्रम्य महाभृङ्गेण साध्यं कबलीकृत्य कालदण्ड-ताड़नेन सुप्तं तं संबोध्य चं इति सपरिवारं तमुन्मूलीकृत्य समिति स्वप्राणशक्तिरूप-महाभ्रमरेण बाधयित्वा हंस इति स्वैक्यं संभाव्य क्रीं ओमिति वश्यादौ जीवनाय प्लावनं कृत्वा यं मृते इत्यादिना स्वमृतां संबोध्य अमुष्य मृतात्मकाः प्राणा इह प्राणा इत्यादिना स्वमृताप्राणानितरमृताप्राणैः संयोज्य रमिति साध्यमृतातन्तुच्छेदं विधाय सकोटयन्त्रहृदयायां पुत्तल्यामात्मनि वा साध्यमृताप्राणान् संस्थाप्य पूर्ववत् आं क्रीं इत्यादि सप्रतिपत्तिकं जपन् साध्यहृदयं गत्वा तस्य मृताजीवा-दिकमप्येवमेवानयेदिति मृताप्राणप्रतिष्ठामन्त्रक्रमः । एवमेव वैवस्वतादिप्राणा अपि स्थापनीयाः । युगपदेव वा मृतादिप्राणान् संस्थापयेत् ।

सुप्तेऽशेषजने निशीथसमये साध्ये स्वपित्यादरा-
दारुह्य स्ववशं निधाय हृदये साध्याकृतेः कीटकम् ।
बद्धा तच्च निपीड़मेव सहसा कालस्य यष्ट्या शिर-
स्याताड्य क्षुभिताखिलेन्द्रियगणं साध्यं स्मरेत् साधकः ॥ १४

वायव्याग्नेयैन्द्रवारीशमहेश-
क्रव्यात्सोमप्रेतराजमध्यगेषु ।
स्थानेष्वेतेष्वष्ट यादीन् सहंसान्
भृङ्गान् ध्यायेत् स्वीयबिन्दुप्रबद्धान् ॥ १५

अथ यादीनिति । अथाऽनन्तरं यादीन् होमन्तानुक्त्वा साध्यस्य धातून् जीवं च सपरिकरं स्वहृदयाम्बुजमध्ये वायुना स्वमण्डले संकोचितं कवलीकृत्य सयादिकदूतीश्च स्वस्य सम्बद्ध्यन्ताः साध्यस्य चामुष्य मृतात्मकान् प्राणानित्यादिक्रमेणोक्त्वा चशब्देन क्रियां चोक्त्वा पुनरपि साध्यनामादिकम् अमुष्य मृतात्मकाः प्राणा इह प्राणा इत्यादिक्रमेणोक्त्वा अथानन्तरं पुनरपि धातून् मृतादींश्च एवं पूर्वोक्तक्रमेण जीवाद्याहरणार्थमुक्त्वा इत्यनुषज्यते । सवीर्यः सप्राणादिकः साध्यस्य जीवो यावत् साधकस्य आत्मा भवति साधकात्मना एकीभवति तावत् यादिके आवर्तिते सति प्रयोगमन्त्रो भवतीति यादीनां त्रयावृत्तिरभिहिता । प्राणजीवसर्वेन्द्रियाकर्षणार्थं केचिद् यादीनां चतुरावृत्तिं वर्णयन्ति । प्राणजीवेन्द्रियसामान्यतद्विशेषाणामाकर्षणार्थं केचित् पञ्चावृत्तिं वर्णयन्ति । प्राणसामान्य जीवेन्द्रियसामान्य तद्विशेष-प्राणविशेषाणामाकर्षणार्थं केचिन्नवावृत्तिं वदन्ति ॥ १३ ॥

मन्त्रोक्तानां सर्वेषां प्रत्येकमाकर्षणार्थं प्राणप्रतिष्ठायाः कालमाह— सुप्त इति । आदरादिति । तात्पर्येणेत्यर्थः । आरभ्येति । साधकः स्वयं पाशादि-पञ्चात्मना निष्क्रम्य साध्यं पाशेन बद्ध्वा शक्त्या वशीकृत्य अङ्कुशेनाकृष्य तस्यान्तः प्रविश्य तस्य हृदयकमलमारुह्य महाभृङ्गेण तं कवलीकुर्वन् वशे निधायेत्यर्थः । साध्याकृतेः कीटकमिति । प्राणप्रतिष्ठारम्भात् प्रागेव साध्य-प्रतिकृतेः हृदये प्राणप्रतिष्ठायन्त्रं लिखित्वा संस्थाप्य वा तत्र किञ्चित् कीटादि सजीवं निक्षिप्याच्छाद्य प्रयोग आरम्भणीयः इत्युक्तम् । तं चेत्यादिना कालदण्डेन ताड़यित्वा तस्य बोधनमुक्तम् । अन्यथा प्राणप्रतिष्ठायोगात् ॥ १४ ॥

स्वहृदये साध्यहृदये पुत्तलीहृदये च मृतादिदूतीनां स्थानमाह— वायव्येति । यादीन् सहंसान् भृङ्गान् ध्यायेदिति । याद्यक्षररूपमृतादिनवकं

स्वीयेऽप्येवं संस्मरेद्धृत्सरोजे
भृङ्गीरूपान्निर्गतान् श्वासमार्गैः।
साध्याब्जस्थान् चञ्चरीकान् गृहीत्वा
स्वीयं स्थानं पूर्ववत् संप्रविष्टः॥ १६

बीजानि रक्तानि तु वश्यकर्मण्यम्भोधराभाण्यभिचारकाले।
धूम्राणि विद्वेषविधौ सहोमे पीतानि संस्तम्भविधौ स्मरेच्च॥ १७
अथवा साध्यप्राणान् मण्डूकाकारधारिणो ध्यायेत्।
स्वीयान् भुजगाकारानभिचारादौ नृशंसकर्मविधौ॥ १८

प्राणप्रतिष्ठाकर्मैवं विधायैकादशावरम्।
पुत्तल्यादौ स्वचित्ते वा तांस्तु संस्तम्भयेद्भुवा॥ १९

आकृष्टानां साध्यदेशादसूनां
पुत्तल्यादावप्ययं स्यात्प्रकारः।
किन्तु स्वीये हृत्सरोजे प्रवेशो
वश्याकृष्ट्योरेव नात्राभिचारे॥ २०

भृङ्गरूपेण साध्यहृदयकमलपत्रेषु कर्णिकायां चोक्तक्रमेण स्मरेदित्युक्तम्। स्वीयबिन्दुप्रबद्धानिति। भृङ्गमस्तकबिन्दुगततन्तुभिः परस्परबद्धानित्यर्थः॥ १५॥

स्वहृदये विशेषमाह—स्वीय इति। निर्गतान् श्वासमार्गैरिति। तदानीं वहन्नासापुटेन निर्गम्य ऋज्व्या नाड्या साध्यहृदयं प्रविश्य पूर्ववत्तत्सर्वमादायान्यया तयैव वा नाड्या निर्गम्य पुत्तल्याम् ऋज्व्या नाड्या प्रविश्य तद्धृदयपङ्कजे सर्वं संस्थाप्य ग्लौंबीजात्मना महाकोटेन संस्तभ्य यथागतं स्वदूतीभिः सह पुत्तल्या निर्गम्य निर्गमननाड्या साध्यहृदयं प्रविश्य प्रवेशनाड्या निर्गम्य निर्गमनाड्या स्वहृदयं प्रविश्य स्वदूतीं स्वहृदयपङ्कजे स्थापयित्वा मयि प्राणा इह प्राणाः मयि तज्जीव इह स्थितः इत्यादिमन्त्रं जपित्वा पुनरप्येवं कुर्यादित्यर्थः। साध्यहृदयाद् यथागतं चेन्निर्गच्छति तर्हि पुत्तल्या निर्गतस्य पुनः न साध्यहृदयप्रवेशः कर्तव्यः। किन्तु स्वहृदयमेव प्रवेष्टव्यम्॥ १६॥ १७॥

मारणे विशेषप्रयोगमाह—अथवेति। भुवेति। ग्लौं बीजेनेत्यर्थः॥१८॥१९॥

पुत्तलीस्वहृदादिष्वप्याकृष्टानां साध्यप्राणानां भुवा स्तम्भनं कार्यमित्याह—आकृष्टानामिति। आभिचारकर्मणि साध्यप्राणाः सर्वात्मना पुत्तल्यामेव स्थापनीयाः। वश्याकर्षणादौ एकमंशं पुत्तल्यां संस्थाप्य अंशान्तरं स्वदूतीभिः

पाशाद्यत्रिकयुक्तमूलहृदयभ्रूमध्यसूचायिता
साग्निः साध्यललाटरन्ध्रपथतोऽप्यामूलमाजग्मुषी ।
योन्यामात्महृदब्जमेवमनिशं भ्राम्यत्यसौ चिन्तिता
शक्तिर्जन्मशतान्यपीह वशयेत् साध्यं तथाकर्षयेत् ॥ २१

प्राणप्रतिष्ठाविधिरेवमुक्तः
साङ्गः सयोगो विनियोगयुक्तः ।
अस्मिन् प्रवीणो गिरिकाननादीन्
प्रचालयेत् किं पुनरात्मयुक्तान् ॥ २२
इति श्रीप्रपञ्चसारे पञ्चत्रिंशः पटलः ।

सह स्वहृदये स्थापनीयमित्याह—किञ्चेति ॥ २० ॥

सर्वाकृष्ट्यादिकरं योगमाह—पाशाद्यत्रिकयुक्तेति । अष्टदलमध्यगतशक्तौ साध्यादिकं लिखित्वा पाशाङ्कुशाभ्यां तां संवेष्ट्य याद्यष्टकमष्टदलेषु लिखित्वाऽवशिष्टेन बहिः संवेष्ट्य भूपुरद्वये पाशाङ्कुशौ लिखेत् । इति यन्त्रविधिः ॥ २१ ॥ ॥ २२ ॥

इति श्रीपद्मपादाचार्यकृते प्रपञ्चसारविवरणे
पञ्चत्रिंशत्पटलः ।

[अतीतपटलोक्तसकलमन्त्रयन्त्रादीनां प्राणप्रतिष्ठाविध्यन्तानां गुरूपदेशलब्धानामेव यथोक्तफलसाधनत्वं न लिखितपठितानामिति शिष्यदेशिकार्थमाह—प्राणाग्निहोत्रमिति । अनलाख्यं त्रिष्टुप्पटलोक्तम् । बलिप्रयोगोऽस्मिन् पटल उक्तः । योगः प्रणवपटलादावुक्तः । इति उपान्त्यश्लोकव्याख्यानावसरे सम्बन्धदीपिकायाम् । एतन्मतेऽत्राधिकः श्लोको विद्यत इति प्रतीयते]।

षट्त्रिंशः पटलः ।

अथ सन्तानसंसिद्धिसमाकुलितचेतसाम् ।
तदुत्पत्तिकरं योगं प्रवक्ष्ये गृहमेधिनाम् ॥ १
नचाऽपुत्रस्य लोकोऽस्ति पितरोऽधः पतन्ति च ।
तस्मात्तु सकलोपायैर्यतेताऽपत्यसिद्धये ॥ २
देवर्षिपितृपूजासु विरतानामभक्तितः ।
गुरुमातृपितृश्राद्धवञ्चकानाञ्च नित्यशः ॥ ३
अर्थिभ्योऽर्थमदातॄणां विद्यमानेऽर्थसञ्चये ।
अदत्त्वैवाऽतिथिभ्योऽन्नं भोक्तॄणां पापचेतसाम् ॥ ४
हरिशङ्करयोः पादपद्मार्चारहितात्मनाम् ।
स्वभार्यानिन्दकानाञ्च लोकवेदविरोधिनाम् ॥ ५
इत्यादिदोषदुष्टानां पापानां गृहमेधिनाम् ।
दुष्प्रतिग्रहदोषाद्वा जायते त्वनपत्यता ॥ ६
एवमादिकदोषापनोदिनी सुतसिद्धिदा ।
अशेषपापहन्त्री च वक्ष्यते यजनक्रिया ॥ ७
पुत्राप्तये गृहस्थो दीक्षाविधिना चतुर्दशीरात्रिम् ।
सह पत्न्या गमयित्वा कृत्वा पौर्वाह्णिकीः क्रियाः सकलाः ॥ ८
संयोज्य किञ्चन यथाविधि पञ्चगव्यं
संकोचकेन मनुना प्रतिमथ्य वारणम् ।
संमन्त्र्य चाऽष्टशतकं समवद्यभूत-
मन्त्रैः पिबेत् स्वयमसावपि गर्भधात्री ॥ ९

उक्तमन्त्रानुष्ठानयोग्यं पुत्रोत्पत्तिकरं प्रयोगविशेषं वक्तुमारभते—अथ सन्तानेति। न केवलं पुत्रानुत्पत्तिहेतुदोषाणामेवाऽयं प्रयोगो नाशहेतुः किन्तु सर्वपापापनोदक इत्याह—अशेषपापेति ॥ १ ॥ २ ॥ ३ ॥ ४ ॥ ५ ॥ ६ ॥ ७ ॥

दीक्षाविधिनेति। ब्रह्मचर्याधःशय्यापयोव्रतादिनियमेनेत्यर्थः। कृत्वा पौर्वाह्णिकीः क्रियाः सकलाः पञ्चदश्यामिति शेषः ॥ ८ ॥

यथाविधि पञ्चगव्यमिति। आम्नाष्टाक्षरस्थमन्त्रैरुक्तमानकृत्या संयोज्येत्यर्थः।

तत्राऽग्निमाधाय चरुञ्च कृत्वा सङ्कल्प्य तद्दक्षिणमुत्तरञ्च ।
भागक्रमात् पैतृकदैविकं तत्प्रीत्यै तु पूर्वं जुहुयात् क्रमेण ॥ १०

स्मृत्वा निजं पितरमप्यधरान्निषण्णं
सान्नाय्यपिण्डयुगलं घृतसंप्लुतं तत् ।
हुत्वा ध्रुवेण घृतसंपुटितं तथैव
मन्त्री पितामहमथ प्रपितामहञ्च ॥ ११

व्याहृतीभिरथ पक्वहोमत: सर्वश: प्रतिजुहोतु सर्पिषा ।
मातृवर्गगुरुतत्पितृद्वयं पूर्ववत्समवदाय साधक: ॥ १२
कलायुतै: षोड़शमूर्तिमन्त्रैर्व्यस्तैरथाऽष्टाक्षरजैश्च वर्णै: ।
अष्टौ समस्तेन च तेन पञ्चाक्षरेण चाऽष्टाक्षरवज्जुहोतु ॥ १३

संकोचकमनुरत्र भविष्यति। पात्रद्वयेऽवदानद्वयं कृत्वा प्रथमं स्वयमेकं हस्ते संगृह्य इतरं गर्भधात्र्या दद्यात्। अस्मिन् प्रयोगे आत्माष्टाक्षरोक्तविधानेनात्मानं सकलीकृत्य स्वयं परशुचक्रगदात्रिशूलधर: सिन्दूरकाञ्चनवर्ण: शङ्करनारायणो ध्येय: पूज्यश्च। अङ्गै: प्रथमावृति:। ईशानादिभिर्द्वितीया। अष्टाक्षराक्षरमूर्तिभि: तृतीया केशवादिषोड़शमूर्तिभिश्चतुर्थी। इन्द्रादिभिरन्त्येत्यावरणक्रम: ॥९॥

तत्राऽग्निमाधायेति। देवस्योत्तरे भागे। दक्षिणे भाग इत्यन्ये। चरुं चोक्तप्रकारेण योग्यपरिमाणं कृत्वा देवपितृभागं विभजयन् पलाशसमिधा देवभागमधिकं कल्पयेत् ॥ १० ॥

निजं पितरमप्यधरान्निषण्णमिति। पित्रादीन् देवोपासकतत्कृतेन पीठसमीपे स्मृत्वेत्यर्थ:। सान्नाय्यशब्देन चरुरुच्यते। घृतसंप्लुतमिति। हविषो घृतबहुलत्वमुक्तम्। घृतसंपुटितमिति। स्रुवेण जुह्वामुपस्तीर्याऽवदानद्वयं तत्र निधाय स्रुवेणाऽभिघार्य होतव्यमित्यर्थ:। ध्रुवेणेति। मन्त्राणां प्रणवादित्वमुक्तम्। अमुकगोत्राय अमुकनाम्ने अस्मत्पित्रे स्वाहेत्यादिमन्त्रा: सूचिता: मन्त्रीति ॥११॥

पक्वहोमान्तरं सप्रणवव्याहृतीभि: होम: कर्तव्य इत्याह—व्याहृतीभिरिति। प्रथमस्तु सप्रणवव्याहृतिहोम: प्रसिद्ध एव। मातृपितामहीप्रपितामह्य: मातृवर्ग:। तद्गुरुर्मातामह:। तत्पितृद्वयं मातु:पितामह मातु:प्रपितामहलक्षणम् ॥ १२ ॥

एवं पितॄणां पक्वनवकं हुत्वा देवभागेन देवहोम: कर्तव्य इत्याह—कलायुतैरिति। षोड़शमूर्तय: केशवाद्या:। अष्टाक्षरवदिति। ओं नम:

पक्वाहुतीनामिति वर्णसंख्यं चतुर्गुणं चापि घृताहुतीनाम् ।
हुत्वाऽवदानद्वितयञ्च पुंस्त्रीभेदप्रभिन्नं हविषा करोतु ॥ १४

पश्चाच्चरेण पुरुषात्मकमन्यदष्ट-
वर्णेन चाऽष्टशतयुग्ममथ प्रजप्य ।
संयोज्य तद्युगलमप्यभिजप्य विष्णु-
र्योन्यादिकेन मनुना च कपर्दिसंख्यम् ॥ १५

पुरुषः पुरुषात्मकं प्रकृत्यात्मकमन्याथ समाहितोपयुज्य ।
अवदानयुगं क्रमान्मनस्वी पुनराचम्य समर्चयेद्धुताशम् ॥ १६
गुरवेऽप्यथ दक्षिणां प्रदत्त्वाऽनलमुद्वास्य च भोजयेद्द्विजातीन् ।
प्रतिपर्वकमेवमेकवृद्ध्या मतिमान् वत्सरकं प्रपूरयीत ॥ १७
एकग्रासादन्यमब्दं द्विजातीन् संभोज्याऽन्नं पूरयेदेकवृद्ध्या ।
संपूर्यमाणादेवमेव त्रिकाब्दादर्वाक् पुत्रो जायते दैवशक्त्या ॥ १८

पितृदेवताप्रसादान्मेधायुःकान्तिसंयुतो विद्वान् ।
लक्ष्मीतेजोयुक्तो धर्मरुचिर्भवति सन्ततेः कर्त्ता ॥ १९

समुनिसुरपितृभ्यो ब्रह्मचर्येण यज्ञै-
स्त्रिविधमृणमपत्यैश्चैव संमोचयेद्यः ।
श्रुतिवचनकृदस्मिन्वाऽपि लोके परस्मि-
न्निति स तु गृहमेधी पूज्यते साधुलोकैः ॥ २०

वर्गादिको हलोमन्तः सङ्कोचाख्यो भ्रुवादिकः ।
मन्त्रः स्याद्भूतमनवः स्युश्च भूतात्मनामभिः ॥ २१

शिवाय स्वाहा इत्यादिक्रमेणाऽक्षरैः हुत्वा ॐ नमः शिवाय स्वाहेत्यपि पञ्चवारं जुहुयादित्यर्थः ॥ ११ ॥

घृताहुतिसंख्यामाह—पक्वाहुतीनामिति । वर्णसंख्यमिति । एकपञ्चाशत्-संख्यातमित्यर्थः । अवदानद्वितयमिति । भागद्वयादामलकप्रमाणं हविरादाय मिश्रीकृत्याऽवदानद्वयं स्त्रीपुंसयोर्विभागेन करोत्वित्यर्थः ॥ १४ ॥ १५ ॥ १६ ॥ ॥ १७ ॥ १८ ॥ १९ ॥ २० ॥

भूतात्मनामभिरिति । भूतबीजैरात्मशब्देन नामभिश्च भूतमनवः स्युरित्यर्थः । लं पृथिव्यात्मने नमः । इत्यादयो भूतमन्त्राः ॥ २१ ॥

अतो हिताय जगतां प्रथितं शितचेतसाम् ।
अथ संक्षिप्य वक्ष्यामि लक्षणं गुरुशिष्ययोः ॥ २२
स्वच्छः स्वच्छन्दचरितोऽतुच्छधीस्त्यक्तहृच्छयः ।
देशकालादिविद्देशे देशे देशिक उच्यते ॥ २३
अग्रगण्यः समग्रज्ञो निग्रहानुग्रहे क्षमः ।
षड्वर्गविजयव्यग्रोऽनुग्रो विगतविग्रहः ॥ २४
शुक्लः शुक्लांशुकोऽक्लिष्टकर्माऽविक्लवमानसः ।
वेदवेदाङ्गविद्यादिवेदिता विदितागमः ॥ २५
दुष्टदोऽनिष्टसंहर्ता दृष्टादृष्टसुखावहः ।
रतोऽविरतमर्चासु परं पुरमुरद्विषोः ॥ २६
दाता दान्तः शान्तमना नितान्तं कान्तविग्रहः ।
स्वदुःखकारणेनापि परं परसुखोद्यतः ॥ २७
ऊहापोहविदध्यात्मव्याकुलो मोहवर्जितः ।
अज्ञानुकम्पी विज्ञातज्ञानो ज्ञातपरेङ्गितः ॥ २८
निरंशः सांशवित् सर्वसंशयच्छिदसंशयः ।
नयविद्विनयोपेतो विनीतनीतिरात्मवान् ॥ २९
व्याधिरप्रापितव्याधिः समाधिविधिसंयुतः ।
श्रुतिशूरोऽतिधीरश्च वीरो वाक्यविशारदः ॥ ३०
वर्गोपेतसमारम्भो गभीरो दम्भवर्जितः ।
आदर्श इव विद्यानां न तु दर्शनदूषकः ॥ ३१
असौ मृग्यश्च दृश्यश्च सेव्यश्चाऽभीष्टमिच्छता ।
शिष्यस्तदावर्जनकृद्देहेन द्रविणेन च ॥ ३२
तस्य पादारविन्दोत्थरजःपटलभूषणः ।
ज्ञानमप्राप्य न प्राप्यं प्रायो बुद्धिमतेप्सितम् ॥ ३३

[गुरुशिष्यलक्षणं सफलमाह—अतो हितायेति ॥ २२ ॥]

[तत्र गुरुलक्षणमाह—स्वच्छ इति । हृच्छयः रागः । शुक्लः शुचिः । आत्मवान् प्रशस्तबुद्धिः । व्याधिः विगतमानसव्यसनः । वीरः अध्यवसायान्तगामी । वर्गोपेतसमारम्भः पुरुषार्थसम्बन्धिव्यापारवानित्यर्थः ॥ २३—३१ ॥]

नित्यशः कायवाक्चित्तैस्त्रिहेायनाब्दाधिकावधि ।
परिचर्यापरः शिष्यः स्यात् सुसंयतमानसः ॥ ३४
तं तथाविधमालक्ष्य तथाऽवितथवादिनम् ।
मातृतः पितृतः शुद्धं बुद्धिमन्तमलोलुपम् ॥ ३५
अस्तेयवृत्तिमास्तिक्ययुक्तं मुक्तिकृतोद्यमम् ।
अकलङ्कं मृषाहीनमहीनद्रव्यमानसम् ॥ ३६
ब्रह्मचर्यरतं नित्यं परिचर्यापरं गुरोः ।
अल्पाशनिद्रं पूजायामनल्पकृतकल्पनम् ॥ ३७
अधीतवेदं स्वाधीनमनाधिं व्याधिवर्जितम् ।
तरुणं करुणावासं परितोषकरं गुरोः ॥ ३८
सुवेषमेषणातीतममलं विमलाशयम् ।
सुप्रसन्नमसन्नाङ्गं सदा सन्निहितं गुरोः ॥ ३९
परोपकारनिरतं विरतं परदूषणे ।
मातृवद्गुरुपत्नीश्च भ्रातृवत्तत्सुतानपि ॥ ४०
स्मरन्तमस्मराबाधं स्मितोपेतमविस्मितम् ।
परिगृह्णीत् परीक्ष्यैवं शिष्यमेवंगुणं गुरुः ॥ ४१
अलसं मलसंक्लिन्नं क्लिष्टं कष्टान्ववायजम् ।
दम्भान्वितमगम्भीरं चण्डं पण्डितमानिनम् ॥ ४२
रागिणं रोगिणं भोगलालसं बालसम्मितम् ।
रौद्रं दरिद्रं निद्रालुमाद्यूनं क्षुद्रचेष्टितम् ॥ ४३
नृशंसमन्धं बधिरं पङ्गुं व्यङ्गममङ्गलम् ।
अतिदीर्घमतिह्रस्वमतिस्थूलं कृशात्मकम् ॥ ४४
परदारपरं भीरुं दारुणं वैरिणं सताम् ।
तुच्छं त्वलब्धवैराग्यं स्तब्धं लुब्धकबान्धवम् ॥ ४५
आदित्सुं कुत्सितं वत्सं वीभत्सं मत्सरात्मकम् ।
सुखिनं मुखरं दुष्टं दुर्मदं मूर्खमानसम् ॥ ४६

[शिष्यलक्षणमाह—शिष्यस्तदिति । एषणा पुत्रवित्तलोकेच्छा ॥३२–४१॥]

[शिष्यत्वेनाऽग्राह्यानाह—अलसमिति । चण्डो मूर्खः । आद्यूनं बह्वाशिनम् ।

प्रत्ययग्रमुग्रं व्यग्रेहमग्रगण्यं दुरात्मनाम् ।
भ्रष्टव्रतं तमःस्पृष्टं क्लिष्टमिष्टापहं नृणाम् ॥ ४७
स्वार्थकृत्ये प्रसक्तार्थं निरर्थारम्भणं शठम् ।
ईदृग्विधं गुरुः शिष्यं न गृह्णीयात् कथञ्चन ॥ ४८
यदि गृह्णाति तद्दोषः प्रायो गुरुमपि स्पृशेत् ।
मन्त्रिदोषो यथा राज्ञि पत्यौ जायाकृतो यथा ॥ ४९
तथा शिष्यकृतो दोषो गुरुमेति न संशयः ।
स्नेहाद्वा लोभतो वापि योऽनुगृह्णाति दीक्षया ।
तस्मिन् गुरौ सशिष्ये तु देवताशाप आपतेत् ॥ ५०
मधुद्विषि महादेवे मातापित्रोर्महीभृति ।
भक्तिर्या सा पदाम्भोजे कार्या निजगुरोः सदा ॥ ५१
छायाछत्रपादुकोपानद्दण्डांश्च शयनासने ।
यानं मनोगतं चाऽन्यदन्तेवासी न लङ्घयेत् ॥ ५२
व्याख्यां विवादं स्वातन्त्र्यं कामितां कामजृम्भिकाम् ।
निद्राकुतर्कक्रोधांश्च त्यजेद्गुरुगृहे सदा ॥ ५३
सग्राम्यधर्मविण्मूत्रोत्सर्गनिष्ठीवनादिकम् ।
परित्यजेत् परिज्ञाता वसिञ्च गुरुमन्दिरे ॥ ५४
ग्राह्योक्तिमनृतं निद्रामृणञ्च क्रयविक्रयम् ।
परित्याज्यं गुरौ तस्य सपत्नैश्च समागमम् ॥ ५५
दुष्टं वाऽनिष्टमादिष्टं गुरुणा यत्तु गुर्वपि ।
त्वरया परया कुर्याद्बुद्ध्या सम्यगजिह्मया ॥ ५६
कर्मणा मनसा वाचा सदा भक्तियुजा गुरुम् ।
निर्व्याजं पूजयेच्छिष्यो निजकार्यप्रसिद्धये ॥ ५७
लोकोद्वेगकरी या च या च मर्मनिकृन्तनी ।
स्थित्युच्छेदकरी या च तां गिरं नैव भाषयेत् ॥ ५८

बीभत्सं जुगुप्सितम् । दुर्मदं दुर्मानम् । प्रसक्तार्थं यथासिद्धप्रयोजनम् । ॥ ४२—५० ॥]

[दीक्षितशिष्यस्याचारमाह—मधुद्विषीति ॥ ५१—६१ ॥]

रम्यमप्युज्ज्वलमपि मनसोऽपि समीहितम् ।
लोकविद्वेषणं वेशं न गृह्णीयात् कदाचन ॥ ५९

इत्याचारयुतः सम्यगाचार्यं यः समर्चयेत् ।
कृतकृत्यः स वै शिष्यः परत्रेह च नन्दति ॥ ६०

देवानृषीनपि पितॄनतिथींस्तथाऽग्नी-
न्नित्योद्यतेन मनसा दिनशोऽर्चयेद्यः ।
इष्टानवाप्य सकलानिह भोगजातान्
प्रेत्य प्रयाति परमं पदमादिपुंसः ॥ ६१

इत्थं मूलप्रकृत्यक्षरविकृतिलिपिव्रातजातग्रहर्क्ष-
क्षेत्राद्याबद्धभूतेन्द्रियगुणरविचन्द्राग्निसंप्रोतरूपैः ।
मन्त्रैस्तद्देवताभिर्मुनिभिरपि जपध्यानहोमार्चनाभि-
स्तन्त्रेऽस्मिन् पञ्चभेदैरपि कमलज ते दर्शितोऽयं प्रपञ्चः ॥ ६२

यदाश्रया विप्रकृतिस्वभावतो
विभिन्नताराादिसमुत्थितौजसः ।
जगन्ति पुष्णन्ति रवीन्दुवह्नयो
नमोऽस्तु तस्मै परिपूर्णतेजसे ॥ ६३

इति श्रीप्रपञ्चसारे षट्त्रिंशः पटलः ।

* ॥ समाप्तोऽयं प्रपञ्चसारः ॥ *

[निगदितं सकलमप्यर्थमनूद्य उपसंहरति—इत्थमिति । मूलप्रकृतिश्चासौ अक्षरं चेति मूलप्रकृत्यक्षरं भुवनेशीबीजम् । लिपिव्रातं मातृका । क्षेत्राणि राशयः । आदिपदेन तिथिकरणग्रहः । गुणाः सत्त्वादयः । क्षेत्राद्यैराबद्धा ये भूतेन्द्रियादयः तैः संप्रोतं रूपं येषां मन्त्रादीनां तैः सह जगत्प्रपञ्चो विस्तारो विज्ञानप्रपञ्चो वा तन्त्रे दर्शित इति योजना । कमलज इति सम्बुद्धौ ॥ ६२ ॥]

[मङ्गलमाचरन् प्रारब्धग्रन्थमुपसंहरति—यदाश्रयेति ॥ ६३ ॥]

इति श्रीपद्मपादाचार्यकृते प्रपञ्चसारविवरणे
षट्त्रिंशत्पटलः ॥

* श्रीरस्तु *

प्रपञ्चसारविवरणव्याख्या

प्रयोगक्रमदीपिका ।

प्रथमः पटलः

देवतायै नमो वृत्तिं वृहद्विवरणस्य तु ।
कुर्मः प्रपञ्चसारस्य प्रयोगक्रमदीपिकाम् ॥

विवरणारम्भे मङ्गलाचरणं विवरणकृत् करोति—अवर्णविग्रहमिति । देवं नमामि स्तौमि संश्रय इत्यन्वयः । देवशब्देन वक्ष्यमाणसर्वमन्त्रदेवतात्मिकैका सती परदेवतोच्यते । अवर्णविग्रहमिति । तस्याः सकलरूपेण विशेषणम् । अ इत्येतद्वर्णो विग्रहस्य यस्येति समासः । अ इति सामान्यवैखरी गृह्यते । वक्ष्यति हि—वर्णजापी अकारजापी वेति । स्ववाच्याविभक्तस्वसामान्यादिपूर्वान्वितश्चाऽयमकारः । तत्र वाचकांशस्य वर्णत्वं वाच्यांशस्य च विग्रहत्वमर्थाद्भवति । वर्णविग्रहवर्जितमिति । निष्कलरूपेण विशेषणम् । वर्णविग्रहवेत्तारमिति । सकलनिष्कलरूपेण विशेषणम् । वेत्ता साक्षी । इह सर्वाऽपि वक्ष्यमाणा मन्त्रदेवतैयतो प्रतिपत्तव्येत्यपि सूचितम् । किञ्च सर्वमन्त्रदेवतासामर्थ्यात्मिकायाः परदेवताया अ इत्ययं मन्त्र इत्यपि सूचितम् । तत्र पीठन्यासः शैवो वैष्णवोऽन्यो वा गोमूर्त्याकारोऽपि व्याप्तिपटलभावीन्यङ्गानि सामान्यपटलोक्ता न्यासाः सर्वमन्त्रन्यासाश्चेह कार्याः । एवं हकारप्रणवशक्तिमातृकाजपापरमात्मगायत्र्यादीनामप्यवबोद्धव्यम् । तेषामपि सामान्यमन्त्ररूपतया सामान्यपटलेष्वभिमतत्वात् । नमामि स्तौमि संश्रय इति कायवाग्बुद्धिभिः परदेवतोपस्थितिः क्रियते । यद्वा क्रियमाणविवरणव्यापारस्य प्रपञ्चसारप्रतिपाद्यायां परदेवतायां समर्पणमेतदारम्भे क्रियते । तत्र वाग्व्यापारस्तावद्विवृतिः । सा च परदेवताया गुणकर्माद्यभिधानतया स्तुतिः स्यात् । तथा च तदेकनिष्ठो मनोव्यापारः संश्रयणं कायव्यापारश्च तत्प्रवणतायोगान्नतिरेवेति । अत्रैतदपि सूचितम् देवतां ध्यात्वा कर्मसमर्पणं विधायेति यन्मन्त्रदेवतायां सकलकायिकादिसमर्पणं वक्ष्यते तदप्येतेन प्रकारेण स्यादिति ।

इह खल्वित्यादि । इह तदनुग्रहाय ग्रन्थं चिकीर्षुरित्येवं सम्बन्धः । ग्रन्थकरणमेतदुचितमिहेत्यनेन सूचितम् । इह हि देशे काले चेति । अयं हि तावत्प्रसिद्धो देशः । नह्यत्र कस्यचिल्लौकिकेनोपायेन दुःखात्यन्तनिवृत्तिर्लभ्यते । एवं कालेऽपि ज्ञेयमिति । लोकानुग्रहैकरसतया कृतशरीरपरिग्रह इति

ग्रन्थकरणे सामान्यहेतुरुक्तः। मीमांसोपनिषत्सांख्ययोगकामसूत्रादिव्याख्यानतः तत्तदधिकार्या(र्थ)नुग्रहयोगाल्लोकग्रहणम्। भगवानिति पूजया स्वगुर्वनुस्मरणं ग्रन्थारम्भे क्रियते। यद्वा भगवदवतारोऽयमिति प्रसिद्धेः तथा तदनुस्मरणमेतत्।

ननु परानुग्रहमात्रार्थतया शरीरपरिग्रहासंभव इत्याशङ्कायां तद्धेतुरुच्यते। स च हेतुः सिद्धितत्साधनलक्षणम्। तत्राऽपरोक्षीकृतपरदेवतात्मतत्त्व इति स्वसाधनलक्षणो हेतुः। परदेवतैव साधकात्मनस्तत्त्वम्। मन्त्रन्यासजपयोगादिभिश्च तदपरोक्षीकरणम्। परमां विभूतिकाष्ठां प्राप्त इति सिद्धिलक्षणो हेतुः। परकैवल्यसिद्धिपर्यन्तां विभूतिमिति भावः। अत्र तदनुग्रहायेति यत्प्रयोजनं दर्शयिष्यते तत्प्रकारोऽपि दर्शितः। परदेवतात्मकत्वापरोक्षीकरणोपायतः परमविभूतिकाष्ठाप्राप्तिरूपोऽयमनुग्रह इति। अथैतद्धेतुक एव ग्रन्थकरणे विशेषहेतुरुच्यते—स्वयमेकाकिसम्पदा लज्जमानो दुःखिजनकारुण्याक्रान्तमानसश्च सन्निति। परमां विभूतिकाष्ठां प्राप्तोऽपर इहासुलभ इत्यसौ स्वसिद्धिरेवैकाकिसम्पद्भवति। तया स्वयं लज्जमान इति। सतां ह्येष स्वभाव इति भावः। चकारः प्रागुक्तहेतोरपि समुच्चयार्थः। तदनुग्रहायेति। दुःखितजनानामनुग्रहसिद्धय इत्यर्थः। नानासिद्धिप्रक्रमा परमकैवल्यपर्यन्ता कृत्स्ना विभूतिः तत्प्राप्तिश्चायमनुग्रहः। ईदृगनुग्रहकरणे पर्याप्तताऽप्याचार्यस्योक्तविशेषणैः सूचिता।

समस्तागमाः सत्त्वसागरसंहितादयः तेषां संग्रहः प्रपञ्चागमः तस्यापि सारसंग्रहरूपमिति प्रपञ्चसार एवायमभिप्रेतः। अनेनाऽस्याप्युक्तानुग्रहसाधने पर्याप्तता साधिता। किञ्च परीक्षाणां भूयसामर्थानां सद्भावोऽपीह सूचितः।

अभिमतसकलप्रयोजनसिद्धय इति। मन्त्रदेवतानां स्वबुद्धौ समवभासः समुचितपदवाक्यादिस्फुरणमित्येवमादीनां फलवदारम्भान्वयिनां सद्भावात् सकलग्रहणम्। परदेवतातत्त्वानुस्मरणमिति। प्रधानपदेन गुणपदेऽश्चेति भावः। आशीर्लक्षणं चेति शिष्याणामभिमतार्थाशासनमुक्तम्। ग्रन्थारम्भौपयिकमिति ग्रन्थारम्भसमये युक्तमुचितं तदप्रतिपत्तौ शिष्याणामिह प्रवृत्त्ययोगादिति भावः।

शारदा व इति। काश्मीरमण्डले प्रसिद्धेयं देवता। तत्र निवसता आचार्येणाऽयं ग्रन्थः कृत इति तदनुस्मरणोपपत्तिः सकलागमानामधिदेवतेयमिति। व इति युष्माकम्। यदनुग्रहायाऽयमारम्भस्तेषां शिष्याणां कालपरम्परयाऽवस्थितानां ग्रहणमेतत्। चेतसः परिशुद्धिमिति। वक्ष्यमाणमन्त्रदेवताप्रतिपत्त्याद्युचितामिति भावः। वितरणं दानम्। यद्यपि शारदाया विश्वयोन्यादिगुणयोगितयाऽनुस्मरणमिह क्रियते तथापि संभाविताशङ्कोत्तरतया

तेषामन्वयो न विरुध्यत इति तथा विशेषणानि योज्यन्ते। तत्र प्रथमं सामान्यजनचार्वाकाद्यभिप्रायेणाऽऽशङ्कामाह—चित्तादिसङ्घातव्यतिरिक्तायाः इति। चित्तादीनां सङ्घातः शरीरमेव। तच्च शारदायाः साधकस्यैव वा गृह्यते। चित्तस्य शुद्धिं हि चित्तादिसङ्घातातिरिक्तैव साधयितुमर्हतीति भावः। तदेव कुत इति। सत्त्वे तावत् सिद्ध एव तस्याश्चित्तशुद्धिवितरणसामर्थ्यं निरूपणीयमिति भावः। विश्वकार्यकारणत्वेनेति। विश्वशब्देनेदं कृत्स्नं जगद्गृह्यते। तत्कार्यं सन्निवेशादियोगात्। कार्यञ्च कारणपूर्वकं प्रसिद्धमिति भावः। इह व्यष्ट्यभिप्रायेणाशङ्का समष्ट्यभिप्रायेण परिहारः। तेन तयोरभेदोऽपीहोपदिष्टो भवतीति ज्ञेयम्। अपूर्वपरिणामत्वाभ्युपगमादिति। सकलकायिकादिकर्मणामनुष्ठितानां यदुत्तरकालं स्थायिरूपं तदपूर्वमुच्यते। कर्मापूर्वस्यैव परिणाम एतद्विश्वमिति जैमिनीयानामभ्युपगमः। कर्मणोऽपीति स्वापूर्वद्वारेति भावः।

अनुमानमिति। यदेतदुपन्यस्तमनुमानं तदिति भावः। कार्यत्वेनाऽनित्यत्वादिति। कर्मापूर्वस्य ह्यनित्यत्वादुपादानान्तरसापेक्षत्वमेव। अतो न तन्मूलकारणं स्यादिति भावः। मूलग्रहणेन कर्मापूर्वस्येह सहकारिकारणत्वमभ्युपगतम्। वक्ष्यति हि—सृष्टिहेतुकर्मोन्मुख्यानन्तर्यार्थोऽयमथशब्द इति।

सर्वसाक्षिण्या इति नित्यत्वे हेतुरुक्तः। साक्ष्यस्यैव ह्यनित्यत्वं युक्तं न तु साक्षिचिद्रूपस्येति भावः। साक्षित्वेऽपि उपादानत्वमिष्यत एव। वक्ष्यति च—शारदैव तद्द्वारेण जगदुपादानं निमित्तं चेति। राद्धान्तः सिद्धान्तः। प्रधानादेरिति परमाण्वादिग्रहणम्। सांख्याभिप्रायेणाशङ्का सांख्यवार्हस्पत्याद्यभिप्रायेण परिहारः। चेतनानधिष्ठितस्येति प्रधानादेरपि कथञ्चित् कारणत्वमभ्युपगतम्। वक्ष्यति हि—प्रकृतिपुरुषकाला द्विविधा इत्यादि। सर्वाधिष्ठानसमर्थेत्यमुमर्थं विवृण्वन् दर्शयति—सकलं कारणमिति। नहीह प्रचितोऽर्थ उपेक्षणीयः सकलस्य जगतोऽधीशेति। परमार्थसत्त्वस्येति। सत्त्वमस्तित्वम्। तच्च द्विविधं परमार्थसिद्धं प्रतीतिसिद्धञ्चेति। निमित्तमात्रत्वमेवेति। न तूपादानत्वमपीति भावः। निरीश्वरसांख्यादिपक्षेषु तु न कर्मणोऽतिरिक्तं निमित्तकारणमस्ति। सेश्वरसांख्यादिपक्षमिति। पाशुपतादिग्रहणम्। सर्ववर्णतदर्थसमष्ट्यात्मकस्येति। परमसमष्टिर्विवक्ष्यते। अध्यस्तत्वेनेति। अध्यास आरोपः। तद्द्वारेणेति। तस्मिन् सति तथा प्रतीत्युपपत्तेरिति भावः। तच्छेषत्वमिति। तदीयकार्यैकनिष्ठत्वम्। विग्रहग्रहणं त्वेतत्प्रतिपादनार्थमेवेति भावः।

विरचितपदं विवृणोति—शरीरवत्त्वेनेति। श्लिष्टपदानि तु स्थूलविषयकथन

एव व्याख्येयानि। स्वातन्त्र्य हेतुमिति। हेतुरिह लिङ्गमेव। सकलजगतोरधीशनेन स्वातन्त्र्यस्वभावता गम्यत इति भावः। तर्ह्यधिष्ठातृत्वेनेति। सकलजगतोरधीशनं हि तयोर्यथेष्टविनियोगं प्रति पर्याप्तत्वं तदेव चाधिष्ठातृत्वम्। अतः प्रवर्तकत्वाद्विकारित्वं स्यादिति भावः।

शाश्वतेति नित्या। स्वसन्निधिमात्रेणैव प्रवर्तकत्वेनाऽविकारित्वादिति भावः। तर्हीति। प्रधानप्रवृत्तौ तदप्रवृत्तौ च निर्विशेषावस्थत्वमेकरूपत्वम्। परमार्थतस्तदभावेऽपीति। वास्तवसमीचायामित्यर्थः। मायाद्वारेणेति। मायैव तावच्चिद्वस्तुनि स्वात्मावभासयति। ततश्च स्वाधिष्ठानस्य स्वतन्त्रस्य तस्य चिद्वस्तुनः कारणत्वमप्यवभासयति। ततस्तस्मात् बुद्ध्याद्यर्थंजातमपीति भावः। पक्षान्तरेष्विति क्रमोपन्यस्तचार्वाकजैमिनीयाद्यभ्युपगमे। एवंविधकारणत्वस्यापीति। प्रातीतिकस्याऽपीति भावः। पारमार्थिककारणत्वस्याऽत्यन्तानुपपत्तिरपिशब्देनोक्ता। सा चाऽनुपपत्तिस्तत्र तत्रैवोक्तैवेति। चित्तशुद्धिवितरणसामर्थ्यं चेति। तस्या हिमाद्रिविग्रहत्वात् सकलजगदधीशेत्यादियोगाच्चेति भावः।

इह शारदायाः स्वरूपतः स्थूलरूपपर्यन्तं तत्त्वस्वरूपपर्यन्तं चाऽवरोहमारोहं च विदधतैतदपि सूचितम्। साधकानामनुष्ठानावशेषकालेषु मन्त्रदेवतायाः स्वरूपतः स्थूलरूपपर्यन्तं ततः स्वरूपपर्यन्तं चाऽवरोहारोहावृत्त्याऽनुसन्धानं कार्यमिति। किञ्च शारदाया ईदृशीं स्थितिं वदन्नेतदपि दर्शयति। परदेवतायास्तत्तदायतनेषु सन्निहितानि विश्वेश्वरमहालक्ष्म्यादिरूपाण्यप्येवमेव प्रतिपत्तव्यानीति।

अथ विषयादिकं वदन् विषयं तावद्विभजते—स्थूलेति। विषयस्तावदभिधीयते। स चैवं पञ्चविध इत्यर्थः। प्रथमार्धेनेति। अकचटतपयेत्यमी वर्णा आद्या येषामिति समासः। ननु कथं विराडत्रोक्त इति तत्राह—मातृकाक्षरन्यासस्थानमिति। यस्याऽवयवक्लृप्तिरियं विराट् स इति भावः। स चेह समष्टिव्यष्टिरूपोऽभिप्रेतः। मूले वाहेति वाङ्घ्रभिधानम्। मध्याख्यं पवर्गस्थानम्। हृच्छब्देन हृत्प्रदेशग्रहणम्। तत्र हि दशदिक्क्रमेण व्यापकानां न्यासः। ककारस्तु समासान्त एव। अत्राऽभिप्रायान्तरं दर्शयति—मध्यशब्द इत्यादिना।

अर्थान्तरमाह—आख्यशब्देनेति। आख्याय्यते एभिरितीति। प्राणादिमात्रभाजामात्मनामनभिव्यक्तानां त्वगादिसङ्घातयोगाच्चैत्रमैत्रादितया ज्ञानं व्यवहारश्च भवतीति भावः। इतीति। सूचित इत्युपरि सम्बन्धः। यादिन्यासस्थानानीति। त्वगादिबुद्ध्या हृदि न्यासो व्यापकन्यासो वा विवक्षितः। यत्तु मातृकापटले वक्ष्यते—हृदोर्मूलेत्यादि। तेन सहाऽस्य विकल्पः। तेषां याथात्म्यमिति तत्त्वम्।

यथा धातूनां सङ्घाततयात्मनां व्यवहारसाधनत्वमिति तत्तदन्वर्थाभिः तत्तद्याथा-त्म्यमनुसन्धेयमित्यप्यनेन सूचितम्। यतो वक्ष्यते—हृदयं बुद्धिगम्यत्वादित्यादि।

धात्वादियोग इति। यं त्वगात्मने नम इत्यादि। हं ब्रह्मात्मने नमः। ई मायात्मने नमः। चं परमात्मने नम इति। त्वगादिस्थानन्यासविधौ चाऽयं तद्योगः।

सर्वमन्त्रजपादेः शेषतयेति। त्वगादीनामाख्यत्वेन सामान्याकृतित्वात् तत्तन्मन्त्राणाञ्च विशेषाकृतित्वादिति भावः। तत्तन्मन्त्रजपध्यानयोगतर्पणोपस्थानादिषु तत्तन्मन्त्रन्यासात् प्राक् तच्छेषतया मातृकान्यासोऽपि कर्तव्य इत्यपीह सूच्यते। तत्प्रकारस्तु सौस्थानिकौत्थानिकेत्यादिना वक्ष्यते। न्यासस्तत्साद्वर्थात् तत्स्थाया मातृकाया इत्यवसेयम्। यद्वा सर्वमन्त्रशेषतया जपादेरिति पाठः। परमात्ममायादीनां मातृकाशेषताभिधानेन तद्वाचकाजपापरमात्मप्रणवहृल्लेखादीनां स्वप्रधानानामपि तत्तन्मन्त्रशेषतया न्यासः सूचित इत्यर्थः। वक्ष्यति च—नित्यलिपिन्यासानन्तरमिति। हंसपूजां सङ्कल्प्येति। सामान्यपटलोक्ता न्यासाः सर्वत्र कार्या इति च। साधकशरीरे सन्निधाने सतीति। सर्वन्यासकार्यमनेनोपदिश्यते। सन्निधानं चैतत्तादात्म्यपर्यवसितमिति बोद्धव्यम्।

देवतावयवविशेषकल्पनार्थमिति। इह त्रिविधो मातृकान्यासः। साधकशरीरोत्पत्त्यर्थन्यासः सर्गन्यासः। यद्वक्ष्यति—मूलाधारात् स्फुरिततटिदाभेत्यादि। तथा शुद्धन्यासेन सकलीकृत्येत्यादि। तत्संहृत्यर्थन्यासः संहारन्यासः। यच्च वक्ष्यति—तत्रोक्तचतुर्विधलिपिन्यासानामिति। साधकशरीरे देवतात्मनस्तादात्म्यस्थित्यर्थन्यासः स्थितिन्यासः। सोऽपि त्रिविधः। अनैश्वरगुणसंहारप्रधानः संहारन्यासः। ऐश्वरगुणोदयप्रधानः सर्गन्यासः। तत्स्थितिप्रधानः स्थितिन्यासः। तत्रैश्वरगुणोदयप्रधानोऽयं न्यासोऽभिप्रेयते। गुणोदयार्थत्वेऽप्यस्याऽऽद्यत्वात्। गुणगुदयार्थत्वमप्यस्तीति कल्पनार्थत्वमित्युक्तम्।

चकारादित्वं स्यादिति। परमात्ममायादिक्रमोपपत्तेरिति भावः। सर्वत्रैव सामान्यविशेषात्मकं हीति कालाभिप्रायम्। हिशब्देनाऽऽगमोपपत्तिसिद्धमेतदिति सूचितम्। न्यासेनोत्पाद्यत इति। यद्यपि समष्टिव्यष्ट्यात्मकं देवताशरीरम् किन्तु साधकशरीरे तथा न रूढिः। यद्वा तत्र समष्टिशरीरतया न रूढिः तदर्थं तस्य सन्निधानं न्यासेनोत्पाद्यत इत्यर्थः।

न च संहारक्रमेणेति। साधकशरीरसंहृत्यर्थः संहारन्यासोऽयं विवक्षितः। उभयोरप्यात्मन्येव संहारादिति। साधकशरीरस्य देवताशरीरत्वारूढावयं संहारः। तदा च सामान्यतो देवताशरीरतावगतौ मातृकया तत्संहारसंभवः।

तदा च कृत्स्नस्य साधकशरीरस्य संहार्यत्वात् तस्य तदधिष्ठानसाक्षिचिद्रूपे देवतातत्त्वे संहार इति ज्ञेयम्। विशेषसंहारक्रमचिन्ताया इति। सामान्यसंहारानन्तरं विशेषसंहार इति क्रमः। कर्तव्यत्वादिति। चिन्ता तावदुभयथापि शक्यत एव किन्तु संहारसंस्कार एवमेव स्यात्। आगमप्रामाण्यादिति भावः। यद्यपि देहोत्पत्त्यर्थो मातृकान्यासः। वक्ष्यति च—तत्रोक्तचतुर्विधलिपिन्यासानामित्यादि। तत्रापि समानमेतत्। न्यासान्तरेऽप्येतत् सर्वं यथायोगं योज्यमिति।

प्राणादिरूपसूक्ष्मादिकथनमिति। प्राणमायापरमात्मानः प्राणादयः सूक्ष्मकारणसामान्यसाक्षिणः सूक्ष्मादय इति नानुपपन्नमित्यर्थः। तेन विनेति। स्थूलादीनां केवलत्वेऽप्येकैकांशेन मिथःसमावेशोऽस्त्येवेति भावः। विराजोऽपि सर्वात्मत्वादिति। विराण्नाम स्थूलमात्राभिमानिन्यपि देवता कृत्स्नैव स्यादिति भावः। प्राणबुद्धिजीवस्थितिकरा इति। स्थूलदेहगत एव कश्चिदंशः प्राणादीनां तस्मिन्नासक्तिं विदधत्तत्स्थितिं प्रतिलभ्नातीति भावः। अन्नादिशब्दवाच्या इति। 'अन्नमयं वै सौम्य मन' इत्यादि प्रसिद्धिरुक्ता। यत् तु वक्ष्यति—अन्न प्राणशब्देनेन्द्रियादिप्रवृत्तिकारणमन्नमुच्यत इत्यादि। तत्र पक्षे हृल्लेति प्राणबुद्धिजीवानां वा ग्रहणं स्यादिति। स्थूलसमावेशिनां त्वितरेषां इहाविशेषं वेत्यभिप्रायेणाह - अस्मिन् पक्ष इति। बिन्दुनादादिभिरिति। सर्ववर्णानां बीजबिन्दुनादशक्तिशान्तांशयोगादिति भावः।

सौस्थानिकानुष्ठान इति। सुस्थानं साधकस्य स्वस्थावस्थतया तदुचितकालसंभवः। उत्थानं तस्यैवावश्यकार्यान्तकार्यान्तरोद्युक्तावस्थतया तदुचितावसरायोगः। स्नानादीति। स्नानतर्पणोपस्थानपूजास्तुतिनमस्कारसवनसपर्यानित्यसेवारम्भावसानमन्त्रोद्धारव्याख्यानश्रवणादिग्रहणम्। स्नानादीनां पृथगुपादानादेतदवसीयते। सौस्थानिकमौत्थानिकं च देहशुद्ध्यादियोगजपपर्यन्तं प्रधानं कर्म विवक्षितमिति। तेन स्नानादीन्युभयोरवस्थयोर्न भिद्यन्ते। भोजने तु स्नानतो विशेष इत्याह—भोजनकाल इति। मातृकायाः स्वप्रधानत्वे मन्त्रान्तरशेषत्वेऽपि समानमेतत्सर्वं भवति। किञ्च मन्त्रान्तराणामपि न्यासभेदसंभवे सौस्थानिकादिष्वेषा रीतिरनुसर्तव्या। देशकालाद्यपेक्षयेति। सौस्थानिकेऽपि कुदेशसंभवे सर्वं लघ्वनुष्ठेयम्। औत्थानिकेऽपि पुण्यायतनसम्भवे सर्वं विततमनुष्ठेयमित्याद्यवबोद्धव्यम्।

अथवेत्यादि। समस्तमन्त्रपारायणोद्धारार्थेति। न केवलमातृकाया एवेह मन्त्रपारायणमिति समस्तमन्त्रग्रहणम्। यतो वक्ष्यते—तत्तन्मन्त्रभेदेनेत्यादि। न च समस्तमन्त्राणामेव पारायणम् किन्तु तेषामपि मन्त्रपारायणमिति। यस्मा

मन्त्रदेवताया यो मन्त्रवर्गो वक्ष्यते ब्रह्मसरस्वतीविष्णुश्रीत्यादि तथा तेषा-मवान्तरवर्गोऽपि कृष्णवर्गो नरसिंहवर्ग इति तस्या मन्त्रानुष्ठानविधौ तद्वर्गजपो मन्त्रपारायणम्। सकलमन्त्राणामप्येकैकस्य वर्गसंसर्गवैचित्र्यतो यावान् विस्तर-स्तज्जपस्तस्य मन्त्रस्यापि मन्त्रपारायणमिति न्यासस्थानकथनादुद्धारग्रहणम्।

मातृकाया मन्त्रपारायणं तावद्द्विविधम् स्वरव्यञ्जनभेदात्। तत्र प्रथमं स्वरपारायणमुच्यते। अकचटतपयाद्यैरित्यादि। अकचटतपयवर्गसम्बन्धिभिरिति षट्सु समासो विहितः। किमिह सिद्धं भवतीत्याह—पञ्चाशद्वर्णानामिति।

प्रयोगप्रकारं दर्शयति—लिपिन्यासस्थानेष्विति। प्रधानं वर्णमिति परितः सतां षोडशस्वराणां तत्परिवारत्वमपि सूचितम्। सकृन्मातृकां विन्यस्ये-तदारब्धव्यम्। जपेच्च जपप्रिय इत्येकं वाक्यम्। ध्यायेदिति। न्यासस्थाने-ष्वेतदित्यवबोद्धव्यम्। वर्णानां तेजोरूपेण शक्तिरूपेण रेखारूपेणैव वा ध्यानम्। ओं अं ओं नमः इत्यादिप्रणवपुटितनमोऽन्तवर्णोपादानेन सर्वमन्त्रन्यास-विधावप्येवं तदीयवर्णपदादिप्रयोग इत्यपि दर्शितम्। ओं अं नम इत्यत्र जघन्य-पक्षोऽपि सूचितः। न्यासादीति जपध्यानग्रहणम्। यद्वा तर्पणपूजाहोमादीना-मपि ग्रहणम्। ननु कदा पुनरेतन्न्यासादि कार्यमिति। उच्यते। मातृकान्यास-विधौ वर्णन्यासे कृते पारायणन्यासः। वक्ष्यति च—तत्तदक्षरन्यासे तत्पारायणव्या-स्यविस्मरणमिति। मातृकाजपे कृते तत्पारायणजपः। ध्यानकाल एव ध्यानमिति।

अथ व्यञ्जनपारायणक्रम इत्यादि। उक्तैरिति। स्थूलं विषयमाहेत्यत्रेति शेषः। विविधरचनमित्यत्राऽयमाशयः। इहाऽकारोऽपि व्यञ्जनत्वेन कल्पनीयः। अकखादिषट्त्रिंशद्वर्णानां प्रत्येकं षोडशस्वरानुषङ्गः। यथा—अ आ इ ई क का कि की इत्यादि। तेषामेकैकस्य तथा षट्त्रिंशता योग इति व्यञ्जनपारायणं षोडशविधम्। तत्र प्रथमं ब्रह्मब्रह्मपारायणम्। ओं अं ओं नम इत्यादि अकखादि षट्त्रिंशद्वर्णस्थानेषु षोडशदलानि पद्मानि विभाव्य तत्कर्णिकायां तं तं प्रधानं वर्णं विन्यस्य दलेष्वेकैकं तत्तदनुबद्धं तत्तद्वर्णयुक्तं स्वरं विन्यस्य तं तं स्वरं परितस्तत्तत्स्वरानुबद्धान् केवलाकारयुक्तान् अकखादिषट्त्रिंशद्वर्णान् विन्यसेदिति प्रकरणार्थः। विसर्गान्तं समानमिति। अकारपद्मस्य षोडशे दले यो विसर्गस्तदन्तमित्यर्थः। इह त्वाकारादिपद्मेषु न न्यासो मन्त्राभेदात्। यद्यपि पूर्वं स्वरपारायणे अकारपद्मदलेषु न क का कीत्यादीनां न्यासोऽस्ति तथापीह तथा न्यासो मन्त्रभेदोपपत्तेरिष्यते। इह ब्रह्मब्रह्मपारायणादिसमाख्यातो वर्गश एष प्रयोगो यथा स्वरपारायणमिति लभ्यते। किञ्च तत्तद्वर्णेषु

तत्तन्मूर्त्यनुसन्धानमपि सूचितम्। कर्णिकायां परा सरस्वती शक्तिः दलेषु तदंशतया ब्रह्मब्रह्मादिषोडशमूर्तयः तत्परितस्तत्तदंशा ब्रह्मब्रह्मकलारूपा इति। एवमुत्तरेष्वप्यवबोद्धव्यम्। स्वरपारायणेऽपि समानमेतत्। अं आं नम इत्यादि। अस्मिन् पारायणे प्रतिदलं षट्त्रिंशद्वर्णानामकारयोग इत्येव भेदः। अः आं नम इत्यादि। अस्मिन्निकारयोगः। एवमुत्तरेष्वपि ज्ञेयम्।

अथेमामेव रीतिं समस्तमन्त्रेष्वपि दर्शयति—पारायणक्रमवदिति। उक्त-पारायणक्रमवन्मन्त्रभेदानामपि पारायणस्याऽचरविरचनारूपत्वात् सोऽपि पारायणक्रमो विरचितेत्यनेन सूचित इति सोपस्कारं योज्यम्। अत्र कचटत-पयाद्यास्तत्तन्मन्त्रसंभविनो वर्णाः मुखबाह्वादिशब्दाश्च तत्तन्मन्त्रवर्णस्थानपराः। अयं भावः समस्तमन्त्रेष्वपि तत्तद्वर्णस्थानेषु यावद्वर्णदलानि पद्मानि विचिन्त्य कर्णिकायां तं तं वर्णं दलेषु तद्वर्णयोगिनः सर्वांस्तत्तन्मन्त्रवर्णान् विन्यसेदिति।

यद्वा समस्तमन्त्राणां सामान्यतोऽयमुद्धार उच्यते—पारायणक्रमवदिति। सोऽपीति। स समन्त्रभेदोऽपीत्यर्थः। अत्र तु मुखबाह्वादिशब्दैः सर्वमन्त्रेषु तत्तदवयवन्यासभाजस्तत्तद्वर्णा गृह्यन्ते।

अथेति समस्तमन्त्रोद्धारानन्तरमित्यर्थः। उक्तैरिति। स्वरपारायणतया व्यञ्जनपारायणतया चोक्तैरिति भावः। वर्णवर्गैरित्येतस्य विवृतिर्मन्त्रवर्गैरिति। कदा पुनस्तत्तन्मन्त्रपारायणमिति। उच्यते। यदि तावत्तत्तन्मन्त्राणां वीर्याधानार्थ-मेतत् स्वतन्त्रतया कर्तव्यम् मातृकान्यासस्यनुस्मरणार्थत्वे तु न्यासविधौ स्यात्। यदि पुनस्तत्तन्मन्त्रविभूत्यर्थं तदा तत्तन्मन्त्रपुटितमातृकान्यासानन्तरमेतत् कार्यमिति। अलमित्यादि स्थूलविषयोपसंहारः। अन्यदप्येवंविधं शक्यं वक्तुमि-त्यलमित्यनेन सूचितम्। तेन सप्तभिर्वर्णवर्गैरिति षडध्वप्रचयोऽपि सूचितः।

वर्णपदमन्त्रास्त्रयः प्रत्यचा मन्त्रवर्गाः कलातत्त्वभुवनानि च त्रयः परोक्षाः तत्समष्ट्यात्मको मूलवर्णाङ्गरूपः सप्तमो वर्गः। तथाविधैर्वर्णवर्गैर्विरचित-तत्तदुचितावयवेति। तस्या बुद्धिगतत्वादपि कलाभिरवयवैरित्यादि वरणोपपत्तिः। लिपिन्यासे कृते चायं न्यास इति। कलाभिरिति। यद्यपि षडध्वानो देवता-विग्रहगताः तथापि व्यष्टिसमष्ट्योरभेदात् साधकविग्रहेऽपि नामावयवादियोगा-देवमभिधानोपपत्तिः। तानि चेति। शून्यात्मने नमः स्पर्शात्मने नम इत्यादयो मन्त्राः। इच्छादीन्यपि मध्यमान्तर्गतान्येव प्रसरपुष्पाञ्जलौ यद्वक्ष्यति —वामायै ज्येष्ठाया इत्यादि। ततोऽर्थादुभयत्रापि स्थानादिविकल्पो वैखरीन्यासात् पूर्वमेवेति। परा पश्यन्ती मध्यमा वैखरीत्यमुना क्रमेणाऽयं न्यास इति भावः।

मातृकान्यासविधौ चैव न्यासः स्यात्। तत्तन्मन्त्रन्यासविधौ तु मूलपुटितमातृकान्यासात् पूर्वमेते परादिन्यासाः स्युः। अथवा भूषणन्यासानन्तरमेतन्न्यासचतुष्टयं कार्यम्। किन्तु तदा जपपूजावसाने गुणितयोगात् पूर्वं वैखरीमध्यमादिक्रमेण संहाररीत्यैते न्यासाः स्युरिति। तपउपचयादिशब्दवाच्यमिति। 'स तपोऽतप्यत' 'तपसा चीयते ब्रह्म' इत्यादि प्रसिद्धिरुक्ता। कारणात्मन इति। सामान्यमेव तावत्कारणम्। किन्तु तस्य सृष्ट्याद्युन्मुखं यद्रूपं तत्कारणाकाराभिव्यक्तेस्तथा व्यपदेश्यं भवतीति भावः। सृष्ट्याद्युन्मुखमित्यादिशब्देन संहारफलोत्पत्त्यादिग्रहणम्। शाश्वतत्वमिह व्यावहारिकमिति। आदिसर्गादीति। ब्रह्मसर्गप्रलयाभिप्रायेण। आदिमहेति। तयोर्विशेषणोपादानम्। सदादिरूपत्वाच्चेति। परस्परव्यावृत्तेषु घटपटाद्यर्थेषु अनुवृत्ततयानवच्छिन्नत्वात् सत्तामात्रमपि शाश्वतं भवति। अत एव महासत्तेति व्यपदिश्यते। एवं चिदानन्दयोरपि ज्ञेयम्।

अथ परातदर्थात्मकमिति। सामान्यरूपं विषयमाहेत्यन्वयः। आत्माविभक्तान्तर्मुखकारणात्मकमिति। देवतात्मनः स्वरूपस्याशेषद्वैतनिर्वाहकं यच्छक्तिमात्रं तत्स्वरूपविश्रान्तिलक्षणायां प्रलयदशायां ततः स्वाधिष्ठानचिद्रूपतो न विभक्तम्। अतएवान्तर्मुखं तत्स्वरूपमात्रविमर्शस्वभावं सत् सकलाद्वैतनिदानतया वस्तुतः कारणं भवति। तदेतत्सामान्यमित्यर्थः। शक्तिरूपमिति। बीजबिन्द्वादिषु मध्य इति भावः। विश्वयोन्यै नम इति मन्त्रः। अवशिष्टमिति साक्ष्यभिप्रायः। अव्यवहार्यमिति लक्षणयोक्तौ हेतुः। साक्षिणस्तु स्वयमेव सिद्धत्वान्न न्यासः। यद्वा शारदायै नम इति प्रथमत एव व्यापकमिष्यते। एवं मन्त्रान्तरेषु तत्तन्मन्त्रेण प्रथमतो व्यापकम्। विश्वेश्वरमहालक्ष्म्यादिष्वपि समानमेतत्। स्थूलादिलक्षणमिति। स्थूलसूक्ष्मकारणं समष्टिव्यष्ट्यात्मकं भोग्यभोगायतनभोक्तृविग्रहाद्यात्मकम्। तद्ददाति। कायिकादिसकलकर्माराधिता सतीति भावः। भुक्तिरूपं फलमेतत्। तत्कारणं चेति मुक्तिरूपं फलम्। तच्छब्देन स्थूलादिग्रहणम्। तत्कारणशब्देन च सामान्यस्य ग्रहणम्। ब्रह्मविद्याधिरूढा सतीति। देवताया यदनारोपितं रूपं तद्ब्रह्म। तद्विषया वक्ष्यमाणा शेषयोगपर्यन्तजन्या मनोवृत्तिर्ब्रह्मविद्या। द्यतीति। दो अवखण्डन इति धातोः श्यनि रूपम्। शारदाशब्दार्थ उभयत्रापि समान एव। व्याख्येयमिति। शारदाशब्दस्य स्वतः सर्वशक्त्यां देवतायामेव वृत्तेरिति भावः। शारदापदमित्थं विवृण्वन्नेतदपि दर्शयति—विश्वेश्वरमहालक्ष्म्यादिपदं भुवनेशीसरस्वत्यादिपदमप्येवं परदेवतार्थतया नेयमिति।

प्रयोजनकथनेनैवेति। प्रयोजनमात्रेऽप्यारम्भेऽभिहिते तदर्थिनस्तत्र प्रवृत्ति-

रवश्यं स्यादेवेति सामान्यतोऽधिकारिसिद्धिः। वितरत्वित्यादिनेति। श्लोकशेषेणेति शेषः। इह केवलकैवल्यार्थी मुख्याधिकारी। भुक्तिक्रमेण तदर्थी मध्यमः। केवलभुक्त्यर्थी अधमः। वश्याकर्षणादिप्रयोगमात्रार्थी क्षुद्राधिकारीति भेदः। कथंविधोऽसावनेन सिद्ध इत्याह—शुद्धान्तःकरण इति।

दीक्षेह द्विविधा लौकिक्यागमिकी च। तत्र लौकिकी वाचिक्यादिदीक्षा। आगमिकी तु त्रिविधा आणवी शाक्ती शांभवी चेति। तत्र वाचिकीयं शारदा वश्चेतसः परिशुद्धिं वितरत्वित्येवमाशीर्लक्षणा स्थूला। तथापि संस्कृतस्य ग्रन्थश्रवणादावधिकारः। अनेनैतदपि सूचितम्। प्रपञ्चसारं व्याचिख्यासुनैतत्श्लोकद्वारेणेयं वाचिकी दीक्षा श्रोतुः कार्येति। यद्यपीयमेका दीक्षैव तथाप्यनयाऽर्थोपलक्षणाभ्यां विशेषाधिकार्यपि सूचितः स्यात्। ततः शुद्धान्तःकरण इत्यर्थितार्थकथनं वक्ष्यमाणार्थश्रवणशेषतया चित्तशुद्ध्याशासनात्। गुरुणेत्यादिनोपलक्षितार्थ उक्तः। दीक्षाभेदलक्षणार्थत्वात् अस्या इति।

अणुभिर्मन्त्रैरिति। यदुक्तं—मन्त्रात्मकवर्णविशेषपरामर्शरूपत्वादाणव इति। संहृत्येति लिपिः संहारन्यासेन संहारः सर्गन्यासेन च सर्ग इति द्रष्टव्यम्। अनेन कदाचिदियतापि कार्या देहशुद्धिरित्यपि सूचितम्। न्यासरूपाणवीदीक्षाप्रकार इति पूर्वार्धेन सूचित इति भावः। स्वशक्तिसूत्रेणेति। स्वात्मतः शिष्यात्मान्तं सूत्ररूपेणानुस्यूतं शक्तितत्त्वं भावयित्वा तेन मार्गभूतेन यद्वा तेन स्वाकारेणेत्यर्थः। प्रविश्येति। सकलजगदधीशेतिपदेन सूचितमेतत्। तत्त्वसंहारं कृत्वेति। शाश्वतेति सूचितम्। तत्त्वग्रहणं षडध्वविकल्पोपलक्षणार्थम्। कलाभिरवयवैरित्याद्युक्तत्वात्। तं परदेवतारूपं भावयेदिति। विश्वयोनिरिति सूचितम्। शुद्धतत्त्वसर्गोऽप्यनेनैव सूचितः। शाक्तदीक्षाप्रकार इति। यदुक्तम्—उच्चारणादिव्यतिरेकेण संविद्विकल्पमात्राकारत्वादिति। द्वारभेदपदेनैतदुक्तम्। स्वशक्तिसूत्रस्य शिष्यात्मान्ततया प्रसृतौ चक्षुःसम्बन्धादीनां द्वारत्वमिति। केवलस्वस्वरूपस्थितिमात्रेणेति गुरोर्यत्स्वरूपं देवतातत्त्वलक्षणं शिष्यस्यापि यत्तदेव स्वरूपं तस्मिन्नखण्डब्रह्मात्मैकत्वलक्षणे स्वस्वरूपे स्थितिरनुच्चलतया स्थानम्। मात्रग्रहणेन यत्नव्युदासः। यदुक्तं—सर्वविकल्पक्षोदव्युदासेन स्वस्वभावमात्रोपपादनप्रवृत्ततया शाम्भव इति। शिष्यसर्वदेहग्रसनरूपेति। समष्टिव्यष्ट्यात्मकस्थूलसूक्ष्मादिः सर्वो देहः स्वस्वरूपस्थितौ तस्यारोपसिद्धस्य ग्रसनं स्यादिति। शारदेत्यनेनेति। शारं द्यतीति विद्रुतत्वादिति भावः। मन्त्राणामिह भूयस्त्वादासां दीक्षाणां यथायोगमुपयोगो द्रष्टव्यः। विषयविषयिभाव इति परस्परनियमरूप उक्तः॥ १॥

गन्थारम्भौपयिकमित्युक्तविषयादिकथनेन किमिह साधितं भवतीति तद्वदन् उत्तरश्लोकसङ्गतिं वक्तुमारभते—विषयादिमत्त्वादिति। भवत्ययमिति वक्ष्यमाणग्रहणम्। तमेवाऽवतारं सङ्गतिरूपमाह—शारदेत्यादिना। पुराणादिष्वेवेति। स्थूलदर्शनाभिप्रायेणाशङ्का सूक्ष्मदर्शनाभिप्रायेण परिहारः। परमकारणत्वानुपपत्तेरिति। कारणत्वं तावदस्त्येवेति भावः। विद्यास्तुत्यादिप्रयोजनयेति। वक्ष्यमाणा मन्त्रा एव विद्याः। आख्यायिका कथा। अथाऽत इत्यत्राऽथशब्दारम्भार्थः। यदारम्भाङ्गतयैतन्मङ्गलाचरणं तस्य चाऽयमारम्भः।

अर्थान्तरमाह—सृष्टिहेत्विति। पुरा प्रलयावसाने प्रधानाद्ब्रह्महरीश्वराख्या अभवन्निति मूलान्वयः। आख्याग्रहणं पुराणागमादिप्रसिद्धिसूचनार्थम्। तदाख्यास्वेत्यर्थान्तरकथनम्। तेषां वाचका मन्त्रास्वेति तदर्थं उक्तः। पदवाक्यादिरूपत्वेऽपि मन्त्राणामाधेयकल्पा एवेत्याख्याग्रहणम्। पुरेति चिरपूर्वकाले। अर्थान्तरमाह—तेषामिति। पुरेति प्रकृत्यादित्वतोया।

यद्यपि तत उत्पन्नमिति प्रधानं शारदातत्त्वमेव तथापि तदिहाभिप्रेतमित्याह—प्रथितमस्तीति। मायाशक्तिमत्साच्चितत्त्वमिह प्रधानम्। तस्यैकत्वेऽपि कार्यभेदतस्त्रिधा विकल्पः। विश्वमिदं प्रतीतत्वाद्विततत्वाच्च प्रथमं तदस्तीति प्रथा। तदेव वर्णव्यापत्त्या प्रधानमिति। तद्वाचको हकारस्वेति। सकलवाचकसंहारादिति भावः। त्रितयहेतुत्वश्रुतेरिति। पुराणादिष्वेवेति भावः। प्राधान्येनेत्याधिकारिकत्वात्। साधकवशात्त्वापेक्षिकमितरत्।

अस्यैव श्लोकस्याभिप्रायान्तरमाह—सृष्ट्यादावित्यादिना। सृष्टिः शरीरसर्गः। यद्वक्ष्यति—निरवद्यादिमन्त्रैर्व्यापय्येति। आदिशब्देन देवताविग्रहान्तस्चतुर्मूर्तिभावना। तेषु पुष्पाञ्जलिं कदाचित् साधकशरीरस्य समष्टीकरणं देहसंहार इति सर्वं गृह्यते। ब्रह्महरीश्वरास्वेत्येकशेषेण सर्वेश्वरसिद्धिः। पुराभिमानिनामिति विश्ववैश्वानरादीनाम्। व्यस्तसमस्तप्रणवानन्तर्यमिति सूचितमित्यनुषङ्गः। प्रलयः सर्वमन्त्रनिदानभूतः प्रणवः। गुणप्रभिन्ना इतीत्यस्येति च योग इत्युपरि सम्बन्धः। रजआदयो गुणा एवं सरस्वत्यादयः। सर्वज्ञत्वं सर्वेषामेको गुणः। सदखण्डसंविदादयोऽपि गुणा एव। अयमिह प्रयोगः। ओं अं क्रीं रजउपाधये स्थूलविराट्शरीराय विश्ववैश्वानरात्मने सर्वस्रष्ट्रे ब्रह्मणे सरस्वतीसहिताय सर्वज्ञाय सदात्मनेऽखण्डसंविदे परमात्मने नम इत्यादि।

पञ्चममन्त्रं दर्शयितुमाह—मूर्त्यपवादमन्त्रस्त्विति। मूर्त्यारोपः सा क्वचिद्रूपे सामान्याद्यारोपतः सर्वेश्वरादिसंभवस्तज्ज्ञानात् केवलता च तदपवादः। अत्र

निरवद्यनिर्गुणायेति गुणांशापवादः। अशरीर्यांशरीरायेति शरीरांशस्येत्यादि प्रतिपत्तव्यम्। इदानीं प्राक्प्रतिज्ञातां विद्यास्तुतिमधिकारिविशेषणेन सह दर्शयति—प्रधानादभवन्नित्यादिना। विद्यानां महत्त्वमध्ययनेनाधिकारिविशेषणेन लभ्यते। महत्त्वकथनं च स्तुतिरिति। किञ्च ब्रह्मादयोऽपि ह्येतन्मन्त्रदेवता भावनादिभिरेव स्वसमीहितं लेभिरे किमुच्यते महाभाग्यमासामित्यपि विद्यास्तुतिः स्यात्। किञ्चाधिकार्युत्पत्तिरपीह सूचिता। प्रलयावसाने प्रधानादभवन्निति। प्रलय इह प्राक्तनदेहच्चयकालः। तदा यत्र स आत्मा सकर्मा पूर्वयुक्तः स्थितः तदेवतातत्त्वं प्रधानम्। तत उद्भवस्य पितृमातृसंबन्धद्वारा विशिष्टकार्यकरणसङ्घातेनोत्पत्तिः। ब्रह्महरीश्वराख्या इति। तेषां स्वतोऽसाधारणत्वमुक्तम्। गुणप्रभिन्ना इति विनयकारुण्यादिगुणैरितरेभ्योऽत्यन्तभेद उक्तः। जगतोऽस्येत्येवं विराडात्मना प्रत्यक्षतोपस्थिता देवतोच्यते। तस्य सृष्टिस्थितिक्षयाः स्वात्मनि न्यासजपयोगलक्षणा एव। तेषु प्राधान्यतो निविष्टचेष्टाः। यदुक्तं—न्यसेन्न्यासप्रिय इत्यादि। प्रधानादेवं त्रिविधोऽधिकारी समुत्पद्यते। तावदिति ग्रन्थकृतोऽभिप्रायः॥ २॥

ते विचिन्त्येति। त्रिविधस्याधिकारिणो व्यवहारदशायां निजनिमित्तादिविचारयोगोऽपि सूचितः। स्वरूपविश्रान्तिस्तावत्परमपुरुषार्थः। नित्यत्वे स्वमेव तत्त्वं स्वरूपम्। अनित्यत्वे तु यतः स्वोत्पत्तिस्तदेव स्वरूपमिति स्वनिष्पत्त्यादिविचारोपपत्तिः। तदापत्तिसाधनमेव तावदनुष्ठेयम्। तदेव च स्वोत्पत्तिकार्यं नान्यदिति स्वकृत्यविचारोपपत्तिः। गुणसाम्योपाधिमिति। माय्यभिधाननिबन्धनमुक्तम्। गुणसाम्योपाधिग्रहणाच्च गुणसामान्यरूपस्य सर्वेश्वरस्य ग्रहणार्थम्। वक्तारमिति स्वनिष्पत्त्यादेरिति शेषः। समाविदन्निति प्रातिभं ज्ञानमुक्तम्। अरूपत्वं तत्रेत्यव्यक्तत्वे हेतुरित्यर्थः। गुणसाम्यस्याऽत्यन्तनिर्विकल्पतया तदधिष्ठानचिद्रूपानतिरिक्तत्वादरूपत्वम्। तदेव च निर्विशेषत्वम्। मायासम्बन्धादिति। गुणसाम्यमात्रं माया भवति। सविशेषत्वमिति। वचनशक्तियोग्याकारत्वमिति भावः। विद्यास्तुत्यादिप्रयोजनयेत्यादिशब्दोक्तमपरमधिकारिविशेषणम्। गुरुविशेषणमप्याह—विचारक्षमा इत्यादिना॥ ३॥

अत्रेत्यस्मिन् प्रकरणे। किञ्चैवमुत्पन्नानां स्वनिष्पत्त्यादिविचारिणामधिकारिणां स्वाधिकारमहिम्नैव तादृग्गुरुसंभवस्तत्प्रतिपत्तियोगश्चेह सूचितः। मायिनोऽपीति न केवलं ब्रह्मादीनामेव। यद्वा मायित्वमात्रेणैव न वचनोपपत्तिरिति भावः। अवक्तृत्वमिति छेदः। तत्सर्वमिति। स्थानविशेष इह

दुग्धार्णवः। मूर्तिविशेषो नीलोत्पलदलप्रख्यामित्यादिलक्षणः। आदिशब्देना-नन्तभोगशय्याग्रहणम्। यद्वा श्वेतद्वीपाद्युपलक्षणार्थमादिग्रहणम्। मूर्त्याभासेन शयितमिति। दुग्धार्णवादीनां स्वबुद्धाववभासेऽपि तच्छयितविग्रहस्य तथाऽनव-भासादाभासग्रहणम्। यद्वा दुग्धार्णवानन्तभोगयोः स्वेच्छामात्रविभावितयोरधुना दर्शनं जातम् न तद्वन्मूर्तेरिति। अतएव पश्चात् स्वमूर्तिं स व्यदर्शयदित्यभि-धानम्। अत्राभिप्रायान्तरं वदन्नन्वयमाचष्टे—मूर्तिरित्यादिना। मूर्तिर्मायेति। निर्विशेषचिन्मात्रस्य मूर्तिप्रख्यत्वात्तस्या इति भावः। आ समन्ताद्भासत इति। यदुक्तं—ओमित्यन्तर्नदति नियतं यः प्रतिप्राणिशब्द इति। विग्रहभूतेनेति। शब्दाविभक्तत्वादर्थस्येति भावः। गायकत्राणकथनादिति। ब्रह्मादयः सूक्तिभिः स्तुतिभिः स्तोतृत्वाद्गायकाः तेषां त्राणं च तदीयसर्गादिकृत्योपदेशतस्त-त्समीहितसाहाय्यकाचरणम्। देवतां चेति विश्वेशेति। सर्वेश्वराभिधानादिति भावः। भों बीजं क्लीं शक्तिः। मूर्तिसंबन्धित्वेनेति। मूर्तिः शक्तिबीजमेव। इह वैष्णव एव पीठन्यासः। सामान्यपटलोक्तन्यासाः सर्वत्र कार्याः। सावरणे-श्वभिर्मूर्तिभिरिन्द्रादिभिश्च पूजा। ब्रह्मादीनामप्येवमङ्गमूह्यम्। ध्यानपूजे तु स्वावसरे भविष्यतः। तस्य चेति। तस्य च यथाश्रुतस्तावदर्थः। स च स्पष्ट एवेत्यर्थः। तत्र लहर्यस्तरङ्गाः। आमर्शः संस्पर्शः। सर्वेश्वरस्य व्याप्यवस्थस्य मूर्त्यवस्थापत्त्यभिप्रायेणैवमेतद्विवृतम्।

गुणोन्मेषावस्थापत्त्यभिप्रायेणाऽप्येतद्विवृणोति—अथान्योऽर्थ इत्यादिना। यदुक्तं —व्याप्तिमात्रं गुणोन्मेषो मूर्तिभाव इति त्रिधेति। यद्वा द्विविधाः साधकाः सकलनिष्ठा निष्कलनिष्ठाश्च। वक्ष्यति च—एवं निर्गुणनिष्ठानामित्यादि। तत्र सकलनिष्ठाभिप्रायेणैवं विवृतः। निष्कलनिष्ठाभिप्रायेणाऽयमारम्भ इति। मायि-नोऽमायिनोऽपि स्थानमूर्तिविशेषाद्यभावे वक्तृत्वमाशङ्क्येत्येतदिहापि समानम्। तत्र ब्रह्मादीनां बुद्धिरेव स्थानविशेषः। तदभिव्यक्तश्चैतन्याभासश्च मूर्तिरिति भेदः। इह मूर्त्याभासेन दुग्धाब्धौ शयितमित्येवमन्वयं दर्शयन् विवृणोति—मूर्तिरिति। तदभिव्यक्त इति। मूर्तावभास इति विग्रहोऽपि दर्शितः। चैतन्याभास इति। अतत्तदिवाभासमानमाभासः। इह चिन्मात्रं मायाशक्तिः। तस्यां सत्त्वलक्षणस्वच्छांशस्तत्र चिदाभासः। तस्मिंश्चित्प्रतिबिम्बं तदतिरिक्तं चिन्मात्रलक्षणमेव च बिम्बमिति षट्कोऽर्थः संभवति। तत्र चित्प्रतिबिम्बन्तु सर्वेश्वरादीनामात्मा चिन्मात्रलक्षणं तु बिम्बं साक्षी किन्तु सर्वेऽपि सर्वेश्वरादयः स्थूलसूक्ष्मकारणसामान्यसाक्ष्यंशयोगिन एव। तेषामपि मन्त्रदेवतात्मत्वात्। तत्र

सर्वेश्वरे बिम्बमिह प्राधान्यतो गृह्यते । कृत्स्नार्थप्रतिवचनयोग्यतोपपत्तेः । एवञ्च अजमव्यक्तमरूपमिति साहं मय्येवेति चैतत् सर्वमुपपन्नं भवति । ब्रह्मादिषु प्रतिबिम्बं प्राधान्यतो गृह्यते । अभिमतार्थप्रश्नयोग्यतोपपत्तेः ।

किञ्चैवं परब्रह्मसाक्षी सर्वेश्वरादिगुरुक्रमोऽपीह सूचितो भवति । आभासिनः शयन इति । यस्य चैतन्यस्याऽयमाभासः स आभासी साक्षिचिद्रूपः सर्वेश्वरः । कृत्स्नेऽपि मायातत्कार्ये तदधिष्ठानतया तत्साक्षितया च व्याप्तस्य साधकबुद्धौ तद्दर्शनयोग्यतयाऽभिव्यक्तिरेव शयनम् । द्वारत्वमिति । आभासे प्रतिबिम्बसंभवात् प्रतिबिम्बस्य च बिम्बतोऽनन्यत्वादिति भावः । ननु बुद्धौ साक्षिचिद्रूपावभासे किमाभासेन । यदुक्तं—ब्रह्मविद्याधिरूढा सतीति । उच्यते । सर्वेश्वरावभासो ह्यत्र वाच्यो न साक्षी चिन्मात्रावभासः । यद्वा ब्रह्मादीनामाभासाः व्यष्टयः सर्वेश्वराभासास्तेषां समष्टिः । गुणसाम्योपाधित्वात् सर्वेश्वरेण स्वव्यष्ट्याभासानां स्वसमष्ट्याभासाकारेणाऽवभासनमिहाऽभिप्रेतम् । सकलमन्त्रन्यासजपयोगानामपीयमेव स्थितिरिति । किञ्च साधकानां निजसमष्टिभूतपरदेवतावबोधप्रक्रियाऽपीह प्रतिपाद्यते । विविक्तज्ञानफलं संसारमान्द्यमित्याद्यभिधानाच्चैतदवगम इति । एवञ्च ब्रह्मोपलक्षणभूतज्ञानक्रियाशक्तिसमाकुलतादिसर्वमुपपन्नं भवति । ननु मायायां तावदेतदाभासे न शयनबुद्धाविति । नैष दोषः । मायाया अपि बुद्धावेवावभासादिति तस्य तद्बुद्धाविति शयनमिह स्वतोऽभिव्यक्तिमात्रम् । ततो विविक्ततोऽभिव्यक्तिविशेषः ततश्चान्ततस्तद्दर्शनमित्येवंविधमभिप्रेयते । मरुतोऽन्तर्यामिण इत्यवस्थाभेदात्तथा निर्देशः । प्रचारप्रकारैरिति । किरणपदविवरणम् । प्रशान्तसंसारोदय इति । विविक्तक्रमस्य परदेवतात्मैकत्वपर्यन्तत्वादिति भावः । परमानन्दाकारेति पूर्णचन्द्रकरपदविवरणम् । जडविषया इति । लडयोरविशेषः । संसारदशाभिप्रायमेतत् ॥ ४ ॥ ५ ॥

अनन्तभोग इत्येतदिह दुग्धाब्धिविशेषणम् । अनन्ताकाराश्चित्तवृत्तय इति । समाधिवृत्तिरियमुक्ता । यदुक्तं—ब्रह्मविद्याधिरूढा सतीति । तस्याः सजातीयप्रत्ययप्रवाहरूपत्वात् पुनः पुनराविर्भावसंभवः । शार्ङ्गिशब्दो मूर्तिपक्षे शार्ङ्गगदाद्यायुधयोगाभिप्रायः । इह तु मायायोगाभिप्राय इत्याह—तत्राभिव्यक्ताविति । सर्वतो व्याप्तस्यैकरूपस्यापि सत इति भावः । शरणादिति । सामान्यकारणादिरूपेण चिदाश्रयतयाऽवस्थानमुक्तम् । यद्वा चिद्रूपहिंसामोहनमुक्तमरणादिविषयभोगसमर्पणम् । गमनादिति । स्वाधिकारविरतौ निवृत्तिः ॥ ६ ॥

तेषु श्रव इति । वेदप्रथितिरुक्ता । विस्तीर्णकीर्तिर्वेति । लोकप्रसिद्धिः ।

सूक्तिभिरुक्तैर्मन्त्रैरित्यकारादिमन्त्राणां सर्वेश्वरप्रणवानां तदङ्गानामपि ग्रहणम्। व्यष्टिमन्त्रैरपि समष्ट्यात्मनि प्रत्ययो न्यासपूजादिषु प्रसिद्ध एव। स्तुतिभिरिति। तासामिहानुपयोगादनुपन्यास:। यद्वा मासयन्त्रपटलभाविन्य एव ग्राह्या:। स्वमूर्तिं स व्यदर्शयदिति निष्कलविषये। दर्शनमपरोक्षीकरणानुग्रहलक्षणम्। यदुक्तम्—अपरोक्षीकृतपरदेवतात्मतत्त्व इति। इह सूक्तिभि: स्तुतिभिरिति मन्त्रस्तुत्यादिप्रयोगस्य समाधिवृत्तिभि: सह तदपरोक्षीभावापकारित्वमुक्तम्॥ ७॥

उन्नसी उन्नतनासिका। विसरणं प्रसरणम्। औदरिकाबन्ध उदरबन्ध एव। राजय: पङ्क्तय:। एषा इयं मूर्ति:। मूर्तिवर्णनं तु सकलमन्त्रमूर्तीनामप्येवं समुचितरूपाभोगप्रतिपत्त्यर्थम्॥ ८॥ ९॥ १०॥ ११॥ १२॥ १३॥ १४॥

भक्तिपरवशचित्ता इति। चित्तशब्देनात्मशब्दो विवृत:। तत्राऽब्रवीदज इति। ब्रह्मगताया: सर्गशक्तेरुद्बुद्धतमत्वादिति भाव:। अज: स्वयंभूर्ब्रह्मा। प्रकारान्तरमाह—अजोऽकारज इति। अकारोऽवर्णविग्रहं देवमित्युक्त: परो देव एव। इह त्रिविधस्य साधकस्य गुरुसमासादनसंभवोऽपि सूचित:॥ १५॥

यद्यनित्या इति। अनित्यत्वे तु यत्कारणं तत्स्वरूपं भविष्यतीति ब्रह्मणोऽभिप्राय:॥ १६॥

मूले परं ज्योतिरिति शार्ङ्गिणो ग्रहणम्। प्रमिताक्षरमिति। प्रमितं परिमितमक्षरं यस्य भाविविस्तारसङ्ग्रहरूपत्वात् तत् प्रमिताक्षरम्। यूयमक्षरसंभूता इत्यादिवाक्यम्। पुन: प्रश्ने कृते सर्वानित्यमुवाच हेति विस्तारोपक्रम:।

अत्र प्रकरणान्तरमाह—प्रमिताक्षरमित्यादिना। प्रकर्षेणेत्येतदाख्यातत्रयेण सम्बन्धनीयम्। मीयत इति मीङ्माङो: साधारणं कर्मणि रूपम्। मिनोतीति कर्मणि डुमिञ् प्रक्षेपणे। कर्मवासनाप्रचयेनाऽविद्यां स्थायिनीं करोतीति तदर्थ:। परिच्छिनत्तीति। माङर्थतो गृहीत:। कालपरिच्छेदोऽत्र विवक्षित:। तदभिन्नमित्यस्याऽयमाशय:। हकारमुवाचेति ह्यनेनोक्तं भवति। तदा च तदभिन्नताभावे प्रकृत्याद्यर्थस्याग्रहणादकृतस्त्रमुत्तरं स्यादिति। सतत्त्वमपि तत्त्वमेव। तस्येति शार्ङ्गिणोऽभिप्राय इत्येतदन्तं वाक्यम्। द्रष्टव्यमिति। साधकैरिति शेष:। अहमेलनरूपिणेवेति। मेलनं द्वयोरहयो: संसर्गरूपो मध्यमांश:। प्रकृत्यादिमन्त्रो हकार इत्येतदपोह सूचितम्। सार्वेश्वरप्रणववद्दृषिच्छन्दसी। प्रकृतिपुरुषकालात्मको देवो देवता। हां हीमित्यादिभिरङ्गानि। अर्धनारीश्वरो ध्येय:। तस्य वामदक्षिणमध्यमभागैरेतत्त्रयात्मकत्वम्। वक्ष्यति च—मुद्राभयशुकवरदकर इत्यादि। मिलित्वेति। प्रकृतिस्वरूपात् कालो भोक्तरि

पुरुषे महदादिभोग्यजातं निष्पादयतीति भावः। तेषु वो जायते लय इति। तदा जिज्ञासितमालक्ष्य उत्तरम्। अभिप्रायान्तरमाह—उपादानत्वमिति। इह त्रिविधस्य साधकस्य स्वात्मपर्याप्तगुरुसमासत्त्यनन्तरं तदुचितप्रश्नोत्तरप्रकारोऽपि सूचितः। अत्र यूयमक्षरसंभूता इति मन्त्रदेवतास्वरूपभूतादक्षरात्तेषा-मुत्पत्तिरुक्ता। तेनैषामक्षरस्वरूपत्वं निर्धारितं भवति। सृष्टिस्थित्यन्तहेतव इति। यथास्वं न्यास इव योगैककार्यत्वमेषां विग्रहोत्पत्तेरुक्तम्। तेषु वो जायते लय इति च न्यासादिभिः स्वस्वरूपभूताक्षराप्ययलक्षणोऽपवर्गोऽप्यभिहित इति।

अथ यत्प्रागुक्तं प्रकृतिपुरुषकाला हकारश्चोक्ता इति यच्चेहापि तदभिन्नं स्वरूपं प्रमिताक्षरमिति तदादिगुरोः शार्ङ्गिणो वचनसिद्धमिति दर्शयन्निहाऽक्षरशब्द-स्येयानभिप्राय इति सोपपत्तिकमाह—अत्रेत्यादिना। अत्रेत्यस्य गम्यत इत्युपरिसम्बन्धः। व्युत्पत्त्या प्रकृतिपुरुषकाला रूढ्या हकार इति विभागः। वाच्यस्य साक्षिचिद्रूपस्यैकत्वेऽपि तद्विभूतिवर्गाणां त्रिधाभिन्नत्वात्प्रकृत्यादितया त्रेधा विकल्पसंभवः। इह वाच्यवाचकयोरक्षराभिधाने।

अयमभिप्रायः वर्णास्तावदक्षराणि प्रसिद्धान्येव। त एव च मन्त्राः। तथा जगदपीदं स्थिरमक्षरं प्रसिद्धमेव। तदेव च तद्वाच्यदेवता। यदेतद्वाच्यवाचकम-क्षरं तदेतदेवाक्षरं स्थूलावस्थमेतत्त्वेव साक्षादक्षरमिति ॥ १७ ॥ १८ ॥

अक्षरशब्दोक्तमिति। वाच्यवाचकयोरभेदस्य स्वयंप्रतिपन्नत्वाद्वाचकैकत्वस्य च हेत्येवं श्रुतत्वाद्वाच्यानां त्रित्वेऽपि तदव्यतिरिक्तत्वादेकीकरणोपपत्तिः। सर्वानित्थमुवाच हेत्यस्यायं स्थूलोऽर्थः। मूलार्णादीन् त्रिमूर्तिप्रश्नोत्तरभूतानित्थं वक्ष्यमाणप्रकारेणोक्तवानिति। हकारः पुराकल्पावद्योतनार्थः ॥ १९ ॥

अत्र सूक्ष्ममर्थं दर्शयति—सर्वेषामित्यादिना। समस्तशब्दानुगतमिति। नित्यत्वसमर्थनार्थमुक्तं वाचकं तावदिह हकार एव। तस्य स्वरूपमूलार्णं शक्तिबीजम्। तच्च नित्यं स्वयंमूलार्णतया तस्यापि मूलार्णान्तरायोगात् समस्तमन्त्रानुगततया तेषामेवानित्यतोपपत्तेरिति मूलार्णग्रहणेऽभिप्रायः। ननु हकारस्यैव कथं शक्तिबीजं स्वरूपमभ्युपगम्यत इति। उच्यते। परावाचस्सा-वच्छक्तिलक्षणं स्वरूपम्। हेति च परावागेव। तदेव स्वान्तस्फुरत्सकल-शब्दार्थमात्रात्मकरेफतदुन्मेषनिमिषेशनरूपेकारविलसितमेव शक्तिबीजम्। तच्च तस्योचितं स्वरूपं स्यादिति इह चतुर्धा विकल्पः संभवति। वाच्यवाचकौ मिथो भिन्नौ। वाच्यं प्रधानमितरस्तद्गुणः। वाचकं प्रधानमितरस्तद्गुणः। वाच्य-वाचकौ परस्पराभिन्नाविति तत्र पूर्वंविकल्पद्वयाभिप्रायेणैतदुक्तम्। वाचकस्य

तावदिति। उत्तरविकल्पद्वयाभिप्रायेणैतदुच्यते। अथवेत्यादि। सर्वेषामेवेति। वाचकस्य वाच्यानां चेत्यर्थः। ननु वाच्यानामुपरि सर्वं वक्ष्यत एव तत इह को विशेष इत्यत आह—संग्रहेणेति। कथं पुनरयमभिप्रायो लभ्यत इत्यत्राह—प्रकृतमित्यादि। उत्तरत्रेति। प्रकृतिः पुरुषश्चेवेत्यस्मिन् प्रकरणे। सर्वात्मत्व-कथनाच्चेति पूर्वत्र सम्बन्धनीयम्। इदानीमुक्तविकल्पचतुष्टयानुगुणतया विवृणोति मूलार्णमित्यादिना। शक्तिबीजं हृल्लेखापटल उद्धरिष्यति। मूलार्णशब्देन प्रणवो वा विवक्षितः। तदुक्तं—मूलार्णमिति प्रणवशक्तिवाचकपक्षाविति।

परतत्त्वस्योदासीनदशायां वाचकमनुत्तरमकारः। यदुक्तम्—अजोऽकारज इति। तस्य निजशक्तिधर्मितया पुंस्त्वावभासदशायां स एव प्रणवः स्यात्। तच्छक्तिधर्मतया स्त्रीत्वावभासदशायामीशानाख्यः शक्तिप्रणवः। तस्यैव शक्तिभावयोग्यतादशायां स एव हकारो भवति। साक्षादेव शक्तिदशायां यथोक्तरूपा भुवनेश्वरीति भेदः। एवमुत्तरत्रापीति। केवलमर्थसहितमेव योजनीयमित्यर्थः। वक्ष्यमाणा इति। शक्तिपटल इति शेषः। कादिक्षान्ता इति तत्रैव वक्ष्यमाणाः। विकृतेर्विकृतय इति मूलपदाभिप्रायः। अङ्गत्वेनेति। गुणतया। तान् सर्वान् ह इतीत्यमाहेति। अत्रेतिशब्दोऽध्याहृतः।

अयमिहार्थः—मूलार्णादयोऽमी हेत्येतदक्षरमित्युवाचेति हेत्येतन्मूलार्णा-द्यात्मकमिति चैतदभिप्रायः। अत्र यत्परोक्षं शार्ङ्गिणो वचनमवभासते मूलार्णो हेत्येवंविधं तदभिप्रायेणोक्तं समस्तशब्दानुगतं स्वरूपमाह मूलार्णमितीत्येतदव-बोद्धव्यम्। इह मूलार्णमिति हकारस्याक्षरस्य नित्यप्रश्नोत्तरं स्वरूपप्रश्नोत्तरं च। अर्णविकृतीरित्यादि सर्वं किमात्मकमित्यस्योत्तरम्। नन्वेवं हकारस्य केवलस्य शक्तिबीजस्यापि वा सतो मूलार्णतया नित्यत्वं नित्यत्वे च नित्यानां प्रकृतिपुरुष-कालानां वाचकत्वं चोक्तं कथं पुनरिह सत्सु वर्णान्तरेषु हकारस्यैवोभयरूपेणापि परावाक्तत्त्वमिति नियमः कथं वैवं नियमेऽप्यस्यार्णविकृतत्वादिसर्वोपपत्तिरिति तदेतदुपपादयति—हकारो हीत्यादिना। प्रत्याहारार्थोऽपि सन्नकारो हकारा-भिव्यक्त्यर्थश्चापि स्यादिति। तदुपरि निविष्ट इत्यभिप्रायेणाऽकारहकारात्मेत्येवं निर्देशः। तयोश्चेति। सर्ववर्णाद्यनुगमादित्युपरि सम्बन्धः। आद्यन्ताक्षरयो-रिति। मातृकाया इति शेषः। गृहीततरवर्णयोरिति। हकारस्त्वेवं कृत्स्नैव मातृका भवति न केवलं तद्वर्णमात्रमिति भावः। इयता हकारस्य वर्णान्त-रेभ्यो विशेष उक्तः। एवमयमेव परावाक्तत्त्वमिति नियमः स्यादिति भावः।

नादाकाररूपेण वेति सर्ववर्णाद्यनुगमादित्यनेनाऽन्वयः। हकारात्मिकाया

मन्त्रदेवतायाः स्थूलसूक्ष्मादिपञ्चविधात्मकत्वात् तदनुरोधेनायं वाच्यवाचक-पञ्चकोपन्यासः। नादबुद्धिज्ञानशक्तिविमर्शचितोऽकारहकारयोः स्थूलाद्यंशेषु क्रमेण वाचकांशा इतरे वाच्यांशा इत्यवसेयम्। वाशब्दः सर्वथापि संभवाद-नियमार्थः। कार्यानुगमे कारणस्य तदनुगमे कार्यानुगमादिति। पारायण-वर्णानामादिशब्देन तत्प्रभिन्नानां मन्त्राणां प्रयोगमन्त्राणां च ग्रहणम्। तथा तद्देवतानां च ग्रहणम्। नादाकाररूपेण वेत्यकारप्राणादिवाच्यांशानामप्यु-पात्तत्वात् हेतुस्तावदित्थमुक्तः। अथ साध्यमुच्यते सर्वशब्दार्थेति। हकारस्य केवलस्य शक्तिरूपस्याप्येवं सावयवद्वारा सर्ववर्णतदर्थसङ्घातरूपत्वात् सवर्णादिषु तदर्थेष्वपि तदवयवद्वारानुगमात् सकलवाच्यवाचकानुगमसिद्धेः सर्वात्मत्वं स्यात्। केनाकारेणास्यैतत्सर्वात्मत्वमित्याह—सर्वशब्दार्थसमष्ट्यात्मकपरावागात्मत्वेनेति। केवलमर्थसहितं वेत्येतदिहापि यथास्वं प्रत्येतव्यम्। यत एतस्य केवलस्य शक्तिरूपस्यापि स्वयंनित्यत्वं नित्यप्रकृतिपुरुषकालवाचकत्वं च सम्यगुपपन्न-मित्याह—प्रकृतीति। तत्क्रमेणेति। नित्यत्वं सर्वात्मत्वं स्वरूपं चेत्यर्थः। क्रमशब्देनैतदाह प्रथमं तावत्प्रकृतिः पुरुषश्चैवेति प्रकृतिपुरुषकालानां नित्यत्वं ततो विभुशब्देन प्रकृतेः स्वरूपमणोरणीयसीत्यादिशेषेण ततः सर्वात्मत्वं ततः साहं यथमिति पुरुषस्य स्वरूपं व्याप्तिश्च ततः सा तु कालात्मनेति कालस्य स्वरूपम् लवादिप्रलयान्तोऽयमित्यादिशेषेण तद्विभूतिरिति।

देवतातत्त्वं हि चिद्रूपमेकमेव। तस्य स्वशक्तिकल्पित एवायं प्रकृतिपुरुष-कालात्मको विकल्प इत्यभिप्रायेण प्रकृतिव्याप्तेरेव प्रबन्धेनाऽभिधानमिति। प्रकृतिः पुरुषश्चैवेत्येवकारस्तेषामेव नित्यतेत्यवधारणार्थः। चकाराविति। तेषां द्वयोर्द्वयो-र्मिथो यः सम्बन्धो भोग्यभोक्त्रादिलक्षणो यश्च मिथोभेदः सोऽपि तद्वन्नित्य एवेति भावः। कालस्य पृथग्ग्रहणमित्यसमासकरणमुक्तम्। निमित्तत्वावद्योतनार्थ-मिति। काल एव साक्षान्निमित्तमिति भावः। यत् तूक्तमितरौ निमित्तमिति तत्र पुरुषो भोक्तृत्वेन निमित्तमात्रमिति विशेषः। ननु प्रकृत्यादीनां तत्सम्बन्धभेदयोश्च नित्यत्वे देवतातत्त्वस्य नानात्वापत्तिरित्याशङ्कायां तस्य साक्षिलक्षणस्यैकत्वेऽपि तत्साक्ष्याणां भेदसंभवात्तद्द्वारा निरूपण एवायम्। तस्मिन् भेदावभासो न तन्मात्र-निरूपण इत्यभिप्रायेण प्रकृतिपुरुषकालान् साक्षिसाक्ष्यरूपाभिप्राये द्वेधा विभजते—प्रकृतिपुरुषकाला इति। एतच्च शार्ङ्गिणो विवक्षितमिति दर्शयन् परावर स्वरूपमपि दर्शयति—विचिकीर्षुरिति। अत्र विचिकीर्षयी युष्मानपि लवादि प्रलयान्त इत्यपरे प्रकृत्यादयः। स्वसंवेद्यस्वरूपा बहुना किं सा तु कालात्मनेति

परे। अत्रापरप्रकृत्यादीनां तद्विभूतिद्वारा प्रतिपत्तिः तद्वारेणैव तु परप्रकृत्यादिसाचिव्यं तद्विग्रहतया चापरप्रकृत्यादिभाव इत्यपि प्रतिपादितम्। वाक्यशेषादिति। द्विविधा इत्यधः सम्बन्धः। मूले सत्त्वमिति त्रिनियवत्तिस्त्वयैव (?) प्रतिपत्तव्येति सूचितम्। त्रयात्मकं ह्येदं जगदिति। यद्वा त्रिविभागफलं त्वयैवावसेयमिति। तत्र सरस्वतीत्रिपुरादयः प्रकृतिप्रधानाः सूर्यसोमादयः पुरुषप्रधानाः विष्णुशिवादयः कालप्रधाना इति। अथवा तेषां मन्त्रसेवायां समन्वयस्त्वयैव निरूपणीय इति। तत्र पूजकः कालः साधको देवता च पुरुषं क्रिया मन्त्रो द्रव्यमिति प्रकृतिरिति यदुक्तं तदाह—

पुरुषो भगवानिहोपहारः प्रकृतिः कालतनुः स्वयं हि कर्ता। इति।

प्रकृतेर्व्याप्तिकथनेन भोग्यद्रव्यत्वादिति सिद्धेरिति। अभिप्रायान्तरमाह—विपर्यय इति। प्रकृत्यादीनामनित्यत्वे तेषामप्यन्यैः प्रकृत्यादिभिरेव भाव्यम्। तेषामप्यनित्यत्वे तेषामप्यपरैरितीयमनवस्थेति ॥ २०॥२१ ॥

प्रकृतेः स्वरूपं व्याप्तिं चाहेति पृथग्विनियोगः क्रियते। वाच्याचराणामपि तदिति हि सामान्यतो विनियोगः। सामान्यतो व्याप्तिमित्यनेनैतदपि सूचितम्। अणोरणीयसो स्थूलात् स्थूलेत्व्अणुमध्यमस्थूलेषु चराचरेषु विशेषतो व्याप्तिकथनमिति। आदित्येन्द्वादीत्यधिज्योतिषं व्याप्तिः। विभुरिति तु प्रकृतेः स्वरूपाभिधानम्। विभावनलक्षणा शक्तिरस्याः स्वरूपमिति ॥ २२ ॥

न श्वेतरक्तेत्यधिविषयं व्याप्तिः। श्वेतरक्तादिपदैस्तद्गुणानां विषयभूतानां तन्मात्राणां ग्रहणम्। सर्ववर्णानुगमादन्यतमवर्णतया निर्धारणायोगः। न गुणेष्वित्यधिगुणं व्याप्तिः। गुणाः सत्त्वादयः। सर्वस्मिन्ननुगमादेकस्मिन् विशेषतो न व्यवस्थितिः। न भूतेष्वित्यधिभूतं व्याप्तिः। पूर्ववदव्यवस्थितिः ॥ २३ ॥

अन्तरान्तरित्यध्यात्मं व्याप्तिः। अधुना तु तद्दर्शनोपदेशसावसरस्वात्मनि व्याप्तेरपीदानीं सिद्धत्वादित्याशयं दर्शयन्नाह—कथं तर्हीति। मूले दैशिकदर्शितैरित्युपायैरित्युपस्कारः। ते चोपाया अनुयागादयः। दर्शनमपरोक्षानुभवः। स्वसंवेद्यस्वरूपेति च नित्यत्वमपि तत्कालविशेषणम्। स्वयैवाऽहंतया वेद्यं स्वरूपं यस्याः सा तथोक्ता। स्वरूपमिह पारमार्थिक आरोपसिद्धश्चाभिप्रेतः। तद्दर्शयति—अपरप्रकृतिसाचिव्येनेति। अत्राऽर्थादेतद्गम्यते। प्रकृतितत्त्वे याथात्म्यतो निरूप्यमाणे किञ्चित्स्वयैव संवेद्यं किञ्चित्तया संवेद्यं चास्तीति। परप्रकृतिरूपसाचिव्येनेति वा पाठः। इह स्वसंवेद्यमस्याः स्वरूपमिति परप्रकृतिस्वरूपमप्युक्तम्। तत्साक्ष्यमचिद्रूपमित्यपरप्रकृतेः स्वरूपमप्युक्तमित्यव-

बोद्धव्यम्। यत् पूर्वमुक्तं विभुरिति तत्सामान्येन स्वरूपकथनमिति भेदः ॥ २४ ॥

सा लब्धेति उपलम्भः परोक्षावभासः। दर्शनं साक्षादनुभवः। लाभस्तद्वृद्धिरिति भेदः। स्वात्मप्रत्ययसाधकमिति। स्वात्मन्येष प्रत्ययः स्पष्टतयाऽवभासः निश्चयो विश्वासो वा। यया आकाशमित्यस्यायमर्थः। यया लब्धया आकाशस्तमो वापि तेन साधकेनोपलभ्यते। सर्वविशेषाणां तस्यामेव निमग्नत्वादिति संभाव्यानुपलम्भत्वादाकाशतमसोर्ग्रहणम्। अभिप्रायान्तरमाह—आकाश इति। बुद्ध्यादीनि सर्वाण्यपि कार्याणि सत्त्वादय इच्छादयश्चेति कारणावस्थाविशेषत्वादुक्तम्। त्रिषु तुल्यापीति। तुल्यग्रहणादित्थं विवृतिरिति भावः। विशिष्यत इत्येतदभिप्रायमाह—अङ्गनास्विति प्रकृतेरिति शेषः ॥ २५ ॥

कथमेतत्त्रिषु तुल्यत्वमित्यत आह—गुणभूतादिरूपेणेति। पुंस्त्रीनपुंसकात्मसु तदीयसत्त्वेच्छादिगुणरूपेण लिङ्गशरीरधात्वादिभूतभौतिकरूपेण वेत्यर्थः। सकलव्याप्तीनां मिथो व्याप्तिरप्यनेन दर्शिता। प्रधानमिति यामाहुरित्यत्र त्रिलिङ्गपदेशब्देषु परोक्षस्त्रीपुंनपुंसकभावेषु व्याप्तिरुच्यते। प्रधानादिग्रहणं तमआदिप्रदर्शनार्थम्। यद्वा प्रकृतेरागमेषु लक्ष्म्युमादिप्रसिद्धेरुक्तव्याप्त्यनुपपत्तिरित्याशङ्कायां प्रधानमिति यामाहुरित्युच्यते। तदाह—शब्दतोऽपीति। या युष्मानपीति चेतनेषु व्याप्तिस्तत्र प्रकारभेदोऽप्युच्यते। एतद्विवृण्वन् प्रकृतिव्याप्त्युपसंहारं पुरुषव्याप्त्युपक्रमं च दर्शयति—किं बहुनेति। व्याप्त्यन्तरमपि बहु संभवति तदुक्तव्याप्तिभिरेवोह्यमिति किं बहुनेत्युक्तम्। जगत्कारणभूतान् युष्मानपीति हिरण्यगर्भाद्यखिलचेतनातिवृत्तिस्तावत् स्यादिति भावः। नन्वचितश्चिदतिवृत्तौ किं निबन्धनमित्यत इदमुक्तम् मां नित्यमवष्टभ्येति। तदेव च मदवष्टम्भादिति हेतुतया विवृतम्। अत्र मच्छब्देन स्वसंवेद्यस्वरूपा सेत्युक्ता पराप्रकृतिः गृह्यते। यद्वा परपुरुषतत्त्वं साहमिति पुरुषस्य प्रकृतौ व्याप्तिरुक्ता। यूयमित्यादिशेषेण तु तद्व्याप्तायास्तस्या ब्रह्माद्यशेषानुगमकथनेन तथा तेषु व्याप्त्यभिधानम्। पुरुषचिद्रूपे कल्पितायां तस्यां ब्रह्मादीनां कल्पितत्वादेतद्व्याप्तिसंभवः। तथा चाह—युष्माकं विषयवदिति। अत्र यूयमिति मूर्तयः। तथैवान्यदिति सकलचराचरचेतनजातम्। यद्वेद्यमिति प्रकृतेर्विभूतितयोक्ताखाद्यखिलार्थग्रहणम्। पुरुषकृतस्तव्याप्तिरेकैव सतीत्यमुक्ता भवति। अत्र वेद्यग्रहणेन पुरुषाणां वेदितृत्वाभिधानात् पुरुषस्वरूपमपि वेदितृचिल्लक्षणमुक्तं भवति। वेदमेव हि भोगः।

अत्र पूर्वोक्तशेषतयाभिप्रायान्तरं दर्शयति—त्वदनतिक्रम इति। मयि कल्पितत्वेन तस्या इति। सर्वेश्वरस्तावदाद्यः पुरुषः स च निजवेदितृत्वाङ्गभूता-

चिदंशविशिष्ट एव। तत्स्वरूपे च याथात्म्यतो निरूप्यमाणे तद्गतं सारभूतं चिद्रूपं स्वसंवेद्यलक्षणं तद्वैद्यमचिद्रूपं चाऽवसीयते। तत्र चिद्रूपमिह परः पुरुषः। तत्प्रतिबिम्बलक्षणमचिद्रूपमपरः पुरुषः। सर्वेश्वरे चापरपुरुषसद्भावेऽपि तस्य साक्षितयैवेह विवक्षितत्वात् ब्रह्मादिष्वेवाऽपरपुरुषांशो दर्शयितव्यः। अतएवाह —युष्माकं विषयवदिति। प्रथमं तावच्चिद्वस्तुन्यचिदारोपः। स च प्रकृतिपुरुषयोः समान एव। नात्र चिद्रूपस्य स्वदृष्ट्या स्वरूपभेदः। अत एव मां नित्यमवष्टभ्य साहं सा तु कालात्मना सम्यङ्मयैवेत्येकचिदनुगमसंभवः। ततस्तस्मिन्नचिदर्थे क्वचित्तदाश्रयस्य चिद्वस्तुन आरोपः। सोऽपरः पुरुष इति। नन्वपरप्रकृति-कालयोरपि चेतनव्यवहारो बहुलमुपलभ्यत इति। नैष दोषः। यथा हि पुरुषेषु तदीयभोक्तृत्वाङ्गतया प्रकृत्यंशानुगमस्तथा प्रकृतिविकारेष्वपि तदीय-भोग्यताङ्गतया चिदंशानुगमोपपत्तेः। एवमपरकालेष्वपि स्यात्। एवं च पीठशक्तीनामिन्द्रियोपहारादिशक्तीनां भूषणायुधादिशक्तीनामपि तदङ्गीभूतदेव-पूजाङ्गतया पूजार्हामतर्पणाद्युपपत्तिरिति। अनित्यैवेयं प्रकृतिपुरुषयोर्व्याप्तिः। किन्तु स्थिता विस्तीर्णा प्रलये संक्षिप्तेति भेदः इत्येत्प्रलये व्याप्यत इत्युच्यते। स्थितिसमय इदं जगदित्थं स्वस्वाकारेण वर्तत इति तावदुक्तम्। प्रलयसमये तु पुनरेतदेव प्रकृतिपुरुषगता चिदंशे संक्षिप्ततया निजनिजशक्तिमात्राकारेण व्याप्यत इत्यस्यायमर्थः। अभिप्रायान्तरमाह—तत्रेति। प्रलये सर्वविकृतीनां सर्वपुरुषाणां च तत्र विलयात् तेषां तत्र कल्पितत्वमवसेयमित्यर्थः॥ २६॥ २७॥

ननु प्रलये सर्वविकृतीनां प्रकृतौ व्याप्तिरयुक्ता बुद्ध्यादेस्तदध्यक्षतयाऽवस्थान-स्याऽभ्युपेयत्वादित्याशयेनाशङ्कामाह—ननु प्रलयेऽपीति। मूले सैव स्वां वेत्ति परमेति। तत्कालविशेषणम्। सैव परमा सती स्वां स्वरूपमुभयविधमपि वेत्तीति। एतद्दर्शयति—परमा साक्षिलक्षणेति। स्वसंवेद्यस्वरूपेति पूर्वोक्तेति योजनीयम्। तस्या नान्य इति षष्ठी। तस्याः पराया अन्य इति पञ्चमी।

वैपरीत्येनेति। अपरप्रकृतिः स्वैर्बुद्ध्यादिभिः स्वस्वरूपं परप्रकृतिं च विद्यादिति भावः। जडत्वलक्षणविशेषद्योतक इति। बुद्ध्यादीनां तदध्यक्षचिदनुप्रवेशादेव बोधशक्त्यवभास इति भावः। कालात्मना ज्ञानात्मनेति। कालेनैवं प्रचोद्यत इत्यसावस्य शेष एव। ज्ञाने तु प्रकृतेर्न लवादिकालापेक्षा प्रचोद्यत्वे च तदपेक्षेति लवादिकथनपूर्वकं कालेनैवं प्रचोद्यत इत्यभिधानम्। सा तु प्रकृतिः कालात्मना मयैव प्रेर्यत इति। कलयति प्रकृतिं जानाति योजयति च पुरुषस्यार्थेष्विति कालः। योजनमेव प्रेरणम्। सम्यग्ज्ञायत इति प्रकृत्यन्तर्गततदीयानेककार्य-

प्रकृतिपुरुषनिचयतदोयापूर्वंजातज्ञानमप्युक्तम्। सदेति स्थितौ प्रलयेऽपि तुल्यमेतदित्यर्थ:। अत्र च प्रकृतिविषयसर्वज्ञानप्रेरणलक्षणचिद्रूपं कालस्य स्वरूपमित्यपि प्रतिपादितमिति।

अत्र सूक्ष्ममर्थं दर्शयति—कालात्मना ज्ञानात्मनेति। सम्यगित्यस्य साक्षितयाऽव्यवधानेनेत्यर्थ:। नात्र बुद्ध्यादिकरणव्यवधानसंभव इति भाव:। ननु परकालस्य स्वोपाधिभूतापरकाललक्षणप्रकृत्यंशविषयमेव साक्षित्वं स्यात् न तूपादानलक्षणप्रकृत्यंशविषयमपीति। नैष दोष:। कालोपाधेर्विशुद्धसत्त्वांशतया विशुद्धसत्त्वांशस्य च सर्वावभासकतया तद्द्वारेण सर्वदृक्त्वात् सर्वसाक्षित्वं स्यात्। यद्वा परप्रकृतिपुरुषयो: स्वोपाधिसाक्षित्वम्। परकालस्य तु तदुभयसाक्षित्वं स्वोपाधिसाक्षित्वं चेति। अथवा कृत्स्नाया: प्रकृते: सूक्ष्मतमो विशुद्धोंऽश: परकालोपाधि:। सा तु प्रकृतिरेव परप्रकृत्युपाधिस्तदंशविशेष: पुरुषोपाधिरिति। परकालस्यापि स्वरूपमिति। कालात्मना ज्ञानात्मनेत्युक्तत्वादिति भाव: ॥ २८ ॥

अभिधायेति। कालस्य स्वरूपं तावदुक्तम्। इदानीमेतद्व्याप्तिकथनावसर इति भाव:। अपरं कालमिति। कार्यकारणरूपमिति भाव:। मूले लवादिप्रलयान्तोऽयमित्यत्राऽयमिति कालात्मनेति प्रकृतस्य ग्रहणम्। अयमेव कालो लवादिप्रलयान्तोऽपि कालो भवतीत्यर्थ:। अस्य कालस्य लवादयो विभूतिरित्यपोद्दोक्तं भवति। अतएव वक्ष्यति - कालपर्वाणीति। नलिनीपत्रसंहत्यामिति लवस्य मानमुक्तम्। तस्य प्रथमतया प्रतिपत्तौ निरालम्बनत्वादित्यवगन्तव्यम्। लववाचक इति बहुव्रीहि:। सोऽङ्गुलिस्फोटतुल्यश्चेति। मूर्तकालानां प्रथमत्वादुक्तम्। कालेन यावतेति। प्राणायामादिषु उपयोगादुक्तम्। मात्रा सेतिच्छेद:। निश्वासैरिति मात्रात्मकैरहोरात्रैर्मास इतिच्छेद:।

अयमहोरात्रं दिवौकसामिति पृथग्वाक्यम्। भिन्नैरित्येतद्विवृणोति—चतुस्त्रिद्व्येकसहस्रैरिति। कालवेदिभिरिति + + + + मासमृक्षसोति। तव मास इति भाव:। त्वमपीति। जगत्कारणभूतोऽपि सन्नित्यर्थ:। अर्थान्तरमाह—एताविति। त्वदायुर्मम नि:श्वास इति पर: कालो ममेत्युक्त:। यस्य कालस्यानाद्यन्तस्य विभोरेतानि पर्वाणि तस्य ब्राह्म: काल: न दिनस्थानीयोऽपीति किन्तु नि:श्वासमात्रमित्यर्थ:। अत्राऽभिप्रायमाह—तेषामिति। परकैवल्याधिकारिणां ब्राह्मकालविभूतितोऽपि वैराग्येण भाव्यमिति भाव:। कालेनैवं प्रचोद्यत इति। कालेनैव मयैवमुक्तलवादिविकल्पोपपत्त्या प्रेर्यते प्रकृतिरित्यर्थ:। एतच्छ्लोकोत्तरत्वेन योजयति—नि:श्वासादिमत इति। विषममायुरिति। मनुष्यदेवब्रह्मसु

भेदादिति भावः। वैषम्यनैर्घृण्ये स्याताम् इति। पुरुषानुग्रहार्थैव हि काला-ख्यस्येश्वरस्य स्वोपाधिपरिग्रहः। तथा च तेषु समेन दयालुना च तेन भाव्यम्। स चोच्चावचतया तेषु जीवितकालमायुर्विदधद्विषमः स्यात्। मनुष्येष्वल्पमायु-र्विदधत्तेषु निर्घृणस्य स्यादिति भावः। पुरुषकर्मानुसारिणीत्येवंशब्दविवरणम्। तस्य प्रथिततया बुद्धिगतत्वाच्चैवमिति ग्रहणोपपत्तिः। वक्ष्यमाणप्रकारेणेत्यत्र नाशङ्का योजनीयेति। एवं तावदकारवाच्याक्षरस्य त्र्यात्मकस्य स्वरूपं सर्वात्मत्वं च वर्णितम्॥ २८—४०॥

अथाऽस्यैव प्रकरणस्याऽर्थान्तरं दृष्ट्वा देशिकदर्शितैरिति सूचितम् अनेक-विधयोगरूपं वक्तुमारभते—प्रकृतिरिति। अकारोकारमकारा इति। वाच्य-वाचकग्रहणमिति भावः। नित्या इति। यदा स्वतन्त्रा एते योगाः स्युः। यतो वक्ष्यति—ततो वाक्यार्थप्रतिपत्तिमाहेति। तदा प्रणवहृल्लेखयोः साधकेच्छया प्रवृत्तिः। यदा तु मन्त्राङ्गभूताः। यतो वक्ष्यति—सयोगान्वक्ष्यमाणन्यासानाचरे-दिति। तदा तत्तन्मन्त्रसंयोगोऽप्यनयोरिष्यते। तत्र च पुंवाचकेषु मन्त्रेषु प्रणवः स्त्रीवाचकेषु हृल्लेखा च स्यात्। प्रणवहृल्लेखयोस्तु मन्त्रत्वे केवलयोरेव तयोः प्रवृत्तिरिति सर्वमवबोद्धव्यम्। योगैश्चित्यैरित्यणुयोगादावकारोकारमकारा एव + + + त्यादि द्रष्टव्यमिति भावः॥ २१॥

अणोरणीयसी स्थूलात्स्थूला व्याप्तचराचरेत्यत्र प्रकृतिः क्रमेण भवतीत्यर्थो-लभ्यते। प्रकृतिर्ध्येया अकाराकारिणीति। प्रकृतिरिहाऽपरोपलक्षिता परा विवक्षिता। कुतः। योगानां साक्षिपर्यन्तताभिधानात्। यदुक्तम्—अपरप्रकृति-साक्षितयेति। वक्ष्यति च—स्वरूपस्थो भवेदिति परमात्मस्वरूपेण सानुभव-नीयेति तत्रात्मनो निर्विशेषत्वचिन्तनमिति च। हेत्येवेह प्रतिपत्तव्यम्। रूपमित्याकारग्रहणेनोक्तम्। प्रभारूपिणीति। प्रकृतेः समन्तादपर्यन्ततया प्रभाप्रसारणमर्थसिद्धम्। तदुपदेशादेव तस्याः प्रकृतेस्तटित्स्वज्योतीरूपत्वम-प्युक्तम्। आकाशादेरपीति। स्थूलस्य ब्रह्माण्डतदावरणादेरपि ग्रहणम्। मज्जनीयमिति। प्रभाया द्रवदमृतमयत्वं तदाविशक्रमेणाकाशादेस्तत्र विलयश्च सूचितः। हृल्लेखाग्रयणी हरमाया इतो योज्याः। योगानां स्वतन्त्रत्वे प्रणवावयवैरेवमनुसन्धानमेव कार्यम्। ध्येया सञ्चिन्त्य ध्यात्वेत्येवंनिर्देशात् प्रणवो-च्चारणसमये होत्येवाभिधानाच्च। मन्त्राङ्गत्वे तु न्यासपुरःसरमेवमनुसन्धानं स्यात्। यतो वक्ष्यति—सयोगान् वक्ष्यमाणन्यासानिति। न्यासयोगे चैवं प्रयोगक्रमः। प्रणवेन मूलाधारे त्रिकोणं विभाव्य तन्मध्ये अमिति न्यासेन प्रकृतिं विचिन्त्य

ओं क्रोमित्युच्चरन् द्वादशान्तादमृतमास्राव्य तन्मयैरुपहारैः संपूज्य पुनः अं उं मं इत्येतैरुक्तानुसन्धानं कुर्यात्। तत्तन्मन्त्रसंयोगोऽपोह्य कार्य इति।

मूल आदित्येन्द्वादीति धामचतुष्टयमुक्तम्। तेजोमदिति मूलाधारत्रिकोण-गतचिदग्निर्तेजोयोग उक्तः। तत्तन्मयोति। कुण्डलिनीरूपायाः प्रकृतेस्तेष्वनु-गतिरुक्ता। विभुरिति। व्यापिन्यादिक्रमेण स्वरूपपर्यन्ततया व्याप्तिरुक्तेति।

चिदग्नीति मूलाधारे प्रणवन्यासेन त्रिकोणं चिदग्न्यधिष्ठितं विभाव्य तदग्ने-रणीयसीं ज्वालासुषुम्नान्तरा द्वादशान्तं प्रवृत्तां प्रणवन्यासेनैव विचिन्त्य तत्र मणिपूरकादिषु अं उं मं ॐ इति न्यासेन धामचतुष्टयं विभाव्य संपूज्य तदनुगतायां कुण्डलिन्यामकारादिभिः क्रमेण विलाप्य बिन्द्वाद्यन्तप्रणवोच्चारणेन व्यापिन्यादिक्रमेण स्वरूपपर्यन्ततया व्याप्तिं भावयेदिति। सर्वयोगेष्वपि विभूत्यर्थ-तायामुन्मनीपर्यन्तत्वं परमकैवल्यार्थतायां साप्तिपर्यन्तत्वमिति विभागः। यतो ह्येषापि वक्ष्यति—परमात्मस्वरूपेण सानुभवनोयेति। स्पर्शव्यापिनीसमन्युन्मनी शक्तिरिति कथ्यत इति च। इह बिन्द्वादयो बिन्दुनादशक्तयः। व्यापिन्याद्या व्यापिनीसमन्युन्मन्यः। ततोऽधिका वा ग्राह्याः। विभुर्भवेदिति ॥ २२ ॥

तयोर्गुणभूतवर्णानामिति। गुणयोगे गुणानां शुक्लरक्तकृष्णवर्णाः। भूतयोगे भूतानां पीतशुभ्रपाटलश्शितिसितावर्णाः। तेषां सतामपि कुण्डलिनीप्रभावेश-वशादनियम इत्यर्थः। गुणादियोगमिति। न गुणेषु विशेषेण व्यवस्थितेति गुणयोगः। न भूतेषु विशेषेण व्यवस्थितेति भूतयोगः। पूर्वोक्तमण्डल-स्थानेष्विति। चिदग्निव्याप्त्येत्यादि सर्वं समानमिति भावः। सत्त्वादिगुण-गणमिति सत्त्वरजस्तमांसि। अत्र ब्रह्मरन्ध्रे गुणसाम्यमपि भावनीयम्। एक-वर्णमिति। स्वानुगतकुण्डलिनीप्रभावेशमहिम्नेति भावः। ज्योतिर्लिङ्गवदिति। प्रतिपत्तव्याकार उक्तः। गुणेषु तदधिष्ठातारो विचिन्तनीयाः। पूर्ववदिति बिन्दुनादादिना व्यापिन्यादिक्रमेणेत्यर्थः। स्वात्मभूते देवतातत्त्वे स्थित इत्यर्थः। हृत्कण्ठेति। चिदग्निव्याप्तसौषुम्नमार्गग्रहणमिहापि तुल्यमेव। मण्डलबीजा-धिष्ठातृसहितानिति। यथा हृदये अकारन्यासेन चतुरस्रं पार्थिवं मण्डलं तन्मध्ये पञ्चोक्तलतादिबीजत्रयं स्ववाच्यसहितम् तत्र च निवृत्तिकलां ब्रह्माणं वा तदधिष्ठातारं चिन्तयेत्। एवमुत्तरेष्वपीति। अत्र कारणं मण्डलं वृत्तम्। प्रणवः शक्तिर्वा बीजम्। परशक्तिः परमात्मा वाधिष्ठातेति ज्ञेयम्। संयोजयेदिति। सर्वानुगतां कुण्डलिनीं ध्यायन् विलाप्यैतद्विदध्यादित्यर्थः॥ २३ ॥

अथास्य योगस्य शेषं दर्शयति—अस्यैवेति। अत्रान्तरा बहिश्चेत्यन्वयः।

व्याप्तेति च शेषः। एतद्दर्शयति—समस्तरन्ध्रद्वारेणेति। कुण्डलिन्याः प्रभां स्वदेहान्तस्ततः सप्तधातुषु चापूर्य समस्तरन्ध्रद्वारेण बहिर्विसार्याकाशादेरपि व्यापिकां विभावयेदिति भावः। इहाकारादिशक्त्यन्तानां पृथिव्यादिषट्सु विनियुक्तत्वात् तच्छेषैर्व्यापिन्यादिभिस्तत्तदवस्थाक्रमेणोन्मनीप्राप्तिरिति ज्ञेयम्। देहसंहर्त्रीति। सङ्कुचितस्य पूर्णतापादनम्। अर्थात्तस्य संहार एवेति भावः। पर्यन्तदशामपि दर्शयति—एवमित्यादिना। देशिकदर्शितैरुपायै-रित्यणुयोगादीनां देवाः सम्भुतय इत्यादियोगानां च ग्रहणम्। सर्वयोगदपर्यन्त-दशा ह्येयं विवक्ष्यते। परमात्मस्वरूपिणीह साक्षिग्रहणम्। पृथक्त्वेनेति। न साक्ष्यरूपिणीत्यर्थः। अत्र विभूतिविषये साक्षिचिद्रूपे तस्या उन्मन्यास्तादात्म्ये-नान्तर्भावकैवल्यविषये तस्या विलापनमिति भेदः॥ २४॥

परमपुरुषार्थत्वमिति। सकलद्वैतानवभासे दुःखात्यन्तनिवृत्तेः स्वरूपावभासे च निरतिशयानन्दप्रवृत्तेरिति भावः। पुंनपुंसकयोस्तुल्यापोत्यमुमंशं विवृणोति—पुंनपुंसकयोरिति। वाचि चेत्यङ्गनासु विशिष्यत इति विशेषाभिधानात् स्त्रिया अप्युपसंग्रह इति भावः। इच्छादिशक्तिरूपेण तुल्यापीति प्रकृतिर्विशिष्यते। तस्मिन् साम्यतेजसि स्थितास्वङ्गनास्वित्युपरि संबन्धः। ननु किमिदं तुल्यत्वमभिप्रेतं कथं वेति तदुभयमिहान्तरा दर्शयति—प्रणवोच्चारणसमये हीति। प्रणवग्रहणं हृल्लेखाविकल्पोपलक्षणम्। हिशब्देन स्वानुभवगम्यमेतदिति सूचितम्।

अयमभिप्रायः। प्रकृतेस्तुल्यत्वं मिथःसमत्वम्। तच्च स्वकीयेच्छादिशक्त्य-वस्थायामेव संभवति। तासां मनआदिषु साम्यञ्च मनआदीनामपि साम्यापत्तिः स्यात्। तत्रेच्छादीनां मनआदीनाञ्च द्वयोर्द्वयोस्तादात्म्येन भाव्यम्। तथाविधा-नाञ्च तत्साम्यमपरशक्ताविव संभवति। तस्यामेवेतरयोः शक्त्योरनुगमोपपत्तेः। तच्च साम्यं परस्परमोतप्रोतभावलक्षणमेकत्वम्। मनआदीनां तदवस्था च वाक्यरूपो ध्वनिरेव। स्वानुभवसिद्धं चैनतदिति। क्रमेणेतीच्छात्मकं मन इत्यादिक्रमेण तादात्म्यमुक्तम्। यदा प्रणवविवक्षायां प्रथममिच्छारूपं मनः ततः क्रियारूपः प्राणः तदा च पूर्वस्य तस्मिन्ननुगमात् तयोः साम्यं विवक्षितस्य च प्रणवस्य च बिन्दुतापत्तिः ततो ज्ञानरूपा वाक् तदा च पूर्वयोस्तस्यामनुगमात् त्रयाणां साम्यमोतप्रोतभावलक्षणमेकत्वम्। स च तदा प्रणवो बीजरूप इत्ययं क्रम उक्तः। एकत्वं तुल्यत्वमिति। तुल्यत्वमेकत्वाकारेण विवृतम्। निबिडेत्यादिना तदेकत्वप्रकारोऽप्युद्दिष्टः। निबिडशब्दस्तेजोध्वन्योर्विशेषणम्। आत्मशब्द आकारवचनः। ज्ञानरूपा वागेव तावद्ध्वनिः। स च नादबिन्दुबीजक्रमोत्पन्न-

त्वान्निबिडः। निबिडध्वनिरूपेण हि तावदेषामेकत्वं भवति। स च निबिडध्वनिरुच्चार्यमाणप्रणवमन्त्राकार एव। तथाविधश्चासौ निबिडतेजोरूप इति तस्य प्रतिपत्तव्याकाराभिधानम्। निबिडतेजोग्रहणादाकाशादेरपि व्यापिनी प्रभा सूचिता। यद्वक्ष्यति—प्रभामत्तीति। किञ्च निबिडतेजोग्रहणादेवेच्छात्मकमनसस्तेजोरूपत्वं क्रियात्मकप्राणस्य ततोऽधिकतेजोरूपत्वमपि सूचितमिति।

इदानीमङ्गनासु विशिष्यत इत्यमुमंशं विवृण्वन् प्राक्प्रकृतशेषमाह—तस्मिन्निति। कुण्डलिनीशक्तेर्मूलाधार एव स्थानम्। साम्यतेजस्त्वार्थान्मूलाधारो देश एव। सैषा परावाग्लक्षणा कुण्डलिनी। तस्यास्तिस्रोऽवस्थाः पश्यन्त्याद्याः ता एवेह परपरापरापरकुण्डलिन्य उक्ताः। तासां क्रमेणेच्छादिभिः सम्बन्धः। अयमिहाभिप्रायः। प्रकृतिरेवेयं साम्यरूपापि विशेषं प्राप्नोति। विशेषो वैषम्यं परस्परत उद्रेकः। तच्चापि स्वकीयेच्छादिदशायामेव संभवति। तत्र केवलेच्छादीनां साम्यम्। तासामेव विभूतयः सकलार्थविषया इच्छादयस्तासां वैषम्यदशेति। विशिष्टा विभिन्ना विषमेति यावत्। सामान्यध्वनिः प्रणवः। तद्विकारा विशेषध्वनयः। वाक्यानि सामान्यान्तर्गताश्च विशेषा इत्येवं क्रमोपपत्तिः॥ २५॥

ततस्तासामिति कुण्डलिनीत्रयग्रहणम्। प्रथितं त्रयमिति। तासां सकलार्थविषयतया विस्तीर्णत्वात् प्रथितत्वम्। तासामपरपरापरपरक्रमेण च संहारः। मनआदिकमिति। मनआदीनां प्रथममेव साम्यरूपं निबिडतेजः। प्रभामिति। प्रथामिति भावः। प्रभायाः स्थूलसूक्ष्मतया द्विविधत्वमपि नादनादान्तग्रहणाद्भवति। सकृत्प्रणवेनैवायं शक्तियोगः। मन्त्राङ्गत्वे त्वेवं प्रयोगः। मूलाधारे प्रणवं शक्तिनादबिन्दुमकारान्ततया विन्यस्यन् क्रमेण प्रकृतिं तस्या मनआद्यात्मकेच्छादिशक्त्यापत्तिञ्च तेजोध्वनिवृद्धिक्रमेण विभाव्य प्रणवन्यासेन तत्सामान्यमपि निबिडतेजोध्वनिरूपं स्वदेहान्तर्विचिन्त्य मकारोकाराकारन्यासेन परपरापरापरकुण्डलिनीरपि तत्तेजोऽन्तर्भागे बहिर्बहिरनुसन्दधीत। पुनरकारादिभिस्तेषामुक्तक्रमेण संहार इति। एवं प्रकृतियोगपञ्चकमुक्तम्। अथ पुरुषयोगं प्रस्तौति—अथ चतुर्मूर्त्यादिचतुर्दशयोगानिति। यद्यप्ययं स्थूलादिसाक्षिनिष्ठतयैक एव चतुर्दशपर्वायोगस्तथापि चतुर्दशयोगानिति नानात्वेनाभिधानम् एषु कतिपययोगस्यापि सूचनार्थम्। तत्र चतुर्मूर्तिचिदवष्टम्भादिशेषैरष्टौ योगाश्चतुर्मूर्तिलिङ्गचिदवष्टम्भसंहाराविकल्पैः पञ्चलिङ्गविरहे चत्वारः संहाराविकल्पयोरेकत्वे त्रय इति ह पञ्चयोगी लिङ्गमेकं वा महत्प्रतिपत्तव्यम्। तदा चतुर्मूर्तेर्योऽप्येकैव महती मूर्तिरिति। युष्मान्मामपीति अतिवर्तत इत्युपरि संबन्धः।

नाभिहृद्भ्रूमध्यद्वादशान्तस्थितानिति। चिदग्निव्याप्तसौषुम्नमार्गग्रहणमिहा-प्यनुवर्तत एव। मां षोडशान्तःस्थितमिति। मामित्यस्य मूलपदस्यावृत्तिरुक्ता।

ब्रह्मयोगं वदन् सकलयोगक्लृप्तिमपि दर्शयति—चतुर्ष्वपीति। पीठचिन्तन-मप्यर्थात्कार्यम्। सपरिवारमिति। विष्णुशिवयोः स्वपटलभाविनः परिवाराः। ब्रह्मणस्तु दिक्षु वेदाः विदिक्ष्वङ्गोपाङ्गोपवेदागमाः तद्बहिश्छन्दांसीति अङ्गानीति। लोकपालास्त्राणि च सर्वत्र समानानि। विष्णुशिवयोर्मूर्तिसद्भावे ब्रह्मणो मोदप्रमोदहंससामगसत्या मूर्तयः। सर्वेश्वरस्य तु ब्रह्मादय एव सावरणा वामाग्र-दक्षिणभागेषु स्युः। सर्व एव लोकेशाद्यावरणमिति भेदाभेदलिङ्गयोगेषु परित एव सर्वेषामावरणानि विविदिषा विभाव्यानीति स्वतन्त्रप्रयोगे चिन्तामात्रम्।

मन्त्राङ्गत्वे त्वयं क्रमः। क्ष्रौमिति मूलाधारनाभिहृद्भ्रूमध्यद्वादशान्तषोड-शान्तेषु न्यसन् बीजानि विभाव्य तेषु ॐ अं उं मं ॐ ओमिति न्यसंश्चिदग्निब्रह्म-विष्णुरुद्रसर्वेश्वरामृतार्णवान् सावरणान् विभाव्य क्ष्रौमित्युच्चरन्नमृतार्णवादमृतमा-स्राव्य तन्मयैर्जलादिभिः सावरणं मूर्तिचतुष्टयं संपूज्य पुनर्ह्रौमित्युच्चरन्नमृतास्रवणेन तांस्तदमृतप्लुतानपि विभाव्य प्रणवेन सर्वानुगतचिदग्न्यात्मककुण्डलिनीतेजोवृद्ध्या ब्रह्मादींस्तस्मिन् संहृत्याऽमृतार्णवादमृतमास्रावयेदिति। एवं ब्रह्मयोगादिष्वपि बोद्धव्यम्। चिदग्नेरावरणयोगे सर्वेश्वरवच्चिदग्निकरणरूपेणावरणकल्पनमेवम-मृतार्णवस्यामृतकरणरूपेणेति च ज्ञेयम्। अभिन्नरूपमिति छेदः। अत्र लिङ्गाकारेणावरणानि। सर्वयोगेष्वपि समोऽयं न्यासः। तत्राणुयोगे तावत् क्ष्रौमिति सत्रिकोणकर्णिकापीठं मूलाधारे विन्यस्य तन्मध्ये अं इति न्यसन् प्रकृतिमप्यणीयसीं विभाव्य तत्रोग्रादिकोणत्रये बीजमन्त्रविद्या आत्मदेवताब्रह्माणि प्राज्ञतैजसविश्वानीश्वरहिरण्यगर्भविराजः परमाणुमध्यमार्धभुवनान्यणुमध्यस्थूल-चराण्यणुमध्यमस्थूलचराण्यपि बहिर्बहिःक्रमेण भावयेत्। धामक्रमयोगेत्यादि धाम्नां वक्ष्यमाणाग्न्यादिवदावरणकल्पना। ब्रह्मधाम्नस्तु वामाग्रदक्षिणभागेषु सावरणान्यग्न्यादिधामानि। गुणयोगे तु सर्वत्र स्वस्वगुणानि तत्त्वानि मनोबुद्ध्य-हंकारचित्तचेतनाः प्राणादयः श्रोत्रादयो वागादयः शब्दतन्मात्रादयोऽपञ्चीकृताः पञ्चीकृताश्चाकाशादयः। गुणसाम्येति गुणत्रयमधिकमिति। भूतयोगे तु तत्तदधिष्ठातॄणां परिवाराः। शक्तियोगे तु कुण्डलिनीत्रयस्य वक्ष्यमाणानि त्रिचतुःपञ्चेत्यादीनि बहिर्बहिः स्युरिति। तेजसेति लिङ्गयोगपर्यन्तसिद्धं तेजो विवक्षितम्। स्थूलादिशरीरमिति व्यष्टिसमष्टिशरीरग्रहणम् ॥ २६ ॥

अत्रैवावान्तरं किञ्चित् कर्मास्तीत्याह—चिदवष्टम्भयोगानन्तरमिति।

पिण्डमिति प्रतिपत्तव्याकाराभिधानम्। पूर्वमिति चतुर्मूर्त्यादियोगेषु। कुण्डलिनीरूपेण स्थितेति। मूलाधारगतः शिखावानग्निरुक्तः। परिवारजातमित्यन्यपदविवरणम्। बाह्यं चेति वेद्यपदविवरणम्। तत्तु सा स्मृतेत्येतद्विवृणोति—तत्सर्वमित्यादिना। तत्सर्वं सैवेति। यदेतत्कुण्डलिन्यमृतसर्वमूर्तितदावरणबाह्यार्थजातमुक्तम् तत्सर्वं सैवेत्यर्थः। यद्यपीह लिङ्गयोगे नास्ति सर्वमूर्तितत्परिवारजातम् किन्तु चतुर्मूर्त्यादियोगगतमेव एतल्लिङ्गयोगेऽपि एवमवस्थितमिति तथानुवादोपपत्तिः। कीदृशी सैव तत्सर्वमित्यत्र स्मृतेत्येतत्पदं सोपस्कारं योजयति—या हि न इति। या हि नः स्थूलादिशरीररूपिणी प्रकृतिविराड्ढिरण्यगर्भकारणरूपेण चिन्तिता सैव तत्सर्वमित्यर्थः। एतदुक्तं—पूर्वं व्यष्टिशरीररूपिणी प्रकृतिः इदानीं समष्टिशरीराकारेण चिन्तनीया। तदा तदन्तर्गतं कुण्डलिन्यमृतार्णवादि सर्वं प्रकृत्यात्मकमेव भवतीति।

प्रलय इति प्रणवे वाचके। तस्यां च वाच्यात्मिकायामितीयता गुणयोग उक्तः। व्याप्यत इत्यादिशेषेण संहारादियोगाः। चराचरमिदं जगदिति वाच्यवाचकरूपमेकपिण्डभूतमुक्तम्। पूर्वं पूर्वमित्यादिना संहारप्रकार उक्तः। एतदादियोगचतुष्टयमप्येवं कारणतापन्नस्य जगतः संहार एवेति तदपीहोक्तमेवेति। तत्र तावद्गुणयोगक्लृप्तिं दर्शयति—अकारोकारेत्यादिना। पूर्वं विराडादित्रयस्येदानीं विराडादिसप्तकस्य पुरा स्थूलादिचतुष्टयस्य चाभिधानादर्थादेषां विकल्प इत्यवसेयम्। तेषां क्रमेणेति। पूर्वोक्तः क्रमोऽभिहितः। एवमधिष्ठानस्यस्येति। चिदवष्टम्भयोगगतचिद्वस्तुस्यस्येत्यर्थः॥ २७॥

ततो वाक्यार्थप्रतिपत्तिमिति। तत्त्वमसि अहं ब्रह्मास्मि इत्यादिवाक्यैस्तदर्थप्रणवहृल्लेखादिमन्त्रैर्वा तदर्थस्य देवतातत्त्वभूतब्रह्मात्मैकत्वलक्षणप्रतिपत्तिमित्यर्थः। मूले स्वैव स्वामिति वाक्यार्थ उक्तः। वेत्तीति तत्प्रतिपत्तिः। एतद्दर्शयति—सा परशक्तिरिति। ननु पुरुषयोगे कथं प्रकृतिः स्वां वेत्तीत्यभिधानमिति। उच्यते। चिदद्वैतदशायां प्रकृतिपुरुषयोरभेदात् यद्वा चतुर्दशयोगैरपि पुरुषविग्रहतया कृत्स्नाया व्यष्टिसमष्टिजगदात्मिकायाः प्रकृतेश्चिल्लक्षणपुरुषतत्त्वे देवतावस्तुनि परमात्मनि तदेकशेषतयाऽवस्थापितत्वादिति। स्वामित्येतदभिप्रायमाह—ब्रह्मात्मरूपतामिति। स्वस्या इति शेषः। परमेति निरतिशयोत्कर्षं प्राप्तेत्यर्थः। तस्या नान्योऽस्ति वेदितेत्यस्यायमर्थः। तत्स्वरूपतोऽन्यद्वेदित्रादिकं कालत्रयेऽपि नास्तीति। एतद्दर्शयति—वेद्येति। वाक्यार्थप्रतिपत्तिः सकलयोगावसानेष्विष्यत एव। मन्त्राङ्गतया प्रयोगे तु न वैतदुपयोग इति। एवं

पुरुषयोग उक्तः। अथ कालयोगमारभते—अथेति। मूले सा त्विति प्रकृतिः। सा च कालात्मना ज्ञायत इति निर्देशात्। परकालचिद्रूपस्योपाधिरपरकालाना-द्यन्तस्वभावादिसकलकार्यकालमूलभूतोन्मनीशक्तिरेव। कालात्मेति। तस्या-स्तदीयलवादिकार्याणां चाध्यक्षभूतः परकालात्मा। सम्यग्ज्ञायत इति। न साक्षतयैव अपि तु स्वात्मतयापीति। सदेति। वस्तुतस्तु कालत्रयेऽपि न त्विदानी-मेवेति। अमुमर्थं दर्शयति—कालस्याऽपरस्येत्यादिना। उन्मनीरूपेणेति। अपरकाल उन्मनी तदुपलक्षितत्वादेवमुक्तम्। यद्वा परोन्मनीचिद्रूपमेवेति। पञ्चदशकालाभिमानिनीत्यपरकाललक्षणोन्मनीरूपा प्रकृतिः। अत्र लवाद्यभि-मानिन्या उन्मन्याः स्वात्मभूतपरकालचिद्रूपेणैकताभिधानात् तथाविधो योगो-ऽप्युक्तो भवति। योगक्लृप्तिमुपदिशति—लवत्रुटीति। मूलाधारमारभ्येति। चिदग्निव्याप्तसौषुम्नमार्गग्रहणमिहाप्यनुवर्तनीयम्। मूलाधारगतत्रिकोणमध्ये प्रणवेन हृल्लेखया वा चिदग्निं प्रागुक्तवत् परिकल्प्य प्रणवांशैर्लवादिपर्वाणि कल्पयेदिति ज्ञेयम्। प्रणवमात्रास्विति। लवादीनां प्रणवमात्रा एव स्ववाचकत्वात् प्रतिपत्तव्याकारा इत्यपि सूचितम्। क्रमेण संहृत्येति। मानसपूजानन्तरं लवादिक्रमेण सर्वानुगतापरकालात्मकोन्मन्यां प्रणवांशैर्विलापनमुक्तम्। अकाल-कलितायामुन्मन्यामिति। उन्मन्या यत् स्वरूपं परकालचिद्रूपं तस्मिन्नित्यर्थः। इहापि प्राग्वदुन्मन्यास्तत्साक्षित्वेन तादात्म्यं तत्र संहारो वा स्यादिति। व्यवतिष्ठेतेति। प्रणवेन हृल्लेखया वेति भावः। उन्मन्यामवस्थितस्येत्याद्यण-प्रयोगादिष्वपि समानमुन्मन्यविशेषादित्येव बोद्धव्यम्॥ २८॥

अप्रयत्नेनैवेति। स्थानकरणादिना मूर्तिध्यानादिना वा प्रसिद्धेन प्रयत्नेन विना मानसमात्रादेव जपात्। यद्वाऽर्थपुरुषकारविनियोगलक्षणेन प्रयत्नेन विनाऽनन्तं फलमिति व्याख्येयम्। लवादिप्रलयान्त इत्यत्रायं काल इत्यस्याय-मर्थः। कालात्मना मयेत्युक्तो योऽयं कालः स लवादिप्रलयान्तः सन्निति। सौस्था-निकानुष्ठाने त्विहापि परिवारसंभवः। तत्र लवस्य निरंशत्वेन परिवाराभावः। त्रुटेस्तु स्वांशाश्चिंशल्लवाः। एवं कालादिष्वपि द्रष्टव्यम्। कालवेदिभिरित्यनेन चैतत्सूचितम्। अत्र मानुषाणां दिव्यानां ब्रह्मणां चाहोरात्रमाससंवत्सराणां पृथक्प्रमाणतो भेदेऽपि जात्यभेदात् पृथगगणनमिति ज्ञेयम्। कल्पो ब्रह्मदिवसः। तथाविधानामब्दानां शतमित्ययं महाकल्पः। स परो व्यावहारिकः काल इति। तदर्धं परार्धं व्यपदिश्यत इति। अत्र त्वदायुर्मम निश्वास इत्येतदन्तेन जपादनन्तं फलमुच्यत इति पूर्वमुक्तम्। इदानीमस्यैवाहोरात्रादियोगार्थत्वमाह—त्वदायु-

रिति। कालयोगेनोन्मन्यामवस्थितस्यायं योगः। यद्वा नासौ तच्छेषभूतः। अत्रात्मनः प्रतिपत्तिः कालेनैवं प्रचोद्यत इतीयमेवेति श्वासोच्छ्वासयोरहोरात्रानुसन्धानमेको योगः। शुक्लकृष्णयोः पैत्रयोरहोरात्रयोरनुसन्धानमपरः। संवत्सरार्धयोर्द्व्ययोरनुसन्धानमन्यः। आदिशब्देन ब्रह्माहोरात्रयोर्द्वयोः परार्धयोरप्यनुसन्धानं योगान्तरमुक्तम्। त्वदायुर्मम निश्वास इत्ययमुक्तः षष्ठो योग इति। आयुषोऽपि त्वद्रूपत्वमिति। त्वदायुर्मम निश्वास इत्यनेनैव सूचितमेतदिति भावः। एतदुक्तं भवति—श्वासयोरहोरात्रयोगे श्वासोच्छ्वासपरिमितमप्यायुरहोरात्रपरिमिततया वर्धत इति। एवं पक्षादियोगेष्वपि। तदावृत्तौ तु तत्संस्कारप्रचय इति। कालेनैवं प्रचोद्यत इतीत्यस्येत्युक्तमित्युपरि संबन्धः। कालेनोन्मन्यात्मकेनैवमहोरात्राद्याकारेण सैवोन्मनी स्वोपाधिरेवं प्रेर्यत इति मूलार्थः। साक्षितयेत्यनेनैतद्दर्शितम्। मूलाधारादाषोडशान्तामतिसूक्ष्मां कुण्डलिनीमुन्मनीशक्तिं ध्यात्वा तदन्तरत्यन्तसूक्ष्मतयात्मानमपि परकालचिह्नलक्षणं तत्साक्षितया संविभावयेदिति। सत्तामात्रेणेति कालसम्बन्धात्यन्तहानार्थमुक्तम्। प्रेरक इत्युन्मन्याः स्वरूपतः श्वासरूपस्याङ्गो बहिर्मुखतया प्रसरः तत उच्छ्वासरूपाया रात्रेरन्तर्मुखतयोन्मन्यन्तं सङ्कोच इत्येवं द्विधा प्रवृत्तिलक्षणं प्रेरणमुक्तम्। नतु कालमध्यवर्तितयेति। एवं कालयोगोऽप्युक्तः।

अथेदानीं स जानाति विपाकांश्चेत्यादि विवरणीयम्। ननु यदिह ब्रह्मादिभिर्जिज्ञासितं तत्सर्वमप्येवं सर्वेश्वरेणोपदिष्टम् तत्र कस्तत्त्वसर्गोपदेशस्य प्रसङ्ग इति। उच्यते। इह तावत् अक्षरं नाम किं नाथेत्यादि यदन्तेन प्रकरणेनाक्षरं तस्य स्वरूपं नित्यत्वं सर्वात्मकत्वं चोक्तम्। तत्र सर्वस्यापि जगतस्तत एवोत्पत्तौ तत्रैव स्थितौ तस्मिन्नेव च प्रलये सिद्ध एव तत्सर्वात्मत्वमुपपन्नं स्यात्। किञ्च तस्य नित्यत्वनियमोऽपि विश्वस्याऽनित्यत्वे सिद्ध एव सिध्येदिति तस्याक्षरस्यैव सर्वात्मत्वाद्युपपादनार्थोऽयं तत्त्वसर्गाद्यारम्भः।

अपि च साधकानामक्षरादुत्पत्तिस्तावदथाऽभवन् ब्रह्महरीश्वराख्या इत्यभिहिता। तेषां विराडादिमयदेवतालक्षणया प्रकृत्यावस्थितिरूपन्यासादिकर्तव्यं च सृष्टिस्थित्यन्तहेतव इत्युक्तम्। ततस्तेषां देवतातत्त्वावस्थितिलक्षणं फलं च तेषु वो जायते लय इत्युक्तम्। तत्सकलमपि देवतातत्त्वस्यैव स्वशक्त्या साधकावस्थोपपत्तावेवोपपन्नं स्यात्। तदुपपत्तिश्च सर्गादिकथन एव सिध्येदिति चायमारम्भः। अतएव अथ व्यवस्थिते त्वेवमस्य शक्तित्वमिष्यत इत्येतदुभयथापि योजयिष्यते। अत्रायं प्रथमः सर्गपटलः। द्वितीयः सर्गशेषपटलः। तृतीयः स्थितिपटलः। तदवसाने संहारसंग्रह इति विभाग इति ॥ २८—३८ ॥

स जानाति विपाकांश्चेत्यस्य कालेनैवं प्रचोद्यत इत्यनेन सह सङ्गतिं दर्शयति—कालः कर्मापेक्षयेति। पूर्वस्मिन् व्याख्यान इति। कालेनैवं प्रचोद्यत इत्यनेनेति शेषः। यतस्तत्र विवृतं पुरुषकर्मानुसारेण तस्य प्रेरकत्वादिति। सूक्ष्मरूपेण कर्मणामवस्थितिमिति। प्राणिचिद्रूपेष्विति भावः। ईश्वरस्येति। कालात्मनः प्रकृतिपुरुषान्तर्यामिण इति भावः। स जानातीत्यत्र स इत्यस्यार्थमाह—अनन्तरोक्त इति। कालेनैवं प्रचोद्यत इति प्रकृत इत्यर्थः। व्यवहितत्वेनोक्तो वेति। लवाद्यनुक्रमणात् प्रागेवोक्तो वेत्यर्थः। ननु कः पुनरनयोर्भेद इति। सा तु कालात्मनेत्युक्तन्याः स्वोपाधेरपि साक्षी परः कालः कालेनैवं प्रचोद्यत इति तद्विशिष्ट एव परः काल इति भेदः। चशब्दात्तां चेति। प्रचोद्यत इति सा त्विति वोक्तां प्रकृतिमिवेत्यर्थः। तद्गतप्राण्याद्युपलक्षणं चैतत्। विपाकानित्येतद्विवृणोति—परिपक्वानीति। सर्वदेति कृत्स्नेऽपि प्रलयकाले। कादाचित्कोति। नादौ मध्येऽपि किन्त्ववसान एवेत्यर्थः। ईश्वरापरकालादिवशादिति। ईश्वरो भोजयता परः कालः परिपाकं प्रदास्यतीति संभावनोक्त्या तस्येच्छावशात् सृष्टिरिति तावद्दर्शितम्। त्वाद्दशामायुरन्वीक्ष्येति। महाकल्पमहाप्रलयकालयोरस्त्यहोरात्रवत्कालनियम इत्यायुरन्वीक्ष्येति दर्शितम्। त्वाद्दशामिति। तव त्वत्सदृशानाञ्च विष्णुरुद्रहिरण्यगर्भविराडादीनामप्यायुः सहस्रकृदुपभोगकालमन्वीक्ष्येत्यर्थः। तत्त्वविकृतिरपीति न केवलं कर्मणामेव विपाक इति भावः।

ईश्वरवशादिति ब्रह्मादिसर्गोऽपीश्वराधीन एवेति भावः। कालत इवेति। कालतोऽल्पत्वं तावदुक्तम्। त्वदायुर्मम निश्वास इति परस्य कालवपुषोऽनाद्यन्तस्यान्तरायं महाकल्प इति कालतोऽल्पत्वम्। तस्यैव प्रकृतिवपुषोऽनाद्यन्तस्य क्वचिदुद्देश एवेयं महदादितत्त्वविकृतिरिति देशतोऽल्पत्वम्। मूले च प्रकृतेश्च क्वचित् काल इति चकारः परिपाकं प्रदास्यतीति समुच्चयार्थः। प्रतिपादयेदिति प्रापयेत्। एवं तावत्सर्गाभिधित्सया परिकरोऽभिहितः ॥ ४० ॥

तत्त्वविकृतिक्रममिति। सा तत्त्वसंज्ञेत्यत्र मूलेऽयमन्वयः। सा प्रकृतिस्तत्त्वसंज्ञैव सती तदा क्वचिद्देशे बिन्दुतामभ्येतीति। तदेति परिपाकावसरे।

सा प्रकृतिरिति। कृत्स्ना प्रकृतिर्विवक्ष्यते। तत्त्वस्येति। चिन्मात्रं यद्देवतातत्त्वमक्षरशब्दोक्तं परप्रकृतिपुरुषकालविकल्पलक्षणमेतत्तदिह तत्त्वमुक्तम्। पारमार्थिकस्येति। प्रकृतिविकृत्यात्मके जगति परमार्थतो वास्तवतो निरूप्यमाणे सिद्धस्येत्यर्थः। साक्षात्तत्त्वमेतदेव। महदादि त्वापेक्षिकं तत्त्वम्। तत्तद्विकृत्यपेक्षयैव पारमार्थिकत्वादिति भावः। संज्ञैव संज्ञेति। देवतातत्त्वं परं ब्रह्मेत्यादि-

पदैरनुपचारतस्तस्या अपि सह गृहीतेति भावः। तदविभक्तत्वादित्यन्तनिर्विकल्पतया तत्तादात्म्यापन्नत्वादित्यर्थः। किञ्चित्स्थौल्यमित्येतद्बिन्दुतामित्यस्य विवरणम्। किञ्चिद्बहिर्मुखतयेति तत्स्थौल्यप्रकारकथनम्। सृष्ट्युन्मुखकर्माविभक्ततयेति तन्निबन्धनाभिधानम्। कर्मणोऽपूर्वावस्थस्य विपाकावस्था तावदुक्ता—स जानाति विपाकांश्चेति। तस्य कार्योन्मुख्यावस्थेयमुक्तेति ज्ञेयम्। तरङ्गमूलभूतेत्यादि। दृष्टान्ताभिधानम्। स्वतः स्तिमितस्य समुद्रस्य यो हि तरङ्गस्तस्य मूलभूतं तावत् सूक्ष्मं व्याप्तं सञ्चलनं तद्वदिति।

विचिकीर्षुर्घनीभूतेति च तत्रावान्तरदशाभिधानम्। तदाह—परिपक्वेति। तत्त्वात्मिकाया अपि प्रकृतेः स्वगतकर्मणामपूर्वावस्थातः परिपक्वावस्थायां भेदात् तदविभक्ततया वर्तनमवस्थानम्। स इह घनीभवेदित्यर्थः। तदर्थमिति। निरतिशयसूक्ष्मेच्छाज्ञानक्रियालक्षणोऽयं व्यापारोऽभिप्रेतः। यद्यपि प्रकृतेः स्वातन्त्र्यावस्थेयं बिम्बादिशक्तिपर्यन्ता ततः परमेवेच्छादिशक्त्यवस्थाः। वक्ष्यति च—बहिर्मुखसत्स्वातन्त्र्येच्छाज्ञानप्रयत्नेति। किन्तु तत्राप्यवान्तरावस्थासमीचायां तदुचितेच्छाद्युपपत्तिरिति। ननु यद्येवमेवंविधो घनीभावस्तर्हि कीदृग्विधोऽसौ बिन्दुरित्यत्राह—बिन्दुः कर्मभिन्नं रूपमिति। प्रकृतेरेव प्रलयावस्थातो यत्परिपक्वदशानन्तरं सृष्ट्युन्मुखैः कर्मभिर्भिन्नं स्वाकारनिरूप्यं रूपं सोऽसौ बिन्दुः। परिपक्वैरेव कर्मभिर्भिद्यमानं रूपं घनीभाव इति भेद इति भावः॥ ४१॥

मूले कालेन भिद्यमानस्त्वित्यादेरयमर्थः। स बिन्दुस्त्रिधा भिद्यते। ते च भेदाः स्थूलसूक्ष्मपरा बिन्दुनादबीजलक्षणा इति। चेतनानां मलिनमिश्रशुद्धभेदतस्तदीयमहदादीनां त्रिधा भेदात् तन्निनाद(दान)भूतायां प्रकृतावप्येवं त्रिभेदसंभव इति। बिन्दुनादबीजानि च शब्दार्थप्रक्रिययोः साधारणपदानीत्यवबोद्धव्यम्।

अर्थान्तरमाह—एवं परस्मादित्यादिना। परस्मादिति तत्त्वादिति शेषः। इच्छासत्त्वादिरूपतामिति। इच्छाज्ञानक्रियारूपतां सत्त्वरजस्तमोरूपतां चेत्यर्थः। तत्रेच्छादिशक्तिभिरुत्तरसर्गेषु तत्तद्विकृतीनां प्रसूतिः सत्त्वादिगुणैश्च तासामुच्चावचो वैचित्र्यमिति विभागः। सम्बध्यमान इति। संभेद इह भेद इति भावः।

तत्र फलं हेतुतया दर्शयति—नहीति। चित्संबन्धमिति। कालस्येश्वरस्य चिद्रूपत्वादेवमुक्तः। अचिद्रूपस्येति च्छेदः। प्रकृतितत्त्वस्येच्छादिरूपस्येति च शेषः। इच्छादीनामिति त्रिशक्तीनामेव ग्रहणम्। यतो वक्ष्यति—नवानामपि भेदानामिति। मायातच्छक्तितत्तत्प्राणिकर्मविषयभेदेनेति। प्रकृतितत्त्वस्यैवान्तर्गतो विकल्पोऽयमुक्तः। तत्राचिच्छक्तिमात्रं तावत्प्रकृतिः। तस्याः

स्वान्तर्गतं स्वेशितृकालप्रयोज्यं स्वकल्पिततदीयत्रिमूर्तिहिरण्यगर्भाद्यखिलचेतनांशेषु नानात्वादिप्रत्ययकरमवान्तरशक्तिमात्रं माया। तथा च वक्ष्यति—मायातत्त्वं स्वरूपाच्छादनविक्षेपात्मकमिति। मायाया अप्यन्तर्गतं तेषां परिच्छिन्नस्वरूपतादिप्रत्ययकरमविद्यालक्षणमवान्तरशक्तिमात्रमिह शक्तिः। माया त्वनयैव स्वकीयकार्यं तेषां संसारित्वलक्षणं विधत्त इति तस्याः शक्तिरियमिष्यते। तस्याः शक्तेरप्यन्तर्गतं यत् तत्तत्प्राणिनां प्राक्तनभवोपार्जितं कर्मजातं तदिह कर्म। न च केवलस्य कर्मणोऽवस्थानमिति तत्समवायी मलिनोऽचिदंशोऽप्यभ्युपेयते। यच्छैवप्रक्रियायां प्रकृतितत्त्वं व्यपदिश्यत इति। किञ्च मायातच्छक्त्योरपि किञ्चित्कर्माभ्युपेयते तद्व्यतिरेकेण तयोरभिव्यक्तौ निमित्तोपयोगादिति। तत्र सकलचेतनानां यानि स्वानि स्वानि कर्मापूर्वाणि तानि परिपाकावस्थायां सामान्यविशेषरूपेण द्विधा भिद्यते। तत्र सामान्यांशेन प्रकृत्याद्युत्पत्तिर्विशेषांशैर्निजनिजभोग्याभोगायतनाद्युत्पत्तिः। सामान्यञ्च विशुद्धतरविशुद्धमिश्रमलिनतया भिन्नं प्रकृतिमायादिसमवायि भवतीति विभागः। ततश्च मायादीनामपि विचिकीर्षुर्घनीभूता क्वचिदभ्येति बिन्दुतामित्यवस्थात्रयं समानमेव च। तथा च मायादिष्वपि बिन्द्ववस्थामापन्नेषु स्वस्वाकारनिरूप्येषु सत्सु कृत्स्नापि प्रकृतिर्बिन्द्ववस्थां प्राप्ता संपद्यत इति। मूले स्थूलसूक्ष्मपरत्वेनेति वृत्तानुरोधार्थमुक्तम्। परसूक्ष्मस्थूलत्वेनेत्येवाभिप्रायः। सर्गप्रकरणौचित्यादिति ॥४२॥

नवानामपि भेदानामिति। प्रकृतेस्तावन्निर्विषयतयैव प्रथममिच्छादीनामभिव्यक्तिः। ततस्तासां मायाविषयतया प्रवृत्तौ क्रियाव्यापारपर्यन्तवेलायां माया स्वोचितसृष्ट्युन्मुखकर्माविभक्ततया स्वाकारनिरूप्योत्पन्ना भवति। ततस्तासां तदीयशक्तिविषयतया प्रवृत्तावेवं तदुत्पत्तिः। ततश्च तासां तदन्तर्गतकर्मविषयतया प्रवृत्तौ तदुचितमलिनाचिदंशयोगतस्तदुत्पत्तिरिति क्रमोऽवबोद्धव्यः। तत्त्वमिति। मायाशक्तिः कर्मेत्येव सिद्धानां याथात्म्यमित्यर्थः। भेदमिति वा पाठः। स्वान्तर्गतं भेदमित्यर्थः। सन्निहितायेति। प्रासङ्गिकमेतदिति भावः। बिन्दुरीश्वर इति। नवस्वपि परिच्छेदादिभेदेषु यश्चित्प्रधानः काललक्षण ईश्वरः स बिन्दुरित्यर्थः। नादस्तस्या इति। प्रकृतेरिति शेषः। चिन्मिश्रमिति। चिदचित्समप्रधानोंऽशो विवक्षितः। बीजमचिदंश इति। प्रकृतिलक्षणोऽचित्प्रधानोंऽशो गृहीतः।

यत्त्वन्यत्रोक्तं—चित्प्रधानं ततः पूज्यं द्रव्यं प्रकृतिबृंहितम्।
तयोः समप्रधानत्वमुपाधिः कालरूपिणः॥

इति। तद्व्यापारप्रधानम्। एतत्तु स्वरूपप्रधानमिति भेदः।

इदानीं मन्त्रिणां हितमेव दर्शयति—एतदिति। परेच्छादिनवके बिन्दुनादादित्रयं तथेच्छादित्रिशक्तिमात्रेऽपि त्रयं तथैव बिन्दुतत्त्वमात्रेऽपि त्रयं सर्वत्रैवं संभवात् तत्सर्वमप्येतदित्युक्तम्। मन्त्रावृत्तिसमय इति निजेष्टमन्त्रजपसमये। वक्ष्यति च हृल्लेखापटले—पुनर्ध्यात्वा संपूज्य जपित्वेति। तथाणुयोगेन जह्वेति। तथोक्तं च कालयोगे—जपादनन्तं फलमिति। तत्सर्वमपोह्याभिप्रेतम्। न सकृदेवैतदनुसन्धानमित्यावृत्तिग्रहणेन सूचितम्। मात्रावृत्तिसमय इति वा पाठः। प्रणवमात्रमावृत्तिवेलायामिति। उक्तं च योगप्रकरणे—योगौचित्येन बिन्द्वादियोगः सूचित इति। तथा बिन्दुनादादिना व्यापिन्यादिद्वारेणेति। तत्रोन्मनोमात्राया यावत्परेच्छादिसंख्यमावृत्तिरपोह सूचिता। स्वानुभवेनेति। परेच्छादीनां स्वकीयपरेच्छाद्याकारेणेत्यर्थः। अनुगन्तव्यमिति। सर्गक्रमेण वा संहारक्रमेण वादेः प्रभृत्यान्तमनुसन्धेयमित्यर्थः। स्वरूपस्थेनेति। मन्त्रदेवतातत्त्वावस्थेन। वक्ष्यति च लिपिपटले—तामिति परं चिदात्मकमिति। हृल्लेखापटले च—तामिति परध्यानमिति। तथा च योगप्रकरणे—पूर्ववत् स्वरूपस्थो भवेदिति। तच्च स्वरूपमियदिह ग्राह्यमिति मूलवचनेनैव दर्शयति वक्ष्यति हीति। शब्दब्रह्मेति शब्दावगम्यमर्थं हि कीर्तितमिति च तद्वचनम्। तत्र चायं जातोऽर्थः। तत्त्वं तावत् स्वरूपं तदभिन्नत्वात्। तत्त्वसंज्ञापि तदहन्तानपायाच्च पश्यन्तीवाग्रूपा बिन्दुशक्तिरपि स्वरूपमेवेति। यद्वक्ष्यति—शब्दब्रह्मणोऽप्यूर्ध्वमित्यादि। तथा शब्दोच्चारणकाले तत्साचितयान्तरत्वेनावगम्यमर्थं बिन्द्वात्मकमिति। अत्रैवं प्रयोगः। मन्त्रजपसमये स्वयमनवच्छिन्नतत्त्वस्वरूपस्थो(पः सो)न्मनीशक्तिविशिष्टतत्स्वरूपो वा समन्त्रजपं विधाय पुनर्बिन्दुस्वरूपः समन्त्रजपं कृत्वा तद्गतबिन्दुनादबीजाकारतया तदन्तर्गतेच्छादिशक्तिमात्रगतबिन्द्वाद्याकारतया पुनर्मायादिविषयोत्तरोत्तरवृद्धेच्छादिगतबिन्द्वाद्याकारतया च जपोऽयं सर्गक्रमः। कर्मविषयक्रियादिगतबीजनादबिन्दुक्रमेण तत्त्वावस्थानिष्ठः संहारक्रमः। एवं योगतः स्वरूपावस्थितावपि प्रणवमात्राभिर्जप्यमानमन्त्रान्विताभिर्वानुसन्धानं कार्यम्। बिन्दुस्वरूपत्वे तु नादनादान्तादिमात्रा अपि स्युरिति ॥ ४३ ॥

मूले बिन्दोस्तस्मादित्यत्र कालेन भिद्यमानस्त्वित्याद्युक्तो भेदोऽभिप्रेतः। अवश्यपश्यन्त्यात्मक एव। परावाग्रूपस्य तु नित्यत्वेनोत्पत्त्ययोगादिति। अत्र सूक्ष्ममर्थमाह—बिन्दुरित्यादिना। उक्त इति। चिन्मात्रज्योतिष इति वा बिन्दुरीश्वर एवोक्तः। उक्तयेति। तत्त्वसंज्ञेति बीजमचिदंश इति वोक्तया। संबध्यमानादिति संभेदः संबन्धः। स चानादिर्नित्य एव। अत्र साक्ष्यादिबिन्दुपर्यन्ता-

र्थंगतयोश्चिदचिदंशयोः सम्बन्धोऽभिप्रेतः। तत्र साक्षिणि नित्यो बिन्दुतत्त्वे तु विकृत इति भेदः। साक्षितत्त्वसंज्ञावस्थयोरप्युन्मनीशक्तियोगादेतदुपपत्तिः। यदुक्तं—ज्ञानक्रियाशक्तिरूपेण प्रकाशविमर्शरूपेण चिदानन्दरूपेण वेति। उभयाभेदलक्षण इति चिदचिन्मेलनात्मकः। यदुक्तं—नादस्तस्याश्चिन्मिश्रं रूपमिति। देदीप्यमान इति। निरावरणचिन्मयत्वादिति भावः। परापश्यन्त्यात्मक इति। परायाः संभवमात्रं पश्यन्त्यास्तूत्पत्तिरिति ज्ञेयम्। मूले त्वव्यक्तात्मको व्यक्तात्मक इति चोभयथा पदमित्यर्थात् सूचितम्। रवो नादः। स एवेति। अव्यक्तात्मकत्वात् कुण्डलिनीव्यक्तात्मकत्वं त्वभिलप्यत इति विवृतमित्यपि द्रष्टव्यम्। कोऽसौ रव इति। गवाश्वादिलक्षणः प्रसिद्धः शब्दः अन्यो वेति। मूले श्रुतिसम्पन्नैरित्युपदेशप्रधानत्वं शब्दरहस्यत्वं चोक्तम्। यद्वा शब्दब्रह्मणोऽप्युपासनादि सूचितम्॥ ४४

मूलेऽन्तरुदितत्रिभेदं सगहनं स्वरूपं महानित्येवं प्रसिद्धस्य तत्त्वस्योक्तम्। तत्र त्रीन् भेदान् विवृणोति—त्रिभेदा इति। प्रकृतितत्त्वे शब्दगुणानामत्यन्तसूक्ष्मतेत्यन्तरुदितपदेन सूचितम्। मूले महतोऽहङ्कृतिस्तथेत्यन्तरुदितत्रिभेदगहनात्मकं भवेदित्यर्थः। ननु कस्तर्हि महदहङ्कारयोर्भेद इत्यत आह—अत्रेत्यादि। सर्वजगदाश्रयभूत इति। तदभावे जगतः प्रलयदशैव स्यादित्यर्थः। ईक्षणादिशब्दार्थ इति। 'स ईक्षत' 'स तपोऽतप्यत'इत्यादिप्रसिद्धिरुक्ता। कस्येदमीक्षणमित्यर्थात् तदध्यक्षस्येश्वरस्येति ज्ञेयम्। इहेक्षणं वृत्तिरेव। तया तद्वतो महतो ग्रहणमित्यवबोद्धव्यम्। तदभिमान इत्यहङ्कृतिशब्दत एवैतत्सिद्धिरिति भावः॥ ४५

मूले भूतादिकेत्यत्र भूतादिकानां भेदानां क्रमो यस्मिन्निति समासः। क्रमशब्देनैतदुक्तम्। पूर्वं भूतादिकादहङ्कारात् शब्दतन्मात्रादीनां सर्ग इति। अत एव वक्ष्यति—तैजसवैकारिकाहङ्कारयोर्भूतानुगतयोरिति। भूतादिकतैजसवैकारिकभेदक्रमादिति क्वचित्पाठः। कालप्रेरितयेति। शक्तेर्नियन्त्रेश्वराख्येन परकालेनापरकालान्वितेन प्रेरितयेत्यर्थः। एतदभिप्रायेणाह—कालो द्विविध इति। गुणघोषयुजेति। सत्त्वादिभिः सूक्ष्मस्थूलभूतानां शान्तघोरमूढादिवैचित्र्ययोगः। घोषेण तु निजनिजवाचकसंवलितत्वम्। यद्वा शब्दसृष्टिमात्रविषयमेवैतत्। प्रागुक्तबैन्दवशब्दतत्त्वस्य विवर्तो विकृतिस्थूलीभावोऽयं शब्दतन्मात्रसर्ग इति। अत एवाह—पूर्वोक्तो रवः शब्दब्रह्मेतीति। शक्त्येत्युपलक्षितादिति शेषः। सर्वत्र स्वकीयकारणजातविशिष्टादेव कार्यात् कार्यान्तरोत्पत्तिरित्यप्यनेन सूचितम्।

शब्दाद्व्योमेत्यत्र धराद्या भूताः क्रमेण गुणोनाः स्युरित्युपस्कारेण सम्बन्धः। स्युरित्युत्पत्त्यभिप्रायम्। तदाह—धराद्या भूता उत्पन्ना इति। स्पर्शतस्तेन

वायुरित्यत्र शब्दादित्यनुषङ्गः। शब्दादुत्पन्नः स्पर्शस्तेन शब्देनान्विताद्वायुरुत्पन्न इति तदर्थः। एवं ताभ्यां रूपाद्वह्निरित्यादिष्वपि द्रष्टव्यम्। क्रमेण गुणोना इति। गन्धरसरूपस्पर्शशब्दैः पञ्चगुणा भूमिर्गन्धं विना चतुर्गुणा आप इत्येवं प्रकारोऽभिप्रेतः। शब्दादीनामेवेति। पञ्चीकरणाभ्युपगमादस्मिन् क्रमवृद्ध्यभ्युपगमे भेदोऽनेनाभिहितः। शब्दस्यैव काठिन्यमाकाशः शब्दान्वितस्य स्पर्शस्य काठिन्यं वायुरित्यादि ज्ञेयम् ॥ ४६॥४७ ॥

खमपि सुषिरचिह्नमित्यादि भूतानां स्वरूपकथनमेव न तु लक्षणाभिधानम्। स्वरूपकथनं चेह प्रकृतमेवेति दर्शयति—विभेदगहनात्मकमित्यादिना। सुषिरचिह्नमसाधारणं स्वरूपात्मकं चिह्नं यस्येति समासः। एवमितरेऽपि स्वरूपपरतया व्याख्येयाः। रसवदिति। रस इह द्रवः। न्यासप्रयोगादिविशेषतयेति। न्यासो निजतत्त्वन्यासो वर्णतत्त्वन्यासश्च। तत्र भूतमन्त्रन्यासे तेषामेवं प्रतिपत्तिः स्यादिति कदाचित्तन्मन्त्रेषु तदनुषङ्गः। यथा ॐ आकाशमण्डलसुषिराकाराय सितवर्णाय सदाशिवाधिष्ठिताय नम इत्यादि।

महदहङ्कारादीनां तु वृत्तमेव मण्डलम्। श्रोत्रादीनां त्वणुमात्रमिति ज्ञेयम्। प्रयोगं तु वक्ष्यति—एतदन्त्यं पार्थिवमण्डलगतं स्तम्भन इत्यादि। आदिशब्देन भूतयोगो भूतसंहारसर्गावित्यादिग्रहणम्। यदुक्तं—मण्डलबीजाधिष्ठातृसहितानिति। सितेत्यादिनेति। वर्णानामाकारविशेषणत्वमिति सूचितम्। सितमाकाशमण्डलम्। शितः श्यामः। श्वेतरक्तस्तु पाटलः ॥ ४८ ॥

स्वस्तिकं कोणत्रययातमिति सम्बन्धः। शेषेण स्वस्तिकलक्षणमुक्तम्। ज्वाला चेयं भवति। तदुक्तं—दहनहेतियुतं त्रिकोणमिति। मूले अब्जोपेतार्धेन्दुमदित्यस्यायमर्थः। मध्ये वोभयकोण्योर्वाम्बुजयुतार्धचन्द्राकारमिति। बिन्दुविनिर्गता इति। शक्त्यन्वितादहङ्काराच्छब्दादितन्मात्रोत्पत्तिरित्युक्तप्रकृतितया तदुत्पन्ना इत्यर्थः। निर्गतपदेन स्वातन्त्र्यादियोगोऽपि तासां ख्यापितः ॥ ४९ ॥

प्रयोगाद्यर्थमेवेति। न्यासप्रयोगादिविशेषतयेत्यर्थः। भूतन्यासे कृते न्यासः मण्डलबीजाधिष्ठातृसहितानित्यादिषु प्रयोगः। आदिशब्देनोत्थानिक आभिः सकलीकरणमित्यादिकमुक्तम्। नादकलादिभूता इत्यस्यायमर्थः। नादबिन्द्वादिभूतकलारूपेण भूता विकृता इमास्तासां प्रकृतय इति। सर्गक्रमाभिप्रायेण नादादिग्रहणम्।

अर्थान्तरमाह—तासामित्यादिना। स्थूलवाचकांशमिति। सूक्ष्मो वाचकः स्वस्वानुगतशब्दतत्त्वमेव। यद्वा नादबिन्द्वादयः। अथवा ऐ औ ऊ ई आ

वाच्यवाचकद्वंश + + य एक एव सर्वः पदार्थ इत्यभिप्रायेणांशग्रहणम्। यद्वक्ष्यति—अभिन्नो रवो वाचकांश इति। नादः कलादयश्चेति समासः। कशब्दस्य मूर्धवाचकत्वादूर्ध्वार्थत्वम्। लादीनामिति। समस्तानामिति भावः। त्रिधा योज्यमित्येकशेषप्रक्रिययेति भावः। कशब्देनैवेति। कमनुस्वारः। तद्योगिनोऽपि कशब्देन गृह्यन्ते। तस्य च नादकशब्देनावयवैकशेषः स्यादिति भावः। नादकलादिशब्दस्य भूतशब्देन योजनां तु वक्ष्यति—तेभ्यो भूता इत्यादि। तन्मात्राभिमानिबीजोद्धार इति। तन्मात्राभिमानिनीनामासां शान्त्यतीतादीनामित्यर्थः। तासां स्थूलवाचकांशमिति द्युक्तम्। तन्मात्राणामप्येतान्येव बीजानि।

अपञ्चीकृतबीजोद्धार इत्याकाशमात्रादीन्यपञ्चीकृतभूतानि तदभिमानिनीनामप्येतान्येव बीजानि। लादीनां सर्वेषामिति व्यस्तानामित्यर्थः। लादय आदयश्चेत्यवयवैकशेषः। ल आदिर्यस्येति सिद्धवर्णातिरिक्तस्यैव लभ्यत्वादिह हकारसिद्धिरिति बोद्धव्यम्। ननु नादकलाग्रहणेनैवैतत्सिद्धमिति नेत्याह—नादशब्दोक्तस्येति। सर्वसम्बन्धादिति। लादीनां सर्वेषामिति विवृतमेतदिति भावः। ह्लां ह्लीमित्यादिसर्वेषु हकारयोगः कारणान्वयादिति बोद्धव्यम्। यद्वा शब्दाद्व्योमेत्येवमुक्तान्येवापञ्चीकृतानि विवक्ष्यन्ते। ततश्च क्रमवृद्धिपक्षेऽप्येतान्येव बीजानि भवन्ति। पञ्चीकृतबीजादीनीति। परस्परयोगेन विकृतानि भूतानि पञ्चीकृतानि। नादकलश्च लादिश्चादिश्चेत्यवयवैकशेषः। तेभ्यो भूता इति। स्ववाचकतो निष्पत्तिरुक्ता। सा च तदभिन्नस्वभावत्वात्तद्रूपेणाभिव्यक्तिरेव। तदाह—तदात्मतयाभिव्यक्त इति। क्व पुनरेषां विनियोग इति। उच्यते। यद्वक्ष्यति—मध्ये पञ्चीकृतभूतबीजं लिखित्वेति। तथा च पञ्चीकृतभूतबीजानि मूर्धादिषु न्यसन्नित्यादि। मण्डलबीजाधिष्ठातृसहितानिति चोक्तमिति॥ ५०॥

पुटयोरुभयोरित्यत्र नस उभयोः पुटयोरित्यन्वयः। नस इति नासिकायाः। दण्डसंस्थेति। मध्यगतदण्डसङ्घट्टनेनोद्भूतो वायुः पृथिव्युदयं सूचयतीत्यभिप्रायः। एवं तोयादीनामपि प्रतिपत्तव्यम्। तोयमध इत्युभयोः पुटयोरिति सर्वत्र योज्यते। तनूद्भवेयमिति। कालोद्भवाप्यस्तीति सूचितम्। वक्ष्यति च—योगाद्यर्थमेवेति।

तदुक्तं—वश्यस्तम्भनयोर्भूमेरपां शान्तिकपौष्टिके।
मारणे मोहने चाग्नेरुदयो देहकालयोः॥
उत्सादोच्चाटयोर्वायोः शान्तिके निर्विशेषकृतौ।
आकाशस्यैवमन्यानि स्थानान्येषां प्रकल्पयेत्॥ इति

आदिशब्देन कार्यारम्भे फलसिद्ध्यादिपरिज्ञानमप्येवं कार्यमित्याद्यपि सूचितम् ॥ ५१

प्रासङ्गिकमिति पूर्वत्र सम्बध्यते। सर्गक्रमेऽनुपयोगात् प्रासङ्गिकत्वम्। वर्णाद्यभिधानेऽपि समानमेतत्। व्योम्नि मरुदित्यस्यायमर्थः। व्योम्नान्तर्भागे क्वचिदेव वायुः तस्मिन्नन्तर्भागे क्वचिदेवाग्निरेवमापः पृथिवी च। पृथिव्यामप्यन्त-र्भागे सर्वभूतानि एवमित्थमुत्पन्नानां स्थितिरिति। परतत्त्वे क्वचिदेव प्रकृतिरिति तावदुक्तम्—क्वचिदभ्येति बिन्दुतामिति। प्रकृतावप्यन्तर्भागे क्वचिदेव महा-नेवमहङ्कार आकाशश्चेति द्रष्टव्यम्।

तदुक्तम्—ब्रह्माण्डं पार्थिवं ह्येतत्सर्वभूतास्पदोदरम्।
जलाद्यावरणैश्चैव सप्तभिर्बहिरावृतम्॥ इति।

अर्थान्तरमाह—पञ्चीकरणमाहेति। व्योम्नीतरेषामंशावेशोऽवोक्तः। तत्सम्बन्ध इति। व्योम्नि यो वायोरंशस्तस्मिन्नित्यर्थः। एतत्प्रागपि तुल्यमेव प्रदर्शनार्थं चैतदिति दर्शयति—मरुति व्योमेत्यादि। लयाद्युपयोगितयेति। भूतसंहार-सर्गादिग्रहणम्। व्याप्यस्यैव हि व्यापके संहारः सुप्रतिपाद्यो भवति। यदुक्तं—पूर्वं पूर्वं वाच्यवाचकरूपमित्यादि॥ ५२॥

भूतानुगतयोरिति। यथा स्पर्शस्य शब्दान्वितस्यैकं कार्यं वायुर्यथा चाकाशस्य वाय्वादिचतुरन्वितस्यैकं कार्यं स्थूलाकाशः तथा तैजसाहङ्कारस्य शब्दान्वितस्यैकं कार्यं श्रोत्रमित्याद्यवबोद्धव्यमित्यभिप्रायः। क्रमेणेति। तैजसाच्छ्रोत्रादीनां वैकारिकाद्वागादीनामित्यर्थः। क्वचित्पाठविपर्ययः।

तथा चोक्तम्—वैकारिकात्तु जातानि श्रोत्रं त्वक्चक्षुषी तथा।
जिह्वा घ्राणं च पञ्चैव तानि बुद्धीन्द्रियाणि हि॥ इति।

बुद्धेस्तत्तदर्थनिश्चयार्थानीन्द्रियाणि बुद्धीन्द्रियाणि प्राणस्य तत्तदर्थकरणार्थानि कर्मे-न्द्रियाणीति भेदः। तन्मात्राणां शब्दस्पर्शाद्याख्यात एव श्रोत्राद्यर्थत्वं सिद्धमिति।

वागाद्यर्थानाह आचार्यो वचनादाने इति। समनो बुद्धिरहङ्कारचित्तमपि करणमिति। श्रोत्रादीनां बहिःकरणत्वादेतदन्तःकरणमर्थाद् भवति। मह-त्तत्त्वस्यांश एव मनश्चित्तमपि। यद्वा तैजसाहङ्कारकार्यमुभयमिति। केचिदु-भयेन्द्रियाण्यपि वैकारिकाहङ्कारकार्याण्याहुरिति॥ ५३॥ ५४॥

मूले भूतेन्द्रियेन्द्रियार्थैरित्याकाशादीनि भूतानि श्रोत्रादीनि वागादीनि चे-न्द्रियाणि शब्दादयो वचनादयश्च तदर्थाः। वचनादीनामपि ग्रहणादापेक्षिकोऽयं सङ्घातः न तु नित्यः। ततश्चाग्निमन्त्रादिषु वर्णतत्त्वार्थमेतत्। महागणपत्यादिषु महदहङ्कारमनोयोगोऽनुष्टुबादिषु त्वगादिधातुयोग इत्येवं सर्वमवबोद्धव्यम्।

तत्त्वपञ्चविंशतिकेति स्वार्थे कः। अभिप्रायान्तरमाह—तत्त्वपञ्चविंशतिकेत्यत्रेति। तत्त्वकल्पनाया इत्यस्या इति शेषः। कुत्सितत्वमिति। (नि)त्यताभ्युपगम एवमिति भावः। व्यानन्दकेश्वेति। गायत्र्यादिषु वर्णतत्त्वापेक्षयायं सङ्घातः। तथा-शब्देनापि पूर्ववदित्यवगमादिति भावः ॥ ५५ ॥

मूले करणोपेतैरिति नित्यः सङ्घातः। मनोऽहङ्कारबुद्धिचित्तानि तु करणानि। चतुर्विंशतितत्त्वाभिप्रायमेवैतत्। अत्रापि सूक्ष्ममभिप्रायान्तरमाह—तत्त्वान्युक्तानी-त्यादिना। इह चित्तशब्देन प्रकृतिर्विवक्षितव्येति भावः। सिद्धमर्थं दर्शयति—तत इति। गायत्र्यादिष्वेवमपि वर्णतत्त्वन्यासः स्यादित्याशयेन विकल्पः। केवल-तत्त्वन्यासे त्वीश्वरादीन्येव तत्त्वानि स्युरिति। व्यवहारशेषतयेति। यथा तथा प्रकृतिभेदादिनो(ने)त्यादि। केषाञ्चिन्मन्त्राणामिति + + योग इह तत्त्वयोगः। अर्थात्सोऽपि तत्तन्मन्त्रोचितो योगावसरे कार्य इति गम्यते। तत्र चैवं प्रयोगः। वर्णतत्त्वानि मूलाधाराद्याषोडशान्तं व्यवस्थितानि सङ्कल्प्य क्रमेण वर्णैः संहृ-त्यामृतमाप्लावयेदिति। आदिशब्देन देहशुद्ध्यादिग्रहणम्। करणोपेतैरव्यक्त-महदहङ्कृतिभूतानीत्यनयोरन्यतरेण देहं संहृत्य सृजेदिति। संहारन्यासेन प्राणा-यामसहितेन वा संहारः। तथा सर्गन्यासेन सर्ग इति। तत्र प्रणवेन परतत्त्वेन वा तत्त्वावस्थां विभाव्य प्रणवेन विचिकीर्षुर्घनीभूतेत्युभयं संभाव्य प्रकृतितत्त्वेन प्रकृति-तत्त्वमुत्पाद्य पुनः प्रणवषट्केनेच्छादिसत्त्वादित्रयद्विकं पुनः प्रणवत्रयेण माया-तच्छक्तितद्गतापूर्वाभिव्यक्तीश्च विधाय महदादितत्त्वमन्त्रैस्तत्तत्सर्गं विभाव्य पञ्ची-करणं भावयेत्। शैववैष्णवादिपाठेष्वपि समानमेतदिति ॥ ५६ ॥ ५७ ॥

मूले सत्त्वं रज इति स बिन्दुर्भवति त्रिधेति प्रागुद्दिष्टत्रिभेदाभिधानम्। तस्या इति परप्रकृतिग्रहणमित्याह—मूलकारणभूताया इति। नैवं विकृताया महदादेरेव वेति भावः। मूले तत्सम्बन्धादिति। गुणविकाराणां प्रागुक्तम-हदाद्यखिलविकारेष्वेवान्तरविभागतयानुगतिकथनम्। तत्सम्बन्धस्तदन्वयः। भेदत्रितयैरिति। शान्तघोरमूढादिलक्षणैरनेकविधैरित्यर्थः। अभिप्रायान्तरमाह—तस्यास्त्रिगुणात्मकत्व इति ॥ ५८ ॥

न्यासयोगविशेषांश्चेति। न्यासयोगान् वक्ष्यमाणन्यासानिति। प्रणवादि-ष्विति। प्रणवहृल्लेखयोः श्रीबीजादीनां च ग्रहणम्। न्यासस्य पृथक्त्वे त्रैपुरगायत्र्यादीनामपि तंत्रशालिनां ग्रहणम्। कामनानुरूपेणेति। स्वेच्छ-यान्यतमकतिपयसमस्तानुष्ठानमुक्तम्। यद्वा देववेदादितत्तदर्थवशीकरणं कामना तदनुसारेणेति। दर्शयन्निति प्रपञ्चयतीत्यधः सम्बन्धः। देवा ब्रह्मविष्णुरुद्राः

सूर्यवाय्वग्नयो वा। स्वरा अनुदात्तोदात्तस्वरिताः। मरुतः प्राणादयः आवहादयो वा। वैश्वानरा अग्नयो गार्हपत्यादयः। काला भूतादयः। शक्तय इच्छाद्या उत्साहप्रभुमन्त्रशक्तयो वा। प्रसिद्धा वेति विवरणम्। पिङ्गलेडासुषुम्ना वेत्यर्थः। अन्यच्चेति। त्रिदोषत्रिलिङ्गादिग्रहणम्। तत् संबध्येति। कारणतानुगम्येत्यर्थः। लोकानां स्थितय इति। सूर्योदयाद्यभावे विश्वक्षयः स्यादिति भावः। चरन्त्य-विरतमिति। प्रसिद्धमण्डलाकारेणोदयादिकमुक्तम्। सूर्येन्दुवैश्वानरा रजःसत्त्व-तमोऽभिमानिन इति। मण्डलत्रयोपेतमिति। अयमिह प्रयोगः। अं सूर्य-मण्डलाय नम इति नाभिपद्मे विन्यस्य ब्रह्मवेदानुदात्तप्राणभूर्लोकगार्हपत्य-भूतेच्छाधर्मपिङ्गलावातानप्यन्यतमकतिपयसमस्ततया तत्र विन्यस्य संपूज्य मूलाधारोत्थितचिदग्निशिखया सहोत्तरोत्तरसंहारक्रमेण षोडशान्तस्थानन्दामृत-मण्डलान्तराविश्याऽमृतमास्रावयेदिति। चरन्तीति। चरगतिभक्षणयोरिति धातुः। परमानन्दमिति। यदुक्तं—मां षोडशान्तस्थितममृतमयमिति ॥ ५८ ॥

* एवं तावदग्निसूर्यादिदेवताविषये तत्त्वान्युक्तानि। इदानीं शिवविष्ण्वादि-विषये तत्त्वानि वक्तुमारभते—ननु सर्वमन्त्रसमानत्वेनेति। नाग्निसूर्यादि-मन्त्रप्राधान्येनेति भावः। साक्षादनभिधानादियान् प्रश्नः संभवति। सत्यमुक्ता-नीति च वक्तुर्वचनं शृणिवति च। चिन्मात्रज्योतिःशब्दाभ्यामिति। चिन्मात्र-मधिष्ठानम्। तदेव स्वपरावभासकतया ज्योतिः साक्षी भवति। अनाहतत्व-मव्याहतिरसङ्गः। अकारलक्षितार्थाविति। सर्वस्वरतन्मात्ररूपोऽकारो बीजमुक्तः। अचिन्मात्रं बीजरूपमाहतशिवः। तस्य चिद्रूपावच्छिन्नत्वादाहतत्वम्। कथ्येत इति सर्वत्रानुषङ्गः। एतच्छुद्धतत्त्वपञ्चकमिति शैव इति शेषः। अत्रैवं मन्त्रप्रयोगः। अं अनाहतशिवाय नमः अं अनाहतशक्त्यै नमः। अं आहतशिवाय चं आहत-शक्त्यै इत्यादि। इत्येवेत्यचिन्मात्रशक्तीच्छाज्ञानक्रियालक्षणत्वन्तु समानमिति भावः। अत्र प्रथमं प्रणवेन परपुरुषतत्त्वमपि ग्राह्यम्। षोयरावलाश्चेति। यथा षों परमेष्ठ्यात्मने वासुदेवाय नम इत्यादि। स्वरूपाच्छादनविक्षेपात्मक-मिति। स्वाधिष्ठानचित्स्वरूपस्याच्छादनमर्थान्तरप्रत्ययश्चास्याः स्वभावो यथा शुक्तिकायामिदं रजतमितीति भावः। ननु शुद्धपञ्चकेऽपि समानमेतदिति नेत्याह —शुद्धपञ्चके त्विति। कुतो विक्षेप इति भावः। तत्र हेतुमाह—तस्येश्वर-रूपत्वाद्विद्यावत्त्वेनेति। विद्या चित्स्वरूपस्वभावः तद्योगत ईश्वररूपाण्येता-नीत्यर्थः। चिन्मात्रस्याचिन्नियन्तृत्वमिह विशेष इतीश्वरग्रहणेन सूचितम्।

ननु मायादीनामपि नियन्तासाविति। सत्यम्। किन्तु जीवचिदेषामधिष्ठा-

नमित्यभिप्रायेणाह—मायादिकं त्विति। नन्वेकमनेकशक्तियोगादद्वैतविरोध इत्यत्राह—एकैवेति। अन्तर्मुखत्वं द्वैतास्फूर्तिः स्वाधिष्ठानचिद्रूपनिष्ठत्वम्। विकासतारतम्याच्च विद्यादितत्त्वोपपत्तिः। बहिर्मुखत्वं चिदाभासनिष्ठत्वम्। सङ्कोचतारतम्याच्च मायादितत्त्वसंभव इति। तदुपहित इति मायादिग्रहणम्। तेषामिति शैवानाम्। वैष्णवेऽपि यथार्हमेतत्प्रतिपत्तव्यम्। मायाविक्षेप इति। जाते सतीति शेषः। ईश्वरेच्छैवेति। शिवचिदधिष्ठानत्वमस्या उक्तम्। अस्य च सप्तकस्येति। शुद्धाशुद्धस्येति भावः। जीवतत्त्व एवेति। तत्त्वं तावत्तदेव व्यपदेशमात्र एव तु भेद इति भावः। अन्तर्भूतमिति यदुक्तं तदुपहित एव जीव इति। पशोरिति। मायादीनां पाशत्वात् पुरुष एव पशुरभ्युपेयते। सुखदुःखमोहलक्षणमिति। सत्त्वादिगुणयोगादिति भावः।

ननु सत्त्वाद्युत्पत्त्यनन्तरं मायातच्छक्त्याद्युत्पत्तिः पूर्वमुक्तेति। सत्यम्। किन्तु शैवमार्गे शक्तितत्त्वेऽपि शुद्धतरसत्त्वादियोगेऽपि तथा न व्यवहार इति भेदः। प्राणतत्त्वेनैवेति। परपुरुषस्य जीवत्वविवक्षायां प्रकृतिरपि प्राणो व्यपदिश्यते। जीवनस्य प्राणधारणरूपत्वादिति बोद्धव्यम्। प्रकृतेः स्थूलांशत्वमपि प्राणस्य सूचितम्। शैवे तु + + + बिन्दोस्तस्माद्भिद्यमानादितीति। कालेन भिद्यमानस्त्वित्यादि शैवे वैष्णवेऽपि समानमिति भावः। बिन्दुः शिव इति। परोऽनाहतशिव उक्तः। स चार्थाच्छुद्धविद्यापर्यन्त इत्याह—तस्मादिति। भिद्यमानात् परिणस्यमानात्। कथं परिणाम इत्येवमुक्तेन प्रकारेण। सोऽपि कथमिति मायादिरूपेणायं परिणाम इति।

अभिन्नो रव इति। मायाद्यर्थाविभक्तः सन्नित्यर्थः। अव्यक्तात्मक इत्यव्यक्तं प्रकृतिरित्याह—प्रकृतितत्त्वात्मक इति। वैष्णवे तु न मायादिरूपेण परिणामोऽस्तीत्येव भेदः। सर्वत्रेति। शैवे वैष्णवेऽपीति। अथ शैवेऽवान्तरभेद एव शाक्तमिति शैवानन्तरं शाक्ततत्त्वाभिधानमित्याह—निवृत्तिसंज्ञा चेत्यत्रेति। कथमेतदिह सूचितमित्यत आह—स्युरिति। त्रयोदशेत्युपस्कारः। तावादिभूताविति। बिन्द्वादयो बिन्दुकलानिरोधिकाः। नादादयश्च नादान्तशक्त्यादयः। उन्मन्यादीनां स्वरूपं गायत्रीपटले वक्ष्यति—पूर्णसंविदात्मना स्थितस्य प्रणवस्येत्यादि ॥ *

इदानीमेष सर्गः समुत्पन्न इत्यमुं वादं विवृणोति—अर्थसृष्टेरिति। कार्यस्येत्यवगमसाधनत्वं विश्वस्योक्तम्। यतः प्रपञ्चस्त्वित्यत्र समुत्पन्नशब्दानुषङ्गः कृतः। तदिति चोपस्कारः। ब्रह्मानवच्छिन्नं देवतातत्त्वम्। इत्थं विश्वमिति। विश्वप्रतीतौ हीत्यनयोः प्रयोजनवाक्ययोरेष सर्गः समुत्पन्न इत्यत्र

सम्बन्धः। तस्मादिति चार्थादध्याहारः। तदाह—तस्मात्सृष्टिरर्थवतीति।

अथवेति। एष सर्ग एव समुत्पन्न इति सम्बध्यते। एष इति प्रत्यक्षसिद्धस्यानुवादः। स एवेति। तस्य परोक्षभूतपरात्मरूपतया विधानम्। सृजतीति सर्गपदं कर्तरि व्याख्यातम्। किमिह्योक्तं भवतीत्याह—योऽसावित्यादि। कुत इति। कथमेतद्गम्यत इति भावः। सत्प्रकाशत इति च सत्तास्फुर्ती परमात्मलक्षणतयोक्ते। किमितीति। किं प्रयोजनमभिसन्धायेत्यर्थः। तत्साक्षितयेत्यर्थादध्याहारः।

एतदेव पद्यमिति। शैवतत्त्वावगतिपूर्विकैव त्रैपुरतत्त्वावगतिरितीदानीं तदारम्भः। अत्रैवमुत्पन्न एष सर्ग इत्यनुवादः। एष इति प्रकृतशैवतत्त्वपरामर्शः। तदाहेत्थं समुत्पन्न इति। विश्वं प्रतीयत इति तत्रापूर्वविधानम्। विश्वपदं विवृणोति—प्रमेयप्रमाणेति। प्रतीयत इति संग्रहसमीचायां श्रुतौ चेति शेषः। तत्र श्रुतिमाह—प्रमेति। त्रैपुरमन्त्रानुष्ठानमपि वैदिकमेवेत्यपीह सूचितम्। वक्ष्यति च—सत्संप्रदायादिति। शैवतत्त्वेऽपि कियत्प्रमेयमात्मतत्त्वमित्याद्यपेक्षायामाह—तत्रेत्यादि। मायान्तमिति पृथिव्यादिमायान्तप्रमेयरूपमिति। प्रमातृशिवतत्त्वकल्पितशक्तावारोपितत्वात्। तदुक्तं—युष्माकं विषयवत्प्रकृतिकार्यत्वेन तस्यां कल्पितत्वादिति। वेद्यस्येति। साक्ष्यतया प्रतीतियोग्यतोक्ता। प्रतीतौ ह्रीत्यर्थात् साक्षिणि सतीति लभ्यते। तदाह—साक्षिणि सतीति। स परमशिवोऽवगम्यत इत्यत्र संबन्धः। यतः प्रपञ्चस्त्वित्यत्र भवतीति शेषः। प्रपञ्चश्चायमुक्तः शैवतत्त्ववर्गत्रयात्मकतत्त्वत्रयरूप इत्यभिप्रायेणाह—यस्मादिति। साक्ष्येव त्वर्थादधिष्ठानमपि सम्पद्यते। किमात्मतयावगम्यत इत्यत उक्तं—सर्वतत्त्वरूप इति। मन्त्रक्लृप्तिस्तु वक्ष्यते—ह्स्रैं आत्मतत्त्वेश्वर्यै इत्यादि। हृल्लेखादिष्वप्येतदिष्यते। प्रासादेऽपि देहोत्पत्तेरकथितत्वादर्थस्य मध्यमान्तत्वाद्वा शब्दसृष्टिमित्यस्यैवैतद्विशेषणम् ॥ ६० ॥

ननु पश्यन्त्यन्त एव शब्दसर्ग उक्तः बिन्दोस्तस्मात् भिद्यमानादिति। उच्यते। गुणघोषयुजेति मध्यमावस्थस्य शब्दस्य ग्रहणम्। तदन्वयविधानाच्च भूतेन्द्रियेष्वपि तदनुगतेः कृत्स्ना मध्यमापीहोक्तैवेति। नन्विह कियन्मध्यमापर्व वैखरीपर्व वेति जिज्ञासायां कृत्स्नां शब्दपर्वक्लृप्तिमुपदिशति—तत्रेत्यादिना। परावाक् तदर्थरूपिणीति तत्त्वसंज्ञा विशेष्यते। यदुक्तं—तत्त्वस्य पारमार्थिकस्य संज्ञैवेत्यादि। प्रकृतितत्त्वान्तमिति। विचिकीर्षाघनीभावेच्छासत्त्वाद्यवान्तरदशायोगादेवमुक्तम्। यद्वा शैववैष्णवयोराहतशिववासुदेवादिप्रकृतिप्राणान्तग्रहणार्थमेतत्। इन्द्रियान्तमिति। महदहङ्कारतन्मात्रोभयेन्द्रियार्थमयमित्यर्थः। पञ्चीकृतमिति।

समष्टिव्यष्टिरूपं गृह्यते इति। मूले तदुद्देश इत्यत्र उद्देश उपदेशः। नासौ स्वाकारेण किन्तु स्वकार्याकारेणेत्याह—तस्य क्रमेणेति। याथात्म्याभिधानमुपदेशः। प्रवर्त्यत इति। महता प्रकरणेन क्रियत इत्यर्थः। बैन्दवतत्त्वरूपशब्दब्रह्मणोऽपीति। यदुक्तं—बिन्दोस्तस्माद्भिद्यमानादिति। याथात्म्योपदेशनमङ्गत्वेति। तद्धि तावत्कर्तव्यं प्रथमप्राप्तत्वात् साररूपत्वाच्चेति भावः। मूलेऽतः परमिति शब्दब्रह्मणोऽप्युत्तरं तत्त्वमुक्तम्। आत्मा स्वसंवेद्यत्वेनेत्यत्रात्मेति साक्षिणो ग्रहणम्। स्वरूपसंवेद्यत्वेनेत्यनन्यगोचरत्वेनेत्यर्थः॥ ६१॥

सूक्ष्मो व्यापीति सामान्यवैखर्यात्मकाकारग्रहणम्। सूक्ष्मतया व्यापित्वं हि ब्रह्मत्वम्। तदेव च ब्रह्मत्वम्। तत्तावदिहास्तीति चाभिप्रायः। शब्दावगम्यमिति सप्तमीसमासः। तत्र चेयानर्थो लभ्यत इत्याह—शब्दोच्चारणकाल इति। अर्थशब्द इह पदार्थवचनः। तदाह—बिन्द्वात्मकमिति। बुधास्तत्त्वनिष्णाताः। इह तावन्मुख्यतया शब्दत्वं ब्रह्मत्वं चैषितव्यम्। तदुभयं च तत्र नास्तीति दर्शयन् विवृणोति—इतरस्येति। शब्दे हि प्रकाशकांशो रहस्यमुपनिषद्भूतं भवति तत्र स्थूलस्य रवस्यास्ति। ब्रह्मत्वं च निरतिशयसूक्ष्मतया व्यापित्वं तदपि नास्तीत्यर्थः॥ ६२॥

सर्वत्र संस्यूत इति। संस्यूतिरान्तरतया व्याप्तिः। कारणत्वादिति। बैन्दवं तत्त्वमेतदिति ह्युक्तमिति भावः। सामान्यवैखरीरूपस्य न कारणत्वम्। विशेषावधारणार्थ इति। त्वदुक्तशब्दादयमिह विशेष इति प्रतिपादनार्थ इत्यर्थः। सामान्यवैखर्यास्तु कार्यत्वात् सर्वत्र संस्यूतिर्न स्यादिति भावः। अत इत्यनेनैतद्दर्शितम्। यस्मात् स सर्वत्र संस्यूतस्तस्मात्स एव देहेषु यावदर्थविस्तृत आविर्भवति। तदभावात्तु नैवं सामान्यवैखरीरूपो रव इति। अत्र यावदर्थं विस्तृत इति ब्रह्मत्वं साधितम्। आविर्भवति प्रकाशत इति प्रकाशकत्वमपि विवेकः। मूले भूताकार इति पञ्चीकृतभूतानि लोकाद्याकाराण्युक्तानि। सङ्कल्पविकल्पनिश्चयविमर्शनात्मनेति विमर्शरूपेणाविर्भावः। विमर्शश्च मनोबुद्ध्यादिधर्मतया सङ्कल्पादिलक्षण इति भावः। सङ्कल्पादिज्ञानभेदो विमर्शस्तु शब्दस्वभाव इत्येवमभिधानमिति॥ ६३॥

तस्याविर्भावप्रकारप्रदर्शनार्थमिति। तस्याविर्भावप्रकार एव तावदिदानीं दर्शयितव्यः। यद्वक्ष्यति—निर्धारितमर्थमेषेत्यादि। मूलाधारात् प्रथममुदित इत्यादि। अव्यक्तं प्रलपतीत्यादि च। स च मूलाधारादिप्रतिपादनसापेक्षतया देहोत्पत्तिप्रकारेऽपि दर्शित एव सुप्रतिपदः स्यादित्यभिप्रायः। किञ्च पर-

देवताया: स्वाविद्ययैव देहित्वमित्यपि दर्शयितव्यम्। यतो वक्ष्यत्याचार्य:—क्रमहृतौ परं ज्योतिष्कला चैतन्नतामियादिति। तथा—बहुना किं परं पुंस इत्यादि। तदनुक्तौ तु—अथ व्यवस्थिते त्वेवमस्य शक्तित्वमिष्यत इत्याद्यनुपपत्ति: स्यादिति। किञ्च स्थावरादिदेहेष्वपि स्याच्छब्दब्रह्माभिव्यक्तिरिति सर्वजातिकथनम्। परदेवतास्वरूपानधिगमे पर्यायेण सर्वजात्यापत्तिरिति। वैराग्योत्पादनार्थं च गर्भावस्थाकथनमप्येतदर्थम् वक्ष्यति च—उत्तमपि गर्भवासमित्यादि इति।

मूले कालनुन्नायामिति ईश्वरस्याशेषकार्यनिष्ठतया प्रेरणमुक्तम्। गुणान्त:-करणात्मनोति समष्टिव्यष्टिग्रहणम्। सर्वतत्त्वात्मकत्वोपलक्षणार्थमिति समष्टितत्त्वानां सर्वेषां ग्रहणम्। व्यष्टितत्त्वानां तु लिङ्गदेहान्तानामिति ज्ञेयम्। सत्यामिति चोपस्कार:। यद्वा देहाधिकरणे सप्तमी ॥ ६४॥६५॥६६ ॥

मूलेऽम्बुयोनीति। योनिर्भूमि:। अदर्शनादितिच्छेद:। स्वेदजोत्पत्तेरिति च शेष:। आप: प्रधानं येष्विति समास:। पञ्चस्वपि भूवक्त्रपां स्वेदो भेद: + + + स्त्रोवल्मीककारिणो। क्षणभङ्गुरा: स्वल्पकालेनैव विनश्वरा:। शुक्लशोणितसंपुटादित्यर्थाद्गवादिमिथुनसंप्रयोगजादिति लभ्यते। कालेन भिन्नादिति। कालोऽपि द्विविध एव। प्रक्रमिष्यतीति सद्यस्त्वरणमुक्तम्। संभावनया प्रायेणैवमिति सूचितम्। वयोभेदा: पक्षिभेदा:। मूले ग्राम्यात: क्रियातो या स्रुतिस्तत: संभवो यस्येति समास:। पुंस्त्रियो: संप्रयोगो ग्राम्यक्रिया। स्रुति: तदा शुक्लशोणितयो: स्रवणम्। सर्वतत्त्वानामिति। पुरुषतत्त्वाभिप्रायम्। यद्वा शैववैष्णवादितत्त्वाभिप्रायम् ॥ ६७॥६८॥६९॥७० ॥

मूले स्वस्थानतश्च्युतादित्यादि जननप्रकाराभिधानम्। स्वस्थानतश्च्युतादिति ग्राम्यक्रियायामिति शेष:। शुक्लस्य स्वं स्थानं पुंसि शुक्लादय:। शुक्लाद्बिन्दुमिति यावति तदाविष्टजीववस्तुव्याप्तिस्तावतो ग्रहणम्। आदायेति योन्यन्तराविष्टलिङ्गाग्रादिति भाव:। मारुत इति स्त्रोगतो गर्भोचितो वायु:। शुक्लशोणितयो: प्रभवदिरभेदाद्वायुभेद:। आर्तवं स्त्रिया रक्ताशयगतं शोणितम्। परमं बीजमिति शरीरपरिणामोचितं बिन्दुमित्यर्थ:। अस्याश्चेति ग्राम्यक्रियाया: प्रकृतत्वात् स्त्रिया इति गम्यते। मूलत इति रक्ताशयप्रदेशादेव न तु योनावपि शुक्लच्युतिप्रदेशादिति भाव:। यदेत्ययं कालो यदा गर्भाशयं प्रविशति तदा गर्भाशयं नेष्यतीत्येवमुक्तो गृह्यते। नेष्यतीति संमिश्रमाणस्य गर्भाशयप्रवेश: सूचित:। अथ संमिश्रयेन्मरुदित्यपर एव गर्भोचितो वायु: ॥ ७१॥७२ ॥

मायीयं नाम योषोत्थमिति मलमिति संबध्यते। त्वगादीनां स्वदेहत्वेन

स्वात्मतयाभिमाने मायैव प्रधानं निमित्तमिति तत्कारणस्य रक्तस्य मायीयत्वम्। मज्जादीनामेवमभिधाने कर्मैव प्रधानं निमित्तमिति तत्कारणस्य शुक्रस्य कार्मत्वम्। तयोरुभयोरप्येवमभिधाने स्वरूपस्य परिच्छिन्नत्वमेव प्रधानं निमित्तमिति तदैक्यस्याणवत्वम्। नामपदेनागमप्रसिद्धिरुक्ता। यद्वा प्रकृतिरेव स्त्री। यदुक्तम्—अङ्गनासु विशिष्यत इति। सैव संप्रयुयुक्षायां माया भवति। तदुत्थत्वान्मायीयम्। पुरुष एव च पुमान् सोऽपि संप्रयुयुक्षायां कर्तृतया भोक्तृतया च कर्ममयः तदुत्थत्वात् कार्मकम्। यस्तु जनिष्यति स प्रागवस्थायां परपुरुषे लीनः सन्नस्यां दशायामविद्योद्बोधादत्यन्तपरिच्छिन्नत्वेनाणुरिति। तत्प्रयुक्तत्वात् तदुभययोगस्याणवत्वमिति। अभिप्रायान्तरमाह—योषोत्थं रक्तमित्यादिना। फलद्वारेह मायीयत्वादिकमुक्तमिति भेदः। अनुशय्यणुत्वहेतुत्वादिति। यो मायादिलक्षणं स्वोपायमनुशेते सोऽनुशयी जनिष्यमाणो जीवः। तस्याणुत्वप्रतीतिः शरीरनिबन्धनेति हेतुरुक्तः। मायीयत्वादिप्रतिपादनस्य वैराग्यार्थत्वात् तदुचिततया शुक्रादीनां मलव्यपदेशः ॥७३॥

मूले सूक्ष्मरूपाणीत्याश्रित्येतदन्तं वाक्यम्। सूक्ष्माणीत्येतच्च तत्कालविशेषणम्। सर्वेषां सर्वोपाधित्वमिति। सर्वेषामपि तत्त्वानां सर्वेऽपि स्थावरादिचतुर्विधा उपाधयो न कतिपयतत्त्वानामेव किन्तु जरायुजे देहे सर्वेषामपि समभिव्यक्तिर्न तत्त्वेवमितरेषु देहेष्वित्येतदुक्तं भवतीत्यर्थः। लब्धवृत्तीनीत्येतद्युक्तिं व्रजन्तीत्यस्य विवरणम्। चतुर्विंशत्तत्त्वसंयुक्तदेहवानिति तत्त्वानां तत्र सद्भावमात्रमुक्तमिति भेदः। हृदयेन्द्रियगोलकाद्युत्पत्तौ स्फुटो वृत्तिलाभः स्यात्। वक्ष्यति च—बहुद्वारेण कुम्भेनेत्यादि। ततस्तद्गर्भमारुतः संक्षोभ्य संवर्धयतीति वाक्यम्। गर्भमारुतः स्त्रिया गर्भाशयगतो वायुः। संक्षोभणं विलोडनम्। संवर्धयतीत्याप्रसवं तद्व्यापार उक्तः। वर्धनसाधनं तु मातुर्भुक्तरसात्मवदित्येतद् भवति। ना स्यादिति नृशब्दस्य प्रथमैकवचनम्। पुमानित्यर्थः। स्वगतैरिति। तस्मिन् मिलिते मले तदीयजीवस्य देहमात्रे युक्तिमाशु व्रजन्तीत्युक्तनयेन विद्यमानैरित्यर्थः। क्लेदनं क्वाथनं च सान्द्रीभावकिट्टादिविक्रियानिबन्धनम्। तदह्नैव सान्द्रीभूतं परेऽहनि विजृम्भत इति मूलान्वयः। कथं विजृम्भत इति मातुरङ्गुष्ठसम्मितमायामि बुद्बुदाकारमिति योज्यम्। मातुर्भुक्तरसात्मवदिति। भुक्तमोदनादि। तस्य रसः सारः। स एव तस्यात्मा स्वरूपमुपचयकरत्वात् तद्युक्तमित्यर्थः ॥ ७४॥७५॥७६॥७७ ॥

मिलितादपीत्यत्र तस्मान्मलद्वयात्पूर्वं किट्टभूतं द्वयं पृथगेव समुन्नमेदित्यन्वयः। बीजयुग्ममिति वृषणफलद्वयमुक्तम् ॥ ७८ ॥

ऊर्ध्वं तु नुन्नमिति। किञ्चिदिति शेषः। नोदनं प्रेरणम्। तच्च सुषुम्नाख्या नाडी संवृत्ता भवेदिति पुनर्योज्यम्। वृत्तेति वृत्ताकारत्वं वोक्तम्। अग्नीषोमात्मिकेति। मूलादाग्रं चिदग्निशिखाया अग्राद्यामूलं सोमामृतधारायाश्च नित्यसद्भावादेवमुक्तम्। प्रकृतिपुरुषाद्यात्मिकी चेति। तत्र सोमाग्न्योः प्रकृतिपुरुषात्मकत्वम्। आदिशब्देन बिन्दुनादात्मिकीत्यादिग्रहणम्॥ ७९॥

नाड्योर्द्वयमिति सम्बन्धः॥ ८०॥८१॥

या वाममुष्कसम्बद्धेत्यादीडापिङ्गलयोर्गतिक्रमाभिधानं प्राणायामेऽनुसन्धानार्थम्। वाममुष्केतिच्छेद इति। यद्यवाममुष्केतिच्छेदस्तदा दक्षिणामित्येव पदमित्येतदपि सूचितम्। तद्वेडापक्षे दक्षिणवृत्ताख्यमांसप्राप्तिः। पिङ्गलापक्षे तु वामांसजत्रन्तरप्राप्तिरिति विशेषः। दक्षिणमुष्कोत्थेतिच्छेद इति। यद्यदक्षिणमुष्कोत्थेति छिद्यते तदा वामरन्ध्रगेत्येव पदं स्यात्। पूर्ववच्च विशेष इति॥ ८२॥८३॥

मूले याः प्रोक्ता इति सप्तान्या नाड्यो मता इत्येवमिति भावः। वामनेत्रजिह्वादक्षिणनेत्रं पायुर्दक्षिणवामश्रवणे प्रजननमित्यासामग्रमिति ज्ञेयम्। व्यापिकास्तनाविति। नेत्रादिगोलकपर्यन्ततया वृत्तेरिति भावः। विद्वद्भिरिति ता एवं प्रोक्ता इति शेषः। काचिन्नाडीति तस्य देहमात्रस्य नाभ्यग्रतया बहिर्मुखो नाडी भवति। त्वगिन्द्रियनाडीयं शङ्खिनो विश्वोदरी वा नामेति काचिदित्युक्तम्।

यया तत्पुष्टिमाप्नोतीति।

तदुक्तम्—मातुराहारवीर्येण षड्विधेन रसेन च।

नाभिस्तत्र निबद्धेन वर्धते स दिने दिने॥ इति।

मातुराहाररसजैरिति पोषणप्रकार उक्तः। मलधातुरसांशेषु धातुरुपचयकरोंऽशः। क्रमादिति कालक्रमो रसासृगादिक्रमश्च गृह्यते॥ ८४॥ ८५॥ ८६॥

परंज्योतिष्कलेति। या परदेवतायाः स्वाविद्याकल्पिता जीवचिन्मात्रलक्षणा कला चतुर्विंशत्तत्त्वसंयुक्तदेहवानित्युक्ता सा क्रमवृद्धे तस्मिन् हृदयायतनसम्पन्ने सति लब्धवृत्तितया कृत्स्नदेहाभिमानयोगित्वेन क्षेत्रज्ञसंज्ञां लभत इत्यर्थः।

सदोषदूष्यमिति। वातपित्तश्लेष्माणः त्रिदोषाः। त्वगसृगादिधातवो दूष्याणीति। न तत्सार्वत्रिकमिति। केषुचिद्देहेष्वनुपलम्भादाशङ्कोपपत्तिः + + शारीरार्थविचारका इति योगविदो भिषजो वोक्ताः॥ ८७॥८८॥८९॥९०॥

येन देहः प्रवर्त्यत इति। नानाविधचेष्टाभिप्रायम्॥ ९१॥

ज्ञानयोगक्रियानिष्ठानां हितायेति। ज्ञाननिष्ठानां तावद्देवतात्मैकतायामवस्थितस्वस्वरूपतस्त्वदायुर्मम निश्वास इत्युक्तरीत्या श्वासेन सकलजगद्द्वैतविकल्प-

लक्षणाहरुन्मेषमुच्छ्वासेन च तदुपरमलक्षणरात्रिनिमिषं चानुसन्दध्यादित्येतदितं भवति। योगनिष्ठानां तु श्वासोच्छ्वासयोरहोरात्रानुसन्धानं क्रियानिष्ठानां त्वहनि रात्रौ वारभणीयस्य कर्मणः श्वास उच्छ्वासे च प्रवर्तमान आरम्भः। एवमयनद्वय-मपि प्रतिपत्तव्यमिति। अपिशब्दोऽभ्युदयसमुच्चयार्थ इति। अत्र समीरणोऽपि समुदेतीत्यन्वयः। अग्निरिह चिदग्निः तस्य त्वस्तमयो द्वादशान्त इत्यवबोद्धव्यम्। बाह्योदयसमुच्चयार्थो वेति। अत्र मूलाधारेऽपीत्यन्वयः। बहिर्द्विषडङ्गुलेऽप्यु-देतीत्यपिशब्दार्थः। मूलाधारे समुदेतीति। ततो यथायोगमिडापिङ्गलाभ्यां गच्छन्नासिकाविवरेणाग्रतो बहिर्द्वादशाङ्गुलपरिमितोद्देशेऽस्तमेति पुनस्तत्रो-देति। ताभ्यामेवागच्छन् मूलाधारेऽस्तमेतीति तात्पर्यार्थः। इनः सूर्यः। इतर-रूपेणेतरेतरदिति। इन्दुरूपेणाधोऽपानवृत्तौ रात्रिरित्यर्थः। सूर्यस्य मूलाधार उदयो बहिर्द्विषडङ्गुलेऽस्तमयः। सोमस्य तु विपरीत इति भावः। चिदग्न्युदय-पक्षे षोडशान्तेऽमृतसोमोदयो मूलाधारेऽस्तमय इति ज्ञेयम्। मूले वामदक्षिण-नाडीभ्यामित्यपरपूर्वपक्षयोरप्युपलक्षणं द्रष्टव्यम् ॥ ८२ ॥ ८३ ॥

चेतनाधातुरिति + + विरोधार्थेनेति। अत्र बहुधा विदुरपीत्यन्वयः। यद्यपि स स तथा तथा वेद तथापि तदनुपपन्नमिति तदभिप्रायः। तदाह— न हीति। यच्चेतनाधातोरपीति वान्वयोऽभिप्रेतः। रेतःशोणितजमिति। ताम्बूल-पूगचूर्णानां योगाद्राग इवेति भावः। तद्द्वारेणेति। मातुरभ्यवहार्यमन्नमनु-प्राप्तस्तदभ्यवहारेण तदुदरगतः सन् तत्पाकजरसाविष्टः काचिन्नाडी बहिर्वक्ष्ये-त्युक्तरीत्या तद्रसेन सह तद्देहमात्रमाविशतीति भावः। केचित्कर्मफलं विदु-रित्यत्र प्रागनुष्ठितपुत्रीयकर्मफलत्वं त्वपत्योत्पत्तेः सर्वपक्षेषु समानमेवेत्यभि-प्रायेणाऽर्थान्तरं दर्शयति—अपत्यार्थिनामिति। यथोक्तेति वैद्यशास्त्रग्रहणम्। आहारोऽभ्यवहारः। विहारोऽभ्यञ्जनस्नानासनादिः। श्रद्धाऽपत्यवाञ्छा। आदि-शब्देनाभिमताकारपुत्रचिन्तादिकमुक्तम्। तदतिशये च तदीयदेहमाविश्य तद्देहमात्रमाविशतीत्यर्थः। परंधाम्नो व्याप्तिमिति। प्राक्तनकर्मणः परदेवतातत्त्वे पूर्वतयावस्थितस्य विपाकसमये तदुचितदेशसंभविनि मातृगर्भे तत्कर्मवशात् तत्कर्मफलोपभोक्तृतयांशावच्छेदावेशसंभव इति भावः। व्याप्तिमिति। तस्य व्याप्तत्वाद्यत्र यत्रोपभोग उचितस्तत्र तत्रांशावेशः स्यादिति सूचितम्। यद्वा व्याप्तिमात्रमेतदिति।

तात्पर्यान्तरमाह—सर्वगस्येति। निसर्गतः स्वगतानां मनोबुद्धीन्द्रियादि-शक्तीनामभिव्यक्तौ तत्कारणस्तन्निमित्तकोऽशावच्छेदसंभव इत्यर्थः। कश्चित्

कर्मप्रकारश्च इत्यत्र दीपाद्दीपान्तरं यथेति दृष्टान्ते समस्तं दार्ष्टान्तिकं प्रतिबिम्बितमित्यभिप्रायेणाह—दीपादिति। कश्चिदेवं ब्रूत इत्येवंशब्देन कृत्स्नो मूलवाक्यार्थो गृह्यते। अत्र पितुरिति दीपस्थानीयमुक्तम्। तत्परं धामेति च दीपान्तरस्थानीयम्। तदर्थमाह—तस्य पितुरात्मेति। आत्मान्तरभूतः सन्निति भावः। सौजस्कमिति चाज्यस्थानीयम्। मारुतेन त्विति दीपयितृस्थानीयमुक्तम्। तदा दीपस्य संक्रमसमुचितो यः संक्षोभस्तत्स्थानीयं देहात्मनेत्यादिनोक्तम्। शुक्लधातुत इति तु वर्तिस्थानीयमिति विभागः। शुक्लधातुत इति शुक्लधातुद्वारेण संक्रान्तमित्यर्थः। देहात्मना सक्तसम्बध्य मदनोद्रेकविलीनादिति संप्रयोगसमये पितुरेव देहाभिमानिजीवचैतन्येन संबध्य शुक्लधातोर्विलयः सक्तज्ञावातिशयप्राप्तिसमये संभवति। स च विलयो मैथुनव्यापारसिद्धमथनप्रकर्षतो भवत्यतीर्थः। + + अस्मिन् पक्षे जीवस्य नित्यत्वमनित्यत्वं वा स्यादिति ॥८४॥८५॥८६॥८७॥

कश्चित्त्वित्यत्र भौतिकव्याप्ते वपुषीति गर्भाशयगतं देहमात्रमुक्तम्। भौतिकग्रहणेन मनोबुद्ध्यादीनामिन्द्रियाणाञ्च भूतविकृतितया तदभ्युपगमः सूचितः। कुतश्चिदेत्येति यत्र कुत्र प्राक्तनं कर्मफलमुपभोगतः क्षयं नीतं तत एत्येत्यर्थः। अभिप्रायान्तरमाह—अनिमित्तमेवेति। न कुतश्चिदप्यागत्य अपि तु तत्रैव सहसाभिव्यज्येति भावः। जन्मकाल इति प्रसवसमय एव न निषेकादिसमयेष्वित्यर्थः॥ ८८

बहुना किमिति मतान्तरमप्येवंजातीयकं बहु वक्तुं शक्यते तेन किं स्यात् फलमित्यर्थः। परं पुंसः सान्निध्यात् प्रविजृम्भिता प्रकृतिरेवमापञ्चत्वात् प्रवर्तत इति संबन्धः। चैतन्याभासोदय इति। चैतन्याभासस्य जीवचिल्लक्षणस्य परंज्योतिष्कलेति प्रागुक्तस्य प्राक्तनदेहापायसमये तस्मिन्नेव परपुंस्यभिन्नतया स्थितस्योदयो मायातच्छक्तितद्गतप्राणिकर्मविषयभेदेनेत्युक्तरीत्याभिव्यक्तिः। पञ्चत्वं कर्मफलोपभोगावसाने देहक्षयो मरणम्। अयं भावः—नात्र गर्भदेहे तदात्मनः प्रवेशः अपि तु स्वोपाधिना प्रकृतिविकृतिलक्षणेन सह पितृशुक्लादिसंपृक्ततया गर्भाशयप्राप्तिः। तस्य चोपाधेरामरणावस्थं प्रवृत्तिरिति।

यद्वा चैतन्याभासस्योदयोऽनादिसिद्ध एव विवक्षितः। ततः प्रकृतेः प्रवृत्तिरपि नित्यैव। सा चाकैवल्यात् भवतीति। यद्वक्ष्यति—आमोक्षादित्यर्थ इति। अत्र प्रकृतेः स्वाधिकारोपरमपर्यन्तमित्थं तत्तज्जवरूपेण पर्यायशो विजृम्भणमित्येव न तु निष्पद्यमाने देहे तदात्मप्रवेशो नामेत्याशयः। गुणभिन्नेत्ते तद्विकृणोति गुणसाम्यावस्थात इति। जीवात्मनः प्राक्तनदेहक्षये प्रकृतेस्तदुपार्जितकर्मापूर्वेण सह गुणसाम्यदशायां स्थितिरित्यर्थादुक्तम्। इत्यादिनेति। पञ्चत्वादौ प्रवर्तत इत्यन्तेनेति

भावः। उक्तसंक्षेप इति। 'कालेन भिद्यमानस्तु' 'देवाः सम्प्रुतयः' 'शब्दादिग्राम' 'सदोषदूष्यमित्यादिविस्तरोक्तानां संक्षेपेणाभिधानमित्यर्थः। महत्त्वं शरीरावस्थाया-मिति। तत्तद्भवेषु पर्यायशो महत्त्वं प्राप्तेत्यर्थः। अनेन भावावसाने सङ्कोचोऽ-प्यर्थात्प्रतिपादितः। पञ्चभिर्भौतिकैश्च गुणैः युक्तेत्यन्वयः। शब्दस्पर्शादयश्च गुणाः। पञ्चेन्द्रियार्थगेत्येतद्विवृणोति पञ्चकर्मेन्द्रियार्थरूपेणेति। बुद्धीन्द्रियार्थानां पञ्चभिश्च गुणैरित्युक्तत्वादेवं विवृतिः। पञ्चबुद्धिप्रभाविनीत्येतद्विवृणोति श्रोत्रादिजन्येति। श्रुतिस्पृश्यादिबुद्धय इहोक्ताः। बाह्यं प्रविजृम्भणमेवमुक्तम् ॥ ९९॥१००॥१०१ ॥

अथाभ्यन्तरमारभते—सैवेति। समनुप्रोपसर्गाणामिति। समनुप्रबद्धेत्यत्र सम्बद्धश्चिद्रूपस्य प्रकृत्या सह साक्षितया सम्बन्धः। अनुबन्धः कारणतया सम्बन्धः। प्रबन्धोऽन्तर्यामितया सम्बन्धः। एतत्त्रयं चाविशेषात् परपुंसः सान्निध्यात् प्रवि-जृम्भितेत्यत्रापि समानमेवेति ज्ञेयम्। यदा तु सङ्कल्पविकल्पकृत्या तदा सा मन इत्यन्वयः। मनसो वृत्तिरिह सङ्कल्पविकल्पेत्युक्ता।

यदा पुनर्निश्चिनुते तदा बुद्धिसंज्ञा च स्यादिति निश्चयज्ञानं बुद्धेः वृत्तिरिति चोक्तम्। यद्यपि महानेव बुद्धिरपि तथापि तदध्यक्षभेदाद्वृत्तिभेदः। यत उक्तं—सर्वजगदाश्रयभूत ईक्षणादिशब्दार्थ इति।

यदा ज्ञातारमात्मानं प्रवेत्ति तदाऽहंकृतिः स्यादित्यन्वयः। नेदं साक्षितया ज्ञातुर्वेदनमित्याह—अहमेवेति। अत्रापि प्रागुक्ताहङ्काराद्वृत्तिभेदः। यदुक्तम्—ईक्षितुस्तदभिमानोऽहङ्कार इति।

यदा सा त्वन्तरभिलीयते तदा चित्तं चेति सोपस्कारमन्वयः। अन्तरित्ये-तदभिप्रायमाह—साक्षिणीत्यर्थ इति। सर्ववृत्तिनिरोधावस्थचित्तमिति भावः। यदुक्तं—योगश्चित्तवृत्तिनिरोधः। तदा द्रष्टुः स्वरूपेऽवस्थानमिति। शरीरान्तं परिणामकदम्बमिति। कदम्बशब्दः समूहवचनः। सचराचरात्मनि चेति। सर्वशरीरोत्पत्तिः। तत्र स्थावरादिशरीरभेदः प्रकृतौ कालनुन्नायामित्या-दिनोक्त इति विवेकः। संग्रहेणेति। विस्तारवचनस्याशक्यत्वाल्लोकादीनां च विस्तारत्वादिति भावः। पूर्वोक्तस्य शब्दब्रह्मण इति। शब्दब्रह्मेति यत्प्रोक्तमित्यत्र यत्प्रतिज्ञातं तदिति भावः। संक्षेपेणेति। द्वितीयपटले विस्तारावसर इति भावः।

मूले निर्धारितमर्थमित्यत्र यदैषा निर्धारितमर्थं स्वयं करणैर्व्यञ्जयितुं यततेत्य-न्वयः। निर्धारितं बुद्ध्या निश्चितम् समीक्षितमर्थम्। यदुक्तम्—आत्मा बुद्ध्या समीक्ष्यार्थान्मनो युङ्क्ते विवक्षयेति। प्रयत्नविशेषैरिति। स्पृष्टत्वमीषत्स्पृष्टत्वं बाह्यौ विवारसंवारावित्येवमादयो गृह्यन्ते। इतरैरेत्यन्तःकरणानां ग्रहणम्। यदुक्तं—

सङ्कल्पविकल्पनिश्चयविमर्शनात्मनाविर्भवतीति। मूले महीयसीत्यस्य महत्त्वं प्राप्ता शरीरावस्थायामित्येवार्थः। तत्कालविशेषणं चैतत्। बिन्दुस्फुटनोद्भवस्येति। स्फुटनं भेदनम्। यदुक्तं—बिन्दोस्तस्मादित्यादि। एव इह परा वागेव। पश्यन्त्यादिक्रमेणेत्युक्तत्वादिह यतेतेत्येतद्यतनं वागिन्द्रियावस्थायास्तस्या व्यापारः। एवस्तु तस्या मनोबुद्ध्यादिवदवस्थान्तरमिति। सा यतेत एवस्य प्रविजृम्भितमिति भेदाभिधानम्। वैखरीपर्यन्त इति। पश्चाशद्वर्णपर्यन्तत्वमुक्तम् ॥१०२॥१०३॥१०४॥

इति प्रयोगक्रमदीपिकायां प्रथमः पटलः।

श्रीरस्तु। अथ द्वितीयः पटलः।

पटलसङ्गतिमाह—उक्तमपीति। सविशेषमिति। वक्ष्यति च—जन्तुः षडङ्गी पूर्वं स्यात्। प्रयात्यूर्ध्वं यदा प्राण इत्यादि। वैराग्यार्थमिति। यतो वक्ष्यति—प्रसूतिसमये सोऽथेत्यादि। द्वितीयपटलारम्भ इत्यनेनाथ व्यवस्थिते त्वित्यथशब्दार्थोऽप्युक्तः। सोपस्कारं विवृणोति—एवमिति। क्षेत्रज्ञप्रवेशे व्यवस्थित इति। शुक्लस्य प्रकृतिविकारात्मकत्वात् तत्सन्निहितस्य क्षेत्रज्ञस्य तत्र प्रवेशोऽपि नैसर्गिक एवेति तावत् गतपटले स्वसिद्धान्ततया व्यवस्थापितम्। तथैव च सति स्वगतैर्मरुदग्न्युक्तिरिति तदीयतत्त्वान्तर्गतवाय्वादिसंभवात् तस्य गर्भस्याधानत एव प्रभृति वर्धनोपपत्तिरिति भावः। केषांचिदवयवानां मासेनाभिव्यक्तिः केषांचित्पक्षेणेत्याद्यभिप्रायेण मूले मासपक्षाद्युपादानम्। यद्वा त्रसरेण्वादिपरिमितिसूक्ष्मांशोपचयप्रतिपादनार्थं क्षणाद्युपादानम् ॥ १ ॥

मूले जन्तुः षड़ङ्गी पूर्वं स्यादिति पूर्वपटलोक्तचतुरस्रदशायामेतदिति ज्ञेयम्। अन्तराधिश्रेति मध्यप्रदेशः। पुनः षड़ङ्गेष्वित्याद्युरःकक्षस्तनाद्यं चेत्यन्तं वाक्यम्। मुखाद्यङ्गेष्वक्षिनासादिप्रत्यङ्गजातप्रवृत्तिकथनमेतत् ॥ २ ॥

ततः सर्वाङ्गवान् विभुरिति वाक्यान्तरम्। कालेनेति यदि तस्मिन् वातादिदोषा अनुगुणाः स्युः ततः कतिपयेन कालेनासौ गर्भो यथोक्तलक्षणो जन्तुर्भवति। यदुक्तम्—मासेन तु शिरो द्वाभ्यां बाह्वङ्घ्र्याद्यङ्गविग्रह इत्यादि। तदनुगुणतायां तत्रैव क्षेत्रज्ञच्युतेरजन्तुत्वं पूयभावो गर्भस्रंसनं वा स्यादिति भावः ॥ ३ ॥ ४ ॥

प्रसूतिसमये स जनित्रीं मुहुः क्लेशयेदिति। प्रसववेदनोत्पादनमुक्तम्। संवृतास्यसुषुम्नाख्य इति मोक्षमेव किलेच्छतीत्युपरि सम्बन्धः। संवृतास्या सुषुम्नाख्या नाडी यत्रेति समासः। सुषुम्नाया मुखं द्वादशान्ते मूलाधारे च। तदुक्तम्—अवाङ्मुखत्वमप्यस्तीति। तेन निरतिशयक्लेशगतस्यापि स्वस्वरूपा-

नवभासोपपत्तिरिति सूचितम्। यद्वा प्राणापानयोस्तस्यां स्वेच्छाचारनिरोधतस्तदा प्रक्षुभितैरिति प्राणादिक्षोभोपपत्तिरिति। अवाङ्मुख इति। प्रसवानुकूलतयाऽवस्थितिरुक्ता। गर्भाशये + + + स्थितिरिति। अनिलचोदित इति। प्रसूतिवायुप्रेरणयावाङ्मुखताद्युपपत्तिरिति भावः। तस्या ग्रहण्यामिति।

वक्ष्यति च—तत्क्षोयमानं विश्राम ग्रहणीं पूरयेन्मुहुः। इति। शकृत् तद्गतं पुरीषम्। पुरा कृतानां पापानामित्यनुभूतदुःखाद्युपलक्षणम्।

तस्याः कायाग्निना दग्ध इति। यथा लोहपात्रे सोदके क्षिप्तोऽग्निना पच्यते तद्वदिति भावः। क्लेदैः क्लिन्नाङ्गबन्धन इति। क्लेदो गर्भोदकमिति विवरणम्। प्रत्युद्गारपरीतश्चेति। दुःसहदुर्गन्धिनाधस्त्योद्गारेण परीतविग्रहः। तत्रायुद्गारगोचर इति प्रत्युद्गारसंभवकथनम्। यद्वैतदप्यपरं वैराग्यनिमित्तमुक्तम् ॥ ५ ॥ ६ ॥ ७ ॥

तदा प्रक्षुभितैरिति। प्रक्षोभवशाद्दशधा गतिरित्येव बोद्धव्यम्। संपिण्डितशरीरस्त्विति। संपिण्डन + + मोक्षमेव किलेच्छतीति। स्मृत्युत्पत्तिस्तावदयुतं संस्मरन्नित्युक्ता। तथा च मोक्षेऽपि स्मृतिसंभवः। यद्यपि सप्तमे मासि स्मृत्युत्पत्तिः।

यदुक्तम्—कललघनावयवास्थित्वग्लोमस्मृतिसमुद्भवाः क्रमशः।

मासेष्वशनोद्वेगप्रसवा गर्भगस्य स्युः॥ इति।

किन्तु तस्या बाह्यवायुपर्यन्तमनुवृत्तिरिति। इदानीं तद्वचनं स्वावस्थाचिन्तयोद्वेगेऽपि समानमेतत्। परोक्षत्वादिति। गर्भावस्थानामिति शेषः। इदानीमिति। प्रजातप्रवृद्धस्याधिकारावस्थायामिति भावः। मोक्षग्रहणं तत्साधनजातोपलक्षणम् ॥ ८ ॥

मूले परस्परमिति प्राणेनापानस्तेन च प्राण इत्यर्थः। समानव्यानयोरपि मिथःसम्बन्धोपलक्षणमेतत् ॥ ९ ॥

प्रयात्यूर्ध्वमिति प्राणापानप्रतिबन्धाभिधानम्। मूलाधारादूर्ध्वं प्रयान्तं प्राणं बहिर्द्विषडङ्गुलेऽपानः प्रतिबध्नाति तं च ततोऽधः प्रयान्तं मूलाधारे प्राणश्च प्रतिबध्नातीति भावः। यदा समान इति समानव्यानसम्बन्धाभिधानम्। कायाग्निर्जाठराग्निः। यद्वक्ष्यति—अधस्तस्याः प्रधानाग्निरित्यादि। सन्धुक्षणं समिन्धनम्। पाचितुमिति। स्वाशयागतमभ्यवहृतं पक्तुमित्यर्थः। वक्ष्यति च—तत्रान्नान्तरसंश्लिष्टं पच्यते पित्तवारिणेति। तत्पक्वमुक्तं त्विति। पूर्वं पक्वं ततो विमुक्तमित्यर्थः। रसमिति। मलांशतो विविक्तः सारांशो धात्वभिधो विवक्षितः। वक्ष्यति च—पच्यमानाद्रसं भिन्नं वायू रक्तादितां नयेदिति। व्यानो रसमादाय तं देहमापादतलमस्तकं धावतीत्यन्वयः। अयमनयोर्मिथः सम्बन्धः ॥ १० ॥ ११ ॥

प्राणसहग इति प्राणोदानयोर्मिथः सम्बन्ध उक्तः। प्राणसहगत्वान्नागादिचतुर्णामपि प्रतिपत्तव्यम्। प्राणेनानुग्रहस्य सर्वेष्वप्यविशेषादिति। मृतं च न विमुञ्चतीति। तदा सशरीरे श्वयथुः शक्तलच्यत इति भावः॥ १२॥ १३॥ १४॥

वह्नयश्च दशान्ये स्युरिति। प्रागुक्तजाठराग्नेरन्ये तदीयकलात्मका इत्यर्थः। तेषामन्वर्थनामानि वदन् प्राणादिव्यापारवत्तद्व्यापारानपि दर्शयति—भ्राजकेति। त्वग्गतोऽग्निर्भ्राजकः सशरीरस्य भ्राजिष्णुतां दीप्तिमावहति। तस्य सम्भुक्षणमपि समान एव स्वांशेन करोति। एवमुत्तरेष्वपि द्रष्टव्यम्। स्वेदक्लेदात्वगाश्च त इति। त्रिदोषगता एवेति भावः। तदुपपत्तिं दर्शयति—पित्तश्लेष्मेति। वक्ष्यति च—यदा पित्तं मरुन्नुन्नमित्यादि। किञ्च प्राणादीनामानुगुण्याभावे तन्मन्त्रजपादिभिस्तदानुगुण्यं साधनीयम्। एवमेषामग्नीनामपीत्यभिप्रायेण चैषामुभयेषां नामोक्तिरिति ज्ञेयम्। किञ्च गुणितयोगी स्यादेषामुभयेषामुपयोगः। यद्वक्ष्यति च + + सा यदा पञ्चगुणितेत्यादि। तथा—दशधा गुणितानां धीर्मर्मांशादिविभेदिनीति। मूले त्रिदोषगा इत्यत्र दोषदूष्यादिजिज्ञासायां त्वगसृगित्याद्यारम्भः। कफपित्तैराश्लेषपित्तवाताः। तत्प्रेरको मरुदिति। दोषाणां दूष्येषु प्रवर्तकः संयोजकः प्राण इत्यर्थः॥ १५॥ १६॥

मरुत इति। यदि प्राणो वातादिदोषैस्त्वगादिधातून् दूषयति धातुसङ्घात एव शरीरं तदवस्थानमेव जीवनम् तथा च तेन प्राणव्यापारेण जीवनमेव दूषितं स्यात्। ततः केवलदुःखेन भवितव्यम्। न चैवं लक्ष्यत इत्याशङ्कोपपत्तिः। समं वयत इति। वयनं सन्तननं संयोजनं दोषाणां दूष्येषु सङ्ख्यापनम्। समत्वं च यथा तेषामानुगुण्यमेव स्यात् तथा व्यापृतिरिति। विश्वात्मेति। विश्वस्येह कृत्स्नस्य शरीरस्य तदन्तर्गतानां च दोषधात्वादीनामात्मस्थानीयः। तस्य शरीरस्थानीयमेव तद्विश्वमतोऽसौ सममेव तस्मिन् वर्ततेति भावः। विश्वग इति। तस्मिन् विश्वपदार्थे व्यापितयावस्थितोऽसौ तस्यात्मस्थानीयः। विश्वकर्मकृदिति। तत्र विश्वपदार्थे यत् किञ्चित्कर्म संभाव्यते तदशेषमसावेव करोति। यदुक्तम्—ईरणः स्याच्चलनपर इति। अतोऽप्यसौ तस्यात्मस्थानीय इति भावः। विषमवयनादिति। कदाचिदाहारविहारादिदोषवशान्न्यूनाधिकतया विषमं वयनं स्यादिति भावः। स दोषो वेति। स प्राणो दोषो वा न्यूनाधिकभावेन धातूनां दूषकत्वात्प्राणोऽपि त्रिदोषेष्वन्तर्भूतः सन् दोषो भवति। स दूष्यो वेति। स एव प्राणो दूष्यो वा धातुषु व्याप्तोऽसौ पित्तश्लेष्मभ्यां दूष्यो भवतीति भावः। क्रियातः संप्रधार्यत इति। क्रिया सहसोत्पद्यमाना पतनसंन्यासादिलक्षणा सन्निपातादिव्याधीनां

विषमवयनसंभविनां कार्यम्। ततस्तदवगतिरिति भावः॥ १७॥

वायुप्रसङ्गेनेति। वायुस्तत्प्रेरको मरुदित्युक्तः। तदुक्तिरेव तत्प्रसङ्गः। ततश्च तद्धर्मकथनस्य तावदयमवसरः। ततश्च तत्सहचारिणां बुद्धिदेहधर्माणां कथनस्याप्ययमेवावसर इति भावः। बुभुक्षापिपासे प्राणस्य शोकमोहौ बुद्धेः जरामृती देहस्येति विभागः। धर्मेष्विति। सन्त्येषां भूयांसो धर्मास्तेष्वन्यतमतयेति। तदाह—धर्मत्वेनेति॥ १८॥

ऊर्मिप्रसङ्गेनेति। क्ले(को)शा ऊर्मिसहचारिण इति कोशकथनोपपत्तिः। षाट्कौशिकमिति षड्भिः कोशैः सम्पन्नः॥ १९॥

धातुगत्वेनेति। प्रकृतिशेष एवायमिति भावः। वक्ष्यश्च दशान्ये स्युरित्यादि धातुगत्वेन तद्वचनं प्रयोजनमिति कार्यं फलमिति यावत्। ततश्च मूले पाक इति तैरग्निभिरिति लभ्यते। रसादित इत्यस्यायमर्थः। कृत्स्नादभ्यवहृताज्जाठराग्निना रसपाकस्तावद्भवति। तत्प्रागुक्तं—यदा समानः कायाग्निमित्यादि। ततस्तस्माद्रसाच्छरीरव्याप्तात्प्रभृति भ्राजकाद्यग्निभिः क्रमेण पाको भवति। कुत्र वा केषां वायं क्रमेण पाक इत्यतः शुक्लान्तेषु धातुष्वित्युक्तम्। रसादिशुक्लान्तेषु धातुषु क्रमात्पाकः रसादीनां शुक्लान्तानां च सारांशानां क्रमात्पाक इति रसधातौ तावद्रसपाकादसृग्धातूत्पत्तिस्तत्र तत्पाकान्मांसधातूत्पत्तिरित्यादि द्रष्टव्यम्। शुक्लपाकस्तावदिहोक्तस्तस्मात् किमुत्पद्यत इत्यत उक्तं शुक्लपाकादिति। स्वयमित्योजसो विशेषणम्। तदभिप्रायमाह—प्रधानमित्यर्थ इति। भिद्येदिति भिद्येतेत्यर्थः। अष्टमी दशेति। नासौ धातुः किन्तु महत्कार्यमित्येवेति भावः॥ २०॥

मूले चैतन्यकृमिकथनानन्तरं चैतन्यकृमिकथनाय चैतन्यस्य तदोजस्त्वित्ययमारम्भः। केवलाश्रयमिति। चैतन्यस्यैवाश्रय ओजस्तद्विशिष्टस्याश्रयः शुक्लान्तधातुसंघातो देह इति भावः। तत्र दृष्टान्तद्वयं यथा स्नेह इत्याद्युच्यते। यथा प्रदीपस्याज्यतैलादि स्थितिकारणमाश्रयः। यथा वा विद्युतो मेघस्फुरणकारणमाश्रयस्तद्वत् चैतन्यस्य तदोजः स्थितिस्फुरणकारणतया केवलाश्रयभूतं भवतीत्यभिप्रायः। समीपालोकशक्तिमदिति। सन्निहितपदार्थप्रकाशनसमर्थमित्यर्थः। महाल्विष इति प्रथमा महत्यः प्रभा इत्यर्थः। अत्र प्रभा ज्ञानकलास्तासां महत्त्वं बुद्ध्याद्युपबृंहितत्वादभिप्रेतम्। स्वं स्वमर्थं ग्रहं प्रतीति शब्दस्पर्शादयः श्रोत्रादीन्द्रियाणामर्थाः॥ २१॥ २२॥ २३॥

नभः श्रोत्र इति श्रोत्रेन्द्रिये स्वांशेन स्थित आकाशः। यदुक्तं—तैजसवैकारिकाहङ्कारयोर्भूतानुगतयोरिति। यद्वा विषयसप्तमीयम्। श्रोत्रेन्द्रियविषय-

तयाकाशस्थित इति। अर्थंप्रवर्तनं स्वे स्वेऽर्थे श्रोत्रादीनां प्रवृत्तिः ॥ २४ ॥

कार्यंतः संप्रधार्यंत इत्युक्तमिति। स दोषो वा स दूष्यो वा क्रियातः संप्रधार्यंते इत्यत्रेति भावः। तदाहेति। तत्र दिङ्मात्रमेतदिति बोद्धव्यम्। यदा पित्त-मित्यस्यायमर्थः। कदाचित् पित्तं वायुना नोदितं विलीनं द्रवीभावं प्राप्तं स्यात्। तदा च तत्तथाविधं पित्तं धातून् प्रविलापयेत्। प्रविलापं व्यापनम् यद्वा द्रवणम्। तदा च स रक्तधातुर्लसीकां चणाद्द्रावयति। लसीका रक्तत्वचोरन्तरालस्थितोऽर्थ-विशेषः। सा द्रुता रोमरन्ध्रैर्बहिः सर्वत्र कणशः प्रवर्तते। तदा देहे स्वेदो लक्ष्यत इति। स्वेदः प्रतीयत इत्यनेनैतावदेव विज्ञ इति दर्शितम् ॥ २५॥२६ ॥

यदा कफ इत्यस्यायमर्थः। कदाचिच्छ्लेष्मा वायुना पित्तेन च प्रेरितः सन् विलीनो द्रवीभावं प्राप्तः सन्नूर्ध्वं प्रवर्तते तदा स + + वाष्पमश्रु नेत्रजलं प्रसेकं लालामास्यजलं च प्रवर्तयेदिति ॥ २७ ॥

कफात्मिकास्त्वित्यस्यायमर्थः। श्लेष्मदोषविकृतिः कर्णशष्कुलीपूर्वकान् गण्ड-मालादिकान् वापि व्याधीन् कुर्यादिति। कर्णशष्कुलिः कर्णपिटकः। पूर्वशब्देन + +। गण्डमाला गलगण्डः। आदिशब्देन + +। कर्मजानिति पूर्वार्जित-कर्मफलभूतानित्यर्थः ॥ २८ ॥

ग्रहणी नामेति। या ग्रहणी नामोक्ता सा प्रसृताञ्जलिसन्निभा पात्री भवति। तस्याः स्थानं तु तत्र किट्टं पृथ(अस्थ)ग्भिन्नमित्यत्रावगम्यं भविष्यति। यदा समानः कायाग्निमित्युक्तयोरग्निसमानयोः स्थानमधस्तस्या इत्युच्यते। प्रधानाग्निरिति। यस्य कला धातुषु त्रिदोषेषु चोक्ताः स प्रधानभूतोऽग्निः। को नामासावित्याह—प्रधानाग्निर्जाठर इति ॥ २९ ॥

ततः सर्वाङ्गवान् विभुरित्यत्रोक्तस्य चेतज्ञस्य स्थानं तस्याधस्तादित्युच्यते। तत्र सङ्गत्यन्तरमाह—तत्कारणमाहेति। जाठराग्नेः कारणं चिदग्निः। यद्वा तैजसो ज्ञानक्रियाशक्तिमयोऽग्निः प्राणलक्षणस्तस्य विकृतिमात्रं जाठरोऽग्निः। प्राणस्य तैजसकारणं च प्राज्ञः स एव चिदग्निरिति। त्रिकोणाभमिति तप्तहाटकप्रख्यातो-पलक्षणम्। ज्योतिराधारमिति चेतज्ञस्वरूपलक्षणस्य ज्योतिषः स्थानमित्यर्थः। सन्त्यन्यान्यपि स्थानानि तेष्वेतत्प्रकृष्टमित्युत्तममित्युक्तम्। मूलाधारं विदुरिति। यदाचक्षते—गुदात्तु द्व्यङ्गुलादूर्ध्वं मेढ्रात्तु द्व्यङ्गुलादधः। इत्यादि ॥ ३० ॥

अथ 'मातुर्भुक्तरसात्मवत्' 'यदा समानः कायाग्निं सन्धुक्षयति' 'तस्या ग्रहण्यां प्रकृतीत्याद्युक्तं सर्वमवबोधयितुमथाह्वतमित्याद्यारम्भः। तत्र फलान्तरं दर्शयति —दोषत्रयमिति। आहारोऽभ्यवहारः। षड्रसमपि मधुरीभवेदित्यन्वयः।

श्लेष्मणानुगतमिति स्वाश्रयगतेनेति शेषः। नाभेरधस्तादापादतलं वाताश्रयः। हृदयादधस्तादानाभि पित्ताशयः। हृदयादूर्ध्वं मूर्धान्तं श्लेष्माशय इति विभागः। तस्य प्रभावादिति पवनप्रेरितस्य तस्य श्लेष्मण इत्यर्थः॥ ३१॥

तत्र स्वाद्विति। स्वादुर्मधुरः। भूतविकृत्येति तत्तद्द्रव्येषु कारणतयानुगतभूत-विक्रियानुसारिणीत्यर्थः। यस्य भूतस्य विक्रियया यो रसस्तं तथा दर्शयति—अबाधिक्य इत्यादिना। द्रव्याणां पाञ्चभौतिकत्वादन्यतमाधिक्येनैव रसभेदोप-पत्तिरिति सर्वत्राधिक्यग्रहणम्। मतान्तरमाह—क्ष्माम्भ इति। 'द्वयोस्त्रयोः क्रमोद्भूतैर्मधुरादिरसोद्भवः' इति तत्पद्यस्योत्तरार्धं भवति॥ ३२॥

तथैवामाशयगतमिति। तथैवेति श्लेष्मणानुगतं तस्य प्रभावान्मधुरीभवेदित्यर्थः। तदा तस्यानुगमनादिति। वायुप्रेरितस्य पित्तस्यानुगमनादित्यर्थः॥ ३३॥

तत्रान्त्रान्तरसंश्लिष्टं पच्यते पित्तवारिणेति। अस्यायमर्थः—तत्र पित्ताशयेऽस्यान्त्रं नामोदर्योऽवयवः। तस्यान्तरं तदाहृतमन्नं प्राप्नोति। तदा तत्र संश्लिष्टं तत् स्वास्पदगतेन पित्तजलेन पाकं प्राप्नोतीति पित्तस्य द्रवद्रव्यत्व-मप्यर्थादुक्तम्। ननु—यदा समानः कायाग्निमधस्तस्याः प्रधानाग्निमित्यादि यदुक्तं तस्य कथमिह संभव इति। उच्यते। तण्डुलपाकवदेतदुपपत्तिः। जाठराग्नि-स्तावत् स्वाश्रयभाजा समानेन सन्धुक्ष्यमाणः पित्तोदकक्लिन्नं तदन्नं पचति। पित्तस्य चाग्नेयत्वात्तेनापि पित्तेन कश्चित् पाकविशेषः स्यात्। तदभिप्रायेणैव च त्रयस्त्रिदोषगाः प्रोक्ता इत्युक्तमिति। पच्यमानादिति। पाकसमये स व्यानो रसांशं ततो विविच्य देहं समन्ततो व्यापयति। यदुक्तं—तदा तत्पक्वमुक्तं त्वित्यादि। ततश्च स रसधातुः स्वास्पदगवाय्वग्निव्यापारतः क्रमेणासृगादिधातुतां भजते। यदप्युक्तं—रसादितः क्रमात्पाक इति॥ ३४॥

तत्र किट्टमिति। रसकिट्टविभागसमये किट्टं रसतः पृथग्भिन्नं संग्रहण्यां नाम पात्र्यां वायुः सञ्चिनुत इति। विष्ठामिति पुरीषतया प्रसिद्धमित्यर्थः॥ ३५॥

सा तथेति। पायुमार्गेणेत्यन्तं वाक्यम्। तयेति विष्ठा। तदेवाह—शकृतेति। बलन + + तत्रैवमवान्तरमाह—तत्पाक इति। तस्याहृतस्य पाकसमय एव तस्य स्वच्छजलरूपेण च कणशो मलं भिद्यते। तदा तैर्जलकणैस्तत्रत्यासु सूक्ष्मसिरास्वाविश्य तन्मुखतो निर्गतैर्वस्तिं नाम पात्रं वायुरापूरयेत्। तदा च स वस्तिस्तया पूर्णः संस्तज्जलं धारारूपेण विसृजतीत्यर्थः।

अङ्गस्वेदवदभ्यन्तर्व्याप्तैरिति कणविशेषणम्। यथाङ्गेषु स्वेदकणा व्याप्ता भवन्ति। यदुक्तं—रोमकूपैः प्रवर्तन्ते बहिः सर्वत्र कणश इति। तथैव कणा

देहाभ्यन्तरभागे व्याप्ता भवन्तीति भावः। वस्तेर्मेहननिर्गतमिति। वस्तेरिति पञ्चमी। मेहनं लिङ्गं भगो वा। वस्तेः सकाशान्मेहनद्वारेण पायुद्वारेण पुरीषमिव निर्गतमित्यर्थः॥ ३६॥ ३७॥ ३८॥

इहापि पायोर्धातुवद्विषमवयनसंभव इत्याह—अपथ्यभाजामिति। अनयोर्मार्गयोरिति। मूत्रमार्गे पुरीषमार्गे च। दोषदुष्टयोरिति। त्रिदोषैर्वायुवशाद्दूषितयोरित्यर्थः। इह प्राक्—तदा प्रक्षुभितैः स्वीयवायुभिरिति तावदासन्नप्रसवावस्था प्रकृता। तत्र प्रसङ्गाद्द्वयोर्दशधा गतस्य व्यापारकथनं तत्प्रसङ्गादन्न्यादीयत्पर्यन्तकथनमिति॥ ३९॥

इदानीं तत्प्रकृतावस्थाशेषं वक्तुमित्थंभूतः स जन्तुस्त्वित्यारम्भः। इत्थंभूत इति। दशधा गतैर्वायुभिः संपिण्डितशरीरावस्थ इति भावः। यद्वादिकर्मणीयं निष्ठा। एवं भवितुं प्रवृत्त इति गर्भेऽन्तरवस्था तावदस्यावसिता। वायुभिर्दशधा गतैरित्ययं बहिरवस्थाया आरम्भो बहिरवस्था चेयं विस्तारेणोक्तेत्येवमभिधानमुपपद्यत इति। जरायुच्छन्नगात्रवानिति। शुक्लशोणितमयेऽतोऽन्तर्भागः शरीरतया प्रवर्तते। बहिर्भागस्तु त्वगाकारेण व्यावर्तते। स जरायुः भवति। यदुक्तं—षड्भिर्जरायुणा वीत इति। अपत्यवर्त्म सङ्गम्येति। प्रजननमार्गमित्यर्थः। यद्वा प्रजननप्रधानं जननमरणावस्थाबहुलं संसारमार्गं प्राप्तः खल्वसौ भवतीति भावः। सज्यत इति। प्रेर्यते पीड्यत इति वार्थः॥ ४०॥

जायतेऽधिकसंविग्न इति। ततोऽधिकं भीतः सन् प्रजातो भवतीत्यर्थः। जूर्त्यौत्स्वणं निश्वसितीति। जूर्तिपदं विवृणोति—जूर्तिः ज्वर इति। भीत्या च परिरोदितीति। यदिदमतिदुःसहं कृच्छ्रमनुभूतमधुनापि तथाविधमनुभवितव्यमिति भयोपपत्तिः॥ ४१॥४२॥

परिरोदनमिदं न भीतिजं विकृतिमात्रमपि तु स्वावस्थाद्योतकमनिर्वचनीयं प्रथमतरं वाचो व्यापारमात्रमित्यभिप्रायेण तत्रैव परिरोदने वाग्व्यापारं कृत्स्नं दर्शयितुं मूलाधारादित्ययमारम्भः। तत्र सङ्गतिमाह—यदर्थं इति। महान् प्रयासस्तावदियता प्रकरणेन कृतः। स चैतदर्थ एव। यत उक्तं—तस्याविर्भावप्रकारप्रदर्शनार्थं देहोत्पत्तिप्रकारमिति। मूलाधारमित्यस्यायं स्थूलोऽर्थः। अस्य जन्तो रुरुदिषोर्मूलाधाराद्यस्तु प्रथममुदितो भावः स पराख्यः पश्चात् स एव पश्यन्ती। अथ हृदयगो बुद्धियुतो मध्यमाख्यः स एव वक्त्रे वैखरीति। रुरुदिषोरिति। स्वावस्थानिर्धारितामभिव्यञ्जितुमिदं रोदनम्। यदुक्तं—निर्धारितमर्थमेषा। यद्वा स्वपदार्थवचनम्। अथ सूक्ष्ममर्थं दर्शयति—मूलं

जगन्मूलभूतेत्यादिना। चिदात्मनो जगन्मूलत्वम्। यदुक्तं—शारदैव तद्द्वारेण जगदुपादाननिमित्तं चेति। अत उक्तं परिणामिनीति। मायाशक्तिरिति तत्त्वाख्यस्तमचिद्रूपं गृह्यते। तस्याभिव्यक्तिस्थानत्वादिति। तदुक्तम्—तस्याधस्तात् त्रिकोणाभं ज्योतिराधारमिति। तस्मादिति। तदुभयमपि सह गृह्यते। प्रथममुदित इति। यः प्रथममुदितोऽर्थः यस्य भावः स पराख्य इति सम्बन्धनीयम्।

भावशब्दार्थमाह—जगद्भावयतीति। किमिह्योक्तं भवतीत्याह—चैतन्याभासविशिष्टतयेति। चैतन्याभासस्य भावस्य चेत्येकतया प्रतिनिर्देशादयमर्थो लभ्यते। चैतन्याभासयोगि फलं प्रकाशिकेत्युक्तम्। चैतन्याभासविशिष्टतया तथाविधस्य स्वरूपस्य प्रकाशिकेति भावः। नित्यसिद्धत्वान्निष्पन्दत्वम्। सस्पन्दावस्था इति। तस्या इति शेषः। स्पन्दः स्यन्दनम् चलनम्। सामान्यस्पन्दप्रकाशरूपिणीमिति। सामान्यशब्दः स्पन्दप्रकाशशब्दाभ्यां सम्बन्धनीयः। अध्यात्ममित्यधिदैवतमभिव्यक्तिः सृ(सृ)ष्टिप्रभृतिनित्यैवाध्यात्मन्तु विवक्षायामेवाभिव्यक्तिभेदः सूचितः। यदुक्तं—निर्धारितमर्थमेषेत्यादि।

मूलाधारादिति। परायास्तु मूलाधार एव स्थानम्। तत्र नित्योदिततयाभिव्यक्तेरित्यवबोद्धव्यम्। सामान्यज्ञानरूपत्वात् पश्यन्तीत्यन्वर्थाभिधानम्। दर्शनमिह स्वार्थस्याऽपरोक्षतयाऽवभासनम्। बाह्यान्तःकरणात्मिकामिति। यदुक्तम्—इन्द्रियान्तं मध्यमा तदर्थात्मकमिति। विशेषस्पन्दसङ्कल्पादिसतत्त्वादिति। तत्तदर्थविशेषतयावभासनाद्विशेषस्पन्दः। सङ्कल्पादिशब्देन सङ्कल्पविकल्पनिश्चयविमर्शात्मनेत्येतदुक्तम्। सतत्त्वमपि तत्त्वमेव। प्रेरकवर्गः सर्वोऽपीति। द्विविधः कालो मनोबुद्ध्यादिस्थानप्रयत्नादिरित्येतत्सर्वमुक्तम्। सुषुम्नावह: पवनप्रेरित इति चोभयं पश्यन्त्यादिष्वपि समानम्।

अथवेत्येकचतुष्टयापेक्षया विकल्पः—सूक्ष्मा परेति। प्रथममुदित इति सूक्ष्मा भाव इति च परेत्यवबोद्धव्यम्। सप्तपद्यपि वागिति। मूलशब्देन संविद आधारशब्देन च तत्पूर्वदशायाः शून्यस्य ग्रहणमित्यवबोद्धव्यम्। परादीनामाकारस्तावदभिहितः। शून्यादीनान्तु दर्शयति—तत्रानुत्पन्नेति। सा तत्त्वसंज्ञेत्युक्तरूपानुत्पन्ना भवति। निष्पन्देत्यनेनेह संविदाद्युत्तरावस्थानां सस्पन्दत्वमपि सूचितम्। उत्पन्नावस्था परेति दर्शयति—मूलाधारात्प्रथममुदिता परेति। पूर्वोक्तैवेयमित्येतावदुपादानम्। इह पञ्चपद्यभ्युपगमे सप्तपद्यभ्युपगमे चाकचटतपयाद्यैरित्यत्र व्यापकत्वेनास्या न्यास इति परान्यासात्पूर्वमेवासां न्यासोऽपि स्वमन्त्रैः कर्तव्य इति ज्ञेयम्। परादिपुष्पाञ्जलावपि समानमेतत्॥४३॥

रोदनव्याजेनेति। स्वावस्थाद्योतकं शब्दरूपमेतदिति स्थितौ रोदनध्वनिस्तदुपाधिमात्रमेव स्यादिति भावः। किमप्युच्यत इति। शब्दरूपमिति भावः किमपीति स्वत एवानिर्वचनीयाकारं वर्णपदाद्यनभिज्ञत्वादुत्पन्नमात्रस्येत्यभिप्रायः। कथं वर्णानभिव्यक्तिरिति। तस्यानिर्वचनीयत्वेऽपि केनचिद्वर्णमात्राकारेणावश्यं भाव्यम्। तस्य कथनमभिव्यक्तिरित्यर्थः। यद्वा किमपीति वर्णानां सद्भावेऽप्यस्माभिरविज्ञानीयमिति भावः। कथं वर्णानभिव्यक्तिरिति तत्र विद्यमानानामपि वर्णानां कथनमभिव्यक्तिरित्यर्थः। ननु कथं वर्णानां सद्भावो रोदनध्वनावनवसीयत इति। उच्यते। वाक्यात्मकस्यैव शब्दरूपस्य स्वावस्थाभिव्यञ्जकत्तोपपत्तेः वर्णपदतदर्थसम्बन्धाद्यनभिज्ञत्वेऽपि स्वैच्छिकवर्णमात्रसंभवात्। श्रूयते हि—बृहस्पते प्रथमं वाचो अग्रं यत्प्रैरतनामधेयं दधाना इति।

स्रोतोमार्गस्येति। वचःस्रोतो वर्णपदाद्याकारेण प्रवाहः। तस्य मार्गः तत्स्थानलक्षण एव। तदाहाक्षराभिव्यक्तिस्थानस्येति। तत्र तावद्वर्णानां प्रकाशो न जायत इति मूलेऽन्वयः। यावत्कण्ठमूर्धादिभेद इति। भेदो विभक्तत्वकृतस्वस्वाकारसंपत्तिः। कण्ठमूर्धाद्यवयवानां सम्यग्भेदे निष्पन्न एव तदन्तर्गतस्रोतोमार्गोऽपि विभक्तः स्यादिति भावः। कुत एवमित्यत्र यतो वर्णव्यक्तिस्थानसंस्था अत इति। यस्माद्वर्णानामभिव्यक्तिः कण्ठमूर्धादिस्थानसंस्था तस्मादित्यर्थः॥ ४४॥

एवं तावज्जातमात्रेऽपि वाचः कृत्स्ना प्रवृत्तिरुक्ता। तदेतद्वैखरीमात्रमेव। स यदा सन्निहितजनसंव्यवहारतो वर्णपदतदर्थसम्बन्धाभिज्ञः स्यात् तदा विवक्षायां कृत्स्ना वैखरी स्यादिति। तदवस्थायां तथाविधाया वाचो व्यापारविशेषमभिधित्सुराचार्यो जातमात्रस्य तत्पर्यन्तामवस्थामाह—ज्ञातास्मीति। तत्राभिप्रायं दर्शयति—गर्भ इति। विविक्तवत इति। यदुक्तं—पुरा कृतानां पापानामयुतं संस्मरन्निति। मोक्षमेव किलेच्छतीति च। मायाभाववशादिति। मायानिमित्तको भावोऽन्तःकरणवृत्तिविशेषो मायाभावः। मूले ज्ञातास्मीत्यादिनाऽहंभावबन्धोऽभिधीयते। जातस्य तावत्तदानीमेव वा स्वल्पकालेनापि वा ज्ञातास्म्यहमित्येवंरूपो मायानिमित्तको भाव उत्पन्नः स्यात्। स यदा तस्योत्पन्नस्तदा स जन्तुरहङ्कारबुद्धिमान् जातो भवेदिति अहङ्कारेण बुद्ध्या चातिशयेन युक्तः। यद्वाहङ्कारेऽहंबुद्धिरहङ्कारबुद्धिः तद्युक्त इति। अत्राहङ्कारग्रहणं प्राणेन्द्रियदेहोपलक्षणम्। एतदाह—तदाहङ्कारादावात्मबुद्धिर्दृढतरा जातेति। तत्र ज्ञातास्मीत्यहङ्कारे बुद्धौ चात्मप्रत्ययः। प्राणिमीति प्राणे। द्रष्टास्मि श्रोता-

स्मीति इन्द्रियेषु। स्थूलोऽस्मि कृशोऽस्मीति देहे। सम्पन्नोऽस्मि विपन्नोऽस्मीति बाह्यार्थेष्विति। मूले चित्पूर्वक इति बन्धुषु च क्रमादित्यन्तं वाक्यम्। तदभिप्रायमाह—अहंकारवशस्येति। अहङ्कारपूर्वक इत्यहङ्कारादिष्वहंप्रत्ययपूर्वको भाव इत्यर्थः। मूले क्रमवर्धित इति। कालक्रमेण परिचयक्रमेण च वृद्धिं प्राप्तः सन्नित्यर्थः। पूर्वं मातापित्रोस्तु बध्नाति ततः क्रमाद्बन्धुषु च बध्नातीत्यन्वयः।

बन्धः सक्तिः ममायं ममायमित्येवं दृढतरप्रत्ययः। स पीत्वेत्यादिना ममभावबन्धस्य पौष्कल्यापत्तिरुच्यते। स्तन्यमिति स्तनभवं क्षीरम्। तां मातरं स्तन्यदायिनीं वीक्ष्य स्तन्यमिच्छन् रोदितीत्यन्वयः। अनेन तत्र स्यादितरेतरबन्ध इत्यत्र निबन्धनमप्युक्तम्। तत्राधिकतरमिति तत्रापीत्यन्तं वाक्यम्। तत्रानुषङ्गमाह—तत्रापि ममत्वबन्ध इति। पितापुत्रयोरितरेतरममत्वबन्ध इति भावः। प्रमोदत इति। ममत्वप्रत्ययकृता प्रीतिर्दर्शिता इति ॥ ४५॥४६॥४७ ॥

विक्षेपशक्तिविलसितमिति। असति सत्त्वप्रत्ययकरी विक्षेपशक्तिः। तस्या विलसितमियमुक्ता प्रमोदनपर्यन्ता स्वच्छन्दतो वृत्तिः। आच्छादनशक्तेरपि तदिति। सत्यसत्त्वकरी पुनराच्छादनशक्तिः। तदिति विलसितम्। गर्भदशाया विस्मरणात्यन्तासंभावनायामपि तद्विस्मरणपर्यन्ता स्वच्छन्दतो वृत्तिः। यद्यप्याच्छादनपूर्वको विक्षेपः स्यात् किन्तु विक्षेपकार्यं यत्संसारफलं नानाविधप्रमोदरूपं तदास्वादक्रमेणाच्छादनप्रचयक्रमो भवतीति विक्षेपपूर्वकमाच्छादनमुक्तम् ॥ ४८ ॥

मूल एवं सम्बद्धसंसारबान्धव इत्यस्यैवं विग्रहः। संसारायैव नतु मोक्षाय। बान्धवा एत एव मातृपितृप्रभृतयस्त एवं संबद्धा येनेति विस्मरणे हेतुरयमुक्तः। यत्रैव बन्धस्तत्रैव मनसः प्रमोदलक्षणाभिरतिरिति विस्मरणोपपत्तिः। विस्मरिष्यतीत्याच्छादनशक्तेर्व्यापार उक्तः। संभावनया त्वेतत् सूचितम्। यद्यपि जातमात्रस्य बुद्धेरेव (व)स्तुतयाभिविस्मरणसंभवः किन्तु स्वानुभूतगर्भवासक्लेशस्य तीव्रतरतया दुर्विस्मरत्वेन बुद्धौ चिरकालानुवृत्तिसंभवात् संसारनैरन्तर्याभिरतिवशादेव तद्विस्मरणेन भाव्यमिति। पूर्वकर्म चेति पुराकृतानां पापानामित्येतदुक्तम्। अयमिह मूलाभिप्रायः। गर्भगतस्यैव तावत्परवैराग्यमुमुक्षातिशयोत्पत्त्या परदेवतात्मतत्त्वाधिगमाधिकारो जातः। किन्तु स एवोत्पन्नस्य मायाभावमहिम्ना तिरोहितः स पुनर्बुधेनोद्बोध्य वर्धनीय इति ॥ ४९ ॥

इदानीं वर्णपदाद्यभिज्ञावस्थायां विवक्षमाणस्य कृत्स्ना वैखरी स्यादिति तत्प्रसरप्रकारं प्रथमतः संभविनं दर्शयितुमथ स्वमित्यारम्भः। अविशदाक्षरमाश्रयेदिति योजनीयम्। उत्तारणमुद्धारणम्। यदा कृच्छ्रशय्याद्यतिनयनम्। तदा

प्रक्रममाणाया वैखर्यवस्थाया मूलभूततया मूलाधार आविर्भवन्त्याः शब्दब्रह्मावस्थाया वाचो वृत्तिप्रकारं दर्शयितुमप्यव्यक्तमित्याद्यारम्भः। यदा स शिशुरव्यक्तमपि प्रलपति तदा कुण्डलिनी मूलाधारे सुषुम्नावेष्टनी मुहुर्विसरतीत्यन्वयः। अपिशब्दोऽव्यक्तप्रलापोपसंग्रहार्थः। किञ्च प्राङ्मूलाधारे प्रथममुदित इत्यनिर्वचनीयावस्थायामव्यक्ततया वेष्टनमपि सूचितम्। कुण्डलिनीति पश्यन्त्यवस्थापर्यन्ता परा वागुच्यते। यदुक्तं—परापश्यन्त्यात्मको रवो भवेत् स एव कुण्डल्यादिशब्दैरभिधीयत इति। प्रत्यक्चित्तत्वं वलयाकारेण परिवेष्ट्योपरि स्वमुखेनावरणात् कुण्डलिनीव्यपदेशः। सकलीकरणे वक्ष्यति—सुषुम्नां कारणशक्तिकबलीकृतजीवामिति। विविधं सरणमिति। कुण्डलिन्यामपि निष्पन्दांशः परा वाक् तस्यांशस्य नानास्पन्दनं प्रसरणम्। कुण्डलिन्या एव पश्यन्त्यंशोऽयं भवति। वक्ष्यति च—नादसङ्गादित्यत्र पश्यन्तीमध्यमाभाव इति। विविधपद्मादिरूपेणेति। विसरणप्रकारस्याभिधानादवस्थानमित्येवं निर्देशः। विविधानि पद्मानि द्विदलचतुर्दलादिपद्मानि त्रिगुणितषड्गुणितादियन्त्रपद्मानि च गृह्यन्ते। वक्ष्यति च—त्रिचतुरित्यादि। यन्त्रमन्त्रदेवतादिसकलजगन्मयीति। मन्त्रदेवतादिशास्त्रीयार्थानां सकललौकिकव्यवहारवाक्यतदर्थानामपि ग्रहणं स्यात्। तद्दलावच्छिन्नकर्णिकाभूपुराद्यंशानां तद्दलगतमन्त्रवर्णानां च तत्प्रसरणेनैव सह प्रसरणमित्येवं सर्वपद्मेषूहनीयमिति। सुषुम्नावेष्टनीति सप्तमीसमासः। वेष्टनं च विसरणविशेषणम्। तदाह—सुषुम्नायामिति। मूलाधारान्वयतः सुषुम्नापीह मूलाधारगतैव गृह्यते। मूलाधारे सुषुम्नाया मूलोद्देशान्तर्भाग एवात्मानं वेष्टयति स्वस्वरूपमेव वलयाकारेण स्पन्दयति। यद्यपि निष्पन्दायाः परावाचा भाविकार्यमूलतया तदवयवसङ्ख्यया प्रसरणमात्रमिह भवति। किन्तु तस्याः कुण्डलिन्याकारेणेहाभ्युपगमात् प्रसरोऽपि वलयाकारेणैवाभ्युपेयते। गुणयतीति। कुण्डलिनीरूपा सती स्वाकारमावर्तयत इत्यर्थः। स्थापयतीति। स्वस्वरूपं तथावस्थापयतीत्यर्थः। वेष्टनमिह न मध्यस्थस्य + + वस्त्वन्तरस्य परिवेष्टनम् किन्तु वलयाकारापत्तिमात्रमेवेत्येतावदुक्तमित्यवसेयम्॥ ५०॥५१॥

मुहुर्वेष्टनमेवेति। मुहुरिति वेष्टनावृत्तिसङ्ख्या। तथाविधवेष्टनसङ्ख्या चाभिप्रेता। तामुभयोमपि दर्शयतीत्यर्थः। मूले गुणयेदिति कुण्डलिनी स्वाकारमिति शेषः॥ ५२॥

यदा त्रिशोऽथेत्यादेस्तात्पर्यमाह—एवमिति। यन्त्रेति त्रिचतुराद्यवयवयुक्तो यन्त्राभिधः शब्दार्थमयोऽर्थः। मन्त्रेति तथाविधः शब्दप्रधानो मन्त्राभि-

धोऽर्थः। देवतेति तथाविध एव देवताभिधोऽर्थप्रधानोऽर्थः। एषामपि शास्त्र-सिद्धानां जगति सद्भावाज्जगदर्थान्तर्भावः। वक्ष्यति चाचार्य एव—इत्थं मूल-प्रकृत्यक्षरविकृतलिपिव्रातेत्यादि। ननु यदा त्रिशोऽथ गुणयेदिति सकृदेव त्रिशो गुणनमुक्तम्। तदाकारस्य त्रिगुणितायनेकविध उक्तः। कथमेतदुपपद्यत इति। उच्यते। येऽमी त्रिगुणितादयस्त्र्यवयवशालिवर्गलक्षणा उच्चावचा अर्था उप-लभ्यन्ते तेषां मूलस्तावत्तिस्रस्तिस्रः शक्तयो भवेयुः। तासां याः सामान्यभूतास्तिस्र एव मूलभूताः शक्तयस्तदाकारापत्तिरिह सकृत् त्रिशो गुणनं भवति। तासामपि मूलभूतं शक्तिमात्रं कुण्डलिनीसतत्त्वं परा वाग् भवति। तत्र तिसृषु शक्तिषु विसृतासु पुनर्यस्य वर्गस्योत्पित्सा तन्मूलभूता एव तिस्रो विशेषशक्तय उद्यन्ति। तदपि सामान्यशक्तिविसरणशेष एवेति सकृत् त्रिशो वेष्टनस्य सकलत्र्यवयववर्गा-त्मकत्वं सिद्धमिति। मूले विभुरिति नानाविभवनसामर्थ्यमुक्तम्। त्रिकोणसम्ब-न्धानिति त्रैपुराभिप्रायम्। अस्या इति। सामान्यशक्तित्रयात्मिकायाः सकृत्त्रिशो गुणनशालिन्या इत्यर्थः। गुप्तमूर्तिरिति। त्रैपुराणामत्यन्तगोप्यत्वमुक्तम्। यद्वा त्रिकोणस्य रहस्यस्थानत्वात् तत्स्थायिनी मन्त्रदेवतापि गुप्ता भवतीति। यद्वा स्व-वचने त्रिपुरोद्धाररूपे गूढस्वरूपेत्यर्थः। लोपामुद्रा नाम निष्कीलविद्या त्रिपुरेयम-भिप्रेता। वक्ष्यति च—सरमार्धचन्द्रैरित्यत्र सकाररूपिणी शक्तिरित्यादि। अथवा-ऽऽचार्यस्यैवायमभिप्रायः स्ववचनेऽकचटतपयाद्यैरित्यत्र गूढस्वरूपेति कामराजा-भिख्या त्रिपुरेयमभिप्रेयते। कामः कामराजबीजमिति। वक्ष्यति च—वागीश्वर्या-तिशयदतयेत्यादि। मध्यमबीजानीति। सर्वाख्यपीति शेषः। अग्निर्वाग्भव इत्यग्नि-र्वाग्भूत्वेति श्रुतेरिति भावः। नादो नादप्रधामानीति। वक्ष्यति च—मन्यदृद्युशीत-करेति। त्रैपुराणां वाग्भवादिकत्वेऽपि वाग्भवमध्यकत्वाभिधानं सर्वप्रकारेणापि गुण-नयोगादिति ज्ञेयम्। वक्ष्यति च—आदिमादिमनादिं चेत्यादि। बीजत्रयतया विव-क्षायां त्रिर्गुणनम्। तदवान्तरवर्णभेदेन विवक्षायां तु यावत्तद्वर्णं गुणनवृत्तिरित्येव बोद्धव्यम्। सर्वमन्त्रेषु सर्वदेवतास्वर्थान्तरेष्वपि समानमेतत्। तारशक्त्योरेकयोरपि त्रिगुणनं सप्तगुणनञ्च मूलोक्तमेवोपपद्यते। मूर्तिमन्त्रोद्धारो वेति। त्रिमूर्तिसर्वेश्वर-मन्त्राणामुद्धार इत्यर्थः। गूढमूर्तिपदस्यार्थोऽप्येवं प्रकटितः। यद्यपि तत्तदाकारा-पत्तिमात्रमिह विवक्षितं तथापि मन्त्रसिद्धिसंभवात्तदुद्धाराविरोध इत्युद्धारग्रह-णम्। गूढमूर्तिरित्यत्र ब्रह्मादि मूर्तेर्गूढत्वं रहस्यत्वमुपदेशलभ्यत्वं तेनेह कामाग्नि-नादात्मनामुपदेशत एव योग इति सूचितम्। तदाह हं हरिहरेत्येवं सिद्धं भव-तीति। मन्त्रत्रयेऽपि वा बिन्दुयोगः स्यात्। हरिहरमन्त्रयोर्हकारो व्यञ्जनमात्र-

मेवेष्यति। मूल ओमात्मेति हरेमात्मेति च मन्त्रस्वरूपकथनम्। बहुश्रुता इति श्रुतिस्मृतिनिष्ठा इत्यर्थः। अपर इति आगमनिष्ठा इत्यर्थः॥ ५३ ॥ ५४ ॥

उक्तविद्यार्थरूपाणीति। पुरा त्रिमूर्तिप्रणवशक्तय उक्ता विद्यास्तासां वाच्यार्थरूपाणीत्यर्थः। रूपग्रहणेन शब्दार्थभेदात्तदंश एवायमर्थ इत्युक्तम्। मूले विशिष्यत इति भिद्यत इत्यर्थः। गुणदोषादिग्रहणमन्येषामपि प्राणाग्न्यादीनां त्रयाणामुपलक्षणार्थम्। तदुक्तम्—सकलजगन्मयीति। चतुर्गुणनादिष्वपि समानमेतत्। वक्ष्यति च—अत्र सप्तात्मकात्तारादेरित्यादि। प्रणवशक्त्योरेकरूपतया विवक्षायां सकृदेव गुणनम्। अजपापरमात्ममन्त्रादिविवक्षायां द्विर्गुणनमित्याद्यप्यवबोद्धव्यम्। त्रिप्रक्रमस्य प्रणवशक्त्यादिप्रथितिनिबन्धनत्वादिति। प्रणवशक्त्योः सर्वमन्त्रानुस्यूतयोः देवतातत्त्वप्रधानत्वं निर्वचनेन दर्शयत्याचार्य एतेषामिति। त्रिगुणितायुक्तार्थानां तारणं स्थूलसूक्ष्मादिरूपाणामपि तन्मूलभूतवस्तुनि कुण्डलिनीसतत्त्वे देवतात्मचिद्रूपे प्रापणं स्वसामानाधिकरण्येन स्वनिष्ठैकपरताकरणं तद्वृत्तिशक्तिरेतेषामेव त्रिगुणितानां तन्मूलभूतवस्तु निर्हरणलक्षणं शकनमिति स्वरूपप्राधान्याच्चानयोर्बिन्दुयोगापत्तिरिति। मूले तदा सूक्ष्मादिस्थानवाचिकीत्यन्वयः। सूक्ष्मादीनि वाचः स्थानानि। तदाह परादीति। केनाकारेण वाचकत्वमिति। सौरचतुरक्षरादिमन्त्ररूपेणेत्यवबोद्धव्यम्। करणं चेत्यन्तःकरणग्रहणम्। तदा पञ्चपञ्चविभेदिनीत्यन्वयः। अयमत्राशयः। भूतेन्द्रियादिरूपेण पञ्चधा गुणनं स्यात्। तथाकाशवाय्वादिरूपेण वाक्पाण्यादिरूपेण चेत्येवं पञ्चधा गुणनं स्यादिति। एवं स्पर्शादिष्वपि ज्ञेयम्। तदाह—पञ्चविंशतितत्त्वादिकमुक्तमिति।

पञ्चानामक्षराणां चेति भेदिनीति सर्वत्रानुषङ्गः। शिवपञ्चाक्षरपञ्चब्रह्मादीनि पञ्चाक्षरपदेन गृहीतानि। यद्वा नादपर्यन्तानां प्रणवशक्त्यंशानां ग्रहणम्। वर्णमरुदादीनां पञ्चाक्षरवाच्यतया ग्रहणम्। यत उक्तमुक्तविद्यार्थरूपाणीति। तदा कोशोर्मिरसभेदिनीत्यन्वयः। त्वगादिषड्धातवः षट्कोशाः। बुभुक्षापिपासादयः षडूर्मयः। षडक्षरादय इह मन्त्राः॥ ५५॥५६॥५७॥५८॥५९॥

अङ्गा(हा)द्यैरित्यकारादिभिर्हकारादिभिश्चेत्यर्थः। अङ्गेभ्योऽस्यास्तु सप्तभ्य इति सप्तधातुगुणनयोगिन्याः षडङ्गान्येतान्येव प्रणवहृल्लेखावयवरूपाणि। तेभ्यस्तद्वाच्यतया विश्वं जगत् सप्तधा भिद्यत इत्यर्थः। तत्तद्गुणितसङ्ख्यात्मन इति। कुण्डलिन्या इति शेषः। तत्तदात्मकजगदुत्पत्तेरिति। तत्तत्सङ्ख्यार्थवर्गात्मकजगदुत्पत्तेरित्यर्थः॥ ५८ ॥ ६० ॥ ६१ ॥ ६२ ॥ ६३ ॥

यदाऽष्टधा सेत्यत्राष्टाक्षरादेर्वाच्यतयाऽष्टप्रकृत्यादय इति ज्ञेयम्॥ ६४ ॥

मूले आशा दिशः। द्वादशार्णाख्यमभिधत्त इति। यद्यपि द्वादशार्णमन्त्रो वाचकमेव किन्तु सवर्णमात्रार्थरूपेणाभिप्रेतसन्मन्त्रान्तरवाच्योऽपि स्यात्। यथा वर्णशब्दादिशब्दैस्तदर्थाभिधानमिति। मन्त्रान्तरेष्वपि समानमेतत्। तत्सङ्ख्यं चेति यन्त्रपदविशेषणम्। तेन चैतत् सूचितम्॥ ६५॥६६॥

* कुण्डलिन्यादिगुणनसद्भावेऽपि त्रिचतुरादिगुणनाभिधानेऽभिप्रायान्तरं दर्शयति—त्रिगुणितादिष्वित्यादिना। मूलाधारं प्रसिद्धम्। स्वाधिष्ठान + + मणिपूरक ++ अनाहत ++ विशुद्धि ++ लम्बिका ++ आज्ञा + + कला + +। ब्रह्मरन्ध्रमूर्धप्रदेशः। तेषु त्रिचतुष्पञ्चेत्याद्युक्तसङ्ख्यापरिमिता वर्णाः स्युः। तदाह ऋष(?) इति। त्रिचतुरादिवर्णानामन्त्यवर्णा इहोपादीयन्ते। अवधिग्रहणायेति ज्ञेयम्। द्वादशदलपद्मे लवशाद्यष्टवर्णा विसर्जनीयजिह्वामूलीयोपध्मानीयदुस्स्पृष्टवर्णाश्च स्युः। तदाह—अः कः पहेति। पञ्चाशद्दले सर्वांश्च वर्णान् स्मरेत्। नात्र विसर्जनीयादिचतुर्वर्णयोगः। तत्परिवारत्वेनोक्तां विभूतिमिति। कर्णिकास्वकारादितारांशवाच्यतया इष्टदेवतादलेऽष्ट चाकारादिलिपिवर्णवाच्यतयोक्ता विभूतय इति ज्ञेयम्। प्रणवांशग्रहणं ह्रींस्वांशविकल्पोपलक्षणम्। तदुक्तम्—अकारोकारहरमाया वेति। संहृत्येति। चिदग्निशिखारूपेण कुण्डलिन्यपि सर्वानुस्यूता विभावनीया। यद्वा सा मूलाधारादि द्वादशान्तावधि सूक्ष्मतयावस्थिता सती तत्तदाधारे तथा तथा गुणिता तत्तद्विभूतिपर्यन्तं प्रसरन्ती विभावनीयेति। किञ्चैतदपि त्रिगुणितादिष्वाशयान्तरम्। मूलाधारगतात् कुण्डलिनीसतत्त्वात्तारहृल्लेखात्रिपुराद्यभिमतमन्त्रस्य तदुचितगुणनेनोदयस्तावद्भावनीयः। 'यदा सा सप्तगुणिता' 'शक्तिः कामाग्निनादात्मे-त्यादि ह्युक्तम्। ततस्तस्योदितमन्त्रस्य तदुचितसङ्ख्यसकलजगद्रूपेण व्याप्तिरप्यनुसन्धातव्या। 'अङ्गेभ्योऽस्यास्तु सप्तभ्यः' 'सूक्ष्मादिस्थानवाचिकेत्यादि ह्युक्तम्। तदेतदुभयमर्थाभिमतमन्त्रपीठन्यासात् पूर्वमेव कार्यमित्यवबोद्धव्यम्। यद्वक्ष्यति—मातृकान्यासं विधाय वक्ष्यमाणक्रमेण पीठन्यासं कृत्वेति। *

शिशुवाक्यगताक्षरन्यासानुसारेणेति शिशोर्वाक्यान्यप्यव्यक्तं प्रलपति यदेत्युक्तान्येकद्वित्राद्यक्षरात्मकानि तद्गतान्यक्षराणि च मातृकाया विकृतिरूपाण्यनित्यस्तेषां स वाक्यरूपसङ्घातस्तदनुसारेणेत्यर्थः। कुण्डलिन्यवस्थानविशेषमिति। तद्वाक्यरूपं प्रणवहृल्लेखात्रिपुरादिरूपं चावस्थानविशेषमित्यर्थः। यद्यपि तद्वाक्यरूपोऽवस्थाविशेषो यदा त्रिशोऽथ गुणयेदित्यादिप्रकरणेऽनुक्त एव किन्त्वप्यव्यक्तं प्रलपति यदेत्यत्रोक्तोऽसाविति तद्वाक्यरूपो ह्यवस्थाविशेष इह गृह्यते।

मनुस्वारग्रहणेनैतदुक्तम्। प्रणवहृल्लेखादिमन्त्राणां तावन्न शिशुवाक्यत्वमसंभवादेव। किन्तु या तन्मूलभूता कुण्डलिनी त्रिचतुरादिगुणनयोगिनी तस्या एव सप्रणवहृल्लेखादिमन्त्रोऽपि तच्छिशुवाक्यवदवस्थानविशेष इति सामान्यशक्तिषु विशेषशक्तिवर्गाणां स्फुर्तावपि यथाविवक्षमेव तत्तदर्थाकारेण स्थूलीभाव इति। नित्यसिद्धमातृकाक्षररूपेणापीति। कुण्डलिन्यवस्थानविशेषमित्यनुषङ्गः। नित्यसिद्धेति मातृकाविशेषणम्। शिशुवाक्यस्यानित्यत्वात् ततो विशेषाभिधानमेतत्। यद्वा शिशुवाक्येषु प्रणवहृल्लेखादिमन्त्रेषु च यथासमनुस्यूततयावस्थितत्वान्नित्यसिद्धत्वमिति। ननु पञ्चाशद्वाग्गुणितेत्येतदपि मातृकाक्षररूपेणैवावस्थानं तत्कोऽत्र विशेष इति। उच्यते। तत्र पञ्चाशदक्षरमात्रलक्षणस्यानित्यस्य शिशुवाक्यस्य मूलभूतायाः कुण्डलिन्या अवस्थानं तद्वाक्यं मातृका च। इह तु मातृकाया एव तदभिन्नेन तेन पुनरक्षरार्थमाणाया मूलभूतायाः कुण्डलिन्या अवस्थानं सैव मातृकेति विशेषः। पञ्चाशदंशगुणितेत्यत्रैव स्पष्टमेतदिति। अथ सा यदा पञ्चाशदंशगुणिता भवेत्तदा पञ्चाशद्वर्णानीरयतीत्यन्वयः। गुणनावृत्तीनां कृत्स्नरूपापेक्षयांशत्वमिति देवी सती ईरयतीति। देवीशब्देनाचिच्छक्तेरपि कुण्डलिन्या ज्ञानैश्वर्यादियोगितया स्वातन्त्र्यमुक्तम्। तत्समर्थकतयात्मविनिविशितदिव्यभावेत्येतत्पदं योजयति कथमित्यादिना विवृणोति। प्राप्तचिदानन्दभावेति। आत्मनि स्वस्वरूपे विनिवेशितस्तादात्म्येन प्रापितो दिव्यभावो यथेति विग्रहः। दिव्यशब्देन कुण्डलिन्याः प्रकृतेरधिष्ठानभूतः पुरुष उक्तः। दिव्यत्वमसाधारणत्वम्। तच्चार्थाच्चिदानन्दलक्षणम्। यद्वा द्युशब्देन दीप्तिसर्गवचनेन चिदानन्दग्रहणम्। दिवि भवो दिव्य इति नित्यसिद्धं चैतत् तादात्म्यमेव बोद्धव्यम्। यद्वा प्राग्वर्णसङ्घातान्तररूपेण निष्पन्ना तद्दिरत्या ततः स्वस्वरूपात्मतया प्रतिनिवृत्ता सती स्वाधिष्ठानचिदानन्दरूपपुरुषतां प्राप्नोतीति प्रतिपत्तव्यम्। मन्त्रोदयसमयेऽप्यनुसन्धेयमेतत्। चिदानन्दापत्तिफलन्तु वर्णानामपि तत्कालानुस्यूतत्वम्। यतो वक्ष्यति—यस्मात्प्राप्तचिदानन्दभावादित्यादि। परा सती कुण्डलिनी कथं स्थूलान्वर्णानीरयतीत्यत्र सौषुम्नवर्त्म सुषिरोदितनादसङ्गादित्युक्तम्। सौषुम्ने वर्त्मनि मूलाधारप्रदेशे स्थिता कुण्डलिनी तस्यास्तद्वर्त्मसुषिराद्वाङ्मार्गप्रक्रमभूतादुदितेन नादेन स्वकार्यभूतेन यः सङ्गः स्वात्मनोऽवच्छेदः तस्मादिति ल्यब्लोपे पञ्चमी। सङ्गं प्राप्य वर्णानीरयतीति सम्बन्धः। नादशब्देन पश्यन्तीमध्यमावस्थस्थूलो नादो विवक्षितः। तदाह—पश्यन्तीमध्यमाभाव इति॥ ६७॥

इति प्रयोगक्रमदीपिकायां द्वितीयः पटलः।

अथ तृतीयः पटलः ।

पटलसङ्गतिमाह—एवमिति । वर्णनिष्पत्तिप्रकारमिति । यद्यपि 'यूयमचरसंभूताः' 'सर्वानित्थमुवाच ह' 'प्रकृतिः पुरुषश्चैव' इति वागर्थरूपतया प्रकृतस्याचरस्योक्तसर्वात्मतोपपत्तये ततः साधकादिशरीरान्तार्थांशोत्पत्तिस्तदभिव्यङ्ग्यमातृकावर्णान्ता शब्दांशोत्पत्तिश्चाभिहिता किन्तु तत्रार्थांशव्याप्तिस्तत्त्वानां विश्वव्यापितयाभिधानेनोक्तैव । शब्दांशव्याप्तिरेव त्विदानीं वक्ष्यत्येवमभिधानम् ।

तद्विभूतिकथनायेति । तेषां निष्पन्नानां वर्णानां विभूतिरग्नीषोमादिरूपेण व्याप्तिः । यदिह वर्णानामीरणादिकथनं तदपि व्याप्त्यन्तराविष्करणार्थमेव । व्याप्तिश्च विद्यमानानामेवेति स्थित्यवस्थैवेयं भवति । तृतीयपटलारम्भ इत्यनेन मूलगताथशब्दोऽपि दर्शितः । अस्यैवार्थान्तरमाह—अथशब्दो हेत्वर्थ इति । गतपटलान्ते देवीतदात्मविनिवेशितदिव्यभावेति यदुक्तं तदेवामुं हेतुं दर्शयति—यस्मादिति । वर्णेषु तदीयपरमकारणस्याग्नीषोमतया तदनुगमात्तेषां तदात्मकत्वमिति भावः । ननु प्राप्तचिदानन्दरूपपुरुषभावेत्यत्रानन्दग्रहणं किमर्थमिति । उच्यते । चिदानन्दावेवाग्नीषोमौ भवतः शक्तेस्तु तन्मात्रत्वमेव न सोमरूपत्वमिति मतान्तरप्रतिपादनार्थमेतत् । अमृतदीधितिग्रहणममृतस्फारतावबोधनार्थम् । तेनैतदपि सूचितम् । प्रकृतकुण्डलिन्याः स्वरूपचिदग्नावु(व)परिमितामृततया तादात्म्यपर्यन्ततया विनियोगं प्रणवेन शक्त्या वा शान्तान्तोच्चारणेन विधाय ततो मातृकारूपेण मन्त्रान्तररूपेण वोदयः समुचितगुणनतो विभावनीय इति ।

मूलेऽग्नीषोमभेदत इति । वर्णतदर्थानामग्नीषोमाभेदाभिप्रायेणोक्तम् । कथमिह विभाग इत्यत्राह—सर्ववर्णेष्वित्यादि । स्वरेष्वारम्भे व्यञ्जनेष्ववसाने चातिसूक्ष्मत्वेनाकारस्य सद्भावादंशद्वयोपपत्तिः । तदुक्तम्—अकारस्य करणावस्थान्यानित्यादि । पुरुषप्रकृतिग्रहणमग्नीषोमयोः स्वरूपभेदप्रतिपादनार्थम् नात्र प्रकृतिपुरुषमात्रतया सोमाग्न्यात्मकत्वम् किन्तु भोग्यभोक्तृरूपेणेति तदभिव्यक्त्यर्थमपि चिदग्न्यमृतदीधितिपदोपादानम् । समविभागतो वेति । प्रायिकमेतत् टठान्ततया सोमांशस्य विभागात् । यद्वक्ष्यति—आदिठान्तमुक्तेति ।

गूढमर्थं दर्शयति—अनेन चेत्यादिना । प्रपञ्चयागादिष्विति प्राणाग्निहोत्रग्रहणम् । निवेद्यविधौ देवनिवेद्ययोरन्तरग्नीन्दुभावनापि गृह्यते । तारशक्त्यादिपूर्वकमिति मूलमन्त्रादिग्रहणम् । नमः स्वः स्वाहेति वेति । तावत्येवांशेऽयं विकल्प इति ज्ञेयम् । इतरोऽवशिष्ट इति । तारशक्त्यादिपूर्वकं डादिफान्तमुक्त्वा अग्नये नमः स्वाहेति वाग्निमन्त्र इत्यर्थः । प्राणाग्निहोत्रे त्व(तू)क्तोविवि(त)वर्णा

वैलोम्येन स्युरिति बोद्धव्यम् । सोमेनाग्निविभागत इत्यत्र इन: सूर्य: । मिश्रं रूपमिति । प्रकृतिपुरुषयोर्वर्णेष्वकारतदितरांशयोरपीति भाव: । प्रकाशकप्रकाश्यांशाभ्यां वेत्यत्रापि समानमेतत् । कालात्मैवेह सूर्योऽभिप्रेयते । स्वरस्पर्शव्यापकभेदेन वेत्यनेनोक्तश्लोकस्य मुख्यार्थोऽपि दर्शित: । अनेन चेत्यादि पूर्ववद्व्याख्येयम् । शोषणादिविधानान्नाभ्यादिषु सूर्यादिमण्डलभावनायामप्येषामुपयोग: ॥ १ ॥

स्वराख्या: षोडशेत्यत्र सूक्ष्ममर्थमाह- अष्टत्रिंशत्कलान्यास इति । सोमसूर्याग्निकलानामेतद्ग्रहणम् । मण्डलमन्त्रा इति व्यापकमन्त्रा: । ते चेह कृत्स्नतया पठिता: । प्राणप्रतिष्ठामन्त्रक्लृप्तिस्तु दीक्षायामेव वक्ष्यते । ननु कश्चिदंश इह सूचित: क्व पुनरंशान्तरमिति तदाह—असूचितमिति । उत्तरत्रेति तत्तत्कलाकथने । किञ्चिदिति । सम्प्रदायलभ्योऽवशेष इति भाव: ॥ २ ॥

एषु स्वरा इत्यत्र मुख्यार्थमर्थान्तरं च दर्शयति—स्वराणामेवेति । अत्रैष्वित्येषु वर्णेषु मध्य इत्यर्थ: । अत्र ह्रस्वदीर्घशब्दाभ्यां मूर्तिशक्त्यात्मकपुंस्त्रीद्योतकाकारग्रहणम् । तथा च मूर्तिशक्तिरूपेण व्याप्तिरियमुक्ता भवति वाच्यवाचकयोरभेदात् । तेषामष्टमूर्तितच्छक्त्यादिवाचकत्वायेत्यनेन चैतावल्लभ्यत इति । शैवे भवादयोऽष्टौ मूर्तयो वामदेवादयश्च शक्तय: । वैष्णवे विष्ण्वादिमूर्तय: + + शक्तय: । आदिशब्देनाष्टप्रकृत्यादिग्रहणम् । मिथुनानामेवेह वाच्यतोपपत्ति: ।

मूले पूर्वौ ह्रस्व इत्यादिना तद्विभागोऽप्युक्त: । स्वराणां द्वये द्वये पूर्व: पूर्वो ह्रस्व: पर: परो दीर्घ इत्यर्थ: । बिन्दुसर्गान्तिकौ च ताविति ह्रस्वानामन्ततोऽनुस्वारो दीर्घाणां विसर्जनीय: । यद्वा यद्वक्ष्यति—दत्तसव्यस्थिते ह्रस्वदीर्घा: पञ्चोदयन्ति चेति । तद्विषयमेतत् । बिन्दुविसर्गौ ह्रस्वदीर्घाणामन्तत: संयुज्येते इति । वक्ष्यति च—बिन्दुविसर्गौ स्त्रीपुरुषाद्यनुगताविति ॥ ३ ॥

आद्यन्तस्वरषट्कस्येति श्लोकेन व्याप्त्यन्तरमुच्यते । तदाह—स्वराणामित्यादि । तद्वर्णानां मध्ये नपुंसकमीरितमिति । अत्रैतदर्थसिद्धमिति दर्शयति—अवशिष्टह्रस्वपञ्चकस्येति । ह्रस्वदीर्घस्वराणां पुंस्त्रीद्योतकाकारतयेत्थं विभागसिद्धिरिति भाव: ।

नन्वाद्यन्तस्वरषट्कस्येतीत्थं विभागाभिधानं किमर्थमिति । उच्यते । केवलं पूर्वषट्कं व्यञ्जनगर्भमध्यमचतुष्कं तत्समवेतयोरेव फलकार्ययोर्व्यञ्जनमात्रतयैवाभिप्रेतत्वात् केवलस्वरसंयोगरूपमुत्तरचतुष्कं स्वरव्यञ्जनपचयो: समौ बिन्दुविसर्गौ स्वरकार्याणि व्यञ्जनानि व्यञ्जनसंयोगरूपश्च चकारस्तस्य सकलसंयोगप्रदर्शनार्थत्वादित्येतत्प्रदर्शनार्थमित्थं विभागाभिधानम् । बिन्दुविसर्गाविति । पुंस्त्रीनपुंसकानामन्तर्मुखतया बिन्द्वनुगमो बहिर्मुखतया विसर्गानुगम इति

विभागः। अथेह स्वराणां पुंस्त्रीनपुंसकव्याप्तौ—देवी तदात्मविनिवेशित-दिव्यभावेत्यसौ हेतुः। अपितु अन्य एवेति तत्प्रतिपादनार्थमिहागमधनै-रीरितमित्येतदित्यभिप्रायेण विवृणोति—आगमधनैरिति अयमर्थ इत्यादिना।

शिवादितत्त्वावस्थास्तावदमी वर्णाः। तदुक्तं प्राक्—सा तत्त्वसंज्ञेत्यत्रेत्यादि। यस्मान्न किञ्चिदुत्तरं तदनुत्तरमन्तत्वं शिव एव। नाऽत्राहतानाहतभेदो विवक्षितः। तस्य वाचकोऽयमकारः। तस्याभिधायकत्वात् तदीयविमर्शशक्तिमूर्तरूपत्वात् तदागमधनपदेनैतदुक्तम्। मूलाधारादकारशिवाच्छक्तौच्छादिपूर्वकं भोग्यार्थस्य ईषत्स्फुर्तावानन्देच्छादिमेलनपूर्वकं विसर्गशक्त्यभिव्यक्तावात्ममायादिक्रमेण भोग्यवस्तुनो घटपटाद्याकारेण दर्शनदशापत्तिः। पुनस्तत्रैव शिवे तच्छक्त्युत्क्रमेण प्रविलय इति। वाच्यवाचकयोरभेदादनुत्तरं तत्त्वमेवायमकारः। स च पुंस्त्रीनपुंसकेषु पुरुषः। स्वानन्दशक्तिधर्मित्वात् स्वतन्त्रत्वाच्च। किञ्च स एवेह पुरुषः। अन्ये तु वर्णाः प्रकृतिरेव। ततश्चानुत्तराकार एव पुरुषः तस्य चिद्रूपस्यानन्दितुरानन्द एव तद्धर्मत्वाच्छक्तिः। यद्यप्यस्य स्वरूपमेवानन्दश्चिदानन्दैकरसत्वात्तस्य किन्तु स आनन्दस्तद्धर्मत्वेन विकल्पनीयः। यदुक्तं—प्रकाशविमर्शरूपेण चिदानन्दरूपेण वेति। यद्वा तस्य स्वातन्त्र्यमेव शक्तिः सा तत्स्वरूपविश्रान्ता। तस्यानन्दलक्षणो विमर्श इत्यानन्दः शक्तिरुपपद्यते। वाच्यवाचकयोः सर्वत्राभेद एव। तद्योगिनः शिवस्य सकलतत्त्वोन्मेषोनतयोरिच्छा प्रथमः शक्तेः प्रसर इकारः। तत्प्रभविष्णुत्वमीशनमीकारः। ततः सकलतत्त्वानामुन्मेषस्फुरणमुत्पत्तिरुकारः। तेषामेव तद्वैलोम्येन ऊनता संहृतिरूकारः। तदाह—पृथिव्यादिविलयादिति। शिवस्यैवाविद्यावशादवस्थाभेदा एत आनन्दादय इत्यवस्थाग्रहणम्। अवशिष्टतत्त्वावस्थारूपाणीति। शिवस्तावदनुत्तरः प्रथमं तत्त्वम् ततस्तस्यानन्दलक्षणा शक्तिः तत इच्छा सदाशिवः ईशनमीश्वरतत्त्वम् ततस्तून्मेष ऊनता च विद्यातत्त्वमेव। ततोऽवशिष्टानि तत्त्वानि मायादीनि तदवस्थारूपाणि इतराक्षराणि तत्र कादीनि पञ्चत्रिंशन्मायादितत्त्वाक्षराणि। तेषामपि पञ्चत्रिंशत्संख्यासम्भवान्मायातः पूर्वमात्मतत्त्वं प्रकृतेरुत्तरं त्रिगुणतत्त्वम् इकारस्तेषां गुणव्यतिकरजन्यभेदावस्थारूपः क्षकारश्च पञ्चीकृतावस्थारूप इति तेषां तत्त्वानां परसामान्येनाचिच्छक्तिमात्रेणान्तस्फुरतोपलक्षणमिच्छादिविशिष्टं शिवशक्ति तत्त्वमेव। ऌवर्णादिचतुष्टयं न तत्त्वान्तरम्। तथानन्देच्छादियोगरूपमेकारादिचतुष्टयम्। तथाविधस्यादितत्त्वस्य कादितत्त्वसंहारावस्थारूपोऽनुस्वारः तत्सर्गावस्थारूपो विसर्जनीयः

नतु तत्त्वान्तरमिति। तत्र कादीनि साक्षादेवावशिष्टतत्त्वरूपाणि। तेषां सामान्यमात्रमृवर्णादिचतुष्टयम्। तस्य संहारसर्गावस्थौ बिन्दुविसर्गौ शक्तिसदाशिवादियोगमात्रमेकारादिचतुष्टयमिति तान्यपि तत्त्वाक्षराणि स्युरिति।

अकिञ्चित्कराणीति। न किञ्चिदपि साधयितुं समर्थानि। स्वयं साध्यत्वात् शिवतत्त्वस्य भोगमोक्षार्थतया मायादितत्त्वसिद्धये शक्तिकलापयोगादिति। अयमाशयः। स्वरेष्वकार एव तावत् पुरुषः। स्वयं साधकत्वादाकारादिपञ्चकं स्त्री तदर्थसाधनशक्तित्वात् एकारादिचतुष्टयमपि स्त्र्येव। तद्‌योगरूपत्वात्। बिन्दुविसर्गौ तु मायाद्यचिन्मात्रस्फुर्तिदशायामूनतोन्मेषरूपत्वात् स्त्रियावेव। व्यञ्जनमात्रलक्षणं लृवर्णादिचतुष्टयं साधकतदीयसाधनशक्तित्वाभावेन पुंस्त्रीत्वाभावान्नपुंसकमिति। व्यञ्जनानामप्येवं नपुंसकत्वमेव। पृथिव्यादिविलयादित्यनेनैतदुक्तम्। तत्तत्स्य शक्त्यादिसाधनपरिग्रहफलस्य जातत्वात् साधनान्तरासम्भव एवेति ॥ ४ ॥

मूले तच्चतुष्कमित्यादिना व्याप्त्यन्तरमुक्तम्। ह्रस्वाणां विभूतिर्दक्षिणायनम्। दीर्घाणामुत्तरायणम्। ऋऌवर्णयोस्तु तत्संक्रमः। बिन्दुविसर्गयोस्तु तन्निवर्त्तकौ सूर्यसोमौ। तत्प्रेरकश्च प्राणः प्रवाहरूप इति। अस्य पूर्वोक्तव्याप्त्युपपादकत्वमप्यस्तीति वदंस्तच्चतुष्कमित्यर्थस्यार्थान्तरं दर्शयति—स्त्रीपुरुषभागयोरित्यादिना। दक्षोत्तरस्थे प्राणाख्य इति। देहस्य दक्षिणोत्तरभागाभिधानम्। तेन दक्षिणवामाख्यौ भागौ पुंस्त्रीविशेषावित्युत्तरपटलेऽवगमात्तयोः पुंस्त्रीभागत्वम्। तयोर्मध्यभागः सुषुम्ना भवति स नपुंसकभाग इति। सुषुम्नाख्ये सति प्राण इति। वर्णचतुष्कस्याप्येतदेवाधिकरणं प्रवहस्थानीयत्वाद्दाक्षश्च प्राणसमवायादित्यवबोद्धव्यम्। अयनयोर्दक्षिणोत्तरगतिरूपयोः स्थितिर्निवृत्तिरूपा। तदाह—अयनसंक्रान्तिरूपां स्थितिमिति। तेषां विनियोगमाहेति यदुक्तं तदपि दर्शयति—तदानीमित्यादिना। ह्रस्वदीर्घाणामुदयाभिधानादेषामप्युदयसिद्धिः। तेषामुदयाभिधानादेव तेषां मन्त्ररूपाणामुदयलाभः। तत्प्रधानानां चेति शास्त्रबीजादिग्रहणम्। नपुंसकात्मकमन्त्राणामप्युपलक्षणमेतत्। तेषां वीर्योद्भवकाल मित्येतद् वक्ष्यमाणमिहापि समानम्। दक्षिणसंक्रमण इति दक्षिणायनारम्भ उक्तः। स एवमुत्तरसंक्रमण इति। अत्रायं विगागः। प्राणस्योत्तरभागसञ्चारिणो यदा दक्षिणभागप्रेप्सया सुषुम्नायां तन्मूलाधारे वृत्तिस्तदा तस्य प्रवेशप्रधान ऋकारो निष्क्रमणप्रधान इतरः। तस्यैव तत उत्तरभागप्रेप्सया यदा सुषुम्नायां तन्मूलाधारे वृत्तिस्तदा तत्प्रवेशप्रधान आकारो निष्क्रमणप्रधान इतर इति।

अथ दक्षोत्तरस्थ इत्यर्थस्यार्थान्तरमाह—अनयनेऽपीति। समप्रकृतेर्नाडी-

पञ्चकपरिमितोऽयमयनकाल इत्यभिप्रायेणाह—बाह्यघटिकापञ्चकेनेति। नारम्भे नाड़ीपञ्चकं दक्षिणायनम् ततो नाड़ीपञ्चकमुत्तरायणमित्येवं तद्व्यवस्था भवति। अनेनैतदपि सूचितम्। विषमप्रकृतेर्नाड़ीकृतं श्वासकृतं वायनं स्यादिति। उत्तरत्वेऽपीति। यद्यप्येतदिहोक्तं तथापीत्यर्थः। विडम्बसम्भवादिति। बाह्ययोरनयोर्विडम्बसम्भवात्तावदान्तरायनाभिधानम्। तत्रापि विडम्बसम्भवादिति भावः। यदैकस्मिन्नयने प्रवृत्ते सतीतरायनकार्यमुपस्थितं स्यात् तदा तत्कार्यप्रयुयुक्षया तदयनप्रतीक्षणे तत्कार्ये कालविडम्बसम्भवः। कालावयवेति सामान्यतो ग्रहणमहोरात्रादिग्रहणार्थम्। अतएवाह—तत्रेत्यादि। श्वासोच्छ्वासात्मकानीत्यहोरात्रादिषु श्वासोच्छ्वाससम्पादनम्। अहोरात्रात्मकौ वेति। श्वासोच्छ्वासयोरहोरात्रादिसंवाचकानुत्तरपदाद्युत्तरपदाद्यचरत्वात् तदुचितानुकरणरूपत्वाद्वाऽस्य तत्प्रतिपादकत्वम्। अत्र श्वासोच्छ्वासग्रहणमिहोक्ताध्यात्मिकायनयोरुपलक्षणम्। मासशब्देन तत्त्ववयवयोर्मासयोर्ग्रहणम्। इच्छावशेनेति। तत्तदुपस्थितकार्यप्रयुयुक्षापेक्षयेत्यर्थः॥५

अथ दक्षसव्यस्थित इत्यर्थस्य गूढ़ार्थमाह—ह्रस्वदीर्घाणामित्यादिना। तत्प्रधाना मन्त्राः ह्रस्वदीर्घप्रधानाः ग्रहाश्च तत्प्रधाना एव। यथा सूर्यः सोमश्च दीर्घादिः सन् दीर्घप्रधानः बुधः शुक्रश्च ह्रस्वादिः सन् ह्रस्वप्रधान इति। एवं नक्षत्रेष्वपि द्रष्टव्यम्। तिथिराश्यादीनामादिशब्देन ग्रहणम्। बाह्यसूर्योदयादिकालस्य विडम्बसंभवे अग्रमान्तरसूर्योदयादिपरिग्रहः। इह ह्रस्वदीर्घप्रधानमन्त्राणां स्वयमेव प्रतिपत्तिरित्यग्नीषोमात्मकान्मन्त्रान् प्रतिपादयति—तत्रेति। चहरादिप्रधाना इति खफादिग्रहणम्। खठादिप्रधाना इति झसादिग्रहणम्। तेषां वीर्योद्भवकालमिति यदुक्तं तत्र किं विषयं तद्वीर्यमित्यपेक्षायामाह—ते चेति। ह्रस्वप्रधानानां सौम्यानां च वश्यशान्तिकर्मसु प्रयोगः। स्त्रैणानां वश्ये पौंस्नानां शान्तौ इतरेषां क्रूरकर्मस्विति विभागः। भूतभूतकलाभिः सहोदय इति व्याप्यन्तराभिधानम्। तेषामुदयावगमोपायोऽप्यनेनैव दर्शितः। वर्णानां भूतसम्बन्धस्तु प्राणाग्नीलाम्बुखात्मका इत्यमुना क्रमेण प्रतिपत्तव्यः। भूतलिपिविषये तु भेदः। स्वोक्ते नाडीपञ्चकात्मकेऽयने भूतोदयं तावद्दर्शयति—तत्रेति। राशिशब्देन स्वाभिहितमयनमुक्तम्। आध्यात्मिके तु कथमेषामुदय इत्याह—केनेति॥ ६॥

स्वराणां सौम्यत्वे हेतुं वदन्निति तिथिकलाव्याप्त्युपपादनविषयमेव। सोमेनाग्निविभागत इत्यत्र तु—देवीतदात्मविनिवेशितदिव्यभावेत्ययमेव हेतुः स्यात्। चिदग्निप्रकृतिसोमतन्मेलनसूर्योत्पन्नतयैव तथात्वादिति। बिन्दुविसर्गयोस्तत्त्वमिति। बिन्दोरादानस्वभावतया चित्सूर्यत्वं विसर्गस्य विसर्जनस्वभावतया

शक्त्यमृताकारत्वं सूर्येन्द्वो रसादानविसर्जनस्वभावत्वादिति भावः। कालनिर्वर्तक-त्वेनेत्ययनद्वयगतदिनमासकरत्वमुक्तम्। इतरस्वरवदित्ययनद्वयगतदिनात्मकत्व-मुक्तम्। पञ्चानामेव दिनानां प्राणाग्नीलाम्बुखात्मकतया तत्स्वभावानां पर्यायतः प्रवृत्तिरयनद्वयेऽपि लक्ष्यत इति। सूक्ष्ममर्थं दर्शयति—अनेनेति। कालरूप-तिथ्यात्मकत्वमिति व्याख्यन्तरम्। कालोऽत्र मासावयवलक्षणः। अत्र बिन्दो-रुभयात्मकत्वमस्ति सोमस्य तिथिनिर्वर्तकत्वे तदङ्गतया सूर्यस्य तत्रोपस्थितत्वा-दित्यवबोद्धव्यम्। कार्यानुसारेणेति। शान्तिकर्मसु बिन्दुयोगः समृद्धिकर्मसु विसर्गयोगः मिश्रप्रयोग उभययोग इति भावः। तयोर्विकारविस्तार इति। केवलयोर्बिन्दुविसर्गयोर्विभूतिविस्तारः ॥ ७ ॥

स्पर्शानां सौरत्वमिति मासकालादिव्याप्त्युपपादनविषयम्। व्याप्तिं च वद-न्निति। तदन्त्य आत्मेत्यतः प्रभृति तत्त्वरूपेण व्याप्तिकथनम्। ततः प्राक् स्पर्शानां तदौचित्यकथनमिति विभागः। तेषां भूतेन्द्रियमात्रादिसम्बन्धयोग्यतार्थमिति। मात्रास्तन्मात्राः। मनोऽहङ्कारबुद्ध्यव्यक्तात्मवर्गस्यादिशब्देन ग्रहणम्। वाच्य-वाचकलक्षणोऽत्र सम्बन्धः। यद्वा कवर्गस्य भूतैरित्यादिलक्षणः तत्सम्बन्धकथनमेव चार्थाद्व्याप्तिकथनं भवति। पाञ्चविध्यमिति। कखादीनां पुंस्त्वादिसाधारणा-कारतया तादृशे पृथिव्यम्ब्वादिसामान्यसम्बन्धे सति तद्वर्गविशेषसम्बन्धस्य तदु-चितपाञ्चविध्याधीनत्वादिति भावः। तदन्त्य आत्मा रविः स्मृत इति। मकारस्य जीवसूर्यात्मकत्वमुक्तम्। चिदादित्य एवाध्यात्मम् जीवात्माधिदैवतं च सूर्य इति। तदुक्तं—जीवादित्यन्तमहमतनुमिति। तदाहाऽन्त्यो मकार इति। परे क्रमादित्यत्र विवक्षितं क्रमं दर्शयन्नाह—भादय इति। चतुर्विंशतितत्त्वयोग इति। योग-स्तद्वाच्यतया सम्बन्धः। यद्वा मन्त्रदशायां संयोगः। तेन स्पर्शाक्षराः सौरा इत्ये-तद्विवृणोति—स्पर्शानामित्यादिना। मासात्मिका व्याप्तिरपोहाभिप्रेता। यद्व-क्ष्यति—शश्यादिकलारूपतिथिमासभ्राजकादिसम्बन्धेनेति। अत्र तपनताप-नादयो मासमूर्तयः तेन कभादिद्विद्विवर्णवाच्याः। वक्ष्यति च—कभाद्या वसुदाः सौरा इति। तेषां पक्षद्वयलक्षणत्वात्तदुपपत्तिरिति। प्राणाग्नीलाम्बुखात्मका इत्येतत्पञ्चपञ्चविभेदत इत्येतद्विभागाभिप्रायम् किमनेनोक्तमित्यत आह—न चतुर्विंशतितत्त्वसम्बन्धक्रम इति। उक्त इति शेषः। तथाहि सति नणादीनां स्पर्शत्वादिभिः सम्बन्ध आपद्येतेति भावः। भूतैः सहोदयक्रम इति। कचटतपा-दिक्रमेण सम्बन्धोऽत्र विवक्षितः। तत्प्रधानमन्त्रग्रहणचक्राद्युदयोऽत्रापि समानः। स्पर्शानां व्याख्यन्तरमेतदर्थादभवति ॥ ८ ॥ ९ ॥

पञ्चशो वर्गद्वयत्वमिति । तदुचितस्थूलसूक्ष्मभूताद्यन्वयार्थमेतत् । तेन तादृग्व्याप्तिर्लभ्यते । प्राणाग्न्यादिक्रम इति । प्राणाग्नीलाम्बुखात्मका इत्ययं क्रम इत्यर्थः । प्राग्वद्व्याप्त्यन्तरमेतत् । तत्प्रधानमन्त्राद्युदय इहापि समान एव । ननु भ्राजकादिदशाग्निरूपेण व्याप्तिरेतदुपपादनार्थतया हेतुरपीह दर्शयितव्य इति । तत्राह—व्यापकानामपीति । कालाग्निरेव नृसिंहरूपः । अत्र चकारस्याग्न्यात्मकत्वं तदंशात्मकत्वं चेष्यते । तस्य कालाग्निरूपतया पूर्वेषां समष्टिरूपत्वेन तेष्वनुगमोऽत्र प्रतिपिपादयिषित इति ज्ञेयम् । पञ्चाशद्वर्णेभ्यः कथमिति तत्त्विभिदसमुद्भूता इति एतावद्वर्णेभ्योऽष्टत्रिंशत्कलोत्पत्तिरुद्देश्या । तदा चेयमाशङ्का स्यादिति भावः । वर्णानां पञ्चाशत्सङ्ख्यत्वेऽपि प्रकारभेदेनाष्टत्रिंशत्सङ्ख्यत्वादिति परिहारः । स च प्रकारः शश्यादिकलारूपेत्यादिनोक्तः । शशीनाग्निकलारूपास्तावत्तिथिमासाग्नयः मासानां मूर्तित्वेन भावप्रधानतया मधुमाधवादित्वेन तपनतापनादित्वेन च व्यवहारः । शक्तिभावप्रधानतया च तपनीतापन्यादिव्यवहारः । एवं तिथीनामग्नीनामप्यवगन्तव्यम् । तत्र भ्राजकादयोऽग्नेर्मूर्तयो धूम्रार्चिरादयः शक्तयः अमृतो मानद इत्यादयः शशिनो मूर्तयोऽमृतामानदेत्यादयः प्रतिपदाद्याश्च शक्तय इति तत्सम्बन्धस्तद्वाचकभावः । मूले स्वरस्पर्शव्यापकाच्चरा इति स्वरस्पर्शव्यापकवर्णानां ग्रहणम् । मण्डलत्रयमन्त्रैर्व्यापकमिति । शशीनाग्न्युत्थिता इति मण्डलानां स्वकलापेक्षया समष्टिताभिधानादेवमुक्तम् । कलानां वर्णसंयोगं चेति तत्त्विभिदसमुद्भूता इति वर्णेभ्यस्तदुत्पत्त्यभिधानात् ॥ १० ॥

मूले स्पर्शयुग्मैरिति कभादिग्रहणम् । वक्ष्यति च—कभाद्या वसुदाः सौरा इति । सोमादिकलारूपेण वर्णानां व्याप्तिरियमुक्ता ॥ ११ ॥

अथ ब्रह्मादिरूपेण तेषां व्याप्तिरुच्यते—वर्णेभ्य एवेति । पञ्चाशत्संख्यकाः कलाः समुत्पन्ना इत्यन्वयः । तारस्य भूतगैः पञ्चभेदैस्त्विति । भिन्नेभ्य इति शेषः । वर्णानां विशेषणं चैतत् । प्रणवस्याकारादिनादान्तैः पञ्चभिरंशैर्वर्णानां समुदितानां पञ्चवर्गतया भेदः । ते च प्रणवांशाः पृथिव्यादिपञ्चभूतात्मका इति भावः । अत्र प्रणवांशानां भूतानां च वर्णकलाभिः समष्टितया सम्बन्ध इत्यवबोद्धव्यम् ।

सर्वगास्त्विति । पञ्चभूतानां सकलपञ्चविधार्थानुगमात् तत्कलात्वाच्चासामिति भावः । गूढमर्थं दर्शयति—पञ्चाशत्कलान्यास इत्यादिना । पञ्चप्रणवांशयोगोऽकारादियोगः । स चार्थात् कलानां समुदायतः स्यात् । भूतयोगः पृथिव्यादियोगः । स च समुदायत एव । तत्सम्बन्धिवर्णयोगः कटपटाकारादियोगः । स तु प्रत्येकमेव संभवति । तत्सम्बन्धिसर्वयोगं चेति । पञ्चप्रणवांशभूतसम्बन्धिनां तन्मात्रेभेन्द्रि-

यभूतकलाबीजानां सर्वेषां योगं चेत्यर्थः। सर्वगा इत्यस्यार्थोऽयमुक्तः। दीक्षापटले तु मन्त्रक्लृप्तिं वक्ष्यति—लं पृथिव्यात्मने इत्यादि। वर्णप्रणवांशभूततत्संबन्धिवर्णयोगमिति वा विवरणपाठः। तदा तत्सम्बन्धिवर्णा लं वमित्यादिबीजानि वर्णास्तु कटवषाकारादय इति। मूले तेभ्य एव त्विति वर्णानां केशवकीर्त्यादिव्याप्तिरुद्दिश्यते ॥ १२ ॥ १३ ॥

तावत्य इति श्रीकण्ठपूर्णोदर्यादिव्याप्तिः। मातृभिरिति रुद्रशक्तीनां तथा प्रथितत्वादुक्तम्। तेभ्य एव त्विति वर्णौषधिरूपेण व्याप्त्यन्तरमुद्दिश्यते। इह सर्वत्र यस्मात्प्राप्तचिदग्निभावाच्छक्त्यमृतदीधितेर्जाता वर्णास्तस्मादिति प्रागुक्त एव हेतुः प्रत्येतव्यः ॥ १४ ॥

याभिस्त्विति कलाद्वयमूर्तिशक्तिद्वयौषधिरूपाणां वर्णविभूतीनां प्रयोगभेदतोऽभिमतसकलसिद्धिरुक्ता। मन्त्रिण इति। वर्णौषधिप्रयोगेऽपि तत्तद्वर्णभावनाजपादि सूचितम्। वाञ्छितार्थदामिति कलादिमन्त्रेषु तत्तत्फलोचितबीजयोगोऽपि सूचितः। वक्ष्यति च—मेधाकामस्य हसौर्योग इत्यादि ॥ १५ ॥

अथ यथोद्देशं कलादीनामाम्नानम्। तत्रामृतामानदेत्यादिना तेजस्त्रयकलाः। इह प्राग्यदुक्तम्—असूचितमंशमुत्तरत्र सूचयिष्यतीति तदाह कामदायिन्य इतीत्यादिना। मूले कभाद्याः ठडान्ता इति वर्णतत्कलानामभेदाभिप्रायेण तद्योगक्लृप्तिरुक्ता। हव्यकव्यवहे अपीति हव्यवहा कव्यवहा च ॥ १६॥१७॥१८॥१९ ॥

सृष्टिर्ऋद्धिरित्यादिना पञ्चमूर्तिकलाः। अत्राकारोत्था इति तारस्य पञ्चभेदैरित्युक्तानुवादः। तत्राभिप्रायमाह—अकारोत्था इति। तत्कलान्यास इति। तत्कलासु प्रत्येकं कखादिवर्णतः पूर्वमकारादिवर्णतोऽभिप्रेयते। कखादिवर्णयोगनियमस्तु नादकलानां षोडशसंख्यतया स्वरयोगप्रतीतेर्बिन्दुकलानां च चतुःसंख्यतयाऽष्टादिशेषवर्णयोगप्रतीतेश्चावसीयते। वक्ष्यति च—कलाः कला नादभवा वदन्त्यजा इत्यादि। ब्रह्मजाता इत्यादिनापीति। ब्रह्मणि सृष्ट्यात्मन इत्येवं समुदायतो योग उक्तः। बिन्दुनादकलासु योज्यमाह—बिन्दुजा ईशजा इत्यादिना। या बिन्दुजास्ता ईशजा अपि स्युः। प्रकरणात्। तथा या नादजास्ताः सदाशिवजा अपि स्युरिति। भुक्तिमुक्तिप्रदायिका इत्युभयासामप्युक्तानां कलानां विशेषणमिति मत्वाह—भुक्तिबिन्दुकलासु योज्येति ॥ २०॥२१॥२२॥२३॥२४॥२५॥२६॥२७ ॥

मूले केशवो नारायण इत्यादिना वैष्णवमूर्तिशक्त्यभिधानम्। मूर्तयो हलामिति व्यञ्जनानामित्यर्थः। मूर्त्याद्या इत्यादिना मन्त्रक्लृप्तिकथनम्। यथा—अं केशवाय कीर्त्यै नम इत्यादि। यद्वा अं केशवकीर्तिभ्यां नम इत्यादि।

सधात्वित्यर्थेन यादिषु विशेष उक्तः। यादिसप्तसु त्वगादिधातुयोगः हादित्रिषु प्राणशक्त्यात्मयोग इति विभागः। यत्तु वक्ष्यति मातृकापटले—केशवादिन्यासे विशेषमाहेत्यादि। तद्विस्तराभिप्रायमित्यवबोद्धव्यम् ॥ २७—३८ ॥

श्रीकण्ठोऽनन्तसूक्ष्मौ चेत्यादिना शिवमूर्तिशक्त्यभिधानम्। मूर्त्याद्या इत्याद्युक्तमिहापि समानम् ॥ ३९—५२ ॥

अथ वर्णौषधिकथनं चन्दनं कुचन्दनेत्यादि। कुचन्दनं रक्तचन्दनम्। घुसृणं कुङ्कुमम्। चोरं कर्चूरम्। ग्रन्थि(?) कर्णौ वर्चिलगुहमूलं तृणं चोर्वेरि फुल्लकुम्भी वदनी गजवदनी। कार्श्मरी अब्दमुस्तमं आदर पुष्पी शङ्खपुष्पी अग्निमन्थं सिंही कृष्णादरपुष्पी शंखपुष्पी रोहिणं बृहती चित्रा तुलसी हिरेफं मुसलिनी अञ्जली श्रीदेवी तलसहं सदाभद्रं(?) ॥ ५३ ॥ ५४ ॥ ५५ ॥ ५६ ॥

इह यत्प्रागुक्तं—याभिस्तु मन्त्रिणः सिद्धिं प्राप्नुयुरिति तत्रौषधिविषये विशेषो गुलिकाकषायेत्यर्थेनोक्तः। तदाह—औषधिकथनप्रयोजनमिति। उत्तरत्रेति लिपिपटले वक्ष्यते—पञ्चाशदौषधिविपाचितपञ्चगव्यजात इत्यादि। कलादीनामुपयोगोऽपि तत्रैव वक्ष्यते कलाः कला नादभवा इत्यादि ॥ ५७ ॥

ननु वर्णानां व्याप्तिकथनमिह प्रकृतम् तत्र कथं यथा भवन्ति देहान्तरिति तदीरणादिकथनं स्यादित्याशङ्क्य एतदपि प्राक् प्रकृतमेव। किन्तु तदवसरे जात इदानीं तत्क्रियत इत्यभिप्रायेणाह—पञ्चाशदंशगुणितेत्यत्रेति। किञ्चेहाप्यवान्तरव्याप्तिरस्त्येव। वक्ष्यति च—अकारेकारयोर्योगादित्यादि। यदुक्तमाचार्येण—तयोर्विकारविस्तारः परस्तात्संप्रवक्ष्यत इति। किञ्च पञ्चाशदंशगुणितेति या कुण्डलिनीव्याप्तिरुक्ता तत्प्रकारोऽप्ययं भवतीति। अपि च शक्त्यंशस्य तत्सारभूतस्य केवलहकारस्य व्याप्तिस्तावदिह पटले प्रतिपिपादयिषिता। सा च व्याप्तिर्वर्णानां व्याप्तौ प्रतिपादितायां ततस्तेषामपि वर्णानां तद्विभूतितायां प्रतिपादितायां कृत्स्नापि प्रतिपादिता स्यादिति वर्णानां विभूतिकथनानन्तरमिदं प्रकरणमारभ्यते। वक्ष्यति च—एवं हकारस्य प्रकृतिपुरुषात्मकत्वमित्यादि। तथा च पटलोपसंहारः—पूर्वोक्ताद्बिन्दुमात्रादित्यादि इति। तदीरणादिप्रकारमिति। पञ्चाशदीरयतीत्यत्राकाङ्क्षिततया प्रकृतमेवेति भावः। देहान्तर्यथा भवन्तीत्येतस्यार्थमाह—स्वरूपतो यथा भवन्तीति। देहान्तरेव येन येन प्रकारेण भवन्तीत्येतद्विवृणोति—स्वरमात्रेति। स्वर उदात्तादिः। मात्रा अर्धमात्रादिः। सन्धिरेत्वादिः। स्थानं कण्ठताल्वादिः। प्रयत्नः स्पर्शनमात्रादिः। भूतं प्राणहुताशादिः। षट्कर्माणि स्तम्भनादीनि। स्वरमात्रादीनां भावी क्रमोऽपोह दर्शितः ॥ ५८ ॥

स्वरूपनिष्पत्तिप्रकारमाहेति। वर्णानामिति शेषः। मूलाधार एव तावद्वर्णाः सूक्ष्मशक्तिमात्रतया निष्पन्नाः। तदुक्तमधस्तात्—अप्यव्यक्तं प्रलपतीत्यादि। तेषां ततस्तत्प्रेरकप्राणवायुप्रयत्नतो निःसरणं सुषुम्नारन्ध्रनिर्गता इत्युक्तम्। पश्यन्त्यादिक्रमेण वदनं प्राप्तानां स्वस्वाकारेणाभिव्यक्तिरुत्तरार्धेनोक्ता। यदुक्तं—मूलाधारात् प्रथममुदित इत्यादि ॥ ५९ ॥

अथोच्चैरुन्मार्गग इति श्लोकेन स्वरविषयः प्रकार उच्यते। अत्र सूक्ष्ममभिप्रायं दर्शयति—वर्णानामिति। उदात्तो वर्णः पुरुषवाचकः अनुदात्तः प्रकृतिवाचकः स्वरित उभयवाचकः। स्वरितविषये च प्रतिपत्तिं वक्ष्यति—मुद्राभयेत्यादि। तत्र पुरुषत्वे प्रकृतित्वे च तदुचितो विशेषः कल्पनीय इत्यवबोद्धव्यम्। प्रयोग इति। प्रयोगस्तु प्राग्दर्शितः। ते च वश्यशान्तिक्रूरकर्मसु प्रायेण प्रशस्ता इति ॥ ६० ॥

अथार्धकेत्यनेन मात्राविषयः प्रकार उच्यते। अत्रार्धमात्रं व्यञ्जनमित्यादि ज्ञेयम्। अत्राप्यभिप्रायमाह—पापच्चयेति। ह्रस्वादीनां पापचयादिषु यथाक्रमं विनियोगः। व्यञ्जनानां तु त्रिष्वपीत्यवबोद्धव्यम् ॥ ६१ ॥

अथाकारेकारयोरित्यादिभिः सन्धिविषयः प्रकार उच्यते। तस्यैवेत्यकारग्रहणम्। एकारयोगेनेति वृद्ध्यादेशादैकारसिद्धिः। एवमौकारयोगेनेत्यत्रापि द्रष्टव्यम्। अत्रापि सूक्ष्ममभिप्रायमाह—सर्वेषामेवेति। यद्यपि सर्वेषामपि द्व्यात्मकं प्रागुक्तम्—सर्वेष्वकारोऽग्न्यात्मकपुरुषांश इतरः प्रकृत्यात्मकसोमांश इति। किन्त्विह तत्तद्वर्णस्यार्धद्वयेन पुरुषप्रकृतिवाचकत्वं सन्ध्यक्षरेषु त्वकारेकाराद्यर्धद्वयेनेत्येवं विभागोऽभिप्रेतः। इहाकारादेरेकारादिषु व्याप्तिरप्युक्ता भवति ॥ ६२ ॥ ६३ ॥

मूले सन्ध्यक्षराणां मन्त्रताभिधानं प्रदर्शनार्थमेव। सर्वेऽपि वर्णाः केवलाः संयुक्ताः समुचिता अपि सर्वार्थसाधका मन्त्रा एवेति। सर्वार्थसाधकपदस्यार्थान्तरमाह—प्रकृतिपुरुषात्मकोऽर्थ इति। मन्त्रत्वादेषामृष्यादिकमप्युपदेष्टव्यमित्याह—एषामिति। तत्तद्वर्णादियुतैः स्वरैरिति। यो यो वर्णमन्त्रो भावनीयस्तेन तेन वर्णेनादौ युक्तैर्द्विचतुःषड्द्वादशचतुर्दशान्त्यस्वरैरित्यर्थः। यथा इकारस्य यांयोमित्यादि। कादीनां कांकीं खांखोमित्यादि इति। मुद्राभयेति। मुद्रया सहाभयं शुक्रेन सह वर इत्येवं द्विभुजतोपपत्तिः। शुक्लरक्तभागद्वय इति। वामदक्षिणभागद्वयाभिप्रायम्। कोऽपीति। ब्रह्मा विष्णुः शिवः सर्वेश्वरो वाऽन्यो वा गणपत्यादिः। अथवा त्रिपुरासरस्वत्यादिरिति भावः। परमात्मनः सर्वदेवसामान्यरूपत्वात् कोऽपि देव इत्येतदुपपत्तिः। तत्र ब्रह्मादिषु स्त्रीभागः कल्प्यते त्रिपुरादिषु पुंभाग इति भेदः। यथा तत्तन्मन्त्राणामपि वर्णाः

पृथङ्मन्त्राः स्युः तदापि समानमेतत् सकलमित्येव बोद्धव्यम्। तत्रर्षादिसर्वं स्वोक्तमेव। स स देव इहोक्तलक्षणो ध्येयः। सकलवर्णमन्त्रभावनासु न्यासप्रपञ्चः तत्तन्मन्त्रसमान एव। पूजा चाङ्गेन्द्रवज्रादिभिरिति। एवमवर्णस्येवर्णादिभिः सह सन्धिरुक्तः। अथ केवलयोॠऌवर्णयोः स्वांशेन सन्धिरुच्यते ऌवर्णॠवर्णयोरिति। व्यक्तिः स्फुटता। लरोस्तदीयस्थूलावस्थारूपत्वादिति भावः। इहायमभिप्रायः। यदेतदृवर्णान्तरमिति सूक्ष्मं किञ्चित्स्वराकारविलक्षणं लक्ष्यते तदेवोद्रिच्यमान मितरांशन्यग्भावादसौ रेफो भवति। एवं लकारोऽपीति। अत्र स्वरमात्राया मध्ये रलमात्रासन्धानमुक्तं भवति। लरोः सम्यगिति। व्यञ्जनान्तरेषु तु न तद्वदिति भावः। तेनैतदपि सूचितम्। सर्वव्यञ्जनतन्मात्रमेव ॠऌवर्णान्तर्गतमिति। चिदानन्दात्मकपुरुषप्रकृत्यंशप्रधानतया तु द्विवर्णोपपत्तिरिति।

अत्रापि सूक्ष्ममभिप्रायमाह—ॠवर्णऌवर्णयोरिति। व्यक्तिरित्यस्य लरोरित्युपरि सम्बन्धः। व्यक्तिपदमन्तरा विवृणोति—व्यज्यतेऽनेनेति। मन्त्रमूर्तिरिति शेषः। अङ्गसामान्यमिति। षडङ्गेष्वादितो योजनीयो वर्णः लरोर्वर्तमानमित्यर्थादुगम्यते। कुत्र दृश्यत इत्याह—मूलागमेष्विति। यकारादिभिरिकाराद्यङ्गान्यपि तेष्वेवेति मूलागमेष्वित्येतावदुक्तम्। अत्र इ ए ऐ इत्येषां यां यीमित्यादि उ ऊ औ इत्येषां वां वीमित्यादि इति॥ ६४॥

अथ बिन्दुविसर्गयोरपि स्वांशेन सन्धिरुच्यते—बिन्दुविसर्गात्मनोरिति। बिन्दुविसर्गवर्णयोः स्फुटं रूपमजपां स्वांशयोः अं अः इत्यनयोर्वदेदिति तदर्थः। बिन्दुविसर्गमात्रयोरकारेण सन्धानमेतदुक्तम्। अत्राप्यभिप्रायान्तरं दर्शयति—बिन्दुविसर्गाङ्गेष्विति। बिन्दुविसर्गस्वरूपयोः अं अः इत्यनयोः स्वरयोरङ्गसामान्यमजपां हकारसकारात्मिकां क्रमेण वदेदिति तदर्थः। यथा बिन्दोः हांहीमित्यादि विसर्गस्य सांसीमित्यादि इति। नन्विकारादीनां यकारादिसम्बन्धे निबन्धनं तावत् स्पष्टमस्त्येव किं पुनरिह निबन्धनमिति तदाह—हकारसकारयोरिति। बिन्दोः कार्यसंहारशक्तितया चिद्रूपनिष्ठत्वात् पुरुषत्वं हकारस्य च घोषवत्त्वात् विसर्गस्य तु कार्यसर्गशक्तित्वेनाचिद्रूपनिष्ठत्वात् प्रकृत्यात्मकत्वं सकारस्य चाघोषत्वादिति। अथोपपत्त्यन्तरमपि दर्शयंस्तदुपपत्तिवशादवर्णमन्त्रयोरप्यङ्गेषु हकारयोगसिद्धिरित्यपि दर्शयति—स्थानसाम्यमकारयोगश्चेत्यादि। तदुक्तम्—अकुहविसर्जनीयानां कण्ठ इति। बिन्दोरपि नासिकया सह कण्ठस्थानत्वमिष्यते। अकाराङ्गेष्वपीत्यवर्णयोर्ग्रहणमिष्यते। प्लुतप्रयोगेऽपि सर्वत्र समानमेतदवबोद्धव्यमिति। इहैवं सन्ध्यभिधानं प्रदर्शनार्थम्। तत्तद्वर्णानामपीत्थं

सन्धिभिस्तत्तन्मन्त्रास्तद्विकाराः स्युरिति। तदुक्तं—मन्त्रभेदानामप्यक्षरविरचनारूपत्वादिति। इदानीं विसर्गस्याकारेण नित्यं सन्धिं वक्तुं तस्य सर्ववर्णनिदानतया प्रथमतः स्थानप्रयत्नं प्रतिपादयितुं च कण्ठादित्याद्यारम्भः। अत्र कण्ठास्त्विति स्थानं निःसरन्निति विसर्जनलक्षणः प्रयत्नः प्राय इति योग्यता द्योत्यते। अचामेकतः पर इति स्वराणामन्यतमः। तत्रापि प्रथमतः परो भवति कण्ठादुद्भवति कण्ठस्यैवोपादानयोगादिति भावः।

इहाकारयोगो बिन्दुविसर्गयोः सम एवेति मन्यमानोऽभिप्रायान्तरमप्याह—मन्वित्यादिना। बिन्दुविसर्गयोः सर्वस्वरसमानत्वं तावदुक्तम्—बिन्दुसर्गान्तिकौ च ताविति। तथा च तयोरकारयोगनियमासंभवः। बिन्दुविसर्गमात्रस्वरूपत्वात् केनचिदपि स्वरेण योगासंभवः। तदसंभवे च कुतोऽजपाया हकारसकारयोग इति आशङ्काभिप्रायः। तयोरिति बिन्दुविसर्गयोर्हि तावत् स्वस्वरूपाभिव्यक्त्यर्थमवश्यमकारयोगः स्यादेव। तन्नियमो हकारसकारयोगोपपत्तिश्च विवृतिसमये दर्शयिष्यत इति भावः। अत्र कण्ठात्तु निःसरन्निति बिन्दोरपि स्थानप्रयत्नोपलक्षणम्। यद्वा कण्ठो बिन्दोरपि स्थानं निःसरणं त्विह मुखविवरतो नासिकाप्राप्तिः। अत्र केन पदेन बिन्दोरुपादानमिति तद्दर्शयति—प्राय इति। प्रैत्यस्मिन् कार्यजातं प्रलीयत इति प्रायशब्दो निर्वक्तव्यः। प्रायमुपाददानस्याभिप्रायमनयोः प्रकृतिपुरुषस्वरूपस्याविष्करणं दर्शयति—सृष्टिरूपप्रकृतिप्रतिभटः संहारात्मकः पुरुष इति। प्रतिभटशब्दः प्रतियोगिवचनः। प्रकृतेः कार्यप्राधान्यं पुरुषस्य स्वरूपप्राधान्यमिति द्वयदेवेह विवक्षितम्। अयमिहाभिप्रायः। न केवलमिह बिन्दुविसर्गमात्रमभिव्यञ्जिजिषितम्। किन्तु तयोः पुरुषप्रकृतिलक्षणस्वभावोऽपि। तत्र तयोः स्वरूपाभिव्यक्त्यर्थमकारयोगस्वभावाभिव्यक्त्यर्थं च हकारसकारयोगः। तयोर्घोषवदघोषरूपेण हरणसर्जनवदाद्यक्षरतया वा पुरुषप्रकृतिसमुचितत्वादिति। प्रधानत इति। अनुत्तरतत्त्वस्वरूपत्वात् प्रधानत्वम्। यदुक्तम्—अवर्णविग्रहं देवमिति। अनेनाकारयोगनियमोऽप्युपपादितः। कुत एतद्योगस्य तदभिव्यक्त्यर्थत्वं लभत इति तद्दर्शयन्नुत्तरपादं विवृणोति—(अ)तत्परत्व इत्यादिना ॥ ६५ ॥

नश्वरः स्यादिति। नाशोऽसद्भावोऽनुपलम्भो वा। एवं च यदाशङ्कितं तत्सर्वं परिहृतं भवति। किञ्चैवं व्यञ्जनानामप्यभिव्यक्त्यर्थं तयोपर्यकारोऽप्युपपादितः। एवं तावद्विसर्गस्य स्थानप्रयत्नमुक्तम्। अथायमेव सकलकार्यमूलकारणभूतो हकारोऽपि भवतीति सोष्मा सप्राणकस्तु ह इत्युच्यते। विसर्ग एवोष्मप्राणविशिष्टः सन्नसौ हकार इति तदर्थः। ऊष्मा बलं प्राणः श्वास एव। अनेन हकारस्यापि

स्थानप्रयत्नमुक्तम्। कण्ठ एव स्थानमूष्मप्राणमयश्च प्रयत्न इति। न चात्र विसर्गविभूतितया हकाराभिधानम्। 'सर्वानित्यमुवाच ह' 'प्रकृतिरथ हसंज्ञा भवेदिति च निर्दिष्टत्वात्। किन्तु प्रकृतिपुरुषात्मकत्वमूलकारणतोचितं दर्शितम्। कथं विसर्गत्वेनास्य प्रकृतित्वमूष्मप्राणलक्षणस्य बिन्दुमयपुरुषभावस्य योगेन पुरुषत्वमिति। अत्रैवाभिप्रायभेदमाह—यद्येवमित्यादिना। प्रकृतिपुरुषवाचकाविति। ननु खल्विह प्रकृतिपुरुषवाचकत्वमप्याचार्येणोक्तमिति। नैष दोषः। प्रकृतिपुरुषं तावदजपावस्थायां प्रथितमेव। ततश्चेहापि तत्सिद्धिः स्यादिति। पूर्वं सर्ववाचकत्वमुक्तमिति। सर्वानित्यमुवाच हेत्यत्रेति भावः। प्राणस्य प्राण इति प्राणस्यापि प्राणनकरत्वमुक्तम्। पुरुष इति चाध्याहारः। हकारे तावद्यावूष्मप्राणांशौ तद्वाच्यतया तदभिन्नाविद्दोष्मप्राणपदवाच्यौ प्रकृतिपुरुषौ भवत इत्यभिप्रायः।

अथ सर्ग इत्यस्यैव वर्णस्य विकृतिरूपेणावर्णकवर्गयोरुत्पत्तेः स्थानस्य चाभिधानम्। तस्य तात्पर्यं दर्शयति—एवं हकारस्येत्यादिना। स हकारलक्षणो विसर्गः कण्ठे वर्तमानोऽपि वर्णसारथिभूतेन प्राणवायुना तत्रैव कण्ठे श्लेषितः सन् तदुचितकरणभेदतोऽकादिमीरयेदिति मूलार्थः। अकादिं वर्गमितिच्छेद इति। अ इत्यवर्णग्रहणम्। कादिपदेन कादिमान्तग्रहणम्। स एव च वर्गः। ननु सर्ववर्णादिकारणत्वं कथमिहोक्तं स्यादिति चेत्। उच्यते। कण्ठे श्लेषितोऽकादिमीरयेत् स्थानान्तरे तु श्लेषितो वर्णान्तराणीत्येवमर्थस्याभिप्रेतत्वादिति। तत्रैवेति कण्ठ एव। यद्वा कण्ठादिस्थानेषु ग्रन्थतत्सामर्थ्याभ्यां प्रतिपादितेष्वित्यर्थः।

वर्गं स्पर्शनमात्रेणेत्यत्र कं वर्गमिति संबन्धः। कचटतपेत्ययं चेह वर्गः। एवं खादिष्वपि प्रतिपत्तव्यम्। ङश्च बहिर्गत इति। मुखविवरतो बहिर्नासिकायां गत इत्यर्थः। अत्र स्वरेष्वर्थादस्पर्शनं प्रयत्न इत्यवसीयते ॥ ६६ ॥ ६७ ॥

विसर्गस्तालुग इति। स एव हकाररूपस्तालुगतो वायुना श्लेषितः सन्नित्यर्थः। सोष्मेशं चवर्गं चेत्यत्र सोष्मेत्येकं पदम्। पुनरिशमिति। सोष्मेत्यर्थं दर्शयति—सोष्मा साग्निरिति। इशमित्येतद्विभजते—इश्च शश्चेतिच्छेद इति। इवर्णशकारग्रहणमेतत्। यन्तथेति यकारः। दन्तगस्तथा लृतवर्गलसानित्येकम्। पु इति पवर्ग उक्तः। उपध्मानग्रहणं प्रदर्शनार्थम्। जिह्वामूलाज्जिह्वामूलीयमिति। तत्तत्स्थानगोऽर्णान् समीरयेदिति। एवमित्युपस्कारः। हकारलक्षणो विसर्ग इति प्रकरणाद्भवति। किमनेन क्रियत इत्याह—उपसंहरतीति। स सर्गः श्लेषित इत्यादाविति। वक्ष्यति च—एवं हकारस्य केवलस्य विश्वयोनित्वमभिधायेति॥६८॥ ६९॥

इदानीं भूतषट्कर्मविषयः प्रकारो वक्तव्यः। तदाह—वर्णानामिति। 'भूत-

भूतकलाभिः' 'प्राणाग्नीलाम्बुखात्मका' इत्येवमुक्तमपीत्यर्थः। विशदयन्निति। तत्रास्पष्टत्वादिह स्पष्टीकरणोपपत्तिः। मूले ह्रस्वाः पञ्चेत्यत्र परे चेति पञ्चेत्यनुषङ्गः। तदाह—परे च दीर्घा आदयः पञ्चेति। सन्धानेन विकृताः सन्धिविकृताः। यदुक्तम्—अकारेकारयोर्योगादिति। बिन्दुसर्गात्मनोर्व्यक्तिममसोरिति च। परोक्तसन्धिर्बिन्दुरित्येव भेदः। बिन्दन्तिका इति विसर्गनिवृत्त्यर्थमुक्तम्। यद्वा चत्वारि सन्ध्यक्षराणीति बिन्दुपरिग्रहार्थमुक्तम्।

मूले काद्या इत्युपलक्षणम्। चाद्याष्टाद्यास्ताद्याः पाद्या इति। कशब्देन जलग्रहणम्। पृथग्भूतात्मकाः क्रमेण कथिता इति सम्बन्धनीयम्। तैस्तैः पञ्चभिरेव वर्णदशकैरिति। तैस्तैरिति पार्थिवैराप्यैरित्याद्युक्तम्। यथा अआएकचटतपयषेतीत्यादि। स्तम्भनाद्यमित्याद्युक्तविवरणम्। स्तम्भनाद्यमिति रक्षादिग्रहणम्।

तदुक्तम्—रक्षास्तम्भनकर्माणि वर्णैः कार्यं धरात्मकैः।
शान्तिकं पौष्टिकं कर्म वर्षणं सलिलात्मकैः॥
दाहमोहाङ्गभङ्गानि चाकृष्टिं दहनात्मकैः।
सेनाभङ्गभ्रमोच्चाटद्वेषकर्माणि वायुजैः॥
कालभस्मानि चूर्णानि विविधान्यथ मारणम्।
क्षुद्राणां स्थापनं वर्णैर्नभसैर्वर्गसंख्यकैः॥ इति।

शून्यता ग्रामनगरादीनामत्यन्तं मनुष्याद्यभावकारणम्। मन्त्रान्तरैरपि स्तम्भनाद्युपपत्तावेतैः संपुटीकरणं कार्यम्। वक्ष्यति च—संयजेन्मन्त्रीति ॥७०॥७१॥७२॥७३॥

स्तम्भनादिप्रयोगप्रकारमिति। स्तम्भनाद्युचितेषु सीसादिषु मध्ये त्रिकोणं तद्बहिः स्तम्भनाद्युचितं पार्थिवादिमण्डलमप्यालिख्य तत्र त्रिकोणमध्ये पञ्चीकृतभूतादि विलिख्य भूतबीजैर्द्वन्द्वशो मध्यादिषु संपूज्य जप्त्वा निखननादि कुर्यादित्येवंविधः प्रयोगप्रकारोऽवबोद्धव्यः। स्तम्भनाद्यर्थं कल्पितेषु कुण्डेष्वप्येवं कल्पनीयः। संयजेदित्येतद्विवृणोति—संलिख्य सञ्चिन्त्य वा पूजयेदिति। लेखयेत् चिन्तयेत् पूजयेदेति वा पाठः। अत्र लेखनं चिन्तनं च विकल्पेनोपलक्षितमिति। सिद्धमन्त्रस्यायं प्रयोग इति। सञ्चिन्तनेनापि स्तम्भनादिकार्यस्य साधनीयत्वादिति भावः। मध्ये पञ्चीकृतभूतबीजमिति। स्वं स्वं भूतबीजमिह विवक्षितम्। भूतबीजानि च नादकलादिभूता इत्यत्र प्रतिपादितानि। तद्बिन्दूर्ध्वाधोभागादिष्विति। भूतबीजस्य मध्योद्देशे तदीयबिन्दुर्लेखनीय इत्यर्थादवसेयम्। तस्य बिन्दोरन्तर्वा बहिर्वोर्ध्वाधोभागग्रहणमिष्यते। तत्रोर्ध्वभागे साधकः। अधोभागे साध्यः। कर्म च यथास्वं तयोर्भागयोः स्यात्। तदसंभवे पार्श्वदिशि कर्म लेखनीयम्। कर्म च

कदाचित् साधकस्य यथा स्यात्। यथा चैत्रो मैत्रं जयत्विति। कदाचित् साध्यस्य। यथा चैत्रार्थे मैत्रो नश्यत्विति। कदाचिद्देवताया एव कर्म भवति। चैत्रं रक्षेति। कदाचित् तु साध्य एवास्ति। यथाऽत्रैवेत्यादि सर्वमूह्यमिति। यन्त्रजीवादियोगश्चेत्यत्र प्रागुक्तमादिपदं संबध्यते। तत्र नियमस्तु वक्ष्यत एव। एतच्चेत्येवमुक्तलक्षणमित्यर्थः। पार्थिवभूतलिपियोगस्त्वर्थाद्भवति। यन्त्राणीत्यभिधानं पार्थिवयन्त्रपरिग्रहनिवृत्त्यर्थम्। तत्तद्भूतयन्त्राणीत्येतदर्थम्।

इदानीं यन्त्रजीवमाह—ह्सौरिति। मध्यबीजाधोभाग इति। तस्यान्तर्बहिर्वाऽधोभागोऽभिप्रेतः। हमिति लिखेदित्यन्तं वाक्यम्। गुणशोऽष्टदिक्ष्विति लेख्येति शेषः। गुणश इति त्रित्रिवर्णाभिप्रायम्। यन्त्रप्राणबहिरेतल्लेखनमिष्यते। दलेष्विति सत्स्वष्टदलेषु तेषु गुणशो लेखनं चतुर्दलेषु षट् च इत्याद्यूह्यम्। तद्बहिरिति यन्त्रद्वयमिति संबध्यते। लेख्यमिति च शेषः। मध्यबीजे गायत्री चेत् तद्बहिरेतद्दलेषु गायत्री चेद्यन्त्रप्राणबहिरेतदित्यवबोद्धव्यम्। प्राणप्रतिष्ठामन्त्र इति। स तु कलासु वक्ष्यमाणप्रक्रियया प्रतिपत्तव्यः। यन्त्रसामान्यमपीति यन्त्रजीवादि। यदुक्तं—तदन्येष्वपि वक्ष्यमाणयन्त्रेषु समानमिति भावः। वक्ष्यति च—व्योमाविःसचतुर्दशस्वरविसर्गान्तस्फुरत्कर्णिकमित्येवमादि। येन येन प्रकारेणेति यत्प्रागारब्धं तदिह परिसमाप्तमिति ॥ ७४ ॥

पूर्वोक्ताद्बिन्दुमात्रादित्यन्त्यश्लोकस्य तात्पर्यं दर्शयति—एवमिति। पटलत्रयोक्तां सृष्टिमिति। 'प्रकृतेश्च क्वचित् काल' इत्येवारभ्योक्तां सृष्टिमित्यर्थः। ततोऽर्वाक् तु हकारस्य सवाच्यार्थस्य नित्यत्वं स्वरूपं व्याप्तिश्चैवोक्तेति। यद्यपीह स्थितिरिह पटलेऽभिहिता तथापि वर्णनिष्पत्त्यभिधानं सृष्टिरेवेति तथाभिधानम्। यद्यपि स्थितिरपीहाभिहिता न सृष्टिरेव किन्तु संहारप्रतिपादनार्थतयैवायं सर्गानुवादस्तद्व्यत्ययरूपत्वात् संहृतेरिति सृष्टिरेव गृह्यते। अत एवानुवदन्निति निर्देशः। प्रकृतिः स्वयं पूर्वोक्ताद्बिन्दुमात्रादथ स्वतन्मात्रतामभ्युपेतेति सम्बन्धनीयम्। स्वयमित्येतदभिप्रायमाह—निस्तरङ्गा तत्त्वसंज्ञेति। प्रकृतेर्यन्नित्यं स्वरूपं तदभिप्रायमेतदिति भावः। परस्मादुत्पन्नस्य प्रकृतितत्त्वस्येति इयमवस्थेह व्यावृत्त्या भवति। यद्वा प्रकृतिरिह 'प्रकृतिः पुरुषश्चैव' 'प्रकृतेश्च क्वचित्काल' इत्युक्तैव स्यात्। स्वयमेवेति तु कालपुरुषयोस्तस्यामन्तर्भावः स्वकीयनिस्तरङ्गाकारस्य बिन्द्वादिविकारापत्तावप्यनपायो विक्रियायामन्यनिरपेक्षत्वमित्यादि सर्वमुक्तम्। शब्दब्रह्मात्मतामिति। तदुक्तं—बिन्दोस्तस्माद्भिद्यमानाद्रव इत्यादि। मूले षकारादीन् हरष्टेत्यत्राप्यभ्युपेतेति सम्बध्यते। तथा तदनुगतान् कादीन्

पञ्चविंशदित्यत्रापि पञ्चविंशदिति पञ्चविंशतिमित्यर्थः। तेषां स्वरैरनुगतिरकारनित्ययोगात् ककादिवैचित्र्याच्च भवति। तथैव संयुक्तधातूनपि यादीनित्यन्वयः। तदनुगतानित्येतत्तथैवेत्युक्तम्। अभ्युपेतेति चानुषङ्ग इति। अत्र 'बिन्दोस्तस्मादित्यत आरभ्य 'पञ्चाशदीरयति पंक्तिश एव वर्णानित्यत उक्ता शब्दसृष्टिरनूदिता। 'यथा भवन्ति देहान्तरित्यादि तु प्रकरणमेतदन्तर्गतमेवेति। गुणसहितैः पञ्चभूतैस्ताभिस्तन्मात्राभिश्चेत्यन्वयः। तदर्थं दर्शयति—अर्थात्मकतामुक्तामित्यादिना। यादीनिति सन्निधानादुक्तम्। यद्वा यादिशब्देन सर्ववर्णग्रहणम्। अथवा गुणसहितैस्तन्मात्राभिश्च सहितैर्भूतैः सह यादीनिति संबन्धनीयम्। गुणसहितैरित्यत्र सकलकरणैरित्युपस्कारः। गुणकरणतन्मात्राभूतान्वितान् बिन्दुवर्णानभ्युपेतेति तात्पर्यार्थः। अत्र 'विचिकीर्षुर्घनीभूतेत्यत आरभ्य 'भीत्या च परिरोदितीत्यत उक्तार्थसृष्टिरनूदितेति सर्गानुवादोऽयमेतावान् भवति।

मूले अथ व्यतीत्य व्याप्य हसंज्ञा भवेदित्यन्वयः। तदभिप्रायं दर्शयति—संहारमाहेति। व्यत्ययो यथोक्तव्यापारविपर्ययः। तदाह—कार्यजातमुक्तं स्वात्मन्येव संहृत्येति। स्वस्वरूपाद्येन क्रमेण कार्यजातमुभयविधमुत्पन्नमुक्तं तत्सर्वं तद्व्युत्क्रमेण स्वस्वरूपोपसंहृतं कृत्वेत्यर्थः। विश्वं व्याप्येत्येतद्विवृणोति—विश्वं सर्वमित्यादिना। परिपूर्णस्वभावत्वाद्विश्वमिति देवतातत्त्वमुक्तम्। अत एव ब्रह्मपदोपादानम्। तेनाभिन्नतामिति। सा तत्त्वसंज्ञेतीमामेव प्रकृतामवस्थामिति भावः। यद्वा विश्वं व्याप्य व्यतीत्य हसंज्ञा भवेदिति सम्बन्धनीयम्। तथाच सृष्टानां व्याप्तिरपीह पटल उक्तोपसंगृहीता भवति। ह इति संज्ञा वाचकं यस्याः सा हसंज्ञा। सर्वानित्यमुवाच ह इति प्रागारम्भ एवोक्ताक्षरलक्षणा प्रकृतिरिति॥७५॥

इति प्रयोगक्रमदीपिकायां तृतीयः पटलः।

अथ चतुर्थः पटलः।

इह 'के वयं केन भाविता' 'यूयमक्षरसंभूता' इत्यादित एवाक्षरस्य तद्विसाधकस्य च प्रकृतत्वादुभयोश्चातोऽनुवृत्तत्वादुभयथापि स्यात् पटलसङ्गतिरिति। पूर्वं तावदक्षरोचितां पटलसङ्गतिमाह—एवमिति। पूर्वोक्ताद्बिन्दुमात्रादित्यनूदितः प्रकार एवमित्युक्तः। हकारस्येति वाच्यवाचकाभेदात्मकस्याक्षरस्य प्रकृतत्वेऽपि वाचकांशस्यैव ग्रहणम्। केवलस्येति रेफाद्यपेक्षयोक्तम्। विश्वयोनित्वमिति। सङ्गतिमात्रमेतदुक्तम् न तु हेतुतया सङ्गत्यभिधानमिति ज्ञेयम्। तेन संहारस्योक्तत्वेऽपि तदनुपादानमिति। आदाविति प्रपञ्चसारारम्भ एव—मूलार्णमर्णविकृतिरित्यत्रेत्यर्थः। प्राप्तस्येति। हकारस्य रेफादियोगतस्तत्प्राप्तिर्भवति।

विश्वयोनित्वमिति। नास्मिन् शक्तिपटले विश्वस्य स्थितिसंहाराभिधानमित्येवमुक्तम्। चतुर्थपटलारम्भ इति मूलगताथशब्दार्थोऽप्युक्तः।

मूल एवं व्यवस्थिते त्वस्य शक्तित्वमिष्यत इत्यन्वयः। विश्वस्य जगतो हलक्षणादुत्पत्तिः तत्र स्थितिः तस्मिन्नेव च प्रलय इत्येतत्तावदेवं व्यवस्थितम्। तथा च सत्यस्य प्रकृतस्य परावाक्तदर्थात्मकस्य हस्याक्षरस्य शक्तित्वमिष्यत इति तदक्षरार्थः। तत्र जगति कृतकृत्यस्य जगत्येव सततं रूढ़संस्थितेरिति हेतुगर्भं विशेषणम्। हादक्षराज्जगत उत्पत्त्यादिनियमे सति तज्जगद्विषयतया यत्किञ्चित्तस्य कर्तव्यं स्यात् तत्सर्वमविकृतमेव। येन न किंचिदकृतमशक्यमवशिष्यते स तथोक्तः। तथा तस्मिन्नेव जगति सततं सर्वस्मिन्नपि काले देशे च रूढाक्षरमेवायं घटशब्दः तदर्थो वेत्येवं निरुढा संस्थितिर्यस्य स तथोक्तः। जगतस्तत्रैव कल्पिताकारत्वमनेनोक्तम्। यत एवमसौ हो भवति अतोऽनेन शक्त्या भाव्यमित्यवसीयत इति भावः। स्वस्मिन्नेव स्वरूपे स्वस्वातन्त्र्येणैव विश्ववैचित्र्योत्पादनतदवस्थापनविलयनकरत्वं हि तावच्छक्तित्वनिबन्धनमिति। साधकाभिप्राये तु विशेषः। हाक्षरमेव जीवतापत्तितो जन्तुभावप्राप्तौ साधकदशां प्रतिपद्यते। तत्स्वरूपभूताच्च तदक्षरतो वाङ्मनसोर्यावद्विश्वमुक्तिप्रतीतिरूपेण प्रसर इत्येतत्तावदेवं व्यवस्थितम्। तथा च सत्यसौ साधको जगति कृतकृत्यो जगत्येव रूढसंस्थितिश्च सच्छक्तिरेवावसीयत इति महतोऽक्षरस्य कलेव तावदसौ साधकस्तस्य चैतावदेव कृत्यम् यत्तेनैव कृते विश्वस्मिन् जगति स्वाधिकारानुरूपतोऽवभासनमभिधानं च। यदुक्तम्—इत्थं विश्वं प्रतीयतेऽप्यव्यक्तं प्रलपतीति। नातोऽधिकं तदयोगात् तत्सर्वमप्यनेन कृतमेव भवति। तत्र च जगत्यस्य सततं निरूढैव संस्थितिः। तत्तदुक्तिप्रतीतिषु स्वरूपचितोऽपि तत्तदर्थेष्वनुगमात्। अन्यथा तत्प्रतीत्यनुपपत्तेः। तथा च स्वस्वरूप एव स्वस्वातन्त्र्येणैव तत्तज्जगद्वैचित्र्योत्पादनतदवस्थापनविलयकरत्वमेतदेव हि शक्तित्वनिबन्धनमिति महतोऽक्षरस्य जगतोऽपूर्वस्यावभासः। साधकाक्षरस्य तु स्वस्वरूपे तस्य विद्यमानस्यैवावभास इति भेदः। एवं च साधकस्य महाशक्त्यंशमात्रत्वात्तद्रूढिसिद्धये तन्न्यासजपध्यानाद्युपदेशस्तावदिह कर्तव्य इति।

अस्यैव श्लोकस्य सूक्ष्ममर्थं दर्शयति—अथशब्दो हेत्वर्थ इत्यादिना। स्वयमेवेति। नेहाक्षरतो जगदुत्पत्त्यादिमात्रं तस्य शक्तित्वसिद्धौ निबन्धनम्। तच्च न स्वयमेव वाच्यमिति भावः। उक्तेन प्रकारेणेत्येवंशब्दविवरणम्। 'प्रकृतेश्च क्वचित्काल' इत्यत आरभ्य 'हसंज्ञा भवेदित्यत उक्तः प्रकारोऽयं गृह्यते। कारणत्वेनेति हाक्षरत्वेनेति विशेषणतयाऽध्याहारः। व्यवस्थित इत्युपपादनेन व्यवस्था

हि सिध्यतीति भावः। तुशब्दोऽवधारणार्थ इति प्रकारान्तरेण जगतः सर्गाद्यनुपपत्तेरवधारणसिद्धिः स्यात्। अस्य हकारस्येति। जगतो निमित्तोपादानकारणतया प्रकृतस्येति भावः। शक्तित्वमिति। ननु ह्यक्षरस्य नित्यतां सर्वात्मतामपि चोपपादयितुं ततो जगतः सर्गाद्युक्तम् तथा च तदुभयमपोहेषितव्यमिति। नैष दोषः। यदुपपादयितुमेतदुक्तं तत्सर्वं प्रकृतिरथ हसंज्ञेत्यत्रार्थादुपपन्नं सिध्यति। किन्तु तत्र शक्तित्वमिह तदीयविभूतिविवक्षयाऽनूद्यत एवेति।

ननु जगतो ह्यक्षरत्वे व्यवस्थितेऽपि कथमस्य शक्तित्वमवसीयतामिति। उच्यते। ह्यक्षरस्य तदुचितशक्तित्वव्यतिरेकेण जगतस्तद्भावानुपपत्तेरेतच्छक्तित्वसिद्धिरिति। अतएव हेतोरपि कारणत्वेन व्यवस्थित इति सप्तम्योपादानम्। शक्तिवाचकमन्त्रत्वमिति। ननु वाच्यवाचकरूपस्य ह्यक्षरस्य शक्तित्वं तावदिहावसीयते। प्रकृतिरथ हसंज्ञेत्युक्तत्वात् रूढसंस्थितेरित्यत्र रेफेकाराभ्यां शक्त्यसाधारणरूपयोः कार्यशक्तितदीशानयोरपि ग्रहणसंभवाच्चेति। नैष दोषः। वाच्यांशस्य शक्तिमात्रत्वमेवावसेयम्। वाचकांशे तु रेफादियोगोऽपि तद्योगोपपत्त्या त्वपि तस्यां वाच्यशक्तौ कार्यशक्तितदीशयोगप्रतीतिः स्यादिति। गुणत्रयात्मकशक्तिवाचकत्वमिति। सत्त्वादिगुणात्मकत्वमक्षरत्वेऽप्यस्या भवेदेव न तच्छक्तित्वनिबन्धनमिति भावः। रेफेकारयो रजस्तमोवचनत्वेऽपि कार्यशक्तितदीशानाभिधानत्वमविरुद्धमेव। वर्णवाचकानामनेकशक्तित्वाभ्युपगमात्। यत उक्तम्—अथोभयात्मका वर्णास्त एव स्युः त्रिधा भूय इत्यादि। वर्णान्तरसंयोग इति कर्तव्यतयाभिप्रेतो विशेषोऽयमुक्तः। मन्त्रत्वेष्टेरिति। मन्त्रत्वस्येष्टत्वादित्यर्थः। हकारं विशिनष्टीति। दुर्विग्रहत्वाद्विशेषणस्यैतदुक्तम्। रेफोढ इति। रेफमूढवान् धृतवानिति यावत्। ईरित्ययमीकारः। संस्थितेरिति आद्गुण इति सन्धौ प्रथमैकवचनमिति ज्ञेयम्। अत्र त्वीकारस्य ङीबादिस्त्रीप्रत्ययमात्रतयाभिप्रेतत्वात् गोस्त्रियोरुपसर्जनस्येति ह्रस्वभावोऽपोह्यत इत्यवबोद्धव्यम्। तथा च रूढसंस्थितेरित्यादिनिर्देशोपपत्तिः। व्याप्तत्वात् तस्येति पूर्वेणान्वय इति।

इदानीं साधकोचितां पटलसङ्गतिमपि दर्शयति—जातस्येत्यादिना। साधकस्याप्यादित आरभ्यानुवृत्तत्वेऽपि गतपटले तस्यादर्शनादस्येति तत्परामर्शानुयोग इत्यत एतावदुच्यते। अत्रायमाशयः। ब्रह्महरीश्वराख्या इत्यादित एव प्रकृतस्य साधकस्य ह्यक्षरांशतयोत्पत्तिस्तथोत्पन्नाच्च ततस्तदक्षरप्रसरतया वर्णानामुत्पत्तिस्तदवस्थायामेव च तेषामग्नीषोमादिरूपेण व्याप्तिरित्येतत्सर्वं गतपटलैरुक्तम्। ततश्च शक्तिपटलेऽपि साधकोऽनुवृत्त इति। जातस्य निर्गतानामिति पदाभ्यामाद्य-

पटलयोरपि तदनुगतिरुक्ता। व्याप्त्यादिकमिति। व्याप्तिस्तदुत्पत्तिर्निष्पत्तिरन्यच्चेत्यर्थः। अभिहितमिति। ततश्च मूल एवमस्येति च निर्देशोपपत्तिरिति भावः। अथैवमिति प्राग्वदथशब्दो हेत्वर्थः। स चैवं व्यवस्थित इति स्वयमेव दर्शितः। एतद्विवृणोति—एवं वर्णानामिति। वर्णास्तावदग्नीषोमादय एव। ते च वर्णा हकारस्यैव विकारो ह्यक्षरमेव साधकस्य स्वरूपमित्यसौ गतपटलगतः प्रकार एवमित्युक्तः। तेन च तथाविधानां वर्णानां ह्यक्षरत्वलक्षणमेव तत्त्वं व्यवस्थितं भवति। तुशब्दोऽवधारणार्थः। तेषां प्रसिद्धाकारमात्रत्वायोगादुक्तव्यवस्थावच्छेदितः स्यात्। वर्णोच्चारकस्येति। एवमनुवृत्तस्य साधकस्येति भावः। यद्यपीह जातः शिशुरेवानुवृत्तस्तथापि ब्रह्महरीश्वराख्या इत्यादित एव प्रकृतस्य साधकस्याक्षरांशतोपपिपादयिषयैव तस्य जीवजन्तुपुरुषतापत्त्यभिधानाच्छिशुत्वेऽपि न्यासयोगादिसमुचितवयोऽवस्थादिप्रतीक्षणोपपत्तेश्च साधकतोपपत्तिरिति।

ननु वर्णानामेवं तत्त्वे व्यवस्थितेऽपि कथमस्य शक्तित्वमिष्यतामिति। उच्यते। साधकस्वरूपस्य शक्तित्वव्यतिरेकेण ततो विसृतानां वर्णानामित्थं व्यवस्था नोपपद्यते। तथा चास्य शक्तित्वमवसीयते। किन्तु मलिनं परिच्छिन्नं चैतत् शक्तितत्त्वमतोऽस्य विशुद्धत्वं महत्त्वं चैषितव्यमेव। एतदभिप्रायेणैव च जगन्मूलकारणशक्त्यात्मकत्वमिष्यत इत्युक्तम्। तथा प्राकृतस्य परिच्छिन्नस्येति चोक्तम्। स्वतो विशुद्धमपरिच्छिन्नमपि हि तत्त्वं भवति। योग्यत्वस्येति। शक्तित्वं हि तावत्साध्यम् तस्य न्यासादिः साधनम्। तेन च स्वशक्तिगतमालिन्यपरिच्छेदादिक्षयतो महाशक्त्याकाराभिव्यक्तिरित्येवमुक्तम्। किञ्च न्यासानां भूयस्त्वात्तेषामेव चावृत्त्यानुष्ठेयत्वात् तद्रूढियोग्यताप्रधानो न्यासादिरिति चैवमुक्तम्। सम्पाद्यमानत्वादित्यस्मिन्नेव शक्तिपटल इति भावः। सम्पादितत्वाच्चेति (गत)पटलेष्विति भावः। तेषु ह्यणुयोगादय उपदिष्टा इति तथा च तत्रोक्तं—दृष्ट्वा देशिकदर्शितैरिति।

ननु स्वस्वरूपे शक्तितत्त्वे महाशक्तेरनन्यतयाऽनुसन्धानमेव कार्यम् नतु न्यास इति। नैष दोषः। क्रमसाध्यमेव ह्येतदनुसन्धानम्। ततश्च प्रथमं तावत्स्वदेहे स्वशक्तिविभूतिरूपे महाशक्तिविभूतिरूपस्य विश्वजगद्विग्रहस्यानन्यतया सन्निधानं न्यासेन कार्यम्। ततस्तथा जपो ध्यानम् ततस्तन्मूलभूतशक्तिमात्रपर्यन्ततया योगश्चेति। एतदभिप्रायेण च मूले जगतीत्येतत्पदमुपात्तमिति मन्यमानो विवृणोति—जगति सर्वतत्त्वात्मके शरीर इति। कृत्स्नमपि स्थूलसूक्ष्माकारेण सामान्यसाक्षिलक्षणमक्षरशक्ते रूपमिह सम्पादयितुमुचितमित्यनेन सूचितम्।

सततं रूढसंस्थितिरित्यनेन न्यासादिभिर्यत्नतो जन्यं शक्तिसिद्धिपूर्वावस्थारूपं

फलमुक्तम्। प्रसिद्धेति। स्वात्मन्येव प्रथितेत्यर्थः। संविद्रूपप्रकृत्यात्मकत्वेनेति। चिद्रूपस्य पुरुषस्य स्वात्मविश्रान्तिलक्षणमानन्दरूपं ज्ञानं संविदुच्यते। तदेव च प्रकृतिशक्तिरूपम्। तदुक्तं—प्रकाशविमर्शरूपेण चिदानन्दरूपेण वेति। चिदानन्दयोरेकार्थत्वेऽपि तथा विकल्प्यत्वादेतदुपपत्तिः। यद्वा जगति सततं रूढसंस्थितेरिति संबन्धनीयम्। व्यष्ट्यात्मके स्वदेहे समष्टिदेहन्यासतस्तत्प्रतीतौ तदनुसन्धानप्रचयतस्तत्र समष्ट्यात्मनि सततं रूढा संस्थितिः स्यात्। ततश्च सततं रूढा प्रसिद्धेत्याद्युक्ता स्थितिर्भवेदिति।

यद्वाथैवं व्यवस्थित इत्यत्राथशब्दः पूर्वोक्तानन्तर्यार्थः। तत्राभिप्रेतं पूर्ववृत्तं तावद्दर्शयति—जातस्येति। वर्णानां व्याप्त्यादिकथनानन्तरमिदानीमस्य तदुच्चारकतयानुवृत्तस्य साधकस्य शक्तित्वमिष्यते। तत्संपिपादयिषया तद्विभूतिकथनमारभ्यत इति तत्र हेतुरेवं व्यवस्थित इत्युक्तः। एतद्विवृणोति—एवं वर्णानां तत्त्वे व्यवस्थित इति। वर्णानां तत्त्वमग्नीषोमाद्यात्मकत्वम्। अयं भावः। वर्णानां तत्त्वं तावत् तेषामग्नीषोमाद्यात्मकत्वम्। तच्च साधकान्तर्गतायास्तत्स्वरूपभूतायाः शक्तेरेव कार्यमर्थादवसीयते। तथा च सति वर्णानां व्याप्तावभिहितायां तेषु वर्णेषु साधकस्याग्नीषोमादिरूपेण स्वान्तर्गतशक्तिकार्यतयाऽवभासमानेषु केवलं सा शक्तिस्तस्य स्वरूपभूता ह्यसती न तथावभासत इत्येतावदेव जातम्। ततस्तत्सिद्धये तस्य साधकस्य शक्तित्वमिदानीमिष्यते। शक्तौ तु तथाऽवभासमानायां स्वविभूतितया मन्त्रन्यासजपादिषु सा वर्णविभूतिरवभासत इति। अनेन पुरा गुणितप्रकरणे हृल्लेखादिविभूतीनामिह च वर्णविभूतीनां तत्तन्न्यासजपादिषु तथावभास उपयोग इत्यपि सूचितम्। तत्र हृल्लेखादीनां विभूतयस्तत्तन्मन्त्रन्यासजपादिविशेषा एव। वर्णानां विभूतयस्तु मातृकान्यासजपादिविशेषाः सर्वमन्त्रन्यासजपादिविशेषाश्चेति भेदोऽवबोद्धव्यः। जगन्मूलकारणशक्त्यात्मकत्वमिष्यत इति। वर्णविभूतीनां समष्टित्वात् तत्कारणशक्त्यापि समष्टिभूतया भाव्यमिति भावः। प्राकृतस्येति। शक्तिविपरीततया निरूढात्मनस्तच्छक्त्युपदेशमात्रेण तदात्मकत्वमुपपन्नमिति भावः। न्यासयोगादिभिरिति। न केवलमिह कृत्स्नायाः शक्तेरभिधानं तदवबोधार्थमेव। अपितु तथा न्यासयोगाद्यर्थमपीति भावः। न्यासयोगादिभिश्चात्मनः प्राकृतरूढिप्रचयपूर्विका कृत्स्ने शक्त्यात्मन्यपरिच्छिन्नाकारे निरूढिः स्यादिति जगति सततं रूढसंस्थितेरित्युक्तम्। ततश्च शक्तिरेवासौ साधकः सम्पद्यत इति ॥ १ ॥

एवं तावत्साधकस्य न्यासयोगादिक्रमेण हृल्लेखात्मकशक्तित्वसिद्धये तद्व्याप्तिकथनन्यासमन्त्रस्थानादिप्रतिपादनं चेह प्रस्तुतं भवति। तत्र प्रथमं तावद्धृल्लेखायाः

त्वंशप्रधाना साधकगतप्राणतद्धर्मांद्यर्थशक्तिलक्षणा व्याप्तिरुच्यते। प्राणात्मकं हकाराख्यमिति। एतदाह—उक्तस्याक्षरत्रयस्येति। रूढसंस्थितेरस्येत्युक्ताया हृल्लेखायास्त्रयाणां वर्णानामित्यर्थः। प्रकृत्यात्मकत्वसिद्धय इति। न्यासयोगादिभिस्तन्निरूढिद्वारा तदात्मत्वसिद्धय इत्यर्थः। कालपुरुषाविभक्ता प्रकृतिशक्तिरिहाभिप्रेयते। षोड़शाङ्गन्यासमिति। वक्ष्यति च—इतीदं षोड़शाङ्गवदिति। प्रथमतोऽस्याभिधानौचित्यमप्यनेन सूचितम्। साधकस्य तावद् बुभुक्षादयः प्रथिताः। ततस्तेषां शक्त्यंशतयाऽनुसन्धानं सुकरं स्यादिति भावः।

मूले हकाराख्यं बीजं प्राणात्मकं स्यात् तदुद्भवाः षड़ूर्मयः स्युरिति योजना। हकार आख्या यस्य हेत्येतस्य तत्तथोक्तम्। बीजशब्देन वाचकवर्णत्वमुक्तम्। प्राण आत्मा स्वं रूपं यस्येति समासः। बुभुक्षा च पिपासा चेत्युक्ताः षड़ूर्मयः। बुभुक्षादीनां हकारकार्यतायां निबन्धनं तस्य प्राणात्मकत्वमेवेति तेनेत्युक्तम्। ननु कथं शोकादीनां प्राणधर्मत्वमित्यत आह—प्राणे सत्येवेति ॥ २ ॥

मूले रेफोत्था गुणा इति। के त इत्यपेक्षायां पवनाद्या इत्युक्तम्। तदाह—गुणचतुष्टयमिति। स्पर्शाद्यैरितीति। स्पर्शादिगुणयोग इति भावः। पारतन्त्र्याद्वा गुणशब्दस्तेष्विति। प्राणस्तावदादिशक्तेः क्रियाशक्तिः। सा च बुभुक्षादिशक्तीनां समष्टिः। तस्या ज्ञानशक्तिर्मनआदीनां समष्टिः। तस्या एव कार्यशक्तिराकाशः। स च वाय्वादीनां समष्टिः। प्राणस्य ग्रहणादाकाशस्य च गुणिष्वगणनाद्रेफिकारस्वरूपतया आकाशज्ञानशक्त्योरपि ग्रहणं लभ्यते। तत्र च ज्ञानक्रियाशक्तितन्त्रत्वं कार्यशक्तेरस्तीति पारतन्त्र्याद्वेत्युक्तम्। तेष्विति। यद्यपीकारस्य गुणा इति मनआदयोऽपि गुणा एव। किन्तु तेषां गुणत्वं मननादिवृत्तिप्रधानत्वात् न तु पारतन्त्र्यादिति दर्शितम्। विशिष्टः कार्यकरणसङ्घात इति। अत्र श्रोत्रादीनां करणेष्वन्तर्भावोऽभिप्रेतः। त्रिशिष्टः शरीराकारेण व्यवस्थितः। अवशिष्ट इति वा पाठः। प्राणाद्यंशेषु गृहीतेषु तेषां सङ्घाताकारमवशिष्यते स इत्यर्थः।

मूले बुधैरिति। बुभुक्षादिशक्तीनां सर्वप्राणिगततयः समष्टित्वं प्राणाकाशज्ञानशक्तीनामादिशक्तेर्व्यष्टित्वम् आदिशक्तेरपि कालपुरुषाविभक्तत्वमित्येतत्सर्वमुक्तम्। वक्ष्यति च—प्रणवशक्तिभ्यां व्यापकमिति। न्यासविषये विशेषः। प्राणात्मकपदेन मन्त्र आत्मपदयोग उक्तः। तदभिप्रायेण विवृणोति—प्राणशरीरमिति। बीजत्वादेव तस्य बिन्दुयोगो लभ्यते। तदाह—बिन्दुसहितमिति। स्यादिति शेषः। किं सिद्धं भवतीत्याह—हं प्राणात्मन इति : कृतकृत्यस्येत्युक्तत्वादेव न्यासो बुधैरिति निर्देशाच्च तस्य स्थानमपि सिध्यतीत्यवसेयम्। तेनेति सहार्थे तृतीया।

तदाह—तेन प्राणात्मकेनेति। यथायोग्यमिति। प्राणस्य देहान्तर्व्यापित्वात्तथा व्यापकतया बुभुक्षापिपासयोर्न्यासः मनसो हृद्गतत्वाद्धृदि शोकमोहयोरितरयोर्देह एव व्यापकतया न्यास इत्यभिप्रायः। करणान्यपीति। अत्रापिशब्दात् ज्ञानशक्तिसिद्धिरिति भावः। मनआदिष्विति। हृद्येव तत्तद्बुद्ध्येति भावः। सङ्घातस्य शरीरे व्यापकं भवतीति। अथ मूल जकारान्तास्वित्यादिना बुभुक्षादिशक्त्यनुगतिभ्यो हकारादिभ्योऽकारादिस्वराणां बुभुक्षादिशक्तिवाचकतयोत्पत्तिरुक्ता।

हकारस्य महात्मन इति। तस्य जात्या प्राणवाचित्वेऽपि व्यक्तिभिर्बुभुक्षादिवाचकत्वमिति सूचितम्। न्यासविषये विशेषः। बुभुक्षादिभ्योऽकाराद्युत्पत्तिकथनेन मन्त्रेषु तत्तद्योग उक्तः। तत्र विशेषस्तुशब्देनोक्तः। तदाह—तुशब्द इति। अत्र केवलहरमायायोगि तद्युतस्वरयोगि च बुभुक्षादिशक्तीनां सूक्ष्मस्थूलतया भेदो द्रष्टव्यः। ऋं वायुस्पर्शाभ्यां नम इत्यत्रापीत्यादयो मन्त्रा इति सम्बन्धनीयम्। येमित्यपीकार एकारादिश्च संहित इति ज्ञेयम्। अत्रापि न्यासे प्राग्वत् प्राणाकाशज्ञानशक्तिन्यास इष्यत एव। मूले हकारस्य महात्मन इति। महात्मत्वं स्वव्यष्टिसहितत्वम्। एतच्च प्रदर्शनार्थम्। तेन रेफमाययोरप्येवं महात्मत्वं लभ्यते। न्यासप्रकरणत्वाच्च न्यासार्थमेतदपि स्यात्। तदाह—हकारस्येत्यादिना। ऋं ॠं ऌं रेफात्मने नमः। यें यैं यों यौं यं यः ईकारात्मने नम इति मन्त्रद्वयमादिग्रहणेनोक्तम्।

मूले इतीदं षोडशाङ्गवदित्यस्यायमर्थः। यदिदमुक्तं तत् षोडशाङ्गवच्च स्यात्। षोडशाङ्गानि यस्य शक्तिबीजस्य तच्च षोडशाङ्गमिति। एतदभिप्रायेण तत्तद्बीजयुतेत्याद्युक्तम्। प्रणवोऽत्रापीष्यते। ॐ हं हां हिं हीं हुं हूं ऋं ॠं ऌं ॡं यें यैं यों यौं यं यः क्षीं नम इत्यसौ महाव्यापकमन्त्र इति॥ ३॥४॥५॥६॥

अथ मूले एभ्यः सञ्जज्ञिर इत्यासां स्थूलानामपि बुभुक्षादिशक्तीनां प्रत्येकं षट्त्रिंशद्विधो द्विधावान्तरभेद उक्तः। हकारादीनामेवैभ्योऽङ्गेभ्य इत्यकारादिविशिष्टानां बुभुक्षादीनां ग्रहणम्। सर्वगा इति। यावन्तो बुभुक्षादीनामवान्तरभेदाः तान् गच्छति वाचकतयेति सर्वगाः। तत्र बुभुक्षाशक्तेस्तावत् सत्त्वरजस्तमोभेदेन त्रयो भेदाः। तत्र सत्त्वभेदेऽपि केवलसत्त्वेन रजःस्पृष्टेन तमःस्पृष्टेन तदुभयस्पृष्टेन च सत्त्वेन भेदचतुष्टयम्। तत्रापि तीव्रमध्यमन्दतया भेदत्रयम्। एवं द्वादशविधा सात्त्विकी बुभुक्षा स्यात्। तथा राजसी तामसी चेति। एवं पिपासादिष्वपि संभव इति। न्यासविषये विशेषः। तदाह—एभ्य उक्तेभ्य इत्यादिना। पूर्वोक्तस्वरपारायणन्यासवदित्यनेन षोडशदलानि पद्मानि सञ्चिन्त्य तेषां दलेषु न्यास उक्तः। तानि च पद्मानि वर्णस्थानेष्वेव चिन्त-

नीयानि नतु प्राणादिस्थानेष्वित्येवकारेणोक्तः। अयमिह प्रयोगः। शिरसि षोडशदलं पद्मं सञ्चिन्त्य तत्कर्णिकायां हं बुभुक्षायै नमः विन्यस्य तत्र पूर्वादिदलेषु हं अं बुभुक्षायै नमः हां आं पिपासायै नमः इत्यादिषोडशमन्त्रान्न्यसेत्। पुनः कामबुज एव न्यासः। कखादिक्षान्ताक्षरसंयुक्ताः स्वरा इत्युक्तत्वात्। तस्मिन् पद्मे कर्णिकायां हं बुभुक्षायै नम इत्येव विन्यस्य पूर्वादिदलेषु हं कं बुभुक्षायै नमः हां कां पिपासायै नम इत्यादि षोडश मन्त्रान् न्यसेत्। एवं क्षान्तमूह्यम्। अयं कर्णिकायां बुभुक्षान्यासेनैकः पर्यायः। एवं पिपासादिन्यासेन पञ्चदश पर्यायाः स्युः। पिपासादिन्यासभेदा इति वक्ष्यमाणत्वादेतदवसीयत इति।

अथ मूले तेभ्यो वर्णान्तराः सर्वे इत्येष्ववान्तरभेदेष्वपि प्रत्येकं विषयावान्तरभेदसंभवादवान्तरभेद उक्तः। वर्णान्तरा अकखादय एव। ते च सर्वे भवन्ति। य एतेषामपि भेदानां विषयेषु प्राग्वद्गुणतत्संसर्गतत्त्वे(ये)वादिभेदतो भूयोऽपि षट्त्रिंशदवान्तरभेदास्तदभेदास्तदभेदात् सर्वत्वमिहाभिप्रेयते। न्यासविषये विशेषः। तदाह—तेभ्य इत्यादिना। अकारपद्मदलेष्विति। शिरसि प्राग्वत् षोड़शदलं पद्मं प्रकल्प्य कर्णिकायां हं बुभुक्षायै नम इति विन्यस्य पूर्वदलमध्ये हं अं बुभुक्षायै नम इति विन्यस्य हं अं अः बुभुक्षायै नम इत्यादि षट्त्रिंशन्मन्त्रान् तत्परिवारत्वेन तत्र परितो न्यसेत्। ततो द्वितीयदलमध्ये हां आं पिपासायै नम इति विन्यस्य परितः हं अं बुभुक्षायै नम इत्यादि षट्त्रिंशन्मन्त्रान् न्यसेदित्यादि प्रतिपत्तव्यम्। काम्बुजदलेष्वित्यत्रापि आकारादिविसर्गान्तस्थानेषु न न्यासः। आदौ हां ह्रिमादियुक्ता इति। पिपासावर्गे हांयोगः। शोकवर्गे हिं योग इत्यादि। आदिस्वरैरेवेति। प्राग्वदेवेति भावः। पिपासावर्गे तावच्छिरसि पद्मे कर्णिकायां हां पिपासायै नम इति विन्यस्य पूर्वदलमध्ये हां अं बुभुक्षायै नम इति विन्यस्य हां अं कं पिपासायै नमः हां आं कं पिपासायै नम इत्यादि षट्त्रिंशन्मन्त्रान् परितो न्यसेत्। द्वितीयदलमध्ये हां आं पिपासायै नम इति विन्यस्य परितः हां आं कं पिपासायै नमः हां आं खं पिपासायै नम इत्यादि षट्त्रिंशन्मन्त्रान् विन्यसेत्। एवं शोकादिवर्गेष्वपि ऊह्यमिति।

द्वितीयदीर्घादिसंयुता इति। द्वितीयो दीर्घ आकारः। आदिशब्देन तृतीयक्रमादिषोडशविसर्गान्तस्वरग्रहणम्। यद्यपि द्वितीयादिस्वरसंयुता इति वाच्यम् तथापि द्वितीयदीर्घादिग्रहणं द्वितीयस्वरयोगेन एको वर्गस्तृतीयस्वरयोगेनैक इत्यादिवर्गविभागस्फूर्त्यर्थमिति ज्ञेयम्। त्रिबीजं ह्येते मन्त्रा भवन्ति। तत्र तृतीयबीजेष्वयं ब्रह्मविष्ण्वादिस्वरयोगो दर्शितः। ततो मूलमिदं विदुरित्यस्यार्थमाह—

प्रतिपर्यायमिति। प्रतिदलन्यासः प्रतिपद्मन्यासो वात्राभिप्रेयते। ततश्च प्रणवशक्तिभ्यां तत्र तत्र व्यापकं भवति। अत एव व्यापकन्यासा इति बहुवचनमिति॥७॥

अथ गतो वो बीजतामिष इत्यस्या एव शक्तेस्त्रिबीजप्रधानेव साधकगतव्यक्ताव्यक्तार्थशक्तिलक्षणव्याप्तिरुच्यते। तदाह—गतो व इति। षडध्वन्यासः सूचित इति। तथा व्याप्तिं वदतीत्यर्थाल्लभ्यते। साधकस्य प्रकृत्यात्मकत्वसिद्धय इत्येतदिह समानम्। गतो वो बीजतामिष इति ब्रह्मादीन् प्रत्यभिधानाद्द इति तेषां ग्रहणम्। एष मन्त्रः खांशैर्हकारादिभिर्ब्रह्मादीनां त्रिमूर्तीनां बीजतां प्राप्तस्तदात्मकः संपृक्त इत्यर्थः। न्यासविषये विशेषः। तदाह—वो युष्माकमिति। ईश्वरसदाशिवयोरपीति। बिन्दुनादयोरेतद्बीजत्वमुक्तम्। यद्यपि त्वंशशकोऽपि विषडध्वा विद्यत एव। किन्तु नात्रातिसंक्षेपो नाप्यतिविस्तार इति पञ्चांशकः षडध्वा परिगृहीत इति ज्ञेयम्।

अयमिह प्रयोगः। हं ब्रह्मणे नमः रं विष्णवे नमः ईं रुद्राय नमः क्लीं ईश्वराय नमः क्लीं सदाशिवाय नमः इति पादगुह्यहृन्मुखमूर्धसु न्यसेत्। यतो वक्ष्यति—मूर्तिस्थानेषु न्यास इति। अथ प्राणिष्वेवं व्यवस्थित इत्यस्य त्रिमूर्त्यात्मकस्याक्षरत्रयस्य सकलप्राणिदेहपर्यन्तं व्याप्तिरुच्यते। एवमित्यनेनैतदुक्तम्। यथा पूर्वं हकारादित्रयं प्राणाद्यात्मकं तत्कार्यैर्म्यादिद्वारा प्राणिशरीरे व्याप्तमेवमिह त्रिमूर्त्यात्मकं तत्कार्यार्थद्वारा प्राणिशरीरे व्याप्तमिति। तदेतदुक्तम्—एवमुक्तेन प्रकारेण पञ्चमूर्त्यात्मकत्वे सतीति। तत्र प्राणाद्यात्मकम् इह तु ब्रह्माद्यात्मकमिति भेदः। कार्याणामनुगमे कार्यार्थानामप्यवश्यमनुगमादेवमुक्तम्। न्यासविषये विशेषः। तदाह—प्राणिष्विति। अध्वषट्कविशिष्टेषु जीवेष्विति। तेषां शरीरस्वभावत एव षडध्वात्मत्वमिति भावः। तथा च सकलजगदधीशेत्यत्रोक्तं कलाभिरवयवैरित्यादि। एवमित्यत्र सतीत्युपस्कारः। पञ्चमूर्त्यात्मकत्वं चेह विशेषः। तदाह—एवमुक्तेन प्रकारेणेति। यद्वा प्राणिष्वस्मिन् युष्माकं बीजे सतीति मूलार्थः। तदाह—एवमुक्तेनेति। बीजस्य पञ्चमूर्त्यात्मकत्वे सतीति भावः। अध्वाभिमानित्वेनेति। मूर्त्यभिमानित्वात् तद्द्वारेतद्विवक्षितम्। किमिह सिद्धं भवतीत्याह—अध्वोपाधिकेति। विस्तरस्याशक्यत्वादिति। षडध्वन्यासस्त्विह संग्रहेण विस्तरेणापि वा कार्य इत्यपि सूचितम्। शिवायै इति वेति सकलशक्तिमन्त्रविषयं द्रष्टव्यम्। सद्योजातादय इति। सद्योजातं प्रपद्यामीत्यादिग्रहणम्। पृथिव्यादीनीति पञ्चभूतग्रहणम्।

अथ ब्रह्माण्डं ग्रस्तमितिनेति सकलप्राणिशरीरात्मकस्य ब्रह्माण्डकबलीकारेण व्याप्तिरुक्ता। न्यासविषये विशेषः। तदाह—प्रणवेन तानिति। क्रमेणेति। वर्णानां तत्त्वेष्वित्यादिक्रम उक्तः। कथमिह वर्णतत्त्वाद्यध्वनामपि संहारो

लभ्यत इत्याह—ब्रह्माण्डमितीति। अथ व्याप्तस्थावरजङ्गममिति ब्रह्माण्डव्यापिनोऽपि तदन्तर्गतसकलप्राणिषु मूर्त्याद्यनुगमव्यतिरेकेणैकरूपतयाऽन्तर्मुखतया प्रसरलक्षणा व्याप्तिरुक्ता। न्यासविषये विशेषमाह—मूर्त्यधिष्ठेयतयेति। तत्तत्तत्त्वादिवर्तिन इति। तत्त्वेषु वा भुवनेषु वा वर्तमानस्येत्यर्थः। तत्रापि पृथिव्यबादीनां भूम्यन्तरिक्षादीनामपि भावात्तत्तच्छब्दोपादानम्। ननु प्राणिष्वध्वषट्कं प्रागुक्तम् ततः कथमिहाध्वसु प्राणिसंभव इति। उच्यते। समष्टिव्यष्टिभेदात् समष्ट्यध्वसु प्राणवस्थानं प्राणिषु च व्यष्ट्यध्वसंभव इति शक्तेर्बिन्दुदशेयमुक्ता॥ ८॥

अथ नादादिदशाभिः स्वरूपपर्यन्तमन्तर्मुखतया व्याप्तिर्नादः प्राणस्येत्यर्धेनोक्ता। न्यासविषये विशेषमाह—मूर्तिलयानन्तरमिति। न्यासयोगाविति। सर्वान् क्रमेण न्यस्योत्तरोत्तरस्मिन् संहारेण योगं कुर्यादिति भाव इति।

अथैष पुंस्त्रीनियमितैरिति। हृल्लेखायास्त्र्यंशप्रधानेव देहाकृतिशक्तिलक्षणा व्याप्तिरुच्यते। अत्रैष इति हृल्लेखामन्त्र उक्तः। लिङ्गैरिति सहार्थे तृतीया॥ ९॥

रेफो माया बीजमिति प्रधानविभूतिकथनम्। तद्विभूतयोऽन्यानि। पुरुषप्रकृत्यादिघटशिलाफलान्ताः सर्वेऽप्युच्चावचपदार्था इति लिङ्गैरिति बहुवचनेन सूचितम्। अत्र रेफपदेन हृल्लेखाया रेफांशवाच्यता पुंशक्तिग्रहणम्। एवं मायाबीजमिति स्त्रीनपुंसकशक्तिग्रहणम्। तच्छक्तीनां कार्यक्रमेण सर्वेऽपि पुंस्त्रीनपुंसकार्या विकाराः स्युः। अत्र तरुवल्ल्यादयो घटशिलादयोऽपि स्ववाचकलिङ्गवशाद् ग्राह्या एव। रेफो माया बीजमित्यभिधानात्। न्यासविषये विशेषः। तदाह—लिङ्गन्यासमाहेति। व्याप्तिं वदन्निति प्रकरणाल्लभ्यते इति। अथ शक्तिः श्रीरित्यादिना शक्तेः सर्वप्रधाना शक्तिलक्षणा व्याप्तिरुच्यते। तदाह—शक्त्यादिन्यासमिति।

मूल इत्याद्यैरित्यत्रैष समभिधीयत इत्यनुवर्तते। शब्दैरिति च विशेष्याध्याहारः। आदिशब्देनान्येऽपि शक्तिवाचिनः सावित्रीश्रद्धादिशब्दा गृह्यन्ते। अत्र शक्तिः स्वयमेव प्रकृतिः। श्रीसन्नत्यादयस्तद्विकारशक्तयः। सावित्र्यादयस्ततोऽपि बाह्याः शक्तय इत्यवबोद्धव्यम्। न्यासविषये विशेषः। तदाह—इत्येताभिरिति।

अथ स्वार्थवाचकैरित्यासामेवास्त्रीलिङ्गशब्दवाच्यशक्तितया व्याप्तिरुक्ता। स्वोऽर्थः शक्त्याद्युक्तलक्षणा स्वयमेव प्रकृतिरेव तद्वाचकाः शब्दाः संवेदनादयः प्रणवादिमन्त्राश्च तैरपि समभिधीयत इति। न्यासविषये विशेषः। तदाह—एतेषामेवेत्यादिना। कुण्डलिन्युच्यत इति शक्त्यादीनां स्वरूपं कुण्डलिन्येवेत्येवमुक्तम्। तारवराः प्रणवादयः। त्रिबीजात्मका मृत्युञ्जयादयः। विद्याश्चेति त्र्यंशशालिन्यस्त्रिपुरादयः। कुण्डलिनीशक्तेर्विश्वयोनित्वादिच्छादित्रिशक्त्यात्मकत्वाच्च त्र्यंशशालिनी

मन्त्रवाचकाः स्युः। प्रथममेकैकबीजमिति। ॐ अं ऐं शक्त्यै नमः। ॐ अं क्लीं शक्त्यै नमः। ॐ अं सौः शक्त्यै नम इत्यादि। एवं प्रणवमृत्युञ्जयादिष्वपि स्यात्। पुनर्द्विद्विबीजमिति संयोज्येत्याद्यनुषङ्गः। ॐ अं ऐं क्लीं शक्त्यै नमः। ॐ अं क्लीं सौः शक्त्यै नम इत्यादि। समस्तसंयोगेनापीति। ॐ अं ऐं क्लीं सौः शक्त्यै नम इत्यादि। अथ नानाविकारतां प्राप्तैरिति। तथाविधानामप्यासां ब्रह्मादितया व्याप्तिरुक्ता। स्वावान्तरभेदैः सह स्वार्थवाचकैः समभिधीयत इति भावः।

न्यासे विशेषमाह—एवं न्यास इति। एकैकबीजादिसंयोगेन न्यासोऽपीति भावः। सर्वमन्त्राणामिति निर्देशेनैतद्दर्शितम्। तत्राक्षरादिसंयोगतो न्यासः सर्वमन्त्रसाधारणः। ब्रह्मादिसंयोगतो न्यासस्तु तत्तन्मन्त्रविषय इति। सर्वमूलमौलिकमन्त्रेष्विति। मूलमन्त्रा एत उक्ताः। मौलिकमन्त्रास्तु तेषामपि विभूतयो ब्रह्माष्टाक्षरद्वादशाक्षरादयः। अत्रैतदप्यर्थादवसीयते। ब्रह्मादीनां बीजानां तु संयोगतो न्यास एकैकं बीजं संयोज्येत्यनेन समान एवेति। अथ स्वैः स्वैर्भावैरिति। ब्रह्मादिभावापन्नानामप्यासां शक्तिश्रीप्रभृतीनां गुणव्यतिरेकनिबन्धनरूपतया व्याप्तिरुक्ता। न्यासविषये विशेषमाह—अथैवंविधानामेवेति। अकारककारादिसंबन्धिभिरिति पञ्चाशद्वर्णग्रहणम्। ॐ अं ऐं नमो ब्रह्मणे शक्त्यै नम इत्याकारपद्मकर्णिकायां ॐ अं अं ऐं नमो ब्रह्मणे शक्त्यै नमः ॐ अं आं ऐं नमो ब्रह्मणे शक्त्यै नम इत्यादि षोड़शमन्त्रांस्तदीयदलेष्वित्यादि। अथ विकल्पितैरित्येवंविधानामप्यासामवस्थादिभेदतो भूयोऽपि व्याप्तिरुक्ता। स्वैः स्वैर्भावैरित्येतद्विशिष्यते सह स्वार्थवाचकैः समभिधीयत इति। पूर्ववदेव न्यासे विशेषमाह—व्यञ्जनपारायण(न्यास)मिति। प्राग्वद्ब्रह्मब्रह्मादिभेदेन षोडशविधो विस्तारः प्रतिपत्तव्यः। सर्वत्र चेष समभिधीयत इत्यनुवृत्तेः मूलेन व्यापकं लभ्यत इति ॥ १०॥११ ॥

अथ तामेनामिति। हृल्लेखायाः केवलहकारप्रधाना मूर्तिशक्तिलक्षणा व्याप्तिरुच्यते। सन्त इत्यनेनैतदुक्तम्। साधकस्य हृदयहमिति रूढियोगादिदं तावच्छक्त्यात्मत्वनिरूढिकरमिति। एके विदुरिति। केचिन्मूलाधारगतां विदुरिति सूचितम्। तथा चाधस्तादुक्तं—कुण्डलिनी तदा मूलाधारे विसरतीति। कुण्डलिन्येकैव तावत् प्रधानविभूतिरिष्यते। न्यासविषये विशेषं दर्शयति—कुण्डलिनीन्यासं वक्तुमिति। व्याप्तिं वदन्निति प्रकरणाल्लभ्यते। अन्य इति मूलाधारादिषु प्रत्येकं योजनीयम्। मूलाधारनाभिहृदयभ्रूमध्यद्वादशान्तानि क्रमेण स्थानानि सिद्धानि भवन्ति। मूलाधारग्रहणात् षोडशान्तोऽपि ग्राह्यः।

अथ सा रौतीति। कुण्डलिन्याः शक्तेर्नादशक्तिरूपेण व्याप्तिरुक्ता। सततमिति।

प्राणिनां बहिर्मुखतया व्यापृतिषु तूष्णीमवस्थासु सुषुप्तावपीति भावः। न्यासविषये विशेषमाह—सा रौतीति। सर्वस्थानानुगतेति सततशब्दाभिप्राय उक्तः। नादज्योतिरिति। रौति देवीत्यनयोरभिप्राय उक्तः। मूलाधारगतत्रिकोणमध्यादतिसूक्ष्मसूत्राकारेण नादज्योतीरूपेणाषोडशान्तं चिन्तनमिति भावः। भृङ्गीसङ्गीतकध्वनिरिति। तस्य ज्योतिष आनन्दामृतात्मकत्वमपि षोडशान्तगतादमृतासारयोगादुक्तम्॥ १२॥

अथाकृतिमिति। नादशक्तेरपि नानाविधमूर्तिशक्तिरूपेण व्याप्तिरुक्ता। तस्या इत्यर्थादुपस्कारः। स्वो भावः स्वकीयनादस्वरूपस्य नानाविधो विकारः। पिण्डनमुपचयः। बहुधेति परब्रह्मसाक्षिचतुर्मूर्त्यादिरूपेण परशक्तिसाक्षिणी चतुर्मूर्त्यादिशक्तिरूपेण चानेकविधतयेत्युक्तम्। तस्या नादशक्तिरूपायाः शक्ते रूपं स्वेन विकारजातेनोपचितं तत्तद्वाच्यनानाविधमूर्तिशक्तिरूपेण बहुधावस्थितं विदुरिति मूलार्थः। अत्र च ब्रह्मसरस्वत्यादीनामपि ये प्रतिस्वं विभूतयः ता अप्युपसंहार्याः। चराचरस्य जगतो मूलत्वादिति निर्देशात्। न्यासविषये विशेषः। तदाह—न्यासमाहेत्यादिना। स्वेन भावेन चेति। समुच्चयार्थश्चकारः। तत्र कुण्डलिनीवाचकहकारेणेति स्वशब्दार्थ उक्तः। कुण्डलिनीबीजेन चेति भावशब्दार्थ उक्तः। भवत्यस्मात्कार्यजातमिति बीजं भावः। पिण्डितामुपचिताम्। स्वमिति कुण्डलिनीबीजम्। ह्स्वं ह्स्रीमिति मूर्तिशक्तितया च तद्द्विधाम्नातम्। तदाह—ब्रह्माणं सरस्वतीञ्च सञ्चिन्त्येति। न्यसेदित्यधःसम्बन्धः। द्वादशान्तभ्रूमध्यहृदयनाभिष्वित्येकः पक्षः। त्रिकोणमध्यकोणत्रयेषु वेति पक्षान्तरम्। प्रकृतनाभिविषयमेतत्। एतच्छेष एव चैवं नाभौ न्यसित्वेत्यादि वक्ष्यते। तत्र द्वादशान्तादिषु न्यासविधावेवं प्रयोगः। द्वादशान्ते त्रिकोणं विचिन्त्य तन्मध्ये सर्वेश्वरं मूलप्रकृतिं च स्मरन् ह्स्वं ह्स्रीमिति विन्यस्य परब्रह्मपरशक्त्यादित्रयं व्यापकतया विन्यस्य सर्वेश्वरमूलप्रकृतिन्यासं कुर्यात्। पुनः रुद्रसर्वेश्वरोमामूलप्रकृत्यादित्रयं कोणत्रये न्यस्य तेषां यथास्वं परिवारत्वेन रुद्ररुद्रोमोमादित्रयत्रिकं विन्यसेत्। ततो भ्रूमध्ये रुद्रसर्वेश्वरोमाप्रकृतिबुद्ध्या बीजद्वयं विन्यस्य परब्रह्मपरशक्त्यादित्रयं रुद्रसर्वेश्वरोमामूलप्रकृतितदावरणत्रयञ्च न्यसेत्। एवं हृदये नाभौ चोहनीयमिति। नाभौ न्यासविधौ तु नाभिहृदयभ्रूमध्यद्वादशान्तेषु समान एव न्यासः। तदाह—हृदयादिष्विति।

अथ कुण्डलिनी सर्वथा ज्ञेयेति सकलमूर्तिशक्त्यात्मिकायाः शक्तेरन्तर्मुखतया स्वरूपपर्यन्तमनेकावान्तरक्रमवती व्याप्तिरुक्ता। सर्वथेति सर्वप्रकारेण। सन्ति तत्र बहवः प्रकाराः तैर्ज्ञेयेत्यर्थः। सुषुम्नानुगतैव सेति। तेषां स्वरूपनिष्ठानां

प्रकारभेदानां सुषुम्नान्तर्वर्तित्वमुक्तम्। ते च भेदाः केवलब्रह्मसर्वेश्वरसरस्वती-मूलप्रकृतिचतुष्कप्रभृतयोऽवबोद्धव्याः। न्यासविषये विशेषमाह—कुण्डलिनी सर्वथेत्यादिना। चतुर्मूर्तियोगस्तावदयमुक्त एव। ब्रह्मयोगादय एव तु पुनः कार्याः। किं च चतुर्मूर्तियोगग्रहणेन तत्रापि योगप्रकारः प्रागुक्तः सूचितः। यदुक्तं—चतुर्ष्वपि स्थानेष्वित्यादि। ननु तत्रोक्ताच्चतुर्दशयोगादस्य कुण्डलिनी-योगस्य को भेद इति। उच्यते। तत्र चिदवष्टम्भादियोगानां व्याप्तत्वम्। तदुक्तम्—तेजसा बाह्यं स्थूलादिशरीरमित्यादि। इह तु सुषुम्नायामेव सर्वं चिन्तनीयम्। तदिहोक्तं—सुषुम्नानुगतैव सेति। चिदवष्टम्भयोगे सुषुम्नानुगतकुण्डलिनीचित्तेजसा स्वदेशावष्टम्भः स्यादिति। योगानुक्तानिति या युष्मानपीत्यत्रेति भावः॥ १३॥

मूले चराचरस्य जगत इति। ततो मूलमिदं विदुरित्यादिवद्विश्वयोनितयोप-संहारः। अनेन बहुधा विदुरित्युक्तमूर्तिशक्तितद्विभूतीनामपि विभूतितान्तर्बहिः-कारणभूतदेहविषयाणां सूचितम्। न्यासविषये विशेषमाह—केन मन्त्रेणैव-मित्यादिना। बीजमेव तदित्यत्रापिशब्दोऽध्याहृतः। तत्र चार्थात्सिद्धं प्रणवस्य तावद्बीजत्वमिति मन्यमानो विवृणोति—न केवलमिति। तदपि बीजमेवेत्यन्वयः। किमिह तदपीत्युक्तमिति तद्दर्शयति—शब्दब्रह्म हकार इति। तच्छब्दलिङ्गोप-पत्तये शब्दब्रह्मेत्युक्तम्। किञ्चात्र बीजमेव तदिति हृल्लेखाप्यभिप्रेयते। तेन योगावसाने हृल्लेखया स्वरूपमनुसन्धेयमित्यपि सूचितम्। षडध्वयोगाद्यवसानेऽपि समानमेतदित्यवबोद्धव्यमिति।

अथ मूलस्य बिन्दुयोगेनेति शक्तेर्हकारप्रधानैव मूर्तिलक्षणा व्याप्तिरुच्यते। मूलशब्देनेह शक्तिगतो हकारो गृह्यते। वक्ष्यति च—हंकाराख्यो भवानित्यादि। शतानन्देति ब्रह्मण आमन्त्रणम्। त्वदुद्भव इति। त्वद्वाच्यत्वादिति भावः। न्यास-विषये विशेषः। तदाह—मूर्तिन्यासमाहेति। व्याप्तिं वदन्निति प्रकरणाल्लभ्यते। त्वदुद्भव इति ब्रह्मशब्दस्य पश्चात्प्रयोगोऽपि सूचितः एवमितरयोरपि॥ १४॥

अथ हंकाराख्यो भवांस्तेनेति ब्रह्मादिविभूतीनामात्मप्रकृतीश्वररूपेण व्याप्ति-रुक्ता। तेनेति यस्माद्बिन्दुयुक्तहकारात् त्वदुद्भवस्तस्माद्भवान् हमित्येवं लोके प्रथित इत्यर्थः। हंकार आख्या प्रसिद्धिर्यस्येति समासः। हमित्येतदहमित्येतदेव। अत एव वक्ष्यति—सोहंभावमुपागतेत्यादि। अहमिति च सकलचराचर-जातस्यात्मनि प्रसिद्धम्। ततश्च त्वं सकलचेतनानामात्मतयाहमिति प्रथितः। अत एवेत्युक्तं भवति—हरिरित्येष शब्दगत इति। लोक इति शेषः। हरति मायारूपेणात्मनां स्वरूपप्रथितिमिति हरिर्मायावी विष्णुः। अनेन तनु-

भुवनाद्यात्मकमायाप्रकृतिविग्रहो विष्णुर्हरिः। तथास्य प्रसिद्धिः। अत एवेत्युक्तं भवति—हरत्वमस्य तेनैवेति। लोकप्रथितमिति शेषः। हरति विश्वं संहरतीति हरः कालतनुरीश्वर एव। तदुक्तम्—ईश्वरस्य सर्वज्ञतां चाहेत्यादि। सर्वात्मत्वं ममापि चेति। हकारस्य इकारबिन्द्वादिसंयोगादहं भवामि अत एवात्मप्रकृतीश्वराणां समष्टितया मम सर्वात्मत्वमपि लोके प्रथितमिति भावः। अनेनैतत् सिद्धं भवति। शक्तेः प्रधानविभूतिः सर्वेश्वरः तद्विभूतयो ब्रह्मादयः तेषां महाविभूतयश्चराचराणामात्मजातं तदुपाधिजातं प्रकृतिलक्षणमीश्वरश्चेति।

ननु रुद्रस्य कथमीश्वरो विभूतिरिति। नैष दोषः। रुद्रत्वेऽपि तावदुच्यासिसंभवात्। तथा चोक्तम्—ईश्वरः शर्व ईशान इति। न्यासविषये विशेषमाह—उक्तेऽर्थं इति। न्यसेदित्यर्थ इति। श्लोकद्वयाभिप्रायोऽयमिति भावः। बीजत्वमेव प्रपञ्चयन्नित्यत्र यदप्यभिप्रेतं तद्दर्शयति—एतदेवेति। ब्रह्मादिकारणत्वादपि कुण्डलिनीवाचकं हकारोऽपि बीजमेवेति एतदभिप्रायः। तेनेहापि प्रणवयोगसिद्धिरिति। इह मूर्तिन्यासमित्याह। हृल्लेखापटले तु योगप्रकरणे हं हरिहरादिचतुष्प्रणवादि वक्ष्यति। तत्रार्थादयं नियमोऽवसीयते। तत्र न्यासविधावित्थं हरिहरादिचतुष्प्रणवन्यासोऽपि कार्यः। न चैकस्योभयथापि प्रयोगायोगः। अजपापरमात्मप्रणवन्यासानित्यजपापरमात्मप्रणवयोगन्यासानिति चोभयथाभिधानात्। तत्रैषां योगविधानादिह न्यासविधानानन्तरं तच्छेषतया योगप्रकारोऽपि कुण्डलिनीयोगवदुपलक्षणीयः। ततश्च मूर्तिलिङ्गचिदवष्टम्भाद्यविकल्पयोगान्तं सर्वं कार्यम्। यद्वा मूर्तियोगमात्रमेव सामान्यसिद्धं कार्यम्। यदुक्तं प्रथमपटल एव—चतुर्ष्वपि स्थानेषु सपरिवारमित्यादि। 'बीजमेव तदित्येतदिहापि समानमेवेति।

अथास्य बिन्दोरित्यादि विवरीतुमारभते—विभूत्यन्तरमिति। मूर्तिन्यासे षडध्वन्यासादिषु चोक्तेषु व्याप्तिरपि दर्शितैवेति विभूत्यन्तरपदेन दर्शितम्। अजपापरमात्मप्रणवन्यासानिति सहाभिधानं सहप्रयोगसूचनार्थम्। तेन यद्वक्ष्यति—हंसपूजां सङ्कल्पेऽत्र। तत्रैषां त्रयाणामपि न्यासयोगौ स्यातामिति। यद्वा स्थूलसूक्ष्मपरत्वमेषां सूचितम्। तेन मन्त्रविग्रहसंहारसर्गविभिः क्रमोत्क्रमन्यासाभ्यां कार्यमिति। तदभिप्रायेण वेह न्यासमात्राभिधानम्। सर्वमन्त्रभावनासु मानसपूजानन्तरमजपापरमात्मप्रणवन्यासैः स्थूलाद्युपाधित्रयं देवतातत्त्वे संहृत्य सच्चित्सुखाद्वैतमात्रस्वरूपो भूत्वा प्रणवपरमात्माजपान्यासैस्तन्मूर्ततामात्रकल्पमुपाधित्रयं सृष्ट्वा सकृन्मन्त्रन्यासं कृत्वा मन्त्रजपं कुर्यात्।

यद्वा बीजबिन्द्वादिक्रमोऽत्र विवक्षितः। तत्र षोडशाङ्गन्यासादित्रयाणामन्य-

तमेन वाचकांशे बीजसंहारः। शक्तिःश्रीरित्यादिन्यासेन बिन्दुसंहारः कुण्डलिनीन्यासेन नादस्य पुनः शक्तिन्यासेन शक्तिसंहारः ततो हं हरिहरादिचतुष्प्रणवन्यासयोरेकतरेण वाच्यांशे स्थूलसंहारः। अजपापरमात्मन्यासाभ्यां सूक्ष्मकारणसंहारः पुनः शक्तिन्यासेन सामान्यसंहारः। ततः प्रणवन्यासेन निरुपाधिकदेवतातत्त्वभावः। तदनन्तरं ताराद्विभक्तादितिन्यासेन वाच्यवाचकात्मकदेवताविग्रहः ततः सकलमन्त्रन्यासं कृत्वा मन्त्रजपं कुर्यादिति। तदुक्तं—मन्त्रात्मा भूत्वा मन्त्रं संहृत्येत्यादि। षोडशाङ्गन्यासादीनां स्थूलसूक्ष्मक्रमोपपत्त्या चायमप्यभिप्रायो लभ्यत इति।

किञ्चाऽजपापरमात्मप्रणवन्यासानिति सहाभिधानं तासां व्याप्तीनां हकारेकारप्रधानत्वादपि भवति। तत्र षोडशाङ्गादिव्याप्तिषु शक्तेर्वर्णत्रयमपि प्रत्यक्षमेव। तथा शक्तिः श्रीरित्यादिव्याप्तौ शक्तिः कुण्डलिनीचतुर्मूर्त्यौस्तु हकारः प्रत्यक्षः। अजपापरमात्मव्याप्तेर्हकारः प्रत्यक्षः। ईकारस्तु परोक्षः। प्रणवव्याप्तावुभयोरपि परोक्षत्वम्। गायत्र्यादिव्याप्तिषु त्रयाणामपीति। यत एवं भेदोऽत एवायं व्याप्तिक्रम आश्रित इति। तत्र प्रथममस्य बिन्दोरिति पुरुषप्रकृतिलक्षणा व्याप्तिरुच्यते। तत्रास्य बिन्दोरिति शक्तेः प्रधानविभूतिवाचकांशोऽभिहितः। अस्येति प्रकृतस्य शक्त्यंशस्य हकारस्य ग्रहणम्। बिन्दुः 'क्वचिदभ्येति बिन्दुतामिति पुरोक्तं बिन्दुतत्त्वं तस्मादस्य समुद्भूतिः। 'तस्माद्भिद्यमानात्' 'तदा तु बिन्दुस्फुटनोद्भवस्येत्याद्युक्तप्रकारेणाभिव्यक्तिः।

यद्यपि परावाक्सतत्त्वमेवायं हकारः तथापि तस्याकारादीतरवर्णवद्बिन्दोरुत्पत्तिसंभवः। तदुक्तं गुणितप्रकरणे—तामेव शक्तिं ब्रुवत इत्यादि। यस्मादस्य हवर्णस्य बिन्दोरुत्पत्तिस्तस्मादसौ स्वकारणानुगमाद्बिन्दन्तः सन् हमित्येवमुच्यत इति। स इत्यत्राप्येतत्सर्वमनुषज्यते। बिन्दोरेव विसर्गावस्थात्समुत्पन्नस्तावदयं सकारः। कुतः। विसर्गस्य स्थूलदशा सकार इत्यभ्युपगमात्।

यदुक्तम्—ओभावश्च विवृत्तिश्च शषसा रेफ एव च।

जिह्वामूलमुपध्मेति गतिरष्टविधोष्मणः॥ इति।

तस्मादसावपि स्वकारणानुगमाद्विसर्गान्तः सन् स इत्येवमुच्यत इति। बिन्दोरेव समुत्पन्नो हकारः। कुतः। बिन्दुतत्त्वादेव सकलवर्णोत्पत्त्यभिधानाद्वर्णेषु हकारस्येतरकारणताभिधानाच्च। यदुक्तं—स सर्गः श्लेषितः कण्ठ इत्यादि। बिन्दुरन्तर्मुखः स एव बहिर्मुखः सन् विसर्गो भवति। निगिरणोद्गिरणप्रयत्नाभ्यां तयोरीर्यमाणत्वादिति॥ १६॥ १७॥

हंकारः पुमानित्येतद्वाच्यप्रधानविभूतिरुक्ता। प्रोक्त इत्यनेनैतदुक्तम्—हमित्येतदहमित्येतदेव। तस्य बिन्दोः स्थूलरूपत्वादहंरूपेण प्रत्यगर्थनिष्ठत्वाच्च

पुरुषत्वमिति। मतेत्यनेन चैतदुक्तं—स इत्यस्य विसर्गस्य स्थूलरूपत्वान्नित्यप्रकृतपरागर्थनिष्ठत्वाच्च प्रकृतत्वमिति। न्यासविषये विशेषः। तदाहास्य हस्येत्यादिना। तत्त्वं वदन्तीति। हृल्लेखायां यः पुरुषः हकारः स एव हंकारो या प्रकृतिरोकारः। स एव स इत्ययं वर्ण इति तयोस्तत्त्वमुक्तम्।

अथाजपेयं स्मृता शक्तिरिति हृल्लेखाशक्तेरियं प्रकृतिपुरुषमयी शक्त्यंशप्रधानैकमूर्तिरूपैव प्रधानविभूतिरित्येतदुक्तम्। शक्तिरियमजपा स्मृतेति योजनीयम्। शक्त्यंशप्रधानत्वादजपेत्येवमभिधेया भवति। तथा दक्षिणवामत इत्येकमूर्तित्वेऽपि प्रकृतिपुरुषविभाग उक्तः। इयं स्मृतेत्यनुषङ्गः।

तत्र व्यवस्था बिन्दुर्दक्षिणभागस्त्वित्युक्ता। अस्याः शक्तेरिति शेषः। बिन्दुशब्देनान्तर्मुखशक्त्यात्मा हंकार उक्तः। विसर्गशब्देन च बहिर्मुखशक्त्यात्मा स इत्ययं वर्णः। तौ च पुरुषप्रकृत्यात्मकाविति। तेन दक्षिणवामाख्याविति तदाकारोऽप्युक्तः। अस्याः प्रधानविभूतेः शक्तेरिति शेषः। तेन बिन्दुविसर्गयोर्दक्षिणवामभागत्वमिह हेतुत्वेनोक्तम्। पुंस्त्रीविशेषिताविति। पुंस्त्रीरूपेण भिन्नावित्यर्थः। न्यासविषये विशेषः। तदाह—देवतात्वेनेत्यादिना। तथा दक्षिणवामत इति न्यास इति शेषः। मूलशिरसोरिति मूलाधारमूर्धाभिप्रायम्। मूलशिरोग्रहणं तु देहस्याधऊर्ध्वार्धांशग्रहणार्थम्। सर्वेषां चेति। सकलप्राणिनामपीत्यर्थः॥ १८॥

अथ बिन्दुः पुरुष इति प्रधानविभूतेरर्धयोर्विभूती पुरुषप्रकृती इत्युक्तम्। पुंप्रकृत्यात्मको हंस इत्येवमियमजपाशक्तिः पृथगपि पुंप्रकृत्यात्मको भवतीत्यर्थः। तदात्मकमिदं जगदिति। बिन्दुविसर्गयोरेव दक्षिणवामभागनियमेनापीत्यर्थः। अत इति। यत एवमतोऽर्धनारीश्वरदैवत्यो हंसमन्त्रः अतएव तथा ध्येयो न्यासविधावित्यर्थः। सर्वात्मकत्वं वदन्तीति। पुंस्त्र्यात्मकत्वादीश्वरस्येति भावः। न्यासफलमिति जगन्मूलशक्त्यात्मकत्वमभिप्रेतम्। यदुक्तं—साधकस्य प्रकृत्यात्मकत्वसिद्धय इति। योगविधौ त्वेकलिङ्गयोगचिदवष्टम्भयोगादि सर्वं कार्यम्। न्यासे तु किञ्चिदभ्यधिकमुपदिशति अयमत्रेति। द्वितीय इति। मूलमूर्धदक्षिणवामभागन्यासानन्तरमयं न्यास इति भावः। द्वितीयशब्देनैतत्सूचितम्। सामान्यन्यास उक्तो विशेषन्यासस्तु तत्रायमुच्यत इति। मूलेनैवान्ततो व्यापकं सामान्यसिद्धम्। तदुक्तं—ततो मूलमिदं विदुरिति॥ १९॥

अथ पुंरूपं सेति पुरुषप्रधाना व्याप्तिरुच्यते। तत्र सङ्गतिमाह—एवमिति। प्रत्यगात्मनो ब्रह्मणैकत्वप्रतिपादकमिति शक्तेरेव प्रत्यक्षपरोक्षावयवत्वेऽपि हंसस्य हं हरिहरादिवाच्यत्वम्। तदा च तद्वर्णयोर्लौकिकपदाकारतया समुचितार्थप्रति-

पादकत्वादात्माष्टाक्षरदशप्रणवगायत्र्यादिवद्वाक्यत्वम्। तदा च तत्पदयोः प्रत्यक्-परागात्मनिष्ठतयान्वये प्रत्यगात्मनोऽनुवादेन तस्य परमात्मताविधानात् प्रत्यगात्मनः परब्रह्मलक्षणदेवतातत्त्वैक्यप्रतिपादकोऽयं भवतीति भावः। शक्तेरीकारस्य सकारपरिग्रह एतदेव निबन्धनं यदुक्तार्थाभिधानम्। अतएव प्रकृत्यंशप्रधानत्वमस्या विभूतेरिति। ननु हं पुरुषः सश्च प्रकृतिरुक्ता तत्कथं प्रत्यगात्मपरब्रह्मात्मत्वमनयोरिति। नैष दोषः। वर्णतया पुरुषप्रकृत्योः पदतया जीवपरयोश्च वाचकत्वात्। यद्वा पुरुषस्यैव प्रकृत्यैक्यापत्तावपि स पुरुषः स्वान्तर्गतं प्रत्यगात्मानं प्रकृत्यन्तर्गते परब्रह्मण्यैक्येनाविशयेत्। तदर्थत्वात्स्वात्मनः प्रकृत्यैक्यप्रतिपादनस्येति। ननु कदा पुनरनेन मन्त्रेणैवमैक्यानुसन्धानमिति। योगावसान इत्यवगन्तव्यम्। तदुक्तं—ततो वाक्यार्थप्रतिपत्तिमाहेति। यद्वाऽजपामन्त्रावृत्तावेतदिष्यते। गायत्र्येव तदावृत्ताविति। तस्यानेन तत्प्रतिपादकमिति। परब्रह्मणः प्रत्यगात्मनैक्यप्रतिपादकमित्यर्थः। योगावसान इदमनुसन्धानमिष्यते। यद्वा प्रत्यगात्मनः परब्रह्मतया तस्य च प्रत्यगात्मतया व्यतीहारेणानुसन्धानमिहाजपापरमात्ममन्त्रवाक्येन विवक्षितम्। हंसपूजां सङ्कल्प्येत्येतदप्येतदर्थमेव।

अथवा सौरपटलेऽजपाविधानानन्तरमेतद्विधानमपि तद्वदभिप्रेतम्। तज्जपविधौ चैतदनुसन्धानं भवति। यत्तावच्छक्त्यवयवयोर्बिन्दुविसर्गयोगाद्युक्तमस्य बिन्दोः समुद्भूतेत्यादिना तत्सर्वमिहापि तदेव। किन्तु हकारपरोक्षेकारयोः क्रम एव भेद इति तन्निबन्धनमेव वदन् तत्सर्वं सूचयति—पुंरूपं सेति। सा हृल्लेखाशक्तिरजपालक्षणा विसर्गः प्रकृतिर्मतेत्युक्ता। स्वावयवेन तेनैव परोक्षेकारलक्षणेन साभिधेया सती स्वावयवेनैव हमाभिधेयं पुरुषलक्षणं बिन्दुः पुरुष इत्युक्तं सत् स्वस्वरूपं प्रतिपद्यमाना स्वात्मनोऽनुवादेन पुरुषताविधानात् तदुपपत्त्या स्वावयवाभ्यां सोहंभावं प्राप्तो भवति। साधकार्थतयैवेयं प्रकृतेः पुरुषैक्यापत्तिः। सकलमन्त्रदेवतोत्पत्तेरशेषजगदुत्पत्तेश्च तथात्वादित्थं विश्वं प्रतीयत इत्यभिधानात्। तथाच साधकप्रतिपत्त्यनुगुणतया प्रकृतिः स इत्यात्मानमहमिति च पुरुषं ब्रूयादिति।

ननु कथं स इति पुंलिङ्गं कृतं स्यादिति। नैष दोषः। प्रकृतिलक्षणस्यात्मनो विवक्षितत्वात्प्रकृतौ पुरुषेश्वरान्तर्भावाच्च प्रकृतेः पुरुषनिष्ठत्वादिह पुरुषांशप्रधानत्वमिति। इह सोहंभावमुपागतेत्युक्तत्वादजपायां हसभावेन स्थितिरपि लभ्यते। अत एव प्रत्यगात्मनो ब्रह्मणैकत्वप्रतिपादकमित्युक्तमिति।

स एष परमात्माख्यो मनुरिति। सेयं प्रधानविभूतिरुभयलक्षणा सती परमात्मा नाम भवति। तदभिन्नतया तदाख्यस्त्वायं मन्त्रो भवतीति मूलार्थः।

प्रकृतिपुरुषयोस्तद्विभूतित्वमशेषस्त्रीपुरुषाणां तद्व्यापित्वं च पूर्ववदेव।

पुंरूपं सेत्यभिप्रायान्तरमाह—सा तावदुपाधिको जीव इति। अत्र सेति हृल्लेखाशक्तिरुच्यते। सा चेह हंस इत्यनेन प्रकृत्यात्मैक्यमापन्नो जीवः। स च तदैक्यमापन्नोऽपि व्युत्थानसंस्कारबलात् ततोभिन्नस्वस्वरूपं पुरुषरूपं विद्वान् स्वात्मतया प्रतिपन्नः प्रकृतेः स्वस्वरूपपर्यन्ततामनुसन्धत्ते सोहमित्येवमित्यर्थः। अस्मिन् पक्षे स इति प्रकृत्यात्मनो यथास्थितं निर्देश उपपद्यत इति। न्यासविषये विशेषः। तदाह—अस्यापीति। सोहंरूपोपपत्त्या मन्त्रो न्यासस्थानं चेति न्यासस्योक्तप्रायत्वम्। व्यापकध्यानादिकमादिशब्देनोक्तम्। तत्र सोहं प्रकृतिपुरुषात्मने नम इति व्यापकम्। परमात्मा देवतात्वेन ध्येयः। व्यापकध्यानादिकमादिशब्देनोक्तम्। अजपायां शक्तिरेवार्धेन पुरुषाकारं धत्ते। इह तु पुरुषार्धेन शक्त्याकारमिति भेद इति।

अथास्य महामनोरिति प्रकृतिपुरुषाभेदलक्षणा विभूतिरुच्यते। तदाह—पुनरेकत्वानुभवसाधनमिति। महामनुशब्देन स्वर्गात्मावध्याततधामशाखेतीयमवस्थानेन पूरितेति सूचितम्। अस्य सकारं च हकारं च लोपयित्वा पूर्वरूपाख्यं सन्धिं प्रयोजयेदिति योजनीयम्। प्रकृतिपुरुषयोरसाधारणरूपहानात् सकारहकारलोपः। तयोर्व्यतिहारमहिम्नैक्यप्राप्तेः सन्धानमित्यवबोद्धव्यम्। पूर्वरूपाख्यमित्येङः पदान्तादतीत्ययं सन्धिरभिप्रेतः। अत्र हृल्लेखाया हकारसकारावुभावपि परोक्षावेव। तद्वाच्यः परमात्मैव प्रधानविभूतिः। तस्य प्रकृत्यभिन्नः पुरुषः तदभिन्ना च प्रकृतिः। तयोरशेषस्त्रीपुरुषजातं भोक्तृभोग्यांशाभिन्नं व्याप्तिरित्यर्थो लभ्यते। न्यासस्तु व्यापकमेव। ज्योतिरेवोभयाभेदलक्षणं ध्येयम्। 'ततो मूलमिदं विदुरित्येतदिहापि समानम्। एकत्वानुभवसाधनमिति एकावसान एतदनुसन्धानम्। यद्वा प्रणवजपविधाविति ज्ञेयमिति ॥ २० ॥ २१ ॥

अथ ताराद्विभक्तादिति शक्तेरर्थप्रकाशविमर्शलक्षणा विभूतिरुच्यते। तदाह उद्धृतस्येति। ननु गुणितप्रकरण उद्धृतस्तावदसौ प्रणवः—तदा तां तारमित्याहुरोमात्मेति बहुश्रुता इति। नैष दोषः। बहुबिन्द्वन्तोऽसौ विवक्षितोऽस्य बिन्दोः समुद्भूतेत्युक्तत्वात्। ततश्च हकारैकारयोरेवेह परोक्षत्वम्। शक्तेर्बिन्दुस्तु स एव। यद्वा सोहंभावमिति मकारान्तत्वमिष्यते। हृल्लेखाविकारतयेहोद्धार इति तु भेदो द्रष्टव्यः। न्यासयोगादिकमित्यादिशब्देन ध्यानादिकं गृह्यते। गायत्रीपटले वक्ष्यति—मन्दानां सप्रपञ्चार्थत्वमाह प्रकाशिताद्राविति। ताराद्विभक्तादित्यादि। विभूतिमित्यर्थप्रकाशविमर्शरूपामिति भावः। ननु कथमिह सकारहकारयोग-

लक्षणस्य प्रणवस्य तंत्रशत्वमिति। उच्यते। हकारात्तावदकारो भवति। सकारादकारस्तु पूर्वविसर्गान्वयादुकारः स्यात्। कुतः। अकारविसर्गयोरौत्वापत्तावनन्तराकारस्य तदन्तर्भावे चाकारस्य पृथग्भावात्। तत्र मध्ये उकारस्यावस्थितत्वात् मकारस्तु चरमांश इति। ततश्च शक्तेरोकारहकारबिन्दव एवैते परोक्षा इति ज्ञेयम्। ताराद्विभक्तादिति। अ उ म इति वर्णरूपेणेह विभागः। ते च वर्णा अर्थप्रकाशविमर्शैः प्रधानविभूतिभिरभिन्नाः। कुतः। भूतानां तेजसां शब्दानां च व्यष्टीनामभिधानात् तदीयसमष्टित्वाच्चैषामिति। प्रभवन्ति लोक इति सकलभौतिकतैजससमासादिशब्दानां तद्व्याप्तित्वमपि सूचितम्। न्यासविषये विशेषः। तदाह—आकाशात्मने नम इत्यादिना। 'ततो मूलमिदं विदुरित्येतदिहापि समानमिति॥ २२॥

अथैवमेषेति हृल्लेखायाः परोक्षसमस्तप्रधाना सवितृलक्षणा व्याप्तिरुच्यते। तदाह—गायत्रीतत्त्वन्यासमिति। गायत्रीदेवताप्येषैव शक्तिरिति प्रधानविभूतिकथनम्। गायत्री नाम देवता गायत्रीदेवता। पुरुषाभिप्रायेण सविता शक्त्यभिप्रायेण गायत्रीति भेदः। सहेतुकमित्यनेनैवमेषां जगत्सूतिरित्येतद्विवृतम्। अत्रैषेति प्रकृता हृल्लेखाशक्तिः। एवं जगत्सूतिरिति नानाविधो विश्वजगत्समुद्भवप्रकारो ह्यत उक्तः। तेन जगतः सवित्रीयं शक्तिर्यतो भवति ततः सा सवितेति प्रथितेति मूलार्थः। सूतिशक्तेः स्वातन्त्र्यप्रधानतायां सवितृत्वमित्यवबोद्धव्यम्। सा च जगत्सूतिरपि सती प्रतिदिनोत्पाद्यार्थयोनितया मण्डलाकारेणावस्थितः सवितेति च प्रतिपत्तव्यम्। वक्ष्यति च गायत्रीपटले—आदित्यमण्डल इत्युपलक्षणं कारणमण्डलस्यापीति। यदेति। यदा सवितेत्यभिधीयत इति पूर्वत्रान्वयः। तदा स्वैस्तत्त्वैश्चतुर्विंशतिधा भिदामेतीति। सवितृविभूतितया प्रकृतिबुद्ध्यादितत्त्वाभिधानम्॥ २३॥

तद्वर्णभिन्नेति सवितृलक्षणा जगत्सूतिर्विशेष्यते। तेषां तत्त्वानां वर्णास्तत्सवितुरित्यादयश्चतुर्विंशतिः तैर्भिन्ना च सा चतुर्विंशतितत्त्वैर्भिदां प्राप्नुवती भवति। हृल्लेखायाः समस्ताया एव परोक्षं रूपं गायत्रीमन्त्रः। तद्वाच्या प्रधानविभूतिः सविता। तस्याश्चतुर्विंशतिवर्णवाच्यानि तत्त्वानि च तद्विभूतयः। जगत्सूतिरित्यनेन तत्त्वविकारस्य जगदर्थजातस्य तद्व्याप्तित्वमपि सूचितम्। गायत्रीत्यत्रापि पूर्ववज्जगत्सूतिर्विशेष्यते। गायकत्राणनाद्वेदिति तदाख्याफलं हेतुतयोक्तम्। गायको जापकः। न्यासकाद्युपलक्षणमेतत्। न्यासविषये विशेषः। तदाह—तत्त्वन्यासमिति। तद्वर्णभिन्नेत्यत्र तच्छब्देन किं विवक्षितमिति तत्राह—तच्छब्द

इति। अयमत्र मन्त्रप्रयोगः। प्रकृत्यात्मने नमः बुद्ध्यात्मने नम इत्यादि। न्यासान्ते कृत्स्नां गायत्रीमुक्त्वा सवित्रे गायत्र्यै नम इति व्यापकम्। 'ततो मूलमिदं विदु-रित्येतदिहापि समानमिति। अथ सप्तग्रहात्मिकेति शक्तेः सप्तांशप्रधाना ग्रहलक्षणा व्याप्तिरुच्यते। तदाह—सप्तग्रहात्मकत्वमिति। यदेयं सप्तभेदिनी तदा सप्तग्रहा-त्मिका प्रोक्तेति मूलान्वयः। न्यासविषये विशेषमाह—हकारादिशान्तान्तैरिति। षट्सु च कोणेषूक्तमन्त्रैः सप्तग्रहन्यासः। ततो व्यापकमन्त्रेण देहे व्यापकं च। षड्ग्रहन्यासे तु मध्ये सूर्यमन्त्रं शक्तिबुद्ध्या विन्यस्य षट्सु कोणेषु तद्विभूति-तया षड्ग्रहमन्त्रान् विन्यस्य तदीयव्यापकमन्त्रेण देहे व्यापयेदिति॥ २४॥

तदा स्वरेश इति। हकाराद्यंशविकृततया स्वरादिसप्तवर्गाणां हकारादिवाच्य-त्वाच्च सूर्यादीनां तदीशत्वमुक्तम्। न्यासे विशेषमाह—मन्त्रशेषमिति। मूल इति सप्तगुणा त्वियमित्युपसंहारः। शक्तिरिति च शेषः। गुणशब्दस्तस्याः प्रधान-भूतायाः विभूतिवचनः। सप्तास्या एवं प्रधानविभूतयः। तद्व्याप्तिश्च तत्तदभिव्य-ङ्ग्यफलमयं चराचरजातमित्यवबोद्धव्यम्। वक्ष्यति च—सर्वव्याप्ता हि सा शक्ति-रिति। न्यासविषये विशेषमाह—इति सप्तगुणेति। अत्रांत्यमित्याद्यन्तग्रहणं सर्ववर्णग्रहणार्थमिति ज्ञेयम्॥ २५॥ २६॥

अथ शक्तेरेव रेफादिषडङ्गप्रधानां षड्ग्रहलक्षणां व्याप्तिं वक्ष्यंस्तेषां सवित्रा-त्मकत्वमिह विशेषं दर्शयति—यथेति। नान्ये स्युरिति। त एव तदनुगता एवेति भावः। व्यञ्जनानामृवर्णकार्यत्वात् तदुगतस्वरांशस्यैव च तदुत्पत्त्युपयोगिशक्तितया तदव्यतिरेकात् तस्य च व्यञ्जनदशायां तेष्वनुगमोपलम्भात् परा नकारोदयवह्नि-वर्त्मेति च स्मरणादेवमुक्तम्। न संशय इति। सोमादीनां सवितुरंशावेशादेव भास्करस्वरूपत्वं तद्वित्सु प्रसिद्धमिति सूचितम्। न्यासविषयेऽभिप्रायभेदमाह—तस्या व्यापकत्वमिति। तस्या इति प्रकृता हृल्लेखाशक्तिः गृह्यते। सूर्यात्मकसंवि-द्व्याप्यत्वमिति। न केवलायास्तस्या व्यापकत्वं किन्तु सवित्रात्मिकाया एव तस्या इत्युक्तम्। सप्तग्रहन्यासविषयमेतत्। यद्वा षड्ग्रहन्यासविषयमेव। तत्र चायं व्यापकमन्त्रः। ह्रीं स्वरानुक्त्वा स्वराधिपतये सर्वेश्वराय संविद्रूपाय सवित्रे नम इति। नान्ये स्युरिति। तत्कार्यतया तदनुगमनित्यत्वात् तत्कार्यत्वं च षोडशाङ्ग-व्याप्तावुक्तम्। तदाह—उक्तं हीति॥ २७॥

अथ सोमादीनां सवित्रात्मकत्वमुक्तं युक्तिसिद्धं वदन् षड्ग्रहलक्षणां व्याप्तिम-प्याह आचार्य—इति संलीनसूर्यांश इति। शक्तेर्यः सूर्यांशो हकाररूपः स एवं सोमादिषु संलीनः तदाकारतां प्राप्तो भवति। तदा सोमादिषड्ग्रहभेदत इयं

शक्तिः षड्गुणापि भवतीति तदर्थः। वर्गषट्क इति। तदीशसोमाद्यभेदाभिप्राये-णोक्तम्। तदा यन्त्रमिति षड्गुणितमर्थादवसीयते। तस्याप्येतद्विभूतित्वमनेनोक्तम्। स्मृतिकोविदैरिति। सोमादिविभूतिभूतयन्त्रावयवविद्भिरिति भावः। न्यासविषये विशेषमाह—समग्रहन्यासार्थमिति। हृदयमध्यमिति। अयमाशयः। हृत्प्रदेशे वृत्तमालिख्यांसद्वयगुह्याग्रं जानुद्वयमूर्ध्वाग्रं च त्रिकोणद्वयं मिथः पुटितं विलिख्य तद्बहिर्देहपर्यन्ते वृत्तं भावयेत्। हृद्वृत्तमध्ये शक्तिं विन्यस्य तां परितः शक्त्या श्रीबीजेन कामबीजेन च व्यापय्य वामजान्वादिषडश्रिषु ह्रीं श्रीं क्लीं इति विन्यस्य तदश्रान्तरालेषु शक्तिं विन्यस्य वृत्तबाह्येऽनुलोमया च मातृकया परितो व्यापयेदिति। यन्त्रग्रहणादियानाशयोऽवसीयत इति ॥ २८ ॥

अथ सर्वव्याप्ता हि सा शक्तिरिति ग्रहाणां व्याप्तिः शक्तेः सर्वजगन्मूलत्वं चोक्तम्। सा शक्तिर्भास्कररूपिणी शश्वत् सर्वव्याप्ता हीति योजनीयम्। भास्कररूपिणीति। जगत्सूतिः सवितेत्युक्तप्रधानविभूतिरूपा सतीत्यर्थः। सा सदापि स्वयमेव च सोमादिषड्ग्रहविभूतिद्वारा च सर्वमपि जगद्व्याप्य स्थितेति मूलार्थः। तस्य तस्य ग्रहस्य यदभिव्यङ्ग्यं शुभाशुभरूपं फलं तन्मयमेव सर्वं जगदिति तथेयं व्याप्तिर्विवक्षिता। हिशब्देन ग्रहवित्सु प्रसिद्धमेतदिति सूचितम्। तस्या सूर्यतया पृथगपि व्याप्तिः स्वभासेत्युक्ता। स भास्करः शक्तिविभूतिस्वभासा यत्र क्रमते तत्रास्याः शक्तेः स्थितिर्व्याप्तिरिष्यत इति मूलार्थः। यत्रेति ग्रहमण्डलानि ब्रह्माण्डोदरभागश्चाभिप्रेतः। पर्यायेण क्रमणेऽपि व्याप्तिर्नित्यैवेति स्थितिरित्युक्तम्। न्यासविषये विशेषमाह—न्यासस्येति। सवितृरूपेण ध्यानम्। स च षड्गुणितयन्त्रव्याप्तविग्रह इति ध्यानप्रकारः। 'ततो मूलमिदं विदुरित्येतदपीह सूचितम्। देवताव्याप्तिं चेति। सर्वन्यासेषु समानमेतदवबोद्धव्यम् ॥ २९ ॥

अथास्यास्तु रजसा चैवेति। हृल्लेखायाश्चतुरंशप्रधानाहोरात्रादिलक्षणा व्याप्तिरुच्यते। तदाह—अहोरात्रन्यासमिति। व्याप्तिं वदन्निति प्रकरणाल्लभ्यते। मूले दिवानिशमित्यहोरात्रे भवत इत्यर्थः। सत्त्वावष्टब्धबिन्द्वात्मेति बिन्दुशब्देन बिन्दुलक्षणं गुणसाम्यं विवक्षितम्। बिन्दुग्रहणाद्रजआद्यात्मतया हृल्लेखाया रेफादयोऽपि ग्राह्याः। तदाह—रेफिकारहकारा इति। सत्त्वस्यावष्टम्भकताभिधानात्तदेव मेरुरिति लभ्यते। सत्त्वेन मेरुरूपेणावष्टब्धोऽवपातादिनिर्मुक्तः स्थिरीकृतो बिन्दुरेवात्मा मण्डलाकारं रूपं यस्य स तथोक्तः। रेफादिरूपा रजआदिलक्षणा अहरादयोऽस्याः प्रधानविभूतय इति मूलाभिप्रायः। 'सर्वव्याप्ता हि सा शक्तिरित्येतदिहापि समानम्। तदीयाहोरात्रयोस्तु पितृदेवाद्यहोरात्रेषु व्याप्तिरिति।

न्यासविषये विशेषमाह—रं अङ्गे नम इति। 'ततो मूलमिदं विदुरित्येतदिहापि समानमिति ॥ ३० ॥

अथास्या विकारादिति शक्तेरेव समस्तप्रधाना राश्यादिलक्षणा व्याप्तिरुच्यते। तदाह—राशिव्याप्तिमिति। तत्रास्या विकारादित्यर्धेन राशिरूपा प्रधानविभूतिरुक्ता। अस्या इति प्रकृता हृल्लेखाशक्तिः गृह्यते। विकाराद्वर्णेभ्य इति सामानाधिकरण्यमभिप्रेतम्। वर्णानां तद्विकारत्वं षोडशाङ्गव्याप्तौ 'स सर्गः स्नेषितः कण्ठ इत्यादौ च प्रतिपादितम्। यद्वा शक्तिस्वरूपादेव सर्ववर्णोत्पत्तिरिहेष्यते। अथ वा राशयस्तावद्गुणलक्षणा ह्रकारादिरूपाः स्युः। वक्ष्यति च—

चरस्थिरोभयात्मानं चातुर्वर्ण्यं गुणात्मकम्। इति।

तथा च यस्य राशेर्ये वर्णा वक्ष्यन्ते तदीयाच्छक्त्यवयवात्तेषामुत्पत्तिः स्यात्। तदा च शक्तेर्विकाराद्धकारादेर्ये वर्णाः स्युस्तेभ्यो जाता इत्ययमर्थः। न्यासविषये विशेषमाह—राशिन्यासे वर्णयोगमिति। लवादिकालोपचितैरिति लवादीनां राशिविभूतित्वं चक्रस्य च तत्कार्यत्वं तस्य च त्रित्वमुक्तम्। न्यासे विशेषमाह—कालचक्रमध्य इति ॥ ३१ ॥

ऋक्षराश्यादियुतयेति नक्षत्रादीनां राशिविभूतित्वमेवं विव + + दर्शितः। गतिर्व्यवगमः संहार एवेति भावः। जगतः स्थितिरित्येतद्विवृणोति—जगतः परमात्मरूपेण स्थितिरिति। चक्रसंहारे तद्विभूतेरपि जगतः संहारादेतदुपपत्तिः। वक्ष्यामीति सुबोधमिति। व्याप्तिविषय एतदुक्तम्। वक्ष्यामि चक्ररूपं चेत्याद्यापटलान्तं कालचक्रप्रकरणम्। तच्च महदित्येतदभिप्रायेणैवमभिधानमिति ज्ञेयम्।

मूले चक्ररूपमिति कालचक्रस्य संस्थानं राशिभिः प्रबद्धं यथा भवति तथा वक्ष्यामीति सोपस्कारमन्वयः। राशिग्रहणं नक्षत्राद्युपलक्षणम् ॥ ३२ ॥

षोडशाङ्गादिविभूतीनां रूपं प्रथितमेव नैवं कालचक्रविभूतेरित्येतदारम्भः। तत्रान्तर्बहिरित्यादिप्रकरणस्य न्यासविषयेऽनुष्ठानसंग्रहप्रतिपत्त्यर्थं तात्पर्यार्थं दर्शयति—अन्तर्बहिरित्ययमर्थ इत्यादिना। चतुरस्रत्रयात्मकं सकोणसूत्रमित्यनेन अन्तर्बहिर्विभागेनेत्यस्यार्थोऽपि दर्शितः। पूर्वं समं चतुरस्रं कृत्वा पुनस्तस्य चतुर्षु कोणेषु बाह्यतः संस्पृष्टं चतुर्दिग्गतकोणावसानरेखा लिखेदिति विवरणाशयः। अत्रान्तर्बहिश्चतुरस्रैस्तज्जन्यैर्वा द्वादशभिस्त्रिकोणैः राशिमण्डलस्य विभागो मूल उक्तः। षट्कोणाद्युपलक्षणं चैतत्। यद्वा षट्कोणादितिथिचक्रान्तं कृत्स्नमप्यन्तर्बहिर्विभागेनेति गृहीतमेव राशिमण्डलग्रहणं चैवमुपपन्नं स्यादिति। राशिचक्र इति। द्वादशत्रिकोणपङ्क्तिलक्षणे भाग इत्यर्थः। तत्र चतुरस्रकोणेष्विति

+ + + + राश्यादि मण्डलरचनाप्रकार इति। राशिनचत्रतिथिलवजादि-मण्डलं तदेव। रचयेद्राशिमण्डलमित्युक्तम्। तस्य चेयानभिप्रायः। तस्मिन् मण्डले च कालत्रयं सुव्यक्तं प्रतिपत्तव्यमिति। मूले भूचक्र एष इति। 'चक्रगति-स्त्रिधेत्युद्दिष्टं भूचक्रं प्रस्तुतम्। एष इति वच्यमाणग्रहणम्। मानुष इति मनुष्याणां शुभाशुभफलाभिव्यञ्जकत्वं मनुष्येषु तथा व्याप्तिश्चोक्ता। न्यासविषये विशेषमाह—भूचक्र इतीति + + + ॥ ३३॥

मूले आद्यैर्मेषाद्यो राशिरित्यादिना वर्णेभ्यो जाता द्वादश राशय इत्येतत्प्रा-गुद्दिष्टं विव्रियते। अमःशवर्गलेभ्यश्च बिन्दुविसर्गौश्चचतुष्टयलकारा उक्ताः। शक्तिजृम्भणादिति हृल्लेखाया मूलशक्तेः स्वस्वरूपावस्थानतो बहिर्मुखतया वर्धना-दित्यर्थः। तदुक्तम्—अस्या विकाराद्दर्णेभ्य इति। मोनग इति। तत्कारणत्वादिति भावः। न्यासविषये विशेषमाह—तेषामेवेति। राशिव्यापकमन्त्राणां तच्छब्देन ग्रहणम्। प्रथमत इत्यारभ्य एव ॥ ३४॥ ३५॥ ३६॥ ३७॥

अथ स्यातामिति राशीनां विभूतितया तत्तदवयवा नाड्य उक्ताः। पादाधिका इति पञ्चनाडिकशब्दोऽनुवर्तनीयः। युगमिति मिथुनग्रहणम्। पादोनाविति पञ्चनाडिकौ। वणिक्कन्ये च पञ्चक इति। तुला कन्या च पञ्चनाडिकेत्यर्थः।

त्रिपादोनाविति पञ्चनाडिकावित्यनुषङ्गः। संख्योक्तेति नाडीनामिति शेषः। न्यासविषये विशेषमाह—संख्याया इति। तेष्वेव मन्त्रेषु राशिनाडिका-संख्याया इत्यर्थः। नीरगो मीनः। युङ्मिथुनम्। वणिक् तुला। कुलीरः कर्कटकः। चरा इति पूर्वत्र सम्बन्धनीयम्। वशिष्टा इत्यकारलोपः। यदुक्तम्—

वष्टिवागुरिरल्लोपमवाप्योरुपसर्गयोः। इति।

वृषसिंहवृश्चिककुम्भानां ग्रहणमेतत् ॥ ३७॥ ३८॥ ३९॥ ४०॥

अथ स्युः कर्कट इति राशीनां ब्राह्मणादिरूपतया तद्रूपेण व्याप्तिरुक्ता। न्यासविषये विशेषमाह—चरादिपीताद्योरिति ॥ ४१॥

अथाङ्गाराविति राशीनामेवाङ्गारकादीनां निजनिजग्रहतया तथा व्याप्ति-रुक्ता। न्यासविषये विशेषमाह—राश्यधिपतिन्यासमिति। गोपतिः सूर्यः। धिषणो बृहस्पतिः। मन्दः शनैश्चरः। बलेश्च कलश इति। दीक्षाकलशपूजायां यो बलिस्त-स्येत्यर्थः। वक्ष्यति च—हुते तु देशिकः पश्चान्मण्डले बलिमाचरेदित्यादि ॥ ४२

अथ लग्न इति। राशीनामेवाभिव्यङ्ग्यफलात्मकतया तथा व्याप्तिरुक्ता। न्यासविषये विशेषमाह—राशिनाम्न इति। राशिव्यापकमन्त्रेष्वेव एतदपि भवति। भूचक्रमेवमुक्तम्। इदानीमित्थं मन्त्राणां निष्पन्नत्वात् तैर्न्यासप्रयोगं

दर्शयति—अयमत्रेत्यादिना। त्रिकोणाग्रकोणस्तेषां मध्ये त्रिकोणानीत्युक्तस्य त्रिकोणस्य शिरोदेशगतकोण उक्तः। एवं सर्वत्रेति। क्लीं ऋषभराशिप्रथमघटिकायै नम इत्याद्यूह्यम्। तत्र चायं विशेषः। क्लीं ऋषभराशिप्रथमपादाय नमः। क्लीं ऋषभराशिद्वितीयपादाय नमः। क्लीं ऋषभराशितृतीयपादाय नमः। इति कोणत्रये न्यासः। मिथुनराशौ तु क्लीं मिथुनराशिपञ्चमघटिकायै नम इति चतुरस्रमध्ये न्यासः। यद्वा पञ्च घटिकाश्चेत् पञ्चाशा राशयः स्युरिति ॥ ४३ ॥

अथ ततस्तदूर्ध्वभागस्थ इति भुवश्चक्रमुक्तम्। खसमाख्ययैवान्तरिक्षवर्तित्वमप्यस्य लभ्यते। सम इति। भूचक्रेणेति शेषः। यस्मिन् पैतृकी नियता गतिरिति तथा व्याप्तिरुक्ता। यदुक्तं—चक्रगत्या जगत्स्थितिरिति। न्यासविषये विशेषमाह—मूलाधारचक्रवदेवेति ॥ ४४ ॥

अथ तदूर्ध्वभागसंस्थः स्यादिति स्वश्चक्रमुक्तम्। तादृश इति भूचक्रतुल्यः। न्यासविषये विशेषमाह—मूर्धस्थस्वश्चक्रेऽपीति। त्रैनाभिकस्त्रयमिति त्रिधोक्तचक्रविशेषणम्। तद्दर्शयन् न्यासविषये विशेषमाह—चक्रत्रयन्यासानन्तरमिति। + + + + ॥ ४५ ॥

धनुस्त्विति धनुषो लग्नतया प्रसिद्धिनिबन्धनकथनेन दैवराशीनां लग्नादिफलं प्रधानमित्युक्तम्। समासादिति संग्रहात् लग्नमित्येव व्यवहारविधौ तत्तद्विशेषव्यवहारे मेषसिंहयोरपि लग्नत्वं मनुष्यलग्नं पितृलग्नमितीति भावः। दैवलग्नादिफलानुगतमितरलग्नादिफलं देवानामितरनियामकतोपपत्तेरित्यनेन सूचितम्। न्यासविषये विशेषमाह—धनुर्मासायेति। समासादित्यत्रापि धनुःशब्दो योज्यः। मासपदसहिताद्धनुःशब्दादनन्तरमित्यर्थः। दैवलग्नत्वादित्यस्याभ्यधिकपदस्य मन्त्रेषु योजने हेतुः। दैवलग्नं हि महन्मासमात्रलक्षणम्। तस्माद्धनुर्मासयोग इति भावः। मकरमासादियोगोपलक्षणमेतत्। तदेतद्दर्शयति—मासादूर्ध्वमिति। बध्युरिति मिथो बध्नीयुरित्यर्थः। येनैकस्य राशेः गुणे दोषेऽपि वा सतीतरेऽपि तदनुविद्धाः स्युः सम्बन्धः स एव च वेधः। न्यासविषये विशेषमाह—वेधन्यासप्रकारमिति। उक्तमित्यथ राशिवेधन्यास इत्यादिना पूर्वमुक्तमित्यर्थः ॥ ४६ ॥

अथ मूलेऽतो वेधस्तु भात्मक इति नक्षत्रप्रकरणारम्भः। तदाह—नक्षत्रन्यासमिति। वदन्नित्यतो वेधस्तु भात्मक इत्यादिप्रकरणेनेति शेषः। व्याप्तिमपि दर्शयन्निति प्रकरणाल्लभ्यते। मूलेऽत इति। राशिवेधो हेतुतया परामृष्टः ॥ ४७

यथा धनुर्मेषसिंहानां मिथो वेधात्तेषु प्रथमनक्षत्राणां मिथो वेधो द्वितीयनक्षत्राणामपि मिथ इत्यादि तदभिप्रायेण वेधसाम्यादित्युक्तम्। धनुर्मेषादीनां मिथो

वेधस्तद्गतनक्षत्राणां मिथो वेध इत्येवं साम्यं विवक्षितम्। इह प्राग्राशिन्यासस्तद्ग्रन्थविवरणपूर्वमुक्तः। इदानीन्तु नक्षत्रन्यासकथनपूर्वकं तु तद्ग्रन्थविवरणं प्रतिपत्तिवैचित्र्यादिति ज्ञेयम्। मूलाश्विन्यादिक्रमेणेति वेधग्रन्थभाविक्रमेणेत्यर्थः।

नक्षत्रन्यासे प्रकारान्तरमाह—राशिचक्र एव चेदिति। मन्वांशा इति शक्तितद्वर्णनमःशब्दाद्ययोगादिति भावः। देवतान्यासस्तावदिह दुर्वह एव। वेधन्यासस्तु राशिवेधन्यासवत्संभवति। तृतीयं प्रकारमपि दर्शयति—प्रथममिति। राशिगतेति। तत्तद्राशौ येऽन्तस्त्रिकोणास्तेषामग्रकोणः पूर्वपादकोणस्ततोऽप्रादक्षिण्येन त्रिपादकोणोऽर्धकोणश्च पूर्वं प्रादक्षिण्येन घटिकापादानां न्यस्तत्वादिति नक्षत्रदेवतावेधन्यासावपि संभवत इति। इदानीं मूलाश्विनीमखा बन्ध्युरिति। एवमिति। त्रित्रिनक्षत्रैरेकैकवेधप्रक्रिययेति भावः। याम्यपूर्वादिषु यथान्यासं वा धनुर्मेषाद्युचितक्लृप्त्या वा त्रित्रिनक्षत्रयोगः। याम्यं भरणी। पूर्वा पूर्वफल्गुनी। अनुपूर्वा पूर्वाषाढा। अहिर्बुध्निरुत्तरप्रोष्ठपदा। पादं पादत्रयैर्बन्ध्यादिति। उत्तराषाढाकृत्तिकोत्तरफल्गुनीषु विशाखापूर्वप्रोष्ठपदापुनर्वसुषु च पादत्रिपादानां पर्यायेण वेधः स्यादिति भावः। योजयेदर्धमर्धकैरिति। अविष्ठामृगशिरश्चित्रास्वर्धानां मिथो वेध उक्तः॥ ४८॥ ४९॥

मूले चरस्थिरोभयात्मानमिति गुणदोषवेधोऽयं ग्रहकृत इत्युच्यते। राश्यधिपा एवं यथोक्तो वेधविधानतो बन्ध्युरिति। यथा धनुषि तदधिपतिः गुरुः स्थितश्चेत् धनुर्मेषसिंहा गुणविद्धाः स्युः। मेषे तदधिपतिरङ्गारकश्चेत् ते दोषविद्धाः स्युरिति राश्यधिपग्रहणम्। वेधतारतम्यसूचनार्थं शुभाशुभग्रहयोगमात्रे वेधमात्रमिति। चरस्थिरोभयात्मानमिति पूर्वोक्तानुवादेन चरादिवेधः सूचितः। तत्कालविशेषणं चैतत्। राश्यधिपाः सर्वराशिं चरात्मानं स्थिरात्मानमुभयात्मानं विध्येयुरिति। यथा धनुषि गुरुः स्थितः तद्राशिवशान्मेषसिंहावप्युभयात्मानौ कुर्यात्। मकरे स्थिते वृषकन्ये चरात्मानौ कुम्भे स्थितो मिथुनतुले स्थिरात्मानौ मीने स्थितश्च कर्कटकवृश्चिकावुभयात्मानावित्यादि। अयं चरादिवेधः। चातुर्वर्ण्यगुणात्मकमिति पूर्ववत् तत्कालविशेषणम्। चातुर्वर्ण्यात्मकमिति वर्णवेधः। नात्र 'स्युः कर्कट इत्याद्युक्तवर्णग्रहणम् किन्तु वर्णग्रहसंसर्गनिबन्धनं वर्णत्वं विवक्षितमित्यवबोद्धव्यम्। यथा बृहस्पतिर्ब्राह्मणग्रहः तत्संसर्गाद्धनुर्ब्राह्मणः तद्वेधान्मेषसिंहावपि ब्राह्मणाविति। गुणात्मकमिति गुणवेधः। स चरादिवेधवद्द्रष्टव्यः। इह राशिग्रहणमुपलक्षणम्। नक्षत्रमपि राश्यधिपास्त्वेवं वेधविधानतो बध्नीयुरिति। अत एवायं नक्षत्रवेधावसितावुक्त इति। न्यासविषये विशेषमाह—पूर्वोक्तराशिव्यापकमन्त्रमिति॥ ५०॥

मूल एभ्य एव त्विति राशीनां विभूतितया नक्षत्राभिधानम्। मेषात्तावदश्विनी भरणी कृत्तिकायाश्च पादो जात इत्यादि प्रतिपत्तव्यम्। न्यासविषये तु नक्षत्रविधोक्तपादत्रिपादार्धप्रयोगसिद्ध्यर्थमेतदिति राशिवर्णानां नक्षत्रेषु तत्कार्यतयानुगमविशेषः स चापीत्यादिनोक्तः। न्यासविषये विशेषमाह—नक्षत्रन्यास इति। अक्षरयोगक्रममाहेति। नक्षत्रोत्पत्तिकथनपूर्वकमित्युपस्क्रियते॥ ५१॥

मूल आभ्यामिति अ आ इत्येताभ्यामित्यर्थः। एर्जातेतीकारात्। लिपित्वयादिति ई उ ऊ इत्यत इत्यर्थः। तदन्याभ्यामित्योकार औकारश्चोक्तः। अमसोरिति बिन्दुविसर्गावुक्तौ। केवलो योग इत्ययमेक एव योग इत्यर्थः। रेवत्यर्थमिति। वक्ष्यति च—ताभ्याममोभ्यामिति॥ ५२॥५३॥

कत इति ककारात्। चतः पूर्वा चेति। चवर्णात् पूर्वफल्गुनीत्यर्थः। झञयोस्तथा हस्त इति वाक्यम्। बतस्तथा पूर्वाषाढेति बकारादित्यर्थः। भतोऽन्येति भकारादुत्तराषाढेत्यर्थः। मत इति मकारात्। शतभिषक् लत इति लकारात्। षसहेभ्यः परा स्मृतेत्युत्तरप्रोष्ठपदोक्ता॥ ५४॥५५॥५६॥५७॥

ताभ्याममोभ्यामिति। यौ पूर्वं रेवत्यर्थं पृथक् स्थितावुक्तौ ताभ्यामित्यर्थः। लकारो रेवत्या वर्णः। बिन्दुविसर्गौ च सूर्याचन्द्रमसौ। तथा च तेषां योगो रेवत्यां सूर्येन्दुसङ्गम एव स्यात्। तथा च विषुवति नक्षत्रमण्डलान्ते तिथिमासान्तसम्पन्न इति भावः। + + वत्स्यत इति संभावनया न नित्योऽयं योग इति सूचितम्। सह वत्स्यत इति चाभिधानमप्यमावास्याव्यवहारनिबन्धनमप्येतदिति सूचनार्थम्। सहार्थोऽमाशब्दो भवतीति॥ ५८॥

अथ क्षकारस्य षसहैः सह वासो भुवनं कषत इत्युक्तम्। कषणमोषदोषहिलापक्रमेण प्रलयप्रापणम्। मत्त इति शार्ङ्गिणः स्वात्मपरामर्शः। वर्णव्यष्टीनामेवोत्पत्तिः गुणितप्रकरणादौ साधकस्वरूपादुक्ता। वर्णसमष्टीनामुत्पत्तिस्तु शार्ङ्गिणः स्वरूपादेव सकलभुवनमूलभूतादखिलक्षेत्रज्ञतत्त्वात्मकाद्भवति। वर्णानां च स्वतोभिन्नानामेकार्थान्वयितया मिथो योगे पदतापत्तिः। ततश्च शार्ङ्गी यदा भुवनं कषामीति प्रलये प्रवृत्तो मन्यते तदा तद्गतौ कषवर्णौ संहृतिक्रियैकार्थान्वयितया पदतापत्तौ कषलक्षणं संयोगं प्राप्नुतः। कषामीत्यत्र कषावयवमात्रं नृसिंहस्तस्य देवतेति तदभिमानी मदंशो नरसिंह एवेति शार्ङ्गिणोऽभिप्रायः।

तदुक्तम्— हंसो वराहो विमलो नृसिंहो मूर्तयो हलाम्। इति

श्वेतो भृगुर्लकुलीशः शिवः संवर्तकस्तथा। इति च॥ ५९॥

स पुनरित्यत्र चायमाशयः। यदा बिन्दुविसर्गयोर्लकारस्य च योगस्तदा

रेवत्याममावास्या स्यादिति तावदुक्तम्। स च तावदब्दान्तः सन् कालस्य कश्चिदवधिर्भवति। तदा चेदसौ चकारोऽप्युपस्थितः स्यात्। तदा विश्वस्य प्रलय आपतेदित्यतोऽयं चकारः ततोऽर्वागवस्थित इति ॥ ६० ॥

अथ कारस्कराख्येत्यादिना नक्षत्रविभूतितया वृक्षकथनम्। अत्राभिप्राया-न्तरमाह—नक्षत्रवृक्षकथनमिति। उत्तरत्रेति यथा ऋक्षवृक्षप्रतिकृतिमित्यादि। कारस्करं काञ्जीरं कृष्णं रोहिणं अम्बष्ठं शबरं वञ्जुलं मधूकम्। अङ्घ्रिपा इति नक्षत्रवृक्षाः। आयुस्कामः स्वर्क्षवृक्षमिति प्रासङ्गिकमुक्तम् ॥ ६०॥६१॥६२॥६३ ॥

अश्वियमेत्यादिना नक्षत्रविभूतितयैव देवताकथनं नक्षत्रेभ्यस्तदधिपतितया देवतोत्पत्तिसंभवात्। सुरेड्यो बृहस्पतिः। इन्द्राग्नी इत्येका देवतेत्यर्थः। भाना-मिति नक्षत्राणाम्। न्यासविषये विशेषमाह—नक्षत्रदेवतान्यासमिति ॥६४—६६

मूल एभ्योऽमावास्यान्ता इति राशीनामेव विभूतितया तिथय उक्ताः। एभ्यो राशिभ्य इति संबन्धः। तत्प्रविभागस्त्वत्र तिथीनामित्युक्तः। न्यासविषये विशेषमाह—तिथिन्यासमिति। राशीनामेव विभूतिं दर्शयन्निति प्रकरणाल्लभ्यते। इह तु ग्रन्थविवरणमध्ये न्यासकथनं प्रतिपत्तिवैचित्र्यादेवेति ज्ञेयम्। हं शुक्ल-पक्षाय नम इति। तदेन्दुसूर्ययोर्योगादित्यर्थाद्धंसवर्णयोरिह पक्षबीजत्वमव-सेयम्। हं अं शुक्लप्रथमकालायै नम इति स्वरव्यञ्जनभेदादेवं पक्षद्वयतिथिष्वन्वयः। तत्र बिन्दुविसर्गयोः हंसावयववर्णतया तिथिद्वयीष्वन्वयेऽपि बिन्दुस्वरान्तराभावात् पञ्चदशीमन्वेति। व्यञ्जनानामर्थाद्द्विद्विशस्तिथियोगः। तत्र वशषाणां पञ्चदश्य-न्वयः। सहौ तिथिद्वयीष्वन्वयं भजेते इति। यद्वा व्यञ्जनानामेव तिथिष्वन्वयः।

तदुक्तम्—तिथयः प्रतिपत्पूर्वाः ककाराद्यक्षरैरिह।

+ न्तेर्जाताः स्वरैः पौर्णमासी तत्सङ्ख्यकैरभूत् ॥

णादिवर्णत्रयोद्भूता प्रतिपत् कृष्णपक्षजा।

परा दादित्रयोद्भूता पवर्णात् तत्परा अपि ॥

चतुर्विधबभार्णेभ्यः पञ्चम्याद्या यथाक्रमम्।

मादिलान्ताक्षरोत्थाः स्युरमावास्या स्वरान्त्ययोः ॥ इति।

राशिचक्र एव वेति प्रकारान्तरमुक्तम्। पूर्वार्धत्रिपादकोणेष्विति पूर्वपादकोणे-ऽर्धकोणत्रिपादकोणे चेत्यर्थः। पूर्वत्रिपादार्धकोणेष्विति वा पाठः। अस्मिन् पक्षे तृतीयाद्या भङ्क्त्वा न्यस्तव्या। हं इं तृतीयार्धकलायै नम इति मेषगतत्रिपाद-कोणे न्यस्य पुनस्तमेव मन्त्रमृषभगतपूर्वपादकोणेऽपि विन्यसेत्। एवमष्टम्यादि-ष्वपि द्रष्टव्यम् इति। तृतीयं प्रकारमाह—अथवेति। अत्र तिथिचक्रे तिथि-

न्यासो विकल्पनीय इति। इदानीमेभ्योऽमावास्यान्ता इत्यत्राभिप्रायान्तरमप्याह—एभ्य इति। अत्रैभ्य इति न्यस्ततया प्रकृतानां राशीनां ग्रहणम्। तेन राशिचक्र एव तिथिन्याससिद्धिरिति भावः॥ ६७॥

तेनेति उक्तस्य हेतुत्वेन निर्देशः। वर्णभेदतो भिन्ना इति। राश्यनुगतवर्णानां तत्कार्यतया तिथिष्वप्यनुगम उक्तः। वर्णविशेषयोगमिति। हंस इति वर्णसामान्ययोगः। पञ्चदशस्वराणामेकत्रिंशद्व्यञ्जनानां च योगो वर्णविशेषयोगः। मूले ता एव स्युरिति तिथीनां पक्षद्वयं विभूतिरित्युक्तम्। अन्त्यपक्षोऽपरपक्षः। न्यासविषये विशेषमाह—ता एवेति॥ ६८॥

पक्षव्याप्तौ नियममाह—पक्ष इति। न्यासविषये विशेषमाह—प्रतिपदादिक इति। न्यासमन्त्रांशा इति। हं अं शुक्लप्रथमाकलायै नम इत्यादावित्यर्थः॥ ६९॥

ननु पञ्चदशभिरेव तिथिभिः पक्षसिद्धिः स्यात् पक्षाभ्यां च माससिद्धिरित्याशङ्कायां संज्ञासाम्ये सत्यपीत्याद्युक्तम्। सौम्यात्तु ह्रासवृद्धित इति। सोमस्य शुक्लपक्षे वृद्धिरपरपक्षे ह्रासः। ततस्तिथयो द्वय्य एवेति मूलार्थः॥ ७०॥

अग्न्यर्कोति तिथिविभूतितया देवताकथनम्। न्यासविषये विशेषमाह—अग्न्यर्कोति॥ ७१॥

मूले राशिभ्य इति तिथिविभूतितया करणाभिधानम्। दिनशब्देनादित्यादिवाराणां ग्रहणम्। राशीनामिव करणपर्यन्तं व्याप्तिरित्यभिप्रायेण राशिभ्यः सदिनेभ्य इत्याद्यभिहितम्। यद्यपि वाराणां कुतश्चिदुत्पत्तिर्नोक्ता तथापीह सदिनग्रहणात् संख्यासाम्याच्च तिथिभ्य उत्पत्तिरित्यवबोद्धव्यम्। शक्तिजृम्भणसमुत्थादिति। हृल्लेखाशक्तेरेव प्रक्षोभाद्राश्याद्युत्पत्तिरकाराद्युत्पत्तिवदित्येवमुक्तम्। अक्षरभेदविकारादित्यक्षरभेदलक्षणाद्विकारादित्यर्थः। अनेन तिथ्यनुगतवर्णानां करणेष्वप्यन्वय उक्तः। न्यासविषये विशेषमाह—करणन्यासमिति। विभूतिं दर्शयन्निति प्रकरणाल्लभ्यते। राश्यादिपदोपादानाभिप्रायमाह—राशिभ्य इतीत्यादिना। करणपञ्चकन्यास इति सप्तानां करणानामष्टावृत्त्या षट्पञ्चाशत् करणानि संपद्यन्ते। ततः पक्षिमृगसर्पकोटैः सह षष्टिः करणानि स्युः। तत्र च पञ्चभिः पञ्चभिः करणैरेकैकराशिसंभव इत्येवमुक्तम्। गत इत्याषष्टिसंख्यापूर्तेरेवमित्युक्तम्। तिथियुक्तराशिमन्त्रेणेति। अं आं इं शुक्लप्रथमाद्वितीयातृतीयार्धकलात्मने मेषराशये नम इत्यादिना प्रागुक्तेनेति भावः। प्रतिपर्यायमिति सप्तानां करणानामष्टाविह पर्यायाः। तेषु सर्वेष्वपि पर्यायेष्वित्यर्थः। सप्तग्रहयोग इति शब्देन तदधिपग्रहणादिति भावः। षष्टिसंख्यानामिति। गुणित-

प्रकरणे तावत् पञ्चपञ्चाशद्वर्णा उक्ताः। तत्र हवर्णानन्तरं चत्वारो यमाख्या वर्णाः सामविद्प्रसिद्धो भकारश्च स्यात्। यद्वा मातृकायामेवावर्णादिपञ्चानामिकारादिचतुर्णां च प्लुतसंभवान्नवप्लुतास्तत्तदनन्तरं स्युः। एवं षष्टिर्वर्णाः सिध्यन्ति ॥७२॥

मूले सिंहव्याघ्रवराहा इत्यत्रान्त्यात्प्रतिपदर्धादिति संबन्धनीयम्। प्रतिपदिह पूर्वपक्षगतैव गृह्यते। कृष्णगोरित्यपरपक्षाभिप्रायम्। चतुर्दश्या इति च तदीयपूर्वार्धग्रहणम्। अभिविधौ चाकारः। प्रतिपच्चक्रापरार्ध इति चक्रशब्देनेह त्रिकोणग्रहणम्। सर्वेषु तिथिचक्रेषु द्व्यर्धतया विभागः कल्पनीयः। तत्र प्रतिपच्चक्रपूर्वार्धे षष्टितमं करणं न्यसनीयमिति तदपरार्ध इह करणन्यासोपक्रम उक्तः। इह च करणचतुष्क एव गते मेषराशिमन्त्रेण व्यापकं स्यात्। पुनर्गजादित्रये सिंहे व्याघ्रे च गत ऋषभराशिमन्त्रेण व्यापकमित्याद्यवगन्तव्यम्। अथ कृष्णचतुर्दश्युत्तरार्धात्प्रभृति यावच्छुक्लप्रतिपदुत्तरार्धतिथ्यर्धेषु करणान्याह—पक्षिमृगसर्पकीटकरणानीति। केतुराहू ग्रहाविति। तयोर्द्वौ पर्यायावित्यवबोद्धव्यम्। अत्र वृषे कुक्कुरे पक्ष्यादित्रये च गते मीनराशिमन्त्रेण व्यापकं भवति। पुनः कीटन्यासः ॥ ७३ ॥

मूल एवं सग्रहेति प्रकृतकालचक्रोपसंहारः। दिनशब्देन नक्षत्रग्रहणम्। प्रभेदकशब्दे स्वार्थे कप्रत्ययः। अस्मात्पञ्चविभागादिति तेषामपि विभूतिकथनम्। पञ्चवर्णनिष्पत्तिरिति। वर्णशब्देन तल्लक्षणानां पञ्चभूतानां ग्रहणम्। अत एव क्काद्या इत्युक्तम्। कुः भूमिः। न्यासविषये विशेषमाह—केवलसमष्टिव्यापकमन्त्रमिति। चक्रत्रयेऽपि व्यापकमिति ॥ ७४ ॥

मूल इति मूलाक्षरविकृतमिति हृल्लेखायाः कालचक्रतयोक्तविभूत्युपसंहारः। मूलाक्षरं हृल्लेखा। तस्य विकृतं विक्रिया। इदमिति—अस्या विकाराद्वर्णभ्य इत्यादि क्काद्या इत्यन्तेनोक्तपरामर्शः। वर्णविकृतिबाहुल्यमिति हृल्लेखायास्तावद्विकारो वर्णस्तदुक्तम्—ऊकारान्तास्त्वकाराद्या इत्यादि। स सर्गः श्लेषितः कण्ठ इत्यादि च। तेषां वर्णानां विकृतयो ग्रहराश्यादयः। तदप्युक्तम्—आद्यैर्मेषाह्वयो राशिरित्यादि। बाहुल्यं विस्तारः। पञ्चभूतानां ग्रहराश्यादिविकारत्वात् तद्विभूतित्वाच्च कृत्स्नस्य जगतो बाहुल्यग्रहणम्। वक्ष्यति च—सचराचरस्य जगत इति। तथा च मूलाक्षरविकृतिरेवैवं ग्रहराश्यादिलक्षणस्तद्विकृतिवर्णविक्रिया विस्तार इत्येवमभिधानोपपत्तिः। न्यासविषये विशेषमाह—सर्वमन्त्रेष्विति। तथा च न्यासारम्भो क्रीं लवाय नम इत्यादि। षोडशाङ्गादिन्यासमन्त्रेषु न तद्योगः तदवयवानां हरमायानां योगादित्यवबोद्धव्यम्। 'ततो मूलमिदं विदुरित्येतदिहापि समानमिति सचराचरस्येत्युक्तम्। भूतविकारत्वाच्चराणां भूतानाञ्च कालचक्र-

विभुतित्वात् सचराचरग्रहणम्। न्यासविषये विशेषमाह—व्याप्तिन्यासकथनफलमिति। अत्रास्येति साधकग्रहणम्। बीजस्येति ह्रल्लेखाग्रहणम्। जगत इति साधकशरीरग्रहणम्। तदुक्तमधस्तात्—जगति सर्वतत्त्वात्मके शरीर इति। चराचरशब्देन कृत्स्ना कालचक्रविस्तृतिरुक्ता। तन्न्यासतो जगतः सचराचरत्वम्। तदेतदाह—अस्य साधकस्येति। बीजशब्दार्थौ मन्त्रस्येत्युक्तः। ह्रल्लेखाभिप्रायं चैतत्॥ ७५॥

मूले यां ज्ञात्वेति शक्तिप्रकरणोपसंहारः। यामिति। 'प्राणात्मकं हकाराख्यमित्यादि 'मूलतास्य बीजस्येत्यन्तमुक्ता. ह्रल्लेखाशक्तिः गृह्यते। ज्ञात्वेति। स्वरूपतः षोडशाङ्गादिकलाचक्रव्याप्तितश्च तद्रूढिपर्यन्ततया विज्ञानमुक्तम्। नन्वेकव्याप्तिकथनेनैव तद्विज्ञानं स्यात् किं बहुव्याप्तिकथनेनेति। नैष दोषः। साधकानां विचित्रा हि प्रतिपत्तिर्भवति। यद्वा कृत्स्नापि व्याप्तिरेवं सिद्धा भवति। यद्वा विज्ञानावृत्तिरेवेयं फलतो भवति। सा चावृत्तिरनेकविधेति भेदः। अथवा प्रकृतिपुरुषकालभेदोऽपीह विवक्षितः। प्रथमपटलोक्तयोगवत् तत्र षोडशाङ्गादिव्याप्तिचतुष्टयं प्रकृतिप्रधानं कुण्डलिन्याद्यष्टकं पुरुषप्रधानं पुनः समग्रहव्यात्यादिचतुष्टयं कालप्रधानमिति। अथवा व्याप्तिन्यासोऽपीहोक्त एव। तदुक्तं—कृतकृत्यस्य जगतीति। न्यासप्रचयजन्यात् संस्काराच्च तद्रूढिसिद्धिरिति बहुव्याप्तिकथनोपपत्तिरिति।

सकलं कर्मबन्धमपास्येति। यत्कर्मजातं प्राग्भवेषूपार्जितं शुभाशुभमिश्रलक्षणं भूयोऽप्युच्चावचभवनिमित्तं तस्य तद्विज्ञानप्रचयमहिम्नैव तद्रूढिलक्षणेन संक्षयोऽयमुक्तः। तदुक्तं—तदधिगम उत्तरपूर्वाघयोरश्लेषविनाशौ तद्व्यपदेशादिति।

ननु किमर्थमेतदुक्तमिति। उच्यते। साधकस्य शक्तिव्याप्तिविज्ञानपूर्वकं तन्न्यासेन तच्छक्तितापत्तिस्तावत्पटलारम्भ उक्ता। तत्र चोच्चावचसंसारोपभोगकरकर्मसद्भावे तदसिद्धिरित्याशङ्कायामेतदुक्तमिति।

तद्विष्णोः परमं पदमिति। तदित्युपनिषत्सु प्रथितम्। यद्वा 'यूयमक्षरसंभूता इत्यादित एव प्रकृतम्। यद्वा 'अस्य शक्तित्वमिष्यत इत्येवेहारम्भे शक्तिपदेनोक्तमिति। विष्णुशब्देन शार्ङ्गिणः स्वात्मन एव परोक्षतयाभिधानम्। शक्तिमतो ममैवेति भावः। शक्तिशक्तिमतोरभेद इह विवक्षितः। तदुक्तं—साहं यूयमिति। पुंरूपं सा विदित्वा स्वमिति च। कृत्स्नाया देवताया ग्रहणार्थमित्यमभिधानमिति ज्ञेयम्। परमपदमिति विभूतिलक्षणमपि पदमेव किन्तु तदवरं चिदानन्दैकरसममृतमभयं परब्रह्मपरदेवतादिपदवाच्यं परमं पदं स्थानमिति शक्तितापत्तेरपि फलावस्थेयमुक्ता। त्रिजगति जन्तुजीवभूतामिति सकलचराचरात्मस्वरूपभूतामित्यर्थः।

जपत च नित्यमर्चयतेति च मध्यमपुरुषबहुवचनम्। शार्ङ्गिणो ब्रह्मादीन्

प्रति नियोजनमितत्। ननु तां ज्ञात्वा तत्परमं पदं प्रयातीति तावदिहोपसंहार उचितः। तद्विज्ञानस्यानन्यशेषत्वात् तद्विज्ञानपूर्वकन्यासेन तद्दृढिवशाच्छक्तित्वसिद्धौ पुनर्व्यापारान्तरायोगाच्च। तथा च कथं यां ज्ञात्वेत्यादिप्रकरणोपसंहार इति। उच्यते। शक्तेर्विज्ञानन्यासतस्तद्दृढिवशात् तदापत्तिस्तत्प्रसादसाध्या भवति। प्रसादश्च जपार्चनाद्याराधनसाध्येत्येतत्प्रतिपादनार्थमित्यमुपसंह्रियते। तत्र जपतार्चयतेति चाभिधानं तयोरेवावृत्तिविस्ताराभ्यामदृष्टप्रचयप्रकर्षकरत्वान्महता यत्नेन भाव्यमित्यवबोधनार्थम्। न्यासविषये विशेषमाह—कालचक्रयोगमिति। जपादिकस्येति हृल्लेखापटलभाविरोत्येति भावः।

त्रिजगतीति। यद्यपि प्रकृतं प्रकरणमनेनोपसंह्रियते किन्तु त्रिजगति जन्तुजीवभूतामित्येतद्विशेषेण तु कालचक्रयोगार्थमेवेति भावः। चक्रात्मके जगत्त्रय इति भूचक्रस्य कृत्स्नायां भूमौ व्याप्तिरित्यादि द्रष्टव्यम्। तदुक्तम्—अस्मात्पञ्चविभागादित्यादि। तत्र ये जन्तव इति पद्यं च भूतविकारात्मकशरीरभाजो राश्याद्यनुगता इति भावः। तेषु प्रविश्येति। तदुक्तम्—अत्रापि चेतनाधातोरागतिं बहुधा विदुरिति। जीवभूतामित्यनेन जीवावस्था ततः पूर्वापरावस्था च गृह्यते। तदाह—जीवात्मतां प्राप्तां परां चिन्मात्ररूपामिति। ननु 'चक्रसंहारेण स्वरूपस्थितिं सूचयतीति तावदुक्तम्। क इह विशेष इत्यत आह—कालचक्रयोगक्रमः सूचित इति। चक्रत्रयन्यासानन्तरं चक्रत्रयात्मकं जगदात्माभेदेनाऽनुसन्धाय तदनुगतशक्तितेजसा तस्य स्थूलांशस्य तद्गतजीवसमष्टितन्मात्रे संहारं विभाव्य तस्यापि तच्छक्तिमात्रसंहारं भावयेदित्यनेनोक्तमिति। सकलं हृल्लेखां ज्ञात्वा जपतेति च। हृद्यमिति। हृद्यं हृदयस्य प्रियोऽभिप्राय इत्यर्थः। हृल्लेखाशक्तिरेव यथोक्तरूपा सती तत्तन्मन्त्ररूपापि भवतीति ज्ञात्वा तत्तन्मन्त्रमपि जपेदिति चात्राभिप्रेतमिति विवरणार्थम्। अत्र जन्तुजीवभूतामिति तत्तन्मन्त्रदेवताया जीवतादात्म्यापन्नाया ग्रहणम्। यामेवमुक्तव्याप्तिमयीमपि तत्तन्मन्त्रदेवतारूपेण सकलजन्तुजीवात्मिकां ज्ञात्वा तत्पदं याति तां जपत चार्चयत चेति मूलार्थः।

ननु शक्तिभावनयैव कृत्स्नं कैवल्यं सिद्धम् किं तदवान्तरभेदभावनयेति। नैष दोषः। साधकानां रुचिवैचित्र्यात् तदनुसारतः शक्तेरवान्तरभेदात्मिका मातृका त्रिपुरादिमन्त्रदेवतास्तावदिह भावनीयाः। तासां प्रतिस्वं सर्वात्मत्वमपि प्रतिपत्तव्यम्। इतरथा कृत्स्नापवर्गप्राप्त्यभावात्। तत्र यत्सकलमन्त्रदेवतानां विशेषरूपं तत् स्वस्वप्रकरणेन वक्तव्यम्। यत्तु सामान्यरूपं तत्तावदिह शक्तिलक्षणं शक्तिपटलेऽभिहितमिति हृल्लेखाशक्तेः सामान्यरूपत्वेऽपि तन्मन्त्रस्यास्ति विशेषरूपत्व-

मिति ह्रल्लेखापटलोपपत्तिः। अत एव—तामेनां जपत च नित्यमर्चयतेत्युक्तम्। तत्तन्मन्त्रजपादिरेवेह प्रधानतयाभिप्रेत इति ह्रद्यशब्दोपादानमिति ॥ ७६ ॥

* इह तत्तन्मन्त्रजपस्यापि विहितत्वात् साधकानां तत्तद्रुचावपि तदानुकूल्यमपि परीक्षणीयमिति तत्प्रतिपादनार्थमारभते—अत्र लग्न इति। राशिनक्षत्रनामार्णानुकूल्यमिति। राश्यानुकूल्यं नक्षत्रानुकूल्यं नामानुकूल्यं कुलानुकूल्यमृणानुकूल्यं चेति पञ्चविधमानुकूल्यमुक्तम्। तत्र राश्यानुकूल्यं तावदाह—यस्मिन् राश्यक्षरगण इत्यादिना। षोडशकोष्ठमण्डलं कृत्वा मध्ये चतुष्पदीं मार्जयेत्। तदा परितो मेषादिराशयः संभवन्ति। तेषु वर्णानाद्यैर्मेषाद्वयो राशिरित्याद्युक्तक्लृप्त्या लिखेत्।

तदुक्तम्—वेलागुरुखरः शोणः शर्मणेवेति भेदिताः।

लिप्यर्णा राशिषु ज्ञेयाः षष्ठे शादींश्च योजयेत् ॥ इति।

तत्रैकस्मिन् राशौ साधकस्य नामाद्यक्षरं स्यात्। कस्मिंश्चिद्राशौ च मन्त्राद्यक्षरमपि स्यात्। तत्र साधकनामाद्यक्षरयुक्तराशिमारभ्य मन्त्राद्यक्षरयुक्तराशिपर्यन्तं लग्नादिरूपेण गणनमिति। तदेतदुक्तम्—यस्मिन् राश्यक्षरगण इति।

यन्मन्त्राद्यक्षरयुक्तराशिवर्णा इति। येषां मन्त्राणामाद्यक्षरैर्युक्ता राशिवर्णाः स्युः ते मन्त्रा ग्राह्याः। धनभ्रात्रादिरूपेणात्मनोऽनुकूलत्वादित्यर्थः।

अन्यथापोत्यत्रैवापरः प्रकारोऽपोत्यर्थः। तत्र गणनक्लृप्तिं दर्शयति—स्वराशिमारभ्य गणनमिति। स्वजन्मराशिमारभ्येत्यर्थः। नक्षत्रानुकूल्यमाह—त्रिनवखण्डमित्यादिना। तेष्वश्विन्याद्यक्षराणीत्याभ्यामश्वयुगित्याद्युक्तानीत्यर्थः।

तदुक्तम्—राज्यलाभोपकाराय प्रारभ्यारि खरः कुरुः।

गोपालककुटीं प्रायात् फुल्लापोत्युदिता लिपिः।

नक्षत्रेषु क्रमाद्योज्या स्वरान्त्यौ रेवतीयुजाम् ॥ इति।

स्वनामाक्षरं स्वनक्षत्राक्षरं चेति प्राग्वत्प्रकारद्वयमुक्तम्। एकैकान्तरमिति। षोडशकोष्ठमपि पदचतुष्टयात्मकावान्तरखण्डचतुष्कतया विभजेत्। तत्र चैशानादिचतुर्षु खण्डेषु यान्यैशानानि पदानि तेषु प्रादक्षिण्यक्रमादकारादिवर्णचतुष्टयं लिखेत्। एवमेकैकपदान्तरितत्वं वर्णानां स्यात्। पुनस्तेषु यान्याग्नेयानि पदानि तेषूकारादिचतुष्टयम्। यानि नैरृतानि तेषु ऌकारादिचतुष्टयम्। यानि वायव्यानि तेष्वोकारादिचतुष्टयमिति स्वरलेखनप्रकारः। पुनः खादीन् थादीनपि लिखित्वा हलन्तानपि ऐशाग्नेयनैरृतखण्डगतेशानपदेषु लिखेदिति विवरणाशयः। खण्डचतुष्टयमिति। पदचतुष्टयात्मकखण्डग्रहणम्। जानीयादिति गणयित्वा धारयेदित्यर्थः। पुनः सिद्धखण्डादिखण्डचतुष्टयेऽपि पदचतुष्टयानि सिद्धादित्वेन ज्ञेयानि। सिद्ध-

सिद्धादिनिर्देशोपपत्तेरित्यवगन्तव्यम् । तत्साध्य इति सुसिद्धसाध्य इत्येवं तत्सुसिद्ध-स्तदरिरित्यत्रापि ज्ञेयम् । अरिसिद्धादय इत्यरिसाध्यतत्सुसिद्धतदरीणां ग्रहणम् ।

नामानुकूल्यं न नित्यमित्याह—नृसिंहार्कवराहाणामिति । वैदिक इति । गायत्रीत्रिष्टुबादयः । पिण्डमन्त्रे चेति चिन्तामणित्रिपुरादयः ।

कुलानुकूल्यमाह—अथ कुलाकुलविभाग इत्यादिना । एकभूतसम्बन्धित्व इति । भूतलिपिक्लृप्तिस्तावद्धसाः पञ्चेत्यादिनोक्तैव । नानाभूतसम्बन्धित्वे तु कुलाभेद इत्यर्थोक्तम् । प्रकारान्तरमाह—आग्नेयानामिति ।

ऋणानुकूल्यमाह—अथर्णधनविभाग इत्यादिना । अज्झल्विभागेनेति । यथा नारायण इत्यस्मिन् नाम्नि नकार आकारो रेफ आकार इत्यादि । अष्टशः परित्यक्त इति । परित्यागापर्याप्तौ तु तान्येव शेषवद्द्रष्टव्यानीत्यवबोद्धव्यम् ।

दोषाणामपि सूचितत्वादिति । न केवलं वक्ष्यमाणानामेव छिन्नरुद्धादिदोषाणां विनाशः किन्तु शत्रुमरणादिदोषाणामपि महता यत्नेन प्रशान्त्यादिति सूचितम् । प्रयोग इति । वीर्ययोजनजननादिरूपो दशविध इत्यर्थः । तत्र प्रथमं वीर्ययोजन-माह—योनिबन्धपूर्वकमिति । बीजबिन्द्वादिक्रमेणेति । स्वात्मनस्तन्मन्त्रसकली-करणं कृत्वा तन्मन्त्रमुच्चरन् तदीयबीजबिन्दुकलानिरोधिकानादनादान्तस्पर्श-व्यापिनीसमन्युन्मनीक्रमेण दुष्टमन्त्रसंहारं विधाय तत्र तदीयस्वरूपे तदभेदेन स्थितः संस्तन्मन्त्रं सहस्रवारमावर्तयेत् । एतन्मन्त्रे तद्वीर्ययोजनम् । तत उन्मन्यादि-बीजान्ततया तस्योत्पत्तिं भावयित्वा मानसपूजामाचरेदिति विवरणाभिप्रायः ।

मातृकापद्ममिति । वक्ष्यति च—व्योमाविःसचतुर्दशस्वरविसर्गविस्फुर-त्कर्णिकमित्यादि । तत उद्धरेदिति । दुष्टसंहारोऽपोष्यत एव । पूर्ववत् स्वात्मनः सकलीकरणं मातृकापद्मे मातृकामिष्ट्वा दुष्टमन्त्रस्य मातृकागतनिजवर्णद्वारा तन्मूलभूतोन्मन्यां विलापनं विभाव्य केवलावस्थां कञ्चित्कालमनुसन्धाय ततो मातृकागतनिजवर्णतयोत्पत्तिं विभाव्यान्यत्र स्वोचितपद्मे स्ववर्णांस्तान् क्रमेणो-द्धरन्नालिख्य तत्र मन्त्रं पूजयित्वात्मनि नयेदिति विवरणाभिप्रायः । प्रणवान्त-रितानिति । प्रणवेन नित्यशुद्धवात्मत्वेन दुष्टमन्त्रस्यानुस्यूतताकरणमेतत् । तेन तत्तेजसा तस्मिन्दोषसंहारः तद्वार्येण मन्त्रवर्णानामुपबृंहणं च कार्यम् । वायु-बीजेनेति । तदीयदोषशोषणकरं ह्येतदिति भावः । अग्निबीजेनेति । तदीयदोष-दहनकरं तदीयतेजउद्बोधकरं च ह्येतदिति भावः । स्वतन्त्रोक्तप्रकारेणेति + + । सञ्चिन्त्य मनसेति । मन्त्रं शिष्यवदग्रतः स्थितमनसा विचिन्त्य ज्योतिर्मन्त्रमुच्चरं-स्तस्य तदनुप्रवेशं विभाव्य तत्तेजसा तस्य मलत्रयदहनं भावनीयम् । प्रतिवर्ण-

मिति। भूर्जपत्रे लेखनमिहापि समानम्। प्रोक्षणमिहाष्टशतवारं स्यात्। नाम्ना स्वेनेति। जले मन्त्रं सन्निधाप्य तत्र तर्पणमेतदिष्यते। प्राग्वत् संख्या स्यात्। सर्वत्रापि स्वात्मनः सकलीकरणं मन्त्रभावनेत्यादि समानमेव। तारमायारमायोग इति। प्रतिवर्णमेतैरष्टशतवारं संपुटीकरणमेतदभिप्रेतम्। अन्येषामप्रकाशनमिति। दीक्षितानामदीक्षितानां च पत्रलेखनेनोष्ठपरिस्पन्दनादिना वा न प्रकाशनमिति। दशधा शोधित इति। दोषभेदानुसारेणान्यतमः कतिपये सर्वे वा प्रयोगाः स्युरिति भावः। छिन्ना रुद्धा इत्यादय इति।

तदुक्तम्—अपूर्णरूपाश्छिन्नाः स्युः स्तम्भिताश्चानुनासिकाः।
दग्धाः षट्कर्णगा मन्त्राः त्रस्ताः स्युरधिकैर्जपात्॥
गर्वितास्त्वविधिप्राप्ताः शत्रवो वैरिकोष्ठगाः।
बाला लघ्वक्षरप्राया वृद्धा गुर्वक्षरान्विताः॥
निर्जिताः कर्मबाहुल्यादंहसाः सत्त्ववर्जिताः।
अकालविनियोगेन मूर्च्छिताः स्वापगा जवात्॥
मत्ताः पत्रेषु पठनादन्यवर्णैस्तु कीलिताः।
रुद्धा विसन्धिताः प्राप्तदुःखा वैरिसमन्विताः॥
खण्डीभूतास्त्वंशजवादङ्गहीनास्त्वसंवृताः।
अपूर्णेनोपदिष्टा ये हीनवीर्यास्तु ते मताः॥
सदा प्रयोगात्कणठत्वं क्लिष्टतातिविडम्बनात्।
रुग्नः प्रलेपनैर्जापादन्यमन्त्रैः सहाविलाः॥
उपेक्षावस्थया जापाद्वैषम्यादवमानिताः।
पञ्चविंशतिरुद्दिष्टा दोषास्ताञ्छमयेद् गुरुः॥ इति।

इति प्रयोगक्रमदीपिकायां चतुर्थः पटलः।

अथ पञ्चमः पटलः।

इह तावत् 'यूयमक्षरसंभूता' इति प्रकृतस्य वाच्यवाचकोभयाभेदरूपस्याक्षरस्य शक्तित्वमित्थं समुत्थितम्। साधकस्य तदापत्तिश्च तद्व्याप्तिन्यासेनोक्ता। ततस्तदापत्तिकरतया जपार्चने चोक्ते। तत्र कथं तन्न्यासजपार्चनादिकार्यमित्यपेक्षायां तत्प्रकारप्रतिपादनार्थमापरिसमाप्तेर्ग्रन्थशेषारम्भः। तत्र प्रथमं दीक्षा। ततोऽपि पूर्वं तदीयाङ्गजातकथनम्। तदाह—अदीक्षितानामिति। तत्सिद्धय इत्यधिकारसिद्धय इत्यर्थः। साङ्गोपाङ्गेति पञ्चमपटलार्थो दीक्षेति षष्ठपटलार्थश्चोक्तः।

अतोक्तन्यासादिष्विति सामान्यन्यासानुवादेन दीक्षाया अपि सामान्यैवेयमित्यपि सूचितम्। सामान्यदीक्षैव च सकलविशेषार्थापि भवतीति।

मूले मनूनां दीक्षाविधानमित्युक्तम्। ननु शक्तेरेव प्रकृतत्वे कथं मनूनामिति तदवान्तरभेदमन्त्रग्रहणमिति। उच्यते। मन्त्रभेदा एव तावदिह प्रतिपिपादयिषिताः। साधकमतिवैचित्र्यात् सर्वानुग्रहार्थत्वाच्चास्य प्रपञ्चसारस्य। तेषु यत्सामान्यं शक्तिलक्षणं तत्पृथगभिहितं तत्तन्मनुषु विशेषणतया विनियोजयिषितम्। वक्ष्यति च—सामान्यपटलोक्ता न्यासाः सर्वत्र कार्या इति। ततश्च सामान्यकथनानन्तरं तद्भेदकथनोपपत्तिरिति। पञ्चमषष्ठपटलारम्भ इति मूलगताथशब्दार्थोऽप्युक्तः। अर्थान्तरमप्याह—अतोऽथशब्द इति। श्लोक्त एवासौ हेतुरित्यत उक्तं—विधिवदिति। मूलागमोक्तरीत्येत्यर्थः। अर्थान्तरमाह—वेदाविरुद्धत्वमुक्तमिति। विधयो वेदगताश्चोदनास्तदर्हतयेति भावः। येनोपलब्धेनेति उपलम्भोऽपीह लाभ एव। यदाह—दीक्षालाभमात्रेणेति। साधकेशा इति तत्कालविशेषणम्। तदभिप्रायं दर्शयति—न केवलमिति ॥ १ ॥

मूले दिव्यभावमिति। मन्त्रदेवतात्मतापत्त्या स्वात्मनोऽसाधारणरूपत्वमुक्तम्। दुरितानीति तत्प्रतिबन्धनिचय उक्तः। तत्त्ववदस्येति। विश्वजगद्वसुभूतं देवतातत्त्वलक्षणं स्वस्वरूपमुक्तम्। भयतस्त्रायत इति च सम्बन्धनीयम् ॥ २ ॥

दैवादिकस्य वत्सरस्येति। दैववत्सरस्येत्यर्थः। एतद्दर्शयति—दैवशब्दादय इति। ते च वत्सराः कालचक्रप्रकरण उक्ताः। वत्सरस्यादिश्च पूर्वपक्ष एव। तदाह—आदिं पूर्वपक्षमिति। समग्रसम्पदिति तदपेक्षितपरिकरजातसमृद्धिरुक्ता। दीक्षाकालार्थतयैतद्विवरणम्। अथाचार्यस्य नियमार्थतया विवृणोति—देवा इति। दैवेत्यत्र स्वार्थे तद्धितः। ब्रह्माद्या ब्रह्मविष्णुरुद्रेश्वरसदाशिवाः। ते च विशेषसामान्यतया बीजद्वयबिन्दुकलानिरोधिकात्मकाः। वत्सरो नाद इति निर्देशात्। हृदयादिस्थानानि हृदयगललम्बिकाभ्रूमध्यब्रह्मरन्ध्राणि। मूर्तयश्चाचार्ये साधके चावगन्तव्याः। वक्ष्यति चाभिषेकविधौ—पटुरवाणां मुखे भवेत्यादि। पित्रेत्यत्रापि स्वार्थे तद्धितः। एषामिति गुरुशिष्ययोस्तदन्तर्गतायाश्च ब्रह्मादिरूपाया मन्त्रदेवताया इत्यर्थः। वत्सान्देवादीनिति कार्यत्वाद्वत्सत्वम्। वक्ष्यति च—कुण्डलिनीमुखान्निष्पततामित्यादि। व्याप्येति। वत्सेषु रीतीत्यर्थाद् व्यापनं सिद्धमिति भावः। रवणं नदनम्। समारभ्येतितत्समाश्रित्येति विवृतम्। समः शिष्यात्मन इति। समिति जीववाचकम् बीजम् शिष्यजीवपरिग्रहस्त्वर्थादिति भावः। तत्साधकेनेतीह यत्नशब्देन समास इत्यपि लभ्यते + + + ॥ ३ ॥

मूले शुभकर्मणीति दीक्षामण्टपकरणाङ्गतया वास्तुपूजाप्रकरणारम्भः। शुभकर्मणीति + + दीक्षायामिति + + मण्टपकरण इतीहैव तावदिति भावः। गृहादिविधिष्विति गृहनिर्माणगृहप्रवेशनादिग्रहणम् ॥ ४ ॥

अभवत् पुरेति। वास्तुपूजानादरेऽप्यापद्दिष्णवादिसम्भवोऽपि सूचितः। विश्रुतो दितिज इति सम्बन्धनीयम्। चतुरस्रसंस्थितिरिति निहितविशेषणम् ॥ ५ ॥

तद्देहसंस्थिता य इति सुरगणैरित्युक्तस्य ग्रहणम्। ते यथा मण्डलमध्याद्यर्चा विश्रुतास्तथा वक्ष्यन्त इति योजना। तत्क्रमेणेति तदुचितः क्रम उक्तः ॥ ६ ॥

अष्टाष्टकोद्यतपदां चेति। अष्टानामष्टकेनोद्यतानि सुनिर्मितानि पदानि यस्यामिति समासः। प्रागग्रैरुदगग्रैश्च नवनवसूत्रैरास्फालितैरष्टाष्टकसंख्यासिद्धिः। अत्र चकारो वृत्तपूरणार्थः। अर्थान्तरमाह--चकारेणेति। कोणचतुष्क इति + + चतुष्पदसमन्वितमध्यकोष्ठ इति चतुर्णां पदानामेकीकरणेन समन्वयः। ब्रह्मा त्विति तुशब्दो वृत्तपूरणार्थः। पद्ममात्रे स्वनाममन्त्रेणैवार्चनं भवति।

अर्थान्तरमाह—तुशब्देनेति। ब्राह्मपीठादिपूजनमिति तदुपरि मूर्तिपूजोक्ता। अणिमादिसर्वसिद्ध्यन्ता इति। अणिमा महिमा लघिमा गरिमा ईशिता वशिता प्राप्तिः प्रकामता सर्वसिद्धिश्चेत्यर्थः। अणिमायै नमः महिमायै नम इत्यादिप्रकारेण प्रयोगः। स्रुक्स्रुवदण्डकमण्डलुधर इति। + + साधकवरेणेत्यनेनैतत्सर्वं सिद्धम् ॥ ७ ॥

प्राग्याम्येति। ब्राह्मखण्डस्य चतुर्दिक्षु चतुष्पदैकीकरणेनैकैकखण्डं कार्यम्। तदा च तत्खण्डस्यार्वागर्धप्रान्तयोर्द्वे अर्धकोष्ठे स्याताम्। परागर्धप्रान्तयोर्द्वे पदे तदनन्तरं द्वे अर्धकोष्ठे स्याताम्। तत्र यदर्धपदं तत्कोणद्वयार्धकोष्ठेष्वित्युक्तम्। यत्तु पदं तदग्रे पार्श्वोत्थपदद्वन्द्वेष्वित्युक्तम्। सर्वत्रापि पद्ममात्रेषु स्वनाममन्त्रैरेव पूजा। ॐ अर्यकाय नमः ॐ विवस्वते नम इत्यादि।

कोणद्वयार्धकोष्ठेष्विति। कोणेषु यानि द्वयान्यर्धकोष्ठानि तेषु द्वौ विशेषलक्षणावयवौ यस्य तत्सामान्यलक्षणं द्वयम्। तदेतदाह—कोणेष्विति। तज्जयो रुद्रजयः। साप आपेन सहितः। अग्रे पार्श्वोत्थपदे द्वन्द्व इति। अग्निशब्देन कोणानां ग्रहणम्। अग्न्याद्या इत्येतदिहानुवर्तनीयम् ॥ ८ ॥ ९ ॥ १० ॥

अर्धपदाद्यन्तासु चेति। बाह्यदिक्चतुष्टयपङ्क्तीनां प्रान्तयोर्द्वे द्वे अर्धपदे स्याताम्। ताभ्यां सह प्रतिदिशं पदान्यष्टावष्टौ स्युरितीत्थमेवमुक्तम्। बहिर्वासवयमजलेशशशिनां चतसृषु दिक्ष्विति च योजनीयम्। मन्त्रिणेत्यत्राभिप्रायान्तरमाह—ब्रह्मण इति। अनयोः पृथक्पूजादिकमपि कार्यम्। पीठमूलाङ्गादि तु सर्वं

स्वस्वपटलात्प्रतिपत्तव्यम्। मूले प्रागुदीरिता इति पूर्वदिश्युक्ता ॥ ११—१५ ॥

इतीरितानामित्यपि शब्दो ब्रह्मकार्यादिसमुच्चयार्थः। अभिप्रायान्तरमाह—अपिशब्द इति। अत्र साध्विति शब्देनैव ब्रह्मादिसर्वोक्तदेवताग्रहणम्। रजसा चित्राणि पदानि कृत्वेति। द्विवर्णैः त्रिवर्णैः पञ्चवर्णैर्वा वृत्त्या संपूरणं स्वस्तिककरणं वोक्तम्। तां तां देवतामावाह्येति। पद्ममात्रे स्वनाममन्त्रैरित्यवबोद्धव्यम्। तेषां च पदैश्चतुर्भिर्मन्त्रार्धाभ्यां च षडङ्गानि न्यसनीयानि। मन्त्रविशेषसिद्धेरिति। पाशुपतादितन्त्रेषु विशेषसिद्धैः प्रतिदेवतमुक्तैरित्यर्थः। अत्र प्रतिवर्गं तन्त्रेषु सिद्धान्युपदिशति—दध्याज्येति। पायसादीनि सप्तान्नानि। आर्यकसावित्रशर्वशानाग्निनिर्ऋतिवाय्वादयश्च सप्त वर्गा इति ज्ञेयम् ॥ १६ ॥

वास्तुबलिस्तावदुक्तः। अथ भूय इति मण्टपाभिधानम्। तदभिप्रायं दर्शयति—रोमादिकमिति। स्नात्वा रोमादिपरिहारो भवति। एककलशपक्ष इति। वक्ष्यति च—प्रोक्तेनैवं कलशविधिनैकेन वानेककुम्भैरित्यादि। पञ्चहस्तमिति। मण्टपोऽयं सर्वोऽप्येकयोनिरित्यवबोद्धव्यम्। ततश्च पञ्चहस्तत्वेऽपि पादोनत्वं दशाङ्गुलाधिकत्वं चैषितव्यम्। एवं सप्तहस्तादिष्वप्यवगन्तव्यमिति। सप्तपञ्चकमिति। सप्त च पञ्च च सप्तपञ्च चेत्येकशेषोऽत्राश्रितः। मूले परीणाहत इति चतुर्दिक्षु पृथग्योजनयेति भावः। मण्टपविस्तारप्रमाणमेवैतदुक्तम् न पर्यन्तपरिमाणमिति ज्ञेयम्। स च षोडशस्तम्भयुत इति। कथमित्याह—मध्य इति। प्रान्तेऽवशिष्टा इति। कोणेषु चत्वारो दिक्षु द्वौ द्वौ संभूय द्वादशेति भावः। तेषामित्युभयेषामपि ग्रहणम्। फलका इति तोरणस्तम्भयोरूर्ध्वोद्देशे तत्प्रोतात्रतया निधेयस्य फलकस्य ग्रहणम्। ध्वजाष्टकमिति। मूले तोरणग्रहणमेतदुपलक्षणमिति भावः। लोकपालप्रभमिति श्वेतरक्तादिवर्णपताकोज्ज्वलत्वमनेनोक्तम्। मूले पयोभूरुहः क्षीरिद्रुमाः। दर्भस्रक्परिवीतमिति। दर्भमालया नीव्रदेशे परिवीतं त्रिगुणसूत्रपरिवीतमपीष्यते। उज्ज्वलतरमिति। वितानसंभवपरिवेष्टनादिभिरिति भावः। संवृतं समन्ततश्छादितम् उपरि च कटादिभिश्छन्नम् ॥ १७ ॥

इदानीं सप्ताहतो वेति मण्टपकरणीयदीक्षोपयोगितया मङ्गलाङ्कुरसम्पादनाभिधानम्। पुण्याहादिपुरःसरमिति। स्थलशुद्धिनान्दीमुखपुण्याहपीठपूजादिसमुचितकर्तव्यजातमुक्तम्। मूले सपालिकेत्यत्र चतुष्टयशब्दः प्रत्येकं संबन्धनीयः ॥ १८ ॥

कथमेतद्बीजवपनमित्यपेक्षायामन्यस्मिन् भवन इत्यारम्भः। तदर्थमाह—अन्यस्मिन्निति। मूले शुद्धे स्थल इति। लौकिकी मुष्ट्यादिकार्या च स्थलशुद्धिरुक्ता। पदचतुष्कोपेतभानूदरमिति। भानुशब्देन द्वादशपदान्यभिप्रेयन्ते। पदचतुष्कै-

मिंथो विभक्तास्त्रिभिरुपेता भानवो द्वादश पदानि उदरे यस्य। अथोक्तं तत्संवाद-प्रकारं दर्शयति—पञ्चहस्तप्रमाणानीत्यादिना। पालिकादिमुखविस्तारस्य द्वादशाङ्गुलत्वात् तदुपपत्त्या द्वादशाङ्गुलान्तरत्वमित्यादि प्रतिपत्तव्यम्। दक्षिणोत्तरसूत्राणीति। तान्यप्येवं द्वादशाङ्गुलान्तराणि भवन्ति। पङ्क्त्या सर्वत इति। पदचतुष्काणां परित इत्यर्थः। एतदुक्तं भवति। तत्र मध्यगतस्याष्टाष्टशालिनः प्रागायतपङ्क्तियुगलस्य परितश्चतुर्दिक्ष्वेकां बाह्यां पङ्क्तिं विलोप्य वीथीं संपाद्य पुनस्तास्वष्टसु तत्पङ्क्तियुगलगतासु उदगायतासु द्विद्विपदशालिषु पङ्क्तिषु तृतीयां षष्ठीं च पङ्क्तिं च विलोप्य बाह्यवीथ्यवगाहिन्या वीथ्या विदध्यादिति। मूले प्रतिपदं पीतारक्तसितासितमित्यन्वयः। वज्रादिशर्वान्तिममिति। तद्रजोविकिरणक्रम उक्तः। तदुक्तम्—ततश्चोक्तरजसापूर्येति। वीथ्यः श्यामेनेति। तस्य पञ्चवर्णास्विहावशिष्टत्वादिति भावः। याम्योदीच्यसमायातमित्यत्राप्येतत्सर्वं योजनीयम्। मन्त्रिण इति + + ॥ १८ ॥

मूले वैरिञ्चश इति। विरिञ्चो ब्रह्मा। जलक्षालिता इत्यस्त्रेणेत्यर्थाल्लभ्यते। पश्चिमादि विन्यसेदिति। पश्चिममध्यमपूर्वं दचतुष्केषु क्रमाद्विन्यसेत्। पालिकादिचतुष्काणीति भावः। वज्रादिशर्वान्तिक इत्येकैकस्मिन् पदचतुष्केऽपीति भावः॥ २०॥

मूले पृथगपीत्यार्यायाः पूर्वार्धं पङ्क्तिष्वित्येतस्य विशेषणम्। पृथगपीति प्रतिपदमित्यर्थः। उत्तरार्धं विन्यसेदित्यनुषङ्गः। विशेषाभिधानं चैतत्। कङ्गुश्यामानिष्पावखल्वाढकीप्ररोहयोग्यानीति। प्ररोहोऽङ्कुरः। योग्यानीत्यभिधानं देवताविशेषानुसारेण यवशिम्ब्याद्युपसंग्रहार्थम्। यद्वा प्ररोहयोग्यानामेवैषामुपादानार्थम् ॥ २१ ॥ २२ ॥

मूले मूलबीजेनाभिमन्त्र्य निर्वपेदित्यन्वयः। मूलबीजं हृल्लेखैव। यदुक्तं—मूलार्णमर्णविकृतोरिति। ननु मनूनां दीक्षाविधानमिति तावदुक्तम्। तत्र कथमिति तत्रापि हृल्लेखयैव बीजावापः। यद्वा तत्तन्मन्त्रोपलक्षणमेतत्। तदुक्तम्—मूलबीजेन तत्तन्मन्त्रेणेति। विप्राशिषेत्यत्र सहार्थे तृतीया। ब्राह्मणानां गोहिरण्यादिसमर्पणेनाशिषः संपादनीयाः। विधिवत्प्रतिपद्यमानैः शङ्खादिभिर्मुख्यतरैः पञ्चमहास्वनैश्चेति समासः। सहार्थं एव तृतीया। प्रतिपादनं शब्दनं मुख्यतरग्रहणमितरेषां यथायोगमुपसंग्रहार्थम्।

शङ्खं च काहलं चैव तालकांसी तथैव च।
ढक्का चेति च संप्रोक्तं पञ्चवाद्यं मनीषिभिः॥

यद्वा—पणवं मर्दलं चैव तालकांसी तथैव च ।
काहलं चैव संप्रोक्तं पञ्चवाद्यं मनीषिभिः ॥

अस्मिन् पक्षे शङ्खादिभिः पञ्चमहास्वनैश्चेति द्वन्द्वः । यद्वा महान् प्रभूतः स्वनः शब्दो येषामिति समासः । नात्र रूढिरिष्यते । तदाह—दुन्दुभ्यादय इति । तत्र दुन्दुभ्यादयश्चर्माघातयोगिनो दुन्दुभिपणवढक्कागोमुखादयः । तालादयः कांस्याघातयोगिनः तालजयमङ्गलादयः । वीणादयस्तन्त्रीशालिनो वीणाविपञ्चीरावणहस्तादयः । मुखवाद्यादयो मुखवाद्यकरवाद्यदण्डवाद्यभूमिदुन्दुभ्यादयः । शङ्खादयस्तु पूरणयोगिनः शङ्खकाहलशृङ्गवंश्यादय इति ।

उचिततालशब्दविशेषेणेति + + + यद्वा विधिवदित्यनेन पात्रेषु विष्ण्वादिपूजनं बीजेषु मूलबीजेनावाह्य पूजनं चोक्तम् ॥ २३ ॥

हरिद्राद्भिः सम्यगभ्युक्ष्य वस्त्रेराच्छाद्येति प्रक्रान्तद्रात्रिकर्तव्यविशेषकथनम् । हारिद्रापो हरिद्राचूर्णविलोलितजलानि । सम्यगिति प्ररोहानुगुणतयेत्यर्थः । वापमन्त्र एव प्रोक्षणमन्त्रोऽपि स्यात् । वापवदेव चात्र क्रमो ज्ञेयः । अद्भिः सिञ्चतां पञ्चघोषैः सायंप्रातरिति । ततो द्वितीयादिदिवसेषु कर्तव्यमुक्तम् । अद्भिरिति हारिद्राद्यभिप्रायम् । पञ्चघोषैरित्युक्तपञ्चमहास्वनग्रहणम् । सायंप्रातरिति कालाभिधानम् । त्रिषवणं प्रोक्षणमेके मन्यन्ते । मूलबीजसपर्या प्रोक्षणदशायामिष्यत एव । शर्वरीष्वित्यादिविशेषेण सर्वरात्रिषु रात्रिदेवतानां बलिदानमुक्तम् ॥ २४ ॥

नवसु वेति । तत्र त्रिरात्रिषु विष्णुग्रहा एव देवताः । वक्ष्यति च—वैष्णवेयं यदि नवरात्रमिति । नक्तरजो हारिद्रचूर्णम् । ईषत्स्फुरिता उडुम्बाः । सम्यक् स्फुरिता लाजाः । केरोदं नालिकेरजलम् । क्रसरं तिलान्नम् । दुग्धान्नं क्रसरं च वैष्णवेयं यदि नवरात्रमिति वाक्यान्तरम् ॥ २५ ॥ २६ ॥ २७ ॥ २८ ॥

पात्राणि त्रिविधान्यपि परित इति । बाह्यवीथ्येरपि बहिः समन्तादित्यर्थः । बलिक्रमिरिति । तिलगन्धाद्यर्चनादुपलक्षितो बलिरित्यर्थः । सार्वकामिकमिति । अथ यत्प्रागुपक्रान्तं भूयो भूमितल इति तच्छेषः प्रागेवेत्यादिनोच्यते । तत्र प्रथमं कुण्डप्रकरणम् । प्रागेवेति प्रथमं तावदित्यर्थः । अर्थान्तरमाह—मण्डलनिर्माणादिति । सम्यगिति कौशलेनेत्युक्तम् । आखण्डलादय इन्द्रयमवरुणसोमाः दिशास्वित्यनेन च सम्बन्धः । + + विलसद्गुणमेखलानीति गुणास्त्रयः ॥ २९॥३० ॥

विधिष्विति । विंशद्भिस्त्रतुरधिकाभिरङ्गुलीभिरिति परिमितं भूमिभागमिति सम्बन्धनीयम् । कुण्डावटस्यायाममानमेतदुक्तम् । ताभिश्चेति विंशद्भिस्त्रतुरधिकाभिरङ्गुलीभिः परिमित + तमेव भूमिभागमित्यर्थः । तत्र विशेषमाह—

मेखलोच्छ्रयेणेति । तावतीभिरित्यङ्गुलीभिः परिमिता इत्यनुषङ्गः । एकामङ्गुलिं त्यक्त्वेति । खातस्य तटोद्देशे परितोऽपीति भावः । तावतीभिरित्युभयतटापेक्षया परिमाणाभिधानम् । यद्वा मेखलात्रयापेक्षयैव । तदाह—मेखलाविस्तार इति । उच्छ्रयश्चैवमेवेत्यन्तर्मेखलोच्छ्रयो द्वादशाङ्गुल इत्यादिप्रकारेणेत्यर्थः ॥ ३१॥३२ ॥

मूले सकलसिद्धिदा इति मेखलात्रयमावश्यकमिति सूचितम् ॥ ३३ ॥

योनिस्तत्पश्चिमस्यामथ दिशीति स्यादित्यनेन सम्बन्धः । तच्छब्देन मेखला-ग्रहणम् । चतुरस्रस्थलारब्धनालेति । चतुरस्रात् स्थलादारब्धो नालो यस्या इति समासः । चतुरस्रशब्देन पृथिवी लक्ष्यते । तदुक्तं—वज्रोद्यच्चातुरस्रं धराया इति । यद्वा मेखलाबाह्यमेकाङ्गुलपरिमितं कुण्डाङ्गतया चतुरस्रं परिकल्पनीयम् । अथ वा मेखलाक्षेत्रबाह्यतोऽङ्गुलमात्रं द्व्यङ्गुलं वोन्नतं चतुरस्रं स्थलं कार्यम्। तदुपर्येव मेखलेत्येतदप्यर्थात् सूचितं भवति । सैवेह कुण्डाङ्गतया भूमिरिष्यते । तदाह—पृथिवीस्थानारब्धनालेति । तन्मध्योल्लासिरन्ध्रेत्यत्र तच्छब्देन नालग्रहणम्। प्रकृतमेखलाग्रहणं वा । तदाह—तस्य नालस्येति । मेखलेह विस्तारत एव गृह्यते । द्वादशाङ्गुला तावद्विस्तारतो मेखला । तस्याः षडङ्गुलावधिप्रदेशयोने रन्ध्रं परि-स्तरणार्थं स्यात् । तच्चार्थान्मध्यममेखलोपरि स्यादिति भावः ।

उपरि परिविततेति । सा योनिरुपरि प्रदेशे सम्यग्विस्तीर्णा च स्यात् । ततोऽर्थादधः किञ्चित् सङ्कुचितेत्यपि गम्यते । अश्वत्थपत्रानुकारेति तदाकृति-कथनम् । यथा सनालमश्वत्थपत्रं तद्वदस्याः संस्थानमिति भावः । नालस्य पश्चिमतोऽभिहितत्वादग्रस्य कुण्डान्तर्भागत्वमपि लभ्यते ।

उत्सेधायामकाभ्यामिति । उत्सेधेन प्रकृत्यङ्गुला आयामेन विकृत्यङ्गुला च । यद्यपि द्वादशाङ्गुलोन्नता मेखला किन्तु तत्र मूले चतुरङ्गुलोत्सेधो नालोऽष्टाङ्गुलश्च योन्युत्सेधः । यद्यपि द्वादशाङ्गुलवितता मेखला किन्तु योनिस्ततः प्राक् पश्चाच्च द्व्यङ्गुलाधिका नालस्य द्व्यङ्गुलनिष्क्रमाद्योन्यग्रस्य कुण्डे प्रवेशादिति । यद्वोत्सेधतः प्रकृत्यङ्गुल आयामस्तु प्रकृतिविकृत्यङ्गुलः सप्ताङ्गुल एव । अस्मिन् पक्षे योनिपृष्ठमुपर्युपर्यन्तरावेशनीयं स्यात् । यद्वाष्टौ प्रकृतयः षोडश विकृतयश्च संभूय चतुर्विंशतिः गृह्यते । समविभागेनोत्सेधायामौ द्वादशाङ्गुलौ भवतः । पक्षत्रयेऽप्यष्टाङ्गुला स्यात् । विस्तृत्येति समानमेव । योनेरुपरीयं विस्तृतिः । यदुक्तमुपरि परिविततेति । द्वादशार्धाङ्गुलमित-नमिताग्रेति । द्वादशार्धशब्देन षण्णां ग्रहणम् । यत्राष्टाङ्गुलविस्तारः ततोऽग्रे षडङ्गुलविस्तारोऽनेन क्रमेणाङ्गुलमितं कुण्डावटेन मितं चाग्रं स्यादिति ।

प्रकारान्तरेण विवृणोति—उत्सेधायामकाभ्यामितीत्यादिना। प्रकृतिविकृतयः सप्त। तासामष्टभिर्योगे पञ्चदशसंख्यासम्पत्तिः। प्रत्येकं पञ्चाङ्गुलेति त्र्यङ्गुल उत्सेध आयामे च मेखलामानतो वर्धनीयमिति। मूले निविष्टैव कुण्ड इति क्रमावनतत्वमप्युक्तमिति। सर्वं चैतदर्धचन्द्राकारादिकुण्डेष्वपि समानम्॥ ३४॥

चतुःकुण्डकरणं कलशादिवृद्धिविषये स्यात्। अन्यत्रैकमेव कुण्डं कार्यम्। तदुक्तमथवा दिशीति। गदितैरपि लक्षणैरिति मेखलादिह्रासो मा भूदिति भावः। अपघनमङ्गम्। दृष्टिमनोहरं च कान्त्येति सर्वकुण्डसमानं ज्ञेयम्। हस्तमितकुण्डमेवमुक्तम्। तस्य हुतसंख्याभेदेनाल्पत्वं महत्त्वं च विवरणकृदभिधत्ते—शतार्धहोम इत्यादिना। + + अथ कुण्डप्रमितभेदेन तदवयवप्रमितिभेदमाह—सर्वेष्वपीत्यादिना। प्रथममेखलोच्छ्रयेण तुल्यमिति। मेखलोच्छ्रयेण सार्धमिति यदुक्तं तत्र विस्मर्तव्यम्। कण्ठोऽष्टयव इति। यन्मूल उक्तमेकां त्यक्त्वा चाङ्गुलिमपीति स इह कण्ठोऽभिप्रेयत इति॥ ३५॥

अथ ततो मण्टपमध्ये त्वित्यादिना मण्डलमुच्यते। यस्त्विह मण्टपसंस्कारादि कर्म तत्सर्वमुत्तरस्मिन् कर्मपटले वक्ष्यते। ईशानकोणावसानत्वमिति अग्न्यादीशान्ततया स्थण्डिलोपलेपनमुक्तम्। अभ्युक्षणादिकं चेति + + +॥ ३६॥

मूले प्राक्प्रत्यगात्ताग्रं सूत्रं निधापयेदित्यात्तं गृहीतम्। सूत्रस्य ह्यग्रद्वयं गृहीत्वास्फालनं क्रियते। तत्प्रमाणं तु चिकीर्षितमण्डलचतुरश्रप्रमाणतोऽधिकमिति ज्ञेयम्। विप्राशीर्वचनैः सहेति पूर्ववत्। गुणितेनेत्यर्धेन दक्षिणोत्तरसूत्रास्फालनोपाय उक्तः। मध्यादारभ्य गुणितेनाभितो मत्स्यौ विन्यसेदित्यन्वयः। तत्सूत्रमध्ये गृहीत्वाग्रद्वययोजनया द्विगुणितं कुर्यात्। तेन गुणितेन सूत्रेण प्रागास्फालितसूत्रमभितो दक्षिणत उत्तरतश्च मत्स्यौ कुर्यात्। तदा तत्सूत्रमूलविधानं तु पूर्वसूत्रे तन्मत्स्योपपत्त्या यत्र संभवति तत्रेति द्रष्टव्यम्। प्रकारान्तरेण विवृणोति—सूत्रमित्यादिना। मध्यादभितोऽभितो मध्यादभितो मत्स्यौ विन्यसेदिति एवमावृत्त्या योजनीयम्। तत्र मध्यादभित इत्यत्र प्रकृतं प्रागास्फालितं सूत्रं संबध्यते। तदाह प्राक्प्रसृतसूत्रस्याभितो मध्यादिति। तस्य मध्यदेशादभितः दक्षिणतश्चोत्तरतश्चेति मत्स्यौ विन्यसेदित्युपरि संबन्धः। कथं तत्र मत्स्यौ संभवत इत्यत्राभितो मध्यादभित इत्युक्तम्। अभितोऽपि कस्य मध्यादित्यत्र प्रागास्फालितसूत्रे पश्चिमार्धस्य पूर्वार्धस्य च मध्यादित्यर्थाल्लभ्यते। तदेतदाह—द्विगुणितस्याप्युभयतो मध्यादारभ्योभयत इति उभयत इत्युत्तरपदं वामदक्षिणभागाभिप्रायम्। मूलयोजनानुसारादेवमभिधानम्। अयमिह प्रयोगः। गुणितसूत्रमूलं प्रागास्फालितसूत्र-

पश्चिमार्धमध्ये निधाय तदग्रेण दक्षिणतो वामतश्च प्रागास्फालितसूत्रस्यैव मध्यो-द्देशमभितो रेखे कुर्यात्। पुनः प्रागास्फालितसूत्रपूर्वार्धमध्ये निधायापि तद्रेखा-भेदिन्यौ रेखे कुर्यात्। तदा तस्य प्राक्पश्चादायतसूत्रस्य मध्यमभितो द्वौ मत्स्यौ भवत इति। यद्वाभितो मध्यादारभ्य मत्स्यौ विन्यसेदिति मूलान्वयः। कस्याभित इत्यत्र प्राक्प्रसृतसूत्रस्य गुणितसूत्रस्य चेत्यर्थात् संबध्यते। तदाह—प्राक्प्रसृत-सूत्रस्येति। प्रागास्फालितसूत्रस्य दक्षिणतश्चोत्तरतश्च यन्मध्यं तत आरभ्य मत्स्यौ कुर्यात्। द्विगुणितसूत्रस्य च यत्प्रागास्फालितसूत्रे पूर्वतः पश्चिमतश्च मध्यं तत्र सूत्रमूलं निधायाग्रेणोभयतस्तौ मत्स्यौ निष्पादयेदिति ॥ ३७ ॥

मूले तन्मध्यस्थितेति। तच्छब्देनोक्तमत्स्यद्वयग्रहणम्। सपदहस्तमानेनेति भाविचतुरश्रोचितमानमुक्तम्। सपदहस्तः पादाधिकहस्तः त्रिंशदङ्गुलम्। दिशं प्रतीति चतसृष्वपि दिक्ष्वित्यर्थः ॥ ३८ ॥

मकरानिति। यथा प्रागायतसूत्राग्रमत्स्यनिहितमूलेन दक्षिणायतसूत्राग्रमत्स्य निहितमूलेन च सूत्रेणाग्निकोणे रेखासम्पाते तत्र मत्स्यसंभव इत्यादि ॥ ३९॥४० ॥

प्राग्याम्येति यथा ततो मध्यादित्युक्तमत्स्येषु मध्ये प्राग्दक्षिणमत्स्ययोरेकं सूत्रं दक्षिणपश्चिममत्स्ययोरेकं सूत्रमित्यादि ॥ ४१॥४२ ॥

एषु प्राग्वारुणान् सूत्रानिति। प्राक्पश्चिमायतसूत्रस्योभयतो द्वे प्राग्वारुणायते सूत्रे पातयेत्। एवं याम्योदगायतमध्यसूत्रस्योभयतो द्वे याम्योदीच्यायते सूत्रे पातयेदिति। बहुवचनं त्वावृत्त्यपेक्षम्। तेनैतत्सिद्धं भवति। पुनरपि कोण-कोष्ठेषूक्तनयेन मत्स्यान् विधाय प्राग्वरुणादिसूत्राणि पातयेत्। पुनरप्येवं पुनरप्ये-वमिति तथा यत्र पूर्वापरा दक्षिणोत्तराश्च मत्स्याः संभवेयुः। तत्रापि सूत्राणि पातयेदिति। षट्पञ्चाशदिति। यदा शतद्वयादधिकानि षट्पञ्चाशत्पदानि स्युरित्यन्वयः। यदा तत्क्षेत्रं षोडशवर्गात्मकं संपद्येतेति भावः। सुधीरितिपदाभि-धाने तदुचितक्षेत्रप्रतिपत्तिकुशल इति भावः।

पदैः षोडशभिरिति चतुर्वर्गात्मकं क्षेत्रमुक्तम्। वृत्तत्रयान्वितमिति + + तैरष्टचत्वारिंशद्भी राशिः स्यादिति। तच्छब्देन पदग्रहणम्। पञ्चक्षेत्रबाह्यपङ्क्ति-द्वयगतपदाभिप्रायमेतत्। वीथ्यशीतिभिरिति। ततोपि बाह्यपङ्क्तिद्वयगतपद-ग्रहणम्। शोभायुग्द्वारकोणकमिति। शोभयोः युगं शोभोपशोभा च। तद्विभागो द्वाराणीत्यादिनोक्तः ॥ ४३॥४४॥४५ ॥

पदषट्कानीति। बाह्यपङ्क्तौ मध्यतश्चतुर्भिः पदैरान्तरपङ्क्तौ द्वाभ्यां च द्वार-मेवं चतुर्दिक्ष्वपि कार्यमित्यर्थः। शोभाख्याः स्युश्चतुष्पदा इति। द्वारपार्श्वयोर्बाह्य-

पङ्क्तौ पदेनान्तरपङ्क्तौ त्रिभिश्च पदैः शोभा स्यादित्यर्थः। चतुष्पदाश्चोपशोभा इति। शोभयोः सन्निधौ तद्विपरीतपदक्लृप्त्योपशोभा स्यादित्यर्थः। षट्पदं कोणकं भवेदिति। पङ्क्तिद्वयेऽपि त्रित्रिपदैरित्यर्थः॥ ४६॥

वृत्तवीथ्योरिति। वृत्तशब्देन वृत्तत्रयान्वितमित्युक्तवृत्तग्रहणम्। प्राग्याम्य-वारुणोदीच्यं सूत्रचतुष्टयमिति कोणसूत्रं वर्जयित्वाष्टचत्वारिंशत्पदानि संमार्ज्य चतुर्दिशं मध्यसूत्राग्रेषु प्राग्याम्यं याम्यवारुणं वारुणोदीच्यं प्रागुदीच्यं च सूत्रचतुष्कमास्फालयेत्। तदा त्र्यस्रा द्वादश राशयो निष्पद्यन्त इति भावः॥ ४७॥

कर्णिकायाः केसराणामिति पद्मविभागोऽप्युक्तः। कर्णिकादीनां मानं तु भवेन्मण्डलमध्यार्धं इत्येतदुपपत्त्या कल्पनीयम्। मध्यराशिमण्डलार्वाचीनवृत्तयो-रन्तरं द्वादशधा विभज्य द्वाभ्यां द्वाभ्यां कर्णिकादिचतुष्टयमेकैकेन दलाग्रादि-चतुष्टयमिति वृत्तशब्देन वृत्तत्रयग्रहणम्। शोभोपशोभाभ्यामेव द्वारकोणयोः सिद्धिरिति तयोरग्रहणमिति। एवं बाह्यमानप्रक्रतितया पद्मादितदंशमानपक्ष उक्तः। यदुक्तं— ततो मध्यात् सपद्मस्तमानेनेति॥ ४८॥

अथ पद्माद्यंशमानप्रक्रतितया बाह्यमानपक्ष उच्यते—भवेन्मण्डलमध्यार्धं इति। तत्पदं विवृणोति—मण्डलस्य मध्यमित्यादिना। राशिमण्डलान्त इति। भाग इति शेषः। तस्याप्यर्धं इति। मध्यसीम्न आरभ्यैकस्मिन्नेव भागे राशिमण्डल-पराचीनवृत्तपर्यन्तमंशमानमेतत्। तद्वदन्यस्मिन् भागेऽपि मानं स्यादिति मध्य इत्यर्थसिद्धमुक्तम्। तत्र मध्यसीमोद्देश इति भावः। तदङ्गुला इति चतुरङ्-गुलाः। तथेति चतुरङ्गुलम्। एवं षोडशाङ्गुलानि गतानि। तदग्रमिति दलानामग्रम्। वृत्तत्रयस्यान्तरालं तत्तदन्तर्भावः। एवं पूर्वैः सह चतुर्विंशति-रङ्गुलानि स्युः। स्वस्ववर्णविभूषितमिति पूर्वोक्तपक्षेऽपि तुल्यमेव। स्वस्वो वर्णः। तदुक्तं कालचक्रप्रकरणे—चापो नीरजयुक्कन्या इत्यादि। षड्भिर्नवभिरेव वेत्येतदर्थमाह—षड्भिरिति। यद्यपीह त्र्यस्रो राशिरुक्तो वृत्तवीथ्योरारचये-दिति। किन्तु षडङ्गुलस्य वृत्ततायां प्रायो नवाङ्गुलं त्र्यस्रं तत्सममिति वृत्तराशिपक्षे षड्भिरित्युक्तम्। षड्भिरष्टाभिरेव वेति पाठान्तरम्। त्र्यस्रे वृत्ते च सम एवायं विकल्पः। द्वात्रिंशदङ्गुलं ह्येतदिति। पूर्वोक्तचतुर्विंशत्यङ्-गुलानां राशिगताष्टाङ्गुलानां च योगादेवं संख्योपपत्तिः। राशेरष्टाङ्गुलत्वं मुख्यमित्यप्यनेन सूचितम्। षड्भिर्नवभिरेव वेत्यत्र त्वेतद्विवृणोति—द्वात्रिंश-दङ्गुलमिति। अत्र द्विशब्दस्य द्वाभावो न लौकिक इति ज्ञेयम्। राशेः षडङ्गुलपक्षेणैतदुक्तम्। नन्वेवं त्रिंशदङ्गुलमेवैकमर्धं भवति। सत्यम्। इत्यर्धं-

मानयोगेनैतदुक्तमिति बोद्धव्यम्। परस्तात्तावदिच्छत इति मण्डलमध्यार्धे हि तावदुभयत एतन्मानमुक्तम्। तस्य बाह्यार्थेऽप्युभयत एतावदेव मानं स्यादित्यर्थः। तत्र पञ्चदशाङ्गुला वीथयः पञ्चदशाङ्गुलमेव द्वारादिकमिति विभागोऽवगन्तव्यः। इह मण्डले पद्मवृत्तत्रययोः वृत्तत्वं तावदुक्तम् ॥ ४८॥५०॥५१॥५२ ॥

अथ राशिभागस्य संस्थानविकल्पो वृत्तश्च + + मित्युक्तः तद्विद इति। तत्र राशिभागस्य वृत्तत्वपक्षे राशीनां संस्थानं यदि वा वर्तुलमित्युक्तम्। यदि वर्तुलं वृत्तं राशिचक्रं स्यादिति तत्राराणामपि द्विधा संस्थानं ते स्युरित्युक्तम्। अथ राशिभागस्य चतुरश्रत्वपक्षे राशीनां संस्थानं चक्रं च चतुरश्रं चेत्युक्तम्। अत्रापि द्विधा संस्थानमुक्तम्। यदिह पूर्वमुक्तं वृत्तराशिपक्षे षड्भिरिति तत्पङ्कजदलनिभा वेत्येतदिति द्रष्टव्यम्। यद्वा पद्मदलाभानामग्रवृत्तत्वमेव वृत्तं पुनरर्धवृत्तं तच्च बुधैः कथिता इत्यत एव लब्धव्यमिति। अथ तद्बहिरिति वीथ्यलङ्काराभिधानम्। चतुरश्र इति प्रतिदिशमिति भावः। वीथीबाह्ये चतुरश्रसंपादनीयमिति तद्बहिः पार्थिवमित्युक्तम्। कृष्णकोणकमिति शुक्लद्वाराद्युपलक्षणमिति ॥५३—५८

मण्डलानि चेति सर्वसामान्यतयोक्तस्य राशिचक्रस्य सकलविशेषमण्डलेष्वन्वय उक्तः। मण्डलानि चेति भाविमण्डलाभिप्रायम्। वक्ष्यति च—व्योमाविःसचतुर्दशस्वरेत्यत्र प्रविधाय पद्ममितीति। तथा—वह्नेः पुरद्वितयवासवयोनिमध्येति। दीक्षावाहयै पुरोक्ते रचयतु विधिवन्मण्डलमित्यादि। रुचिराष्टपत्रमथ वारिरुहं गुणवृत्तराशिचतुरश्रयुतमिति च। तत्त्वज्ञ इति। कालात्मिकं मन्त्रदेवतां विद्वानित्यर्थः। राश्यन्तान्येवेत्येवकारोऽयोगव्यवच्छेदार्थः। राशावन्यत्रेति। विपर्यये दोषोऽप्यभिहितः। राशेरन्यत्रेति राशिचक्रव्यतिरेकेणेत्यर्थः। उभाभ्यामित्युत्तरत्र संबन्धः। आवाह्येति दृष्टान्तार्थमुक्तम्। उभाभ्यामिति देवताभ्यामित्यर्थः। राशावन्यत्रेत्यत्रोभाभ्यामिति मण्डलशक्तिभ्यामित्यर्थः। तरलश्चञ्चलः स एव दुर्मतिश्च तरलदुर्मतिः। यदिह तत्त्वज्ञ इत्युक्तं तस्यैव विवरणम् ॥ ५९ ॥ ६० ॥

कालात्मकस्येत्येतत्++तस्मादित्युपसंहारः। राशीन् साधिपतीन् मण्डलानि चानुरूपाण्यवगम्य सर्वदेवतामर्चयितुं होतुं वोपक्रमेदिति योजनीयम ॥ ६१॥६२ ॥

अथ मण्डलोपयोगिनां स्वस्ववर्णविभूषितमिति प्रसक्तरजसां तत्त्वं रजांसि पञ्चवर्णानीत्युक्तम्। भूतशः पञ्चपञ्च द्रव्यात्मकानि चेत्यन्वयः। रजसां साधनं हारिद्रं स्यादित्यनेनोक्तम्। ताण्डुलं तण्डुलानां विकारः। दोषारजो रजनीचूर्णम्। सार + + दग्धपुलाकोत्थमिति + + विपश्चितेति सात्त्विकत्वं सूचितम्। शुक्लपीतरक्ताश्च केसरा इति + + दलान्यच्छानीति सितानि। चित्राकाराश्चेति।

पूर्वोक्तचतुर्दिग्गतकल्पद्रुमावशेषभागेषु विचित्रलतादिलेखनेनेति भावः। सितरक्त-निशासिता इति। निशाशब्देन पीतवर्णग्रहणम्। राशिचक्रावशिष्टानीति। ननु राशिवीथ्योरन्तराभावात् कथमेतत्संभव इत्यत्राह—वृत्तराशिपच्च इति। वृत्तं चक्रमुशन्त्येक इत्यस्मिन् पच्च इत्यर्थः। तत्र चतुरश्रतया सूत्रिते पुनः वृत्तता-मापादिते कोणदेशाना बहिरेवावस्थानादिति ॥ ६३॥ ६४॥ ६५॥ ६६॥ ६७॥ ६८॥ ६९ ॥

वैष्णवादाविति दुर्गाश्रीप्रभृतीनां ग्रहणम्। इह सपदहस्तमानेनेति सार्धद्वि-हस्तमानं मण्डलमुक्तम्। द्वात्रिंशदङ्गुलं ह्येतदिति पञ्चहस्तमानम्। यद्वा तत्रापि कर्णिकाचतुरङ्गुलेत्यादीनामुभयार्धयोगतोऽभिधाने सार्धद्विहस्तमानं स्यात्। तदेतदेककलशविषये भवति। नवकलशादौ तु मण्डलमेतद्वर्धयितव्यम्। तदुक्तं —पञ्चहस्तं मण्डलं नवहस्ते मण्टप इति। कदाचिद्राश्यन्तमेव मण्डलं स्यात्

तदुक्तम्—असंभवे तु स्थानानि नेम्यन्तानि न ह्यापयेत्। इति।

तदभिप्रायेणैव च राश्यन्तानीत्युक्तम् + + ॥ ७० ॥

इति प्रयोगक्रमदीपिकायां पञ्चमः पटलः।

अथ षष्ठः पटलः।

पटलसङ्गतिस्तावत् प्रागुक्तैव साङ्गोपाङ्गदीक्षाकथनायेति। साङ्गदीक्षाकथना-रम्भार्थोऽयं मूलेऽथशब्दः। अर्थान्तरमाह—एवमिति। मूले पुनराचम्येति गुरो-र्दीक्षाप्रक्रमे तदङ्गतया द्वितीयमाचमनमुक्तम्। स्नानमपि तदङ्गतया कार्यमेव। स्मृतिप्राप्तत्वादिति ज्ञेयम्। विष्टरोपविष्टः सन्निति। मण्टपे प्रविश्य तत्र नैरृते स्वायतन आसन उपवेशनमभिप्रेतम्। प्राणायामं सलिपिन्यासमिति। प्राणायामो देहशुद्ध्यर्थः। वक्ष्यति च हृल्लेखापटले—अग्नीन्दुयोगविकृता इत्यादि। प्रणव-पटलेऽपि—अथवा शोषणदहनेत्यादि। यद्यपीहैव तावत्प्राणायामो वक्तव्यः। किन्तु सोऽनेकविधः संस्तत्तन्मन्त्रप्रकरणे वक्तुमुचितः संप्रदायान्तरसिद्धोऽप्यसाविह ग्राह्य एवेत्यभिप्रायेण हेयदेवोक्तं लिपिन्यासस्त्वसौ मन्त्रन्यासाङ्गतयैवाभिप्रेतः। न्यसेत्त-दृष्यादीनिति। तच्छब्देन मनूनामिति प्रकृतस्य दीक्षान्वयिनोऽभिमतमन्त्रस्य ग्रहणम्। न्यासान्तरसंभवेऽपि ऋष्यादिमात्रकथनं तस्यावश्यतमत्वप्रतिपादनार्थम्।

पुनराचम्येत्यत्राभिप्रायान्तरमाह—पुनराचम्येत्यादिना। ब्राह्मे मुहूर्त इति। रात्र्यां दशमो मुहूर्तोऽसौ भवति। तल्पतलान्निद्रातश्चैतदुत्थानमभिप्रेतम्। पूर्वेद्युर्निद्रावसरेऽभिमतमन्त्रदेवतामनुसन्धायाऽजपापरमात्मप्रणवमन्त्रैर्देवतातत्त्वेऽ-स्थाय हि निद्रा कृता। ततः प्रबोधे तदवस्थानुसन्धानपूर्वकं मन्त्रेणोत्थानं

कार्यम्। देवतां ध्यात्वेति। कृताचमनः स्वासने समुपविश्याभिमतमन्त्रदेवतामनुसन्दधीत। कियदत्र ध्यानमभिप्रेतमिति नातिसंक्षिप्तम्। तदुक्तमधस्तात्—स्नानादावकया(चा)दिवर्गत्रयस्य मुखमध्यपादेष्विति। तदुपपत्त्या गुरुवन्दनादिकं चतुर्मूर्तिभावनादिकं च कार्यम्। यद्वा विस्तारोऽपीच्छया स्यात्। तदप्युक्तमधस्तात्—देशकालाद्यपेक्षया सर्वं वा सर्वत्र प्रयोक्तव्या इति। तदेतदभिप्रेयता ध्यात्वेत्येतावदेवाभिहितम्। कर्मसमर्पणं विधायेति। ह्यस्तनं श्वस्तनं च लौकिकं शास्त्रीयं च कायिकं वाचिकं मानसं च सकलमपि कर्मजातमिह समर्पणीयमभिप्रेतम्। तन्मन्त्रेण समर्पणं भवति। यद्वा तन्मन्त्रपूर्वं पूर्वदिने कृतमद्य करिष्यमाणं च सकलमपि कर्माऽस्मत्स्वामिने सदाशिवाय नारायणाय वा समर्पयामीति। यद्वा विभज्य कार्यमेतत्। तदा च भोजनवद्देवतां ध्यात्वोक्तमन्त्रेण ब्रह्मार्पणमन्त्रेण वा ह्यस्तनकर्मसमर्पणं करिष्यमाणस्य तु न वा समर्पणमित्येतदभिप्रायेणैव च कर्मसमर्पणमित्येवोक्तम्। हंसपूजां सङ्कल्प्येति। हंसशब्देनाऽजपात्मिका देवतोच्यते। तदुक्तम्—अस्य बिन्दोः समुद्भूत्येत्यादि। तथा—सर्वमन्त्रशेषतया जपादेर्न्यासश्चेति। तस्य पूजा मानसी। सपर्यायन्तु हृल्लेखापटले वक्ष्यति—अजपापरमात्मप्रणवयोगन्यासानिति। तत्र योगः प्रधानम् इह तु पूजाऽवश्यकार्येति पूजाग्रहणम्। ततश्च तज्जपोऽपि सिद्धो भवति। परमात्मप्रणवावपि वा ग्राह्यौ। अजपापरमात्मप्रणवन्यासानित्येवमभिहितत्वात्। ततश्चायं प्रयोगः। स्वाभिमतमन्त्रदेवतामनुसन्धाय संपूज्य कर्मसमर्पणं विधायासंहरन्नमृतमास्राव्य तन्मन्त्रयुक्ताजपाव्यापकेन हंसो भूत्वा मानसीं पूजां विधाय स्वात्मनि देवतातत्त्वपर्यन्तं व्याप्तिमनुसन्दधानः तद्युक्तमन्त्रं चतुर्वारं जप्त्वा संहरन्नमृतमास्राव्य परमात्ममन्त्रेणाप्येवं कुर्यात्। तत्र देवतातत्त्वस्य स्वात्मपर्यन्तं व्याप्तिरनुसन्धेया। पुनः प्रणवेनाप्येवं कार्यम्। तत्राखण्डा मिथो व्याप्तिरनुसन्धेया। ततस्तं रूपं संहरन्नमृतमास्राव्याङ्गन्यासं विदध्यादिति। पृथक् समर्पणसंभवे हंसपूजापि पृथगिष्यत इति। सुशुद्ध इत्यावश्यकशौचाचमनमुक्तम्। स्वाचान्त इति। भाविरीत्या मन्त्राचमनमुक्तम्। सकलीकृत्येति। स्नानाङ्गतया सकलीकरणमुक्तम्। यदुक्तम्—स्नानादावकया(चा)दिवर्गत्रयस्येत्यादि। तत्र च स्नानकाले स्नानं भवति। धृत्वेति स्थापनमुक्तम्। मूलेनाभिमन्त्र्येति। भागत्रयमपीति शेषः। भागिनेत्यन्यतमेनेति भावः। आपादमस्तकमिति संबोध्यम्।

हृन्मन्त्रानीत इति। सूर्यमण्डलाद्धृन्मन्त्रेण तीर्थावाहनमुक्तम्। साङ्गेन मूलेनेति। तत उन्मज्य तत्रैव तिष्ठन्निति ज्ञेयम्। सकलीकृत्येति। जले मन्त्रदेवतायाः सकलीकरणमभिप्रेतम्। यद्वा स्वात्मनि मानसपूजापूर्वकं पूजां समा-

पयेत्। पुनस्तर्पणार्थमपि सकलीकुर्यात्। पूजाक्रमेण सन्तर्प्येति। पीठमन्त्रैः मूलमन्त्रेणान्तर्मूर्तिमन्त्रैरावरणमन्त्रैः मूलमन्त्रेणावृत्त्या पुनर्ब्रह्मार्पणमन्त्रेणापि तर्पणमुक्तम्। उद्वास्येति। प्रागावाहनाद्यपि गम्यते। सूर्यमुपस्थायेति। तन्मन्त्रेणार्घ्यं दत्त्वा तन्मन्त्रमावृत्य जप्त्वा पुनरपि तेनार्घ्यं दद्यादित्यभिप्रायः। ततोऽर्थात्तीर्थोद्वासनपूर्वकमात्मनि निष्कलीकरणमपि स्यात्। मन्त्रजप्तजलपानमपीष्यते। वक्ष्यति च। इदानीं पुनराचमनक्लृप्तिं दर्शयति—वेदमन्त्रैरित्यादिना। ऋग्वेदाय स्वाहेत्यादिभिस्त्रिभिरप आचम्य अथर्ववेदाय नमः अङ्गेभ्यो नम इत्योष्ठमार्जनम् अग्नये नम इति मुखमार्जनं च कृत्वा सूर्याय सोमाय प्राणायापानाय दिग्भ्यो विदिग्भ्य इति नेत्रनासिकाश्रोत्राणि उपस्पृश्य जीवात्मने नमः परमात्मने नम इति हृदयं ब्रह्मरन्ध्रं चालभेतेति प्रयोगक्रमः। पुनः सवित्रेऽर्घ्यं दत्त्वेति। ॐ सवित्रे नम इत्येव मन्त्रः। सामान्यार्घ्येणेति। गन्धपुष्पमात्रान्वितेन मन्त्रमात्रजप्तेनोदकेनेत्यर्थः। द्वारपूजां कुर्यादिति। कथमित्याह—अस्त्रजप्तोदकेनेति। ऊर्ध्वभागेऽपि दक्षसव्यभागयोरेव पूजा मध्ये गणपतिक्षेत्रपालयोरधश्च गङ्गायमुनयोरित्येव बोद्धव्यम्। देहल्यामित्यलिन्दग्रहणम्। द्वाराभ्यन्तरभागे स्थण्डिल एतद्विवक्षितम्। दिव्यादिव्यविघ्नानिति। दिव्यान्तरिक्षभौमानां क्रमेण ग्रहणम्।

देहलीं लङ्घयित्वेति + +। निर्ऋतिकोण इति। प्रदक्षिणतयालिन्ददेशेन गत्वा नैर्ऋतकोणोद्देशे स्थित आसीनो वा सन्निति भावः। मण्टपमिति। मण्डपवेदिकाभिप्रायम्। कुण्डोपलक्षणं चैतत्। तोरणादीनां मण्टपालङ्कारत्वान्न विशेषतः पूजोक्ता। यद्वा वास्त्वीशब्रह्मपूजानन्तरं बहिर्निष्क्रम्य प्रणवेन हृल्लेखया वा दर्भमालाबन्धनतोरणध्वजपूजामपि विधायान्तरागत्य वेद्यभ्युक्षणं कार्यम्।

पुण्याहं वाचयित्वेति। वास्तुदेवताः प्रीयन्तामिति तत्र देवतापरिग्रहः। गुरुरितीति गौणोऽयं गुरुशब्दः। क्रियाविज्ञानतो गरिम्णाढ्यः सन्नितीत्यभिप्रायः।

प्राग्वदनो विष्टरोपविष्टः सन्नित्यभिप्रायमाह—पुनरस्त्रप्रोक्षित इत्यादिना। सन्निति शुद्धत्वं देवताविग्रहत्वं च गुरोरुक्तम्। तत्र शुद्धत्वमस्त्रप्रोक्षित इत्यादिनोक्तम्। देवताविग्रहत्वं च लिपिपद्ममध्यगेत्यादिनोक्तम्। बिन्दूपरि तदीयनादादिमूर्त्याकारतयाऽवस्थानमिहाभिप्रेतम्। लिपिपद्मकर्णिकायामभिमतमन्त्रपद्ममपि वा चिन्तनीयम्। यद्यपीह मध्ये प्रणवो नास्ति 'व्योमाविःसचतुर्दशस्वरविसर्गेति निर्देशात् किन्त्विह तद्बीजहृदयतया प्रणवोऽप्यत एव निर्देशात् कल्पनीय इति बोद्धव्यम्। प्रणवमध्ये चेह बिन्दुरिष्यते। एतच्च प्रागघमर्षणसमयेऽपि समानम्। यदुक्तं—निमज्ज्य मूलं शक्तितोऽनुसन्धायेति। जलपानेऽपि करतल एतत्पद्मं भाव-

नीयम्। वक्ष्यति च—लिपिपद्मं हस्ते सङ्कल्प्येत्यादि। बद्धासन इत्यासनक्लृप्तिः। प्रणवपटले वक्ष्यते—ऊर्वोरुपरि विन्यस्येत्यादि। कथं विष्टरोपविष्टपदे गुरुवन्दनादिचतुष्टयप्रतीतिरिति। तद्दर्शयति—विष्टर इति। विष्टरपदस्य गौणार्थेषु मुख्यमध्यमादिभेदक्रमेण परमात्मादिग्रहणमित्यवबोद्धव्यम्। अत्र ॐ ह्रीं परमात्मादीत्ययं गुरुसमष्टिमन्त्रः। व्यष्टिमन्त्रास्तु परमात्मसाक्षिसर्वेश्वर(?)चतुष्टयं हिरण्यगर्भसदाशिवेश्वरादित्रयं विराड्गिरीशोन्मत्ता गोविन्दशङ्करानन्दाः स्वगुरुत्रयं चेति ज्ञेयम्। तदेतदक्षारमजमव्यक्तमित्यत्र सूचितम्। प्रणवानुष्ठाने चैवमुक्तम्। त्रिपुरापटले चैतदभिप्रायेण वक्ष्यति—परप्रकाशानन्दनाथश्रीपादुकामित्यादि। अंसोर्विति। वामदक्षिणांसयोर्दक्षिणवामोर्वोश्च ग्रहणम्। अग्रेति। पुरोदेशग्रहणम्। विधिवदित्युभयकनिष्ठादिषु करतलयोस्तत्पृष्ठयोश्चास्त्रव्यापकमूलेन करपुटयोर्व्यापकं चोक्तम्। अकारादिमन्त्रैरिति। अथाभवन् ब्रह्महरीश्वराख्या इत्यत्रोद्धृतानां पञ्चमन्त्राणां ग्रहणम्। यदुक्तं—सृष्ट्यादौ विनियुक्ता इति।

प्राणायामं सलिपिन्यासमित्यत्राप्यभिप्रायान्तरमाह—अथ प्राणायाम इत्यादिना। प्राणायामान्तर्गतोऽप्यस्ति लिपिन्यास इत्यपोह सलिपिन्यासमिति सूचितम्। यतो वक्ष्यति—स्पर्शवर्णान् विन्यस्येत्यादि। तथा यादिन्यासेन तान् सञ्चिन्त्येत्यादि। पुनरप्यस्ति प्रथितरीत्या लिपिन्यास इत्यपि सूचितः। तदपि वक्ष्यति—सर्वं सृष्ट्वा मातृकान्यासं विधायेति। सूर्यमण्डलद्वयं विवक्षितम्। रेचकादिषु मन्त्रो वायुबीजम्। मात्राश्च षोडशतद्द्विगुणतद्द्विगुणाः स्युः। वक्ष्यति च प्रणवपटले—मुञ्चेद्दक्षिणयाऽनिलमित्यादि। अग्निमण्डल इति द्वयोरपि ग्रहणम्। तस्यामिति मूर्धनि चेत्युपस्कारः। मूर्धस्थेनामृतमण्डलेनेति तत्रापि स्वरा न्यसनीयाः। यद्वा त एव प्रागपि बाह्य एव। सूर्यमण्डलेऽग्निमण्डले च स्पर्शव्यापकन्यासो भवेदिति।

सधातुप्राणशक्त्यात्मस्तु न्यसन्निति संहाररीत्याऽयं न्यासो विवक्षितः। नात्र प्राणादिशब्दानां मुख्यार्थग्रहणम्। पञ्चीकृतभूतेषु संहारायोगादित्यभिप्रायेणाह—अत्र प्राणशब्देनेति। कथमयं संहार इति। तद्दर्शयति—यादिन्यासेनेति। उत्कृष्येत्युत्कर्षणमूर्ध्वं कारणाभिमुखतयाकर्षणं योजनम्। संहारव्यापकेनैतदिष्यते। पञ्चीकृतभूतबीजानीति। तान्यधस्तान्नादकलादिभूता इत्यत्रोद्धारितानि ह्लौं ह्लैं ह्लूं ह्लीं ह्लां इति। आप्याय्येति सर्गव्यापकमिहेष्यते। प्राणायामपञ्चकमिति। प्रणवेन कुम्भकप्राणायामोऽयमुक्तः। मनणजङादिपञ्चकान् न्यसन्निति। तत्तत्स्थानेष्वेवायं न्यासः। तत्र नाभिः हृदन्तं समानः। उदरान्नेत्रान्तमुदानः। देहे व्याप्तो व्यानः। नासिकादिपादतलान्तं पृष्ठतोऽपानः। पादतलादिनासिकान्तमग्रतः

प्राण इति मादिस्थानानि। देहान्तर्व्याप्तो धनञ्जयो बहिर्व्याप्तो देवदत्तो नासिकायां कृकलो नेत्रे कूर्मो वदने नाग इति नागादीनां स्थानानि। अन्तःकरणानि मनोबुद्ध्यहंकारचित्तचेतना हृदय एव। अपञ्चीकृतभूतबीजानि हौं ह्रीं क्रूं ह्रौं ह्मामित्येतानि। प्राणायामपञ्चकमिति पूर्ववत्। नाभ्यादिगतब्रह्मब्रह्मादिष्विति। तदुक्तं कुण्डलिनीव्याप्तिकथने—द्वादशान्तभ्रूमध्यहृदयनाभिष्वित्यादि। अकारादित्रयं नाभिहृदयभ्रूमध्येषु ओंकारादिचतुष्टयं मूर्धनीति तेषां स्थानानि। प्राणायामषट्कमित्यपि प्राग्वत्। निरवद्यादिमन्त्रैरिति पञ्चभिरिति शेषः। मूर्तिं सङ्कल्प्येति व्यापकेन कल्पनमुक्तम्। वक्ष्यति च—पीठन्यासमूर्तिन्यासानन्तरमिति। न्यासप्रकारोऽपि तत्रैवावगन्तव्यः। तदृष्यादीनित्यत्राप्यभिप्रायान्तरमाह— अङ्गर्ष्यादिकं न्यसेदिति। हृदयशिरसोरित्याद्यनन्तरकथनादेतदवगमः॥ १॥

मूल ऋषिः गुरुत्वादिति सोपपत्तिकमृष्यादिन्यासस्थानमुच्यते। मन्त्रस्य द्रष्टृत्वादादिगुरुस्तावदृषिः। ननु परमात्माद्यशेषगुरुपारंपर्यक्रमेणेति हि गुरुमन्त्रः समाम्नात इति। सत्यम्। परमात्मैव हि तत्तदवस्थायां स स ऋषिर्भूत्वा मन्त्रं पश्यति। स एव परमात्मा साक्ष्यादिक्रमेण मन्त्रसंप्रदायं प्रवर्तयते। श्रूयते च—तस्मादृग्टत्वमदमाचचत एतमेव सन्तिरित्यादि। वक्ष्यति चेहैव—स गुरुः स्यादृषिवाचक इति। गुरुत्वादिति। तं प्रत्यात्मनो नित्यप्रवणत्वाच्छिरसि तन्न्यास इति सूचितम्। धार्य इति जपाद्यवसानपर्यन्तं तदनुसन्धानमपि सूचितम्।

छन्दोऽक्षरत्वादिति। संख्यादिनियमितोऽक्षरसङ्घातश्छन्दो नाम तद्विद्भिर्व्यपदिश्यते। जपविधौ रसनायां तस्य नित्यप्रवृत्ततयावस्थानात् तत्र तन्न्यास इति भावः। रसनागतमिति धार्य इतिवद्द्रष्टव्यम्।

धियाऽवगन्तव्यतयेति। बुद्ध्याह्यंभावेनानुसन्धेयत्वादित्यर्थः। बुद्धौ तस्याः समुपारूढत्वात्तत्र न्यास इति भावः। हृदि प्रविष्टेत्यपि पूर्ववदिति॥ २॥

अथैषामनुसन्धिविशेषप्रतिपादनार्थं निर्वचनमृषिवर्णादिकावित्यादिनोच्यते। तत्रर्षिवर्णादीतिपूर्वार्धं विवृणोति ऋगतावित्यादिना। मूल ऋषि इति च वर्णावादी ययोरिति समासः। ऋधातोराद्यन्तवदेकस्मिन्निति तदादिकत्वसंभवः। आभ्यामिति पृथक्पदपूर्वार्धानन्तरं योज्यम्। तदुपस्कारेण विवृणोति आभ्यां निष्पन्न इति।

शेषमपि पूर्वोत्तरार्धयोः संबन्धं वदन् विवृणोति—अथेत्यादिना। यातीत्येतत्प्राप्नोतीत्यस्याप्युपलक्षणमेव बोद्धव्यम्। ततश्च द्वयोस्तत्स्वरूपापत्तिर्भवति। तदभिप्रायेणाह—शिष्यो गुरुश्चेति। यत्स्वरूपमिति। यच्छब्दोपात्तस्यैव स गुरुरिति तच्छब्देन परिग्रहः। तदभिप्रायं दर्शयति—स परमात्मैवेति। गुरोर्मन्त्रयोगतः

परमात्मतापत्तावजपापरमात्मप्रणवोक्तनयेन तस्य पुनः गुरुतापत्तिरपि स्यात्। यद्यपि शिष्यस्यापि सममेतत्। किन्तु गुरुः सिद्ध एव। शिष्यस्तु साधकः। स इदानीं तन्न्यासेन तदापत्तिभाग्भवतीति तद्रूपेण न न्यासोपपत्तिः। अतएव गुरुरूपेण स्थित एवेत्युक्तम्। ननु मन्त्रदृशि गुरौ कथमेतदुपपत्तिरिति। उच्यते। स हि तदवस्थायां साधकः संस्तन्मन्त्रयोगतः परमात्मतापन्नः तस्य पुनः स्वतापत्तौ सिद्धः सन् गुरुतामेवापन्नो भवति। अतएव शिष्यो गुरुश्चेत्ययं क्रमो गृहीतः। तदीयैकात्म्यस्य गुरुपरम्परासु नित्यत्वात्। गुरुरूपेणेति सामान्यतो गुरुग्रहणम्। मन्त्रं प्रतिपत्ता शिष्यः प्रयोक्ता साधकः। मन्त्रदृशस्तु न शिष्यत्वम्। स्वयंभातमन्त्रतत्प्रयोगत्वादिति। देवतागुर्वात्मनामैक्यमुक्तमिति तथानुसन्धानं कार्यमिति भावः। तथाविधस्य वस्तुनः + स्वात्मता तन्न्यासेन साध्यते। ननु यद्येवं व्यापकेन भवितव्यमिति। नैष दोषः। शिरसि विशेषतः सन्निधानात् तत्र न्यासंभवः। तदुक्तम् ऋषिः गुरुत्वाच्छिरसैव धार्य इति। तद्द्वारेण चेयतोऽनुसन्धेः संभव इति यत्स्वरूपं याति प्राप्नोति च शिष्यः स गुरुः स्यादिति। स गुरुरिति गुरुदेवतयोरैक्यमुक्तम्।

अयमिहाशयः। शिष्यस्य मूलाधारादात्मतेज उद्धृत्य द्वादशान्तस्थं परमात्मानमेव गुरुं प्राप्नोति। तत एव च तन्मन्त्रं प्राप्नोति। पुनस्तथा स्वायतनमूलाधारमायातीति मन्त्रोदयक्रमोऽनेन सूचितः॥ ३॥

इच्छादानार्थकाविति पूर्वार्धं विवृणोति—छदु इत्यादिना। मूले छदाद्यो दादिकश्च धातू स्त इत्यन्वयः। तयोरित्येतद्विदुपस्कारेण विवृणोति—तयो रूपमिति। शेषं विवृणोति—समुदायार्थमिति। साधकाभिमतसकलफलामृतमयाक्षरात्मकत्वं छन्दसोऽनुसन्धेयमित्यनेन सूचितम्। यद्वा यत्स्वरूपं याति प्राप्नोति च शिष्यः स गुरुरिच्छां ददातीति छन्द इत्यत्रायमादेशः। शिष्यस्यात्मतेजो मूलाधारादुद्धृत्य द्वादशान्तस्थं परमात्मानमेव गुरुं प्राप्नोति। ततः तस्माच्चिदादित्यरूपान्मन्त्रमयममृतं प्राप्नोति। तेन च तदायतने मूलाधारे हृदये वा स्रवता कृत्स्नं वपुर्व्याप्नुवता सकलाघसंचयं सकलफलसिद्धिं च लभत इति मन्त्रोदयात्प्रागियमधिकारभावना स्यादिति॥ ४॥

आत्मनो देवताभावेत्यत्रापेक्षितं देवतापदावयवार्थमभिधत्ते—दिवु क्रीडेत्यादिना। समुदायार्थस्तु सुप्रतिपाद एव। देवतालक्षणो भावविशेष इह देवताभाव इत्युक्तः। देवतापदे देवतेत्येतत्क्रीडाद्यर्थस्य दीव्यते रूपम् तेति च तस्य भावस्त्वतलाविति तलस्तनोतेश्चैकं रूपम्। तननं च कृत्स्नं प्रदानमेव। देवतायाः स्वरूपत्वेनाविर्भवत्तयात्मन्यवस्थानमप्यनुसन्धेयमित्यप्यनेन सूचितम्।

यद्वा अयमिह प्रकरणाभिप्रायः। शिष्यस्यात्मतेजो मूलाधारादुद्धृत्य द्वादशान्तस्थं परमात्मानं गुरुं प्राप्नोतीति ऋषिन्यासे विभाव्य तस्मान्मन्त्रमयं महो लब्ध्वा वाक्पथमवतरतीति छन्दोन्यासे विभाव्य तन्महो देवतात्मकं सच्छिष्यहृद्यवतीर्य तस्मिंस्तदात्मतयावस्थितं भवतीति देवतान्यासेऽपि भावयेदिति। मन्त्रोदये कृते पुनः कार्यमेतत्। समस्ततन्त्रेष्वित्यादि सर्वं पूर्वत्रापि समानम्। तन्त्राण्यागमाः। यदुक्तं—समस्तागमसारसंग्रहेत्यादि। अनेनर्ष्यादितत्त्वानुस्मरणमावश्यकमिति सूचितम्। हृदयादिष्वपि समानमेतदवबोद्धव्यम् ॥ ५ ॥

मूले हृदयशिरसोरित्यङ्गमन्त्रेषु सामान्यांश उक्तः। अत्रापि नेत्रम्। हृदयादिचतुर्थ्यन्तपदेषु नत्यादिपदैर्योजितैः हृदयादिषडङ्गप्रयोग इत्यर्थः ॥ ६ ॥

षडङ्गानामेव प्रतिपाद्यार्थं वक्तुं हृदयं बुद्धिगम्यत्वादित्याद्यारम्भः। तत्र हृदयं बुद्धिगम्यत्वादित्यत्रायं प्रसिद्धोऽर्थः। हृदयमिह देवताया एव। तेन च तद्गम्यस्य तदात्मनो ग्रहणम्। तदाह—हृदयं बुद्धिगम्यत्वादिति। तं प्रति साधकस्य सर्वात्मना प्रवणता नमःशब्दार्थः। तदाह—प्रणामः स्यान्नमःपदमिति। तथा च हृदयमन्त्रेण देवताया निजहृदयगम्याय चैतन्यभूतायात्मने साधकेन नमस्कारः क्रियते। तदाह—क्रियत इति। अत्र सूक्ष्ममर्थं दर्शयति—हृदयमितीत्यादिना। परमात्मेति देवतायास्तत्त्वमात्रं हृदोऽयं हृदयम् इण् गतावित्यस्याऽयमिति रूपम्। हृच्छब्देन च तत्स्था बुद्धिः गृह्यते। तदाह—हृत्स्थबुद्धिगम्यत्वादिति। बुद्धिश्चेह साधकस्यैवाभिप्रेयते। शब्दगम्यत्वं तावदवगतिमन्त्रेण बुद्धिगम्यत्वं त्वन्वयव्यतिरेकैरनेकविधैरेव। तथा तस्मिन्नवगते तस्योपादेयत्वेन तदभिमुखतया गतिर्नतिः। सा चात्मनो देवतात्मनश्चैकत्वात्तस्याहंभावेन प्राप्तिरेव। तदाह—हृदयमन्त्रेणेति। विविच्येति बुद्ध्यावगतिरप्युक्तैवेति ज्ञेयम्। ततश्चायं हृदयमन्त्रार्थः। मम हृदोयदयं बुद्धैव यदन्वयव्यतिरेकैरवगतं तस्मै नमः तं प्रति प्रह्वो भवामि तदात्मतापत्त्या तत्र मग्नभवामि तदेवाहं भवामीति। सर्वमन्त्रेषु तदच्चरन्यासादिषु नतेरेवमुभयथार्थोऽवगन्तव्यः। स्वाहाकारादिष्वपि समानमेतत् ॥ ७ ॥

तुङ्गार्थं स्यादित्यत्रायं स्थूलोऽर्थः। शिरःशब्देन देवताया देहो गृह्यते। शिरसः प्रधानाङ्गतया कृत्स्नाङ्गोपलक्षकत्वात्। यद्वा निरतिशयसौन्दर्यादियोगितया सकलदेहतो विप्रकृष्टत्वात्। तदाह—तुङ्गार्थं स्याच्छिर इति। तस्मिन्नात्मीयं सर्वमुपभोग्यतया समर्पयितुं स्वाहाकारः। तदाह—स्वे स्व इति। आत्मीयस्यार्थजातस्य नानाविधविषयात्मकत्वात् तदुपभोगस्य च मतिश्रुत्यादिभेदात् स्वे स्व इत्युक्तम्। विषयस्याहरणमुपाहरणम्। द्विठ इति स्वाहाकार उक्तः। उक्तुङ्गविषयाहृतिरिति।

देवतादेहे स्वीयार्थजातस्य सत उपाहृतिरित्यर्थः। सूक्ष्ममर्थं दर्शयति—तुङ्गार्थमित्यादिना। पूर्वं हृदा विवेके देवतातत्त्वस्योपादेयतया प्रतिपन्नत्वाद्धेयापेक्षया तस्योत्तुङ्गत्वं भवति। स्वे स्व इत्यनात्मार्थस्य स्थूलसूक्ष्माद्यनेकविधत्वात् तत्तदुपाहरणे भेदादुक्तम्। तदुक्तम्—उभयोरप्यात्मन्येव संहारादिति। आहरणं च फलतो विलापनमेव। तदाह—छन्नमन्येन विविक्तस्येति। हेयतया पृथगवस्थितस्येत्यर्थः॥ ८॥

शिखा तेज इत्यत्रायं प्रसिद्धोऽर्थः। शिखाशब्देन देवतायाः केशकिरीटाद्युपाङ्गजातं गृह्यते। शिखायाः प्रधानोपाङ्गतया सकलोपाङ्गोपलक्षकत्वात्। यद्वा विग्रहोत्थतेजोरूपत्वात्। तदाह—शिखा तेजः समुद्दिष्टेति। तस्यां स्वदेहमप्युपभोग्यतया समर्पयितुं वषट्कारः। तदाह—वषडित्यङ्गमुच्यत इति। अङ्गस्याहरणमिति भावः। स्वाहाकृतौ प्रदीयमानं द्रव्यमात्रमिह तु द्रव्यं महदिति भेदः। यद्वा नम इत्यत्र देवतात्मशक्तेः स्वदेहाप्यायनं तापाद्युपशमनं वापि हुमित्यत्र कवचशक्तेः साधकं प्रति बलवतां बाधकानां दहनमपीति भेदः। तत्र नत्यादिषु साक्षादात्मात्मीयसमर्पणं मदीयोऽसावित्यादिविशेषोत्पत्तिस्तु परोक्षेण हुंफडित्यनयोस्तु समर्पणं परोक्षेण बाधकानां व्यवासनम् दहनविशेषोत्पत्तिस्तु साक्षादिति भेदः। प्रणामादेरनुष्ठीयमानत्वाच्च समर्प्यमाणस्यात्मादेरनुपादानम्। यथा नमो महद्भ्यां स्वाहाग्नये वरुणायेति चावबोद्धव्यम्। तत्तेजोऽस्य तनुरिति। तदात्मतया तदुपभोगोऽपि सूचितः। समर्पणदशापेक्षया शिखायै वषडिति समर्पितदशापेक्षया तत्तेजोऽस्य तनुरिति च निर्देश इत्यवबोद्धव्यम्। सूक्ष्ममर्थं दर्शयति—एवमित्यादिना। तत्त्वस्य ह्यध्यारोपापवादाभ्यां स्वरूपसिद्धिः स्यात्। तदुक्तम्—अध्यारोपापवादाभ्यां निष्प्रपञ्चं प्रपञ्च्यत इति। नन्वेवं पूर्वमारोपेण भाव्यमिति। नैष दोषः। स्वात्मतत्त्वे परमात्मनि जगतो नाद्यारोपिततया तदपवादस्यैव त++स्वकार्यतया प्राप्तत्वात्। तदुक्तम्—विश्वप्रतीतौ हि यतः प्रपञ्चस्त्ववगम्यते॥ इति। पुनरारोपश्चैतदनारोपिततत्त्वस्थितये स्यात्। यद्वा कृतेऽप्यपवादे पूर्वसंस्कारेणोद्बुद्ध्यमानस्य जगतस्तत्रारोपमात्रसिद्धताप्रतिपत्तिः पुनः क्रियत इति। तेजश्चिदात्मकमिति। यस्मिन् सर्वविषयहुतिः कृता तस्य महती दीप्तिः स्यादित्येवमुक्तम्। कार्यकारणात्मकं शरीरमिति कृत्स्नस्य देहाद्यर्थग्रहणार्थमुक्तम्। यद्यपि वषडिति समर्पणं किन्तु कृतेऽपवादे देहादेरभावात् समर्पणं नाम तस्मिंस्तदध्यास एवेति शरीरं वषडित्युक्तम्। स्वरूपभूतं तेजस्तनुरिति चिदचिद्भेदापेक्षया शिखायै वषडिति नानात्वम्। तदन्यतापेक्षया चाभेद इति प्रतिपत्तव्यम्। ननु कुत इहाध्यासलब्धिरिति तत्तेजोऽस्य तनुरिति सामानाधिकरण्यस्यान्यथानुपपत्तेरित्याह—तनोस्तत्रेति॥ ९॥

कवग्रहण इत्यत्रायं प्रसिद्धोऽर्थः। कवयति सर्वतो गृह्णाति देहमिति कवचम्। तदाह—कव ग्रहण इति। तत्र स्वदेहमात्मीयं च सर्वं रक्ष्यतया समर्पयितुं हुंवौषट्फडित्येतत्त्रयं भवति। तत्र परभीतिकरमभिमतपरिगुप्तिप्रधानं तेजो हुमिति प्रवर्तते। तदाह—हुन्तेज इति। तेजसा देहो गृह्यत इति। तेजसेति सहार्थे तृतीया। तेनैतदपि लभ्यते। हुमित्येतत्कवचस्यैवोक्तविधं तेजोऽभिधत्त इति। गृह्यत इति कवचेनेत्यर्थाल्लभ्यते। साधकस्य देहः कवचेनोक्तविधतेजसा सह सर्वतो गृह्यत इत्यर्थः। अत्र कवचायेति प्रयोगः। समर्पणं समर्प्यमाणस्य च। तेन सर्वतो ग्रहणमिति ज्ञेयम्। सूक्ष्ममर्थं दर्शयति—आत्मनोत्यादिना। मुक्तानां परमात्मनश्च नास्त्यारोपः। जीवन्मुक्तानां साक्षिण्यात्मन्यनारोपोऽस्ति। बद्धानां ब्रह्मादीनां च तस्मिन्ननात्मन्यारोपितेऽपि पुनरात्मारोपोऽप्यस्ति। देहादाविवाहमाद्यभिमानोपपत्तेः। तदुक्तमधस्तात्—मयि कल्पितत्वेनेति। युष्माकं विषयवत् प्रकृतिकार्यत्वेन तस्यां कल्पितत्वादिति च। कवचेनाहेति योज्यम्। अत्र कर्मणि कवचशब्दः स्यात्। देहः पूर्वोक्त इति। तत्तेजोऽस्य तनुरित्यात्मन्यध्यस्ततयोक्त इत्यर्थः। कवचाय हुं तेजसा देहो व्याप्यत इति च भेदः पूर्ववद्द्रष्टव्यः। कवचमित्युच्यत इति कवचमन्त्राभिप्रायम्॥ १०॥

नेत्रं दृष्टिरित्यत्रायं प्रसिद्धोऽर्थः। देवताया दृगिन्द्रियं नेत्रमित्युच्यते। तदाह—नेत्रं दृष्टिः समुद्दिष्टेति। तत्र स्वदेहार्थमुपभोग्यतया रक्ष्यतया च समर्पयितुं वौषट्कारः। स च प्रदानार्थोऽपि तस्य यत्साधकदेहाद्याह्लादपरं तद्बाधकतापादिकरं सोमाग्न्याद्यात्मकरं तेजस्तदप्यभिधत्ते। ततश्च तदुभयवृत्तिमुभयविधं दर्शनमप्यभिधत्ते। तदाह—वौषड्दर्शनमुच्यत इति। दर्शनं दृशोति। येन तेजसा देवताया दृगिन्द्रिये साधकतद्बाधकसमुचितं दर्शनं स्यात् तस्य नेत्रमन्त्रो वाचकमित्यर्थः। नेत्राभ्यां वौषडित्यादि भेदः प्राग्वदेव।

सूक्ष्ममर्थं दर्शयति—अथाध्यासनिवर्तकमित्यादिना। ननु अपवादेनैव तन्निवृत्तिः स्यात्। यदुक्तम्—अन्वयव्यतिरेकैरनात्मनो विविच्यात्मप्रतिपत्तिरिति। नेत्युच्यते। वस्तुमात्रविषयं तद्यौक्तिकज्ञानम्। इदन्तु शाब्दं तदीययाथात्म्यविषयं ज्ञानम् अतएव दर्शनम् तदाकारं ज्ञानमित्यभिधानम्। तेनैव च तन्निवृत्त्युपपत्तिरिति। नेत्रमन्त्रेणाहेति योज्यम्। दृष्टेः दृष्टिरिति। दृष्टौ तत्त्वतः समीक्ष्यमाणायामस्ति तदन्तरतिसूक्ष्मं तदीयं तत्त्वं साक्षिचिद्रूपं तदेव तस्या दृष्टिकार्यमावहति तदित्यर्थः। दृष्टिरूप इति साक्षाद्दृष्टिरूप इत्यर्थः। येन स्यादिति दर्शनं यस्य वृत्तिस्तस्य ग्रहणम्॥ ११॥

असुत्वसादिकाविल्यत्वायं प्रसिद्धोऽर्थः। अस्यति बाधकं स्वविषय आक्षिपति त्रासयति च तं स्वावस्थातश्चालयतीत्यस्त्रम्। तदाह—असुत्वसादिकाविति। ताभ्यामित्यस्त्रसंभव इति शेषः। तत्र स्वदेहाद्यर्थं रक्ष्यतयैव समर्पयितुं फट्कारः। स च प्रदानार्थोऽपि तस्य यत्साधकदेहाद्यव्यापत्तिपरं तद्बाधकदाहादिप्रधानं तेजस्तदप्यभिधत्ते। तत्त्विह फट्पदाग्निनेत्येवोक्तम्। अनिष्टमाक्षिप्येति। साधकोऽस्त्रमन्त्रेण स्वदेहाद्यर्थमस्त्रशक्तौ रक्ष्यतया समर्पयंस्तेन स्वबाधकं चेतनसकलं तद्विषयेऽवपात्य फडग्निना स्वावस्थातः संहारान्ततया चालयतीत्यर्थः। अत्राक्षेपं चलनं चास्त्रस्य स्वाभाविको व्यापारः। चालनस्य च दाहसंहारपर्यन्तत्वं फडग्नियोगाल्लभ्यते।

सूक्ष्ममर्थं दर्शयति—उत्पन्नज्ञानस्येत्यादिना। अस्त्रेणाहेति योज्यम्। ताभ्यामित्यादि सर्वं विवृतप्रायमित्यभिप्रायेण नेह विव्रियते। अत्रानिष्टं संसार एव तापत्रयास्पदत्वादिति बोद्धव्यम्। ननु किमिहास्त्रं विवक्षितमिति। उच्यते। फडग्निस्तावत्परमात्मन एव सकलसंसारदाहकं तेजः। तस्यैवाक्षेपचलनरूपो व्यापारोऽस्त्रमित्युक्तम्। अत एव फट्पदाग्निनाक्षिप्य चालयेदित्येवोक्तम्। फडग्निना स्वव्यापारेणैवास्त्रेणाक्षिप्य प्रचाल्य संहरेदिति। ननु देवतातादात्म्यं हि तावदिहाङ्गन्यासेऽपि साध्यम् 'अस्य शक्तित्वमिष्यत इत्याद्यभिधानात्। तथा च पुनः स्वकीयोऽसावित्याद्युक्तविशेषोत्पत्तिरनुपपन्ना। पुनर्भेदावभासमन्त्रस्याङ्गमन्त्रेष्वविवक्षितत्वादिति। नैष दोषः। सकलदेवताविषयतयाङ्गमन्त्राणां प्रवृत्तौ फलभावनाद्युपपत्तेः। तदुक्तम्—प्रकृतिं पुनरद्वये तदन्तःस्फुरित इत्यादि। ननु मन्त्रभावनायामात्मन्यनात्मारोपापवादादिति प्रतिपत्तिर्नोपपद्यते। अन्वयव्यतिरेकादीनामसंभवादिति। नैष दोषः। तथाप्यनुसन्धानस्य तदा शक्यत्वात् विविक्ततयापि प्रतिपत्तिसंभवात्। तदुक्तमधस्तात्—उक्तविवेकप्रकारेण स्वां वेत्तीति।

यद्वा ऋषिवर्णादिकाविल्यादि फट्पदाग्निनेत्यन्तस्य प्रकरणस्यायमभिप्रायः। शिष्यस्यात्मतेजो मूलाधारादुद्धृत्य द्वादशान्तस्थपरमात्मानं गुरुं प्राप्य ततो वर्णसङ्घातदेवताभेदलक्षणं मन्त्रं प्राप्य स्वायतनं प्राप्नुवन्मुखोद्देशे तदीयवर्णाभिव्यक्तिं हृदुद्देशे तद्वाच्यदेवतातत्त्वाभिव्यक्तिं च लब्ध्वा तदैकात्म्याच्चिदचिद्विवेकसमर्थः संस्तत्तेजोंऽशैः हृदयाद्यङ्गानि संपादयन् हृदयेनात्मचितः स्थितिं शिरसा कार्याचिदंशस्य शिखया कारणाचिदंशस्यात्मन्येव संहारं कृत्वा कवचेन विग्रहग्रहणं नेत्रेण सर्वज्ञत्वमस्त्रेणाऽज्ञानानैश्वर्याद्यनिष्टक्षपणञ्च करोति। तत्र हृदयादिपदैरङ्गसंपादनं तदनुगतनमःस्वाहादिपदैरात्मचितः स्थापनादिकमिति विवेक इति ॥१२॥

मूले प्रोक्ता इत्युपसंहारः। सर्वतन्त्रेष्विति सर्वागमग्रहणम्।

मन्त्रिभिरित्येतद्विवृणोति—मन्त्रिभिरितीत्यादि। सर्वज्ञादिपदयोग इति। सर्वज्ञादिपदानां हृदयाद्यङ्गमन्त्रेषु योग इत्यर्थः। कानि सर्वज्ञादिपदानीति। उच्यते। सर्वज्ञो नित्यतृप्तोऽनादिबोधः स्वतन्त्रोऽलुप्तशक्तिरनन्तशक्तिरिति। वक्ष्यति च पञ्चब्रह्मप्रकरणे—इन्द्रियतारसमेतं सर्वज्ञायेत्यादि। अयमिह प्रयोगः। हृदयादिविहितमन्त्रांशमुक्त्वा सर्वज्ञाय हृदयाय नमः तथा नित्यतृप्ताय शिरसे स्वाहेत्यादि। देवतालिङ्गान्येतानि पदानि। न तु हृदयादिलिङ्गानीत्यवबोद्धव्यम्। तेन हृल्लेखादिषु भेदः यथास्वद्वारा हृत्स्थबुद्धिगम्यताद्युचितं निष्कलज्ञानमात्रं लक्षयति। एवं नित्यतृप्तादिष्वपीति भावः। तत्र सर्वज्ञपदेन ज्ञानमात्रं नित्यतृप्तपदेनानन्दमात्रमनादिबोधपदेन स्वातन्त्र्यमात्रमलुप्तशक्तिपदेन कालाद्यनवच्छिन्नत्वम् अनन्तशक्तिपदेन च देशाद्यनवच्छिन्नत्वमिति। इह ज्ञानादेः हृदयादेश्च सामानाधिकरण्यसंभवः। कवचे तु इहैतदप्यर्थादवसीयते। निष्कलनिष्ठस्य मन्त्रेण तदंशैरपि वर्णपदादिभिस्तदङ्गभूतैश्च षोडशाङ्गन्यासादिमन्त्रैरपि देवतायास्तत्त्वमेव तत्तदुचितं लक्ष्यमिति। देवताया ध्यानेऽपि समानमेतत्। वक्ष्यति लिपिपटलादिषु—तामिति परं चिदात्मकमित्यादि। गायत्रीपटलेऽपि—एवं केवलनिर्गुणनिष्ठानामित्यादि। प्रागप्युक्तम्—एवं वागर्थात्मकचतुर्विधविषयकथनेनैवेत्यादि। ततश्चैवं प्रयोगः। तत्तद्वर्णादिन्यासे तत्तदर्थद्वारा तत्साक्षिणि प्रतिपत्तिः। यथा 'मूलपुटितां मातृकां विन्यस्येत्यादि। तत्तन्मन्त्रैर्देवताभिधानेऽपि लक्षणया तत्तत्स्थूलादिरूपान्तर्गतसाक्षिणि प्रतिपत्तिः 'यथाङ्गमन्त्रेष्विति। सगुणनिष्ठस्य त्विति तैरुच्यत इत्यन्तं वाक्यम्। सर्वज्ञत्वादिशक्त्यात्मकत्वमिति। ज्ञानानन्दादीनामखण्डावस्था देवतातत्त्वं परं ब्रह्म। तेषामेव सर्वार्थभाजामखण्डावस्था स्थूलादि च रूपः सकलो देवतात्मा। तथाविधानां च ज्ञानादीनामुपाधयः सर्वज्ञत्वादिशक्तयः। ताभिर्विभक्ता ज्ञानादयस्तदंशाः सर्वज्ञत्वादिशक्त्यात्मानः सर्वज्ञनित्यतृप्तादिपदवाच्या विवक्षिताः।

केचित्तत्त्वत एव निर्देशात् सर्वज्ञात्मने हृदयायेत्यादिरीत्या हृदयादिमन्त्रान् वदन्ति। तदात्मकत्वमिह ज्ञानानन्दानामिति बोद्धव्यम्। शक्तिग्रहणेनैतदपि सूचितम्। देवतायाः सर्वज्ञत्वशक्तिः हृदयाङ्गतां प्रतिपद्यते। नित्यतृप्तत्वशक्तिः शिरोऽङ्गतामित्यादिशक्तिताभ्युपगमे च तेषामावरणभावोऽपि संभवति। वक्ष्यति च— हृदयं सशिरस्तथा शिखेत्यादि। धर्माधर्मादीनामपि समानमेतत्।

हृदयादिशब्दैरपीति। ननु हृदयादिशब्दानामर्थस्तावदिहोक्त एवेति। सत्यम्। किन्तु त्रिविधो ह्यत्र मन्त्राणामर्थः स्वतन्त्रः कर्मभाङ्नित्यश्च। तत्र यः शब्दतः स्वरसतयाऽवगम्यते स स्वतन्त्रः। यथा हृल्लेखायां हरतीति। महागणपतौ सर्वजनं

मा वक्ष्यमाणयेति। क्रियमाणकर्मान्वयी कर्मभाक्। यथा हृल्लेखायामाकर्षणादा-वाहरतीति। महागणपतौ नित्यसेवायां सर्वजनशब्देनेन्द्रियाद्यभिधानमिति। वर्णाव्यभिचारी नित्यो यथा हृल्लेखायां प्राणात्मकं हकारमित्यादि। महागणपतौ च तद्वर्णानां पदाद्यनपेक्षयापि तद्देवतात्मनिवृत्तिरिति।

तत्र हृदयादिशब्दानां स्वतन्त्रोऽर्थोऽयमुक्तः—हृदयं बुद्धिगम्यत्वादिति। हृद-याद्यङ्गतया प्रसिद्धानामर्थानामनुपादानात् तदुपादानेऽपि नित्यादीनामङ्गन्यासेऽनु-पयोगित्वात्। अयं तु कर्मभागर्थोऽभिप्रेयते। हृदयादिशब्दैरिति। हृदयाय नमः शिरसे स्वाहेत्येवमादीनां वाक्यात्मकानां ग्रहणम्। सर्वज्ञादिपदानां यदुभयथोक्तं तदन्वयार्थश्चापिशब्दः। अत एवेह सर्वज्ञत्वादिशक्त्यैक्यमित्युक्तम्। साधकगतत्वेन परिच्छिन्नानां देवतागतत्वेनापरिच्छिन्नानां च सर्वज्ञत्वादिशक्तीनामैक्यं परिच्छेद-क्षपणेन तदात्मत्वमुच्यत इति। तत्र हृदयादिशब्दैरपरिच्छिन्नशक्तिग्रहणम्। नमः स्वाहादिपदैः स्वात्मनस्तासु तादात्म्येन समर्पणम्। तच्चार्थत्वात् स्वगतपरिच्छिन्न-शक्तिसमर्पणं भवतीति। ननु हृदयादिशब्दैरपि कथं सर्वज्ञत्वादिशक्तिग्रहणम्। उच्यते। सर्वदेवतात्मनि याः सर्वज्ञत्वादिशक्तयस्ता एव तस्य हृदयाद्यङ्गतयाव-स्थिताः। तथा चाङ्गेषु हृदयाद्यर्थानां तेषु सर्वज्ञत्वादिशक्तीनां तासु च ज्ञानानन्दा-दीनामपि सद्भावः। तथा हृदयादिपदैर्यावदपेक्षं विवक्षेति सर्वज्ञाय हृदयाय नम इति सर्वज्ञपदेन देवतायाः सर्वज्ञत्वशक्त्यात्मलक्षणमंशमुक्त्वा हृदयपदेन तमेव हृदयावस्थस्यात्मनोऽन्तर्गतत्वमुक्त्वा नमःशब्देन तत्र स्वं तथाविधमंशं तदात्मतया समर्पयतीत्येवं सर्वाङ्गेषु ज्ञेयम्। ननु यद्येवं नमःस्वाहादिशब्दभेदेन किं प्रयोजन-मिति। तथा तथा संस्कारार्थमिति ब्रूमः। यदुक्तं—विशेषसंहारक्रमचिन्तायाः कर्तव्यत्वादिति। सामान्येनैतदुक्तम्। तेन निष्कलनिष्ठस्य परिच्छिन्नापरिच्छिन्न-ज्ञानानन्दाद्यैक्यमित्यपि लभ्यते। अत्र हृदयादीनां ज्ञानादिलक्षणायामुपयोग इति सकलनिष्ठस्य त्वङ्गैक्यमेवोच्यत इति। पूर्वोक्तान्तु सकलनिष्कलनिष्ठविषयम्। वक्ष्यति च मातृकापटलादिषु—भारतीमिति नादाद्यात्मकं सूक्ष्मरूपं कथितमि-त्यादि। यद्वा कृत्स्नदेवतात्मनिष्ठविषयम्। यदुक्तं—स्थूलसूक्ष्मकारणसामान्यसाक्षि-लक्षणः पञ्चविध इति। अथवा स्थूलादिसाक्षिपर्यन्ततया प्रतिपत्तृविषयम्। यद्वक्ष्यति—सगुणद्वारा निर्गुणपर्यन्तं गच्छतामिति। सकलनिष्ठस्य त्विति केवल-सकलनिष्ठो विवक्षितः। अङ्गैक्यमिति। सर्वज्ञत्वादिशक्त्यवस्थारूपाणां हृदयाद्य-ङ्गानामैक्यं स्वकीयहृदयादीनां देवताहृदयाद्यात्मतेत्यर्थः।

मूले पञ्चैव यस्येति। पञ्चाङ्गविषये नेत्रलोपविधानम्। तस्य नेत्रलोप

इत्यध्याहारेण योजनीयम्। मन्त्रिण इत्येतदभिप्रायमाह—मन्त्रिण इतीति। न मन्त्रित्वहानिरिति। नेत्रशक्तिकार्यस्याह्लादेः शिखास्त्रशक्तिभ्यामपि लब्धेरलुप्तशक्तेस्थानन्तशक्तावन्तर्भावसंभवादिति भावः॥ १३॥ १४॥

मूलेऽङ्गुलिषु क्रमादित्यादिना संक्षिप्तं सकलीकरणमुक्तम्। करयोरङ्गुष्ठादिष्वङ्गुलिष्वित्यन्वयः। करयोरित्युभयोः युगपन्न्यास उक्तः। तद्वाह्यतलयोरिति। तच्छब्देन करयोर्ग्रहणम्। अस्त्रन्यासोऽयमुक्तः। पञ्चाङ्गविषये तु नायं न्यास इत्यवबोद्धव्यम्। सुधीरित्येतद्विवृणोति—कस्यचिदिति। कस्यचिन्मन्त्रस्येत्यर्थः। एतच्च कनिष्ठादिक्रमत्वमित्यादिषु प्रत्येकं संबध्यते। यथा + + ॥ १४॥ १५॥

मूले तेनैव दश दिशः क्रमाद्बन्धयेदित्यन्वयः। क्रमशब्दाभिप्रायमाह—दिशो दशेति। चकारेण कस्यचिदित्येतदाकृष्यते। तत्तदुचितक्रमेण बध्नीयात्। सर्वमन्त्राणां पूर्वाग्नेयादिक्रमेण बन्धनम्। कस्यचित् तु दिगूर्ध्वविदिगधोभागक्रमेणेति मूलाशयोऽत्र दर्शितः। पञ्चकमेवेति। पञ्चाङ्गयोगिष्वेतदिति। सामान्येयं प्रकल्पनेति। कर्माङ्गतयाचमनं विष्टरोपवेशः प्राणायामलिपिन्यासावृष्यादिन्यासोऽङ्गुलिष्वङ्गुलिन्यासस्तालत्रयदिग्बन्धनं हृदयादिष्वङ्गन्यास इत्येतत्सर्वं सर्वमन्त्राणां समानम्। क्वचित्तत्सर्वमेकैकस्य सामान्यम्। विशेषास्तु वर्णन्यासादयस्तत्र तत्रावगन्तव्या इत्यभिप्रायः। क्रमोऽन्य इत्यनेन विष्टरोपवेशनानन्तरमेव तालत्रयादिकरणमित्यसौ वा क्रमोऽभिप्रेतः। तदुक्तम्—विष्टरोपविष्ट इत्यनेनैवेत्यादि॥ १६॥

किञ्चिज्जपित्वेति + + मूले शङ्खमित्यस्यायमर्थः। शङ्खं सपादमस्त्रेण प्रक्षाल्यात्मनो वामभागे मण्डले निधाय तस्मिन् मूलेन पुष्पगन्धाक्षतं निक्षिप्य जलेनापूर्य मूलेनावाहनाङ्गन्यासादि विधाय पूजयेदिति। गुरूपदशेनेति। साङ्गमन्त्रन्यासे विशेषो वोक्तः। तदुक्तं—मूलेन संपूर्य हृदयेण चन्दनं शिरसा पुष्पाक्षतक्षेपः शिखयाङ्गुष्ठेन विलोलनं कवचेनावकुण्ठनं नेत्रेणावलोकनमस्त्रेण दिग्बन्धनं पुनर्जलं संशोध्यादित्यात्तेजोऽमृतमावाह्याङ्गानि च कृत्वा मूलं जप्त्वेति। गुरूपदशेनेत्यत्राभिप्रायभेदमाह--वामस्यामाग्रत इत्यादिना। अर्घ्यमण्डलमर्घ्यपात्रस्य शङ्खस्योचितं मण्डलम्। तच्च वृत्तम्। तत्र शङ्खपादवलये। गन्धाक्षतादिकमिति पुष्पग्रहणम्। गालिनीं प्रदर्श्येति। मुद्रालक्षणं तूक्तम्---

अन्योन्यमाबध्य कनिष्ठिकाद्वयं ज्येष्ठाद्वयं चाप्यथ शेषिताङ्गुलीः।
अधोमुखीकृत्य निकुञ्चिताग्रिकाः परिभ्रमय्य प्रकरोतु गालिनीम्॥
हस्तौ परावृत्त्य कनिष्ठिकाद्वयं तर्जन्द्वयं च प्रकरोतु गारुडीम्।
बध्नातु मुद्रामवलम्बिताग्रजां चलत्तदन्याङ्गुलिकॢप्तपत्रिकाम्॥

कनिष्ठिकानामिकयोः करद्वये प्रदेशिनीमध्यमयोर्युगं मिथः।

व्यत्यस्तवज्राग्रमधोमुखोक्तं प्रकल्प्य मुद्रां प्रकरोतु सौरभीम् ॥ इति।

तीर्थमावाह्येति अर्कबिम्बाद्धादशान्तादेत्यवबोद्धव्यम्। लोलिन्येति। गालिन्येव परिभ्रममात्ररूपा लोलिनी भवति। नेत्रेणावलोक्येति। पञ्चाङ्गसंभवे तु जलादिभिः संपूज्येति मूलेन पूजोक्ता। भगवन्तमिति। लब्धत्वेऽप्यादरार्थमुक्तम्। करकोदक इति। सामान्यार्घ्यपात्रं करकी गृह्यते। ततः किञ्चिदादायेति। करकादेव शङ्खे जलं किञ्चिन्निषिच्येत्यर्थः। त्रिधा प्रोक्षयित्वेति। पूर्वं फडन्तकारेण पूजोपकरणानां गन्धपुष्पादीनां प्रोक्षणमिष्यते। सर्वं सच्चिदानन्दरूपमिति। प्रणवाम्यमृतबीजैरभिमर्शनमुक्तम्। यद्वा गन्धपुष्पादिकं सद्रूपेण दीपादिकं चिद्रूपेण निवेद्यादिकमानन्दादिरूपेण भावनीयमित्युक्तम् ॥ १७ ॥ १८ ॥

लौकिकमात्मालङ्करणम्। यद्वा यथावत् प्रयजेदिति सूचितम्। तदाह—निजसव्यत इति। न्यासस्थानेष्विति। यथावदित्यात्मपूजापूर्वकमित्यनेनोक्तम्। लिपितत्त्ववर्णाङ्गादिन्यासस्थानेषु तत्तन्मन्त्रैरिति भावः। पीठन्यासस्थानेष्वपि पूर्वं पूजा क्रियते चेत्तदनन्तरं मूर्तिमिष्ट्वावाहनाद्यपि कृत्वा मन्त्रन्यासस्थानेषु पूजा कार्येत्यवबोद्धव्यम्। आत्मानमलङ्कृत्येति। मूलेन चन्दनेन ललाटादिष्वनुलेपनादिकमुक्तम्। सासनमूर्तिपूजापूर्वकमिति। पूर्वं गुरुगणेशस्थाने ॐ गुर्वासनाय नमः ॐ गणपत्यासनाय नमः इत्यासनपूजां कृत्वा तद्वन्मूर्तिपूजामपि कृत्वा तत्तन्मन्त्रेण तांस्तत्र सङ्कल्प्य पूजयेदिति भावः। यथावदित्यनेनैवैतदपि सूचितम्। देवमयानिति। 'यात्याभ्यां यत्स्वरूपं स गुरुः स्यादित्येतदेवाभिप्रेतम्। अभिप्रायान्तरमाह—गुरुध्यानमुक्तमिति। स्वान् महागुरूनिति। महद्ग्रहणं तथानुसन्धानार्थम्। अभिप्रायान्तरमाह—गुं परमगुरुभ्यो नम इत्यादिना। गुरुसमष्ट्यादयोऽप्यत्र यथाक्रमं पूजनीया एव। स्वशब्देनास्मद्गुरुपूजनमिति ज्ञेयम्। अयमिह प्रयोगः। गुरूणां चत्वारि स्थानानि विभाव्य पूर्वोक्तसमष्टिमन्त्रेण सामान्येन पूजयित्वैभिश्चतुर्भिश्चतुर्षु स्थानेषु पूजयित्वा परषट्कादिभिरपि तत्तत्स्थानेषु यथास्वं पूजयेदिति। मूलेऽन्यतश्चेति निजदक्षिणत इत्युक्तम् ॥ १९ ॥

रक्तं धर्मं वृषतनुमिति। धर्मादिभिरेव पीठपूजोक्ता। अत्रापि वा यथावदित्यनुषङ्गः। यथावद्यजत्विति सम्बध्यते। तदभिप्रायमाह तत्रेत्यादिना। मूलेऽग्नौ धर्ममित्यन्वयः। वृषतनुर्ऋषभाकृतिः रक्षोदिशि ज्ञानमित्यन्वयः। हरिमिति सिंहाभिप्रायम्। मरुति भूताकारं वैराग्यमित्यन्वयः। अत्राधारशक्त्यै नमः धर्माय नमः इत्यादयो मन्त्रा ऊह्याः। गात्रग्रहणाद्धर्मादीनां पीठपादत्वं लभ्यते। गात्राणीषीकाः ॥ २०

तारवर्णैर्विभिन्नैरिति। ॐ सूर्यमण्डलाय नमः इत्यादिमन्त्रा उक्ताः। सत्त्वाद्यैश्चेति चकारेण तारवर्णैर्विभिन्नैरित्येतदनुकृष्यते। आत्मयुक्तानित्यत्रापि समानमेतत्। आत्मशब्देनात्मान्तरात्मपरमात्मान उक्ताः। शक्तीरिति नवशक्तिष्वष्टौ केसरेषु। नवमी मध्ये कर्णिकायामित्यर्थः। शक्तयस्तत्तत्प्रकरणे वक्ष्यन्ते। यथा लिपिपटले—मेधा प्रज्ञा प्रभा विद्येत्यादि। सूर्यमण्डलादिवर्णाः सिद्धा एव। श्वेता कृष्णेति सर्वपीठं सामान्येन नवशक्तिवर्णाभिधानम्॥ २१॥ २२॥

विन्यस्य कर्णिकोपरीति सनियमं कलशनिधानमुक्तम्। तत्र प्रयोगक्रमं दर्शयति—शालिविन्यसनादिकमिति। मूले तदुपरीति वस्त्रान्तरितत्वं सर्वत्र द्रष्टव्यम्। त्रिगुणेन चेति सत्त्वादिग्रहणम्। तेन तन्मन्त्रैस्तन्तुवेष्टनं लभ्यते। यथावदिति तिलयवमाषमात्रान्तरेणेत्यर्थः। यद्वास्त्रचालनमूलगन्धालेपनादि सूचितम्। लघुनेति गुग्गुलुग्रहणम्। अलघ्विति पदं + तारजापीति तेन पूजापि कार्या। शोषणाद्यनन्तरं चैतद्भवति॥ २३॥ २४॥

न्यस्येति कुम्भस्योत्तानीकरणमर्थसिद्धम्। अक्षताद्यायुतमिति गन्धपुष्पाक्षतशुद्धधान्ययुतमित्यर्थः। सनवरत्नकमिति। नव रत्नानि प्राणाग्निहोत्रन्यासे वक्ष्यन्ते—चाद्यास्ते सप्त वर्गा इत्यादि। सहकषादिकान्तगैरिति। कषेति चकारो विवक्षितः। अ इत्ययमन्ते गता येषां त आन्तगाः। कषादिकाश्च त आन्तगाश्चेति समासः। लिपिवर्णानां प्रतिलोमपठितानां ग्रहणमेतत्। तैः सह जलैः पूरयेदिति तेषां सकृदुच्चारणमुक्तम्। अभिप्रायान्तरमाह—त्रिश इति। कषादिकान्तगेन मातृकामन्त्रेण सह पूजयेत्। बहुवचनं तु तस्य त्रिरुच्चारणार्थमित्यभिप्रायः। अष्टरौषधिविपाचितैरिति। तदुक्तं व्याप्तिपटले—चन्दनकुचन्दनेत्यादि॥ २५॥

दशमूलपुष्पदुग्धाङ्घ्रिपचर्मोत्क्वथितैरिति। दशमूलानि + + दुग्धाङ्घ्रिपचर्माणि क्षीरवृक्षाः अश्वत्थवटोदुम्बरप्लक्षाः तेषां त्वचः उत्क्वथनमग्नौ पचनम्। त्रयाणां मूलपुष्पत्वग्वर्णानां पृथक् सह वा कषायजलमभिप्रेतम्। तेषां च यावत्तुरीयांशं क्वथनं भवति। स्तनजद्रुमचर्मसाधितैर्वेति। क्षीरवृक्षत्वग्भीरुषितं जलमभिप्रेतमिति ज्ञेयम्। संयतधीरित्येतदाशयं दर्शयति—विनापीति।

मूले कषायोदकपूरित इत्युपलक्षणम्। येन कलशपूरणं कृतं तदवशेषेण पूरित इति। विलोड्य सम्यगिति यथावद्विलोडनमुक्तम्। विधिना विलोड्येति शङ्खपूरणोक्तप्रकाराभिप्रायम्। तदाह—समूलेन हृदयेनेत्यादिना। शङ्खपादन्यासादिसूर्यमण्डलमर्शनान्तं गालिनीप्रदर्शनादिसोममण्डलाभिमर्शनान्तं च न कार्यम्। अन्यत् सर्वमानन्दरूपान्तं कार्यमित्यभिप्रायः। क्वाथोदकापूर्णमुख इति। कषाया-

युक्तजलानामन्यतमेनापूर्णमुखे ईषत्पूर्णमुख इत्यर्थः ॥ २६ ॥ २७ ॥

त्रिविधमिति। वक्ष्यमाणमन्त्रदेवतानां शक्त्यादित्रयेऽन्तर्भावादिति भावः। मन्त्रिणा गन्धाष्टकेन कृते कलशेऽनन्ता तस्य शक्तिः स्यादिति। गन्धाष्टकेन करणं सम्पादनं तज्जलविनिक्षेपेण तन्मयीकरणम्। कपि कण्ठीकर्चूरम्। सान्निध्यकरमिति प्रतिमाद्यभिप्रायम्। लोकरञ्जनकृदिति साधकस्यानुलेपनाद्यभिप्रायम्। क्षौबेरं बाला असृक् कुङ्कुमम्। अपरं वैष्णवम्। दलं + रुधिरं कुङ्कुमं कुशीतं रक्तचन्दनं रोगं जलम्। अपरं शैवम्। सान्निध्यकरं चेत्येतदिहापि समानमवबोद्धव्यम् ॥२८—३०॥

प्रागुदीरिता इति व्याप्तिपटल इति भावः। गुरूपदेशक्रमत इति न प्रागुदीरित इह क्रम इति भावः। तद्दर्शयति—आग्नेयसौरसौम्यक्रमेणेति। विद्वानित्यावाहनप्रतिपत्त्यभिज्ञत्वमुक्तम्। अभिप्रायान्तरमाह—मण्डलमन्त्राणामिति। मूले विनियोजयेदिति। कषायोदकपूरित इत्युक्ते शङ्खोदक इति शेषः ॥ ३१ ॥

याः पञ्चाशत्कला इति ता अपि शङ्खोदके विद्वान् विनियोजयेदित्यभिप्रेयते। ताश्चापि प्रागुदीरिता एव। तारपञ्चभेदसमुत्थिता इति। तदुक्तं—वर्णेभ्य एव तारस्येति। अनेन तारांशैः शङ्खोदके कलात्रयतया पूजनमपि सूचितम्। अभिप्रायान्तरमाह—अकारादिकलान्यासानन्तरमिति। तत्त्ववेदिन इत्यनेन 'भूतेन्द्रियार्थैरुद्दिष्टस्तत्त्वपञ्चविंशतिक इत्येतत्पञ्चपञ्चकं लभ्यते। यथा ब्रह्मकलासु पृथिवीवाग्घ्राणवचनगन्धयोग इत्यादि। केचिद्वचनादि हित्वा मनोबुद्ध्यहंकारचित्तचेतनां योजयन्ति। मतान्तरमाह—लं पृथिव्यात्मन इत्यादिना ॥ ३२ ॥

मूले सप्तात्मकस्येत्यस्यायमर्थः। सप्तात्मकस्तावत्प्रणवस्तस्य यौ पञ्चभेदत उत्तरौ भेदौ शक्तिशान्ताख्यौ तौ यतः परावत्यन्तसूक्ष्मौ तत इतरैः स्थूलसूक्ष्मांशैः सह न सर्वत्र पठ्येते। इह तु तावपि विनियोजनीयाविति।

अभिप्रायान्तरमाह—शक्तिशान्तकलावाहनमिति। यतः परौ ततः शक्तिशान्ताख्याविति यतोऽत्यन्तसूक्ष्मौ ततः शक्तिशान्ताख्यावेव। शक्तय इच्छाज्ञानक्रियाः शान्तौ चिदानन्दौ त एवानयोराख्याः। न लकारादीनामिव सृष्टि कृद्विरित्याद्या आख्या इति। तदेतद्दर्शयति—एवमिति। विनापि मन्त्रैरिति स्थूलैर्मन्त्रैरित्यर्थः। न पठ्येते परैः सहेत्यत्राप्यभिप्रायान्तरमाह—तत्रेति। प्रागुक्तकलानामपराणि पञ्चकान्यपि सन्ति शक्तिशान्तयोस्त्वपराणि न सन्तीति मूलाशयः ॥ ३३ ॥

मूले प्रथमप्रकृतेरिति। शक्तिशान्तयोः पञ्च मन्त्रा उक्ताः। प्रथमप्रकृतिरिति शक्तिग्रहणम्। प्रथम इति वा पदम्। हंस इति हंसः शुचिषदित्येष उक्तः। चतुर्थस्तत्पदादिक इति शान्तस्य मन्त्रद्वयमुक्तम्। तत्पदादिकस्तत्सवितुरित्येषः।

इच्छादिकलाभ्युपगमे त्वकारादिपञ्चानामिवैते मन्त्राः स्युः। तत्र प्रथमप्रकृतिरकारः तारस्य प्रथमोंऽश इत्यवबोद्धव्यम्।

चतुर्णवतीत्युपसंहारः। इहाष्टत्रिंशत्पञ्चाशच्च कला उक्ताः पञ्च च मन्त्राः। तथा च त्रिणवतिरेव मन्त्राः सन्ति। अत्रापरापि कलार्थाद् ग्राह्या सा मातृकैव। यद्वा बिन्दुकलानामन्त्या चकारकलानन्ता। अथवा सोमकलास्वमाकलान्त्येति।

अभिप्रायान्तरमाह—त्रिणवतिकलावाहनानन्तरमिति। अयमिह मूलार्थः। चतुर्णवतिशब्देन चतुर्णवतितमस्य ग्रहणम्। त्रिनवतिमन्त्रावाहनानन्तरं चतुर्णवतितमः। तेषामात्मा सती स्वयं देवतापि शङ्खे आवाह्य कलशे पूर्यतामिति। देवताग्रहणं च मूलाभिप्रायम्॥ ३४॥ ३५॥

मूले अत्र या इति हंसः शुचिषदित्याद्यृचां विनियोगक्रमिरुक्ता तास्तारस्य पञ्चभिः कलाप्रभेदैः पृथग्युज्यन्त इति सम्बन्धनीयम्। एकैककलावाहनानन्तरमिति। पृथगित्यस्यार्थोऽयमुक्तः। अकारकलादिष्वित्यकारकलासु ब्रह्ममन्त्रे तदीयपञ्चकमन्त्रे चेत्यर्थः। यद्वैकैककलाशब्देनैकैककलावर्गो गृह्यते। अत्र पृथगिति पञ्चानां पृथगेव योगो न संभूयैकैकत्रेत्यर्थः। अकारकलादिष्विति विकल्पाभिप्रायम्। अकारकलासु ब्रह्ममन्त्रे तदीयपञ्चकमन्त्रे वा योग इति॥ ३६॥

मूले कुर्यादिति। तत्र तत्र प्राणप्रतिष्ठामन्त्रेण प्राणप्रतिष्ठां च कुर्यादित्यन्वयः। समाहित इति + + ॥ ३७॥

प्रोक्तापूर्वमिति प्राणप्रतिष्ठामन्त्रोद्धारः। अत्रामुष्येति यस्य प्राणाः प्रतिष्ठाप्यास्तस्य तथा निर्देशार्थमुक्तम्। यथाऽकारकलानामित्यादि। एतच्च सकलीकरणेऽप्युक्तं भविष्यति। यथा तत्रैव व्यापककलानामग्नेश्च प्राणप्रतिष्ठां कुर्यादित्यादि। प्राणका इति प्राणा इत्युक्तम्। यथा अकारकलानामित्यादि। अमुष्यशब्दं प्रोच्येत्यर्थः। स्थितेति स्थित इत्युक्तम्। तथेत्यमुष्यशब्दं प्रोच्येत्यर्थः। तद्वदित्यपि तथा। एवं चतुर्भागोऽयं मन्त्र उक्तः। अत्रार्थभेदं दर्शयति- प्रोक्तेत्यादिना। आपूर्वमित्याकारः पाशमन्त्रः तत्पूर्वकं भावमुक्त्वेत्यर्थः। तत्तत्पदद्योतनार्थ इति साध्यनामाभिप्रायम्। तथा सर्वेन्द्रियाणीत्यपि तथेति वाक्यम्। तथेत्यापूर्वं तत्तत्पदं चोक्त्वेत्यर्थः। वाङ्मनसग्रहणमिति। यथा वाङ्मनश्चक्षुःश्रोत्रघ्राणप्राणा इति॥ ३८

सुत्रामवस्त्रव्रीतण्डुलानीति चक्रिकागतानां ग्रहणम्॥ ३९॥

मूले पुनस्तोयगतं देवमिति। चतुर्नवतिमन्त्रात्मा देवतावाह्य पूर्यताम् इत्युक्तस्य तथावाहितस्य ग्रहणम्। साध्यमन्त्रानुरूपत इति तोयगतमित्यधःसंबन्धः। यो मन्त्रस्तदा साधयितुमिष्यते तदानुरूप्येण कलश आवाहितमिति मन्त्रवाच्य-

त्वाद्देवस्येत्थं निर्देशोपपत्तिः। सकलीकृत्येति सर्वमपि न्यासजातमुक्तम्। तत्र कलान्यासः सकलीकरणभाविरीत्या कर्तव्य इति ज्ञेयम्। अभिप्रायभेदमाह—सकलीकृत्येतीत्यादिना। आवाहनादिन्यासान्तमिति हृल्लेखापटलभाविप्रक्रिययेति भावः। कलान्यासस्त्विह कलावाहनानन्तरमिष्यते। तत्पूजानन्तरमेतदावाहनं भवति। इह मूर्तिकल्पना तु कलावाहनतोऽपि पूर्वं स्यात्। यदुक्तं—तत्तन्मूर्तिमन्त्रेण मूर्तिं सङ्कल्प्यावाहनेत्यादि। उपचारानित्यर्घ्यादिग्रहणम्। शङ्खपूरणवदिति। तदुक्तं—समूलेन हृदयेनापूर्येत्यादि। अर्घ्यादिपुरणक्रम इत्यनुष्ठानक्रम उक्तः। द्रव्यदेवतासम्बन्धश्चैकात्म्यलक्षण इति। द्रव्याणामर्घ्यादीनां देवतया तैरुपचर्यमाणाया यः संबन्धः स तया तेषामेकात्मभावात्मक इत्यर्थः। + + + ॥ ४० ॥

मूल आसनस्वागत इत्युपचाराभिधानम्। पूजितं पीठमासनतया प्रयोजयेत्। आचम आचमनीयमेव। वसनं + सुमनः पुष्पम्। वन्दनं नमस्कारः। यत्तु सपर्यासप्तकमुक्तम् तज्जलाद्यमुपहारविधानमिति तद्विकल्पाभिप्रायम्। तदा च स्वागतस्य न षोडशसु ग्रहणमिति ज्ञेयम्। तासामेकांशमाश्रयेदिति। देशकालाद्यनुसारेण पूज्यभेदानुसारेण चेति भावः। श्यामाकं [श्यामा]। अब्जं पद्मम्। पङ्कशब्देन पिष्टमार्द्रभूतमुक्तम्। तुलस्याविति + + एतानि दश पुष्पाणीति + + तथेति रक्तनीलोत्पलाभ्यां सह द्वादशसंख्यार्थमुक्तम्। पार्थं +। स्वागमोक्तानि यानि चेति।

तथा चोक्तम्—श्वेतार्कं करवीरकं च कमलं धुत्तूरकारग्वधे
राजार्कं च सिताम्बुजं च तुलसीसाशोकसच्चम्पकैः।
कह्लारं बकपाटले वकुलकं द्वे मल्लिके मालती
पालाशस्थलपद्मदर्भदमनापामार्गदूर्वाङ्कुरैः॥
तद्वद्ग्रन्थिशमीद्रुहन्मरुवकैः पुन्नागनागासनै-
र्नन्द्यावर्ततमालकुब्जविजयामन्दारकाश्मीरकैः।
शस्तान्युत्पलकर्णिकारकुसुमैः कादम्बबिल्वान्यथो
नीलं चोत्पलमित्यमूनि कुसुमान्युक्तानि शैवान्यलम्॥
अम्भोजोत्पलबन्धुजीवविजयापुन्नागनागान्यथो
जातीकुन्दकुरण्टचम्पकजपायूथीरमापाटलैः।
बिल्वाशोकहयारिकुब्जदमनैर्मन्दारदूर्वादलै-
र्नन्द्याह्वाप्यपराजितेति कुसुमान्युक्तानि शाक्तान्यलम्॥
शस्ते द्वे तुलसी सिताम्बुजमथो रक्ताब्जपालाशके
जातीकुब्जकमाधवीदमनकैः पन्नागनागासनैः।

नन्द्यावर्तशमीस्थलाब्जविजयासन्मल्लिकाचम्पकै-
र्बिल्वं चोत्पलकेतकानि च नवं कुन्दं तथा पाटलम् ॥
लक्ष्मीदेविसहासभृङ्गमुसलीभीतेन्द्रवल्ल्यः सदा-
भद्रा श्रीपतिलङ्घिता च दशमी दूर्वाथ जम्बुच्छदम् ।
कह्लारं करवीरमेकदलकं पद्मं कुशं कैरवं
रक्तं चेति विलोमतोऽधिकफलं पुष्पं भवेद्वैष्णवम् ॥
सूर्याग्न्योस्त्रिविधानि चापि कुसुमानीष्टानि विघ्नेशितुः
शाक्तान्यप्यथ शाम्भवानि च तथा स्कन्दार्यचण्डादिषु ।
शाक्तान्येव मनोजवाग्गिरिसुतादुर्गाष्टमातृप्रिया-
ण्यम्भोजासनदेवराजकमलाः पूज्यास्तथा वैष्णवैः ॥ इति ।

तत्तन्मन्त्रैरेव सर्वत्र पूजा भवति ॥ ४१—५२ ॥

मन्त्रो नोक्तैरित्यत्राभिप्रायमाह—धूप इति । अत्र ॐ नमः परायेत्यत्र मूलं वा प्रयोक्तव्यम् । गन्धादिदान इत्यन्तं वाक्यम् । आसनाद्युपचारेषु तु सर्वत्र मूलमेव भवति । अभिप्रायान्तरमाह—अथवेत्यादिना । शक्तिषु तु स्वात्मसंस्थामजां शुद्धामित्याद्यूह्यम् । अयमत्र स्नानक्रम इति । यदा मण्डले सा सा प्रतिमा कल्प्यते तदैवं प्रयोगोऽर्थाल्लभ्यते । यानेनेति । यानमप्यश्वादिकं प्रतिमार्हं तैजसं गृह्यते । सोपचारमिति । स्नानोपचारैर्वक्ष्यमाणैः सहेत्यर्थः । पीठं समर्प्येति । पूजितं स्नानपीठमित्यर्थः । अर्घ्यादिकमित्यर्घ्यादित्रयग्रहणम् । प्रागुपचाराणां यत्षोडशानां विधानं तत्प्रधानतयैवेत्यवबोद्धव्यम् । तेन तेषामन्याङ्गतया प्रयोगोऽन्येषामपि केशप्रसाधनादीनामवान्तराणां प्रयोगोऽपि स्यादेव । केशप्रसाधनादीनि लौकिकान्येव । तानि पञ्च दत्त्वा कषायोदकेन स्नापयेत् । तच्च कलशपूरणोक्तमेव । पञ्चगव्यपञ्चामृताभ्यां स्नानमित्युभयोः कलशतया पूजापि सूचिता + + गन्धशब्देन चन्दनग्रहणम् । यद्वा "चन्दनागुरुकर्पूरपङ्कं गन्धमिहोच्यते" इत्येतदभिप्रेतम् । अष्टगन्धशब्देन प्रागुक्तं स्वं स्वमष्टगन्धं गृह्यते । दिव्यगन्धशब्देन + + पुष्पादिशब्दैः पञ्चभिरुदकशब्दः सम्बन्धनीयः । पुष्पाणि पद्मानीति । फलानि कादलादीनि । मन्त्रोदकमब्लिङ्गशुद्धवाक्याद्यभिमन्त्रितमुदकम् । अर्घ्यादिपूर्वकमिति । यथा केशप्रसाधनादिपञ्चकं दत्त्वार्घ्यादित्रयं दत्त्वा कषायोदकेन स्नापयित्वार्घ्यादित्रयं दत्त्वा पञ्चगव्येन स्नापयेदित्यादि । गन्धानुलेपनगन्धोदकस्नानादिषु सकृदेवार्घ्यादित्रयं भवति । मन्त्रोदकस्नानानन्तरमप्यर्घ्यादि देयम् । कलशपूजायान्तु तत्रैव भावनया स्नानप्रयोगः । स्नानानन्तरं यानमारोप्य स्वस्थानप्रापणमर्थसिद्धं भवति ।

इतिशब्दः स्नानप्रकरणसमाप्त्यर्थः। भूषणन्यासानन्तरमिति। यत्र तु भूषणानि न संभवन्ति तद्विषयमेतत्। यद्वा त्रिपुरोक्तक्रमेण भूषणन्यासमाचरेदित्येतद्विवक्षितम्। तेनैतदपि सूचितम्। यत्र भूषणानि समर्पयितुमुचितानि तत्रैव भूषणन्यासो न न्यासावसान इति। यद्वा अयमपर एव तत्तत्कल्पप्रसिद्धो भूषणन्यासः। तदुक्तम् + + +। मूले सुसितेनेति प्रसङ्गादिह निवेद्यमुक्तमित्यवबोद्धव्यम्। कृते निवेद्ये चेति वक्ष्यमाणत्वात्॥ ५४॥ ५५॥ ५६॥

वर्णैर्मनुप्रपुटितैरिति। दीपमुच्चैः प्रदापयेदिति यद्देवे दीपेन मूलमन्त्रेण वा पूजनमुक्तं तदनन्तरं मूलपुटितैर्मातृकाक्षरैर्गन्धादिभिर्न्यासक्रमात् पूजयेदित्यर्थः।

सकलासु मनुदेवतास्विति। विष्णुशिवशक्त्यादिषु सर्वासु समानमेतदिति भावः। मन्त्रीति वर्णानां बिन्द्वन्तत्वं मूलपुटने प्रणवादित्वं प्रणवनमोन्तत्वं चोक्तम्। प्रथमत इति परिवारपूजातोऽपि पूर्वमित्यर्थः। अनेन परिवाराणामपि गन्धादिभिः स्वस्वमन्त्रेण पूजा सूचितेति ज्ञेयम्। अयं प्रयोगस्त्रैलोक्यमोहनमिति प्रथित इत्युपस्कारेण सम्बन्धनीयम्। सौम्यपूजास्वेतदुचितं न क्रूरास्वित्यनेन सूचितम्। यद्वा काम्यपूजास्वावृत्तिरपि सूचिता। अत्र मातृकायां केवलवर्णैरेव पूजनमर्थाद्भवति। अत्राभिप्रायान्तरं दर्शयति—पुनः पुष्पाञ्जलिमित्यादिना। पुष्पाञ्जलिरयं मूलेनावृत्त्या स्यात्। यद्वान्यैरपि स्वागमाम्नातमन्त्रे स्ववाचकपारायणादिभेदैरप्यभिप्रेयते। प्रसरपुष्पाञ्जलिमिति। स्वावयवशक्तीनां स्वान्तर्मूर्तिशक्तीनां स्वावरणशक्तीनामपि क्रमेण स्वात्मतः प्रसरकृते तु पुष्पाञ्जलिमिति भावः।

एकाक्षरादिमन्त्रैरिति परादिमन्त्रोपलक्षणम्। यद्वा यद्यपि वर्णैर्मनुप्रपुटितैरित्युक्तम् तथाप्येकाक्षरादिमन्त्रैः पुष्पाञ्जलिरवश्यकार्यः। समष्टिमूर्तेर्निष्पन्नत्वाद्व्यष्टिमूर्तिनिष्पत्त्यर्थत्वाच्चास्य पुष्पाञ्जलेरिति। यद्वैकाक्षरेण परादिमन्त्राणामपि प्रणवप्रभृतीनां ग्रहणम्। परादिक्रम इति। पूर्वं परापुष्पाञ्जलिस्ततः पश्यन्तीपुष्पाञ्जलिरित्येवंविधः क्रम इत्यर्थः। परादिकलायोग इति। विश्वयोनिमहासत्त्यादयाः कलाः। अत्र प्रणवादीनां व्यापकबुद्ध्या हृदये पुष्पाञ्जलिः। महासत्तादीनां मूर्धादीन्येव स्थानानि। तदभिधानं तु प्राप्तस्थानानवसानार्थं तेन यत्प्रागुक्तं मूर्धस्तनद्वयमूलाधारेष्विति तस्यापि विकल्पेन परिग्रहो भवति। शक्तिषु वा स्तनद्वयनियम इति अं नम इति पूर्ववद्धृदये हं नम इत्यप्येवमेव। तथेति मूर्धादिष्वेवेत्यर्थः। शून्यादीनां पुरोक्तान्येव स्थानानि। तानि च मूलाधारलिङ्गमूलनाभिहृत्कण्ठलम्बिकाभ्रूमध्यललाटेषु न्यस्तव्यानीति। मूर्धादिष्विति मूर्धभ्रूमध्यहृन्नाभिग्रहणम्। पुनः समस्तव्यस्तेति। अत्र तत्सवितुरित्येषैव ब्रह्मगायत्र्युच्यते।

वक्ष्यतीति। नरसिंहपटलेऽनुष्टुप्पटले चेति भावः। तत्सामान्यमन्त्रैरित्यङ्गेभ्यो नमो लोकपालेभ्यो नम इत्यादिभिरित्यर्थः। प्रसरपुष्पाञ्जलिरिति। इह गन्धादिभिरभियजेदित्यभिधानात् पुनः पूजापि कार्येति ज्ञेयम्॥ ५७॥

मूले हृदयं सशिर इत्याद्यावरणप्रकरणम्। दिशास्वस्त्रं चेत्यस्त्रस्य चतुरावृत्तिर्भवति। मन्त्रीत्यङ्गमन्त्राणामन्ते नतियोगोऽप्युक्तः॥ ५८॥

हारो मौक्तिकम् कलायं + ललनाशब्दः स्त्रीवचनः। प्रधानतनवः प्रधानाभिमुखाः। यद्वा प्रधानदेवताकृतयः। तदाह—पक्षान्तरमिति। निशाचरो निर्ऋतिः। अहिपतिरनन्तः। जात्यधिपेति सुरतेजःप्रभृतयो जातयः। अयमिह प्रयोगः। इन्द्राय सुराधिपतये वज्रायुधायैरावतवाहनाय सपरिवाराय नम इत्यादि॥ ५९—६२॥

रथचरणं चक्रम्। अचिरप्रभा विद्युत्। करविन्दं [नीलवर्णम्]। आवरणपूजानन्तरमिति। परादिपूजामन्त्रमूर्तिपूजामपि कृत्वा पुनरावरणपूजेत्यपि सूचितम्। यद्वान्तर्मूर्तीनामपि स्यादावरणपूजा। प्रसरपुष्पाञ्जलिर्वैलोक्येनेति। यथा लोकपालेभ्योऽङ्गेभ्यो नमः। पुनर्व्यस्तसमस्तानुष्टुप्त्रयमित्यादि यावद्विश्वयोन्यै नमः। अहन्नम ॐ नमः। पुनर्मूलेन पुष्पाञ्जलिरिति। अर्घ्याद्यष्टकमित्यर्घ्यादित्रयं जलगन्धादिपञ्चकं चोक्तम्। निवेद्यपात्रमिति। देवताग्रतो निधानमर्थाल्लभ्यते। मूलमन्त्रतेजसीति। पात्रोदरे मूलाभिमर्शनमूलयन्त्रभावना वोक्ता। लिपियन्त्रकर्णिकायां वा मूलयन्त्रं भवति। अमृतीकरणमिति। पूर्वमस्त्रेण प्रोक्षणमपि कार्यम्। शङ्खपूरणवदमृतीकरणादि कार्यम्। कवचास्त्राभ्यामिति। कवचेनावकुण्ठनमस्त्रेण सतालत्रयदिग्बन्धनं चेति विभागः। परिषिकादिकमिति। परिषेकोपस्पर्शनाचमनग्रहणम्। सुरभिसंहारेति। तदुक्तम् + + ॥ ६३॥ ६४॥

मूले कृते निवेद्ये चेति परिषिकादिकं प्राणाहुतयश्चेत्येतावदेव प्रसिद्धेर्लभ्यत इति। अङ्कुरार्पणगतक्रमेणेति। यदुक्तं—वज्रादिशर्वान्तिममिति। यद्वा येन क्रमेण तत्र न्यस्तानि तेनैव क्रमेणेहानीय प्रागादिपरितः स्थापनीयानीति। विष्णवे नम इत्यादिमन्त्रैरिति। यदुक्तं—वैष्णव्यस्त्वथ पालिकाः वैरिञ्चो घटिकाः शैवाः शरावाह्वा इति॥ ६५॥

मूले उपलिप्य कुण्डमिति होमप्रकरणमारभ्यते। प्रधानकुण्ड उपलेपनमात्रमेव संस्कार उक्तः। अत्राभिप्रायं दर्शयति—उपलिप्येत्यादिना। चकारेणेत्युपलिप्य चेति मूले पदान्वयोऽप्युक्तः। खननोद्धाराविति। वज्राकारेण कोष्ठेन कुण्डतले खननं तदुद्भूतमृदस्योद्धरणमभिप्रेतम्। पूरणं हृदेति। शुद्धमृदा खातपूरणमुक्तम्। समीकरणमस्त्रेणेति। पूरितमृदो हस्ताग्रेण समीकरणमेतत्। अस्त्रेण कुट्टनमिति।

दृढीकरणम्। वर्मणेत्यादि चेत्यन्तं वाक्यम्। कलारूपतत्त्वकल्पनमिति। शान्त्यतीताद्याः पुरोक्ताः पञ्च कलास्तद्रूपाणां तत्त्वानां कल्पनं तत्त्वर्थात्तन्मन्त्रैर्भवति। अस्त्रेण वज्रीकरणमिति + + हृदयेन चतुष्पथीकरणमिति + + कवचेनाक्षपाटनमिति + + कुण्डसंस्कारा इति। विस्तारोऽयमिति भावः। मूले त्वतिसंक्षेप उक्तः। मध्यमक्लृप्तिमाह—अथवेति। मूलेन वीक्षणमस्त्रेण प्रोक्षणमस्त्रेण कुट्टनं वर्मणाभ्युक्षणमित्येषामिह ग्रहणम्। स्वचरणयोग्या इति। तदुक्तम्—उदगायतां पश्चादित्यादि। प्रकल्पयेद्योगविष्टरमिति दर्भनिर्मितविष्टरन्यासः। तत्र शाक्तपीठपूजाप्युक्ता। योगग्रहणान्मन्त्रिशब्दाच्चैतदवगमः। अभिप्रायान्तरमाह—योगविष्टरमित्यादिना। पीठसमष्टिर्वायं मन्त्रो विवक्षितः। तदा तु शाक्तपीठे तेन पूजनं स्यात्॥६६

मूलेऽथवेति। प्रकारान्तरेण रेखाविधानमुक्तम्। प्रकल्पयेद्योगविष्टरमित्यनुषङ्गः। यद्वा समुच्चयोऽत्राभिप्रेतः। षट्कोणावृतत्रिकोणके स्वचरणयोग्या रेखा विलिख्येति तदनुषङ्गेण संबन्धः। गुप्तोक्तविधिनेति। गुप्तं त्रैपुरम्। वक्ष्यति च—वक्षः पुरहितयेत्यादि। महागणपतिपटलोक्तविधिना चेति। वक्ष्यति च—त्रिषट्कोणोल्लसित इति। त्रिकोणत्रयमिति। + + + मन्त्रविशेषानुसारेणेति + + + प्राणाग्निहोत्रविधिनापीत्ययमपि विकल्प एव। वक्ष्यति च—शक्तेः सत्त्वनिबन्धनमित्यादि। अनलस्थाने योगविष्टरं कल्पयेदित्यनुषङ्गः। यद्वा स्वचरणयोग्या रेखा विलिख्येत्यनुषङ्गेण संबन्धः।

अत्राभिप्रायान्तरमाह—मूलाधारेऽपीत्यादिना। अत्र त्वपिशब्दः समुच्चयार्थः। मूलाधारे हि तत्रानलस्थानमुक्तम्। ततश्चायमर्थः। न केवलं कुण्ड एव योगविष्टरं कल्पयेत् अपि तु मूलाधारे प्राणाग्निहोत्रन्यायसिद्धे आवसथीयकुण्डेऽपीति॥ ६७॥

मूले तत्राथो सद्दतुमतीमिति। हृल्लेखया शक्तेरेवावाहनसकलीकरणादि पूर्वमुक्तम्। सद्दतुमतीमिति। विशिष्टफलयोग्यतुयुक्तामित्यर्थः। सौन्दर्यकान्त्याद्यतिशयेनातीन्द्रियाभा भवति। सकलजगन्मयीमिति। शक्तिपटलोक्तलक्षणामित्यर्थः। गुरुरेव वागीश्वर इहाभिप्रेतः। अत्राभिप्रायान्तरमाह—उभयत्रापीति। अत्र वागीश्वरोऽपि पृथक् तत्र विष्टरे मूलमन्त्रेणावाहनसकलीकरणपूर्वकं कल्प्यते। सद्दतुमतीं बाह्य इति। सच्छन्देनैव तदीयाकारवेषावुक्ताविति भावः। मूले तद्योनाविति। प्रणवेनैव देवभूतस्वेन्द्रियात्मकानुसन्धानमग्नेर्गम्यते। अत्राभिप्रायान्तरं गुरुजनोपदेशेनेत्येतदनुषङ्गसिद्धं दर्शयति—मण्यादिजमित्यादिना। पात्रेणानीयेति शरावेणानीय नाभौ दर्भसंस्तरे निधायैतत्सर्वं क्रियते। क्रव्यादांशं परित्यज्येत्यङ्गारकणं दर्भोद्योतं वा क्रव्यादांशबुद्ध्या नैर्ऋतभागे जह्यादित्युक्तम्। वीक्षणादिभिरिति।

वीक्षणप्रोक्षणताडनाभ्युक्षणग्रहणम्। शिवशक्त्यात्मककुण्डलिन्येति। यदुक्तम्— उभयत्रापि वागीश्वरी कल्पयेदिति। तत्र प्रथमं वागीश्वरान्तर्नीत्वा ततो वागीश्वर्यां निषिक्तं तत उत्पन्नं च विभावयेदित्यभिप्रायः। प्राणाग्निहोत्रविधिनेति। ॐ ह्रीं चं मूलमुक्त्वा परंज्योतिषि जुहोमि सोऽहं हंसः स्वाहेत्याद्युकारान्तं होम उक्तः। तमग्निमिति कुण्डलिन्यात्मकस्य ग्रहणम्। बैन्दवाग्निनेति त्रिकोणान्तर्गतावसथीयाग्निरुक्तः। यद्वक्ष्यति—मूलाधारत्रिकोणशक्तिबिन्दुमध्येत्यादि। तदग्निमध्ये कुण्डलिनीशक्तिरवस्थिता। सैव शिवः शक्तिश्च भवतीत्येषां भेदः। शिवग्रहणं तत्तच्छक्तिमदभिप्रायमेव। यदुक्तं—शक्तिमत्समुच्चयार्थं इति। वागीश्वरीवागीश्वरासनाय नम इति च। अमृतमास्राव्येति। तारशक्त्युच्चारणेन द्वादशान्तादेतदित्यवबोद्धव्यम्। पात्राग्नाविति। इदानीं पात्रगतोऽग्निः कुण्डकल्पितवागीश्वरान्तस्तदिन्द्रियरूपेण कल्पनीयः। गुरुरेव वागीश्वरश्चेत् तदन्तरिन्द्रियरूपेण कल्पयेदिति ज्ञेयम्। परिभ्राम्येति। तदिन्द्रियमथनबुद्धेरिति प्रतिपत्तव्यम्। शिवबीजबुद्धेरिति। शिवोऽसौ वागीश्वर एवेति। अत्र गुरूपदेशेनेत्यन्यो वाभिप्रायः। प्राणाग्निहोत्रविधिनेत्येतच्छिष्ये गुरौ च विवक्षितम्। ततश्च तमग्निं शिष्यस्य नासिकाद्वारेण तदीयमूलाधारं नीत्वा तत्रोक्तप्रकारेणामृतस्रावणान्तं विधाय तमग्निं शिष्यस्य क्रियाशक्त्यभिमान्यात्मरूपं श्वासमार्गेणानीय स्वान्तर्मूलाधारं नीत्वैतत्सर्वं कृत्वा वागीश्वरान्तर्नीत्वा तदिन्द्रियरूपेण विभाव्योक्तप्रकारेण देव्या योनौ क्षिपत्विति। यदुक्तं तत्साधकेन यत्नविशेषणयुक्तः सन्निति ॥ ६८ ॥ ६९ ॥ ७० ॥

ततः प्रविन्यसेदित्यादि ससर्वाङ्गेष्वित्यन्तं वाक्यम्। अत्र विभावसोर्जिह्वामन्त्रैर्देहे गुरोः स्वदेहे विन्यसेदित्येतदपि अभिप्रेतम्। तेनाधुना स्वात्मन्यग्नेः पीठन्यासमूर्तिकल्पनावाहनादिपूर्वकं जिह्वाङ्गमूर्तिन्यासं मानसपूजाञ्च कृत्वाग्न्यात्मा संस्त्स्मिन्नग्नावपि सर्वं कुर्यादिति सिद्धं भवति। तदुक्तं—पूर्वसाध्यमन्त्रन्यस्तदेहोऽग्निमन्त्रजिह्वादिन्यासं च कृत्वारभतेति। कल्याणरेतस इत्यग्नेः।

अनलेरार्घीत्यादिपदं जिह्वानां विशेषणम्। अनलो रेफः। ईरो यकारः। अर्घी अर्घीश ऊकारः। यथा स्र्यूं हिरण्यायै। ष्र्यूं गगनायै इत्यादि। दिव्यपूजास्विति। तत्तन्मन्त्रदेवतैकात्म्यसिद्ध्यर्थासु पूजास्वित्यर्थः। यदुक्तम्—अस्य शक्तित्वमिष्यत इत्यादि। सर्वव्यापिन्यादिशक्तिं समारभ्येत्यादि च। विपश्चितेति। तास्वप्यवान्तरभेदत्वमुक्तम् ॥ ७१ ॥ ७२ ॥ ७३ ॥ ७४ ॥ ७५ ॥ ७६ ॥ ७७ ॥

सुरा इति। जिह्वासु देवादीनां क्रमेण पूजनमप्युक्तम्। जिह्वास्विति काम्यक्रूरकर्मविषयमेतत्। दिव्यकर्मस्वीश्वरस्यैव पूजा। तदा चाग्नेरास्यगतायां कृष्णा-

ख्यायामेव जिह्वायां होमः। कुतः। वह्नेकोकरणादेर्वक्ष्यमाणत्वात्। काम्यादिष्वपी-श्वरविषय एवमेव स्यात्। देवादिविषये तु तां तु जिह्वां कृष्णायाः स्थाने कृष्णां चेतरस्याः स्थाने कल्पयेत्। तदुक्तं—यद्देवतात्वेन विवक्षिता या जिह्वा तद्देवतार्चने तां मध्ये संस्थाप्येति। मध्ये च कोणषट्के चेत्यत्रापि समानमेतत् सर्वमित्यवगन्तव्यम्। मता इति तत्तन्मन्त्रजपपूर्वकत्वं सूचितम्। इहैतदपि सिद्धं भवति। यत् कल्पान्तरसिद्धं तत्तदभिप्रेतफलकरं देवपितृगन्धर्वादिवाचकं मन्त्रान्तरं तदपीहोपलक्षणीयम्। किन्तु सामान्यपटलोक्ता न्यासा न कार्याः। तेषामीश्वरात्मकत्वादिति। ततश्च यन्त्रवर्णमन्त्रादीनां प्रयोग एव वक्ष्यते तदप्युपपन्नं भवति इति। प्राय इति विश्वमूर्त्यादीनामनिर्वाच्याभत्वमपि सूचितम् ॥७८॥७९॥८०॥

मन्त्री प्रविन्यसेदित्यङ्गन्यास उक्तः। मन्त्रीति वक्ष्यमाणाग्निमूलमन्त्राभिज्ञत्वमुक्तम्। यद्वा हृदयाय नम इत्यादीनां पटलारम्भ उक्तानां योग उक्तः। अभिप्रायान्तरमाह—सर्वज्ञादिप्रयोग इति। सहस्रार्चिषे सर्वज्ञाय हृदयाय नम इत्यादि। यद्वा मन्त्रीत्यग्निमूलमन्त्रस्य षण्णां खण्डानां योगोऽपि सूचितः। यथा ॐ वैश्वानरसहस्रार्चिषे सर्वज्ञाय हृदयाय नम इत्यादि। पीठमूर्तिपूजादिकं चाङ्गन्यासात् पूर्वमिति वाक्यम्। कर्तव्यमिति शेषः। आदिशब्देनाग्निमूलमन्त्रेणावाहनादिकमुक्तम्। सर्वं चैतदिह सकलीकरणविधिनैवार्थादवसेयमिति ज्ञेयम् ॥ ८० ॥ ८१ ॥

मूले विन्यसेदित्यष्टमूर्तीरिति भावः। यथावदिति चतुर्थीयोग उक्तः। अभिप्रायान्तरमाह—यथावदित्यादिना। अग्न्यादिपदाष्टकम् 'अग्निं प्रज्वलितमित्येतन्मन्त्रगतसुबन्तपदाष्टकम्। यथा ॐ क्रौं अग्नये जातवेदसेऽग्नये नमः। क्रौं अग्नये सप्तजिह्वाय प्रज्वलिताय नम इत्यादि। यद्वा ॐ क्रौं अग्निं वन्दे अग्नये जातवेदसे नमः। ॐ क्रौं प्रज्वलितं वन्देऽग्नये सप्तजिह्वाय नम इत्यादि। विश्वदेवमुखाह्वयाविति। विश्वमुखो देवमुखश्चोक्तः ॥ ८२ ॥ ८३ ॥ ८४ ॥ ८५ ॥

पुनरित्यादि यजेदित्यन्तं वाक्यम्। सम्यगिति परिस्तृतौ परिसमूहनपर्युक्षणयोः पुनः परितो गन्धपुष्पाराधनमग्नेः समूलमन्त्रेण पूजा चोक्ता। अभिप्रायान्तरमाह—सम्यगितीत्यादिना। परिषेको दक्षिणादिदिक्त्रये जलेन सेचनपूर्वकमैशानादि परितः सेचनम्। तेष्विति पूर्वदिशि न परिधानम्। ततस्तत्र परिस्तरण एव पूजा स्यात्। सर्वेश्वर इह चतुर्थी भवति। मध्ये च कोणषट्के च जिह्वाभिरिति वाक्यम्। गन्धादिभिर्यजेदिति चानुषङ्गः। केसरेषु चाङ्गमन्त्रैरिति वाक्यम्। तेषां क्रमश्च 'हृदयं सशिर इत्यत्रोक्तः। ततो बाह्य इति दलाभिप्रायम्। इह षट्कोणावृतत्रिकोणक इत्यत्र षट्कोणाः सन्ति। तद्बहिस्त्वष्टौ दलानि

चिन्तनीयानि। यद्वा तान्यपि पूर्वमेव षट्कोणादिलेखनसमय एव लेखनीयानि। यदा तु स्वचरणयोग्याः प्राणाग्निहोत्रविधिनापीति वा तत्र सर्वाण्यपि भावनीयान्येवेति बोद्धव्यम्।

ततोऽग्निं मनुनानेनेति पुनरपि प्रधानपूजोक्ता। सा त्वर्वागेव कार्येति दर्शयति—पुनर्वैश्वानरमन्त्रेणेति। मातृभैरवाहुतिरपीति। वक्ष्यति च त्रिपुरापटले—संपूज्य योनिषु च मातृगणमित्यादि। तद्वद्दिर्लोकपाला इति सामान्यसिद्धमेतद्दिति भावः। मन्त्रीति प्रणवयोग उक्तः। अभिप्रायभेदमाह—मनुनेति। वैजाङ्लोमशा इत्यादिवर्णैः षडङ्गानि कल्प्यानि ॥ ८५ ॥ ८६ ॥ ८७ ॥ ८८ ॥

शाशब्दो जटावचनः। नमतेति शार्ङ्गिणस्त्रिमूर्तीन् प्रति वचनमिति ज्ञेयम्।

जिह्वा ज्वालारुचः प्रोक्ता इति। नतु प्रागुक्तहारस्फटिकादिवर्णा इति भावः। वराभययुतानि चाङ्गानीति वाक्यम् ॥ ८९ ॥ ९० ॥

संस्कृतेन घृतेनेति स्वचरणोक्तसंस्काराभिप्रायम्। यत्र चरणेऽभिद्योतनाभावस्तत्राप्यभिद्योतनार्थमभिद्योतनोद्योतितेन चेत्युक्तम्। स्रुवादिसंस्कारोऽपि स्वचरणोक्त एव। अत्राभिप्रायभेदं दर्शयति—आवरणपूजानन्तरमित्यादिना। निरुह्य वायव्येऽङ्गारानिति वाक्यम्। आज्ये चिद्वेति तत्र संस्पर्शनमुक्तम्। सर्वत्राज्यसंस्क्रियायामेव मन्त्रोऽवबोद्धव्यः। एतदेवेति ताभ्यामेव कुशाभ्यामस्त्रेणेवेति ज्ञेयम्। आज्य इति आज्यस्य मध्य इत्यर्थः। हृदा सहेति। + + सर्वे मन्त्रा इत्युक्तानां सोमादिमन्त्राणां ग्रहणम्। स्वाहेतीति + + संस्कृतेन घृतेनेत्याज्यस्य संस्कारषट्कमुक्तम्। अभिद्योत्यत इत्यभिद्योतनम्। नेत्रं वक्त्रं च तदुद्द्योतितं प्रकाशितमुद्घाटितं येन घृतेन तत्तथोक्तम्। तेन मनुनेति। पूर्वोद्धृताग्निमन्त्र उक्तः। त्रिश इति नात्र नियमः। तेनाष्टादिसंख्यापि भवति।

वेदव्रतचतुष्टयेति। महान + + महाव्रतमौपनिषदं गोदानमिति तत्तच्चरणवशादूह्यम्। समुद्वाहावसानिका इति समुद्वाहोऽवसानिको यासामिति समासः। समुद्वाहेऽग्न्याधानमुपलक्षणीयमिति केचित्। अभिप्रायान्तरं दर्शयति—तत्तत्कर्मसमाप्तय इति। समुद्वाहश्चावसानिकाश्चेति समासः। समुद्वाहोऽपि कार्य एव। न समावर्तनमात्रमिति समुद्वाहग्रहणम्। आवसानिका गर्भाधानादीनामवसानभाविन्यः पूर्णाहुतयः। तदाह—तत्तत्कर्मसमाप्तय इति। कार्या इति च शेषः। क्रियाशब्देन तु पञ्चदशानामेव ग्रहणम्। पूर्णाहुतिस्तु मूलेन भवति। ततः पितराविल्यग्नेरिति च शेषः। वागीश्वरं वागीश्वरीं चेत्यर्थः। आत्महृदये स्थापयित्वेति। नात्मन्युद्वासनमात्रमपि तु + + + ॥ ९१ ॥ ९२ ॥

मूले जिह्वाङ्गमूर्तिमनुभिरिति। पीठपूजा प्रागग्नेः कृता चेत्पीठमन्त्रैरपि पूर्वं सकृत्सकृज्जुहुयात्। पुनरग्नेः मूलेन हुत्वा जिह्वाङ्गमूर्तिमन्त्रैर्होमः। पुनर्लोकपालादिमन्त्रैरपि कार्यं इत्यवगन्तव्यम्। जिह्वायामित्यादि दशाहुतीरित्यन्तं वाक्यम्। जिह्वायां मध्यसंस्थायामिति। मध्ये च कोणषट्के च जिह्वाभिरित्युक्तत्वाद्धिरण्या मध्यसंस्था भवति। तथा सलिङ्गगुदमूर्धास्वेत्याद्युक्तत्वात् कृष्णा च मध्यसंस्था भवति। ततश्चायमर्थः। हिरण्यायां तत्रापि तन्मध्यस्थाग्निमूर्त्यास्यवर्तिन्यां कृष्णायामिति। यत उक्तम्—इदं नेत्रवक्त्रोद्घाटनमिति। ज्वालावलीतनाविति तस्या विशेषणम्। ज्वालावलय इतरा जिह्वाः। तास्तनुरेव यस्या मध्यसंस्थाया आत्मस्थानीयाया जिह्वायाः सा तथोक्ता। ज्वालाग्रहणेनेतरासां ज्वालात्वेनावस्थानम्। मध्यस्थायास्तु रसनात्वेनेत्यपि उक्तम्। अत एव जिह्वायां मध्यसंस्थायामिति जिह्वाग्रहणम्। ज्वालानामावलिग्रहणमनेकधाऽवस्थानप्रतिपत्त्यर्थम्। अयमिहाशयः। यदिदं स्वायतनस्थमग्निमण्डलं तत्तावदग्नेर्विग्रहस्तत्र मध्ये या ज्वालोर्ध्वा व्यवस्थिता हिरण्या सा तदात्मा तन्मध्यगता त्वग्निर्देवतात्मा तत्रापि मध्यस्था या जिह्वा तदास्यवर्तिनी कृष्णा सैवात्मा। इतरास्तद्विग्रह एव। तस्यां च होम इति। मन्त्रिशब्देन तन्मन्त्रेण तदानुसन्धानं सूचितम्। अभिप्रायान्तरमाह—समस्ताग्निमन्त्रैरिति। न केवलमिहैव प्रागुदष्टतैन अपि तु तत्पटले वक्ष्यमाणैरपि सप्तद्वरादिमनुभिरन्यैरपि यथायोगमग्निमन्त्रैरित्यर्थः। यद्वा मन्त्री ज्वालावलितनाविति जिह्वामन्त्रैस्तदधिष्ठात्सुरपित्रादिमन्त्रैश्च हुत्वा षण्णां मध्योचितजिह्वयैकीकरणमिह प्रतिपादितम्। तदुक्तं—पुनरन्यजिह्वामध्यजिह्वायामायोज्येति। सर्वा जिह्वास्तनुः स्वाकृतिरेव यस्या इति समासः इति।

गाणपत्येन मनुनैवंभूतेन दशाहुतीः जुहुयात्। कथंभूतेनेति। ताराद्यैर्दशभिर्भेदैः सतेति योज्यम्। पूर्वैः पूर्वैः संभवद्भिर्भेदैः समन्वितैरिति तेषां विशेषणम्। तत्र प्रणवादीनि षड्बीजानि षड्भेदाः स्पष्टा एव। शेषान् भेदानभिधत्ते—गणपतय इत्यन्त इत्यादिना। अयमिह प्रयोगः। ॐ स्वाहा। ॐ ह्रीं स्वाहा। ॐ श्रीं स्वाहा। ॐ श्रीं ह्रीं स्वाहेत्यादि। अत्र वशमानय स्वाहेत्ययं दशमो भेदः। स च पूर्वैः समन्वितः सन् समस्त एव संपद्यत इति ॥ ८३ ॥ ८४ ॥

सकृदेतदबुद्ध्या हुत्वा पुनर्जुहुयाच्च चतुर्वारमित्येतत्कर्तव्यमिति ज्ञेयम्। पुनः साध्येन मनुनेत्येतन्मूलमन्त्रपूजां विधाय कर्तव्यम्। 'पूजायामप्यग्निकार्ये हिठान्त इत्यभिधानादिति। सर्वहोमेष्विति। + + अनलत्वमय इत्यग्न्यात्मकदेवस्य तर्पणमेतदिति भावः। अत्र विशेषमाह—ततश्चर्वर्थमित्यादिना। चरुहोमार्थः।

वक्ष्यति च—सर्पिःसंयुतेन पयोऽन्धसेति। साज्यचरुणा वेति च। यद्वा चरुरन्य एवायमभिप्रेतः। वक्ष्यति च—ततश्चर्वर्थं स्थापितेऽग्नाविति। पीठपूजादिकमिति मूर्तिकल्पनमादिशब्देनोक्तम्। अग्निरूपान्तामिति। जिह्वाङ्गमूर्तिन्यासं मूलाक्षरादिन्यासं च कुर्यात्। जिह्वाङ्गाद्यावरणं मन्त्रदेवतावरणं चार्चयेदित्यप्युक्तम्। वह्नैकीकरणमित्यग्निमन्त्रदेवतयोरिति भावः।

सुधीशब्देनैतत्सर्वं लब्धव्यमित्यभिप्रेयन्नाह—सुधीरितीति। तस्यैवार्थान्तरमाह—आत्मवर्तिदेवतैक्यमिति। वह्निदेवतैक्यं तावत् पूर्वं कल्पितम्। तेनात्मनो नाडीद्वारैक्यमेतदिति भेदः। जिह्वाङ्गादिमन्त्रैरित्यग्नेर्देवस्य च परिवारमन्त्रैर्होम उक्तः। महाव्याहृतिपश्चिममित्यादिसमापनमिहापि समानमेव। तदुक्तं—परिवारमन्त्रहोमव्याहृतितारहोमानन्तरं पूर्णाहुतिं कृत्वाग्निजननसमाप्तिरिति। पुनः सावरणां देवतां तेषु संपूज्येति विधानादिह प्रसन्नपूजादिक्रमेण प्रागारब्धपूजापरिसमाप्तिरपि कार्येत्यवबोद्धव्यम्। मूले तान्त्रिकाणामिति + +।

पुनः साध्येन मनुनेति दीक्षाङ्गतया प्रधानहोम उक्तः। तदर्थं पुनरपि विधिवत्पूजा कार्या। होमबहुत्वे तु तमग्निं विहृत्य पृथक् पूजयित्वायं होमो भवति। तदाह—कुण्डान्तरेष्वग्निमिति। कुण्डान्तराणि प्रागुक्तानि कुण्डानि। कारयतु सम्यगिति मूलेन। पञ्चविंशतिसंख्यं हुत्वेति पीठमन्त्रहोमानन्तरमेतत्। पुनर्जिह्वाङ्गादिहोम उक्तवत् पूर्णाहुत्यन्तं कर्तव्यः। यद्वा प्रधानद्रव्यहोमानन्तरमेव जिह्वाङ्गादिहोमः स्यात्। विवरण आज्येनेत्यादि हुनेदित्यन्तं वाक्यम्। प्रागुक्तस्याज्येन साध्यमनुनेत्याज्यस्यानुवर्तनात्तद्विकल्पोऽत्रोक्तः। इत्यादीति विधानप्रोक्तद्रव्यहोमविकल्पो महाव्याहृतिहोमादिकं चाभिप्रेयते। मूले सुधीरनलदृश्य इति सुधीशब्दः साध्येन मनुना हुनेदित्यत्रापि सम्बन्धनीयः। तेनैतत् सूचितं भवति। हूयमानं द्रव्यं रसामृतरूपेण देवविग्रहे त्वगाद्यात्मान्तं समर्प्यमाणं ततश्च फलामृतरूपेण त्वदादित्वगन्तं निःसरत्तदिन्द्रियरोमकूपेभ्यो बहलसुधाधारारूपेण प्रवर्तमानं स्मरंस्तदाप्लाव्यमानविग्रहं देवपादाब्जगतमौलिं साध्यं च स्मरन् जुहुयादिति। यद्वा पूर्वोक्तनाडीसन्धानप्रक्रियया साध्यं देवेनैकीभूतं स्मरंस्तेन फलामृतेनाप्लुतं विभावयेदिति। द्रव्यमपि तदीयसामान्यरूपं वा तदीयान्तःकरणादिवर्गविशिष्टं वा प्रतिपत्तव्यम्। मूले त्वियती शुद्धिः साधकस्यार्थादुक्ता। विवरणे तु पृथग्विस्तारेण शुद्धिकथनमित्यवगन्तव्यमिति ॥ ८५ ॥ ८६ ॥ ८७ ॥

द्रव्यैर्विधानप्रोक्तैर्वेति। सर्वास्वपि मन्त्रदीक्षासु सर्पिःसंयुतेन पयोऽन्धसेत्येतत् सामान्येनोक्तम्। तन्मन्त्रविधानप्रोक्तैर्द्रव्यैर्वेति विशेषेणेति भेदः। ततश्च यत्र क्वचि-

धाने द्रव्यभावस्तत्र सामान्यद्रव्यमेवैतद्धोम्यं भवति। यथा मातृक ++ ति। अथ तत्तद्विधानेषु विविधानि सन्ति द्रव्याणि। तेषां केन परिमाणेन होमः स्यादित्यपेक्षायामेतद्विवरणमारभ्यते—द्रव्यैर्विधानप्रोक्तैरित्यत्रेति। अथ यजमाननाशादिदोषसूचनसंभवे तद्दोषनिवृत्तिकरं नैमित्तिकं दर्शयति—एवंविधेष्विति। पञ्चविंशतिवारमित्युपलक्षणम्। दोषगरीयस्त्वे संख्यावृद्धिरिति॥ ९७॥ ९८॥

मूले भूर्भुवःस्वरिति महाव्याहृतीनामुद्धारः। प्रथमं भूः भुवः स्वरिति पदानि त्रीणि पुनरेकमिति ज्ञेयम्। तेषामग्नये चेत्यादि चतुर्णामर्धानां च क्रमेण योजना। अयमिह मन्त्रप्रयोगः। भूरग्नये च पृथिव्यै च महते च स्वाहेत्यादि। सर्वशो देवतामया इति + +॥ ९९॥ १००॥ १०१॥

पुनरष्टाविति। महाव्(व्याहृ)तिहोमानन्तरमित्यर्थः। कर्मबन्धविमुक्ताय इति + +। इतः पूर्वमिति ब्रह्मार्पणमन्त्रोद्धारः॥ १०२॥ १०३॥ १०४॥ १०५॥

हुते त्विति। बलिकरणारम्भः। मण्डल इति। यत्र मण्डले कलशो वर्तते तत्रैव। वक्ष्यति च—बलिस्त्वेवं संप्रोक्तः कलशात्मक इति। तत्र नक्षत्राणामिति। बलिदेवताद्युक्तम्॥ १०६॥ १०७॥

ताराणामिति। बलिमन्त्रोज्जिहीर्षयैकैकराश्यन्वयितया नक्षत्राणां प्रविभाग उक्तः। ताराणां पादाधिकं द्वयं राशिः स्यात्। द्वे कृत्स्ने नक्षत्रे तृतीयस्य चैकः पादः। अयमेतावानेको राशिरिति। परिमाणप्रदर्शनार्थं चैतत्। तेन पादत्रयमेकं कृत्स्नं तृतीयस्य चार्धमेको राशिरित्येवं सर्वमपि सिद्धं भवति। मेषादिमुक्त्वेति यावदन्तराल इति। विनियोगोऽयमुक्तः। अत्र व्यवहितमन्वयमाह—नक्षत्रसंज्ञामिति। नक्षत्रसंज्ञापूर्वमिति समासपदं वा। तदा नक्षत्रसंज्ञापूर्वं राशिमुक्त्वानन्तरं देवताभ्यः पदं प्रोच्येत्यन्वयः। सिद्धं मन्त्रमाचष्टे—अश्विनीति। इत्यादय इति। कृत्तिकात्रिपादरोहिणीमृगशीर्षापूर्वार्धनक्षत्रवृषभराशिदेवताभ्यः मृगशीर्षोत्तरार्धार्द्रापुनर्वसुत्रिपादनक्षत्रमिथुनराशिदेवताभ्यः। पुनर्वसुपादपुष्याश्लेषानक्षत्रकर्कटकराशिदेवताभ्य इत्यादि। शेषमूह्यमिति भावः।

केचिदन्यथा योजयन्ति। मेषादिमुक्त्वानन्तरं नक्षत्रसंज्ञापूर्वं देवताभ्यः पदं प्रोच्येति। तदैवं मन्त्रः। मेषाश्विनीभरणीकृत्तिकापाददेवताभ्यः। वृषभकृत्तिकात्रिपादरोहिणीमृगशीर्षार्धदेवताभ्य इत्यादि॥ १०८॥ १०९॥

मूल एवं राशौ तु संपूर्णे तस्मिन्निति। राशिमण्डले संपूर्ण इत्यर्थः। तद्वदित्यादि तत्र तत्र त्वित्यन्तं वाक्यम्। बलिं प्रयोजयेदित्यध्याहारेण योजनीयम्। तद्वदिति गन्धपुष्पादिपूजोक्ता। तथेति मन्त्रप्रकार उक्तः। तं दर्शयति—राश्यधिप-

मन्त्रेष्विति। अयमिह प्रयोगः। अश्विनीभरणीकृत्तिकापादमेषराश्यधिपत्यङ्गारकदेवताभ्य इत्यादि। तथा राश्यधिपानां चेत्यत्र च न राश्यादियोगः। अङ्गारकदेवताभ्यो दिवानक्तंचारिभ्यः शुक्रदेवताभ्य इत्यादि तत्तद्राशिष्वेव बलिः राश्यधिपलिङ्गाद्भवति। यद्वा मेषाधिपत्यङ्गारकदेवताभ्य इत्यादि। केचित्त्वाचक्षते। राशिचक्र एव चेन्नक्षत्रकल्पना। तदैवं तन्मन्त्राः स्युः। यदा तु पृथङ्नक्षत्रचक्रं भवति तदा पृथङ्मन्त्रा ऊह्याः। यथा मेषराशिदेवताभ्य इत्यादि। अश्विनीनक्षत्र इत्यादि तदा च पृथगेव तिथिमन्त्रैरपि भाव्यम्। वारमन्त्रा अप्येवं स्युरिति। नक्षत्राणां सराशीनामित्येतन्मूलं साधारणं भवति॥ ११०॥

मूले सप्तानामित्याद्यन्तराल इत्यन्तं वाक्यम्। सिंहकरणदेवताभ्य इत्यादि करणबलौ कृते तत्रैव वारबलिरित्येके हरदुर्गागुहविष्णुब्रह्मलक्ष्मीधनदवार + + देवताभ्य इत्यादिश्च मन्त्रो भवति। शुद्धान्नेन चायं बलिरिति ज्ञेयम्। बलिस्त्वेवमित्युपसंहारः। कलशात्मक इति कलशगतदेवताप्रधानकं तच्छेषत्वेनैता देवताः प्रतिपत्तव्या इति भावः॥ १११॥

पुनर्निवेद्यमुद्धृत्येति कलशगतदेवतायामर्धकृतपूजाशेष उच्यते। तत्रार्थसिद्धं सर्वं दर्शयति—पानीयमित्यादिना। यथाविधानमिति स्वचरणविहितवदित्यर्थः। गण्डूषदन्तधावनादिकमिति पुनराचमनहस्तमृज्जानुलेपमाल्यभूषाग्रहणम्। पूर्ववत् परिपूज्य चेत्येतदभिप्रायं दर्शयति—दर्पणादिकमिति। अत्र मुखवासकरवासताम्बूलादिदानं गण्डूषाद्यनन्तरं वेहैव वा स्यात्। दर्पणादिकं त्विहैवेति मूलाशयः। दर्पणादिसद्भावे तेषां तदा तदा प्रदानमपि कार्यम्। तदसंभवे तथा कल्पनमात्रमेव भवति। राजोपचारं दत्त्वेति दर्पणादीनामेव तथा प्रतिपत्त्यर्थमुक्तम्। तद्युक्तया स्तुत्या पुनः स्तुत्वेति समुचितपुष्पाञ्जल्याद्युपलक्षणम्। तदाह—पुष्पाञ्जलिं विधायेति। यद्वा यथावत् स्तुत्वेति सम्बन्धनीयम्। तदभिप्रायश्चायमुक्तः। पूजायां प्रवरौ त्विमाविति। यथायोगमनयोरन्यतरः कार्य इति भावः। किञ्च प्रवरशब्देन निवेद्यतोऽपि श्रेष्ठत्वमस्य नैवेद्यवन्दनानीति प्रागुद्दिष्टस्य चरमोपचारस्याभिहितमिति॥ ११२॥११३॥११४॥११५॥

मूले गुर्वाद्या इत्यस्मिन् पूजाप्रकरणे पूजनीयतयोक्तानां मन्त्रप्रकार उक्तः। गुर्वाद्या लोकेशान्ताः सर्वे पूजामन्त्रास्ते ताराद्याश्चतुर्थीनमोऽन्ताः पूजायामपीतियोजना। बलावपीत्यपिशब्देनोक्तम्। यद्वाप्यग्निकार्ये द्विठान्ता इति सम्बध्यते। तदा निवेद्ये बलावपीत्युक्तम्। पूजा स्याद्विभक्त्या वियुक्तैरिति वाक्यान्तां + + मूले तु तदेवाभिषेकारम्भ उक्तः। यद्वा यद्वक्ष्यति 'अभिषिञ्चेद्यथावदिति' तत्राय-

माशय:। पूर्वेद्यु: स्नातमुपोषितं शिष्यं वाससी च पुनरित्यादिप्रकारेण दत्तदक्षिणमात्मसमीपमानीय संहारक्रमेण संहृत्य दिव्यं देहं समुत्पाद्य सकलीकृत्याभ्यर्च्य भद्रासने संस्थाप्याभिषिञ्चेदिति।

अत्रैवाभिप्रायभेदं दर्शयति—देवतानुज्ञया त्वित्यादिना। उत्तरत इत्येतदेव ऐशानकोण इत्युक्तम्। तत्र स्वस्तिकलेखनसामान्यसिद्धम्। हेमवस्त्रादिसंयुक्तामिति। हेमरत्नादि तस्यां सकूर्चं निक्षेप्तव्यम्। वस्त्रं तु पीठार्थं परिवेष्टनार्थं च। अस्त्रदेवतामिति। तत्तन्मन्त्रास्त्रदेवतामिति भाव:। तत्र पीठपूजा निजैव। अस्त्रस्याङ्गानि + + अङ्गलोकपालादिरावरणपूजेत्यवबोद्धव्यम्। चलासनेनेति। प्रागावाहनसमये प्रतिपत्तिसिद्धमेतदिति ज्ञेयम्। प्रदक्षिणं नयन्निति। मण्टपालिन्दपर्यन्तदेशे तां कर्करीं नयन्निति भाव:। लोकपालानामिति + + श्रावयित्वेति तत्तद्दिग्भावप्राप्तिसमय इति भाव:। तत्राभिघारमित्याज्येनोपस्तरणमुक्तम्। मण्डल इति तदर्थं स्वस्तिकादिमण्डलं कार्यमिति गम्यते। सकलीकृत्येति प्रागुक्तरीत्येति भाव:। शिखाबन्धाभिरक्षितं कृत्वेति + + नैमित्तिकीमपि मण्डलगतकलशे पूजोक्ता। शुद्धं शिष्यमिति कर्माङ्गतया स्नानादिकृतवन्तमित्यर्थ:। दिव्यदृष्ट्या विलोक्येति। + +। मूले तत: परात्मने तनुभृते गुरवे स्वं दत्वा निजतनुमर्पयेदित्यन्वय:। स्वमित्येतदिह सर्वस्वपदेन विवृतम्॥ ११६॥११७॥११८॥

संक्षेपतोऽध्वशुद्धिमभिधत्ते—मन्त्रपदेत्यादिना। संहारक्रमेणेहाध्वानस्तेषां + + न्यासस्थानान्यप्युक्तानि। सघृतैस्तिलैरिति। पीठपूजादिसर्वमर्थात् कार्यम्। अमुकमिति। ॐ मन्त्राध्वानं शोधयामि स्वाहा। ॐ पदाध्वानं शोधयामि स्वाहेत्यादि। पूर्वं पदाध्वादिस्मरणेऽपि ॐ मन्त्राध्वने नम इत्यादि प्रयोगो द्रष्टव्य:। क्रमेण विलाप्येति मन्त्राध्वनि होमेन शुद्धे तं पदाध्वनि विलापयेदित्यादि ज्ञेयम्। तत्रेति शिष्यशरीर इति भाव:। देवतामिति कुण्डगतोक्ता। जिह्वाङ्गादीनामित्यग्निसंबन्धिनां पूर्वपूजितानामिति भाव:। पुष्पाञ्जलिमित्यमन्त्रकमिति ज्ञेयम्। मूले वाससी चेत्यादि यदुक्तं तदिदानीं भवेदित्याह—सर्वस्वादिक्रमेणेति। यथावदित्येतस्याभिप्रायतयैतावत्कर्मोक्तम्। पुनरपि तदभिप्रायतयैव कर्मशेषमाह—तं दर्भसंस्तर इति। आत्मयागक्रमेणेति। पुनरस्त्रप्रोक्षिते शुद्धे विष्टर इत्याद्युक्तं सर्वं गृह्यते। साध्यमन्त्रन्यासादिकमिति स्नानावधिसर्वमभिप्रेयते।

मूलेऽथ पटुरवेत्यभिषेक उक्त:। मुख्यवाद्यान्यादौ व्याख्यातानि। द्विजहोमकृतोऽन्ये च दत्तादाना: + + सहार्थे च तृतीया। अत्राभिप्रायान्तरं दर्शयति—अभिषिञ्चतो गुरोरित्यादिना + + +॥ ११९—१२५॥ इति षष्ठ: पटल:।

अथ सप्तमः पटलः ।

अथ विशेषप्रकरणं वितत्वन्मन्त्रविशेषेषु मातृकायाः प्रथमतोऽभिधेयतामाह —सर्वमन्त्रजपादेरिति । पूजाहोमादीनामादिशब्देन ग्रहणम् । न्यासेऽपि लिपेरनुगमाज्जपस्यैवादितयाभिधानम् । लिपिन्यासादिपूर्वकत्वादिति । तदुक्तं – प्राणायामं सलिपिन्यासमिति । प्राणाग्निहोत्रादीनामादिशब्देन ग्रहणम् । सर्वमन्त्रमयज्ञानशक्तिरूपत्वेनेति । ज्ञानशक्तिस्तावदियं मातृका ज्ञानं च सकलपदवाक्यादिमयमर्थावभासकत्वात् । तथा च तत्सर्वमन्त्रमयमपि भवति । समस्तबोधस्थितिदीपिकाया इति । मन्त्रग्रहणेनैतदुक्तम् । मन्त्रविशेषास्तावदिहाभिधेयास्तेषामियं मातृकासमष्टिरिति । प्राधान्याच्चेति स्वव्यष्ट्यपेक्षयेति भावः । वक्तुमारभत इति । मूलगताथशब्दार्थोऽप्युक्तः । अर्थान्तरं वदन् प्रकरणसङ्गतिमप्याह —सर्वमन्त्रसामान्यदीक्षाकथनानन्तर्यमिति । सामान्यदीक्षायामुक्तायां हि तत्र विशेषस्तत्पूर्वको न्यासजपादिश्च वक्तुमुचित इति भावः । प्रदर्शनार्थं चैतत् । तेन सर्वमन्त्राणां स्वरूपव्याप्तिन्यासजपेषु दीक्षापूजाहोमेषु च सामान्यं तावदुक्तम् । विशेषस्त्विदानीं वक्तुमुचित इति । पञ्चाशदक्षराणामधिदेवता तदभिमानिनी शक्तिः । ननु यद्येवं कथं मातृकाविधानमित्युक्तमिति । नैष दोषः । ज्ञानशक्तेः स्वयं मूर्तभावः सामान्यवैखरीरूपोऽकारः । यदुक्तं—अवर्णविग्रहं देवमिति । तस्या एव सर्वमन्त्रविशेषलक्षणव्यष्ट्यावित्सायां तत्पर्यास्यवस्था स्यात् । तदवस्थायास्तस्य मूर्तभाव एव मातृकाव्यापिनो मूर्ध(र्त)दशा नार्थान्तरम् । तदुक्तम्—व्याप्तिमात्रं गुणोन्मेषो मूर्तिभाव इति त्रिधा । इति । अत एव वक्ष्यति –वर्णजाप्यकारजापी वेति ।

समस्तबोधस्थितिदीपिकाया इत्यधिकारफलमुक्तम् । त्रिविधं देवतातः फलं भवति । तत्र यदवश्यं स्यात् तदधिकारफलम् । साधकाधिकारानुरूपतया विभूत्यपवर्गसिद्धिर्नित्यफलम् प्रयोगजन्यं काम्यफलमिति । समस्तानां बोधानां विज्ञानानां स्थितयो वेदागमकाव्यप्रभृतयस्तेषां दीपिका साधकचित्ते प्रकाशिका तस्या इति सकलवेदागमकाव्याद्यभिज्ञत्वादिरूपं फलमुक्तम् । अभिप्रायान्तरमाह—समस्तबोधेत्यादिना । कस्या एतदक्षराधिदेवतात्वमुपपाद्यत इति । तस्या अक्षराधिदेवताया एव । का पुनः सा भवतीति तदिहोन्मनीशक्तिरित्युच्यते । ज्ञानशक्तिप्रसरात्मका इति । ज्ञानशक्तिरेव स्वान्तर्गतं तत्तदर्थाकारं स्वाकारेणाभिव्यञ्जती । तत्तद्विमर्शशब्दाकारेण प्रसरतीति भावः । स्थितय इति तन्मात्रसामान्यविशेषमूर्ततया क्रमेण व्यवस्थितानि पर्वाणि । तासां दीपिकेति । स्वान्तर्गतानां तासां स्वेच्छया

बहिर्भावेन प्रकाशिकेत्यर्थः। उन्मनीशक्तिरिति। भवतीति शेषः। स्वेच्छयाच्चराणां तदीयावस्थाविभावनया प्रसारिका हि तदधिदेवता भवतीति भावः। समस्तानां बोधानामिति। पूर्ववज्ज्ञानशक्तिप्रसरात्मकानां शब्दानामित्यर्थः। तस्य प्रकाशिकाया इति। कथमित्याह—अस्ति हीति। वाक्यशब्देन तदनुगता वर्णपदात्मकज्ञानशक्तिप्रसरसमष्टिलक्षणा ज्ञानशक्तिर्विवक्ष्यते। समस्ता बोधा इति। ज्ञानव्यक्तीनामिव ग्रहणम्। तस्य सर्वस्य दीपिकाया इति। कथमित्याह—शब्दानुविद्धं हीति। शब्दनं च तस्याः स्वाभाविको व्यापार इति भावः। स्वेच्छयाचरैर्देवतातत्त्वं परं ब्रह्म कृत्स्नं विश्वं चाभिधापयन्ती तदधिदेवता भवतीत्यभिप्रायः। विनियोगोक्तिरिति। मातृकालौकिकदुःखप्रशमने कृत्स्नदुःखप्रशमने चापवर्गे विनियोगोऽयमुक्त इत्यर्थः। बिन्दुविसर्गाविति। पञ्चदशषोडशौ स्वरावित्यर्थः। हसाविति त्रयस्त्रिंशद्वात्रिंशयोर्व्यञ्जनयोर्ग्रहणम्। स्वसंप्रदायमाह—तत इति। मूले प्रवरमित्यन्यदप्यस्ति कर्मेति सूचितम्। तद्यथावसरं वक्ष्याम इति। यदिह नित्यफलमधिकारफलं चोक्तम् तदुचितमर्थान्तरमप्याह—अथवेत्यादिना। अत्र जपादेः समस्तबोधस्थितिदीपिकायाश्चाधिदेवतायाश्च अथाच्चराणामिति योजनीयम्। जपादिशब्दश्चावर्तनीयः। प्रणवानन्तर्यमपीति। जपानामादिः प्रथमो ह्यसौ भवतीति भावः॥१॥

मूले सुमतिभिरीरित इत्यनुवादमात्रम्। अभिप्रायान्तरमाह—सुमतिभिरिति। मातृकासरस्वतीति। तन्त्रेष्वित्यस्याभिप्रायान्तरमेतदवबोद्धव्यम्। आद्यन्तेति। आदिस्वरषट्केऽन्तस्वरषट्के च यौ लघ्ववरौ ह्रस्वदीर्घौ तयोरन्तर्मध्ये स्थितैरिति। यथा अकखगघङ अं हृदयाय नम इत्यादि सर्वज्ञादिपदयोगोऽपि स्यात्। तदुक्तं—मन्त्रिभिरिति सर्वज्ञादिपदयोगः सूचित इति। ह्रामादियोग इति। ह्रां ह्रीमित्यादिग्रहणम्। नचायं योगो मातृकाङ्गेषु नित्य इत्याह—भुवनेश्वर्यादियोगे चेति। ननु प्रणवादियोगे चेति वक्तव्यमिति। नैष दोषः। व्यस्तयोगस्यापीहाभिप्रेतत्वात्॥२॥

मूले भास्वत्कपर्देति दीप्तिमद्ग्रहणम्। चिन्ता व्याख्यानमुद्रा लिखितं परं पुस्तकमेव दक्षिणवामोर्ध्वयोरधःकरयोश्चैतच्चतुष्टयमवबोद्धव्यम्। अच्छाकल्पामिति। स्वच्छाभरणाम्। अतुच्छशब्दो महद्वचनः। भारतीमिति मातृकासरस्वती।

अर्थान्तरमाह—भारतीमितीति। भासि नादनादान्तप्रभृतिसमनीपर्यन्तावस्थायां रमत इति भारतीति भावः। परमिति रूपमित्यनुषङ्गः। किं तदित्याह—चिन्तात्मकमिति। उन्मनीस्वरूपलक्षणमित्यर्थः। तामित्यव्यपदेश्यरूपाभिधानादिति भावः। भुवनेश्वर्यादियोगे विशेषं दर्शयति—भारतीं तामिति।

तच्छब्देन भुवनेश्वरी गृह्यत इति भुवनेश्वरीरूपिणीमित्युक्तम् ॥ ३ ॥

मूले काननवृत्तेति। कं शिरः। न इति नासिका। अपरगलो गलपृष्ठभागः। जठराननयोरित्यत्रापि हृदयादिपदानुषङ्गः। व्यापकसंज्ञानिति हृदयादिपदैरन्वयः।

सन्दीक्षित इति दीक्षापटलादनुष्ठानक्रमः। पूजा त्विह वक्ष्यत इत्यवबोद्धव्यम्। विमलधीरिति शुद्धचित्तः। अभिप्रायान्तरमाह—विमलधीरितीति। चित्तस्याप्यक्षेपेण हि स्मृतिसंभव इति भावः। तत्पारायणव्याख्यवस्थानमिति पारायणमपि प्रथमपटलोक्तमक्षराणां व्याप्तिरेव तदविस्मरणेन तत्प्रतिपत्तिर्यथावसरं तन्न्यासश्च लक्षितः। गुरुणानुशिष्ट इति। मन्त्रोपदेशानन्तरं तज्जपक्लृप्त्याद्यप्युपदेशनीयमिति सूचितम्। करयोरङ्गन्यासस्तु प्रागुक्त एवाङ्गुलिषु क्रमादङ्गैरिति।

अभिप्रायान्तरमाह—गुरुणेत्यादिना। तलादिष्विति। तलयोः पृष्ठयोः पार्श्वयोश्चेत्यर्थः। दक्षकनिष्ठाद्यङ्गुलिष्विति। व्यतीहारेणेति ज्ञेयम्। दक्षज्येष्ठाद्यङ्गुलिषु वायं न्यासः। अङ्गुलिपर्वस्वित्यग्रोपलक्षणम्। यद्वाङ्गुलिपर्वाग्रेष्विति पाठः। कासामेवाङ्गुलीनां पर्वाग्रेषूभयाङ्गुष्ठपर्वद्वयाग्रेषु चेति भावः। व्यतीहारेण क्रमेणैव वायं न्यासः। सृष्टिन्यासोऽयं भवति। क्षादिव्युत्क्रमेण संहारन्यासः। यादिकाद्यादिक्रमेण स्थितिन्यासः इति चावबोद्धव्यम्। एवं काननवृत्तेत्यत्रापि स्यात्। भूतलिपिन्यासे तु विशेषः। अ इ उ ऋ ऌ ए इत्यादि पञ्चकं कादिषान्तं च ल सहेत्यर्थं वर्णक्रमः। तेषां स्वे स्वे स्थाने न्यासः। बिन्दोस्तु विसर्गाभावादुभयत्र सह न्यासः। यवर्गकादिपञ्चवर्गैः षडङ्गविधिरिति।

न्यासान्तरमाह—सामान्यपटलोक्ता इति। सर्वत्रेति सर्वेष्वपि मन्त्रेषु न केवलमिहैवेति भावः। तत्क्रमस्तु हृल्लेखानुगमौचित्यात्तदीयपटले वक्ष्यते। तेषु च न्यासेष्वकारो योजनीयः। तत्तन्मन्त्रयोगेन तद्विधानादकारस्य मातृकासंग्रहरूपत्वात्। यद्वक्ष्यति। गुरुणानुशिष्ट इति। ब्राह्मे मुहूर्त उत्थायेत्यादि सर्वमपि सिद्धं भवति। गुरुसमष्टिमन्त्रेण शिरसि वन्दनं कृत्वा स्नानादावित्युक्तनयेनाकथादिवर्गत्रयेण मुखमध्यपादेषु व्यापय्याऽङ्गन्यासादि कृत्वा शक्तिमायारेफहकारैरकारान्वितैर्हृदशान्तादिषु चतुर्मूर्तीरपि विभाव्य मानसपूजां विधाय कर्मसमर्पणादि विदधीत। तथा स्नानादावपि द्रष्टव्यम्। नित्यलिपिन्यासे कृते प्राणाग्निहोत्रादित्रयं विधाय मन्त्रोदयादि सर्वं देहन्यासे मातृकान्यासं पञ्चविंशतितत्त्वन्यासं च कृत्वा शक्तिःश्रीःसन्नतिरित्यादिन्यासं कुर्यादित्यादि। श्रीकण्ठादिन्यासं केशवादिन्यासं च कुर्यात्। यद्वा शुद्धस्यापि सबिन्दुक इत्यादिन्यासाः कार्याः। ततो मातृकायाः सर्गादिन्यासं शाक्ततत्त्वन्यासं चेत्यादि प्रणवन्यासानन्तरं षड्भिर्वर्गैः शैववद्गोलक-

न्यासं सप्तमवर्गेण तत्र तत्र व्यापकान्वितं कृत्वाङ्गर्ष्यादिन्यासं विदध्यात्। पुनरावरणन्यासः। परादिन्यासमेकाक्षरादिन्यासं च कृत्वा चतुर्मूर्तयः स्वशक्त्या भावनीयाः। जपानन्तरं गुणितयोगादिसर्वमप्याचरेदिति। लक्षं न्यसेदिति सर्वन्यासजातं कृत्वा प्रागङ्गादिन्यासादयं न्यासः कार्य इत्यवबोद्धव्यम्। यावता कालेन चतुर्मासादिलक्षणेन संख्या सम्पादयितुं शक्यते। तावतः कालस्य यावद्दिनं सा संख्या विभज्य प्रतिदिनन्यासजपयोः संख्या सम्पादनीयेत्यवबोद्धव्यम्।

अभिप्रायान्तरमाह—सुनियत इतीति। स्थानासनयोर्जपे विकल्पः। आदिशब्देन मूलेऽन्तेऽयुतमिति जपसंख्यायां पूरितायां जपशेषतया होम उक्तः। अपि यजेदिति। न जपमेव केवलं कुर्यादिति भावः। अभिप्रायान्तरमाह—अपि यजेदितीति। पुष्पाञ्जलिनमस्कारादीनामादिशब्देन ग्रहणम् ॥ ४॥५॥६ ॥

मूले व्योमाविःसेति यजनार्थं पद्ममुच्यते। व्योम्नि हकारे आविर्भूतः सकारो व्योमाविःसः। तदाह—हकारसकारावुद्दिष्टताविति। हसौरिति बीजेन व्यक्ततया दीप्तकर्णिकमिति पदार्थः। किञ्जल्कालिखितस्वरमित्यष्टदलेष्वित्यर्थाल्लभ्यते। तेषु केसरस्थाने द्वन्द्वशः स्वरा लेखनीया इति भावः। प्रतिदलं प्रारब्धवर्गाष्टकमिति। प्रतिदलं प्रारब्धानां वर्गाष्टकं यत्रेति समासः। किञ्जल्कालिखितस्वरमित्येवं प्रारब्धानां वर्णानामष्टौ वर्गाः अष्टसु दलेषु लेखनीया इत्यर्थः। कचटतपयशादयः सप्तवर्गा लक्षावष्टम इत्यवबोद्धव्यम्। प्रारब्धशब्दस्याभिप्रायान्तरं दर्शयति—प्रतिदलमिति। वर्गाष्टकमुक्तमेव। वर्गाष्टकस्यारम्भः क्रमेण तेन तद्व्याप्त्यादिरूपशेषवर्णस्वभावोऽपि गम्यत इति भावः। किञ्जल्कालिखितस्वरमित्यत्रापि समानमेतदर्थाद्भवति। यन्त्रान्तरेष्वपि समानमेतत्। यथा 'आख्यां मध्ये सतारे मनुमथ शतसंयुक्तविंशत्पुटेष्वित्यत्र प्रतिवर्णं परितः स्वान्मन्त्रवर्णानपि शक्तितो लिखेदिति। ऋग्वेदादिगतेत्यत्र लेखनं सूचितमिति चशब्दार्थः। यद्वा किञ्जल्कालिखितस्वरमिति किञ्जल्कशब्देन तत्स्थानीयदलानां ग्रहणम्। तेनैतदपि सूचितम्। केसरदलसन्धिदलतदग्रस्थानीयाश्चतस्रोऽत्र दलपङ्क्तयः सन्ति। कर्णिकां परितो वह्निर्बहिरिति स्वरशब्देन स्वराः स्पर्शा व्यापका लक्षाविति चत्वारोऽपि वर्णभेदा लक्ष्यन्ते। चतुर्षु दलेष्वमी चत्वारो वर्गा इति भावः। प्रतिदलमिति। तद्बहिरष्टसु दलेष्वकचटतपयशाद्यष्टवर्गलेखनमुक्तम्। किञ्च प्रतिदलं प्रकर्षेण अ आ इत्यारब्धवर्गाष्टकं यत्रेति समासः। प्रकर्षस्त्वाष्टानां द्वन्द्वानामपि पृथक्त्वम्। तेन तद्बहिः षोडशदलेष्वकारादिविसर्गान्तलेखनमुक्तम्। प्रकर्षेण प्रारब्धानां वर्गाष्टकं यत्रेति च समासः। वर्गाणामष्टकं वर्गाष्टकम्। वर्गाश्चतुर्वर्गाः द्वात्रिंशद्वर्णाभिप्राय-

मेतत्। तेन तद्वहिर्द्वात्रिंशद्दले कादिसान्तलेखनमुक्तम्। तथारब्धानामेवं प्रक्रान्तानां वर्णानां वर्गाष्टकमित्थं लिखितमलिखितं च यत्रेति समासः। प्रकर्षश्च वर्गवर्णानां पृथक्त्वम्। तेन तद्वहिश्चतुःषष्टिदले चतुःषष्टिवर्णलेखनमुक्तम्। तत्र षोडशसु स्वरेषु त्रयोदश प्लुता अधिकाः व्यञ्जनेषु चत्वारो यमा जिह्वामूलीयोपध्मानीयौ चाधिकाविति चतुःषष्टिः ऌकारदीर्घाभावे लकारो योग इति। अश्रासु च सप्तमार्णवयुजा क्ष्माबिम्बेन संवेष्टितमित्यन्वयः। चतुर्ष्वश्रिषु सप्तमार्णः। कोऽसौ तदाह—ठकार इति। दिक्षु वकारः। वर्णाब्जमित्यन्तमेकं वाक्यम्। शेषं प्रासङ्गिकं वाक्यान्तरं वर्णाब्जमित्यनुवर्तते। सर्पदष्टस्य शिरसि स्मृतं विषध्वंसी-त्यादि द्रष्टव्यम्। स्मरणं चैतत् स्रवदमृतधाराप्लुतसाध्यविग्रहमित्यवबोद्धव्यम्। अथार्थमिदं विशेषमाह—विषध्वंसे गारुडयोग इति। क्षिौमिति गरुडबीजाभि-प्रायमेतत्। कुत्रास्य योग इति कर्णिकायामेव वा दलेषु प्रतिवर्णमपीति ज्ञेयम्। गदो व्याधिः। उपलक्षणं चैतत्। यथोष्णार्तस्यामृतबीजयोगः शिरोरुजार्तस्य चिन्तामणियोग इत्यादि। स्मृतमिति केवलं स्मृतिमात्रं वा वामकरतले यन्त्रमा-लिख्य तदभिमर्शने स्मरणं वा स्वर्णपट्टादिषु विलिख्य तद्धारणे स्मरणं वा जल-तैलादिषु यन्त्रं विभाव्य तदा सेकादौ स्मरणं वा स्यादिति ॥ ७ ॥

प्रविधाय पद्ममितीत्येवमित्यर्थः। दलबाह्ये राशिचक्रमालिख्य तद्वहिर्भूपुरादि कल्पनीयम्। मण्डलानि च तत्त्वज्ञो राश्यन्तानीति ह्युक्तम्। कथितक्रमेणेति। प्रथमं निजसव्यतो यथावदित्याद्युक्तक्रमेणेत्यर्थः। विधिनेति। तत्रोक्तमनुष्ठान-मुक्तम्। अभिप्रायान्तरमाह—पृथिव्यनन्तरमिति। विधिनेत्येतत् प्रविधायेत्यत्रापि संबन्धनीयम्। तदाभिप्रायमाह—प्रविधायेति। विधिनेत्यनुषज्यते। यन्त्रजीवादि सर्वं तृतीयपटलान्तेऽभिहितम्—ह्सौरिति यन्त्रजीवमित्यादि। अमुत्रेति पूजिते पीठ इत्यर्थः। अर्थान्तरमाह—अमुत्रेतीति। नित्यपूजाविधिरयमुच्यते। यदुक्तं—यजेद्दिनशोऽक्षरेशीमिति। दीक्षापूजायां तु कलशं पूजयित्वा तत्र पूजेति भेदः। मूर्तिपूजेति सूचितेत्यनुषङ्गः। तनुशब्दस्य मूर्त्यर्थत्वादिति भावः। अं सरस्वती-मूर्तये नम इति मूर्तिमन्त्रः ॥ ८ ॥ ९ ॥

तदनु च कलायुग्मश इति कलाः स्वराः। यथा अं आं नमः। इं ईं नम इत्यादि। चकारः समुच्चयार्थः। अष्टवर्गांश्चेति वान्वयोऽभिप्रेतः। तदाभिप्राया-न्तरमाह—चाष्टवर्गानितीति। अष्टवर्गाश्च पूर्ववत्। कचटतपयशाद्या लक्षौ च। यथा कं खं गं घं ङं नम इति। अत्र स्वरद्वन्द्वशक्तीनां व्यञ्जनवर्गशक्तीनां च प्रधानवदाकारोऽभिप्रेतः। ब्रह्माण्यादीरिति। मातृरित्यध्याहारः। तासामाकारं

दर्शयति—अच्चवलयेत्यादिना। शतमखमुखानप्यथो लोकपालानितीन्द्राद्या-
नित्यर्थः। शतमखमुखाद्यानिति वा पाठः। तद्विवृणोति—शतमखमुखा इति।
वर्णान् जापोति वर्णानाभीच्ण्येन जपितुं शीलमस्येति तथोक्तः। सुनियतः
प्रजपेच्च तावदित्यस्यैव अयमनुवादः। अर्थान्तरमाह—वर्णान् जापोति। कृत्स्नां
मातृकां वा जपेत्। यद्वा तत्समष्ट्यात्मकमकारमेव जपेदित्यर्थः। लच्चं न्यसेदि-
त्येतत् कृत्स्नाया एव। तथा होमोऽपीति ज्ञेयम् ॥ १० ॥ ११ ॥

वर्गस्वरेत्यादि प्रयोगप्रकरणम्। वर्गशब्देन स्पर्शग्रहणम्। स्पर्शस्वरयाद्यंशा
इति वा पाठः। कलधौतं सुवर्णं स्पर्शवर्णान्मानं सुवर्णमित्यादि द्रष्टव्यम्।
इतीत्युक्तोन्मानानुवादः। रुचकमङ्गुलीयकम्। रुचकत्वादेव बालानां ग्रीवाया-
मितरेषामङ्गुलौ च धार्यमवसीयते। तस्य च शोधनपूजाजपसंपातयोगोऽर्थसिद्ध
एव। साधकसर्वार्थदायीति।

तदुक्तं—इयं रचःचुद्ररोगविषज्वरविनाशिनी।

व्यालचोरमृगादिभ्यो रचां कुर्याद्विशेषतः।

युद्धे विजयमाप्नोति धारयन्मनुजेश्वरः॥ इति ॥ १२ ॥

त्रिवारमम्भ इत्यत्र हि तया विद्यया त्रिवारमपि परिजप्तमम्भ इत्यन्वयः।
मातृकयेत्यर्थः। सुधीरिति। देव्याः पादपद्मगलदमृतमयध्यानमुक्तम्। विद्यये-
त्यत्राभिप्रायान्तरमाह—कर्णिकाबीजयोग इति। व्योमाविःसेत्याद्युक्तेन बीजेन
योग इत्यर्थः। सहार्थे तृतीयेत्यपि सूचितम्। योगश्चायं कृत्स्नायास्तद्वर्गाणां
वर्णानामेव वोभयतो योजनम्। पुनरप्यभिप्रायान्तरं दर्शयति—अथवेति।
दशाचरीयोग इति। वच्यति च—मध्ये वद्यचरयोरित्यादि। त्रैपुराणामिति।
शुद्धादिभेदभिन्नानामिति भावः। आधारेष्विति। मूलाधारादिग्रहणम्। स्वयं
देवताविग्रहो भूत्वेत्यादि पूर्वोक्तेऽपि समानम्। परिजप्तमित्यत्र परेः सर्वतोऽर्थत्वात्
विसर्गादियोगतस्त्रिर्जपेन सकृत्पानं भवति। त्रिवारमित्यनेन चैवं त्रिवारं
पानावृत्तिरपि भवतीति ज्ञेयम्। सप्त तेऽकवर्गैर्वेति। क्रमेण वा प्रत्येकं वा त्रिवार-
जप इत्यनेन संबन्धः स्यात्। अनेडमूकोऽपीति। जात्या मूकः + + ॥ १३ ॥

मूले कमलोद्भवौषधिर्ब्राह्मी। सर्पिरपीति न केवलमुक्तारम्भः। पानेनेति भावः।
अभिप्रायान्तरमाह—अप्ययुताभिजप्तमितीति। पूजाहोमादिकमितीति +++
दशाचर्यादियोगोऽत्रापि जपे यथार्थमुचित एव। इह वचा कल्कत्वेन विवचिता।
ब्राह्मीरसं पयोयुक्तं वचापङ्कं वा पयोयुक्तं प्रतिदिनमयुतसंख्यं विभज्य जप्त्वा पिबेत्।
यद्वा ब्राह्मीघृतान्तरोपलचणमेतत्।

यदुक्तम् पलं श्वेतवचाचूर्णं कर्षं तुरगगन्धिनी ।
कृष्णा हरिद्रासिन्धूत्थं धात्री रुग्विश्वभेषजम् ॥
प्रतिनिष्कन्तु संयोज्य घृतप्रस्थे विनिक्षिपेत् ।
ब्राह्मीरसचतुष्प्रस्थे पचेन्मृद्वग्निना शनैः ॥ इति ।

सिद्धार्थसिन्धूत्थकणामयोग्राब्राह्मीसुगन्धोत्पलकल्कसिद्धम् ।
ब्राह्मीरसे सर्पिरिदं तु रक्षामेधाधृतिश्रीस्मृतिकान्तिदं स्यात् ॥ इति ।

लेहोपलक्षणं चैतत् । यदुक्तम्—

ब्राह्मी वचा हिरण्यं सरसिजकन्दं च सर्पिषा मधुना ।
पृथगथवाद्यावन्त्या मेधार्थे लेहयेदलं बालम् ॥ इति ।

कविर्भवतीति । कवित्वमेतीत्यर्थः ॥ १४ ॥

वर्णौषध्या शृताभिरिति । वर्णौषधयो व्याप्तिपटल उक्ताः । शृताभिः पक्वाभिः । अमलधीरिति सावधानत्वमुक्तम् । अभिप्रायान्तरमाह—कमलमित्यादिना । कामना इह मेधेन्दिरायुरित्याद्युक्ता एव । दशशतपरिजप्तेनेत्यत्रैषां योगः स्यात् । पूजाभिषेकयोरपि तद्योगो भवति । आदिशब्देन बीजैर्मातृकया च पृथक्पूजादिकं गृह्यते । जूंसःयोग इति मृत्युञ्जयोपादानम् । कामनान्तरेष्वपि तत्तदुचितबीजोऽभिप्रेयते । यथा अगदे नृसिंहबीजयोगः । + + इत्यादि । नानागुणगणनिलयमिति । मेधेन्दिराप्रभृतय उक्ता अनुक्ता अप्यारोग्यादयो गुणा विवक्षिताः । सर्वयोग इति । क्ष्रौं कलशेऽपि होमादिकार्यमिति ज्ञेयम् । नानागुणेत्यत्रैवामलधीपदयोजनायामभिप्रायान्तरं दर्शयति—अथवेत्यादिना । सर्वैर्बीजैरिति । मेधेन्दिरादिसर्वगुणानुगुणतया सप्तभिस्तद्बीजैः दुंबीजेन चेत्यर्थः । प्रागुक्तवत् तद्युक्तमातृकया पृथग्वा पूजा भवति । शान्तिन्या + + + इत्यष्टमी शक्तिरुक्ता । तस्या अनुक्तगुणानुगुणतया दुंबीजेन पूजा भवति । +++ नवरत्नमुद्रिकायामप्यस्य कलशस्य विनियोग इति तद्वदन् प्रागुक्तत्रिलोहमुद्रिकायामपि । तदाह—त्रिलोहमुद्रिकेति । मुद्रिकाङ्गुलीयकम् । नवरत्नानीहोक्तान्येव मुक्तामाणिक्यादीनि । तेषां क्रमोऽप्ययमेव भवति । अकलितसङ्गतेति + + + कलशजपपूजा होमसहिता चेति । स्यादिति शेषः । + + पटलारम्भे प्रवरं विधानमित्यन्यदपि विधानं सूचितम् ।

यदुक्तम्—शान्तिके तु पयःसर्पिस्तिलक्षीरद्रुमेध्मकाः ।
अमृताशकलां चैव पायसं तत्र कीर्तिताः ॥
गोक्षीरमधुसर्पिर्भिरष्टाष्टाहुतयः पृथक् ।
तैर्मिश्रितैस्तथाष्टौ च खादिरेध्मैश्च पौष्टिके ॥ इति ।

राज्यं बिल्वदलैः सजातिकुसुमैः कन्याश्च लाजैः श्रियं
दध्नाधोनिधिमाज्यबिल्वसतिलैर्धान्यान्धसो स्वेन तु ।
सम्पत्तिं पयसा घृतेन मधुनार्द्राब्जैश्च कीर्तिं लभे-
ताज्येन श्रियमम्बुजैरमृतया त्वायुर्लिपेर्होमतः ॥
वशयेज्जातीकुसुमैराकर्षेल्लवणकङ्गुभिर्हन्यात् ।
गरलाक्तोन्मत्तफलैर्बीजैर्विद्वेषयेच्च कार्पासैः ॥ इति
हुत्वा लक्षं तिलैः शुद्धैर्मुच्यते सर्वपातकैः ।
पायसान्नेन जुहुयान्मन्त्री सर्वसमृद्धये ॥ इति ॥ १५ ॥

मूल आधारोद्यदित्यादिश्लोकेन योग उक्तः । मूर्धेन्दुं ग्रसन्त्याः प्रभाया वक्त्रे पातयेदिति योजनीयम् । मूलाधारचतुर्दलकमलकर्णिकायां त्रिकोणे प्रादुर्भवन्ती शक्तिः भुवनेशीरूपा । तस्या मध्ये गताद्बिन्दोरुत्थिताऽतिसूक्ष्मरूपा या प्रभा । सा सुषुम्नान्तर्वर्त्मना मूर्धानं तन्नचितं द्वादशान्तं वा प्राप्ता मतो तत्र साधोमुखसहस्रदल-कमलकर्णिकागतं सोमं वेधपूर्वकं व्याप्नोति । तदेव तस्य ग्रसनम् । तस्या वक्त्रं च तदा तदधोभाग एव । तत्र तस्मात्सोमान्मातृकां प्रतिलोमामुच्चरन् क्षकाराद्यकारा-न्तवर्णान् पातयेत् । तेषां विशेषणं वह्निसोमप्रोतानित्येतत् । प्रोतत्वं व्याप्तत्वम् । तदाह—अग्नीषोमात्मकानिति । द्विद्विबिन्दुतया वर्णानां पातनम् । यद्वैकैक-बिन्दुतयैव तदा चार्धद्वयेनोभयात्मकत्वमिति ज्ञेयम् । मन्त्रीति । सकृच्छक्तेर्लिपि-प्रतिलोमस्य चोच्चारणमुक्तम् । अभिप्रायभेदमाह—मन्त्रीतीति । अत्र प्रतिवर्ण-मावृत्तो रेफवकारयोगश्चेति भेदः । मुच्यते रोगजातैरिति । जातशब्दः समूह-वचनः । अत्र पतद्भिर्वर्णैः मूलाधारपर्यन्तं तस्याः प्रभाया दीप्तिरपि विभावनीया । ततश्चाशेषदेहव्याप्तिरपि । तत्राग्न्यंशेन दुरितरोगदाहः सोमांशेनाप्यायनमित्य-वबोद्धव्यम् । लिपेः सकलीकरणं कृत्वायं प्रयोगः कर्तव्यः । किं च गुणितयोगा-त्पूर्वमपि नित्यतयायं योगः स्यादिति ॥ १६ ॥

मूले विन्यासैरथेति फलान्तराभिधानेनोपसंहारः । लक्षं न्यसेदित्युक्तत्वाद्वि-न्यासैरिति बहुवचनोपपत्तिः । ध्यानैश्चेति । पञ्चाशद्वर्णभेदैरिति परसूक्ष्मध्यान-योरप्युक्तत्वादाधारोद्यच्छक्तीति च नित्ययापि योगस्याभिप्रेतत्वात् बहुवचनसंभवः । जरापमृत्युरोगैरिति विमुक्तो भवतीति शेषः । अभिप्रायान्तरं दर्शयति—विन्या-सैरितीत्यादिना । अथ विन्यासैरिति संबन्धनीयम् । वक्ष्यमाणन्यासभेदापेक्षया च बहुवचनम् । तदाह—शुद्धविसर्गेति । वक्ष्यति च—शुद्धश्चापि सबिन्दुक इत्यादि । कलाः कला इत्यादि च । अन्यैश्चेत्यात्माक्षरयोगः कामरत्यादियोग इत्यादिग्रह-

णम्। सजपैरित्येतद्विवृणोति—जपाश्चेति। केवलन्यासा एवेति चकारेणोक्तम्। न्यासजपयोः संख्यापि पूर्वोक्तैव भवति। हुतार्चनाद्यैरित्येतदाशयमाह—हुतार्चनाविधौ इति। आद्यशब्देन + + + ध्यानेश्चैतदभिप्रायं न्यासे विशेषञ्च दर्शयति—शुद्धन्यास इत्यादिना। सरस्वत्येवेति। न तु मातृकासरस्वतीति भावः। अवशिष्टाः शक्तय इति। देव्यै इत्येतस्य स्थाने पठनीया इति भावः। शक्तेः ऋष्यादिकमिति तद्भृल्लेखापटले—शक्तिः स्यादृषिरस्य त्वित्यादि। द्विरुक्तैर्बीजैरिति। ह्रीं श्रीं क्लीं ह्रीं श्रीं क्लीमित्येभिः षड्भिः क्रमेणेत्यर्थः। इदानीं स श्रीमानित्यादिशेषस्याभिप्रायमाह—स श्रीमानितीत्यादिना। ज्वरापमृत्युरोगादिजय इति बहुवचनाशयोऽप्युक्तः। सर्वं सर्वत्र वेति। तत्तदुचितबीजयोगोऽपि वेष्यते॥ १७॥

वर्णयोगक्रममिति। व्याप्तिपटलोक्तादयमिह भेद इति भावः। सर्वत्र संयोज्येत्युपस्कारः। कलाः संयोज्य नादभवाः कला वदन्तीत्येवं सर्वत्रान्वयः। कलाः संयोज्येति अकारादिस्वरान् संयोज्येत्यर्थः। कचादिवर्णान् संयोज्याजा इत्यकारजाः कला वदन्तीत्यर्थः। षादिकान् संयोज्यानन्तावधिका बिन्दुजाः कला वदन्तीत्यन्वयः। पीताश्वेतारुणाऽसिता अनन्तेतीमान् कला इति भावः। प्रसङ्गात्वान्यदिति सान्निध्यकृदित्यादेर्मन्त्रोद्धारविधान इत्यादेश्चेह निबन्धनमुक्तम्॥ १८॥

पाशाङ्कुशवरचरादियोग इत्यजपापरमात्मादिमन्त्राणां ग्रहणम्। मूले सान्निध्यकृत् स इति तच्छब्देन न्यासग्रहणम्। कस्य सान्निध्यकृदिति प्रकृतत्वात् कलाशक्तेरिति गम्यते। प्रतिमाग्रहणात्तु तत्तन्मन्त्रसंयोगतस्तत्तद्देवताया अपीत्यवसीयते। मर्त्यः साधकः। प्रतिमाशिवविष्ण्वादिबिम्बकलशे दीक्षायामभ्युदयार्थोऽपि ग्राह्यः। आदिशब्देन यन्त्राज्यादिग्रहणम्। सान्निध्यफलाभिधानान्न्यासावृत्तिरपि लक्षपर्यन्ता लभ्यते॥ १९॥

मन्त्रोद्धारविधान इति। तत्तन्मन्त्रस्य वर्णाब्जादुद्धारानुष्ठान उद्धाराभिधाने चेत्यर्थः। आभिर्वर्णव्यत्यासक्लृप्तिर्विशेषज्ञैरुद्दिष्टेत्यन्वयः। आभिरिति कलाग्रहणम्। वर्णानां व्यत्यासो विनियमः। तत्तन्मन्त्रवर्णस्य स्थाने नामान्तरयोजनम्। यथा—घनवर्त्मकृष्णगतिशान्तिबिन्दुभिरिति। श्रीकण्ठादिप्रोक्तैर्नामभिर्वेति। वर्णव्यत्यासक्लृप्तिरित्यनुषङ्गः। यथा तारोमायामरेशोद्रिपीठ इति। मन्त्रोद्धारकथनं त्वन्यैरपि नामभिः स्यात्। यथा घनवर्त्मकृष्णगतिशान्तिबिन्दुभिरिति। कदाचित्तु न व्यत्यासः। यथा मध्ये बद्धक्षरयोरिति। मन्त्रोद्धारानुष्ठाने त्वयं नियमो भवति। यथा वर्णाब्जादकारं निवृत्त्यै नम इति वा श्रीकण्ठाय नम इति वोच्चरन् सपुष्पमादानमुद्रयान्यत्र निपानमुद्रया न्यसेत्। तत्र त्वकारं च लिखेदिति। मलसंहार-

रूपत्वमिति मन्त्रवर्णानां छित्वा रुद्वा इत्यादिरूपं मलं कलाशक्तिभिः श्रीकण्ठादि-मूर्तिभिर्वा तादात्म्यापत्तौ संहृतं प्रतिपत्तव्यमिति भावः ॥ २० ॥

केशवादिन्यासे विशेषमिति ध्याने विशेष इहोक्तः। मन्त्रितमो यथावदिति वर्णयोगो नाम्नां चतुर्थीनतियोगश्चोक्तः। अभिप्रायान्तरमाह—अष्टाक्षरपटल इति। अष्टाक्षरपटलयोगोऽपीति न केवलं ध्येयाकार एवेति भावः। त्रिपुटादियोग इति। त्रिपुटा वक्ष्यते—अथ रमाभुवनेशिमनोभवैरिति। आदिशब्देनाजपादिग्रहणम्। यथा ॐ श्रीं ह्रीं क्लीं हंसः सोऽहं अं नमो नारायणाय कीर्त्यै नम इत्यादि। ध्येयत्व-मिति सूचितमिति शेषः। मूले पुरेव चेति व्याप्तिपटलोक्तरीत्येत्यर्थः। कीर्त्यादि-शक्तिभिरपि युतैरित्यनेनोक्तं विशेषमाहेत्येतद्रुद्रादीनित्यत्रापि समानमेव ॥ २१ ॥

श्रीकण्ठादौ न्यासे रुद्रादीन् शक्तियुताञ्न्यसेदिति सोपस्कारमन्वयः। रुद्र-शब्देन श्रीकण्ठग्रहणम्। पूर्णोदर्यादयस्तु तेषां शक्तयः। विद्वानिति मन्त्रोचित-तयाऽर्धनारीश्वरं शक्तियुतमीश्वरं वा ध्येयं जानन्नित्यर्थः। वर्णानां योगस्तु प्रकरणा-दिभिर्भवति। वर्णान् प्राग्बीजसंयुतान् वापीति श्रीकण्ठादावित्यनुषङ्गः। बीज-मिह प्रासादः। अभिप्रायान्तरमाह—रुद्रादीनितीति। रुद्रादीन्वर्णानित्यन्वयः। सर्वन्यासेष्विति कलान्यासे केशवादिन्यासे च तथा शुद्धादिन्यासेष्वपि चेत्यर्थः। पञ्चाक्षरीविद्यायोग इति विद्याग्रहणं देवीमन्त्रस्यापीच्छया परिग्रहार्थम्। अज-पादियोग इति परमात्ममन्त्रादिपरिग्रहार्थम्। यथा ॐ ह्रीं हंसः सोऽहं अं नमः शिवाय शिखायै श्रीकण्ठाय पूर्णोदर्यै नम इत्यादि ॥ २२ ॥ २३ ॥ २४ ॥

अथ मूल आत्माष्टाक्षरन्यासः अथानयेत्यादिप्रकरणेनोच्यते। स च मन्त्रो द्विविधो ब्रह्मयागमन्त्रः प्राणाग्निहोत्रमन्त्रश्चेति। तत्र ब्रह्मयागमन्त्रस्य द्विधा प्रयोगः। प्रपञ्चयागो न्यासमात्रं च। तत्र प्रथमं प्रपञ्चयागः प्रस्तूयतेऽथानयेति। पञ्चविभेदभिन्नयेति पृथिव्यादिभूतलिपिविभेदेन बीजबिन्द्वाद्यंशविभेदेन च भिन्न-येत्यर्थः। कथं मातृकयैवानया प्रपञ्चेन योगोपपत्तिरिति तदर्थमेतदुक्तम्। तेन वर्णहोमे कृत्स्ना प्रतिपत्तिरपि सूचिता भवति। अभिप्रायान्तरमाह—पञ्चाश-दिति। पञ्चाशदादिपञ्चसंख्याभेदयुक्तयेत्यर्थः। प्रपञ्चयागस्येत्यनेन प्राणाग्निहोत्रे तु शुद्धादिसप्तविभेदभिन्नयेत्यपि सूचितम्। वक्ष्यति च—शुद्धसबिन्द्वादिमातृकाभेद-संयोगक्रमविदामिति। मूल इह कृत इति न जन्मान्तरापेक्षेत्युक्तम्। प्रपञ्चया-गादाविति द्विविधः प्रपञ्चयागो द्विविधश्च प्राणाग्निहोत्रं गृह्यते। तत्त्वस्पृहा-मिति। परदेवतात्मतत्त्वं परमपुरुषार्थतयाधिजिगमिषतामिति भावः ॥ २५ ॥

मूले पूर्वं महागणपतिमिति तदङ्गतया पुरस्ताद्गणपतिभावनोक्ता। द्विविधोऽयं

प्रपञ्चयागोऽभिप्रेयते। स्वतन्त्रोऽभिमतमन्त्रन्यासाङ्गभूतश्च। तत्र स्वतन्त्रतया प्रपञ्चयागेऽभिमतमन्त्रन्यासजपादौ कृत एतद्भवति। मन्त्रन्यासाङ्गभावे तु कालो वक्तव्य इति। तदर्थमभिप्रायमाह—पूर्वमितीति। समुनिच्छन्दोदैवतमित्याद्युच्यमामाल्लिपिन्यासात्पूर्वमित्याद्युक्तावर्थादन्यस्माल्लिपिन्यासात्पश्चादित्यपि गम्यत इति भावः। मूले स्वविधानसिद्धरूपमिति। वक्ष्यति च—मन्दाराद्यैरित्यादि। निजेष्टविषय इति। यजनस्य वाचिकत्वात्तदङ्गतया गणपतिपूजापि वाचिकीति भावः। अवहितो यथावदिति प्राप्तानुवादः। अभिप्रायान्तरमाह—अवहित इतीति। सिद्धरूपमिति बीजस्य। साङ्गमिति ऋचः। साङ्गमित्यङ्गावरणपर्यन्तं विवक्षितम्। सावरणमिति मालामन्त्रस्य। स च महागणपतिमन्त्र एवेति ज्ञेयम्। अङ्गादिन्यासपूर्वकत्वमिति निजोऽङ्गन्यास इत्यवबोद्धव्यम्। तत्र तु ऋचः पादैरर्धाभ्यां चाङ्गानि। आदिशब्देनर्ष्यादीनां संभवे सति वर्णन्यासादेरपि ग्रहणम्॥ २६॥

मन्त्रितम इति स्वपटलभाविमन्त्रज्ञ इत्यर्थः। अभिप्रायान्तरमाह—मन्त्रितम इतीति। सकृदस्य जपः स्यात्॥ २७॥

मूले प्रागभिहितेनेति। यथा ब्रह्मा स्यादृषिरस्येत्यादि। ध्यानमपि तदेव भवति। मूले तथेति। विन्यसेदिति भावः। नवग्रहन्यास इति। सप्त च न्यसेदित्युक्तौ तत्प्रतीतेरिति भावः। प्राणाग्निहोत्रार्थमित्यधःसंबन्धः॥ २८॥

मूले वदन इत्यत्रैवं मन्त्रः स्यात्। ॐ स्वराधिपतये सूर्याय नम इत्यादि। अत्राभिप्रायान्तरं वदन् प्रथमं प्रयोगक्लृप्तिं दर्शयति—अयमत्रेत्यादिना। मङ्गलायेत्यादिषु चवर्गन्यासतद्वचनादिसर्वं प्रकरणाद्गम्यत एव। प्रणवशक्तिमूलमन्त्रादियोग इत्यजपादिग्रहणम्। स्वतन्त्रेऽपि प्रपञ्चयागेऽभिमतमन्त्रभाजा मूलयोगः स्यादेव। यथावदित्यस्यैवाभिप्रायान्तरमाह—स्वरानुक्तेत्यादिना। ग्रहांश्च सप्त तथेत्यनेनैव प्राणाग्निहोत्रार्थं नवग्रहादिन्यासोऽपि सूचित इति मन्यमानो नवग्रहादिन्यासमपि दर्शयति—अथ नवग्रहन्यास इत्यादिना। प्रणवशक्तिमूलमन्त्रादियोगोऽत्रापि समानः। पूर्वोक्तवैपरीत्येनेति। यथा प्रणवशक्तिमूलाद्यनन्तरं चादियान्तमुक्त्वा अग्निमण्डलाय नम इति पादादिनाभ्यन्तं व्यापयेदित्यादि। हंसन्यासे तु भेदः। चाद्यकारान्तमुक्त्वा सोहं प्रकृत्यात्मने नम इति पादादिशिरोऽन्तं व्यापकत्वेन न्यसेत्। वैपरीत्याभिधानादेवैतदपि लभ्यत इति प्राणाग्निहोत्रप्रपञ्चयागन्यासक्रममूलसिद्धमभिधत्ते—हुत्वेत्यादिना॥ २९॥

मूले सप्तग्रहन्यासं कृत्वा प्रपञ्चयागं कुर्यादिति तारश्च शक्तिरित्यनेनोक्तम्। परमात्मबीजमिति सोहमित्येतदुक्तम्। तृतीयलिपिभिरिति। यथा ॐ ह्रीं अं

हंसः सोहं स्वाहा। ॐ ह्रीं भ्रां हंसः सोहं स्वाहेत्यादि। सकलार्थदायीति गुणफलाभिधानम्। तत्त्वसङ्ग्रहामधिकार इति स्फुटम् ॥ ३० ॥

ब्रह्मा स्यादृषिरस्येत्येषां पञ्चमन्त्राणां योगस्य मन्त्रान्तरतामापन्नस्येत्यर्थः। सकलपदार्थसदर्थ इति परंज्योतिषो विशेषणम्। सकलः पदार्थोऽयमेव शुद्धषितः प्रपञ्चः। तत्र यत्सन्मात्ररूपं वस्तु तत्साक्षितयाऽनुगतं तदित्यर्थः। अत्रास्येत्यभिप्रायान्तरमाह—अस्येति। परमान्विता चेत्यत्र चकारः समुच्चयार्थः। तदभिप्रायमाह—स्वयमन्वितेति। प्रकरणसिद्धमभिप्रायं दर्शयति—स्वयं ज्योतिरिति। ब्रह्मा स्यादित्यत्राप्येतदुभयं प्रकरणसिद्धमभ्युपेयम्। वक्ष्यति च—परमपदेन प्रकाशितः प्रवर इति। यथा परंब्रह्मा ऋषिः परमगायत्री छन्दः परंज्योतिर्देवता। स्वयं ब्रह्मा ऋषिः स्वयं गायत्री छन्दः स्वयं ज्योतिर्देवतेति ॥ ३१ ॥

मूले जायाग्नेरित्यात्माष्टाक्षरस्याङ्गकथनम्। स्वयं च वर्मेति शक्त्यभिप्रायम्। हरिहरवर्णमस्त्रं स्यादित्यन्वयः। इह मूल एकमेवाष्टाक्षरं विनियोगमात्रे तु भेदः। ततोऽङ्गर्यादा न विशेष इत्यर्थोऽवगम्यते। अङ्गमन्त्रेष्वप्यभिप्रायान्तरमाह—शिरस्येत्यादिना। सोहं च शिर इत्यन्वयः। चकारः समुच्चयार्थः। तदभिप्रायमाह—प्राणाग्निहोत्र इति। हंसात्मा त्वथ च शिखेत्यत्राप्येवमेव चकाराभिप्रायः। तदाह—अथ चेति। अयमिहाङ्गमन्त्रप्रयोगः। स्वाहा हृदयाय नमः। सोहं शिरसे स्वाहा। हंसः शिखायै वषट्। ह्रीं कवचाय हुम्। ॐ नेत्रत्रयाय वौषट्। हरिहर अस्त्राय फडिति। तथा स्वाहा हृदयाय नमः। हंसः शिरसे स्वाहा। सोहं शिखायै वषट्। ह्रीं कवचाय हुम्। ॐ नेत्रत्रयाय वौषट्। हरिहर अस्त्राय फडिति। शक्तेः ध्येयत्वमिति। तारश्च शक्तिरित्युक्तशक्तेरेव। जायाग्नेः हृदयमित्यादि व्युत्क्रमतो गम्यमानायाः स्वयमिति मन्त्रात्माभिधानादिति भावः। ततश्च 'उद्यद्भास्वत्समाभामित्येतदेव ध्यानमिति लभ्यते ॥ ३२ ॥

मूलेऽत्राकारहकाराद्यावित्याद्युक्तमन्त्रव्याप्तिप्रकरणम्। अत्राद्यौ मनू अकारहकाराद्यौ शान्तान्तिकावित्यन्वयः। आद्याविति। तारश्च शक्तिरित्युक्तयोः ग्रहणम्। व्याप्त्यर्थतयैतत्सप्तांशकथनम्। व्याप्तिश्च गुणितप्रकरण उक्तैव। यथाङ्गेभ्योऽस्त्वासु सप्तभ्य इत्यादि। अत्राभिप्रायान्तरमाह—मन्त्राणामिति। ततश्चेह प्रणवस्य तन्मात्रमहदहङ्काराः शक्तेस्त्वगादिधातवश्च समुचिता ग्राह्याः। अयमत्र मन्त्रप्रयोगक्रमः। अं शब्दतन्मात्रात्मने नमः। उं स्पर्शतन्मात्रात्मने नमः। मं रूपतन्मात्रात्मने नमः। रं असृगात्मने नमः। ईं मांसात्मने नमः। ह्रीं मेदआत्मने नमः। ह्रीं अस्थ्यात्मने नमः। ह्रीं मज्जात्मने नमः। ह्रीं शुक्लात्मने

नम इति तत्तत्स्थानेषु न्यासः। सर्गी च साक्षरः साकारश्चेति। सकारोऽकारो विसर्गश्चेत्यर्थः। आत्ममन्त्रो जीवमन्त्रोऽजपेति यावत्। षडिन्द्रियात्मक इति श्रोत्रादीनां मनसश्च ग्रहणम्। हं श्रोत्रात्मने नमः। अं त्वगात्मने नमः। अं चक्षुरात्मने नमः। सं जिह्वात्मने नमः। अं घ्राणात्मने नमः। अं मनआत्मने नम इति। हकारेति ह अ इत्यनयोर्ग्रहणम् ॥ ३३ ॥ ३४ ॥

करणात्मसमायुक्त इति। सं मनआत्मने नमः। ओं बुद्ध्यात्मने नमः। हं अहंकारात्मने नमः। अं चित्तात्मने नमः। अं आत्मात्मने नम इति। सवाकारैरिति स व आ इत्येषां ग्रहणम्। वागादीन्द्रियसंभिन्न इति। सं वागात्मने नमः। वं पाण्यात्मने नमः। आं पादात्मने नमः। हं पाय्वात्मने नमः। आं उपस्थात्मने नम इति। ते चेति। गुर्वादिशब्देन गणपत्यादिग्रहणम्। करशुद्ध्यादिकमिति तालत्रयादिग्रहणम्। प्राणायामादिकमिति। मन्त्रप्राणायामाभिप्रायम्। शोषणादीनामिहासंभवात्। आदिशब्देन कराङ्गुलिषु प्रणवशक्त्यादिन्यासोऽङ्गन्यासो देहे व्यापकमात्माष्टाक्षरपुटितलिपिन्यास इत्येतत्सर्वमुक्तम्। प्रपञ्चयागमन्त्रानुसारेणेह न्यास उक्तः। तेनैव प्राणाग्निहोत्रेऽपि न्यासः कृतो भवति। यद्वा प्राणायामादि सर्वं यथाक्रमं पृथक् कर्तव्यम्। यद्वा पीठन्यासमूर्तिकल्पनावाहनाद्यपीष्यत एवेति ॥ ३५ ॥ ३६ ॥

मूले ब्रह्मा बृहत्तया स्यादित्यादि ऋष्यादिनिर्वचनप्रकरणम्। यत् पूर्वमृष्यादिपदनिर्वचनेन तेषां तत्त्वमुक्तमृषिवर्णादिकाविति तदन्वयोचितं ब्रह्मादिपदवाच्यमिहोच्यते। ततश्च गुरुणा प्राप्तस्वरूपः अतएव गुरुरूपः शिष्येण च प्राप्यमाणस्वरूपः सन् परमात्मा तावदृषिः स एव बृहत्तया ब्रह्मा स्यात्। तस्य च विश्वोत्कृष्टत्वात् परमत्वमिति। ब्रह्मा बृहत्तयेत्यत्र प्रतिपत्तव्योऽर्थः। एवं छन्दोदेवतयोरप्यवबोद्धव्यम्। प्रवर इति। ब्रह्मणो विशेषणतया पुंलिङ्गनिर्देशः। गायत्रीविशेषणत्वेऽपि स एवार्थः। गायकसन्त्राणनत इति। यत् पूर्वमुक्तमिच्छां ददातीति छन्द इति तत्सामान्यम्। इदं त्वस्या विशेषफलमिति तयोरन्वयोपपत्तिः ॥ ३७ ॥

परमन्यदतिशयं वेति। परशब्दो विकल्पेन निरुक्तः। अतिशेत इत्यतिशयः। कर्तरि प्रत्ययः। ज्योतिस्तेज इति ज्योतिःशब्दार्थ उक्तः। निरूपित इत्यादिना तयोर्वाक्यार्थ उक्तः। तेजःशब्दस्त्विह विशेष्यतयानुवर्तनीयः। यन्निरूपितेऽन्यत् नितरामतिशायि च निरूपिताद्भवति तदित्येवं परं ज्योतिर्देवता कथितेत्यन्वयः। निरूपित इति बुद्ध्यैवमिदमित्येवं निरूप्ये विश्वस्मिंस्तेजसीत्यर्थः। तत्र हि तदनिरूप्यतयान्यदेव ज्योतिर्देवतातत्त्वं भवति। तस्य तस्मादिश्वतस्तेजसोऽतिशयश्च

स्वतःसिद्धचित्प्रकाशयोगात् स्यात्। मन्त्रान्तरेष्वप्येवमृष्यादि निर्वक्तव्यमित्यपीह दर्शितमिति ॥ ३८ ॥

अथाङ्गमन्त्राणां निर्वचनम्। स्वेति स्वर्ग इति स्वाहेत्यत्रेति शेषः। स्वर्गशब्देनेह स्वतो निरतिशयानन्दरूपं परमसिद्धानां तदानन्दानुभवस्थानं देवतातत्त्वं विवक्षितम्। स्वेति चात्मेति। स्वशब्दस्यात्मात्मीयादिवचनत्वादिति भावः। आत्मा चेह साधकस्य प्रत्यगात्मा भवति। तदेतदभिप्रयन् स्वशब्दं हाशब्देन योजयन् विवृणोति—हेत्याहुतिरितीति। स्वाहेति युगपत् क्रमेण वैतदुभयं क्रियत इति भावः। वाक्यार्थस्तावदेवं लब्ध एव। तात्पर्यार्थस्तूत्तरार्धेनोच्यत इति दर्शयति —हृदयमन्त्रेणेति। मूले धामशब्दश्चिन्मात्रवचनः। तस्य साधकगतव्यतिहारदृष्ट्या प्रत्यक्परागात्मपर्यन्ततया व्याप्तिः। सैव च तस्य धाम्नः शिखाभिप्रेयते। शाखाशब्द इह शिखावचनः। हृदयमन्त्रेणेत्यनेनैतत् सूचितम्। यत् प्रागुक्तं 'हृदयं बुद्धिगम्यत्वादिति तेन सहान्वयोऽप्यस्यैवमुपपन्नो भवतीति। सोऽहमित्यादिष्वप्येतत् प्रतिपत्तव्यम्। होमेष्वपि स्वाहाकारस्येयमेव प्रक्रिया। देवतायाः द्रव्यरस आहुतिः द्रव्यरसस्य देवतायां गतिरित्येवं व्यतिहारस्य तादात्म्यं सम्बन्धनिष्ठत्वात्। उपपत्तिमिति। स्वाहाकारो हि होमादिकरणोद्देशपूर्वकं तत्र द्रव्यविनियोगार्थो होमेषु प्रसिद्धः। प्रत्यग्ब्रह्मणोर्व्यतीहारादेकत्वे सति तत्र तदुव्यवधानलक्षणं विश्वमपि जगद्धोमतया क्षपयितव्यं भवतीति देवतायामपि रसवतो द्रव्यस्यैवं विनियोगसम्भव इति च ज्ञेयम् ॥ ३९ ॥

त्वंपदार्थपर्यन्ततत्पदार्थत्वमिति। तत्त्वमसीति एतावन्महावाक्यं प्रसिद्धम्। तच्चाचार्यस्य शिष्यं प्रत्युपदेशरूपम्। तत्र त्वमिति शिष्ये प्रत्यगात्मा गृह्यते। तदिति च तदा प्राग्वर्णितः परमात्मा। तयोरेकमसीत्युपदिश्यते। ततश्च त्वंपदार्थः प्रत्यगात्मा प्रथितः। तत्पदार्थश्च परमात्मेति ज्ञेयम्। ननु ब्रह्मणः प्रत्यगात्मनैकत्वप्रत्यगात्मप्रतिपादिकत्वमिति हि वाच्यम्। यथा शक्तिपटलेऽजपापरमात्मप्रणवप्रकरण इति। नैष दोषः। तत्त्वमसीत्याद्युपनिषन्महावाक्यव्यापार एव। एवं तत्त्वस्त्वहामनुसन्धानानुगुणतया परिणत इति प्रतिपादयितुमेवमभिधानम्। मूले परिततमिति सर्वतो व्याप्तम्। परं तु तेजस्त्विति। तुशब्दो विशेषद्योतनार्थः। परिततत्वं परत्वं चेह विशेषः। तदुक्तं—परमन्यदतिशयं वेति। मय्यदितेऽस्य मनो यत्र सोऽहमित्युपस्कारेण संबन्धः। तदहमित्येव वा योजनीयम्। मयीति शार्ङ्गिणो वक्तुः स्वात्मपरामर्शः। एतद्दर्शयन् विवृणोति—देहेन्द्रियादिभ्य इति। प्रत्यग्ब्रह्मणोः शबलशुद्धान्वयैकत्वभेदेन चतस्रोऽवस्थाः। तत्र प्रत्यगात्मनो देहेन्द्रियादितादात्म्यं परब्रह्मणो विराडादितादात्म्यं च

शबलावस्थात: स्वोपाधित उद्गतिरितरा:। तत्रोपाधित: पृथग्भावे यद्यप्येकत्व-मेवाखण्डचिल्लक्षणं भवति किन्तु तदुपाधिद्वारेतरदवान्तरावस्थाद्वयं स्यात्। तत्र स्वस्वोपाधिसाचिततया स्थिति: शुद्धावस्था तदान्योन्यैकतान्वयावस्था तदन्योन्याकार-विलयादेकत्वमिति भेद:। तत्र देहेन्द्रियादिशबलस्य तत: पृथग्भावे निष्पन्नैकत्वा-वस्था मय्युदित इत्युक्ता। मनोऽस्य यत्रेति तत: पूर्वतरा शुद्धावस्थोक्तं परिततं परन्तु तेज इत्यपि शुद्धावस्थैव तदर्थं परग्रहणम्। यद्यप्युपाधिपृथग्भाव एकमेव देवता-तत्त्वमर्थान्निष्पद्यते किन्तु तत्रापि यत्र मनो वर्तते सोऽहमर्थो यत्र माया वर्तते स सोऽर्थ इति भाव:। तयो: शुद्धयोरयत्नसिद्धमेकत्वमिति मय्युदित इत्युक्तम्। मूले तदिति सकलचित्प्रकाशरूपमिति वाक्यार्थकथनम्। सकलचित्प्रकाशपदेन परि-ततपरतेजोग्रहणम्। तस्य रूपमेव रूपं यस्येति समास:। ब्रह्मणो रूपमेवास्यापि रूपम्। ब्रह्मैवोक्तप्रकारेण तदहंवस्त्विति मूलार्थ:। कथितमित्याद्युपसंहार:।

प्रकारभेदेन विवृणोति—सकल इति। मूलयोजना त्वेवम्। इत्येवं तदिदं सकलचित्प्रकाशरूपं शिरसोऽपि मन्त्रे कथितमिति। अत्र य: परिपूर्णश्चित्प्रकाश: परिततं परं तु तेज इत्युक्त: तं रूपयति। साधकचिद्रूपतयाहमर्थतयाभिव्यनक्तीत्यर्थो विवक्ष्यते। सोऽर्थ एव च वाक्यार्थमाहेत्यभिप्रेत इति ज्ञेयम्। सोऽहमर्थस्य सकल-चित्प्रकाशत्वात्तुङ्गार्थं स्याच्छिर इति शिरसे स्वाहेत्यनेनान्वयोपपत्तिरिति॥ ४०॥

अजपाया इति प्रत्यगात्मन: परमात्मपर्यन्ततापतिपादकत्वमित्यर्थ:। अह-मिति पूर्ववच्छाङ्गिण: स्वात्मनिर्देश:। मनोऽस्य यत्रेत्येतदिहापि समानम्। सकल-प्रकाशनिर्वाणमिति। सकल: परितत: प्रकाश: परं तेजस्तदेव च निर्वाणमुप-शान्तरूपम्। अतुलमिति। तदतुलममुष्णमशीतं यत्तदित्युपस्कारेण मूलान्वय:। तच्छब्देनाहमर्थग्रहणम्। तस्यातुलादिरूपं परब्रह्मत्वमनेनोक्तम्। पूर्ववच्छिखायै वषडित्यनेनान्वय इति॥ ४१॥

न केवलमनयोरर्थकथनमङ्गोपयोगि। किन्तु प्रपञ्चयागहुतेष्युपयुज्यत इति दर्शयन्नाह—एवमिति। परदेवतात्मतत्त्वं तावदिहाग्निरिष्यते। स चाग्नि: स्वाहाकृतौ प्रतिपत्तव्य:। स एव च प्रपञ्चयागहुतेऽधिकरणं भवति। यत्र हूयते तद्धोमाधिकरणम्। स चाग्निर्देवतातत्त्वस्य साधकात्मनश्च भेदेनावभासान्मलिनो वर्तते। तस्य शोधनं चात्मैव देवतातत्त्वं न ततो भिन्नमन्यत्तदेव चात्मा न ततो भिन्नोऽन्य इत्येवमवस्थापनम्। तत्र यद्भेदनिबन्धनं स्थूलसूक्ष्मादिलक्षणं प्रपञ्चवस्तु तच्च होमद्रव्यं भवति। नन्वग्निशोधनमपि तावत् स्वाहाकृतावस्त्येव। यदुक्तं—स्वेति स्वर्ग इत्यादि। नैष दोष:। क्रमेणान्योन्यात्मतया संहितयो: युगपत्तथानुसन्धान-

मखण्डैकत्वरूपमेवैतत्। अतएवोक्तं—स्वर्गात्मावध्याततता धामशाखेति। द्रव्यसंशोधनार्थस्येति। न केवलं कवच एवास्योपयोग इति भावः। होमद्रव्यं तावत्प्रपञ्चरूपम्। तस्यामृतभावे सत्येवाग्नौ होमः स्यात्। अवरप्रकृतितायामेव च ब्रह्मणि विलापनसंभव इति तदापादनमिह शोधनमभिप्रेतम्। मूले स्वगुणैः गुणत्रयानुबद्धं सकलं प्रतिमथ्येत्यनेनैतदपि दर्शितम्। हरतीति शक्तिबीजं निर्वाच्यमिति। स्थावरजङ्गमाभिपूर्णमित्येतज्जगदित्युक्तम्। निजबिन्दुसन्ततात्माखिललोकस्थितीति। निजबिन्दौ सन्तत आत्मा स्वरूपं यस्या इति समासः। तादृश्यखिललोकस्थितिर्यत्रेति पुनः समासः। बिन्दुग्रहणं संहारक्रमेण नादाद्युपलक्षणम्। अखिललोकस्य प्रतिमथ्येत्युक्तस्य स्थितिस्तन्मात्रतयावस्थानं यत्र तदाश्रयत्वात्तत्तथोक्तम्। तदाह—सर्वलोकेति। प्रकरणादमृतत्वसिद्धिरित्यवबोद्धव्यम् ॥ ४२ ॥

प्रणवस्येति। न केवलं नेत्र एवास्योपयोग इति भावः। अमृतरूपद्रव्योत्पादकस्येति। प्रकृतिरेव तावदमृतं तत्कार्यं तत्तल्लिपिवर्णतदर्थजगद्रूपं द्रव्यमपि तत्स्थूलाकारत्वादमृतरूपमेव। तस्योत्पादकं प्रणवोऽनुग्राहकत्वात्। यद्वा अवतीति निर्वचनं स्यात्। अवनं चेह भावनं स्यात्। अनेकार्थत्वादवतेः। तथाच वक्ष्यति—अवरक्षणगतिप्रीतीत्यादि। सर्वभावक इति च। ननु यद्यमृतरूपमेव द्रव्यमुत्पद्यते। तदा शक्तिमन्त्रेण तस्य शोधनासंभवः शुद्धोत्पन्नत्वादिति। नैष दोषः। सत्यप्यमृतत्वे स्थावरजङ्गमादिरूपेणान्यथाभिमानात् पुनः शोधनोपपत्तिः। ब्रह्मत्वेऽपि द्रव्यतयाभिमानाद्धोमोपपत्तिरात्मब्रह्मतया भेदाभिमानाच्च तस्यापि शोधनोपपत्तिरिति।

मूले आद्यैरित्यकारोकारमकारा उक्ताः। तपनान्तिकैरित्यग्नीषोमसूर्याणां नेत्रत्रयशक्त्यात्मनां ग्रहणम्। गुणात्मान एते। तैरेव चास्य प्रपञ्चस्य भावः। स्थावरजङ्गमाद्यात्मकं स्वरूपं तत्कारणात्मा सृजति। सर्वथाप्यर्थानामुत्पत्तियोगादजस्रमित्युक्तम्। सन्ततमिति च तदर्थः। अभिप्रायभेदमाह—प्रतिहोममिति। मातृकान्यासवदिति पञ्चाशद्वारं होमविधानात् प्रतिहोमं चाष्टाक्षरावृत्तेरेतदुपपत्तिः ॥ ४३

मूले हृङ्काराख्य इत्यस्यांशनिर्वचनम्। हृञ् हरण इति धातुरयमुक्तः। साधकस्यानभीष्टान्यनिष्टान्येव। हरिहरेति हृञावृत्तिरेव। सा च सर्वानिष्टसंहरणार्थेति चार्थादुक्तम्। तस्यास्त्राय फडित्यनेन संबन्ध इति। तारश्च शक्तिरिति तावत्प्रणवादीनां पञ्चमन्त्रतया लिपिसंयोगेन प्रपञ्चयागार्थत्वमुक्तम्। तेषामेव स्वप्रधानतयैकमन्त्रत्वं यदा लिपिविहीनोऽयमित्युच्यते। सर्वप्रपञ्चस्य मूलमित्यस्य विनियोगसूचनार्थम्। सकलपुरुषार्थकरमेतदिति भावः। प्रपञ्चयागस्त्वमुनेति पूर्वोक्तानुवाद एव। तस्य द्विधा प्रयोगो वर्णैर्देहे इत्युक्तः। प्रपञ्चात्मकैरित्यर्थाल्लभ्यते ॥ ४४॥४५॥४६ ॥

मातृकान्यासवदित्यात्माष्टाक्षरयोगेन लिपिन्यास उक्तः। यदुक्तं—शुद्धसविसर्गेत्यत्रान्यैश्चेति। पञ्चाशद्वारमुत्तममिति त्रिमसादिवारमधमादिकमित्यप्यर्थात् सूचितम्। शुद्धादिन्यासेऽपि समानमेतत्। अभिप्रायान्तरमाह—पञ्चाशन्मन्त्रैरिति। यद्यप्येक एवायं मन्त्रः किन्तु पञ्चाशल्लिपिवर्णसंयोगभेदतः पञ्चाशदेव मन्त्राः स्युरिति भावः। पञ्चाशद्वारमित्यस्यार्थोऽनेनोक्तः। यद्देहापि लिप्यपेक्षयैव पञ्चाशद्वारत्वं स्वप्रधाने प्रपञ्चयागे त्वेवं संभवतीति चावबोद्धव्यम्। प्रपञ्चयागस्वरूपं तावदेभिस्तृतीयलिपिभिरित्युक्तम्। तत्र मातृकान्यासवदित्यकारादिक्रमोऽत्रोच्यते। तदाह—प्रपञ्चयागक्रममिति। सप्तग्रहमण्डलत्रयादिहोममिति। तुशब्दस्य विशेषसूचनार्थत्वादिति भावः। प्राणाग्निहोत्रप्रपञ्चयागयोरिति तदीयमन्त्राभिप्रायम्। ऋष्यादिकमिति। ब्रह्मा स्यादृषिरस्येत्यत्र विस्तरोत्येति भावः। मूलाधारेति। मूलाधारे चतुर्दलपद्मे कर्णिकात्रिकोणं तन्मध्ये शक्तिः हृल्लेखा। तस्या मध्ये तदीयबिन्दुः वृत्ताकारस्तत्रापि मध्यभागे मध्यादिपञ्चदिक्षु कुण्डानि। वक्ष्यति च—शक्तेः सत्त्वनिविष्टमध्यमित्यादि। मध्येन्द्रवरुणेत्यादि च। अग्नीन् प्रज्वाल्येति। चिदग्निस्वाहाकारगोचरतयोक्त एकोऽपि सन् होमद्रव्याणां पञ्चत्वात्तथा विह्नतो गृह्यते। वक्ष्यति च—कल्पान्ताग्निशिखास्फुरत्कुहरकेष्वित्यादि। पादादिमस्तकान्तं व्याप्येति। तदावृतिमाह—स्वशरीरात्मकमिति। परमामृतेनेत्यवरप्रकृत्यात्मनेति प्रागुक्तरूपेणेति भावः। एकीकृत्येति + + + ॐ क्रीं चमिति। अत्रैवं प्रतिपत्तिः। प्रणवेन परामृतभूतात् स्वदेहादकारतद्वाच्यरूपं वस्तूत्पाद्य शक्त्या तस्य प्रतीतिसिद्धार्थास्तरताविलापनेनामृतात्मकतामापद्य तदेव चमिति होम्यतया प्रतिपद्य परं ज्योतिषि जुहोमीति विनियुञ्जानः सोऽहं हंस इति तद्द्रव्याश्रयचिद्रूपं ततो विविक्तं प्रत्यग्ब्रह्मरूपं विभाव्य स्वाहेति तस्मिन्नेकवस्तुन्यग्नौ जुहुयादिति। मध्यादिकुण्डेष्विति। मध्यप्राग्वारुणसौम्यदक्षिणकुण्डेष्वित्यर्थः। शाद्याकारान्तमिति। पञ्चपञ्चभिर्वर्णैरेकैकपर्यायेणेति भावः। अकारमिति। स ह्येकपञ्चाशो वर्ण इति भावः। प्रणवशक्तिबीजाभ्यामिति। प्रणवव्यापकेनोत्पादनं शक्तिव्यापकेन तस्यामृतोपादानमिति भेदः। शरीरशब्देनानभिव्यक्तावयवस्य ग्रहणम्। ताभ्यामेव वर्णाभ्याममृतपिण्डमिति। अग्नीनेकीकृत्येति। कुण्डैकीकरणेनेति भावः। ॐ क्रीं अमिति कृतहोमद्वयेऽपि योऽवशेषितोऽकारस्तस्यायं होमो विवक्षितः। इत्यादिनेति। सोऽहं हंसः स्वाहेत्ययमेव मन्त्रशेषोऽभिप्रेतः। नवग्रहन्यासमन्त्रैर्विधिवद्धुत्वेति। ॐ क्रीं चं लं हं मरकतवर्णाधिपतिं केतुं भगवन्तं परं ज्योतिषोऽस्मादिरूपेण मन्त्राम्नानमुक्तम्। एवमग्न्यादिमण्डलत्रयन्यासमन्त्रैर्विधिवदित्य-

त्रापि द्रष्टव्यम् । अग्नीषोमन्यासमन्त्राभ्यां हंसन्यासमन्त्रेण चेत्यत्रापि समानमेतत् । मूलमन्त्रादियोगस्तु सर्वहोमेष्वपेक्ष्यत एव । सप्तग्रहन्यासवदित्यत्रापि विधिवदिति संबन्ध इष्यते । मण्डलत्रयादिष्वपि समानमेतत् । प्रणवेन स्वात्मस्थो भवेदिति सकृत् प्रणवमुच्चरन्निति भावः ॥ ४७ ॥

इह प्रपञ्चयागे प्रणवशक्त्यादिषु प्रतिपत्तिस्तावदुक्ता—आद्यैस्त्रिभेदैरिति । न तु तद्गतवर्णेषु प्रतिपत्तिरिति प्रतिपादनार्थं पञ्चज्ञानेन्द्रियाबद्धा इत्याद्यारभ्यते । यद्यपि वर्णानां काननवृत्तद्वाचीत्यत्र स्थानसम्बन्ध उक्तः किन्त्वग्रमेवेन्द्रियसम्बन्धोऽपि स्यात् । तत्र इई इत्यनयोश्चक्षुषा सम्बन्धः । उऊ इति श्रोत्रेण । ऋ ॠ इति घ्राणेन । विसर्गस्य रसेन । एतेषां सर्वेषां त्वगिन्द्रियेण सम्बन्धः । तस्य व्यापित्वात् बहुवर्णसम्बन्धसंभवः । वर्णानामेवेन्द्रियसम्बन्धात् तद्ग्राह्यसकलार्थसम्बन्धोऽपि स्यात् । ततश्च तथाविधैर्लिपिवर्णैः स्वसंबन्धात्तदिन्द्रियगोचरं सदूरे भवमितरदपि सर्वं वस्तु ब्रह्माग्नौ जुहुयादिति सम्बध्यते । प्रदर्शनार्थं चैतदुक्तम् । यत्तावदथानया पञ्चविभेदभिन्नयेति वर्णानां पञ्चभूतरूपत्वं तेषां प्रत्येकं स्थूलसूक्ष्मादिरूपत्वं चोक्तम् तदेव प्रतिपत्तव्यम् । यद्वाध्यात्मिकाधिदैवतविग्रहयोरैक्यतया काननवृत्तादिस्थानामेवापरिमितत्वं प्रतिपत्तव्यमिति सोऽग्निरपि व्याप्त एव । तस्य मुखमात्रमेतद्धोमादिकरणत्वेनाभिप्रेतमित्यभिप्रायेण विशेषणमुक्तम् ।

स्मर्तव्येति । स्मर्तव्याशेषलोकशब्देन तत्तदिन्द्रियगोचरस्यैव ग्रहणम् । यावान् स्मर्तुं शक्योऽशेषो लोकस्तावानेवायं तत्तदिन्द्रियगोचरोऽर्थो भवतीति तदभिप्रायः । यदैश्वरं तेजस्तस्मिन् ब्रह्माग्नाविति सम्बन्धः । देवतैवेश्वरस्तदीयं चिल्लक्षणं स्वरूपमेव च तेजः । यदुक्तं—स्वर्गात्मावध्याततता धामशाखेति । सदा सर्वत्र वर्तिनीति कालदेशाभ्यां तस्यानवच्छिन्नत्वमुक्तम् । यदुक्तं—स इति परिततं परन्तु तेज इति ।

अभिप्रायान्तरं दर्शयति—एवं समन्त्रकमित्यादिना । विदुषामयत्नसाध्यमिति । मन्त्रन्यासजपयोगादिभिर्विदितदेवतात्मसतत्त्वा विद्वांसः । अनेन तैरप्येवमवश्येयं यत्नेनानुसन्धेयमनुष्ठानावशिष्टकालेष्वित्यपि सूचितम् । मूले पञ्चज्ञानेन्द्रियाबद्धा इत्यस्यायमर्थः । श्रोत्रादीन्द्रियगोचर एवायं विश्वः प्रपञ्चः स च वैखरीवाच्य इति सर्वेऽपि लिपिवर्णाः प्रपञ्चवदिन्द्रियसम्बद्धा इति । यद्वानाहतशिवादिविषयान्ततया वर्णसम्बन्धोऽत्र विवक्ष्यते । तदाह—वाचकवर्गस्येति । वाच्यवाचकभेदेन वर्गद्वयमिहाभिप्रेतम् । वाच्यस्यापीति । वर्गस्येत्यनुषङ्गः । स च तत्त्वगणरूप इति तत्त्वगणस्येत्युक्तम् । तदितीन्द्रियसम्बन्धमिति भावः । त्विति विशेषार्थः । समुच्चयार्थो वा । यश्च शब्दस्तथा चैतल्लभ्यत इति भावः । तत्तदिन्द्रियगोचरमिति

श्रूयमाणमस्पृश्यमानादिलक्षणम्। ततः प्रपञ्चमिति मूलार्थः। आरात्तनं सर्वमिति तद्विशेषणम्। तद्व्याचष्टे—दूरात्तनमिति। दूरभवमिति तदर्थः। दूरग्रहणमन्तिकोपलक्षणमाराच्छब्दस्योभयार्थत्वादिति दर्शयंस्तद्विभागमपि दर्शयति—दूरमन्तिकं चेति। दूरमधिदैवतमन्तिकमध्यात्ममिति च द्रष्टव्यम्। श्रोत्रादिभिरुभयथाऽप्यर्थग्रहणादेवमुक्तम्। घटादिविषयदर्शनसमय इति प्रचुरसंभवादेतदुपादानम्। श्रवणादिसमयेऽप्येतत् सर्वमिष्यत एव। तत्त्वगणस्येति वर्णविशिष्टस्येति च द्रष्टव्यम्। ननु कथं स्वस्मादुत्पत्तिः कथं वा लय इति। तत्राहतशिवतत्त्वमिति स्वयमवाच्यमवाचकं ब्रह्मेति यदुक्तं तदनाहतशिवतत्त्वमित्यवबोद्धव्यम्। तदुक्तमधस्तात्—अधिष्ठानसाक्षिलक्षणावनाहतशिवशक्ती अकारलक्षितार्थाविति। प्रमातेत्यनाहतदशायां न प्रमातृत्वमपीति भावः। तदप्युक्तं—विश्वं प्रमेयप्रमाणप्रमातृरूपात्मविद्याशिवतत्त्वरूपमिति। प्रमातृप्रमाणादिक्रमप्रतिपत्त्यर्थं च प्रमातृग्रहणम्। तद्विभागश्च तत्रैवोक्तः—तत्र मायान्तं मेयरूपमात्मतत्त्वं सदाशिवान्तं ज्ञानरूपं विद्यातत्त्वमाहतशिवान्तं प्रमातृरूपं शिवतत्त्वमिति। अकारवाच्यार्थ इति तत्त्वप्रसरक्रमेण सह तदविभक्ततद्वाचकवर्णप्रसरक्रमोऽपि सूचितः। तेन सदाशिवादीनामिहादिवर्णयोगोऽपि लभ्यते। तदुक्तं—इह सवाचकानि सदाशिवेश्वरशुद्धविद्यातत्त्वानीत्यादि। ननु तत्रैव तावत्तत्त्वानां रूपं सिद्धान्ततः किमिह तदभिधानेनेति। नैष दोषः। + + +। परिणामिन्यपरशक्तिरिति धर्म्यभिप्रायः। परशक्तिरनाहतं वस्त्वित्यवरग्रहणम्। परिणामसामर्थ्यमिति धर्माभिप्रायम्। चकारतदर्थरूपिणीति वाच्यवाचकाविभागाभिप्रायम्। विमर्शप्रकाशाभ्यां वेति + + + वेति। तत्तद्विक्षेप इति। मत्तः परिणममानार्थतया विक्षेप इत्यर्थः। अन्याच्छादन इत्यनुवर्तमानस्य चिद्रूपाच्छादन इत्यर्थः। विषयसप्तम्येषा। अवस्थितमिति चान्वयः। एतदुत्तरत्रापि समानम्। सर्वविषयेष्वित्यवस्थितं प्रसिद्धमेवेत्यनुषङ्गेण सम्बन्धनीयम्। तत्तदवस्थितिव्यपगमेन विलयक्रमोऽप्यूहनीय इति ॥ ४८ ॥ ४९ ॥

मूले ब्रह्मात्मभिरिति प्रपञ्चयाग एव सूक्ष्मा प्रतिपत्तिरुक्ता। मन्त्रकर्त्रग्निद्रव्येषु ब्रह्मतया प्रतिपत्तिरियं भवति। मन्त्राणामर्थतोऽपि महत्त्वान्महामन्त्रैरित्युक्तम्। तदुक्तं—स्वेति स्वर्ग इत्यादि। ब्रह्मविद्भिरिति। देवतातत्त्वं ब्रह्म तदेवात्मानं विद्वद्भिरित्यर्थः। ब्रह्मार्पणमिति साक्षादेवेति शेषः। अभिप्रायान्तरमाह—अमन्त्रक इति। सर्वेषां वस्तुतो ब्रह्मरूपत्वादिति भावः ॥ ५० ॥

मूले एवं वर्णविभेदभिन्नमिति प्रपञ्चयागोपसंहारेणाभिमतमन्त्रजपाद्यधिकारो

दर्शितः। वर्णविभेदभिन्नमिति। यदुक्तं—मातृकान्यासवत् सार्धं लिपिनेत्यादि। बाल्याद्यवस्थायोगाद्देहस्याष्टढत्वम्। मांसान्त्रमज्जावृतमिति जुगुप्सितत्वमुक्तम्। तत्तदिन्द्रियेभ्यो ज्ञानक्रियाप्रसरणात् चरत्वम्। अनेन होमद्वारा देहस्य तद्विपरीते ब्रह्मात्मनि विलापनमुचितमित्युक्तम्। सुविशदत्वं निर्मलत्वम्। विमलधीरिति + + +। तेजःस्वरूपी स्वयं भूत्वेति। तद् ब्रह्मैवेह तेजः। सर्वमन्त्रं जपेदिति प्रपञ्चयागानन्तरं तदङ्गर्ष्यादि विन्यस्याभिमतमन्त्रोदयाद्यारब्धव्यम्।

अभिप्रायभेदमाह—एवमित्यादिना। तेजःशब्देनेह कलानां ग्रहणम्। तदाह—सकलीकरणन्यासेनेति। परतेजसेति। तदुदरभाग इति भावः। ताभ्यामेव सुषुम्नामिति। सुषुम्नाकारेण न्यासोऽभिप्रेतः। कारणशक्तिकबलीकृतजीवामिति। सुषुम्नान्तर्गते मूलाधार एवैतद्भवति। ताभ्यामेव वर्णात्मकमिति। व्यापकेनेत्यवबोद्धव्यम्। तावद्दलानीति दशद्वादशषोडशदलानि। न्यासेनेयं चिन्ता स्यात्। व्यापककलाय धूम्रार्चिषे नम इत्याद्याः। पादयोर्न्यसित्वेति। तच्चतुःसन्ध्यग्रेष्विति भावः। एवं हस्तयोरित्यत्रापि द्रष्टव्यम्। गलास्यनेत्रादिष्विति मूर्धग्रहणम्। विसर्गाद्यकारान्तस्थानेष्विति। मुखे काननवृत्तेत्येतद्वैलोम्येनेत्यर्थः। शक्तिशान्तकलान्यासस्तु विकल्प्यत इत्यर्थादवसीयते। मूलाधारे त्रिकोणकोणेषु शक्तिकलान्यासः। मूर्धनि द्विदलपद्मे शान्तकलान्यासः। प्राणप्रतिष्ठा चोभयविधा कार्येति। जीवकलानामिति जीवस्योपलक्षणम्। तासामिति परस्योपलक्षणम्। पाशाङ्कुशत्वगचरेति। न कलास्वेवैतद्योगोपि तु ऋक्समष्टिप्राणप्रतिष्ठासु वा कलास्वपीति ज्ञेयम्। मातृकां न्यसित्वेति। यदादावेव कृतं समुनिच्छन्दोदैवतमित्यादि तस्यैवानुसन्धानार्थमेतत्। तेन तदङ्गर्ष्यादिन्यासो गणपतेरङ्गर्ष्यादिन्यासोऽपि स्यात्॥ ५१॥

प्राणाग्निहोत्रप्रपञ्चयागशेषत्वेनेति स्वतन्त्रयोरभिमतमन्त्रशेषभूतयोरप्येतत् संभवति। नन्वभिधायेति तस्वे तदभिहितमिति। उच्यते। सशक्तिकमलामारन्यासादीनां तावदथानया पञ्चविभेदभिन्नयेत्यत्राभिधानम्। शुद्रादीनां त्वथ हितविधये विदुषामित्यत्र। यद्यप्येतद्भाव्येव किन्तु तस्यापीह गतत्वेनाभिमान इत्यभिधायेत्युक्तमिति बोद्धव्यम्। स्वातन्त्र्येणापीति। ननु स्वातन्त्र्येण फलसम्बन्धोऽपि तावदुक्त एव। यथा—विन्यासैरथ सजपैरित्यादि। केशवादियोगे श्रीबीजयोगे च श्रीरेव फलमित्यादीति। नैष दोषः। तत्र तत्तदर्थिनां तत्तन्न्यासजपादिकमभिप्रेतमिह तु फलविशेषार्थिनां दशविधन्यास इति भेदः। केशवाद्य इति केशवादियुतः। शक्तिकमलामारैस्सेति युतशब्दोऽनुवर्तते। कमला श्रीबीजम्। मारः कामबीजम्। एकैकश इति तेषां पृथगपि योग उक्तः। वाकारो विकल्पार्थः। सविसर्गः सबिन्दु-

सर्गो मारकमलाशक्तियुतश्चेत्येषां योगः। तेषां पृथग्योगो न ग्राह्य इत्येवं वा दशधा न्यास इति भावः। पृथङ्निगदिता इति। न प्राणाग्निहोत्रप्रपञ्चसहिततया किन्तु स्वतन्त्रतयेति भावः। न्यास एवैवं स्यात्। प्रबन्धेन चैषामावृत्तिरिति ज्ञेयम् ॥५२॥

मूले तेजःस्वरूपी स्वयं भूत्वेति प्रपञ्चयागस्याभिमतमन्त्रविशेषतया प्रयोग उक्तः। स्वतन्त्रतया प्रयोगः प्रपञ्चयागस्त्वित्युच्यते। तदाह—समन्त्रकप्रपञ्चयागस्येति। विशेषत इति शुद्धादिन्यासादितोऽभिमतमन्त्रतोऽप्यतिशय उक्तः। मूलेऽपि यत् प्रपञ्चस्य यापको विनाशकः संसारविशेषस्य सम्पद्रूपस्य यापको नेता परस्य चार्थस्य परो निवेदक इति योजनीयम्। परोऽर्थो मोक्ष एव। प्रकारान्तरेण विवृणोति—विपत्प्रपञ्चयापनमिति। मोक्षापेक्षया विपत्प्रपञ्चो बन्धक + + + तत्कार्यप्रपञ्चः। परस्येत्यर्थः। अमन्त्रकप्रपञ्चयागपरतया विवृणोति—अमन्त्रकप्रपञ्चयागस्येति। वर्णैः प्रपञ्चयागस्तावदेवमुक्तः। अथ द्रव्यैः प्रपञ्चयाग उच्यते—द्रव्यैर्यथेति। तानीति द्रव्याणि। तथैवेति तत्प्रकारः ॥ ५३॥५४ ॥

षष्ठपटलोक्तक्रमेणेति। ताराद्यैर्दशभिर्भेदैरित्याद्युक्तक्रमेणेत्यर्थः। मातृकाविधानेनाग्निजननं पूजा च। तदुक्तं—हुताचनाविधौ मातृकोक्ताविति। तत्र कलायुग्मशश्चाष्टवर्गानित्यावरणद्वये प्रतिवर्णमात्माष्टाक्षरयोगो विशेषः। सन्त्रितम इत्येभिस्तृतीयलिपिभिरित्येतद्विधानित्यर्थः। अभिप्रायान्तरमाह—बीजेनेति। जुहुयाच्च चतुर्वारमित्यतोऽर्वागेतदर्थादवसीयते। संख्या तु सचतुश्चत्वारिंशद्वारमित्युक्तैव। यद्वा विघ्नान्तिकमिति साध्यमन्त्रस्य पीठपूजादिकं कृत्वेत्यादि मूलेन पञ्चविंशतिसंख्यं हुत्वेत्यतो यदुक्तं तत् सर्वं कृत्वा ततो गणपतिमन्त्रेण चतुर्वारं होमोऽयमभिप्रेतः। ततः पूर्वमयं बीजेन ऋचा च होमो भवति। पश्चाद्विभूतिमन्त्रेणापि सकृद्धोमः स्यादिति। मूल एकावृत्त्येति मातृकावृत्त्यभिप्रायम् ॥ ५५ ॥ ५६ ॥

नियुताधिकलक्षसंख्यमिति। नियुतं विंशतिसहस्रम्। लक्षसंख्यमित्येव वा पाठः। मन्त्रीत्यनुवादः। अभिप्रायान्तरमाह—सिद्धिकामस्येति। स स्वैहिकीं सकलसिद्धिमवाप्येत्येतदभिप्रायमेतत्। वाञ्छायोग्यामिति। पुत्रार्थाद्यभिमतविशेषप्रधानामिति भावः। मुक्तिकामस्येति। परतरं च परत्र यातीत्येतदभिप्रायम्। सिद्धिपदमनुषज्यते। प्रणवादित्वं सर्वमन्त्रेषु नित्यमिति तत्पुटनमुक्तम्। मातृकावृत्तिभिरिह सर्वत्र लक्षादिसंख्या भवतीत्यवबोद्धव्यम् ॥ ५७ ॥

एकद्विकेति पञ्चशताद्यपि ग्राह्यमेव। अभिवृत्तिरावृत्तिः। विकृतिमिति क्षुद्रग्रहादिकारितामिति शेषः। प्रकोप इति शरीरेन्द्रियादिविक्रियावेगः ॥ ५८ ॥

द्वादशसहस्रमथवेति पूर्वोक्तशेषः एव। तदाह—होमविधिमिति ॥ ५९ ॥

अयथाप्रतिपत्ति प्रजपादिति। तत्तद्विहिता प्रतिपत्तिर्यथाप्रतिपत्तिः। न तथेत्ययथाप्रतिपत्तीति क्रियाविशेषणं चैतत्। सहस्रवृत्त्येति सहस्रावृत्त्येत्यर्थः। वसुशब्दो द्रव्यवचनः। रात्रौ तिलहोमश्चेति + + + नृसिंहयोगश्चेति सूचित इत्यनुवर्तते। सविस्मृतीश्चेति दुर्दैवतादिकारिता इति शेषः। सापस्मृतिरित्यपस्मृतिरपस्मारः। शापभवानिति गुर्वादिकोपकृताः शापाः। मूले यो मन्त्रीत्यनुवादः। अभिप्रायान्तरमाह—मन्त्रीति। सूचित इत्यनुवर्तत एव। मूले महद्भेरति। महत्या ऋद्धेरत्यर्थः। लक्षं तदर्धकं वेत्यत्र + + + ॥ ६०—६३ ॥

सद्द्रव्यैरिति सद्भिर्द्रव्यैरित्ययमनुवादः। अभिप्रायान्तरमाह—सद्रव्यैरितीति। समुचितद्रव्यविशेषसहितैरेभिरित्यर्थः। तत्तत्कर्मयोग्येति। यथा + + + कार्येत्यत्र व्यञ्जनशिथिलोच्चारणेन मात्रापूरणमित्यवबोद्धव्यम्। योग्यपरिमाणमिति संख्याभिप्रायम्। जुहुयादिति च संबन्धः॥ ६४॥६५ ॥

मूले शितधीरिति महदवधानमुक्तम्। न्यासोक्तक्रमत इति तत्तत्स्थानं भङ्क्त्वाभङ्क्तेति भावः। मंक्ष्विति क्षिप्रमित्यर्थः। विधिना तेनैव लोणेन वेति। सप्तरात्रं त्रिमधुराक्तया लवणपुत्तल्या वेत्यर्थः॥ ६६ ॥

पञ्चाशदोषधिविपाचितेति। जनिते कुण्डाग्नौ घटे पञ्चगव्यं योजयित्वा तत्र वर्णौषधीर्निक्षिप्य यावत्तस्मिन्नग्निरुत्पद्यते तावत्तत् पाचयेत्। तस्मिन्नग्नौ होमः। तदापि पूजादिसर्वं कर्तव्यमेव। तद्यावद्भस्म संपद्यते तावत्तूष्णीमवस्थाय तस्मिन् भस्मनि विधिनाभिसमर्चनं जपश्च भवति। जपोऽप्यस्यैव मन्त्रस्यैति ज्ञेयम्। विधिनेत्येतत् सूचितम्। वर्णौषधीनां तत्तद्वर्णेन संपूज्य जपः कार्यः। फलविशेषापेक्षायान्तु तस्मिन् भस्मनि तदनुरूपमन्त्रस्य यन्त्रविलेखनं पूजा तस्यैवायुतजपोऽपि कार्य इति॥ ६७ ॥

मूल एकादशार्धकणिकेत्येकं पदम्। सार्धैकादशकणिकामित्यर्थः। अभिप्रायान्तरमाह—एकेति। दशार्धशब्देन सार्धदशग्रहणम्। दशार्धकणिकां दद्यात्। सैका दक्षिणेत्येवं योजनीयम्। अर्धेऽर्धपञ्चकणिकेति। सार्धपञ्चग्रहणम्। द्विकणा च सार्धेति। सार्धद्विकणिकेत्यर्थः। निजेप्सितमिति द्रव्यप्रपञ्चयागोपसंहारः। तथा प्रपञ्चयागादपि करप्रचेया इति सम्बन्धः। प्रचयनमुपार्जनम्। यथा करेण वृक्षशाखातः फलान्युपार्ज्यन्ते तद्वदितोऽपीति भावः। प्रभूतत्वमश्रमलभ्यत्वं चानेनोक्तम्॥ ६९॥ ७०॥

इति प्रयोगक्रमदीपिकायां सप्तमः पटलः।

अथ अष्टमः पटलः ।

लिपिरेव पटलद्वयेऽपि प्रतिपाद्या । अत इह प्रकरणसंगतिरेव वक्तव्ये-त्यभिप्रायेणाह—प्रपञ्चयागादिति । क्रमगोपनार्थमिति । परमरहस्यत्वादनयो-रिति भावः । मूलगताथशब्दार्थोऽप्यनन्तरमित्युक्तम् । मूले विदुषां हितविषय इति । स्वेति स्वर्ग इत्याद्युक्तविदामित्यर्थः । अभिप्रायान्तरमाह—शुद्धेति । मूले बद्ध्वा पद्मासनमिति तदुचिततया विशेषत आसनमुक्तम् । यद्वा स्वतन्त्रप्राणाग्नि-होत्रापेक्षमेतत् । स्वासनपूजनमिति + + + ॥ १ ॥

मूले शक्तेः सत्त्वनिबद्धमध्यमित्यग्निहोत्रानुसन्धानमुक्तम् । शक्तिः हृल्लेखा । तस्याः सत्त्वं हकारः । तेन निबद्धं संबद्धं मध्यं यस्य तत्तथोक्तम् । मूलाधारमित्यनेन सम्बन्धः । तस्या एव माया ईकारः स तमोरूपः रजो रेफरूपं ताभ्यां परितो वेष्टितम् । प्राग्रक्षोनिलदिक्षु गतास्त्रिकोणस्याश्रयो यत्र तत्तथोक्तम् । त्रिकोणमध्ये हकारः । त्रिकोणबहिर्मायारजोवेष्टनं तदन्तरेव वा । जठरं मध्य इति जठरस्य मध्य इत्यर्थः । तदभिप्रायमाह—अशनकाल इति । वक्ष्यति च—अनुदिनममुना भजतामित्यादि । योगकाल इति प्राणाग्निहोत्रहुताभिप्रायम् । नाभेरित्यत्र निष्कर्ष-माह नाभिर्लिङ्गमिति । लक्षणयेति भावः । त्रिकोणान्तर्भागे शक्तेर्बिन्दुस्तदन्तरेव कुण्डानीति ज्ञेयम् । तदुक्तं—मूलाधारत्रिकोणशक्तिबिन्दुमध्येत्यादि । कुण्डैरित्युप-लक्षितमिति शेषः । अनारतमित्याहोमान्तमित्यर्थः । अभिप्रायान्तरमाह—अने-नेति । क्रियादिशक्त्यात्मनेति पञ्चवृत्त्यात्मनो ग्रहणार्थमेतत् । क्रियाभेदा एव हि पञ्च वृत्तयः । आदिशब्देन ज्ञानेच्छादिग्रहणम् । तदुक्तमधस्तात्—ज्ञानक्रियाशक्त्या-त्मकः प्राण इति । प्राणानामेवात्राग्निभावः । तेषां समष्टिरेकोऽग्निरिति चाव-बोद्धव्यम् । समतलमृजुतलमित्यर्थः । अभिप्रायान्तरमाह—समो जीवस्येति । सं श इत्याभ्यामुभयोर्ग्रहणमित्यर्थः । तदुक्तं—स्वेति स्वर्गः स्वेति चात्मा समुक्त इति । तयोरेकतत्त्वमेव प्राणरूपेणाग्न्यात्मनावस्थितमित्यर्थादवसीयते । प्रपञ्चयागे तु समयोर्देहे व्याप्ततयावस्थानमत एव लभ्यते । तयोरेकतत्त्वे हि स योगी भवति । तदुक्तं—सर्वत्र वर्तिन्यथ हुत्वा ब्रह्म हुताशन इति । मूले योगीति प्राणाग्निहोत्रा-धिकार्यभिप्रायम् । सिद्धय इति । ते रत्नैरित्यादिसकलफलाभिप्रायम् ॥ २ ॥

मूले मध्येन्द्रेत्याद्यभिधानं वैदिकपञ्चाग्नितयैषां प्रतिपत्त्यर्थम् । कुण्डनाम-कथनमित्यभिप्रायान्तरमुक्तम् ॥ ३ ॥

मूले सकलप्रभाप्रभवकादिति । सकलानामर्केन्द्वादिप्रभाणामुत्पत्तिस्थानभूता-दित्यर्थः । कल्पार्कादिति । प्रलयकालीनादित्याद्द्वादशान्तस्थादित्यर्थः । आत्मा-

वितां जुहुयादिति च सम्बन्धः। अमृतमयीमित्यानन्द एवामृतं भवति। चिदि-वार्कोऽग्निरिति। तदाह—आनन्दमयीमिति। मूलेऽच्छामिति। निर्मलामित्यर्थः। त्विति प्रतिकुण्डं क्रमतो हुतावकाशोऽवशिष्यत इति सूचितम्। तदभिप्रायमाह—त्वितीति। कल्पान्ताग्निशिखास्फुरत्कुहरकेष्विति। मूलाधारे तावच्चिदग्नि-र्वर्तते। तदुक्तं—तस्याधस्तात् त्रिकोणाभमित्यादि। तस्य पञ्च शिखा एव पञ्च-कुण्डोदरेषु स्फुरन्तीति भावः ॥ ४ ॥

चाद्यास्त इति वर्णहोमानन्तरं ग्रहहोम उक्तः। पञ्चानामग्नीनामेकीकरणा-मर्थसिद्धम्। अत्राभिप्रायान्तरमाह—नवग्रहहोममिति। अन्त्यशवर्गेति द्वितीय-होमः। त्विति तृतीयहोमः। मन्त्रीति चतुर्थहोमः। अयं पञ्चम इति ज्ञेयम्। चाद्यग्रहणं प्रतिलोमप्रयोगाभिप्रायम्। पशुमेदो गोमेदः। व्यापकस्पर्शसंज्ञा इति चाद्यानां विशेषणम्। अभिप्रायान्तरमाह—व्यापकेत्यादिपदैरिति। स्वराख्या इत्येतदादिशब्देनोक्तम्। सुमतिरिति मन्त्रप्रयोगाभिज्ञत्वमुक्तम्। अभिप्रायान्तर-माह—परमानन्दतत्त्वविज्ञिरिति ॥ ५॥६ ॥

मूल इत्येवमित्युपसंहारः। दिनादाविति। प्रातरित्यर्थः। शतार्धमिति। पञ्चा-शद्वारमित्यर्थः। वर्णसंयोगतोऽष्टाचराद्वृत्तिरियमुक्ता। तदुक्तं—पञ्चाशन्मन्त्रैरिति। यद्वा मातृकावृत्तिरियमभिप्रेयते। स्वतन्त्रे प्राणाग्निहोत्र एव संभवतीत्यवबोद्धव्यम्। गुणफलमिति। प्रधानफलं तु वक्ष्यति—नित्यानन्दमयस्त्वनादिनिधन इति ॥ ७ ॥

मूलेऽन्त्यशेति कुण्डेषु तेषु क्रमादित्युक्तस्यैव विशदीकरणम्। अभिप्रायान्तर-माह—दशभिर्दशभिरिति। अन्त्यः चकारः। वर्गान्त्या मनणञङाः। असिति विसर्गः। वामश्रवणमूकारः। असिता लकारः। अं इत्यनुस्वारः। हलयुतेति हकारलयुतेत्यर्थः। औ इत्यौकारः। परा + + कारः। फादिपञ्चकं फथठ-छखाः। वर्गादिकाः पतटचकाः ॥ ८॥९॥१० ॥

व्योम्ना मध्यस्थितेऽग्नाविति तस्मिन्नेव वर्णहोमे प्रतिपत्तिरुच्यते। व्योम्ना शब्दमध्यस्थितेऽग्नौ हुनेदिति सम्बन्धः। तन्मात्राणां स्थूलभूतैर्वेह होम उच्यते। सकलजगद्धोमसिद्धिरेवं स्यादिति। प्रपञ्चयागेऽप्येवमुक्तम्—पञ्चज्ञानेन्द्रियाबद्धा इत्यादि। स्वेनैव रूपमित्यग्नाविति प्रकृतापेक्षम्। अग्निना सह रूपमित्यर्थः। अभिप्रायान्तरमाह—व्योम्नेत्यादिनेति। भूतमन्त्रोद्धार इति। भूतमन्त्रैर्होम-मित्युक्तानामित्यर्थः। कथमविरतशब्देन सामान्यमुक्तमित्याहाविरतमिति। स्पर्शा-दिष्वपि समानमेतद्द्रष्टव्यम्। इह व्योम्ना शब्दमिति प्रदर्शनार्थम्। तेन तत्त-द्वर्गभाजामिन्द्रियादीनामपि ग्रहणं भवति। तदुक्तम्—आकाशशब्दश्रोत्रेत्यादि।

उभयरुचिरुचिरेष्विति कुण्डेष्वित्यर्थाद्भवति। तद्विवृणोति—चिदानन्दात्मकेति। चिदात्मकः कल्याग्निः मूलाधारगतः आनन्दात्मकः कल्यार्को द्वादशान्तगतः। ननु तस्यापि चिदात्मकत्वमुक्तम्—चिद्रूपात्सकलप्रभाप्रभवकादिति। नैष दोषः। ज्योतीरुचा स्पृष्टामृतमयीमास्राविताभित्यभिहितत्वादिति। उभयो रुचिभी रुचिरेष्विति विग्रहः। कल्यान्ताग्नियोगेऽपि कुण्डानां कल्यार्कप्रकाशयोगादतीव परिदीप्तत्वमनेनोक्तम्। पुनरप्यभिप्रायान्तरमाह—उभयरुचिरुचिरेष्विति। चिदानन्दात्मकाग्नीषोमदीप्तेष्वित्यग्नीषोममन्त्राभ्यां सप्तहोमः सूचितः। अक्षरौघैरिति। समस्तया मातृकयाष्टमो होम इति भावः। मूले स स्यादित्युपस्कार उत्तरपदेन चान्वयः। सर्वेषां वेद्यानामर्थानां प्रतिमथनं होमतो विलापनं तेन समुल्लासितोऽपरोक्षतया प्रकाशितो ब्रह्मलक्षणः प्रत्यगात्मा यस्येति समासः॥ ११॥

सतारशक्त्यादीति प्राणाग्निहोत्रमन्त्रोद्धारस्तदनन्तरं प्रपञ्चयागस्योक्तः। प्रणवशक्त्याद्यनन्तरमित्येभिः तृतीयलिपिभिरित्युक्तमातृकाग्रहणम्। मूलमन्त्रादियोग उक्त इत्येतद्ग्रहणं च। सूक्ष्ममात्राकृतिरिति। यद्वेद्यार्थेषु सूत्रमनुगतवस्तुमात्रं चिन्मात्रं तदाकारः। नित्यतनुरिति तस्यैव विग्रहत्वान्नित्यतनुत्वं वेद्यं ह्यनित्य + तनुरिति। तदुक्तं—मांसान्त्रमज्जावृतं देहं तत् क्षरमिति। अनयोरभिप्रायान्तरमाह—सूक्ष्ममात्राकृतिरिति + + पूर्वमेवोक्तमिति। कथमित्याह—स्वयं च वर्मेतीति। तदुक्तं—शक्तेर्ध्येयत्वं सूचितमिति। ध्यातस्यैव फलत्वादिति नित्यफल एव नियमादिति भावः। अनेनेति सूक्ष्ममात्राकृतिर्नित्यतनुश्च भूयादित्येतदभिप्रायं सकलापत्तिरपि फलमेवेष्यते। अस्य शक्तित्वमिष्यत इति कृत्स्नशक्त्यापत्तेरभिहितत्वात्। अत एवोक्तं—परमां विभूतिकाष्ठां प्राप्त इति॥ १२॥

समुच्चित्येति तथानुसन्धानस्य कार्यत्वादिति भावः। मूले कल्यादित्यमुख इति पदं मुखशब्दोऽग्रवचनः। चन्द्रार्कयोर्ग्रहतया मण्डलतया चान्तःस्फुरणं भूततत्कार्यसकलजगत्तद्वर्गान्तर्गतब्रह्मादिमूर्तीनां द्वितीयहोमभाजामप्यन्तःस्फुरणं भवति। संहारोन्मुखतया संक्षियमाणया वैतद्विवक्ष्यते। कल्यादित्यमुखादिरूपत्वेऽपि तस्य कल्पितत्वाद्वस्तुतस्तु तदभावादव्यक्तत्वं लिपिसमष्टित्वादनश्वरत्वाच्चाक्षरत्वम्। तेजोद्वयोद्यत्प्रभ इति + + + नित्यानन्दमयस्त्विति तत्राप्यन्तररूपमुक्तम्। यः स्यात् स हंसात्मक इति। हंसशब्देन हंसः सोऽहमर्थरूपं देवतातत्त्वं ब्रह्मोच्यते। य एवमनुसन्धानदृढतया स्यात् स हंसस्वरूपो भवतीत्यर्थः। अत्र स्थूलाद्यं दर्शयति—विष्ण्वादिक इत्यन्तेनेति॥ १३॥

मूले अनुदिनमिति। प्राणाग्निहोत्रान्तरारम्भः। तत्राभिप्रायभेदमप्याह—

उक्तेति। अस्ति ह्यशनकालेऽपि प्राणाग्निहोत्रम् तत्रोक्तप्राणाग्निहोत्रयोगिनामेवाधिकारोऽप्यनेनोक्त इत्यर्थः। अनुदिनममुना विधिना देवतां भजतामिति सोपस्कारमन्वयः। प्राणाद्याः स्युरिति। प्राणापानादय एव गार्हपत्याद्यग्नयो भावनीया इत्यर्थः। केचन मन्त्रा इति। यथान्नं प्राणमन्नमपानमाहुरित्यादि। यद्यपि मूलविवरणपूर्वकं प्रयोगक्रमो वक्तव्यः किन्तु प्रयोगक्रमे प्रतिपाद्यमाने मूलोऽर्थोऽपि स्फुटो भवेत्। न विवरणापेक्षेत्यभिप्रयन्नाह—अयमत्रेति। स्वेष्टदेवतोपस्थितेऽशने पादप्रक्षालनमन्त्राचमनपूर्वकमेतद्भवति। लिपिन्यासस्तु प्रागुक्त एव—भोजनकाले समस्तस्येत्यादि। इत्यारभ्येति। यथा—श्रद्धायामपाने निविष्टोऽमृतं जुहोमीत्यादि। दक्षिणोत्तरेति षष्ठमन्त्रेणापि मध्यकुण्ड उज्ज्वलनम्। सप्रणव इति स्वाभीष्टमन्त्रस्यापि यन्त्रलिपिपद्मकर्णिकायां कल्पनीयम्। परिषिच्योपस्पृश्येति स्वकल्पोक्तरीत्येति भावः। ओन्तद्ब्रह्मेत्यारभ्याचमनमन्त्रः। ॐ गार्हपत्ये प्राण इति। मूले तु गच्छत्वित्यन्ते तदन्ते स्वाहाकारोऽभिहितः। मन्त्रविदामित्यनेन तु मन्त्रविशेषोऽपि सूचितः। नारायणेत्यत्र स्वाभीष्टदेवताख्या चतुर्थ्यन्ता प्रयोक्तव्या।

मूले पञ्चाग्नीनित्यादिना पञ्चाग्नीनामेकीभाव उक्तः। ततः पञ्चाग्नीन् संयुक्तरोचिषः स्मरेदित्यन्वयः। तदर्थोऽग्नीनेकीकृत्योक्तः। मूले गार्हपत्यादिकमिति पञ्चानामग्नीनां प्राणानां च समासेनोच्चारणम्। ततो हिरण्यादिसमासपूर्वं वर्णशब्दोच्चारणम्। शुचयः पावका अग्नीनित्याद्युपचर्येत्यन्तमुच्चारणं चोक्तम्।

मन्त्रं सर्वमनुक्रम्येति ऊर्ध्वादिसा[स्वाहा ?]न्तोच्चारणमुक्तम्। जिह्वाः संस्मृत्येति तासामनुसन्धानमुक्तम्। बहुरूपां तु सङ्कल्प्येति षष्ठीप्रधानजिह्वानुसन्धेयोक्ता इत्येवंविधानेन हुत्वापूर्णं तूष्णीं हुत्वेति योजनीयम्। मूले पचाम्यन्ते स्वाहाकारः प्रकरणसिद्ध एवेति ज्ञेयम्। आपूर्णमिति पूर्णान्तमीषत् पूर्णमिति वार्थः।

उपस्पृश्य विधानत इत्येतदर्थमाह—गण्डूषादिकमिति। वृष्टिरसीत्यादि सर्वं मन्त्रविदामिति सूचितमेव। उद्वयं चित्रमित्यादिनेति। उद्वयं तमसस्परीत्यादिना चित्रं देवानामुदगादित्यादिना च ऋङ्मन्त्रेणेत्यर्थः। मूल आरभ्येत्यस्यायमर्थः। तमग्निमात्मानं स्वमूलाधारगतमपि तत आरभ्यामस्तकमाद्वादशान्तं सूक्ष्मसूत्राकारेणानुस्मरेदिति। अत्राभिप्रायभेदमाह—अथ प्रणवेनेति। मूलादारभ्येति द्वादशान्तस्थेन्दुमण्डलान्तर्मूलाधाराग्नेः सूक्ष्मशिखारूपेणोद्गमनमुक्तम् ॥१४—२१

चैतन्यसंज्ञकमित्यनेन तस्य व्याप्ततयानुसन्धानमुक्तम्। चैतन्यसंज्ञितममुना मस्तकमुद्गतमपि व्याप्तद्विसप्तभुवनात्मकमुक्तहोमतर्पितमनुस्मरेदित्यर्थः। प्रकृतिस्थमिति प्रकृतावस्थानाद्धि प्राणादिभावोपपत्तिरिति भावः। आद्यमिति साक्षात्

देवतातत्त्वमेवेति भावः। अनन्यमित्यनारोपितरूपम्। पञ्चाननेति पञ्चाननानि कुण्डानि। तेष्वग्नय एव रसना जिह्वास्तासु दत्तेन प्रकृतमयतया शुद्धेन सान्नाय्येन तदुचितहविषा तथा भुक्तेन स्वरूपानन्दपर्यन्तं व्याप्तिमुपगतेन तर्पितमिति व्याख्येयम्। केन तर्पितमिति। साधकेनेत्यर्थाद् गम्यते। अतर्कितमिति। तर्कयितुमशक्यम्। युक्तिभिरपरिच्छेद्यमित्यर्थः। आत्मरूपं चेतन्नमिति। हंसः सोऽहमर्थभूतमित्यर्थप्रतिपत्तिमात्रमत्रोक्तम्। प्रकृतिस्थमिति। तत्र सोमेऽग्रेणावेशनम्। पञ्चाननाम्नीति पदेन तस्याग्नस्य तच्छिखाद्वारतां प्रकृत्यवस्थामुपगतस्यामृततयास्रावणं तेन तस्याग्नेः सन्तर्पणं चोक्तम्। व्याप्तद्विसप्तेति पदेन तस्य तदमृतसंपर्कतो वर्धमानस्य व्याप्तिरप्युक्ता। प्रणवो मन्त्रस्तु मन्त्रविदामित्येव सिध्येदिति चेतन्नसंज्ञकममुमिति श्लोकेन सह सम्बन्ध इत्यारभ्येत्यादिनेत्येवमुक्तम्॥ २२॥

सञ्चिन्त्येति पदस्यार्थं दर्शयति—मातृकयापीति। यत्तद्धविस्तस्मिन् चेतन्ने हुतं तमेवं तर्पयद्वर्तते तत् पुनरमृतरूपाणामक्षराणां शतार्धमयेनाभ्यसावसिक्तं सिञ्चेदिति व्याख्येयम्। मूलादारभ्येत्याद्युक्तावस्थयैव द्वादशान्तां मातृकया तद्वर्णरूपेणामृतास्रावणमेतदभिप्रेतमिति विवरणाशयः। तैर्जुह्वित्यक्षरैर्जप उक्तः। प्रयोगान्तरमाह—तत इति। मूले जुह्वित्यत्रोपसंहरेदित्यध्याहार्यम्। अकुटिलान्तराधिः भोज्यानि नित्यं भजन्नित्यनेन संबन्धः। मध्यशरीरमन्तराधिरित्युच्यते। सोऽकुटिल ऋजुर्यस्येति समासः। भोजनोचिततयासनमनेनोक्तम्। सन्दीप्तपञ्चानल इत्यग्नीनां सुलक्षणा लौकिकी सन्दीप्तिरुक्ता भोजनोचिततयावस्थानेनोक्ता। सायं प्रातरिति। नक्तं दिवा चेत्यर्थः। प्राणी न प्रमदोदरं प्रविशतीति। य एवमुभयविधं प्राणाग्निहोत्रं नियमेनानुतिष्ठति स पुनः प्राणी सन् स्त्रिया उदरं गर्भतया न प्रविशति। पुनरावृत्तिहीनां सिद्धिमेव प्रपद्यत इति मूलार्थः॥ २३॥

मूल इति तवेति मातृकोपसंहारः। विरिञ्चेत्यामन्त्रणम्। तदाह—शार्ङ्गी ब्रह्माणं प्रत्याहेति। मूले शास्त्रादीत्यागमकाव्यादिग्रहणम्। तैरुपहिताः सर्वे विकारास्तद्वाच्यार्थास्तेषां सङ्घः समूहो वाचकवाच्यप्रपञ्चः। तस्य माता जननी मूलप्रकृतिः। विश्वस्थितिलयसर्गकरीति + + + ॥ २४॥

मूल इति जगदनुषक्तामित्युक्तानुष्ठानोपसंहारः। तामिमां वर्णमालामित्युक्तप्रकारेण न्यसेदिति योजनीयम्। बहुवचनं त्रिमूर्त्यभिप्रायम्। तदाह—सर्वान् प्रत्याहेति। शार्ङ्गीत्यनुषङ्गः। जगदनुषङ्गो व्याप्तिः। यदुक्तं—सषडङ्गवेदशास्त्राद्युपहितेति। अथोभयात्मका वर्णाः स्युरित्यादि च॥ २५॥

वर्णमालाग्रहणाशय इतीरितेत्युक्तम्। इतीरितार्णमालिका क्रमोत्क्रमक्रम-

गुणिता मनुप्रतिपुटिता मन्त्रिणामभीष्टसाधनविधयेऽक्षमालिका भवेदिति योजना। क्रमोत्क्रमाभ्यां क्रमेण गुणितेति। गुणनमिह द्विरावर्तनम्। तत् प्रथमं क्रमात् पुनरुत्क्रमाच्च क्रमेण भवेदिति भावः। मनुप्रतिपुटितेति प्रत्यक्षरं मन्त्रेणाभिमतेन प्रतिपुटनञ्च कर्तव्यम्। प्रतिपुटनं चैतद्वर्णद्वयापेक्षया सकृत्प्रयोगरूपमेव न प्रतिवर्णापेक्षया द्विःप्रयोगरूपमिति ज्ञेयम्। यथा मन्त्राकारो मन्त्र इकार इत्यादि।

अत्र विशेषमुपदिशति—अक्षमालाया इति। मेरुत्वेनेत्यक्षरमालानां मद्दक्षं मध्ये न्यस्यते। स मेरुरित्युच्यते। मन्त्रसंयोग इति। तत्प्रतिपुटनाभिप्रायेणेति भावः। मन्त्रिणामित्यभिमन्त्रजापिनामित्यर्थः। अभीष्टसाधनविधय इति। शीघ्रसिद्धय इति भावः। इह लिपिवर्णाः शतं संपद्यन्ते। तदन्वयेन मन्त्रस्यैकशतमावृत्तिः स्यादेवमक्षरमालाया मन्त्रावृत्तिः कार्येति ॥ २६ ॥

मध्ये वद्यक्षरयोरिति। ननु मातृकाप्रकरणमुपसंहृतम्। ततः कथं तत्पटलशेषतयाऽयमारम्भ इत्याशङ्क्याह—सरस्वतोदैवत्यामिति। अवश्यं क्वचिद्वक्तव्यमेतत्। तथा चायमेव तदवसर उचित इति भावः। सदवदवाग्वाक्षराणीति दव इत्याभ्यां सहितानि दवाग्वा इत्यक्षराणीत्यर्थः। चन्द्रयुगमिति। चन्द्रष्ठकारः तद्द्वयं स्वाहाकार इति यावत्। ऋषिप्रमुखा इति ऋषिच्छन्दोदेवताः ॥ २७ ॥

श्रोत्रेति। श्रोत्रनयननासानां द्वयं द्वयं ग्राह्यम्। अन्धुः गुह्यम्। ब्राह्मे मुहूर्त उत्थाय देवतां ध्यात्वेत्यादि सर्वमिह योजनीयम्। चतुर्मूर्तिषु हरमायासमस्तयोगि वदेत्यादिपदयोगः स्यात्। करन्यासे प्रणवपुटितैर्दशभिर्वर्णैर्दक्षिणाङ्गुष्ठादि-वामाङ्गुष्ठान्तमङ्गुलिषु न्यासः। पञ्चपदान्युभयाङ्गुष्ठादिकनिष्ठान्तन्यासः। देहन्यासे मन्त्रन्यासावसरेऽयं न्यासो भवति। सृष्टिन्यासोऽयमुक्तः। विपर्ययेण संहारः। नासादिनयनान्ता स्थितिः। ईश्वरपुरुषाष्टप्रकृतयोऽक्षरतत्त्वानि। वदाद्यष्टवर्णैर्दशाङ्गन्यासः स्वाहाकारेण तत्र तत्र व्यापकं चेति विशेषः। भूषणावरणन्यासानन्तरं संपूज्य जपः पुनर्गणितयोगादि सर्वं कर्तव्यम्। सामान्यपटलोक्ता न्यासाः सर्वेच कार्या इति ह्युक्तम्। सर्वत्र दशाक्षरयोगो विशेष इति। स्वरपुटितैरथ हल्भिरिति मातृकाङ्गान्येव अस्या अप्यङ्गानि इत्युक्तम्। मन्त्रीति सर्वत्रादियोगः। अभिप्रायान्तरं दर्शयति—अङ्गानीति। अङ्गेषु मन्त्रयोगः सूचित इत्युपरि संबन्धः। यथा अकखगघङ आं वदहृदयाय नम इत्यादि ॥ २८ ॥

मूले भवभयानां भङ्गिनोति विनियोगोऽपि सूचितः ॥ २९ ॥

अक्षरलक्षमिति। पुरश्चरणमुक्तम् ॥ ३० ॥

मातृकोक्तविधिनेति। पीठं विनियुज्येति संबन्धः। अक्षराम्बुज इति + +

+ शक्तिभिरिति मेधादि नव शक्तय उक्ताः। पीठमूर्तिमन्त्राविति। वर्णाब्जासनाय नम इति पीठमन्त्रः + + + मूर्तिमन्त्रः। मूले मनोजदूर इति कामविवर्जितः। वनितां गीरवेण वागधिपेत्यवगच्छन्नित्यन्वयः ॥ ३१ ॥ ३२ ॥ ३३ ॥

न्यासान्वितमिति। न्यासेऽपि सहस्रवारमिष्यते। तन्मन्त्रिता अप इति तथेति सहस्रपदानुकरणार्थः। तथाशब्देन ध्यानं वोक्तम्। बालया सहेति बालायोगोऽनुलोमविलोमबालापुटितत्वं वोक्तम्। मूले हृदयद्वयस इति हृदयमात्रे। चतुरङ्गुलं को + + कमलोद्भवो ब्रह्मा ॥ ३४ ॥ ३५ ॥ ३६ ॥ ३७ ॥ ३८ ॥

आद्यन्तप्रणवगेति मन्त्रान्तरमुक्तम्। आदिप्रणवगाया अन्तप्रणवगायाश्च शक्तेर्मध्यसंस्थिता वाग्वाग्भव ऐकारः तारशक्तिवाग्भवशक्तितारा इत्यर्थः। भुवि भजमानपारिजात इति। भूमावयं तावद्भजतामभिमतफलदतया पारिजातइत्यर्थः ॥ ३९ ॥

नवक इति दृक्श्रुतिनासाद्वयवदनगुह्यपायूनां ग्रहणम्। दक्षिणाङ्गुष्ठादिवामाङ्गुष्ठान्ताङ्गुलिषु तलद्वये युगपच्च करन्यासः। सुषुम्नाग्रादिषु सृष्टिः पार्श्वादिषु संहारः नासादिश्रुत्यन्ता स्थितिः। परमात्मेश्वरपुरुषाष्टप्रकृतयोऽक्षरतत्त्वानि पूर्ववत्पदैर्दशावृत्तिन्यासः। अङ्गानि षट्क्रमाद्वाचेति वाग्भवेनैवेत्यर्थः। अभिप्रायभेदमाह—ऐं क्लामिति। तदा च तद्युक्तेन तेनाङ्गानीत्यवबोद्धव्यम् ॥४०॥

भसितं भस्म। हरहासः शिवस्य हसितम्। सर्वेषामवदातेत्यनेन सम्बन्धः। विद्यावीणेति। दक्षिणवामाधः करयोरेतदुभयम्। विद्या ज्ञानमुद्रा वा। अमृतमयघटाक्षस्रगिति दक्षिणवामोपरि करयोः। भवदभिमतप्राप्तय इति सकलभोगकैवल्यलक्षणं नित्यफलमुक्तम् ॥ ४१ ॥

संयतेन्द्रियो मन्त्रीति मन्त्रश्रवणमुक्तम्। गूढमर्थमाह—बालायोग इति। वाग्भवानन्तरमितरयोर्बीजयोरपि योग इति भावः। तदा च त्रयोदशाक्षरोऽयं मन्त्रो भवति। तदा च न्यासे भ्रूयुगमध्य इति स्थानत्रयं प्रत्येतव्यम्। सितसरसिजनागचम्पकैरिति विकल्पाभिप्रायम् ॥ ४२ ॥

पूजायामिति पीठमन्त्रास्त + + + ष्टिमूर्तिमन्त्रश्च मातृकोक्ता एव च लिपिपद्म एव च पूजा भवति। संस्कृता प्राकृता शक्ती भवतः।

तदुक्तम्—दक्षिणे संस्कृता पूज्या योगमुद्राकरद्वया।
सन्ततं निःसरच्छब्दवदनाऽन्या च वामतः ॥ इति

केवलवाङ्मयरूप इति तयोर्विशेषणम्। प्रधानदेवतारूप इत्यर्थः। लिपिपद्माभिप्रायं वैतत् ॥ ४३ ॥ ४४ ॥

इह वागीश्वर्या मन्त्रद्वयमुक्तम्। तयोरिति निगदित इति सद्योपसंहारः। तेन

न्यासान्वितं निश्चितधीरित्यादि यद्दशाक्षर्याः प्रयोगजातमुक्तम् तदिहापि योजनीयं भवति। सकलदुरितैः परिमुच्यत इति सम्बन्धनीयम्। परमपरमां भक्तिमित्यत्यन्त-परमामित्यर्थः। मन्त्रीति मन्त्रद्वयग्रहणार्थमुक्तम्। अभिप्रायान्तरमाह—दुरित-मोच इति। प्रणवशक्तिवाग्भवानामन्यतमानन्तरं योग इष्यते। लक्ष्म्यास्तद्बीज-स्येति लक्ष्म्या लाभे श्रीबीजस्य योग इत्यर्थः। प्रदर्शनार्थं चैतत्। फलान्तरविषये तत्तदुचितबीजयोगः स्यादिति ॥ ४५ ॥

मातृकाविभेदानिति। केवला शुद्धसबिन्द्वादिभेदा भूतलिपिरित्येतत् सर्वं गृह्यते। मन्त्रद्वयं चेति वागीश्वरीमन्त्रद्वयम्। चकारस्याभिप्रायान्तरं दर्शयति—मन्त्रान्तरेष्वपीति।

तदुक्तम्—हृदयान्ते भगवति वदशब्दयुगं ततः।

वाग्देविवह्निजायान्तं वाग्भवाद्यं समुद्धरेत् ॥ इति

षड्भिः पदैरङ्गानि।

शुभ्रां स्वच्छविलेपमाल्यवसनां शीतांशुखण्डोज्ज्वलां
व्याख्यामक्षगुणं सुधाढ्यकलशं विद्यां च हस्ताम्बुजैः।
बिभ्राणां कमलासनां कुचनतां वाग्देवतां सुस्मितां
वन्दे वाग्विभवप्रदां त्रिनयनां सौभाग्यसम्पत्करीम् ॥

वसुलक्षं जपस्तद्दशांशमाज्याक्ततिलैर्होमः। मातृकापद्मे दशाक्षरीवत् पूजाक्रमः। तद्वत्प्रयोगास्तज्जप्तजलपानादभिषेकात् तर्पणाच्च मेधा भवति। तज्जप्तगन्ध-पुष्पादिधारी सभायां पूज्यते वादे विजयी जायते चेति।

वाचस्पतेऽमृते भूयः प्लुवः प्लुरिति कीर्तयेत्।
वागाद्यो रुद्रसंख्यार्णो वागाद्यैस्त्वङ्गपञ्चकम् ॥ इति।

आसीना कमलोत्करे जपपटीं पद्मद्वयं पुस्तकं
बिभ्राणा तरुणेन्दुनद्धमकुटा मुक्तेन्दुकुन्दप्रभा।
भावोन्मीलितलोचना कुचभरक्लान्ता भवद्भूतये
भूयाद्वागधिदेवता मुनिगणैरासेव्यमानाऽनिशम् ॥

रुद्रलक्षं जपस्तद्दशांशं घृतेन च होमः। एकादशाक्षरीवत्पूजाक्रमः। पलाश-पुष्पैर्होमे परावाक्सिद्धिः। कदम्बपुष्पैर्बिल्वफलैर्वा होमे वाचः श्रीर्भवति। कुन्दनन्द्यावर्तपुष्पैर्होमे वाग्वल्लभो भवति।

ब्राह्मीरसे स्वकल्काढ्ये कपिलाज्यं पचेज्जपन्।
पिबेद्दिनादौ तन्नित्यं सर्वशास्त्रार्थविद्भवेत् ॥ इति।

बिन्द्वर्घीशयुतो वह्निर्बिन्दुसद्योम्बुमान् भृगुरिति तत्त्वरीद्विरुक्तैर्बीजैरङ्गानि ।

मुक्ताहारावदातां शिरसि शशिकलालङ्कृतां बाहुभिः स्वैः
व्याख्यावर्णाक्षमालामणिमयकलशं पुस्तकं चोद्वहन्तीम् ।
आपीनोत्तुङ्गवक्षोरुहभरविनमन्मध्यदेशामधीशां
वाचामीडे चिराय त्रिभुवनविनतां पुण्डरीके निषण्णाम् ॥

त्रिलक्षं जपः तद्दशांशं पायसेन च होमः । प्राग्वत्पूजाक्रमः । जातिपद्मनन्द्यावर्तकुन्दपुष्पैश्चन्दनार्द्रैर्होमेन वाक्सिद्धिर्भवति इति । एवमन्यदपि ग्राह्यमिति । प्रतिश्लोकं वाग्भवयोग इत्यादावाद्यन्तयोरादिमध्यान्तेषु वेति बोद्धव्यम् । वाक्सूक्तादिजपो वेति । चत्वारि वाक् सप्तपरी द्वे । यद्वाग्वदन्ती द्वे । बृहस्पते प्रथममहं रुद्रे + + दिति वाक्सूक्तानि । नमो वाचे या चोदितेति । वाग्यजुःसारस्वतसूक्तानामादिशब्देन ग्रहणम् । पावका नः सरस्वतीति । यस्ते स्तनः सरस्वति त्वमियमददादिति सूक्तम् । प्रक्षोदसेति सूक्तद्वयम् । सरस्वतीन्देवयन्तस्तिस्त्र इति । ध्यानमिति तत्तत्सारस्वतमन्त्रोचितमुक्तम् ॥ ४६ ॥

मूले अचलात्मजा पार्वती । कमला श्रीः । श्रोतुं वक्तुमशिक्षितोऽनेडमूकः ।

मूलाधारमुखं तदुगतशक्तिमुखम् । प्रभावशब्दो व्याप्तिवचनः । व्रातशब्दः समूहवचनः । योगीन्द्रैरपीति सम्बन्धः ॥ ४७—५४ ॥

अविद्यानाशनीतिच्छेदः । त्रिमुखो त + + + त्रयीस्वरूप इति । त्रयी वेदः । षडङ्गानीन्द्रियाणि चेति ज्ञेयम् । तदुक्तं—छन्दःपादौचित्यादिति । भक्तिं प्रसीदेति सम्बन्धः । सकर्मकोऽयमिहेष्यते । जपार्चनाहवनवृत्तिष्विति ध्यानाद्युपलक्षणम् । देहापदीति । स्वदेहक्षयसमये नित्यशुद्धं पदं स्थानमेति । यन्मन्त्रजपादिशेषतयायं स्तोत्रजपस्तस्य सकलसिद्धिसाधनत्वादेवमुक्तम् ॥ ५४—६० ॥

इति प्रयोगक्रमदीपिकायामष्टमः पटलः ।

अथ नवमः पटलः ।

एवं ज्ञानशक्तिप्रधानानिति । ज्ञानशक्तिस्तावत् सरस्वती । तदुक्तम्—समस्तबोधस्थितिदीपिकाया इति सर्वमन्त्रमयज्ञानशक्तिरूपत्वेनेति च । तस्याः स्वरूपभूता सा शक्तिः परादिक्रमेण स्थूलार्थविषयतया कार्यदशापन्नेह ज्ञानशक्तिर्विवक्षिता । तत्प्रधानानिति । यद्यप्येवं ज्ञानशक्तिरूपा एवामी मन्त्राः । यत उक्तं—ज्ञानशक्तिप्रसरात्मकानां शब्दानामिति । किन्त्विच्छाक्रियाशक्त्योरपि तेषु गुणतया सद्भाव इति प्रधानग्रहणम् । तेन ज्ञानशक्तावपि सरस्वत्यां तयोर्गुणतया सद्भावोऽ-

वसीयते। मातृका भूतलिपिः सबिन्द्वादिविकाराः कलादियोगिन्यः शक्त्यादियुक्ता वागीश्वर्यादय इति सर्वापेक्षं बहुवचनम्। वागीश्वर्या वदवदादियोगेऽप्यर्थाभिधानप्रधानतया ज्ञानशक्तिप्रधानत्वमिति ज्ञेयम्। मन्त्रानिति। सारस्वतानिति शेषः। यद्यप्येवं ज्ञानशक्तिप्रधानां सरस्वतीमित्येव वाच्यम्। किन्त्वेवमक्षराणामधिदेवताया इति प्रक्रमात्केवलमातृकैव स्वप्रधाना स्यादिति सर्वेषामप्यमीषां समं सामान्यमिति प्रतिपादनार्थमित्थमभिधानम्। क्रियाशक्तिप्रधानानिति सर्वं पूर्ववदेव। क्रियाशक्तिस्तावत् त्रिपुरा। वक्ष्यति च—त्रिमूर्तिसर्गाच्चेत्यादि। प्रधानग्रहणात् तस्यामिच्छाज्ञानशक्त्योः गुणतया सद्भावोऽवसीयते। हृल्लेखायामपि समानमेतत्। यतो वक्ष्यति—इच्छाशक्तिप्रधानां भुवनेशीमिति।

ततश्चैतदपि लभ्यते। एकैवोन्मनीशक्तिरिच्छाशक्तिप्रधाना भुवनेशी ज्ञानशक्तिप्रधाना सरस्वती क्रियाशक्तिप्रधाना च त्रिपुरेति। क्रियाशक्तिप्रधानानां श्यादीनां सद्भावात् त्रिपुरग्रहणम्। मध्यमपञ्चकूटः शुद्धा बालेत्यादिसर्वापेक्षं बहुवचनम्। यद्यप्येवं क्रियाशक्तिप्रधानां त्रिपुरामित्येव वाच्यम्। किन्त्वेवं त्रिपुराभिधानां विद्यामिति प्रक्रमान्मध्यमपञ्चकूट एव स्वप्रधानः स्यादिति सर्वेषामपि त्रैपुराणां समं प्राधान्यमिति प्रतिपादनार्थमित्थमभिधानम्। ननु यद्येवं किं मध्यमपञ्चकूटस्य विधानं परिगृहीतमिति। उच्यते। शुद्धा मिश्रा द्विकूटेत्येवमाद्यास्त्रिपुरास्तासां मध्येवर्तिनीयं विद्या। किं च ताः समकूटा विषमकूटाश्च भवन्ति। तथा च मध्यमपञ्चकूटपरिग्रहे सर्वासामप्यासां त्रिपुराणां विधानमुपसंगृहीतं भवतीति ज्ञेयम्। ननु त्रिपुरायाः श्रियश्चास्ति क्रियाशक्तित्वम्। तत्र कुतस्त्रिपुरायां विशेष इति। उच्यते। यत्तावदुक्तं—समस्तबोधस्थितिदीपिकाया इति। तत्र या क्रियाशक्तिः सेयं त्रिपुरा भवति। सा च विमर्शलक्षणा। तदुक्तं—संविदाख्या विमर्शशक्तिरिति। मूलार्णमर्णविकृतिरित्यत्र चोक्तम्—ज्ञानक्रियाशक्तिरूपेण प्रकाशविमर्शरूपेणेति। ततश्च त्रिपुरायाः सर्वमन्त्रमयविमर्शशक्तिरूपत्वेन प्राधान्याच्छ्रीत्रिपुटादिभ्यो पूर्वमभिधानं ज्ञानान्तर्गतत्वाच्च विमर्शस्य सरस्वत्याः पश्चादित्यवसेयम्। सर्वमन्त्रमयत्वाच्चैवं त्रिपुरायाः सामान्यविशेषमन्त्रत्वमपि मातृकादिवद्भवति। सर्वमन्त्रेषु हृल्लेखायाः शक्तिमात्रतया प्रवृत्तिः। तदुक्तम्—अस्य शक्तित्वमिष्यत इति चराचरस्य जगत इत्यादि च। मातृकायास्तु स्वाविभक्तार्थवाचकतया सर्वमन्त्रेषु प्रवृत्तिः। तदप्युक्तम्—त्वगादिपरमात्मान्तस्येत्यादि। स च मातृकायाः स्वार्थवचनव्यापारो विमर्शमयज्ञानलक्षण एवेति गतपटलेषु प्रस्तुतैवार्थादियं त्रिपुरा भवति। किन्तु सरस्वत्याः स्वरस्पर्शादिक्रमनियमो नैवं त्रिपुरायाः कूटाकूटादीनामेव विधाना-

दिति। किञ्च त्रिपुराशक्तिरेव शब्दब्रह्म भवति। प्रस्तुतं—स एवः श्रुतिसम्पन्नै-रित्यादि शब्दोच्चारणकाले तत्साच्चितयेत्यादि चेति। तथा सर्वमन्त्रेषु सामान्य-तया प्रवृत्तानां हृल्लेखादीनां स्वस्वप्रधानतायां विशेषमन्त्रतेति सर्वमुपपन्नमिति।

प्रस्तौतीति मूलगताथशब्दार्थोऽप्युक्तः। मूले विद्यामिति मन्त्रविशेषा-भिप्रायम्। यदुक्तं—उत्तार्थभाजः पिण्डबीजात्मानः पंवाच्याध्यासिताश्च मन्त्राः संवेद्यमानस्फुटार्थरूपा मालामन्त्राः स्त्रीरूपवाच्याध्यासिताश्च विद्या इति। या त्रिभेदा इति तां विद्यामित्यधः सम्बन्धः। त्रिबीजतया त्रिप्रभेदत्वम्। तदुक्तम्—यदा त्रिशोऽथ गुणयेदित्यादि। तद्व्याप्त्यपेक्षया त्रिंशत्प्रकारत्वम्। तदप्युक्तम्—त्रिगुणा सा त्रिदोषा सेत्यादि। तथा—देवाः सस्तुतय इत्यादि। इह त्रिंशत्सङ्ख्या तु यथेच्छं सम्पादनीया। त्रिप्रधानत्वात्तु त्रिपुरायास्त्रिंशत्प्रकारेत्यभिधानम्। व्याप्ते-र्जगदात्मकत्वाज्जगत्यवाप्तेति विशेषणम्। अभिप्रायान्तरमाह—बीजत्रयरूपेणे-त्यादिना। तद्गतबीजबिन्द्वादिभिरिति बीजबिन्दुकलानिरोधिकानादनादान्त-शर्वव्यापिनीसमन्तुन्मनीनां ग्रहणम्। त्रयाणां दशभिर्विभागे त्रिंशत्सङ्ख्या-सम्पत्तिः। बीजबिन्द्वादीनां जगद्व्यापित्वाज्जगत्यवाप्तेत्येतदुपपत्तिः। यदुक्तम्—जगति सततं रूढसंस्थितेरिति। त्रिपुरेह मध्यमपञ्चकूटैव। तस्या बीजरूपेण बिन्दुकलाद्यवसानतया पृथगुच्चारणसंभवात् प्रकारनानात्वोपपत्तिः। यत उक्तं—योगौचित्येन बिन्द्वादियोगः सूचित इति। सर्वास्वपि त्रिपुरास्वेतत्संभवति। सर्वे-ष्वपि मन्त्रान्तरेष्वेवमुपपद्यत इति चाववोद्धव्यम्। मूले सुदुर्लभाप्तिमिति। सुतरां दुर्लभा यस्या उपदेशसिद्धिः गूढमूर्तित्वादिति समासः।

अभिप्रायान्तरमाह—अथवेति। त्रिंशत्प्रकारविषयतयैवायं विकल्पो भवति। त्रिप्रभेदत्वं प्राग्वदेव। वक्ष्यति च—सर्वेषां त्रिबीजात्मकत्वेनेत्यादि। व्याप्तिरुच्चा-रणमिति। वाचा व्यापनमस्य विवक्षितत्वादिति भावः। केवलेति मध्यमपञ्च-कूटाया विवक्षितत्वात् सैव गृह्यते। स्वरान्ततयावस्थानात् केवला सा भवति। कूटस्थपृथग्गती वेति। द्वित्रादिव्यञ्जनमुपर्यधोभावेन संपिण्डितं कूटो व्यपदिश्यते। कूटे सकृदुच्चार्यतया वर्णानां स्थितौ स मन्त्रः कूटस्थो भवति। यथा ह्स्रैं इति। कूट एव पृथगुच्चार्यतया वर्णानां स्थितौ स मन्त्रः पृथग्गतो भवति। यथा ह्स्रैं इति। कूटस्थो दुर्वाच्यः पृथग्गतः सुवाच्य इत्यर्थाद्भवति। कूटाकूटपक्षयोरपीति कूटस्थ-पक्षे पृथग्गतपक्षे चेत्यर्थः। पञ्चानां षड्भिः संभेदे त्रिंशत्सङ्ख्यासम्पत्तिरिति मन्य-मान आह—पुनश्चेति। आदिमादिमनादिं चेति त्रिपुरायामादिं वर्णं वाग्भवमादिं प्रथममनादिं च मध्यमोत्तमयोरन्यतरं च कुर्यादित्यर्थः। कामराजशाक्तवर्णयोस्तु

तदितरस्थानयोः वृत्तिरर्थात् सिद्धा भवति। एवमितरपादद्वयमपि व्याख्येयम्। तथा च प्रतिपादं मिथो भिन्नौ द्वौ द्वौ मन्त्रौ सिध्यतः। संभूय च षट्प्रकारभेदा भवन्ति। यथा आदिमादिमनादिं चेत्यत्र तावद्वाग्भवकामराजशाक्तानि शाक्त-वाग्भवकामराजानि च। मध्यं मध्यममध्यममित्यत्र शाक्तकामराजवाग्भवानि वाग्भवशाक्तकामराजानि। अन्त्यमन्त्यमनन्त्यं चेत्यत्रापि कामराजवाग्भवशाक्तानि कामराजशाक्तवाग्भवानीति। त्रिपुरा शीघ्रसिद्धिदेति सर्वाप्येवं क्रमभेदभिन्ना त्रिपुरा शीघ्रसिद्धिदैव। न त्वेकैवोद्धारक्रमेतिन्यायेनेति केवलसबिन्द्वादिपक्षस्य व्यापित्वादुक्तम्। कूटपक्ष इति कूटस्थपक्षे। अकूटपक्ष इति पृथग्गतपक्षे। सर्वेषा-मिति द्विविधानामप्येषां त्रिंशन्मन्त्राणामित्यर्थः। सिद्धमिति। सुदुर्लभापि या त्रिभेदापीति संबन्धादिति भावः। जगत्त्रयाप्तेति तु तथा मन्त्रवित्सु प्रथित-त्वमभिप्रेतम्। मूले विशिष्टामिति प्रशंसार्थमुक्तम्।

अभिप्रायान्तरमाह—विशिष्टामितीत्यादिना। भेदपदेन विशिष्टामित्यत्र विशेषांशो विवृतः। चकारोऽध्याह्रियते। न केवलं त्रिपुराभिधानां प्रधानभूतां त्रिपु-राम् किन्तु विशिष्टां च विद्यामभिवक्ष्यामीति। विशिष्टामित्येतदुपलक्षणमिति मन्यमान इहाभिप्रेतान्मन्त्रानाह—अविशिष्टेति। केनापि व्यञ्जनेनासंपृक्ता त्रिष्वपि स्थानेषु केवलस्वररूपेत्यर्थः। व्योमेन्दुवज्रधरबिन्दुभिरित्यत्राधरादिस्वरैरियं भवति। शुद्धा बालेत्यन्यापि बालास्तीति सूचितम्। सा च गतपटले त्रैपुराणामन्यतमयोग इत्यत्रोपदिष्टा। अतएवास्याः प्राधान्यमपि गम्यते। शुद्धा सङ्केतविद्या। अन्या तु कुलसुन्दरीति भेदः। हकारादिव्यञ्जनविशिष्टेति। सैव बालेति शेषः। हका-रादिग्रहणेनैतदुक्तम्। रक्ताच्छकेन्द्रशिखिभिरित्यमीभिर्हसकलरेफैरेकद्व्यादिक्रमेण संयोगो विवक्षितः। स चायं व्यञ्जनसंयोगस्त्रिधा भवति। त्रिष्वपि स्वरेषु संयोगो द्वयोरपि संयोगेनैकस्मिन् प्रथमे मध्यम उत्तमे वा एकस्मिन्नेव संयोगः न द्वयोरा-द्यन्तयोराद्ययोरन्त्ययोर्वेति। तथा च सप्तधा विशिष्टा एका च शुद्धेत्यष्टौ भेदा भवन्ति। तत्र द्वित्र्यादिव्यञ्जनसंपिण्डितरूपं कूटाक्षरं व्यपदिश्यते। ततश्च शुद्धा सैकव्यञ्जना कूटस्था पृथग्गतेति चतुर्भेदसंभव इति। सभेदानामेतेषामिति भेदपदेन विशिष्टानां ग्रहणम्। ते चाविशिष्टा च संभूय बहवो मन्त्रा इति बहुवचनम्। यद्वा भेदशब्देनैकस्मिन् द्वयोस्त्रिषु वा स्वरेषु व्यञ्जनसंयोगसंभावि-नामवान्तरभेदानां ग्रहणम्। कूटाकूटत्वमिति द्वित्र्यादिसंयोगे कूटत्वमसंयोग एकसंयोगे चाकूटत्वं सिद्धमिति शेषः। विशिष्टामित्यत एवैतत्सिद्धिरिति बोद्ध-व्यम्। यद्वा समानमित्यनेन संबन्धनीयम्। यथोक्तम्—कूटस्थपृथग्गतौ वा

सुदुर्वाचौ मन्त्राविति। यथायोगमिह कूटस्थपृथग्गतविवक्षेति ज्ञेयम्। सुदुर्वचत्व-मिति। यदुक्तं—सुलभा दुर्लभा चाप्तिरित्यादि। सर्वेषामिति विशिष्टामित्यभि-प्रेतानामित्यर्थः। सिद्धमिति या त्रिभेदापीत्याद्यन्वयादिति भावः।

पारायणभेदेन चेति शुद्धादीनामेषामवान्तरसकलभेदोपसंग्रहार्थमेतत्। लिपि-पारायणवच्चैतदूहनीयम्। तत्राकूटद्विकूटादिष्वेव पारायणसंभवो न शुद्धायाम् केवलस्वरूपत्वात्। तत्राकूटे तावत् ऐकारं कादित्रयस्त्रिंशद्व्यञ्जनयुतमुच्चरेत्। एवमौकारमिति। शुद्धादिभेदोऽत्रापीष्यत एव। द्विकूटे तु कै इत्येतत् कादि-त्रयस्त्रिंशद्व्यञ्जनपिण्डितमुच्चरेत्। एवं ख्वै गै प्रभृति सै है पर्यन्तम्। एवमुत्त-रबीजयोरपीति। त्रिकूटे तु तेषामेकैकस्यापि त्रयस्त्रिंशद्व्यञ्जनपिण्डनमित्याद्यू-हनीयम्। पारायणन्यासो वेहाभिप्रेतः। मूलाधारहृदयमूर्धसु दशद्वादशषोडश-दलकमलकर्णिकासु त्रिकोणानि विभाव्य तेषां रेखासु तिसृषु बहिरेकादशैकादश त्रिकोणानि स्मृत्वा मध्ये शुद्धायास्त्रीन् वर्णान् क्रमेण विन्यस्य परितस्त्रिकोणेषु तत्त-दनुबद्धानि कठबाद्येकादश व्यञ्जनानि न्यसेत्। एवमकूटपारायणन्यासः। द्विकूट-पारायणन्यासे तु बाह्यत्रिकोणरेखात्रयेषु बाह्यतस्त्रयस्त्रिंशत्त्रिकोणानि विभाव्य तत्तदकूटानुबद्धानि त्रयस्त्रिंशद्व्यञ्जनानि तेषु न्यसेत्। यथा खकैं खखैमित्यादि। एवमुत्तरेष्वप्यूह्यम्। ललितायां पञ्चदशवर्णात्मकस्य कूटस्य विधानाद्द्विचशादि-पञ्चदशान्तं कूटसंभव इत्यवबोद्धव्यम्। व्यञ्जनमध्ये स्वरोऽपि कूटतया गृह्यते कामराजविद्यायां तथा दर्शनादिति। अनन्तप्रकारत्वमिति। लिपिपारायणे तावत्परब्रह्मपारायणपर्यन्तत्वात् कथंचित्पर्यन्तो दृष्ट एव। तथा बुभुक्षादि-पारायणेऽपि। त्रिपुरापारायणे तु नैवम्। प्रतिकूटं तत्तन्मन्त्राणां त्रयस्त्रिंशद्-व्यञ्जनानुबन्धयोगादिति भावः। जपो ध्यानमप्येवं भवति। तदुक्तं—न्यसेच्च न्यासप्रिय इत्यादि। त्रिपुरायोगतस्तु यल्लिपिपारायणं यदुक्तमुक्तपारायणमन्त्रान्ते तांस्तान्मन्त्रानुद्धार्य न्यासादिकं कर्तव्यमिति तदन्यदेवेति। त्रिपुराभिधानामित्य-त्राप्यभिप्रायान्तरमाह—पुनरपीत्यादिना। सत्त्वादिपदेन त्रिगुणशक्त्यादिग्रहणम्। विष्ण्वादिपदेन च त्रिमूर्तीनां लक्ष्म्यादीनामपि ग्रहणम्। तत्तन्मन्त्रपदेन बीज-मन्त्राणामेकाक्षरद्व्यक्षरादीनां सर्वेषामपि ग्रहणम्। त्रिप्रभेदादिसर्वं तदनुगत-त्रिपुराश्रयमेव। न तु स्वस्वाश्रयमसंभवादिति प्रतिपत्तव्यम्। संयोगिनेत्यत्र भिन्नामित्युपस्कारः। भेदमाहेति प्रक्रमादेतल्लभ्यते। किंचेह सर्वत्रादिमादि-मनादिं चेति क्रमभेदे फलभेदो भवति। तत्र वाग्भवकामराजशाक्तक्रमः सर्गक्रमो विपरीतः संहारक्रम इतरः सर्वस्थितिक्रमः। तेषु फलभेद उक्तः—

धर्मवाक्सिद्धिकामानां जपे सृष्टिक्रमो भवेत्।
अर्थकामार्थिनां गीतो जपे सद्भिः स्थितिक्रमः॥
मुमुक्षूणान्तु सर्वेषां संहारक्रम ईरितः।
मन्त्राचरन्यासविधावपि न्यायमिमं विदुः॥ इति।

केवलादिष्वपि फलभेदः। यदोक्तफलं प्रतिबन्धप्रचुरं तदा बिन्द्वन्ता मकारान्ता च स्यात्। यदा तत्फलं मन्दं तदापि सर्गान्ता। उभयसंभवे बिन्दुविसर्गान्ता। सामान्येन न तु केवलेति शुद्धा कूटद्वित्रिकूटादिषु च यथोत्तरं फलवृद्धिर्भवति। किञ्च सङ्केतविद्यादिषु विजयादिषु च फलभेदः। पारायणसिद्धेष्वपि च समानमेतत्। पारायणन्यासे तु वीर्यप्रकर्षो भवति। त्रिमूर्त्यादिमन्त्रयोगे तु तत्तत्फलयोग इति॥ १॥

त्रिमूर्तिमन्त्रेष्विति। ननु विद्यायां त्रिमूर्तिमन्त्रयोग इति वाच्यम्। विद्याशेषतयैषामुक्तत्वादिति। नैष दोषः। विद्यायां त्रिमूर्त्यादिशेषत्वमपि स्यादितीह सूच्यते। तेन त्रिपुरान्यासे त्रिमूर्त्यादिमन्त्रयोगः तन्न्यासेषु त्रिपुरायोगश्च यथासंभवं सिद्धो भवति। यद्वा स्वतन्त्रतया मन्त्रभेदोऽयं विद्यात्रिमूर्त्यादिसंयोगरूपो विवक्षितः तदा चोभयथापि वचने नास्ति विरोध इति। त्रिमूर्तिसर्गाच्चेति। तदुक्तम्—अथाभवन् ब्रह्महरीश्वराख्या इत्यादि। त्रिमूर्तयो विश्वसृष्ट्यादिशक्तिविशिष्टात्मानः तेषां सर्गादपि पुरा सती ह्येषा। अतोऽस्यास्त्रिपुरेति नाम प्रायो भवति। त्रिमूर्तिभ्यः पुराभवत्वात्तन्मन्त्रेभ्यः प्रागस्याः प्रयोगः स्यात्। यद्वा त्रिमूर्तिषु कारणत्वेनानुगमात्तन्मन्त्रेष्वस्या अनुगमः स्यादिति विवरणाभिप्रायः। प्रायोग्रहणेनैतदुगम्यते। तेनैतावता नामनिबन्धनं परिपूर्णमिति। तेनैतदवसीयते। न केवलं बाह्यैस्त्रिभिरेव संबन्ध एव त्रिपुरात्वे निबन्धनम् किन्तु तदर्थगम्यं स्वान्सर्गतं चित्वमपीति। तेनायमिहार्थः। त्रिभ्यः पुराभवाः स्वयं च त्रयः सती त्रिपुरेति। त्रिमूर्तिसर्गात् पुरा सती तदीयसृष्ट्यादिशक्तिः। समष्टिशक्तिः तच्छक्तीनामाद्यवस्थायोगिनी स्वयमपि त्र्यंशा भवति। तदुक्तं—यदा त्रिधोऽथ गुणयेदित्यादि। त्रयीमयत्वाच्चेति। देवताकर्माद्यभिधायिन ऋग्यजुःसामलक्षणा वेदास्त्रयी। सा च स्वार्थाभिधानक्रियायोगिनी क्रियाशक्त्यात्मिका भवति। पुरैव त्रयीमयी ह्येषा। शेषं पूर्ववत्। तत्समष्टिशक्तावस्थां तदाद्यवस्थासद्भावात् त्र्यंशयोगः। लय इति। भूर्भुवः स्वरिति लोकाः त्रिलोकी। सा च महत्यपि प्रत्येकं देशकालादिपरिच्छिन्नैव। तस्याः प्रलयदशायां पूरणी ह्येषा। शेषं पूर्ववदेव। प्राक् स्वस्वरूपतया परिपूर्णत्वेनावस्थितस्यार्थस्य देशकालादिविशिष्टतया परिच्छिन्नत्वेन व्यवहार-

योग्यतापादनमेव सर्गः। तदुक्तम्—एष सर्गः समुत्पन्न इत्यादि। तस्य पुनस्तद्वि-पर्ययेण प्रागिव परिपूर्णतापादनमेव संहारः। वक्ष्यति च—एवमुच्चारणात् पूर्वं पूर्णसंविदात्मना स्थितस्य प्रणवस्येत्यादि। तत्समष्टिशक्तौ तदाद्यवस्थासद्भावात् तस्याः त्र्यंशयोगः तदाद्यवस्थापादनमेव हि त्रयीति भावः। परशक्तिविवक्षायां सच्चिदानन्दरूपत्वम्। तदुक्तम्—स्वसंवेद्यस्वरूपा सेति। स्वापरप्रकृतियोगविवक्षायां गुणसाम्यात्मकत्वम्। तदप्युक्तं—पुरा प्रधानादिति। यद्वा त्रिमूर्तिसर्गाच्चेति वामा-शक्तिरुक्ता। विश्ववमनयोगात् तस्या विश्वस्रष्ट्रादिसर्गशक्तियोगतः त्र्यंशयोगः। त्रयीमयत्वाच्चेति ज्येष्ठा शक्तिः। सा हि कर्माद्युपचयतो विश्वं पुष्णती तदुचित-देवताकर्मादिसर्वमनुष्ठानपर्यन्ततयोपदिशन्ती त्रयीशक्तिर्भवति। सा च पुरुषाणां नियोगकारिणी ज्येष्ठाभिधीयते। लये त्रिलोक्या अपीति रौद्री शक्तिः। विश्व-निरोधयोगात् पूर्ववत् त्र्यंशयोगः। तस्यां समष्टिरम्बिका। सा च वामादित्र्यंश-योगतस्त्रिपुरेति। अथवा त्रिमूर्तिसर्गाच्चेति त्रिमूर्तिशब्देन वागर्थज्ञानप्रपञ्चानां ग्रहणम्। तेषां परशक्तौ व्याप्ततया स्थितानां मूर्तावस्था हि सा भवति। तत्र वाचः स्वार्थं प्रतिवचनं व्यापारस्तच्च ज्ञानं तद्विमर्शमयमेव वाक्प्रधानाश्चेते भवन्ति। तेषां सर्गः परशक्तेः परादिक्रमेण स्वस्वारनिरूप्यतयोत्पत्तिः। ततोऽपि पुरा सती ह्येषा। शेषं प्रागुक्तवत्। वागादिसमष्टिशक्तेश्च तदादिदशायोगितया त्र्यंशयोगः। वाक्प्रधानानामर्थानां प्रभवस्थानत्वादस्या वाग्भवत्वं चार्थादुक्तम्। वाग्भवत्वे चार्थात् स्वयं वाग्रूपत्वं स्वरूपप्रकाशविमर्शस्वभावत्वम्। अतएव चिद्रूपत्वमपि सिद्धं भवति। तदुक्तम्—प्रकाशविमर्शरूपेण चिदानन्दरूपेण वेति। त्रिपुरायाः परविमर्शशरीरिण्या इति च। त्रयीमयत्वाच्चेति स्वरूपरसविषयानन्दास्त्रयस्त्रयी पुरे-वानन्दत्रयीमयी ह्येषा। शेषं प्राग्वत्। सर्वानन्दकरत्वाच्चास्याः कामराजत्व-मप्यर्थादुक्तम्। कामराजत्वे चार्थं स्वयमानन्दत्वं च सिद्धं भवति। विमर्शचिदेव स्वात्मविश्रान्तावानन्दः सम्पद्यत इति वाग्भवात्परं कामराजोपपत्तिः। लय इति। त्रिलोक्या वागर्थज्ञानप्रपञ्चत्वेऽप्यर्थप्रधानत्वं भेदः। प्रलये त्रिलोक्या अपि पूरणी ह्येषा। शेषं प्राग्वदेव। तदादिदशायोगतश्चास्याः त्र्यंशयोगः। स्वयं पूर्णैव सती स्वापत्या त्रिलोकीमपि पूर्णां विदध्यादिति तस्याः पूर्णत्वम्। त्रिलोक्या अपीत्युक्त-विधार्थप्रपञ्चनिदानतया शक्तित्वमप्यर्थादुक्तं भवति। विमर्शचिदानन्दतां प्राप्तः अतएव तत्रैव पर्यवसितः पूर्णो भवतीति कामराजात्परं शाक्तोपपत्तिः। वागा-नन्दपूर्णतायोगाद्वाग्भवकामराजशाक्तयोगाच्च त्रिपुरात्वम्। वागादयः शक्ते रूपाणि। तेषु च चिल्लक्षणस्य शिवस्य चिदानन्दरूपाण्यविशिष्टानि। तेषां स्वैरावस्था वा

वासास्यदत्वाद्वागादिरूपाणां पुरत्वम् त्रिमूर्त्यादीनामावासास्पदत्वाद्वाग्भवादीनामपि पुरत्वम्। ननु वाग्भवादीनां प्रत्येकं त्रिपुरात्वमिहोक्तमिति। नैष दोषः। शक्तेस्त्रिपुरात्वे तदंशानामपि तथात्वं संभवदुचितमेव हि भवतीति। प्रायोग्रहणेनान्यान्यपि सन्ति त्रिपुराभिधाननिबन्धनानीति सूचितम्।

तदुक्तम्—शिवशक्त्यात्मसंज्ञेयं तत्त्वत्रितयपूरणात्।

त्रिलोकजननी वाथ तेन सा त्रिपुरा स्मृता॥ इत्यादि॥ २॥

मूले व्योमेन्दुवह्न्यधरबिन्दुभिरिति प्रस्तुतमध्यमपञ्चकूटविद्योद्धारः। व्योमेन्दुवह्न्योऽधरबिन्दू चेति समासः। इन्दुः सकारः। एकमिति प्रकरणाद्बीजमिति लभ्यते। एवमन्यदित्यपि। रक्तो हकारः। अच्छः सकारः। क इति स्वरूपग्रहणम्। इन्द्रो लकारः। रमा ईकारः। अन्यदित्यपि बीजम्। द्युशीतकरौ मन्वमन्तौ चेति समासः। द्यौर्हकारः। शीतकरः सकारः। मनुरौकारः। अमन्तो विसर्जनीयः। बीजैरमीभिरिति कूटस्थतया पृथग्गततया वा योजितैरिति भावः। अत्रैकमन्यदपीत्येवं निर्देशेनैतदपि सूचितम्। यद्यपीह वाग्भवकामराजशाक्तक्रमः परिगृहीतः तथापि नैवं नियम इति तेनैषां बीजानां व्युत्क्रमोपक्रमस्य सिद्धो भवति। तदुक्तम्—आदिमादिमनादिं चेत्यादि। अत्रामन्तेति विन्दुविसर्गयोर्वा ग्रहणम्। विकल्पाभिप्रायं चैतत्। तेन तृतीयबीजस्तभेदेन बिन्द्वन्तमप्युक्तं भवति। इहाधरबिन्दोरमार्धचन्द्रयोर्मन्वमन्तयोश्च पृथक्करणात् शुद्धोद्धारोपिता (पपत्तिः ?) सेयं सङ्केतविद्येत्युच्यते। इह सन्मात्रं परशिवः स एवापरशक्तिप्रवृत्तिद्वारा निरूप्यमाणः परशक्तिर्भवति। तदपरशक्तिमात्रं शब्दार्थपरसमष्टिः स एव स्वाधिष्ठानपरशिवशक्तिविमर्शलक्षणः सत्कारः। तदुक्तम्—अनाहतशिवशक्तौ अकारलक्षितार्थाविति। स चैवं परशिवशक्तिविमर्शमात्रतयान्तर्मुखोऽपि संस्तदा ह। अनेनैव त्रिमूर्तिसर्गाच्चेति उक्तविधवाक्प्रपञ्चप्रसवस्थानतया तदुचितयोन्या खेकारपरिग्रहोऽपि सन् वाग्भव ऐकारो भवति। विमर्शयोगितया च सद्रूपः परशिवः प्रकाशलक्षणोऽपि भवति। स च प्रकाशविमर्शस्य स्वरूपविश्रान्ततयानन्दो भवति। तदीयो विमर्श एवानन्दनम् तदुचिततया सोऽकारो वाङ्मात्ररूपोऽवस्थान्तरं प्राप्नुवन्निकारः। स चैवमन्तर्मुखोऽपि संस्त्रयीमयत्वाच्चेत्युक्तस्वरूपरसविषयानन्दतया विप्लवत्वाच्छक्त्यात्मकत्वाच्च तदुचितमोकारं परिगृह्णन् कामराज ईकारो भवति। स चानन्दरूपः प्रकाशस्तदीयानन्दनरूपविमर्शस्य तत्रैव पर्यवसितत्वात्पूर्णो भवति। तदीयश्च सविसर्श इकाररूपोऽवस्थान्तरं प्राप्नुवन्नुकारः स चैवमन्तर्मुखोऽपि सन् लये त्रिलोक्या अपीत्युक्तरूपसकलार्थनिदानशक्तिस्तत्स्वभावभूतोन्मेषोनतारूपत्वाच्छक्तित्वाच्च तदु-

चितमूकारं तथानुवृत्तस्वप्रकाशरूपा + + रोधित्सयादितोकारं वाङ्मात्ररूपं च परिगृह्णन्नौकारः शक्तिर्भवति। सेयं शुद्धा सकलवर्णेषु स्वस्वार्थप्रत्ययपरेषु नित्यत्वादेकद्वित्र्यादिवर्णयोगिनी स्यात्। सर्वन्यासेषु च वर्णपदादिवाचकाना-मियान् त्रिरूपो विमर्शव्यापारोऽभिप्रेत एव।

तदुक्तम्—कृतकृत्यस्य जगति सततं रूढसंस्थितेः॥ इति।

वागैश्वर्यातिशयदत्येत्यत्र बालासिद्धिः वाग्भवं बीजमित्युक्तविधे वाग्भवं प्रतीयते। कामराजमुक्तमिति चाजकलाप्रथमावशान्तिभिरिति वक्ष्यमाणं कामबीजमपि प्रतीयते। शाक्तमिति च शक्तिसमूहस्य सकारौकारविसर्गरूपस्य प्रतीतिरिति। यदुक्तं —सकाररूपिणी शक्तिरिति। विसर्गः प्रकृतिर्मतेति च। सेयं कुलसुन्दरीत्युच्यते।

बालायास्त्रिषु बीजेषु विजयोपरि ह्री यदि।
जीवविद्या सकारश्चेच्छिवविद्या ह्यसौ यदि॥
सह्रौ चेच्छक्तिविद्यैषा कामाख्या त्रिष्वपि युक्।
मायाद्या मोहनी बाला तन्मध्या क्षोभणी मता॥
तदन्ता क्लेदनी सैव श्रीकण्ठाद्या महोदया।
शोधनीत्वं प्रतिष्ठाद्या क्लेमन्ता मोहनी तु चेत्॥
मालिनी पञ्चकूटं चेत् सिद्धा बीजेष्वपि त्रिषु।
शुद्धा त्रिष्वपि बीजेषु निष्कला वाग्भवे तु वाक्॥
सिद्धैर्वोर्ध्वं त्रिरेफेभ्यो उकारे त्वंबिका भवेत्।
सिद्धा याष्टककारोर्ध्वं भूमेरेवोनलान्मरुत्॥
त्रिषु बीजेष्वपि स्याच्चेत् + + + +।
बालेव कामवाक्छक्तिष्वनन्तानुत्तरारुणाः॥
प्राक्छान्तियोनिशूलेभ्यो यदि सम्पत्करी भवेत्॥

[अत्रादर्शपुस्तके श्लोकैकः पतितः]

सरमार्धचन्द्रैरित्यत्राभिप्रायान्तरं दर्शयति—सकाररूपिणीत्यादिना। सो रमतेऽस्मिन्निति सरो हकारः। कथमियता हकारसिद्धिरिति। तत्प्रकारोऽपोह्योच्यते। सस्तावच्छक्तिः। तदुक्तम्—स इति प्रकृतिर्मतेति। शक्तिश्च शिवे रमते। हकारश्च शिवः। तदप्युक्तम्—हकारः शिव इत्युक्त इति। तथा च सरो हकारो भवतीत्यर्थः। निष्कीलविद्योद्धारप्रकार इति। कीलमाविलम्। तदुक्तम्—वाग्भवः सन्निराविल इति। तद्रहिता निष्कीलविद्या सा च प्रकृतविद्यैव। सा च मध्य-मपञ्चकूटा विश्वविद्योच्यते। त्रिंशत्प्रकारापोत्युक्तनयेन सर्वपञ्चकूटा सिद्धा विद्यापि

निष्कीला संभवति। तस्यामुत्पत्तिसिद्धायामपि कीलयोगः अत एव गम्यते। तदुद्धारे तद्विपरीतवर्णयोगे च कृते सैव निष्कीला भवति। यथा वनदुर्गायां वक्ष्यति—वातम्म इत्यक्षराणीत्यादि। मन्त्रशक्तीनां नित्यावदाततया कीलासंभवेऽपि कार्यविशेषापर्याप्तिर्वर्णविशेषतः स्यात्। तत्र तत्कार्यकरवर्णयोगोऽपि कार्य एवेति कीलोद्धारोपपत्तिः। इह सरद्वयस्य तन्मन्त्रेणोपादानमित्यवबोद्धव्यम्। सरः सर इति रेफान्वितः सन् हकार इति च तदर्थः। तस्य चेकारबिन्दुयोगः। तथा चेयं भुवनेशी भवति। तदवयवेन क्रमेण केवलरेफस्य कीलतयोद्धार इह विवक्षितः। वक्ष्यति च अङ्गाभिधाने—हसकलह्रामित्यादि। यद्वा निष्कीलविद्याग्रहणं ललिताभिप्रायम्। त्रिपुरसुन्दरीविद्यायामिह कीलोद्धारः। ललिताया वाग्भवमात्रमेतदुद्धृतम्। शेषं समानमेवेति।

तदुक्तम्—द्वावन्त्यौ कामशक्त्याख्यौ वर्णौ निष्कीलकौ मतौ॥ इति।

यद्वा कामराजशाक्तयोरपोह्योद्धारोऽभिप्रेत एव। रक्ताच्छकेन्द्रशिखिभिरित्येतदावर्तनीयम्। क्वचिद्रक्ताच्छकेन्द्रशिखिभिः सद्वो रक्ताच्छकेन्द्रशिखिभिरिति च योजना। क्वचिदिति चास्यामेव मध्यमबीजाभिप्रायम्। रक्तः सकारः। तेन शक्तिस्तृतीयबीजं लक्ष्यते। शक्तिबीजे यो हकारो रक्ताच्छकेन्द्रशिखिभिरिति सामान्यविधानप्राप्तः सोच्छेरक्तो रक्ताच्छः स के शिरस्युपरि यस्य स रक्ताच्छकः। इन्द्रशिखी चेन्द्रशिखिरक्ताच्छक इन्द्रशिखी येष्विति विशेषणपदस्य समासः। तेनैतदुक्तं भवति। ललितायां शाक्तबीजे नास्त्यादितो हकारः। कामराजबीजे तु स लकारात्पूर्वमधिकृतोऽस्तीति। ततश्च कृत्स्ना ललितेह सिद्धा भवति। तदेतदधस्ताद्गुणितप्रकरणे सूचितम्—शक्तिः कामाग्निनादात्मा गूढमूर्तिः प्रतीयते। इति। किञ्च तत्र सकलजगदधीशा शाश्वता विश्वयोनिरित्यत्र कामराजविद्योद्धारोऽपि सूचितः। तत्र सकलजगदधीशेति शाक्तमुक्तम्। सकारादिवर्णत्रयं भुवनेशी चेति। शाश्वतेति विशेषणयोगे कामराजमप्युक्तम्। सकौ लजगदधीशेति समासः। शाश्वतेत्यावृत्त्या विशेषणद्वयं भवति। शाश्वतं शिवो हकारस्तद्योगादियं शाश्वता भवति। तद्योगश्च सति पृथक्करणात् तदुपरीत्यवसीयते। पुनः शाश्वत + यस्याः सा शाश्वतेति समासनीयम्। अ इति तरत्स्थानस्य शिरसो ग्रहणम्। तेनादावपि हकारयोगः सिद्धो भवति। वाग्भवोद्धारे तु शाश्वता विश्वयोनिरेकारो यस्यामिति समासः। तद्योगश्चानेनो + क्तति च + कारोपरि भवति। सका ककारसहिता लजगदधीशेति समासः। अत्र कारस्य पृथक्करणात्तदुपरि तद्योगोऽवसीयत इति॥ २॥

मूले वागीश्वर्यातिशयदतयेति त्रिबीजानां वाग्भवादितया प्रसिद्धिस्तन्निबन्धनं चोच्यते। त्रैलोक्यक्षोभणेत्यादिपदमपि हेतुगर्भं विशेषणम्। त्रैलोक्यपदं वशता-कृष्टीत्यत्रापि सम्बध्यते। क्ष्वेलापहरकविताकारकमित्येतदपि हेतुगर्भमेव। क्ष्वेलग्रहणं दुष्प्रतिहरसकलदुरितरोगभयाद्युपलक्षणम्। तथा चात्राप्यतिशय उक्तो भवति। अत्राभिप्रायान्तरमाह—व्यस्तविनियोगोक्तिर्वागीश्वर्येतीति। त्रिपुराबीजानां त्रयाणां व्यस्तानामपि साधनमस्तीत्यप्यनेनोक्तम्। विश्वविद्यायां बालायां शुद्धा-यामन्या + मपि त्रैपुरविद्यानां वाग्भवबीजं केवलमेव वागीश्वर्यातिशयार्थिभिः साधनीयम्। तासामेव कामराजं विश्वक्षोभणाद्यर्थिभिरित्यभिप्रायः। त्रिपुर-सुन्दर्यामपि समानमेतत्। किन्तु कामराजप्रधाना सा भवति। तदुक्तमियं मध्यमबीजप्रधाना विद्या बीजत्रयेऽपि कामराजसंयोगादिति। तत्र वाग्भवशाक्तयो-रपि जगत्क्षोभणादिसमुच्चयो द्रष्टव्यः। मन्त्रमित्यादिविशेषस्याभिप्रायमाह—धर्मेति समस्तविनियोगोक्तिरिति। त्रिपुरसुन्दरी तु + + समस्ता द्विधा भवति। तत्र त्रिबीजोक्ताया भुवनेश्वर्याः सकृदन्त एव योग एकबीजा भवति। तच्च सरमार्धचन्द्रैरिति सकृद्योजनायां सिद्धं भवति। तदुक्तं + + ॥ ४ ॥

मूले नाभिरथाचरणमित्यादिन्यासप्रकरणम्। तत्र यत्सामान्यकर्तव्यं तद्दीक्षा-पटल उक्तम्—अथ पुनराचम्य गुरुरित्यादि। तत्र लिपिन्यासानन्तरमङ्गुलीषु क्रमादङ्गैरित्यादिन्यासानन्तरं नाभिरथाचरणमित्यादि सर्वं कार्यम्। पुनरङ्गर्ष्यादि-न्यासः। तदाह—अङ्गषट्कममुना विधायेति। मूले त्वृष्यादिन्यासो नावश्यक इति तदकथनम्। किं पुनस्तदिति तदाहादिनाथेति। त्रिपुराभैरवी सर्वेषां त्रैपुराणां देवता। यद्वा मध्यमपञ्चकूटस्यैव + + बालादीनां तु सा सा देवता ग्राह्या। यथा बालायाः कुलसुन्दरी शुद्धाया अपि सैव। विजयायास्त्रिपुरविजया मोहिन्यास्त्रिपुरमालिनी सिद्धायास्त्रिपुरसिद्धा कामराजनिष्कीलविद्ययोस्त्रिपुर-सुन्दरीत्याद्यूह्यमिति। तथा ब्रह्मादिमन्त्रयोगेऽपि ब्रह्मरूपिणी त्रिपुरभैरवीत्या-द्यूह्यम्। वक्ष्यति च श्रीपटले। वाग्भवकामराजाविति। ह्सैं बीजम्। [मध्यमन्त्यं वा] शक्तिरिति भावः। तत्तन्मन्त्रेषु तत्तद्वाग्भवकामराजयोरेवं भवति। नाभिरथा-चरणमित्यथशब्दो न्यासप्रकरणारम्भार्थः। अभिप्रायान्तरमाह—पीठमूर्तिन्यासे-त्यादिना। ब्राह्मे मुहूर्ते उत्थाय देवतां ध्यात्वेत्यादि सर्वमिह समानम्। तत्र प्रबोधसमये स्वनाममहावाक्यमूलमन्त्राजपापरमात्ममन्त्रप्रणवैरात्मानुसन्धानं कृत्वोत्थानं कार्यम्। पुनर्गतदिनकर्मसमर्पणविधौ च गुरुसमष्टिमन्त्रेण शिरस्यञ्जलिं कृत्वा ऋष्यादिन्यासं विधाय देवतां ध्यात्वा मानसपूजां कृत्वा गतदिनकृतकर्म-

समर्पणं कृत्वा योगं विधायोपसंहरेत्। पुनस्तथा शिरस्यञ्जलिं कृत्वा गुरुगणपतिमन्त्रं स्वास्त्रेण तालत्रयादि च कृत्वा प्रणवप्राणायामं सकृन्मातृकान्यासं मूलप्राणायामं तदङ्गैरुभयाङ्गुष्ठादिकलान्तन्यासं मूलेन देहव्यापकं च कृत्वा मूलं समस्तव्यस्तसमस्तसमस्तं मूलाधारादिषु न्यस्याङ्गर्ष्यादिन्यासं विधाय मानसपूजापूर्वकं मूलं त्रिवारं परिजप्य प्रागुक्तवैलोम्येन षोडशान्तादिष्वानन्दार्णवादीन् विभावयेत्। सर्वेश्वरादयः सर्वत्र स्वशक्तिभिर्मूलप्रकृत्युमालक्ष्मीसरस्वतीभिर्युक्ताः स्युरिति विशेषः। मानसपूजां कृत्वा त्रिवारं मूलं परिजप्य तद्दिनकरिष्यमाणकर्मसमर्पणमपि विधाय योगं विधायाजपापरमात्मप्रणवयोगानपि कृत्वाङ्गर्ष्यादि कुर्यात्। स्नानेऽप्येवं सर्वं योजनीयम्। जपस्थानं कृत्वा लिपिपद्मकर्णिकागतत्रैपुरमध्ये तज्जीवतज्जीवतयोपविश्य गुरुवन्दनमाचरेत्। तत्र ॐ क्लीं परप्रकाशानन्दाद्यशेषगुरुपारम्पर्यक्रमेण स्वगुरुपादाम्बुजं यावत्तावत् प्रणमामीति गुरुसमष्टिमन्त्रेण शिरस्यञ्जलिं कृत्वा ॐ क्लीं परगुरुपादुकाभ्यो नमः। ॐ क्लीं परावरगुरुपादुकाभ्यो नमः। ॐ क्लीं अपरगुरुपादुकाभ्यो नमः। इति त्रिगुरुमन्त्रैरपि। ॐ क्लीं परप्रकाशानन्दनाथश्रीपादुकां पूजयामीत्यादि वक्ष्यमाणगुरुव्यष्टिमन्त्रैरपि शिरस्यञ्जलिं विधाय गुं अस्मद्गुरुभ्यो नमः। गं गणपतये नमः। दुं दुर्गायै नमः। सां सरस्वत्यै नमः। क्षं क्षेत्रपालाय नमः इत्यंसोर्वंशेषु। क्लीं परशक्त्यै नम इति हृदये च नत्वास्त्रेण कराङ्गुलिशोधनतालत्रयादिसर्वं कृत्वा करादिमन्त्रैः पादादिमस्तकान्तं व्यापकं विधाय जीवरक्षां विभाव्य + + प्राणायामं सलिपिन्यासमित्यत्र विहितप्रकारेण वा वक्ष्यमाणवेधकप्राणायामैर्वा भुवनेश्वर्यादिपटलभाविरीत्या वा देहशुद्धिं विधाय नित्यलिपिन्यास + + प्राणाग्निहोत्रप्रपञ्चयागसकलीकरणान्यपि कुर्यात्। तत्र च मूलमनुवर्तनीयम्। तदुक्तं—प्रणवशक्तिमूलमन्त्रादियोग इत्यादि। ततो मन्त्रोदयमन्त्रप्राणायामाद्यष्यादिन्यासबीजादिप्रतिपत्तिमन्त्रव्याप्त्यनुस्मरणानि च कृत्वा पीठन्यासमारभेतेति दीक्षापटलेऽतः सिद्धमिति। पीठन्यासादिषु विशेषमभिधत्ते—पीठन्यासमित्यादिना। यद्दीक्षापटल उक्तमाधारशक्तिमूलप्रकृतीत्यादि तत्सर्वमिह प्राप्तम्। तत्रामृतार्णवादिविशेषोऽयमभिधीयते। यद्वा सर्वविधानेषु विकल्पाभिप्रायमेतत्। धर्मादिकं वरदान्तमिति धर्मादिचतुष्कं वरदं चेत्यर्थः। पीठमध्ये पादौ वरद इति ज्ञेयम्। अधर्मादिकमित्यवरदान्तमित्यर्थादवसेयम्। पीठमध्यफलकमवरद इति ज्ञेयम्। मूले तु वरदावरदौ नोक्ताविति पुनरनन्तपद्ममण्डलगुणात्मत्रयन्यासं कृत्वा नवशक्तीर्न्यसेत्। तदाहेच्छाज्ञानेति। वक्ष्यति च—वामादि-

शक्तिसहितं परिपूज्य पीठमित्यादि। मूलबीजैरिति यस्या विद्याया मन्त्रोदयादि कृतं तस्या वाग्भवादिबीजैस्त्रिभिरित्यर्थः। तेषां व्युत्क्रमे प्रक्रमे च तदुपपत्त्या न्यासो द्रष्टव्यः। हृदीति। हृदि हि पीठपद्मकर्णिका भवति। तत्र च नवयोनिचक्रं तन्मध्ये च त्रिकोणमित्येवमुक्तम्। त्रिकोणरेखात्रय इति। प्रागादिरेखासु प्रादक्षिण्येनेति भावः। कोणबाह्येष्विति। अग्न्यादिकोणानां बाह्यप्रदेशेष्विति भावः। कोणत्रितय इति। अग्न्यादिकोणप्रदेशेष्वन्तरिति भावः। वामादीनामष्टाश्रमध्ययोगिस्थानपक्षे तु तथा न्यासः स्यात्। पुनश्चतुष्पीठन्यास इति। समस्तयोगादीड्याणपीठस्य प्राधान्यमवसीयते। इह धर्मादीनां नवयोनीनां चतुष्पीठानां च यद्यप्यन्यथा स्थितिर्भवति किन्तु तेषामेषु स्थानेषु सन्निधानमित्येव न्यासोपपत्तिः। पूजितानां योगो युक्तानां पूजेति विशेषसंभवः। पीठसमष्टिमन्त्रमाह—ऐं परायै इति। एवं पीठन्यास उक्तः। अथान्तरा पादुकान्यासमाह—पादुकाः समेत्यादिना। न्यसेदित्यस्य कुत्रेत्यपेक्षायां मन्त्राम्नानानन्तरमाह—शिरसीति। संप + ते। अथ मूर्तिन्यासमाह—ऐं क्लीं सौः इति।

तत आवाहनादिकमिति। तदुक्तमावाहनस्थापनेत्यादि। ततः करन्यासाङ्गुलिन्यासाविति। करयोस्तलपृष्ठपार्श्वेषु मूलेन व्यापय्य बीजैस्त्रिभिर्न्यसत्वित्यमुं न्यासं च कुर्यात्। अयं करन्यासः। तत्राङ्गुलिन्यास इति। मध्यमादिकनिष्ठान्तमङ्गुष्ठतर्जनीतलेषु च त्रिबीजानां न्यासः पूर्वं कार्यः। त्रिपुरसुन्दर्यान्तु विशेषः।

> न्यसेद्बीजानि विद्यायाः पञ्च शङ्खतलद्वये।
> पृष्ठयोर्मूलमध्याग्रस्थानेषु तलयोरपि॥ इति।

मध्यबीजस्थक्लकारेणेति। निष्कीलपञ्चकूटाभिप्रायमेतत्। अन्यत्र तु ह्स्रकारो गृह्यते। यद्वा सर्वास्वपि भुवनेश्यात्मकतया क्लकार एव ग्राह्यः। विनपुंसकक्लस्वयुतेनेति ओ ए उ इ अ इत्येषां ग्रहणम्। मन्त्रानप्यप्रतिपत्त्यर्थं पठति क्लौं ईशानेति। ननु यद्येवं किमेषां लक्षणकथनेनेति चेत्। उच्यते। देहन्यासे मन्त्रसिद्ध्यर्थमेतदित्यवगन्तव्यम्। वक्ष्यति च—मूर्तय ईशानमनोभवाद्या इत्यादि। पुनः षडङ्गेनेति। तत्प्रकारमपि दर्शयति—सवाग्भवमध्यदीर्घेणेति। मध्यबीजगतैः आ ई इत्यादिदीर्घैः षडङ्गानि। ते दीर्घा वाग्भवान्ताः स्युरित्यर्थः। यद्वक्ष्यति—मूलबीजमध्यबीजदीर्घानन्तरमिति। तेन सहायं विकल्प इत्यवबोद्धव्यम्। यथा ह्सकलह्रां ह्सैं हृदयाय नम इत्यादि। शुद्धादिषु स्वानि स्वान्यङ्गानीति ज्ञेयम्। मूलपुटितमातृकां न्यसित्वेति। तदुक्तं—बीजत्रयानुलोमप्रतिलोममध्यगतां मातृकामिति। प्रत्येकं बीजैः पुटिता द्विधा ग्रस्ता च मातृका न्यस्यते। श्रीकण्ठादि-

न्यासं कुर्यादिति। यच्छ्रीकण्ठादिन्यासानन्तरमित्युक्तं तदिति भावः। ननु छन्नलेखापटले वक्ष्यति—शैवतत्त्वन्यासशक्तिश्रोसन्नतिरित्यादिन्यासवुभुचादिन्यास-श्रीकण्ठादिन्यासेति। तच्च सर्वमन्त्रसामान्यतया विवचितम्। तेनेह कथं भाव्य-मिति। उच्यते। नेह तदुपेच्यते। किन्तु यदिहावश्यकं तदुच्यत इति। इहै-तदपि गम्यते। शैवतत्त्वादीनां सर्वमन्त्रेष्वपि यावदिच्छान्यास इति। मूले नाभेरथाचरणमिति मूलबीजन्यास उक्तः। बीजैस्त्रिभिर्न्यसत्विति संबध्यते। सव्ये दचान्यये च हस्ततले द्वितयमपीति संबन्धः। बीजद्वयन्यासोऽयमुक्तः। तृतीयं बीजमुभयोर्हस्ततलयोः सह न्यसत्विति योजनीयम्। त्रिखण्डन्यासोऽयमुक्तः।

मूर्धनि गुह्यहृदोरपीति पञ्चावृत्तिन्यासः ॥ ५ ॥ ६ ॥

वाग्भवेन पुनरित्यङ्गन्यास उक्तः। पुनर्वाग्भवेनाङ्गुलिषु न्यसेत्। अथो पुनरुक्तमार्गत इत्यन्वयः। पुनरिति पृथक् पदम्। तालत्रितयादि कुर्यादिति च शेषः। तदुक्तमधस्तात्—अङ्गुलीषु क्रमादङ्गैरित्यादि। इह यत्प्रागुक्तं हस्त-तले च सव्य इत्यादि यच्चेदमङ्गुलिष्वङ्गन्यासादिकमुक्तं तद्यथोक्तकालं कार्यम्। यद्वा प्रागेवाङ्गुलिन्यासविधाविति ज्ञेयम्। वाग्भवेन पुनरिति प्रथमबीजेनैव षडङ्गमुक्तम्। अभिप्रायान्तरमाह—वाग्भवेन पुनरितीति। पुनर्वाग्भवेनेति संबध्यते। मूलबीजानि द्विरुक्त्वा षड्बीजानि संपादनीयानि। तैरेव षड्भिरङ्गान्येके वदन्ति। मध्यमबीजस्य दीर्घा आ ई इत्यादयः षड्गृह्यन्ते। तान्येव सुप्रति-पत्त्यर्थं पठति—ह्स्रैमित्यादिना। निष्कीलविद्याविषयेऽयमङ्गपाठः। बालादि-ष्वप्यनेन न्यायेनाङ्गानि कल्प्यानि। पुनरुक्तमार्गत इत्येकं पदमभिप्रयन् विवृणोति —पुनरुक्तं पुनर्वचनमिति। वाग्भवेन विन्यसेदित्यत्र विशेषणमेतत्। वाग्भवस्य पुनःपुनरावृत्तिरेव षट्स्वङ्गेषु स्यात्। न त्वाकारादि तदुचितदीर्घयोग इति तदाशयः। चशब्देनेति। विन्यसेच्चेत्यमुनेति भावः। प्रा(बा)णादिन्यासा इति मूर्तिन्यासो गृह्यते। बहुवचनं तु बीजन्यासाद्यभिप्रायमित्यवबोद्धव्यम्। मूले तद्देवतां विशदधीरिति। स्वच्छमतिः समाहितः सन्न्यस्तमन्त्रदेवतां ध्यायेदित्यर्थः।

अभिप्रायान्तरमाह—धीवैशद्यहेतुभूतेत्यादिना। न्यासविशेषणमेतत्। न्यासे हि नानाविधे क्रियमाणे देवतायामास्तिक्यबुद्धौ तदनुसन्धानयोग्यता धियः स्यादिति न्यासानां धीवैशद्यहेतुत्वमुक्तम्। न्यासान्तरोपलचणं चैतत्। तेन श्रीकण्ठन्यासानन्तरं कामरत्यादिन्यासः—

कामश्च कामदः कान्तः कान्तिः कामाङ्ग एव च।
कामचारः कामकल्पः कामुकः कामबन्धकः ॥

रामणो रामरमणो रतिनाथो रतिप्रियः ।
रात्रिनाथो रमाकान्तो रममाणो निशाचरः ॥
नन्दको नन्दनश्चैव नन्दी नन्दयिता ततः ।
पञ्चबाणो रतिसखः पुष्पधन्वा महाधनुः ॥
भ्रमणो भ्रामणश्चैव भ्रममाणो भ्रमस्तथा ।
भ्रान्तश्च भ्रामकश्चाथ भ्रान्ताचारो भ्रमावहः ॥
मोहनो मोहको मोहो मोही मोहविवर्धनः ।
मन्मथो मदनश्चैव मातङ्गो भृङ्गनायकः ॥
स्याद्गायको गीतिकरो नर्तकः च्खे(खे)लकस्तथा ।
उन्मत्तो नृत्तजश्चैव विलासी कामवर्धनः ॥
रतिः प्रीतिः कामिनी च मोहिनी कमलप्रिया ।
विलासिनी कल्पलता श्यामवर्णा शुचिस्मिता ॥
विस्मिताविस्मिता चैव लेलिहाना दिगम्बरा ।
वामा कुब्जा परा नित्या कल्याणी मोहनोत्तमा ॥
सुरोत्तमा सुलावण्या मालिनी कलहप्रिया ।
एकाक्षी चैव जटिलाजटिला नीलिमालिके ॥
शिखा दग्धा रमा पश्चाद्भ्रामिणी चारुलोचना ।
रतिप्रिया पलाशाक्षी रटहिणी विकटापि च ॥
मदारूपधरा माला ह्लादिनी विश्वतोमुखी ।
नन्दिनी चरमा काली का(क)लकण्ठा च कन्दरा ॥
मेघश्यामा मदोन्मत्ता लिपिवर्णैः सह न्यसेत् ॥ इति ।

गणपतिविधानवद्विघ्नेशादिन्यासः । पुनर्ग्रहन्यासः ।

सूर्यः सोमोऽङ्गारकश्च बुधः शुक्रो बृहस्पतिः ।
शनैश्चरश्च राहुश्च केतुश्चैषां तु शक्तयः ॥
रेणुका च सुधा धात्री ज्ञानरूपा यशस्विनी ।
शाङ्करी चैव शक्तिश्च धूम्रा कृष्णाः नव क्रमात् ॥
स्वरान्तस्थाः पञ्च वर्गा ऊष्माणो लक्ष एव च ।
हृदधश्च शिरोनेत्रहृदये हृदुपरि न्यसेत् ।
ग्रीवानाभिमुखेष्वेव क्रमात्पादद्वयेऽपि च ॥ इति ।

पुनर्नक्षत्रन्यासः । द्विशो वर्णा योज्या हलचास्त्वेकश एव ।

भाले नयनयोः कर्णद्वये नासापुटद्वये ।
कण्ठे स्कन्धद्वये पश्चात्क[रयो]र्मणिबन्धयोः ।
स्तनयोर्नाभिकट्यूरुजानुजङ्घापदद्वये ॥ इति ।

ततो योगिनीन्यासः ।

कामरूपं वाराणसी नेपालं पौण्ड्रवर्धनम् ।
वरस्थिरं कान्यकुब्जं पूर्णशैलमथार्बुदम् ॥
आम्रातकेश्वरैकाम्रे त्रिस्रोतं कामकोट्टकम् ।
कैलासं भृगुकेदारं पीठं चन्द्रपुरं पुनः ॥
श्रीपीठमेकवीरं च जालन्धमथ मालवम् ।
कुलान्तं देवीकोट्टं च गोकर्णं मारुतेश्वरम् ॥
अट्टहासं च विरजं राजगृहं महापथम् ।
कोल्लागिरिरलकपुरमोंकारं च जयन्तिका ॥
उज्जयिनी विराबा च चीरकं हस्तिनापुरम् ।
ओड्डीशपुरं प्रयागं षष्ठीशं मायापुरं तथा ॥
गौरशैलं च मलयं श्रीशैलं मेरुसंज्ञकम् ।
गिरिवरं महेन्द्रं च वामनं हिरण्यपुरं पुनः ।
महालक्ष्मीपुरोड्याणं छायाच्छत्रमिति क्रमात् ॥ इति ।

ततो नाभेरथाचरणमित्युक्तम् । त्रिखण्डन्यासः । स च संहारक्रमेणोक्तः । तत्र मूर्ध्नस्तथा हृदयमित्यादिक्रमेण सर्गः । नाभेराचरणं मूर्ध्न आहृदयं हृदयादानाभि च स्थितिरित्यवबोद्धव्यम् । मूलन्यासान्तरमप्याह—तत्रेति । स्थितिन्यासोऽयम् । सर्गसंहारावपीहेष्यते । ततः शाक्ततत्त्वन्यासः । तदाह—ह्स्रैंमित्यादिना । निष्कीलविद्याविषयमेतत् । शुद्धादिषु तु स्वबीजानि ग्राह्याणि । स्वविलोमेनाप्येषां न्यास इष्यते । पुनरहोरात्रत्रिलिङ्गाजपापरमात्मप्रणवन्यासानन्तरमावृत्तिन्यासः । स इह त्रिविधः । तदाह—पादजानुगुह्येत्यादिना । नाभिहृत्कण्ठेषु आस्यभ्रूमस्तकेषु च विभागः । मूर्धगुह्यहृत्स्वित्यादिन्यासस्तु मूलोक्त एव । नवावृत्तिन्यासो नवयोनिवदिति । तदुक्तम्—मूलबीजैः श्रोत्रद्वयचिबुकेष्वित्यादि । ततश्चतुर्दशावृत्तिन्यासः । तदुक्तम्—शिरोऽपरभागे दक्षोत्तरब्रह्मरन्ध्रेषु मूलबीजानि व्यस्तानि विन्यसेत् । एवं तैरेव दक्षादिशङ्खद्वयभ्रूमध्येषु नेत्रद्वयघ्राणेषु श्रोत्रद्वयास्येष्वंसद्वयहृत्सु स्तनद्वयनाभिषु प्रपदद्वयाधारेषु जानुद्वयस्वाधिष्ठानेषु कटिद्वयजठरेषु पार्श्वद्वयहृत्सु स्तनद्वयकण्ठेषु अंसद्वयास्येषु श्रोत्रद्वयमस्तकेषु नेत्रद्वय-

भ्रूमध्येषु विन्यसेदिति। पुनः शृङ्खलान्यासः।

केशान्ते चिबुके वक्त्रे वक्त्रे कण्ठे च चैबुके।
चिबुके हृदये कण्ठे कण्ठे नाभौ तथा हृदि॥
हृदि गुह्ये तथा नाभौ नाभौ गुह्ये च मूलके।

मूलबीजत्रयं न्यसेदिति। अमृतेश्वर्यादिन्यासमाह—ह्स्रौमिति। रत्यादिन्यासमाह—ह्स्रैमिति। मूर्तिन्यासमाह—मूर्तय इति। सुप्रतिपत्त्यर्थं मन्त्रप्रयोगं दर्शयति—ह्स्रौमिति। पुनरङ्गानि विन्यस्येत्यावरणभूतान्यभिप्रेतानि। वक्ष्यति च—तेनैव चाङ्गानि विदिग्दिशास्वित्यादि। मूर्तिन्यासवदिति। मूर्धास्यान्येव स्थानानि। सुभगादिन्यास इति। ललाटभ्रूमध्यलम्बिकागलहृदयनाभिलिङ्गमूलमूलाधाराण्यष्टाधाराणि विन्यस्येत्यनेन संबन्धः। बीजपञ्चकं च प्रत्येकं संयोजनीयम्। यथा ऐं क्लीं ब्लूं स्त्रीं सः सुभगायै नम इत्यादि। आवरणान्तरसद्भावे केषामप्यनया दिशा न्यासः स्यात्। तदुक्तम्—या + +। मूलाधाराद्यष्टाधारेष्वित्यत्राधाराणामेव वैलोम्येन ग्रहणम्। भूषणन्यासं विधायेति। यत्तु हृल्लेखाविधाने वक्ष्यति—त्रिपुरोक्तक्रमेण भूषणन्यासमाचरेत् अथावरणन्यास इति। ततश्चोभयत्रापि क्रमविकल्पोऽवसीयते। ननु किमिहैव भूषणन्यासोऽभिधीयत इति। उच्यते। इहैव भूषणन्यास आवश्यको मन्त्रान्तरेषु तु प्रकारान्तरेण भूषणन्यासोऽपि स्यादित्येतत्प्रतिपादनार्थमेतत्। विशदधीर्ध्यायेदिति। मूलगतविशदधीपदाभिप्राय इयानुक्त इति भावः। अतएवेत्यर्थं इत्युक्तमिति। भूषणन्यासं दर्शयति शिरोललाटेत्यादिना। तत्पृष्ठेति। पाणिपृष्ठद्वयमेकमेव गृह्यते। कटकद्वयमप्येकमेव। भूषणन्यासानन्तरमायुधन्यासोऽपि कार्यः। तदुक्तं विधृतजपवटीत्यादि॥ ७॥

मूल आताम्रार्कायुताभामित्याताम्रं रक्तम्। सटाशब्दो जटापर्यायः। जपवटी माणिक्याक्षमाला दक्षिणोपरिहस्त एतत् पुस्तकं वामोर्ध्वहस्ते। अभीतिरभीष्टं चेतरयोः। बलिलसितविलग्नामिति बलित्रयशोभितमध्यप्रदेशाम्। असृक्पङ्कराजन्मुण्डस्रङ्मालिताङ्गीमिति। मुण्डानामेवासृग्रक्तं सान्द्रमसृक् पङ्कः। तेन राजतां मुण्डानां स्रग्भिरलङ्कृतशरीरामिति। यद्वा असृक् कुङ्कुमं तस्य पङ्क इव: तद्वद्विराजतां मुण्डानां स्रग्भिरिति। अत्राभिप्रायान्तरमाह—असृक्पङ्केत्यादिना। मुण्डपदेनोत्तमाङ्गं लक्ष्यते। तदाह—उत्तमाङ्गरूपाभिरिति। तेन च सर्वोर्ध्ववर्तिनीनां शक्तीनां ग्रहणम्। तदाह—शक्तिव्यापिनीसमनोभिरिति। बिन्द्वाद्युपलक्षणमेतत्। बिन्द्वादिसमन्यन्तस्य सूक्ष्मतया विवक्षितत्वात्। अतएव लिपिपटल उक्तम्—भारतीमिति नादाद्यात्मकं सूक्ष्मरूपं कथितमिति। त्रिधा विभागे

हि वैराजं स्थूलमितरद्वयं त्रयं वा सूक्ष्मं तदुत्तरं परं च रूपं स्यादिति। ननु तर्हि शक्त्यादिग्रहणं किमर्थमिति यावदिच्छं बिन्द्वादीनां संख्यापरिग्रहः शेषाणां च तदन्तर्भाव इति प्रतिवादार्थमेतत्। परपरापरध्यानकथनमेतदिति परं परापरं च ध्यानं समुच्चयेनोक्तमित्यर्थः। परं देवतातत्त्वमुन्मनीशक्तिरेव परं रूपम्। तदुक्तं —सामिति परं चिदात्मकमिति। तदेव त्रिपुरायाः स्वरूपम्। तस्या रूपमिह शरीरं विवक्षितम्। तत्र सम्बन्मूर्धादिपादान्तमविच्छिन्नतया वर्तमानाः शक्ति-व्यापिनीसमन्यस्तासामाकारस्य कुङ्कुमसान्द्रीपम इत्येतदिह सिद्धं भवति। तच्च परं रूपं स्थूलरूपहृत्कमलेऽतिसूक्ष्मतद्रूपाभं चिन्तनीयम्। शरीरग्रहणादिति। प्रकारान्तरं दर्शयति—अथवेति। अस्रगिति अस्रजतीति कृदन्तमेतत्। तदा-द्याकारः स्रष्टेति। परावागकार इष्यते। तदुक्तम्—अनुत्तराकारपुरुषस्येति। तस्य सर्गस्तु चिन्मात्रापेक्षया संभवति। तदुक्तम्—वैखरीमध्यमापश्यन्तीपरालक्षणा-स्तासां दीपिकोन्मनीशक्तिरिति। पर इति परमात्मेत्यर्थः। परग्रहणमेतदेव चिन्मात्रात्मकं परं रूपमिति प्रतिपादनार्थम्। सान्द्रीभाव इति। चिन्मात्रपरा-वाक्तदर्थगतविशुद्धांशवलनतः सान्द्रीभावः स्यादिति भावः। आभास इति। चैतन्याभासाभिप्रायम्। तदुक्तं—मूर्तिर्माया आभासस्तदभिव्यक्तश्चैतन्याभास इति। तेन राजन्तीति तद्योगः। सापि चिन्मयी परिदीप्ता स्यादिति भावः। मुण्डकुण्ड-लिनीति। मुण्डमुत्तमाङ्गरूपत्वात् परापश्यन्त्यात्मिका हि शक्तिरध्यात्मवर्तिनी कुण्डलिनी। सा च स्थूलप्रपञ्चशिरःस्थानीया भवति। अस्रगित्यकारोऽपि सैव भवति। तस्यामिति मूलाधारान्तर्वर्तिन्यामिति भावः। सम्बदविच्छिन्नतयेति। समन्यादीनां मन्त्रजपवेलायामविच्छिन्नतया प्रसरोपरमयोः सद्भावादिति भावः। तदुक्तम्—अव्यक्तं प्रलपतीत्यादि। शक्तिभेदा इति। सामान्यशक्तिः कुण्डलिनी तस्या विशेषांशा बिन्द्वादिसमन्यन्ताः शक्तय इत्येवमुक्तम्। मुण्डस्रज इति। मुण्डानां स्रजो मुण्डस्रज इति समासः। तैरलङ्कृतशरीरामिति कुण्डलिन्यन्तर-तिसूक्ष्मतया व्यवस्थितोन्मन्यभिप्रायमेतत्। पूर्वस्मिन् विवरणे सूक्ष्मशरीर-वत्युन्मनी। तस्याः सम्बत्सामान्यादयः। इह तु विवरणे सूक्ष्मतेजोरूपोन्मनी। तस्याः समन्तादविच्छेदेन प्रसरोपरमभाजस्तेजोमात्राः समन्यादय इति भेदः।

पुनरपि प्रकारान्तरं दर्शयितुमारभते—यथा श्रुतो वार्थ इति। स्थूलरूपविषय-मेव ह्येतत्। परादिरूपमस्तु पदान्तरगम्यमिति भावः। आताम्रेत्यनेनैवेति। एकमे-वैतत्पदं रूपद्वयपरमित्येवकारेणोक्तम्। आताम्राभामर्कायुताभां चेत्येवं विवरणीय-मेतत्। तत्रार्कायुताभामिति स्थूलविषयम्। निरतिशयरक्ता तदपेक्षयेति न्यूनतया

च रक्ता आभा ज्योतिर्यस्याः सैवमातात्राभित्युक्ता । तत्र निरतिशयरक्तं स्थूलरूपच्छदन्तर्वर्तिज्योतिरुन्मनो चिन्मात्रं परं रूपम् । तदुक्तं—तदन्त स्फुरिति तेजसि बोधमात्ररूप इति । तत ईषनन्यूनस्थूलरूपाभापेक्षया च प्रकर्षाढ्यं रक्तं पररूपप्रभास्थानीयं परापरं रूपम् । तदप्युक्तम्—भगवत्यनलात्मके विदध्यादित्यादि । तदेतत् सर्वं भारतीं तामम्बिकां तामित्यत्रापि समानमेव ध्यानमित्यवबोद्धव्यम् । निष्कीलपञ्चकूट इति । पञ्चकूटविद्या द्विविधा मध्यमपञ्चकूटं सर्वपञ्चकूटं चेति । तयोर्द्वयोः सहेदं ग्रहणम् । ललिता तु पञ्चकूटग्रहणान्न गृह्यते । सा तु पाशाङ्कुशेक्षुधनुःपुष्पशरधरा भवति । पाशाङ्कुशशूलकपालधरा वेति + इदं ग्रहणम् । ललिता तु पञ्च । सर्वासामपि रूपभेदविकल्पोपलक्षणमेतत् । शुद्धायास्तावत्—

शुभ्राब्जस्थां त्रिणेत्रामभयवरकरां कुन्दमन्दारगौरां
पद्माचीमङ्गदाढ्यामतिरुचिरविचि त्राकल्पवस्त्रभूषाम् ।
वन्दे देवीं कुमारीं शशिशकलसमोपेतमौलिं वहन्तो-
मज्ञानोच्छेदिनीं तां प्रवरधनधान्यप्रदां कान्तिदां च ॥ इति ।

बालायास्तु मूलोक्त एव धवलत्वं विशेषः । यद्वा—

पीयूषकुम्भवरदाभयपुस्तकोद्यद्दाहामयुग्मनयनाममलाम्बुजस्थाम् ।
अच्छाङ्गरागवसनापघनां नमामि बालेन्दुमौलिमनिशं वचसामधीशाम् ॥ इति ।

व्यस्तविधाने तु वाग्भवे ।

धवलनलिनराजच्चन्द्रसंस्थां प्रसन्नां धवलवसनभूषामाल्यदेहां त्रिनेत्राम् ।
कमलयुगवराभीत्युल्लसद्बाहुपद्मां कुमुदरमणचूड़ां भारतीं भावयामि ॥ इति ।

कामराजे च + + शाक्ते च ब्रह्मादिमन्त्रयोगे तु तत्तदायुधादियोगो विशेषः । मिश्रणयोगे तु ब्रह्मादीनां रक्ताभानां वामाङ्के सरस्वत्याद्याका द्विकरा देवी ध्येया । त्रिपुरसुन्दरीयोगेष्वपि समानमेतत् सर्वमिति ॥ ८ ॥

मूले दीक्षां प्राप्येति पुरश्चरणमुक्तम् । विशिष्टलक्षणयुत (ज) इति + + सत्संप्रदायादगुरोरिति । द्विविधः त्रैपुरः संप्रदायः साधुरसाधुश्च । तत्र देव्याः स्थितो प्रेतासनयन्त्रबन्धः पूजायामासवादिसंयोगः सन्ध्यां त्रैपुरगायत्रीप्रवृत्तिरिति सर्वमस्ति सोऽसाधुः । श्रुतिस्मृतिविरोधात् प्रत्यवायकरत्वाच्च । यत्र सरस्वत्यादिदेवतान्तरोचितमेव सर्वं स साधुः वैदिकपरिग्रहात् । स संप्रदायो यस्य स सत्संप्रदायो गुरुः । अभिप्रायान्तरमाह—वैदिकादितीत्यादिना । वेदसंप्रदायेनैव सार्धं प्रवृत्तः संप्रदायोऽयमभिप्रेतः । तद्दर्शयति—परप्रकाशानन्दनाथेत्यादिना । त्वरितादिनित्यास्वप्ययमेव गुरुक्रमः । नित्यानां विद्यानामविशेषात् । यद्वा

तासु प्रागुक्त एव सर्वसामान्यभूतः क्रमो भवति। ननु कथमिह गुरुसमष्टिमन्त्रः स्यादिति। ॐ क्लीं परप्रकाशानन्दनाथाद्यशेषगुरुपारम्पर्यक्रमेणेत्येवमूह्यम्। परगुरुश्रीपादुकां पूजयामीत्यादि च प्रतिपत्तव्यमिति। मूले सुनियत इति सकलनियमजातमुक्तम्। अभिप्रायभेदमाह—ब्रह्मचर्यादिमानिति। कामराजबीजादियोगतो मन्त्रमहिम्नैव कामचोदसंभवात् तत्परिहाराद्यवश्यविधानार्थमेतदुक्तम्। तत्त्वार्धलक्षावधीति द्वादशलक्षग्रहणम्। अभिप्रायान्तरमाह—तत्त्वानीति। तत्त्वशब्देन चतुर्विंशतिसंख्याग्रहणम्। तत्त्वार्धलक्षावधीति द्वादशलक्षग्रहणम्। व्यस्तसाध[नेऽ]पि समस्तोक्तैव संख्या त्रिमूर्त्यादिमन्त्रयोगे तु सर्वेषां द्वादशलक्षमेव स्यादिति ज्ञेयम्। मूले स्वाद्वक्तैरिति। त्रिमधुराद्रैरित्यर्थः। सम्यक्‌समिद्ध इति जननाद्यभिप्रायम्। अश्वारि करवीरम्। अपिशब्दो विकल्पार्थः। अभिप्रायान्तरमाह—अपिशब्देनेति। भानुसहस्रकमपीति योजनीयम्। द्वादशलक्षजपापेक्षत्वे तद्भानुसहस्राभिधानमिति भावः। काम्यहोमेष्विति। पुरश्चरणाङ्गहोमे मन्त्रविशेषवित्त्वस्यानुपयोगादिति भावः। तत्तत्कामनोचितबीजयोग इति। पलाशपुष्पैर्मधुरत्रयाक्तैरित्यादिवक्ष्यमाणहोमविषयमेतत्। तत्र सौभाग्ये + + लक्ष्म्यां श्रीबीजयोग इत्यादि। यद्वा स्वाद्वक्तैश्च नवैरितीहोक्तमेव होमद्वयं तत्तत्कामनयापि कार्यम्। तत्र तत्तदनुगुणबीजयोगोऽयमभिप्रेतः। तत्र लक्ष्म्यां श्रीबीजयोगो मृत्युञ्जये तद्योग इत्यादि॥ ८॥

मूले प्राणायामैरित्यन्तर्यागाभिधानम्। दोचितमात्रस्य योनिमुद्रादिबन्धासमर्थत्वान्न्यासानन्तरमेतदभिधानमिति ज्ञेयम्। प्राणायामैरिति। प्रणवपटलभाविभिरन्यत्र सिद्धैश्च शोषणादिरूपैरित्यर्थः। अभिप्रायान्तरमाह—वेधकप्राणायामसूचनमिति। वर्णवेधः कलावेधो योगिनीवेध इत्येतदपेक्षं मूले बहुवचनम्। वर्णादीनां वेधो नाम शक्तिचिदावेशेन तद्व्याप्तिः। तत्र वर्णभेदमाह—मूलेनेति। प्रागुक्तरीत्या जीवरक्षान्तं विधायैतदारब्धव्यम्। कुम्भकोऽपि प्रतिलोमवर्णपूर्वकेण मूलेन स्यात्। वर्णाश्च काननवृत्तादिव्यापिनः। तेषां स्ववाच्यार्थैः सह संहारः। पर इति प्रकाशमात्रे शिव इत्यर्थः। कलावेधचिकीर्षया सर्गमाह—पुनरिति। बीजानि तु 'नादकलादिभूता इत्यत्रोक्ताः। भूतस्थानेष्विति शिरोमुखहृदयगुह्यपादेषु। सर्वं स्पष्टेति तत्तन्न्यासे तथानुसन्धानमुक्तम्। इदानीं कलावेधमाह—पञ्चीकृतापञ्चीकृतबीजानीति। इतरा अपीति। रसतन्मात्राबीजं जान्वादिनाभ्यन्तं विन्यसेत्। रूपतन्मात्राबीजं नाभ्यादिकण्ठान्तं स्पर्शतन्मात्राबीजं कण्ठादिकर्णान्तं शब्दतन्मात्राबीजं कर्णादिमूर्धान्तम्।

प्रतिन्यासं मूलेनैव प्राणायामेन संहारः। परे सर्वं संहरेदित्येतस्मिन्नेव च सर्वं संहार्यमिति। योगिनीवेधचिकीर्षयापि पुनस्तत्त्वा वा पश्चोक्तत्यायुक्तरीत्या सर्वं स्रष्टव्यम्। योगिनीवेधमाह—पूर्वोक्तेति। पूर्वशब्देन 'प्रकृतिः पुरुषश्चैवेत्यत्र भूतयोगो गृह्यते। तत्र चैवमुक्तम्—हृत्कण्ठतालुभ्रूमध्यब्रह्मरन्ध्रद्वादशान्तेषु मण्डलबीजाधिष्ठातृसहितान् पृथिव्यादिकारणान्तान् कुण्डलिनीप्रभाविनैकवर्णां ध्यात्वेति। तेष्वधिष्ठातारो निवृत्त्यादिशक्तयः। तदुक्तम्—भूताभिमानिनीरिति। कारणे तु शक्तिरेवाधिष्ठात्री। तासामेव च योगिनीवेध इति योगिनीपदेन ग्रहणम्। मूलयुक्तैर्लक्षितवृत्त्यै नम इत्यादिमन्त्रैस्तन्न्यासेन तासां तेषु यथोक्तं कल्पनं षडाधारेषु योगो दृढमनुसन्धानम्। मूलयुतैः स्वैर्मन्त्रैः प्राणायामः संहारश्च षोडशान्तस्थिताधोमुखकमलकर्णिकागतेन्दुमण्डलानन्दसंविद्रूपे परे शिवतत्त्वे। यदुक्तम्—अकारलक्ष्ये पर इति। प्रागपि समानमेतत्। तत्तु द्वादशान्त एवैवं कल्पनीयम्। यद्वा पूर्वशब्देन 'त्रिवारमथ परिजप्तमितयेत्येतद्गृह्यते। तत्र चैवमुक्तं—मूलाधाराद्याधारेषु चतुःषड्दशद्वादशषोडशद्विदलपद्मेषु वर्णानां वादिबादिडादिकाद्यादिहादीनां दीपशिखावद्ध्यानमुक्तमिति। योगिनीवेधग्रहणाच्च तत्कर्णिकास्वधिष्ठात्र्यो योगिन्योऽपि भावनीयाः। ताश्च सकलरडहाद्या [योगि]न्यो हसकलरडाद्या [योगि]न्यो वा प्रथिताः। ब्रह्मरन्ध्रे तु प्राग्वदानन्दसंविन्मात्रं कल्पनीयम्। योगिनीनां षट्कोणान्तस्त्रिकोणे स्थितिश्चेत् षट्स्वपि कोणेषु स्वादिवर्णाः षड्दीर्घयुता आवरणशक्तयः स्युः। नवयोनिमध्ययोनौ स्थितिश्चेदीकारवह्निः युग्मस्वरैरन्विताः स्वादिवर्णा नवस्वपि योनिषु स्युरिति चावबोद्धव्यम्। सं कं लं रं डं हं मूलं च न्यसंस्तासां सप्तानामपि कल्पनं कृत्वा तन्मन्त्रैः प्राणानायच्छन्नानन्दसंविच्छक्तिलक्षणे परशिवे संहरेत्। सं षं शं वं सां सीं सूं सृं सॢं सें सैं सौं सः मूलं साकिन्यै नम इत्येवं मन्त्रप्रयोग इति। डरलकसहाद्या [योगि]न्यो वा योगिन्यः स्युरिति। प्राणायामत्रयमिति वेधकप्राणायामत्रयाभिप्रायम्। प्राणायाममन्त्रैरेवेति। योगिनीवेधप्राणायाममन्त्रैरित्यर्थः। व्युत्क्रमेणेति मन्त्रावयवानामाधाराणां व्युत्क्रमो विवक्षितः। न्यासश्चेहार्थाद्भवति। अयमिह प्रयोगः। मूलं ब्रह्मरन्ध्रे विन्यस्य मूलं हाकिन्यै हां हीं हूं हैं हौं हौं हं हं क्षं नम इत्याज्ञायां न्यसेत्। यद्वा मूलं हाकिन्यै नम इति मध्ययोनौ हां हीमित्यादि वर्णान्नव योनिषु हं क्षमिति दलद्वये च न्यसेदित्यादि। यद्वा पुनस्तत्त्वात्वापश्चोक्तभूतबीजन्यासं सकृत्स्रिपिन्यासमपि विदध्यात्। वेधकप्राणायामद्वयमेकमेव वा कार्यम्। तदा तु तत्तन्मन्त्रैरेव सर्गन्यासेन सृष्टिरिति ज्ञेयम्। यद्वा निरवद्यादिमन्त्र-

व्यापकैरेव सृष्टिः स्यादिति। मूले निजाधारराजद्योनिस्थामिति मूलाधारे नवयोनिमध्ययोनौ स्थितां विभाव्येत्युक्तम्। परादिमन्त्रन्यासमेकाक्षरादिमन्त्रन्यासं च कृत्वा पुनस्तामेव मूलाधारे सावरणां कल्पयित्वा जलादिभिरन्तर्यागः कार्य इति। दिव्यरूपामिति निरतिशयसौन्दर्यादियोग उक्तः। अभिप्रायान्तरमाह—व्यापिन्यादिप्रभाभिरिति। सर्वमन्त्रेष्वपि समानमेतत्। न चैतत्परापरध्यानम्। अपि तु सकलरूपस्यैव व्याप्तिरित्यवबोद्धव्यम्। प्रभाग्रहणं चात एवेति। मूले प्रमुदितमनसेति हर्षादियोग उक्तः। जलगन्धादय इहोपचाराः। यद्वावरणन्यासानन्तरमेव परादिन्यासमेकाक्षरादिन्यासं च कृत्वा मूलाधारे विभाव्यासनस्वागतार्घ्याद्युपचारान्दद्यादिति। पुनः प्राग्वदेव ध्यात्वा योनिमुद्रामाबध्य जपं कुर्यात्। योनिमुद्रा च द्विविधेत्याह—बाह्येऽभ्यन्तरे चेति। तत्र मूले निजगुदलिङ्गान्तरस्थामित्याभ्यन्तरलक्षणम्।

तदुक्तम्—गुदमेढ्रान्तरे योनिस्तामाकुञ्च्य प्रपञ्चयेत्॥ इति।

बाह्ये च—मध्यमे कुटिलाकारतर्जन्युपरि संस्थिते।

अनामिकामध्यगते तथैव हि कनिष्ठिके॥

सर्वा एकत्र संयोज्या अङ्गुष्ठपरिपीडिताः।

एषा तु प्रथमा मुद्रा योनिमुद्रेति सा स्मृता॥ इति।

ओड्याणजालन्धरखेचरीबन्धार्थं इति। बाह्ये खेचरी।

सव्यं दक्षिणदेशे तु दक्षिणं सव्यदेशतः।

बाहुं कृत्वा महेशानि हस्तौ संपरिवर्त्य च॥

कनिष्ठानामिके देवि युक्ता तेन क्रमेण तु।

तर्जनीभ्यां समाक्रान्ते सर्वोर्ध्वमपि मध्यमे॥

अङ्गुष्ठौ तु महेशानि कारयेत् सरलावपि।

इयं सा खेचरी नाम्ना मुद्रा सर्वोत्तमा प्रिये॥ इति।

आभ्यन्तरे तु—चिबुकं योजयित्वा तु षोडशस्वरमण्डले।

चन्द्रसूर्यनिरोधेन मूलशक्तिनिकुञ्चनात्॥

रसनामन्तरा कृत्वा अ[व्यक्तं] धारयेन्मनः।

एषा सा खेचरी ख्याता उन्मनात्वं प्रयच्छति॥ इति।

मानसयोगान्तेऽनुष्टुबादिन्यासं वैखर्यादिन्यासं च कृत्वा चक्रलेखाभाविरीत्या योगान् विदधीत। तत्र प्रथमं स्तोया योगाः स्युः। वक्ष्यति च—जप्त्वाऽर्चयित्वेत्यादि। सर्वयोगान्तेऽन्त्ययोगेन जप्त्वान्तर्यागं समापयेदिति। इदानीं बहिर्यागं वक्तुमार-

भते—भूयो द्रव्यैरिति। वक्ष्यमाणप्रकारेणेति नवयोनिविरचनपीठसपर्यादिसर्वं देवतायागार्थं हि भवतीति तस्यारम्भरूपत्वमुक्तम् ॥ १० ॥

मूले वामादिशक्तिसहितमिति विशेषणं संपद्यते। तदाह—वामादिशक्तिसाहित्यमिति। पीठमित्यत्र नवयोनिचक्रान्तमेव पीठमभिप्रेतम्। पुनस्तद्गतनवयोनेरप्रथितत्वात्तन्मध्ययोनौ कलशनिधानस्य च वाच्यत्वादत्र प्रकल्प्येत्यादिवचनसम्भव इति। वामाद्या द्वादश शक्तयो वक्ष्यन्ते। तास्त्वष्टावष्टदलेषु तिस्रो मध्ययोनिकोणेष्वन्त्या मध्यत इति ज्ञेयम्। अभिप्रायान्तरमाह—वामादिशक्तिसाहित्यमिति। तत्प्रकारस्तु प्रागुक्तः—द्वादशशक्तिन्यासं कुर्यादित्यादि। यद्वा वामाद्यष्टौ प्रागाद्यष्टयोनिषु तिस्रो मध्ययोनिकोणेष्वन्त्या मध्यत इति। नवशक्तयस्त्विहान्या एव स्युः। तदुक्तं प्राक्—इच्छाज्ञानाक्रियेत्यादि। ननु पीठं परिपूज्यात्र नवयोनिचक्रं प्रकल्प्येत्येवमभिधानं कथं संभवतीति। नैष दोषः। नवयोनिचक्रान्तमेवैतत् पीठमभिप्रेतम्। तस्य चक्रस्य त्वप्रथितत्वादत्र प्रकल्प्येत्याद्यभिधानं स्यात्। नवयोनिकथनानन्तरमेव वामादिकथनं चैवमुपपद्यत इति। विधिवदिति वह्नेः पुरद्वयेत्याद्यभिप्रेतम्। अभिप्रायान्तरमाह—विधिवदित्यादिना। मातृभैरवबीजानामिति श्रां श्रामित्यादीनां ग्रहणम्। राशिचक्रविरचनन्तु सामान्यसिद्धमेव। चतुरस्र इति तस्याष्टदिक्षु लेखनमिति। यन्त्रान्तरम्—

मध्याद्यन्नवयोनिषु प्रविलिखेद्बीजानि वर्णांस्त्रिशो
गायत्र्याः पुनरष्टपत्रविवरेष्वालिख्य लिप्याहृतम्।
भूबिम्बद्वितयेन मन्मथयुजा कोणेषु संवेष्टितं
यन्त्रं त्रैपुरमीरितं त्रिभुवनप्रक्षोभकं श्रीप्रदम् ॥
युद्धे वादे च जयं कवितामायुर्विवृद्धिमारोग्यम्।
पुत्रसुहृद्धनवृद्धिं कुर्यादेतदद्भुतं यन्त्रम् ॥ इति।

कामं षट्कोणमध्ये लिखतु पुनरिमं षट्सु कोणेषु पश्चात्
पत्रेष्वप्यष्टसंख्येष्वमुमथ परतो व्योमबीजेन वीतम्।
क्षौणीबिम्बान्तरस्थं भुजदललिखितं रोचनाकुङ्कुमाभ्यां
प्रोक्तं सौभाग्यसम्पन्निरुपमकविताकीर्तिदं यन्त्रमेतत् ॥ इति।
शुद्धा षोडशभिः स्वरैः सुमिलिता तावद्द्विधा स्यान्निवृत्
तान्तः शक्त्युदरे बुधो लिखतु तास्त्वाद्यां द्वितीये ततः।
वृत्ते भूतलिपिर्दशाभिमतकार्या[त]स्तृतीये पुनः
लिप्या वेष्टयतु प्रकार इतरासामप्यसाविष्यताम् ॥

सा मिश्रा यदि षोडशस्वरयुतं स्यात् तत्स्वरव्यञ्जनं
प्राग्वत् षोडश तान्यथ प्रथम आलेख्यः स्वरः पूर्ववत् ।
कृत्वा वृत्तमथाधिकं स्वरपुरोभागे लिखेद्व्यञ्जनं
द्वे चेत्ते दलयोर्द्वयोर्यदि पुनस्त्रीणि त्रिकोणाश्रिषु ॥
चत्वार्यब्धिदलेषु पञ्च शरपत्रेष्वेव षट् चेत्पुनः
षट्कोणेष्वथ सप्त पर्वतदलेष्वष्टावथाष्टाश्रिषु ।
शेषाणामियमेव रीतिरुदिता नाप्तत्तवर्णः पुनः
गण्यः स्यादिह भूपुरालि तु बहिः स्याद्वा फलौचित्यतः ॥
औदर्योऽथ शिरोऽक्षिकर्णकरजाः पादान्तराध्युद्भवा
धीकर्मेन्द्रियजाश्च वातजनिताः पित्तोद्भवाः श्लेष्मजाः ।
नाशं यान्त्यथ सन्निपातजनिता रोगाः पिशाचादयो
यन्त्रैः षोडशभिर्धृतैरथ महारोगा अकाले मृतिः ॥ इति ।

यन्त्राणां धारणं वा स्याद्यन्त्रेष्वर्चनमेव वा ।
अभिषेकोऽथ वा तेषां स्थापनं वा विधीयते ॥ इति ॥ ११ ॥

मूले वह्नेरित्यस्यायमाशयः । अष्टदलपद्मकर्णिकायां पूर्वापरं सूत्रमास्फाल्य तत्षोडशधा समं भङ्क्त्वा प्रागारभ्य चतुःसप्तद्वादशभागान्तसीमासु दक्षिणोत्तराणि सूत्राण्यास्फालयेत् । तत्र द्वितीयसूत्राग्रद्वयात् पूर्वापरसूत्रपश्चिमाग्रावधि सूत्रद्वयं तृतीयसूत्राग्रद्वयात् तत्पूर्वाग्रावधि च सूत्रद्वयमास्फालयेत् । तदा पुटितं वह्निपुरद्वितयं संपद्यते । यत्तु प्रथमं सूत्रं तत्पूर्वदिग्गतत्रिकोणमध्यगतमेवं भवति । तद्वासवयोनिसंबद्धेत्युक्तम् । पुनस्तदग्रद्वयात् पूर्वापरसूत्रे यत्र तृतीयसूत्रं संलग्नं तदवधि सूत्रद्वयमप्यास्फालयेत् । पूर्वनिष्पन्नदक्षिणोत्तरगतत्रिकोणपुरोभागे परं त्रिकोणद्वयं मध्यभागे पश्चिमाग्रं योन्याकारं नवमं त्रिकोणं च संपद्यते । तद्वह्निवरुणेशसमाश्रिताश्चेत्युक्तम् । मुनिभिः पुरैव विहितमिति वैदिकपरिग्राह्यत्वमुक्तम् । लोकेऽतिदुर्लभमिदमिति गोप्यतरत्वमुक्तम् ॥ १२ ॥

मूले वामा ज्येष्ठेति वामादिशक्त्यभिधानम् । तासां न्यासस्तु प्रागुक्तः 'द्वादशशक्तिन्यासं कुर्यादित्यादि । यद्वा वामाद्यष्टौपप्रागाद्यष्टयोनिषु । वि[षम्रा]दि तिस्रो मध्ययोनिकोणेषु सर्वानन्दा मध्य इति ॥ १३ ॥

प्राङ्मध्ययोन्योरित्यन्तरा पादुकापूजोक्ता । वाग्भवादिमिति सर्वासां वामादीनामपि च विशेषणम् । तदुक्तम्—ऐं वामादये नम इत्यादि । यद्वा पराभिधानामित्यत्रैवैतत्संबध्यते । तदाह—वाग्भवादित्वमिति । परावरादिपङ्क्त्योरिति

क्रमोऽप्यर्थसिद्ध उक्तः। मूले परावराख्यामपीत्यपिशब्देनाण्डजा[दि] चतुष्टयं वा सूचितम्। तदुक्तमधस्तात्—पादुकासप्तकं न्यसेदित्यादि। चतुष्पीठपूजा च प्रागिष्यते। ततो दीक्षायां योनौ निधायेत्यादि कार्यम्। नित्यपूजायां त्वावाह्य तामित्याद्येव कार्यम्। तत् सर्वं प्रागभिहितम्। त्रिपुरभैरवीमूर्तये मम इत्यादि। कामेश्वर्यादौ रत्यादौ च सति देव्या वामदक्षिणाग्रकोणेष्वग्रबीज-क्रमेण तदर्चनमिति ज्ञेयम्। तदुक्तं—वामकोणे यजेद्देव्या इत्यादि ॥ १४ ॥

ततोऽङ्गावरणमाह—तेनैव चेति। वाग्भवग्रहणमेतत्। तत्र वाग्भवेन पुन-रङ्गुलिष्वित्युक्तम्। यथोक्तक्रमत इति। तदुक्तम्—हृदयं सशिरस्तथा शिखे-त्यादि। मूलयोग इति षट्स्वप्यङ्गेषु समस्तमूलयोगोऽभिप्रेतः। यत्तु प्रागुक्तं 'मूलबीजमध्यमबीजदीर्घानन्तरमिति। तत्र व्यस्तयोग इति भेदः। तन्मध्ययोने-रिति बाणावरणमुक्तम्। अभित इति बहिः परितः प्रागादिदिक्ष्विति यावत्। भगाभगसर्पिणिभगमालिनीरित्येकं समासपदम्। तत्पूर्वेत्यत्रानङ्गकुसुमा अनङ्ग-मेखला अनङ्गमदना चोक्ता। प्रागादि योनिषु चेत्यधः संबध्यते। त्रिपुरा-म्बिकायां त्रिपुरसुन्दर्यां चावरणान्तरौचित्यसंभवे तत्पूजापि कार्या। तत्र त्रिपुरसुन्दर्यामष्टयोनिषु वशिन्याद्यष्टौ स्युरिति ज्ञेयम्। दलेषु मातृगणं सचण्डि-कान्तमसिताङ्गकाद्यैः सहाभियजेदिति संबन्धः। दलेषु ब्रह्माण्यादिचण्डि-कान्ता मातरः। दलाग्रेष्वसिताङ्गभैरवादयः। सह चैषां द्वन्द्वशः पूजा स्यात्। तदुक्तम्—आं ब्रामादिदीर्घयुता इत्यादि। तैरङ्गबाणादिभिर्भैरवैश्च सह भगवती-मभियजेदित्यपि योजनीयम्। कृत्स्नापि पूजा सामान्यसिद्धेति ज्ञेयमिति ॥१५-१८

मूले क्रमाप्त्येति। सहेति शेषः। गुरुसकाशादेव जपपूजादिक्रमस्य प्राप्ति-रभिषेकसमये कार्येति। तदाह गुरोरिति। मूल उक्तवतेति जपार्चाहुतेषु संबध्यते। ततश्चैतदपि लभ्यते। योगेषु फलाभिधानेऽपि नित्यतयापि ते कार्या इति। व्यस्त-साधनेऽपि समानमेतदवबोद्धव्यम् ॥ २० ॥

वाग्भवसाधनक्रममिति जपहोमादिसद्भावात् क्रमग्रहणम्। मूलेऽच्छाभ इति देहनिर्मलतोक्ता। धरणिमयगृह इति गुहापवरकाद्यभिप्रायम्। वाग्भवमिति केवलवाग्भवाभिप्रायम्। यद्वा तत्प्रधानस्य कृत्स्नस्य ग्रहणम्। तदाह तदादिक-मिति। शुद्धादिसर्वसाधारणमेतत्। केवलवाग्भवजपे तु ध्यानविकल्पः—

नवकुम्भनिभां देवीं मुक्ताजालविभूषणाम्।
मुद्राकपालविद्याक्षमालाराजच्चतुर्भुजाम् ॥ इति।

मन्त्रजप्ताञ्जनादिरिति तिलककुसुमचूडनादिग्रहणम् ॥ २१ ॥

मूले रत्नाकल्प इति कामराजसाधनक्रम उक्तः। भूसद्मनि पूर्ववद्‌गुह्यादि-ग्रहणम्। रतिपतिमयं बीजं यो जपतीति संबन्धनीयम्। केवलकामराजाभिप्राय-मेतत्। मन्त्रिपदस्याभिप्रायान्तरमाह मन्त्रस्येति। केवलकामराजे ध्यानविकल्पः—

रक्तां सुरतरोर्मूलविलसन्मणिपीठगाम्।

सृणिपाशकपालेक्षुमातुलङ्गधनुष्कराम्॥ इति।

शुद्धकामराजस्य तु प्रतिपत्त्यन्तरम्—

ऊर्ध्वबिन्द्वात्मकं वक्त्रमधोबिन्दुद्वयात्मकम्।

कुचद्वयं च तच्छेषैः शेषाङ्गानि च भावयेत्॥ इति॥ २२

मूले ससुरासुरेत्याद्यपि प्रकृतफलप्रकरणमेव। तदाह—मध्यमबीजस्येति। मूले ससुरासुरादीनां प्रमदा एवमवस्थाः सत्यः तद्‌दृष्टिपातमपि सन्नमन्तीत्येवं योजनीयम्। मदवेगत इति कामजमदग्रहणम्। प्रथितान्तरित्यत्रान्तर्व्याप्तत्व-मुक्तम्। घनेति भूमाभिप्रायम्। घर्मजतोयेति खेदजलग्रहणम्। औत्सुक्यभाराद्यः पृथुर्वेपथुः ततो यः खेदस्तेन भिन्नस्य + + निभृत(हरिण)शावलोचना इति + + ॥ २३॥२४॥२५॥२६॥२७॥

मूले धरापवरक इति शाक्तसाधनक्रम उक्तः। अन्त्यं मनुमिति केवलशाक्तबीज-ग्रहणम्। तत्प्रधानग्रहणं वा। तदाह—अन्त्यबीजादिकमिति। केवलशाक्तजपे ध्यानविकल्पः—अक्षमालासुधा[कुम्भमुद्रा]पुस्तकधारिणीम्।

नवकुन्देन्दुसङ्काशां राजन्मौक्तिकभूषणाम्॥ इति।

सकारयुतं शाक्तं पराभिधीयते। तत्र निष्कामविषये ध्यानभेदः—

अकलङ्कशशाङ्काभां त्र्यक्षां चन्द्रकलावतीम्।

मुद्रापुस्तलसद्बाहां मुक्तामणिविभूषिताम्॥ इति।

मूले वशीति जितेन्द्रियत्वमुक्तम्। विचित्रपदपङ्क्तिभिर्भारतीत्यन्वयः॥ २८॥

मूले पलाशपुष्पैरिति समस्तस्य प्रयोगप्रकरणारम्भः। अयुतावधिमित्ययुतम्। सौभाग्यलक्ष्म्योश्चेति मन्दिरपदं संबन्धनीयम्। मन्त्रजापीति मूलमन्त्रं नित्यं जपत एव सर्वत्र प्रयोगाधिकार उक्तः। यद्वा तत्तदुचितप्रतिपत्त्या जपोऽपि कार्य इति सूचितम्। तदुक्तम्—

पाशाङ्कुशोद्यतकरामरुणां त्रिनेत्रां माणिक्यवज्रहरितैरपि भूषिताङ्गीम्।

मूर्तिं विचिन्त्य विदधीत पुरोक्तमार्गाद्वश्यक्रियानयनसं[वन]नादि मन्त्री॥

मातुलङ्गनिधिपङ्कजैः शिवां शोभमानकरपङ्कजामिह।

संविचिन्त्य खलु पौष्टिकीं क्रियां कुर्वतो भवति भूतिरुत्तमा॥ इति।

अभिप्रायान्तरमाह—स मन्त्रजापीतीति। सर्वत्र + जप इति योजनीयम्। सर्वत्रेति। सर्वमन्त्रविधानेष्वपि होमानन्तरमिति भावः ॥ २९ ॥

करञ्ज + शमि वह्नि। बिल्वदलप्रसूनैरिति बिल्वस्य पत्रैः पुष्पैश्चेत्यर्थः ॥३०॥

दलद्दलैरित्येतद्विवृणोति—विकसद्दलैरिति। कुसुमकैरिति संबध्यते ॥ ३१ ॥

अनुलोमविलोमेत्यत्र वाचकमित्युपस्कारः। साध्याह्वग्रहणं कर्मणोऽप्युपलक्षणम्। यथा अनुलोममुक्त्वा देवदत्तं वश्यं कुर्विति पुनः प्रतिलोमं ब्रूयादिति। कर्मसाधकयोरपीत्यत्राभिप्रायान्तरम्। देवदत्तस्य यज्ञदत्तं वश्यं कुर्विति। पटुसंयुतयेति। पटुश्चन्दनम्। विकल्पोऽत्र विवक्षितः। नरपो राजा। जनता जनसमूहः। कमलाकरी श्रीकरी ॥ ३२ ॥ ३३ ॥

सुधालता अमृता। मन्त्रितम इत्यभिप्रायमाह—अन्त्यबीजादित्वमिति। व्यस्तैरपि बीजैः स्यात् तत्तदुचितफलकृते होम इत्यप्यनेन गम्यते। यथा पलाशपुष्पैरित्यत्र वाग्भवेनेत्यादि। यदुक्तं—वागैश्वर्यातिशयदतयेत्यादि ॥ ३४ ॥

मूले फुल्लैर्बिल्वप्रसूनैरितीन्दिरायै जुहुतेत्युपरि संबन्धः। त्रिमूर्तीः प्रति वचनमेतत्। + + + सर्पिषा पायसेनेति च बिल्वप्रसूनादिवद्विकल्पः। सर्वत्रायुताधिकमिति संख्या ज्ञेया इति ॥ ३५ ॥

पूर्वसूचितानिति। 'युञ्जीत योगांश्च गुरूपदिष्टानित्यमूनित्यर्थः। मूलाधारादिति समस्तयोग उच्यते। मूलाधारादा + + स्फुरन्तीमित्यन्वयः। मूलाधारादुत्पद्य द्वादशान्तस्थसूर्यमण्डलं प्राप्नुवन्तीं स्फुरद्रूपामित्यर्थः। शिखिपुरपुटवीतामिति षट्कोणमध्यगतामित्यर्थः। तन्मध्यगेन्दोरित्यर्कमध्यगतात्सोमादित्यर्थः। वक्ष्यति च—सार्धसोमादिति। स्रवदमृतमुचा धारयेति + + +। मन्त्रमय्येति तदा मन्त्रजपोऽपि सूचितः। तत्सङ्ख्या चायुताधिकं तत्त्वार्धलक्षावधीत्येतदेव वा भवति। सद्यः संपूर्यमाणामिति क्रमेणेति ज्ञेयम्। पूर्वं तस्यां प्रभायामाप्लावनं पुनः समस्तसिराभिर्देहपूरणमित्यादिक्रमेणेति भावः। तन्मयत्वेनेति तदमृतमयत्वमुक्तम्। मन्त्रीति समस्तमन्त्रविदित्यर्थः। अभिप्रायान्तरमाह—शिखिपुरपुटेष्वित्यादिना। मन्त्रन्यासमिति चाह मन्त्री ध्यायन्नित्युपरि संबन्धः। नित्यतया योगी वैश्वर्यादिसङ्कोचन्यासानन्तरमिताख्यासं विधाय योगं कुर्यात्। वैरूप्यादिक्षयार्थतया योगी तु सकलीकरणपूर्वकमिति ज्ञेयम्। अयमिह प्रयोगः। मूलाधारेऽष्टदलं कमलं तत्कर्णिकायां षट्कोणम्। तदन्तस्त्रिकोणं परिचिन्त्य त्रिकोणोदरे श्रुद्रादीनामन्यतमं मन्त्रं विन्यस्य षट्सु कोणेषु तं मन्त्रं द्विरावृत्त्या विन्यसेत्। त्रिपुराम्बिकायां तु षट् स्ववर्णा एव विन्यसनीयाः। भूपुरे मध्यबीजयोगमिति

बहिश्चतुरस्रस्याष्टदिक्ष्विति भावः। बीजविशेषयोगं चेति वक्ष्यमाणाः परिवारवर्णा इत्युक्तानां ग्रहणम् + + + वैरूप्यादिष्वयार्थतया यन्त्रधारणमप्येवं कर्तव्यमिति चेह विवरणाशयोऽवबोद्धव्यः॥ ३६॥

वह्नेर्बिम्बेत्यादि व्यस्तयोगाभिधानम्। तदाह—वाग्भवयोगमिति। स्वरगण-समावेष्टितमिति षोडशदलं पद्ममप्यर्थादवसीयते। वह्निबिम्बमप्यर्थाद्दलगतं भवति। स्वीयादिति साधकसंबन्धिन इति भावः। मूलाधारगताया वाग्भव-शक्तेः परावाग्लक्षणायाः पश्यन्त्यादिक्रमेण वैखर्यापत्तावेवं तस्या निःसृतिरित्य-र्थादवसेयम्। प्रततकिरणप्रावृतमिति। प्रततिस्त्रिभुवनव्याप्तिः। तस्या वास्याः प्रततेः किरणैः समन्तात्परिवृतं वाग्भवाख्यमिति संबन्धः। मन्त्री ध्यायेदित्य-त्राभिप्रायमाह—षट्कोणेष्विति। भूपुरे इत्यादिबीजविशेषयोगः सर्वत्र समान एव। दुःखशान्त्या इत्यत्रार्थात् कवितासिद्ध्यै चेति लभ्यते। यन्त्रधारणेऽप्येतत् फलमभिप्रेतम्॥ ३७॥

मूले इत्यत्रेति द्वादशदलपद्माभिप्रायम्। तत्र दलगतं भानुबिम्बम्। योनिरिह न त्रिकोणमात्रम्। तदाह—योनिः षट्कोणमिति। यद्वा षट्कोणं प्रकरणसिद्धम्। तन्मध्यगतं त्रिकोणमिह योनिरुक्ता। इह मध्ययोनौ षट्कोणेषु च कामराजं न्यसनीयम्। तदाह—अत्र षट्कोणेष्विति। एवकारो यथाश्रुतार्थाबाधनार्थः। योनिष्वन्तरालं मध्यमबीजं यत्र तद्योन्यन्तरालं तत्रोदितम्। तत्रापि कु + स्त्रिमु-द्वेश उदितमिति योनीनामन्तरालेऽभ्यन्तरभाग उदितमित्येवं योजना। कभा-द्यन्तकैरिति कादिभान्तैरित्यर्थः। कभादि + + + मस्तु सूर्यमण्डलवर्णत्वादेव भवति। तदुक्तमधस्तात्—कभाद्या वसुदाः सौरा इति। भूपुरादिसर्वमिहापि समानमेव। यन्त्रधारणमप्येवमभिप्रेतम्॥ ३८॥

मूले मूर्ध्नं इति। तत उपरीति भावः। शशधरबिम्बं दशदलपद्मे दलगतं भवति। प्राग्वद्योनिशब्दः। तदाह—योनिः षट्कोणमेवेति। नवयोनिर्वेति। पूर्वेष्वपि समानो यो विकल्पः। स्फुरन्तमिति बीजविशेषणम्। संवीतं व्याप-कार्णैरिति। दलगतैरिति शेयम्। मकारस्थितमिति स्पर्शान्त्यस्य कभादिसमष्टि-भूतस्य सूर्यमण्डलतया शशधरबिम्बासदलेन चिन्तनमुक्तम्। वक्ष्यति च—सार्धं-सोमादिति। सारस्वताच्छामृतजललुलितमिति त्रिभुवनस्य तत्प्रवाहेण पूरण-मपीष्यते। तदुक्तम्—सद्यःसंपूर्यमाणां त्रिभुवनमखिलमिति। यन्त्रधारणमप्ये-वमभिप्रेतम्। योगस्तत्तद्बीजजपेन कार्यः। जपसंख्या तु पूर्वोक्तैव। अथ समस्तस्य त्रिस्थानं योगान्तरम्।

मूलाधारस्य मध्याज्ज्वलदनलनिभं वाग्भवं ज्योतिरुद्य-
द्धृत्पद्मं प्राप्य दीव्यद्द्युमणिनिभमतोऽप्युद्गतं कामराजम्।
प्राप्तं भ्रूमध्यपद्मोदरममृतकराकारमच्छामृताद्भिः
शान्तं संपूर्यमाणां खलु तनु भुवनं चिन्तयेद्गू + + + ॥

किं च 'त्रिमूर्तिसर्गाच्चेत्यत्रापि प्रतिबीजं योगत्रयं सूचितम्। त्रिमूर्तिसर्गात्पुराभवत्वाच्चेति चकारेण त्रिमूर्तिविसर्गात् पश्चाद्भवत्वमप्युक्तम्। सर्गविसर्गौ च प्रतिपत्त्या साक्षाच्च संभवतः। तत्र सर्गप्रतिपत्त्यैहिको योगः। विसर्गप्रतिपत्त्या चामुष्मिकः। तयोः साक्षाद्भावे त्वामुष्मिक एवेति विभागः। त्रिमूर्तिरिह शब्दप्रधानो वागर्थज्ञानप्रपञ्चः। तदुत्पत्तेरपि पुराभवा शक्तिरिति मूलाधारगताया वाग्भवशक्तेः स्वरूपविमर्शस्थूलीभाववशात् पश्यन्त्यादिक्रमेण वैखरीरूपेण सकलवेदागमकाव्यव्यवहारादेः शब्दप्रधानस्य प्रपञ्चस्य प्रतिपत्तिरभिप्रेता।

तदुक्तम्— ध्यायेद्वागीश्वरीं पराम्।
बीजरूपामुल्लसन्तीं ततोऽनङ्गपदावधि।
ब्रह्मग्रन्थिं विनिर्भिद्य जिह्वाग्रे दीपरूपिणीम्॥ इति।

त्रिमूर्तिविसर्गात्पश्चाद्भवामिति शब्दप्रधानस्य प्रपञ्चस्य संहारानन्तरभाविनी शक्तिरिति। तत्र वाग्भवे व्यञ्जनं शब्दप्रधानं प्रपञ्च ऐकारस्तद्विमर्शः। बिन्दुस्तन्मूलभूतो वि + + ष्टा ततो वाग्भवोच्चारणे वाक्प्रधानस्य जगतो विमर्शे तस्य तत्कर्तरि संहारः। तदन्ते च तदीयं साक्षिचिद्रूपमवतिष्ठत इति। साक्षात्त्वे तु विशेषः। वेदागमादिप्रसरसमये स्वसाक्षिचिद्रूपतो विमर्शस्थूलीभाववशात् पश्यन्त्यादिक्रमेण तदभिव्यक्तिः तदवसाने च तद्विपर्ययेण साक्षिचिद्रूपावस्थितिरपि भावनीयेति। तथा च प्राणाग्निहोत्रप्रकरण उक्तम्—सर्वसाक्षित्वेन स्वयमवाच्यमवाचकं ब्रह्म भूत्वेत्यादि। पुरैव त्रयीमयत्वाच्चेति। चकारेण पश्चादपि त्रयीमयत्वादित्युक्तम्। पूर्ववच्च सर्वं योजनीयम्। स्वरूपरसविषयानन्दास्त्रयस्त्रयी तदवस्थातः प्रागपि तत्तन्मात्रमयी स्वरूपमहानन्दलक्षणेति। त्रयी चेह भोगप्रधानः प्रपञ्च एव। हृदयगतायाः कामराजशक्तेः स्वरूपानन्दस्थूलीभाववशात् परसूक्ष्मस्थूलक्रमेण सकलविषयरसाद्यानन्दस्य सोपकरणस्य प्रतिपत्तिरियमभिप्रेता। पश्चादपि त्रयीमयत्वादिति सकलभोगप्रधानप्रपञ्चो व्यञ्जनम् तदुपभोग ईकारः। तदानन्दिता च बिन्दुः ततश्च कामराजोच्चारणे सकलभोग्यप्रपञ्चस्योपभोगि तस्य तदानन्दितरि संहारः। तदन्ते तदीयसाक्ष्यानन्दरूपमवतिष्ठत इति। साक्षात्त्वे तु विशेषः। विषयोपभोगसमये स्वसाक्ष्यानन्दरूपत उपभोगशक्तिस्थूली-

भाववशात् परसूक्ष्मस्थूलक्रमेण तद्विषयप्रपञ्चाभिव्यक्तिस्तदवसाने तद्विपर्ययेण साक्ष्यानन्दरूपावस्थितिरिति। लयेऽपि त्रिलोक्याः पूरणत्वादित्यपिशब्देन सर्गेऽप्युक्तम्। त्रिलोकी चार्थप्रधानः प्रपञ्चः। तस्य सर्गे पूरणं स्वस्वाकारतयावस्थापनम्। भ्रूमध्यगतायाः तृतीयबीजशक्तेः ज्ञानशक्तिस्थूलीभाववशात् कारणसूक्ष्मक्रमेण स्थूलजगद्रूपतया प्रतिपत्तिरित्युक्ता। लये त्रिलोक्या अपि पूरणत्वादिति शाक्तबीजे व्यञ्जनमर्थप्रपञ्चः। औकारस्तदुचितं ज्ञानम्। विसर्गो ज्ञाता। ततश्च तदुच्चारणे तत्स्वस्यातिप्रधानप्रपञ्चतदवच्छेदलक्षणे ज्ञाने तस्य च ज्ञातरि संहारः। तदन्ते साक्षिपूर्णरूपमवतिष्ठत इति। साक्षात्त्वे तु विशेषः। तत्तदर्थप्रतीतिसमये साक्षिस्वरूपात् पूर्णादवच्छेदज्ञानशक्तिवशात् कारणसूक्ष्मादिक्रमेण तदर्थप्रत्ययः तदवसाने च तद्विपर्ययेण साक्षिपूर्णरूपावस्थितिरिति ॥ ३९ ॥

पुनर्वश्यप्रधानमिति सकृद्वाग्भवयोगस्योक्तत्वात् पुनःशब्दः। योनेरिति मूलाधारगतनवयोनिग्रहणम्। मध्य इति च शेषः। यद्वा योनिरुच्यतीमित्युपस्कारः। परिभ्रमितकुण्डलिरूपिणीमिति। नवयोनिमध्ययोनिमध्ये परिभ्रमणशीलां कुण्डलिनीरूपामित्यर्थः। तदुक्तं—कुण्डलिनी तदा मूलाधारे विसरतीत्यादि। कुण्डलिग्रहणौचित्यादेव वाग्भवयोगोऽयमित्यवगमः। रक्तामृतद्रवमुचेति। तेजसा रक्तत्वात् स्वरूपं रक्तं लभ्यते। तदुक्तम्—रक्तवर्णध्यानयुक्तामिति। व्योमस्थलमिति। त्रैलोक्यान्तर्भागाभिप्रायम्। + + तस्मिन्नाविश्येति स्त्रियं पुरुषं वा साध्यमाविश्य मङ्क्षु द्रुतं वशयेत्। तस्मिन् साध्यस्याविशन + + ॥ ४० ॥

+ कामबीजस्य स्थानभेदेनेति पूर्वं हृत्पद्मे तद्योगस्योक्तत्वादेवमभिधानम्। मूले गुह्यस्थितमिति गुह्यपदेन लिङ्गमुच्यते। तथा च कामपटले—शिवज्वालातनुमिति। यद्वा गुह्यशब्देन त्रिपुरात्मभूतस्य साधकस्य योनिग्रहणम्।

तथा चोक्तम्—तथा कामकलारूपां मदनाङ्कुरगोचर इति।

मदनस्य बीजमिति कामराजग्रहणम्। निजतेजसैव व्योमस्थलं सकलमप्यभिपूर्य तस्मिन्नित्येतदिहापि समानम्। तस्मिन्निति + + विदग्धलोक इति + ॥ ४१ ॥

[निकल]योगमिति। निष्कलानां योगानामुक्तत्वादेवमभिधानम्। इतरयोगेष्वपीति कल्पेन सकलदेवताध्यानमुक्तम्। तेनेह सकलयोगेऽपि विकल्पेन निष्कलध्यानमपि सिद्धं भवति। चित्ताम्बुज इति हृदयपद्माभिप्रायम्। तद्भूतामिति बीजात्मिकमित्यर्थः। नानारसस्रोतसा निर्यान्तमिति + + + निरस्तसंसृतिभय इति सामान्यफलमुक्तम्। सर्वत्रापि समानमेतदवबोद्धव्यम्। ननूक्ततया गुरुत्रययोगानिति तावदुक्तम्। ततः क इह भेद इति। उच्यते।

तत्र निष्कामस्यानुष्ठानम् इह तु सकामस्यापि मुमुक्षोरिति। वक्ष्यति च—विद्येशोमित्यादि ॥ ४२ ॥

मूले संक्षेपतो निगदितेत्युपसंहारः। विद्येशोमिति तु शास्त्रफलेनोपसंहारः। प्रतिभजन्निति भक्तिमान् नियमवानिति वार्थः। तस्यैवंभूतोऽन्दिरा भवेदिति च योजनीयम्। ततयशःपूरेति व्याप्तयशःसमूहेत्यर्थः। सर्वमुनिभिः संप्रार्थनीयं पदमिति त्रैपुरं चिदानन्दपूर्णस्वरूपमुक्तम् ॥ ४३ ॥ ४४ ॥

इति प्रयोगक्रमदीपिकायां नवमः पटलः।

श्रीश्रीगणेशाय नमः।

श्रीश्रीशारदायै नमः।

शिवपञ्चाक्षरीभाष्यम्।

श्रीगणेशाय नमः।

नमः शिवाय इति मन्त्रः। तस्य व्याख्यानम्।

त्यागो हि नमसो वाच्य आनन्दः प्रकृतिस्तथा।
फलं प्रत्ययवाच्यं स्यात् त्याज्यं पत्रफलादिकम्॥ १
त्यजामीदमिदं सर्वं चतुर्णामिह सिद्धये। (१म व्याख्यानम्)
नमः शिवाय।

अथवा नमसो वाच्यः प्रणामो दैन्यलब्धये॥ २
दैन्यं सेवा तथा ज्ञप्तिः सिद्धिः सर्वस्य वस्तुनः।
नमामि देवदेवेशं सकामोऽकाम एव वा॥ ३ (२य व्याख्यानम्)
नमः शिवाय।

नञा निषिध्यते भावविकृतिर्जगदात्मनः।
मसनं देवदेवेश नेह नानास्तिशब्दतः॥ ४
अथेति गमयेत्यर्थे तस्माच्छुद्धोऽस्मि नित्यशः।
प्रणामो देहगेहादेरभिमानस्य नाशनम्॥ ५
शिवो ब्रह्मादिरूपः स्याच्छक्तिभिस्तिसृभिः सह।
अथवा तूर्यमेव स्यान्निर्गुणं ब्रह्म तत्परम्॥ ६
नमसो नमने शक्तिर्नमनं ध्यानमेव च।
चतुर्थ्या तादात्म्यसम्बन्धः कथ्यते प्रत्यगात्मनोः॥ ७
अहं शिवः शिवोऽहं च मन्ये वेदान्तनिष्ठया।
इत्येवं नम इत्युक्तं वेदैः शास्त्रैश्च सर्वशः॥ ८
अथवा दास एवाहमहं दास इतीरणम्।
इत्येव नम इत्युक्तं वेदैः शास्त्रैश्च सर्वशः॥ ९
अथवेदमिदं सर्वं त्यजामि परमात्मने।
अर्थं धर्मं च कामं च वाञ्छंश्च जगदीश्वरम्॥ १०
एतन्मन्त्रार्थतत्त्वज्ञैर्वेदवेदान्ततत्परैः।
निर्णीतं तत्त्वगर्भं यद्‌विज्ञेयं मुक्तिलब्धये॥ ११

अथवा भुक्तिलाभाय ध्येयं तत्त्वविवेकतः।

भिन्नं बुद्ध्वा सदा देवं मन्त्रेणेशं जगद्गुरुम्॥ १२ (३य व्याख्यानम्)

नमः शिवाय।

नमेरपि नमः प्रोक्तो जन्तास्याज्जगदीश्वरे।

तस्माद् दासोऽहमित्येवं मत्वा मां प्रापयात्मनि॥ १३

अस्मिञ्छेते जगत् सर्वं तन्मयं शब्दगामि यत्।

तद्वानाच्छिव इत्युक्तं कारणं ब्रह्मतत्परैः॥ १४

न मा यस्यास्ति लक्ष्मीश सोऽहं देवो न संशयः।

तस्मान्मे प्रापयेहैव लक्ष्मीं विद्यां सनातनीम्॥ १५

यस्मादानन्दरूपस्त्वं देवैर्वेदैर्निगद्यसे।

तस्मान्मे देहि योगीश भद्रं ज्ञानं सुभावनम्॥ १६ (४र्थ व्याख्यानम्)

नमः शिवाय।

यस्मात् त्वं नेति नेतीति नञर्थं मासि वेदजम्।

तस्मान्नमोसि भद्रं मे यतो जातोऽनमो नमः॥ १७

शिवं शिवमथाप्रासः शिवायेति निगद्यसे।

शिवाय मे तथा प्राप्तया शिवायं कुरु सर्वदा॥ १८ (५म व्याख्यानम्)

नमः शिवाय।

शिवां यातो महाभद्र नमोऽहं मायया ध्रुवम्।

ततो नमाय मह्यं मः शिवायं कुरु सर्वथा॥ १९ (६ष्ठ व्याख्यानम्)

नमः शिवाय।

शिव मेषियतो ज्ञप्तया शिवायस्त्वं प्रपद्यसे।

नते माया यतो ज्ञप्तया नमो वेदैः प्रपद्यते॥ २०

नमोऽहं च शिवायोऽहं नमो मह्यं नमो नमः।

नमो नमाय शुद्धाय मङ्गलाय नमो नमः॥ २१

नमो नमस्तनं शम्भो निराकाराय ते नमः।

निर्गुणं निष्क्रियं शान्तमित्याद्याः श्रुतयो जगुः॥ २२

नमो ब्रह्म निराकारं शिवायं शिव सर्वदा।

अतोऽहं च नमा भद्र शिवायोऽहं न संशयः॥ २३ (७म व्याख्यानम्)

इति पद्मपादाचार्यविरचितं शिवपञ्चाक्षरीभाष्यं सम्पूर्णम्।

श्लोकानुक्रमणिका

अ

अं स्वादात्मा कुधरा १४३
अकचटतपयाद्यैः १
अकारप्रभवा ब्रह्म ४१
अकारेकारयोर्योगा ४५
अक्षीबदादयाम् २४८
अक्षतयवकुशदूर्वा १९२
अक्षरं नाम किं नाथ १०
अक्षरपादत्रिष्टुब् २५४
अक्षरलक्षचतुष्कं २९८
अक्षरलक्षजपान्ते १२४
अक्षिनासास्यकर्णभ्रू २९
अक्षोभ्यासव्यवादिन्यौ १५३
अग्निं प्रज्वलितं वन्दे ९२
अग्निः पूषा च वितथो ६९
अग्नीन्दुयोगविक्रमा १४०
अग्नीषोमात्मकममरि २८५
अग्न्यश्व्यमाः सविघ्ननागा ६४
अग्न्यादिकमपि सर्वं २५७
अघगणः समयज्ञी ३७७
अथाद्यावामोदः प्रमोद २१०
अग्रेऽथ बिल्वमभितश्च २०९
अग्रे समयवलसुय २८७
अङ्कुशशरबाणानां १८०
अङ्गबाह्याहुतिरूर्ध्वं २१९
अङ्गमन्त्रा इमे प्रोक्ता ८१
अङ्गमन्त्रान् क्रमादष्ट ९१
अङ्गमन्त्रैस्ततो चाद्ये ९१
अङ्गस्वेदवदभ्यन्तर्व्याप्ति ३२
अङ्गानि कर्णिकायां २६७
अङ्गानि दिक्षवर्णानि २६८
अङ्गानि पूर्वं त्वथ २३८
अङ्गाग्न्यादौ तदनु च १०२
अङ्गाहुतिरनु च हेति २०४
अङ्गाग्रेड् वक्ष्याद्यैः २२२
अङ्गिराः स्यादृषिश्छन्दो २४१
अङ्गुल्यग्रससन्धि २५६
अङ्गुष्ठगुल्फजङ्घासु २२७
अङ्गुष्ठसन्धिप्रपद २४४
अङ्गैः प्रथमावरणं यष्ट्वे १९६
अङ्गैः प्रथमावरणं मूर्त्ति २४०
अङ्गैः प्रथमाहृतिरपि पश्चौ २७७
अङ्गैः प्रथमाहृतिरपि च पूज्या २५६
अङ्गैः प्रथमाहृतिरपि मूर्त्तौ १६१
अङ्गैः शक्तिभिराभि १७८
अङ्गैः समाहृभिर्मन्त्री ३१५
अङ्गैः स्यादाहृतिः पूर्वा १८२
अङ्गैरष्टभिरहिभि २५९
अङ्गैराद्याऽर्काद्यैः २४९
अङ्गैस्तंत्रौहरिर्गिरि १७०
अङ्गैर्हुतवहमूर्त्तिभि २०५
अचलात्मजा च दुर्गा १२६
अच्छस्वच्छारविन्द २४८
अच्छांशुकाभरण २५६
अच्छाभः स्वच्छभूषो १३४
अच्युतकामिनि भानु २४९
अजकला प्रथमा २१८
अज प्रसीद भगवन् २५१
अजाद्रीड्गुहालाच १५९
अजाधीशजवीचया १५७
अजेश शर्व सोमेश्वराह्वा ४३
अणिमा महिमा च २३३
अणोरणीयसो स्थूलात् ११
अतिदुःसहमन्मथमथनाभि १३५
अतिविमलं अरस्य २६६
अतो हिताय जगतां १७७
अथ याः पञ्च संप्रोक्ता ८४
अथाक्षारहकारान्ता ११०
अचार्चौ मधुसूदन २४७
अथापि चेतनाधातो २६
अथोत्तरस्यां दिशि १३५
अथ कथयामि विधानं २७१
अथ कथयिष्ये मन्त्रं १९१
अथ कृतपुष्पाञ्जलिरपि १९१
अथ कुङ्कुमहावीर २१४
अथ गजलिप्सु २११
अथ गौरि रुद्रदयिते १५५
अथ चन्द्रमनुं वक्ष्ये २००
अथ तु हविष्यप्राशो १४७
अथ द्वितीयावरणेऽर्चती २१९
अथ पटुरवमुख्य ९९
अथ परराष्ट्रजयेच्छो २७९
अथ पापकृतां शरीरभाजा ११
अथ पुनरभिवक्ष्ये २१४
अथ पुनरसुमभि २१६
अथ पुनराचम्य ह ७७
अथ पुरुषार्थचतुष्टय १७२
अथ प्रणवसंज्ञकं २२४
अथ प्रवक्ष्यति च ३०२
अथ प्रवक्ष्यामि च मास २४१
अथ प्रवक्ष्यामि नृसिंह २७६
अथ प्रवक्ष्यामि सुदर्शनस्य २५४
अथ प्रवक्ष्यामि सुदुर्लभा १२८
अथ प्रवक्ष्ये विधिवन्मनूना ६८
अथ मन्मथमन्त्रविधिं २१८
अथ यम्बिरथगाभि १५८
अथ रमाभुवनेश्वियमौ १६९

अथ लवणमनुं वदामि ३४१
अथ वक्ष्यामि दुर्गाया १८१
अथ वक्ष्यामि विद्याया ३२७
अथ वक्ष्ये संग्रहतो १५१
अथ वदाम्यजपा १९३
अथवा कुसुमैर्जवा २९४
अथवा त्रिवलयबिन्दु २३०
अथवा त्रिमधुरसिक्तै ३२६
अथवा दशमूलपुष्प ८३
अथ वादिशीजमी २३०
अथवा दिशि कुण्डमुत्तरस्यां ७३
अथवा पञ्चगव्योत्थ ३३१
अथवा बिन्दुं वर्तुल २३०
अथवाऽमलकमल ३०८
अथवा योगोपेताः २३१
अथ वारिदरगदा १८७
अथवाऽरुणानि दलानि ७६
अथवा लवणैः पराग ३४७
अथवा शक्तिस्वस्तिक २०३
अथवा शोषणदाहन २२७
अथवा षट्कोणाहत ९१
अथवा षोडशयुग्म ३१०
अथवा सघृतैरन्नैः १९८
अथवा सप्तभिरेतै ३०८
अथवा साध्यप्राणान् ३७२
अथ व्यवस्थिते त्वेवं २९
अथ व्यवस्थिते त्वेव ४९
अथ श्रियो मन्त्रविधिः १६०
अथ संग्रहेण २०८
अथ सन्तानसंसिद्धि ३७४
अथ संप्रति विष्णु २८३
अथ सजपहुतादौ ३१०
अथ स्वमुत्तारयितु ३४
अथ हितविषये विदुषां ११८
अथाक्षराणामधिदेवताया १०१
अथाखिलार्थानुगतैव ११७
अथाग्निमन्त्रा २०२
अथानया पञ्चविभेद १०७
अथाभवन् ब्रह्महरीश्वराख्या ६
अथाभिवक्ष्यामि मनुं २९३
अथाभिवक्ष्ये महितस्य ३४८
अथाभिवक्ष्ये सकलप्रपञ्च १२९
अथाहृतं षडरसं ३२
अथोच्यते द्वादश २५३
अथोच्यते श्रीकर २७०
अथोभयात्मका वर्णा ३८
अद्रिः क्षिणा कालकर्णं ३०२
अद्रिर्मीनस्य मेषस्य ४३
अधीतवेदं स्वाधीन ३७८
अधो गुह्यादभेदः ३४३
अधोभागस्तु षष्ठः स्या ३४५
अनङ्गरूपा सानङ्ग २१८
अनङ्गशिशिराऽनङ्ग २१८
अनङ्गानङ्गमदना १५३
अनन्तब्रह्मपर्यन्तैः १६४
अनन्तभोगविमले ८
अनन्तसूक्ष्मौ च शिवौ २९५
अनयैव च पूर्वसेवया १६२
अनयेव जपाभिषेक १८२
अनुदिनमघशान्त्यै ३५१
अनुदिनमनुलिम्पे ११७
अनुदिनमसुना भजतां १२०
अनुदिनमर्चयितव्यं १९३
अनुदिनमर्चयितव्यो २१०
अनुदिनमष्टशतं यो ३१६
अनुदिनमादित्याभि २७१
अनुपमसौन्दर्येण २६६
अनुरागी विसंवादी १६४
अनुलोमजपेऽङ्गाना ३३०
अनुलोमविलोमगतै १५५
अनुलोमविलोमगेय २८५
अनुलोमविलोममन्त्र १२६
अनुष्टुबन्त्ये प्रस्तार १६५
अनेन ज्वलितं मन्त्रे ९२
अनेन विधिना वाऽथ २६९
अन्तपादप्रतीपे हि ३३०
अन्तराग्निश्रियोः क्रमं १४९
अन्तराथ पुनरात्म १८९
अन्तरान्तर्बहिश्चैव ११
अन्तरा योजयेन्मन्त्रो २८५
अन्तरालं पृथग्वृत्त ७५
अन्तर्बहिर्विभागेन ५८
अन्त्यं बीजमथेन्दु १३८
अन्त्यतुरीयतदादिक २५४
अन्त्यशवर्गान्त्यासे ११९
अन्त्यावुभस्वमून् १४०
अन्त्याम्बोन्दुकादिति १२१
अन्त्यासनोऽथ सूक्ष्मो २१६
अन्तेऽवशिष्टमचर २७५
अन्नं मह्य[य्य]न्नं मे १६२
अन्नघृताभ्यां जुहुयात् १६६
अन्नाद्यर्थश्चैरपि १२६
अन्यस्मिन् भवने ७०
अन्या धमन्यो याः प्रोक्ता २५
अन्योन्यतस्संक्रमार्थे २९०
अन्वहमङ्गामादौ २१७
अपत्रपो युवा कामी २१९
अपथ्यभाजामनयो ३२
अपमृत्युरोगपाप २३०
अपरकराभयमुद्रा १९६
अपाङ्गभ्रूविलासी च २२०
अप्यव्यक्तां प्रलपति ३५
अभवत् पुराथ किल ६८
अभिध्येयं सदानन्दं ३२०
अभिनवैः सुमनोभि २२२

अभिषिच्य गुरुः शिष्यं २१८
अभिषिच्य पुनः शिष्यं ३२९
अभिषिच्य यन्त्रकलशं २५०
अभीष्टार्थी स्मरणादपि २२२
अभ्यर्च्य पीठं नवशक्ति १५०
अभ्यर्च्य पूर्ववत् पीठे २८६
अभ्यर्च्य वैष्णवमयी २२५
अमलकमलसंस्था १२४
अमलकमलाधिवासिनि १२६
अमितां श्रियमाप्नोति २०२
अमुना विधिना कृताभि १८२
अमुना विधिनाऽर्चनाहुता १९८
अमुना विधिना महेश २९५
अमुमेव मनुवरं ३००
अमृतमयजलावसिक्त १९३
अमृतावटतिलदूर्वाः ३०८
अमृतोद्भवो मकर २१९
अम्बिका ह्लादिनी चैव १५२
अम्बुयोन्यग्निपवन २३
अम्भस्युरोजहृदयसे १६२
अम्भोधाराः सदा भिन्ने २६७
अयथा प्रतिपत्तिमन्त्र ११६
अयुतं जपेन्मनुमिमं ३६७
अयुतं तिलैर्वनोत्थै १८४
अयुतं नियतो मन्त्री ३४२
अयुतं प्रजपेच्च ३६६
अयुतं प्रजपेज्जुहुयाद ३६२
अयुतं प्रजपेन्मन्त्री २००
अयुतद्वितयावधिर्जप २२२
अरिदरकृपाणखेटक १८४
अरिदरगदाब्जहस्ताः २३९
अरिदरगदाब्जहस्ता १४६
अरिशङ्खकृपाणखेटबाणा १८३
अरिशङ्खकृपाणखेटसंज्ञान् २७२
अरुणकनकवर्णं १९४
अरुणकमलसंस्था १६५
अरुणतरवसन २१९
अरुणमरुणवासो २१८
अरुणसरोरुहसंस्थ १९६
अरुणारविन्दकर्णिका २६६
अरुणा शिखिदीर्घयुता १९५
अरुणैः पुनरुत्पलैः २०६
अरुणैश्चन्दनकुसुमै १७३
अरुणोत्पलैश्च पुष्पै १७४
अरुणोऽरुणपङ्कज ३४२
अरुणोऽरुणपङ्कजे १९८
अर्कद्विजाङ्घ्रिपमयूर १९७
अर्कस्यन्दनबद्धपन्नग ३३७
अर्कानलोज्ज्वल २८७
अर्काभरुजसासौ १४८
अर्केऽजस्थेऽब्धिगाया ३३९
अर्केन्दुधरणितोया ३४९
अर्केन्दुवह्निनिलय २८९
अर्कौघाभं किरीटा २३४
अर्घपदाद्यन्तासु च ६९
अर्घ्यपाद्याचमन ८६
अर्चयित्वा दण्डदीर्घं ३४५
अर्चयेदङ्गमूर्त्तीश्च २०४
अर्चयेद्विधिनाऽनेन १६६
अर्चा कार्या नित्यशः ३०६
अर्च्या कृत्स्नवयक्तीव १८१
अर्थिभ्योऽर्थमदातृणां ३७४
अर्धैकद्विद्विसंख्याभि ४५
अलङ्कारा तथा सूर्या १६७
अलदतनिशाकुशोतै ३५९
अलसं मलसंक्लिन्नं ३७८
अलिकांसपार्श्वकुक्षिषु १४४
अवनिजलानलमारुत २३२
अवनिपगुपुत्र २५०
अवाङ्मुखी सा तस्याश्च २४
अव्यक्तमहदहङ्कृति १९
अव्यक्तादन्तहृदित १७
अव्यात् कपर्दक ३१५
अव्याद्भास्करसप्रभाभि २५५
अव्यान्निर्व्याजरौद्रा ३८०
अव्यान्नीलत्कलाप ३२१
अशोकोद्भवबिल्वोत्थ ८६
अश्रेः पार्श्वोत्थपदे ६९
अश्वत्थचूतपनस ८५
अश्वत्थविपाङ्घ्रिपबिल्व १४७
अश्वत्थोडुम्बरप्लक्ष ११५
अश्वारूढा कराग्रे २६७
अश्विशमानलधात्र ६२
अश्वेभाजभुजङ्ग ६१
अश्वोदरजसंज्ञश्च ९१
अष्टचत्वारिंशता तैः ७४
अष्टत्रिंशत्प्रभेदेन ८३
अष्टपवगुणवृत्त २९४
अष्टपत्रमथ पद्म २७२
अष्टप्रकृत्यात्मकश्च २३६
अष्टभिः सप्तभिः षड्भि २५६
अष्टभिरेतैर्विहितौ २१७
अष्टसाहस्रसंख्येन १८१
अष्टसु शूलेषु तथा २७५
अष्टद्वारविघ्नसिंहासने १७१
अष्टाक्षराक्षरविधान २४०
अष्टाक्षरादराष्टक २२९
अष्टाक्षराङ्गैरष्टार्णं २२७
अष्टाक्षरान्तरित २६०
अष्टाक्षरेण व्यस्तेन २३४
अष्टाक्षरोक्तमनुवर्यं १०७
अष्टादशन्तु चक्रस्य २९०
अष्टार्णचक्रमनुमध्य २८८
अष्टाशात्तगजाविह्वल १५४
अष्टैश्वर्यसमेतौ ३२१

अष्टोत्तरं शतमथो २०५
अष्टोत्तरशतजप्तं १८५
अष्टोत्तरशतावृत्त्या २०२
अष्टोर्ध्वंशतं मन्त्री २७४
अष्टोर्ध्वंशतं हविषा २०६
असकलशशिराज १६२
असिखेटकराऽर्कस्था १८६
असितचन्द्रदंष्ट्रा १८६
असिताङ्गाद्यौ रुद्ररपि १३४
असृग्वसादिको धातू ८०
असौ मन्त्रस्य हृत्स्थस्य १७७
अस्तेयहत्तिमास्तिक्य १७८
अस्त्रमन्त्रप्रवस्राय २३५
अस्पृष्टकं तीम. १८९
अस्य तु वेदादित्वात् २२९
अस्य यन्त्रमभिलिख्य २८१
अस्याचाराण्यमूनि च २९८
अस्या विकाराद्धर्यैभ्यो ५७
अस्यास्तु रजसा चैव ५७
अस्यैकप्रज्ञो हृदयं २७२
अहं वैश्वानरो भूत्वा १२२
अहरहरष्टशतं २१६
अहिमूषिकहंसिका १८९
अहिशशधरगङ्गा २१०
अहोरात्रमिनेन्दुभ्या २६

आ

आकृतिं स्वेन भावेन ५२
आकृष्टानां साध्यदेशा २७२
आख्यां मध्यगतामले १७५
आख्यां मध्ये समारे १७५
आग्नेयो वक्ष्यमाणेन २९०
आज्ञारावज्रहंसिको ५९
आज्यतिलराज्यानित्यक १८६
आज्याक्तैर्जुहुयाच्छ्रिये २५८
आज्यापामार्गसमित् २०४
आज्येनाष्टसहस्रं २२९
आज्यैरयुतं जुहुयात् २०६
आज्यैरष्टोर्ध्वंशतं २०२
आताम्राकायुताभा १३१
आत्मनो देवताभाव ७९
आत्मन्यधश्चोपरि च २२४
आत्मानं मदनं ध्यायेत् २२०
आत्मानमार्यां प्रतिपद्य १८९
आत्मान्तरात्मपरम २२५
आदावङ्गावरणं मन्त्र ९०
आदावङ्गावरणमनु १५२
आदित्यं रविभानू १९८
आदित्याभिमुखो भूत्वा २२१
आदिरसं कुत्सितं वत्सं २७८
आदौनामिति कथिता ४४
आदौ तारं विलिखतु २०७
आदौ तार: प्रकृति २१८
आदौ विधानेषु समेत २४२
आ[घ्रा]द्यं घ्राणेन्द्रियं २२०
आद्यन्तप्रणवगशक्ति १२५
आद्यन्तस्वरषट्कस्य २९
आद्य: स्वर: समेतो २२४
आद्या मिथुनैराहृति २११
आद्ये सूक्तवये छन्दो १६५
आद्यैरावीतबीजं २४७
आद्यैर्मेषाद्ययो राशि ५८
आद्यैस्त्रिभेदैस्तपनान्तिके १११
आर्द्राशुकोऽग्निमनुना २२७
आर्द्रा प्रज्ञा प्रभा मेधा २४९
आधाय वाणे निशिते १८९
आधाय वैश्वानरमत्र २१२
आधाय वैश्वानरमादरेण २२८
आधारहृद्वदनदौ: २२५
आधारोद्यच्छक्तिबिन्दू १०४
आनन्द: कर्दमश्चैव १६५
आनित्यकसमिद्धोमात् १८६
आपोहिष्ठामयाद्याभि २२१
आप्यायितोऽग्निना २०७
आप्यायिनी शशियुता २०१
आबद्धरत्नमुकुटां १६९
आभाष्य चटप्रचटी २०२
आभि: सर्वाभिरपि च २२२
आभ्याममृयुगीर्णाता ६२
आयामि बुद्बुदाकारं २४
आयुष्काम: स्वर्चहचं ६२
आरक्तोत्सरचि २८२
आरण्यकोऽत्यनुष्टुब् १८२
आरभ्य कर्मक्रमन्त्री २४२
आरभ्याच्छां प्रतिपद १६५
आरभ्यादिज्ज्वलनं २११
आरम्भे मानुषाणि स्यु २२२
आराध्य च विसृज्याऽग्नि २८७
आराध्य चाष्टोर्ध्वंशतं २७२
आराध्य चैवं विधिना २७०
आरेणारभ्य मन्त्रेन २२२
आर्कैर्मन्त्री त्रिमधुरयुते १९०
आर्कै: समित्सहस्रै: १८५
आर्त्तवात् परमं बीज २४
आर्या दुर्गा भद्रा १८४
आलिख्य वीरपट्टे २६०
आलिख्यात् कर्णिकाया २१८
आलिङ्गेदग्निसंस्पर्शं २२१
आलोड्य गुडमध्वाज्यै २४२
आवाहादिविसर्गान्ते २६४
आवाह्य देवतामर्च्या ७५
आवाह्य विघ्नेश्वर २१२
आवाह्य सम्यक्कलशे १६१
आवाह्य हार्लेखिक १९२
आहुति: कथिता चेति २२६

आहुतिरङ्गैराद्या २०१
आहुतिराद्या मूर्त्तिभि २९८
आहुतेर्बहिरग्न्यादि ३२८
आद्यान्तिद्वयवाम २१८
आयोपायान्तराशासु २९१
आसनस्थागते साध्यं ८५
आहाराचारनियती २०१
आहाराद्रसजं प्राहुः २६

इ

इच्युमकलैः समुद्रैः १७४
इचोः सितस्य शकलै ३५६
इत्थन् रोदिति तां वीक्ष्य ३४
इच्छादानार्थको धातू ७९
इतःपूर्वं प्राणबुद्धि ९६
इति कृतकलशोऽयं १५५
इति कृतदलसुभूषित ७
इति कृतदोषः प्रजपे २८१
इति कृतयन्त्रविभूषित ३०७
इति क्रमाप्त्या विहिता १३४
इति चक्षुमन्त्रविहितं ३१६
इति जगदनुपक्तां १२३
इति जपहुतपूजातर्पणै २१७
इति जपहुतपूजाध्यान २९९, ३०१
इति जपहुतार्चनादिभिः ३०६
इति जपहुतार्चनाद्यैः २११, २२८
इति जपहुतार्चनाभि २६०
इति तव षडङ्गवेद १२३
इति दीक्षितविहित २३७
इति निगदितकॢप्त्या १७७
इति निगदितो वागीश्वर्या १२५
इति परमरहस्यं ३२६
इति परिपूज्य च कलशं १९४
इति परिपूज्य महेशं २४९
इति पृष्टः परं ज्योति ९
इति मदनयोगकॢप्त्या २२०
इति मन्त्रजपाहुतधी १६२
इति मातृकाविभेदा १२६
इति मूलाचर ६५
इति यन्त्रकॢप्तकलशी २१९
इति योगमार्गभेदैः २३३
इति लवणमनोर्विधान ३४७
इति विरचितयन्त्र २८१
इति शताचरमन्त्र ३५१
इति संलीनसूर्याग्नि ५७
इति सिद्धमनुर्मनोज १२४
इति सिद्धमनुर्मन्त्री २०१
इति सोममन्त्रविधिः २०२
इति हवनजपार्चा २५२
इति हृल्लेखाविहितो १५९
इतीरितानामपि ७०
इतीरिता लोकहिताय १७९
इतीरिताश्चापि किरीट २४२
इतीरिता सकलजगत् १२३
इतोऽह दिनकृन्मनुं १९९
इत्थं जपार्चनाहुत १८४
इत्थंभूतः स जन्तुस्तु ३३
इत्थं मन्त्री तारमनुं १२६
इत्थं मूलप्रकृत्यक्षर ३८०
इत्थं संप्रार्थितं सं २६७
इत्यजपामन्त्रविधिः १९५
इत्याचारयुतः सम्य ३८०
इत्यादिदोषदुष्टानां ३७४
इत्यादिवादि[वि]नोभिः १७४
इत्युक्तविधिचतुष्के २२९
इत्येवं प्रणवविधिः २३३
इत्येवं प्रविगदितो २७५
इत्येवं हुतविधि ११९
इन्दुकलाकलितोज्ज्वल १७८
इन्दुदयोदितसुधा १९४
इन्द्राग्नियमनिशाचर ९०
इन्द्राग्निरक्षोवरुण १५९
इन्द्राणी कौमारिका २४५
इन्द्राणी चैव रुद्राणी १५२
इन्द्राद्यस्त्रकदम्बिय २१८
इन्द्रियतारसमेतं १९६
इमाः पश्चाद्यदुद्दिष्टा ४३
इयमेवाहुतिरधिका २२९
इष्टं वाऽनिष्टमादिष्टं ३७९
इष्टदोऽनिष्टसंहर्त्ता ३७७
इह दिनेशमथ १९२
इह यथोक्तमिति १५२

ई

ईकारस्य गुणाः प्रोक्ताः ५०
ईश्वस्व देहि वाचं १७४
ईदृशं गणपं ध्यात्वा २१५
ईशाग्निनिर्ऋति १५१
ईशानस्तत्पुरुषाघोरा २९२
ईशानाख्यः सपर्ज्यन्यो ६९
ईशानादीन्मन्त्रवित् २९२
ईशे शर्वरि शर्वाणि ३४४
ईशोऽनुष्टुब्भूरो १९६

उ

उकारयोगात्तस्यैव ४५
उक्तैः किमत्र बहुभि २८०
उक्तैवमत्र गायत्री ३२२
उग्रं वीरयुतं महान्तिक २७६
उच्चार्योच्चार्य च तं २३०
उच्चैरुन्मार्गगो वायु ४५
उत्क्रान्ती परकाय २३२
उत्तरभागे तस्याः २१३
उत्तानां दारवीं कुण्डे ३४३
उत्तिष्ठपदं प्रथमं १८२
उत्तुङ्गाद्रिः प्रचेता १६६
उत्पलानि च नीलानि ८६
उत्पाते सति महति २७८

उत्पूर्वात्तिष्ठशब्दात् २०४
उदानः प्राणसङ्गी ३०
उद्घूर्णैः प्रकरणके १८९
उद्दिश्य यद्यदिह ३५५
उद्दिश्य यद्यदेनं १८४
उद्बुद्धभावे नलिने १६६
उद्यदादित्यकिरण ८
उद्यदिनेन्दुपयोद २६६
उद्यद्भास्वत्समाभां १४३
उद्यद्भास्वत्सहस्र २७७
उद्यद्दिक्कृतिभुजाढ्या १८३
उद्यद्विद्युत्कराला ३२७
उन्मत्तस्खेलनेच ३३७
उपक्रमेदर्चयितुं ७६
उपलिप्य कुण्डमव ९१
उपलिप्तेऽथ कुण्डे ३४४
उपस्थितेऽर्धरात्रे तु ३४६
उमा चण्डेश्वरी नन्दी २९५
उरः कुक्षिस्तनाद्यं च २९
उष्मार्णाष्टाचरावेष्टित २४६

ऊ

ऊदद्गादिलला: कीर्णं ४७, ३३६
ऊर्ध्वं तु मरुता नुन्नं २४
ऊर्ध्वाधः क्रमशः कुर्यात् २९९
ऊर्ध्वाधः प्रोतपद्म ३०६
ऊर्ध्वाधस्तिर्यगूर्ध्वाध १२१
ऊर्ध्वादिमेखलासु २१३
ऊर्ध्वेन्द्रयाम्यसौम्य १४५
ऊहापोहविदध्यात्म ३७७

ऋ

ऋक् च तदाद्यादिः २२९
ऋक्पञ्चकं पञ्चविंशत् ३४३
ऋचराश्यादियुतया ५७
ऋगियम्नणमोचनो ३५६
ऋग्भिराभिस्तु पञ्चाङ्गं ३४१
ऋग्वारुणी ध्रुवाख्याद्या ३५६
ऋतवसुवरनरसंज्ञा १९४
ऋद्धिः समृद्धिः शुद्धिश्च ४३
ऋषिः प्रजापतिश्छन्दो २५३
ऋषिर्देवते तु पूर्वे २१६
ऋषिरपि गणकोऽस्य २०८
ऋषिरपि काश्यप ३१०
ऋषिरपि वराह उक्त १७०
ऋषिरपि संवलनोऽस्या ३५२
ऋषिरभिहितो वशिष्ठ ३४८
ऋषिरस्य कहोलाख्य ३०५
ऋषिरस्य मनोः साध्य २३४
ऋषिरस्य वामदेवः २९३
ऋषिरस्याघोराख्यः ३०३
ऋषिरस्याजश्छन्दो १९१
ऋषिरस्याहिर्बुध्न २५४
ऋषिर्गुरुत्वाच्छिरसैव ७९
ऋषिर्दीर्घतमाश्छन्दः १८८
ऋषिर्भृगुश्छन्दसि १६०
ऋषिवर्णादिको धातू ७९
ऋषिश्च नारदोऽस्य स्याद २२२
ऋषिस्तु जैमिनिः प्रोक्त २६४
ऋषिस्तु भार्गवः प्रोक्तो २७२
ऋष्यादिकमपि पूर्वं २७८
ऋष्यादिकाश्च सम्मोहन २१८
ऋष्याद्याः पूर्वोक्ता ३५०, २०३
ऋष्याद्याः स्युः २०५
ऋष्याद्या ब्रह्मदेव्यादि १९३

ऌ

ऌतवर्गलसानोष्ठा ४६

ए

एकद्विकत्रिकचतुष्क ११६
एकमपि नारिकेलं २१६
एकङ्गासादन्यमब्दं ३७६
एकां साध्यर्चनेचैण ३४२
एकाग्रचित्तो रविलच ३५६
एकादशांसभिन्नैर्वा ३४५
एकादशार्धकर्णिकां ११७
एकारादिविसर्गान्तं ५०
एकीकृत्य समस्तवस्तु १९३
एकैकं विसहस्रं ३२६
एकैकं त्रिस्त्रिशतं १६६
एकैकान्तरितास्तासु १४९
एकैकेषु दलेषु १५४
एतत्तु वेदसारस्य ३२२
एतत्त्रयं विप्रः कुर्या ३२४
एतद् यन्त्रं मदालिप्तं १८०
एता द्विषट् प्रतिदलं १५०
एतानि केसरेष्वता ११९
एतावत्यस्तु जातास्तद ३३१
एतेषां तारणात्तार: ३५
एतैः सहस्रद्वितया ११६
एतैर्जुहोति च[नि]युता ११५
एदैतौ: कर्कटी राशि ५८
एदैतौमृगशीर्षार्द्रे ६१
एनस्ता: प्रतिनिघ्नन्ति ३२३
एभिर्विधानैर्धरणी २५०
एभिर्विधानैर्भुवनेश्वरीं १५६
एभिर्विधेया: कलशाश्च २५०
एभिस्त्रिभिर्मनुवरैस्तु ३५०
एभ्यः संजज्ञिरेऽङ्गेभ्यः ५१
एभ्य एव तु राशिभ्यो ६२
एभ्योऽमावास्यान्ता ६४
एवं काले कीलमभ्य २७३
एवं कृतेन मन्त्रोष्टं ३४५
एवं कृत्वा तु सिद्धार्थे ३२५
एवं जपहुतार्चाभिः ३१५
एवं दिशासु दशसु ३४७
एवं देवं पूजयन्मन्त्र २२३
एवं प्रोक्तैः प्रतिजप २७१

एवं प्रोक्तैर्योगे २३३
एवं प्रोत्थापयति च २४०
एवं मदुपलयोरथ ३३९
एवं राशौ तु सम्पूर्णे ९७
एवं वर्णविभिदभिन्न ११३
एवं विचिन्त्य पुनरच्चर १८८
एवं सप्तदशात्मिक ६५
एवं सम्पूज्य देवीं १५५
एवं सम्पूज्य पीठं १४४
एवं सम्बद्धसंसार ३४
एवमभ्यर्चिते विष्णौ २३८
एवमादिकदीषाप ३७४
एवमेषा जगत्सूतिः ५६
एष: सर्ग: समुत्पन्न २१
एषां यागविधौना २५०
एषु स्वरा ह्रस्वदीर्घं ३८

ऐ

ऐच्चवज्जलनिधि २०९
ऐन्द्रं घृतेन यमदिक् १४५
ऐन्द्रीं समारभ्य दिशन्वथ २५४

ओ

ओंकारो गुणबीजं २२९
ओं नमो भगवते सर्वं २८९

औ

औदार्यकान्तिसौरभ २६६
औद्भिज: स्वेदजोऽण्डोत्थ २३

क

कण्ठे कैनावरुद्धा ३१३
कण्ठे भ्रूमध्ये हृदि २३२
कतस्तिष्यस्तयाऽश्लेषा ६२
कथयामि मनोर्विधान २९८
कट्टगास्यकराळ्हन्नाभ्य ३०३
कनकविदूरजविद्रुम २९५
कनिष्ठान्तासु तद्वाद्य ८१
कन्धराचिबुकास्येषु ३४४
कफात्मिकास्तु विकृतौ: ३२
कभाद्या वसुदा: सौरा: ४१
कमलोद्भवौषधिरसैम १०४
कम्प: पुलकानन्दौ २३३
कम्बुग्रीवां पृथुहंस ९
करकमलविराज ३४२
करचरणपार्श्वमूल २६६
करणात्मसमायुक्त: ११०
करणेन्द्रियरसधातु ३६४
करणोपेतैरेते १९
करतलकल्पित २६७
करदेहमुखन्यासं २९६
करपादमुखादि २२६
करपुष्करधृत २०९
करालो विकरालो च १५२
करिकलभा: करिणीभि: २१३
करेण तेनैव जलाभि १९५
कर्णिकाया: केसराणां ७४
कर्त्तव्यो वाञ्छितावाप्तै ३२९
कर्मणा मनसा वाचा ३७९
कर्षोन्मिते च हाटक २५०
कला: कला नादभवा १०६
कलाहतं याहि २५९
कवग्रहण इत्यस्मात् ८०
कलायुते: षोडश ३७५
कल्पादित्यमुख: १२०
कश्चित् कर्मप्रकारज्ञ: २६
कश्चित्तु भौतिकव्याप्ति २७
कश्रीचनयननासा १२३
कषती भुवनं मत्त: ६३
कांसोऽस्मोत्यनया १६७
कातपूर्वं हसलिपि ३११
काननहत्तहद्दःचि १०२
कान्तां दुर्गासरस्वत्यौ ३२५
कालात्मकस्य देवस्य ७५
कारस्करस्य पत्रै १८५
कालाभाभ: कराग्रै: ३०३
कालिकगलहन्नाभि १७२
कालिकस्रुतिहृग्गुग्ध ३०२
कालीमाररमालोका १७५
कालेन भिद्यमानस्तु १६
कालेन भिन्नात् पूर्णात्मा २३
कालेन यावता स्त्रोयौ १३
काष्ठा तावत्कला ज्ञेया „
काश्मर्यदारुसमिधां ३५०
कुञ्चितकुन्तलविलस १७३
कुडवं पीतलवणं ३४३
कुरु कुर्विति ठद्वन्द्वा ३६३
कुर्यात् कलाभिराभि १०६
कुर्यात् प्रयोगानपि १९०
कुर्यात् प्राणप्रतिष्ठां च ८५
कुर्यादनेन मन्त्रेण २९९
कुसुमरसलुलित ३३८
कुह्वरिति च विद्वद्भि: २५
कूर्मादिभ्यां द्वाभ्यां १७२
कृतसंदीचो मन्त्री १९६, ३१५
कृत्तिकादि च कृत्यान्तं ३३३
कृताभिषेकदीचस्तु १८१
कृते निवेद्ये च ततो ९१
कृत्वा नश्यति तस्य ३३८
कृत्वा त्रिगुणितादीना २३७
कृत्वा पिष्टेन शाल्या: ३१५
कृत्वा मण्डलमष्ट १९७
कृत्वाऽवनिं समतलां ९९
कृत्वा वह्ने: पुरमनु ३१३
कृत्वा समाप्य मण्डलमव ३०४
कृत्वा स्थण्डिलमङ्गणे ३३८
कृत्वा स्थण्डिलमस्मि २३७
क्रन्दामध्यगता: षाय २२२
कृपाभं प्राणगेह ३११

कृणा शूलासिकरा ३२६
कृसरं च वैणवीयं ७२
कीरोदसक्तुपिष्टं „
केशवमेषादीनां २४१
केशवस्वरवर्णान्ते २६४
केशवादिप्रदिष्टानां २३६
केसरेषु लिखेत् पाश १८०
केसरेष्वङ्गपूजा २०१
कोणद्वयार्धकोष्ठे ६९
कोणमत्स्यस्थिताग्राणि ७४
कोणोल्लसितसुधा ३५८
कोष्ठेषु षोडशस्वथ १५४
कौमोदकिं महान्ते तु २६५
क्रमवृद्धो परं ज्योतिः २५
क्रमात्तारादिमन्त्राणा ३२३
क्रमादष्टायुधाः प्रोक्ता १८२
क्रमेण तद्वर्णविकार २८३
क्लीबा सुखद्वयोपेता ३३२
क्वाथैः पयोभूरुह २५६
क्षरितमदनवारि २६६
क्षाद्यास्ते सप्तवर्गा ११९
क्षान्तिः पुष्टिः स्मृतिः शान्ति ५३
क्षीरद्रुमत्वगभिपक्व २०६
क्षुत्क्षत् क्षकरको देव ३०
क्षेत्रसंज्ञकममुं १२२
क्षेत्रज्ञस्य तदोजस्तु ३१
क्षोभणसर्वपदान्ते २६१
क्षौमाम्बरपरिधाने १२६

ख

खड्गं सखड्गशिरसं २८६
खण्डेष्वेकाशीतिषु १७६
खण्डैः सुधालतोत्थे १३६
खण्डैश्च सप्तदिन २०६
खदिरः कृष्णवंशौ च ६३
खमपि सुषिरचिह्न १८
खरमञ्जरीसमुत्थं २८१
खरमञ्जर्याः समिधा २५८
खसप्तमः कर्णयुतो ३०५

ग

गजमृग...रोचनायुक्तैः ३६०
गजमदविलिखित ३६०
गजमृग...रोचनोपेतैः १५६
गणकः स्यादृषिश्छन्दो २१४
गणाधिपं गणेशं च २१४
गतो वो बीजतामेष ५२
गदितं निजपाणितलं १९५
गन्धपुष्पाक्षतयव ८६
गन्धर्वदैत्यरक्षो २६६
गर्भाधानादिका वह्ने ९४
गव्यान्तैर्जुहुयात् ३०५
गव्यैर्वा पञ्चभिः क्वाथ ३२५
गात्रविवर्णपरिपूर्णं ३५०
गायत्रीं न्यसतु गले १४४
गायत्रीं प्रतिलोमतः १५२
गायत्रीं शतमखजे १४६
गुरवेऽप्यथ दक्षिणां ३७६
गुरुणा समनुगृहीतं १००
गुरुमपि परिपूज्य १५६
गुरोर्गरीयः सर्वेश २५१
गुर्वाद्यास्तारादिका ९७
गुह्यस्थितं वा मदनस्य १३७
गुह्यादाचरणतलं १९६
गृहपरिमितमिष्टा १९७
गोमयविहितां गुलिकां १८९
गोमूत्रगोमयोदक १४५
गोरोचनासतिल १९७
गोसर्पिषा वा तैलेन ८७
गौरी त्रैलोक्यविद्या च ४४
गौरीन्दिरा रतिधृती २४४
ग्रहक्षुद्रपिशाचाद्या २९२
ग्रहणी नाम सा प्राची ३२
ग्रहपरिहृतमिष्टा १९७
ग्रामं गच्छन्नगरमपि २१२
ग्राहोक्तिमनृतं निद्रा ३०९

घ

घनघर्मक्षयगति ११९
घृतावसिक्तैस्तिल ३०४
घोरज्वरगराः शोषं २०१

च

चक्रं च चक्राङ्क २८६
चक्रदरखड्गखेटक १८२
चक्रमनुग्रहसंज्ञं १७७
चक्रशङ्खगदाम्बुज २१७
चक्रशङ्खगदापद्म २५६
चक्रस्य प्राक्तने कुण्डे २९१
चक्रस्य नाभिसंस्थं २५८
चक्राय नम इत्येव २६५
चक्रे चाष्टाष्टपदे १७६
चण्डचण्डाय चेत्युक्त्वा ३१५
चतसृषु दिक्षु निखन्या ३५९
चतुःषष्ट्यंशे वा १७७
चतुःसहस्रसंयुक्तं ३२९
चतुरङ्गुलजैः समित् १२४
चतुरङ्गुलिपरिमाणे ३०८
चतुरश्रमर्धशशि ७२
च-तुरीयो विलोमेन २१४
चतुर्थ्यां नारिकेलैस्तु २१५
चतुर्थ्यामावृती पूज्या २२०
चतुर्भिर्यादिभिः सार्धं ५८
चतुर्भिश्च शिखावर्णैः २५१
चतुर्भुजा [illegible] १२५
चतुर्वक्त्रयुक्ता लसद्धंस १५८
चतुर्विंशतितत्त्वाख्या ४०
चत्वारिंशच्चतुःपूर्वं २१५
चत्वारि चत्वारिंशच्च ३२९

चन्दनकर्पूरागुरु ८३
चन्दनकुचन्दनागुरु ४४
चन्दनागुरुकर्पूर ८६
चन्दनक्षीवेरागुरु ८३
चन्द्रमसे नक्षत्रेभ्यो ९६
चरणाग्रसन्धिगुह्या ३४८
चरन् वने दुष्टमृगाहि २७८
चरस्थिरोभयात्मान ६२
चराचरस्य जगती ५४
चरैर्विंशज्ज्योभयकै ३३२
चामरमुकुरसमुद्गक १६९
चित्तात्मैक्यधृतस्य २२७
चित्पिङ्गलपदमुक्ता ९१
चिद्रूपा चिन्मया चिन्ता २४८
चिद्रूपात् सकलप्रभा ११८
चिन्तारत्नाश्रितासि ३५९

छ

छन्दस्तु देवी गायत्री ३२३
छन्दस्त्वनुष्टुप् त्रिष्टुप् च २८७
छान्तं मरुत्तुरियवर्ण १८७
छायाग्नापादुकोपान ३७९
छिन्नरुहां समिधां २८१
छुरिकाक्षपाणनखरा १८९

ज

जङ्घाचरणयोर्न्यस्येत् ३२७
जटाबद्धचन्द्राहिगङ्गा १५८
जन्तुः षडङ्गी पूर्वे स्यात् २९
जन्मर्क्षाणां त्रितये ३०८
जपः पुरोक्तसंख्यः स्या ३३१
जपहुतपूजाभेदे १७४
जपाद्दशांशं जुहुया १४७
जपावसाने दिनकृत् १६१
जपेच्चतुर्विंशतिलक्ष १५६
जपेत्तथा हि मन्त्रोऽयं ३२९
जपेदिमं मनुमतु २०२
जप्तमघोसुखमेतत् १७६
जप्तव्योऽयं मन्त्रवर्यं २०६
जप्तेनाष्टसहस्रं २७८
जप्त्वैवं मन्त्रमेनं ३०३
जप्यः स्यादिह परलोक ३१७
जप्याच्च लक्षमानं २०५
जम्बुभिः स्वर्णाभैर् १७४
जम्भयस्तम्भयो वीप्स्य ३४७
जय चक्रगदापाणे २५१
जय पक्षिपतिच्छाया २५१
जय सुन्दर सौम्यात्मन् २५१
जया दुर्गा प्रभा सत्या ४३
जरायुजस्तु ग्राम्यात: २३
जया सविजया भद्रा ३२८
जाग[ग्र]ता तपनो वेद ३२८
जाग्रत् स्वप्नसुषुप्तो २३१
जातवेदो महादेव ३४४
जातीपलाशकरवीर २०६
जान्वीरापादमुद्यत् २७२
जान्वीरासक्ततीक्ष्ण २७६
जायतेऽधिकसंविग्नो ३३
जायाग्नेर्हृदयमथो १०९
जिह्वाङ्गमूर्त्तिमनुभि ९५
जिह्वा ज्वालारुचः प्रोक्ता ९४
जिह्वासु विदशादीनां ९२
जीवशिखिकर्णरेफान् ३०३
जुहुयाच्च चतुर्वारं ९५
जुहुयात् कलाचतुष्कैः ३५३
जुहुयात्तिलैः सुगुडैः २०३
जुहुयात् सर्वहोमेषु ९५
जुहुयादशोकदहने १६२
जुहुयादष्टभिर्द्रव्यै २३८
जुहुयाद गुग्गुलुगुलिका २५८
जुहुयाद दुग्धहविर्भि २२२
जुहुयाद्व्रीहिणासमिधा १८५
ज्ञाताश्नोति यदा भावी ३४
ज्येष्ठा धकारान् मूलाख्या ६३
ज्वरार्तैः श्वसद्भिः पतद्भिः २६७
ज्वरादिकां रोगपर २५७
ज्वलज्ज्वालारुचः प्रोक्ताः २२५
ज्वलितशिखिशिखान्ते २९६

झ

झिण्टीशो भौतिकः सद्यो ४१

ट

टङ्काचाभयवरान् १४६
टान्ते लिख्यात् कलाभि ३१४

त

तं तथाविधमालिख्य ३७८
तच्च तुरीयातीतं २३२
तच्चतुष्कं सुषुम्नास्थे ३९
ततः कृत्वा जपक्रासं १४७
ततः क्रमेण चक्रादीन् २९१
ततः क्रोधीशचण्डेश ४३
ततः स्युर्मन्त्रवर्णेभ्य ३३१
तत उद्वास्य देवेशं २९१
ततश्चक्री गदी शार्ङ्गी ४२
ततश्च मनसा वाचा ९६
ततश्छिन्नोद्भवानां च ३०७
ततस्तदुर्ध्वभागस्थो ६०
ततो मण्डपमध्ये तु ७१
ततो महामुसलकं २८५
ततो लक्षत्रयं जप्त्वा २६७
ततो विदर्भितं भूमे १४९
ततोऽष्टाक्षरपूर्त्यर्थं २१५
ततोऽस्य प्रत्ययास्त्वेवं १४७
तत्कर्णरन्ध्रजापात् १७५
तत् त्रिभेदसमुद्भूता ४०
तत्पञ्चकं च प्रत्येकं ३३१
तत्परं धाम सौजस्कं २६
तत्पुरुषाद्याः सर्वे २९८

तत् प्रविचिन्त्य च तस्मिं २२७
तत्र किंद्रमस्तृग्भिन्नं ३२
तत्र या प्रथमा नाडी २५
तत्र विशन्ति न चौरा २६०
तत्र स्वाद्वम्ललवण ३२
तत्राग्निमाधाय ३७५
तत्राग्निमाहृतं सुवं ७४
तत्राथो सहतुमती ९१
तत्रान्त्यान्तरसंसृष्टं ३२
तत्राधाय घटं गव्य ३२८
तथा दण्डादिकानष्टौ २९१
तथा दिव्यैरहोरात्रे १३
तथा देहावृतस्यापि ३१
तथा दोषा रजःसार ७६
तथाविधैर्दशभि १३
तथा शिष्यकृतौ दोषौ ३७९
तथैवामाशयगतं ३२
तदन्तरिक्षा पीठस्य २९१
तदा तत्पक्षमुक्तं तु ३०
तदा तां तारमित्याहु ३५
तदात्मकं जगत् सर्वं ३२२
तदा प्रत्युभितिः स्वीय २९
तदायुधैः पञ्चमी च १८२
तदा षड्गुणिताख्यस्य ३६
तदा स्वरैश्च सूर्योऽयं ५६
तदूर्ध्वभागसंस्थः स्यात् ६०
तद्द्वितीयैकवचन ३२०
तद्देहसंस्थिता ये ९९
तद्बहिः शरमायाश्च १४९
तद्बहिर्मण्डलं सर्वं २८५
तद्बाह्ये मनुवर्णै २७५
तद्भेदांश्च बहूनाहु २६
तद्यन्त्रयुगं विलिखे ३५८
तद्वद्घटं प्रतियोज्य ३५३
तद्वद्घटार्गलाख्यं ३६०
तद्वद्विधाय कलशं ३६०
तद्वर्णभिन्ना गायत्री ५६
तनुदीर्घाङ्गुलीभास्व ९
तनुमध्यलतां पृथुल १७३
तन्नखण्ड इति प्रोक्ता ३१५
तन्मध्यगतं प्रणवं २२८
तन्मध्यगतं शुद्धं २२८
तन्वी श्रीकण्ठाद्यं २६२
तन्मध्यस्थितयाम्योद ७३
तपिनी तापिनी धूम्रा ४१
तपो ज्ञानतया चैव ३१९
तमोपहारिणीं सूक्ष्मां ३२५
तमोमयि महादेवि ३४४
तरणिजलचममुं मनु २१८
तवर्गोत्थः सुरगुरुः ५६
तस्मात् सर्वप्रयत्नेन ७५
तस्मादघोरास्त्रमनुं ३०५
तस्मादिनाय दिनशो १९३
तस्मादेनं मनुवर ३४०
तस्मिन्निधाय चित्तं २३०
तस्य पादारविन्दोत्थ ३७७
तस्य पुरस्ताद् विधिवम् २८०
तस्यां च स्थापयेत् प्राणान् ३४३
तस्यां रात्रावुपोष्याथ ३४६
तस्याः कालाग्निना दग्धः २९
तस्या ग्रहणां शक्ति २९
तस्याधस्तात् विकीर्णाभं ३२
तां दृष्ट्वा तरलात्मानो ९
ताः स्युः पञ्च चतस्रोऽष्टौ २९६
तानि विषड्द्वादश २४१
ताभ्यां करोति दिनकृत् ३३४
ताभ्याममीभ्यां लार्णोऽयं ६३
तामेनां कुण्डलीत्येके ५३
तामेवाथ प्रतिकृति ३६०
तारं तु मूर्ध्न्येथ सिता २५४
तारं सहृदयं मध्ये २५३
तारं हृदन्ते भगवत् २८३
तारः शक्त्युत्थतया २३४
तारः श्रीशक्तिमारा २०८
तारमालमथ मध्य ३०६
तारभवाभिरर्णगैभिः १४५
तारयुञ्जा त्वमुनाऽग्नौ २११
तारमामायाः श्रीः १६४
तारव्याहृतयश्चाग्रे २०३
तारशक्त्यादिकैर्ज्ञा ३०२
तारस्य शक्तिरजपा १०९
ताराणामश्विनादीनां ९७
तारादिकं नतिमपि २९४
तारादैर्दशभिर्भेदै ९५
तारादिभक्ताक्षरमांशतः स्युः ५६
तारान्तेऽस्त्रादावपि १७२
ताराह्वयी व्याहृतयश्च ३१७
तारेण लक्ष्म्याद्रिसुता ३१३
तारेऽमुमपि लिखित्वा २७४
तारो मायाऽमरेशोऽद्रि १८१
तालस्य पत्रे भुज ३३८
तावती तत्र रात्रिश्च १३
तावत्यो मातृभिः सार्धं ४१
तावदष्टतेन जुहुया १८६
तावद्वह्निर्द्विजवरैर्द्विज ३४९
तासु हृदेशलिखित ३४३
तास्ताश्च देवता अपि ३३९
तिथिनक्षत्रवारेषु ९३
तिथिषु तु कालाष्टम्यां ३३९
तिर्यञ्चो भौतिकाः प्रोक्ता ३३१
तिलतण्डुलकैर्लोणै ३६२
तिलसिद्धार्थैर्जुहुया २८७, १८९
तिलैः सराजीक्षर २८२
तिष्ठसि तावद् यावत् २६२
तीक्ष्णा रौद्री भया निद्रा ४२

तीव्रा ज्वालिनी मन्दा २११
तीव्रे ज्वरे घोरतरे ३०८
तुङ्गार्थं स्याच्छिरः ८०
तुलस्यौ पङ्कजे जात्यौ ८६
तुष्टिः पुष्टिश्च धनदा १६७
तुष्टुवुर्हृष्टमनसो ८
तुहैः नीलोत्पलकैः १७४
तूष्णीं कृत्वा पिधायाऽङ्घ्रि १२२
तृतीयाष्टाक्षरस्यापि ३२२
तेजस्यनन्यगे चिति २३१
तेन विंशत्तिथ्यंशो ६४
तेनैव चाङ्गानि विदिग् १३४
ते स्युः पिपीलिका मध्या ७५
तेषां मातङ्गानां २१४
तेषां शङ्खकुलदशीत्य ३१७
तेषु प्राग्वारुणां ७४
तैरेव विकृतिं याता १०
तोयात्मिका तथा नित्या ३२८
त्यजन्त्वार्यसूर्यर्णा १९८
त्रिंशद्धिरण्यहोरात्रै १३
त्रिकालमेवं परिचिन्त्य २२३
त्रिगुणा सा त्रिदोषा सा ३५
त्रिगुणितमपि यन्त्र २४१
त्रिगुणितविहिता विधयः ३५९
त्रिगुणितसंज्ञे माया ३५८
त्रिगुणेन च तन्तुरूप ८३
त्रिचतुःपञ्चषट्सप्त ३५
त्रितयं मण्डलानान्तु २०१
त्रिनयनमरुणाभा ९३
त्रिपादीनो मीनमेषौ ५९
त्रिभिस्तु...शिरश्च ३४८
त्रिभिस्तु...शिरोपि १६४
त्रिभुवनवशङ्करीति ३६२
त्रिभुवनेश्वरसर्वान्ते २६४
त्रिमधुरयुतैरानित्यक १८६
त्रिमधुरयुक्तैः पावे ३६०
त्रिमधुरसिक्तैश्च तिलै १८९
त्रिमुखि वयोस्वरूपे १२६
त्रिमूर्त्तिसर्गाच्च पुरा १२८
त्रिवारमभ्यः परिजप्तमेतया १०३
त्रिविधं गन्धाष्टकमपि ८३
त्रिष्टुब्जगत्यौ छन्दांसि ३२३
त्रैकाल्यज्ञानीहो २३३
त्रैलोक्यं रक्ष रक्षेति २५४
त्र्यक्षरस्य जपो यावत् ३१५
त्वगसृङ्मांसमेदोऽस्थि ३०
त्वच्चरणसरसिजन्मस्थिति १२७
त्वच्चरणाम्भोरुहयोः १२६
त्वदायुर्मम निश्वासः १२
त्वमाननमभिवन्द्य ३४४

द

दंष्ट्राग्रलग्नवसुधं २८६
दंष्ट्रायां वसुधा २७२
दक्षः सव्यस्थिते हस्त ३९
दक्षहस्तं तृतीयं स्या ३४५
दक्षिणां सप्तकर्षं तु ३४५
दक्षोऽस्य स्यादृषि १६२
दण्डादिकांस्तथाष्टौ २८६
दण्डादीनामथाष्टाना २८५
दण्डाग्रौशी व्योमासनस्तु २७४
दद्याच्च दिव्यभावं ६८
दधि दुग्धेति दशैतान्याज्य ३४९
दध्यक्ताक्षीणमुद्राभि २१५
दध्यक्ताभिर्जुहुया २२२
दन्तानां धावनं चैव ३२३
दरचक्रगदामुसलाः २६८
दरचापमुसलपाशान् २६६
दलाग्रेषु ग्रहानष्टौ २०१
दले दले तु यः कालः १२
दशधा गुणिता नाडी ३६
दशभिः सप्तभिश्चैव ३६१
दशभिर्दशभिरमोभि ४७
दशांशेन हुनेत् सिद्धैः ३४२
दशाधिकशतैः पशौ २८२
दशाहमेवं कृत्वा तु २०४
दाता दान्तः शान्तमना ३७७
दारिद्र्यरोगदुःखै १७९
दिक्क्रमात् संररिस्तौर्य ९२
दिक्पत्रेषु श्रीरति २७०
दिक्षु प्राग्याम्यवारोड् २९७
दिग्दिक्संस्थमस्त्र १७६
दिनकरलक्षं प्रजपेत् १२५
दिनमनु दिननाथं २७९
दिनमनु स चतुश्चत्वारिंशत् २१०
दिनशः सर्ववश्यं स्यात् २१५
दिनशोऽष्टोर्ध्वसहस्रं २७९
दिनावतारे मनुमेन २०५
दिशो दश क्रमादङ्ग ८१
दीक्षाख्याचरणादौ ३२८
दीक्षां प्राप्य गुरोरथ १७३
दीक्षां प्राप्य विशिष्ट १३२
दीक्षाकृत्ये पुरोक्ते १४३
दीक्षा जपहुतार्चाभिः १८८
दीक्षान्ते जपं १६३
दीक्षा प्रवर्त्यते पूर्वं ३२८
दीक्षाभिषेकयुक्तः २११
दीक्षायुक्तः प्रजपेल्लक्षं २१६
दीक्षितः प्रजपेन्मन्त्री २००
दीक्षितः प्रजपेल्लक्षं १७९
दीक्षितः प्रजपेल्लक्ष २१४
दीक्षितो मनुमिमं २२५
दीप्त्वेकादशसंख्य : स्यु ३२८
दीर्घं करालदहन २५९
दीप्तज्वलज्ज्वालिनिभि ३१५
दीप्ता सूक्ष्मा जया भद्रा १९२

दोर्भिस्तुक्त्वा करायेति २३७
दोर्भिरुपाय चेत्युक्त्वा २५५
दीर्घभाजा स्वबीजेन २००
दीर्घायुषी सुख्यतरे २५०
दीर्घौ विषी विसर्गी २९८
दुःस्वप्नेष्वपि दृष्टेष्वव २७८
दुग्धतरूत्थाः समिधः २८७
दुग्धहुताच्छान्तिः स्यात् ३५०
दुग्धाक्तैर्जुहुयात् सहस्र ३५१
दुग्धाब्धिद्वीपवर्यं २७०
दुग्धाब्धौ रूप्यवप्रा ३६४
दुर्गा च वरदां बिभ्य १८८
दुर्गास्य देवता छन्दो १८१
दुर्गे सर्गादिरहिते ३४४
दुर्भगो बहु सहस्र २६८
दुरितोच्छेदनविधये ३२६
दुष्टां कष्टान्ववायां १६८
दूर्वां घृतप्रसिक्तां २७१
दूर्वाविकैरष्टसहस्र २७८
दूर्वात्रितयैर्जुहुयात् ३०८
दूर्वाभिः सतिलाभिः ३२६
दूर्वायुतेन जुह्वन् ३५०
दृश्यो हिरण्मये देव ३२१
देवतां प्रतिपाद्यार्घ्यं ३४४
देवताभ्यः पदं प्रोक्त्वा ९७
देवभाग ऋषिस्तस्य १९८
देवमाता भगवती १५३
देवर्षिपितृपूजासु ३७४
देवस्य वृष्टिदानादि ३२१
देवानृषीनपि पितॄन् ३८०
देवाश्च श्रुतयः स्वराः २०
देवोऽथाष्टशतं प्रसून ३६३
देवेश कर्म सर्वं मे २५२
देहेऽपि मूलाधारे तु २६
दैवादिकस्याप्यथ ६८
दोर्धृतदाड़िमसायक १७८
दोर्भ्यां पदाभ्यां जानु ९७
दौग्धान्नैर्भृगुवारे ३५७
दौर्भाग्यव्याधिदारिद्र्य २६१
द्रव्यैर्यथा यैः क्रियते ११५
द्रव्यैर्विधानप्रोक्तैर्वा ९५
द्रव्यैस्तैः प्रतिजुहुया २७१
द्राविणी मोहिनी चेति ३४८
द्रुता सा तु लसिकाह्वा ३१
द्वाविंशतिकसहस्रे २७७
द्वाविंशदयुतमानं ३०३
द्वाविंशदिति निर्दिष्टाः ३४९
द्वाविंशदेताः श्रोदेव्या १६७
द्वादशगुणितेऽखिलसन्तू ३५९
द्वादशमध्यमवर्त्तुल १५१
द्वादशसहस्रमथवा ११६
द्वादशाक्षरजपं तु २५४
द्वादशाक्षरमन्त्रं च २३६
द्वादशाक्षरमन्त्रान्ते २८३
द्वादशानां तु संयोगी २३६
द्वाभ्यां वा चैकेन द्वाभ्यां १९८
द्वारगकुम्भघृतैरथ १४६
द्वारशोभोपशोभास्या ७६
द्वाराणि पदषट्कानि ७४
द्वारेषु मण्डपस्य द्वौ १४५
द्विजभूरुहं महान्तं १८६
द्वितीयवर्त्तुलाश्लिष्ट १४९
द्वितीयौ दक्षिणकर ३४५
द्व्यङ्गुलाः केशराश्च स्युः ७४

ध

धनुस्तु देवलग्नत्वात् ६१
धवलनलिनराजचन्द्र ३५२
धरापवरके तथा १३५
धर्मवित्तसुखमोक्ष २६१
धातू द्वौ स्त्री रक्षण १४३
धातोरिह विनिष्पन्नं ३२०
धावयंममित्याख्या २४२
धियो बुद्धोर्मनोरस्य ३२१
धूम्रा तर्जनिशूलाढ्य ३३५
धर्या दुर्विषहा चैव ३२९
धृतपाशाङ्कुशकल्प २१६
ध्यातः सन् भूगृहेऽसौ २७३
ध्यात्वा त्रिशूलहस्तां १८४
ध्यात्वा देवीमेवं ३६९
ध्यात्वा धूम्रां मुसल ३३५
ध्यात्वैवं विघ्नपतिं २१०
ध्यात्वैवं श्रियमपि १६३
ध्यानस्य केवलस्यास्य ३२४
ध्यानादपि धनसिद्धि २७३
ध्यानी मन्त्री मन्त्रजापी २२३
ध्येयाः षट्कोणाश्रिषु २१०
ध्येयौ च पद्मयुग २१०
ध्येचिन्तायामतो धातो ३२१
ध्वजः श्यामो विपो रक्तो २३७
ध्वजश्च वैनतेयश्च २३७

न

न इति प्रोक्त आदेश ३२२
नक्षत्रवृक्षसमिधां ३३६
नक्षत्रवृक्षसमिधो ३३६
नक्षत्राणां सराशीनां ९७
न च रिपवो न च रोगा ३०५
न चापुत्रस्य लोकोऽस्ति ३७४
नत्यन्ते कामदेवाय २१९
नत्यादिभगवत्यन्ते ३६४
नत्वा ततस्तनुभृते ९८
नन्दाख्यारभ्य रिक्तासु ३३२
नन्दिन्यन्ते रक्षयुगं १८८
नन्द्यावर्त्तैर्जुहुत भगभे १६३
नपुंसकस्य किञ्चित्तु २५
नभःश्रोत्रेऽनिलश्चर्मे ३१

नमः शब्दरूपे १५७
नमः श्रीवचर्मा „
नमः संहृतसर्वात्मन् २५१
नमश्चतुर्धा प्रोद्भूत २९९
नमस्ते दह शत्रून् मे ३४४
नमस्ते नलिनापाङ्ग २५१
नमस्ते समस्तेशि बिन्दुरूपे १५७
नमस्ते समस्ते समस्त १५९
नमो देहार्धकान्ताय ३००
नमोऽन्तकान्धकरिपवे „
नमो भगवते प्रोक्ता २५५
नमो ललाटनयन २९९
नमो विभिन्नशेषांश २५१
नमो विरिञ्चिविष्ण्वीश २९९
नमोऽस्तु स्थाणुभूताय २९९
नयनं पञ्चदशार्णैः ३५१
नरसिंहममुं धियेव २७०
नरहरिवपुषात्मना २७९, २७९
नवकनकभासुरोर्वीं १६९
नवनीते नवे लिख्या २१५
नवभिः सप्तभिः षड्भिः ३२७
नश्वरः सर्ग एव स्यात् ४६
न श्वेतरक्तपीतादि ११
नाकारजेऽङ्गतोऽन्ते २४०
नादः प्राणश्च जीवश्च ५२
नादश्च शक्तिः शान्तश्च ३६
नादजाः षोडश प्रोक्ता ४२
नाभिहृदयं ग्रीवा २३२
नाभेरथाचरणमाहृदयाच्च १२९
नाभेर्देशादापदं ३६८
नाभ्यक्तोऽध्यान्न नग्नः १६७
नारिकेलान्वितैर्मन्त्री २१५
नारीं नरान् वा नगरं नृपान् ३४७
नारी नरो वा विधिना १९५
निचिप्य कलशमथिन् १९४
निखन्यात्तत्र कुण्डस्य ३४२
निजजन्मदिने पश्चो ३५०
निजजन्मदिने शतं शतं ३०८
निजनामगर्भमथ ३१२
निजरिपुमचलाद्यैः ३६६
निजवर्णविकीर्णकोष ३११
निजशिवशिरःश्रितं ३१२
निजां प्रियां भजेदेवं २२१
निजेप्सितं दिव्यजनैः ११७
निजोदितो होमविधिश्च २८७
नित्यं चादित्यगतां ३६२
नित्यशः कायवाक्चित्त ३७८
नित्यशः प्रजपेन्मन्त्रं २०१
नित्यानन्दा[न्ता] व्यापिनी २४४
नित्या निरञ्जना क्लिन्ना १७९
नित्याभिः सहस्रतरा „
निद्रयोरन्तरा व्यक्ति „
निद्रां बालिनमाभाष्य २६२
निधाय कलशं तव २३७
निरंशः सांशवित् ३७७
निरवद्या विशालाक्षी ३२९
निर्ऋतिर्दौवारिकाश्च ६९
निर्दिष्टः स्कन्धविटप २३
निवृत्तिश्च प्रतिष्ठा च ४२
निवृत्तिसंज्ञा च तथा १८
निहितायायुगं सूत्र ७४
नीलतरांशुककेशकलापा ३४२
नीलोत्पलदलप्रख्यां ८
नृपतरुसमिधामयुतं २७४
नृपफणिकृतकेयूरां १७३
नृशंसमन्धं बधिरं ३७८
नैवं तारादिकाः सर्वे २६४
नैवं दृष्टिः समुद्दिष्टा ८०
नैचकरयत्तुदिनकर १३९
नैधात्निरताङ्गाय ३०२
न्यग्रोधापुत्तरांभा ३४९
न्यसेच्च दक्षभागे ८२
न्यसेत्तत्पुरुषाघोर २९८
न्यस्य दर्भमयकूर्चं ८३
न्यस्येवं पञ्चभिर्ब्रह्मभि २९७
न्यासक्रमेण देहे मन्त्री २९४
न्यासान्वितं निश्चितधीः १२४
न्यासोक्तेषु स्थानेष्वपि २७९

प

पञ्चाक्षरीणामपि वर्णं १७६
पञ्चः पञ्चदशाङ्कः ६४
पञ्चज्ञानेन्द्रियाख्याः ११३
पञ्चभिरथो सषड्भि ३०३
पञ्चभिश्च विभिरपि ३४१
पञ्चभूतमयो सप्त २७
पञ्चममपि विश्वंशु २४२
पञ्चमयाथ षष्ठश्च ३२९
पञ्चम्यात्ततिरुक्ता ३५१
पञ्चाचरविहितविधिं २९७
पञ्चाचरेण पुरुषा ३७६
पञ्चानामक्षराणां च ३६
पञ्चार्णोक्ताङ्गाय: ३०१
पञ्चाशदंशगुणिताय ३७
पञ्चाशदात्मकोऽपि च ३२७
पञ्चाशदोषधिविपाचित ११७
पञ्चाशद्वर्णभेदे १०२
पञ्चेन्द्रियार्थगा भूयः २७
पतत्सन्धिषु पुनर्द्वाभ्यां ३०२
पदद्वयसन्धिगुदाभ्या १८३
पद्मं चरोभक्षिर २४१
पद्मनाभस्तथा दामो ४१
पद्मरागा सुवर्णा च ९२
पद्मस्था पद्मनेत्रा १६३
पद्मासनः प्राग्वदनो २३८
पद्मा सपद्मवर्णा १६६

पद्मोत्पलकुमुद १८७
पद्मैर्भूपतिमुत्पलै २११
पयसि हृदयदघ्ने २०६
पयोद्रुमार्या च समित् १५६
पयोव्रतोऽर्चाजप २६९
परदारपरं भीरुं ३७८
परमन्यदतिशयं वा ११०
परैकगर्भधृत ३१२
परा परायणा सूक्ष्मा ४३
परिभोजयीत विप्रां २७१
परिलसद्दृढावरणं २१३
परिषिञ्चेन्निशो नित्यं १६६
परेण धाम्ना समनुप्रबद्धा २७
परोपकारनिरतं ३७८
पलं पलार्धं त्वथ १४७
पलाशपाटलीपार्थ ८६
पलाशपुष्पैर्मधुर १३६
पलाशबिल्वप्रसवै १२४
पवनाद्याः पृथिव्यन्ताः ५०
पश्चिमसन्ध्यासमये ३५७
पश्यति परं यदात्मा २३२
पाटलपीतसितारुण २९५
पाठानि विविधान्यपि ७२
पादसन्धिचतुर्ष्वास्तु ३२४
पादाधिका मकरयुक् ५९
पादाष्टकमिदं विद्यात् ३२९
पाद्यं श्यामाकदूर्वाब्ज ८६
पानीयाम्भःपाणिमार्यां १९०
पायसेन मधुरत्रय ३५३
पारिभद्रसुमनो ३१२
पालाशैः कुसुमै २०४
पालाशैः पुनरिध्मकैः २०३
पालाशैर्वा स्तनज २५७
पाशनिबद्धं वैरिण २५७, ३५७
पाशश्रीशक्तिस्मर १५५
पाशाङ्कुशमध्यगया १५३
पाशाङ्कुशान्तरित २८०, ३६९
पाशाङ्कुशाहतमनु १५४
पाशाद्यचिकयुक्त ३७३
पाशाद्यष्टाक्षरार्णं २४५
पाशाष्टाक्षरबीज ३५९
पिङ्गलया प्रतिमुञ्चे २२८
पिञ्जरां पृथुलशालि १७१
पितरं वीक्ष्य तत्रापि ३४
पितृदेवताप्रसादा ३७६
पिप्पलबिल्वगुहारुण ४४
पीठं पूर्ववदभ्यर्च्य १७९
पीठे तनूनपातः २०३
पीठे तीव्रादिभिः २१४
पीठे पूर्वप्रोक्ते पूज्याऽङ्गैः १८४
पीठे विष्णोः पूजयेत् १७१
पीठे हरेरथाङ्गैः २५४
पीतः पिङ्गः कृष्णो धूम्रः ९०
पीतशुक्लारुणशिति ७६
पीतहिमजलदगगना ९०
पीताभा कर्णिका स्या २५६
पीताऽयोमुष्टिगदा ३३५
पीता श्वेतारुणा कृष्णा २०१
पीता स्यात् कर्णिका ७६
पुंरूपं सा विदित्वा स्वं ५५
पुटितनलिनसंस्थं ३०५
पुटयोरुभयोश्च १९
पुत्रभृत्यार्थिनी युद्ध २६१
पुत्राप्तये गृहस्थो ३७४
पुनः प्रतिकृतेरङ्ग ३४५
पुनः समस्तेन च मन्त्र २१३
पुनः साध्येन मनुना ९५
पुनराशिशास्तदनु च २९५
पुनरुद्धृत्य निवेद्यादिकं २१४
पुनर्गगनवेगाख्या १५३
पुनर्निवेद्यमुद्धृत्य ९७
पुनस्तत्पद्ममुद्धृत्य १६६
पुनस्तत्प्रतिपत्त्यर्थं २३६
पुनस्तोयगतं देवं ८५
पुरारातिदेहार्धभागा १५८
पुरुषः पुरुषात्मकं ३७६
पुरुषोत्तमत्रिभुवन २६४
पुष्टिस्तुष्टिर्धृतिरपि २४६
पुष्पैः प्रियङ्गोर्मधुर १७१
पुस्तकजपवटहस्ते १२६
पूजायां पार्श्वयुगे १२५
पूज्याः सितघृतपायस २१६
पूज्या गदा गदाङ्कित २८६
पूज्याश्च वासवाद्या २९९
पूर्णसुषुम्नारन्ध्रां साध्य ३५८
पूर्णेषु षोडशस्वेव २८९
पूर्णोदरी च विरजा ४१
पूर्वं महागणपतिं १०८
पूर्वं स्थाने हृषीकेश २८९
पूर्वंतरे मृत्युपदे २७९
पूर्वप्रोक्तैः क्वाथै १५५
पूर्वमिडाया वदने २२८
पूर्ववत् पुत्तलीं तेन ३४५
पूर्वस्मिन् पङ्क्तौपेते २०१
पूर्वस्याष्टाक्षरस्यैवं ३२१
पूर्वोक्त एव पीठे २९९
पूर्वोक्तमानक्रमशा १५१
पूर्वोक्तलक्षणोपेतं १५०
पूर्वोक्ताद बिन्दुमात्रात् ४८
पूर्वोक्ताभिः पुत्तलीभिः ३४६
पूर्वोद्दिष्टैर्दिक्षु च २५७
पृथगपि शालीतण्डुल ७१
पृथगष्टशतं क्रमेण हुत्वा २७१
पृथगष्टोत्तरशतावृत्त्या ३४६
पृथिव्यम्बनलैरान ३२८

प्रणुवन्तीवमापूर्णं ९
प्रकाशितादौ प्रणव ३१८
प्रकृतिर्विकृतिः सृष्टिः १५३
प्रकृतिसहस्रजपोऽयं ३६६
प्रकृतौ कालनुमायां २३
प्रक्षाल्य तानि ७१
प्रजपेत् प्रमदां विचिन्त्य १७९
प्रजपेदथवा सहस्रसंख्यं २०४
प्रजपेह्लादशलक्षं १९४
प्रजपेल्लक्षावत्या ३४९
प्रज्ञा मेधा स्मृतिरपि १२५
प्रज्वाल्य साध्वीत्तु ३४४
प्रणवं हृदयं चैव २३५
प्रणवयुगलं भूयुग्मान्तस्थितं ३४७
प्रणवव्याहृत्याद्या ३५२
प्रणवस्य व्याहृतीनां ३२०
प्रणवस्य व्याहृतीना ३१९
प्रणवश्चदभगवदयुतङे २५६
प्रणवादिशोजपोठ २०८
प्रतप्यं विभवैः सुसम् २९१
प्रतिपत्तिरस्य चोक्ता २७६
प्रतिपत्तिविशेषाश्च ३३०
प्रतिपादमथकंपादं ३५४
प्रतिपाद्य निजं शरीर २९४
प्रतिपूज्य शक्तिमपि १९२
प्रतिमध्य गुणत्रयाणु १११
प्रतिमन्त्रं च तां वहती २६९
प्रतिमासश्च षण्मासात् २०२
प्रतिसीनाया मध्ये सा १८५
प्रत्यगाननमासीनी २९१
प्रत्ययमुयं व्यदेह ३७९
प्रत्यङ्मुखोऽथ मन्त्री ३५७
प्रत्यब्दसीकाङ्कविता १४८
प्रत्येकं कादिवर्गः ३६८
प्रत्येकं पीडमाना तु ३२१

प्रथमं केशवधात् २४२
प्रथमं हृतकं ततः कषायं १४६
प्रथमं निजसव्यतो ८२
प्रथमं प्रकृतेर्हंसः ८४
प्रधानमिति यामाहु १२
प्रपञ्चयागस्तु ११५
प्रपञ्चयागस्त्वमुना १११
प्रभा कीर्तिकान्ती १५९
प्रभा माया जया सूक्ष्मा १८१
प्रभेदेभ्यः समुत्पन्ना ५०
प्रयजेच्चतुर्भिरेवं २६९
प्रयजेदथ प्रभूतां १९१
प्रयात्यूर्ध्वं यदा प्राण ३०
प्रविधाय पद्ममथ १०२
प्रसादनत्वान्मनसो २९३
प्रसारितं वामकरं २२८
प्रसीद तुङ्ग तुङ्गानां २५१
प्रसीद प्रपञ्चस्वरूपे १५७
प्रसीद भगवन्ब्रह्म २५०
प्रसीदाव्यक्तविस्तीर्ण २५१
प्रसूतिसमये सोऽथ २९
प्रह्लादिनीं प्रभां नित्यां ३२५
प्राक्प्रत्यगर्गेऽक्षि १५४
प्राक्प्रत्यग्यमशशिनां २७७
प्राक्प्रत्यग्याम्यसौम्ये ३४८
प्राक्प्रोक्तविधानेन च ३०२
प्राक्प्रोक्तान् भूतवर्णान् ३३६
प्राक्प्रोक्तैश्चकाद्यै २४७
प्रागच्छन्माच्चभिख्या २४५
प्रागभिहितेन विधिना १९६
प्रागादिदिशा संस्थाः ७
प्रागीरितैरथ जुहोतु २२८
प्रागेव लक्षणयुतानि ७२
प्रागुदक्षिणप्रत्यगुदग् २७२
प्राग्भाषितामपि २१७

प्राग्या पवारुणो ६९
प्राङ्मध्ययोन्योः १३४
प्राणप्रतिष्ठाकर्म वं ३७२
प्राणप्रतिष्ठानमनी ३६८
प्राणप्रतिष्ठाविधिरेव ३७३
प्राणात्मकं हकाराख्यं ४९
प्राणाद्या वायवस्तस्मिन् ३०
प्राणायामैः पवित्रीकृत १३२
प्राणे जीवे चैव हंस ३६८
प्रादक्षिण्येन विन्यसेद ९३
प्रानुप्रोद्यत्स्वराष्ट २४४
प्रालेयत्विषि च स्वरा ३१२
प्राश्रितसम्पातस्य ३३८
प्रासादोक्ते च पीठे ३४९
प्रोक्तक्रमेण विघ्नान्तिक ११५
प्रोक्तमध्यादिकं पूर्वं १९८
प्रोक्तस्त्वेवं दशभुज २१४
प्रोक्तानि वर्णास्त्रान्तानि २८५
प्रोक्तेनैवं कलश १००
प्रोक्तैर्ध्यानजप ३०९
प्रोक्ताय कामदेवाय २१९
प्रोक्ता पूर्वमसुष्य ८५, ३६७
प्रोक्ता सुदर्शनायेति २५५
प्लचाग्निमन्थसिंहो ४४

फ

फलार्थी फलमाप्नोति ३२२
फुल्लैर्बिल्वप्रसूनै १२६

ब

बद्ध्वा माध्यं पाशबीजेन ३७०
बध्नाति मातापित्रोस्तु ३४
बलाकी विमला चैव १६१
बलिसिद्ध्यर्थिनश्चैव २६१
बहिः षोडशयुक्ताङ्कं १४९
बहिरथ षोडशपत्रं १५२
बहिरष्टदलं पद्मं ३२८

बहुवारैश्च कुम्भेन ३१
बहुना किं परं पुंसः २७
बहुना किमनेन मन्त्री ३५७
बहुनेति भाषितेन ३६०
बालं नीलाम्बुदाभं २२२
बाहुभ्यां च सजानुभ्यां ९७
बाह्यरेखामन्तरा १४९
बाह्ये षोडशपत्रं २७४
बिन्दुः पुरुष इत्युक्तो ५५
बिन्दुर्दक्षिणभागस्तु ,,
बिन्दुर्मध्यस्तथा नादो ३२०
बिन्दुसर्गात्मनोर्व्यक्ति ४६
बिन्दुसर्गौ च यौ प्रोक्तौ ४०
बिन्दोस्तस्माद् भिद्यमाना १७
बिन्द्वन्तिका प्रतिष्ठा १५५
बिभ्रद् दोर्भिः कुठारं २९८
बिभ्राणा शूलबाणास्यरि १८८
बिम्बवन्दे श्मशाने ३१४
बिम्बादम्बुदवत् २१७
बिल्वं श्रीसूक्तजापी १६२
बीजानि रक्तानि तु ३७१
बीजापूरगदेक्षुकार्मुक २०९
बीजैस्त्रिभिर्हि रक्तैः १६९
बुभुक्षा च पिपासा च ३१
बोधात्मिके बुधानां १२७
ब्रह्मचर्यरतं नित्यं ३७८
ब्रह्मद्रुमफलकान्ते ३३८
ब्रह्मविष्णुशिवात्मकं १९२
ब्रह्माख्यो हृदयमनुः ३५२
ब्रह्माणमथ च १५०
ब्रह्माणी माहेशी १०२
ब्रह्माण्याद्यास्तद्बहि १४६
ब्रह्मात्मभिर्महामन्त्रे ११३
ब्रह्मा प्रजापतिर्वा २७६
ब्रह्मा ह्यहन्तया स्यात् ११०
ब्रह्मापर्णाख्यमनुना ९६
ब्रह्मश्रीमन्त्रसंप्रोक्ता ३६३
ब्रह्माऽस्या ऋषिरीरितः १०१
ब्रह्मा स्यादृषिरस्य च १०९
ब्राह्मणान् भोजयित्वाऽथ २०४
ब्राह्मीं वशां वाष्ट २८०
ब्राह्मीमाहेश्वर्यौ १३४

भ

भक्तियुतानां त्वरया १७२
भद्रकालि भवाभीष्टे ३४४
भया भारेन्दुयुक् सैव ३६५
भवति नरः सिद्धमनु ३४९
भवत्वन्ते द्विठश्चायं ९६
भवेद् द्वादशसाहस्रे ११
भवेयुः पङ्कजदलनिभा ७५
भक्ष्याभ्यक्ताय भक्तानां ३००
भारती पार्वती चान्द्री १६४
भावहावमधुरस्मित २६६
भासुरभूषणदीप्ती २१६
भास्वद्रत्नौघमौलि १९१
भिक्षावृत्तिर्दिनमनु २२३
भिन्दद्वयस्य पाशेन २६२
भुक्तिप्रदाय भक्तानां २५२
भुजङ्गेशः पिनाकी च ४३
भूःपदाद्या व्याहृतयो ३१८
भूतत्वात् कारणत्वाच्च ३१९
भूतपिशाचनाग ७१
भूतादिकवैकारिक १७
भूतानां शक्तित्वाद् २९५
भूतिर्विभूतिरुन्नति २४६
भूतेन्द्रियेन्द्रियार्थे १९
भूत्वा शक्तिः स्वयमथ १४७
भूधरो विश्वमूर्तिश्च ४२
भूयश्च सुन्दरीजन २६१
भूयस्त्वचरलक्षं ३२६
भूयाद् भूयो द्विपद्मा १६०
भूयोऽनन्तायेति च २९४
भूयोऽपि केशवेन्द्रा २८७
भूयो भूमितले ७०
भूयोऽभ्यर्च्य सुधामये १९२
भूर्जे वा क्षौमपट्टे २६०
भूर्भुवःस्वर्भूर्भुवस्वः ९६
भृगुः ससद्यः सार्धेन्दु २००
भृगुरपि तद्दक्षिणस्कन्दो २०२
भृगुवारे च सुखेऽङ्गः २७४
भृगोस्तु वारे निजसाध्य १७१
भेदैरष्टाद्यैः शान्तान्तं २६
भौमे वारेऽथ भानू २७३

म

मकरान्ते कुण्डलं च २३६
मकारप्रभवा रुद्र ४२
मज्जात्वग्वर्गादिक ११९
मज्जास्थिस्नायवः शुक्रा ३१
मण्डलयुगयुगलं १५१
मण्डलानि तु तत्त्वशो ७५
मत्स्यः कूर्मवराहौ २४०
मदजललोलुप २०९
मदनविधानमितीत्थं २२०
मधुद्विषि महादेवे ३७९
मधुना महता रवेण १४५
मधुपर्कं च सक्षौद्रं ८६
मधुरत्रयसंयुतेन ३१३
मधुरत्रयसिक्ताभि २१५
मधुरत्रयावसिक्ते ११६
मधुरत्रयेण सह १३६
मधुसूदनसंज्ञश्च ४२
मध्यवर्तुलसंस्थाया १४९
मध्यस्थायाः परीतौ २४९
मध्ये च दिग्दलानां २११
मध्ये च मूलमनुना ३३९

मध्ये तारं तदनु च २५९
मध्ये दिशाधिपाङ्का १६६
मध्येऽनन्तं पद्ममखि ८२
मध्येऽनन्तादैरपि २३५
मध्येन्द्रवरुणशशि ११८
मध्ये वदंचरयो: १२३
मध्येऽष्टाशान्तासु च ३३९
मनुनाऽमुनाष्टशत २०७
मनुमन्त्रितैश्च वारिभि १७५
मनुममुमथ शान्त्ये ३५२
मनोरथार्कात्मतया १९१
मनोहृत्तिरस्तु स्मृतिस्ते १५९
मन्त्रं च द्वादशार्णाख्य ३७
मन्त्रं सर्वमनुक्रम्य १२२
मन्त्रं सुदर्शनं चेत्य २९०
मन्त्रपदानि द्वादश २६२
मन्त्रस्य मध्यमनुना १९६
मन्त्रस्यास्य मुनि: २२४
मन्त्रस्यास्य विधिर्हरिय २६८
मन्त्राचरत्रयोद्दल ३०४
मन्त्राचरसहस्रन्तु ३२९
मन्त्रान्ते साध्याख्यां ३०७
मन्त्रिण: कृतकृत्यत्वं २६७
मन्त्री कुर्यात् षडङ्गानि ३०२
मन्त्रीन्दिरावान् भवति १८२
मन्त्री वटसमिद्व्रीहि २०४
मन्त्री समाख्याय २७५
मन्त्री सर्वजनख्याने ३६३
मन्त्री सुनियतचित्त २५८
मन्त्रेणाथ पुरा २११
मन्त्रेणाऽनेन सर्पि २७४
मन्त्रे मन्त्रगुरावपि १००
मन्त्रैरेतैर्घृतयुत ३६४
मन्त्रोद्धारविधानेन १०७
मन्दारकुन्दकुमुद १६६
मन्दाराद्यै: कल्पक २०९
मन्दाराह्वयरोचना ३२५
मरिचं चौद्रसमेतं ३३६
मरीचि: काश्यपो नाम ३२७
मरुत: कपोलबिन्दु ४७, ३३७
मस्तकारचितदोर्द्वयाञ्जलि १३५
महत्त्वाच्च महत्त्वाच्च ३१९
महासिंहाय चेत्युक्ता १८१
मातृकान्यासवत् सार्धं १११
मातृकोक्तविधिना १२४
मातृभि: सारुणान्ताभि: ३२६
मातृभिररुणान्ताभि: १९९
मायाद्विठान्तिको ३६२
मायाविह्नितषड्ङ्गी ३६४
मायाहृदोरथान्ते ३६२
मायोयं नाम योषोत्थं २४
मारणोच्चाटनद्वेष २६१
मारसायकनिपात १३५
मालतीवकुलजे १३६
मितेन्द्रौ निर्ऋतिजले ६३
मिथुनानां गणपानां २१४
मिलितादपि तस्मात्तु २४
मुकुन्दो नन्दको नन्दो ४२
मुकुलै: पतितैर्म्लानै ८६
मुखनासाचिकर्णेषु ३२७
मुख्याम्भोजे निविष्टा १७१
मुख्यार्थवाचो वरशब्द १४३
मुद्रां भद्रार्थदात्रीं ३०२
मुनिव्रातावीतं विमल ३६६
मूवाशयो धनुर्वक्रो ३३
मूतैर्णेन्द्रं गोमयेनापि १४५
मूर्त्याभासेन दुग्धाब्धौ ७
मूर्धनि गुह्यहृदोरपि १२९
मूर्धाचिकण्ठहृदयो २७०
मूर्धाचिकर्णनासामुख १६५
मूर्धाननहृद्गुह्यक २९४
मूर्धास्यनेत्रघ्राणेषु २९९
मूर्धेचणास्यहृदयो २३५
मूर्ध्नोऽथ द्वादशान्तो १३७
मूलमन्त्रचतुर्वर्णं २२२
मूलाधारमुखोद्गत १२६
मूलाधारात् प्रथममुदितो ३३
मूलाधारात् स्फुरन्तीं १३६
मूलाधारात् स्फुरित १४१
मूलार्णमर्णविकृतौ १०
मूलाश्विनीमघाज्येष्ठा ६१
मूषिकलूतावृश्चिक २७९
मृता वैवस्वता चैव ३७०
मृत्काराङ्गुलिकात्तया ३६१
मेखला द्राविणी चैव १७८
मेधा च हर्षा श्रद्धाह्वा ४२
मेधा प्रज्ञा प्रभा विद्या १०३
मेधा हर्षा श्रद्धा क्षपा २४९
मेषादिकं यत्र चतुष्क २४१
मेषादिकेषु त्रिगुणात्मकानि „
मोकारजे रतिधृतौ २३९
मोदकपृथुकसलाजा २१०
मोहनी चोभणी त्रासी २१८

य

य: सूक्ष्म: सोऽहमित्येवं ३२१
य इमं भजते मनुं १७०
यकारजेऽरिशङ्खौ च २४०
यजेत् पुराङ्गैश्च ३५३
यत्तु तेजो निरुपमं ३२१
यथा पुरा पूरितमत्सरै ९९
यथा भवन्ति देहान्त ४४
यथा स्वरेभ्यो नान्ये स्यु ५७
यथोक्तमार्गेण समर्च्य २७७
यथोक्तसंख्यं विधिवत् २५६
यदा कफो मरुत्पित्त ३१

यदा तदार्थो विभजेत् ७४
यदा विशोऽथ गुणयेत् ३५
यदानन्दात्मकं ब्रह्म ३२२
यदा पित्तं मरुद्गुल्मं ३१
यदालिपिविभिन्नोऽयं १११
यदाश्रया विप्रकृति ३८०
यदाष्टधा सा गुणिता ३६
यदा स्वयं व्यञ्जयितुं २८
यदि गृह्णाति तद्दोषः ३७९
यदि नवकलशा १४६
यद् यद् वाञ्छति पुरुष ३४०
यद्येककालशक्तो १४५
यन्त्रं तदेव मन्दिर ३६०
यन्त्रं तदेव शाखा ३६०
यन्त्रममुं रचयेत् २७५
यन्त्रस्य बीजेषु चतुर्षु २८४
यमनियमासनपवना २२६
यमापाटपामाय १७५
यथाकाशसमो वापि ११
यया तत्पुष्टिमाप्नोति २५
यष्टव्याः सुवर्णसुदेवा २३८
यस्तु वक्ष्ये गुडोत्थेवं ३०७
यस्मिन् देशे विहिता १८७
यां च दिशं प्रति २७९
यां ज्ञात्वा सकल ६६
यां प्रमदामभिकाङ्क्षति २६८
याः पञ्चाशत् कला ८४
याभिस्तु मन्त्रिणः सिद्धिं ४१
या मूर्तिरर्च्यतेऽस्य २२९
यावज्जितारिरेष्यति २८०
या वामस्तुष्कसन्नद्धा २५
यूकमत्कुणकीटाण २२
यैः कुर्युं रिष्टाप्ति २४१
योगाग्निदूषणपरं २२६
योगा सत्या विमला १२४
योजयित्वा जपेत् २८९
योजयित्वा नृसिंहात् २८५
योनिं कुण्डस्यान्तः १७४
योनिर्मायावती चेति २१९
योनिर्विंयत् समेतं ३६६
योनिस्तत्पश्चिमाया ७२
योनेः परिभ्रमित १३७
योऽमुमर्चयति मुख्य १५०
यो मेऽग्निगतः ३४६
यो मे दिविगतः "
यो मे पूर्वगत "
योऽर्चयेत् सकृदप्येवं २६८

र

रचोभिरचलवक्षे २९२
रक्तं धर्मं वृषतनु ८२
रक्तमाल्याम्बरो मन्त्री ३४३
रक्ताकल्पारुणतर १३५
रक्ता पाशाङ्कुशिनी ३३५
रक्तामनङ्गकुसुमां १५०
रक्ताम्भोधिस्थपोतो ३६९
रक्ता रक्तांशुक... १७९
रक्ता रक्ताकल्पा १४६
रक्ता रमा कराली २४६
रक्तारविन्दनयना ९
रक्तोत्पलैः प्रतिदिनं २८१
रक्तो रक्ताङ्गरागांशुक २१४
रक्षानिग्रहकर्मणो ३२५
रत्नमये मणिवज्रप्रवाल २०९
रत्नस्वर्णांशुकादो ३६५
रथचरणदरगदाम्बु ३४०
रथचरणशङ्खपाशा २८१
रथाङ्गशङ्खासिगदा १८८
रन्ध्रेष्वङ्गमनूनपि २७४
रमा राका प्रभा ज्योत्स्ना ३४९
रम्यमप्युज्ज्वलमपि ३८०
रविकोणेषु दुरन्तां १५१
रविलेन भूत्वा १५७
रविबिम्बगतामरुणां १८६
रसादितः क्रमात् पाकः ३१
रागिणं रोगिणं भोग ३७८
राजस्यः कथिता जिह्वा ९२
राजोत्साष्टोत्तरशतं २६८
राजोरस्योऽङ्घ्रिपो ३६५
राज्या पट्टसंयुतया १५६, ३६१
राशिभ्यः सदिनेभ्यः ६५
राशिकाङ्गुलकैः कुर्यात् ७५
रुचिरं द्वादशदलं १४९
रुचिराष्टपत्रमथ १६१
रुद्रताण्डवविलोकन ३६४
रुद्रवीर्या प्रभा मन्दा १५२
रुद्रादीन् शक्तियुक्तान् १०७
रूपमन्मथसर्वस्त्रो २६४
रेचकपूरककुम्भक २२६
रेफान्वितेकाराकार ५४
रेफो मायाबीजमिति ५२
रेवता ... ...
रोमाञ्चकञ्चुकित १३५
रोमाञ्चहर्षनिर्गत २६६

ल

लक्षं जपेन्मनुमिमं १६४
लक्षं तदर्धकं वा ११६
लक्षं तिलैर्वा जुहुया "
लक्षायता च सदर्शांश १७१
लक्षायता जपविधि ३५१
लक्ष्मीः सरस्वती चाथ २५६
लक्ष्मीगौरीमनस्विनथ १७०
लक्ष्मीश्च व्यापिनी माये ४४
लक्ष्म्यायुःपुष्टिकरं ३१४
लक्ष्म्यायुष्करमतुलं २५८
लप्ती धर्म भ्रातृबन्धु ५९

लम्बयेदम्बरे सिक्थ २४२
ललाटजठरांस २९९
ललाटोदरहृत्कण्ठ २३६
ललितान् रूढकुसुमान् ७५
लवणाम्भसि चैत्याद्या ३४१
लवणैस्त्रिमधुरसिक्तै ३३५
लवादि प्रलयान्तोऽयं १२
लसच्छङ्खचक्रा चलत् १५८
लसत्कौस्तुभोद्भासिते „
लसदोदरिकाबन्ध ९
लाक्षाभिः कुङ्कुमैर्वा १७७
लाजातिलनखारजो ७२
लाजाभिस्त्रिमधुर २८२
लिपिन्यासादिकान् सर्वान् २२४
लोकाद्रिद्वीपपाताल २६
लोकेश्वरीमिति विचिन्त्य १६९
लोकोद्वेगकरी या च २७९
लोहिता च करालाख्या ९२

व

वकुलः सरलः सर्जो ६१
वक्त्रहृत्पादगुह्याख्य २९८
वक्रतुण्डैकदंष्ट्रो २१५
वक्ष्यामि शैवागम २९५
वक्ष्ये विधानमन्यन् २१९
वचनादाने सगतौ १९
वज्रं सशक्तिर्दण्डः ९०
वणिङ्मकरमेषाङ्क ४९
वत्सरादिचतुर्दंष्ट्रां २०४
वदनामृतकरबिम्ब २३०
वदने च बाहुपाद १०८
वदेद्यक्षेश्वरायेति ३१५
वन्दे हरं वरदशूल ३०१
वन्द्यं देवैर्मुकुन्दं २२३
वययोरन्तरास्त्वं मे २६५
वरदा ह्लादिनी प्रीति ४१
वराहपारावतयोः ३४५
वरेण्यं भजतां पाप ३२२
वरेण्यं वरणीयत्वात् ३२०
वर्गं स्पर्शनमावेश ४६
वर्गस्वरयाद्यंशाः १०२
वर्णार्पितसमारम्भो २७७
वर्णांतनोऽमृतवर्णो १२६
वर्णादिर्वाङ्मन्त्रो २६२
वर्णादिको हली मन्त्रः २७६
वर्णान्त्यानलभुवनबिन्दु २७८
वर्णान् न्यस्य शिरोभू ३४८
वर्णैरादौरमन्त्रैः २४४
वर्णैर्मनुप्रपुटितैः ८९
वर्णैश्चतुर्भिरुदितं २७६
वर्णैर्विध्याश्रिताभि १०४
वर्तुलं तावता भूय १४९
वर्मध्ये च तदन्यः १७२
वर्मासुरमर्दिनी च १८८
वशमुक्ता कुरुं वौषट् २१९
वशिष्ठादिकमित्येव ३४८
वश्याकृष्टिद्वेषण २७९
वश्यादिकानि कर्मा ११६
वसतावुपविश्य कैटभारेः १६२
वसुभिः प्रसाद्य देशिक ३५६
वसुसाहस्रजापश्च २६५
वह्नयश्च दशान्ये स्यु ३०
वह्निरामौ वरे स्यातां ३४२
वह्नेस्तु वह्निपचीये १४९
वह्नेः कोणत्रये श्रीमत् „
वह्नेः पुरद्वितयवास १३३
वह्नेर्बिम्बद्वयपरिवृता १३७
वह्नेर्बिम्बे वह्निवत् ३११
वह्नेर्विखिम्बनिर्यास १७५
वाक्यं प्रोक्ता हृदाख्यं २७१
वागादीन्द्रियसंभिन्नः ११०
वागीशोत्सवमिति यो १२७
वागीश्वरी मदवहा ३२८
वागैश्वर्यातिशय १२९
वाग्भवेन पुनरङ्गुली १३०
वाचिका आयदादीनां ३५
वाणीकरश्चाह्वयमी १३६
वाणी स्यात्ताररूपा २६७
वादिमघोषबहुलं २९१
वामांशगस्वस्तरगा २५
वामाद्याः प्रतिलिख्य २६२
वामाङ्गन्यस्तवामेतर ३०१
वामा ज्येष्ठा रौद्री काल्या २९४
वामा ज्येष्ठा रौद्रिका १३४
वामादिशक्तिसहितं १३३
वामोरुजङ्घगतया २६६
वायवे चान्तरिक्षाय ९६
वायव्याग्नेयैन्द्रवारी ३७१
वायुर्नागश्च मुख्यश्च ७०
वारुणेन्द्रयाम्यप्रा ३२५
वाससी च पुनरङ्गुली ९८
वासुदेवः ... स्फटिक २२५
वासुदेव ... दमकः १६१
वासुदेवाय सर्वात्म २३५
वासो भूषणगन्धान् १६६
वास्तौ पुरे वा ग्रामे वा २९०
विंशत्या चतुरधिकाभि ७२
विकृतिद्विगुणसहस्रे २७७
विकृतिर्दण्डिमुण्डिन्यौ १५२
विक्रान्त्या ध्वस्तवैरि २२२
विघ्नविनायकवीराः २१६
वित्तेशस्यान्तराले २६४
विदारणपदं तस्मात् २६४
विदारयद्वयान्ते तु २६५
विद्ययानुदिनहृद्यया २६७
विद्याचरैः षडङ्गं वा २४१

विद्याधर्यो यक्ष्य:	१७४
विद्यारूपेऽविद्याविनाशिनि	१२६
विद्युद्वर्णोऽथ वेदाभय	२९५
विद्ये विद्यापदे प्रोक्ता	२०२
विद्येशीं त्रिपुरामिति	१३८
विधानमेतत् सकलार्थ	१५३
विधाय तद्बीजविशिष्ट	२७७
विधाय लिपिपङ्कजं	१९५
विधाय विधिनाऽनेन	१८२
विधिना ज्वरविद्ध:	३१६
विधिनाऽनेन तु सद्य:	३५८
विधिनाऽमुना विराचा	३६०
विधिनेति विधातु	२०४
विधिवदथ विहित	२५३
विधिवदभिज्वाल्या	३३८
विधिवदिति कृताभिषेको	१४६
विन्यस्य कर्णिकोपरि	८३
विन्यास: प्रतिमाकृती च	२९७
विन्यासैरथ सञ्जपे	१०५
विपञ्चमियद्दं तेजो	२४६
विप्रक्षीरद्रुमत्वङ्	२५८
विप्रान् प्रतर्प्य विभवे	२३८
विभवानुरूपतोऽस्मै	१७८
विभूतिरुन्नति: कान्ति:	१६१
विमलकमलसंस्थ:	२००
विमले परिधाय वाससी	९९
विमलोत्कर्षणी ज्ञाना	२३७
विमुक्तपातको भूत्वा	३४६
वियतो दशमोऽर्घि	२०२
वियत्तुरीयस्तु विलोमतो	१६०
वियन्मरुज्ज्वलवह्नि	३००
विराजत् किरीटा	१५८
विलसदहङ्कारतनु	२२०
विलिखेच्च कर्णिकायां	१५४
विलिखेत् क्रमेण मन्त्रा	३३९
विलोड्य तामेव मृदं	२७४
विवाससे कपर्दान्त	३००
विशिखानां विंशत्कं	१८५
विश्वग्रासाय विलसत्	२९९
विश्वामित्री वशिष्ठाख्य	३२३
विश्वामित्रस्तु गायत्र्या	,,
विश्वात्र विश्ववन्द्याद्य	२५१
विश्वेदेवा इति प्रोक्ता:	३२३
विषतरुमयीं च शवी:	१८५
विषतरुसमिदयुत	१८६
विषपावकोदादभि	३१३
विष्णवे विदशारति	२५१
विष्णुं भास्वत्किरीटं	२८६
विष्णुं भास्वत्किरीटा	२२५
विष्णुं लिखेन्मध्य	२८३
विष्णु: प्राच्यादिकमथ	२८८
विष्णुपदं ससुधाकर	१९३
विष्णुर्योनिरितीत्यादि:	८४
विष्णो: सान्निध्यलब्धो	२८९
विसर्गस्तालुग: सोम	४६
विस्तारै: किं प्रति	२८२
विस्पष्टजघनवर्चो	१७४
विहितार्चनविधि	३१०
वीक्षयित्वा ज्वलपदं	२१९
वीप्सा देवि महादेवि	३६३
वृते स्वाहापदेनापि	१८०
वृत्तं चक्रमुशन्त्येके	७५
वृत्तं व्योम्नो बिन्दुषट्का	१८
वृत्तवीथ्योरगारचये	७४
वृत्तानि चतुरश्राणि	,,
वृषहरिहयिककलशा	२४३
वेतससमिदयुत	३५७
वेदात्मिके निरुक्ता	१२६
वैखरी मञ्जरी चैव	४४
वैदिकांस्तान्त्रिकांश्चापि	११
वैश्रवण: पक्वाश्य	३६४
वैश्वानरं जातवेद	९३
वैणव्यस्त्वथ पालिका	७१
व्यञ्जनकिञ्जल्केऽन्ये	२७५
व्यन्वेष्यद् ह्रस्वदीर्घा	२५०
व्यस्तैरपि च समस्तै:	१६६
व्यस्तैर्द्वादशभिर्मन्त्रै	२६५
व्याख्यां विवादं स्वातन्त्र्य	३७९
व्याघातसमिद्भिर्वा	३१५
व्याघ्रत्वक्परिधाना	१८३
व्याधिरप्रापितव्याधि:	३०७
व्यापकाश्च द्विवर्गा: स्यु:	४०
व्याहृतीभिरथ पक्व	३७५
व्याहृत्यावीतशक्ति	१५१
व्योमानुगेन वसुधा	१९४
व्योमावि:सचतुर्दश	१०२
व्योमेन्दुवक्राधर	१२८
व्योम्ना मध्योत्थिते	११९
व्योम्नि मरुदग्नि दहन	१९
व्रीहिभिरन्नै: क्षीरै:	३४०
व्रीहीणां जुहुयान्नरो	१८७

श

शक्राय: फुल्लकुन्दाभा	२०१
शक्तिं साध्यचंद्रच	३६३
शक्तिपीठे पूज्या देवी	१७८
शक्तिप्रयत्नसाध्यं	१४८
शक्तिभि: प्राक् समुक्ताभि	३२५
शक्तिशान्ती च संप्रोक्ता	३६
शक्तिश्रीकामबीजै:	२४९
शक्तिस्थं निजनाम	३६१
शक्तिस्वस्तिकपाशान्	२०२
शक्ते: सत्त्वनिबद्धमध्य	११८
शक्तेर्द्वादशगुणिते	२८३
शक्त्यन्त:स्थितसाध्य	३६१
शक्त्यात्मकं तुरीयं	२३२

शत्यावि:साध्यमिन्द्रा १४४
शत्या शक्तिश्रीभ्यां १०७
शक्ति: स्याद्वषिरस्य तु ११९
शक्यमशक्यं वीक्षा १८२
शङ्खं सुगन्धपुष्पाचत ८१
शङ्खं समग्रशिरसं २८६
शङ्खः सनन्दकोऽरिः १८६
शङ्खहलमुसलशूला २८४
शङ्खारिचापशरभिन्न १८१
शङ्खिनी गर्जिनी काल ४४
शङ्खे कषायोदकपूरिते ८३
शङ्खोक्तचिह्नभूषान् २८६
शतं दधि घृतं पयः २६७
शतं वाऽथ सहस्रं वा ३२४
शतं शतं प्रातः ३५१
शतभिषजि समुदितेऽर्के ३५७
शतमूलिखलादिरिफा ४४
शताचरमनीरयं ३५२
शब्दब्रह्मेति यत् प्रोक्तं २२
शब्दब्रह्मेति शब्दा ”
शब्दाद् व्योम स्पर्शतस्तेन १७
शशिनी चन्द्रिका कान्ति ४१
शस्यर्द्धिर्गोसम्वृद्धिश्च २९२
शाक्ते पीठे देवीं ३६९
शाखोपशाखतां प्राप्ता २५
शान्तः शश्वत्स्मितमधुर १६८
शार्ङ्गं शार्ङ्गाङ्कितकं २८६
शार्ङ्गस्य खड्गतोऽप्यन्ते २६५
शालीकङ्गुश्यामाक ७१
शालीतण्डुलकैः सितैश्च २०५
शालीतण्डुलचूर्णकै ११७
शालीभिः शुद्धाभिः २०६
शालीघृतसंसिक्ताः ३५७
शिखा तेजःसमुद्दिष्टा ८०
शिखाललाटहृक्कर्णं ३२७
शिखाललाटनेत्रास्य २५२
शिखा सुभगशब्दन्तु २६४
शिखिशूलकराऽग्नि ३३५
शिरसि निपतिता या १४१
शिरसोऽवतरन्निशेश ३११
शिरोभ्रूमध्यनयन ३२५
शिश्ना च यत् स्मृतं प्रोक्ता ९६
शीतांशुमण्डलस्थं ३५८
शुकः प्रोक्तो मुनिश्छन्दो ३०२
शुक्लास्ये शुक्लपुष्पे ३६५
शुक्लं रक्तं वेष्टितश्च २६८
शुक्लः शुक्लांशुकोऽक्लिष्ट ३७७
शुक्लपुष्करपत्रेषु २९१
शुक्लादिः शुक्लभाः ३११
शुद्धस्यापि सबिन्दु ११५
शुद्धाङ्गिरदणवासी १९८
शुद्धान्नैर्घृतसिक्तैः २०३
शुद्धाभिः शालीभिर्दिन ”
शुद्धैः सारैरिभै १८५
शुद्धैश्च तण्डुलैरथ ३१८
शुभकर्मणि दीक्षायां ६८
शुभ्रसितपीतशुक्ला १९६
शूलाशनिशरचापौ २९५
शूलासिशक्तिवज्राद्यै ३४४
शूलाढ्यौ टङ्कघण्टासि २९३
शेषो वासुकितक्षक २४०
शैवोक्तपीठाङ्गपदे ३१०
शोणतराधरपल्लव १७३
श्यामलतनुमरुण ”
श्रद्धा मेधा मतिः कान्ति १५२
श्रद्धा मेधा स्मृतिरपि ८१२
श्रद्धा स्वाहा स्वधाख्या च ११२
श्रविष्ठाख्या च यरयी ९३
श्रीकण्ठोऽनन्तसूक्ष्मौ च ४३
श्रीकामः श्रीप्रसूते २८०
श्रीधरपौर्णं नवमं २४२
श्रीधरश्च हृषीकेशौ १६४
श्रीफलैः मञ्जुहुयात् २६८
श्रीमन्त्रभक्तः श्रित १६८
श्रीमन्त्रेष्विति गदितेषु १६५
श्रीलक्ष्मीर्वरदा विष्णु १६७
श्रीवत्साङ्कितमाभाष्य २३६
श्री सा माया यामा सा श्री १७७
श्रीवल्गच्चिशिक्षा १९
श्लथमानांशुकचिकुरा १७४
श्वेता कृष्णा रक्ता पीता ८२

ष

षट्कोणस्थसुदर्शनं २८१
षट्कोणान्तःस्थतारं २५५
षट्कोणावद्धवाणा २४८
षट्कोणे कर्णिकायां ३०५
षडक्षराश्च चत्वारः ३२२
षडङ्गुलप्रमाणेन १४८
षड्मयः पञ्चमं स्यात् ३३०
षड्भिश्चतुर्भिरष्टभि १८३
षड्भ्यः कचटतेभ्यश्च ५८
षड्विंशच्छतसम्मिते २५७
षण्मासं तु ततस्तेजो २६८
षण्मासादगुभ्रगु १७१
षड्युत्तरैस्तु विंशते १३
षष्ठस्वरो हुतवह ३१४
षोडश द्वादश दश ४१

स

संक्षेपतो निगदितो १३८, १५६
संक्षेपतो हृदय १७१
संक्षेपादिति गदिता १००
संक्षोभ्य संवर्धयति २४
संचिन्त्य चरितामृता १२१
संचिन्त्य भर्त्तारमिति ३२५
संस्मारच्छितैरपि ते २२१

संज्ञासाम्ये सत्यपि	६४
संतर्प्य विप्रान् पुनरेव	३००
संदीक्षितोऽथ गुरुणा	१६०
संदीक्षितोऽथ प्रजपेच्च	१९१
संदीक्षितोऽथ मन्त्री	१९८
संदीक्षितो मनुमिमं	१३५
संदीक्षितो विमलधी	१०२
संपातितैःलिन च	१८५
संपूज्य चैवं विधिना	२५६
संपूज्य योनिषु च मातृगणं	१३४
संपूज्यैवं दिनेशं	१९९
संपूज्यैवं विधिना	१९६
संपूज्यैवं श्रियमनुदिनं	१६४
संपूरयेत् सुधामय	२२८
संपूरयेद् यथावत्	२११
संप्रीणयित्वा गुरु	२७८
संभोजयेद्धोमदिनेषु	३०८
संयतचित्तो लक्षचतुष्कं	१८३
संयोज्य किंचन	३७४
संवर्त्तकान्ते सुकल	२६५
संवादसूक्तविहितं	३५२
संवादसूक्ते विधिने	३५३
संस्कृतेन घृतेन	९४
संस्थापयेच्च तवेत्येवं	२२७
संस्थापयेच्च नाडेा	"
संस्थापितानिलां तां	१८६
संस्थाप्य दक्षिणस्यां	२५७
संस्थाप्य राजतं तत्र	२०१
संस्थाप्य समोकृत्य च	१८६
संहृतेर्दोषसंहार:	२५३
संहृत्य चोत्पाद्य	१४२
स इति परिततं	११०
सकण्ठहृदयोरोज	३४३
सकपालशूलपाशा	३३५
सकारं च हकारं च	५५
सकुम्भयुग्मवणिजो	६१
सग्राम्यधर्म्मविच्युती	३७९
सगुग्गुलगुरुश्रोर	८६
सघृतेन केशवाद्यै	२८७
स चतुर्दशभिर्दशभि	३६२
स चतुश्चत्वारिंशत्सहस्र	२१३
सचतुश्चत्वारिंशद्वारं	१०८
स च लौकिकवायुत्वात्	३०
सचिन्ताक्षमाला सुधा	१५८
सजया विजया तथा	१४४
सजलाम्बुवाहनिभ	२७२
सज्वालोल्काभ्रिया विद्या	४३
सतारराजमुख्यन्ते	३६३
सतारशक्त्याद्यजपा	१२०
सतारैश्चिटिमन्त्राणं	३४३
स तु सर्वत्र संस्तुतो	२२
सत्त्वं रजस्तम इति	२०
सत्त्वपूर्वकगुणान्विता	७२
सत्यब्रह्मविष्णुरुद्रैः	१९८
सत्यमहिंसासमता	२२६
स विट्भा वह्निगृहेण	२८५
सदोषदूष्यसम्पन्नं	२५
सद्यो वेदाक्षमाला	२९४
स द्वादशाक्षरान्तं	२३७
सन्तोषश्च सध्रीची	२२६
सनिम्बतिलसिद्धार्थ	३४५
सन्ध्यक्षरा: स्युश्चत्वारो	४५
सपादजानुयुगल	२५३
स पुन: षड्भि: सार्धं	६३
सपृथुकशक्तुकला	२१६
सप्तमं वामपादं स्या	३४५
सप्तममपि लोकेशे	२४०
सप्तम्यन्तां च कुण्डाख्या	१२०
सप्तात्मकस्य तारस्य	८४
सप्तानां करणानां च	९७
सप्ताहृती वा	७०
सप्रणवहृदय	२८४
सबिन्दुनादबीजत्व	१७
सब्रह्मविष्णुरुद्रैश्च	३२५
समधुरनलिनानां	१६२
समर्चयेन्मातृवर्गं	२१५
समवायो स विश्वात्मा	३०
समस्तपरमसुभगं	२६२
समहागणपतियुक्तै	२१७
समाराध्या नन्दिनी च	३२९
समापयेद्दक्षपादे	३४६
समिद्भिरथ बोधिजै	२६८
समिधामथ दुग्धवृक्ष	२५४
समीरणं प्रतिष्ठाप्य	२१६
समीरिता: समीरेण	४५
समुद्यद् दिवाकृत्सहस्रा	१५९
समुद्रगायामवतीर्यं	१६३
समुद्रतीरेऽप्यथवाऽद्रि	२५६
समुनिस्कन्दी देवतमपि	१०८
समुनिसुरपितृभ्यो	३७६
सर्गादर्कः चतो	३७०
सर्गाद्यान्ताद्यमन्ते	२४७
सर्पमयवलयनपुर	१८३
सर्पि:पायसशालो	२२५
सर्पि:सिक्तै: क्रमाद्धोम	३२९
सर्पिषाष्टशतहोमतो	१८९
सर्वगाश्च समुत्पन्ना:	४१
सर्वर्त्तुनिर्वृतिकरान्	७५
सर्वयुतं शक्तिपदं	२११
सर्वव्याप्ता हि सा शक्ति:	५७
सर्वान् कामानवाप्नोति	३५१
सर्वेष्वपि च मन्त्रेषु	८१
सलक्ष्मीदयितेत्येवं	२६४
सलिङ्गगुदमूर्धास्य	९२
सलिलानलपवन	२३४

सवासुदेवादिक २३८
सव्यापसव्यभागे २१०
सशान्ती श्रीसरस्वत्यौ २२५
सशिरोच्चिकर्णहृद २७९
सशिरोमुखगल १९८
सशिरोललाटदृग् २७६
सश्रीबीजा लोकेशा १७३
ससप्तभिः पुनः षड्भि २७२
ससर्पिषा पायसेन २००
ससिद्धसुरपूजितः ३१४
ससुप्रभाभिः सहितं १२१
ससुरासुरमौलि १२६
ससुरासुरसिद्धयच १३५
ससुवर्णगटका[प्रभा]स्वर्ण १६७
ससुषुम्नायगयोरपि २३२
सस्वर्णवेत्रयष्टी १७३
स हंकारः पुमान् प्रोक्तः ५५
सहस्रकाणां दशकै ३५३
सहस्रारपदं पूर्वं २८४
सहस्रार्चिः स्वस्तिपूर्णं ९३
सहिरण्मयौ च घन्टा १६५
सहृदयभगवत्यै १७०
साकारस्यात्ममन्त्रः ११०
साङ्गः सप्रतिपत्तिकः ३३०
सा तत्त्वसंज्ञा चिन्मात्रा १६
सा तया शक्तता पूर्णा ३२
सात्त्विका दिव्यपूजासु ९२
साध्यं संस्मृत्य शितधी ३४५
साध्यर्चाङ्घ्रिपचर्मणां ३१६
साध्याख्यां शक्तिवक्त्री ३५९
साध्याख्याकर्मयुक्तं ३१४
साध्याख्याचरदर्भितं १८७
साध्याख्या कामवर्णैः २२१
साध्याख्यागर्भमेनं ३१३
साध्याया हृदय ३१२
सानन्तलोहितवक्त्रौ २६५
साम्नं शिखीलवयुतं ३६१
सामुद्रे च सहिङ्गु ३३७
सार्ण[न्तं]वायसवर्णं २५९
साहं यूयं तथैवान्यद् १२
सिकता चरुगव्याश्म ३३९
सिकता षोडशकुडवं „
सितकिंशुकनिर्गुण्डी ३०४
सितरक्तासितैर्वर्णै ७६
सितसिद्धार्थैः सहस्रा ३०९
सितेन रजसा कार्या ७६
सिद्धार्थायुतहोमैर्वैरिणा ३४९
सिद्धिसमृद्धी चान्या २१०
सिन्दूरकाञ्चनसमौ १०७
सिन्दूरकुन्दकरविन्द २३९
सिंहमुखपादपीठ २०९
सिंहव्याघ्रवराहाः ६५
सिंहस्थां शरनिकरै ३३८
सुगन्धसुमनोधूप ८५
सुजीर्णमितभोजनः २२८
सुदर्शनगदाचक्र २६५
सुदीर्घसुखिमोसुख्यौ ४३
सुधामयीं च तद्योनिं २२०
सुप्तेऽशेषजने निशीथ ३७१
सुभगां भगां भगान्ते १७४
सुरता वारुणी लीला २१९
सुरभिद्वयमहिष २४५
सुराः सपित्तगन्धवं ९२
सुरुचिरसिंहासनगां १७३
सुरूपा बहुरूपा च १५३
सुरौद्रसितदंष्ट्रिका ३४२
सुलम्बोष्ठ्यूर्ध्वकेश्यौ च १५३
सुवर्णगोचीरजवा २४२
सुवर्णवासौ धान्यानि २०४
सुविमलचरितः १६८
सुविमलनखदन्त १२४
सुविशदमतिरथ १७७
सुत्रैषमेषणातीत ३७८
सुश्रीः सुरूपा कपिला ४१
सुसिता पाशाङ्कुश ३३५
सुसितेन सुशुद्धेन ८८
सूक्तैरेतैर्जपत १६७
सूक्ष्मरूपाणि तत्त्वानि २४
सूक्ष्मामरमहासेन २६५
सूक्ष्मा सूक्ष्मामृता ज्ञाना ४२
सूत्रं प्राक् प्रत्यगात्तायं ७३
सूत्रेषु मकरान् न्यस्ये ७४
सूर्यश्चेत्यनुवाकेन ३२३
सृष्टिर्ऋद्धिः स्मृतिर्मेधा ४१
सेनां संस्तम्भयितुं १८५
सैव प्रतिकृतिरस ३३६
सैव स्वां वेत्ति परमा १२
सोऽन्वीक्ष्य त्वाहशामायुः १३
सोमादीनां दिशि दिशि १९७
सौ चौ [वौ] हौ बिन्दुयुतं २९६
सौदर्शनीयं गायत्री २५५
सौरे पीठे पूजा ३५१
सौवर्णे राज्यसिद्धिं २७५
सौषुम्नाये भ्रूयुगमध्ये १२५
स्कन्दयोरुभयोर्मध्ये ३२७
स्तम्भनाद्यमथ पार्थिवै ४७
स्तुतिर्वाक्यबद्धा पदात्मैव १५७
स्तुत्वा यथावत् प्रणमेत् ९७
स्तुत्वेन्दुखण्डपरिमण्डित ३००
स्थानेषु पूर्वमुक्तेषु ३२४
स्थानस्थापनकर्म २२७
स्थानेष्विष्वात्ममनः २३२
स्थाने हृषीकेश २५९
स्थूलाय मूलभूताय ३००
स्नात्वाऽर्काभिमुखः १८४

स्नात्वा चाऽर्कमुखोऽम्भसि ३५०
स्नेहाद्वा स्त्रीमती वापि ३७९
स्पर्शाख्या अपि ये वर्णाः ४०
स्मरदीर्घेऽस्वरकान्त्यौ १७८
स्मरत्नमस्मराद्यं ३७८
स्मरशरविह्वलिताङ्गी १७४
स्मराय धीमहीत्युक्ता २६५
स्मर्तव्याखिललोक ३५१
स्मर्तव्याशेषलोकान्त ११२
स्मृतिपीठः पिनाकी २१४
स्मृते यथा संस्तुति १४२
स्मृत्वा निजं पितर ३७५
स्मृत्वा नित्यां देवीमेवं १७८
स्याद्बुद्धिसंज्ञा च यदा २७
स्युः कर्कटी वृश्चिक ५९
स्युरष्टमूर्तयो वक्रे ९२
स्रवत्सुधावर्षिंच २५९
स्रोतोमार्गस्याविभक्त ३४
स्वक्षेत्रवर्त्तिनः स्यु २४९
स्वगतैर्मरुदभ्यङ्गिः २४
स्वच्छः स्वच्छन्दचरितो ३७७
स्वच्छो मुमुक्षोस्तु ३०४
स्वनामसदृशाकाराः ९२
स्वनिष्पत्तिं च कृत्यस्य ७
स्वराख्याः षोडश प्रोक्ताः ३८
स्वयंपट्टेऽथवा भूर्जे १८०
स्वर्णाप्त्यै मधुना च २११
स्वसारक्तोपेते १८६
स्वसंवेद्यस्वरूपात्म २५१
स्वस्थानतश्च्युताच्छुक्रा २३
स्वाती शतभिषाद्रा च ६१
स्वामिनि संहृत्यैवं २३१
स्वामिन् प्रसीद विश्वेश ९
स्वार्थकृत्ये प्रसक्तार्थं ३७९
स्वाहान्तः पक्षिराजाय २६५
स्वीयेऽप्येवं संस्मरे ३७२
स्वेति स्वर्गं स्वेति चात्मा ११०

ह

हंससारसकारस्थ ७५
हंसास्थाकाररूपं १९५
हंसारूढा हरहसित १२५
हंसारूढी मदन २२१
हंसी वराही विमली ४२
हमिति प्रकाशितोऽहं १११
हयगजरथभृत्या २४४
हयारिकुसुमैर्दरिं २६८
हरत्वमस्य तेनैव ५४
हरिपूर्वं वाहनाय २८५
हरिमुज्ज्वलचक्रदराल २५२
हरिशङ्करयोः पाद ३७४
हरिस्थेऽर्केऽष्टम्या २७३
हरे बिन्दुनादैः १५९
हर्षाढ्या सुनदारुणा २४८
हलयुतवर्गद्वतीयो ११९
हवनक्रिया सपदि ३६७
हस्तश्चित्रा च टठयोः ६१
हस्तश्रवणमघासु ३३९
हस्तोद्यद्वसुपावपङ्कज १६४
हानिं न कुर्याज्जीवस्य २२१
हान्ताः षचलसाः ४७
हारताराबलीराजत् ९
हारस्फटिककलाया ९०
हारिद्राद्भिः सम्यगभ्युत्य ७१
हावभावललितार्धं ३१०
हिरण्या गगना रक्ता ९२
हुंकाराख्या खेचरि १७३
हुंकारे साध्यसञ्ज्ञां १७७
हुतक्रियैवं दिवसैश्च २७४
हुतसंख्यासाहस्रो १७५
हुताहुतिसमुद्दीप्तः १२१
हुत्वा परराष्ट्रेभ्यः २८०
हुत्वा मनुवर्णसमं २८७
हुनेदरुणपङ्कजे २०७
हृङ्काराख्यो धातु १११
हृत्कुक्षिनाभिषु तथा २५३
हृत्पद्मभिस्सदर्णौ ३०३
हृत्पद्मस्थितभानु ११७
हृत्स्थं सर्वस्य लोकस्य ३२३
हृदयं बुद्धिगम्यत्वात् ८०
हृदयं सशिरस्तथा ८९
हृदयकमलवर्णतः १६२
हृदयहयसी स्थितोऽथ १२४
हृदयपुरुषोत्तमान्ते २६१
हृदयशिरसोः शिखायां ७९
हृदयान्ते बन्धनानि २६४
हृदयान्ते विष्णुपदं २५७
हृदयाम्भोजसंस्थं तं २०१
हृदये वदने च रिपो ३१६
हृदयेऽधस्तयोर्ध्वंश्च ३२४
हृदाननपरश्रेणा २९९
हृद्दोर्मूलापरगल १०२
हृन्मूलाधोदृग्गुह्येषु २९८
हृष्टिर्व्युष्टिस्तुष्टिरिष्टा २५०
हृल्लेखया स्वनाम्ना च २२०
हृल्लेखा क्लेदिनी नन्दा १७८
हृल्लेखाख्यां गगनां १४४
हृल्लेखाग्निस्थसाध्या २६१
हृल्लेखाजपविधिमर्चना १५९
हृल्लेखाद्याः पञ्च १९२
हृल्लेखान्तःस्थसाध्यं २८१
हृल्लेखास्थितसाध्याचर ३०४
हेमप्रख्यं पार्थिवे २७२
हेमप्रख्यामिन्दुखण्डात्त १८३
हैमाश्वत्थसुरद्रुमौ २०५
ह्रस्वत्रयक्लीबवियोजिताभिः १९१
ह्रस्वाः पञ्च परे च ४७
ह्रीः श्री रतिः सपुष्टि २४०